MINDTAP
From Cengage

Fit your coursework into your hectic life.

Make the most of your time by learning your way. Access the resources you need to succeed wherever, whenever.

 Study with digital flashcards, listen to audio textbooks, and take quizzes.

 Review your current course grade and compare your progress with your peers.

 Get the free MindTap Mobile App and learn wherever you are.

Break Limitations. Create your own potential, and be unstoppable with MindTap.

MINDTAP. POWERED BY YOU.

cengage.com/mindtap

A People & A Nation

A HISTORY OF THE UNITED STATES

Eleventh Edition

Jane Kamensky
Harvard University

Carol Sheriff
College of William and Mary

David W. Blight
Yale University

Howard P. Chudacoff
Brown University

Fredrik Logevall
Harvard University

Beth Bailey
University of Kansas

Mary Beth Norton
Cornell University

 CENGAGE

Australia • Brazil • Mexico • Singapore • United Kingdom • United States

CANADA

Lake Superior

WISCONSIN
1848

~NESOTA
~858

Lake Michigan

Lake Huron

MICHIGAN
1837

Lake Ontario

St. Lawrence R.

MAINE
1820

VT.
1791

N.H.

MASS.

IOWA
1846

Lake Erie

NEW YORK

CONN.

R.I.

PENNSYLVANIA

NEW
JERSEY

ILLINOIS
1818

INDIANA
1816

OHIO
1803

MASON-DIXON LINE

1790

COLONIES

DELAWARE

MARYLAND

ATLANTIC

MISSOURI
1821

WEST
VIRGINIA
1863

KENTUCKY
1792

VIRGINIA

THIRTEEN

OCEAN

THE ORIGINAL UNITED STATES
(By Treaty with Britain, 1783)

MISSOURI
COMPROMISE
LINE
36°30'N

2000

TENNESSEE
1796

NORTH
CAROLINA

THE ORIGINAL

ARKANSAS
1836

Mississippi R.

SOUTH
CAROLINA

THE

MISSISSIPPI
1817

ALABAMA
1819

GEORGIA

Territorial Growth
of the
United States

LOUISIANA
1812

(Seized from Spain,
1810, 1813)

1820 Date of states admission to the Union

● Geographic center of population by decade

FLORIDA
(By Treaty with
Spain, 1819)

0	150	300 Km.
0	150	300 Mi.

Gulf of Mexico

FLORIDA
1845

BAHAMAS

PUERTO RICO
(Acquired from
Spain, 1898)

VIRGIN IS.
(Acquired from
Denmark, 1916–1917)

19°N

68°W

PUERTO RICO

VIRGIN
ISLANDS

18°N

0 25 50 Km.

67°W

0 25 50 Mi.

66°W

65°W

CUBA

DOMINICAN
REPUBLIC

HAITI

90°W   80°W   70°W   60°W

N

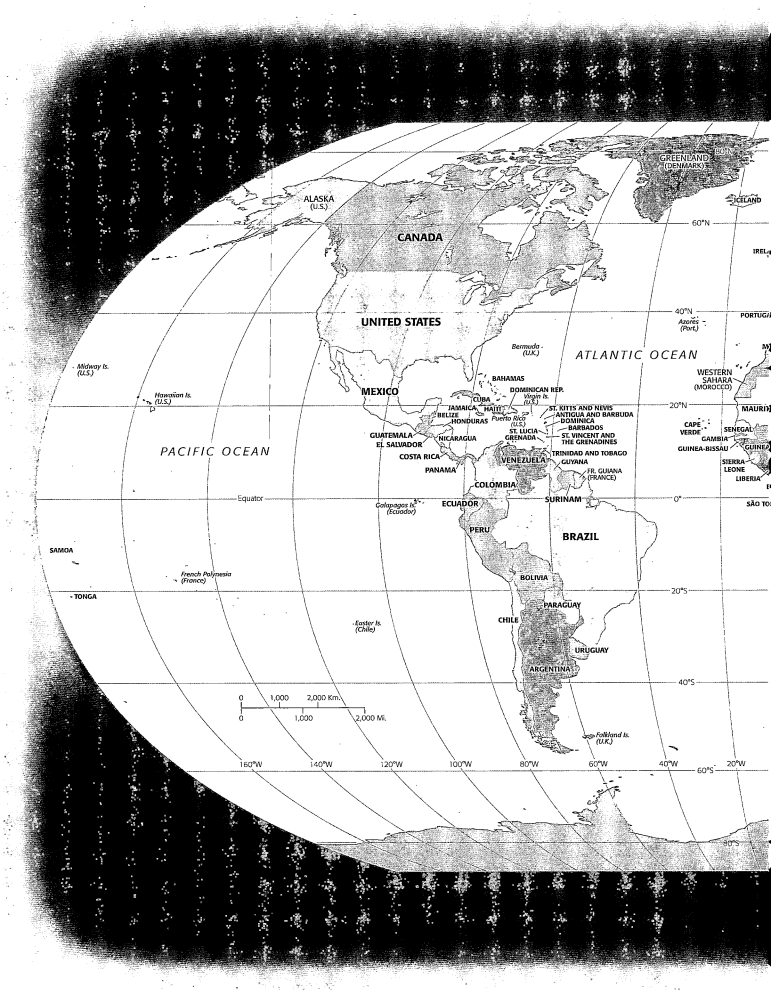

GREENLAND (DENMARK)

ICELAND

IREL

60°N

PORTUGA

40°N

Azores (Port.)

ALASKA (U.S.)

CANADA

UNITED STATES

Bermuda (U.K.)

ATLANTIC OCEAN

WESTERN SAHARA (MOROCCO)

Midway Is. (U.S.)

BAHAMAS

MEXICO

CUBA

DOMINICAN REP.

Virgin Is. (U.S.)

20°N

CAPE VERDE

MAURIT

SENEGAL

Hawaiian Is. (U.S.)

JAMAICA HAITI

BELIZE

HONDURAS

Puerto Rico (U.S.)

ST. KITTS AND NEVIS

ANTIGUA AND BARBUDA

DOMINICA

ST. LUCIA

BARBADOS

GUATEMALA

EL SALVADOR

NICARAGUA

GRENADA

ST. VINCENT AND THE GRENADINES

GAMBIA

GUINEA-BISSAU

GUINEA

PACIFIC OCEAN

COSTA RICA

PANAMA

VENEZUELA

TRINIDAD AND TOBAGO

GUYANA

SIERRA LEONE

LIBERIA

COLOMBIA

FR. GUIANA (FRANCE)

Equator

Galapagos Is. (Ecuador)

ECUADOR

SURINAM

0°

SÃO TO

PERU

BRAZIL

SAMOA

French Polynesia (France)

BOLIVIA

TONGA

20°S

PARAGUAY

Easter Is. (Chile)

CHILE

URUGUAY

ARGENTINA

40°S

| 0 | 1,000 | 2,000 Km. |
| 0 | 1,000 | 2,000 Mi. |

Falkland Is. (U.K.)

160°W   140°W   120°W   100°W   80°W   60°W   40°W   20°W

60°S

80°S

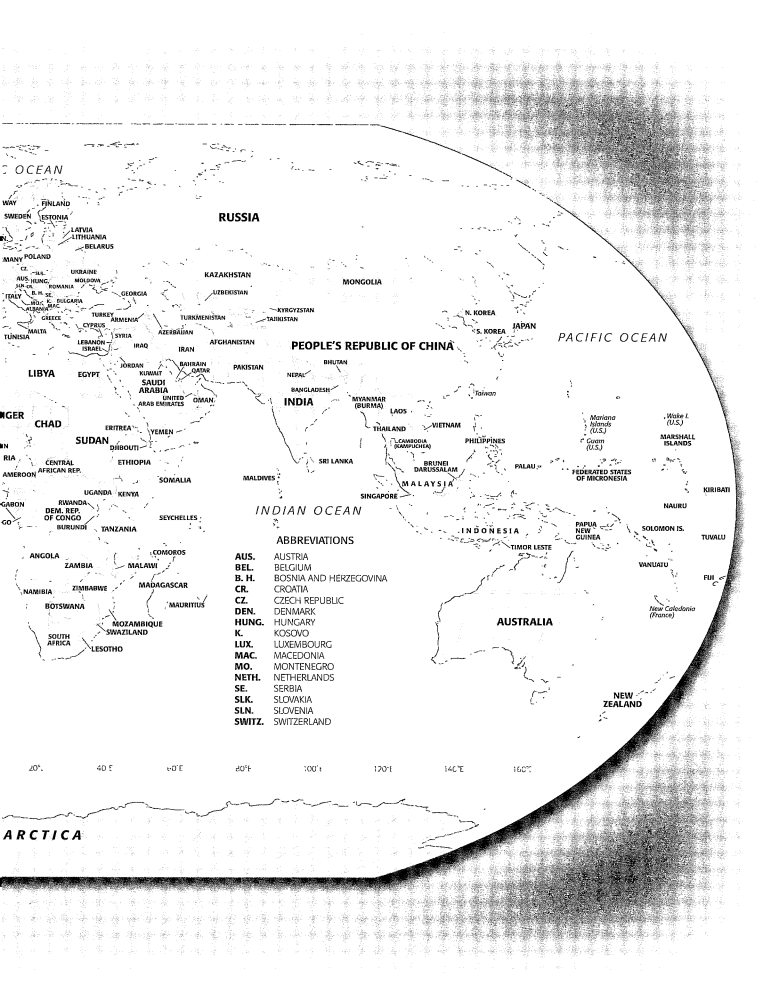

: OCEAN

WAY FINLAND
SWEDEN ESTONIA
LATVIA
LITHUANIA
BELARUS
MANY POLAND
CZ.
SLK. UKRAINE
AUS. HUNG. MOLDOVA
SLN. CR. ROMANIA
B. H. SE.
ITALY MO. K. BULGARIA
ALBANIA MAC.
GREECE TURKEY
CYPRUS ARMENIA
MALTA SYRIA AZERBAIJAN
TUNISIA
LEBANON IRAQ
ISRAEL

RUSSIA

KAZAKHSTAN

MONGOLIA

UZBEKISTAN

KYRGYZSTAN
TAJIKISTAN
TURKMENISTAN

N. KOREA
S. KOREA JAPAN

PACIFIC OCEAN

AFGHANISTAN

PEOPLE'S REPUBLIC OF CHINA

JORDAN BAHRAIN
LIBYA EGYPT KUWAIT QATAR PAKISTAN
SAUDI
ARABIA
UNITED OMAN
ARAB EMIRATES

BHUTAN
NEPAL

BANGLADESH
INDIA MYANMAR
(BURMA) LAOS

Taiwan

IGER
CHAD ERITREA
SUDAN YEMEN
DJIBOUTI

THAILAND VIETNAM

Mariana
Islands
(U.S.)

Wake I.
(U.S.)

MARSHALL
ISLANDS

CAMBODIA
(KAMPUCHEA) PHILIPPINES

Guam
(U.S.)

IN
RIA CENTRAL ETHIOPIA
AMEROON AFRICAN REP.
SOMALIA

SRI LANKA

BRUNEI
DARUSSALAM

PALAU

FEDERATED STATES
OF MICRONESIA

MALDIVES

MALAYSIA

KIRIBATI

UGANDA KENYA
GABON RWANDA
DEM. REP.
OF CONGO
GO BURUNDI TANZANIA

SINGAPORE

SEYCHELLES

INDIAN OCEAN

NAURU

PAPUA
NEW
GUINEA

SOLOMON IS.

INDONESIA

ANGOLA COMOROS
ZAMBIA MALAWI
NAMIBIA ZIMBABWE MADAGASCAR
BOTSWANA MAURITIUS
MOZAMBIQUE
SOUTH SWAZILAND
AFRICA
LESOTHO

TIMOR LESTE

TUVALU

VANUATU

FIJI

New Caledonia
(France)

AUSTRALIA

ABBREVIATIONS

AUS.	AUSTRIA
BEL.	BELGIUM
B. H.	BOSNIA AND HERZEGOVINA
CR.	CROATIA
CZ.	CZECH REPUBLIC
DEN.	DENMARK
HUNG.	HUNGARY
K.	KOSOVO
LUX.	LUXEMBOURG
MAC.	MACEDONIA
MO.	MONTENEGRO
NETH.	NETHERLANDS
SE.	SERBIA
SLK.	SLOVAKIA
SLN.	SLOVENIA
SWITZ.	SWITZERLAND

NEW
ZEALAND

20° 40 E 60°E 80°E 100°E 120°E 140°E 160°E

ARCTICA

CENGAGE

A People & A Nation, Eleventh Edition
Jane Kamensky /Carol Sheriff/
David W. Blight/ Howard P. Chudacoff/
Fredrik Logevall/ Beth Bailey /Mary
Beth Norton

Product Manager: Joseph Potvin

Senior Content Developer: Kate MacLean

Associate Content Developer: Claire Branman

Product Assistant: Alexandra Shore

Senior Marketing Manager: Valerie Hartman

Senior Content Project Manager: Carol Newman

Manufacturing Planner: Julio Esperas

IP Analyst: Alexandra Ricciardi

IP Project Manager: Betsy Hathaway

Production Service/Compositor: MPS Limited

Senior Art Director: Cate Rickard Barr

Text and Cover Designer: tani hasegawa, TT EYE.

Cover Image: *Pastoral Visit* by Richard Norris
Brooke, 1881. Granger, NYC—All rights reserved.

For product information and technology assistance, contact us at
Cengage Customer & Sales Support, 1-800-354-9706

For permission to use material from this text or product,
submit all requests online at **www.cengage.com/permissions.**
Further permissions questions can be emailed to
permissionrequest@cengage.com.

Library of Congress Control Number: 2017955520

Student Edition:
ISBN: 978-1-337-40271-2

Loose-leaf Edition:
ISBN: 978-1-337-40448-8

Cengage
20 Channel Center Street
Boston, MA 02210
USA

Cengage is a leading provider of customized learning solutions with
employees residing in nearly 40 different countries and sales in more
than 125 countries around the world. Find your local representative at
www.cengage.com.

Cengage products are represented in Canada by Nelson Education, Ltd.

To learn more about Cengage platforms and services, visit
www.cengage.com.

To register or access your online learning solution or purchase materials for
your course, visit **www.cengagebrain.com.**

Printed in the United States of America
Print Number: 01   Print Year: 2017

BRIEF CONTENTS

CONTENTS

1 | Three Old Worlds Create a New, 1492–1600   2

2 | Europeans Colonize North America, 1600–1650   32

3   North America in the Atlantic World, 1650–1720   60

4   Becoming America? 1720–1760   88

The Ends of Empire, 1754–1774   118

American Revolutions, 1775–1783   146

7 Forging a Nation, 1783–1800   174

8 Defining the Nation, 1801–1823   208

9 The Rise of the South, 1815–1860   240

10 The Restless North, 1815–1860   272

The Contested West, 1815–1860   306

Politics and the Fate of the Union, 1824–1859   336

Transforming Fire: The Civil War, 1860–1865   370

Reconstruction: An Unfinished Revolution, 1865–1877   410

The Ecology of the West and South, 1865–1900   440

Building Factories, Building Cities, 1877–1920   466

Gilded Age Politics, 1877–1900 — 496

The Progressive Era, 1895–1920 — 522

The Quest for Empire, 1865–1914   548

Americans in the Great War, 1914–1920   572

The New Era, 1920–1929   600

The Great Depression and the New Deal, 1929–1939   630

The Second World War at Home and Abroad, 1939–1945   664

The Cold War and American Globalism, 1945–1961   694

America at Midcentury, 1945–1960   724

The Tumultuous Sixties, 1960–1968   754

27 A Pivotal Era, 1969–1980   786

28 Conservatism Revived, 1980–1992   816

Into the Global Millennium: America Since 1992   844

Appendix   A-1

Index   I-1

MAPS

FIGURES

TABLES

LINKS TO THE WORLD

LEGACY FOR A PEOPLE AND A NATION

VISUALIZING THE PAST

With this eleventh edition, *A People and A Nation* consolidates the last edition's broad structural changes, fine-tuning the streamlining and chapter combinations that made the text easier to assign over the course of an average academic semester. In this edition the authors introduced new interpretations, updated content to reflect recent research, and thought hard about what new features might engage our readers. This edition also more fully embraces the possibilities offered by digital platforms, as you will learn about in the MindTap description that follows later in this introduction.

A People and A Nation represents our continuing rediscovery of America's history—our evolving understandings of the people and the forces that have shaped the nation and our stories of the struggles, triumphs, and tragedies of America's past.

Key Themes in *A People and A Nation*

Published originally in 1982, *A People and A Nation* was the first U.S. history survey textbook to move beyond a political history to tell the story of the nation's people—the story of *all* its people—as well. That commitment remains. Our text encompasses the diversity of America's people and the changing texture of their everyday lives. The country's political narrative is here, too, as in previous editions. But as historical questions have evolved over the years and new authors have joined the textbook team, we have asked new questions about "a people" and "a nation." In our recent editions, we remind students that the "*A People*" and "*A Nation*" that appear in the book's title are neither timeless nor stable. European colonists and the land's indigenous inhabitants did not belong to this "nation" or work to create it, and Americans have struggled over the shape and meaning of their nation since its very beginning. The people about whom we write thought of themselves in various ways, and in ways that changed over time. Thus we emphasize not only the ongoing diversity of the nation's people, but their struggles, through time, over who belongs to that "people" and on what terms.

In *A People and A Nation,* the authors emphasize the changing global and transnational contexts within which the American colonies and the United States have acted. We pay attention to the economy, discussing the ways that an evolving market economy shaped the nation and the possibilities for its different peoples. We show how the meaning of identity—gender, race, class, sexuality, as well as region, religion, and family status—changes over time, and we find the nation's history in the mobility and contact and collision of its peoples. We discuss the role of the state and the expanding role and reach of the federal government; we pay attention to region and emphasize historical contests between

federal power and local authority. We trace America's expansion and rise to unprecedented world power and examine its consequences. And we focus on the meaning of democracy and equality in American history, most particularly in tales of Americans' struggles for equal rights and social justice.

In *A People and A Nation*, we continue to challenge readers to think about the meaning of American history, not just to memorize facts. More than anything else, we want students to understand that the history of the American nation was not foreordained. Ours is a story of contingency. As, over time, people lived their day-to-day lives, made what choices they could, and fought for things they believed in, they helped to shape the future. What happened was not inevitable. Throughout the course of history, people faced difficult decisions, and those decisions mattered.

What's New in This Edition

Planning for the eleventh edition began at an authors' meeting near Cengage headquarters in Boston. Authors' meetings are always lively, and we discussed everything from recent scholarship and emerging trends in both U.S. and global history to the possibilities offered by digital platforms and the needs of the students who would be reading our work.

This edition continues to build on *A People and A Nation*'s hallmark themes, giving increased attention to the global perspective on American history that has characterized the book since its first edition. From the "Atlantic world" context of European colonies in North and South America to the discussion of international terrorism, the authors have incorporated the most recent globally oriented scholarship throughout the volume. We have stressed the incorporation of different peoples into the United States through territorial acquisition as well as through immigration. At the same time, we have integrated the discussion of such diversity into our narrative so as not to artificially isolate any group from the mainstream.

We have continued the practice of placing three probing questions at the end of each chapter's introduction to inspire and guide students' reading of the pages that follow. Additionally, focus questions and key terms have been added to this edition. The focus questions appear beneath each section title within every chapter to further support students in their reading and comprehension of the material. Key terms appear near the first mention of a term and are placed throughout each chapter.

Chapter-level Changes for the Eleventh Edition

For this edition, the authors reexamined every sentence, interpretation, map, chart, illustration, and caption, refined the narrative, presented new examples, updated bibliographies, and incorporated the best new scholarship. What follows here is a description of chapter-level changes for the eleventh edition:

1. **Chapter 2: Europeans Colonize North America, 1600–1650**
   - New chapter-opening vignette on an episode of inter-racial violence in 1630 New England

2. **Chapter 3: North America in the Atlantic World, 1650–1720**
   - New *Legacy for a People and a Nation* feature: "Fictions of Salem: Witch-Hunting in the American Grain"

3. **Chapter 4: Becoming America? 1720–1760**
   - Increased attention to Canadian maritime provinces in King George's War

4. **Chapter 5: The Ends of Empire, 1754–1774**
   - New information on Caribbean colonies' response to the Stamp Act and other imperial tax laws from rare pamphlets published in Barbados
   - New primary source material about the Stamp Act repeal and Boston Massacre trials
   - The *Legacy for a People and a Nation* feature, "Women's Political Action," has been updated to reflect the 2016 presidential election

5. **Chapter 6: American Revolutions, 1775–1783**
   - Increased attention to the Spanish empire and the war in the Gulf of Mexico
   - More attention is given to African American soldiers in the American Revolution
   - New *Visualizing the Past* feature: "A British View of the Colonial Army"

6. **Chapter 8: Defining the Nation, 1801–1823**
   - New *Legacy for a People and a Nation* feature: "The Star-Spangled Banner"

7. **Chapter 9: The Rise of the South, 1815–1860**
   - New section on slavery and capitalism
   - New material on the domestic slave trade
   - Additional information on slave religion
   - Additions to discussion of "planter paternalism"
   - Updated *Legacy for a People and a Nation* feature on reparations

8. **Chapter 11: The Contested West, 1815–1860**
   - New topic ("The Mexican-United States Border") for *Legacy for A People and a Nation* feature

9. **Chapter 12: Politics and the Fate of the Union, 1824–1859**
   - Includes additional information about states' rights under nullification
   - Features a revised map for the Mexican War
   - Added material on Fremont, California, and the coming of the Mexican War

- New scholarship on the underground railroad in New York
- Increased attention to voter turnout in the Jackson era
- The *Legacy for a People and a Nation* feature on coalition politics has been updated

10. **Chapter 13: Transforming Fire: The Civil War, 1860–1865**
    - Chapter-opening vignette has been revised
    - Clarified discussion of secession crisis
    - Added discussion of Native Americans fighting in the Civil War
    - New discussion of the importance of the "Union Cause" to Northerners

11. **Chapter 14: Reconstruction: An Unfinished Revolution, 1865–1877**
    - Revised discussion of Radical Republican vision of Reconstruction
    - New scholarship on the military occupation of the South
    - New scholarship on the movement West
    - Revised discussion of railroad growth and expansion
    - Updated *Legacy for a People and a Nation* feature on the Lost Cause

12. **Chapter 21: The New Era, 1920–1929**
    - New *Links to the World* feature on Margaret Mead

13. **Chapter 22: The Great Depression and the New Deal, 1929–1939**
    - Added section on the voyage of the *St. Louis* and FDR responses to Nazi Germany

14. **Chapter 23: The Second World War at Home and Abroad, 1939–1945**
    - Revised discussion of U.S. path to war
    - Discussion of attack on Pearl Harbor has been recast to emphasize Japan's broader attack on U.S. and U.K. Pacific possessions
    - New scholarship on financing the war

15. **Chapter 25: America at Midcentury, 1945–1960**
    - Discussion of GI Bill updated to incorporate recent scholarship
    - Added material on relative income equality and tax rates
    - Updates made to recast Levvittown in the *Visualizing the Past* feature
    - New *Links to the World* feature: Sputnik

16. **Chapter 26: The Tumultuous Sixties, 1960–1968**
    - Added material on federal spending on social welfare programs

- New section on Mexican American and Chicano activism
- Updated and revised *Legacy for a People and a Nation* feature: "The Immigration Act of 1965"
- Minor updates to the Vietnam section.

17. **Chapter 27: A Pivotal Era, 1969–1980**
    - New chapter-opening vignette on the Iran hostage crisis
    - A section on Puerto Rican nationalism has been added
    - Updated *Legacy for A People and a Nation* feature: "The All-Volunteer Force"
    - Information on Pentagon Papers case has been added.

18. **Chapter 28: Conservatism Revived, 1980–1992**
    - New chapter-opening vignette on 1980 "Washington for Jesus" rally
    - New scholarship on rise of conservatism
    - Revised discussion of economic policies and results.
    - Additional material on computer technology

19. **Chapter 29: Into the Global Millennium: America Since 1992**
    - Added discussion of Obama's presidency and accomplishments
    - Fully recast and updated final section on Americans in the new millennium
    - Information added on the digital revolution
    - Significant changes to the section on Obama's foreign policy, including in the second term, including the rise of ISIS and the civil war in Syria

Format for Each Chapter

Opening Vignette

Each chapter opens with a brief story about a person, place, or event and includes an image related to the story. The stories highlight specific events with historical significance while bringing attention to the larger themes in U.S. History during that period.

Focus Questions

Each chapter section is accompanied by a set of focus questions that guide students in absorbing and interpreting the information in the section that follows. This is a new pedagogical feature added in this edition to help students retain the information they are learning as they move through the book.

Chapter Features: *Legacies, Links to the World,* and *Visualizing the Past*

The following three features— *Legacy for* A People and a Nation, *Links to the World,* and *Visualizing the Past*—are included in each chapter of *A People and A Nation,* eleventh edition. These features all illustrate key themes of the text

and give students alternative ways to experience historical content.

Legacy for A People and A Nation features appear toward the end of each chapter and offer compelling and timely answers to students who question the relevance of historical study by exploring the historical roots of contemporary topics. New *Legacies* in this edition include "Fictions of Salem: Witch-Hunting in the American Grain," "The Star-Spangled Banner," and "The Mexican-United States Border."

Links to the World features examine ties between America (and Americans) and the rest of the world. These brief essays detail the often little-known connections between developments here and abroad, vividly demonstrating that the geographical region that is now the United States has never been isolated from other peoples and countries. Essay topics range broadly over economic, political, social, technological, medical, and cultural history, and the feature appears near relevant discussions in each chapter. This edition includes new *Links* on anthropologist Margaret Mead and on Sputnik and American education. Each *Link* feature highlights global interconnections with unusual and lively examples that will both intrigue and inform students.

Visualizing the Past features offer striking images along with brief discussions intended to help students analyze the images as historical sources and to understand how visual materials can reveal aspects of America's story that otherwise might remain unknown. New to this edition is "A British View of the Colonial Army" in Chapter 6.

Summary

The core text of each chapter ends with a brief summary that helps students synthesize what they have just read and directs students to see long-term trends and recurring themes that appear across chapters.

Suggested Readings

A list of secondary sources appears at the end of each chapter for students and instructors who want to dig deeper into the content of the chapter.

Key Terms

Within each chapter, terms are boldfaced for students' attention with brief definitions appearing on the same page. Terms highlighted include concepts, laws, treaties, movements and organizations, legal cases, and battles.

MindTap for *A People and A Nation*

- MindTap 2-semester Instant Access Code: ISBN 9781337402750
- MindTap 2-semester Printed Access Card: ISBN - 9781337402767
- MindTap 1-semester Instant Access Code: ISBN 9781337404686
- MindTap 1-semester Printed Access Card: ISBN 9781337404693

MindTap for *A People and A Nation* is a flexible online learning platform that provides students with an immersive learning experience to build and foster critical thinking skills. Through a carefully designed chapter-based learning path, MindTap allows students to easily identify learning objectives; draw connections and improve writing skills by 1) completing unit-level essay assignments; 2) reading short, manageable sections from the ebook: 3) and testing their content knowledge with map-based critical thinking questions.

MindTap allows instructors to customize their content, providing tools that seamlessly integrate YouTube clips, outside websites, and personal content directly into the learning path. Instructors can assign additional primary source content through the Instructor Resource Center and Questia primary- and secondary-source databases that house thousands of peer-reviewed journals, newspapers, magazines, and full-length books.

The additional content available in MindTap mirrors and complements the authors' narrative, but also includes primary-source content and assessments not found in the printed text. To learn more, ask your Cengage sales representative to demo it for you—or go to www.Cengage .com/MindTap.

Supplements for *A People and A Nation*

- **Instructor's Companion Website.** The Instructor's Companion Website, accessed through the Instructor Resource Center (login.cengage.com), houses all of the supplemental materials you can use for your course. This includes a Test Bank, Instructor's Manual, and PowerPoint Lecture Presentations. The Test Bank, offered in Microsoft® Word® and Cognero® formats, contains multiple-choice, true-or-false, and essay questions for each chapter. Cognero® is a flexible, online system that allows you to author, edit, and manage test bank content for *A People and a Nation*, 11e. Create multiple test versions instantly and deliver through your LMS from your classroom, or wherever you may be, with no special installs or downloads required. The Instructor's Resource Manual includes chapter summaries and outlines, learning objectives, suggested lecture topics, discussion questions class activities, and suggestions for additional films to watch. Finally, the PowerPoint Lectures are ADA-compliant slides collate the key takeaways from the chapter in concise visual formats perfect for in-class presentations or for student review.

- **Cengagebrain.com.** Save your students time and money. Direct them to www.cengagebrain.com for a choice in formats and savings and a better chance to succeed in your class. Cengagebrain.com, Cengage's online store, is a single destination for more than 10,000 new textbooks, eTextbooks, eChapters, study tools,

and audio supplements. Students have the freedom to purchase à la carte exactly what they need when they need it. Students can save 50 percent on the electronic textbook and can purchase an individual eChapter for as little as $1.99.

- *Doing History: Research and Writing in the Digital Age,* 2e ISBN: 9781133587880 Prepared by Michael J. Galgano, J. Chris Arndt, and Raymond M. Hyser of James Madison University. Whether you're starting down the path as a history major or simply looking for a straightforward, systematic guide to writing a successful paper, this text's "soup to nuts" approach to researching and writing about history addresses every step of the process: locating your sources, gathering information, writing and citing according to various style guides, and avoiding plagiarism.

- *Writing for College History,* 1e ISBN: 9780618306039 Prepared by Robert M. Frakes of Clarion University. This brief handbook for survey courses in American, western, and world history guides students through the various types of writing assignments they may encounter in a history class. Providing examples of student writing and candid assessments of student work, this text focuses on the rules and conventions of writing for the college history course.

- *The Modern Researcher,* 6e ISBN: 9780495318705 Prepared by Jacques Barzun and Henry F. Graff of Columbia University. This classic introduction to the techniques of research and the art of expression thoroughly covers every aspect of research, from the selection of a topic through the gathering of materials, analysis, writing, revision, and publication of findings. They present the process not as a set of rules but through actual cases that put the subtleties of research in a useful context. Part One covers the principles and methods of research; Part Two covers writing, speaking, and getting one's work published.

- *Reader Program.* Cengage publishes a number of readers. Some contain exclusively primary sources, others are devoted to essays and secondary sources, and still others provide a combination of primary and secondary sources. All of these readers are designed to guide students through the process of historical inquiry. Visit www.cengage.com/history for a complete list of readers.

- *Custom Options.* Nobody knows your students like you, so why not give them a text that is tailor-fit to their needs? Cengage offers custom solutions for your course—whether it's making a small modification to *A People and a Nation*, 11e, to match your syllabus or combining multiple sources to create something truly unique. Contact your Cengage representative to explore custom solutions for your course.

Acknowledgments

The authors would like to thank Timothy Cole, David Farber, Mark Guerci, Anna Daileader Sheriff, and Benjamin Daileader Sheriff for their assistance with the preparation of this edition.

We also want to thank the many instructors who have adopted *APAN* over the years. We have been very grateful for the comments from the historian reviewers who read drafts of our chapters. Their suggestions, corrections, and pleas helped guide us through this revision. We could not include all of their recommendations, but the book is better for our having heeded most of their advice. We heartily thank:

Dawn Cioffoletti, *Florida Gulf Coast University*

Charles Cox, *Bridgewater State College*

Mary Daggett, *San Jacinto College – Central*

Jesse Esparza, *Texas Southern University*

Miriam Forman-Brunell, *University of Missouri, Kansas City*

Amy Forss, *Metropolitan Community College – South*

Devethia Guillory, *Lonestar College – North Harris*

Gordon Harvey, *Jacksonville State University*

Kathleen Gorman, *Minnesota State University, Mankato*

Jennifer Gross, *Jacksonville State University*

Donna Hoffa, *Wayne County Community College*

Richard Hughes, *Illinois State University*

Lesley Kauffman, *San Jacinto College – Central*

Karen Kossie-Chernyshev, *Texas Southern University*

Mary Hovanec, *Cuyahoga Community College*

Yu Shen, *Indiana University – Southeast*

Michael Swope, *Wayne County Community College*

Nancy Young, *University of Houston*

The authors thank the helpful Cengage people who designed, edited, produced, and nourished this book. Many thanks to Joseph Potvin, product manager; Kate MacLean, senior content developer; Claire Branman, associate content developer; Pembroke Herbert, photo researcher; Charlotte Miller, art editor; and Carol Newman, senior content project manager.

J. K.
C. S.
D. B.
H. C.
F. L.
B. B.
M. B. N.

Jane Kamensky

Born in New York City, Jane Kamensky earned her BA (1985) and PhD (1993) from Yale University. She is now Professor of History at Harvard University and the Pforzheimer Foundation Director of the Schlesinger Library on the History of Women in America. She is the author of *A Revolution in Color: The World of John Singleton Copley* (2016), winner of the New York Historical Society's Barbara and David Zalaznick Book Prize in American History and the Annibel Jenkins Biography Prize of the American Society for Eighteenth-Century Studies; *The Exchange Artist: A Tale of High-Flying Speculation and America's First Banking Collapse* (2008), a finalist for the 2009 George Washington Book Prize; *Governing the Tongue: The Politics of Speech in Early New England* (1997); and *The Colonial Mosaic: American Women, 1600–1760* (1995); and the coeditor of *The Oxford Handbook of the American Revolution* (2012). With Jill Lepore, she is the coauthor of the historical novel *Blindspot* (2008), a *New York Times* editor's choice and *Boston Globe* bestseller. In 1999, she and Lepore also cofounded *Common-place* (www.common-place.org), which remains a leading online journal of early American history and life. Jane has also served on the editorial boards of the *American Historical Review*, the *Journal of American History*, and the *Journal of the Early Republic*, as well as on the Council of the American Antiquarian Society, the Executive Board of the Organization of American Historians, and as a Commissioner of the Smithsonian's National Portrait Gallery. Called on frequently as an advisor to public history projects, she has appeared on PBS, C-SPAN, the History Channel, and NPR, among other media outlets. Jane, who was awarded two university-wide teaching prizes in her previous position at Brandeis, has won numerous major grants and fellowships to support her scholarship.

Carol Sheriff

Born in Washington, D.C., and raised in Bethesda, Maryland, Carol Sheriff received her BA from Wesleyan University (1985) and her PhD from Yale University (1993). Since 1993, she has taught history at the College of William and Mary, where she has won the Thomas Jefferson Teaching Award; the Alumni Teaching Fellowship Award; the University Professorship for Teaching Excellence; The Class of 2013 Distinguished Professorship for Excellence in Scholarship, Teaching, and Service; and the Arts and Sciences Award for Teaching Excellence. Her publications include *The Artificial River: The Erie Canal and the Paradox of Progress* (1996), which won the Dixon Ryan Fox Award from the New York State Historical Association and the Award for Excellence in Research from the New York State Archives, and *A People at War: Civilians and Soldiers in America's Civil War, 1854–1877* (with Scott Reynolds Nelson, 2007). In 2012, she won the John T. Hubbell Prize from *Civil War History* for her article on the state-commissioned Virginia history textbooks of the 1950s, and the controversies their portrayals of the Civil War era provoked in ensuing decades. Carol has written sections of a teaching manual for the New York State history curriculum, given presentations at Teaching American History grant projects, consulted on an exhibit for the Rochester Museum and Science Center, and appeared in The History Channel's Modern Marvels show on the Erie Canal. She worked on several public-history projects marking the sesquicentennial of the Civil War, and is involved in public and scholarly projects to commemorate the Erie Canal's bicentennial. At William and Mary, she teaches the U.S. history survey as well as upper-level classes on the Early Republic, the Civil War Era, and the American West.

David W. Blight

Born in Flint, Michigan, David W. Blight received his BA from Michigan State University (1971) and his PhD from the University of Wisconsin (1985). He is now professor of history and director of the Gilder Lehrman Center for the Study of Slavery, Resistance, and Abolition at Yale University. For the first seven years of his career, David was a public high school teacher in Flint. He has written *Frederick Douglass's Civil War* (1989) and *Race and Reunion: The Civil War in American Memory, 1863–1915* (2000), which received eight awards, including the Bancroft Prize, the Frederick Douglass Prize, the Abraham Lincoln Prize, and four prizes awarded by the Organization of American Historians. His most recent books are a biography of Frederick Douglass (forthcoming in 2018); *American Oracle: The Civil War in the Civil Rights Era* (2011) and *A Slave No More: The Emancipation of John Washington and Wallace Turnage* (2007), which won three book prizes. His edited works include *When This Cruel War Is Over: The Civil War Letters of Charles Harvey Brewster* (1992), *Narrative of the Life of Frederick Douglass* (1993), W. E. B. Du Bois, *The Souls of Black Folk* (with Robert Gooding Williams, 1997), *Union and Emancipation* (with Brooks Simpson, 1997), and *Caleb Bingham, The Columbian Orator* (1997). David's essays have appeared in the *Journal of American History* and *Civil War History*, among others. A consultant to several documentary films, David appeared in the 1998 PBS series, *Africans in America*. David also teaches summer seminars for secondary school teachers, as well as for park rangers and historians of the National Park Service. He has served on the Executive Board of the Organization of American Historians, and in 2012, he was elected to the American Academy of Arts and Sciences. In 2013–2014 David was Pitt Professor of American History and Institutions at the University of Cambridge in the United Kingdom.

Howard P. Chudacoff

Howard P. Chudacoff, the George L. Littlefield Professor of American History and Professor of Urban Studies at Brown University, was born in Omaha, Nebraska. He earned his AB (1965) and PhD (1969) from the University of Chicago. He has written *Mobile Americans* (1972), *How Old Are You?* (1989), *The Age of the Bachelor* (1999), *The Evolution of American Urban Society* (with Judith Smith, 2004), and *Children at Play: An American History* (2007) and *Changing the Playbook: How Power, Profit, and Politics Transformed College Sports* (2015). He has also coedited (with Peter Baldwin) *Major Problems in American Urban History* (2004). His articles have appeared in such journals as the *Journal of Family History, Reviews in American History*, and *Journal of American History*. At Brown University, Howard has cochaired the American Civilization Program and chaired the Department of History, and served as Brown's faculty representative to the NCAA. He has also served on the board of directors of the Urban History Association and the editorial board of *The National Journal of Play*. The National Endowment for the Humanities, Ford Foundation, and Rockefeller Foundation have given him awards to advance his scholarship.

Fredrik Logevall

A native of Stockholm, Sweden, Fredrik Logevall is Laurence D. Belfer Professor of International Affairs at Harvard University, where he holds appointments in the Department of History and the Kennedy School of Government. He received his BA from Simon Fraser University (1986) and his PhD from Yale University (1993). His most recent book is *Embers of War: The Fall of an Empire and the Making of America's Vietnam* (2012), which won the Pulitzer Prize in History and the Francis Parkman Prize, and which was named a best book of the year by the *Washington Post* and the *Christian Science Monitor*. His other publications include *Choosing War* (1999), which won three prizes, including the Warren F. Kuehl Book Prize from the Society for Historians of American Foreign Relations (SHAFR); *America's Cold War: The Politics of Insecurity* (with Campbell Craig; 2009); *The Origins of the Vietnam War* (2001); *Terrorism and 9/11: A Reader* (2002); and, as coeditor, *The First Vietnam War: Colonial Conflict and Cold War Crisis* (2007); and *Nixon and the World: American Foreign Relations, 1969–1977* (2008). Fred is a past recipient of the Stuart L. Bernath article, book, and lecture prizes from SHAFR, and a past member of the Cornell University Press faculty board. He serves on numerous editorial advisory boards. A past president of SHAFR, Fred is a member of the Society of American Historians and the Council of Foreign Relations.

Beth Bailey

Born in Atlanta, Georgia, Beth Bailey received her BA from Northwestern University (1979) and her PhD from the University of Chicago (1986). She is now Foundation Distinguished Professor of History and director of the Center for Military, War, and Society Studies at the University of Kansas. Beth served as the coordinating author for the tenth and eleventh editions of *A People and A Nation*. She is the author of *America's Army: Making the All-Volunteer Force* (2009), which won the Army Historical Foundation's Distinguished Writing Award; *The Columbia Companion to America in the 1960s* (with David Farber, 2001); *Sex in the Heartland* (1999); *The First Strange Place: The Alchemy of Race and Sex in WWII Hawaii* (with David Farber, 1992); and *From Front Porch to Back Seat: Courtship in 20th Century America* (1988). She also co-edited *Understanding the U.S. Wars in Iraq and Afghanistan* (2015); *America in the Seventies* (2004); and the reader *A History of Our Time* (multiple editions). Beth has lectured in Australia, Indonesia, France, Germany, the Netherlands, Great Britain, Japan, Saudi Arabia, Lebanon, and China. She is a trustee for the Society of Military History and was appointed by the Secretary of the Army to the Department of the Army Historical Advisory Committee. Beth has received several major grants or fellowships in support of her research. She teaches courses on the history of gender and sexuality and on U.S. Military, War, and Society.

Mary Beth Norton

Born in Ann Arbor, Michigan, Mary Beth Norton received her BA from the University of Michigan (1964) and her PhD from Harvard University (1969). She is the Mary Donlon Alger Professor of American History at Cornell University. Her dissertation won the Allan Nevins Prize. She has written *The British-Americans* (1972); *Liberty's Daughters* (1980, 1996); *Founding Mothers & Fathers* (1996), which was one of three finalists for the 1997 Pulitzer Prize in History; and *In the Devil's Snare* (2002), one of five finalists for the 2003 *L.A. Times* Book Prize in History and won the English-Speaking Union's Ambassador Book Award in American Studies for 2003. Her most recent book is *Separated by Their Sex* (2011). She has coedited three volumes on American women's history. She was also general editor of the *American Historical Association's Guide to Historical Literature* (1995). Her articles have appeared in such journals as the *American Historical Review, William and Mary Quarterly*, and *Journal of Women's History*. Mary Beth has served as president of the American Historical Association and the Berkshire Conference of Women Historians, as vice president for research of the American Historical Association, and as a presidential appointee to the National Council on the Humanities. She has appeared on Book TV, the History and Discovery Channels, PBS, and NBC as a commentator on Early American history, and she has lectured frequently to high school teachers. She has received four honorary degrees and is an elected member of both the American Academy of Arts and Sciences and the American Philosophical Society. She has held fellowships from the National Endowment for the Humanities; the Guggenheim, Rockefeller, and Starr Foundations; and the Henry E. Huntington Library. In 2005–2006, she was the Pitt Professor of American History and Institutions at the University of Cambridge and Newnham College.

A People & A Nation

Three Old Worlds Create a New, 1492–1600

ycpolínhq̃ mexica

A generation after Columbus crossed the Atlantic, a Spanish soldier named Hernán Cortés traded words with the ruler of the Aztec empire. Motecuhzoma II was among the most powerful men in the Americas (as Europeans had recently named their "new" world). Thousands of loyal courtiers accompanied him to the gates of Tenochtitlán, the capital, one of the largest cities in the world. Cortés, his Spanish troops, and their Native allies approached on horseback, flying the flag of Charles V, the king of Spain and Holy Roman Emperor, one of the most powerful men in the "old" world. The conquistador and the Aztec ruler bowed to each other, and spoke. "Montezuma bade him welcome," recalled Bernal Díaz del Castillo, a soldier on the expedition. "There is nothing to fear," Cortés told his host. "We have come to your house in Mexico as friends."

This mixture of ceremony, half-truths, and outright lies was among the first exchanges between two great civilizations from two sides of a great ocean. It was not an easy conversation to have. Motecuhzoma spoke Nahuatl and had never heard Spanish; Cortés spoke Spanish and knew no Nahuatl. (The Spanish could not even pronounce the Aztec emperor's name, garbling "Motecuhzoma" as "Montezuma.") But in fact the conversation between Cortés and Motecuhzoma was not a dialogue but a three-way exchange. As Bernal Díaz explains, Cortés addressed the Aztec emperor "through the mouth of Doña Marina."

Who was Doña Marina? Born at the eastern edge of Motecuhzoma's dominion around the year 1500, she grew up at the margins of Aztec and Maya territories, worlds in motion and often at war. Her parents were Nahuatl-speaking nobles. The name they gave her is lost to history. As a child,

◁ Perched on a throne and wearing elaborate plumes in his hat, Cortès accepts the surrender of the Cuauthemoc in August 1521. Seated behind him in traditional dress, Doña Marina translates the negotiation, with gestures that exactly mirror his. The image, from a mural created by Tlaxcalan artists in the 1550s, shows the complex role of the interpreter in the meeting of worlds. AKG Images

Chronology

13,000–10,000 BCE	Paleo-Indians migrate from Siberia to western North America, some by boat and some across the Beringia land bridge
7000 BCE	Cultivation of food crops begins in America
ca. 2000 BCE	Olmec civilization appears
ca. 300–600 CE	Height of influence of Teotihuacán
ca. 600–900 CE	Classic Mayan civilization
1000 CE	Ancient Pueblos build settlements in modern states of Arizona and New Mexico
	Bantu-speaking peoples spread across much of southern Africa
1001	Norse establish settlement in "Vinland"
1050–1250	Height of influence of Cahokia
	Prevalence of Mississippian culture in modern midwestern and southeastern United States
14th century	Aztec rise to power
Early 15th century	Portuguese establish trading posts in North Africa
1450s–80s	Portuguese colonize islands in the Mediterranean Atlantic
1477	Marco Polo's *Travels* describes China
1492	Columbus reaches Bahamas
1494	Treaty of Tordesillas divides land claims in Africa, India, and South America between Spain and Portugal
1497	Cabot reaches North America
1499	Amerigo Vespucci explores South American coast
1513	Ponce de León explores Florida
1518–30	Smallpox epidemic devastates indigenous populations of West Indies and Central and South America
1519	Cortés invades Mexico
1521	Aztec Empire falls to Spaniards
1524	Verrazzano sails along Atlantic coast of North America
1534–35	Cartier explores St. Lawrence River
1539–42	De Soto explores southeastern North America
1540–42	Coronado explores southwestern North America
1587–90	Raleigh's Roanoke colony vanishes
1588	Harriot publishes *A Briefe and True Report of the New Found Land of Virginia*
	English defeat of the Spanish Armada

she was either stolen from her family or given by them to indigenous slave traders. She wound up in the Gulf Coast town of Tabasco, in the household of a Maya cacique. There, in addition to her native Nahuatl, she learned Yucatec, the local strain of the Mayan language. She spoke both tongues well when she encountered the Spanish, who brought yet a third civilization into her changing world in the spring of 1519.

The leaders of Tabasco showered Cortés with tribute, offerings they hoped would persuade the Spanish to continue west, into the heart of their enemies' territory. In addition to gold and cloth, the caciques gave the invaders twenty Native women. The young bilingual slave was one of them. The invaders baptized her under the Christian name "Marina."

Marina learned Spanish quickly, and her fluency in this third language greatly increased her value to the would-be conquerors. As Cortés and his troops progressed inland, Marina's way with words proved as vital to the success of the expedition as any other weapon they carried. Díaz called her "a person of the greatest importance." Cortés, reluctant to share credit for his triumphs, rarely mentioned her in his letters. But she bore him a son, Martín. Sometime before her death in 1527 or 1528, Marina married another Spanish officer.

A speaker of Nahuatl, Yucatec, and Spanish; the mother of one of the first *mestizo* or mixed-race children; the wife of a conquistador: Marina was a young woman in whom worlds met and mingled. The Spanish signaled their respect by addressing her as "Doña," meaning lady. Nahuatl speakers rendered *Marina* as *Malintzin*, using the suffix *–tzin* to denote her high status. Spaniards stumbled over the Nahuatl *Malintzin* and often called her *La Malinche*: a triple name, from a double mistranslation.

The legacy of Doña Marina/Malintzin/La Malinche remains as ambiguous as her name. Her fluency helped the invaders to triumph—a catastrophe for the Aztecs and other indigenous peoples. Their descendants consider Doña Marina their foremother and their betrayer, at once a victim and a perpetrator of the Spanish conquest. Today in Mexico, the word *malanchista* is a grave insult, equivalent to "collaborator" or even "traitor." Though she lived for less than thirty years, nearly half a millennium ago, Marina continues to embody the ambiguities of colonial American history, in which power was shifting and contested, and much was lost in translation.

Experience an interactive version of this story in MindTap®.

What happens when worlds collide? For thousands of years before 1492, human societies in the Americas developed in complex relation to each other, yet in isolation from the rest of the world. The era that began in the Christian fifteenth century brought that long-standing isolation to an end. As Europeans sought treasure and trade, peoples from two sides of the globe came into regular contact for the first time. Their interactions involved curiosity and confusion, trade and theft, enslavement and endurance. All were profoundly changed.

By the time Doña Marina held Cortés's words in her mouth, the age of European expansion and colonization was already under way. Over the next 350 years, Europeans would spread their influence across the globe. The history of the tiny colonies that became the United States must be seen in this broad context of European exploration and exploitation, of Native resistance, and of African enslavement and survival. Even as Europeans slowly achieved dominance, their fates continued to be shaped by the strategies of Americans and Africans. In the Americas of the fifteenth and sixteenth centuries, three old worlds came together to produce a new.

The continents that European sailors reached in the late fifteenth century had their own histories, internal struggles that the intruders sometimes exploited and often ignored. The indigenous residents of what came to be called *the Americas* were the world's most skillful plant breeders; they developed crops more nutritious and productive than those grown in Europe, Asia, or Africa. They had invented systems of writing and mathematics, and created more accurate calendars than those used on the other side of the Atlantic. In the Americas, as in Europe, societies rose and fell as leaders succeeded or failed to expand their power. But the arrival of Europeans altered the Americans' struggles with one another, just as the colonization of the Americas repeatedly reshaped the European balance of powers.

After 1400, European nations not only warred on their own continent but also tried to acquire valuable colonies and trading posts elsewhere in the world. Initially interested primarily in Asia and Africa, Europeans eventually focused mostly on the Americas. Their designs changed the course of history on four continents.

"In the beginning, all the world was America," wrote the English philosopher John Locke at the end of the seventeenth century. But in fact, America wasn't "America" until Europeans renamed the ancient homelands of hundreds of nations after one of their own explorers. The continent was not innocent, empty, and waiting, as Locke implied, but densely peopled and engaged in its own complex history. The collision of old and new worlds changed that history. New opportunities for some meant new risks for others. Every conquest contained a defeat. Every new place name was layered upon an older history. And a great deal was lost in translation.

> *What were the key characteristics of the three worlds that met in the Americas?*

> *What impacts did their encounter have on each of them?*

> *What were the crucial initial developments in that encounter?*

1-1 American Societies

▷ **How were the Americas settled?**

▷ **How did the first Americans—the Paleo-Indians— adapt to their environment?**

▷ **How did Native peoples who began to domesticate and cultivate food crops develop socially and culturally?**

Human beings originated on the continent of Africa, where hominid remains about 3 million years old have been found in what is now Ethiopia. Over many millennia, the growing population slowly dispersed to the other continents. Because the climate was then far colder than it is now, much of the earth's water was concentrated in huge rivers of ice called glaciers. Sea levels were accordingly lower, and landmasses covered a larger proportion of the earth's surface than they do today. Scholars long believed that the Clovis people, Siberians who were among the earliest inhabitants of the Americas, crossed a land bridge known as Beringia (at the site of the Bering Strait) approximately twelve thousand to fourteen thousand years ago. Yet striking new archaeological discoveries in both North and South America suggest that parts of the Americas may have been settled significantly earlier, perhaps by seafarers. Some geneticists now theorize that three successive waves of migrants began at least thirty thousand years ago. About 12,500 years ago, when the climate warmed and sea levels rose, Americans were separated from the peoples living on the connected continents of Asia, Africa, and Europe.

1-1a Ancient America

The first Americans, now called **Paleo-Indians,** were nomadic hunters of game and gatherers of plants. They spread throughout North and South America, probably moving as bands composed of extended families. By about 11,500 years ago, the Paleo-Indians were making fine stone projectile points, which they attached to spears and used to kill and butcher bison (buffalo), woolly mammoths, and other large mammals. As the Ice Age ended and the human population increased, the large American mammals except the bison disappeared. Scholars disagree about whether overhunting or the change in climate caused

Paleo-Indians The earliest peoples of the Americas.

their extinction. In either case, deprived of their primary source of meat, Paleo-Indians found new ways to survive.

By approximately nine thousand years ago, the residents of what is now central Mexico began to cultivate food crops, especially maize (corn), squash, beans, avocados, and peppers. In the Andes Mountains of South America, people started to grow potatoes. As knowledge of agricultural techniques improved and spread through the Americas, vegetables and maize proved a more reliable source of food than hunting and gathering. Except in the harshest climates, most Paleo-Indians started to stay longer in one place, so that they could tend fields regularly. Some established permanent settlements; others moved several times a year among fixed sites. They used controlled burning to clear forests, which created cultivable lands by killing trees and fertilizing the soil with ashes, and also opened meadows that attracted deer and other wildlife. Although they traded such items as shells, flint, salt, and copper, no society became dependent on another group for items vital to its survival.

Wherever agriculture dominated the economy, complex civilizations flourished. Such societies, assured of steady supplies of grains and vegetables, no longer had to devote all their energies to procuring sufficient food. Instead, they were able to accumulate wealth, trade with other groups, produce ornamental objects, and create rituals and ceremonies to cement and transmit their cultures. In North America, the successful cultivation of nutritious crops, especially maize, beans, and squash, seems to have led to the growth and development of all the major civilizations: first the large city-states of Mesoamerica (modern Mexico and Guatemala) and then the urban clusters known collectively as the Mississippian culture and located in the present-day United States. Each of these societies reached its height of population and influence only after achieving success in agriculture. Each later declined and collapsed after reaching the limits of its food supply, with dire political and military consequences.

1-1b Mesoamerican Civilizations

Archaeologists and historians know little about the first major Mesoamerican civilization, the Olmecs, who about four thousand years ago lived near the Gulf of Mexico in cities dominated by temple pyramids. The Mayas and Teotihuacán, which developed approximately two thousand years later, are better recorded. Teotihuacán, founded in the Valley of Mexico about 300 BCE (Before the Common Era), eventually became one of the largest urban areas in the world, housing perhaps 100,000 people in the fifth century CE (Common Era). Teotihuacán's commercial network extended hundreds of miles in all directions; many peoples prized its obsidian (a green volcanic glass), used to make fine knives and mirrors. Pilgrims traveled long distances to visit Teotihuacán's immense pyramids and the great temple of Quetzalcoatl— the feathered serpent, primary god of central Mexico.

On the Yucatan Peninsula, in today's eastern Mexico, the Mayas built urban centers boasting tall pyramids and temples. They studied astronomy and created an elaborate writing system. Their city-states, though, engaged in near-constant battle with one another, much as Europeans did at the same time. Warfare and an inadequate food supply caused the collapse of the most powerful cities by 900 CE, thus ending the classic era of Mayan civilization. When the Spaniards arrived 600 years later, only a few remnants of the once-mighty society remained, in places like the town where Doña Marina was enslaved.

1-1c Pueblos and Mississippians

Ancient Native societies in what is now the United States learned to grow maize, squash, and beans from Mesoamericans, but the nature of the relationship among the various cultures remains unknown. (No Mesoamerican artifacts have been found north of the Rio Grande, but some items resembling Mississippian objects have been excavated in northern Mexico, suggesting the presence of trade routes.) The Hohokam, Mogollon, and ancient Pueblo peoples of the modern states of Arizona and New Mexico subsisted by combining hunting and gathering with agriculture in an arid region. Hohokam villagers constructed extensive irrigation systems, occasionally relocating settlements when water supplies failed. Between 900 and 1150 CE in Chaco Canyon, the Pueblos built fourteen "Great Houses," multistory stone structures averaging two hundred rooms. The canyon, at the juncture of perhaps four hundred miles of roads, served as a major regional trading and processing center for turquoise, used then as now to create beautiful ornamental objects. Yet the sparse and unpredictable rainfall eventually caused the Chacoans to migrate to other sites.

At almost the same time, the unrelated Mississippian culture flourished in what is now the midwestern and southeastern United States. Relying largely on maize, squash, nuts, pumpkins, and venison for food, the Mississippians lived in substantial settlements organized hierarchically. The largest of their urban centers was the **City of the Sun** (now called **Cahokia**), which was located near modern St. Louis. Located on rich farmland near the confluence of the Illinois, Missouri, and Mississippi rivers, Cahokia, like Teotihuacán and Chaco Canyon, served as a focal point for both culture and trade. At its peak (in the eleventh and twelfth centuries CE), the City of the Sun covered more than five square miles and had a population of about twenty thousand: small by Mesoamerican standards but larger than any other northern community—indeed, larger than London in the same era.

Although the Cahokians never invented a writing system, these sun-worshippers developed an accurate calendar, evidenced by their creation of a woodhenge—a large circle of tall timber posts aligned with the solstices and the equinox. The tallest of the city's 120 pyramids, today called Monks Mound, covered sixteen acres at its base and stood 100 feet high at its topmost level. It remains the largest earthwork ever built in the Americas. It sat at the northern end of the Grand Plaza, surrounded by seventeen other mounds, some used for burials. Yet following 1250 CE, the city was abandoned, several decades after a disastrous earthquake. Archaeologists

△ Archaeologists discovered this effigy bottle near Cahokia in present-day Illinois. The statue, which was made c1200–1400 CE, depicts a woman sitting cross-legged and nursing an infant.

Nursing-mother-effigy bottle, Cahokia Culture, Mississippian Period, 1200–1400 (ceramic), American School / St. Louis Museum of Science & Natural History, Missouri, US/Photo © The Detroit Institute of Arts/The Bridgeman Art Library

believe that climate change and the degradation of the environment, caused by overpopulation and the destruction of nearby forests, contributed to the city's collapse. Afterwards, warfare increased as large-scale population movements destabilized the region.

1-1d Aztecs

Far to the South, the Aztecs (also called Mexicas) migrated into the Valley of Mexico during the twelfth century CE. The ruins of Mayan Teotihuacán, deserted for at least two hundred years, awed and mystified the migrants. Their chronicles record that their primary deity, Huitzilopochtli—a war god represented by an eagle—directed them to establish their capital on an island where they saw an eagle eating a serpent, the symbol of Quetzalcoatl. That island city became Tenochtitlán, the nerve center of a rigidly stratified society composed of warriors, merchants, priests, common people, and slaves.

The Aztecs conquered their neighbors, demanding tribute in textiles, gold, foodstuffs, and human beings who could be sacrificed to Huitzilopochtli. The war god's taste for blood was not easily quenched. In the Aztec year Ten Rabbit (the Christian 1502), at the coronation of Motecuhzoma II, thousands of people were sacrificed by having their still-beating hearts torn from their bodies.

City of the Sun (Cahokia) Area located near modern St. Louis, Missouri, where about twenty thousand people inhabited a metropolitan area.

IRA BLOCK/National Geographic Creative

△ Even today, many centuries after the peak of its ceremonial and economic power, the central mound of the Cahokia settlement, known as the Monk's Mound, still dominates the flat landscape around it, as this 2010 photo shows.

The Aztecs believed they lived in the age of the Fifth Sun. Four times previously, they wrote, the earth and all the people who lived on it had been destroyed. They predicted their own world would end in earthquakes and hunger. In the Aztec year Thirteen Flint, volcanoes erupted, sickness and hunger spread, wild beasts attacked children, and an eclipse of the sun darkened the sky. Did some priest wonder whether the Fifth Sun was approaching its end? In time, the Aztecs learned that Europeans knew the year Thirteen Flint as 1492.

1-2 North America in 1492

▷ What factors contributed to the diversity of indigenous peoples in North America?

▷ What role did gender play in the development and organization of indigenous societies?

▷ What role did warfare play in pre-Columbian American society?

Over the centuries, the Americans who lived north of Mexico adapted their once-similar ways of life to very different climates and terrains, thus creating the diverse culture areas (ways of subsistence) that the Europeans encountered when they arrived (see Map 1.1). Scholars often delineate such culture areas by language group (such as Algonquian or Iroquoian), because neighboring indigenous nations commonly spoke related languages. Societies that lived in environments not well suited to agriculture—because of inadequate rainfall or poor soil, for example—followed a nomadic lifestyle. Within the area of the present-day United States, these groups included the Paiutes and Shoshones, who inhabited the Great Basin (now Nevada and Utah). Because of the difficulty of finding sufficient food, such hunter-gatherer bands were small, usually composed of one or more related families. The men hunted small animals, and women gathered seeds and berries. Where large game was more plentiful and food supplies therefore more certain, as in present-day central and western Canada and the Great Plains, bands of hunters were somewhat larger.

In more favorable environments, larger indigenous groups combined agriculture with gathering, hunting, and fishing. Those who lived near the seacoasts, like the Chinooks of present-day Washington and Oregon, consumed fish and shellfish in addition to growing crops and gathering seeds and berries. Residents of the interior (for example, the Arikaras of the Missouri River valley) hunted large animals while also cultivating maize, squash, and beans. The peoples of what is now eastern Canada and the northeastern United States also combined hunting, fishing, and agriculture. They used controlled fires both to open land for cultivation and to assist in hunting.

Extensive trade routes linked distant peoples. For instance, hoe and spade blades manufactured from stone mined in modern southern Illinois have been found as far northeast as Lake Erie and as far west as the Plains. Commercial and

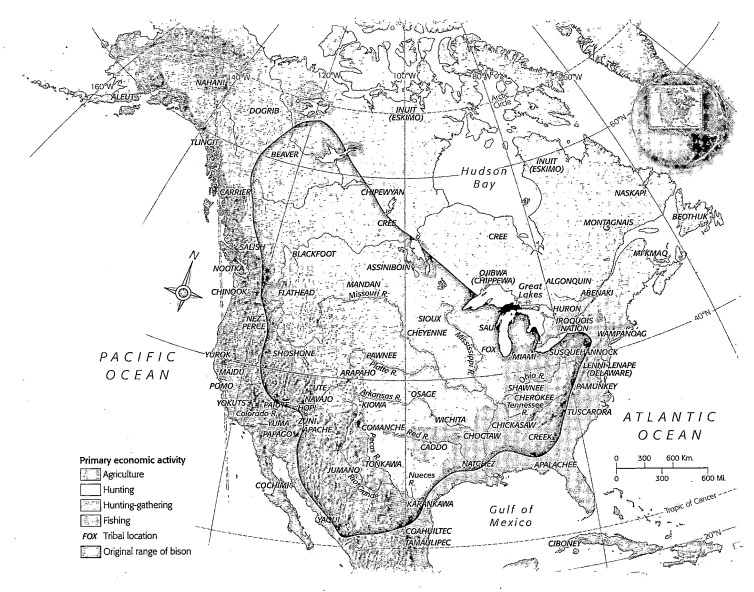

Map 1.1 Native Cultures of North America

The Native peoples of the North American continent effectively used the resources of the regions in which they lived. As this map shows, coastal groups relied on fishing, residents of fertile areas engaged in agriculture, and other peoples employed hunting (often combined with gathering) as a primary mode of subsistence.

other interactions among disparate groups speaking different languages were aided by the universally understood symbol of friendship—the calumet, a feathered tobacco pipe offered to strangers at initial encounters. Across the continent, Native groups sought alliances and waged war against their enemies when diplomacy failed. Their histories, though not written, were complex and dynamic, long before Europeans arrived.

1-2a Gendered Division of Labor

Societies that relied primarily on hunting large animals, such as deer and buffalo, assigned that task to men, allotting food preparation and clothing production to women. Before such nomadic bands acquired horses from the Spaniards, women—occasionally assisted by dogs—also carried

the family's belongings whenever the band relocated. Such a sexual division of labor was universal among hunting peoples, regardless of location. Agricultural societies assigned work in divergent ways. The Pueblo peoples, who lived in sixty or seventy autonomous villages and spoke five different languages, defined agricultural labor as men's work. In the east, large clusters of peoples speaking Algonquian, Iroquoian, and Muskogean languages allocated most agricultural chores to women, although men cleared the land. French colonizers often commented on Native gender roles that were very different from their own. "Men leave the arrangement of the household to the women, without interfering with them; they cut, and decide, and give away as they please, without making the husband angry," noted Father Paul le Juene of the Algonquian peoples he missionized along the shores of the St. Lawrence River. In the six nations of the Haudenosaunee (whom French called "Iroquois"), women held positions of political and cultural authority. This too Europeans found striking. "Amongst the Huron nations," wrote Father Pierre de Charlevoix, "the women name the counselors, and often chuse persons of their own sex." Indeed, he said, "the women have the chief authority amongst all the nations of the Huron language," excepting the Oneida. In general, he thought, they handled this surprising power ably.

Everywhere in North America, women cared for young children, while older youths learned adult skills from their same-sex parent. Children had a great deal of freedom. Young people commonly chose their own marital partners, and in most societies couples could easily divorce if they no longer wished to live together. In contrast to the earlier Mississippian cultures, populations in these societies remained at a level sustainable by existing food supplies, largely because of low birth rates. Infants and toddlers nursed until the age of two or even longer, and taboos prevented couples from having sexual intercourse during that period.

1-2b Social Organization

The southwestern and eastern agricultural peoples had similar social organizations. They lived in villages, sometimes with a thousand or more inhabitants. The Pueblos resided in multistory buildings constructed on terraces along the sides of cliffs or other easily defended sites. Northern Iroquois villages (in modern New York State) were composed of large, rectangular, bark-covered structures, or longhouses; the name Haudenosaunee means "People of the Longhouse." In the present-day southeastern United States, Muskogeans and southern Algonquians lived in large houses made of thatch. Most of the eastern villages were surrounded by wooden palisades and ditches to fend off attackers.

In all the agricultural societies, each dwelling housed an extended family defined matrilineally (through a female line of descent). Mothers, their married daughters, and their daughters' husbands and children all lived together. Matrilineal descent did not imply matriarchy, or the wielding of power by women, but rather served as a means of reckoning kinship. Matrilineal ties also linked extended families into clans. The nomadic bands of the Prairies and Great Plains, by contrast,

△ Jacques Le Moyne, an artist accompanying the French settlement in Florida in the 1560s (see Section 1-9b, p. 28), produced some of the first European images of North American peoples. His depiction of Native agricultural practices shows the gendered division of labor: men breaking up the ground with fishbone hoes before women drop seeds into the holes. But Le Moyne's version of the scene cannot be accepted uncritically: unable to abandon a European view of proper farming methods, he erroneously drew plowed furrows in the soil.

Collection of Mary Beth Norton

were most often related patrilineally (through the male line). They lacked settled villages and defended themselves from attack primarily by moving to safer locations when necessary.

1-2c War and Politics

The defensive design of Native villages points to the significance of warfare in pre-Columbian America. Long before Europeans arrived, residents of the continent fought one another for control of prime hunting and fishing territories, fertile agricultural lands, or sources of essential items, such as salt (for preserving meat) and flint (for making knives and arrowheads). Native warriors protected by wooden armor battled while standing in ranks facing each other, the better to employ their clubs and throwing spears, which were effective only at close quarters. They began to shoot arrows from behind trees only when they confronted European guns, which rendered their armor useless. People captured in such wars were sometimes enslaved and dishonored by losing their previous names and identities, but slavery was not a primary source of labor in pre-Columbian America.

Indigenous political structures varied considerably. Among Pueblos, the village council, composed of ten to thirty men, was the highest political authority; no larger organization connected multiple villages. Nomadic hunters also lacked formal links among separate bands. The Iroquois, by contrast, had an elaborate political hierarchy incorporating villages into nations and nations into a confederation. A council of representatives from each nation made crucial decisions of war and peace for the entire confederacy. In all the North American cultures, civil and war leaders divided political power and wielded authority only so long as they retained the confidence of the people. Autocratic rulers held sway only in southeastern chiefdoms descended from the Mississippians. Women more often assumed leadership roles among agricultural peoples, especially those in which females were the primary cultivators. Female sachems (rulers) led Algonquian villages in what is now Massachusetts, but women never became heads of hunting bands. Iroquois women did not become chiefs, yet clan matrons exercised political power, including the power to start and stop wars.

1-2d Religion

The continent's Native peoples were polytheistic, worshipping a multitude of gods, sometimes under one chief creator. The major deities of agricultural peoples like the Pueblos and Muskogeans were associated with cultivation, and their main festivals centered on planting and harvest. The most important gods of hunters like those living on the Great Plains were associated with animals, and their festivals were related to hunting.

A wide variety of cultures, comprising more than 10 million people, inhabited America north of Mexico when Europeans arrived. The hierarchical kingdoms of Mesoamerica bore little resemblance to the nomadic hunting societies of the Great Plains or to the agriculturalists of the Northeast or Southwest. The diverse inhabitants of North America spoke well over one thousand distinct languages. They are "Americans" only in

retrospect, grouped under the name the Europeans assigned to the continent. They did not consider themselves one people, just as the inhabitants of England, France, Spain, and the Netherlands did not imagine themselves as "Europeans." Nor did they think of uniting to repel the invaders who washed up on their shores beginning in 1492.

1-3 African Societies

▷ **How did the environment affect the development of societies in Africa?**

▷ **What was the influence of Islamic culture on African societies?**

▷ **What roles did gender play in the organization of African societies?**

Fifteenth-century Africa, like fifteenth-century America, housed a variety of cultures adapted to different terrains and climates (see Map 1.2). Many of these cultures were of great antiquity. Like the ancient cultures of North America, the diverse peoples of Africa were dynamic and changing, with complex histories of their own.

In the north, along the Mediterranean Sea, lived the Berbers, who were Muslims—followers of the Islamic religion founded by the prophet Mohammed in the seventh century CE. On the east coast of Africa, Muslim city-states engaged in far-ranging trade with India, the Moluccas (part of modern Indonesia), and China. In these ports, sustained contact and intermarriage among Arabs and Africans created the Swahili language and culture. Through the East African city-states passed the Spice Route, the conduit of waterborne commerce between the eastern Mediterranean and East Asia; the rest followed the long land route across Central Asia known as the Silk Road.

South of the Mediterranean coast in the African interior lie the great Saharan and Libyan deserts, vast nearly waterless expanses crisscrossed by trade routes passing through oases. The introduction of the camel in the fifth century CE made long-distance travel possible, and as Islam expanded after the ninth century, commerce controlled by Muslim merchants helped to spread similar religious and cultural ideas throughout the region. Below the deserts, much of the continent is divided between tropical rain forests (along the coasts) and grassy plains (in the interior). People speaking a variety of languages and pursuing different subsistence strategies lived in a wide belt south of the deserts. South of the Gulf of Guinea, the grassy landscape came to be dominated by Bantu-speaking peoples, who left their homeland in modern Nigeria about two thousand years ago and slowly migrated south and east across the continent.

1-3a West Africa (Guinea)

The inhabitants of West Africa's tropical forests and savanna grasslands supported themselves with fishing, cattle herding, and agriculture for at least ten thousand years before Europeans set foot there in the fifteenth century. The northern region of West Africa, or Upper Guinea, was heavily influenced by

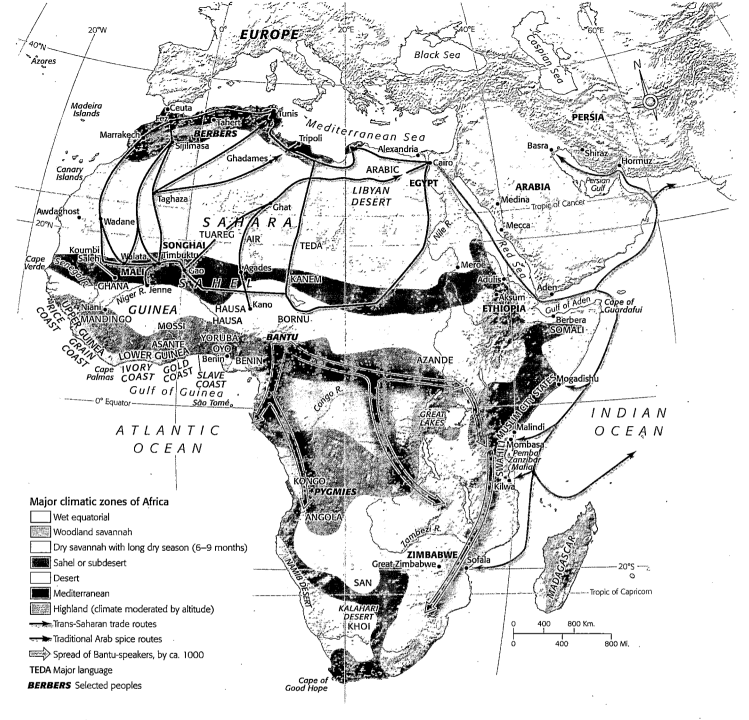

Map 1.2 Africa and Its Peoples, ca. 1400

On the African continent resided many different peoples in a variety of ecological settings and political units. Even before Europeans began to explore Africa's coastlines, its northern regions were linked to the Mediterranean (and thus to Europe) by a network of trade routes.

Major climatic zones of Africa

- Wet equatorial
- Woodland savannah
- Dry savannah with long dry season (6–9 months)
- Sahel or subdesert
- Desert
- Mediterranean
- Highland (climate moderated by altitude)
- Trans-Saharan trade routes
- Traditional Arab spice routes
- Spread of Bantu-speakers, by ca. 1000

TEDA Major language
BERBERS Selected peoples

the Islamic culture of the Mediterranean. By the eleventh century CE, many of the region's inhabitants had become Muslims. Trade via camel caravans between Upper Guinea and the Muslim Mediterranean connected sub-Saharan Africa to Europe and West Asia. Africans sold ivory, gold, and slaves to northern merchants to obtain salt, dates, silk, and cotton cloth.

Upper Guinea runs from Cape Verde in the northeast to Cape Palmas in the southwest. The people of its northernmost region, the so-called Rice Coast (present-day Gambia,

Senegal, and Guinea), fished and cultivated rice in coastal swamplands. The Grain Coast, to the south, was thinly populated and not readily accessible from the sea because it had only one good harbor (modern Freetown, Sierra Leone). Its inhabitants concentrated on farming and raising livestock.

In Lower Guinea, south and east of Cape Palmas, most Africans were farmers who practiced traditional religions, rather than Islam. Believing that spirits inhabited particular places, they invested those places with special significance. Like

△ This brass depiction of a hunting scene with a man and animals was employed by the Akan peoples of the modern Ivory Coast to weigh gold. An otherwise mundane object required for domestic and foreign trade thus was decorative as well as useful, providing for today's viewers a sense of ancient African life.

the agricultural peoples of the Americas, they developed rituals intended to ensure good harvests. Throughout the region, villages composed of kin groups were linked into hierarchical kingdoms. At the time of initial European contact, decentralized political and social authority characterized the region.

1-3b Complementary Gender Roles

In the societies of West Africa, as in those of the Americas, men and women pursued different tasks. In general, both sexes shared agricultural duties. Men also hunted, managed livestock, and did most of the fishing. Women were responsible for child care, food preparation, manufacture, and trade. They managed the extensive local and regional networks through which families, villages, and small kingdoms exchanged goods.

Despite their different economies and the rivalries among states, the peoples of Lower Guinea had similar social systems organized on the basis of what anthropologists have called the dual-sex principle. Each sex handled its own affairs: male political and religious leaders governed men, and females ruled women. In the Dahomean kingdom, for example, every male official had his female counterpart; in the thirty Akan states on the Gold Coast, chiefs inherited their status through the female line, and each male chief had a female assistant who supervised other women. Many West African societies practiced polygyny (one man's having several wives, each of whom lived separately with her children). Thus, few adults lived permanently in marital households, but the dual-sex system ensured that their actions were subject to scrutiny by elders of their own sex.

Throughout Guinea, both women and men served as heads of the cults and secret societies that directed the spiritual life of the villages. Young women were initiated into the Sandé cult, young men into Poro. Neither cult was allowed to reveal its secrets to the opposite sex. Unlike some of their Native American contemporaries, West African women rarely held formal power over men.

1-3c Slavery in Guinea

Africans, like North America's Native peoples, created various forms of slavery long before contact with Europeans. Enslavement was sometimes used to punish criminals, but more often slaves were enemy captives or people who voluntarily enslaved themselves or their children to pay debts.

West African law recognized both individual and communal landownership, but men seeking to accumulate wealth needed access to laborers—wives, children, or slaves—who could work the land. People enslaved for life composed essential elements of the economy. Slaveholders had a right to the products of the men and women they held in bondage, although the degree to which slaves were exploited varied greatly, and slave status did not always descend to the next generation. Some slaves were held as chattel; others could engage in trade, retaining a portion of their profits; and still others achieved prominent political or military positions. All, however, found it difficult to overcome the social stigma of enslavement, and could be traded or sold at the will of their owners.

West Africans, then, were agricultural peoples, skilled at tending livestock, hunting, fishing, and manufacturing cloth from plant fibers and animal skins. They were accustomed to a relatively egalitarian relationship between the sexes, especially within the context of religion. Carried as captives to the Americas, they became essential to transplanted European societies that used their labor but had little respect for their cultures.

1-4 European Societies

▷ **What were the similarities in the everyday lives of Europeans across the continent?**

▷ **What roles did gender play in the social and cultural development of European society?**

▷ **What developments drove Europeans to engage in the exploration of the wider world?**

In the fifteenth century, Europeans, too, were agricultural peoples. Split into numerous small, warring peoples, the continent of Europe was divided linguistically, politically, and economically. Yet the daily lives of ordinary men and women exhibited many similarities. In most European societies, a few families wielded autocratic power over the rest. English society in particular was organized as a series of interlocking hierarchies; that is, each person (except those at the very top or bottom) was superior to some, inferior to others. At the base of such hierarchies were people held in various forms of bondage. Although Europeans were not subjected to perpetual slavery, Christian doctrine permitted the enslavement of "heathens" (non-Christians), and some Europeans' freedom was restricted by such conditions as serfdom, which tied them to particular plots of land if not to specific owners. In short, Europe's kingdoms resembled those of Africa or Mesoamerica but differed greatly from the more egalitarian societies found in America north of Mexico (see Map 1.3).

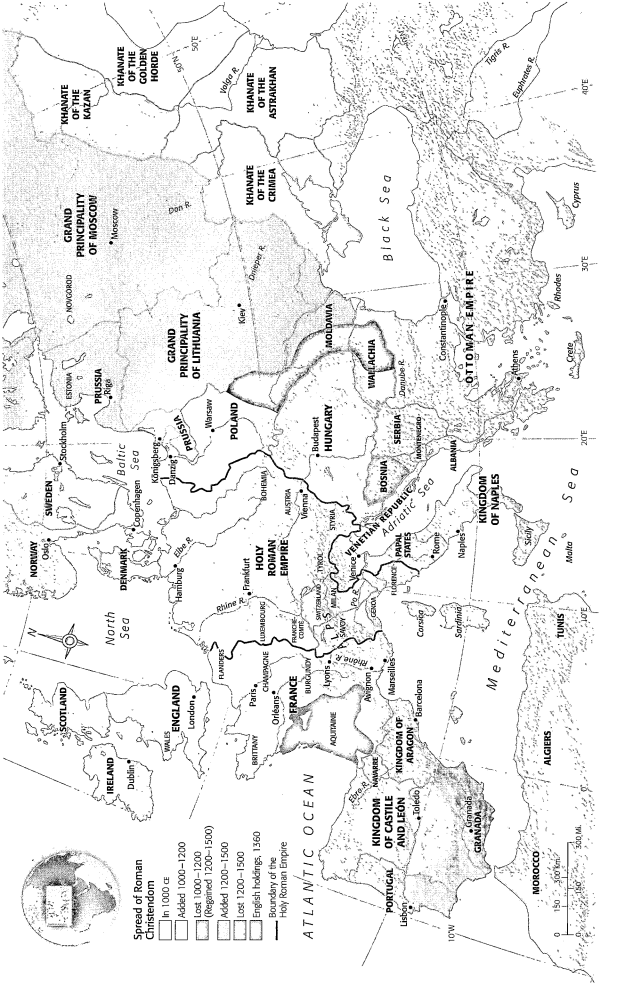

Map 1.3 Europe in 1453

The Europeans who ventured out into the Atlantic came from countries on the northwestern edge of the continent, which was divided into numerous competing nations.

Spread of Roman Christendom

☐ In 1000 CE
☐ Added 1000–1200
☐ Lost 1000–1200 (Regained 1200–1500)
☐ Added 1200–1500
☐ Lost 1200–1500
☐ English holdings, 1360
━━ Boundary of the Holy Roman Empire

1-4a Gender, Work, Politics, and Religion

Most Europeans, like most Africans and Americans, lived in small villages. Only a few cities dotted the landscape, most of them seaports or political capitals. European farmers, called peasants, owned or leased separate plots of land, but they worked the fields communally. Men did most of the field-work; women helped out chiefly at planting and harvest. In some regions men concentrated on herding livestock while women cared for children, prepared and preserved food, milked cows, and kept poultry. A woman married to a city artisan or storekeeper might assist her husband in business. Because Europeans kept domesticated animals (pigs, goats, sheep, and cattle) for meat, hunting had little economic importance in their cultures, and served instead primarily as a sport for male aristocrats.

Unlike in Africa or the Americas, men dominated all areas of public life in Europe. A few women—notably Queen Elizabeth I of England—achieved status or power by right of birth, but the vast majority were excluded from positions of authority. European women also generally held inferior social, religious, and economic positions, yet they wielded power in their own households over children and servants. In contrast to the freedom children enjoyed in Native American families, European children were tightly controlled and subjected to harsh discipline.

Christianity was the dominant European religion. In the West, authority rested in the Catholic Church, based in Rome and led by the pope, who then as now directed a wholly male and officially celibate clergy. Although Europeans were, until the sixteenth century, nominally Catholic, many adhered to local belief systems that the church deemed heretical but failed to extinguish. Kings allied themselves with the church when it suited them, but often acted independently. Yet even so, the Christian nations of Europe from the twelfth century on publicly united in a goal of driving non-Christians (especially Muslims) not only from the European continent but also from the holy city of Jerusalem, which caused the series of wars known as the Crusades. Nevertheless, in the fifteenth century, Muslims dominated the commerce and geography of the Mediterranean world, especially after they conquered Constantinople (capital of the Christian Byzantine empire) in 1453. Few would have predicted that Christian Europeans would ever challenge that dominance.

1-4b Effects of Plague and Warfare

When the fifteenth century began, European nations were slowly recovering from the devastating epidemic known as the Black Death, which first struck in 1346. This plague seems to have arrived in Europe from China, traveling with long-distance traders along the Silk Road. The disease then recurred with particular severity in the 1360s and 1370s. Although no precise figures are available and the impact of the Black Death varied from region to region, the best estimate is that fully one-third of Europe's people died during those terrible years. A precipitous economic decline followed—in some regions more than half of the workers had died—as did severe social, political, and religious disruption because of the deaths of clergymen and other leading figures.

As plague ravaged the population, England and France waged the Hundred Years' War (1337–1453), which began after English monarchs claimed the French throne. The war interrupted overland trade routes connecting England and Antwerp (in modern Belgium) to Venice, and thence to India and China. England, on the periphery of the Mediterranean commercial core, exported wool and cloth to Antwerp in exchange for spices and silks from the East. Needing a new way to reach their northern trading partners, eastern Mediterranean merchants forged a maritime route to Antwerp. Using a triangular, or lateen, sail (rather than then-standard square rigging) improved the maneuverability of ships, enabling vessels to sail north around the European coast. Maritime navigation also improved through the acquisition of a Chinese invention, the compass, and the perfection of instruments like the astrolabe and the quadrant, which allowed sailors to gauge their latitude by measuring the relationship of the sun, moon, or certain stars to the horizon.

Everyday scenes, illuminated page from Book of Hours of King Don Manuel I, manuscript, Portugal 16th Century/DE AGOSTINI EDITORE/Bridgeman Images

△ Daily life in early sixteenth-century Portugal, as illustrated in a manuscript prayer book. At top a prosperous family shares a meal being served by an enslaved African. Other scenes show male laborers clearing land and hunting birds (left) and chopping wood (right), while at bottom a woman plants seeds in a prepared bed and in the top background female servants work in the kitchen.

1-4c Political and Technological Change

After the Hundred Years' War, European monarchs forcefully consolidated their previously diffuse political power and raised new revenues by increasing the taxes they levied on an already hard-pressed peasantry. The long military struggle led to new pride in national identity, which began to eclipse prevailing regional and dynastic loyalties. In England, Henry VII in 1485 founded the Tudor dynasty and began uniting a divided land. In France, the successors of Charles VII made the kingdom more cohesive. Most successful of all were Ferdinand of Aragón and Isabella of Castile, who married in 1469, founding a strongly Catholic and increasingly unified Spain. In 1492, they defeated the Muslims who had lived in Spain and Portugal for centuries, and expelled all Jews and Muslims from their domain.

The fifteenth century also brought technological change to Europe. **Movable type** and the **printing press**, invented in Germany in the 1450s, made information more accessible over wider distances. Printing stimulated Europeans' curiosity about fabled lands across the seas, lands they could now read about in books. The most important such works were Ptolemy's *Geography*, a description of the known world written in ancient times, first published in 1475; and Marco Polo's *Travels*, published in 1477. The *Travels* recounted the Venetian merchant's adventures in thirteenth-century China and intriguingly described that nation as bordered on the east by an ocean. Polo's account circulated widely among educated elites, first in manuscript and later in print. The book led many Europeans to believe they could reach China in oceangoing vessels instead of relying on the Silk Road or the Spice Route overland across East Africa. A transoceanic route, if it existed, would allow northern Europeans to circumvent the Muslim and Venetian merchants who had long controlled their access to Asian goods.

1-4d Motives for Exploration

Technological advances and the growing strength of newly powerful national rulers catalyzed the European explorations of the fifteenth and sixteenth centuries. Each country craved easy access to African and Asian goods—silk, dyes, perfumes, jewels, sugar, gold, and especially spices. Pepper, cloves, cinnamon, and nutmeg were desirable not only for seasoning food but also because they were believed to have medicinal and magical properties. Their allure stemmed largely from their rarity, their extraordinary cost, and their mysterious origins. They passed through so many hands en route to London or Seville that no European knew exactly where they came from. (Nutmeg, for example, grew only on nine tiny islands in the Moluccas, now eastern Indonesia.) Avoiding intermediaries in Venice and Constantinople, and acquiring such valuable products directly, would improve a nation's balance of trade and its standing relative to other countries, in addition to supplying its wealthy leaders with coveted luxury items that bolstered their power.

A concern for spreading Christianity around the world supplemented these economic motives. The linking of material and spiritual goals may seem contradictory, but fifteenth-century Europeans saw no necessary conflict between the two. Explorers and colonizers—especially Roman Catholics—sought to convert "heathen" peoples to Christianity. At the same time, they hoped to increase their nation's wealth by establishing direct trade with Africa, China, India, and the Moluccas.

1-5 Early European Explorations

▷ **What navigational tools and techniques enabled Europeans to engage in exploration?**

▷ **What were the consequences of early European exploration?**

To establish that trade, European mariners first had to explore the oceans. Seafarers needed not just the maneuverable vessels and navigational aids increasingly used in the fourteenth century but also knowledge of the sea, its currents, and especially its winds, which powered their ships. Where would Atlantic breezes carry their square-rigged ships, which, even with the addition of a triangular sail, needed to run before the wind (that is, to have the wind directly behind the vessel)?

1-5a Sailing the Mediterranean Atlantic

Europeans honed new navigation techniques in the region called the Mediterranean Atlantic, the expanse of ocean located south and west of Spain and bounded by the islands of the Azores (on the west) and the Canaries (on the south), with the Madeiras in their midst (see Map 1.4). Europeans reached all three sets of islands during the fourteenth century—first the Canaries in the 1330s, then the Madeiras and the Azores. The Canaries proved a popular destination for mariners from Iberia, the peninsula that includes Spain and Portugal. Sailing to the Canaries from Europe was easy, because strong winds known as the Northeast Trades blow southward along the Iberian and African coastlines. The voyage took about a week, and the volcanic peaks on the islands made them easy to spot.

The problem was getting back. The Iberian sailor attempting to return home faced a major obstacle: the winds that had brought him so quickly to the Canaries now blew directly at him. Confronted by contrary winds, mariners had traditionally waited for the wind to change, but the Northeast Trades blew steadily. So they developed a new method: sailing "around the wind." That meant sailing as directly against the wind as was possible without being forced to change course. In the Mediterranean Atlantic, a mariner would head northwest into the open ocean, until—weeks later—he reached the winds that would carry him home, the so-called Westerlies.

---

movable type Type in which each character is cast on a separate piece of metal.

printing press A machine that transfers lettering or images by contact with various forms of inked surface onto paper or similar material fed into it in various ways.

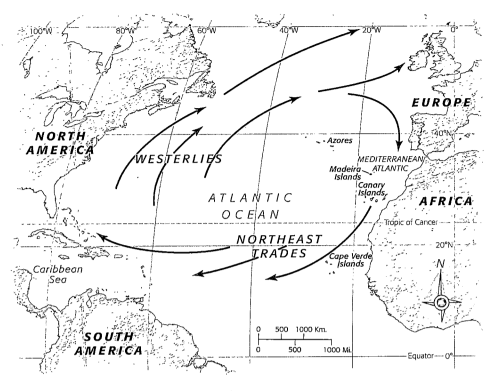

Map 1.4 Atlantic Winds and Islands

European mariners had to explore the oceans before they could find new lands. The first realm they discovered was that of Atlantic winds and islands.

Those winds blow (we now know) northward along the coast of North America before heading east toward Europe.

This solution must at first have seemed to defy common sense, but it became the key to successful exploration of both the Atlantic and the Pacific oceans. Once a sailor understood the winds and their allied currents, he no longer feared leaving Europe without being able to return.

1-5b Islands of the Mediterranean Atlantic

During the fifteenth century, armed with knowledge of the winds and currents of the Mediterranean Atlantic, Iberian seamen regularly visited the three island groups, which they could reach in two weeks or less. The uninhabited Azores were soon settled by Portuguese migrants, who raised wheat for sale in Europe and sold livestock to passing sailors. The Madeiras also had no Native peoples, and by the 1450s Portuguese colonists were employing slaves (probably Jews and Muslims from Iberia) to grow sugar for export to the mainland. By the 1470s, Madeira had developed a colonial **plantation** economy. For the first time in world history, a region was settled explicitly to cultivate a valuable crop—sugar—to be sold elsewhere. Moreover, because the work involved in large-scale plantation agriculture was so backbreaking, only a supply of enslaved laborers (who could not opt to quit) could ensure the system's continued success.

The Canaries did have indigenous residents—the Guanche people, who began trading animal skins and dyes with their European visitors. After 1402, the French, Portuguese, and Spanish began sporadically attacking the islands. The Guanches resisted vigorously, even though they were weakened by their susceptibility to alien European diseases. One by one, the seven islands fell to Europeans who then carried off Guanches as slaves to the Madeiras or Iberia. Spain conquered the last island in 1496 and subsequently converted the land into sugar plantations. Collectively, the Canaries and Madeira became known as the Wine Islands because much of their sugar production was used to fortify sweet wines.

1-5c Portuguese Trading Posts in Africa

While some European rulers and traders concentrated on exploiting the islands of the Mediterranean Atlantic, others used them as stepping-stones to Africa. In 1415, Portugal seized control of Ceuta, a Muslim city in North Africa (see Map 1.2). Prince Henry the Navigator, son of King John I of Portugal, knew that vast wealth awaited the first European nation to tap the riches of Africa and Asia directly. Repeatedly, he dispatched ships southward along the African coast, attempting to discover an oceanic route to Asia. But not until after Prince Henry's death did Bartholomew Dias round the southern tip of Africa (1488) and Vasco da Gama finally reach India (1498).

plantation A large-scale agricultural enterprise growing commercial crops and often employing coerced or slave labor.

At Malabar, da Gama located the richest source of peppercorns in the world.

Long before that, Portugal reaped the benefits of its seafarers' voyages. Although West African states successfully resisted European penetration of the interior, they allowed the Portuguese to establish coastal trading posts. Charging the traders rent and levying duties on goods they imported, the African kingdoms benefited considerably from easier access to European manufactures. The Portuguese gained, too, for they no longer had to rely on trans-Saharan camel caravans. Their vessels earned immense profits by swiftly transporting African gold, ivory, and slaves to Europe. By bargaining with African masters to purchase their slaves and then carrying those bondspeople to Iberia, the Portuguese introduced black slavery into Europe.

1-5d Lessons of Early Colonization

An island off the African coast, previously uninhabited, proved critical to Portuguese success. In the 1480s, the Portuguese colonized São Tomé, located in the Gulf of Guinea (see Map 1.2). By that time, Madeira had reached the limit of its capacity to produce sugar. The soil of São Tomé proved ideal for raising that valuable crop, and plantation agriculture there expanded rapidly. Planters imported large numbers of slaves from the mainland to work in the cane fields, thus creating the first economy based primarily on the bondage of black Africans.

By the 1490s, even before Christopher Columbus set sail to the west, Europeans had learned three key lessons of colonization in the Mediterranean Atlantic. First, they had learned how to transplant their crops and livestock successfully to exotic locations. Second, they had discovered that the Native peoples of those lands could be either conquered (like the Guanches) or exploited (like the Africans). Third, they had developed a viable model of plantation slavery and a system for supplying nearly unlimited quantities of such workers. The stage was set for a pivotal moment in world history.

1-6 Voyages of Columbus, Cabot, and Their Successors

▶ **What was the relationship between explorers and European monarchs?**

▶ **What knowledge of the wider world did European explorers gain?**

Christopher Columbus was well schooled in the lessons of the Mediterranean Atlantic. Born in 1451 in the Italian city-state of Genoa, this largely self-educated son of a wool merchant was by the 1490s an experienced sailor and mapmaker. Like many

Christopher Columbus Genoese explorer who claimed the island of San Salvador in the Bahamas and other places in the Caribbean and Central America for the king and queen of Spain.

mariners of the day, he was drawn to Portugal and its islands, especially Madeira, where he commanded a merchant vessel. At least once he sailed to the Portuguese outpost on Africa's Gold Coast. There he became obsessed with gold, and there he came to understand the economic potential of the slave trade.

Like all accomplished seafarers, Columbus knew the world was round. But he differed from other cartographers in his estimate of the earth's size: he thought that China lay only three thousand miles from Europe's southern coast. Thus, he argued, it would be easier to reach Asia by sailing west than by making the difficult voyage around the southern tip of Africa. Experts scoffed at this crackpot notion, accurately predicting that the two continents lay twelve thousand miles apart. When Columbus in 1484 asked the Portuguese rulers to back his plan to sail west to Asia, they rejected what appeared to be a crazy scheme.

1-6a Columbus's Voyage

Jealous of rival Portugal's successes in Africa, Spain's Ferdinand and Isabella were more receptive to Columbus's ideas. Urged on by some Spanish noblemen and a group of Italian merchants residing in Castile, the monarchs agreed to finance most of the risky voyage—Columbus himself would have to pay a quarter of the costs. They hoped the profits would pay for a new expedition to conquer Muslim-held Jerusalem. And so, on August 3, 1492, Columbus set sail from the Spanish port of Palos in command of three ships—the *Pinta*, the *Niña*, and the *Santa Maria*.

The first part of the journey was familiar, for the ships steered down the Northeast Trades to the Canary Islands. There Columbus refitted his ships, adding triangular sails to make them more maneuverable. On September 6, the flotilla weighed anchor and headed into the unknown ocean. The sailors were anxious about the winds, the waves, and the distance. To stave off panic, Columbus lied, underreporting the number of nautical miles the convoy covered each day. He kept two sets of logbooks, an early chronicler remembered, "one false and the other true."

Just over a month later, the vessels found land approximately where Columbus thought Cipangu (Japan) was located (see Map 1.5). On October 12, he and his men anchored off an island in the present-day Bahamas, called Guanahaní by its inhabitants. The admiral and members of his crew went ashore with guns drawn. Planting a flag bearing a Christian cross and the initials of Ferdinand and Isabella, Columbus claimed the territory for Spain and renamed Guanahaní San Salvador. (Because Columbus's description of his landfall can be variously interpreted, several different places today claim to be his landing site.) Later, he went on to explore the islands now known as Cuba and Hispaniola, which the Native Taíno people called Colba and Bohío. Because he thought he had reached the East Indies (the Spice Islands), Columbus referred to the inhabitants of the region as "Indians," a mistake that continues to reverberate even today. The Taínos thought the Europeans had come from the sky, and wherever Columbus

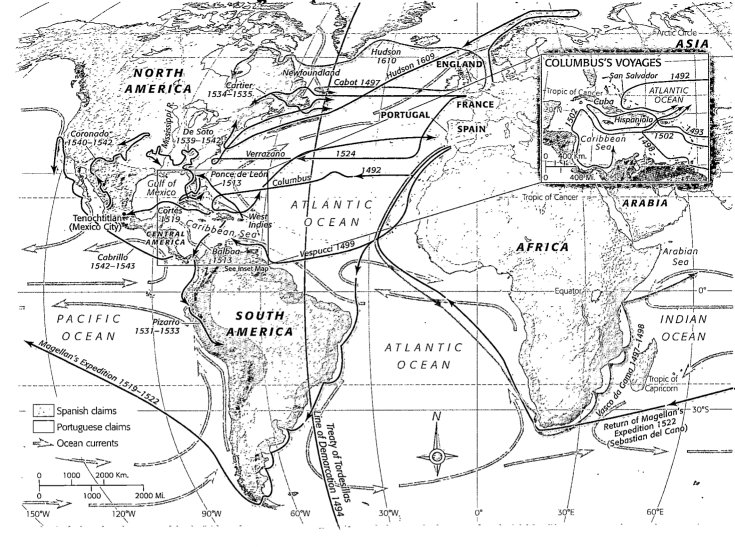

Map 1.5 European Explorations in America

In the century following Columbus's voyages, European adventurers explored the coasts and parts of the interior of North and South America.

went crowds of curious Taínos gathered to meet and exchange gifts with him.

1-6b Columbus's Observations

Three themes predominate in Columbus's log, the major source of information on this first recorded encounter between Europe and what would come to be called the Americas. First, he was eager to exploit the region's natural resources. He insistently asked the Taínos where he could find gold, pearls, and spices. Each time, his informants replied (via signs) that such products could be obtained on other islands or on the mainland. Eventually, he came to mistrust such answers, noting, "I am beginning to believe . . . they will tell me anything I want to hear."

Second, Columbus was amazed by the strange and beautiful plants and animals he encountered. "Here the fishes are so unlike ours that it is amazing . . . . The colors are so bright that anyone would marvel," he noted. "The song of the little birds might make a man wish never to leave here." Yet Columbus's interest was not only aesthetic.

"I believe that there are many plants and trees here that could be worth a lot in Spain for use as dyes, spices, and medicines," he observed, adding that he was carrying home to Europe "a sample of everything I can," so that experts could examine them.

Included in his cargo of curiosities were some of the islands' human residents, whom Columbus also evaluated as resources to answer European needs. The Taínos were, he said, handsome, gentle, and friendly, though they told him of the fierce Caniba (today called Caribs) who lived on other islands, raided their villages, and ate their captives (hence today's word *cannibal*). Although Columbus feared and distrusted the Caribs, he saw the Taínos as likely converts to Catholicism, remarking that "if devout religious persons knew the Indian language well, all these people would soon become Christians." In his mind, conversion was the ally of enslavement. The islanders "ought to make good and skilled servants," Columbus declared. It would be easy to "subject everyone and make them do what you wished."

Naming America

In 1507, German cartographer Martin Waldseemüller created the first map to label the newly discovered landmass on the western side of the Atlantic as "America." He named the continent after Amerigo Vespucci, the Italian explorer who realized he had reached a "new world" rather than islands off the coast of Asia. Waldseemüller's map appeared in a short book called *Cosmographiae Introductio, or Introduction to Cosmography*—the study of the known world. The globe he illustrated was both familiar and new. The sun revolved around the earth, as scholars had believed for a millennium. Yet the voyages of Columbus, Vespucci, and others had reconfigured the earth.

When the twelve sheets of Waldseemüller's map are put together, the image stretches nearly five by eight feet. One of the largest printed maps ever then produced, it includes an astonishing level of detail.

CRITICAL THINKING

☐ What symbols indicate European territorial claims in America and Africa?

☐ Why might Africa be shown as the center of the known world?

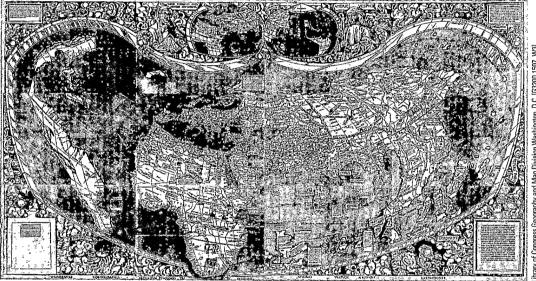

◁ *Waldseemüller map*

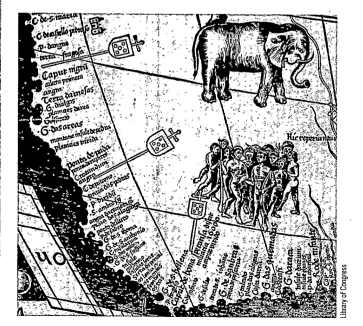

△ *African peoples*

△ *America*

The records of the first encounter between Europeans and Americans revealed themes that would be of enormous significance for centuries to come. Europeans marveled at the new world, and they wanted to extract profits by exploiting American resources, including plants, animals, and people alike. Later explorers would follow Columbus's tendency to divide Native peoples into "good" (Taínos) and "bad" (Caribs).

Columbus made three more voyages, exploring most of the major Caribbean islands and sailing along the coasts of Central and South America. Until the day he died, in 1506 at the age of fifty-five, he believed he had reached Asia.

Others knew better. The Florentine merchant Amerigo Vespucci, who explored the South American coast in 1499, was the first to promote the idea that a new continent had been discovered. In 1502 or 1503, versions of Vespucci's letters were printed in Florence under the title *Mundus Novus*—"new world." By then, Spain, Portugal, and Pope Alexander VI had signed the Treaty of Tordesillas (1494), confirming Portugal's dominance in Africa—and later Brazil—in exchange for Spanish preeminence in the rest of the Western Hemisphere.

1-6c Norse and Other Northern Voyagers

Five hundred years before Columbus, about the year 1001, a **Norse** expedition under Leif Ericsson sailed to North America across the Davis Strait, which separated Greenland from Baffin Island (located northeast of Hudson Bay; see Map 1.1) by just 200 nautical miles. They settled at a site they named "**Vinland**," but attacks by local residents forced them to abandon it after just a few years. In the 1960s, archaeologists determined that the Norse had established an outpost at what is now L'Anse aux Meadows, Newfoundland. Vinland was probably located farther south.

Later European explorers knew nothing of the earlier Norse voyages, but some historians argue that during the fifteenth century, whalers and fishermen from the Basque country (modern southern France and northern Spain) located rich fishing grounds off Newfoundland but kept the information secret. Whether or not fishermen crossed the entire Atlantic, they thoroughly explored its northern reaches, sailing regularly between Europe, England, Ireland, and Iceland. The mariners who explored the region of North America that was to become the United States and Canada built on their knowledge.

The winds that the northern sailors confronted posed problems on their outbound rather than on their homeward journeys. The same Westerlies that carried Columbus back to Europe blew in the faces of northerners looking west. But mariners soon learned that the strongest winds shifted southward during the winter. By departing from northern ports in the spring, they could make adequate headway if they steered northward. Thus, whereas the first landfall of most sailors to the south was somewhere in the Caribbean, those taking the northern route usually reached North America along the coast of today's Maine or Canada.

1-6d John Cabot's Explorations

The European generally credited with "discovering" mainland North America is Zuan Cabboto, known today as **John Cabot**. Cabot brought to Europe the first formal knowledge of the northern continental coastline and claimed the land for England. Like Columbus, Cabot was a master mariner from the Italian city-state of Genoa; the two men probably knew each other. Calculating that England—which traded with Asia only through a long series of intermediaries—would be eager to sponsor exploratory voyages, he gained financial backing from King Henry VII. He set sail from Bristol in May 1497 in the *Mathew*, reaching North America about a month later. After exploring the coast of modern Newfoundland for a month, Cabot rode the Westerlies back to England, arriving just fifteen days after he left North America.

The voyages of Columbus, Cabot, and their successors brought the Eastern and Western Hemispheres together. Portuguese explorer Pedro Álvares Cabral reached Brazil in 1500; John Cabot's son Sebastian followed his father to North America in 1507; France financed Giovanni da Verrazzano in 1524 and Jacques Cartier in 1534; and in 1609 and 1610, Henry Hudson explored the North American coast for the Dutch West India Company (see Map 1.5). All were searching primarily for the legendary "Northwest Passage" through the Americas, hoping to find an easy water route to the riches of Asia. (Nonexistent in early modern days, the Northwest passage may soon become a reality because of global warming.) But in a sign of what was to come, Verrazzano observed, "the [American] countryside is, in fact, full of promise and deserves to be developed for itself."

1-7 Spanish Exploration and Conquest

▶ Why did Spaniards conquer parts of the Americas?

▶ What was the Spanish method of colonization in the Americas?

▶ What was the impact of the Spanish discovery and control of silver deposits in the Americas?

Only in the areas that Spain explored and claimed did colonization begin immediately. On his second voyage in 1493, Columbus brought to Hispaniola seventeen ships loaded with twelve hundred men, along with seeds,

Norse Also known as Vikings, they were members of a warrior culture from Scandinavia.

Vinland The site of the first known attempt at European settlement in the Americas.

John Cabot Italian explorer who established English claims to the "New World."

plants, livestock, chickens, and dogs—as well as microbes, rats, and weeds. The settlement he named Isabela (in the modern Dominican Republic) and its successors became the staging area for the Spanish invasion of America, an often brutal and highly centralized conquest. On the islands of Cuba and Hispaniola, the Europeans and the animals they imported learned to adapt to the new environment. When the Spaniards moved on to explore the mainland, they rode island-bred horses and ate island-bred cattle and hogs.

1-7a Cortés and Other Explorers

At first, Spanish explorers fanned out around the Caribbean basin. In 1513, Juan Ponce de León reached Florida, and Vasco Núñez de Balboa crossed the Isthmus of Panama to the Pacific Ocean, followed by Pánfilo de Narváez and others who traced the coast of the Gulf of Mexico. In the 1530s and 1540s, **conquistadors** traveled farther, exploring many regions claimed by the Spanish monarchs: Francisco Vásquez de Coronado journeyed through the southwestern portion of what is now the United States at approximately the same time that Hernán de Soto explored the Southeast. Juan Rodríguez Cabrillo sailed along the California coast. Francisco Pizarro, who ventured into western South America, acquired the richest silver mines in the world by conquering the Incas. But the most important conquistador was Hernán Cortés, a Spanish notary who first arrived in the Caribbean in 1506. In 1519, he led a force of roughly six hundred men from Cuba to the Mexican mainland to search for rumored wealthy cities.

1-7b Capture of Tenochtitlán

As he traveled on horseback toward the Aztec capital, Cortés, speaking through Doña Marina and other interpreters, recruited peoples whom the Aztecs had long subjugated. The Spaniards' huge domesticated beasts and noisy weapons awed their new allies. Yet the Spaniards, too, were awed. Years later, Bernal Díaz del Castillo recalled his first sight of Tenochtitlán, built on islands in Lake Texcoco: "We were amazed and said that it was like the enchantments ... on account of the great towers and cues [temples] and buildings rising from the water, and all built of masonry." Soldiers wondered "whether the things that we saw were not a dream."

The Spaniards came to Tenochtitlán not only with horses and guns but also with smallpox, transmitting an epidemic that had begun on Hispaniola. The disease peaked in 1520, fatally weakening Tenochtitlán's defenders.

"It spread over the people as great destruction," an Aztec later remembered. "There was great havoc. Very many died of it." Largely as a consequence, Tenochtitlán surrendered

conquistadors Spanish conquerors or adventurers in the Americas.

encomienda Spanish system which awarded Native peoples' labor to wealthy colonists.

in 1521, and the Spaniards built Mexico City on its site. Cortés and his men seized a fabulous treasure of gold and silver. Thus, less than three decades after Columbus's first voyage, the Spanish monarchs—who treated the American territories as their personal possessions—controlled the richest, most extensive empire Europe had known since ancient Rome.

1-7c Spanish Colonization

Spain established the model of colonization that other countries later imitated, a model with three major elements. First, the Crown tried to maintain tight control over the colonies, imposing a hierarchical government that allowed little autonomy to remote jurisdictions. That control included, for example, carefully vetting prospective emigrants and limiting their number. Settlers were then required to live in towns under the authorities' watchful eyes, and to import all their manufactured goods from Spain. Roman Catholic priests dispatched to the new territories attempted to ensure the colonists' conformity with orthodox religious views.

Second, men comprised most of the first colonists. Although some Spanish women later immigrated to America, the men took primarily indigenous—and, later, African—women as their wives or concubines, a development more often than not encouraged by colonial administrators. They thereby began creating the racially mixed population that characterizes much of Latin America to the present day.

Third, the colonies' wealth was based on the exploitation of both the Native population and slaves imported from Africa. Spaniards took over the role once assumed by Native leaders who had exacted labor and tribute from their subjects. Cortés established the **encomienda system**, which granted indigenous villages to individual conquistadors as a reward for their services, thus legalizing slavery in all but name.

In 1542, after stinging criticism from a colonial priest, Bartolomé de las Casas, the Spanish monarch formulated a new code of laws to reform the system, forbidding the conquerors from enslaving Native peoples while still allowing them to collect money and goods from tributary villages. In response to the restrictions and to the declining indigenous populations, the *encomenderos*, familiar with slavery in Spain, began to import kidnapped Africans in order to increase the labor force under their direct control. They employed Native peoples and Africans primarily in gold and silver mines, on sugar plantations, and on huge horse, cattle, and sheep ranches. African slavery was far more common on the larger Caribbean islands than on the mainland.

Many demoralized residents of Mesoamerica accepted the Christian religion brought to New Spain by Franciscan and Dominican friars—men who had joined religious orders bound by vows of poverty and celibacy. The friars devoted their energies to persuading indigenous peoples to

Snark/Art Resource, NY

△ An image from the Codex Azcatitlan, an account of the Aztec (Mexica) people's history from their arrival in the Valley of Mexico through the conquest by Cortés. Printed European-style in the late sixteenth century—that is, about seven decades after the conquest—the codex nonetheless presents a Native viewpoint on the cataclysmic events. Here Cortés and his men are preceded by Malinche, his interpreter and mistress, and followed by their Native allies bearing food supplies. Also in the crowd is Cortés's black slave.

move into towns and to build Roman Catholic churches. Spaniards leveled existing cities, constructing cathedrals and monasteries on sites once occupied by Aztec, Incan, and Mayan temples. In such towns, Native peoples were exposed to European customs and religious rituals designed to assimilate Catholic and pagan beliefs. Friars deliberately juxtaposed the cult of the Virgin Mary with that of the corn goddess, and Native peoples adeptly melded aspects of their traditional worldview with Christianity, in a process anthropologists call *syncretism*. Thousands of indigenous men and women residing in Spanish territory embraced Catholicism, at least partly because it was the religion of their new rulers and they were accustomed to obedience.

1-7d Gold, Silver, and Spain's Decline

The New World's rich deposits of gold and silver, initially a boon, ultimately brought about the decline of Spain as a

major power. China, a huge country with silver coinage, insatiably demanded Spanish silver, gobbling up an estimated half of the total output of New World mines while paying twice the price current in Europe. In the 1570s, the Spanish began to dispatch silver-laden galleons annually from Acapulco (on Mexico's west coast) across the Pacific Ocean to trade at their new settlement at Manila, in the Philippines. This gave Spaniards easy access to luxury Chinese goods such as silk and Asian spices.

But the influx of wealth led to rapid inflation, which caused Spanish products to be overpriced in international markets and imported goods to become cheaper in Spain. The once-profitable Spanish textile industry collapsed. The seemingly endless income from American colonies also emboldened Spanish monarchs to spend lavishly on wars against the Dutch and the English. Several times in the late sixteenth and early seventeenth centuries, the monarchs repudiated the state debt, wreaking havoc on the nation's finances. When the South American gold and silver mines started to give out in the mid-seventeenth century, Spain's economy crumbled, and the nation lost much of its international importance.

1-8 The Columbian Exchange

▶ **What was the Columbian Exchange?**

▶ **What were the consequences of the Columbian Exchange for the peoples on both sides of the Atlantic?**

A broad mutual transfer of diseases, plants, and animals (called the **Columbian Exchange** by historian Alfred Crosby; see Map 1.6) resulted directly from the European voyages of the fifteenth and sixteenth centuries and from Spanish colonization. Separated for millennia, the

Columbian Exchange The widespread exchange, both deliberate and accidental, of animals, plants, germs, and peoples between Europe, Africa, and the Americas.

Eastern and Western Hemispheres had developed widely different life forms. Many large mammals, such as cattle and horses, were native to the connected continents of Europe, Asia, and Africa, while the Americas contained no domesticated beasts larger than dogs and llamas. The vegetable crops of the Americas—particularly maize, beans, squash, cassava, and potatoes—were more nutritious and produced higher yields than Europe's and Africa's wheat, millet, and rye. In time, Native peoples learned to raise and consume European livestock, and Europeans and Africans became accustomed to planting and eating American crops. (About three-fifths of all crops cultivated in the world today were first grown in the Americas.) The diets of ordinary people in all three parts of the globe were consequently vastly enriched. Partly as a result, the world's population doubled over the next three hundred years. The pressure of increased population in Europe propelled further waves of settler colonists westward, keeping the exchange in motion.

1-8a Smallpox and Other Diseases

Diseases carried west from Europe and Africa had a devastating impact on the Americas. Native peoples fell victim to microbes that had long infested the other continents and had

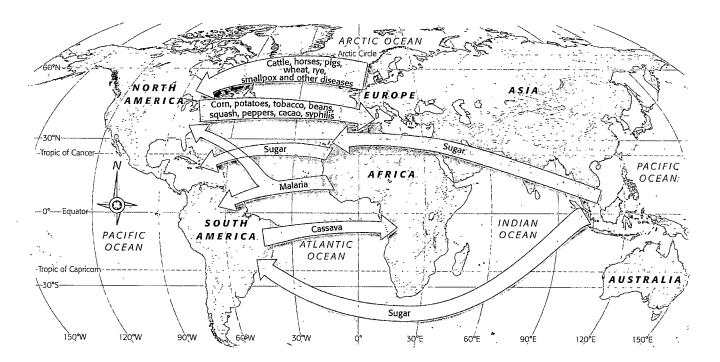

Map 1.6 Major Items in the Columbian Exchange

As European adventurers traversed the world in the fifteenth and sixteenth centuries, they initiated the "Columbian Exchange" of plants, animals, and diseases. These events changed the lives of the peoples of the world forever, bringing new foods and new pestilence to both sides of the Atlantic.

repeatedly killed hundreds of thousands but had also often left survivors with some measure of immunity. It was not only their isolation that made the indigenous populations of the Americas vulnerable, however. Non-biological processes, especially contacts forged through slave-trading and other forms of long-distance commerce, exacerbated the power of microbes and furthered the dramatic depopulation trend. When Columbus landed on Hispaniola in 1492, approximately half a million people resided there. Fifty years later, that island had fewer than two thousand Native inhabitants. Within thirty years of the first landfall at Guanahaní, not one Taíno survived in the Bahamas.

Although measles, typhus, influenza, malaria, and other illnesses severely afflicted the Native peoples, the greatest of the new infectious killers was smallpox, spread primarily by direct human contact. Epidemics recurred at twenty- or thirty-year intervals, when bouts often appeared in quick succession, so that weakened survivors of one wave would be felled by a second or third. Large numbers of deaths further disrupted societies already undergoing severe strains caused by colonization, rendering Native peoples more vulnerable to droughts, crop failures, and European invaders.

Even far to the north, where smaller American populations encountered only a few Europeans, disease ravaged the countryside. A great epidemic, probably viral hepatitis, swept through the villages along the coast north of Cape Cod from 1616 to 1618. Again, the mortality rate may have been as high as 90 percent. An English traveler several years later commented that the people had "died on heapes, as they lay in their houses." Bones and skulls covered the ruins of villages. Just a few years after this dramatic depopulation of the area, English colonists were able to establish settlements virtually unopposed. Disease made a powerful if accidental ally.

The Americans, though, seem to have taken an unintended revenge. They probably gave the Europeans syphilis, a virulent sexually transmitted disease. The first recorded European case of the ailment occurred in 1493 in Spain, shortly after Columbus's return from the Caribbean. Although less likely than smallpox to cause immediate death, syphilis was dangerous and debilitating. Carried by soldiers, sailors, and prostitutes, it spread quickly through Europe and Asia, reaching China by 1505.

1-8b Sugar, Horses, and Tobacco

The exchange of three commodities had significant impacts on Europe and the Americas. Sugar, first domesticated in the East Indies, was being grown on the islands of the Mediterranean Atlantic by 1450. The ravenous European demand for sugar—a medicine that quickly became a luxury foodstuff—led Columbus to take Canary Island sugar canes to Hispaniola on his 1493 voyage. By the 1520s, plantations in the Greater Antilles worked by African slaves regularly shipped cargoes of sugar to Spain. Half

△ A male effigy dating from 200–800 CE, found in a burial site in Nayarit, Mexico. The lesions covering the figurine suggest that the person it represents is suffering from syphilis, which, untreated, produces these characteristic markings on the body in its later stages. Such evidence as this pre-Columbian effigy has now convinced most scholars that syphilis originated in the Americas—a hypothesis in dispute for many years.

a century later, the Portuguese colony in Brazil (founded 1532) was producing sugar for the European market on an even larger scale. After 1640, sugar cultivation became the crucial component of English and French colonization in the Caribbean.

Horses—which, like sugar, were brought to America by Columbus in 1493—fell into the hands of Native peoples in North America during the seventeenth century. Through trade and theft, horses spread among the peoples of the Great Plains, reaching most areas by 1750. Lakotas, Comanches, and Crows, among others, came to use horses for transportation and hunting, calculated their wealth in number of horses owned, and waged war primarily on horseback. Some groups that previously had cultivated crops abandoned agriculture. Because of the acquisition of horses, a mode of subsistence that had been based on hunting several different animals, in combination with gathering and agriculture, became one focused almost wholly on hunting buffalo.

In America, Europeans encountered tobacco, which at first they believed to have beneficial medicinal effects. Smoking and chewing the "Indian weed" became a fad in Europe in the sixteenth century. Despite the efforts of

△ The mysterious illustrated text known as the Drake Manuscript and formally titled *Histoire Naturelle des Indies* (*Natural History of the Indies*) contains many depictions of the culture of the indigenous people of Spanish America in the 1580s. This delightful scene shows the end of a successful courtship: the woman's father sits under a tree while giving his blessing to the young couple. The future husband has proved his prowess as a hunter (note the rabbit in his hand) and the future wife her ability as a cook (she is grinding corn). Both are well dressed, and the pot boiling in the house in the background suggests a prosperous future for the happy pair.

such skeptics as King James I of England, who in 1604 pronounced smoking "loathsome to the eye, hatefull to the Nose, harmfull to the brain, [and] dangerous to the Lungs," tobacco's popularity soared. By the early seventeenth century, Englishmen could smoke the leaves at as many as seven thousand tobacco "houses" in London alone. At that point, the supply of the noxious weed came entirely from the colonies of New Spain.

The European and African invasion of the Americas therefore had a significant biological component, for the invaders carried plants and animals with them in both directions. Some creatures, such as livestock, they brought intentionally. Others, including rats (which infested their ships), weeds, and diseases, arrived unexpectedly. And the same process occurred in reverse. When Europeans returned home, they deliberately took crops including maize, potatoes, and tobacco, along with that unanticipated stowaway, syphilis.

1-9 Europeans in North America

▷ **What kinds of economic exchanges occurred between Native peoples and Europeans?**

▷ **How did exploration and engagement with the American continent and its peoples affect the relationship between Spain and England?**

▷ **Why did early English attempts at colonization fail?**

Europeans were initially more interested in exploiting North America's natural resources than in establishing colonies there. John Cabot had reported that fish were extraordinarily plentiful near Newfoundland, so Europeans rushed to take advantage of abundant codfish, which were in great demand as an inexpensive source of protein.

Maize

Mesoamericans believed that maize was a gift from Quetzalcoatl, the plumed serpent god. Cherokees told of an old woman whose blood produced the prized stalks after her grandson buried her body in a cleared, sunny field. For the Abenakis, the crop began when a beautiful maiden ordered a youth to drag her by the hair through a burned-over field. The long hair of the Cherokee grandmother and the Abenaki maiden turned into corn silk, the flower on the stalks that Europeans called "Indian" corn. Both tales' symbolic association of corn and women intriguingly supports archaeologists' recent suggestion that—in eastern North America

at least—female plant breeders substantially improved the productivity of maize.

Maize was a major part of the ancient American diet, sacred to the Native peoples who grew it. Ground into meal, dried maize was cooked as a mush or shaped into baked flat cakes, the forerunners of modern tortillas. Native peoples also heated the dried kernels of some varieties until they popped open, just as is done today. Although the European invaders of North and South America initially disdained maize, they soon learned it could be cultivated in a wide variety of conditions—from sea level to elevations of twelve thousand feet, from regions with abundant rainfall to lands with very little rainfall. Corn was also highly productive, yielding almost twice as many calories per acre as wheat. So Europeans, too, came to rely on corn, growing it not only in their American settlements but also in their homelands.

Maize cultivation spread to Asia and Africa. Today, China is second only to the United States

in corn production. In Africa, corn is grown more widely than any other crop. Still, the United States produces over 40 percent of the world's corn, almost half of it in the three states of Illinois, Iowa, and Nebraska. Heavily subsidized by the federal government, corn is the nation's largest crop. More than half of American corn is consumed by livestock. Much of the rest is processed into syrup, which sweetens carbonated beverages and candies and has been linked to the spread of obesity and Type II diabetes in the modern United States. Corn is ubiquitous: an ingredient in light beer, toothpaste, and gasolines. It is used in the manufacture of tires, wallpaper, cat litter, and aspirin. Remarkably, of the ten thousand products in a modern American grocery store, about one-fourth rely to some extent on corn.

Today, this crop bequeathed to the world by ancient American plant breeders provides one-fifth of all the calories consumed by the earth's peoples. The gift of Quetzalcoatl has linked the globe.

CRITICAL THINKING

☐ The dramatic ways Europeans changed the "New World" when they arrived are well known. But the currents of change ran in the reverse direction as well. This article describes the importance of maize or corn in the Americas as well as Europe. What other ideas or products that originated in the Americas made an impact on Europe?

◁ Painted by the Englishman John White, who accompanied an expedition to the new Virginia plantation in 1585 and was later named governor of that colony, this watercolor shows three stages of the cultivation of maize in the village of Secotan. "Rype corne" appears at the top right, with "greene corne" below it, beside orderly rows of "corne newly sprong." In all three fields, the crop is carefully fenced. White's painting was a study for a printed engraving, sold to satisfy the many English readers curious about American lifeways.

French, Spanish, Basque, and Portuguese sailors regularly fished North American waters throughout the sixteenth century; Verrazzano and Cartier, in 1524 and 1534, respectively, each encountered vessels already fishing along the American coast. In the early 1570s, after Spain opened its markets to English shipping, the English (who previously had fished near Iceland for home consumption only) eagerly joined the Newfoundland fishery, thereafter selling salt cod to Spain in exchange for valuable Asian goods. The English soon became dominant in the region, which by the end of the sixteenth century was the focal point of a European commerce more valuable than that with the Gulf of Mexico.

1-9a Trade Among Native Peoples and Europeans

Fishermen quickly realized they could increase their profits by exchanging cloth and metal goods, such as pots and knives, for Native trappers' beaver pelts, used to make fashionable hats in Europe. Initially, Europeans traded from ships sailing along the coast, but later they set up outposts on the mainland to centralize and control the traffic in furs. Such outposts were inhabited chiefly by male adventurers, who aimed to send as many pelts as possible home to Europe.

The Europeans' demand for furs, especially beaver, was matched by Native peoples' desire for European goods that could make their lives easier and establish their superiority over their neighbors. Some Native groups began to concentrate so completely on trapping for the European market that they abandoned their traditional economies and became partially dependent on others for food. The intensive trade in pelts also had serious ecological consequences. In some regions, the beaver were wiped out. The disappearance of their dams led to soil erosion, which increased when European settlers cleared forests for farmland in later decades.

1-9b Contest Between Spain and England

English merchants and political leaders watched enviously as Spain was enriched by its valuable American possessions. In the mid-sixteenth century, English "sea dogs" like John Hawkins and Sir Francis Drake began to raid Spanish treasure fleets sailing home from the Caribbean. Their actions caused friction between the two countries and helped foment a war that in 1588 culminated in the defeat of a huge Spanish invasion force—the Armada—off the English coast. As part of the contest with Spain, English leaders started to think about planting colonies in the Western Hemisphere, thereby gaining better access to valuable trade goods while preventing their enemy from dominating the Americas. By the late sixteenth century, world maps labeled not only "America" but also vast territories designated "New Spain" and "New France." The glaring absence of a region called "New

England" would have been a sore spot for Queen Elizabeth I and her courtiers.

Encouraging the queen to fund increased exploration across the Atlantic was Richard Hakluyt, an English clergyman who became fascinated by tales of exploratory voyages while he was a student in the 1560s. He translated and published numerous accounts of discoveries around the globe, insisting on England's preeminent claim to the North American continent. In *Divers Voyages* (1582) and especially *Principall Navigations* (1589), he argued for the benefits of English colonization, contending that "there is none, that of right may be more bolde in this enterprice than the Englishmen."

The first English colonial planners saw Spain's possessions as a model and a challenge. They hoped to reproduce Spanish successes by dispatching to America men who would exploit the Native peoples for their own and their nation's benefit. A group that included Sir Walter Raleigh began to promote a scheme to establish outposts that could trade with Native groups and serve as bases for attacks on Spain's new world possessions. Approving the idea, Queen Elizabeth authorized Raleigh to colonize North America.

1-9c Roanoke

After two preliminary expeditions, in 1587 Raleigh sent 118 colonists to the territory that tens of thousands of Native peoples called Ossomocomuck. Raleigh renamed it Virginia, after Elizabeth, the "Virgin Queen." The group, which included a small number of women and children, established a settlement on Roanoke Island, in what is now North Carolina. Their powerful neighbors included Secotans, Weapemeocs, and Chowanocs: Algonquian-speakers who had recently suffered war and drought. In this unstable environment, Native translators—kidnapped and taken to England on earlier voyages—once again played vital roles in colonial diplomacy. Negotiation was crucial, since the small band of settlers depended heavily on Native assistance; the ships scheduled to resupply them were delayed for two years by England's war with Spain. When resupply ships finally reached the tiny village in August 1590, the colonists had vanished, leaving only the word *Croatoan* (the name of a nearby island as well as one of the area's powerful Native groups) carved on a tree. Tree-ring studies show that the North Carolina coast experienced a severe drought between 1587 and 1589, which would have created a subsistence crisis for the settlers and could have led them to abandon the Roanoke site. Recent examination of a sixteenth-century watercolor map using modern imaging techniques reveals an inland fort to which the settlers may have retreated in a desperate attempt to survive.

England's first effort at planting a permanent settlement on the North American coast failed, as had earlier ventures

△ John White identified his subjects as the wife and daughter of the chief of Pomeioc, a village near Roanoke. Note the woman's elaborate tattoos and the fact that the daughter carries an Elizabethan doll, obviously given to her by one of the Englishmen.

by Portugal on Cape Breton Island (early 1520s), Spain in modern Georgia (mid 1520s), and France in South Carolina and northern Florida (1560s). All three enterprises collapsed because of the hostility of neighboring peoples and colonists' inability to be self-sustaining in foodstuffs. The Portuguese, the Spanish, the first French settlers, and the English failed to maintain friendly relations with indigenous peoples, and Spanish soldiers destroyed the Florida French colony in 1565 (see Section 2-1, "Spanish, French, and Dutch North America").

1-9d Harriot's *Briefe and True Report*

The reasons for such failings become clear in Thomas Harriot's *A Briefe and True Report of the New Found Land of Virginia*, published in 1588 to publicize Raleigh's colony. Harriot, a noted scientist who sailed with the second of the preliminary voyages to Roanoke, described the animals, plants, and people of the region. His account reveals that, although the explorers depended on nearby villagers for most of their food, they needlessly antagonized their neighbors by killing some of them for what Harriot admitted were unjustifiable reasons.

Harriot advised later colonizers to deal more humanely with Native peoples. But his book also reveals why that advice would rarely be followed. *A Briefe and True Report* examined the possibilities for economic development in America. Harriot stressed three points: the availability of valuable commodities, the potential profitability of exotic American products, and the relative ease of manipulating the Native population. Should the Americans attempt to repel the invaders, Harriot asserted, England's disciplined soldiers and superior weaponry would deliver easy victory.

Harriot's *Briefe and True Report* depicted for his English readers a bountiful land full of opportunities for quick profit. The Native people residing there would, he thought, "in a short time be brought to civilitie" through conversion or conquest—if they did not die from disease, the ravages of which he witnessed. If Thomas Harriot anticipated key elements of the story, the fate of Roanoke demonstrates that his prediction was far off the mark. European dominance of North America would be difficult to achieve. Indeed, it never was fully achieved, in the sense Harriot and his compatriots intended.

Summary

The process of initial contact among Europeans, Africans, and Americans began in the fourteenth century, when Portuguese sailors first explored the Mediterranean Atlantic and the West African coast. Those seamen established commercial ties that brought African slaves first to Iberia and then to the islands the Europeans conquered and settled. The Mediterranean Atlantic and its island sugar plantations nurtured the ambitions of mariners who, like Christopher Columbus, ventured into previously unknown waters—those who sailed to India and Brazil as well as to the Caribbean and the North American coast. When Columbus reached the Americas, he thought he had found Asia. Later explorers knew better but, except for the Spanish, regarded the Americas primarily as a barrier that prevented them from reaching their long-sought goal of an oceanic route to the riches of China and the Moluccas. Ordinary European fishermen were the first to realize that the northern coasts had valuable products to offer: fish and furs, both much in demand in their homelands.

Revitalizing Native Languages

If knowledge is power, then language is power. Words make us human, and languages carry the DNA of cultures. From one generation to the next, humans use language as a tool to maintain the distinct identities of individuals and groups. Like peoples, languages evolve. And like all living things, they are fragile. Their lives depend upon the regular nourishment that new speakers provide.

On the eve of European contact, the indigenous peoples of the Americas spoke a dizzying variety of languages. Continental North America was home to the speakers of as many as 1,200 distinct tongues, grouped into over a dozen major language families. (For comparison, linguists sort the languages of Europe into just four main families.)

Over the last five centuries, many of those languages— a crucial part of the biodiversity of humankind—have been silenced by the violence of colonialism, by dispersal and disease, by informal pressures to assimilate to increasingly dominant European cultures, and in some cases by formal campaigns to suppress their usage.

Today an estimated 139 native languages are spoken in the United States; the fluent speakers of perhaps 70 of these tongues are elderly, leaving those languages at risk.

Since the 1970s, however, a native language revitalization movement has grown in strength and visibility across the United States. From Hawai'i to the Florida everglades, cultural survival activists have created immersion schools and nests, language camps, computer programs, even video games to preserve and transmit indigenous languages. Such efforts have trained many fluent speakers of languages once endangered, such as Hawaiian, for example: in 1984, there were fewer than thirty fluent speakers of O'lelo Hawai'i under the age of twelve. Today, there are tens of thousands.

One of the most extraordinary language reclamation programs instructs students in Wôpanâak, the Algonquian-family language of the Wampanoag nation of Massachusetts. Founded in 1993 by Jessie "Little Doe" Baird (Mashpee) and the late Helen Manning, the Wôpanâak Language Reclamation Project (WLRP)

faced especially formidable obstacles: although Wôpanâak was the first indigenous American language to be expressed in alphabetic characters, its last speakers had died in the mid-nineteenth century. Using a range of documents—including sermons and scripture printed in Wôpanâak in the seventeenth century by English missionaries, and colonial land records using the language well into the eighteenth—the WLRP has created a dictionary of over 11,000 words, as well as first- and second-language curricula, an apprenticeship program, and immersion camps. A young Mashpee girl fluent in Wôpanâak and English is the language's first native speaker in seven generations.

CRITICAL THINKING

☐ Why are the efforts to reclaim or preserve indigenous languages important to the survival of indigenous peoples and their cultures in the modern world?

☐ How can new respect for indigenous cultures translate to an effort to right some of the social and economic wrongs of centuries?

The Aztecs predicted that their Fifth Sun would end in earthquakes and hunger. Hunger they surely experienced after Cortés's invasion, and even if there were no earthquakes, their great temples tumbled to the ground, as the Spaniards used their stones (and indigenous laborers) to construct cathedrals honoring their God and his son, Jesus. The conquerors coerced Native peoples and, later, relied on enslaved African workers to till the fields, mine the precious metals, and herd the livestock that earned immense profits for themselves and their mother country.

The first contacts of old world and new devastated the Western Hemisphere's Native inhabitants. European diseases killed millions; European livestock, along with a wide range of other imported animals and plants, forever modified the American environment. Flourishing civilizations were markedly altered in just a few decades. Europe, too, was changed: American foodstuffs like corn and potatoes improved nutrition throughout the continent, and American gold and silver first enriched, then ruined, the Spanish economy.

A century after Columbus landed, many fewer people resided in North America than had lived there in 1491. And the people who did live there—Native, African, and European peoples—together made a world that was indeed new, a world engaged in the unprecedented process of combining religions, economies, ways of life, and political systems that had developed separately for millennia.

Suggestions for Further Reading

David Abulafia, *The Discovery of Mankind: Atlantic Encounters in the Age of Columbus* (2008)

Alfred W. Crosby, *The Columbian Exchange: Biological and Cultural Consequences of 1492* (1972)

John H. Elliott, *Empires of the Atlantic World: Britain and Spain in America, 1492–1830* (2006)

Elizabeth A. Fenn, *Encounters at the Heart of the World: A History of the Mandan People* (2014)

Alison Games, *The Web of Empire: English Cosmopolitans in an Age of Expansion, 1560–1660* (2008)

Paul Kelton, *Epidemics and Enslavement: Biological Catastrophe in the Native Southeast, 1492–1715* (2007)

Peter C. Mancall, *Hakluyt's Promise: An Elizabethan's Obsession for an English America* (2007)

Charles C. Mann, *1491: New Revelations of the Americas Before Columbus* (2005); *1493: Uncovering the New World Columbus Created* (2011)

Daniel K. Richter, *Before the Revolution: America's Ancient Pasts* (2011)

John K. Thornton, *Africa and Africans in the Making of the Atlantic World, 1400–1680* (1992)

MINDTAP
From Cengage

MindTap® is a fully online personalized learning experience built upon Cengage Learning content. MindTap® combines student learning tools—readings, multimedia, activities, and assessments—into a singular Learning Path that guides students through the course and helps students develop the critical thinking, analysis, and communication skills that are essential to academic and professional success.

Europeans Colonize North America, 1600–1650

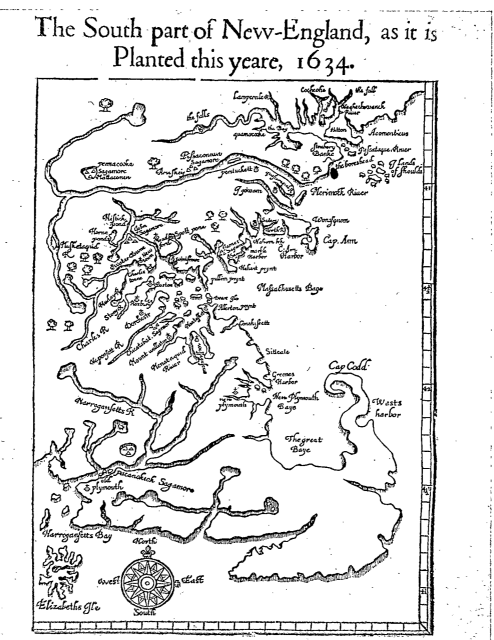

The South part of New-England, as it is Planted this yeare, 1634.

T he timber of the country grows straight and tall, some trees being twenty, some thirty foot high, before they spread forth their branches," wrote the aptly-named William Wood in 1634. Printed in London, Wood's *New England's Prospect* was at once a travelogue and a recruitment brochure for England's new plantations. A rhyming verse inventoried the region's forests: proud stands of chestnut and walnut, oak and cypress, maple and hawthorn, elm and alder, and especially those "sky-towering pines," which made peerless masts.

Having set sail from a land largely deforested centuries before, English travelers marveled at New England's trees, a "commodity" Wood deemed second only to the region's waterways. In the 1620s and 1630s, soon after staking their claims to the Nauset territory they called Cape Cod, the Wampanoag lands they rechristened Plymouth, and the Massachusett harbors they renamed Salem and Boston, the transplants began to fell the forests. They built houses to shelter their fledgling villagers, churches to honor their God, and ships to sustain their way of life.

Theirs was a maritime culture. They had crossed a great ocean to plant their "new" world on its western shores. They huddled along that coastline, and along rivers that flowed toward it, for generations. They depended on the sea for food, for trade, for people, and for power. Shipbuilding was one of the region's first industries, and long remained one of the most important.

The *Desire* was one of the first large ships fashioned in New England. Holding 120 tons of cargo, it would have had two masts and a length of about 90 feet, making it only a little smaller than the

◁ William Wood's "The South Part of New-England," which appeared in his book *New England's Prospect* (London, 1634), was the first printed map of the region by an Englishman who had settled there. English place names and icons indicating churches dot the map, illustrating the colonists' desire to remake the territory in the image of their homeland. But Wood also records many Native place names—including those of particular Algonquian leaders or sagamores—reminding the viewer of the power of local Native groups and their proximity to English settlement. He is careful, too, to indicate the stands of trees crucial to the region's maritime economy.

Map including Massachusetts Bay (litho)/American School/PETER NEWARK'S PICTURES/Private Collection/Bridgeman Images

Chronology

1558	Elizabeth I becomes queen of England
1565	Founding of St. Augustine (Florida), oldest permanent European settlement in present-day United States
1598	Oñate conquers Pueblos in New Mexico for Spain
1603	James I becomes king of England
1607	Jamestown founded, first permanent English settlement in North America
1608	Quebec founded by the French
1610	Santa Fe, New Mexico, founded by the Spanish
1614	Fort Orange (Albany, New York) founded by the Dutch
1619	Virginia House of Burgesses established, first representative assembly in the English colonies
1620	Plymouth colony founded, first permanent English settlement in New England
1622	Powhatan Confederacy rebels against Virginia
1624	Dutch settle on Manhattan Island (New Amsterdam)
	James I revokes Virginia Company's charter
1625	Charles I becomes king of England
1627	English colonize Barbados
1630	Massachusetts Bay colony founded
	Providence Island founded
1630s–1640s	"Sugar revolution" in the West Indies
1634	Maryland founded
1636	Roger Williams expelled from Massachusetts Bay, founds Providence, Rhode Island
	Connecticut founded
1636–1638	Pequot War in New England
1638	Anne Hutchinson expelled from Massachusetts Bay
1642	Montreal founded by the French
1646	Treaty ends hostilities between Virginia and Powhatan Confederacy

Mayflower that famously landed on Plymouth Rock in 1620. Loath to waste anything, the craftsmen who built the *Desire* fitted it out with equipment salvaged from the wreck of the English barque *Warwick*, which had run aground at Natasket, just beyond Boston Harbor. The *Desire* inherited the *Warwick*'s rigging, its ironwork, and its mounted guns. It was a merchant vessel, but commerce and conquest were never very far apart. The same ships that brought families of New England settlers who considered themselves religious refugees also carried muskets, bandoliers, swords, and pikes by the dozen.

Experience an interactive version of this story in MindTap®.

By the time the *Desire* was built, in the fall of 1636, the colonization of New England had been revealed for the violent enterprise that tracts like Wood's *New England Prospect* did much to disguise. Tensions with the Pequots, who controlled trade in much of present-day Connecticut, ran high, and English settlers began to talk of war. The following May, English soldiers and Narragansett warriors allied to rain devastation on Pequot country. Many of the survivors were taken captive. Pequot women and "maid children" should be "disposed aboute in the townes," the Massachusetts governor wrote, describing human spoils of war, distributed as slaves. Captive men and boys were deemed more dangerous; they were to be transported to the English plantations of the West Indies, which were just beginning to experiment with the cultivation of sugar, a labor-intensive crop.

The *Desire* headed south that June, likely its maiden voyage, its new-cut timbers still smelling sharply of pine. No bill of lading survives, so we do not know everything Captain William Pierce crammed into the ship's hold. His cargo likely included salted fish and imported rum, which Governor John Winthrop called "the only commodities for those parts." We do know that among the goods Pierce meant to peddle in Bermuda were seventeen Pequot captives, all but two of them boys.

Pierce, an experienced mariner, had crossed the Atlantic several times already. But on this trip, he missed his mark, fetching up in the English settlement known as Providence Island, off the coast of present-day Nicaragua. He spent the summer and fall trading there, and in some of the other islands dotting those crystal blue waters, before returning north.

In January, the *Desire* sailed back into Boston Harbor, its hold stuffed with the fruits of the Indies trade. Pierce unloaded cotton, tobacco, and salt, along with an unspecified number of "negroes": men and women first taken from Africa by Spanish slave traders, then stolen from Spanish ships by English privateers, and now peddled for sale in the cold new world of New England. Though never the predominant labor system in New England, chattel slavery would continue to be a crucial part of the region's economy and culture, fueling its vital trade with the West Indies for nearly two centuries.

By the time the *Desire* plied the waters of the Caribbean, Spain no longer predominated in the Americas. France, the Netherlands, and England all had permanent colonies in North America by the 1640s. Like the conquistadors, French and Dutch merchants (on the mainland) and planters (in the Caribbean) hoped to make a quick profit and then perhaps return to their homelands. As Thomas Harriot had made clear in the 1580s, English colonists were just as interested in profiting from North America. But they pursued profit in a different way.

Most of the new world's English colonists—including those who settled in New England—came to America intending to stay. They were settlers, whose every success in claiming land and creating community meant the permanent displacement of Native populations. Along the northeast Atlantic coast, settler-colonists arrived in family groups, sometimes accompanied by friends and relatives. They re-created the European agricultural economy and family life to an extent impossible in colonies where single men predominated, as they did in the English colonies of the Chesapeake region and the Caribbean, which focused on the large-scale production of cash crops for export.

Wherever they settled, the English, like other Europeans, prospered only where they learned to adapt to the alien environment. Settlers had to learn to grow such unfamiliar American crops as maize and squash. They also had to develop extensive trading relationships with Native peoples and with other English and European colonies. Needing laborers for their fields, they first used English **indentured servants**. But even in New England, they experimented with enslaving Native peoples and soon began to import Africans to hold in bondage. The early history of England's America is best understood not as an isolated story of English settlement but rather as a series of complex negotiations among European, African, and American peoples.

🔲 *Why did different groups come to the Americas? Which people came by choice, and which were forced to migrate?*

🔲 *How did different Native peoples react to the colonists' presence?*

🔲 *In what ways did the English colonies in North America and the Caribbean differ, and in what ways were they alike?*

2-1 Spanish, French, and Dutch North America

▶ **How did the Spaniards and the French interact with Native American populations?**

▶ **What economic developments emerged in the early European settlements in North America?**

▶ **Why did European powers come into conflict with one another in North America?**

Spaniards established the first permanent European settlement within the boundaries of the modern United States, but others had initially attempted that feat. Twice in the 1560s Huguenots (French Protestants), who were seeking to escape persecution, planted colonies on the south Atlantic coast. A passing ship rescued the starving survivors of the first colony, located in present-day South Carolina. The second, near modern Jacksonville, Florida, was destroyed in 1565 by a Spanish expedition under the command of Pedro Menéndez de Avilés. To ensure Spanish domination of the strategically important region (located near sea-lanes used by

indentured servants Young men and women, usually unemployed and poor, who were given free passage to America, plus basic needs such as food, shelter, and clothing, in exchange for labor after their arrival, usually for four to seven years.

Spanish treasure ships), Menéndez set up a fortified outpost named St. Augustine—now the oldest continuously inhabited European settlement in the United States.

The local Guale and Timucua nations initially allied themselves with the powerful newcomers and welcomed Franciscan friars into their villages. The relationship did not remain peaceful for long, though, because the Guale and Timucua nations resisted the imposition of Spanish authority. Still, the Franciscans offered these indigenous peoples spiritual solace for the diseases and troubles besetting them after the Europeans' invasion, and eventually gained numerous converts at missions that stretched westward across Florida and northward into the islands along the Atlantic coast.

2-1a New Mexico

More than thirty years after the founding of St. Augustine, conquistadors ventured anew into the present-day United States. In 1598, drawn northward by rumors of rich cities, Juan de Oñate, a Mexican-born adventurer whose *mestiza* wife descended from both Cortés and Motecuhzoma, led about five hundred soldiers and settlers to New Mexico. At first, the Pueblo peoples greeted the newcomers cordially. But when the Spaniards began to use torture, murder, and rape to extort supplies from the villagers, the residents of Acoma killed several soldiers, among them Oñate's nephew. The invaders responded ferociously, killing more than eight hundred people and capturing the remainder. All captives above the age of twelve were enslaved for twenty years, and men older than twenty-five had one foot amputated. Not surprisingly, the other Pueblo villages surrendered.

Yet Oñate's bloody victory proved illusory, for New Mexico held little wealth, and it was too far from the Pacific to assist in protecting Spanish sea-lanes. Officials considered abandoning the isolated colony, which lay 800 miles north of the nearest Spanish settlement. But for defensive purposes, the authorities decided to maintain a small military outpost and a few Christian missions in the area, with the capital at Santa Fe (founded 1610) (see Map 3.2, Section 3-2c). As in regions to the south, Spanish leaders were granted *encomiendas*, giving them control over the labor of Pueblo villagers. In the absence of mines or fertile agricultural lands, however, such grants yielded small profit. After most of the Spanish departed, their horses remained, transforming the lives of the indigenous inhabitants.

2-1b Quebec and Montreal

The French turned their attention to the area that Jacques Cartier had explored in the 1530s. Several times they tried to establish permanent bases along Canada's Atlantic coast but failed until 1605, when they founded Port Royal. Then in 1608, Samuel de Champlain set up a trading post at an interior site that the local Iroquois called Stadacona. Champlain renamed it Quebec. He had chosen well: Quebec was the most defensible spot in the entire St. Lawrence River valley, a stronghold that controlled access to the heartland of the continent. In 1642, the French established a second post, Montreal, at the falls of the St. Lawrence (and thus at the end of navigation by oceangoing vessels), a place the Iroquois knew as Hochelaga.

The new posts quickly took over the lucrative trade in beaver pelts (see Table 2.1). The colony's leaders granted

Table 2.1 The Founding of Permanent European Colonies in North America, 1565–1640

Colony	Founder(s)	Date	Basis of Economy
Florida	Pedro Menéndez de Avilés	1565	Farming
New Mexico	Juan de Oñate	1598	Livestock
Virginia	Virginia Co.	1607	Tobacco
New France	France	1608	Fur trading
Bermuda	English sailors	1609	Tobacco, ship-building
New Netherland	Dutch West India Co.	1614	Fur trading
Plymouth	Separatists	1620	Farming, fishing
Maine	Sir Ferdinando Gorges	1622	Fishing
St. Kitts, Barbados, et al.	European immigrants	1624	Sugar
Massachusetts Bay	Massachusetts Bay Company	1630	Farming, fishing, fur trading
Maryland	Cecilius Calvert	1634	Tobacco
Rhode Island	Roger Williams	1636	Farming
Connecticut	Thomas Hooker	1636	Farming, fur trading
New Haven	Massachusetts migrants	1638	Farming
New Hampshire	Massachusetts migrants	1638	Farming, fishing

Acoma Pueblo

Today, as in the late sixteenth century when it was besieged and eventually captured by the Spanish, the Acoma Pueblo sits high atop an isolated mesa. The Ancient Pueblo selected the location, 365 feet above the valley floor, because they could easily defend it. Building the complex was a massive undertaking. Over forty tons of sandstone had to be cut from the surrounding cliffs and pulled up the mesa to make each of the pueblo's hundreds of rooms. Roofing Acoma and the other dwellings in Chaco Canyon consumed some 200,000 trees. Much of the labor was likely provided by other Native groups enslaved by the Ancient Pueblos. The buildings for which they gave their labor and their lives endured; some structures dating to the eleventh century still stand in the middle of the village.

In addition to making construction difficult, situating the city so high above the plains created problems with water supply. To this day there is no source of water in the village. Acoma's residents had to carry water up a steep set of stairs cut into the mesa's side (today there is an almost equally steep road). The women of Acoma were and are accomplished potters. Some pots, like the one shown here, were designed with a low center of gravity.

CRITICAL THINKING

▫ How would that design help women to reach the top of the mesa with much-needed water?

▫ How would they carry such pots?

△ Acoma Pueblo today. The village is now used primarily for ritual purposes; few people reside there permanently, because all water must be trucked in.

Kevin Fleming/Corbis/VCG/Getty Images

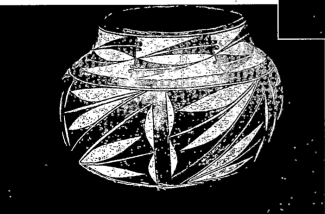

Richard A. Cooke III/Getty Images

△ A pot designed for carrying water to the top of the mesa.

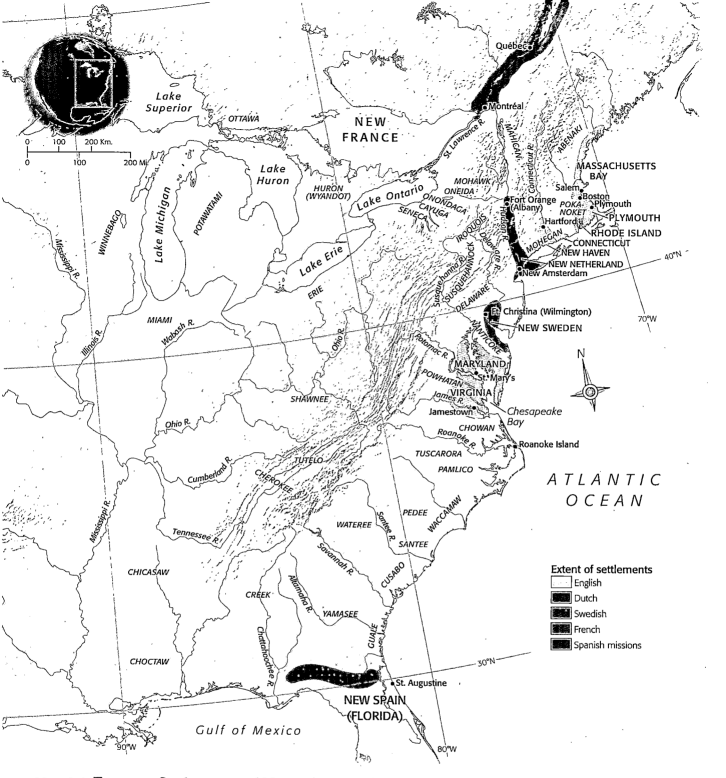

Map 2.1 European Settlements and Native American Tribes in Eastern North America, 1650

The few European settlements established in the East before 1650 were widely scattered, hugging the shores of the Atlantic Ocean and the banks of its major rivers. By contrast, America's Native inhabitants controlled the vast interior expanse of the continent, and Spaniards had begun to move into the West.

land along the river to wealthy *seigneurs* (nobles), who then imported tenants to work their farms. Only a few Europeans resided in New France; most were men, some of whom married Native women. A small number of Frenchmen brought their wives and took up agriculture. Even so, more than twenty-five years after its founding, Quebec had just sixty-four resident families, along with traders and soldiers. Northern New France never grew much beyond the confines of the river valley between Quebec and Montreal (see Map 2.1). Thus, it differed significantly from New Spain, characterized by scattered cities and direct supervision of indigenous laborers.

2-1c Jesuit Missions in New France

French missionaries of the Society of Jesus (Jesuits), a Roman Catholic order dedicated to converting nonbelievers to Christianity, also came to New France. First arriving in Quebec in 1625, the Jesuits, whom the Huron, Iroquois, and Abenaki peoples called Black Robes, tried to persuade indigenous peoples to live near French settlements and to adopt European agricultural methods. When that effort failed, the Jesuits concluded that they could introduce their new charges to Catholicism without insisting that they fundamentally alter their traditional ways of life. Accordingly, the Black Robes learned indigenous languages and traveled to remote regions of the interior, where they lived in twos and threes among hundreds of potential converts. Fluent linguists and careful observers, the Jesuits wrote in great detail about the ways of the Huron, Iroquois, and Abenaki men and women whose souls they attempted to "harvest" for the Christian God.

Jesuits used various strategies to gain the confidence of influential men and to undermine the authority of traditional religious leaders. Trained in rhetoric, Jesuits won admirers with their eloquence. Immune to smallpox (for all had survived the disease already), the Black Robes said epidemics were God's punishment for sin, their arguments aided by the ineffectiveness of traditional remedies against the new pestilence. Drawing on European science, Jesuits predicted solar and lunar eclipses. They further amazed villagers by communicating with each other over long distances through marks on paper. Native peoples' desire to harness the extraordinary power of literacy was one of the factors that made them receptive to the missionaries.

Jesuits slowly gained thousands of converts, some of whom moved to reserves set aside for Christian Native peoples. Catholicism offered women in particular the inspiring role model of the Virgin Mary, personified in Montreal and Quebec by Ursuline nuns who ministered to indigenous women and children. Many male and female converts followed Catholic teachings with fervor, casting off native customs allowing premarital sex and easy divorce, which Catholic doctrine prohibited. In the late 1670s, one convert, a young Mohawk named Kateri Tekakwitha, inspired thousands with her celibacy and other ascetic devotional practices. Known as "the Lily of the Mohawks," her grave was said to be the site of miracles. In October 2012, the Roman Catholic Church made her the first Native American saint.

If they embraced some Christian doctrine, most Native converts resisted Jesuits' attempts to foster strict European child-rearing methods, instead retaining their more relaxed practices. Jesuits, unlike Franciscans in New Mexico, recognized that such aspects of Native cultures could be compatible with Christian beliefs. Their efforts to attract converts were further aided by their lack of interest in labor tribute or land acquisition.

2-1d New Netherland

Jesuit missionaries faced little competition from other Europeans for Native people's souls, but French fur traders had to confront a direct challenge to their economic designs. In 1614,

only five years after Henry Hudson explored the river that now bears his name, his sponsor, the Dutch West India Company, established an outpost (Fort Orange) at the site of present-day Albany, New York. Like the French, the Dutch sought beaver pelts, and their presence so close to Quebec threatened France's interests in the region. The Netherlands, the world's dominant commercial power, aimed primarily at trade rather than at colonization. Thus **New Netherland**, like New France, remained small, confined largely to a river valley offering easy access to its settlements. The colony's southern anchor was **New Amsterdam**, founded in 1624 on an island at the mouth of the Hudson River that the Lenape called Manahatta.

New Netherland was a small outpost of a vast commercial empire that extended to Africa, Brazil, and modern-day Indonesia. Autocratic directors-general ruled the colony for the Dutch West India Company. With no elected assembly, settlers felt little loyalty to their nominal leaders. Few migrants arrived. Even an offer in 1629 of large land grants, or patroonships, to people who would bring fifty settlers to the province failed to attract many takers. (Only one such tract—Rensselaerswyck, near Albany—was ever fully developed.) As late as the mid-1660s, New Netherland had only about five thousand European inhabitants. Some were Swedes and Finns who resided in the former colony of New Sweden (founded in 1638 on the Delaware River; see Map 2.1), which the Dutch seized in 1655.

The Native American allies of New France and New Netherland clashed in part because of fur-trade rivalries. In the 1640s the Iroquois, who traded chiefly with the Dutch and lived in modern upstate New York, went to war against the Huron, who traded primarily with the French and lived in present-day Ontario. The Iroquois wanted to become the major supplier of pelts to Europeans and wanted to ensure the security of their hunting territories. They achieved both goals by using guns supplied by the Dutch to virtually exterminate the Huron, whose population had been decimated by smallpox. The Iroquois thus established themselves as a major force in the region, one that Europeans could ignore only at their peril.

2-2 England's America

▷ **What factors contributed to the migration of English men and women to the North American colonies?**

▷ **What religious changes emerged in European society because of the Reformation?**

▷ **How did the Reformation reshape English society and government?**

The failure of Sir Walter Raleigh's Roanoke colony ended English efforts to settle in North America for nearly two decades. When the English decided in 1606 to try once more, they again planned colonies that imitated the Spanish model. Yet greater success came when

New Netherland Dutch colony in America.

New Amsterdam Dutch seaport that would become New York City.

they abandoned that model. Unlike Spain, France, or the Netherlands, England eventually sent large numbers of men and women to set up agriculturally based colonies on the mainland. Two major developments prompted approximately two hundred thousand ordinary English men and women to move to North America in the seventeenth century and led their government to encourage their emigration.

2-2a Social and Economic Change

The first development was the onset of dramatic social and economic change. In the 150-year period after 1530, largely as a result of the importation of nutritious American crops, which raised the caloric intake of ordinary Europeans, England's population doubled. All those additional people needed food, clothing, and other goods. The competition for goods led to inflation, and the increased number of workers caused a fall in real wages. In these new circumstances, some people— especially those whose sizable landholdings could produce food and clothing fibers for the growing population—grew richer. Others, particularly landless laborers and those with small amounts of land, fell into poverty. When landowners raised rents, took control of lands that peasants had long used in common (enclosure), or combined smallholdings into large units, they displaced their tenants. Geographical as well as social mobility increased. England's cities swelled to bursting. Approximately seventy-five thousand people lived in London in 1550. A century later, nearly four hundred thousand people packed its narrow alleys and cramped buildings.

As "masterless men"—the landless and homeless— crowded the streets and highways, wealthy English people reacted with alarm. Obsessed with maintaining order, officials came to believe England was overcrowded. They hoped that colonies in North America would siphon off England's "surplus population," easing social strains at home. Many ordinary people decided they could improve their circumstances by migrating from a small, land-scarce, apparently overpopulated island to a boundless, land-rich, apparently empty new world. Among those tempted to emigrate were men like William Rudyerd: the younger sons of gentlemen, excluded from inheriting land by the practice of primogeniture, which reserved all real estate for the eldest son. Such economic considerations were rendered even more significant in light of the second development: a major change in English religious practice.

2-2b English Reformation

The sixteenth century witnessed a religious transformation that eventually led large numbers of English dissenters to leave their homeland. In 1533 Henry VIII, wanting a male heir and infatuated with Anne Boleyn, asked the pope to annul his nearly twenty-year marriage to the

Protestant Reformation Split of Christian reformers from Roman Catholic church; triggered by Martin Luther.

Martin Luther (1483–1546) German theologian who critiqued the practices of the Catholic church, including the authority of the pope.

Jean Calvin (1509–1554) French Protestant theologian who believed in the "predestination" of individuals for either heaven or hell, regardless of their behavior.

Spanish-born Catherine of Aragón. When the pope refused, Henry broke with the Roman Catholic Church. He founded the Church of England and—with Parliament's concurrence— proclaimed himself its head.

At first, the Church of England differed little from Catholicism. Under Henry's daughter, Elizabeth I (child of his second marriage, to Anne Boleyn), though, currents of religious belief that had originated on the European continent early in the sixteenth century dramatically affected England's recently established church.

These currents constituted the **Protestant Reformation,** led by **Martin Luther,** a German monk, and **Jean Calvin,** a French cleric and lawyer. Challenging the Catholic doctrine that priests were intermediaries between laypeople and God, Luther and Calvin insisted that people could interpret the Bible for themselves. That notion stimulated the spread of literacy: to understand and interpret the Bible, people had to learn how to read. Both Luther and Calvin rejected Catholic rituals, denying the need for elaborate ceremony and church hierarchy. They also asserted that the key to salvation was faith in God, rather than—as Catholic teaching had it—a combination of faith and good works. Calvin went further, stressing God's omnipotence and emphasizing the need for people to submit totally to God's will.

2-2c Puritans, Separatists, and Presbyterians

Elizabeth I tolerated diverse forms of Christianity as long as her subjects acknowledged her authority as head of the Church of England. During her long reign (1558–1603), Calvin's ideas gained influence in England, Wales, and especially Scotland. (In Ireland, also part of her realm, Catholicism remained dominant.) The Scottish church eventually adopted Presbyterianism, an organizational structure that dispensed with bishops and placed religious authority in bodies of clerics and laymen called presbyteries. By the late sixteenth century, though, many Calvinists—including those called Puritans (a nickname used to insult those who wanted to purify the church), or Separatists (because they wanted to leave it entirely)—believed that reformers in England and Scotland had not gone far enough. Henry had simplified the church hierarchy, and the Scots had altered it; Puritans and Separatists wanted to abolish it altogether. Henry and the Scots had subordinated the church to the interests of the state; the dissenters wanted a church free from political interference. The established churches of England and Scotland, like the Catholic Church or the official Protestant churches of continental European countries, continued to encompass all residents of the realm. Calvinists in England and Scotland wanted to confine church membership to those God had chosen for salvation.

Paradoxically, though, dissenters insisted that people could not know for certain if they were "saved." Mere mortals could not comprehend or affect their predestination to heaven or hell. Thus, pious Calvinists confronted serious dilemmas: if the saved (or "elect") could not be identified with certainty, how could proper churches be constituted? And if you were predestined and could not alter fate, why attend church or respect civil law? Calvinists dealt with the

Table 2.2 Tudor and Stuart Monarchs of England, 1509–1649

Monarch	Reign	Relation to Predecessor
Henry VIII	1509–1547	Son
Edward VI	1547–1553	Son
Mary I	1553–1558	Half-sister
Elizabeth I	1558–1603	Half-sister
James I	1603–1625	Cousin
Charles I	1625–1649	Son

first dilemma by admitting that their judgments about church membership only approximated God's unknowable decisions. They resolved the second by reasoning that God gave the elect the ability to accept salvation and to lead a moral life. Though good works would not earn you a place in heaven, pious behavior might signal that you belonged there.

2-2d Stuart Monarchs

Elizabeth I's Stuart successors, her cousin James I (1603–1625) and his son Charles I (1625–1649), exhibited less tolerance for Calvinists (see Table 2.2). As Scots, they also had little respect for the traditions of representative government that had developed in England. The wealthy landowners who sat in Parliament had grown accustomed to wielding considerable influence over government policies, especially taxation. But James I, taking a position later endorsed by his son, publicly declared his belief in the divine right of kings. The Stuarts insisted that a monarch's power came directly from God and that his subjects had a duty to obey him. They likened the king's absolute authority to a father's authority over his children.

Both James I and Charles I believed their authority included the power to enforce religious conformity. Because Calvinists—and remaining Catholics in England and Scotland—challenged many of the most important precepts of the Church of England, the Stuart monarchs authorized the removal of dissenting clergymen from their pulpits. In the 1620s and 1630s, some Puritans, Separatists, Presbyterians, and Catholics decided to move to America, where they hoped to practice their diverse religious beliefs unhindered by the Stuarts or their bishops. Some fled hurriedly to avoid arrest and imprisonment.

2-3 The Founding of Virginia

▶ How did the early settlers of Jamestown interact with local Native American populations?

▶ How did the competing viewpoints of one another impact the relationship between the English and Native American populations?

▶ What impact did the Virginia Company have on the Jamestown settlement?

The impetus for England's first permanent colony in the Western Hemisphere was both religious and economic. The newly militant English Protestants were eager to combat "popery" both at home and in the Americas. They concurred with the English writer Richard Hakluyt, who remarked that if Spaniards, "in their superstition," had "don so greate thinges in so shorte space," surely the adherents of "our true and sincere Religion" could achieve even more remarkable results.

Accordingly, in 1606, a group of merchants and wealthy gentry—some of them aligned with religious reformers—obtained a royal charter for the Virginia Company, organized as a **joint-stock company**. Such forerunners of modern corporations, initially created to finance trading voyages, pooled the resources of many small investors through stock sales. Yet the joint-stock company ultimately proved to be a poor vehicle for establishing colonies, which required significant continuing investments of capital. The lack of immediate returns generated tension between stockholders and colonists. Although investors in the Virginia Company anticipated great profits, neither settlement the company established—one in Maine that collapsed within a year and Jamestown—ever earned much.

2-3a Jamestown and Tsenacommacah

In 1607, the Virginia Company dispatched 108 men and boys to a region near Chesapeake Bay called Tsenacommacah by its Native inhabitants. That May, the colonists established the palisaded settlement called **Jamestown** on a swampy peninsula in a river they also named for their monarch. Ill equipped for survival in the unfamiliar environment, the colonists attempted to maintain traditional English hierarchies, but soon fell victim to dissension and disease. Familiar with Spanish experience, the gentlemen and soldiers at Jamestown expected to rely on local Native peoples for food and tribute, yet the residents of Tsenacommacah refused to cooperate. Moreover, the settlers had the bad luck to arrive in the midst of a severe drought (now known to be the worst in the region for 1,700 years). The lack of rainfall made it difficult to cultivate crops and polluted their drinking water. The arrival of hundreds more colonists over the next several years only added to the pressure on scarce resources.

The powerful weroance (chief) of Tsenacommacah, Powhatan, had inherited rule over six Algonquian villages and later gained control of some twenty-five others (see Map 2.1). Late in 1607, Powhatan tentatively agreed to an alliance negotiated by Captain **John Smith**, one of the English colony's leaders. In exchange for foodstuffs, Powhatan hoped to acquire guns, hatchets, and swords, which would give him a technological advantage over his enemies. Each side in the alliance wanted to subordinate the other, but neither succeeded.

The fragile relationship soon foundered on mutual mistrust. The weroance

joint-stock company Business partnership that amasses capital through sales of stock to investors.

Jamestown First enduring English colony, established in 1607.

John Smith (1580–1631) English soldier and adventurer who become one of the early leaders of Jamestown.

relocated his primary village in early 1609 to a place the new-comers could not access easily. Without Powhatan's assistance, Jamestown experienced a "starving time" (winter 1609–1610). Hundreds perished and at least one survivor resorted to digging up corpses for food. When spring came, barely 60 of the 500 colonists who had come to Jamestown remained alive. They packed up to leave on a newly arrived ship, but en route up the James River encountered ships carrying a new governor, male and female settlers, and added supplies, so they returned to Jamestown.

Sporadic skirmishes ensued as the standoff with the Powhatans continued. To gain the upper hand, the settlers in 1613 kidnapped Powhatan's daughter, Pocahontas, and held her hostage. In captivity, she converted to Christianity and married a colonist, John Rolfe. Their union initiated a period of peace between the English and her people. Funded by the Virginia Company, she and Rolfe sailed to England to promote interest in the colony. Pocahontas died at Gravesend in 1616, probably of dysentery, leaving an infant son who returned to Virginia as a young adult.

Although their royal charter nominally laid claim to a much wider territory, the Jamestown settlers saw their "Virginia" as essentially corresponding to Tsenacommacah. Powhatan's dominion was bounded on the north by the Potomac, on the south by the Great Dismal Swamp, and on the west by the fall line—the beginning of the upland Piedmont. Beyond those boundaries lay the Powhatans' enemies and (especially in the west) lands the Powhatans feared to enter. English people relied on the Powhatans as guides and interpreters, traveling along rivers and precontact paths in order to trade with the Powhatans' partners.

2-3b Algonquian and English Cultural Differences

In Tsenacommacah and elsewhere on the North American coast, English settlers and Algonquians focused on their cultural differences—not their similarities—although both groups held deep religious beliefs, subsisted primarily through agriculture, accepted social and political hierarchy, and observed well-defined gender roles. From the outset, English men regarded Native men as lazy because they did not cultivate crops and spent much of their time hunting (a sport, not work, in English eyes). Native men thought English men effeminate because they did the "woman's work" of cultivation. In the same vein, the English believed Algonquian women were oppressed because they did heavy field labor.

Algonquian and English hierarchies differed. English political and military leaders tended to rule autocratically, whereas Algonquian leaders (even Powhatan) had more limited authority. Accustomed to the powerful kings of Europe, the English overestimated the ability of chiefs to make treaties that would bind their people.

Furthermore, Algonquian and English concepts of property differed. Most Algonquian villages held their land communally. Land could not be bought or sold outright, although certain rights to use it (for example, for hunting or fishing)

△ During her visit to London, the Powhatan princess—called "Pocahontas" or Matoaka in her childhood and Rebecca as an adult—sat for a portrait by Simon Van de Passe, a young Dutch artist. This image, based on de Passe's engraving, was completed by an anonymous painter roughly a century later. Both the seventeenth-century original and the eighteenth-century copy depict Pocahontas wearing pearl earrings and an elaborate cloak topped by a gorgeous lace ruff. The ostrich fan she holds symbolizes royalty, but her hat is of a type more commonly worn by Puritan men. Van de Passe did not "Europeanize" Pocahontas's features in the image he drew from life in the 1610s, but the later artist did, lightening her skin and hair, and making her cheekbones less prominent.

could be transferred. Once, most English villagers, too, had used land in common, but enclosures in the previous century had made them accustomed to individual farms and to buying and selling land. The English also refused to accept the validity of Native peoples' claims to traditional hunting territories, insisting that only land intensively cultivated or "improved" could be regarded as owned or occupied. As one colonist put it, "salvadge peoples" who "rambled" over a region without farming it could claim no "title or propertye" in the land. Ownership of such "unclaimed" property, the English believed, lay with the English monarchy, whose flag John Cabot had planted in North America in 1497.

Above all, where native belief systems tended readily to absorb new ideas, the English settlers believed unwaveringly in the superiority of their own civilization. If they often anticipated living peacefully alongside indigenous peoples, they always assumed that they would dictate the terms of such coexistence. Like Thomas Harriot at Roanoke, they expected Native peoples to adopt English customs and to convert to Christianity. They showed little respect for the Native Americans when they believed English interests were at stake, as was demonstrated by developments in Virginia once the settlers found the salable commodity they sought.

2-3c Tobacco Cultivation

That commodity was tobacco, the American crop introduced to Europe by the Spanish. In 1611, John Rolfe planted seeds of a variety from the Spanish Caribbean, which was considered superior to the strain Virginia Algonquians grew. Nine years later, Virginians exported forty thousand pounds of cured leaves; by the late 1620s, annual shipments had jumped to 1.5 million pounds. The great tobacco boom had begun, fueled by high prices and high profits for planters who responded to escalating demand from Europe and Africa. The price later fell almost as sharply as it had risen, fluctuating wildly from year to year in response to a glutted market and growing international competition. Nevertheless, tobacco made Virginia prosper.

The spread of tobacco cultivation altered life for everyone. Farming tobacco required abundant land because the crop quickly drained soil of nutrients. Planters soon learned that a field could produce only about three good crops before it had to lie fallow for several years to regain its fertility. As eager applicants asked the Virginia Company for land grants on both sides of the James River, small English settlements began to expand rapidly. Lulled into a false sense of security by years of peace with their Powhatan neighbors, Virginians established farms along the riverbanks at some distance from one another—a settlement pattern convenient for tobacco cultivation but dangerous for defense.

2-3d Opechancanough's Rebellion

Opechancanough, Powhatan's brother and successor, watched the English colonists' expansion and witnessed their attempts to convert Native peoples to Christianity. Recognizing the danger, the war leader launched coordinated attacks along the James River on March 22, 1622. By the end of the day, 347 English men, women, and children (about one-quarter of the colony) lay dead. Only a timely warning from two Christian converts saved Jamestown from destruction.

△ A comparison of the portrait of Sir Walter Raleigh and his son (left), with that of an Algonquian man drawn by John White, from Raleigh's Roanoke expedition (right), shows a dramatic difference in standard dress styles that, for many, must have symbolized the apparent cultural gap between Europeans and Americans. Yet the fact that both men (and the young boy) were portrayed in similar stances, with "arms akimbo," demonstrated that all were high-status individuals. In Europe, only aristocrats were represented in such a domineering pose.

Virginia reeled from the blow but did not collapse. Reinforced by new shipments of migrants and arms from England, the settlers repeatedly attacked Opechancanough's villages. A peace treaty was signed in 1632, but in April 1644 the elderly Opechancanough assaulted the invaders one last time, though he must have known he could not prevail. In 1646, survivors of the Powhatan Confederacy formally subordinated themselves to England. Although they continued to live in the region, their efforts to resist the spread of European settlement ended.

2-3e End of Virginia Company

The 1622 assault that failed to obliterate the colony did succeed in destroying its corporate parent. The Virginia Company never made any profits from the enterprise, for internal corruption and heavy costs offset all its earnings. But before its demise, the company developed two policies that set key precedents. First, to attract settlers, its leaders in 1617 established the "headright" system. Every new arrival paying his or her own way was promised fifty acres; those who financed the passage of others received similar headrights for each person. To ordinary English farmers, many of whom owned little or no land, the headright system offered a powerful incentive to move to Virginia. To wealthy gentry, it promised even more: the possibility of establishing vast agricultural enterprises worked by large numbers of laborers. Two years later, the company introduced a second reform, authorizing the landowning men of the major Virginia settlements to elect representatives to an assembly called the **House of Burgesses**. English landholders had long been accustomed to electing members of Parliament and controlling their own local governments; they expected the same privilege in the nation's colonies.

When James I revoked the charter in 1624, transforming Virginia into a royal colony, he continued the company's headright policy. Because he distrusted legislative bodies, the king abolished the assembly. But Virginians protested so vigorously that by 1629 the House of Burgesses was functioning again. Only two decades after the first permanent English settlement was planted in North America, the colonists successfully insisted on governing themselves at the local level. Already, the political structure of England's American possessions differed from those of the Spanish, Dutch, and French colonies—all of which were ruled autocratically.

2-4 Life in the Chesapeake

▶ How did English settlers in the Chesapeake fulfill their demand for labor?

▶ What were the conditions of indentured servitude in the Chesapeake?

▶ What were the main features of social and political development in the Chesapeake?

House of Burgesses This first elected representative legislature in North America began meeting in 1619.

By the 1630s, tobacco was firmly established as the staple crop and chief source of revenue in Virginia.

It quickly became just as important in the second English colony planted on Chesapeake Bay: Maryland, given by Charles I to George Calvert, first Lord Baltimore, as a personal possession (proprietorship), which was colonized in 1634. (Because Virginia and Maryland both border Chesapeake Bay—see Map 2.1—they often are referred to collectively as "the Chesapeake.") Members of the Calvert family intended the colony as a haven for their persecuted fellow Catholics. Cecilius Calvert, second Lord Baltimore, became the first colonizer to offer freedom of religion to all Christian settlers; he understood that protecting the Protestant majority could also ensure Catholics' rights. Maryland's Act of Religious Toleration codified his policy in 1649.

In everything but religion, the two Chesapeake colonies resembled each other. In Maryland as in Virginia, tobacco planters spread out along the riverbanks, establishing isolated farms. The region's deep, wide rivers offered dependable water transportation in an age of few and inadequate roads. Each farm or group of farms had its own wharf, where oceangoing vessels could load or discharge cargo. Consequently, Virginia and Maryland had few towns, for their residents did not need commercial centers in order to buy and sell goods.

2-4a Demand for Laborers

Planting, cultivation, harvesting, and curing tobacco were repetitious, time-consuming, and labor-intensive tasks. Clearing land for new fields also demanded heavy labor. Above all else, successful Chesapeake farms required workers. But where and how could they be found? Neighboring Powhatans, their numbers reduced by war and disease, could not supply such needs. Nor were enslaved Africans widely available: traders could more easily and profitably sell slaves to Caribbean planters. By 1650, only about seven hundred blacks lived in Virginia and Maryland—roughly 3 percent of the population. Most were enslaved, but a few were or became free. Northampton County's Anthony Johnson, called "Antonio a Negro" when first sold to the English at Jamestown in 1621, earned his freedom in 1635. Two decades later, he and his wife had saved enough to purchase 250 acres of land. Like many of his fellow colonists, Johnson frequently landed in court. But the judges never threatened his freedom. Accused by a local grandee of idleness, Johnson replied, "I know myne owne ground and I will worke when I please and play when I please." While the practice of slavery constrained the lives of all Africans in the Chesapeake, their status in these early years was often quite fluid.

At first, Chesapeake tobacco farmers looked primarily to England to supply their labor needs. The headright system (which Maryland also adopted) allowed a tobacco planter anywhere in the region to obtain both land and labor by importing workers from England. Good management would make the process self-perpetuating: a farmer could use his profits to pay for the passage of more workers, thereby gaining title to more land, and even movement into the ranks of the emerging planter gentry.

Because men did the agricultural work in European societies, colonists assumed that field laborers—at least white field laborers—should be men. Such laborers, along with a few women, immigrated to America as indentured servants, paying their passage by contracting to work for periods ranging from four to seven years. Indentured servants accounted for 75 to 85 percent of the approximately 130,000 English immigrants to Virginia and Maryland during the seventeenth century.

Males between the ages of fifteen and twenty-four composed roughly three-quarters of the servants; only one immigrant in five or six was female. Most of these young men came from farming or laboring families, and many originated in regions of England experiencing severe social disruption. Often they came from the middling ranks of society—what their contemporaries called the "common sort." Most had not yet established themselves in their homeland.

2-4b Conditions of Servitude

From a distance at least, the Chesapeake seemed to offer such people chances for advancement unavailable in England. Servants who fulfilled the terms of their indenture earned "freedom dues" consisting of clothes, tools, livestock, casks of corn and tobacco, and sometimes even land. Yet immigrants' lives were difficult. Servants typically worked six days a week, ten to fourteen hours a day, in a disease-riddled semitropical climate. Malaria—unknown in England—was rampant, as were typhoid and dysentery. As Richard Freethorne, a young servant from Jamestown, explained to his parents back in England, "the nature of the country, is such that it causeth much sickness." Freethorne was also starving. "I have eaten more in [one] day at home than I have allowed me here for a week," he reported. "[I]f you love or respect me as your child," he begged, "release me from this bondage and save my life."

Servants like Freethorne faced severe penalties for running away. But the laws offered them some protection. Their masters were supposed to supply them with sufficient food, clothing, and shelter, and they were not to be beaten excessively. Cruelly treated servants could turn to the courts for assistance, sometimes winning verdicts that transferred them to more humane masters or released them from their indentures.

Servants and their owners alike contended with epidemic disease. Immigrants first had to survive the process the colonists called "seasoning," a bout with disease (probably malaria) that usually occurred during their first Chesapeake summer. About 40 percent of male servants did not survive long enough to become freedmen. Young men of twenty-two who successfully weathered their seasoning could expect to live only another twenty years.

But for those who survived, the opportunities for advancement were real. Until the last decades of the seventeenth century, former servants often became independent farmers ("freeholders"), living a modest but comfortable existence. Some assumed positions of political prominence, such

as justice of the peace or militia officer. But in the 1670s, tobacco prices entered a fifty-year period of stagnation and decline. Good land grew increasingly scarce and expensive. In 1681, Maryland dropped its requirement that servants receive land as part of their freedom dues, forcing large numbers of freed servants to live for years as wage laborers or tenant farmers. By 1700, the Chesapeake was no longer the land of opportunity it once had been.

2-4c Standard of Living

Life in the early Chesapeake was hard for everyone, regardless of sex or status. The imbalanced sex ratio (see Figure 2.1), the incidence of servitude, and the high rates of mortality combined to produce small and fragile households. Schooling was haphazard at best; whether Chesapeake-born children learned to read or write depended largely on whether their parents were literate and took the time to teach them.

Farmers (and sometimes their wives) toiled in the fields alongside servants. Because hogs could forage for themselves, Chesapeake households subsisted mainly on pork and corn, a filling but not nutritious diet. Families supplemented this monotonous fare with fish, shellfish, and wildfowl, in addition to the vegetables they grew in small gardens. The near impossibility of preserving food for safe winter consumption magnified the health problems caused by epidemic disease.

Few households had many material possessions beyond farm implements, bedding, and basic cooking and eating utensils. Chairs, tables, candles, knives, and forks were luxury items. Most people rose and went to bed with the sun, sat on crude benches or chests, and held plates or bowls in their hands while eating with spoons. Their ramshackle houses commonly had just one or two rooms. Chesapeake colonists devoted their income to buying livestock and purchasing more laborers instead of improving their standard of living. Rather than making clothing or tools, families imported necessary manufactured goods from England.

2-4d Chesapeake Politics

Throughout the seventeenth century, immigrants composed a majority of the Chesapeake population. Most of the members of Virginia's House of Burgesses and Maryland's House of Delegates (established in 1635) were immigrants; they also dominated the governor's council, which simultaneously served as each colony's highest court, part of the legislature, and executive adviser to the governor. A cohesive, native-born ruling elite emerged only in the early eighteenth century.

In the seventeenth-century Chesapeake, most property-owning white males could vote, and such freeholders chose as their legislators (burgesses) the local elites who seemed to be their natural leaders. But because most such men were immigrants lacking strong ties to one another or to the region, the assemblies remained unstable and often contentious.

Age and Sex Composition

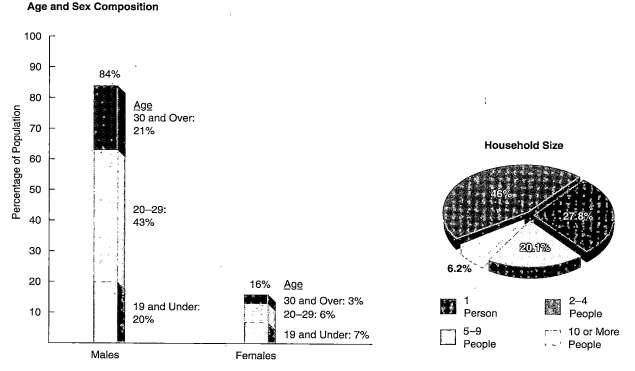

Figure 2.1 Population of Virginia, 1625

The only detailed censuses taken in the English mainland North American colonies during the seventeenth century were prepared in Virginia in 1624, with more detail added in 1625. The colony's population then totaled 1,218 people, arranged in 309 "households" and living in 278 dwellings. (Some houses contained more than one family.) The bar graph on the left shows the age and gender distribution of the 765 individuals for whom full information was recorded; in the pie chart on the right we see the variation in the sizes of the 309 households. The approximately 42 percent of the residents of the colony who were servants were concentrated in 30 percent of the households. At the time of these censuses, less than 2 percent of Virginia's inhabitants were of African descent. Data from *Wells, Peter S.* The Population of the British Colonies in America Before 1776.

2-5 The Founding of New England

▶ How did the demographic patterns and religious experience of settlers in New England differ from those of the Chesapeake?

▶ To what extent did religion shape the founding and development of settlements in New England?

▶ How did the relationship between New England settlers and Native American peoples evolve over time?

The mingled economic and religious motives that lured English people to the Chesapeake also drew men and women to New England, the region the English called North Virginia until Captain John Smith renamed it in 1616 (see Map 2.2). But because Puritans organized the New England colonies, and because of environmental factors, the northern settlements developed very differently from their southern

counterparts. The divergence became apparent even as the would-be colonists left England.

2-5a Contrasting Regional Religious Patterns

Hoping to exert control over a migration that appeared disorderly (and which included dissenters seeking to flee the authority of the Church of England), royal bureaucrats in late 1634 ordered port officials in London to collect information on all travelers departing for the colonies. The resulting records for the year 1635 are a treasure trove for historians. They document the departure of fifty-three vessels—twenty to Virginia, seventeen to New England, eight to Barbados, five to St. Christopher, two to Bermuda, and one to Providence Island. Almost five thousand people sailed on those ships—two thousand bound for Virginia, about twelve hundred for New England, and the rest for island destinations. Nearly three-fifths of the passengers were between fifteen and twenty-four years old, reflecting the predominance of

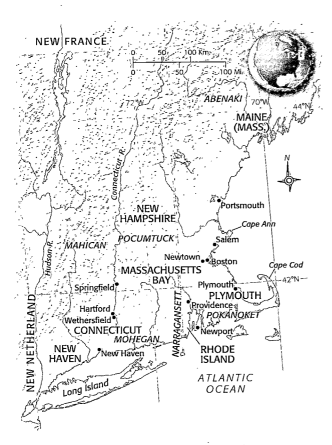

Map 2.2 New England Colonies, 1650

The most densely settled region of the mainland was New England, where English settlements and the villages of the region's indigenous Algonquian-speaking peoples existed side by side.

young male servants among migrants to most colonies in British America.

But among those bound for New England, such youths constituted less than one-third of the total; nearly 40 percent were older, and another third were younger. Whereas women made up just 14 percent of those headed to Virginia, they composed almost 40 percent of the passengers to New England. New England migrants often traveled in family groups. They also brought more goods and livestock with them, and tended to travel with others from the same towns. More than half the passengers aboard one vessel came from York; on another, nearly half came from Buckinghamshire. In short, people migrated to New England with their close associates. This must have made their lives in North America more comfortable and less lonely than those of their southern counterparts.

2-5b Contrasting Regional Demographic Patterns

Puritan congregations quickly became key institutions in colonial New England. Anglican worship had less impact on the early development of the Chesapeake colonies, where

spread-out settlement patterns made it difficult to organize a church. Catholic and Anglican bishops in England paid little attention to their coreligionists in America, and Chesapeake congregations languished in the absence of sufficient numbers of ordained clergymen. (In 1665, only ten of Virginia's fifty Church of England parishes had resident clerics.) Not until the 1690s did the Church of England plant deeper roots in Virginia; by then, it had also replaced Catholicism as the established church in Maryland.

In both New England and the Chesapeake, religion affected the lives of pious Calvinists who were expected to reassess the state of their souls regularly. Many devoted themselves to self-examination and Bible study, and families often prayed together under the guidance of the husband and father. Yet because even the most pious could never be certain they were among the elect, anxiety about their spiritual state troubled devout Calvinists. This anxiety lent a special intensity to their religious beliefs and to their concern with proper behavior—their own and that of others.

2-5c Separatists

Separatists who thought the Church of England too corrupt to be salvaged became the first religious dissenters to move to New England. In 1609, a Separatist congregation relocated to Leiden, in the Netherlands, where they found the freedom of worship denied them in Stuart England. But they soon found the Netherlands too permissive; the nation that tolerated them also tolerated religions and behaviors they abhorred. Hoping to isolate themselves from worldly temptations, these people, known today as Pilgrims, received permission from the Virginia Company to colonize the northern part of its territory.

In September 1620, more than one hundred people, only thirty of them Separatists, set sail from England on the old and crowded *Mayflower*. Like a few English families that had settled along the coast of Newfoundland during the previous decade, the Pilgrims expected to support their colony through profits from codfishery. In November, they landed on Cape Cod, farther north than they had intended. Given the lateness of the season, they decided to stay put. They moved across Massachusetts Bay to a fine harbor (named Plymouth by John Smith, who had visited it in 1614) and into the empty dwellings of a Pautuxet village whose inhabitants had died in the epidemic of 1616–1618.

2-5d Pilgrims and Pokanokets

Even before they landed, the Pilgrims had to surmount their first challenge—from the "strangers," or non-Separatists, who sailed with them to America. Because they landed outside the jurisdiction of the Virginia Company, some of the strangers questioned the authority of the colony's leaders. In response, the **Mayflower Compact**, signed in November 1620 on shipboard, established a "Civil Body Politic" as a temporary substitute for a charter. The male settlers elected

Mayflower Compact
Agreement signed by Mayflower passengers to establish order in their new settlement.

a governor and initially made all decisions for the colony at town meetings. Later, after more towns had been founded and the population increased, Plymouth colony, like Virginia and Maryland, created an assembly to which the landowning male settlers elected representatives.

Like the Jamestown settlers before them, the residents of Plymouth were poorly prepared to subsist in the new environment. Only half of the *Mayflower*'s passengers lived to see the spring. That the others survived owed much to the Pokanokets (a branch of the Wampanoags) who controlled the area. As many as two hundred thousand Algonquian-speaking peoples had lived in the region before contact. But Pokanoket villages had suffered terrible losses in the recent epidemic. To protect themselves from the powerful Narragansetts of the southern New England coast, the Pokanokets allied themselves with the newcomers. In the spring of 1621, their leader or sachem, Massasoit, agreed to a treaty, and during the colony's first years the Pokanokets supplied the settlers with essential foodstuffs. The colonists also relied on Tisquantum (or Squanto), a Pautuxet who served as a conduit between Native peoples and Europeans, as Cortés's Doña Marina had in Mexico. Captured by fishermen in the early 1610s and taken to Europe, Tisquantum had learned to speak English. On his return, he discovered that the epidemic had wiped out his village. Caught between worlds, Tisquantum became the settlers' interpreter and a major source of information about the environment.

2-5e Massachusetts Bay Company

Before the 1620s ended, another group of Puritan dissenters, who hoped to reform the Church of England from within rather than to abandon it, launched the colonial enterprise that would come to dominate New England. (They would later come to be known as Congregationalists, for their insistence on a local level of church governance.) Charles I, who became king in 1625, was more hostile to Puritans than his father had been. Under his leadership, the Church of England drove dissenting clergymen from their pulpits, forcing congregations to worship secretly. Some Congregationalist merchants, concerned about their long-term prospects in England, dispatched a group of colonists to Cape Ann (north of Cape Cod) in 1628. The following year, the merchants obtained a royal charter, constituting themselves as the Massachusetts Bay Company.

The new joint-stock company quickly attracted the attention of Puritans who were increasingly convinced that they no longer would be able to practice their religion freely in their homeland. They remained committed to the goal of reforming the Church of England but concluded that they should pursue that aim in America. In a dramatic move, the Congregationalist merchants decided to transfer the Massachusetts Bay Company's headquarters to New England. The settlers would then be answerable to no one in the mother country and would be able to handle their affairs—secular and religious—as they pleased. Like the Plymouth settlers, they expected to profit from the codfishery; they also planned to export timber products.

2-5f Governor John Winthrop

In October 1629, the Massachusetts Bay Company elected John Winthrop, a member of the lesser English gentry, as its governor. Winthrop organized the initial segment of the Puritan migration to America. In 1630, more than one thousand English men and women moved to Massachusetts—most of them to Boston. By 1643, nearly twenty thousand more had followed.

Winthrop and his company were eager to avoid the failures that beset previous English settlements. Caught up in the currents of European utopian thought that overswept England in the sixteenth and seventeenth centuries, the colony's backers envisioned a utopia across the ocean—a new Jerusalem. Some time before the colonists embarked, Winthrop set down his expectations for the new colony in an essay called "Christian Charitie."

"Christian Charitie" stressed the communal nature of the colonists' endeavor. God, Winthrop explained, "hath so disposed of the condition of mankind as in all times some must be rich, some poor, some high and eminent in power and dignity, others mean and in subjection." But differences in status did not imply differences in worth.

△ This unsigned likeness of John Winthrop is believed to be of English origin, painted in the seventeenth century by a follower of Anthony van Dyck, the leading portraitist of the day. Born in 1588, Winthrop would have seen such stiff lace collars, known as ruffs, during his youth under the reign of Queen Elizabeth I. A generation later, van Dyck and his imitators used them as a kind of Elizabethan masquerade, a style of costume popular among fashionable sitters.

John Winthrop, c.1630-91 (oil on canvas)/AMERICAN ANTIQUARIAN SOCIETY/American Antiquarian Society, Worcester, Massachusetts, USA/Bridgeman Images

Turkeys

As they neared the end of their first year in North America, the Plymouth colonists held a traditional English feast to celebrate the harvest. Famously, they invited Massasoit's Pokanokets to join them, and just as famously, they probably consumed the bird known even then as the "wild turkey." But why was this bird, originally from America and still commonly eaten by Americans at Thanksgiving, given the name of a region of the then-Ottoman Empire? The Native peoples of the Americas had named the fowl in their own languages; Aztecs, for example, called a male bird *huexoloti* and a female *totolin*, while some northeastern Native peoples termed both *nehm*.

When Columbus returned from his first voyage, the birds were among the items he carried to Spain. The Iberian Peninsula had long served as a focal point for Mediterranean commerce, and Spanish mariners sailed frequently to ports in the Middle East. Before long, one of those Spanish vessels took some *huexoloti* and *totolin* to the Ottoman Empire. There, farmers already familiar with distant Asian relatives of the bird began to improve the breed. Within a few decades, they succeeded in producing a plumper and tamer version of the American fowl. By the 1540s, that bird had arrived in England, and by the end of the century "turkeys" were widely consumed for food throughout the British Isles.

Accordingly, when Thomas Harriot in his 1588 *Briefe and True Report* mentioned the wild North American version of the birds, he termed them "Turkie cockes and Turkie hennes." He failed to give the names local Native peoples used because—unlike the many other new plants and animals he encountered—these birds were already familiar to him and his reading audience.

The settlers at Jamestown and Plymouth recognized the birds they saw in their new homelands as relatives of the fowls they had consumed in England. But they regarded the wild American birds as inferior to English ones. Swift and hungry foragers, they ravaged young crops and were viewed primarily as pests. (Of course, any colonist fortunate enough to shoot one of them could have a tasty meal.) So the settlers in both Virginia and New England soon imported English turkeys, which they raised for meat along with chickens and pigs.

The origin of the "turkeys" most likely consumed at the so-called First Thanksgiving remains a mystery. Were they the wild American birds or the tame Ottoman-English variety? No matter; that they were termed "turkeys" linked these fowls of American origin to the Mediterranean, Europe, and the Middle East as a prime example of animals in the Columbian Exchange.

CRITICAL THINKING

- Using the colonists' preference for "English" turkeys over "American" turkeys as an example, describe the ideological underpinnings of English colonization. Did English colonizers always presume their own superiority?
- Have you encountered evidence of exceptions to this pattern?

A turkey-cock, brought to Jahangir from Goa in 1612, from the Wantage Album, Mughal, c.1612 (gouache on paper/Mansur (Ustad Mansur) (fl.c.1590-1630)/Victoria & Albert Museum, London, UK/Bridgeman Images

◁ Turkeys from the Americas quickly traveled around the world, as is illustrated by this Mughal painting from the Islamic empire in India. The local artist Ustad Mansur painted a "turkey-cock" brought to the emperor Jahangir in 1612 from Goa—a Portuguese enclave on the west coast of the Indian subcontinent. Presumably the turkey had been transported from the Iberian Peninsula to that European outpost, whence the fowl made its way to Jahangir's court—where it was immortalized by an artist to whom it was an unusual sight.

On the contrary, God had planned the world so that "every man might have need of others, and from hence they might be all knit more nearly together in the bond of brotherly affection." In New England, Winthrop warned, "we shall be as a city upon a hill, the eyes of all people are upon us." If the Puritans failed to carry out their "special commission" from God, "the Lord will surely break out in wrath against us," and the colony would become "a story and a by-word through the world."

Almost unknown in its day, Winthrop's essay became famous two centuries later. In 1838, one of his descendants published it for the first time, under its now-familiar title, "A Model of Christian Charity," recasting the discourse as a sermon preached en route to New England, and as a parable about uniquely American virtues.

Many modern-day politicians—most famously Ronald Reagan—have quoted Winthrop's speech to underline what they see as the exceptional destiny of the United States. But Winthrop of course could not have imagined an American nation. Rather, he envisioned a biblical commonwealth in which each person worked for the good of the whole. As in seventeenth-century England, this ideal society would be characterized by clear hierarchies of status and power. But Winthrop hoped its members would live according to the precepts of Christian love. Of course, such an ideal was beyond human reach. Early Massachusetts and its Caribbean counterpart, Providence Island, had their share of bitter quarrels and unchristian behavior. Remarkably, though, in New England the ideal persisted for generations.

2-5g Covenant Ideal

The Puritans expressed their communal ideal chiefly in the doctrine of the covenant. They believed God had made a covenant—that is, an agreement or contract—with them when they were chosen for the special mission to America. In turn, they covenanted with one another, promising to work together toward their goals. The founders of churches, towns, and even colonies in Anglo-America often drafted formal documents setting forth the principles on which their institutions would be based. The Pilgrims' Mayflower Compact was a covenant, as was the Fundamental Orders of Connecticut (1639), which laid down the basic law for the settlements established along the Connecticut River valley.

The leaders of Massachusetts Bay likewise transformed their original joint-stock company charter into the basis for a covenanted community. Under pressure from landowning male settlers, they gradually changed the General Court—officially the company's small governing body—into a colonial legislature. They also granted the status of freeman, or voting member, to all property-owning adult male church members. Less than two decades after the first large group of Puritans arrived in Massachusetts Bay, the colony had a functioning system of self-government composed of a governor and a two-house legislature.

2-5h New England Towns

The colony's method of distributing land helped to further its communal ideal. Unlike Virginia and Maryland, where individual planters acquired headrights and sited their farms separately, in Massachusetts groups of men—often from the same English village—applied together to the General Court for grants of land on which to establish towns (novel governance units that did not exist in England). Understandably, the grantees copied the villages whence they had come. First, they laid out lots for houses and a church. Then they gave each family parcels of land scattered around the town center—a pasture here, a woodlot there, an arable field elsewhere—reserving the best and largest plots for the most distinguished residents, including the minister. The "lower sort" received smaller and less desirable allotments. Still, every man and even a few single women obtained land, which sharply differentiated these villages from their English counterparts. When migrants began to move beyond the territorial limits of Massachusetts Bay into Connecticut (1636), New Haven (1638), and New Hampshire (1638), the same pattern of town formation persisted.

Town centers developed quickly, evolving in three distinct ways. Some, chiefly isolated agricultural settlements in the interior, tried to sustain Winthrop's vision of harmonious community life based on diversified family farms. A second group, the coastal towns like Boston and Salem, became bustling seaports, serving as focal points for trade and places of entry for thousands of new immigrants. The third category, commercialized agricultural towns, grew up in the Connecticut River valley, where easy water transportation made it possible for farmers to sell surplus goods readily. In Springfield, Massachusetts, for example, the merchant-entrepreneur William Pynchon and his son John began as fur traders and ended as large landowners with thousands of acres. Even in New England, then, the entrepreneurial spirit characteristic of the Chesapeake found expression. Yet the plans to profit from exports did not materialize quickly or easily; the new settlements lacked both the infrastructure necessary to support such enterprises and a climate conducive to staple crops.

2-5i Pequot War and Its Aftermath

Migration into the Connecticut valley ended the Puritans' relative freedom from clashes with nearby Pequots and Mohegans. The first English people in the valley moved there from Massachusetts Bay under the direction of their minister, Thomas Hooker. Although their new settlements were remote from other English towns, the wide river promised ready access to the ocean. The site had just one problem: it fell within the territory controlled by the powerful Pequot nation.

The Pequots' dominance stemmed from their role as intermediaries in the trade between New England Algonquians and the Dutch in New Netherland. The arrival of English settlers ended the Pequots' monopoly over regional trading networks. Clashes between Pequots and English colonists began even before the establishment of settlements in the Connecticut valley, but their founding tipped the balance toward war, and resulted in a series of exceptionally violent clashes that came to be known as the **Pequot War.** The Pequots tried unsuccessfully to enlist local Mohegan, Niantic, and Narragansett groups in resisting English expansion. After two English traders were killed in 1636 (not by Pequots), the English raided a Pequot village. In return, Pequots raided Wethersfield, Connecticut, in April 1637, killing nine and capturing two. That May, Englishmen and their Narragansett allies burned the main Pequot town on the Mystic River, slaughtering at least four hundred men, women, and children. John Underhill, one of the leaders of the English raid, said it was terrible "to see so many soules ... gasping on the ground so thicke in some places, that you could hardly passe along." Nonetheless, he insisted, the colonists had "sufficient light from the word of God for our proceedings," since "Scripture declareth women and children must perish with their parents." By September 1638, when the violence abated, most survivors of the slaughter were enslaved, some in New England and more in the cane fields of the Caribbean.

For the next four decades, the Native peoples of New England accommodated themselves to the European invasion. They traded with the newcomers and sometimes worked for them, but for the most part they resisted acculturation, or incorporation into English society. Native Americans continued to use traditional farming methods, which did not employ plows or fences, and women rather than men remained the chief cultivators. The one European practice they consistently adopted was keeping livestock, for domesticated animals provided excellent sources of meat once the English had turned traditional hunting territories into farms and wild game had disappeared.

2-5j Missionary Activities

Although the official seal of the Massachusetts Bay colony featured a Native figure crying, "Come over and help us," only a few Massachusetts clerics, most notably John Eliot and Thomas Mayhew, seriously undertook missionary work among the Algonquian. Eliot believed that Native people could not be properly Christianized unless they were also "civilized." He insisted that converts live in towns, farm the land in English fashion, take English names, wear European-style clothing and shoes, cut their hair, and discard a wide range of their own customs. Because Eliot demanded cultural transformation from his adherents, he met with little success. At the peak of Eliot's efforts, only eleven hundred Native people (out of many thousands) lived in the fourteen "Praying Towns" he established, and just 10 percent of the town residents had been formally baptized.

Eliot's failure to win converts contrasted sharply with the successful missions in New France. Puritan services lacked Catholicism's beautiful ceremonies and special appeal for women, and Calvinists could not promise believers a heavenly afterlife. Yet on the island of Martha's Vineyard, Thomas Mayhew showed that it was possible to convert substantial numbers of Native peoples to Calvinist Christianity. He

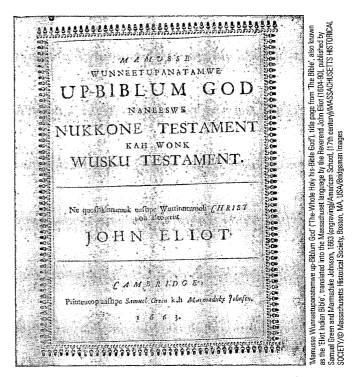

△ The first Bible printed in the English colonies in North America was this translation into the Algonquian dialect spoken by the Native peoples of Massachusetts. The Puritan minister John Eliot arranged for its translation and publication as part of his efforts to convert the Native peoples to Christianity. He did not succeed in gaining many adherents, but today this Bible is serving as a vocabulary source for Wampanoag activists who are revitalizing their language, Wôpanâak, the knowledge of which had been lost by the nineteenth century.

allowed Wampanoag Christians there to lead traditional lives, and he trained men of their own community to minister to them.

What attracted Native peoples to such religious ideas? Many must have turned to European religion to cope with the dramatic changes the intruders had wrought. The combination of disease, alcohol, new trading patterns, and loss of territory disrupted customary ways of life to an unprecedented extent. Shamans had little success restoring traditional ways. Many Native people must have concluded that the Europeans' own ideas could provide the key to survival in the new circumstances.

John Winthrop's description of a great smallpox epidemic that swept through southern New England in the early 1630s reveals the relationship among smallpox, conversion to Christianity, and English land claims. "A great mortality among the Indians," he noted in his journal in 1633.

Pequot War a series of violent clashes (c. 1636–1638) between English colonists and their Native allies and Pequot groups struggling to hang onto their lands in the Connecticut Valley.

"Divers of them, in their sickness, confessed that the Englishmen's God was a good God; and that if they recovered, they would serve him." Most did not recover: in January 1634, an English scout reported that smallpox had spread "as far as any Indian plantation was known to the west." By July, most of the Native peoples within a 300-mile radius of Boston had died of the disease. Winthrop noted with satisfaction, "the Lord hath cleared our title to what we possess."

2-6 Life in New England

▷ How did family life in New England differ from that in the Chesapeake?

▷ What were the characteristics of the New England economy and labor?

▷ What were the consequences of the institution of a Puritan legal code and behavioral expectations?

New England's colonizers adopted modes of life different from those of both their Algonquian neighbors and their Chesapeake counterparts. Algonquian bands usually moved four or five times each year to take full advantage of their environment. In spring, women planted the fields, but once crops were established, the plants did not need regular attention for several months. Villages then divided into small groups, women gathering wild foods and men hunting and fishing. The villagers returned to their fields for harvest, then separated again for fall hunting. Finally, the people wintered together in a sheltered spot before returning to the fields to resume the cycle the following spring.

Unlike the mobile Algonquians, English people lived year-round in the same location. And unlike residents of the Chesapeake, New Englanders constructed sturdy dwellings intended to last. (Some survive to this day.) Household furnishings and house sizes resembled those in the Chesapeake, but without a cash-crop monoculture, New Englanders' diets were more varied. They replowed the same fields, believing it was less arduous to employ manure as fertilizer than to clear new fields every few years. Furthermore, they fenced their croplands to prevent them from being overrun by the cattle, sheep, and hogs that were their chief sources of meat. Animal crowding more than human crowding caused New Englanders to spread out across the countryside; their livestock constantly needed more pasturage.

2-6a New England Families

Because Puritans often moved to America in family groups, the age range in early New England was wide; and because many more women migrated to New England than to the tobacco colonies, the population could immediately begin to reproduce itself. New England was also healthier than

△ Cradles like this one, made by a joiner living in the English plantations on Cape Cod in the third quarter of the seventeenth century, would have seen a lot of use in New England, where an even ratio of male to female settlers, early marriages, and relatively long life expectancies meant that large families—of five or more surviving children—quickly became the norm.

the Chesapeake and even the mother country. Adult male migrants to the Chesapeake lost about a decade from their English life expectancy of fifty to fifty-five years; their Massachusetts counterparts gained five or more years.

Where Chesapeake population patterns gave rise to families that were few in number, small in size, and transitory, New England's demographics made families there numerous, large, and long-lived. More even sex ratios allowed most to marry. Immigrant women married young (at age twenty, on the average); and marriages lasted longer and produced more children, who were more likely to live to maturity. New England women could anticipate raising five to seven healthy children.

The presence of so many children, combined with Puritans' stress on the importance of reading the Bible, led to widespread concern for the education of youth in New England. That people lived in towns meant small schools could be established; girls and boys were taught basic reading by their parents or a school "dame," and boys could then proceed to learn writing and eventually arithmetic and Latin.

Further, New England in effect invented grandparents. In England people rarely lived long enough to know their

▲ Elizabeth Eggington was eight years old when an unknown artist recorded her likeness in 1664. Among the earliest known paintings from New England, it shows the girl's high status. Her sumptuous clothing, edged with costly lace and decorated with red, yellow, and green ribbons, reveals the Puritans' surprising love of ornament. There is a picture within the picture: Elizabeth sports a tiny miniature portrait tied to her collar. Miniatures commemorated dead or absent loved ones. Elizabeth's portrait, too, may have been a mourning picture; the girl died soon after, or possibly before, the artist painted her.

sale overseas. On the large estates of the Connecticut River valley, where the microclimate allowed farmers to grow tobacco, landless male tenants served as hired hands. In eastern New England villages, poorer sons and daughters were often "put out" or apprenticed in the households of richer neighboring families. But family labor was the norm. Sons took up the callings of their fathers and daughters, their mothers.

The prevalence of family labor should not blind us to the presence of slavery in New England. As the 1638 voyage of the *Desire* to sell captive Pequots in the Caribbean, and Africans in Massachusetts demonstrates, Puritan principles did not rule out chattel slavery. John Winthrop himself kept a Narragansett man and his wife as slaves; upon his death, he bequeathed them to one of his sons. Another early Boston settler, Samuel Maverick, purchased three of the people Pierce brought to Massachusetts, two women and one man. Maverick, who wanted from this purchase "to have a breed of Negroes," compelled his enslaved man to rape one of the women. One of Maverick's houseguests heard her scream during the assault.

Like cotton, tobacco, and salt, African men, women, and children were Atlantic commodities, bought and sold in Boston and other ports around the ocean's rim. Pierce's human cargo numbered among the first Africans trafficked in New England. By mid-century, roughly four hundred people of African descent lived in the region, the great majority enslaved. Their number increased slowly but steadily, hovering around two in every hundred New Englanders for most of the colonial era, with higher concentrations in seaports like Boston and, later, Newport, Rhode Island. In 1650, the scale of New England's black population, and the legal status of those forced migrants, closely resembled that of the Chesapeake.

2-6c Impact of Religion

Puritanism gave New England a distinctive culture. Puritans controlled the governments of Massachusetts Bay, Plymouth, Connecticut, and the other early northern colonies. In Massachusetts Bay and New Haven, church membership was a prerequisite for voting in colony elections. All the early English colonies, north and south, taxed residents to build churches and pay ministers' salaries, but only in New England were provisions of criminal codes based on the Old Testament. Massachusetts's first bodies of law (1641 and 1648) drew heavily from scripture; New Haven, Plymouth, New Hampshire, and Connecticut later copied them. All New Englanders were required to attend religious services, whether or not they were church members. Their leaders also believed the state was obliged to support and protect the one true church—theirs.

Puritan legal codes dwelled heavily on moral conduct. Children who dishonored their parents broke the Fifth Commandment and thus risked execution, though only one young man, Salem's John Porter, Jr., was ever prosecuted

children's children. And whereas early Chesapeake parents commonly died before their children married, New England parents exercised a good deal of control over their adult offspring. Young men could not marry without acreage to cultivate, and they depended on their fathers for that land. Daughters, too, needed a dowry of household goods supplied by their parents. These needs sometimes led to conflict between the generations.

2-6b Labor in a New Land

The large number of young people in New England also shaped the region's labor force. Where Chesapeake planters—who had small families and large cash-crop farms—relied chiefly on bound workers, New England settlers—who farmed smaller lots with larger families—shaped a different economy to fit their different society. Early New England farms produced chiefly for subsistence and local sale; the region's climate generally did not support the production of staple crops intended for large-scale

for this offense. (He was not convicted.) Laws forbade drunkenness, card playing, dancing, or even cursing—yet the frequency of such offenses demonstrates that New Englanders regularly engaged in these banned activities. Couples who had sex before marriage (as revealed by the birth of a baby less than nine months after their wedding) faced fines and public humiliation. Nonetheless, roughly one bride in ten was pregnant. Sodomy, usually defined as sex between men, was punishable by death. Yet only two men were executed for the crime in the seventeenth century; though not accepted, "sodomitical" conduct was often overlooked. "Considering their Actions," J. W., one of New England's many critics, quipped in 1682, "their Laws look like but Scarecrows."

It is easy to think of the Puritans as killjoys and hypocrites, as many people did at the time. (They had "God in their mouths, but the Devil in their hearts and actions," J. W. said.) But New England's social conservatism stemmed from its radical views on the nature of true religion and the relationship of true religion to just government. A central irony of Puritan dissent—and a central dilemma of the early New England colonies—was that their godly experiment tended to attract people more radical than the colonies' leaders. Although they came to America seeking freedom to worship as they pleased, New England preachers and magistrates saw no contradiction in refusing to grant that freedom to those who held different religious beliefs.

2-6d Roger Williams

Roger Williams, a young minister trained at Cambridge, England, migrated to Massachusetts in 1631 trailing a reputation as "a godly and zealous preacher." Zealous he was. The Bay Colony, he believed, had gone too far in some areas, and not far enough in others. Williams preached that the Massachusetts Bay Company had no right to land already occupied by Native peoples, that church and state should be entirely separate, and that Puritans should not impose their ideas on others. The bond between God and the faithful was intimate and individual, Williams said; policing it was not the role of government.

For years, the colony's leaders tried without success to wean Williams from his "dangerous opinions," which began to "infect" many others. Called before the General Court in October 1635, he refused to retract his claim that the colony's churches were "full of Antichristian pol[l]ution," among other statements. Fearful that his beliefs tended to anarchy, the magistrates banished him from the colony. When soldiers came to escort him to a ship back to England, they discovered that he had already fled.

Williams trekked through the hard winter

Roger Williams A minister who advocated complete separation of church and state and religious tolerance.

Anne Hutchinson Dissenter who was feared not only for her theology but also because she challenged gender roles; banished from Massachusetts in 1638.

of 1636 to the head of Narragansett Bay, where he founded the town of Providence on land he obtained from the Narragansetts and Wampanoags. Providence and other towns in what became Rhode Island adopted a policy of tolerating all faiths, including Judaism. In the following years, the tiny colony founded by Williams became a haven for other dissenters whose ideas threatened New England orthodoxy. Some Puritans called it "Rogue's Island."

2-6e Anne Hutchinson

No sooner was Williams banished than Mistress **Anne Hutchinson** presented another sustained challenge to Massachusetts leaders. The daughter of an English clergyman—the title *Mistress* signaled her high status—Hutchinson was a skilled medical practitioner popular with the women of Boston. She greatly admired John Cotton, a minister who emphasized the covenant of grace, or God's free gift of salvation to unworthy human beings. (By contrast, most Puritan clerics stressed the need for believers to engage in good works in preparation to receive God's grace.) After spreading her ideas when women gathered during childbirths, Hutchinson began holding meetings in her home to discuss Cotton's sermons. Proclaiming that the faithful could communicate directly with God, she questioned the importance of the institutional church and its ministers. Such ideas—along with Hutchinson's model of female authority—posed a dangerous threat to Puritan orthodoxy.

In November 1637, officials charged her with maligning the colony's ministers. During her trial, Hutchinson cleverly matched wits with her learned adversaries, including Winthrop himself. But after two days of holding her own in debate, she boldly declared that God had spoken to her directly. That assertion assured her banishment. The clergy also excommunicated her—thus in their view, consigning her to hell. "You have stepped out of your place," one preacher told her, "you have rather been a Husband than a Wife and a preacher than a Hearer; and a Magistrate than a Subject." Civil authorities were concerned enough about the revolutionary potential of Hutchinson's ideas that they disarmed scores of her male supporters and exiled Hutchinson, her family, and some of her followers to Rhode Island in 1638.

2-7 The Caribbean

▶ In what ways was the Caribbean at the center of the "Americas" in the seventeenth century?

▶ How did sugar cultivation develop in the Caribbean?

New England and the Chesapeake often dominate histories of colonial America. Projecting backward in time from the establishment of the United States, we find in those regions of the North American mainland seedbeds of the American nation: the passion for self-government revealed in the Mayflower Compact and the House of Burgesses, the family culture of the Puritans, the tolerance of Rhode Island and Maryland. But if we look forward from the seventeenth century instead of backward from 1776, or if we imagine ourselves in the counting houses of London rather than the meetinghouses of Boston, New England and the Chesapeake recede in importance, and the Caribbean looms large (see Map 2.3). In many respects, the island colonies of the West Indies lay at the center, rather than the margins, of what Europeans meant by "America."

France, the Netherlands, and England collided repeatedly in the Caribbean. The Spanish concentrated their colonization efforts on the Greater Antilles—Cuba, Hispaniola, Jamaica, and Puerto Rico. The tiny islands Spain ignored attracted other European powers seeking bases from which to attack Spanish ships loaded with American gold and silver. In the late sixteenth century, as England and Spain warred continually, treasure seized by privateers in the Spanish West Indies added between £100,000 and £200,000 per year to England's treasury.

England was the first northern European nation to establish a permanent foothold in the smaller Caribbean islands (the Lesser Antilles), colonizing St. Christopher (St. Kitts) in 1624, then later other islands, such as Barbados (1627), Providence (1630), and Antigua (1632).

France defeated the Caribs to colonize Guadeloupe and Martinique, and the Dutch gained control of tiny St. Eustatius (strategically located near St. Christopher). In addition to indigenous resistance, tropical diseases, and devastating hurricanes, Europeans in the West Indies worried about conflicts with one another. Like Providence Island, many colonies changed hands during the seventeenth century. For example, the English drove the Spanish out of Jamaica in 1655, and the French soon thereafter took over half of Hispaniola, creating the colony of St. Domingue (modern Haiti).

2-7a Sugar Cultivation

At first, most English planters in the West Indies grew fiber crops including cotton and flax (for linen), dye plants such as indigo, food crops like cacao, and tobacco. But beginning in the 1630s, what historians call a "sugar revolution" remade the West Indies and changed the center of gravity in England's America.

Europeans loved sugar, which offered sweetness and calories. The crop greatly enriched those who grew and processed it for international markets. Entering Europe in

Map 2.3 Caribbean Colonies ca. 1700

English, Spanish, French, Dutch, and other European powers fought for territory in the Caribbean basin throughout the colonial period. At stake were prized shipping routes and the high value of the cash crops produced on the islands, especially sugar, which brought in far more revenue than any other colonial product. Sugar demanded a huge labor force, and so the Caribbean was also the center of the transatlantic slave trade. Many of the enslaved people in mainland British North America were first brought in chains to Jamaica or Barbados.

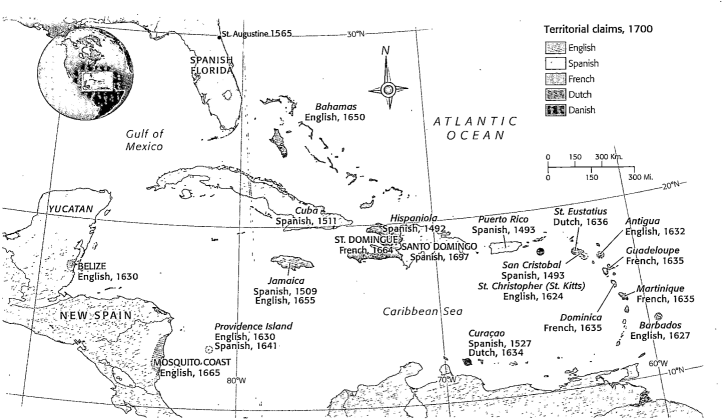

substantial quantities at approximately the same time as coffee and tea—stimulating, addictive, and bitter Asian drinks—sugar quickly became crucial to the European diet. By 1700, the English were consuming four pounds of sugar per person each year—a figure that would more than quadruple by the end of the century.

Until Columbus, Europe's sugar came primarily from the wine islands of the Mediterranean Atlantic and from São Tomé, the Portuguese colony located off West Africa's Slave Coast. The first sugar grown in the West Indies reached Spain in 1517. By the 1530s, some thirty-four sugar mills operated on the island of Hispaniola alone. (Columbus's son Diego owned the largest one.) These were factory-like complexes, with grinding mills, boiling houses, refineries, warehouses, and round-the-clock workforces. Sugar cane had to be processed within two days of being harvested, or the juice would dry, so producers rushed their cane to be crushed, boiled down, and finally refined into brown and white sugars. The work was backbreaking, even lethal. The Spanish population of Hispaniola was relatively small, and warfare and disease had virtually wiped out the indigenous Taíno. The island's sugar was processed by large numbers of enslaved Africans—perhaps 25,000 of them by 1550. "[A]s a result of the sugar factories," one chronicler noted in 1546, Hispaniola had become "an image of Ethiopia itself."

By 1600, Brazil had come to dominate the West Indies sugar trade. Connections between Portuguese planters in the northeastern province of Pernambuco and the Portuguese merchants who controlled the slaving forts of Angola gave Brazilian sugar growers a competitive advantage. Eager to seize that advantage for themselves, the Dutch conquered both ends of this supply chain in the 1630s.

The English colonizers of Barbados discovered in the early 1640s that the island's soil and climate were ideal for cultivating sugar cane. Several of them had visited Dutch Brazil, and Dutch capital, technology, and slaving routes would prove crucial to Barbados's sugar revolution. In the 1640s and 1650s, Barbadian tobacco growers and other small farmers sold out to sugar planters, who used the profits from their crop to amass enormous landholdings. The sugar planters staffed their fields and furnaces with large gangs of bound laborers—African slaves, English and Irish servants, Portuguese convicts—any man who could be bought and worked for six or eight years, until sugar used him up.

But as the Atlantic trade in Africans grew cheaper and more efficient, race-based slavery came to prevail. By the last quarter of the seventeenth century, 175 large planters, each of whom owned more than 100 acres and 60 slaves, controlled the economy of Barbados. So much of the island's arable land was devoted to sugarcane that the planters had to

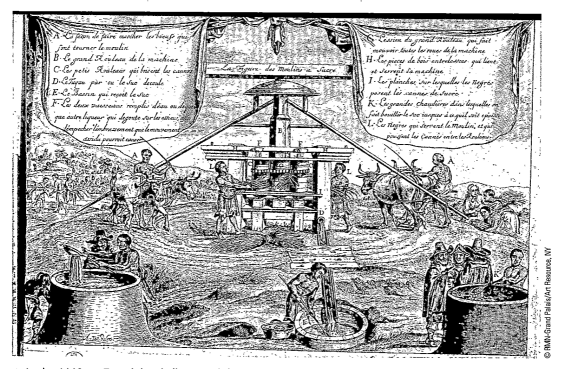

△ In the 1660s, a French book illustrated the various phases of sugar processing for curious European readers. Teams of oxen (A) turned the mill, the rollers of which crushed the canes (C), producing the sap (D), which was collected in a vat (E), then boiled down into molasses (K). African slaves, with minimal supervision by a few Europeans (foreground), managed all phases of the process.

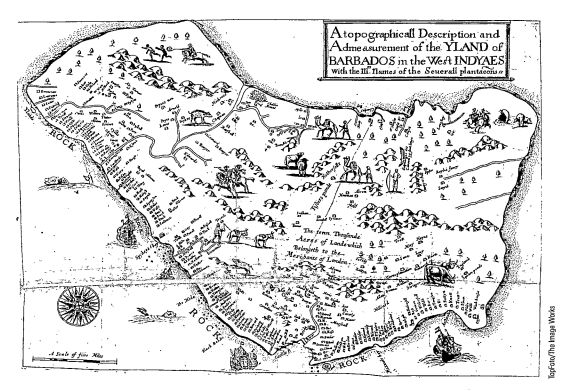

△ First printed in 1657, Richard Ligon's map of Barbados depicts the colony in the midst of its transition to a sugar-growing monoculture. English plantations line the island's Leeward Coast. At the top left corner of the map, a planter on horseback fires his musket at two enslaved Africans attempting to escape. Ligon had seen such cruelty first-hand, and he wrote about it in his *True and Exact History of Barbados*.

import their food; farmers and fishermen on the mainland grew rich shipping grain, cod, and beef to the Caribbean. Barbados, like West Indies more broadly, had become a slave society. The island's English population fell from 30,000 in the 1640s to less than 20,000 in 1680, while the number of the enslaved rose from 6,000 to more than 46,000. Guadeloupe, Jamaica, St. Kitts, and Antigua witnessed similar transitions.

Life for servants and slaves in the West Indies was vicious and short. In Barbados, the English traveler Richard Ligon observed in 1647, "I have seen an overseer beat a servant with a cane about the head till the blood has followed for a fault that is not truly worth the speaking of." The planter aristocracy had learned that such brutality paid. By 1680, Barbados had become the most valuable colony in British America, the jewel in the empire's crown. Sugar exports from that small island alone were worth more than all of the exports from the rest of British America—*combined*.

Summary

By the middle of the seventeenth century, Europeans had come to North America and the Caribbean to stay, a fact that signaled major changes for the peoples of both hemispheres. These newcomers had indelibly altered not only their own lives but also those of Native peoples. Europeans killed Native peoples with their weapons and diseases and had varying success in converting them to Christianity. Indigenous peoples taught Europeans to eat new foods, speak new languages, and to recognize—however reluctantly—the persistence of other cultural patterns. The prosperity and even survival of many of the European colonies depended on the cultivation of American crops (maize and tobacco) and an Asian crop (sugar), thus attesting to the importance of post-Columbian ecological exchange.

Political rivalries once confined to Europe spread around the globe, as England, Spain, Portugal, France, and the Netherlands vied for control of the peoples and resources of Asia, Africa, and the Americas. In South America, Spaniards reaped the benefits of their gold and silver mines, while French colonists earned their primary profits from the fur trade (in Canada) and cultivating sugar (in the Caribbean). Sugar also enriched the Portuguese in Brazil and the English in Barbados. The Dutch concentrated on commerce, trading in furs in North America and sugar in the West Indies.

To a greater extent than their European counterparts, the English transferred the society and politics of

"Modern" Families

Since the late twentieth century, "family values" has been a catchphrase in American politics. Organizations such as Focus on the Family and the American Family Association (both founded by Christian evangelicals in 1977) lobby Washington to protect so-called traditional families from what they see as the modern plagues of premarital sex, fatherless households, and easy divorce. But not much about the "traditional" American family is in fact traditional. In many ways, the families created by seventeenth-century English migrants to the Chesapeake look remarkably modern.

English women were scarce in early Virginia and Maryland. In the first decades of colonization, men outnumbered women by as much as six to one; by mid-century, there were still as many as three male settlers for every female. Young women who made the journey typically migrated as servants, owing five to seven years of labor after they docked. By law, they could not marry during that time; masters did not want to lose working hands to pregnancy. Roughly one in five servant women became pregnant while under indenture nonetheless. Many did so shortly after their contracts ended. In parts of Maryland, one woman in three was pregnant when she married, more than double the rate in most English parishes. Servant women were often punished for bearing an illegitimate child. But marriage itself could be informally contracted. With few ministers around to solemnize their vows, some couples simply declared themselves wed—or, on occasion, divorced.

Both more valuable and more vulnerable than they would have been in England, women in the Chesapeake had their pick of husbands. But indenture delayed marriage, and the region's high rates of endemic disease meant that families easily formed were also easily broken. Only one marriage in three lasted as long as a decade before a spouse died—typically the man. Widows remarried quickly, often within a few months of a husband's death. Men planned for this eventuality, giving their wives an unusual degree of control over their property and their children.

What did early Chesapeake families look like, then? With two or three children, they were smaller than American families in the post–World War II era. Households formed when parents remarried and combined the remnants of previous families included a motley array of blood kin and step-kin. Children routinely grew up with orphaned cousins, half-siblings, and stepparents. One Baltimore County boy had three different stepfathers within a decade.

As the region's demography slowly stabilized, these decidedly modern households of English descent began to police family boundaries more zealously—especially as people of African descent were brought in chains to the Chesapeake. Those boundaries, too, were modern innovations, not time-honored traditions. Then as now, new worlds made extraordinary demands on families, and tradition was a luxury few could afford.

CRITICAL THINKING

◻ When sex ratios were imbalanced in colonial America, family life was much more fluid. As the ratio of men to women, and with it the number of marriages, began to stabilize, English colonists began to police familial boundaries more closely. Similarly, modern groups like Focus on the Family and the American Family Association police modern families in an effort to prevent the erosion of what they deem traditional family values. Are the motivations of both efforts similar?

◻ Why or why not?

---

their homeland to a new environment. Their sheer numbers, coupled with their hunger for vast quantities of land on which to grow crops and raise livestock, brought them into conflict with their indigenous neighbors. New England and the Chesapeake differed in the structure of their populations, the nature of their economies, their settlement patterns, and their religious culture. Yet they resembled each other in the conflicts their expansion engendered, and in their tentative experiments with the use of slave labor. In years to come, both regions would become embroiled in increasingly fierce rivalries besetting the European powers.

Suggestions for Further Reading

Richard S. Dunn, *Sugar and Slaves: The Rise of the Planter Class in the English West Indies, 1624–1713* (1972)

Alison Games, *Migration and the Origins of the English Atlantic World* (1999)

David D. Hall, *A Reforming People: Puritanism and the Transformation of Public Life in New England* (2011)

Jane Kamensky, *Governing the Tongue: The Politics of Speech in Early New England* (1997)

Karen O. Kupperman, *The Jamestown Project* (2007)

Mary Beth Norton, *Founding Mothers & Fathers: Gendered Power and the Forming of American Society* (1996)

Stephan Palmié and Francisco Scarano, eds., *The Caribbean: A History of the Region and Its Peoples* (2011)

Christopher L. Tomlins, *Freedom Bound: Law, Labor, and Civic Identity in Colonizing English America, 1580–1865* (2010)

Wendy Warren, *New England Bound: Slavery and Colonization in Early America* (2016)

David J. Weber, *The Spanish Frontier in North America* (1992)

MINDTAP
From Cengage

MindTap® is a fully online personalized learning experience built upon Cengage Learning content. MindTap® combines student learning tools—readings, multimedia, activities, and assessments—into a singular Learning Path that guides students through the course and helps students develop the critical thinking, analysis, and communication skills that are essential to academic and professional success.

3

North America in the Atlantic World, 1650–1720

heir journey began in Mohawk country, where western New York met eastern Iroquoia. As European settlements in the region grew in size and power, each of the four men had sought a new birth under the Christian God. Tejonihokarawa, from the Wolf Clan, became Hendrick. Sagayenkwaraton, whose Mohawk name meant Vanishing Smoke, would be called Brant. Onigoheriago was baptized John. Etowaucum, a Mohican, took the name Nicholas. They may have found solace in their adopted faith; they also found in the English new allies against old enemies.

Now, in a season of war—part of England's decades-long struggle to wrest the heart of North America from the French—those allies tapped the four Christian Native Americans for a diplomatic mission. Peter Schuyler, a fur trader of Dutch descent who had become a leading citizen of English Albany, directed the operation. His cousin, who knew Mohawk, would serve as interpreter. A British army officer advised the Native emissaries on delicate matters of protocol.

Hendrick, Brant, John, Nicholas, and their retinue traveled overland from Albany to Boston, the capital of another English colony. At Boston's Long Wharf, they boarded one of the vessels that regularly sailed the Atlantic, carrying English manufactures to New England and returning east loaded with timbers, fish, and furs. Six weeks later, after what they called "a long and tedious Voyage," the delegation landed "on the other side of the Great Water." From Portsmouth, coaches took them to London, a city housing three-quarters of a million people—more than twice as many as lived in all of mainland British America.

In the teeming metropolis, the go-betweens were groomed for their task. A theater company's costumers fitted them out "in black under clothes after the English manner." Scarlet cloaks trimmed

◁ Images of the "Indian Kings" circulated widely during and after their visit to London. Queen Anne commissioned these formal state portraits, painted by the Dutch artist John Verelst. Their likenesses were also reproduced in formats ranging from mezzotint engravings to woodcuts on ballads and broadsides affordable by the masses of people who followed their story. Etow Oh Koam, King of the River Nations, 1710 (oil on canvas)/Verelst, Johannes or Jan (b.1648-fl.1719)/Private Collection/Bridgeman Images/Sa Ga Yeath Qua Pieth Ton, King of the Maguas, 1710 (oil on canvas)/Verelst, Johannes or Jan (b.1648-fl.1719)/Private Collection/Bridgeman Images/No Nee Yeath Tan no Ton, King of the Generath, 1710 (oil on canvas)/Verelst, Johannes or Jan (b.1648-fl.1719)/Private Collection/Bridgeman Images/Tac Yec Neen Ho Gar Ton, Emperor of the Six Nations, 1710 (oil on canvas)/Verelst, Johannes or Jan (b.1648-fl.1719)/Private Collection/Bridgeman Images

Chronology

1642–46	English Civil War
1649	Charles I executed
1651	First Navigation Act passed to regulate colonial trade
1660	Stuarts (Charles II) restored to throne
1663	Carolina chartered
1664	English conquer New Netherland; New York founded
	New Jersey established
1670	Marquette, Jolliet, and La Salle explore the Great Lakes and Mississippi valley for France
1672	England's Royal African Company chartered; becomes largest single slave-trading enterprise
1675–76	Bacon's Rebellion disrupts Virginia government; Jamestown destroyed
1675–78	King Philip's War devastates New England
1680–1700	Pueblo revolt temporarily drives Spaniards from New Mexico
1681	Pennsylvania chartered
1685	Charles II dies; James II becomes king of England, Ireland, and Scotland
1686–88	Dominion of New England established, superseding charters of colonies from Maine to New Jersey
1688–89	James II deposed in Glorious Revolution; William and Mary ascend English throne
1689	Glorious Revolution in America; Massachusetts, New York, and Maryland overthrow royal governors
1688–99	King William's War fought on northern New England frontier
1691	New Massachusetts charter issued
1692	Witchcraft crisis in Salem; nineteen people hanged
	Earthquake ravages Port Royal, Jamaica
1696	Board of Trade and Plantations established to coordinate English colonial administration
	Vice-admiralty courts established in America
1701	Iroquois Confederacy adopts neutrality policy toward France and England
1702–13	Queen Anne's War fought by French and English
1707	Act of Union unites Scotland and England as Great Britain
1710	Four "Indian Kings" visit London
1711–13	Tuscarora War (North Carolina) leads to capture or migration of most Tuscaroras
1715	Yamasee War nearly destroys South Carolina

in gold replaced their blankets. Their feet were encased in soft yellow slippers and their long hair tucked beneath turbans. They were given grand new titles to match their elaborate costumes: not even lesser sachems at home among the nations of the Iroquois Confederacy, in London the four men became "Indian Kings."

Finally, on the morning of April 19, 1710, they arrived at St. James Palace. Queen Anne—ruler of Scotland and England, newly unified as Great Britain—received the American ambassadors with "more than ordinary solemnity," one observer noted. The diplomats presented the "Great Queen" with gifts of wampum, pledged·their help against "her Enemies the *French*," and asked her to commit more men and materiel to prosecute the war at the western edges of her dominion.

The Four Indian Kings stayed in London for two weeks, making a royal progress. They sat for state portraits that would hang in Kensington Palace. They dined with dukes and admirals; they met with American merchants and British officials; they visited inmates in the madhouse and paupers in the workhouse; they watched plays and cockfights. Crowds trailed them everywhere, and thousands more read about them in the newspapers, which reported that the visitors loved "*English* Beef before all other Victuals" and preferred English ales to "the best *French* wines." Before they left, the Four Kings sailed down the Thames to Greenwich, where they toured the dockyards that made the ships that were knitting together the Crown's growing blue-water empire.

Experience an interactive version of this story in MindTap®.

H endrick, Brant, John, and Nicholas were far from the first Native Americans to cross the Atlantic. Encounters between new world peoples and the courts of Europe had begun in 1493, when Columbus brought half a dozen Taíno back from his first voyage "so that they can learn to speak," as he put it. In 1616, Pocahontas sailed from Jamestown to St. James, where she was greeted as Lady Rebecca.

But the Four Indian Kings came as tributaries from a *new* new world. In the near-century between Pocahontas's Atlantic crossing and theirs, England's tentative plantations overseas had become a coherent international network: an empire. North America, like England itself, was embedded in a worldwide matrix of trade and warfare. The web woven by oceangoing vessels—once composed of only a few strands spun by Columbus and his successors—now crisscrossed the globe, carrying European goods to America and Africa, Africans to the Americas, Caribbean sugar to New England and Europe, and New England fish and timber (and occasionally Native American slaves) to the Caribbean. Formerly tiny outposts, the North American colonies expanded their territorial claims and diversified their economies after the mid-seventeenth century. Mohawk country was closer to the British metropolis than ever before.

Three developments shaped life in the mainland English colonies between 1650 and 1720: escalating conflicts with Native peoples and with other European colonies in North America; the expansion of slavery, especially in the southern coastal regions and the Caribbean; and changes in the colonies' relationships with England.

The explosive growth of the slave trade significantly altered the Anglo-American economy. Carrying human cargoes paid off handsomely, as many mariners and ship owners learned. Planters who could afford to buy slaves also reaped huge profits. At first involving primarily Native peoples and already enslaved Africans from the Caribbean, the trade soon came to focus on men and women kidnapped in Africa and brought directly to the Americas. The arrival of large numbers of captive West African peoples expanded agricultural productivity, fueled the international trading system, and dramatically reshaped every facet of colonial society.

The burgeoning North American economy attracted new attention from English administrators. Especially after the Stuarts were restored to the throne in 1660 (having lost it for a time because of the English Civil War), London bureaucrats attempted to supervise the American settlements more effectively to ensure that the mother country benefited from their economic growth. By the early eighteenth century, following three decades of upheaval, a new stability characterized colonial political institutions.

Neither English colonists nor London officials could ignore other peoples living on the North American continent. As English settlements expanded, they came into conflict not only with powerful American Indian nations but also with the Dutch, the Spanish, and especially the French. By 1720, war—between Europeans and Native Americans, among Europeans, and among the Native allies of different colonial powers—had become an all-too-familiar feature of American life. No longer isolated from one another or from Europe, the people and products of the North American colonies had become integral to the world trading system and inextricably enmeshed in its conflicts.

▨ *What were the consequences of the transatlantic slave trade in North America and Africa?*

▨ *How did English policy toward the colonies change from 1650 to 1720?*

▨ *What were the causes and results of heightened friction between Europeans and Native peoples?*

3-1 The Growth of Anglo-American Settlements

▶ **How did the English Civil War, and then the Restoration, affect the development of the colonies?**

▶ **What forms of government did settlers establish in the Restoration colonies?**

▶ **How did colonists interact with Native American populations in the Restoration colonies?**

Between 1642 and 1646, civil war between supporters of King Charles I and the Puritan-dominated Parliament engulfed England. Parliament triumphed, leading to the execution of the king in 1649 and interim rule by the parliamentary army's leader, Oliver Cromwell, during the so-called Commonwealth period. But after Cromwell's death late in 1658, Parliament agreed to restore the monarchy if Charles I's son and heir agreed to restrictions on his authority. Charles II did so, and the Stuarts were returned to the throne in 1660 (see Table 3.1).

The Restoration, as the period following the coronation of Charles II was known, transformed the king's realm, including England's overseas plantations. After two decades of Puritan plainness, the restored Stuart monarchy reveled in pomp and splendor. The king's jeweled coronation suit was said to cost £30,000. But Charles also lavished funds beyond the grandeur of his court. Royal patronage buoyed literature, art, philosophy, and science. The intellectual life of England faced outward, from a small island to an expanding world. The money for the government's growing expenditures was to come from overseas commerce as well. More than his predecessors, Charles II and his ministers saw trade as the wellspring of England's greatness. Merchants won new charters for trading ventures around the world. Increasingly, England's America lay at the heart of a grand commercial design.

Table 3.1 Restored Stuart Monarchs of England, 1660–1714

Monarch	Reign	Relation to Predecessor
Charles II	1660–1685	Son
James II	1685–1688	Brother
Mary	1688–1694	Daughter
William	1688–1702	Son-in-law
Anne	1702–1714	Sister, Sister-in-law

The new king rewarded nobles and others who had supported him during the Civil War with vast tracts of land in North America and the West Indies. The colonies thereby established made up six of the thirteen provinces that eventually would form the United States—New York, New Jersey, Pennsylvania (including Delaware), and North and South Carolina (see Map 3.1)—as well as Jamaica, the richest of the thirteen colonies that would remain loyal to the Crown. Collectively, these became known as the Restoration colonies, because they were created by the restored Stuart monarchy.

3-1a New York

In 1664, Charles II deeded the region between the Connecticut and Delaware rivers, including the Hudson Valley and Long Island, to his younger brother James, the duke of York. That the Dutch had settled there mattered little; the English and the Dutch were engaged in sporadic warfare, and the English were also attacking other Dutch colonies. In August, James's warships anchored off Manhattan Island, demanding New Netherland's surrender. The colony complied without resistance. Although in 1672 the Netherlands briefly retook the colony, the Dutch permanently ceded it in 1674.

In New Netherland, James acquired a heterogeneous possession, which he renamed after himself, as New York (see Table 3.2). In 1664, a significant minority of English people (mostly Puritan New Englanders on Long Island) already lived there, along with the Dutch and sizable numbers of Algonquians, Mohawks, Mohicans, Iroquois, Africans, Germans, Scandinavians, and a smattering of other Europeans. The Dutch West India Company had imported slaves into the colony; at the time of the English conquest, almost one-fifth of Manhattan's approximately fifteen hundred inhabitants were of African descent. Slaves then made up a higher proportion of New York's urban population than of the Chesapeake's rural people.

James's representatives moved cautiously in their efforts to establish English authority over this diverse population. The Duke's Laws, a legal code proclaimed in 1665, applied solely to the English settlements on Long Island, only later extended to the rest of the colony. James's

Table 3.2 The Founding of English Colonies in North America and the West Indies, 1661–1681

Colony	Founder(s)	Date	Basis of Economy
Jamaica	Oliver Cromwell Charles II	1655/1661	Cacao, indigo, beef, sugar
New York (formerly New Netherland)	James, Duke of York	1664	Farming, fur trading
New Jersey	Sir George Carteret John Berkeley (Lord Berkeley)	1664	Farming
North Carolina	Carolina proprietors	1665	Tobacco, forest products
South Carolina	Carolina proprietors	1670	Rice, indigo
Pennsylvania (incl. Delaware)	William Penn	1681	Farming

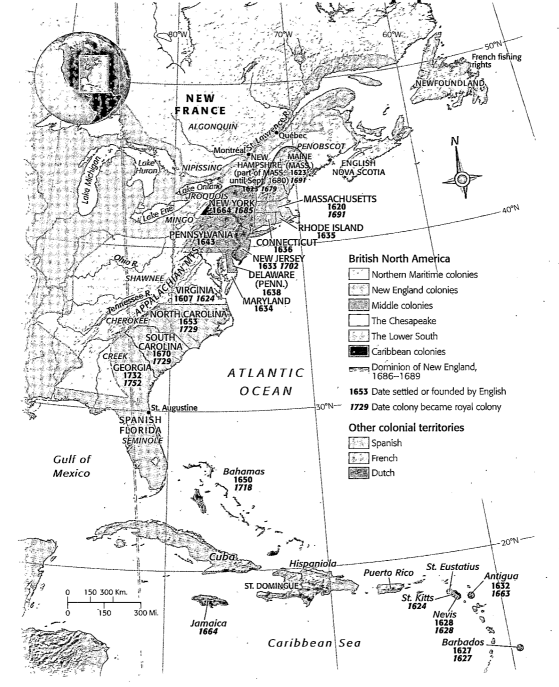

Map 3.1 The Anglo-American Colonies in the Early Eighteenth Century

By the early eighteenth century, the English colonies nominally dominated the Atlantic coastline of North America. But their formal boundary lines are deceiving. The western reaches of each colony were still largely unfamiliar to Europeans. Much of the land was still inhabited and controlled by Native Americans.

policies initially preserved Dutch forms of local government, confirmed Dutch land titles, and allowed Dutch residents to maintain customary legal practices. Each town was permitted to decide which church (Dutch Reformed, Congregational, or Anglican) to support with its taxes. Like other Stuarts, James distrusted legislative bodies, and not until 1683 did he agree to the colonists' requests for an elected legislature. Before then, an autocratic royal governor ruled New York.

The duke did not promote migration, so the colony's population grew slowly, barely reaching eighteen thousand by the time of the first English census in 1698. Until the second decade of the eighteenth century, Manhattan remained a commercial backwater within the orbit of Boston.

3-1b New Jersey

The English conquest brought so little change to New York primarily because the duke of York in 1664 regranted the land between the Hudson and Delaware rivers—East and West Jersey—to his friends Sir George Carteret and John Berkeley (Lord Berkeley). That grant left the duke's own

◁ The Dutch artist Johannes Vingboons painted this view of New Amsterdam/New York in 1665, shortly after the English takeover. Note the windmill, the tall government buildings, and the small row houses, which made the settlement resemble European villages of its day.

The New York Public Library/Art Resource, NY

colony hemmed in between Connecticut to the east and the Jerseys to the west and south, depriving it of much fertile land. Meanwhile, the Jersey proprietors acted rapidly to attract settlers, promising generous land grants, limited freedom of religion, and—without authorization from the Crown—a representative assembly. Large numbers of Puritan New Englanders migrated southward to the Jerseys, along with some Barbadians, Dutch New Yorkers, and eventually Scots. New Jersey grew quickly; in 1726, at the time of its first census as a united colony, it had 32,500 inhabitants, only 8,000 fewer than New York.

Within twenty years, Berkeley and Carteret sold their interests in the Jerseys to separate groups of investors. The purchasers of all of Carteret's share (West Jersey) and portions of Berkeley's (East Jersey) were members of the Society of Friends, also called **Quakers**. That small radical sect rejected earthly and religious hierarchies. With no formally trained clergy, Quakers allowed both men and women to speak in meetings and become "public Friends" who traveled to preach God's word. Quakers proselytized throughout the Atlantic world in the 1650s, recruiting followers in all of England's colonies from a base in Barbados. The authorities did not welcome the Quakers' radical egalitarianism, and Friends encountered persecution everywhere. Mary Dyer—a follower of Anne Hutchinson in the 1630s—became a Quaker, returned to Boston as a missionary,

Quakers Properly known as the Society of Friends, Quakers embraced egalitarianism and rejected traditional religious hierarchies. They believed that the Holy Spirit or the "inner light" could inspire every soul.

William Penn The first proprietor of the last unallocated tract of American territory at the king's disposal, which would become Pennsylvania.

and was hanged in 1660 (along with several men) for preaching Quaker doctrines.

3-1c Pennsylvania

The Quakers obtained their own colony in 1681, when Charles II granted the region between Maryland and New York to his close friend **William Penn**, a prominent member of the sect. Penn was then thirty-seven years old; he held the colony as a personal proprietorship, one that earned profits for his descendants until the American Revolution. Even so, Penn, like the Roman Catholic Calverts of Maryland before him, saw his province not only as a source of revenue but also as a haven for persecuted coreligionists. In widely distributed promotional tracts printed in German, French, and Dutch, Penn offered fertile land to all comers on liberal terms. He promised to tolerate all religions—although only Christian men could vote—and to establish a representative assembly. He also guaranteed such legal protections as the right to bail and trial by jury, prized and ancient rights known then and after throughout England's American realm as "English liberties."

Penn's activities and the Quakers' attraction to his lands gave rise to a migration whose magnitude equaled the Puritan exodus to New England in the 1630s. By mid-1683, more than three thousand people—among them Welsh, Irish, Dutch, and Germans—had moved to Pennsylvania. By 1688, the population had quadrupled, to twelve thousand. (It took Virginia more than three decades to grow as large.) Philadelphia, sited on the Delaware River and planned as the major city in the province, drew merchants and artisans from throughout the English-speaking world. From mainland and Caribbean colonies alike came Quakers with well-established trading connections. Pennsylvania's plentiful and fertile lands soon enabled its residents to export surplus flour and other foodstuffs to the

William Penn (1644-1718) in Armour, aged 22, 1666 (oil on canvas)/English School, (17th century)/PHILADELPHIA HISTORY MUSEUM AT THE ATWATER KENT/© Philadelphia History Museum at the Atwater Kent./Bridgeman Images

△ William Penn, later the proprietor of Pennsylvania, as he looked during his youth in Ireland. In numerous pamphlets printed in the late seventeenth century, Penn spread the word about his new colony to thousands of readers in England and its other colonial possessions.

West Indies. Practically overnight, Philadelphia acquired more than two thousand citizens and began to challenge Boston's commercial dominance on the mainland.

A pacifist with egalitarian principles, Penn attempted to treat Native Americans fairly. He learned the language of the Delawares (or Lenapes), from whom he purchased land to sell to European settlers. Penn also established strict regulations for trade and forbade the sale of alcohol to Native peoples. His policies attracted Native peoples who moved to Pennsylvania near the end of the seventeenth century to escape repeated clashes with English colonists in Maryland, Virginia, and North Carolina. Tuscaroras migrated northward, and Shawnees and Miamis moved eastward from the Ohio valley. Yet the same toleration that attracted Native Americans also brought non-Quaker Europeans who disregarded Native American claims to the soil. The Scots-Irish (Irish Protestants), Germans, and Swiss who settled in Pennsylvania in the early eighteenth century clashed repeatedly over land with the Delaware, Shawnee, and other Native groups who had recently migrated there.

3-1d Carolina

The southernmost proprietary colony, granted by Charles II in 1663, stretched from the southern boundary of Virginia to Spanish Florida. The area had great strategic importance: a successful English settlement there would prevent Spaniards from pushing farther north. The fertile, semitropical land also held forth the promise of producing such exotic and valuable commodities as figs, olives, wines, and silk. The proprietors named their new province Carolina in honor of Charles (whose Latin name was Carolus). The "Fundamental Constitutions of Carolina," which they asked the political philosopher John Locke to draft for them, set forth an elaborate plan for a colony governed by landholding aristocrats and characterized by a carefully structured distribution of political and economic power.

But Carolina failed to follow the course the proprietors laid out. Instead, it quickly developed two distinct population centers, which in 1729 split into separate colonies under direct royal rule. Virginia planters settled the Albemarle region that became North Carolina. They established a society much like their own, with an economy based on exporting tobacco and such forest products as pitch, tar, and timber. Because North Carolina lacked a satisfactory harbor, planters there relied on Virginia's ports and merchants to conduct their trade. The other population center, which eventually formed the core of South Carolina, developed at Charles Town, founded in 1670 near the juncture of the Ashley and Cooper rivers. Many of its early residents migrated from Barbados, where land was increasingly consolidated under a small number of large holders as the sugar revolution advanced.

Carolina settlers raised corn and herds of cattle, which they sold to Caribbean planters to feed their growing enslaved workforces. Like other colonists before them, they also depended on trade with nearby Native peoples to supply commodities they could sell elsewhere. In Carolina, those items were deerskins, sent to Europe, and enslaved Native Americans, who were shipped to Caribbean islands and northern colonies. Nearby Native American nations hunted deer with increasing intensity and readily sold captured enemies to the English settlers. During the first decade of the eighteenth century, South Carolina exported over fifty thousand skins annually. Before 1715, Carolinians additionally exported an estimated thirty thousand to fifty thousand Native American slaves.

3-1e Jamaica

Like Carolina, Jamaica absorbed numerous migrants from Barbados in the late seventeenth century. First colonized by Spain in 1494, the enormous island—at nearly 4,500 square miles, it is the third largest in the Caribbean, twenty-six times the size of Barbados—was still thinly settled when English troops seized it in 1655, as part of Oliver Cromwell's Western Design. Intended as a base from which to plunder Spanish treasure ships, the English garrison fared poorly at first. After the Restoration, however, powerful merchants in London convinced Charles II there was money to be made by converting it to a royal colony. In 1664, the king appointed Sir Thomas Modyford, a wealthy Barbadian planter, to govern Jamaica. Modyford, who brought nearly a thousand experienced planters with him from Barbados, treated the fledgling colony as a personal fiefdom, awarding key offices to his family and generous tracts of land to his friends. He summoned an assembly only once before the Crown ended his tenure in 1671. In those early years, Jamaica was a haven for privateers, transported convicts, and smugglers.

But for all its anarchic tendencies, the colony soon began to grow and even flourish after a fashion. A census taken in 1673 put the island's population at about 17,000, more than ten times what it had been when the English captured it. More than half the inhabitants—over 9,500—were enslaved Africans, forced to grow crops including cacao, indigo, and, increasingly, sugar. As the sugar revolution took hold in Jamaica, the number of the slaves soared. By 1713 the island's enslaved population reached 55,000, more than eight times the number of white settlers. The enslaved rebelled frequently; six organized revolts rocked the colony before 1693. In the mid-eighteenth century, as sugar and slavery exploded in tandem, Jamaica's slave rebellions escalated into full-scale wars.

Jamaica proved as profitable as it was volatile, however. Nowhere was the combustible mixture more visible than in the city of Port Royal. Located on a finger of sand reaching into the Caribbean, Port Royal was a provincial English boomtown. By 1680, it had nearly three thousand inhabitants, including one in six of the island's white settlers. In all of English America, only Boston housed more people. But Port Royal was no Boston. Here wealthy planters, privateers, and the merchants who fenced their loot lived in opulent brick houses standing four stories high, while their slaves—a third of the town's population—crowded into huts. "The Merchants and Gentry live here to the Hight of Splendor, in full ease and plenty," reported one traveler in 1688. Taverns and brothels lined the wharves. Dueling and brawling were common. Those who thought of Port Royal as a new world Sodom—as many did—saw divine justice in the cataclysm that struck in June 1692, when an earthquake buried the city and hundreds of its inhabitants beneath the sea. The news reached Boston by the beginning of August, and London shortly afterwards. "Was there not in this American Island a short representation of the great Day of Tryal?" wrote one English clergyman who saw in Port Royal's fate an intimation judgment day.

An island of extremes unvarnished by piety, Jamaica was easy to scorn. In a pamphlet published in London in 1698 and frequently reprinted, the Grub Street hack Ned Ward called it the "Dunghill of the Universe, the Refuse of the whole Creation … The Place where *Pandora* fill'd her Box." Yet Port Royal, no less than Boston, and Jamaica, no less than Pennsylvania, epitomized British America. The island slowly recovered from the heavy blows of the late seventeenth century to achieve matchless prosperity by the mid-eighteenth. On the eve of the American Revolution, Jamaica was the most valuable British colony, if not the economic capital of the Anglo-Atlantic world.

3-1f Chesapeake

The English Civil War retarded the development of the earlier English settlements. In the Chesapeake, struggles between supporters of the king and Parliament caused military clashes in Maryland and political upheavals in Virginia in the 1640s. But once the war ended and immigration resumed, the colonies again expanded. Settlers on Virginia's eastern shore and along that colony's southern border raised grain, livestock, and flax, which they sold to English and Dutch merchants. Tobacco growers imported increasing numbers of English indentured servants to work their farms, which had begun to develop into plantations. Freed from concerns about Native American attacks by the defeat of the Powhatan Confederacy in 1646, they—especially recent immigrants—eagerly sought to enlarge their landholdings.

Although they still depended primarily on English laborers, Chesapeake tobacco planters continued to acquire small numbers of enslaved workers. At first, almost all of them were people whom historian Ira Berlin has termed "Atlantic creoles": widely traveled people (sometimes of mixed race) who came from other European settlements in the Atlantic world, primarily from Iberian outposts. Not all the Atlantic creoles who came to the Chesapeake were enslaved; some were free or indentured. With their arrival, the Chesapeake became what Berlin calls a "society with slaves," or one in which slavery does not dominate the economy but coexists with other labor systems.

3-1g New England

Migration to New England essentially ceased when the Civil War began in 1642. While English Puritans were first challenging the king and then governing England as a commonwealth, they had little incentive to leave their homeland, and few emigrated after the Restoration. Yet the Puritan colonies' population continued to grow dramatically by natural increase. By the 1670s, New England's population had more than tripled to reach approximately seventy thousand. Such rapid expansion placed pressure on available land. Colonial settlement spread far into the interior of Massachusetts and Connecticut, and many members of the third and fourth generations migrated—north to New Hampshire or Maine, southwest to New York or New Jersey—to find sufficient farmland for themselves and their children. Others abandoned agriculture and learned such skills as blacksmithing or carpentry to support themselves in the growing towns. By 1680, some 4,500 people lived in Boston, which was becoming a genuine city, if not the utopian "city on a hill" that John Winthrop had imagined.

New Englanders who remained in the small, yet densely populated older communities experienced a range of social tensions. Far from being "knit together . . . as one man," as Winthrop had urged in "Christian Charitie," New England

△ Map from A *New Description of Carolina*, by John Ogilby, 1671 (with south at the top). Ogilby's tract, illustrated by a map drawn from information supplied by John Lederer, a German Indian trader, was intended to attract settlers to the new Carolina colony. He filled his text with information supplied by the Lords Proprietors, stressing the colony's pleasant climate, abundant resources, and friendly Native peoples, a message underscored by the peaceful scenes in the corner cartouches.

The Colonial Williamsburg Foundation. Museum Purchase

towns were intensely fractious. Men and women frequently took to the courts, suing their neighbors for slander, debt, and other offenses. After 1650, accusations of witchcraft—roughly 100 in all before 1690—landed suspects in courtrooms across Massachusetts, Connecticut, and New Hampshire. (Though most seventeenth-century people believed witches existed, those suspected were subjected to very few formal trials in other regions.) Most suspects were middle-aged women who had angered their neighbors. Daily interactions in these close-knit communities, where the same families lived nearby for decades, fostered long-standing quarrels that led some colonists to believe their neighbors had used occult means to cause misfortunes ranging from infant death to crop failure. Legal codes influenced by the Old Testament made witchcraft a capital offense in New England, yet judges and juries remained skeptical of such charges. Few of those accused of witchcraft were convicted, and fewer still were executed.

3-1h Colonial Political Structures

That New England courts halted questionable witchcraft prosecutions suggests the maturity of colonial institutions.

By the last quarter of the seventeenth century, almost all the Anglo-American colonies had well-established governments and courts. In New England, property-holding men or the legislature elected the governors; in other regions, the king or the proprietor appointed such leaders. A council, either elected or appointed, advised the governor on matters of policy and served as the upper house of the legislature. Each colony had a judiciary with local justices of the peace, county courts, and, usually, an appeals court composed of the councilors.

Local political institutions also developed. In New England, elected selectmen initially governed the towns, but by the end of the seventeenth century, town meetings—held at least annually and attended by most free adult male residents—handled matters of local concern. In the Chesapeake and the Carolinas, appointed magistrates ran local governments. At first, the same was true in Pennsylvania, but by the early eighteenth century, elected county officials began to take over some government functions. And in New York, local elections were the rule even before the establishment of the colonial assembly in 1683.

The Pine Tree Shilling

The early settlers of Massachusetts shipped most of the coins they had brought with them back across the Atlantic, to pay for goods imported from England and Europe. The resulting trade deficit meant that money was always in short supply. Colonists made do by conducting local and regional trade with a variety of tokens, including musket balls and wampum, the clamshell beads Algonquian and Iroquois peoples prized for ceremonial exchanges. But in the 1640s, the value of wampum collapsed, just as Bostonians entered Caribbean trade.

Long-distance commerce demanded a circulating medium whose value held stable across space and time. That meant coins made from precious metal, whose weight governed their worth. Trade brought silver coins to New England from the Spanish mines at Potosí, but they were often shaved or debased—worth less than their face value. So in 1652, Massachusetts began to mint its own higher-quality coins. Mint master John Hull, a staunch Puritan, designed them without a human face, since the Bible's commandments forbade the worship of graven images. For the king's profile, he substituted a tall pine tree: the only figure to grace these New England shillings.

When Charles II was restored to the throne, he began to question colonial laws that departed from English norms. In 1665, his royal commissioners directed Massachusetts to close its mint, since "Coyning is a Royal prerogative." By minting money, Boston was acting like a city-state; the Crown would have it behave like a colony. Yet Massachusetts kept producing silver shillings until the colony's charter was revoked in the late 1680s.

CRITICAL THINKING

- What did the pine tree signify in Atlantic commerce?
- How did the colonists identify themselves on the shilling?

△ Pine Tree Shilling front

△ Pine Tree Shilling back

Fritz Goro The LIFE Picture Collection/Getty Images

Fritz Goro The LIFE Picture Collection/Getty Images

3-2 A Decade of Imperial Crises: The 1670s

▷ Why did conflict emerge between European powers and Native American peoples in the 1670s?

▷ What impact did warfare and violence have on Native American populations?

▷ How did conflict over land shape the societies of New England and Virginia?

As the Restoration colonies were extending the range of English settlement, the first English colonies and French and Spanish settlements in North America faced crises caused primarily by their changing relationships with America's indigenous peoples. Between 1670 and 1680, New France, New Mexico, New England, and Virginia experienced bitter conflicts as their interests collided with those of America's original inhabitants. All the early colonies changed irrevocably as a result.

3-2a New France and the Iroquois

In the mid-1670s Louis de Buade de Frontenac, the governor-general of Canada, decided to expand New France's reach into the south and west, hoping to establish a trade route to Mexico and to gain direct control of the valuable fur trade. Accordingly, he encouraged the explorations of Father Jacques Marquette, Louis Jolliet, and René-Robert Cavelier de La Salle in the Great Lakes and Mississippi Valley regions. Frontenac's goal, however, brought him into conflict with the powerful Iroquois Confederacy, then composed of five nations—the Mohawks, Oneidas, Onondagas, Cayugas, and Senecas. (In 1722, the Tuscaroras became the sixth.)

Under the terms of a unique defensive alliance forged in the sixteenth century, a representative council made decisions about war and peace for the entire Iroquois Confederacy, although no nation could be forced to comply with a council directive against its will. Before the arrival of Europeans, the Iroquois waged wars primarily to acquire captives. Contact with foreign traders brought ravaging disease as early as 1633, devastating traditional structures of authority in Iroquoia, and intensifying the need for captives. The Europeans' presence also created an economic motive for warfare: the desire to dominate the fur trade and to gain unimpeded access to imported goods. In the 1640s, bloody conflict between the Senecas and the French-allied Hurons soon touched off a series of broader conflicts now known as the **Beaver Wars**, in which the nations of the Iroquois confederacy fought for control of the lucrative peltry trade. Between 1643 and 1647, western Iroquois battled Hurons in engagements that claimed large numbers of warriors and civilians on both sides. Firearms provided as trade goods by colonial powers made the conflicts far deadlier than traditional warfare. "So far as I can divine," wrote a Jesuit priest captured in one such engagement, "it is the design of the Iroquois to capture all the

△ Don Diego de Vargas, leader of the expedition to reconquer the Pueblo peoples in 1692. This is the only known portrait of him; today it hangs in the Palace of the Governors in the New Mexico History Museum.

Hurons, . . . to put the chiefs and a great part of the nation to death, and with the rest to form one nation and one country." By the 1650s, the Iroquois league had indeed consolidated its power, and replenished its population with war captives.

In the mid-1670s, as Iroquois dominance grew, the French intervened, seeking to preserve their own trade channels with

Beaver Wars A series of conflicts over trade in the 1640s between the Huron (and other Native peoples) and Iroquois.

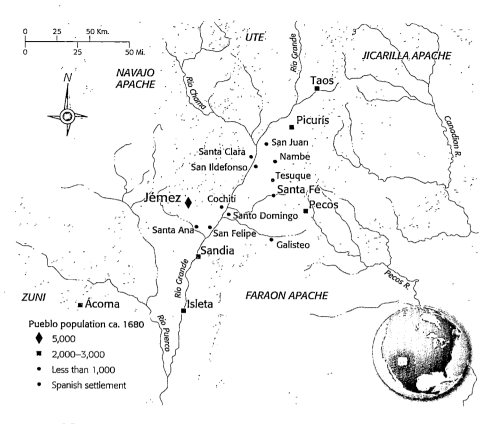

Map 3.2 New Mexico, ca. 1680

In 1680, the lone Spanish settlement at Santa Fe was surrounded and vastly outnumbered by the many Pueblo villages nearby. *Source: Adapted from Apache, Navaho, and Spaniard, by Jack D. Forbes. Copyright © 1960 by the University of Oklahoma Press. Reprinted by permission of the University of Oklahoma Press.*

the western Native peoples. Over the next twenty years, the French launched repeated attacks on Iroquois villages. Although in 1677 New Yorkers and the Iroquois established a formal alliance known as the Covenant Chain, the English offered little beyond weapons to their trading partners. Without much aid, the Confederacy held its own and even expanded its reach, enabling it in 1701 to negotiate neutrality treaties with France and other Native groups. For the next half-century, Iroquois nations maintained their power through trade and skillful diplomacy rather than warfare. The mission of the "Indian Kings" to London belonged to this diplomatic tradition.

3-2b Pueblo Peoples and Spaniards

In New Mexico, too, events of the 1670s led to a crisis with long-term consequences. After years under Spanish domination, the Pueblo peoples had added Christianity to their religious beliefs while retaining traditional rituals, engaging in syncretic practices as Meso-americans had done. But as decades passed, Franciscans adopted increasingly brutal

Popé Leader of the Pueblo Revolt against the Spanish in 1680.

and violent tactics, attempting to erase all traces of the native religion. Priests and secular colonists who held *encomiendas* placed heavy labor demands on the people, who were also suffering from Apache raids and food shortages. In 1680, the Pueblos revolted under the leadership of **Popé**, a respected shaman, successfully driving the Spaniards from New Mexico (see Map 3.2). Even though Spain managed to restore its authority by 1700, imperial officials had learned their lesson. After the rebellion, Spanish governors stressed cooperation with the Pueblos, relying on their labor but no longer attempting to violate their cultural integrity. The Pueblo revolt constituted the most successful and longest-sustained indigenous resistance movement in colonial North America.

Spanish military outposts (*presidios*) and Franciscan missions offered some protection to Pueblos, but other Native peoples' desire to obtain horses and guns from the European colonizers led to endemic violence throughout the region. Navajos, Apaches, and Utes attacked each other and the Pueblos, gaining captives and hides to trade to the Spanish. Captured Native American men might be sent to Mexican silver mines, whereas Spaniards often retained women and children as domestic laborers. When Comanches migrated west from the

Great Plains in the late seventeenth century, Utes allied with them, and after the Pueblo revolt that alliance dominated New Mexico's northern borderlands for several decades.

In the more densely settled English colonies, hostilities developed in the decade of the 1670s, not over religion (as in New Mexico) or trade (as in New France), but over land. Put simply, the rapidly expanding Anglo-American population wanted to seize more of it. In both New England and Virginia, settlers began to encroach on territories that had belonged for centuries to Native Americans.

3-2c King Philip's War

By the early 1670s, the growing settlements in southern New England surrounded Wampanoag ancestral lands on Narragansett Bay. The local chief, Metacom—whom the English called "King Philip"—was troubled by the impact of European culture on his land and people. Philip led his warriors in attacks on nearby communities in June 1675. Other Algonquian peoples, among them Nipmucks and Narragansetts, soon joined Metacom's forces. That fall, the allied Native American nations attacked settlements in the northern Connecticut River valley; the war spread to Maine when the Abenakis entered the conflict. In 1676, Metacom's Native allies devastated villages like Lancaster, and even attacked Plymouth and Providence; Abenaki assaults forced the abandonment of most settlements in Maine. Altogether, the Native alliance wholly or partially destroyed twenty-seven of ninety-two English towns and attacked forty others, pushing the colonizers back toward the coast.

The tide turned in the summer of 1676. As the Native American coalition in southern New England ran short of food and ammunition, colonists began to use indigenous Christian converts as guides and scouts. On June 12, the Mohawks—ancient Iroquois enemies of New England Algonquians—devastated a major Wampanoag encampment while most of the warriors were away attacking an English town. King Philip was shot to death near Plymouth that August; the settlers' captain, Benjamin Church, had his body quartered and decapitated. They mounted the sachem's head on a tall pole, much as the English staked the heads of traitors on London Bridge. After Philip's death, the southern alliance crumbled. But fighting on the Maine frontier continued for another two years. There the English colonists never defeated the Abenakis; both sides, their resources depleted, simply agreed to end the conflict in 1678.

After the war, hundreds of Wampanoags, Nipmucks, Narragansetts, and Abenakis were captured and sold into slavery; many more died of starvation and disease. New Englanders had broken the power of the southern coastal tribes. Thereafter the southern Native peoples lived in smaller clusters, subordinated to the colonists and often working as servants or sailors. Only on the island of Martha's Vineyard did Christian Wampanoags (who had not participated in the war) substantially preserve their autonomy.

The settlers paid a terrible price for their victory: an estimated one-tenth of New England's able-bodied adult male population was killed or wounded. Proportional to population, King Philip's War—which the Native peoples called Metacom's

Rebellion—was the most lethal conflict in American history on a per capita basis. The colonists' heavy losses caused many Puritans to wonder if God had turned against them. New Englanders did not fully rebuild abandoned interior towns for another three decades, and not until the American Revolution did the region's per capita income return to pre-1675 levels.

3-2d Bacon's Rebellion

Conflict over land simultaneously wracked Virginia. In the early 1670s, ex-servants unable to acquire land greedily eyed the territory reserved by treaty for Virginia's Native peoples. Governor William Berkeley, the leader of an entrenched coterie of large eastern landowners, resisted starting a war to further the aims of backcountry settlers who challenged his authority. Dissatisfied colonists then rallied behind the leadership of a recent immigrant, the gentleman Nathaniel Bacon. Like other new arrivals, Bacon had found that all the desirable land in settled eastern areas had already been claimed. Using as a pretext the July 1675 killing of an indentured servant by some members of the Doeg tribe, Bacon and his followers attacked not only the Doegs but also the more powerful Susquehannocks. In retaliation, Susquehannock bands raided outlying farms early in 1676.

Berkeley and Bacon soon clashed. The governor outlawed Bacon and his men; the rebels then held Berkeley hostage, forcing him to authorize their attacks on the Native peoples. During the chaotic summer of 1676, Bacon alternately waged war on Native villages and battled the governor. In September, Bacon's forces attacked Jamestown, burning the capital to the ground. But when Bacon died of dysentery the following month, the rebellion began to collapse. Even so, the rebels had made their point. Berkeley was recalled to England, and a new treaty signed in 1677 opened much of the disputed territory to settlement. The end of **Bacon's Rebellion** thus pushed most of Virginia's Native peoples farther west, beyond the Appalachians. And elite Virginians would increasingly rely on laborers forbidden by law to become free and demand land of their own.

3-3 The Atlantic Trading System

▷ **What factors contributed to the emergence of African slave labor in the British colonies?**

▷ **How did the Atlantic trading system operate?**

▷ **What role did the slave trade play in the Atlantic trading system?**

▷ **What impact did the slave trade have on West African people and their governments?**

King Philip's War Devastating war between several allied Native American nations and New England settlers.

Bacon's Rebellion Uprising that resulted from many conflicts, among them an increasing land shortage and settlers' desires for Native American lands.

In the 1670s and 1680s, the prosperity of the Chesapeake rested on tobacco, and successful tobacco cultivation depended, as it always had, on an ample labor supply. But ever fewer English men and women proved willing to indenture themselves for long terms of service in Maryland and Virginia. Population pressures had eased in England, and the founding of the Restoration colonies, along with the boom in Caribbean sugar, gave migrants many American destinations to choose from. Furthermore, fluctuating tobacco prices in Europe and the growing scarcity of land made the Chesapeake less appealing to potential settlers. That posed a problem for wealthy Chesapeake planters. Where could they obtain the workers they needed? They found the answer in the Caribbean sugar islands, where Dutch, French, English, and Spanish planters were accustomed to purchasing African slaves.

3-3a Why African Slavery?

Slavery had been practiced in Europe and in Islamic lands for centuries. European Christians—both Catholics and Protestants—believed that the Bible justified enslaving heathen peoples, especially those of exotic origin. Muslims, too, thought infidels could be enslaved, and they imported tens of thousands of black Africans into slavery in North Africa and the Middle East. Some Christians argued that holding those they termed "heathens"—people with beliefs other than Christianity, Judaism, or Islam—in bondage would lead to their conversion. Others believed that any heathen taken prisoner in wartime could be justly enslaved. Consequently, when Portuguese mariners reached the sub-Saharan coast and encountered African societies holding slaves, they purchased men and women along with gold and other items. From the 1440s on, Portugal imported large numbers of slaves into the Iberian Peninsula; by 1500, enslaved Africans composed about one-tenth of the population of Lisbon and Seville, the chief cities of Portugal and Spain. In 1555, a few of them were taken to England. Others followed, and residents of London and Bristol soon became accustomed to seeing enslaved black people on the streets.

Iberians exported African slavery to their American possessions, New Spain and Brazil. Because the Catholic Church prevented the formal enslavement of Native peoples in those domains, and because free laborers saw no reason to work voluntarily in mines or on sugar plantations when they could earn better wages under easier conditions elsewhere, enslaved Africans (who had no choice) quickly became mainstays of the Caribbean and Brazilian economies. European planters throughout the West Indies began purchasing slaves soon after they settled in the Caribbean. The first enslaved Africans in the Americas were imported from Angola, Portugal's major early trading partner, and the

△ Nicholas Pocock made this engraving of the frigate *Southwell*, a former privateer from Bristol, England, turned into a slave-trading vessel, about 1760. The images at the bottom show the ship's company trading for slaves on the coast of West Africa.

Portuguese word *Negro*—for "black"—came into use as a common descriptor.

English people had few moral qualms about enslaving other humans. Slavery was sanctioned in the Bible, and it was widely practiced by their contemporaries. Until the eighteenth century, few questioned the decision to hold Africans and their descendants—or captive Native peoples—in perpetual bondage. Yet colonists did not inherit the law and culture of slavery fully formed. Instead, they fashioned the institution of chattel slavery and its supporting concepts of "race" to suit their economic and social needs.

The 1670 Virginia law that first tried to define which people could be enslaved notably failed to employ the racial terminology that would later become common-place. Instead, awkwardly seeking to single out imported Africans without mentioning them, the statute declared, "all servants not being christians imported into this colony by shipping shall be slaves for their lives." Such phrasing reveals that Anglo-American settlers had not yet fully developed the meaning of *race* or the category of *slave*. They did so in tandem over decades, through their experience with slavery itself.

3-3b Atlantic Slave Trade

The planters of the North American mainland could not have obtained the people they wanted to enslave without the rapid development of an Atlantic trading system, the linchpin of which was the traffic in enslaved human beings. Although this elaborate Atlantic economic system has been called the triangular trade, people and products did not move across the ocean in easily diagrammed patterns. Instead, their move-ments created a complicated web of exchange that inextricably tied together the peoples of the four continents bordering the Atlantic (see Map 3.3).

Though enslavement was ancient, the oceanic slave trade belonged to the Atlantic world that began with Columbus. The expanding network of commerce between Europe and its colonies was fueled by the sale and transport of slaves, the exchange of commodities produced by slave labor, and the need to feed and clothe the escalating number of bound laborers. Previously oriented around the Mediterranean and Asia, Europe's economy tilted toward the Atlantic. By the late seventeenth century, commerce in slaves and slave-made commodities and goods to clothe and feed slaves had become the basis of the European economic system.

Map 3.3 Atlantic Trade Routes

By the late seventeenth century, an elaborate trade network linked the countries and colonies bordering the Atlantic Ocean. The most valuable commodities exchanged were enslaved people and the products of slave labor.

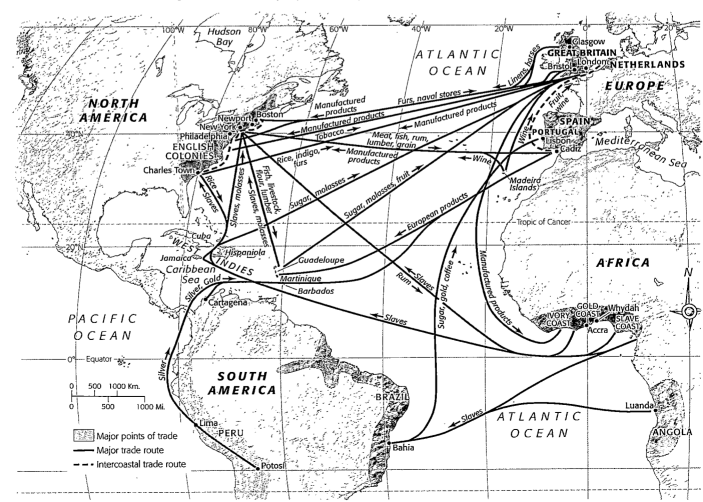

The various elements of the trade had different relationships to one another and to the wider web of exchange. Chesapeake tobacco and Caribbean and Brazilian sugar were in great demand in Europe, so planters often shipped those products directly to their home countries. The profits paid for the African laborers who grew their crops and for European manufactured goods. The African coastal rulers who ran the entrepôts where European slavers acquired their human cargoes took payment in European manufactures and East Indian textiles; they had little need for most North American products. Europeans purchased slaves from Africa for resale in their colonies and acquired sugar and tobacco from the Americas, in exchange dispatching their manufactures everywhere.

European nations fought bitterly to control the lucrative Atlantic trade. The Portuguese dominated at first, but were supplanted by the Dutch in the 1630s. Between 1652 and 1674, England and the Netherlands fought three wars—conflicts over naval supremacy that largely centered on the slave trade. The Dutch lost out to the English, who controlled the trade through the Royal African Company, chartered by Charles II in 1672. Holding a monopoly on all English trade with sub-Saharan Africa, the company became the largest single business in the Atlantic slave trade. The company built and maintained seventeen forts and trading posts, dispatched to West Africa hundreds of ships carrying English goods, and transported thousands of slaves every year to the Caribbean colonies. Some of its agents made fortunes, yet even before the company's monopoly expired in 1712, many individual English and North American traders had illegally entered the market for slaves. By the early eighteenth century, such independent traders carried most of the Africans imported into the colonies. In the fifty years beginning in 1676, British and American ships transported an estimated 689,600 captured Africans, more than 177,000 of them in vessels owned by the Royal African Company. From the founding of the Royal African Company until long after its demise, British slaving voyages dwarfed the trafficking controlled by France, Portugal, and the Netherlands, combined.

3-3c West Africa and the Slave Trade

Most of the enslaved people carried to North America originated in West Africa. Some came from the regions Europeans called the Rice Coast and the Grain Coast, but even more had resided in the Gold Coast, the Slave Coast, and the Bight of Biafra (modern Nigeria) and Angola (see Map 1.2, Section 1-3a). Certain coastal rulers—for instance, the Adja kings of the Slave Coast—served as intermediaries, allowing the establishment of permanent slave-trading posts in their territories and supplying resident Europeans with slaves to fill ships that stopped regularly at coastal forts. Such rulers controlled Europeans' access to enslaved laborers and simultaneously controlled inland Africans' access to desirable trade goods, such as textiles, iron bars, alcohol, tobacco, guns, and cowry shells from the Maldive Islands (in the Indian Ocean),

which were widely used as currency. At least 10 percent of all slaves exported to the Americas passed through Whydah (or Ouidah), Dahomey's major slave-trading port. Portugal, England, and France established forts there.

As the scale of the trade grew, slaving forts became more extensive and elaborate. From simple storerooms housing captured men, women, and children along with trade goods, the coastal forts expanded into full-blown prisons, where shackled captives might be kept for months. Despite thicker walls and a steady provision of "short irons" to bind wrists and "long irons" to shackle ankles, desperate prisoners regularly escaped. In July 1682, one official reported, a group of fourteen captives, including one woman, "undermined the prison walls" and slipped past a guard in the middle of the night.

The slave trade had varying consequences for the nations of West Africa. The trade's centralizing tendencies helped to create such powerful eighteenth-century kingdoms as Dahomey and Asante (formed from the Akan States). Traffic in slaves destroyed smaller polities and disrupted traditional economic patterns. Goods once sent north toward the Mediterranean were redirected to the Atlantic, and local

Tobacco label featuring Virginia planter and distillery (woodcut/English School, (18th century)/VIRGINIA HISTORICAL SOCIETY/Virginia Historical Society, Richmond, Virginia, USA/Bridgeman Images

△ By the middle of the eighteenth century, American tobacco had become closely associated with African slavery. An English woodcut advertising Virginia tobacco and distilled spirits depicted a pipe-smoking English man watching Africans hoe tobacco in the hot Virginia sun.

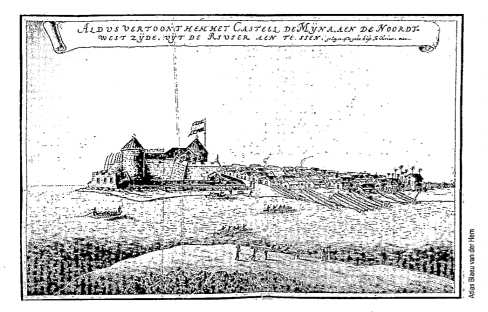

◁ In the fifteenth century, Portuguese explorers renamed the town of Elmina—a trading village on the coast of present-day Ghana—after the gold they exported from the site. (*El mina* means "the mine.") The construction of the massive fort or "castle" depicted in this watercolor began in 1482. At first, its primary purpose was to protect the precious metal trade along what Europeans called Africa's Gold Coast. But during the seventeenth century, enslaved Africans became the primary exports of ports like Elmina, which the Dutch acquired in 1637. Captive men, women, and children were held in the fortress's dungeons before beginning the long voyage to the Americas. The fort's export gate, facing the sea, came to be known as the Door of No Return.

Atlas Blaeu van der Hem

manufactures declined in the face of European competition. Agricultural production intensified, especially in rice-growing areas, because of the need to supply hundreds of slave ships with foodstuffs for transatlantic voyages. Because prisoners of war constituted the bulk of the exported slaves, the most active traders were also the most successful in battle. Some nations initiated conflicts specifically to acquire valuable captives. For example, the state of Benin sold captive enemies to the Portuguese in the late fifteenth century, did not do so at the height of its power in the sixteenth and seventeenth centuries, and renewed the sale of prisoners in the eighteenth century, when its waning power led to conflicts with neighboring states.

Rulers in parts of Upper Guinea, especially modern Gambia and Senegal, largely resisted involvement with the trade; the few slave vessels that departed from that area were much more likely than others to experience onboard rebellions. Despite planters' preference for male slaves, women predominated in cargoes originating in the Bight of Biafra. In such regions as the Gold Coast, the trade had a significant impact on the sex ratio of the remaining population. There a relative shortage of men increased work demands on women, encouraged polygyny, and opened new opportunities to women and their children.

3-3d New England and the Caribbean

New England had a complex relationship to the trading system. The region produced only one item England wanted: tall trees to serve as masts for sailing vessels. To buy English manufactures, New Englanders therefore needed to earn profits elsewhere. The Caribbean colonies lacked precisely the items that New England could produce in abundance: cheap food (primarily corn and salted fish) to feed the burgeoning slave population, and wood for barrels to hold sugar and molasses. The sale of foodstuffs and wood products to Caribbean sugar planters provided New England farmers and merchants with a major source of income. By the late 1640s, decades before the Chesapeake

economy became dependent on *production* by slaves, New England's commerce rested on *consumption* by slaves and their owners. Pennsylvania, New York, and New Jersey later participated in the lucrative West Indian trade as well.

Shopkeepers in the interior of the northern and middle colonies bartered with farmers for grains, livestock, and barrel staves, then traded those items to merchants located in port towns. Such merchants dispatched ships to the Caribbean, where they sailed from island to island, exchanging their cargoes for molasses, sugar, fruit, dyestuffs, and slaves. Once they had a full load, the ships returned to Boston, Newport, New York, or Philadelphia to sell their cargoes (which often included enslaved people). Americans began to distill molasses into rum, a crucial aspect of the only part of the trade that could accurately be termed triangular. Rhode Islanders took rum to Africa to trade for slaves, whom they carried to Caribbean islands to exchange for molasses, which they carried north to produce more rum.

3-3e Slaving Voyages

Tying the system together was the voyage commonly called the **middle passage**, which brought Africans to the Americas. Slaving ships were specially outfitted for the trade, with platforms built between decks to double the surface area to hold human cargo. In its contract with the *Barbados Merchant* for a slaving voyage in 1706, for example, the Royal African Company directed the owners to provide "platforms for ye Negroes, Shackles, bolts, firewood," and beans, as well as "a sword & fire lock, Muskett and ammunition for each of ye ships Comp[any]." Foodstores were priced "per 100 Negroes." Brought aboard in small groups, drawn from many inland nations, speaking diverse languages, an average of 300 men, women, and children comprised what slave merchants called

middle passage The brutal and often fatal journey of enslaved Africans across the Atlantic.

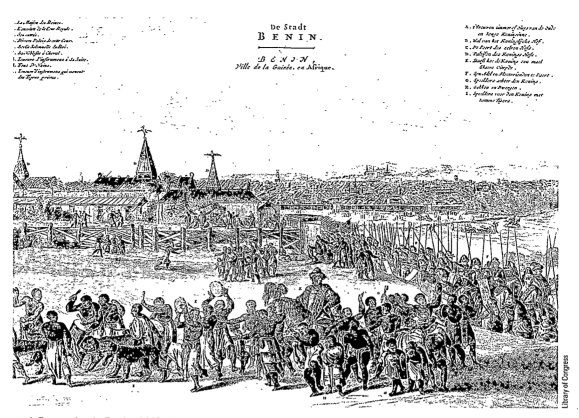

△ A Procession in Benin, 1668. A contemporary European engraving shows a royal procession leaving the city of Benin, capital of the prosperous West African kingdom. During the seventeenth century, the power of Benin's rulers scared off would-be challengers, and so the kingdom did not engage in frequent warfare. In the fifteenth and eighteenth centuries, by contrast, when the kingdom was weaker, it did capture and sell its enemies.

a "full complement" of human merchandise, though voyages transporting 400 or 500 Africans were not uncommon, and cargoes exceeding 600 were not unheard of.

On shipboard, men were shackled in pairs in the hold except for periods of exercise on deck. During the day, women and children were usually allowed to move around, and made to work at such tasks as food preparation and cleaning. At night, men and women were confined to separate quarters. The best evidence of the captives' reaction to their plight comes from secondhand accounts of their behavior, since few ever had the chance to record their experiences. Many resisted enslavement by refusing to eat, jumping overboard, or joining in revolts, which rarely succeeded. Their communal singing and drumming, reported by numerous observers, must have simultaneously lifted their spirits and forged a sense of solidarity. But conditions on board were hellish, as captains packed as many people as possible into holds that were hot, crowded, and reeking with smells from vomit and the "necessary tubs."

The traumatic voyage unsurprisingly brought heavy fatalities to captives and crew alike. An average of 10 to 20 percent of the newly enslaved died en route; on unusually long or disease-ridden voyages, mortality rates could run much higher. Another 20 percent or so died either before the ships left Africa or shortly after their arrival in the Americas. Merchants tallied lost lives in pounds sterling.

Sailors also died at high rates—one in four or five—chiefly through exposure to such diseases as yellow fever and malaria, which were endemic to Africa. Just 10 percent of the men sent to run the Royal African Company's forts in Lower Guinea lived to return home to England. Sailors signed on to slaving voyages reluctantly; indeed, many had to be coerced or tricked. Slave merchants were notoriously greedy and captains notoriously brutal. Some crew members were themselves slaves or freedmen. Unfortunately, the sailors, often the subject of abuse, in turn frequently abused the African captives in their charge. Yet at the same time, through intimate contact with the enslaved, they learned the value of freedom, and sailors became well known throughout the Atlantic world for their fierce attachment to personal independence.

3-4 Slavery in North America and the Caribbean

▷ **What were the primary features of "slave societies" in Britain's American colonies?**

▷ **What were the similarities and differences among African slave labor in the Chesapeake, the Carolinas, and Northern colonies?**

Exotic Beverages

American and European demand for tea (from China), coffee (at first from Arabia), chocolate (from Mesoamerica), and rum (distilled from sugar, which also sweetened the bitter taste of the other three) helped to reshape the world economy after the mid-seventeenth century. One historian has estimated that approximately two-thirds of the people who migrated across the Atlantic before 1776 were involved in one way or another, primarily as slaves, in the production of tobacco, calico, and these four drinks for the world market. As they moved from luxury to necessity, the exotic beverages had a profound impact on custom and culture.

Each beverage had its own pattern of consumption. Chocolate, brought to Spain from Mexico and enjoyed there for a century before spreading throughout Europe, became the preferred drink of aristocrats, who took it hot, at intimate gatherings in palaces and mansions. Coffee, by contrast, became the preeminent morning beverage of English and colonial businessmen, who praised it for keeping drinkers sober and focused. Coffee was served in new public coffeehouses, patronized chiefly by men, where politics and business were the topics of conversation. The English called them "penny universities"; government leaders thought coffeehouses were nurseries of subversion. The first coffeehouse opened in London in the 1660s; Boston had several by the 1690s. By the mid-eighteenth century, though, tea had supplanted coffee as the preferred hot, caffeinated beverage in England and America. It was consumed in the afternoon in private homes at tea tables presided over by women. Where tea embodied genteel status and polite conversation, rum was the drink of the masses. Distilled from sugar, this inexpensive, potent spirit was enthusiastically imbibed by free working people everywhere in the Atlantic world.

The American colonies played a vital role in the production, distribution, and consumption of each of these beverages. Chocolate originated in America, and cacao plantations in the tropics multiplied in size and number to meet the rising demand. Coffee and tea (particularly the latter) were as avidly consumed in the colonies as in England. By the eighteenth century, coffee was grown increasingly in the Caribbean and South America. And rum involved Americans in every phase of its production and consumption. The sugar grown on French and English Caribbean plantations was transported to the mainland in barrels and ships made from North American wood. There the syrup was turned into rum at 140 distilleries. The Americans themselves drank a substantial share of the distilleries' output—an estimated four gallons per person each year. Much of the rest they transported to Africa, where the rum purchased more slaves to produce more sugar to make still more rum, beginning the cycle again.

CRITICAL THINKING

◻ Tea, chocolate, coffee, and rum were all integral parts of the Columbian Exchange between the Americas and Europe. How did these luxury commodities affect Africans, Euro-American colonists, and continental Europeans?

◻ What evidence might document their impact on the Native peoples of the Americas?

England: The Coffee House Mob, frontispiece to Part IV of Vulgus Britannicus, or the British Hudibras (London, 1710)/PICTURES FROM HISTORY/Bridgeman Images

◁ This print entitled "The Coffee House Mob," the frontispiece *Vulgus Britannicus, or the British Hudibras* (1710), illustrates the culture of debate and dispute associated with coffee drinking in the Anglophone world. A wide variety of written and printed materials—books, newspapers, and letters—is visible, the range of public (and published) opinion perhaps fueling the heated debates that unfold among the coffee drinkers. Most of the customers are well-dressed men, though a young boy imbibes in the foreground, and a woman serves from the counter.

▶ **How did Africans and their descendants shape their lives in slavery and the character of "slave societies"?**

Barbados, America's first "slave society" (an economy wholly dependent on enslavement), spawned many others. As the island's population expanded and large planters consolidated their landholdings, about 40 percent of the early English residents dispersed to other colonies. The migrants carried their laws, commercial contacts, and slaveholding practices with them; the Barbados slave code of 1661, for example, served as the model for later statutes in Jamaica, Antigua, Virginia, and South Carolina. Moreover, a large proportion of the first Africans imported into North America came via Barbados. In addition to the many Barbadians who settled in Carolina, others moved to the southern regions of Virginia (where they specialized in selling foodstuffs and livestock to their former island home), New Jersey, and New England, where they already had slave-trading partners.

3-4a African Enslavement in the Chesapeake

Newly arrived Africans in the Chesapeake tended to be assigned to outlying parts of plantations (called quarters), at least until they learned some English and the routines of American tobacco cultivation. The crop that originated in the Americas was also grown in various locations in West Africa, so Chesapeake planters could well have drawn on their laborers' expertise. Such Africans—the vast majority of them men—lived in groups of ten to fifteen housed together in one or two buildings and supervised by an Anglo-American overseer. Each man was expected to cultivate about two acres of tobacco a year. Their lives must have been filled with toil and loneliness, for few spoke the same language, and all were expected to work for their owners six days a week. On Sundays, planters allowed them a day off. Many used that time to cultivate their own gardens or to hunt or fish to supplement their meager diet. Only rarely could they form families because of the scarcity of women.

Enslaved workers usually cost about two and a half times as much as indentured servants, but they could repay the greater investment with a lifetime of service, assuming they survived—which large numbers did not. Planters with enough money could take the chance and acquire slaves, accumulate greater wealth, and establish large plantations worked by tens, if not hundreds, of slaves. The less affluent could not even afford to purchase indentured servants, whose price rose because of scarcity. As time passed, the gap between rich and poor planters steadily widened. The introduction of large numbers of Africans into the Chesapeake accordingly had a significant impact on the structure of Anglo-American society.

So many Africans were imported into Virginia and Maryland so rapidly that, as early as 1690, those colonies contained more slaves than English indentured servants. By 1710, people of African descent comprised one-fifth of the region's population. Even so, and despite sizable continuing imports, a decade later American-born slaves already outnumbered their African-born counterparts in the Chesapeake, and the American-born proportion of the enslaved population continued to increase thereafter.

3-4b African Enslavement in South Carolina

Africans came with their owners from Barbados to South Carolina in 1670, totaling one-quarter to one-third of the colony's early population. The Barbadian slave owners quickly discovered that African-born slaves had a variety of skills well suited to the semitropical environment of South Carolina. African-style dugout canoes became the chief means of transportation in the colony, which was crisscrossed by rivers and bordered by large islands. Fishing nets copied from African models proved more efficient than those of English origin. Baskets that enslaved laborers wove and gourds they hollowed out came into general use as containers for food and drink. Africans also adapted their traditional techniques of cattle herding for use in America. Because meat and hides initially numbered among the colony's chief exports, Africans contributed significantly to South Carolina's prosperity.

In 1693, as slavery was taking firm root in South Carolina, officials in Spanish Florida began offering freedom to runaways who would convert to Catholicism. Over the years, hundreds of South Carolina fugitives took advantage of the offer, although not all won their liberty. Many settled in a town founded for them near St. Augustine, Gracia Real de Santa Teresa de Mose, headed by a former slave, Francisco Menendez.

After 1700, South Carolinians started to import slaves directly from Africa. From about 1710 until midcentury, the African-born constituted a majority of the enslaved population in the colony, and by 1750, enslaved men and women comprised a majority of its residents. The similarity of the South Carolinian and West African environments, coupled with the substantial African-born population, ensured the survival of more aspects of West African culture than elsewhere on the North American mainland. Only in South Carolina did enslaved parents continue to give their children African names; only there did a dialect develop that combined English words with terms from Wolof, Bambara, and other African languages. (Known as Gullah, it has survived to the present day in isolated coastal areas.) African skills remained useful, so techniques lost in other regions when the migrant generation died were instead passed down to the migrants' children. And in South Carolina, African women became the primary petty traders, dominating the markets of Charles Town as they did those of Guinea.

3-4c Rice and Indigo

The importation of Africans coincided with the successful introduction of rice in South Carolina. English people knew nothing about growing and processing rice, but captives taken

△ This watercolor, entitled "The Old Plantation" (c. 1785), has been attributed to John Rose, a slaveholder in the Beaufort district of South Carolina. It depicts a group of ten enslaved people, young and old, male and female, playing music and dancing without ostensible European presence. Many details in the scene, from the banjo-like instrument known in Yoruba as a molo, to the small drum, to the stick dance, to the styles of headdress worn by the women, demonstrate the survival of African culture ways amidst the devastating institution of chattel slavery.

from Africa's Rice Coast had spent their lives working with the crop. Productive rice-growing techniques known in West Africa, especially cultivation in inland swamps and tidal rivers, both of which involved substantial water-control projects,

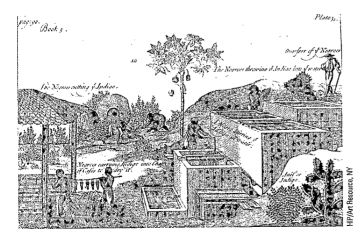

△ This 1761 engraving illustrates an indigo manufactory in French Guyana, on the northern coast of South America. Raw plants were fermented and distilled in a series of descending tanks until they yielded the deep blue dyestuff that cloth-dyers, painters, and others greatly prized.

were widely adopted and combined with European technologies. Enslaved men dug ditches and prepared fields for planting, but as in West Africa, women were responsible for sowing and weeding the crop. Because English grindstones damaged rice kernels, South Carolinians continued to employ the West African system of pounding rice by hand to remove the hulls and bran; planters assigned men as well as women to that task.

On rice plantations, which were far larger than Chesapeake tobacco quarters, every field worker was expected to cultivate three to four acres of rice a year. Most of those field workers were female because many enslaved men were assigned to jobs like blacksmithing or carpentry. To cut expenses, planters also expected slaves to grow part of their own food. By the early eighteenth century, a "task" system of predefined work assignments prevailed. After enslaved people had finished their set tasks for the day, they could rest or work their own garden plots or undertake other projects. Experienced laborers could often complete their tasks by early afternoon; after that, as on Sundays, their masters had no legitimate claim on their time. One scholar has suggested that the **task system,** which gave slaves more autonomy than gang labor, resulted from negotiations between slaves

task system Labor system in which each slave had a daily or weekly quota of tasks to complete.

familiar with rice cultivation and masters who needed their expertise.

Developers of South Carolina's second cash crop also used the task system and drew on slaves' specialized skills. Indigo, the only source of blue dye for the growing English textile industry, was much prized. Eliza Lucas, a young woman born in Antigua, began to experiment with indigo cultivation on her father's Carolina plantations during the early 1740s. Drawing on the knowledge of slaves and overseers whom the family brought with them from the West Indies, Lucas developed planting and processing techniques later adopted throughout the colony. Indigo grew on high ground, and rice was planted in low-lying regions; rice and indigo also had different growing seasons. Thus, the two crops complemented each other. South Carolina indigo never matched the quality of that from the Caribbean, but the crop was so valuable that Parliament paid Carolinians a bounty on every pound exported to Great Britain.

3-4d Enslavement of Indigenous Peoples in North and South Carolina

Among the enslaved people in both Carolinas were indigenous captives who had been retained rather than exported. In 1708, enslaved Native peoples comprised as much as 14 percent of the South Carolina population. The widespread and lucrative traffic in indigenous slaves significantly affected South Carolina's relationship with its indigenous neighbors. Native Americans knew they could always find a ready market for captive enemies in Charles Town, so they took that means of ridding themselves of real or potential rivals. Yet the Westos and other indigenous nations in the region soon learned that Carolinians could not be trusted. As Anglo-American settlers and traders shifted their priorities, first one set of Native allies, then another, found themselves the enslaved rather than the enslavers.

The trade in Native American slaves began when the Westos (originally known as the Eries) migrated south from the Great Lakes region in the mid-1650s, after the Beaver Wars. Expert in the use of European firearms, the Westos began raiding Spain's lightly defended Florida missions and selling the resulting indigenous captives to Virginians. The Carolina proprietors took for themselves a monopoly of trade with the Westos, which infuriated settlers shut out of the profitable commerce in slaves and deerskins. Carolina planters secretly financed attacks on the Westos, essentially wiping them out by 1682. Southeastern Native peoples reacted to such slave raids—continued by other Native peoples after the defeat of the Westos—by trying to protect themselves either through subordination to the English or Spanish, or by coalescing into new, larger political units, such as those known later as Creeks, Chickasaws, or Cherokees.

At first, the Carolinians did not engage directly in conflicts with neighboring Native peoples. But in 1711 the Tuscaroras, an Iroquoian people, attacked a Swiss-German settlement at New Bern, North Carolina, which had expropriated their lands. South Carolinians and their indigenous allies then combined to defeat the Tuscaroras in a bloody war. Afterward, more than a thousand Tuscaroras were enslaved, and the remainder migrated northward, where they joined the Iroquois Confederacy but were not allotted a seat on the council.

Four years later, the Yamasees, who had helped Carolina to conquer the Tuscaroras, turned on their onetime English allies. In what seems to have been long-planned retaliation for multiple abuses by traders as well as threats to their own lands, the Yamasees enlisted the Creeks and other Muskogean peoples in coordinated attacks on outlying English settlements. In the spring and summer of 1715, English and African refugees by the hundreds streamed into Charles Town. The Yamasee-Creek offensive was thwarted only when reinforcements arrived from the north, colonists hastily armed their African slaves, and Cherokees joined the fight against the Creeks. After the war, Carolina's involvement in the Native American slave trade ceased, because all their indigenous neighbors moved away for self-protection: the Creeks migrated west, the Yamasees went south, and the Tuscaroras and other groups moved north. In the war's aftermath, the Native peoples of the Carolinas were able to rebuild their strength, for they were no longer subjected to slavers' raids.

3-4e Enslavement in the North

Atlantic creoles from the Caribbean and Native peoples from the Carolinas and Florida, along with members of local tribes who had been sentenced to slavery for crime or debt, composed the diverse group of enslaved laborers in the northern mainland colonies. The involvement of northerners in the web of commerce surrounding the slave trade ensured that many people of African descent lived in America north of Virginia and that "Spanish Indians" became an identifiable component of the New England population. Some slaves resided in urban areas, especially New York, which in 1700 had a larger black population than any other mainland city. Women tended to work as domestic servants, men as unskilled laborers on the docks. At the end of the seventeenth century, three-quarters of wealthy Philadelphia households included one or two slaves.

Yet even in the North most enslaved men and women worked in the countryside. Dutch farmers in the Hudson Valley and northern New Jersey were especially likely to rely on enslaved African field hands, as were large landowners in the Narragansett region of Rhode Island. Some slaves toiled in new rural enterprises, such as ironworks, working alongside hired laborers and indentured servants at forges and foundries. Slavery made its most dramatic contribution to the northern economy at one remove, through the West Indies provision trade. But although relatively few northern colonists owned slaves, some individual northern slaveholders benefited directly from the institution and had good reason to want to preserve it.

3-4f Slave Resistance

As slavery became an integral part of the North American and Caribbean landscapes, so too did slaves' resistance to their bondage. Most commonly, resistance took the form of work slowdown or escape, but occasionally enslaved people planned rebellions. Seven times before 1713, the English Caribbean experienced major revolts involving at least fifty slaves and causing the deaths of both whites and blacks. In 1675 and 1692, Barbados authorities thwarted plots shortly before they were to be implemented, afterward executing more than sixty convicted conspirators. Jamaica, where a mountainous terrain offered ideal hideouts for runaways, experienced frequent slave mutinies. A 1685 uprising beginning in the northern part of the island lasted nearly a year, and involved more than 250 slaves, before colonial authorities suppressed the rebels with horrific punishments.

The first slave revolt in the mainland English colonies took place in New York in 1712, at a time when enslaved

△ This advertisement for a sale of slaves of African descent appeared in the New York Journal in 1768. The expertise of two of the people described would have appealed to urban buyers: a cooper would have been useful to a barrelmaker or shipper, and the seamstress might have attracted attention from dressmakers. The other men, women, and girls mentioned could have been purchased by people who wanted house servants or laborers.

people constituted about 15 percent of the city's population. The rebels, primarily recent arrivals from the Akan States of the Gold Coast, set a fire and then ambushed those who tried to put it out, killing eight and wounding another twelve. Some rebels committed suicide to avoid capture; of those caught and tried, eighteen were tortured and executed. Their decapitated bodies were left to rot outdoors as a warning to others.

3-5 Forging and Testing the Bonds of Empire

▷ **What was mercantilism and how did English mercantilist policies affect the colonies?**

▷ **How and why did the English seek to exercise more political authority and control over the North American colonies?**

▷ **What internal and external issues threatened to destabilize Britain's American colonies?**

English officials seeking new sources of revenue decided to tap into the profits of the expanding Atlantic trading system in slaves and the products of slave labor. Caribbean sugar had the greatest value, but other colonial commodities also had considerable potential. Parliament and the Stuart monarchs accordingly drafted laws designed to harness the proceeds of the trade for the primary benefit of the mother country.

3-5a Colonies into Empire

Like other European nations, England based its commercial policy on a series of assumptions about the operations of the world's economic system, collectively called *mercantilism*. The theory viewed the economic world as a collection of countries whose governments competed for shares of a finite amount of wealth. What one nation gained, another lost. Each nation sought to become as economically self-sufficient as possible while maintaining a favorable balance of trade with other countries by exporting more than it imported. Colonies played an important role, supplying the mother country with valuable raw materials and serving as a market for the parent country's manufactured goods.

Parliament's Navigation Acts—passed between 1651 and 1673—established three main principles that accorded with mercantilist theory. First, only English or colonial merchants and ships could legally trade in the colonies. Second, certain valuable American products could be sold only in the mother country or in other English colonies. At first, these "enumerated" commodities included wool, sugar, tobacco, indigo, ginger, and dyes; later acts added rice, naval stores (masts, spars, pitch, tar, and turpentine), copper, and furs to the list. Third, all foreign goods destined for sale in the colonies had to be shipped through England, paying English import duties. Some years later, new laws established a fourth principle: the colonies could not export items (such

The Granger Collection, NYC

as wool clothing, hats, or iron) that competed with English manufactures.

These laws adversely affected some colonies, like those in the Chesapeake, because planters there could not seek foreign markets for their staple crops. The statutes initially helped the sugar producers of the English Caribbean by driving Brazilian sugar out of the home market, but later prevented those English planters from selling their sugar elsewhere. In some places, the impact was minimal or even positive. Builders and owners of ships benefited from the monopoly on American trade given to English and colonial merchants; the laws stimulated the creation of a lucrative shipbuilding industry in New England. And the northern and middle colonies produced many unenumerated goods—for example, fish, flour, meat and livestock, and barrel staves. Such products could be traded directly to the French, Spanish, or Dutch Caribbean islands as long as they were carried in English or American ships.

3-5b Mercantilism and Navigation Acts

English authorities soon learned that it was easier to write mercantilist legislation than to enforce it. The many harbors of the American coast provided ready havens for smugglers, and colonial officials often looked the other way when illegally imported goods were offered for sale. In Dutch Caribbean ports like St. Eustatius, American merchants could easily exchange enumerated goods for foreign items on which no duty had been paid. Because American juries tended to favor local smugglers over customs officers (a colonial customs service was instituted in 1671), Parliament in 1696 established several American vice-admiralty courts, which operated without juries and adjudicated violations of the Navigation Acts.

The Navigation Acts imposed regulations on Americans' international trade, but by the early 1680s mainland governments and their residents had become accustomed to a considerable degree of political autonomy. Local rule was most firmly established in New England, where Massachusetts, Plymouth, Connecticut, and Rhode Island operated essentially as independent entities, subject neither to the direct authority of the king nor to a proprietor. Virginia was a royal colony and New Hampshire (1679) and New York (1685) gained that status, but all other mainland settlements were proprietorships, over which the Crown exercised little control. Everywhere in the English colonies, free adult men who owned more than a minimum amount of property expected to have a voice in their governments, especially in decisions concerning taxation.

After James II became king in 1685, such expectations clashed with those of the monarch. The new king and his successors sought to bring order to the apparently chaotic state of colonial administration by tightening the reins of government and by reducing the colonies' political autonomy. English officials targeted New England, which they saw as a hotbed of smuggling. Moreover, Puritans refused to allow

freedom of religion to non-Congregationalists and insisted on maintaining laws incompatible with English practice. New England thus seemed an appropriate place to exert English authority with greater vigor. The charters of all the colonies from New Jersey to Maine were revoked, and a royal Dominion of New England was established in 1686. (For the boundaries of the Dominion, see Map 3.1, Section 3-1.) Sir Edmund Andros, the Dominion's governor, had immense power: Parliament dissolved all the assemblies, and Andros needed only the consent of an appointed council to make laws and levy taxes.

3-5c Glorious Revolution in America

New Englanders had endured Andros's autocratic rule for more than two years when they learned that James II's hold on power was crumbling. The king had angered his subjects by levying taxes without parliamentary approval and by announcing his conversion to Catholicism. In April 1689, Boston's leaders jailed Andros and his associates. The following month, they received definite news of the bloodless coup known as the Glorious Revolution, in which James had been replaced on the throne in late 1688 by his daughter Mary and her husband, the Dutch prince William of Orange.

The Glorious Revolution affirmed the supremacy of Protestantism and Parliament. The new king and queen acceded to Parliament's Declaration of Rights "vindicating and asserting their ancient rights and liberties" as Englishmen. Codified as a Bill of Rights in 1689, this revolutionary document confirmed citizens' entitlement to free elections, fair trials, and petition, and specified that no monarch could ignore acts of Parliament on key issues of taxation and defense. The English Declaration inaugurated a century of heated rhetoric on rights in England, in the colonies, and on the continent. In 1776, the American Declaration of Independence would borrow heavily from Parliament's 1689 Declaration of Rights.

Across the mainland colonies, the Glorious Revolution emboldened people for revolt. In Maryland, the Protestant Association overturned the government of the Catholic proprietor, and in New York a militia officer of German origin, Jacob Leisler, assumed control of the government. Bostonians, Marylanders, and New Yorkers alike allied themselves with the supporters of William and Mary. They saw themselves as defending English liberties by carrying out the colonial phase of the revolt against Stuart absolutism.

But like James II, William and Mary believed England should exercise tighter control over its unruly American possessions. Consequently, only the Maryland rebellion received royal sanction, primarily because of its anti-Catholic thrust. In New York, Leisler was hanged for treason. Massachusetts (incorporating the formerly independent Plymouth) became a royal colony with an appointed governor. The province retained its town meeting system and continued to elect its council, but the new 1691 charter eliminated the traditional religious test for voting and office holding. A parish of the Church of England appeared in the heart of Boston. The **"city upon a hill,"** as John Winthrop had envisioned it, had fallen.

3-5d King William's War

A war with the French and their Algonquian allies compounded New England's difficulties. After King Louis XIV of France allied himself with the deposed James II, England declared war on France in 1689. (This war is today known as the Nine Years' War, but the colonists called it King William's War.) Even before war broke out in Europe, Anglo-Americans and Abenakis clashed over settlements in Maine that colonists had reoccupied after the 1678 truce. Abenaki attacks wholly or partially destroyed a number of towns, including Schenectady, New York, and Falmouth (now Portland) and York, Maine. Expeditions organized by the colonies against Montreal and Quebec in 1690 failed miserably, and throughout the rest of the conflict New England found itself on the defensive. The Peace of Ryswick (1697) formally ended the war in Europe but failed to bring much respite to North America's northern frontiers. New Englanders understandably feared a repetition of the devastation of King Philip's War.

3-5e The 1692 Witchcraft Crisis

For eight months in 1692, witchcraft accusations spread like wildfire through the rural communities of Essex County, Massachusetts, a heavily populated area directly threatened by the Native American attacks to the north. Earlier incidents in which personal disputes occasionally led to witchcraft charges bore little relationship to the witch fears that convulsed the region beginning that February. Before the outbreak ended, fourteen women and five men were hanged, one man was pressed to death with heavy stones, fifty-four people confessed to being witches, and more than 140 suspects were jailed, some for many months. The worst phase of the crisis concluded when the governor dissolved the special court established to try the accused. During the final trials, which took place in regular courts, judges and juries discounted so-called spectral evidence, offered by witnesses who claimed to be afflicted by specters of witches. Almost all the defendants were acquitted, and the governor quickly reprieved the few found guilty. If frontier warfare and political turmoil had created an environment where witch fears could become epidemic, the imposition of a new imperial order on the colony helped to cure the plague.

3-5f New Imperial Measures

In 1696, England created the fifteen-member Board of Trade and Plantations, which thereafter served as the chief organ of government concerned with the American colonies. The board gathered information, reviewed Crown appointments in America, scrutinized legislation passed by colonial assemblies, supervised trade policies, and advised successive ministries on colonial issues. Still, the Board of Trade did not have any direct powers of enforcement. It also shared jurisdiction over American affairs with the customs service, the navy, and a cabinet minister. Although the Board of Trade improved the quality of colonial administration, supervision of the American provinces remained decentralized and haphazard.

Lax enforcement surely made it easier for the English colonies to accommodate themselves to the new imperial order. Most colonists resented English "placemen" who arrived in America determined to implement the policies of king and Parliament, but they adjusted to their demands and to the trade restrictions imposed by the Navigation Acts. They fought another of Europe's wars—the War of the Spanish Succession, called Queen Anne's War in the colonies—from 1702 to 1713. The "Four Indian Kings" journeyed to London to seek greater Crown support for an offensive against the French on the northern front of Queen Anne's War.

Colonists who allied themselves with the royal government received patronage in the form of offices and land grants and composed "court parties" that supported English officials. Others, who were either less fortunate in their friends or more zealous in defense of colonial autonomy, made up the opposition, or "country" interest. By the end of the first quarter of the eighteenth century, most men in both groups had been born in America, along the western margins of Britain's emerging empire.

Summary

The period from 1650 to 1720 established economic and political patterns that would structure subsequent changes in mainland colonial society. England's first attempt to regulate colonial trade, the Navigation Act of 1651, was quickly followed by others. By 1720, essential elements of the imperial administrative structure that would govern the English colonies until 1775 had been put in place.

In 1650, just two isolated centers of English settlement, New England and the Chesapeake, existed along the seaboard, along with the tiny Dutch colony of New Netherland. In 1720, nearly the entire East Coast of North America was in English hands, and Native American control east of the Appalachian Mountains had largely been broken by the outcomes of King Philip's War, Bacon's Rebellion, the Yamasee war, the Tuscarora war, and Queen Anne's War. To the west of the mountains, though, Iroquois power reigned supreme. What had been an immigrant population was now mostly American-born, except for the many African-born people in South Carolina and the Chesapeake; economies originally based on trade in fur and skins had become far more complex and more closely linked with the mother country; and a wide variety of political structures had

"city upon a hill" John Winthrop's biblical phrase describing the Puritan settlement of Massachusetts Bay in 1630 as a model for the world.

Fictions of Salem: Witch-Hunting in the American Grain

Like a nightmare that evaporates upon waking, Salem's witchcraft crisis ended as quickly as it began. Prisoners who outlasted the ordeal trudged home from the fetid village jail. The most tormented of the bewitched accusers went on to marry and live seemingly normal lives, beyond the glare of written records. Some of those responsible came to regret their roles in what was soon widely acknowledged as a grave miscarriage of justice. In early 1697, Judge Samuel Sewall, an educated Bostonian who had served on the special court that arraigned the suspects, publicly lamented his share of "the Blame and Shame of it." Sewall may have cleared his conscience, but Salem did not recover its reputation. The trials had inflicted a lasting, "smutty deformity," wrote the merchant Joshua Scottow, who worried that "New-England will be called, new Witch-land," the sweet smell of its pine forests replaced by the stink of hemlock and brimstone.

History has proved Scottow right. In the centuries since the Salem trials, spirals of false accusation, imprisonment, destruction, and regret have often evoked comparisons to 1692. After an alleged and almost certainly imaginary slave conspiracy in New York City resulted in thirty-four gruesome executions in 1741,

one observer said that the "bloody Tragedy" put him "in mind of our New England Witchcraft in the year 1692," already two generations gone but not forgotten.

It wasn't until the nineteenth century that writers began to make art of Salem's witch panic, which was dramatized in stories, plays, paintings, and novels. Many of these fictions contrasted the rational temperament of the young United States with the supposedly bygone superstitions of the Puritans, who were both beloved and mocked for their stern, ancient faith, so quaintly out of step with a polity that had largely ceased to believe in witches. But in a country that readily fastened on new enemies—immigrants, bankers, laborers, enslaved and emancipated African Americans—it was not quite so easy to remain smug about 1692. As the poet Emily Dickinson wrote, "Witchcraft was hung, in History, / But History and I / Find all the Witchcraft that we need / Around us, every Day—."

The most enduring allegory of Salem was created in 1953, at the height of the anti-communist hysteria fueled by Wisconsin Senator Joseph McCarthy. That year, McCarthy began using a senate subcommittee to root out suspected subversives in the entertainment industry, the government, and finally the military.

Playwright Arthur Miller never referred to McCarthy's purges in The Crucible, which he both painstakingly researched and freely adapted from the historical record. "This play is not history," Miller insisted. Instead of a truth of the past, Miller hoped the reader would discover in his fiction of Salem "the essential nature of one of the strangest and most awful chapters in human history."

More than sixty years after its first Broadway run, and more than three centuries after the events it so memorably depicts, The Crucible has become iconic. Two feature-length versions have been filmed, and it remains one of the most produced plays in high schools and colleges across the United States. In 2016, it was revived on Broadway to rave reviews. Ben Brantley, critic for the New York Times, said the play "feels perfectly timed in this presidential election year, when politicians traffic in fears of outsiders and otherness."

CRITICAL THINKING

▫ The legacy of the Salem witchcraft trials reverberates throughout American history in historical moments like the McCarthy era of the twentieth century. Ben Brantley, critic for the New York Times, implied a more recent comparison can be seen in the election of 2016. What merit do you see in Brantley's criticism?

---

been reshaped into a more uniform pattern. Yet at the same time the adoption of large-scale slavery in the Chesapeake, the Carolinas, and the West Indies differentiated their societies from those of the colonies to the north. They had become true slave societies, heavily reliant on a system of perpetual servitude, not societies with slaves, in which a relatively small number of enslaved people mingled with indentured servants and free wage laborers.

Yet the economies of the northern colonies, much like their southern counterparts, rested on profits derived from the Atlantic trading system, the key element of which was traffic in enslaved humans. New England sold corn, salt fish, and wood products to the West Indies. Slaves subsisted on these foodstuffs, and Caribbean planters shipped their sugar

and molasses in barrels made from staves crafted by northern farmers. Pennsylvania and New York, too, found in the Caribbean islands a ready market for their livestock, grains, and flour. The rapid growth of Atlantic slavery drove all the English colonial economies in these years. The colonies of the West Indies, especially Barbados and Jamaica, were the economic engine of the empire. In 1720, their exports to Britain—chiefly 705,000 tons of sugar—were worth more than double what the combined mainland colonies produced.

Spanish settlements in America north of Mexico remained largely centered on Florida missions and on New Mexican presidios and missions during these years. The French had explored the Mississippi valley, but had not yet planted many settlements in the Great Lakes or the west.

Both nations' colonists depended on indigenous people's labor and goodwill. The Spanish could not fully control their indigenous allies, and the French did not even try. Yet the extensive Spanish and French presence to the south and west of the English settlements meant that future conflicts among the European powers in North America were nearly inevitable.

Suggestions for Further Reading

David Eltis and David Richardson, *Atlas of the Transatlantic Slave Trade* (2010)

Eric Hinderaker, *The Two Hendricks: Untangling a Mohawk Mystery* (2010)

Malcolm Gaskill, *Between Two Worlds: How the English Became Americans* (2014)

Andrew Knaut, *The Pueblo Revolt of 1680* (1995)

Jill Lepore, *The Name of War: King Philip's War and the Origins of American Identity* (1998)

Edmund S. Morgan, *American Slavery, American Freedom: The Ordeal of Colonial Virginia* (1975)

Mary Beth Norton, *In the Devil's Snare: The Salem Witchcraft Crisis of 1692* (2002)

Daniel K. Richter, *The Ordeal of the Longhouse: The Peoples of the Iroquois League in the Era of European Colonization* (1992)

Brett Rushforth, *Bonds of Alliance: Indigenous and Atlantic Slaveries in New France* (2012)

Stephanie E. Smallwood, *Saltwater Slavery: A Middle Passage from Africa to American Diaspora* (2007)

Owen Stanwood, *The Empire Reformed: English America in the Age of the Glorious Revolution* (2011)

MINDTAP
From Cengage

Becoming America?
1720–1760

D r. Alexander Hamilton was a learned man. The son of a theologian, he studied medicine at the University of Edinburgh, which boasted the best medical school in the world. But if Edinburgh was crowded with genius, it was hardly brimming with opportunity. So many Scots left "to range about to all parts of the world," Hamilton wrote, because his country offered "cold comfort … nothing is to be got." Like thousands of other émigrés, the doctor sought a stage on which his talents might loom larger and fetch more. In 1739, he lit out for the colonies, settling in Annapolis, where his older brother preached.

Maryland's capital offered plenty of work to a university-trained physician, and Dr. Hamilton quickly established himself among the town's elite. But like many migrants to the Chesapeake, he sickened in the climate. By 1744, he was suffering from "an Incessant cough." He thought travel might improve his health. Late that May, he and an enslaved man named Dromo set off to tour the countryside from Maryland to Maine. Their four-month journey wound through eight colonies, scores of villages, numerous towns, and the burgeoning cities of Philadelphia, New York, Newport, and Boston. An avid reader of polite literature, including the new books called *novels* then flooding British presses, the doctor recorded his impressions of this strange new world in a journal to which he gave the Latin title *Itinerarium*.

The diversity of the colonists astonished Hamilton, who had known in Scotland a far narrower range of humanity. In one Philadelphia tavern, he dined "with a very mixed company of different nations and religions. There were Scots, English, Dutch, Germans, and Irish; there

◁ Dr. Hamilton said he had "a foolish Sort of a Genius for drawing." In this sketch, "Mr. Neilson's Battle with the Royalist Club," he shows the raucous civic life of Annapolis in the late 1740s. To illustrate American roughness, Hamilton used a British model: the engravings of London's William Hogarth, which were popular throughout the English-speaking world. John Work Garrett Collections of the Milton Eisenhower Library of Johns Hopkins University.

Chronology

1690	Locke's Essay *Concerning Human Understanding* published, a key example of Enlightenment thought
1718	New Orleans founded in French Louisiana
1721–22	Smallpox epidemic in Boston leads to first widespread adoption of inoculation in America
1732	Founding of Georgia
1733	Printer John Peter Zenger tried for and acquitted of "seditious libel" in New York
1737	"Walking Purchase" of Delaware and Shawnee lands in Pennsylvania
1739	Stono Rebellion (South Carolina)
	George Whitefield arrives in America; Great Awakening broadens
1739–48	King George's War affects American economies
1740s	Black population of the Chesapeake begins to grow by natural increase
1741	New York City "conspiracy" reflects whites' continuing fears of slave revolts
1745	Fall of Louisbourg to New England troops; returned to France in 1748 Treaty of Aix-la-Chapelle
1751	Franklin's *Experiments and Observations on Electricity* published, important American contribution to Enlightenment science
1760–75	Peak of eighteenth-century European and African migration to English colonies

were Roman Catholicks, Church [of England] men, Presbyterians, Quakers, Newlightmen, Methodists, Seventh day men, Moravians, Anabaptists, and one Jew," all talking politics, while a "knott of Quakers" debated the price of flour. He met rich planters from Jamaica, Antigua, and Barbados. He saw Africans everywhere, Mohawks now and again. In Boston, he watched "a parade of Indian chiefs" decked out in fine linens. Their leader, the Mohawk sachem Hendrick Theyanoguin, urged the assembled Native people to "brighten the chain with the English, our friends, and take up the hatchet against the French, our enemies."

Hamilton called Hendrick a "bold, intrepid fellow." Why did so many of these provincials act bold when they should be humble? In Scotland, a better man commanded deference from his inferiors. Here, there was little respect on offer. He and Dromo watched "a boxing match between a master and his servant," who had called the master a "shitten elf." On Long Island he met a shoemaker who had "laid aside his awls and leather" to practice medicine; the self-taught physician now cobbled "bodies" instead of "soals." These "infant countrys of America" bred "aggrandized upstarts," Hamilton wrote. About the "different ranks of men in polite nations" they knew little, and cared less.

But for all their "nastiness, impudence, and rusticity," there was a strange worldliness about "the American provinces." Farmers' wives wore fine imported cloth, and tradesmen talked philosophy. Hamilton viewed botanical engravings in rural Maryland and a plaster copy of the Venus de Medici in Boston. He purchased Montaigne's essays and Henry Fielding's latest novel in Philadelphia, and heard Italian concerti played on German flutes in an Albany tavern. He drank tea in every hamlet, coffee in every town, and rum at every crossroads. Always, there was talk of international politics, especially "the dreaded French war"—King George's War—that once again drew the raw edges of the empire into the maelstrom of European rivalries.

Experience an interactive version of this story in MindTap®.

Dr. Hamilton encountered a mobile and fast-changing world on his tour of Britain's American provinces. What he saw there changed him in turn. The boorish multitude convinced him that authority rested "upon the Strong and brawny Shoulders of that gyant called popular opinion." The many—"the vulgar," he called them—were ultimately more powerful than the great.

As many European travelers to North America in the eighteenth century noticed, they did things differently in the colonies. People didn't stay within their stations. Property was held more widely, and opinions voiced more readily, in more languages, than anywhere in Europe. After 1720, a massive migration of European and African peoples changed the North American landscape. Ethnic diversity became especially pronounced in the cities where Hamilton drank and disputed. The British colonies south of New England drew by far the largest number of newcomers, many to the fertile countryside. Their arrival altered political balances and introduced new religious sects. Unwilling immigrants (slaves and transported convicts) likewise clustered in the middle and southern colonies. The rough equality Hamilton witnessed among whites was everywhere built upon the bondage of Africans and their descendants.

This polyglot population, with its distinctive customs and mores, hardly resembled the places from which its peoples had been drawn. But in some ways, the America Hamilton encountered was more British than ever. A flood of European and especially British goods allowed genteel and middling folks to style themselves in the image of fashionable Britons. Educated colonists participated in transatlantic intellectual life; Hamilton found Enlightenment ideas wherever he traveled. Yet most colonists, whether free or enslaved, worked with their hands daily from dawn to dark. The social and economic distance among different ranks of Anglo-Americans had widened noticeably. Workhouses sprang up alongside coffeehouses—just as in London.

In 1720, much of eastern North America remained under Native peoples' control. Four decades later, indigenous peoples still dominated the interior of the continent, yet their lives had been indelibly altered by the expansion of European settlements. France extended its reach from the St. Lawrence to the Gulf of Mexico. Spanish outposts spread both east and west from a New Mexican heartland. The British colonies, the largest and most prosperous on the continent, stretched from the Atlantic coast to the Appalachian Mountains, where they threatened French and indigenous claims. North America's resources were worth fighting for, and Europe's balance of power was always precarious. As European conflicts crossed the Atlantic once again during the 1740s (see Table 4.1), many colonists in British North America defended King George II's empire against other nations jockeying for control of the continent.

▣ **What were the effects of demographic, geographic, and economic changes on Europeans, Africans, and American Indian nations alike?**

▣ **What were the key elements of eighteenth-century provincial cultures?**

▣ **In what ways was North America becoming less like Britain at midcentury? In what ways were colonists more British than before?**

4-1 Geographic Expansion and Ethnic Diversity

▷ **What patterns of settlement did forced and voluntary migrants create in French, British, and Spanish American territories?**

▷ **How did the socioeconomic demographic makeup of the British North American colonies shift over the course of the eighteenth century?**

▷ **How did colonists relate to peoples already present in French, British, and Spanish settlements, and to one another?**

Europe's North American possessions expanded both geographically and demographically during the middle decades of the eighteenth century. The most striking development was the dramatic population growth of the British mainland colonies. In 1700, only about 250,000 European Americans and African Americans resided in the colonies. Thirty years later, that number had more than doubled; by 1775, it would reach 2.5 million.

Migration from Scotland, Ireland, England, Germany, and especially Africa accounted for a considerable share of the growth. Between 1700 and 1780, an estimated 350,000 European immigrants and roughly 280,000 forced migrants from Africa came to Britain's mainland colonies. But even more of the gain stemmed from natural increase. Once the difficult early decades of settlement had passed, the population of Britain's mainland colonies doubled approximately every twenty-five years. Such a rate of growth, unparalleled in human history until very recent times, had a variety of causes, chief among them women's youthful age at first marriage (early twenties for Euro-Americans, late teens for African Americans). Because married women became pregnant every two to three years, they normally bore five to ten children. Since the colonies, especially those north of Virginia, were relatively healthful places to live, a large proportion of children who survived infancy reached maturity and began families of their own. The result was a young, rapidly growing population; about half the people in Anglo America were under sixteen years old in 1775. (By contrast, about one-fifth of the U.S. population today is under sixteen.)

4-1a Spanish and French Territorial Expansion

The rapidly expanding population of mainland British North America was sandwiched between the Atlantic coast (on the east) and Appalachian Mountains (on the west). Older settlements in New England had come to feel crowded. By contrast, Spanish and French territories expanded across much of North America while their populations increased only modestly. At the end of the eighteenth century, Texas had but three thousand Spanish residents and California less than one thousand; the largest Spanish colony, New Mexico, included twenty thousand or so settlers. The total European population of the mainland French colonies increased from approximately fifteen thousand in 1700 to about seventy thousand in the 1760s, but those colonists clustered in a few widely scattered locations. If the population of most French and Spanish settlements remained small, their geographic expansion had far-reaching effects on Native peoples.

Still seeking the rewards that had motivated their American designs for centuries—an inland waterway to the Pacific, fat veins of gold and silver, an advantage over their European rivals—the French by water and the Spanish by land ventured separately into the Mississippi valley in the early eighteenth century. There they encountered powerful American Indian nations like the Quapaws, Osages, and Caddos. A few Europeans—priests, soldiers, farmers, traders, ranchers—found themselves surrounded by Native peoples who wanted access to manufactured goods, and who accordingly sought friendly relations with the newcomers. The Spanish and French invaders of these territories had to accommodate themselves to Native peoples' diplomatic and cultural practices in order to achieve their objectives. French officials, for example, often complained of being forced to endure lengthy calumet ceremonies; Spaniards, unaccustomed to involving women in diplomacy, had to accede to Texas Native peoples' use of female representatives. The European nations established neighboring outposts in the lower Mississippi region in 1716—the French at Natchitoches (west of the Mississippi), the Spaniards at nearby Los Adaes (see Map 4.1). France had already founded a settlement on Biloxi Bay (in the modern state of Mississippi) in 1699, and later strengthened its presence near the Gulf of Mexico by establishing New Orleans in 1718, a move the Spanish could not counter because the overland distance from Santa Fe was too great.

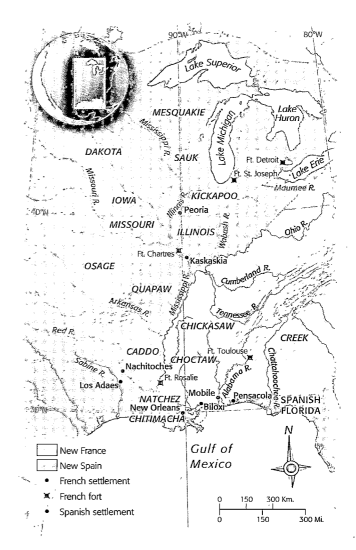

Map 4.1 The North American Interior, ca. 1720

By 1720, French forts and settlements dotted the Mississippi River and its tributaries in the interior of North America. Two isolated Spanish outposts were situated near the Gulf of Mexico.

Instead, Spaniards focused their attention first on Texas (for instance, establishing San Antonio in 1718), and later on the region they called Alta (upper) California. After learning that Russians who hunted sea otters along the Pacific coast were planning to colonize the region, they sent expeditions north from their missions in Baja California. From a base at San Diego, where the Franciscan Junipero Serra set up the first mission in Alta California in 1769, they traveled north by land and sea to Monterey Bay. There, in 1770, they formally claimed Alta California for Spain. Over the next decades, they established presidios and missions along the coast from modern San Francisco south to San Diego. In those centers, Franciscan friars from Spain and a few settlers from Mexico lived amid thousands of Native peoples who had converted to Christianity.

4-1b France and the Mississippi

French settlements north of New Orleans served as the glue of empire. *Coureurs de bois* (literally, "forest runners") used the rivers and lakes of the American interior to carry goods between Quebec and the new Louisiana territory. At such sites as Michilimackinac (at the junction of Lakes Michigan and Huron) and Kaskaskia (in present-day Illinois), Native peoples traded furs and hides for guns, ammunition, and other valuable items. The Osages were so eager to acquire firearms that they became, in effect, commercial hunters; witnesses reported that their women were sometimes so fully occupied processing hides that older men prepared the communities' meals. The population of the largest French settlements in the region, known collectively as *le pays de Illinois* ("the Illinois country"), never totaled much above three thousand. Located along the Mississippi south of modern St. Louis, the settlements produced wheat for export to New Orleans.

French expansion reshaped native alliances far from the Mississippi. For example, the equestrian Comanches of the Plains, able to trade with the French through Native American intermediaries, no longer needed Spanish goods—or their previous allies, the Utes. Deprived of such powerful partners, the Utes negotiated peace with New Mexico in 1752. Once commonly enslaved by Spaniards, Utes instead became the enslavers of Paiutes and other nonequestrian peoples living to the north and west of the colony. They exchanged hides and slaves—mostly young women—for horses and metal goods. That commercial relationship endured until the end of Spanish rule in the region.

In French officials' minds, Louisiana's paramount goals were protection of the valuable Caribbean islands and prevention of Spanish and British expansion. They accordingly did not focus their attention on the colony's economic development. But the profit-seeking farmers and Native traders from Canada who settled there soon demanded that the French government supply them with slaves. In 1719 officials acquiesced, dispatching more than six thousand Africans, mostly from Senegal, over the next decade. But Louisiana's residents failed to develop a successful plantation economy. They did raise some tobacco and indigo, which, along with skins and hides obtained from Native peoples, composed the colony's major exports for most of the eighteenth century. Some enslaved Africans were carried north to the Illinois country, as farm laborers and domestic servants. They made up nearly 40 percent of the region's population in the 1730s.

Louisiana's expansion angered the Natchez, whose lands the French had usurped. In 1729, the Natchez, assisted by newly arrived slaves, attacked northern reaches of the colony,

△ A Russian artist in 1816 painted this view of Ohlone/Costanoan men dancing in front of Mission Delores and Spanish spectators. Today the building shown at the left still stands in the middle of the city of San Francisco. The scene conveys a sense of the religious syncretism characteristic of the missions, as native customs combined with the friars' Catholicism to create a fertile blend of spiritual beliefs.

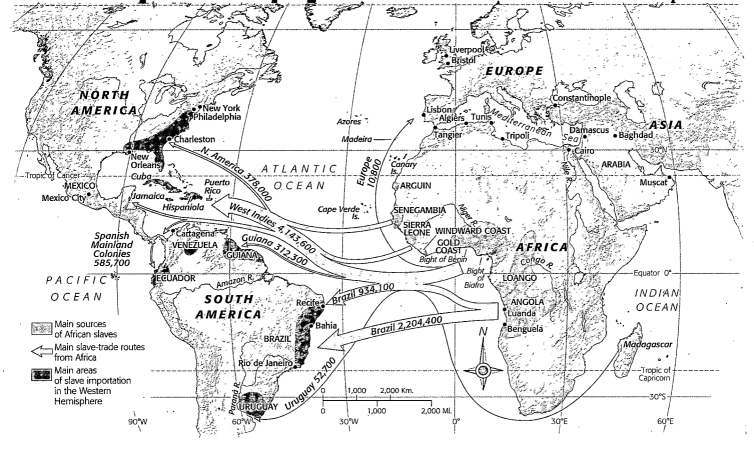

Map 4.2 Major Origins and Destinations of Africans Enslaved in the Americas

Enslaved Africans were drawn from many regions of western Africa (with some coming from the interior of the continent) and were shipped as captives to areas throughout the Americas.

killing more than 10 percent of its settlers. The French struck back, slaughtering the Natchez and their enslaved allies, but Louisiana remained a fragile and neglected colony as long as French rule continued.

4-1c Involuntary Migrants from Africa

Across the Americas, slavery took hold more firmly during the eighteenth century. In all, more Africans than Europeans came to the Americas, the overwhelming majority of them as slaves and about half between 1700 and 1800. Most Africans were transported to Brazil or the Caribbean, primarily in British or Portuguese vessels. The estimated 280,000 people imported before 1780 into the region that became the United States amounted to less than 3 percent of the approximately 12.3 million enslaved people brought to the Americas during the existence of slavery. Rice, indigo, tobacco, and sugar plantations all expanded rapidly in these years, steadily increasing the demand for slaves. In the slaveholding societies of South America and the Caribbean, a surplus of enslaved males over females and appallingly high mortality rates meant that only a continuing influx of new captives could maintain and expand the workforce. On the North American mainland, only South Carolina, where malaria-carrying mosquitoes in the swamps made rice cultivation especially unhealthful,

relied on an inflow of Africans to sustain and expand its labor force.

The involuntary migrants came from many different ethnic groups and regions of Africa (see Map 4.2). More than 40 percent embarked from West Central Africa (modern Congo and Angola), nearly 20 percent from the Bight of Benin (modern Togo, Benin, and southwestern Nigeria), about 13 percent from the Bight of Biafra (today's Cameroon, Gabon, and southeastern Nigeria), and approximately 9 percent from the Gold Coast (modern Ghana and neighboring countries). Smaller numbers of enslaved migrants came from East Africa, the Windward Coast, and the Rice Coast (modern Senegal, Gambia, and Sierra Leone).

Standard slave-trading practice, in which a vessel loaded its human cargo at one port and sold it in another, meant that people from the same broad area (enemies as well as allies) tended to arrive in the Americas together. That tendency was heightened by planter partiality for particular ethnic groups. Virginians, for example, favored Igbos from the Bight of Biafra, whereas South Carolinians and Georgians selected Senegambians and people from West Central Africa. Louisiana planters first chose slaves from the Bight of Benin but later bought many from West Central Africa. Rice planters' desire to purchase

Senegambians, who cultivated rice in their homeland, is easily explained, but historians disagree about the reasons underlying the other preferences.

Thousands, possibly tens of thousands, of these enslaved Africans were Muslims. Some were literate in Arabic, and some came from noble families. Job Ben Solomon, for example, arrived in Maryland in 1732. A slave trader from Senegal, he had been captured by raiders while selling slaves in Gambia. A letter he wrote in Arabic so impressed his owners that they liberated him the next year. Abd al-Rahman, brought to Louisiana in 1788, was less fortunate. Known to his master as "Prince" because of his aristocratic origins, he was not freed until 1829.

Despite the hundreds of thousands of Africans brought to the eighteenth-century mainland, American-born people of African descent, came to dominate the mainland's enslaved population numerically because of high levels of natural increase, especially after 1740. Although about 40 percent of the Africans were male, women and children together composed a majority of slave imports; planters valued girls and women for their reproductive as well as productive capacities. All of the colonies passed laws to ensure that the children of enslaved women were born into slavery. This meant that a planter who owned adult female slaves could engineer the steady growth of his labor force without additional major purchases of workers. The slaveholder Thomas Jefferson later observed, "I consider a woman who brings a child every two years more profitable than the best man of the farm. What she produces is an addition to the capital, while his labors disappear in mere consumption."

In the Chesapeake, the number of people held in bondage grew rapidly as imported African people joined an enslaved population that had begun to sustain itself through natural increase. The work routines involved in cultivating tobacco, coupled with a roughly equal sex ratio, reduced slave mortality and increased fertility. Even in unhealthful South Carolina, where substantial imports continued, American-born slaves outnumbered the African-born as early as 1750.

4-1d Newcomers from Europe

In addition to the new Africans, a roughly equal number of Europeans—about 350,000—moved to mainland British North America between 1700 and 1780, most of them after 1730. Late in the seventeenth century, English officials decided to recruit German and French Protestants for their overseas plantations in order to prevent further large-scale emigration from England itself. Influenced by mercantilist thought, they had come to regard a large, industrious population at home as an asset. Thus, they discouraged emigration, except for the deportation of such "undesirables" as vagabonds and Jacobite rebels (supporters of the deposed Stuart monarchs). They offered foreign Protestants free lands and religious toleration, even financing the passage of some. After 1740, they relaxed citizenship (naturalization) requirements,

△ In December 1729, probably in New York's Hudson Valley, an unknown artist portrayed J. M. Stolle, son of a Palatine immigrant who came to North America from Germany in 1709. The young man's fancy clothing and the column and balustrade in the background suggest that the artist wanted to convey an image of the family's economic success, though whether that image was accurate is unknown.

demanding only the payment of a small fee, seven years' residence, Protestantism, and an oath of allegiance to the British Crown. Such policies created an ethnic diversity unknown outside Britain's American colonies.

Early arrivals wrote home, urging others to come; those contacts created chains of migration from particular regions. The most successful migrants came well prepared, having learned from their American correspondents that land and resources were abundant, especially in the inland areas known as the backcountry, but that they would need capital to take full advantage of the new opportunities. People who arrived penniless did less well; approximately 40 percent of the newcomers fell into that category, for they immigrated as bound laborers of some sort.

Worst off among European emigrés were the roughly fifty thousand migrants who arrived as convicted felons sentenced to transportation for two to fourteen years instead of execution. Typically unskilled and perhaps one-third female, they were dispatched most often to Maryland, where they labored in the tobacco fields, or as ironworkers or household servants. Little is known about the ultimate fate of most, but some who committed further crimes in the colonies became notorious on both sides of the Atlantic.

Slaves' Symbolic Resistance

Although revolts and escapes have been the focus of many studies of enslaved Africans' resistance to bondage, archaeological finds from the mid-eighteenth century such as those illustrated here reveal important aspects of slaves' personal lives and other forms of resistance. The set of objects found in Annapolis constitutes a *minkisi,* or West African spiritual bundle. Africans and African Americans placed such groupings of objects, each with a symbolic meaning (for example, bent nails reflected the power of fire), under hearths or sills to direct the spirits who entered houses through doors or chimneys. The *minkisi's* primary purpose was to protect the enslaved from the power of their masters—for example, by preventing the breakup of a family. The statue of a man was uncovered in an enslaved blacksmith's quarters. It too reflects resistance, but of a different sort: the quiet rebellion of a talented craftsman who used his master's iron and his own time and skill to create a remarkable object.

CRITICAL THINKING

▢ How can such material evidence compliment the written records of enslaved people's lives, which were typically written by their owners?

△ *This iron figure, a product of skilled artisan-ship, was discovered during the excavation of an enslaved blacksmith's quarters.*

Photograph courtesy of Archaeology in Annapolis, University of Maryland, College Park

△ A minkisi *from the eighteenth century found under the floor of the Charles Carroll house in Annapolis, Maryland.*

4-1e Scots-Irish, Scots, and Germans

One of the largest groups of immigrants—about 143,000—came from Ireland or Scotland, largely in family units. About 66,000 Scots-Irish, descendants of Presbyterian Scots who had settled in the north of Ireland during the seventeenth century, joined some 35,000 people who came directly to America from Scotland (see Figure 4.1). Another 42,000, both Protestants and Catholics, migrated from southern Ireland. High rents, poor harvests, and religious discrimination (in Ireland) combined to push people from lands their families had long occupied. Many of the Irish migrants had worked as linen weavers in their homeland, but linen prices declined significantly in the late 1710s. Because the flax used for linen weaving was imported from Pennsylvania, and Irish flaxseed was exported to the same place, vessels regularly sailed between Ireland and Pennsylvania. By the 1720s, the migration route was well established, fueled by positive reports of the prospects for advancement in North America.

Irish immigrants usually landed in Philadelphia, Pennsylvania or New Castle, Delaware. Many moved into the Pennsylvania backcountry along the Susquehanna River, where the colonial government created a county named Donegal for them. Later migrants traveled farther west and south, to the backcountry of Maryland, Virginia, and the Carolinas. Frequently unable to afford any acreage, they squatted on land belonging to Native communities, land speculators, or colonial governments. In the frontier setting, they gained a reputation for lawlessness, hard drinking, and ferocious fighting among themselves and with neighboring Delaware and Shawnee villagers.

Migrants from Germany and German-speaking areas of Switzerland numbered about 85,000, most of them leaving the Rhineland between 1730 and 1755. They, too, usually came in family groups and landed in Philadelphia. Like the English indentured servants of the previous century, many paid for their passage by contracting to work as servants for a specified period. Germans tended to settle together when they could; they composed up to half of the population of some counties. Many Germans moved west into Pennsylvania and then south into the backcountry of Maryland and Virginia. Others landed in Charles Town and settled in the Carolina interior. The Germans belonged to a wide variety of Protestant sects—primarily Lutheran, German Reformed, and Moravian—and added to the already substantial religious diversity of Pennsylvania. Late in the century, they and their descendants comprised one-third of Pennsylvania's residents. Benjamin Franklin, for one, feared as early as 1751 that they would "Germanize" Pennsylvania.

The years between 1760 and 1775 witnessed the colonial period's most concentrated immigration to Britain's American colonies. Tough economic times in Germany and the British Isles led many to seek a better life in America;

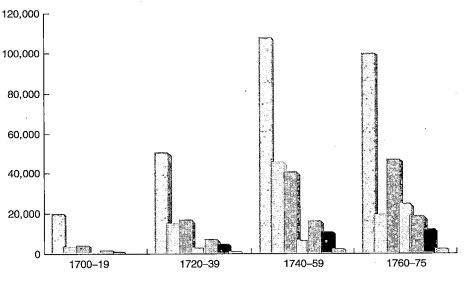

□ Africa □ Germany ▩ Ireland □ Scotland ▨ England ■ Wales ▨ Other European

Figure 4.1 Atlantic Origins of Migrants to Thirteen Mainland Colonies of British North America, 1700–1775

Immigrants from Ireland, Scotland, and Germany significantly outnumbered those from England throughout the eighteenth century. But as this figure shows, forced migrants from Africa comprised by far the largest number of new arrivals in the mainland British colonies. In the Caribbean colonies, the pattern was yet more pronounced. *Data for European numbers: Aaron Fogelman, "Migrations to the Thirteen British North American Colonies, 1700–1775: New Estimates," The Journal of Interdisciplinary History, vol. 22, no. 4 (Spring 1992), pp. 691–709. Data for African numbers: The Trans-Atlantic Slave Trade Database, available online at: http://www .slavevoyages.org. Accessed August 1, 2012.*

simultaneously, the slave trade burgeoned. In those fifteen years alone, more than 125,000 free migrants and 100,000 enslaved people arrived—nearly 10 percent of the entire population of mainland British North America in 1775. Late-arriving free immigrants had little choice but to crowd into the cities or move to the edges of settlement; land elsewhere was occupied (see Map 4.3). In the peripheries they became the tenants of, or bought property from, land speculators who had purchased giant tracts in the (usually vain) hope of making a fortune.

4-1f Maintaining Ethnic and Religious Identities

The migration patterns of the eighteenth century made British North America one of the most diverse places on earth. Even in New England, the most homogeneous region of the mainland provinces, nearly a third of inhabitants had non-English origins by 1760. In the mid-Atlantic, non-English Europeans predominated; less than half of New York's inhabitants, and less than a third of Pennsylvania's, were of English descent. Farther south, settlers of English origin remained a minority. By 1760, Irish and Scots-Irish migrants comprised roughly 15 percent of the region's population; Africans and their descendants accounted for more than half.

How readily migrants assimilated into Anglo-American culture depended on patterns of settlement, the size of the group, and the strength of the migrants' ties to their common culture. For example, in the late seventeenth century, the French Protestants (**Huguenots**) who migrated to Charles Town or New York City were unable to sustain either their language or their religious practices for more than two generations. Yet the Huguenots who created rural communities in the Hudson valley remained recognizably French and Calvinist for a century. By contrast, small groups of colonial Jews maintained a distinct identity regardless of where they settled. In places like New York City, Newport, Savannah, and Kingston, Jamaica, they established synagogues and worked actively to preserve their faith and culture.

Larger groups of migrants (Germans, Irish, and Scots) found it easier to sustain European ways. Some ethnic groups dominated certain localities. Near Frederick, Maryland, a visitor would have heard more German than English; in Anson and Cumberland counties, North Carolina, the same visitor might have thought she was in Scotland. Many New Yorkers continued to speak Dutch. In Coney Island, Dr. Hamilton and an enslaved man Dromo met a Dutch-speaking African woman, with whom Dromo conversed in a kind of pidgin. "Dis de way to York?" he asked. "Yaw, dat is Yarikee… Yaw, mynheer," she replied.

Where migrants from different countries settled in the same region, ethnic antagonisms often surfaced. One German clergyman in Pennsylvania, for example, claimed that "it is very seldom that German and English blood is happily united in wedlock." Anglo-American

Huguenots French Calvinist dissenters from that country's dominant Catholicism.

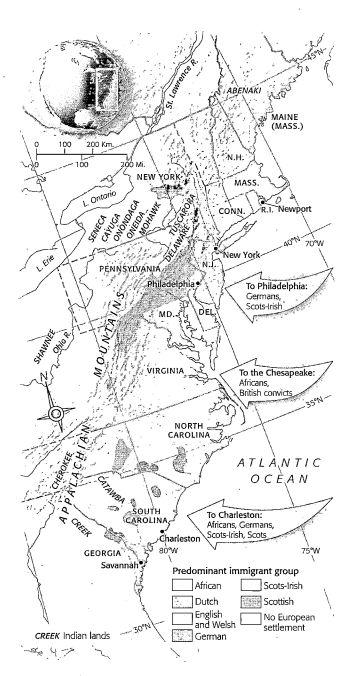

Map 4.3 Non-English Ethnic Groups in the British Colonies, ca. 1775

Non-African immigrants arriving in the years after 1720 were pushed to the peripheries of settlement, as is shown by these maps. Scottish, Scots-Irish, French, and German newcomers had to move to the frontiers. The Dutch remained where they had originally settled in the seventeenth century. Africans were concentrated in coastal plantation regions.

elites fostered such antagonisms in order to fracture opposition and maintain their political and economic power, and they frequently subverted the colonies' generous naturalization laws, depriving even long-resident immigrants of a voice in government. The elites probably would have preferred to ignore the British colonies' growing racial and ethnic diversity, but ultimately they could not do so. In the political crises of the 1770s, they needed the support of non-English Americans.

4-2 Economic Growth and Development in British America

▷ **How did the coastal trade and the internal economy of the British North American economy develop in the eighteenth century?**

▷ **What role did overseas trade play in the British North American colonial economy?**

▷ **What was the impact of the growth of the colonial economy in the eighteenth century?**

Despite the vagaries of international markets, the dramatic increase in the population of British America caused colonial economies to grow. A comparison with French and Spanish America is instructive. The population and economy of New Spain's northern Borderlands stagnated, for the isolated settlements produced few items for export. French Canada exported large quantities of furs and fish, but the government's monopoly on trade ensured that most of the profits ended up in the home country. The Louisiana colony required substantial government subsidies just to survive. Of France's American possessions, only the Caribbean islands flourished economically, largely on the profits of sugar and slaves.

4-2a Commerce and Manufacturing

In British North America, by contrast, the rising population generated ever-greater demand for goods and services, leading to the development of small-scale colonial manufacturing and a complex network of internal trade. Colonists built roads, bridges, mills, and stores to serve new settlements. A lively coastal trade developed; by the late 1760s, more than half of the vessels leaving Boston harbor sailed to other mainland colonies. Such ships not only collected goods for export and distributed imports but also sold items made locally. The colonies no longer wholly depended on European manufactured goods. For the first time, the American population created sufficient demand to support local manufacturing.

Iron making became British America's largest industry. Ironworks in the Chesapeake and the middle colonies required sizable investments and substantial workforces—usually indentured servants, convicts, and slaves—to dig the ore, chop trees for charcoal, and smelt and refine the ore into iron bars. Because the work was dirty, dangerous, and difficult, convicts and servants often tried to flee, but iron making offered enslaved men new avenues to learn valuable skills and accumulate property when they were compensated for doing

more than their assigned tasks. By 1775, Anglo America's iron production surpassed England's.

Foreign trade nevertheless dominated the colonial economy. Settlers' prosperity depended heavily on overseas demand for American tobacco, rice, indigo, salted fish, and timber products. The sale of such items earned the colonists the credit they needed to buy English and European goods. Between 1700 and 1775, colonists' purchases of British manufactures grew fivefold, from 5 percent to 25 percent of Britain's total exports. The English politician Edmund Burke told Parliament that in 1772, the "Export trade to the colonies alone" approached what "the whole trade of England" had been in 1700. But whenever British demand for American products slowed, the colonists' income dropped, along with their ability to buy imports. Colonial merchants were particularly vulnerable to economic downswings, and bankruptcies were common.

4-2b Wealth and Poverty

Despite fluctuations, the American economy grew during the eighteenth century. That growth in turn produced better standards of living for all property-owning colonists. Early in the century, as the price of British manufactures fell in relation to colonists' incomes, more households began to acquire amenities such as chairs and earthenware dishes. Diet also improved as trading networks brought access to more varied foodstuffs. After 1750, luxury items could be found in the homes of the wealthy, and the "middling sort" began to purchase imported English ceramics. Even the poorest property owners had more and better household goods. The differences lay not so much in *what* items people owned, but rather in the quality and quantity of those possessions.

The benefits of economic growth were unevenly distributed: wealthy Americans improved their position relative to other colonists. The American-born elite families who dominated the colonies' political, economic, and social life by 1750 had begun the century with sufficient capital to take advantage of the changes caused by population growth. They were the urban merchants who exported staples and imported luxury goods, the large landowners who rented small farms to immigrant tenants, the slave traders who supplied planters with forced migrants from Africa and the Caribbean, and the rum distillers who processed the sugar grown and refined by slaves in the West Indies. The rise of this group of moneyed families helped to make the social and economic structure of mid-eighteenth-century America more stratified than before. New arrivals had less opportunity for advancement than their predecessors. Even so, few free settlers in rural areas (where about 95 percent of the colonists lived) appear to have been truly poor. By 1750, at least two-thirds of rural householders owned their own land.

4-2c City Life

Nowhere was the maturation of the colonial economy more evident than in the port cities of British North America. By 1760, Boston (with a population holding steady around

15,600), New York (18,000), and fast-growing Philadelphia (nearly 24,000) had become provincial British cities on the scale of Bristol and Liverpool. Life in these cities differed considerably from that on northern farms, southern plantations, or southwestern ranches. City dwellers purchased their food and wood. They lived by the clock rather than the sun, and men's jobs frequently took them away from their households.

Early American cities also saw growing extremes of wealth and poverty. By the last quarter of the eighteenth century, some of the largest merchant families—such as the Hancocks and the Apthorps in Boston or the Allens and the Drinkers in Philadelphia—had amassed trading fortunes their forebears could not have imagined. Yet roughly one-fifth of Philadelphia's workforce was enslaved, and blacks composed nearly 15 percent of the population of New York City. White or black, the families of urban laborers lived on the edge of destitution. As applicants for assistance overwhelmed traditional poor-relief systems, cities began to build workhouses or almshouses to shelter growing numbers of the poor, elderly, and infirm. Between 1758 and 1775, more than 1,800 people—two-thirds of them women and children—were admitted to Boston's almshouse. "Mary Pilsbery came into the house Wednesday May 5, 1762 and brought with her Only the Cloaths on her Back," reads one entry in the town's poor relief records. Three days later, Pilsbery was dead.

City people were in many ways more cosmopolitan than their rural counterparts. Even some of the poorest among them—common sailors, prostitutes—had extensive contact with worlds far beyond their homes. By 1760, most substantial towns had at least one weekly newspaper, and some had two or three. The press offered the latest "advices from London" (usually two to three months old) and news from other colonies, as well as local reports. Newspapers were available (and often read aloud) at taverns and coffee-houses, so people who could not afford or even read them could learn the news. Contact with the outside world, however, had its drawbacks. Sailors sometimes brought deadly diseases into port. Boston, New York, Philadelphia, and New Orleans endured epidemics of smallpox and yellow fever, which Europeans and Africans in the countryside largely escaped.

4-2d Regional Economies

Within this overall picture, broad regional patterns emerged, heightened by **King George's War**, the western front of the War of the Austrian Succession (1739–1748). New England's economy rested on trade with the Caribbean: northern forests supplied the timber for building the ships and the barrels that carried salt fish to feed the slaves on island sugar plantations. The outbreak of war created strong demand for ships and sailors, thus

King George's War Also known as the War of Austrian Succession; started out as a conflict between Britain and Spain, but then escalated when France sided with Spain.

invigorating the economy, but when the shipbuilding boom ended, the economy stagnated.

By contrast, the war and its aftermath brought prosperity to the middle colonies and the Chesapeake, where fertile soil and a long growing season produced an abundance of grain, much of which likewise was shipped to the Caribbean. After 1748, when a series of poor harvests in Europe caused flour prices to rise sharply, Philadelphia and New York took the lead in the foodstuffs trade. Some Chesapeake planters converted tobacco fields to wheat and corn. Tobacco remained the largest single export from the mainland colonies, yet the beginnings of grain cultivation caused a significant change in Chesapeake settlement patterns by encouraging the development of port towns (like Baltimore) where merchants and shipbuilders established businesses to handle the new trade.

South Carolina's staple crop, rice, shaped its distinctive economic pattern. The colony's rice and indigo fields—like cane fields in the Caribbean—were periodically devastated by Atlantic hurricanes, causing hardship and bankruptcies. Yet after 1730, when Parliament removed rice from the list of products enumerated by the Navigation Acts, South Carolinians prospered by trading directly with Europe. The outbreak of war disrupted that trade. The colony entered a depression that did not end until the 1760s brought renewed European demand. Overall, though, South Carolina experienced more rapid economic growth than did Britain's other mainland colonies. By the time of the Revolution, its free-holders had the highest average wealth in continental Anglo America, though the wealth of Barbadian and Jamaican planters dwarfed even theirs.

Closely linked to South Carolina was the newest British settlement, Georgia, chartered in 1732 as a haven for English debtors released from prison. Its founder, James Oglethorpe, envisioned Georgia as a garrison province peopled by sturdy farmers who would defend the southern flank of English settlement against Spanish Florida. To ensure that all adult men in the colony could serve as its armed protectors, Georgia's charter prohibited slavery. But Carolina rice planters won the removal of the restriction in 1751. Thereafter, they essentially invaded Georgia, which—despite remaining politically independent and becoming a royal colony in 1752—developed into a rice-planting slave society.

King George's War initially helped New England and hurt South Carolina and Georgia, but in the long run those effects reversed. In the Chesapeake and the middle colonies, the war ushered in a long period of prosperity. Such variations highlight the mainland colonies' disparate experiences within the British empire, and their economic distance from each other. Despite an increasing coastal trade, each province's fortunes depended less on neighboring colonies than on the shifting markets of Europe and the Caribbean. Had it not been for an unprecedented crisis in the British imperial system (discussed in Chapter 5), it is unlikely they could have been persuaded to join in a common endeavor.

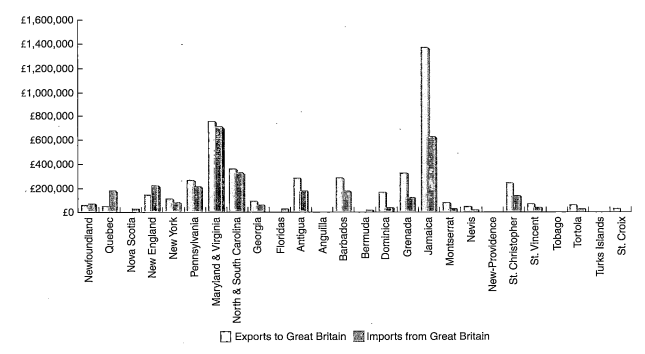

£1,600,000
£1,400,000
£1,200,000
£1,000,000
£800,000
£600,000
£400,000
£200,000
£0

Newfoundland · Quebec · Nova Scotia · New England · New York · Pennsylvania · Maryland & Virginia · North & South Carolina · Georgia · Floridas · Antigua · Anguilla · Barbados · Bermuda · Dominica · Grenada · Jamaica · Montserrat · Nevis · New-Providence · St. Christopher · St. Vincent · Tobago · Tortola · Turks Islands · St. Croix

☐ Exports to Great Britain   ▨ Imports from Great Britain

Figure 4.2 Trade Revenue from the British Colonies in 1769

As this figure shows, the different regions of the British mainland colonies had distinct trading patterns with Britain. New England imported more than it exported; much of its export trade was with the Caribbean. The exports of the Chesapeake colonies (especially tobacco) and the Carolinas (rice and indigo) were more significant, but the value of sugar from Jamaica dwarfed the produce of all the other British colonies. *Data from David MacPherson*, Annals of Commerce, Manufactures, Fisheries and Navigation, with Brief Notices of the Arts and Sciences Connected with them, Containing the Commercial Transactions of the British Empire and Other Countries *(1805), volume III, p. 495.*

4-3 "Oeconomical" Households: Families, Production, and Reproduction

▷ How did European settlement in British North America affect Native American families?

▷ What were the meanings and functions of the family to eighteenth-century European settlers?

▷ How did enslaved African Americans resist and ameliorate their bondage through family roles?

Throughout the colonial era and well into the nineteenth century, the household was the basic unit of economic production, and economic production was the overriding concern of American families. Indeed, the Greek word *oikos*, meaning "household," is also the root of the English word *economy*. Seventeenth-century English writers often used the term *oeconomie* to discuss household and family matters. People living together as families, commonly under the direction of a marital pair, everywhere constituted the chief mechanisms for both production and consumption. Yet family forms and structures varied widely in the mainland colonies.

4-3a Native American and Mixed-Race Families

As Europeans consolidated their hold on North America, Native peoples had to adapt to novel circumstances. Ethnic groups reduced in numbers by disease and warfare recombined into new units; for example, the Catawbas emerged in the 1730s in the western Carolinas from the coalescence of earlier peoples including Yamasees and Guales. Likewise, European **secular** and religious authorities reshaped Native family forms. Whereas many Native societies had permitted easy divorce, European missionaries frowned on such practices; societies that had allowed polygynous marriages (including New England Algonquians) redefined such relationships, designating one wife "legitimate" and others "concubines."

Once Europeans established dominance in any region, it became difficult for Native communities to pursue traditional modes of subsistence. That led to unusual family structures as well as to a variety of economic strategies. In New England, Algonquian husbands and wives often could not live together, for adults supported themselves by working separately (perhaps wives as domestic servants, husbands as sailors). Some Native women married African American

secular Not specifically relating to religion or to a religious body.

men, unions encouraged by sexual imbalances in both populations. And in New Mexico, detribalized Navajos, Pueblos, Paiutes, and Apaches employed as servants by Spanish settlers clustered in the small towns of the Borderlands. Known collectively as *genizaros,* they lost contact with indigenous cultures, instead living on the fringes of Hispanic society.

Wherever the population contained relatively few European women, sexual liaisons (both within and outside marriage) occurred between European men and Native women. The resulting mixed-race people, whom Spanish colonists called *mestizos* and French settlers labeled *métis,* often served as go-betweens, navigating the intersection of two cultures. In New France and the Anglo-American backcountry, such families frequently resided in Native villages, and many children of these unions became Native American leaders. For example, Peter Chartier, son of a Shawnee mother and a French father, led a pro-French Shawnee band in western Pennsylvania in the 1740s. By contrast, in the Spanish Borderlands, the offspring of Europeans and *genizaros* were considered inferior. Often denied the privilege of legal marriage, they bore generations of "illegitimate" children of various racial mixtures, giving rise in Latino society to a wide range of labels describing degrees of skin color with a precision unknown in English or French America.

4-3b European American Families

Eighteenth-century Anglo-Americans referred to all the people who occupied one household (including servants or slaves) as a family. European men or their widows headed households considerably larger than American families today; in 1790, the average home in the United States contained 5.7 free people. Few such households included grandparents or other extended kin. Bound by ties of blood or servitude, family members worked together to produce goods for consumption or sale. The head of the household represented it to the outside world, voting in elections, managing the finances, and holding legal authority over the rest of the family—his wife, his children, and his servants or slaves. In the eyes of the law, wives were *femes covert,* their personhood "covered" by their husbands.

de Arvarrasado è Yndia

△ People in eighteenth-century Spain were fascinated by the topic of *mestizaje:* race mixing or, pejoratively, miscegenation. Such curiosity created a market for so-called *casta* paintings, which illustrated different sorts of multiracial households, focusing on the gradations of color in people's skin. This anonymous painting, one of a series (it's labled *Escena de mestizaje n° 13,* or thirteenth miscegenation scene) illustrates the children of parents from different Mesoamerican groups, the Arvarraso and the Barsino.

In English, French, and Spanish America, the vast majority of European families supported themselves through farming and raising livestock. The production of cash crops such as indigo in Louisiana and South Carolina, or tobacco in the Chesapeake, required different kinds of labor from subsistence farming in New England or cattle ranching in New Mexico and Texas. But regardless of the scale and the crop, household tasks were allocated by sex. The master, his sons, and his male servants or slaves performed one set of chores; the mistress, her daughters, and her female servants or slaves, a different set.

The mistress took responsibility for what Anglo-Americans called "indoor affairs." She and her female helpers prepared food, cleaned the house, and washed and often made clothing. Preparing food involved planting and cultivating a "kitchen" garden, harvesting and preserving vegetables, salting and smoking meat, drying apples and pressing cider, milking cows and making butter and cheese, not to mention cooking and baking. Women's work—often performed while pregnant, nursing, or sometimes both—was unremitting. Mary Cooper, a farm wife from Long Island, wrote in her diary in 1769, "This day is forty years sinc I left my father's house and come here, and here have I seene little els but harde labour and sorrow."

The head of the household and his male helpers, responsible for "outdoor affairs," also had heavy workloads. They planted and cultivated fields, built fences, chopped wood, harvested and marketed crops, tended livestock, and butchered cattle and hogs. So extensive was the work involved in maintaining a farm household that no married couple could do it alone. If they had no children to help them, they hired servants or purchased slaves.

4-3c African American Families

Most African American families lived as components of European American households. More than 95 percent of colonial African Americans were held in bondage. Although many lived on farms with only one or two other enslaved people, others lived and worked in a largely black setting. In South Carolina, a majority of the population was of African descent; in Georgia, about half; and in the Chesapeake, 40 percent. Portions of the Carolina low country were nearly 90 percent African American by 1790.

The setting in which African Americans lived determined the shape of their families, yet wherever possible slaves established family structures in which youngsters carried relatives' names or—in South Carolina—followed African naming patterns. In the North, the scarcity of other blacks made it difficult for enslaved men and women to form households. In the Chesapeake, men and women who regarded themselves

London Coffee House, printed by Kennedy & Lucas's Lithography, 1830 (litho)/Breton, William L. (fl.1830)/LIBRARY COMPANY OF PHILADELPHIA/ Library Company of Philadelphia, PA, USA/Bridgeman Images

London Coffee House.

△ This 1830 lithograph of "The Old London Coffee House" in eighteenth-century Philadelphia shows a slave auction taking place on its porch. That such a scene could have occurred in front of such a prominent and popular meeting place serves as a reminder of the ubiquity of slavery in the colonies, north as well as south.

as married (slaves could not legally wed) frequently lived in different quarters or even on different plantations. Children generally resided with their mother, seeing their father only on Sundays. The natural increase of the population created wide American-born kinship networks among Chesapeake slaves. On large Carolina and Georgia rice plantations, enslaved couples usually lived together with their children, and could accumulate property by working for themselves after they had completed their daily "tasks." Everywhere, slave family ties were forged against the threat of sale that separated husbands from wives and parents from children.

4-3d Forms of Resistance

Because all the British colonies permitted slavery, bondspeople had few options for escaping servitude other than fleeing to Florida, where the Spanish offered protection. Some recently arrived Africans stole boats to try to return home or ran off in groups to frontier regions, to join Native communities or establish independent communities. Others made their way to cities like Philadelphia, where they might melt into small populations of free black laborers and artisans. Masters paid for advertisements in Philadelphia newspapers to reclaim runaways thought to be working as blacksmiths, tanners, barbers, brick makers, ironworkers, and sailors. The revenue from runaway ads underwrote the printing of many newspapers.

Among American-born slaves, family ties strongly affected the decision to steal oneself by running away. South Carolina planters soon learned, as one wrote, that slaves "love their families dearly and none runs away from the other," so many owners sought to keep families together for practical reasons. Most escaped slaves advertised in the newspapers were young men; it was harder for women with children to flee.

Although colonial slaves rarely rebelled collectively, they resisted enslavement in other ways. Enslaved men and women rejected owners' attempts to commandeer their labor on Sundays without compensation. Extended-kin groups protested excessive punishment of relatives and sought to live near one another. The links that developed among African American families who had lived on the same plantation for several generations helped to ameliorate the uncertainties of existence under slavery. If parents and children were separated by sale, other relatives could help with child rearing. Among African Americans, just as among Native Americans, the extended family thus served a more crucial function than it did among European Americans.

Most slave families managed to carve out a small measure of autonomy, especially in their working and spiritual lives, and particularly in the Lower South. Enslaved Muslims often preserved their Islamic faith, a pattern evident in Louisiana and Georgia. Some African Americans maintained traditional beliefs, and others converted to Christianity (often retaining some African elements), finding comfort in the Bible's promise that all would be free and equal in heaven. Slaves in South Carolina and Georgia jealously guarded their customary ability to control their own time after completing their

"tasks." On Chesapeake tobacco plantations, enslaved people planted their own gardens, trapped, and fished to supplement the minimal diet their owners supplied. Late in the century, some Chesapeake planters with a surplus of laborers began to hire slaves out to others, often allowing some enslaved men and women to keep a small part of their earnings. Such wages could buy desired goods or provide a legacy for children.

4-4 Provincial Cultures

▷ **What kinds of cultural exchanges and rituals emerged in eighteenth-century British North America?**

▷ **What value did colonists find in the expansion of consumption activities in the eighteenth century?**

▷ **How did "genteel culture" differ from "everyday culture" in eighteenth-century British North America?**

In addition to serving as the basic unit of economic production and social reproduction, the early American household was a nursery of culture, a term with many, sometimes competing definitions. When anthropologists speak of culture, they typically mean the customs and rituals that define a community—its folkways, in other words. Where folkways belong to the many, learned or "high" culture—art, literature, philosophy, and science—may be the realm of the few, especially in a premodern society, where learning was hardly democratic. Yet folkways interact with the life of the mind, and cultures are always plural. This was particularly the case in eighteenth-century North America, with its dizzying diversity of peoples and its growing social stratification. There were then (and are now) many American cultures. In some respects, these cultures grew more British as the disparate colonies became more fully integrated provinces of empire. But in other ways, as Dr. Hamilton learned on his progress along the eastern seaboard, the ragged outer margins of the British realm fashioned very distinctive cultures indeed.

4-4a Oral Cultures

Most people in North America were illiterate. Those who could read—a small proportion in French and Spanish America, about two-thirds of Anglo-Americans—often could not write. Parents, older siblings, or widows who needed extra income taught youngsters to read; middling boys and genteel girls might then learn to write in private schools. Few Americans other than some Anglican missionaries in the South tried to instruct enslaved children; indeed, masters feared literate slaves, who could forge documents in order to pass as free. And only the most zealous Indian converts learned European literacy skills.

Thus, the everyday cultures of colonial North America were primarily oral and—at least through the first half of the eighteenth century—intensely local. Face-to-face conversation was the chief means of communication. Information tended to travel slowly, within relatively confined regions. Different locales developed divergent traditions, and racial and ethnic variations heightened those differences. Household and public rituals served as the chief means through which the colonists forged cultural identities and navigated the boundaries among them.

4-4b Rituals on the "Middle Ground"

Particularly important rituals developed on what the historian Richard White has termed the "middle ground"—the psychological and geographical space in which Native peoples and Europeans encountered each other, especially but not only in the upper Midwest. Most of those cultural encounters occurred in the context of trade or warfare.

When Europeans sought to trade with Native peoples, they encountered indigenous systems of exchange that stressed gift giving rather than buying and selling. Successful bargaining required French and English traders to present Native individuals with gifts (cloth, rum, gunpowder, and other goods) before negotiating with them for pelts and skins. Eventually, those gifts would be reciprocated. Only then could formal trading proceed.

Intercultural rituals also developed to deal with crime. Both Native peoples and Europeans believed that murder required a compensatory act, but they differed over what the act should be. Europeans sought primarily to identify and punish perpetrators. To Native peoples, such "eye for an eye" revenge was just one of many remedies, including capturing a Native person from an enemy group or a colonist to take the dead person's place, or "covering the dead" by providing the family of the deceased with compensatory goods. The French and the Algonquians evolved elaborate rituals for handling frontier murders that encompassed elements of both societies' traditions.

4-4c Civic Rituals

Ceremonial occasions reinforced identities within as well as boundaries between cultures. New England governments proclaimed days of thanksgiving (for good harvests, military victories, and other "providences") and days of fasting and prayer (to lament war, drought, or epidemic). Everyone was expected to participate in the church rituals held on such occasions. Because able-bodied men between the ages of sixteen and sixty were required to serve in local militias—the only military forces in the colonies—monthly musters also brought townsfolk together.

In the Chesapeake, widely spaced farms meant that communities came together less frequently. Ritual life centered on court and election days. When the county court met, men came to file lawsuits, appear as witnesses, or serve as jurors. Attendance at court functioned as a method of civic education; men watched the proceedings to learn what their neighbors expected of them. Elections served a similar purpose, for property-holding men voted in public. An election official, often flanked by the candidates for office, called each man forward to declare his preference. The gentleman for whom the ballot was cast would then thank the voter. Later, the candidates repaired to nearby taverns, where they plied supporters with rum, a custom called "treating."

Everywhere in colonial North America, the punishment of criminals served to remind the community of proper behavioral standards. Public hangings and whippings, along with orders to sit in the stocks, expressed a community's outrage and restored harmony to its ranks. Judges often devised shaming penalties that mirrored a particular crime. In San Antonio, Texas, for example, one cattle thief was led through the town's streets "with the entrails hanging from his neck." When a New Mexico man assaulted his father-in-law, he was directed not merely to pay medical expenses but also to kneel before him and beg forgiveness publicly.

4-4d Rituals of Consumption

By 1770, Anglo-Americans spent roughly one-quarter of their household budgets on consumer goods, chiefly of British manufacture. Since similar imports flooded shop counters from Maine to Georgia, such purchases established cultural links among the various residents of North America, creating what historians have termed "an empire of goods." The governor of New York scarcely exaggerated when he reported, in 1774, "more than Eleven Twelfths of the Inhabitants of this province ... are cloathed in British Manufactures." Their houses were likewise furnished with Britain's bounty, from the plates on their tables to the very paint on their walls.

Seventeenth-century settlers had acquired necessities by bartering with neighbors or ordering products from a home-country merchant. By the middle of the eighteenth century, specialized shops proliferated in colonial towns and cities. In 1770, Boston had more than five hundred stores, offering a vast selection of cloth wares, exotic groceries, tobacco, ceramics, and metalwork. Most small towns had one or two retail establishments. Colonists would take time to "go shopping," a novel and pleasurable leisure activity in Anglo America as in Britain. Buyers confronted a dazzling array of possibilities and fashioned their identities by choosing among them. Some historians have termed this shift a "consumer revolution."

The purchase of an object—for example, a teapot, a mirror, or some beautiful imported fabric—initiated a complex series of consumption rituals. Consumers would deploy their purchases: hanging the mirror prominently on a wall, displaying the teapot on a sideboard, sewing the fabric into a special piece of clothing. Colonists proudly showed off their acquisitions (and thus their status and taste). Moralists fretted about encroaching luxury. "If we are now *poorer* than we were thirty Years ago, we are at the same Time *finer*," proclaimed a Boston pamphleteer in 1753. "Our Beds, our Tables and our Bodies are covered" with cloth "from foreign Countries." (Instead, he proposed, the poor should be put to work weaving linen.)

A prosperous man might hire an artist to paint his family using imported objects and wearing fine clothing, thereby creating a pictorial record to be admired and passed down as

Mrs. James Smith (Elizabeth Murray), 1769 (oil on canvas)/Copley, John Singleton (1738-1815)/MUSEUM OF FINE ARTS, BOSTON/Museum of Fine Arts, Boston, Massachusetts, USA/Bridgeman Images

△ Elizabeth Murray, the subject of this 1769 painting by John Singleton Copley, was the widow of James Smith, a wealthy rum distiller. She commissioned this likeness after her husband's death. Her fashionable dress and pose would seem to mark her as a lady of leisure, yet before, during, and after her marriage this Scottish immigrant ran a successful dry goods shop in Boston. She thus simultaneously catered to and participated in the new culture of consumption.

a kind of cultural inheritance. In the early eighteenth century, most portraitists active in the colonies were itinerants from Britain. But by midcentury, a small number of American-born painters were gaining prominence. Benjamin West, born in rural Pennsylvania, attracted ever-wealthier patrons in Lancaster and Philadelphia before embarking for Europe in 1760. John Singleton Copley, the son of a Boston tobacco-seller, became the leading artist in the colonies, making a good living by taking likenesses of merchant families grown rich in Atlantic trade. His reputation (and his art) preceded him to London in 1774.

Poor and rural people also participated in the new trends, taking obvious pleasure even in inexpensive purchases. Backcountry storekeepers accepted bartered goods from customers who lacked cash. One Virginia woman traded hens and chickens for a pewter dish; another swapped yards of handwoven cloth for a necklace. Slaves exchanged cotton they grew in their free time for ribbons and hats they must have worn with pride. Some also purchased mirrors so they could see themselves bedecked in their acquisitions.

4-4e Tea and Madeira

Tea drinking, a consumption ritual largely controlled by women, played an important role throughout Anglo America. Households with aspirations to genteel status purchased the items necessary for the proper consumption of tea: pots and cups, strainers and sugar tongs, even special tables. Tea provided a focal point for socializing and, because of its cost, served as a crucial marker of cosmopolitan status. Tea drinking bridged the miles between the East Indies (tea), the West Indies (sugar), and North America, uniting the edges of Britain's empire.

Gentlewomen regularly entertained male and female friends at afternoon tea parties. Even poor households consumed tea, although they could not afford the fancy equipment used by their better-off neighbors. In Connecticut, Dr. Hamilton met a "wild and rustic" family living in a log cabin whose meager possessions included a teapot. Some Mohawk people adopted the custom, much to the surprise of a traveler from Sweden, who observed them drinking tea in the late 1740s.

Madeira wine, imported from the Portuguese islands by merchants with extensive transatlantic familial connections, also connoted gentility. By 1770, Madeira had become a favored drink of the elite. Serving the wine required specialized accoutrements and elaborate ceremony; purchasing it involved considerable expense. In 1784, one Philadelphia merchant's spending on Madeira and other exotic liquors equaled the combined annual budgets of two artisan families.

4-4f Polite and Learned Culture

Colonists who acquired such wealth through trade, agriculture, or manufacturing spent their money ostentatiously, drinking and dressing fashionably, traveling in horse-drawn carriages, and throwing lavish parties. They built large brick homes of the neoclassical style newly fashionable in England, with columns, symmetrical floor plans, and an array of specialized rooms. The grandest houses in the colonies—William Byrd's Westover and Landon Carter's Sabine Hall, both in Virginia; or Thomas Hancock's mansion overlooking Boston Common—would barely have qualified as outbuildings of England's great country houses. Yet they were far more elaborate than the homes of earlier settlers.

Sufficiently well-off to enjoy "leisure" time (a first for North America), genteel Euro-Americans cultivated polite manners, adopting stylized forms of address and paying attention to "proper" comportment. In the late 1740s, a young George Washington, son of an aspiring Virginia planter, copied into his school exercise book a list of 110 "Rules of Civility and Decent Behaviour" taken from an English courtesy manual. Politeness had to be learned, and earned.

Although the effects of accumulated wealth were most pronounced in British America, elite families in New Mexico, Louisiana, and Quebec also fashioned genteel cultures that distinguished them from the "lesser sort." One historian has termed these processes "the refinement of America."

△ This British conversation piece, "A Family of Three at Tea," painted by Richard Collins (c. 1727), depicts a genteel husband, wife, and daughter at the tea table, surrounded by the specialized imported silver and porcelain that accompanied the drinking of tea among the elite. Tea-drinking was often associated with women, family, and home; it was considered feminine and domestic where coffee was masculine and public. The dog in the scene, known then as now as a Cavalier King Charles spaniel, might have identified the family with Tory politics.

Refined gentlemen prided themselves not only on their possessions, but also on their education and on their intellectual connections to Europe. Many had been tutored by private teachers; some even attended college in Europe or America. (Harvard, the first colonial college, founded in 1636, was joined by William and Mary in 1693, Yale in 1701, and later by several others, including Princeton in 1747.) In the seventeenth century, only aspiring clergymen attended college, where they studied ancient languages and theology. But in the eighteenth century, college curricula broadened to include mathematics, the natural sciences, law, and medicine. By the 1740s, aspiring colonial gentlemen regularly traveled to London and Edinburgh to complete their educations in law or medicine, and to Italy to become connoisseurs of art and antiquities.

American women were largely excluded from advanced education, with the exception of female religious who joined nunneries in Canada or Louisiana and engaged in sustained study within convent walls. Instead, genteel daughters perfected womanly accomplishments like French (rather than Latin), needlework, and musicianship. Even relatively educated women including John Adams's wife Abigail and Benjamin Franklin's sister Jane—women who regularly read books and wrote letters—bemoaned their scant learning and poor spelling.

Yet women, like their brothers, sons, and husbands, took part in a burgeoning world of print in Anglo America. There were more than a thousand private libraries in seventeenth-century Virginia, some of them encompassing hundreds of volumes. In Boston, the Mather family's collection numbered several thousand titles by 1700. More than half of free white Marylanders owned books by the middle of the eighteenth century. Booksellers in cities and towns offered a wide selection of titles imported from England and an increasing number printed in the colonies. The number of newspapers grew rapidly as well. In 1720, only three journals were published in Anglo America. By 1770, there were thirty-one, printed in every colony from Massachusetts to Georgia. Those who

△ Built in 1730, William Byrd's grand home, which he called Westover, reflects the genteel aspirations of a new generation of British Americans. Byrd, one of Virginia's wealthiest planters, had spent time in London, and he designed his James River plantation according to the most current English tastes, with an emphasis on symmetry and a highly theatrical entrance. Byrd's diaries reveal the uneasy combination of cosmopolitan refinement and slave-holding barbarism that marked the daily lives of elites in the southern colonies.

could not afford to buy newspapers perused them in coffee-houses, and those who could not afford to buy books might read them in new civic institutions called libraries. Benjamin Franklin, a candle-maker's son who made his living as a printer, founded the Library Company of Philadelphia, the first subscription library in North America, in 1731. Works of fiction made up a large percentage of social library collections and numbered among the most highly circulated titles. One Philadelphia library served a nearly equal number of male and female readers.

4-4g The Enlightenment

Spreading through travel and print and polite conversation, the intellectual currents known as the **Enlightenment** deeply affected American provincials. Around 1650, some European thinkers began to analyze nature in order to determine the laws governing the universe. They conducted experiments to discover general principles underlying phenomena like the

Enlightenment Intellectual revolution in eighteenth-century Europe and America that elevated reason, science, and logic.

John Locke British philosopher and major Enlightenment thinker; known for his emphasis on the power of human reasoning.

motions of planets, the behavior of falling objects, and the characteristics of light. Enlightenment philosophers sought knowledge through reason, taking particular delight in challenging previously unquestioned assumptions. **John Locke's** *Essay Concerning Human Understanding* (1690), for example, disputed the notion that human beings are born already imprinted with innate ideas. All knowledge, Locke asserted, derives from one's observations of the external world. Belief in witchcraft and astrology, among other occult phenomena, thus came under attack in this new empirical order.

The Enlightenment supplied educated Europeans and Americans with a common vocabulary and world-view, one that insisted the enlightened eighteenth century was better, and wiser, than ages past. It joined them in a shared effort to make sense of God's creation. American naturalists like John and William Bartram supplied European scientists with information about new world plants and animals for newly formulated universal classification systems. So, too, Americans interested in astronomy took part in an international project to learn about the solar system by studying a rare occurrence, the transit of Venus across the face of the sun in 1769. A prime example of America's participation in the Enlightenment was **Benjamin Franklin**, who retired from his successful printing business in 1748 when he was just forty-two, thereafter devoting himself to scientific experimentation and public service. His *Experiments and Observations on Electricity* (1751) established the terminology and basic theory of electricity still used today.

Enlightenment rationalism affected politics as well as science. Locke's *Two Treatises of Government* (1691) and other works by French and Scottish philosophers challenged previous concepts of a divinely sanctioned, hierarchical political order originating in the power of fathers over families. Men created governments and so could alter them, Locke declared—a philosophy that aligned with the life experience of many who lived under the locally-created governments in the colonies. A ruler who broke the social contract and failed to protect people's rights could legitimately be ousted by peaceful—or even violent—means. A proper political order could prevent the rise of tyrants; God's natural laws governed even monarchs. The rough and tumble political philosophy Dr. Hamilton found on his 1744 journey through the colonies offers evidence of a vernacular enlightenment bubbling up from the lower orders as well as trickling in from Europe.

4-5 A Changing Religious Culture

▷ **How did eighteenth-century religious revivals affect the practice of religion?**

▷ **How did the eighteenth-century religious revivals contribute to new ideas and practices within society?**

Religious observance was perhaps the most pervasive facet of eighteenth-century provincial culture. In New England's Congregational (Puritan) churches, church leaders assigned seating to reflect standing in the community. By the mid-eighteenth century, wealthy men and their wives sat in privately owned pews; children, servants, slaves, and the less fortunate still sat in sex-segregated fashion in the rear, sides, or balcony of the church. Seating in Virginia's Church of England parishes also mirrored the local status hierarchy. In Quebec City, formal processions of men into the parish church celebrated Catholic feast days; each participant's rank determined his place in the procession. By contrast, Quaker meetinghouses in Pennsylvania and elsewhere used an egalitarian but sex-segregated seating system. The varying rituals surrounding colonial churches symbolized believers' place in society and the values of the community.

While such aspects of Anglo-American religious practice reflected traditions of long standing, the religious culture of the colonies began to change significantly in the mid-eighteenth century. From the mid-1730s through the 1760s, waves of revivalism—today known collectively as the First **Great Awakening**—swept over British America, especially New England (1735–1745) and Virginia (1750s–1760s). In the colonies as in Europe, orthodox Calvinists sought to combat Enlightenment rationalism, which denied innate human depravity. Simultaneously, the uncertainty accompanying King George's War made colonists receptive to **evangelists'** messages. Moreover, many recent immigrants and residents of the backcountry had no strong religious affiliation, thus presenting evangelists with numerous potential converts.

America's revivals began in New England. In the mid-1730s, the Reverend Jonathan Edwards, a noted preacher and theologian, observed a remarkable reaction among the youthful members of his church in Northampton, Massachusetts, to sermons based squarely on Calvinist principles. Sinners could attain salvation, Edwards preached, only by recognizing their depraved nature and surrendering completely to God's will. Moved by this message, parishioners of both sexes experienced an intensely emotional release from sin, which came to be seen as a moment of conversion, a new birth.

4-5a George Whitefield

Such ecstatic conversions remained isolated until 1739, when **George Whitefield**, an Anglican clergyman already renowned for leading mass revivals in Britain, crossed the Atlantic. For fifteen months, he toured the British colonies, concentrating his efforts in the major cities: Boston, Newport, New York, Philadelphia, Charles Town, and Savannah. One historian has termed Whitefield "the first modern celebrity" because of his skillful self-promotion. Everywhere he traveled, his fame preceded him. Readers snapped up books by and about him, and newspapers advertised his upcoming appearances and hawked portrait engravings of his famous face. Thousands of free and enslaved folk turned out to listen—and to experience conversion. Whitefield's preaching tour, the first such ever undertaken, created new interconnections among far-flung colonies.

Established clerics initially welcomed Whitefield and the American-born itinerant evangelist preachers who imitated him. Soon, however, many clergymen began to realize that, although "revived" religion filled their churches, it challenged their approach to doctrine and practice. They disliked the emotional style of the revivalists, whose itinerancy also disrupted normal patterns of church attendance. Particularly troublesome to the orthodox were the dozens of female exhorters who took to streets and

Benjamin Franklin American thinker, printer, and politician who embodied the experimental spirit of the Enlightenment.

Great Awakening Protestant revival movement that emphasized each person's urgent need for salvation by God.

evangelists Preachers or ministers, often traveling beyond a fixed congregation, who enthusiastically promote the Christian gospels to gain new converts.

George Whitefield English preacher who toured the colonies and played a major role in the Great Awakening on both sides of the Atlantic.

Smallpox Inoculation

Smallpox, the world's greatest killer of human beings, repeatedly ravaged the population of North America. Thus, when the vessel *Seahorse* arrived in Boston from the Caribbean in April 1721 carrying smallpox-infected passengers, New Englanders feared the worst. The authorities quarantined the ship, but smallpox escaped into the city, and soon dozens caught the dread disease.

The Reverend Cotton Mather, a member of London's Royal Society (chartered during the Restoration to promote Enlightenment approaches to science), had read in its journal several years earlier two accounts by physicians—one in Constantinople and one in Smyrna—of a medical technique unknown to Europeans but widely employed in North Africa and

the Middle East. Called inoculation, it involved scraping material from the pustules (or poxes) of an infected person and inserting it into a small cut on the arm of a healthy individual. With luck, that person would experience a mild case of smallpox, followed by lifetime immunity from the disease. Mather's interest in inoculation was further piqued by his slave, Onesimus, a North African who had been inoculated as a youth and who described the procedure in detail. "How many Lives might be saved by it, if it were practised?" Mather wondered in his diary that May, as the epidemic spread.[1]

The next month, Mather wrote up what he called "a little Treatise on the *Small-pox*." His strategy blended science and religion: "first awakening

Sentiments of *Piety*," then "exhibiting the best Medicines and Methods," and "finally, adding the new Discovery": inoculation. But when Mather circulated the manuscript, the city's doctors ridiculed his ideas. "They rave, they rail, they blaspheme; they talk not only like Ideots but also like *Franticks*," he wrote. He feared, not least, for his own children. Mather won only one major convert, Zabdiel Boylston, a physician and apothecary, who wanted to publish Mather's arguments. The two men inoculated their own children and about two hundred others, despite bitter opposition, including an attempt to firebomb Mather's house. But by late fall, as the epidemic abated, Bostonians could clearly see the results: of those inoculated, just 3 percent had died, a fraction of the 15 percent mortality experienced by those who took the disease "in the natural way."[2] Even Mather's most vocal opponents were convinced, thereafter supporting inoculation as a remedy for the disease. Mather wrote reports for the Royal Society, and following their publication even Britain's royal family was inoculated.

In the twentieth century, global campaigns for vaccination—a modern cousin of inoculation—eliminated smallpox worldwide. Yet in twenty-first-century America, childhood vaccination has become newly controversial, as New Age religion battles Enlightenment science some three centuries after Mather's time.

CRITICAL THINKING

◻ Aside from general fear of the disease, what other factors may have contributed to the colonists' aversion to adopt inoculation, a common practice in non-Western parts of the world?

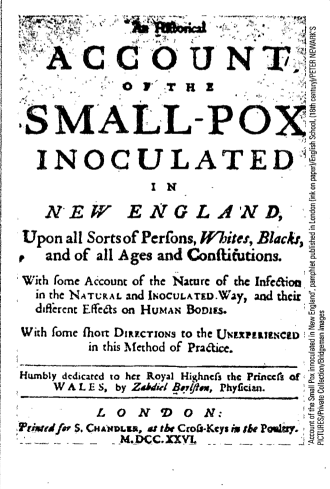

An Pictorical ACCOUNT OF THE SMALL-POX INOCULATED IN NEW ENGLAND, Upon all Sorts of Persons, *Whites, Blacks,* and of all Ages and Constitutions.

With some Account of the Nature of the Infection in the NATURAL and INOCULATED Way, and their different Effects on HUMAN BODIES.

With some short DIRECTIONS to the UNEXPERIENCED in this Method of Practice.

Humbly dedicated to her Royal Highness the Princess of WALES, by *Zabdiel Boylston*, Physician.

LONDON: *Printed for* S. CHANDLER, *at the* Cross-Keys *in the* Poultry. M.DCC.XXVI.

(Account of the Small Pox Innoculated in New England', pamphlet published in London (ink on paper)/English School, (18th century)/PETER NEWARK'S PICTURES/Private Collection/Bridgeman Images)

◁ Several years after he and Cotton Mather combated a Boston smallpox epidemic by employing inoculation, Zabdiel Boylston published this pamphlet in London to spread the news of their success. The dedication to the Princess of Wales was designed to indicate the royal family's sup-. port of the procedure.

[1] *Mather Diary,* II: 621

[2] Ibid, quotations at II: 627–38, 632

pulpits, proclaiming their right (even duty) to expound God's word.

4-5b Impact of the Awakening

Opposition to the Awakening mounted rapidly, causing congregations to splinter. "Old Lights"—orthodox clerics and their followers—engaged in bitter disputes with "New Light" evangelicals. Already characterized by numerous sects, American Protestantism fragmented further as Congregationalists and Presbyterians split into factions, and as new evangelical groups—Methodists and Baptists—gained adherents. After 1771, Methodists sent "circuit riders" (preachers on horseback) to the far reaches of settlement, where they achieved widespread success in converting frontier dwellers. Paradoxically, the proliferation of distinct denominations eventually fostered a willingness to tolerate religious pluralism. Where no sect could monopolize orthodoxy, denominations had to coexist if they were to exist at all.

The Awakening challenged traditional modes of thought. Itinerants offered a spiritual variant of the choices colonists found in the world of goods. Revivalists' emphasis on emotion over learning undermined received wisdom about society and politics as well as religion. Some New Lights began to defend the rights of groups and individuals to dissent from a community consensus, thereby challenging one of the fundamental tenets of colonial political life.

4-5c Virginia Baptists

The egalitarian themes of the Awakening tended to attract ordinary folk and repel the elite. Nowhere was this trend more evident than in Virginia, where taxes supported the established Church of England, and the plantation gentry dominated society. By the 1760s, Baptists had gained a secure foothold in Virginia; inevitably, their beliefs and behavior clashed with the refined lifestyle of the genteel.

Strikingly, almost all Virginia Baptist congregations included both free and enslaved members, and some congregations had African American majorities. Church rules applied equally to all members; interracial sexual relationships, divorce, and adultery were proscribed for all. In addition, congregations forbade masters' breaking up slave couples through sale. Yet it is easy to overstate the racial egalitarianism

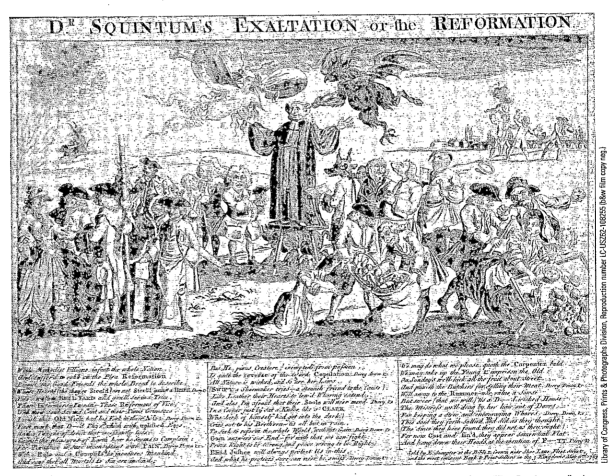

△ This cartoon, printed in London in 1763, mocks George Whitefield, who was cross-eyed, as "Dr. Squintum." The satirist sets him on a stool, preaching outdoors, as he often did. An imp or small devil feeds words into his ear, while Fame—depicted as part woman, part serpent—listens through an ear-trumpet, and barks Whitefield's words to the crowd. Under the preacher's stool, the Devil snatches up gold coins.

of Virginia evangelicals and the attractiveness of the new sects to black members. Masters censured for abusing their slaves were quickly readmitted to church fellowship. Even later in the century, African Americans continued to make up a minuscule proportion of southern evangelicals—roughly 1 percent of the total.

The revivals of the mid-eighteenth century were not a dress rehearsal for Revolution. Still, the Great Awakening had important social and political consequences. In some ways, the evangelicals were profoundly conservative, preaching an old-style theology of original sin and divine revelation that ran counter to the Enlightenment's emphasis on human perfectibility and reason. In other respects, the revivalists were recognizably modern, using the techniques of Atlantic commerce, and calling into question habitual modes of behavior in the secular as well as the religious realm.

4-6 Stability and Crisis at Midcentury

▷ What internal crises challenged the peoples of eighteenth-century British North America?

▷ How did imperial disputes affect the British North American colonists?

▷ How did Native American peoples respond to imperial disputes that emerged in British North America?

The spiritual foment of the Great Awakening points to the unsettled nature of provincial life in the mid-eighteenth century. A number of other crises—ethnic, racial, economic, and military—further exposed lines of fracture within North America's diverse settler society. In the 1740s and 1750s, Britain expanded its claims to North American territory and to the obligations of provincials within the empire. At the same time, Anglo-American colonists—as veterans, citizens, and consumers—felt more strongly entitled to the liberties of British subjects. And Britain and France alike came to see North America as increasingly central to their economic, diplomatic, and military strategies in Europe.

4-6a Colonial Political Orders

Men from genteel families dominated the political structures in each province, for voters (free male property holders) tended to defer to their "betters" on election days. Throughout the Anglo-American colonies, these political leaders sought to increase the powers of elected assemblies relative to the powers of governors and other appointed officials. Colonial assemblies began to claim privileges associated with the British House of Commons, such as the

John Peter Zenger New York printer whose trial in the 1730s challenged prevailing restrictions on the press.

Glorious Revolution Overthrow of James II in favor of William and Mary in 1688.

rights to initiate tax legislation and to control the militia. The assemblies also developed ways of influencing Crown appointees, especially by threatening to withhold their salaries. In some colonies (Virginia and South Carolina, for example), members of the assembly presented a united front to royal officials, while in others (such as New York), provincials fought among themselves. To win hotly contested elections, New York's leaders began to appeal directly to "the people," competing openly for votes. Yet in 1735, the colony's government imprisoned a newspaper editor, **John Peter Zenger**, who had too vigorously criticized its actions. Defending Zenger against the charge of "seditious libel," his lawyer argued that the truth could not be defamatory, thus helping to establish a free-press principle later found in American law.

Assemblymen saw themselves as thwarting encroachments on colonists' British liberties—for example, by preventing governors from imposing oppressive taxes. By midcentury, they often compared the structure of their governments to Britain's mixed polity, which reputedly balanced monarchy, aristocracy, and democracy in ways admired since the days of ancient Greece and Rome. Drawing rough analogies, political leaders equated their royally-appointed governors with the monarch, their councils with the aristocracy, and their assemblies with Britain's House of Commons. All three were believed essential to good government, but Anglo-Americans did not regard them with the same degree of approval. Increasingly, they viewed governors and their appointed councils as potential threats to colonial liberties. Many colonists saw the assemblies as the people's protectors, and the assemblies regarded themselves as representatives of the people.

Yet such beliefs should not be equated with modern practice. Colonial assemblies, often controlled by dominant families whose members were reelected by voters year after year, rarely responded to the concerns of poorer constituents. Although settlements continually expanded, assemblies failed to reapportion themselves, which led to grievances among backcountry dwellers, especially those from non-English ethnic groups. In the ideal, the assembly was the representative defender of liberty. In reality, the most ardently defended and ably represented were wealthy male colonists, particularly the assembly members themselves.

At midcentury, the political structures that had stabilized in a period of relative calm confronted a series of crises. None affected all the mainland colonies, but no colony escaped untouched. Significantly, these upheavals demonstrated that the political accommodations forged in the aftermath of the **Glorious Revolution** had become inadequate to govern Britain's American empire.

4-6b Slave Rebellions and Internal Disorder

Early on Sunday, September 9, 1739, about twenty enslaved men, most likely Catholics from the Kongo region of West Africa, gathered near the Stono River south of Charles Town. September fell in the midst of South Carolina's rice harvest (and thus at a time of great pressure for male Africans), and September 8 was, to Catholics, the birthday of the Virgin Mary, venerated by Kongolese converts with special fervor. Seizing guns and ammunition, the rebels killed storekeepers and nearby planter families. Joined by other enslaved people, they then headed toward Florida in hopes of finding refuge. By midday, however, slaveholders in the district had sounded the alarm. That afternoon a troop of militia attacked the fugitives, who numbered about a hundred, killing some and dispersing the rest. The colony quickly captured and executed the survivors, but rumors about escaped renegades haunted the colony for years.

News of the **Stono Rebellion** reverberated far beyond South Carolina. The press frequently reported on slave uprisings in the West Indies—in Danish St. John's in 1733, in Antigua in 1736, and in Jamaica throughout the 1720s and

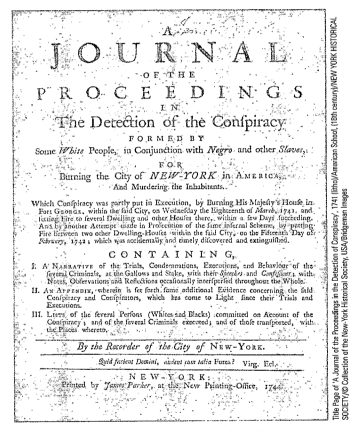

Title Page of 'A Journal of the Proceedings in the Detection of Conspiracy', 1741 (litho)/American School, (18th century)/NEW YORK HISTORICAL SOCIETY,/© Collection of the New-York Historical Society, USA/Bridgeman Images

△ Daniel Horsmanden played a leading role in the prosecution of alleged conspirators who so terrified white inhabitants of New York City in 1741. He expected many buyers for his *Journal of the Proceedings in the Detection of the Conspiracy,* an exacting and often sensationalist account of the trials that had resulted in the execution of thirty-four people, thirteen of whom were burned at the stake. But by 1744, public opinion had begun to turn against the trials, which some compared to the Salem witchcraft hysteria. Horsmanden was mocked in the newspapers, and in 1748 the *Journal's* printer slashed its price, noting, "as he has been a considerable Loser by printing that Book, he proposes to sell 'em very cheap."

1730s, for examples—but on the mainland, where slaves did not so vastly outnumber their masters, such an organized revolt was remarkable, and terrifying. Throughout British America, laws governing the behavior of African Americans were stiffened after Stono. The most striking response came in New York City, which had witnessed the first mainland slave revolt in 1712. The news from the South, coupled with fears of Spain generated by the outbreak of King George's War, set off a reign of terror in Manhattan in 1741. Colonial authorities suspected a biracial gang of illicit traders of conspiring to foment a slave uprising under the guidance of a Spanish priest. Thirty blacks and four whites were executed—gruesomely—for participating in the alleged plot. The Stono Rebellion and the New York "conspiracy" not only exposed and confirmed Anglo-Americans' deepest fears about the dangers of slaveholding but also revealed the assemblies' inability to prevent serious internal disorder.

4-6c European Rivalries in North America

In addition to their internal divisions, Britain's mainland colonies were surrounded by hostile, or potentially hostile, neighbors: Native peoples everywhere, the Spanish in Florida and along the Gulf coast, the French along the great inland system of rivers and lakes that stretched from the St. Lawrence to the Mississippi. Despite the fevered imagination of New Yorkers during the 1741 "conspiracy," the Spanish posed little direct threat. The French were another matter. Their long chain of forts and trading settlements made them the dominant colonial power in the continent's interior. In none of the three Anglo-French wars fought between 1689 and 1748 was Britain able to shake France's hold on the American frontier (see Table 4.1; see also Map 5.1, Section 5-1).

4-6d The Fall of Louisbourg

In the North American theater of King George's War, hostilities largely played out along the northern border between British and French America. Built after Queen Anne's War, the massive French fortress at Louisbourg, on Cape Breton Island, quickly became the largest French town on the continent, with more than 4,000 settlers and some 1,500 soldiers. Privateers based in the fortified port regularly menaced New England merchants and fisherman. In 1744, William Shirley, the royal governor of Massachusetts, hatched a scheme to advance Britain's war aims—and boost New England's prosperity—by seizing the fort for the Crown. New Hampshire, Connecticut, and Rhode Island raised significant sums of money and smaller numbers of recruits; some 3,000 Massachusetts men comprised three-quarters of the expedition force.

Many thought Shirley's plan to conquer Louisbourg foolhardy. As Benjamin Franklin wrote to his brother John in Boston, "Fortified towns are hard nuts to crack; and your teeth are not accustomed to it." But New England merchants, sailors, and militiamen prosecuted the empire's errand with gusto

Table 4.1 The Colonial Wars, 1689–1763

American Name	European Name	Dates	Participants	American Sites	Dispute
King William's War	Nine Years' War	1689–97	England, Holland versus France, Spain	New England, New York, Canada	French power
Queen Anne's War	War of Spanish Succession	1702–13	England, Holland, Austria versus France, Spain	Florida, New England	Throne of Spain
King George's War	War of Austrian Succession	1739–48	England, Holland, Austria versus France, Spain, Prussia	West Indies, New England, Canada	Throne of Austria
French and Indian War	Seven Years' War	1756–63	England versus France, Spain	Ohio country, Canada	Possession of Ohio country

Siege of the French fortress of Louisbourg in 1745 by British vessels and New England colonials (colour litho)/English School, (18th century)/PETER NEWARK'S PICTURES/Private Collection/Bridgeman Images

△ This anonymous painting depicts the siege of the French fortress at Louisbourg by British and provincial troops in 1745, in the middle of King George's War. The British capture of the fortress—sometimes called the Gibraltar of America—was considered a major strategic victory, because Louisbourg guarded access to the valuable North Atlantic fisheries to the east and the St. Lawrence waterway to the west.

that amazed their allies and their enemies alike. In June 1745, after a two-month-long siege, Louisbourg fell to ragtag regiments of colonial soldiers. As news of the victory trickled south, bells pealed in celebration from Boston to Philadelphia. In London, too, the New Englanders' surprising triumph was greeted with astonishment. But when the war ended in 1748,

Britain returned the fortress to France in exchange for concessions in India and the Low Countries, the imperial priorities of the moment. As its wartime shipping boom went bust, Massachusetts was left with staggering debt and hundreds of new widows and orphans, as well as needy soldiers crippled in the futile fight.

4-6e The Ohio Country

By the time King George's War ended, the crucible of North America's imperial rivalries could be found farther south, in lands west of the Appalachians and east of the Mississippi that came to be known as the Ohio Country. The trouble started in the 1730s, as Anglo-American traders pushed west from the Carolinas and Virginia, challenging French power beyond the Appalachians. French officials' fear of British incursions increased when the Delawares and Shawnees ceded large tracts of land to Pennsylvania. In 1737, two sons of William Penn and their Iroquois allies persuaded the Delawares to sell off as much land as a man could walk in a day and a half. Then the Pennsylvania negotiators rigged the deal, sending trained runners down prepared trails to multiply the acreage. Delawares derided the deceitful Walking Purchase as "ye Running Walk." This betrayal by the English and the Iroquois rankled for decades, and other fraudulent land cessions followed. On isolated farms in Delaware territory, backcountry squatters—mostly Scots-Irish and Germans—had coexisted peacefully with their Native neighbors, sometimes even paying rent to Indian leaders who owned the acres on which they farmed. But the agreements reached by the Penn family and the Iroquois ignored the claims of both the local Native communities and the squatters, all of whom were told to move. Disgruntled Delawares and Shawnees migrated west, where they joined other displaced eastern Native peoples who nursed similar grievances.

Claimed by both Virginia and Pennsylvania, the region to which they migrated was coveted by wealthy Virginians. In 1745, a group of land speculators organized as the Ohio Company of Virginia received a grant of nearly a third of a million acres from the House of Burgesses. The company's agents quickly established trading posts that aimed to dominate the crucial area where the Allegheny and Monongahela rivers join to form the Ohio (see Map 5.1, Section 5-1). But that region was also strategically vital to the French, because the Ohio River offered direct access by water to French posts along the Mississippi. By the early 1750s, Pennsylvania fur traders, Ohio Company representatives, the French military, Scots-Irish and German squatters, Iroquois, Delawares, and Shawnees all jostled for position in the region.

4-6f Iroquois Neutrality

Maintaining the policy of neutrality they developed in 1701, the Iroquois Confederacy skillfully manipulated the European rivals and consolidated their control over the vast regions northwest of Virginia and south of the Great Lakes. During Queen Anne's War and again in King George's War, they refused to commit warriors exclusively to either side, and so were showered with gifts by both. Ongoing conflict with Cherokees and Catawbas in the South gave young Iroquois warriors combat experience and allowed them to replace population losses by acquiring new captives. They also cultivated peaceful relationships with Pennsylvania and Virginia; their role in treaties like the Walking Purchase furthered Iroquois domination of the Shawnees and

△ The Swedish-born portraitist Gustav Hesselius painted this half-length canvas depicting the Delaware leader Lapowinsa in 1735. Hesselius did not Europeanize the headman, whose weary, tattooed face and steady gaze confronts the viewer directly. The squirrel-skin pouch hanging from his neck would have held tobacco. Two years after this portrait was made, Lapowinsa was among the negotiators who agreed to the fraudulent "Walking Purchase" ceding Delaware lands to William Penn's sons and their Iroquois allies.

Delawares. And they forged friendly ties with Algonquians of the Great Lakes region, thwarting potential assaults from those allies of the French and making themselves indispensable go-betweens for commerce and communication between the Atlantic coast and the West. But even the Iroquois could not fully control the Ohio Country as clashes there escalated in the early 1750s. Later that decade, in a distinct reversal of previous patterns of imperial rivalry, conflict would spread from the Ohio Country to Europe, and then around the globe.

When he traveled the colonies in 1744, Dr. Hamilton described "America," but he never once referred to the people who lived there as *Americans*. Nor did colonial settlers much use that term to identify themselves at the time. But after King George's War, and especially after the French and Indian War, the most convulsive of the century's Anglo-French wars, Britain's subjects in mainland North America began increasingly to imagine themselves as a group with shared and distinct

"Self-Made Men"

American culture celebrates the "self-made man" (always someone explicitly *male*) of humble origins who gains wealth or prominence through extraordinary effort and talent. Those most commonly cited include such successful nineteenth-century businessmen as Andrew Carnegie (once a poor immigrant from Scotland) and John D. Rockefeller (born on a hardscrabble farm in upstate New York).

The first exemplars of this tradition lived in the eighteenth century. Benjamin Franklin's *Autobiography* chronicled his method for achieving success after beginning life as the seventeenth child of a Boston candle-maker. From such humble origins Franklin became a wealthy, influential man active in science, politics, education, and diplomacy. Yet Franklin's tale is rivaled by that of a slave who became one of the eighteenth century's leading antislavery activists. He acquired literacy, purchased his freedom, married a wealthy Englishwoman, and published

a popular autobiography that predated Franklin's in print. His first master called him Gustavus Vassa, the name he primarily used. But when publishing his *Interesting Narrative* in 1789, he called himself Olaudah Equiano.

In that *Narrative*, Equiano said he was born in Africa in 1745, kidnapped at the age of eleven, and transported to Barbados and then to Virginia, where a British naval officer purchased him. For years, scholars and students have relied on that account for its insights into the experience of the middle passage. But evidence recently uncovered by Vincent Carretta, although confirming the accuracy of much of Equiano's autobiography, shows that Equiano twice identified his birthplace as Carolina and was three to five years younger than he claimed. Why would Equiano reinvent his origins and alter his age? Carretta speculates that the *Narrative* gained part of its credibility from Equiano's African birth and that admitting his real age would have

raised questions about the account of his early life by revealing his youth at the time of the reputed kidnapping.

Equiano, or Vassa, thus truly "made himself," just as Benjamin Franklin and many others have done. (Franklin tended to omit, rather than alter, inconvenient parts of his personal history—for example, his illegitimate son and his ownership of slaves.) Equiano used information undoubtedly gleaned from acquaintances who *had* experienced the middle passage to craft an accurate depiction of the horrors of the slave trade. In the process, he became one of the first Americans to explicitly remake himself.

CRITICAL THINKING

- Does knowing that Equiano and Franklin altered or even fabricated some details about their lives change their import as self-made men in the lexicon of American culture?
- Does it make their autobiographies any less compelling or impressive? Why or why not?

---

concerns. In addition to calling themselves "His Majesty's subjects in America," colonial writers began occasionally to refer to "Americans," "American colonists," or "continentals." These newly labeled Americans were not yet a people, and they were certainly not a nation. They continued to pledge their allegiance to Britain. But the more these overseas Britons came to prize their liberties as the king's subjects, the more some of them began to wonder whether Parliament and the Crown fully understood their needs and, indeed, their rights.

Summary

The decades before 1760 transformed North America. French and Spanish settlements expanded their geographic reach dramatically, and newcomers from Germany, Scotland, Ireland, and Africa brought their languages, customs, and religions with them to the British colonies. European immigrants settled throughout Anglo America but were concentrated in the growing cities and in the backcountry. By contrast, most enslaved migrants from Africa lived and worked within one hundred miles of the Atlantic coast. In many areas of the colonial South, 50 to 90 percent of the

population was of African origin. In the West Indies, the enslaved black majority was far larger.

The economic life of Europe's mainland North American colonies proceeded simultaneously on local and transatlantic levels. On the farms, plantations, and ranches on which most colonists resided, daily, weekly, monthly, and yearly rounds of chores dominated people's lives, providing goods consumed by households and sold in markets. Simultaneously, an intricate international trade network affected colonial economies. The bitter wars fought by European nations during the eighteenth century inevitably involved the colonists, creating new opportunities for overseas sales and disrupting their traditional markets. Those fortunate few who—through skill, control of essential resources, or luck—reaped the profits of international commerce comprised the wealthy class of merchants and landowners who dominated colonial political, intellectual, and social life. At the other end of the economic scale, poor colonists, especially city dwellers, struggled to make ends meet.

A century and a half after European peoples first settled in North America, the colonies mixed diverse European, American, and African traditions into a novel cultural blend that owed much to Europe but just as much, if not more, to North America itself. Interacting regularly with peoples of African and American origin—and with Europeans from nations other than their own—colonists developed new methods of accommodating intercultural differences. Yet at the same time, they continued to identify themselves as French, Spanish, or British rather than as Americans. That did not change in the West Indies, Canada, Louisiana, or in the Spanish territory, but in the 1760s some Anglo-Americans began to realize that their interests did not necessarily coincide with those of Great Britain or its monarch.

Suggestions for Further Reading

Richard R. Beeman, *The Varieties of Political Experience in Eighteenth-Century America* (2004)

Catherine A. Brekus, *Sarah Osborn's World: The Rise of Evangelical Christianity in Early America* (2013)

Richard Bushman, *The Refinement of America: Persons, Houses, Cities* (1992)

Kathleen DuVal, *The Native Ground: Indians and Colonists in the Heart of the Continent* (2006)

Rebecca Anne Goetz, *The Baptism of Early Virginia: How Christianity Created Race* (2012)

Ellen Hartigan-O'Connor, *The Ties That Buy: Women and Commerce in Revolutionary America* (2009)

Rhys Isaac, *The Transformation of Virginia, 1740–1790* (1982)

Jill Lepore, *New York Burning: Liberty, Slavery, and Conspiracy in Eighteenth-Century Manhattan* (2005)

Paul W. Mapp, *The Elusive West and the Contest for Empire, 1713–1763* (2011)

David Waldstreicher, *Runaway America: Benjamin Franklin, Slavery, and the American Revolution* (2004)

MINDTAP
From Cengage

MindTap® is a fully online personalized learning experience built upon Cengage Learning content. MindTap® combines student learning tools—readings, multimedia, activities, and assessments—into a singular Learning Path that guides students through the course and helps students develop the critical thinking, analysis, and communication skills that are essential to academic and professional success.

The Ends of Empire, 1754–1774

A spectacular victory demanded a stirring celebration, and the British capture of Quebec from the French in September 1759 was indeed a spectacular victory. When news of this latest British triumph reached Boston, in October, town fathers proclaimed a "Day of general Rejoicing." Church bells started ringing at dawn and pealed through the day. Preachers thundered praise from the pulpits. Troops paraded down King Street, pausing to blast "Rejoicing Fires" from their muskets. Ninety cannons sounded at the fort called Castle William, after William of Orange; guns mounted on the batteries in nearby Charlestown and on the decks of warships in the harbor echoed the salute.

As night fell, public buildings blazed with candlelight. The hills surrounding the town glowed with "large bonfires formed in a pyramidal manner." An "abundance of extraordinary Fire-Works were play'd off in almost every Street," the *Boston Gazette* reported, "the greatest Quantity of Sky-Rockets ever seen on any Occasion." In the seaport's lanes and alleys, "Persons of all Ranks" joined in the revelry. At the Concert Hall on Hanover Street (named after the dynasty whose rule of Britain had begun with George I, in 1714), His Excellency Thomas Pownall, the royally appointed governor, heard a musical tribute. Then he and his council and members of both houses of the provincial assembly headed to the Town House, a brick building topped by golden statues of the English lion and the Scottish unicorn. Together the politicians toasted the wisdom of the king and the health of the royal family.

Experience an interactive version of this story in MindTap®.

◁ Images of the death of British General James Wolfe at the Battle of Quebec were popular in Britain and America. Pennsylvania-born Benjamin West painted the most celebrated of them in London in 1770. It features an idealized Mohawk warrior, a kilted Scottish Highlander, and a colonial Ranger as well as English officers: a harmonious fantasy of Britain's empire. George III commissioned a copy for himself in 1771. World History Archive/Image Asset Management Ltd/Alamy Stock Photo

Chronology

1754	▦ Albany Congress fails to forge colonial unity
	▦ George Washington defeated at Fort Necessity, Pennsylvania
1755	▦ Braddock's army routed in Pennsylvania
1756	▦ Britain declares war on France; Seven Years' War officially begins
1759	▦ British take Quebec, ending a military *annus mirabilis*—a "year of wonders"—for the British
1760	▦ American phase of war ends with British capture of Montreal
	▦ George III becomes king
1763	▦ Treaty of Paris ends Seven Years' War
	▦ Pontiac's allies attack forts and settlements in American West
	▦ Proclamation of 1763 attempts to close land west of Appalachians to settlement
1764	▦ Sugar Act lays new duties on molasses, tightens existing customs regulations
	▦ Currency Act outlaws colonial paper money
1765	▦ Stamp Act requires stamps on all printed materials in colonies
	▦ Sons of Liberty forms in resistance to the Stamp Act
1765–66	▦ Hudson River land riots pit tenants and squatters against large landlords
	▦ Regulator movement begins in North Carolina

1766	▦ Parliament repeals Stamp Act
	▦ Declaratory Act insists that Parliament can tax the colonies
1767	▦ Townshend Acts lay duties on trade within the empire, send new officials to America
1767–69	▦ Regulator movement in South Carolina tries to establish order in backcountry
1768–70	▦ Townshend duties resisted; boycotts and protests divide merchants and urban artisans
1770	▦ Townshend duties repealed except for tea tax
	▦ Five colonial rioters killed by British regulars; patriots call this the Boston Massacre
1771	▦ North Carolina regulators defeated by eastern militia; six executed for treason
1772	▦ Boston Committee of Correspondence formed
1773	▦ Tea Act aids East India Company; spurs protest in Boston
1774	▦ Coercive Acts punish Boston and Massachusetts
	▦ Quebec Act reforms government of Quebec
	▦ "Lord Dunmore's War" between Shawnees and backcountry settlers in Virginia
	▦ First Continental Congress convenes in Philadelphia, adopts Articles of Association
1774–75	▦ Provincial conventions replace collapsing colonial governments

B oston's "Rejoicing" was "the greatest ever known ... an universal Joy," the *Gazette* declared. As word of Britain's stunning victory in the long conflict that would come to be known as the Seven Years' War spread through the colonies in the waning days of 1759, similar festivities took place across Anglo America. In Flushing, New York, proud British subjects raised their glasses to "the paternal Tenderness of our Most Gracious Sovereign for these infant Colonies." In Philadelphia, a writer in the *Pennsylvania Gazette* joked, dour Quakers feared that the incessant bonfires would "put out the Sun." One Albany correspondent predicted—correctly—that the rest of Canada would quickly follow Quebec, and "hope[d] soon to hear all this Country is to be English."

The celebratory mood would not last. Within months, the war in North America would be over, and the wartime business boom in the port towns would go bust. By the end of the 1760s, many of those who had toasted the health of George II in 1759 would come to suspect that his grandson George III had turned tyrant, bent upon reducing his colonies to slavery. From Nova Scotia to Antigua, protestors against the Crown's new taxes—taxes designed to pay for costly British victories like the one at Quebec—would flood the streets. Of course, the inhabitants of Anglo America knew none of this in the fall of 1759. Proud subjects living on the western edge of His Majesty's empire, they had little reason to anticipate that "this country" would ever be anything but British.

The American Revolution required a thorough transformation in consciousness: a shift of political allegiance from Britain to a polity that was called, at first, the United Colonies. "The Revolution was effected before the war commenced,"

John Adams later wrote. The true Revolution was not the war, he said, but a fundamental change "in the minds and hearts of the people." Between 1760 and 1775, huge numbers of ordinary Americans transferred their obligations and affections from their mother country to their sister colonies. Yet Adams spoke of a singular Revolution, when in fact there were many. Rich and poor, free and enslaved, indigenous and European, urban and rural, mainland and Caribbean, even male and female Americans experienced the era's upheavals differently.

In the long history of British settlement in the Western Hemisphere, considerable tension had occasionally flared up between individual provinces and the mother country. But except for the crisis following the Glorious Revolution in 1689, such tension had rarely endured or expanded. The primary divisions affecting Britain's American colonies had been internal rather than external. In the 1750s, however, a series of events began to draw colonists' attention from local matters to their relations with Great Britain. It started with the conflict in which Britain captured Quebec: the **Seven Years' War.**

Britain's overwhelming victory in that war dramatically altered the balance of power in North America and in Europe. France was ousted from the continent and Spain was ejected from Florida, shifts with major consequences for the indigenous peoples of the interior and for the residents of the British colonies. Native peoples, who had become expert at playing European powers against one another, found one of their major diplomatic tools blunted. Anglo-Americans no longer had to fear the French on their northern and western borders or the Spanish in the Southeast. Had France controlled the interior in 1776, some historians contend, the colonies along the coast would never have dared to break with Britain.

The British victory in 1763 also transformed Great Britain's colonial policy. Britain's massive war-related debt—the price of the country's victory—needed to be paid. Parliament saw the colonies as the chief beneficiaries of British success, and for the first time imposed revenue-raising taxes on the North American territories, in addition to the customs duties that had long regulated trade. That decision exposed differences in the political thinking of Britons in mainland America and Britons in the home islands and the West Indies—differences long obscured by a shared political vocabulary centered on English liberties.

During the 1760s and early 1770s, a broad coalition of Anglo American women and men resisted the new tax levies and attempts by British officials to tighten their control over provincial governments. The colonies' elected leaders grew ever more suspicious of Britain's motives. They laid aside old antagonisms to coordinate responses to the new measures, and they slowly began to reorient their political thinking. As late as the summer of 1774, though, most continued to seek a solution within the framework of the empire.

🔲 *What were the causes and consequences of the Seven Years' War?*

🔲 *What British policies did Americans protest, and what theories and strategies did they develop to support those protests?*

🔲 *Why did the Tea Act of 1773 dramatically heighten tensions between the mainland colonies and Great Britain?*

5-1 From the Ohio Country to Global War

▶ **How did the imperial conflicts of the 1750s and 1760s, and the resulting influx of European settlers into the Ohio Country and other areas, affect the lives and strategies of Native American peoples?**

▶ **Why did the Albany Plan of Union fail?**

In the early 1750s, the Six Nations of the Iroquois Confederacy—despite their considerable diversity—were far more politically integrated than Britain's North American colonies. British officials drafted plans to better coordinate what one writer called "the Interior Government" of their American territories. It was not only the fractiousness of the colonial legislatures, or even the rampant evasion of the Navigation Acts that worried these imperial reformers. Their concerns were also strategic; the disunity of the colonies made it hard to construct an effective bulwark against the French, who were once again on the march in the continent's interior. The unchecked incursions of backcountry traders and squatters had alienated Native allies vital to the British colonies' defense (see Map 5.1). In the summer of 1753, as the French erected a chain of forts in the Ohio Country, the Mohawk leader Hendrick Theyanoguin declared the Covenant Chain binding his people to the English broken. "So brother you are not to expect to hear of me any more," he told New York's governor, "and Brother we desire to hear no more of you." When news of the Iroquois alliance breakdown and the French buildup reached London,

Seven Years' War Major French-English conflict that was the first worldwide war.

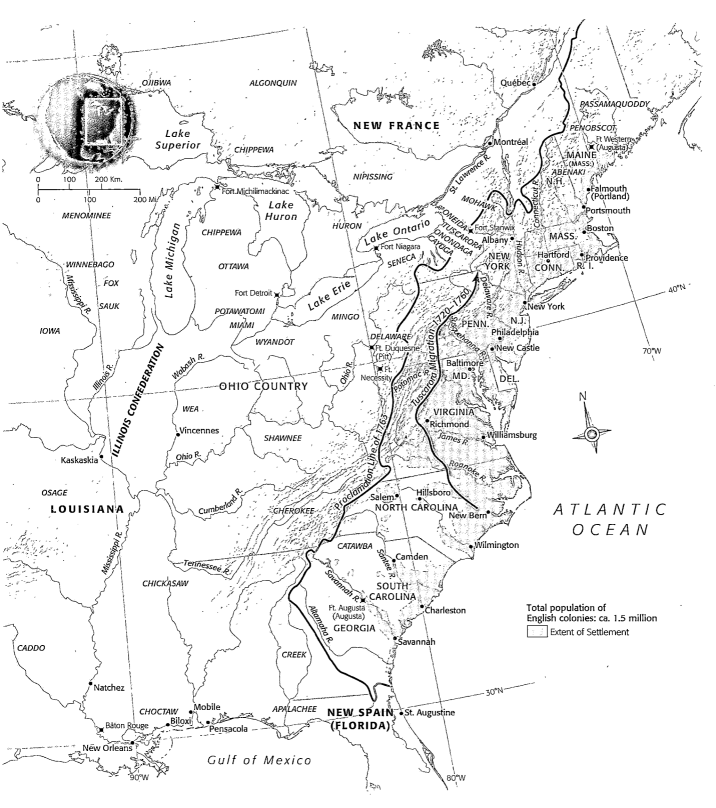

Map 5.1 European Settlements and Native Peoples, 1754

By 1754, Europeans had expanded the limits of the English colonies to the eastern slopes of the Appalachian Mountains. Few independent Indian nations still existed in the East, but beyond the mountains they controlled the countryside. Only a few widely scattered English and French forts maintained the Europeans' presence there.

△ This engraving, labeled "The brave old Hendrick, the Great Sachem or Chief of the Mohawk Indians . . . now in Alliance with & Subject to the King of Great Britain," was sold in London in late 1755, just after the war chief Hendrick Theyanoguin died fighting for the British at the Battle of Lake George. Though he holds a hatchet and a wampum belt, Hendrick wears a fine English-style coat edged with braid, and elegant ruffled linens. This costume matches the finery Alexander Hamilton described when he saw Hendrick parade through the streets of Boston a decade before (see Chapter 4 introduction).

the Board of Trade directed the colonies to assemble in conference and bury the hatchet.

5-1a Albany Congress

In response to the board's instructions, twenty-five delegates from the seven northern and middle colonies and more than two hundred Native individuals from the Six Nations gathered in Albany, New York, in June 1754. The colonists had two goals: to forge a stronger alliance with the Iroquois and to coordinate plans for intercolonial defense. They failed on both counts. Hendrick's Mohawks renewed their support for the British, but the other Iroquois nations reaffirmed the neutrality policy that had served them well for half a century. The colonists, too, remained divided. Connecticut land speculators battled the Pennsylvania proprietors; New England commissioners refused funds

to defend western New York; New York's delegates fought even among themselves.

Before they dispersed in July, the delegates endorsed the Plan of Union crafted by Pennsylvania's Benjamin Franklin, then postmaster general of British America. Franklin's plan called for an unprecedented level of cooperation among the disparate provinces. It proposed the creation of an elected intercolonial legislature with the power to tax and outlined strategies for a common defense. The plan met with quick and universal rejection in the provincial legislatures, which wanted to safeguard their autonomy more than their citizens. Virginia, which had much to lose in the Ohio Country, had declined to attend the Albany Congress and refused even to consider the plan. Other assemblies failed to vote on it. Franklin despaired that the colonies would ever find the common ground they so clearly needed. "[I]f ever there be an Union," he told a correspondent in London, "it must be form'd at home by the Ministry and Parliament." (By "home," this would-be architect of colonial cooperation meant London.) The British ministry agreed, preferring to create a commander in chief for North America rather than an intercolonial legislature.

While the Albany Congress deliberated, the war for which the delegates struggled to prepare had already begun. In the fall of 1753, Governor Robert Dinwiddie of Virginia dispatched a small militia detachment to build a palisade at the forks of the Ohio River—a backstop against the French advance. Reinforcements quickly followed. When a substantial French force arrived at the forks the following April, the first contingent of Virginia militia surrendered,

△ Benjamin Franklin published this cartoon, labeled "Join, or Die," in his newspaper, The Pennsylvania Gazette, in May 1754. The woodcut depicts the British provinces from South Carolina to New England as segments of a snake that had perished because of its violent division. The cartoon promoted Franklin's Plan of Union, which would have created an intercolonial legislature. Though the Albany Congress endorsed the plan, it was roundly rejected by the legislatures of those colonies that considered it.

abandoning the site, and the French began to construct the larger and more elaborate Fort Duquesne. Upon learning of the confrontation, the inexperienced young major who commanded the Virginia reinforcements pressed onward instead of awaiting further instructions. He soon engaged a French detachment. Hoping to start a war that would force the British to defend the Ohio Country against the French, Tanaghrisson, the leader of the major's Ohio Native scouts, murdered the French commander and allowed his warriors to slay the wounded French soldiers. Pursuing French troops then trapped the Virginians and their Native allies in the crudely built Fort Necessity at Great Meadows, Pennsylvania. After a day-long battle during which more than one-third of his men were killed or wounded, the Virginia militia commander, twenty-two-year-old Major George Washington, surrendered on July 3, 1754.

5-1b Seven Years' War

Tanaghrisson's plan to set the British against the French succeeded beyond anything he could have dreamed. His attack, and Washington's blunder, ignited what became the first global war. The fighting at the forks of the Ohio helped to reignite a long-simmering conflict between Austria and Prussia. European nations scrambled for allies. Eventually England, Hanover, and Prussia lined up against France, Austria, and Russia, which were joined by Sweden, Saxony, and, later, Spain. Fighting spread from the American interior to the Caribbean, Europe, Africa, and Asia. That the conflict eventually embroiled combatants around the world attests to the growing importance of European nations' overseas empires, and to the increasing centrality of North America to their struggles for dominance.

The war began disastrously for the British. In February 1755, Major General Edward Braddock arrived in Virginia, followed by two regiments of British soldiers, or "regulars." His orders assigned him the command of all British forces from Nova Scotia to South Carolina. That July, French and Native warriors attacked Braddock's troops as they prepared for a renewed assault on Fort Duquesne. Braddock was killed and his forces decimated. It was a shocking defeat—a rout. Convinced that the British could not protect them, many Ohio Native peoples joined the French. The Pennsylvania frontier bore the brunt of repeated attacks by Delaware warriors for two more years; over a thousand residents of the backcountry—nearly 4 percent of the population in some counties—were captured or killed. Settlers felt betrayed because the Native warriors attacking them had once been (as one observer noted) "familiars at their houses [who] eat drank cursed and swore together" with their Euro American neighbors.

In 1756, after news of the debacle reached London, Britain declared war on France, thus formally beginning what came to be known as the Seven Years' War. Even before then, Britain, poised for renewed conflict with old enemies, took a fateful step. New Englanders lobbied London, insisting that France would try to retake Nova Scotia, where most of the population was descended from seventeenth-century French settlers who had intermarried with local M'ikmaqs. Afraid that the settlers, known as Acadians (after the province's name, Acadie), would abandon their long-standing posture of neutrality, British commanders in 1755 forced about seven thousand of them from their homeland—the first large-scale modern deportation, now called ethnic cleansing. Ships crammed with Acadians and outfitted with irons, in the manner of slaving vessels, sailed to each of the mainland colonies, where the refugees encountered hostility and discrimination. "About a thousand of them arrived in Boston, just in the beginning of the winter, crowded almost to death," recalled Thomas Hutchinson, soon to become lieutenant governor of Massachusetts. Dispersed to widely scattered communities, many of the transported families were separated, some forever. After the Peace of Paris in 1763, the survivors relocated. Some returned to Canada, others traveled to France or its Caribbean colonies, and many eventually settled in Louisiana, where they became known as Cajuns (derived from *Acadian*).

Despite such brutal precautions, one calamity followed another for three years after Braddock's defeat. British officers met with scant success coercing the colonies to supply men and materiel to the army. William Pitt, the Member of Parliament placed in charge of the Crown's war effort in 1757, changed tactics. Pitt agreed to reimburse the colonies for their wartime expenditures. He placed recruitment in local hands, thereby gaining greater American support for the war. Large numbers of colonial militiamen served, not always happily, alongside equally large numbers of red-coated regulars from Britain. Even so, Virginia's burgesses appropriated more funds to defend against slave insurrections than to fight the French and their Native allies.

The actions of Anglo-American merchants added to the tension. During the war, firms in Boston, Philadelphia, and New York continued trading with the French West Indies. Seeking markets for their fish, flour, timber, and other products, they bribed customs officers to look the other way while cargoes nominally bound for such neutral ports as Dutch St. Eustatius or Spanish Monte Cristi (on Hispaniola) actually ended up in the French Caribbean. Colonial merchants acquired valuable French sugar in exchange. British officials failed to stop the illicit commerce, some of which was conducted under the guise of exchanging prisoners of war using flags of truce. North American merchants in fact supplied not only the French Caribbean but also France itself with vital materiel during the war.

Pitt's strategy turned the tide. In July 1758, British forces recaptured the fortress at Louisbourg—returned to the French just a decade before—thus severing the major French supply artery down the St. Lawrence River. That fall, the Delawares and Shawnees accepted British peace overtures, and the French abandoned Fort Duquesne. Then, in a stunning attack in September 1759, General James Wolfe's forces defeated the French on the Plains of Abraham and took Quebec. The capture of Quebec, which

△ This image, by the preeminent British seascape painter Dominic Seres, shows the British capture in 1761 of Belle Isle, a French island off the coast of Brittany. The victory was hard fought; French forces repulsed an earlier attack, and withstood a British siege for six weeks. British forces held the island until the end of the Seven Years' War, when it was returned to the French in exchange for Minorca, which France had taken from Britain early in the conflict. Such images and the battles they commemorate remind us of the importance of island fortresses in an age of naval war.

followed British victories in the Caribbean and eastern India, was hailed as the culmination of an *annus mirabilis*—a year of wonders—for the British. "[O]ur bells are worn threadbare with ringing for victories," wrote one English politician. Many colonists could have said the same. A year later, the British captured Montreal, the last French stronghold on the continent. The North American phase of the Seven Years' War had ended.

In the **Treaty of Paris** (1763), France surrendered to Britain its major North American holdings (excepting New Orleans), as well as several Caribbean islands, its slaving prisons in Senegambia, and all of its possessions in India. Spain, an ally of France toward the end of the war, granted parts of Florida to the victors. France, meanwhile, ceded western Louisiana to Spain, in compensation for its ally's losses elsewhere. No longer would the English seacoast colonies have to worry about the threat posed by France's extensive North American territories (see Map 5.2).

Britain's triumph stimulated some provincial Britons to think expansively. Men like Benjamin Franklin, who had long touted the colonies' wealth and dynamism, predicted a glorious new future for North America—a future that included not just geographical expansion but also economic and demographic growth. Some such thinkers would lead the resistance

to British measures in the years after 1763. For ultimately, the winners as well as the losers would be made to pay for this first worldwide war.

5-2 1763: A Turning Point

▷ **How did the French and Indian War contribute to instability in the North American interior?**

▷ **How did British American colonists interpret the political ideas of representation and power?**

▷ **What did British American colonists dislike about the Sugar Act and Currency Act?**

Britain's great victory had a wide-ranging impact on North America, felt first by the indigenous peoples of the interior. With France excluded from the eastern half of the continent and Spanish territory confined west of the Mississippi, the Native Americans' time-tested diplomatic strategy of playing European nations against one another became obsolete. The consequences were immediate and devastating.

Treaty of Paris Treaty by which France ceded most of its North American provinces to Great Britain and some smaller territories to Spain.

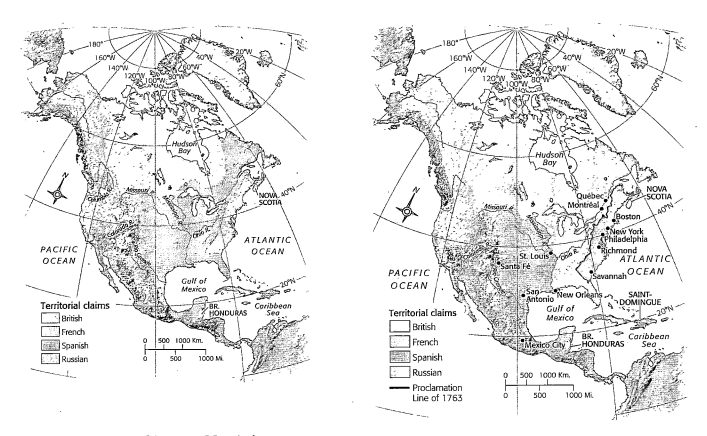

Map 5.2 European Claims in North America

The dramatic results of the British victory in the Seven Years' (French and Indian) War are vividly demonstrated in these maps, which depict the abandonment of French claims to the mainland after the Treaty of Paris in 1763.

Even before the Treaty of Paris, southern Native peoples had to adjust to new circumstances. After Britain gained the upper hand in the American theater of war in 1758, the Creeks and Cherokees lost their ability to force concessions by threatening to turn to France or Spain. In desperation, and in retaliation for British atrocities, Cherokees attacked the Carolina and Virginia frontiers in 1760. Though initially victorious, the Native warriors were defeated the following year by a force made up of British regulars and colonial militia. Late in 1761, the two sides concluded a treaty under which the Cherokees allowed the construction of British forts in their territories and opened a large tract to European settlement.

5-2a Neolin and Pontiac

In the Ohio Country, the Ottawas, Chippewas, and Potawatomis reacted angrily when Great Britain, no longer facing French competition, raised the price of trade goods and ended traditional gift-giving practices. As settlers surged into the Monongahela and Susquehanna valleys, a shaman named Neolin (also known as the Delaware Prophet) urged Native peoples to oppose European incursions on their lands and cultures. For the first time since King Philip in 1675, an influential Native leader called for the unity of all tribes in the face of an

Anglo-American threat. Contending that Native peoples were destroying themselves through dependence on European goods (especially alcohol), Neolin advocated resistance, both peaceful and armed. If Native peoples west of the mountains united against the invaders, he declared, the Master of Life would once again look kindly upon his people. Ironically, Neolin's call for a revival of native traditions itself revealed European influence; his reference to a single powerful deity bore traces of his people's encounter with Christianity.

Pontiac, war chief of an Ottawa village near Detroit, became the leader of a rebellion based on Neolin's precepts. In spring 1763, Pontiac forged an alliance among Hurons, Chippewas, Potawatomis, Delawares, Shawnees, and Mingoes (Pennsylvania Iroquois). Pontiac's forces besieged Fort Detroit while war parties attacked other British outposts in the Great Lakes. Detroit withstood the siege, but by late June, the other forts west of Niagara and north of Fort Pitt (the renamed Fort Duquesne) had fallen to Pontiac's warriors. Native forces then raided the Virginia and Pennsylvania frontiers throughout the summer, killing at least two thousand settlers. Native raiders carried off many enslaved African Americans, raising fears of a Native-black alliance. Still, those who had rallied to Pontiac's cause failed to take Niagara, Fort Pitt, or Detroit. In August, colonial militiamen soundly defeated a combined Native force at Bushy Run, Pennsylvania. Pontiac broke off the siege of Detroit in late October. A treaty ending the war was finally negotiated three years later.

The warfare on the Pennsylvania frontier in 1755–1757 and 1763 ended what had once been a uniquely peaceful relationship between European settlers and Native peoples in that province. For nearly eighty years, the many peoples who lived in "Penn's Woods" had avoided major conflicts with each other. But first the Native attacks and then the settlers' responses—especially the massacre of several defenseless Conestoga families in December 1763 by Scots-Irish vigilantes known as the Paxton Boys—inaugurated violence that would become endemic in the region. In fact, one historian has argued, such acts of violence toward Native peoples helped the disparate European settlers of the Pennsylvania backcountry forge a common American identity in the years ahead.

5-2b Proclamation of 1763

Pontiac's war demonstrated that the huge territory Britain acquired from France would prove a curse as well as a blessing. London officials had no experience managing such a vast territory, particularly one inhabited by restive peoples: the remaining French settlers along the St. Lawrence, the many Native communities, as well as growing numbers of eastern settlers and speculators. In October, George III's ministry issued the **Proclamation of 1763**, which designated the headwaters of rivers flowing into the Atlantic from the Appalachians as the western boundary for colonial settlement (see Map 5.1 and Map 5.2). The crown expected the proclamation line to prevent clashes by forbidding colonists to move onto Native American lands until further treaties had been negotiated. Instead, it infuriated two groups of colonists: settlers who had already squatted west of the line (among them many Scots-Irish immigrants), and investors in land speculation companies from Pennsylvania and Virginia.

In the years after 1763, the speculators (who included George Washington, Thomas Jefferson, Patrick Henry, and Benjamin Franklin) lobbied vigorously to have their claims validated by colonial governments and London administrators. At a treaty conference in 1768 at Fort Stanwix, New York, they negotiated with Iroquois representatives to push the boundary line farther west and south, opening modern-day Kentucky to British settlement. Still claiming to speak for the Delawares and the Shawnees (who used Kentucky as their hunting grounds), the Iroquois agreed to the deal, which brought them valuable trade goods and did not affect their own territories. Yet even though the Virginia land companies eventually gained the support of the House of Burgesses, they never made any headway where it really mattered—in London—because administrators there realized that significant western expansion would require funds they did not have.

5-2c George III

In the Seven Years' War, Britain captured immense territory at immense cost. The country's hard-won hegemony, in Europe as well as in North America, was both isolating and expensive. The British national debt doubled during the war, to £137 million.

The Granger Collection

△ Benjamin West, the first well-known American artist, was living in London when he painted the picture that served as the basis of this engraving. It illustrates a treaty conference at the end of Pontiac's Rebellion. Colonel Henry Bouquet negotiates with a Shawnee leader who holds an elaborate wampum belt. West drew from his own life in Pennsylvania for many of the details of native dress, but he also incorporated poses from ancient works he had seen in Italy.

Having tightened their belts to finance an overseas conflict, Britons in the home islands anticipated a peace dividend, not further austerity in the service of faraway colonies. From the perspective of London, America's imperial crisis was Britain's American problem, and solutions were hard to come by.

The challenge of paying the war debt, and of finding the money to defend the newly acquired territories, bedeviled young George III, who succeeded his grandfather, George II, in 1760. The twenty-two-year-old monarch, an intelligent, passionate man with a mediocre education, proved to be a poor leader of his government. During the crucial years between 1763 and 1770, as the rift between Britain and the American colonies widened, the king replaced cabinet ministers with bewildering rapidity. Although determined to assert the power of the monarchy, George III stubbornly regarded adherence to the status quo as the hallmark of patriotism. His lack of flexibility in the face of changing conditions would have enormous consequences.

Proclamation of 1763
England's attempt to end clashes over Native American lands by preventing westward movement by colonists.

Like many imperial reformers, the man the king selected as prime minister in 1763, George Grenville, believed the colonies should be more firmly administered. Grenville confronted a financial crisis. Before the war, annual government expenditures had totaled no more than £8 million; now the interest on the national debt came to £5 million per year. Grenville's ministry had to find new sources of funds, and the British people were already heavily taxed. Because the colonists had benefited greatly from wartime outlays, Grenville concluded, Anglo-Americans should shoulder a larger share of the cost of running the expanded empire.

5-2d Theories of Representation

Grenville did not doubt Great Britain's right to levy taxes on the colonies. Like his countrymen, he believed that government's legitimacy derived ultimately from the consent of the people. But he defined consent differently than many colonists did. Grenville and many of his English contemporaries believed that Parliament—king, lords, and commons acting together—by definition represented all British subjects, wherever they resided and whether or not they could vote. Many who lived in the North American provinces, by contrast, had come to believe that their interests could be represented only by men who lived nearby, and for whom they (or their property-holding neighbors) actually voted.

Britons in England, Scotland, and Ireland saw Parliament as collectively representing the entire nation. When voters elected a member of the House of Commons, they did not imagine that he would advance the specific interests of their specific district, nor that they would have any special claim on that member's vote. Indeed, members of Parliament did not even have to live near their constituents. According to this theory, called *virtual representation*, each member of Parliament worked for the entire British nation, and all Britons—including colonists—were represented in Parliament. Their consent to its laws could thus be presumed.

In the colonies, however, members of the lower houses of the assemblies were viewed as *actually* representing the regions that had elected them. Voters cast their ballots for those they believed would advance the particular interests of a given district and province. Before Grenville proposed to tax the colonists, no conflict had exposed the contradiction between the two notions. But events of the 1760s revealed the incompatibility of these two understandings of representation.

5-2e Real Whigs

The same events threw into sharp relief Americans' attitudes toward political power. The colonists had grown accustomed to a faraway central government that affected their daily lives very little. Consequently, they believed a good government was one that left them alone, a view in keeping with the theories of British writers known as the Real Whigs or Commonwealth

thinkers. Drawing on a tradition of dissent that reached back to the English Civil War, the Real Whigs stressed the dangers posed by a powerful government, particularly one headed by a monarch. Some of them even favored republicanism, which proposed to eliminate monarchs and vest political power more directly in the people. Real Whig writers warned people to guard against government's attempts to threaten their liberty and seize their property. Political power was always to be feared, wrote John Trenchard and Thomas Gordon in essays entitled *Cato's Letters* (published in London in 1720–1723 and reprinted many times thereafter in the colonies).

Britain's efforts to tighten the reins of government and to raise revenues from the colonies in the 1760s and early 1770s convinced many colonists that Real Whig logic applied to their circumstances. Excessive and unjust taxation, they believed, could destroy their freedoms. By 1775, a large number of mainland colonists would come to see the actions of Grenville and his successors as tyrannical. In the mid-1760s, however, colonial leaders did not accuse Parliament of conspiring to oppress them. Rather, they questioned the wisdom of the particular laws Grenville proposed.

5-2f Sugar and Currency Acts

Parliament passed the first such measures, the Sugar Act and the Currency Act, in 1764. The **Sugar Act** (also known as the Revenue Act) revised existing customs regulations and laid new duties on some imports into the colonies. North American colonists differed sharply with those in the West Indies over its key provisions, revealing a division of interests between Britain's thirteen provinces on the mainland and the equal number located in the Caribbean. As the imperial crisis unfolded, that division would become a chasm. Influential Caribbean sugar planters lobbied for the Sugar Act, which protected their commerce against cheaper smuggled sugar products from the French islands. The act also established a vice-admiralty court at Halifax, Nova Scotia, to adjudicate violations of the law. Although the Sugar Act resembled the earlier Navigation Acts, which the colonies considered legitimate, it was explicitly designed to raise revenue, not to channel American trade through Britain.

The Currency Act effectively outlawed most colonial paper money, something the Crown had tried to do for decades. British merchants had long complained that Americans paid their debts in local currencies of indeterminate value. The Currency Act forced them to pay their debts in pounds and pence—real money, as the British saw it. But Americans imported more than they exported, and so could accumulate little sterling; colonists complained that the act deprived them of a vital medium of exchange.

The Sugar Act and the Currency Act were imposed on an economy already reeling from depression. A business boom accompanied the Seven Years' War, but the brief spell of prosperity ended abruptly in 1760, when fighting moved overseas. Urban merchants found fewer buyers for imported goods, and the loss of the military's demand for everything from food to horseshoes hurt farmers and city dwellers alike. The bottom dropped out of the European tobacco market,

Sugar Act Act passed by British Parliament in 1764 that sought to raise revenues by taxing colonial imports, notably sugar products like molasses and rum.

threatening the livelihood of Chesapeake planters. Sailors were thrown out of work, and artisans found fewer customers. In such circumstances, the prospect of new import duties and inadequate supplies of currency panicked merchants.

Individual essayists and incensed colonial governments protested the new policies. But lacking any precedent for a campaign against acts of Parliament, colonists in 1764 took only hesitant and uncoordinated steps. Eight provincial legislatures sent separate petitions to Parliament requesting the Sugar Act's repeal. They argued that its commercial restrictions would hurt Britain as well as the colonies and insisted that they had not consented to its passage. The protests had no effect. The law remained in force, and Grenville proceeded with another new revenue plan.

5-3 The Stamp Act Crisis

▷ **Why did many British colonists perceive the Stamp Act as a threat?**

▷ **How did North American colonial argumentation against parliament's power to tax them develop amid the Stamp Act Crisis?**

▷ **What were the competing goals and methods of demonstrators who protested the Stamp Act?**

The **Stamp Act** (1765), Grenville's most important proposal, was modeled on a law that had been in effect in Britain for almost a century. It touched nearly every colonist by requiring tax stamps on printed materials, but it placed the heaviest burden on members of the colonial elite, who used printed matter more intensively than did ordinary folk. Anyone who purchased a newspaper or pamphlet, made a will, transferred land, earned a diploma, bought playing cards, applied for a license, accepted a government post, or took a loan would have to buy a stamp. Adding injury to insult, the act also required that scarce coin be used to purchase tax stamps. Never before had a revenue measure of such scope been proposed for the colonies. The Stamp Act broke with the colonial tradition of self-imposed taxation. Violators were to be tried by vice-admiralty courts, in which judges alone rendered decisions, leading Americans to fear for their right to trial by jury. And since the revenues would pay for British peacekeepers in North America, the tax also mobilized long-established fears of a standing army.

5-3a James Otis's *Rights of the British Colonies*

The most important colonial pamphlet protesting the Sugar Act and the proposed Stamp Act was *The Rights of the British Colonies Asserted and Proved,* by James Otis Jr., a brilliant young Massachusetts attorney. Otis starkly exposed the dilemma that confounded the colonists for the next decade. How could they oppose particular acts of Parliament without fundamentally questioning Parliament's authority? On the one hand, he asserted, colonists were "entitled to all the natural, essential, inherent, and inseparable rights" of Britons, including the

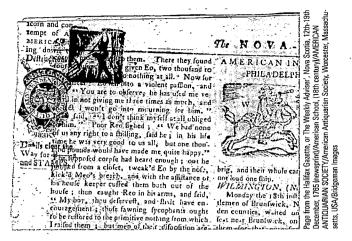

△ This page from the Halifax Nova Scotia *Gazette* in November 1765 shows printers' fury at the Stamp Act. The new law stipulated that newspapers had to be printed on stamped paper; the official seal or stamp appears in red. The printer has created a crude illustration of a devil, who appears to spear the detested stamp with a pitchfork. Below the stamp, he has printed, "Devils clear the way for STAMPS."

right not to be taxed without their consent. This logic followed colonial notions of representation. But Otis also conceded that "the power of parliament is uncontrollable but by themselves … Let the parliament lay what burthens they please on us, we must … submit and patiently bear them." Here Otis accepted the prevailing theory of British government: Parliament was the supreme authority in the empire. To resolve the dilemma, Otis proposed colonial representation in Parliament, an idea that was never taken seriously on either side of the Atlantic.

Like many Enlightenment thinkers, Otis reasoned from natural rights. He argued that the colonists and "their brethren of Great-Britain" were "children of the same Creator," born into "a state of equality and perfect freedom." But like very few writers of his day, Otis extended this natural rights logic to the enslaved. "The Colonists are by the law of nature free born, as indeed are all men, white or black," he wrote. Slavery debased everyone connected with it; the institution threatened "to reduce both Europe and America to the ignorance and barbarity of the darkest ages." It was common, in the 1760s, for colonists to protest that Britain's tyranny enslaved them. To receive the stamps "is Death—is worse than Death—it is slavery!" proclaimed Pennsylvania's John Dickinson. James Otis went further. Not only did unfair taxes reduce people to slavery; chattel slavery itself was the basest tyranny. He warned: "It is a clear truth, that those who every day barter away other mens liberty, will soon care little for their own." Slowly, in small corners of the colonies and in England, the era's talk of liberty would begin to erode the intellectual foundations of human bondage.

Stamp Act Obliged colonists to purchase and use special stamped (watermarked) paper for newspapers, customs documents, various licenses, college diplomas, and legal forms used for recovering debts, buying land, and making wills.

When Otis published his pamphlet, the Stamp Act was rumored, but not yet passed. When Americans first learned of the act's adoption, in the spring of 1765, they reacted indecisively. Few colonists—even appointed government officials—publicly favored the law. But colonial petitions had failed to prevent its passage, and further lobbying appeared futile. Perhaps Otis was correct: Americans had to pay the tax, reluctantly but loyally. Acting on that assumption, colonial agents in London sought the appointment of their American friends as stamp distributors so that the law would at least be enforced equitably.

5-3b Patrick Henry and the Virginia Stamp Act Resolves

Not all colonists resigned themselves to paying the new tax. A young attorney serving his first term in Virginia's House of Burgesses was appalled by his fellow legislators' complacency. The son of a prosperous Scots immigrant, Patrick Henry had little formal education. But his oratorical skills made him a formidable advocate.

Near the end of the legislative session, when many burgesses had already departed for home, Henry introduced seven proposals against the Stamp Act. The few burgesses remaining adopted five of Henry's resolutions by a bare majority. Although they repealed the most radical of the five the next day, their action had far-reaching effects. Some newspapers printed Henry's original resolutions as if the House had passed them all, even though one was rescinded and two others were never even debated or voted on.

The four propositions adopted by the burgesses echoed Otis's arguments about taxation, asserting that colonists had never forfeited the rights of British subjects. The other three resolutions went much further. The repealed resolution claimed for the burgesses "the only exclusive right" to tax Virginians. The final two (never considered) asserted that Virginians need not obey tax laws passed by other legislative bodies—namely, Parliament.

5-3c Continuing Loyalty to Britain

The burgesses' decision to accept only some of Henry's resolutions anticipated the position most mainland colonists would adopt throughout the following decade. Though willing to fight for their liberties as Britons within the empire, they did not seek independence. The Maryland lawyer Daniel Dulany, whose *Considerations on the Propriety of Imposing Taxes on the British Colonies* was the most widely read pamphlet of 1765, expressed the consensus: "The colonies are dependent upon Great Britain, and the supreme authority vested in the king, lords, and commons, may justly be exercised to secure, or preserve their dependence." But, warned Dulany, a condition of "dependence and inferiority" was very different from one of "absolute vassalage and slavery."

Over the next decade, colonial leaders searched for a formula that would let them control their internal affairs, especially taxation, while retaining the many benefits of British rule. But British officials could not compromise on the issue of parliamentary power. Even the harshest British critics of the ministries during the 1760s and 1770s questioned only specific policies, not the principles on which they rested.

In effect, the American rebels wanted British leaders to revise their fundamental understanding of how government worked. That was simply too much to expect.

The effectiveness of Americans' opposition to the Stamp Act rested on more than ideological arguments over parliamentary power. The battle was waged on the streets as well as on the page. The decisive and inventive actions of some colonists during the summer and fall of 1765 gave the resistance its primary force.

5-3d Anti–Stamp Act Demonstrations

In August, the Loyal Nine, a Boston artisans' social club, organized a protest against the Stamp Act. Hoping to show that people of all ranks opposed the act, they approached the leaders of the city's rival laborers' associations, groups of unskilled workers and poor tradesmen based in Boston's North End and South End neighborhoods.

Early on August 14, the demonstrators hung an effigy of Andrew Oliver, the province's stamp distributor, from a tree on Boston Common. The crowds viewing the straw man swelled throughout the day. At dusk, a large group led by about fifty well-dressed tradesmen paraded the effigy around the city and through the Town House, the seat of government. Demonstrators then built a bonfire near Oliver's house and fed the effigy to the flames: a kind of proxy murder. They also broke most of Oliver's windows and threw stones at officials who tried to disperse them. Two days later, Oliver publicly renounced the duties of his office. One Bostonian jubilantly wrote, "I believe people never was more Universally pleased."

Twelve days later, another crowd action—aimed this time at Oliver's brother-in-law, Lieutenant Governor Thomas Hutchinson—drew no praise from Boston's respectable citizens. On the night of August 26, a mob destroyed Hutchinson's elegant townhouse. The lieutenant governor reported that by the next morning, nothing was left of his mansion "but the bare walls and floors." His fine imported furniture was broken to bits, his trees and garden ruined, his valuable library lost. But Hutchinson took some comfort in the fact that the leaders of the resistance "never intended matters should go this length and the people in general express the utmost detestation of this unparalleled outrage."

5-3e Americans' Divergent Interests

The differences between the two Boston crowds of August 1765 exposed divisions that would characterize subsequent protests. Few colonists sided with Britain during the 1760s, but various colonial insurgents had divergent goals. Skilled craftsmen as well as merchants, lawyers, and other educated elites preferred orderly demonstrations centered on political issues. For the city's laborers, by contrast, economic grievances were often paramount. Certainly, their "hellish Fury" as they wrecked Hutchinson's house suggests resentment of his ostentatious display of wealth.

Colonists, like other Britons, had a long tradition of crowd action in which disfranchised people—including women—took to the streets to redress economic grievances. But the Stamp Act controversy for the first time drew ordinary folk into transatlantic politics. Matters that previously had been of

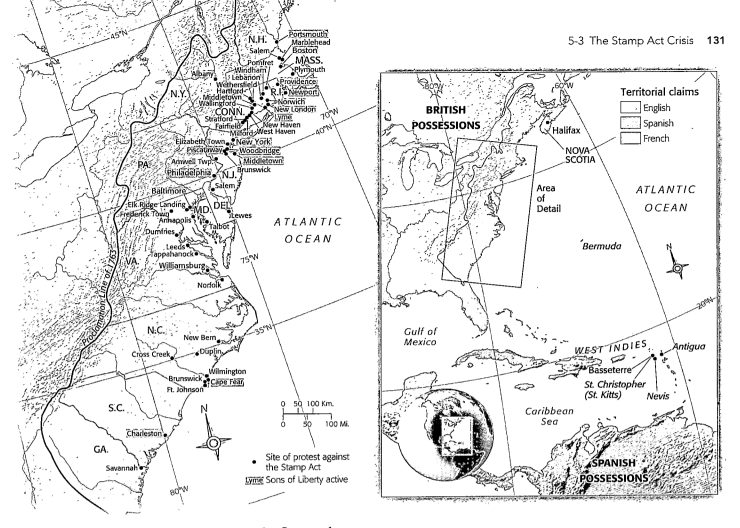

Map 5.3 Colonial Resistance to the Stamp Act

All of the towns and islands labeled on this map witnessed crowd actions protesting the Stamp Act of 1765; British colonies outside the eventual United States joined in the nearly universal opposition to the hated measure.

concern only to an elite few were now discussed in every tavern and coffeehouse. As Benjamin Franklin's daughter told her father, then serving as a colonial agent in London, "nothing else is talked of, the Dutch [Germans] talk of the stompt act the Negroes of the tamp, in short every body has something to say."

Anti–Stamp Act demonstrations took place from Nova Scotia to the West Indies (see Map 5.3). But though the act placed the heaviest tax burden on the Caribbean colonies— levying double or triple duty on large island land transfers, for example—protests there were muted. As on the mainland, West Indian pamphleteers argued for the local imposition of taxes and against their virtual representation in Parliament. But only the Leeward Islands—those most dependent on mainland American merchants for their food—actively resisted the act. Like their counterparts in Massachusetts, rioters in St. Kitts and Nevis burned effigies, torched stamps, and attacked officials' houses. In Montserrat and Antigua, stamp collectors were shunned and the tax largely ignored.

But Jamaica and Barbados, the largest, most populous, and richest islands, complied with the tax. Since the wealthiest sugar planters were sojourners more than settlers, they had strong personal ties to Britain. They also depended on mercantilist legislation to favor their sugar exports over the cheaper French

product. Finally, they relied upon British military might to protect them from the enslaved workforces whose labor made them both obscenely rich and acutely vulnerable. Slaveholders who comprised a tiny ruling minority amidst an enormous enslaved African population saw British troops as a bulwark of liberty, not a threat to it. In such circumstances, abstract principle seemed less important than self-interest. "The Privilege of being taxed by our immediate Representatives, is indeed a most valuable one," supposed one pamphleteer in Barbados. But that privilege was enjoyed by "a very small, not a tenth Part of the People." American provincials were not among those lucky few, yet they were "connected with the Mother Country in point of Interest," and thus well enough represented. The planters grumbled, but they paid the tax. Over three-quarters of the revenues collected during the Stamp Act's brief life came from the West Indies. Jamaica alone paid more stamp duty than the rest of the empire combined.

On the mainland, street protests were so successful that by November 1, when the law was scheduled to take effect, not one stamp distributor was willing to enforce the act. But the entry of unskilled workers, slaves, and women into the realm of imperial politics both aided and troubled the elite men who wanted to mount effective opposition to British measures.

Δ This British cartoon, called "The repeal, or the funeral procession of Miss Americ-Stamp," satirizes the death of Parliament's attempt to tax the colonies via stamped paper. George Grenville, who carries the small wooden coffin holding the repealed act, looks crestfallen, as do the politicians processing behind him. The merchants who owned the warehouses full of goods at the right of the frame would have been overjoyed by the repeal and the attendant boost to transatlantic trade.

Crowd action clearly had a stunning impact. Yet wealthy men recognized that mobs composed of the formerly powerless—whose goals were rarely identical to their own—posed a threat in their own right. What would happen, they wondered, if the "hellish Fury" of the crowd turned against them?

5-3f Sons of Liberty

Elites attempted to channel resistance into acceptable forms by creating an intercolonial association, the **Sons of Liberty.** New Yorkers organized the first such group in early November 1765, and groups emerged rapidly in other coastal cities, eventually coordinating their actions. By early 1766, the Sons of Liberty, composed of merchants, lawyers, and prosperous tradesmen, linked protest leaders from Charleston, South Carolina, to Portsmouth, New Hampshire. The central role of taverns in the exchange of news and opinions makes it unsurprising that a considerable number of members owned taverns.

The Sons of Liberty could influence events but not control them. In Charleston (formerly Charles Town) in October 1765, a crowd shouting, "Liberty Liberty and stamp'd paper" forced the resignation of the South Carolina stamp distributor. The subsequent victory celebration—the largest demonstration the city had ever known—featured a British flag emblazoned with the word "Liberty." But the Charleston Sons of Liberty were horrified when in January 1766 local slaves paraded through the streets similarly proclaiming, "Liberty!" Freedom from slavery was the last thing elite slave owners had in mind, but the language of liberty could easily slip its channels.

Sons of Liberty Groups formed in many colonial port cities to resist the Stamp Act.

No Sons of Liberty chapters emerged in the West Indies. Indeed, mainland Sons groups organized protests against Caribbean colonists as well as British officials. The *Boston Gazette* called on merchants to boycott "the SLAVISH Islands of Barbados and Antigua—Poor, mean spirited, Cowardly, Dastardly Creoles." The sugar islands should receive no "Fresh or Salt Provisions from any Son of LIBERTY on the Continent." Such starvation tactics may only have deepened the rift between continental and Caribbean British Americans.

5-3g Opposition and Repeal

During the fall and winter of 1765–1766, opponents of the Stamp Act pursued several different strategies. Colonial legislatures petitioned Parliament to repeal the hated law, and courts closed because they could not obtain the stamps now required for all legal documents. In October, nine mainland colonies sent delegates to New York to attend a general congress, the first since the Albany Congress of 1754. The Stamp Act Congress met to draft a remonstrance stressing the law's adverse economic effects. At the same time, the Sons of Liberty held mass meetings, rallying public support for the resistance movement. Finally, American merchants organized nonimportation associations to pressure British exporters by refusing to buy their goods. By the 1760s, one-quarter of all British exports went to the colonies, and colonial merchants reasoned that London merchants whose sales suffered from their boycotts would lobby for repeal. Because times were bad and fewer customers were buying imported goods anyway, a general moratorium on future purchases would also help colonial merchants reduce their bloated inventories.

Writing and Stationery Supplies

In the seventeenth century, colonists stressed the importance of teaching children to read the Bible; writing was not seen as nearly so necessary, and many who could read never learned to write. Yet as the eighteenth century progressed, and especially during the era of the American Revolution, writing skills acquired heightened significance. Family members parted by the war needed to communicate with each other, and new opportunities arose for merchants who could deal with distant correspondents. Such experiences led Americans to place increased emphasis on teaching youngsters to write as well as to read.

Most books were either imported from England or printed in the colonies (and later the new United States), but writing drew on a wide range of items from around the world. Paper was either imported from Britain or manufactured at an increasing number of American paper mills; more than thirty were built between 1750 and 1780. The quill pens (goose feathers) that Americans used as writing implements often originated in Germany or Holland. The feathers would be heated to remove fat and to harden their points before they were shipped by the thousands across the Atlantic. Penknives, needed to sharpen blunt quills, and inkpots (typically made of brass, glass, or pewter), largely came from Britain. But the Americans could not write readily without additional items obtained from international trade.

For example, to absorb ink properly, paper needed to be treated with pounce, a powder made from a combination of gum sandarac (a tree resin from North Africa) and pumice, a powdered volcanic glass. Lacking envelopes, eighteenth-century writers folded their sheets of paper, addressed them on the outside, and sealed them with wax made in Holland or Britain from a combination of lac (a resinous secretion of insects, still used today for shellac) from India and cinnabar, a red quartz-like crystal, from Spain. Ink was compounded from a set of diverse ingredients: oak galls from Aleppo (in Syria), gum arabic (sap from acacia trees) from Sudan, and alum and copperas (derived from different stones) from Britain. Most ink was shipped from Britain in powdered form; in America, another key ingredient, urine, would be added to blend the alum with the other substances to create the liquid ink. (Printers' shops famously reeked of piss.) Merchants who sold such supplies sometimes touted the virtues of the "Best Dutch Sealing Wax" or "Aleppo ink" they stocked.

When colonial elites drafted petitions to remonstrate against the Stamp Act that taxed their printed materials, the implements they employed connected them to a long commercial chain stretching to Great Britain, the European continent, North Africa, and the Middle East.

CRITICAL THINKING

◻ For their writing materials, American colonists depended on many products they obtained through international trade. How else was their literary culture dependent upon international imports?

Desk and Bookcase, c.1762 (mahogany, white cedar, yellow poplar, yellow pine, silvered glass & gilded brass)/American School, (18th century)/PHILADELPHIA MUSEUM OF ART/Philadelphia Museum of Art, Pennsylvania, PA, USA/Bridgeman Images

◁ This writing desk, made in Pennsylvania in the mid-to-late eighteenth century, would have been owned by a well-to-do family from the mid-Atlantic states. The pigeonholes would hold incoming and outgoing letters; the many drawers could store paper, ink, seals and sealing wax, and other supplies. The new importance of writing thus produced a perceived need for novel types of furniture.

In March 1766, Parliament repealed the Stamp Act. The nonimportation agreements had indeed created allies for the colonies among wealthy London merchants. But boycotts, petitions, and crowd actions were less important in winning repeal than was the appointment of a new prime minister, chosen by George III for reasons unrelated to colonial politics. Lord Rockingham, who replaced Grenville in the summer of 1765, had opposed the Stamp Act, not because he believed Parliament lacked authority to tax the colonies, but because he thought the law needlessly divisive. Although Rockingham championed repeal, he linked it to passage of a **Declaratory Act**, which asserted Parliament's authority to tax and legislate for Britain's American possessions "in all cases whatsoever."

That spring, crown officials of the provinces waited anxiously as rumors of repeal swirled. "Thinking Men know not which will bring most danger, a Repeal or a Confirmation," Massachusetts Governor Francis Bernard wrote. Upholding the act would "make the People mad with desperation." But repeal, he worried, would make the rebels "insolent with Success."

Bernard's concerns proved prophetic. News of the repeal reached New England in late April, and the Sons of Liberty quickly dispatched messengers to carry the welcome tidings throughout the mainland colonies. They organized celebrations commemorating the glorious event and Americans' loyalty to Britain. Their goal achieved, the Sons of Liberty dissolved. Few colonists yet saw the ominous implications of the Declaratory Act.

5-4 Resistance to the Townshend Acts

▷ How did the Townshend Acts differ from earlier parliamentary acts?

▷ How did individual colonies and colonists begin to join forces in protesting the Townshend Acts?

In the summer of 1766, another change in the ministry in London revealed how fragile the colonists' victory had been. The new prime minister, William Pitt, had fostered cooperation between the colonies and Britain during the Seven Years' War. But Pitt fell ill, and Charles Townshend became the dominant force in the ministry. An ally of Grenville and a supporter of colonial taxation, Townshend decided to try again to obtain badly needed funds from Britain's American possessions (see Table 5.1).

The duties Townshend proposed in 1767 would be levied on trade goods like paper, glass, and tea, extending the existing Navigation Acts. But the Townshend duties differed from previous customs levies in two ways. First, they applied to items imported into the colonies from Britain, rather than

---

Declaratory Act Affirmed parliamentary power to legislate its colonies "in all cases whatsoever."

Table 5.1 British Ministries and Their American Policies

Head of Ministry	Major Acts
George Grenville	Sugar Act (1764)
	Currency Act (1764)
	Stamp Act (1765)
Lord Rockingham	Stamp Act repealed (1766)
	Declaratory Act (1766)
William Pitt/Charles Townshend	Townshend Acts (1767)
Lord North	Townshend duties (except for tea tax) repealed (1770)
	Tea Act (1773)
	Coercive Acts (1774)
	Quebec Act (1774)

to those from foreign countries. Accordingly, they violated mercantilist theory. Second, the revenues would be used to pay some provincial officials. Assemblies would no longer be able to threaten to withhold salaries in order to win those officials' cooperation. Townshend's scheme also established an American Board of Customs Commissioners and created vice-admiralty courts at Boston, Philadelphia, and Charleston. Those moves angered merchants, whose profits would be threatened by more vigorous enforcement of the Navigation Acts. Significantly, Townshend exempted the West Indies from key provisions of the new duties, a divide-and-conquer tactic revealing that Parliament had learned from the Stamp Act protests.

5-4a John Dickinson's *Letters*

The passage of the Townshend Acts drew a quick response. One series of essays in particular, *Letters from a Farmer in Pennsylvania*, by the prominent lawyer John Dickinson, expressed a broad consensus. All but four mainland newspapers reprinted Dickinson's essays; in pamphlet form, they went through seven American editions. Dickinson contended that Parliament could regulate colonial trade but could not use that power to raise revenue. By distinguishing between regulation and taxation—or "external" and "internal" taxes—Dickinson avoided the sticky issue of Parliament's authority. But his argument created an equally knotty problem, suggesting the colonies should assess Parliament's motives in passing any law pertaining to trade before deciding whether to obey it.

The Massachusetts assembly responded to the Townshend Acts by drafting a letter to the other colonial legislatures, suggesting a joint protest petition. What ultimately united the mainland colonies, however, was less the letter itself than the ministry's reaction to it. When Lord Hillsborough, recently named to the new post of secretary of state for America, learned of the Massachusetts circular letter, he ordered the colony's governor, Francis Bernard, to demand that the assembly recall it. He also directed other governors to prevent their assemblies from discussing the letter. Hillsborough's order gave colonial assemblies an incentive to join forces. In late 1768, the Massachusetts legislature rejected Bernard's recall order by a vote of 92 to 17. Bernard dissolved the assembly in response, and other governors followed suit when their legislatures debated the Massachusetts circular letter.

5-4b Rituals of Resistance

The number of votes cast against recalling the circular letter—92—assumed ritual significance in the resistance movement. The number 45 already had symbolic meaning because **John Wilkes**, a radical Londoner sympathetic to the American cause, had been jailed for publishing a pamphlet entitled *The North Briton*, No. 45. In Boston, the silversmith Paul Revere made a punchbowl weighing 45 ounces that held 45 gills (half-cups) and was engraved with the names of the "glorious 92" opposition legislators; James Otis, John Adams, and others publicly drank 45 toasts from it. In Charleston, tradesmen decorated a tree with 45 lights and set off 45 rockets. They adjourned to a tavern where 45 tables were set with 45 bowls of wine, 45 bowls of punch, and 92 glasses.

Such rituals served important political functions. Just as pamphlets by Otis, Dulany, Dickinson, and others acquainted literate colonists with the philosophical issues raised by British actions, so public rituals enlisted common people in the argument. Boston's Sons of Liberty invited hundreds of city residents to dine with them each August 14 to commemorate the first Stamp Act demonstration. Songs supporting the American cause also helped to spread the word.

The Sons of Liberty and other resistance leaders made a deliberate effort to involve ordinary folk in the campaign against the Townshend duties. They urged colonists of all ranks and both sexes to sign agreements not to purchase or consume British products. The consumer revolution that had previously linked colonists culturally and economically now linked them politically as well, supplying them with a ready method of displaying their allegiance. As "A Tradesman" wrote in a Philadelphia paper in 1770, it was essential "for the Good of the Whole, to strengthen the Hands of the Patriotic Majority, by agreeing not to purchase British Goods."

5-4c Daughters of Liberty

As the primary purchasers of textiles and household goods, women played a central role in the nonconsumption movement. More than three hundred Boston matrons publicly promised not to buy or drink tea, "Sickness excepted." The women of Wilmington, North Carolina, burned their tea after walking through town in a solemn procession. Throughout the colonies, women exchanged recipes for tea substitutes

or drank coffee instead. The best known of the protests, the so-called Edenton Ladies Tea Party, had little to do with tea. It was a meeting of prominent North Carolina women who pledged formally to work for the public good and to support resistance to British measures.

Women also encouraged home manufacturing. In many towns, young women calling themselves Daughters of Liberty met to spin in public squares to encourage colonists to end the colonies' dependence on British cloth by wearing homespun. These symbolic displays of patriotism—publicized by newspapers and broadsides—served the same purpose as the male rituals involving the numbers 45 and 92. When young ladies from well-to-do families sat outdoors at spinning wheels all day, eating only American food, drinking local herbal tea, and listening to patriotic sermons, they served as political instructors. Many women took great satisfaction in their newfound role. When a satirist hinted that women discussed only "such triffling subjects as Dress, Scandal and Detraction" during their spinning bees, three Boston women replied angrily, "Inferior in abusive sarcasm, in personal invective, in low wit, we glory to be, but inferior in veracity, sincerity, love of virtue, of liberty and of our country, we would not willingly be to any."

5-4d Divided Opinion over Boycotts

Colonists were by no means united in support of nonimportation and nonconsumption. The Stamp Act boycotts had helped to revive a depressed economy by creating a demand for local products and reducing merchants' inventories. But by 1768 and 1769, merchants were again enjoying boom times and had no financial incentive to support a boycott. Many signed the agreements reluctantly and violated them flagrantly. In contrast, artisans supported nonimportation enthusiastically, recognizing that the absence of British goods would increase demand for their own manufactures. Tradesmen formed the core of the crowds that picketed importers' stores, publicized offending merchants' names in the press, and sometimes destroyed their property.

Such tactics were effective: colonial imports from England dropped dramatically in 1769, especially in New York, New England, and Pennsylvania. But the pressure exerted by the rebels also aroused heated opposition. Even some Americans who supported resistance to British measures began to question the use of violence to enforce the boycott. In addition, the threat to private property inherent in the campaign frightened wealthier men and women. Political activism by ordinary colonists challenged the ruling elite's domination, just as its members had feared in 1765.

Colonists were relieved when news arrived in April 1770 that the Townshend duties had been repealed, with the exception of the tax on tea. A new prime minister, Lord North, persuaded Parliament that duties on trade within the empire

John Wilkes British Whig politician and frequent opponent of King George III who became a hero to American colonists.

◁ In 1775, an English cartoonist satirized American women's involvement in the resistance movement by depicting the women of Edenton, North Carolina, as grotesque, flirtatious figures who neglected their responsibilities as mothers when they dared to enter the political arena. In the background, he showed them discarding their tea.

Library of Congress Prints and Photographs Division Washington, D.C. [LC-US262-12711]

were ill advised. Although some argued that nonimportation should continue until the tea tax was rolled back, merchants quickly resumed importing.

5-5 Confrontations in Boston

▶ What were the origins of the "Boston Massacre"?

▶ How did patriot organizers use the "Boston Massacre" as evidence of the oppression of American colonists?

▶ How did the emergence of Committees of Correspondence alter the resistance movement?

On the very day Lord North proposed repeal of the Townshend duties—news the colonists would learn weeks later—a confrontation between Boston civilians and British soldiers led to five Americans' deaths. The seeds of the event that patriots labeled the "Boston Massacre" were planted years before, when Parliament decided to base the American Board of Customs Commissioners in Boston.

Mobs had targeted the customs officials from the day they arrived in November 1767. In June 1768, their seizure of the patriot leader John Hancock's sloop *Liberty* on suspicion of smuggling caused a riot. The riot in turn helped to convince

Boston Massacre Confrontation between colonists and British troops in which five colonists were shot and killed.

the ministry that troops were needed to maintain order in the unruly port. That October, two regiments of British regulars—about 700 men—marched up Long Wharf toward the Common, "with muskets charged, bayonets fixed, colours flying, [and] drums beating," the *Boston Evening Post* reported. These "lobster-backs," as Bostonians called the red-coated soldiers, served as constant visible reminders of the oppressive potential of British power. Patrols roamed the streets at all hours, questioning and sometimes harassing passersby. Parents feared for the safety of their daughters, whom soldiers subjected to coarse sexual insults. But the greatest potential for violence lay in the uneasy relationship between the troops and Boston laborers. Many redcoats sought employment in their off-duty hours, competing for unskilled jobs with the city's workingmen. Members of the two groups brawled repeatedly in taverns and on the streets.

5-5a Boston Massacre

On the evening of March 5, 1770, a crowd of laborers began throwing hard-packed snowballs at troops guarding the Customs House. Goaded beyond endurance, the sentries ignored their orders and fired on the crowd, killing four and wounding eight, one of whom died a few days later. Reportedly, the first to fall was Crispus Attucks, a sailor of mixed Nipmuck and African ancestry. Rebel leaders idealized Attucks and the other dead rioters as martyrs for liberty, holding a solemn funeral and later commemorating March 5 with patriotic orations. Paul Revere's engraving entitled "The Bloody

Massacre Perpetrated in King Street," which Revere pirated from a rival image by Henry Pelham) was part of a hugely effective propaganda campaign by the rebels. "The prints exhibited in our houses have added wings to fancy; and in the fervour of our zeal, reason is in hazard of being lost," warned Samuel Quincy, the colony's solicitor general, who prosecuted the officer in charge at the time of the massacre.

As the trials unfolded that fall, cool reason carried the day. John Adams and Josiah Quincy Jr., both unwavering patriots, acted as the soldiers' defense attorneys. Almost all the accused were acquitted, and the two men convicted were released after being branded on the thumb.

5-5b A British Plot?

The outcome of the soldiers' trials persuaded London officials not to retaliate against Boston. For more than two years after the massacre, the imperial crisis seemed to quiet. But the most outspoken newspapers, including the *Boston Gazette* (which British officials called the "Weekly Dung Barge"), continued to accuse Great Britain of scheming to oppress Americans. After the Stamp Act's repeal, the protest leaders had praised

Parliament; following repeal of the Townshend duties, they warned of impending tyranny. What had seemed

Committee of Correspondence Local committees established throughout colonies to coordinate anti-British actions.

to be a single ill-chosen stamp tax now appeared part of a coordinated plot against American liberties. Essayists pointed to the stationing of troops in Boston, and the growing number of vice-admiralty courts as evidence of plans to enslave the colonists. Indeed, patriot writers played repeatedly on the word *enslavement*—though they rarely questioned the institution of race-based chattel slavery, as James Otis had done in 1764.

Still, almost no one advocated American independence. Although some colonists were becoming convinced that they should seek freedom from parliamentary authority, they continued to trumpet their British liberties and to acknowledge their allegiance to George III. But they began to envision a system that would enable them to be ruled by their own elected legislatures while remaining subordinate to the king. Of course, any such scheme violated Britons' conception of the nature of government, which accepted Parliament's sole, undivided sovereignty. Furthermore, in the British mind, Parliament encompassed the king as well as lords and commons; separating the monarch from the legislature was impossible.

Then, in the fall of 1772, the North ministry began to implement the Townshend Act that provided for governors and judges to be paid from customs revenues. In early November, voters at a Boston town meeting established a **Committee of Correspondence** to publicize the decision by exchanging letters with other Massachusetts towns.

△ Offering visual support for the patriots' version of events, Henry Pelham rushed this drawing into print in April 1770. Entitled "The Fruits of Arbitrary Power," the engraving depicted British soldiers firing on an unresisting crowd, instead of the aggressive mob described at the soldiers' trials. Pelham anticipated economic as well as political success from the image, and was furious when Paul Revere copied his drawing and beat him to market.

△ Shortly after the Boston Massacre, Paul Revere pirated this illustration of the confrontation near the Customs House from Pelham's version, adding inflammatory details such as a gun firing from a nearby building, which he labeled "Butcher's Hall." He replaced Pelham's quotation from Psalms with a sensationalized doggerel verse about the events of March 5, 1770. Both engravings call the chaotic events a "Bloody Massacre."

Phillis Wheatley, Enslaved Poet in the Cradle of Liberty

In July 1761, the *Phillis* docked at Boston's Long Wharf after a long voyage during which nearly a quarter of its human cargo died. The captain placed an advertisement in the papers hawking "prime young SLAVES, from the Windward Coast." One of the least valuable among them was a little girl still missing her two front teeth. A merchant named John Wheatley purchased her as a gift for his wife, naming the child after the boat that brought her from Africa.

Phillis Wheatley grew up in a genteel house on King Street, part of a prosperous family that included at least one other slave. The Wheatleys, influenced by the ideas of the Great Awakening, recognized her talents and educated her beyond the station of nearly all slaves and, indeed, of most white girls and women. At a young age, she began to write poetry. In 1770, several months after the Boston Massacre took place just steps from the Wheatley mansion, Phillis's elegy on the death of George Whitefield made her famous on both sides of the Atlantic. In 1773, as the crisis over tea engrossed Boston, a volume of her poems was published in London.

Wheatley's *Poems on Various Subjects* included an "elegant engraved likeness of the Author." In an era when books seldom featured portraits of female authors and almost never bore the likenesses of people of African descent, Wheatley's image—probably based on a painting by the black Boston artist Scipio Moorhead—is a striking exception.

CRITICAL THINKING

- What attributes does the portrait give the poet?
- How do the title page and the frontispiece depict her race, age, gender, and genius?

△ Wheatley frontispiece

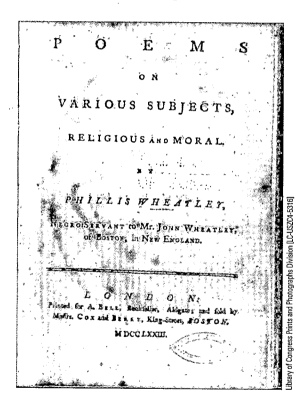

△ Wheatley title page

Heading the committee was Samuel Adams, who had proposed its formation.

5-5c Samuel Adams and Committees of Correspondence

Aged fifty-one in 1772, Samuel Adams was about a decade older than other leaders of American resistance, including his distant cousin John. The Harvard-educated son of a wealthy maltster, he had been a Boston tax collector, a clerk of the Massachusetts assembly, and one of the Sons of Liberty. Adams drew a sharp contrast between a corrupt, vice-riddled Britain and the simple, liberty-loving folk of the mainland colonies. His Committee of Correspondence undertook the task of creating consensus among the residents of Massachusetts.

Such committees, which were eventually established throughout the colonies, opened a new chapter in the American resistance. Until 1772, the protest movement was confined almost entirely to the mainland, largely to the seacoast, and primarily to major cities and towns (see Map 5.3). An experienced political organizer, Adams sought to involve more colonists in the struggle. Accordingly, the Boston town meeting directed the Committee of Correspondence to send copies of its report to other towns in the province.

The statement prepared by the Boston Committee declared, "All persons born in the British American Colonies" had natural rights to life, liberty, and property. The idea that "a British house of Commons, should have a right, at pleasure, to give and grant the property of the colonists" was "irreconcilable" with "natural law and Justice" and with "the British Constitution." Their grievances included taxation without representation, the increased presence of troops and customs officers on American soil, the expanded jurisdiction of vice-admiralty courts, and the nature of the instructions given to American governors by their superiors in London. The document exhibited none of the hesitation that had characterized colonial claims in the mid-1760s. No longer were resistance leaders—at least in Boston—preoccupied with defining the limits of parliamentary authority. No longer did they mention the necessity of obedience to Parliament. They placed colonial rights first, loyalty to Britain a distant second.

The responses to the committee's pamphlet confirmed this shift in thinking. Some towns disagreed with Boston's assessment, but most aligned themselves with the city. The town of Holden declared, "the People of New England have never given the People of Britain any Right of Jurisdiction over us." Pownallborough warned, "Allegiance is a relative Term and like Kingdoms and commonwealths is local and has its bounds."

5-6 Tea and Turmoil

▷ **How did Parliament respond to Boston's reaction against the Tea Act?**

The tea tax was the only Townshend duty still in effect by 1773. In the years after 1770, some Americans had continued to boycott English tea, while many resumed drinking it. Tea figured prominently in both the colonists' diet and their cultures, so observing the boycott required them not only to forgo a favorite beverage but also to alter their everyday rituals. Tea thus retained an explosively symbolic character even after the boycott began to disintegrate.

5-6a Reactions to the Tea Act

In May 1773, Parliament passed an act designed to save the East India Company from bankruptcy. The company, which held a monopoly on British trade with the East Indies, was vital to the British economy and to the

prosperity of many British politicians who invested in its stock. According to the **Tea Act**, tea would be sold in America only by agents of the East India Company. This would enable the company to avoid intermediaries in Britain and the colonies, and thus to price its tea competitively with that sold by smugglers. The net result would be cheaper tea for American consumers. But since the less expensive tea would still be taxed under the Townshend law, resistance leaders interpreted the new measure as another attempt to make them admit Parliament's right to tax them. Others saw the Tea Act as the first step in creating an East India Company monopoly on colonial trade. Residents of the four cities designated to receive the first shipments of tea accordingly prepared to respond to this perceived new threat to their freedom.

A tea ship sent to New York City never arrived. In Philadelphia, Pennsylvania's governor persuaded the captain to sail back to Britain. Tea bound for Charleston was unloaded and stored there; some was destroyed, and the rest was later sold by the new state government. The only confrontation occurred in Boston.

The first of three tea ships, the *Dartmouth*, entered Boston harbor on November 28. Customs laws required cargo to be landed and the appropriate duty paid by its owners within twenty days of a ship's arrival; otherwise, customs officers would seize the cargo. After a series of mass meetings, Bostonians voted to post guards on the wharf to prevent the tea from being unloaded. Hutchinson refused to permit the vessels to leave the harbor. On December 16, a day before the cargo was to be confiscated, more than five thousand people crowded into Old South Church. The meeting, chaired by Samuel Adams, made a final attempt to convince Hutchinson to return the tea to England. (The merchants who had consigned the tea had long since refused to do so.) But the governor remained adamant. In the early evening Adams reportedly announced "that they had now done all they could for the Salvation of their Country." Cries rang out from the crowd: "Boston harbor a tea-pot tonight! The Mohawks are come!" Within a few minutes, about sixty men—merchants and doctors as well as Boston artisans and country farmers—crudely disguised as Native men assembled at the wharf. Moving quickly, they boarded the three ships and dumped their cargo into the harbor. By 9:00 P.M., 342 chests of tea worth approximately £10,000 floated in splinters. John Adams praised the crowd's action. "There is a Dignity, a Majesty, a Sublimity in this last Effort of the Patriots, that I greatly admire," he wrote in his diary. "This Destruction of the Tea is so bold, so daring, so firm, intrepid and inflexible, and it must have so important Consequences, and so lasting, that I cant but consider it as an Epocha in History." He also recognized the violence of the moment, noting that "Many Persons wish, that as many dead Carcasses were floating in the Harbour, as there are Chests of Tea."

Tea Act England's attempt to bail out the East India Company that heightened tensions between the British and the colonies.

5-6b Coercive, or Intolerable Acts and the Quebec Act

The North administration reacted with outrage when it learned of the events in Boston. In March 1774, Parliament adopted the first of four laws that colonists referred to as the **Coercive, or Intolerable, Acts**. It ordered the port of Boston closed until the tea was paid for, prohibiting all but coastal trade in food and firewood. Later that spring, Parliament passed three other punitive measures. The Massachusetts Government Act altered the province's charter, substituting an appointed council for the elected one, increasing the governor's powers, and forbidding most town meetings. The Justice Act allowed a person accused of committing murder in the course of suppressing a riot or enforcing the laws to be tried outside the colony where the incident had occurred. Finally, the Quartering Act permitted military officers to commandeer privately owned buildings to house their troops. The Coercive Acts punished not only Boston but also Massachusetts as a whole, alerting other colonies to the possibility that their residents, too, might face retaliation if they opposed British authority.

Parliament next turned its attention to much-needed reforms in the government of Quebec. The Quebec Act became linked with the Coercive Acts in the minds of the colonial insurgents. Intended to ease strains that had arisen since the British conquest of the formerly French colony, the Quebec Act granted greater religious freedom to Catholics, alarming Protestant colonists who equated the Church of Rome with despotism. In an attempt to provide northern Indians with some protection against Anglo-American settlement, the act also annexed to Quebec the area west of the Appalachians, east of the Mississippi River, and north of the Ohio River. That region, still with few European inhabitants, was thus removed from the jurisdiction of the seacoast colonies. The wealthy speculators who hoped to develop the Ohio Country to attract additional settlers would now have to deal with officials in Quebec.

Members of Parliament who supported the punitive legislation believed they had finally solved the American problem. But resistance leaders saw the Coercive Acts and the Quebec Act as proof of what they had long feared: that Britain had embarked on a deliberate plan to oppress them. If the port of Boston could be closed, why not the ports of Philadelphia or New York? If the royal charter of Massachusetts could be changed, why not the charter of South Carolina? If certain suspects could be tried in distant locations, why not any violator of any law? If troops could be forcibly quartered in private houses, did that not portend the occupation of all America? If the Catholic Church could receive protection in Quebec, why not everywhere? It seemed as though the plot against American rights and liberties had at last been laid bare.

The Boston Committee of Correspondence urged all colonies to join an immediate boycott of British goods. But other provinces hesitated to take such a drastic step. In the West Indies, even opponents of Parliament's evolving American policy thought the "Boston firebrands" had gone too far and hoped the Coercive Acts might restore order. Rhode Island, Virginia, and Pennsylvania each suggested convening another intercolonial congress like the one that had followed the Stamp Act. Few people wanted to take hasty action; even the most ardent patriots remained loyal Britons and hoped for reconciliation. So the colonies agreed to send delegates to Philadelphia in September to attend a Continental Congress.

5-7 The Unsettled Backcountry

▶ **What disputes emerged between elites and common folk during the imperial crisis?**

▶ **How did these internal struggles develop during the imperial crisis?**

In the same years that residents of British North America wrestled over deepening divisions between the colonies and the mother country, they confronted divisions *within* colonial society. For a century, historians have debated the relative importance of struggles over home rule—the imperial crisis—and battles over who should rule at home—social crises within the colonies—to the coming of the Revolution. Rifts between elites and common folk were visible everywhere in the mainland and island colonies: between merchants and the laboring poor in the cities, between tenants and landlords in the backcountry, between slaves and planters in the South and the Caribbean. Along the western edges of British settlement in the 1760s and 1770s, these internal struggles sometimes verged on civil war.

5-7a Land Riots in the North

By midcentury, most of the fertile land east of the Appalachians had been purchased—sometimes fraudulently—or occupied—often illegally. Conflicts over land grew in number and frequency. As early as 1746, some New Jersey farmers clashed violently with agents of the East Jersey proprietors, who claimed the farmers' land and demanded annual payments for the use of the property. Similar violence occurred in the 1760s in the region that later became Vermont.

The most serious land riots took place along the Hudson River in 1765–1766. Late in the seventeenth century, the governor of New York had granted huge tracts in the lower Hudson Valley to prominent families. The proprietors in turn divided these estates into small farms, which they rented to

Coercive, or Intolerable, Acts A series of restrictive laws comprised of the Boston Port Bill, the Massachusetts Government Act, the Justice Act, the Quartering Act, plus the subsequent Quebec Act. Intended by the British Parliament to primarily punish Massachusetts, the acts instead pushed most colonies to the brink of rebellion.

poor Dutch and German migrants who saw tenancy as a step on the road to independent freeholder status. But in the eighteenth century, newcomers from New England and Europe resisted this tenancy system. Many squatted on vacant portions of great estates, rejecting attempts to evict them. In the mid-1760s, the Philipse family sued farmers who had lived on Philipse land for two decades. The courts upheld the landlords' claim, ordering the squatters to make way for tenants with valid leases. A diverse group of farmers rebelled, terrorizing proprietors and loyal tenants, freeing their friends from jail, and on one occasion battling a county sheriff and his posse. The rebellion lasted nearly a year, ending only when British troops captured its leaders.

Such clashes increased in intensity and frequency after the Seven Years' War. Ignoring the Proclamation of 1763, pronouncements by colonial governors, and the threat of Native attacks, land-hungry folk—many of them recent immigrants from Ireland or soldiers who demobilized after the war—swarmed into the Ohio River valley. Sometimes, they purchased property from opportunists with grants of dubious origin; often, they simply claimed land, squatting in hopes that their titles would eventually be honored. Britain's 1771 decision to abandon (and raze) Fort Pitt rendered the Proclamation of 1763 unenforceable, and thus removed the final restraints on settlement in the region. By the mid-1770s, thousands of new homesteads dotted the backcountry from western Pennsylvania south through Virginia and eastern Kentucky into western North Carolina. Their presence provoked confrontations with eastern landowners and Native peoples alike.

5-7b "Regulators" in the South

The Regulator movements of the late 1760s and early 1770s pitted backcountry farmers in the Carolinas against wealthy eastern planters who controlled the colonial governments. In South Carolina, Scots-Irish settlers protested their lack of an adequate voice in colonial political affairs. For months, they policed the countryside in vigilante bands known as Regulators, complaining of lax and biased law enforcement. North Carolina Regulators objected primarily to heavy taxation by the colonial legislature. In 1769, they seated men who held their views in the provincial assembly. The backcountry legislators proposed more equitable tax policies and greater freedom from the established Anglican Church. But their grievances were soon sidelined by battles over the Townshend duties. In September 1770, the Regulators took vigilante action, dragging a justice from the Rowan County Courthouse and then ransacking his home. In form, the crowd's action echoed the destruction of Thomas Hutchinson's Boston mansion in 1765. But in content, the farmers' grievances were very different, focused on local inequality rather than imperial tyranny. The following spring, insurrection became war. Several thousand Regulators fought and lost a battle with eastern militiamen at Alamance in May 1771. A month later, six of the insurgents were hanged for treason.

5-7c Renewed Warfare with Native Peoples

In addition to distrusting their wealthy eastern rulers, few of the backcountry folk viewed the region's Native peoples positively. (Rare exceptions were the Moravian missionaries who settled with their Native converts in small frontier communities in the upper Ohio Valley.) The frontier dwellers had little interest in the small-scale trade that had once helped to sustain an uneasy peace in the region; they wanted only land on which to grow crops and pasture their livestock.

In 1774 Virginia, headed by a new royally appointed governor, **Lord Dunmore**, moved vigorously to assert its title to the colony's rapidly developing backcountry. Tensions mounted as Virginians surveyed land on the south side of the Ohio River—territory claimed by the Shawnees. In April, armed settlers attacked a Shawnee canoe carrying women and children as well as one man, murdering and scalping all nine. John Logan, a Mingo leader whose kin died in the attack, gathered warriors to retaliate against frontier settlements. When the governor dispatched some two thousand troops to move against Native villages along the Ohio, these skirmishes escalated into a conflict known as **Lord Dunmore's War**. Delawares, Miamis, Chippewas, and Wyandots allied with the Shawnee, and fighting continued throughout the summer. When the peace was settled in October, the Shawnee leader Cornstalk ceded the enormous territory that became the state of Kentucky to Dunmore's forces. Thousands of settlers then flooded across the mountains.

5-8 Government by Congress and Committee

▶ What did it mean to be "American" on the eve of the First Continental Congress?

▷ What tasks did the First Continental Congress complete?

▶ How did the First Continental Congress encourage and facilitate shared resistance to parliamentary actions by many of the seaboard colonies?

In the summer of 1774, while the Virginia backcountry bled and Boston suffered, fifty-six delegates from twelve very different mainland colonies readied for a "Grand Continental Congress" in Philadelphia. Because colonial governors had forbidden regular assemblies to conduct formal elections, most of the delegates had been chosen

Lord Dunmore Royal governor of Virginia who promised freedom to the slaves of rebel owners who fought to restore royal authority.

Lord Dunmore's War Confrontation between Virginians and the Shawnee people in 1774. During the peace conference that followed, Virginia gained uncontested rights to lands south of the Ohio country in exchange for its claims on the northern side.

by extralegal conventions. Thus the very act of designating representatives to attend the Congress asserted colonial autonomy in defiance of British authority. The lawyer John Adams, one of four delegates from hard-hit Massachusetts, anticipated that the Congress would serve as "a School of Political Prophets I Suppose—a Nursery of American Statesmen."

But what were American statesmen and what, indeed, was America? New England merchants, many of whom were descendants of stringent Puritans, and southern planters, with their slaves and their horse races and their finery, shared little common culture. (One Rhode Islander complained that because "Southern Gentlemen have been used to do no Business in the afternoon," Congress had to adjourn by three o'clock.) So distinct were the interests of the British West Indies that those thirteen colonies sent no official delegates—nor did Georgia. British North America had no capital city but London; until Congress met, more of the delegates had probably visited the English metropolis than had journeyed to Philadelphia. On the road to Pennsylvania, John Adams paused to admire the statue of the king looming over Battery Park in New York City, a town he had never before visited. Even in the fall of 1774, as tavern talk throughout the colonies turned to the imminence of civil war, Great Britain remained the only nation the congressmen shared. They called themselves "the Inhabitants of the English colonies," descendants of "free and natural-born subjects, within the realm of England." They pledged their fealty to George III. They pressed their claims not for American freedom but for "English liberty"; an image of the Magna Carta adorned the journal of their proceedings. "We uphold this, we lean upon this," read the Latin motto around the seal.

5-8a First Continental Congress

The colonies' leading political figures—most of them lawyers, merchants, and planters—attended the Philadelphia Congress. In addition to John Adams, the Massachusetts delegation included his elder cousin Samuel Adams. Among others, New York sent John Jay, a talented young attorney. John Dickinson, author of the homespun *Letters from a Farmer in Pennsylvania*, arrived in Philadelphia in a resplendent coach with four horses. Virginia elected Richard Henry Lee and Patrick Henry, both noted for their patriotic zeal, as well as George Washington. Most of these men had never met, but in the weeks, months, and years that followed they became the chief architects of a new nation.

The congressmen faced three tasks when they convened at Carpenters' Hall. The first two were explicit: defining American grievances and developing a plan for resistance. The third—articulating their constitutional relationship with Great Britain—was less clear-cut and proved nettlesome. The most radical congressmen, like Lee of Virginia, argued that colonists owed allegiance only to George III; Parliament had no legitimate authority over them. The conservatives—Pennsylvania's Joseph

Galloway and his allies—proposed a plan of union that would require Parliament and a new American legislature jointly to consent to laws governing the colonies. After heated debate, delegates narrowly rejected Galloway's proposal, but they were not prepared to embrace the radicals' position either.

Finally, they accepted wording proposed by John Adams. The crucial clauses in the Congress's Declaration of Rights and Grievances asserted that Americans would obey Parliament, but only voluntarily, and that they would resist all measures that were taxes in disguise. Only a few years before, such a position would have seemed radical. By the fall of 1774, it represented a compromise. The Americans had come a long way since the failure of the Albany Plan of Union in 1754, and even since their protests against the Sugar Act ten years later.

5-8b Continental Association

With the constitutional issue resolved, the delegates readily agreed on the laws they wanted repealed (notably the Coercive Acts) and decided to implement an economic boycott while petitioning the king for relief. They adopted fourteen Articles of Association calling for nonimportation of British goods (effective December 1, 1774), nonconsumption of British products (effective March 1, 1775), and nonexportation of American goods to Britain and the British West Indies (effective September 10, 1775).

The Articles of Association (also known as the Continental Association) were designed to appeal to different groups and regions. The nonimportation agreement banned commerce in slaves as well as manufactures, which accorded with a long-standing desire of the Virginia gentry to halt, or at least to slow, the arrival of enslaved Africans on their shores. (Leading Virginians were not opposed to slavery, but rather worried that continuing slave importations discouraged skilled Europeans from immigrating to their colony. They also knew that their enslaved workforce would continue to grow by natural increase.) Delaying nonconsumption for three months after implementing nonimportation gave merchants time to sell off the inventory they had acquired legally. The novel tactic of nonexportation and its postponement for nearly a year served other interests. In 1773, many Virginians had vowed to stop exporting tobacco in order to decrease supply and thus raise prices in a then-glutted market. Now, two years later, they welcomed an association that declared but delayed the export ban, allowing them to profit from higher prices for their current crop. Postponing the nonexportation agreement also benefited northern exporters of wood and foodstuffs to the Caribbean, giving them a final season of sales before the embargo began.

For all these concessions, the Continental Association was far more comprehensive than any previous economic measure adopted by the colonies, and it asked a great deal of the public. "We must change our Habits, our Prejudices, our Palates, our Taste in Dress, Furniture, Equipage, Architecture etc.," John Adams wrote. "Will, Can the People bear a total Interruption of the [We]st India Trade?" fretted one New York delegate. "Can [they] live without Rum, Sugar, and [Mo]lasses?" West Indian grandees worried about more than impatience. Severing their supply lines from North America could mean famine, and famine could provoke widespread slave insurrection. The *Antigua Gazette* chided the mainland colonists for "their folly, madness, and ingratitude" in adopting the new resolutions. "I look at them as dogs that will bark but dare not stand when opposed," wrote one Jamaican sugar planter who hoped Congress would prove "loud in mouth but slow to action."

5-8c Committees of Observation

To enforce the Continental Association, Congress recommended that every mainland locale elect committees of

A New Method of MACARONY MAKING, as practifed at BOSTON.

△ This British cartoon, entitled "A New Method of Macaroni-Making, as Practised at Boston," satirizes the violence of patriot resistance. The practice of tarring and feathering those seen as enemies of American liberty was first recorded in 1766. Incidents multiplied after the Boston Tea Party. By the summer of 1774, vigilante justice against loyalists included many terrifying rituals: horses were poisoned, wives and children harassed. "One person was put in a coffin, and was near buried alive," a Boston customs official wrote.

observation and inspection. By specifying that committee members be chosen by all men qualified to vote for members of the lower houses of assembly, Congress guaranteed the committees a broad popular base. The seven to eight thousand committeemen—some experienced officeholders, some new to politics—became the local leaders of American resistance.

Such committees were officially charged only with overseeing implementation of the boycott, but during the next six months they became de facto governments. They examined merchants' records, publicizing the names of those who continued to import British goods. They promoted home manufactures, encouraging Americans to adopt simple modes of dress and behavior to symbolize their commitment to liberty. Because expensive leisure-time activities were believed to reflect vice and corruption, Congress urged Americans to forgo dancing, gambling, horse racing, card playing, cockfighting, and other forms of "extravagance and dissipation." Some committees extracted apologies from people caught gambling, drinking to excess, or racing. Everywhere, private activities acquired public significance.

The committees gradually extended their authority over many aspects of colonial life. They attempted to root out and sometimes terrorize opponents of American resistance, developed elaborate spy networks, and investigated reports of questionable activities. Suspected dissenters were urged to support the colonial cause publicly; if they refused, the committees had them watched, restricted their movements, or even tried to force them into exile. People engaging in political banter with friends one day could find themselves charged with "treasonable conversation" the next. One Massachusetts man was called before his local committee for maligning the Congress as "a Pack or Parcell of Fools" that was "as tyrannical as Lord North." When he refused to recant, the committee put him under surveillance.

5-8d Provincial Conventions

While the committees of observation expanded their power, the regular colonial governments edged toward collapse. By late 1774, only a few legislatures continued to meet without encountering challenges to their authority. In most colonies, popularly elected provincial conventions took over the task of running the government. In late 1774 and early 1775, these conventions approved the Continental Association, elected delegates to a Second Continental Congress (scheduled for May), organized militia units, and gathered arms and ammunition. British-appointed governors and councils saw their authority crumble. Royal officials suffered repeated humiliation. Courts were prevented from meeting, taxes were paid to convention agents rather than to provincial tax collectors, and militiamen mustered only when committees ordered. During the six months preceding the battles at Lexington and Concord, ordinary Americans forged independence at the local level, without formal acknowledgment and for the most part without bloodshed.

Women's Political Activism

In the twenty-first century, female citizens of the United States participate at every level of American public life. In 1984, Geraldine Ferraro was the Democratic candidate for vice president, the first woman on a major party ticket. In 2007, Nancy Pelosi was elected Speaker of the House, and Senator Hillary Rodham Clinton (D-NY) began her first run for the presidency. A record number of women were elected to the 114th Congress, whose term began in 2015: twenty serve in the Senate, and eighty-four in the House, or nearly 20 percent of each branch of the legislature. Three women currently serve as Supreme Court justices. After her losing presidential bid in 2008, Hillary Clinton was appointed Secretary of State from 2009-2013, and in 2016 accepted the Democratic nomination for president, the first woman to head a major party ticket. Often, the opposition to Clinton's failed bid to "shatter the highest glass ceiling," as she often put it, defaulted gendered stereotypes that would have been familiar to the men assembled in Congress in 1776.

Though the existence of female politicians today would have shocked those "founding fathers," the entrance of American women onto the political stage in some ways links back to the changes of the revolutionary era. Before the 1760s, women were seen as having no legitimate public role. A male essayist expressed the consensus in the mid-1730s: "Governing Kingdoms and Ruling Provinces are Things too difficult and knotty for the fair Sex." But when colonists began to resist British taxes and laws in the 1760s, traditional forms of protest (for example, assemblies' petitions to Parliament) came to seem too limited. Because women made purchasing decisions for American households, and because their labor in spinning and textile manufacture could replace imported clothing, it was vital for them to participate in the cause. For the first time in American history, women began to take formal political stands. Women of all ranks had to decide whether they would join or oppose the movement to boycott British goods. The groups they established to promote home manufactures—dubbed "Daughters of Liberty"—constituted the first American women's political organizations.

By the mid-nineteenth century, women's political involvement would begin to coalesce into a national "woman movement." In 1848, the leaders of a woman's rights convention at Seneca Falls, New York, drafted a Declaration of Sentiments, closely modeled on the language of the Declaration of Independence. The radical Victoria Woodhull, the first woman to run for president, declared her candidacy in 1871.

The legacy of revolutionary-era women for the nation continues today in such diverse groups as Emily's List and Concerned Women for America. Indeed, contemporary Americans would undoubtedly find it impossible to imagine their country without female activists of all political and partisan affiliations.

CRITICAL THINKING

□ Despite great progress in terms of women's involvement in American politics, do vestiges of that consensus of the mid-1730s—the sense that "Governing Kingdoms and Ruling Provinces are Things too difficult and knotty for the fair Sex"—still remain? If so, provide examples.

Living in the muddle of the everyday without the clarity of hindsight, few Americans realized the extent of this political evolution. The vast majority still proclaimed their loyalty to Great Britain, denying that they sought to leave the empire. "Some People must have Time to look around them, before, behind, on the right hand, and on the left, then to think, and after all this to resolve," wrote John Adams in June 1776. "Others see, at one intuitive Glance into the past and the future, and judge with Precision at once. But remember you cant make thirteen Clocks, Strike precisely alike, at the Same Second." Even on the eve of the Declaration of Independence, each of the thirteen rebel colonies moved in its own way and time.

Summary

In 1754, at the outbreak of the Seven Years' War in the Ohio Country, no one could have predicted that the next two decades would bring such dramatic change to Britain's mainland colonies. Yet that conflict simultaneously removed France from North America and created a huge debt that Britain had to find means to pay, developments with major implications for the imperial relationship.

After the war ended in 1763, colonists experienced momentous changes in the ways they imagined themselves and their allegiances. The number who considered themselves political actors increased substantially. Once linked unquestioningly to Great Britain, many mainland colonists began slowly to develop a sense of their shared identity as Americans. They started to realize that their concept of the political process differed from that of people in the mother country, and that they held a different definition of what constituted representation and appropriate consent to government actions. Many also came to understand their economic interests as distinct from those of Great Britain. Colonial political leaders reached such conclusions only after a long train of events, some of them violent.

While many colonists questioned the imperial relationship with Britain, violence in the backcountry revealed persistent divisions *within* American society. From New England to the Carolinas, small western farmers sporadically battled large eastern landowners. In the 1760s and early 1770s, Regulator movements in the Carolinas assumed the proportions of guerilla warfare, as did battles between frontier settlers and displaced Native peoples in Virginia in 1774.

In late 1774, many Americans were committed to resistance but almost none to independence. Even so, they had begun to sever the bonds of empire. Over the next decades, they would forge a new American nationality to replace frayed Anglo-American ties.

Suggestions for Further Reading

Fred Anderson, *The War That Made America: A Short History of the French and Indian War* (2005)

Richard Archer, *As If an Enemy's Country: The British Occupation of Boston and the Origins of Revolution* (2010)

Christopher Leslie Brown, *Moral Capital: Foundations of British Abolitionism* (2006)

Nick Bunker, *An Empire on the Edge: How Britain Came to Fight America* (2014)

Stephen Brumwell, *Redcoats: The British Soldier and War in the Americas, 1755-1763* (2002)

Vincent Caretta, *Phillis Wheatley: Biography of a Genius in Bondage* (2011)

Benjamin H. Irvin, *Clothed in Robes of Sovereignty: The Continental Congress and the People out of Doors* (2011)

Marjoleine Kars, *Breaking Loose Together: The Regulator Rebellion in Pre-Revolutionary North Carolina* (2002)

Andrew Jackson O'Shaughnessy, *An Empire Divided: The American Revolution and the British Caribbean* (2000)

Peter Silver, *Our Savage Neighbors: How Indian War Transformed Early America* (2008)

MINDTAP
From Cengage

MindTap® is a fully online personalized learning experience built upon Cengage Learning content. MindTap® combines student learning tools—readings, multimedia, activities, and assessments—into a singular Learning Path that guides students through the course and helps students develop the critical thinking, analysis, and communication skills that are essential to academic and professional success.

American Revolutions, 1775–1783

The Mohawks knew her as Konwatsitsiaenni, a leader in the Turtle clan. To the British, she was Molly Brant, common-law wife of the continent's most powerful Native American agent, Sir William Johnson. Their union—never formalized by a preacher or a judge—was a diplomatic alliance from which he gained as much as she did. After the Seven Years' War, Molly Brant became the first lady of Mohawk country, one of the busiest trading regions in the Atlantic world. Her power and influence, wrote one British official, was "far superior to that of all their Chiefs put together."

In the 1760s, people of all nations journeyed to Johnson Hall, the English-style manor that Brant shared with Johnson and their growing biracial family. Perched high above the Mohawk River, the house was the nerve center of an estate that stretched for miles. Iroquois diplomats, British officials, Dutch traders, Anglo-American speculators and politicians: all flocked to a place where they might smoke the calumet and drink tea served by African slaves, bury the hatchet and play billiards, and view a collection including English silver and Algonquian wampum. Worlds met and mingled at Johnson Hall, and in Molly Brant. She wore Mohawk dress and refused to speak English; Johnson spoke Mohawk and sometimes painted his face in the manner of Native warriors. Yet Brant and Johnson named four of their eight mixed-race children after British monarchs: Mary, Elizabeth, Anne, and George.

William Johnson died in 1774, on the eve of a war that would destroy the world he and Molly Brant had built at the western edge of Britain's empire. As Brant returned to her home village of Canajoharie, Mohawk country was transformed from a meeting ground into a battleground. When American rebels took up arms against King George, Molly and her younger brother Joseph rallied the Mohawks behind the British, who were grateful for her support. A leading loyalist noted, "one word from her is more taken notice of by the Five Nations than a thousand from any white man." The Oneidas threw in with

◁ No likeness of Molly Brant survives, but her brother Joseph was depicted by several leading artists. The American-born Gilbert Stuart painted this portrait in London, where Brant journeyed twice to plead the cause of his people. Brant wears the costume of a high-ranking Mohawk, along with a gorget (throat armor) and locket bearing the profile of George III. Fine Art/Getty Images

Chronology

1775	▣ Battles of Lexington and Concord; first shots of war fired
	▣ Siege of Boston begins
	▣ Second Continental Congress begins
	▣ Washington named commander-in-chief of Continental army
	▣ "Olive Branch" petition seeks reconciliation with Britain
	▣ Dunmore's proclamation offers freedom to Virginia patriots' slaves who join British forces
1776	▣ Thomas Paine advocates American independence in *Common Sense*
	▣ British evacuate Boston
	▣ Second Continental Congress directs states to draft constitutions
	▣ Declaration of Independence adopted
	▣ Great Jamaica slave revolt
	▣ New York City falls to British
1777	▣ Articles of Confederation sent to states for ratification
	▣ Philadelphia falls to British
	▣ Burgoyne surrenders at Saratoga
1778	▣ French alliance brings vital assistance to America
	▣ British evacuate Philadelphia
1779	▣ Sullivan expedition destroys Iroquois villages
1780	▣ Charleston falls to British
1781	▣ Articles of Confederation ratified
	▣ Americans take Yorktown; Cornwallis surrenders
1782	▣ British victory over French at Battle of the Saintes secures Jamaica
	▣ Peace negotiations begin
1783	▣ Treaty of Paris grants independence to the United States

the patriots, who professed themselves "afraid" that Brant's "influence may give us some trouble."

Through the summer of 1777, Mohawk country burned and bled. Johnson Hall stood empty, abandoned. As the Continentals advanced through the valley, Molly Brant apprised the British of the rebels' movements. Tipped off by Brant, pro-British militia and Mohawk warriors ambushed American forces and their Oneida allies at the village of Oriskany (Oriske) that August. The daylong battle left two hundred patriots and fifty loyalists dead. Joseph Brant's Mohawks torched what remained of Oriskany; Oneida and American troops razed Canajoharie. Soldiers plundered Molly Brant's house and carried off wagonloads of her possessions. Her people became refugees, hounded and sometimes horsewhipped by

patriot forces as they marched north to seek shelter at Fort Niagara.

After the war, Molly Brant settled in the town of Kingston, in the new British colony of Upper Canada. She later told Britain's Loyalist Claims Commission that she was "not at all reconciled to this place & Country," where she found herself "an entire stranger." But there was no going back. In compensation for all she had done and for all she had lost, the British government awarded her an annual pension of £100. Her daughters married Canadian officials. Only her surviving son chose to live among the Iroquois, in the new Six Nations reserve on Grand River, north of the new national border dividing what had once been his mother's homeland.

Experience an interactive version of this story in MindTap®.

The American Revolution created an enduring republic from thirteen separate colonies—the "thirteen clocks" John Adams described in June 1776. But as Molly Brant's experience shows, it was also a bloody civil war affecting much of North America, often in unpredictable

ways. The fighting uprooted countless families and forced roughly sixty thousand loyalists—black, white, and Native—into exile. The rupture of trading relationships between colonies and empire wreaked havoc upon the American economy. Much more than a series of clashes between armies, the war for independence marks the beginning of the history of the United States and, indeed, a significant turning point in the shaping of the modern world.

The struggle for independence required revolutionary leaders to accomplish three closely related aims. The first was political and ideological: transforming a loyal resistance into a movement demanding separation from Britain. Pursuing a variety of measures ranging from persuasion to coercion, the colonies' elected officials worked to enlist all European Americans in the patriot cause, and to ensure the neutrality of Native peoples and slaves in the conflict.

To win independence, patriot leaders also needed to secure international recognition and aid, particularly from France. Thus they dispatched to Paris the most experienced American diplomat, Benjamin Franklin, who had served for years as a colonial agent in London. Franklin skillfully negotiated the Franco-American alliance of 1778, which proved crucial to the American war effort.

Only the third task directly involved the British. George Washington, named commander-in-chief of the American army in the summer of 1775, soon recognized that his primary goal should be not to win battles so much as to avoid losing them decisively. The outcome of any one battle was less important than preserving his army to fight another day. Consequently, the story of the Revolutionary War often unfolds in British action and American reaction, British attacks and American defenses and withdrawals.

The challenges the rebellion presented to the British army aided the American war effort. King George's fighting forces—at least 100,000 men over the course of the war—had to cross 3,000 miles of ocean. Over such vast distances, men, materiel, and vital news traveled achingly slowly. The theater of war was immense, stretching from the Caribbean to the North Atlantic, and from the seacoast to the Appalachians. And the colonial disunity John Adams noted created challenges of its own. The United Colonies had no single capital whose conquest would crush the rebellion; instead of fighting a dragon, the British army confronted a many-headed Hydra. Against an enemy so various and dispersed, priorities were difficult to assign, especially after the entry of the French on the American side. Was it more important to punish Massachusetts than to preserve Jamaica? Faced with such strategic complexities, British military planners made grave errors. In the end, the Americans' improbable triumph owed as much to their geography, their endurance, and their enemy's missteps as to their own military prowess.

American victories on the battlefield violently severed the political bonds tying thirteen of the former colonies to Great Britain. But military success does not alone make a nation. To make thirteen clocks strike as one, as John Adams and other patriot leaders knew, required profound changes in politics, culture, and society. Through the years of war and long after the signing of the peace, Americans experimented with everything from the structure of their governments to the appearance of their money. The new nation layered new rituals and new identities atop older bonds of kin, church, and community. The triumph of the Continental army only began the long work of creating the United States.

▭ *What choices of allegiance confronted residents of North America after 1774? Why did people make the choices they did?*

▭ *What strategies did the British and American military forces adopt, and why?*

▭ *How did the United States win independence and forge the outlines of a new national government?*

6-1 Toward War

▷ **How did the military conflict between the British and the American colonies unfold in 1775–1776?**

▷ **What beliefs guided the British in prosecuting the war, and what were the consequences of those?**

▷ **What issues did the Second Continental Congress need to address?**

On January 27, 1775, Lord Dartmouth, Britain's secretary of state for America, addressed a fateful letter to General Thomas Gage in Boston, urging him to act. Opposition could not be "very formidable," Dartmouth wrote. Even if it were, "better that the Conflict should be brought on, upon such ground, than in a riper state of Rebellion." Gage, in short, should take the offensive. Now.

6-1a Battles of Lexington and Concord

Gage, the commander-in-chief of Britain's forces in America and, since the departure of Thomas Hutchinson, also the governor of Massachusetts, received Dartmouth's letter on April 14. He quickly dispatched an expedition to confiscate the stockpile of colonial military supplies at Concord. Bostonians learned of the impending seizure and sent two messengers, William Dawes and Paul Revere (later joined by Dr. Samuel Prescott), to rouse the countryside. When the vanguard of several hundred British regulars (a commonly used term for soldiers in the British Army) approached Lexington at dawn on April 19, they found a ragtag group of seventy

△ In 1775, an unknown artist painted the redcoats entering Concord. The fighting at North Bridge, which occurred just a few hours after this triumphal entry, signaled the start of open warfare between Britain and the colonies.

militiamen—about half the town's adult men—mustered on the common. Realizing that their small force could not halt the redcoats' advance, the Americans' commander ordered his force to withdraw. But as they dispersed, a shot rang out. British soldiers then fired several volleys. When they stopped, eight Americans lay dead, and another ten had been wounded. The British marched on to Concord, five miles away.

There the contingents of colonial militia were larger, reinforced by men from nearby towns. An exchange of gunfire at the North Bridge spilled the first British blood of the Revolution: three regulars were killed and nine wounded. Then thousands of militiamen hidden in houses and behind trees fired at the British forces as they retreated toward Boston. By day's end, the redcoats had suffered 272 casualties, including 70 deaths. The Americans suffered just 93 casualties.

The outbreak of war, long anticipated, was nonetheless shocking to those who experienced it. Subtle and shifting allegiances resolved, sometimes suddenly, into sides. Patriot printers decried the "Bloody Butchery" perpetrated by the British troops and eulogized "the deceased worthies, who died gloriously fighting in the cause of liberty." Others lost sympathy for the insurgents. "My hand trembles while I inform you that the Sword of Civil War is now unsheathd," wrote the engraver Henry Pelham to his half-brother, the painter John Singleton Copley, then in Italy. Pelham thought the British regulars "the Bravest and best Disciplined troops that ever Europe Bred," while the patriot militia were bloodthirsty "Rebels" who "skulk'd behind trees."

6-1b The Siege of Boston

By April 20, some twenty thousand American militiamen had gathered around Boston. Many soon went home for spring planting, but those who remained, along with newer recruits, were organized into formal units. Officers under the command of General Artemas Ward of the Massachusetts militia ordered that latrines be dug, foodstuffs purchased, military discipline enforced, and defensive fortifications constructed.

Boston, which the colonists and the British alike saw as the cradle of the rebellion, was thus besieged by patriot militia whose presence effectively confined Gage's forces within the beleaguered town. Within weeks, some ten thousand of the city's sixteen thousand inhabitants—most of them patriot sympathizers—had fled into the surrounding countryside. "You'll see parents that are lucky enough to procure papers, with bundles in one hand and a string of children in the other, wandering out of the town … not knowing whither they'll go," wrote one man who hoped he too might "escape with the skin of my teeth." As supporters of the rebellion streamed over the narrow neck separating Boston from the mainland, loyalist refugees—subject to vigilante assaults in the countryside— flowed in the opposite direction, straggling into town to seek the protection of British troops. By late May, fresh food was running low. In August, smallpox claimed dozens; dysentery ravaged hundreds more. As winter descended, Gage's troops tore down houses, bridges, boardwalks, even the Old North Church, burning the lumber for fuel.

For nearly a year, the two armies eyed each other across the battlements. The redcoats attacked their besiegers only once, on June 17, when they drove the Americans from trenches atop Breed's Hill in Charlestown. In that misnamed Battle of Bunker Hill, the British incurred their greatest casualties of the entire war: more than 800 wounded and 228 killed. Though forced to abandon their position, the Americans lost less than half that number.

6-1c First Year of War

During the same eleven-month period, patriots easily captured Fort Ticonderoga, a British outpost on Lake Champlain, acquiring much-needed cannon. Trying to bring Canada into the war on the American side, they also mounted a northern campaign that ended in disaster at Quebec in early 1776. But the chief significance of the war's first year lay in the long lull in fighting between the main armies at Boston. The delay gave both sides a chance to organize and plan their strategies.

Prime Minister Lord North and his new American secretary, Lord George Germain, made three central assumptions about the war they faced. First, they forecast that patriot forces could not long withstand the assaults of trained British regulars, and that the 1776 campaign would therefore prove decisive. Accordingly, they dispatched to America the largest fighting force Great Britain had ever assembled: 370 transport ships carrying 32,000 troops, accompanied by 73 naval vessels and 13,000 sailors. Among the troops were thousands of professional German soldiers (many from the state of Hesse); the rulers of their principalities had hired them out to Britain. Second, British officials and army officers believed that capturing major cities—a central aim in European warfare—would defeat the rebel army. Third, they assumed that a clear-cut military victory would regain the colonies' allegiance.

All three assumptions proved false. North and Germain vastly underestimated Americans' commitment to armed resistance. Battlefield defeats did not lead patriots to abandon their political aims and sue for peace. London officials also failed to recognize the significance of the American population's dispersal over an area 1,500 miles long and more than 100 miles wide. Although Britain would control each of the largest mainland ports at some time during the war, less than 5 percent of the American population lived in those cities. The coast offered so many excellent harbors that essential commerce was easily rerouted. Capturing cities consumed vital British resources, but did relatively little damage to the American cause.

Most of all, London officials did not initially understand that military triumph would not bring political victory. Securing the colonies would require hundreds of thousands of rebel Americans to resume their allegiance to the empire. After 1778, King George's ministry determined to achieve that goal by expanding the use of loyalist forces and restoring civilian authority in occupied areas. But the new policy came too late. Britain's leaders never fully realized they were fighting an entirely new kind of conflict: not a conventional European war, but the first modern war of national liberation.

6-1d Second Continental Congress

At least Britain had a bureaucracy ready to supervise the war effort. The Americans had only the Second Continental Congress, originally convened to consider the ministry's response to the Continental Association. But much had changed between the fall of 1774 and the spring of 1775. The delegates who gathered in Philadelphia on May 10, 1775, had to assume the mantle of intercolonial government. As spring gave way to summer, Congress organized the United Colonies to prosecute the war that had escalated since the skirmishes in Lexington and Concord. The delegates authorized the printing of money, established a committee to oversee relations with foreign countries, strengthened the militia, and ordered ships built for a new Continental navy. In July, Pennsylvania's John Dickinson, who drafted Congress's Declaration on Taking Arms, proclaimed, "We are reduced to the alternative of chusing an unconditional submission to the tyranny of irritated ministers, or resistance by force.—The latter is our choice."

Yet for many delegates, hesitation remained. That same month, Dickinson drafted a petition beseeching the king to halt the growing conflict. Approved by Congress on July 5, 1775, the address, now known as the Olive Branch petition, began with the assertion that its 48 signatories remained "your Majesty's faithful subjects in the colonies," and concluded with a "sincere and fervent prayer" that the king would "enjoy a long and prosperous reign, and that your descendants may govern your dominions with honor to themselves and happiness to their subjects."

Even while preparing the Olive Branch petition—which the king would ultimately reject—Congress pursued the urgent task of creating the Continental army and appointing its leadership. In the first weeks after Lexington and Concord, the Massachusetts provincial congress supervised General Ward and the troops encamped at Boston. But that army, composed of men from all over New England, constituted a heavy drain on limited local resources, and Massachusetts soon asked Congress to take over. This meant Congress had to choose a commander-in-chief, and many delegates recognized the importance of naming someone who was not a New Englander. In mid-June, John Adams proposed the appointment of a fellow delegate to Congress, a Virginian (Adams later recalled) "whose Skill and Experience as an Officer, whose independent fortune, great Talents and excellent universal Character, would command the Approbation of all America": George Washington. Congress unanimously concurred.

6-1e George Washington

Neither a radical nor a reflective political thinker, Washington had played a minor role in the pre-revolutionary agitation. Devoted to the American cause, he was dignified, conservative, and respectable—a man of unimpeachable integrity. The early death of his older brother and his marriage to the landed, slave-owning widow Martha Custis had made him one of the wealthiest planters in Virginia. Hundreds of enslaved men, women, and children worked his Mount Vernon estate. Though a slaveholding aristocrat, Washington was unswervingly committed to representative government. After his mistakes at the beginning of the Seven Years' War, he had repaired his reputation by maintaining a calm demeanor under fire.

Washington both looked and acted like a leader. Standing more than six feet tall in an era when most men were five inches shorter, he displayed a stately and commanding presence. Even a loyalist admitted that Washington could "atone for many demerits by the extraordinary coolness and caution which distinguish his character."

Washington took command of the army surrounding Boston in July 1775. The new general continued Ward's efforts to organize and sustain those troops. In March 1776, the arrival of the cannon captured at Ticonderoga finally enabled him to put direct pressure on the redcoats, yet an assault on Boston proved unnecessary. Sir William Howe, Britain's new commander, had been considering an evacuation of the city; he wanted to transfer his men to New York, where he expected a warmer welcome in a city said to be well supplied with "friends to government," as the British called **loyalists**. The patriots' cannon mounted on Dorchester Heights decided the matter. On March 17, the British and more than a thousand of their supporters abandoned Boston forever.

6-2 Forging an Independent Republic

▷ What were the main features of republican thought in the late eighteenth century?

▷ What values and principles guided the formation of new state constitutions and the Articles of Confederation?

▷ What role did the publication of Thomas Paine's *Common Sense* play in the imperial dispute?

Well before the British fleet (along with many loyalist exiles) sailed north to await reinforcements in Halifax, the colonies were moving inexorably toward independence. By the late summer of 1775, Congress had begun to mold republican ideals into the structures, rituals, and symbols of a nation.

---

loyalists Colonists who retained their allegiance to the British crown through the upheavals of the revolution.

6-2a Varieties of Republicanism

Since its first meeting, in the autumn of 1774, Congress's actions had been strongly influenced by republican thought. The strenuous discipline required by the Articles of Association, for example, depended on Real Whig conceptions of self-sacrificing virtue. As John Dickinson recalled many years later, "We knew that the people of this country must unite themselves under some form of Government and that this could be no other than the republican form."

But *which* "republican form"? Three different definitions of republicanism animated Congress's thinking and continued to jockey for preeminence in the new United States. Despite their differences, the three strands shared many assumptions. All three contrasted the industrious virtue of America with the decadence of Britain and Europe. Most agreed that a virtuous country would be composed of hardworking citizens who would dress simply, live plainly, and elect wise leaders to public office.

Ancient history and political theory informed the first concept, embraced chiefly by members of the educated elite (such as the Adamses of Massachusetts). The histories of Greece and Rome suggested that republics fared best when they were small and homogeneous. Unless a republic's citizens were willing to sacrifice their private interests for the public good, government would collapse. A truly virtuous man, classical republican theory insisted, had the temperament—and the resources—to forgo personal profit and work for the best interests of the nation. Society would be governed by members of a "natural aristocracy," men whose talent elevated them to positions of power. Rank would not be abolished, but would be founded on merit rather than birth.

A second definition, advanced by other members of the elite and also by some skilled craftsmen, drew more on contemporary economic theory. Instead of perceiving the nation as an organic whole composed of people nobly sacrificing for the common good, this version of republicanism followed the Scottish thinker Adam Smith, whose treatise entitled *An Inquiry into the Nature and Causes of the Wealth of Nations* was published just weeks before Congress declared America's independence. Smith saw the pursuit of rational self-interest as inevitable and even salutary. Republican virtue would be achieved through the pursuit of private interests, rather than through the subordination of personal profit to communal ideals.

The third notion of republicanism was more egalitarian. Men who advanced this version—including many with scant formal education—wanted government to respond directly to the needs of ordinary folk, and rejected the notion that the "lesser sort" should defer to their "betters." They were, indeed, democrats in more or less the modern sense, in an era when "democracy" was typically a term of insult, roughly equivalent to mob rule. For them, the untutored wisdom of the people embodied republican virtue. The most prominent advocate of this variety of republicanism was a radical English printer named Thomas Paine, who

△ That America's patriot leaders read Thomas Paine's inflammatory *Common Sense* soon after it was published in early 1776 is indicated by this first edition, owned by George Washington himself.

sailed to Philadelphia in 1774 bearing letters of introduction from Benjamin Franklin. Throughout 1775, Paine scribbled in obscurity, publishing essays railing against the bloody excesses of English officials in India and attacking the "savage practice" of African slavery in America. In 1776, he would become one of the best-known writers in the world.

6-2b Common Sense

First printed in January 1776, Thomas Paine's *Common Sense* sold for as little as a shilling—about $7.50 in today's money. Perhaps 100,000 Americans bought copies or read sections of *Common Sense* reprinted in newspapers. Thousands more heard it read aloud in taverns, coffeehouses, and public squares. An estimated one in five American adults became familiar with Paine's arguments, far more than had read or

debated any previous patriot writings. Within months, copies surfaced not just in London and Edinburgh but also in Berlin and Warsaw.

Paine's best-seller did not create American independence, but it transformed the terms of debate. Even after they had been at war for months, many American leaders hesitated fully to break with Great Britain. "[D]o We aim at independency? or do We only ask for a Restoration of Rights putting of Us on Our old footing?" one South Carolina delegate asked Congress in May 1775. As late as March 1776, John Adams called independence "an Hobgoblin, of so frightful Mein, that it would throw a delicate Person into Fits to look it in the Face."

Thomas Paine was not a delicate person. He wrote with passion verging on rage, in straightforward prose that reflected the oral culture of ordinary folk. *Common Sense* took the Bible—the only book familiar to most Americans—as its primary source of authority. As its title suggested, *Common Sense* aimed to cut through a fog of received wisdom—to see clearly and speak plain.

Paine insisted that America's independence was inevitable. Just as all children one day grow up, the "authority of Great Britain over this continent, is a form of government, which sooner or later must have an end." Rejecting the widespread assumption that a balance among monarchy, aristocracy, and democracy preserved liberty, Paine said monarchs were "ridiculous," and aristocrats greedy and corrupt. No tender parent, Britain had exploited the colonies unmercifully, Paine argued. And for the frequently heard assertion that an independent America would be weak and divided, he substituted boundless confidence in its future. "The sun never shined on a cause of greater worth," he wrote. Independence was "not the affair of a City, a County, a province, or a kingdom; but of a continent—of at least one-eighth part of the habitable globe." America's struggle was "not the concern of a day, a year, or an age" but of "posterity . . . even to the end of time."

It is unclear how many were converted to the cause of independence by *Common Sense*. But by late spring, Adams's "hobgoblin" had become a given. Towns, grand juries, and provincial legislatures drafted at least ninety different statements demanding American independence. Then, on June 7, Congress confirmed the movement toward separation. Virginia's Richard Henry Lee introduced the crucial resolution: "that these United Colonies are, and of right ought to be, free and independent States, that they are absolved of all allegiance to the British Crown, and that all political connection between them and the State of Great Britain is, and ought to be, totally dissolved." Congress postponed a vote on Lee's resolution to allow time for consultation and public reaction. In the meantime, they directed a five-man committee—including Thomas Jefferson, John Adams, and Benjamin Franklin—to draft a declaration of American independence. The committee

Common Sense A pamphlet written by Thomas Paine that advocated freedom from British rule.

assigned primary responsibility for writing the document to Jefferson, a thirty-four-year-old Virginia lawyer known for his eloquence.

6-2c Jefferson and the Declaration of Independence

Thomas Jefferson had been educated at the College of William and Mary and trained in the law offices of a prominent attorney. A member of the House of Burgesses, he had read widely in history and political theory. That broad knowledge was evident not only in the Declaration of Independence but also in his draft of the Virginia state constitution, completed a few days before his appointment to the committee. An intensely private man, Jefferson loved his home and family deeply. This early stage of his political career was marked by his wife Martha's repeated difficulties in childbearing. Not until after her death in 1782, from complications following the birth of their third surviving child, did Jefferson fully commit himself to public service. He would not marry again. In the late 1780s, he began a long-lasting relationship with one of his slaves, Sally Hemings. Hemings was Martha Jefferson's half-sister, born of another relationship between a slave owner and enslaved woman. Between 1790 and 1808, Hemings bore seven children whose father was almost certainly Thomas Jefferson.

Jefferson's draft of the **Declaration of Independence** was laid before Congress on June 28, 1776. The delegates voted for independence four days later, on July 2, and then refined the wording of the Declaration for two more days, adopting it with some changes on July 4. Since Americans had long since ceased to see themselves as legitimate subjects of Parliament, the Declaration of Independence (see appendix) concentrated on the actions of George III. The document accused the king of attempting to destroy representative government in the colonies and of oppressing Americans through the use of excessive force.

The Declaration's chief long-term importance, however, did not lie in its lengthy catalogue of grievances against George III (including, in a section deleted by Congress, Jefferson's charge that the British monarchy had forced African slavery on America). It lay instead in the first lines of its second paragraph, ringing statements of principle that have served ever since as the ideal to which Americans aspire: "We hold these truths to be self-evident: That all men are created equal; that they are endowed by their Creator with certain unalienable rights; that among these are life, liberty and the pursuit of happiness; that, to secure these rights, governments are instituted among men, deriving their just powers from the consent of the governed; that whenever any form of government becomes destructive of these ends, it is the right of the people to alter or to abolish it, and to institute new government." These phrases have echoed down

the centuries like no others: a clarion call taken up by many groups struggling for their rights within the United States, and well beyond it.

The congressmen who voted to accept the Declaration of Independence could not predict the consequences of their audacious act. By signing the Declaration, they committed treason, a capital offense. When they concluded with the assertion that they "mutually pledge[d] to each other our lives, our fortunes, and our sacred honor," they spoke no less than the truth. The real struggle lay before them, and few had Thomas Paine's confidence in their success.

6-2d Colonies to States

The Declaration dissolved an ancient set of political bonds with the stroke of a pen. Creating political entities to supplant the individual colonies, and to knit the newly united states together, would take much longer. Shortly before adopting the Declaration, Congress directed the individual provinces to replace their colonial charters with state constitutions, and to devise new republican bodies to supplant the conventions and committees that had governed since 1774.

The supporters of American independence wanted to create tangible documents specifying the fundamental structures of government, but at first legislators could not decide how to accomplish that goal. Political leaders eventually concluded that regular legislative bodies should not draft the constitutions that defined their powers. Following the models of Vermont in 1777 and Massachusetts in 1780, states began to elect conventions for the sole purpose of drafting constitutions. In this fashion, states sought authorization directly from the people—the theoretical sovereigns in a republic—to establish new governments. Delegates then submitted the constitutions they had drafted to voters for ratification.

Americans' experience with British rule permeated every provision of their new constitutions, which varied considerably in specifics while remaining broadly comparable in outline. Under their colonial charters, Americans had learned to fear the power of governors—usually the appointed agents of the king or proprietor—and to see their legislatures as defenders of the people. Accordingly, the first state constitutions typically provided for the governor to be elected annually (commonly by the legislature), limited the number of terms he could serve, and gave him little independent authority. The most radical of the state constitutions, adopted by Pennsylvania in late 1776, closely followed Paine's egalitarian thinking, and featured no executive or upper legislative house.

In every case, the state constitutions expanded the powers of the provincial legislatures. Each state except Pennsylvania and Vermont retained a two-house structure, with members of the upper house serving longer terms and required to own more property than their counterparts in the lower house. But they also redrew electoral districts to more accurately reflect population patterns and increased the number of members in both houses. Finally, most states

Declaration of Independence Proposed by the Second Continental Congress, this document proclaimed independence of the Thirteen Colonies from British rule.

lowered property qualifications for voting. As a result, state legislatures came to include members who earlier would not even have been eligible to cast a ballot. Thus, the revolutionary era witnessed the first deliberate attempt to broaden the base of American government, a process that continues in the present day.

6-2e Limiting State Governments

The authors of state constitutions knew that governments designed to be responsive to the people would not necessarily prevent tyrants from being elected to office. To protect what they regarded as the natural rights of citizens, they included explicit limitations on government authority in the documents they composed. Seven state constitutions contained formal bills of rights, and others had similar clauses. Most guaranteed freedom of the press, fair trials, the right to consent to taxation, and protection against general search warrants; an independent judiciary was charged with upholding such rights. Most states also safeguarded freedom of religion, but with restrictions. Seven states required that all officeholders be Christians, and some continued to support churches with tax revenues. (Not until 1833 did once-Puritan Massachusetts become the last state to remove all vestiges of a religious establishment.)

In general, state constitution makers put greater emphasis on preventing tyranny than on wielding political power effectively. Their approach was understandable, given the American experience with Great Britain. But establishing such weak political units, especially in wartime, all but ensured that the constitutions would require revision. Even before the war ended, some states began to rewrite the frameworks they had drafted in 1776 and 1777. Invariably, the revised versions increased the powers of the governor and reduced the legislature's authority.

American politicians initially concentrated on drafting state constitutions and devoted little attention to their national government. While officials were consumed with the military struggle against Britain, the powers and structure of the Continental Congress evolved by default. Not until late 1777 did Congress send the **Articles of Confederation**—the document outlining a national government—to the states for ratification, and those Articles simply wrote into law the unplanned arrangements of the Continental Congress.

6-2f Articles of Confederation

Under the Articles, the chief organ of national government was a unicameral (one-house) legislature in which each state had a single vote. Its powers included conducting foreign relations, mediating interstate disputes, controlling maritime affairs, regulating Native American trade, and setting the value of state and national money. Congress could request but not compel the payment of taxes. The United States of America was described as "a firm league of friendship" in which each state retained "its sovereignty, freedom and independence, and every Power, Jurisdiction and right, which is not by this confederation expressly delegated to the United States" (see the appendix for the text of the Articles of Confederation).

The Articles required the unanimous consent of state legislatures for ratification or amendment, and a clause concerning western lands quickly proved troublesome. The draft Congress accepted in 1777 allowed states to retain all land claims derived from their original charters. But states whose charters established definite western boundaries (such as Maryland and New Jersey) wanted the others to cede to the national government their landholdings west of the Appalachian Mountains, lest states with large claims grow to overpower their smaller neighbors. Maryland refused to accept the Articles until 1781, when Virginia finally surrendered its western holdings to national jurisdiction (see Map 7.1).

6-2g Funding a Revolution

In the 1770s as in the present day, fighting a war cost an enormous amount of money, of which the former colonies had precious little. To finance the American war, Britain possessed a well-developed fiscal-military state that could collect taxes effectively and issue sovereign debt in great quantity. It also had a stable national paper currency backed by substantial reserves of gold and silver coins, also known as hard money or specie. Because the newly created United States had none of these resources at its disposal, finance posed the most persistent problem faced by both state and national governments.

Congress borrowed what it could at home and abroad—from the American people, from Dutch investors, from Spain, and especially from France. But such mechanisms went only so far. The certificates purchased by domestic borrowers funded roughly 10 percent of the cost of the war, and the combined value of all foreign loans and gifts received between 1777 and 1783 totaled less than $10 million—about 7 percent of the Revolution's cost. With limited credit and even less power to tax, Congress turned to the only remaining alternative: printing money.

Through 1775 and the first half of 1776, these paper dollars—dubbed "Continentals"—passed at face value. But in late 1776, as the American army suffered reverses, prices rose, confidence in the nation's credit fell, and the Continental began to depreciate. State governments tried to prop up the ailing currency by controlling wages and prices and by requiring acceptance of paper money on an equal footing with specie. States borrowed funds, established lotteries, and levied taxes. But they also printed their own competing currencies, which further cluttered an already confusing monetary landscape. State currencies—issues totaling roughly $209 million—funded nearly 40 percent of the cost of the war. But as the conflict dragged on, they too plummeted in value.

Articles of Confederation The first document that framed the limited powers of an American national government. It reserved substantial powers for the states, granting to each state its "sovereignty, freedom and independence."

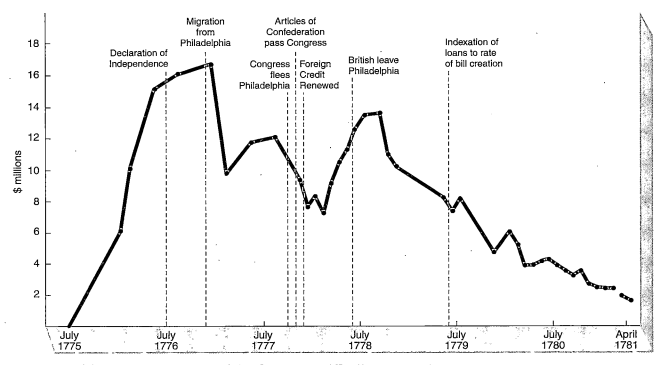

Figure 6.1 The Changing Value of the Continental Dollar, 1777–1781

This graph, illustrating the total value in silver coin of congressional bills of credit issued during the Revolution, shows that confidence in the new American currency was high at the beginning of the war. In 1777 and early 1778, the Continental's value sank with American defeats and rose with American victories. But after July 1778, the enormous number of bills in circulation caused their value to plummet. By the end of the war, they were virtually worthless. *Source: Adapted from Charles W. Calormis, "Institutional Failure, Monetary Scarcity, and the Depreciation of the Continental," Journal of Economic History, Vol. 48, No. 1 (Mar., 1988), p. 56.*

By the end of 1780, the value of the Continental had fallen so far that it took 100 paper dollars to purchase one Spanish silver dollar (see Figure 6.1). Congress responded by devaluating its notes, accepting Continental dollars in payment of taxes at one-fortieth of their face value. This scheme succeeded in retiring much of the "old tenor" paper, at an enormous cost to people who had taken the notes. All told, Congress issued more than $200 million worth of Continental dollars—funding about 40 percent of the cost of the war—before stopping the presses.

By the war's end, the phrase "not worth a Continental" had entered the American vernacular. Yet in many ways, the printing presses had offered the best possible answer to an impossible question: how could a new, underdeveloped nation finance a continental war with such limited powers of taxation? Benjamin Franklin—long a proponent of colonial paper money—called the Continental "a wonderful Machine": "it pays and clothes Troops, and provides Victuals and Ammunition; and when we are obliged to issue a Quantity excessive, it pays itself off by Deprecation," extracting a kind of tax on everyone who passes it. For better or worse, the new nation that created itself with a paper declaration also financed the great bulk of its war of independence with paper money.

6-2h Symbolizing a Nation

In addition to passing laws and mustering troops, Congress devised a wide array of symbols and ceremonies to embody the new nation in the daily lives of its citizens. The Continental dollar, for example, tried out a dizzying variety of images, including a harp with thirteen strings, a chain with thirteen links, and a beaver gnawing an enormous, unyielding oak. Some critics mocked the ever-changing face of American money as evidence of congressional fecklessness. But promoting a sense of "we" in the everyday interactions of ordinary citizens was one of Congress's most crucial tasks. The United States shared no common language or lineage. The Declaration of Independence called the new nation into being after a political crisis that had lasted barely a dozen years—an eye blink in historical time. When they printed money, coined medals, invented seals, designed uniforms, and proclaimed festivals, members of Congress worked to create unity from the astonishing diversity of former British subjects who must now become Americans. The crest for a proposed national coat of arms commissioned in September 1776 featured a scroll reading *E Pluribus Unum*: "out of many, one." Congress rejected the design, but the motto would reappear on the great seal of the United States in 1782.

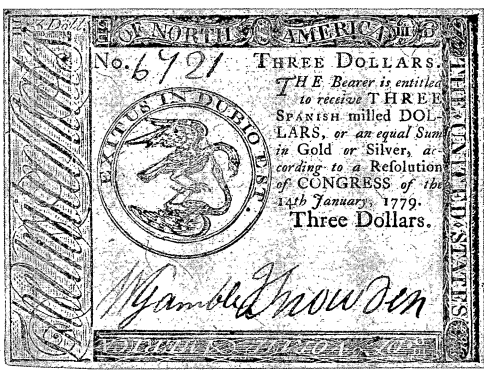

◁ Among the first designs for Continental currency was this three-dollar bill, which featured the image of an eagle battling a crane. When it began circulating in 1776, people were unsure what the scene represented. Noted the *Pennsylvania Magazine*, "The eagle, I suppose, represents Great-Britain, the crane America." Benjamin Franklin, thought by some to have created the bill, later lamented that the eagle had come to symbolize the United States, calling it "a Bird of bad moral character." The turkey, he said, was "much more respectable." Not only was the national symbol up for grabs early in the war, so too was the result of the fighting. The motto on the bill, EXITUS IN DUBIO EST., translates to "*the outcome is in doubt.*"

6-3 Choosing Sides

▷ **What motivated American colonists to remain loyal to Britain or remain neutral during the war?**

▷ **How did Native American and African American populations respond to the war?**

▷ **How did the United States and the British seek to engage Native American and African American populations in the war?**

The endurance—and, indeed, the eventual global dominance—of the United States can obscure the chaos and tentativeness of its beginnings. American mythology sketches a conflict in which virtuous patriots, clearly in the right, squared off against villainous loyalists, clearly in the wrong, with the outcome preordained. In fact, the war of American independence was a long, bloody, and multi-sided conflict in which allegiance was often unstable and virtue often uncertain. Where patriots saw Sons of Liberty acting "with manly firmness" (as the Declaration put it) against British tyranny, those loyal to the Crown saw armed insurgents—"Sons of Anarchy," some called them—taking vigilante action against "Friends of Government" who defended the very notion of order. To Native Americans, land meant liberty, and the rise of the new nation threatened it. To African Americans—roughly a fifth of the mainland population—liberty meant freedom from slavery; their loyalty belonged to whoever would help them secure it. For Britain's ministers, the fate of twenty-six American colonies, not just the thirteen rebellious ones, hung in the balance.

And Spain and France knew that the balance of power in Europe as well as North America must change with the outcome of the rebels' fight for independence.

6-3a Patriots

Many though by no means most residents of the thirteen rebel colonies supported resistance and then backed independence. Active revolutionaries accounted for no more than two-fifths of the European American population. Among them were small and middling farmers, members of dominant Protestant sects (both Old and New Lights), Chesapeake gentry, merchants handling American commodities, urban artisans, elected officeholders, and people of English descent. Wives usually, but not always, fell in with their husbands about politics. Although such groups supported the Revolution, they pursued divergent goals within the broader coalition, much as they had in the 1760s. Some patriots sought more sweeping political reform than others; many fought for social and economic change instead or as well.

Some colonists, though, could not endorse independence. Like their patriot friends and neighbors, most had objected to parliamentary policies in the 1760s and 1770s, but they favored imperial reform rather than rupture. The events of the crucial year between the passage of the Coercive Acts in 1774 and the outbreak of fighting in 1775 crystallized their thinking. Their objections to violent protest, their desire to uphold legally constituted authority, and their fears of anarchy combined to make them sensitive to the dangers of independence.

6-3b Loyalists

Like patriots, loyalists comprised a diverse group of ordinary colonists, male and female, white, black, and Native. But loyalism, unlike patriotism, required no dramatic political conversion; those who supported the Crown merely sought to remain what they were born—subjects of the British sovereign and his empire—rather than to become something entirely new to modern history—citizens of an extensive republic.

Between one-fifth and one-third of the European American population rejected independence. Most who remained loyal to Great Britain had long opposed the men who became patriot leaders, for varying reasons. British-appointed government officials; Anglican clergy everywhere and lay Anglicans in the North; tenant farmers, particularly those whose landlords sided with the patriots; members of persecuted religious sects; backcountry southerners who had rebelled against eastern rule in the late 1760s and early 1770s; and non-English ethnic minorities, especially Scots: all these groups believed that the colonial assemblies had shown little concern for their welfare in the past. Joined by merchants whose trade depended on imperial connections, and by former officers and enlisted men from the British army who had settled in America after 1763, they formed a loyalist core who retained a political identity that revolutionaries proved willing to abandon.

Whole regions of British America, lying to the north and south of the familiar roster of thirteen colonies represented in Congress's many symbols (including the American flag), continued within the empire. Halifax, Quebec, and St. John (Prince Edward Island) in what became Canada; as well as East and West Florida, the Bahamas, Barbados, Dominica, Grenada, Jamaica, the Leeward Islands, and St. Vincent remained loyal to Britain, while Bermuda steered a precarious neutral course. The unfolding war cannot be understood without accounting for Britain's desire to protect its valuable Caribbean possessions, especially Jamaica.

Both Nova Scotians and West Indians had economic reasons for supporting the mother country. In the mid-1770s, the northerners had broken New England's domination of the northern coastal trade and entered the Caribbean market with their cargoes of dried, salted fish. Once the shooting started, they benefited greatly from Britain's retaliatory measures against rebel commerce. Sugar producers relied on Parliament's mercantilist trade laws for their profits, and counted on the British army's might for their security in a society where the enslaved, whom they brutalized, hugely outnumbered them. Neither Caribbean planters nor Nova Scotians had reason to believe they would be better off independent.

During the war, loyalists in the thirteen rebel colonies congregated in cities held by the British army. When those posts were evacuated, loyalists scattered to different parts of the empire—to Britain, the Bahamas, West Africa, and especially the Canadian provinces of Nova Scotia, New Brunswick, and Ontario. All told, roughly sixty thousand Americans

△ Bernardo de Gálvez, shown here in a twentieth-century copy of an earlier portrait, became governor of Spanish Louisiana in 1777, as the war between the United States and Britain moved south. Though Louisiana lay well to the west of the battle lines, its border with British West Florida made it strategically important to both the United States and the English crown. When representatives of the American Congress sought his assistance, Gálvez faced a delicate choice: to support the Americans—the enemy of his British enemies—might encourage colonial uprising in his own territories. He elected to throw in with the United States, recruiting Native allies to the cause, and attacking British ships in the Gulf to open supply lines to the fledgling American navy.

preferred exile to life in a republic independent of British rule. Their number included some eight to ten thousand escaped slaves who survived to the end of the war, a fraction of those who had trusted the British promise of freedom. In addition, slave-owning loyalists carried an estimated fifteen thousand enslaved African Americans along the varied paths of their exodus from the United States.

6-3c Neutrals

Between the patriots and the loyalists, there remained in the uneasy middle two-fifths to three-fifths of the European American population—a number equal to or greater than the patriots. Some who tried to avoid taking sides were committed pacifists, such as Quakers. Others shifted their allegiance to whichever side appeared to be winning, or cared little about politics and deferred to those in power. Their patriot neighbors

New Nations

The American Revolution that created the United States also led directly to the formation of three other nations: Canada, Sierra Leone, and Australia.

In modern Canada before the Revolution, only Nova Scotia had a sizable number of English-speaking settlers. Those people, largely New Englanders, had been recruited after 1758 to repopulate the region forcibly taken from the exiled Acadians. During and after the Revolution, many loyalist families, especially those from the northern and middle colonies, moved to the region that is now Canada, which remained under British rule. The provinces of New Brunswick and Upper Canada (later Ontario) were established to accommodate them, and some displaced loyalists settled in Quebec as well. In just a few years, the refugees transformed the sparsely populated former French colony, laying the foundation of the modern Canadian nation.

Sierra Leone, too, was founded by colonial exiles—African Americans who fled to the British army to seek their freedom during the war. Many of them ended up in London. Seeing the refugees' poverty, a group of charitable merchants—calling themselves the Committee for Relief of the Black Poor—developed a plan to resettle the African Americans elsewhere. After refusing to be sent to the Bahamas, where they might be re-enslaved, the refugees concurred in a scheme to return them to the continent of their ancestors. In early 1787, vessels carrying about four hundred settlers reached Sierra Leone in West Africa, where representatives of the Black Poor committee had acquired land from local rulers. The first years of the new colony were difficult, and many of the newcomers died of disease and deprivation. But in 1792, several thousand loyalist African Americans left Nova Scotia to join the struggling colony. The influx ensured Sierra Leone's survival; it remained a part of the British Empire until achieving independence in 1961.

△ An early view of the settlement of black loyalists in West Africa, the foundation of the modern nation of Sierra Leone.

While the Sierra Leone migrants were preparing to sail from London in late 1786, British prison ships were being readied for Australia. At the Paris peace negotiations in 1782, American diplomats refused to allow the United States to continue to serve as a dumping ground for British convicts. Needing another destination for the felons its courts sentenced to transportation, Britain decided to send them halfway around the world, to the continent Captain James Cook had explored and claimed in 1770. Britain continued to dispatch convicts to some parts of Australia until 1868, but long before then voluntary migrants also began to arrive. The modern nation was created from a federation of separate colonial governments on January 1, 1901.

Thus, the founding of the United States links the nation to the formation of its northern neighbor and to new nations in West Africa and the Pacific.

CRITICAL THINKING

☐ The nations of Canada, Sierra Leone, and Australia were, in different ways, outgrowths of the American Revolution. How have the ideological underpinnings of the American Revolution affected other nations in the centuries since it occurred?

△ Thomas Rowlandson, an English artist, sketched the boatloads of male and female convicts as they were being ferried to the ships that would take them to their new lives in the prison colony of Australia. Note the gibbet on the shore with two hanging bodies—symbolizing the fate these people were escaping.

The New York Public Library/Art Resource, NY

National Library of Australia

sometimes derided them as "flexibles." On the whole, neutrals believed what the Boston-born painter John Singleton Copley wrote to his family from Europe in 1775: whether the new country would be "free or Dispotick is beyond the reach of human wisdom to decide." In such fluid circumstances, not taking sides might prove the best form of self-preservation. Thus Copley urged his kin to resist entreaties to take up arms and "be neuter at all events." Neutral colonists resisted British and Americans alike when the demands on them seemed too heavy—when taxes became too high or when calls for militia service came too often or lasted too long.

Found in every colony, neutrals made up an especially large proportion of the population in the backcountry, where Scots-Irish settlers had little love for either the patriot gentry or the British authorities. Understanding that backcountry settlers were likely to follow whichever side would better serve their interests, the Continental Congress moved to reoccupy the site of Fort Pitt and to establish other garrisons in the Ohio Country. Relying on such protection, as many as twenty thousand settlers poured into Kentucky and western Pennsylvania by 1780. Yet frontier affiliations were not clear: the growing town of Pittsburgh, for example, harbored many active loyalists.

To patriots, apathy or neutrality was as heinous as loyalism: those who were not with them were surely against them. In the winter of 1775–1776, the Second Continental Congress recommended that all "disaffected" persons be disarmed and arrested. State legislatures began to require voters (or, in some cases, all free adult men) to take oaths of allegiance; the penalty for refusal was usually banishment to England or extra taxes. After 1777, many states confiscated the property of banished persons, using the proceeds to fund the war effort. Enmities remained long after the fighting stopped. Some loyalists returning to the United States in the early 1780s were welcomed with tar and feathers, whippings, or even the noose.

The patriots' policies helped to prevent their opponents from banding together to threaten the revolutionary cause. But loyalists and neutrals were not the patriots' only worry, for revolutionaries could not assume that their longtime indigenous allies, or their enslaved laborers, would support their cause.

6-3d Native Americans

Their grievances against the tide of European American newcomers flooding the backcountry predisposed many Native Americans toward an alliance with Great Britain. Yet some chiefs urged caution: after all, Britain's earlier abandonment of Fort Pitt (and them) suggested that the Crown lacked the will—and perhaps the ability—to protect them. Moreover, Britain hesitated to make full, immediate use of its potential Native allies. Officials on the scene understood that neither the Native Americans' style of fighting nor their war aims necessarily coincided with British goals and methods. Accordingly, they at first sought from Native peoples only a promise of neutrality.

Patriots also sought to keep Native warriors out of the conflict. In 1775, the Second Continental Congress sent a general message to Native communities, describing the war as "a family quarrel between us and Old England" and requesting that Native warriors "not join on either side" because "you Indians are not concerned in it." The Iroquois Confederacy responded with a pledge of neutrality that proved short-lived. But a group of Cherokees led by Chief Dragging Canoe took advantage of the "family quarrel" to regain some land. In summer 1776, they attacked settlements in western Virginia and the Carolinas. After a militia campaign destroyed many Cherokee towns, along with crops and supplies, Dragging Canoe and his followers fled west, establishing new villages. Other Cherokees agreed to a treaty that ceded still more of their land to the United States. Bands of Shawnees and Cherokees continued to attack settlements in the backcountry throughout the war, but dissent within their ranks crippled their efforts.

The British victory over France in 1763 had restricted many Native American nations' most effective means of maintaining their independence: playing European powers against one another. Successful strategies were difficult to envision under these new circumstances, and Native leaders no longer concurred on a unified course of action. Communities split as older and younger men, or civilian and war leaders, disagreed over what policy to adopt. Only a few communities (among them the Stockbridge of New England and the Oneidas in New York) unwaveringly supported the American revolt; most Native villages either remained neutral or sporadically aligned with the British.

Warfare between settlers and Native peoples persisted in the backcountry long after fighting between patriot and redcoat armies had ceased. Indeed, the Revolutionary War constituted a brief chapter in the ongoing struggle for control of the region west of the Appalachians, which continued through the next century.

6-3e African Americans

So, too, the African Americans' Revolution formed but one battle in an epic freedom struggle that began with the first stirrings of race-based slavery and continues in the twenty-first century. Revolutionary ideology exposed one of the primary contradictions in colonial society. Both European Americans and African Americans saw the irony in slaveholders' claims that they sought to prevent Britain from "enslaving" them. Some patriot leaders, including Boston's James Otis and Philadelphia's Dr. Benjamin Rush, voiced the theme in their published writings. Common folk also pointed out the contradiction. When Josiah Atkins, a Connecticut soldier, saw George Washington's plantation, he observed in his journal: "Alas! That persons who pretend to stand for the rights of mankind for the liberties of society, can delight in oppression, & that even of the worst kind!"

African Americans did not need revolutionary ideology to tell them that slavery was wrong. But the pervasive talk of liberty added fuel to their struggle. Above all, the goal of bondspeople was *personal* independence—liberation from slavery. But could they best escape bondage by fighting with or against their masters? African Americans in different regions made different decisions. In New England, where blacks comprised the smallest share of the population, many joined the patriot ranks. Although they made up only 2 percent of the inhabitants of Massachusetts, African Americans comprised more than 12 percent of the militiamen who battled the British at Breed's Hill. During the crushing winter of 1777–1778, Washington, bogged down at Valley Forge, approved Rhode Island's plan to raise an enslaved regiment to reinforce his beleaguered troops. That state's legislature declared, "History affords us frequent precedents of the wisest, the freest, and bravest nations having liberated their slaves and enlisted them as soldiers to fight in defense of their country."

Most slaves in most colonies thought they stood a better chance by considering Britain to be "their country." As talk of war increased, groups of enslaved men from Massachusetts to South Carolina offered to assist the British army in exchange for freedom. Slave owners' worst fears were realized in Virginia, the mainland colony with the largest enslaved population. In late 1774, some Virginia slaves began meeting to discuss their response to the British troops who were soon expected to arrive. The following April, several Williamsburg slaves sent word to the royal governor, Lord Dunmore, that they were prepared to "take up arms" on his behalf. Dunmore quickly began to formulate the policy he announced in November 1775, with a proclamation offering to free any Virginia slaves and indentured servants who abandoned their patriot masters to join the British. In the months that followed, an estimated 2,500 enslaved Virginians—among them numerous women and children—rallied to the British standard. The surviving men (many perished in a smallpox epidemic) were organized into the British Ethiopian Regiment. White sashes across their uniforms bore the inscription, "Liberty to Slaves."

As other commanders renewed Dunmore's proclamation, and as the war and its attendant disruptions moved southward, thousands of escaped slaves—including people owned by George Washington and Thomas Jefferson—eventually joined the British. The best recent estimates suggest that some thirty to forty thousand people, more than two-thirds of whom were women and children, escaped their bondage during the conflict. Many died of battle wounds, starvation, and disease; those who survived till the war's end left with the redcoats, joining the global loyalist diaspora.

While the British sought to capitalize on the military potential of African Americans' freedom struggle, patriots turned rumors of slave uprisings to their own advantage. In South Carolina, resistance leaders argued that unity under the Continental Association would protect masters from their slaves at a time when royal government was unable to muster adequate defense forces. Georgia sent no delegates to the First Continental Congress and reminded its representatives at the second to remember the colony's circumstances, "with our blacks and tories [loyalists] within us," when voting on the question of independence.

In the Caribbean, the very real fear of slave uprising was a major determinant of the region's loyalism. In the summer of 1776, as news of American independence spread through the Atlantic world, more than one hundred Jamaican slaves—among them skilled artisans and house servants—led a carefully coordinated revolt that spread across much of the island. Sugar planters suspected that some of the rebels had overheard talk of revolution among their masters. "Can you be surprised that the Negroes in Jamaica should endeavour to Recover their Freedom," wrote one Kingston merchant, "when they dayly hear at the Tables of their Masters, how much the Americans are applauded for the stand they are making for theirs?" The conspirators, some of whom were burned alive for their crimes, demonstrated that there was ample reason for masters to fear the impact of the language of liberty upon their slaves.

◁ This watercolor appears in a diary kept by Jean Baptiste Antoine de Verger, a French officer serving in Rochambeau's army during the American campaigns of 1780 and 1781. The sketch depicts soldiers in varying uniforms, including a black infantryman and a scout in fringed buckskins with a tomahawk tucked in his belt.

Patriots could never completely ignore the threats posed by loyalists and neutrals, or the particular aims of Native peoples and African Americans. But only rarely did fear of these groups directly hamper the revolutionary movement. Occasionally, backcountry militiamen refused to turn out for duty on the seacoast because they worried that Native peoples would attack at home in their absence. Sometimes southern troops refused to serve in the North because they (and their political leaders) were unwilling to leave their regions unprotected against a slave insurrection. But the difficulties of a large-scale slave revolt on the mainland, coupled with dissension in Native communities and the patriots' successful campaign to disarm and neutralize loyalists, generally allowed the revolutionaries to remain in control of the countryside as they fought for independence.

6-4 The Struggle in the North

▷ **How did the British implement their military strategy in the North in 1776–1777?**

▷ **What were the consequences of the Battle of Saratoga?**

▷ **What were the outcomes of the French and American alliance?**

In June 1776, three months after they evacuated Boston, the first ships carrying Sir William Howe's troops from Halifax appeared off the coast of New York City (see Map 6.1).

Map 6.1 The War in the North, 1775–1778

The early phase of the Revolutionary War was dominated by British troop movements in the Boston area, the redcoats' evacuation to Nova Scotia in the spring of 1776, and the subsequent British invasion of New York and New Jersey.

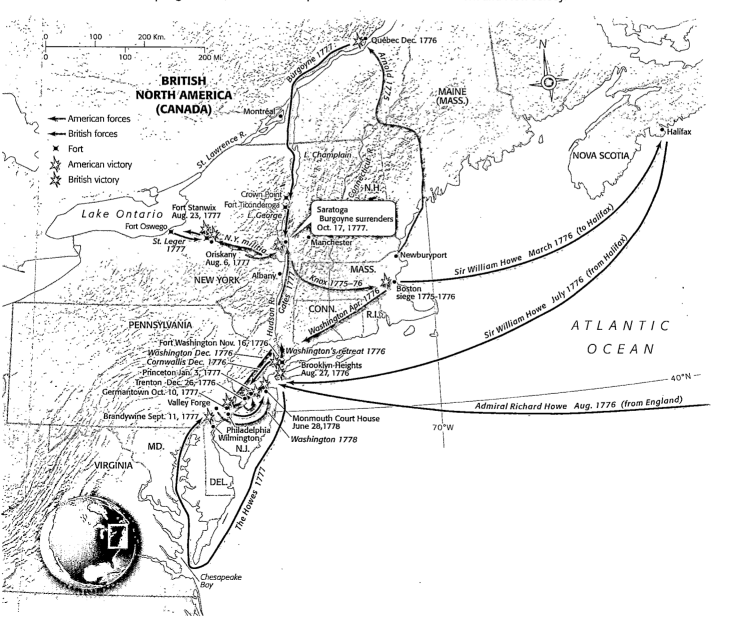

Howe staked a great deal on "getting Possession of the Town of New York," his "principal Object" of the British campaign that year. Taking New York, home to numerous loyalists, would allow the British to consolidate their colonial allies and isolate New England, which they saw—not without reason—as the flinty soil from which the rebellion had sprung. The British also hoped that victory there would ensure their triumph in the psychological war—the struggle, as Howe's successor put it, to "gain the hearts & subdue the minds of America." On July 2, the day Congress voted for independence, redcoats landed on Staten Island, but Howe waited until more troops arrived from England before attacking. The delay gave Washington time to march his army of seventeen thousand south from Boston to defend Manhattan. "We expect a very bloody summer," he told his brother.

6-4a New York and New Jersey

Bloody it was. By August, when British forces reached full strength, they comprised some twenty-four thousand men at arms, including at least eight hundred fugitive slaves from as far south as Virginia. Washington and his men, still inexperienced in fighting and maneuvering, made major mistakes, losing battles at Brooklyn Heights—the war's largest, measured by number of participants—and on Manhattan. In September, New York City fell to the British, who captured nearly three thousand American soldiers. (Those men spent most of the rest of the war on British prison ships anchored in New York harbor, where many died of smallpox and other diseases.) As the British army remade New York into its military nerve center, the patriot population fled into the countryside, much as Boston's had done the previous year. The long occupation fostered intense, small-scale violence in and around the city. Vigilante loyalists lynched suspected rebel spies, and British and Hessian soldiers systematically raped female civilians in Westchester, Staten Island, and New Jersey.

As Washington and his men slowly retreated into Pennsylvania, British forces took control of most of New Jersey. Occupying troops met little opposition; the revolutionary cause appeared to be in disarray. "These are the times that try men's souls," read the opening line of Thomas Paine's periodical *The Crisis*, whose first issue was published on December 23, 1776.

Washington determined to strike back. Moving quickly, he crossed the Delaware River at night to attack a Hessian encampment at **Trenton** early on the morning of December 26, while the Germans were sleeping off their Christmas celebrations. The patriots captured more than nine hundred Hessians and killed another thirty; only three Americans were wounded. Several days later, Washington attacked again at Princeton, defeating a British fighting force of nearly 10,000 men. Having gained command of the field and buoyed American spirits with the two swift victories, Washington set up winter quarters at Morristown, New Jersey.

6-4b The Campaign of 1777

British strategy for 1777, sketched in London over the winter, still aimed to cut off New England from the other colonies. General John Burgoyne, a subordinate of Howe, would lead an invading force of redcoats and Native warriors down the Hudson River from Canada to rendezvous near Albany with a similar force moving east along the Mohawk River valley, through Molly Brant's homeland. The combined forces would then presumably link up with Howe's troops in New York City. Meanwhile, Howe simultaneously prepared his own plan to capture Philadelphia—the seat of Congress and functionally the patriot capital—and then pursue General Washington into Pennsylvania. Thus in 1777 the British armies in America would operate independently; the result would be disaster for the empire.

Howe delayed beginning the Philadelphia campaign for months, and then took precious weeks to transport his troops by sea. By the time British forces advanced, Washington had had time to prepare his defenses. The two armies clashed twice on the outskirts of the city, first at Brandywine Creek in September, and then at Germantown a month later. Although the British won both engagements, the Americans acquitted themselves well. The redcoats captured Philadelphia in late September, forcing Congress to move inland. But the campaign season was nearly over, and the Continental army had gained skill and confidence.

Far to the north, Burgoyne was headed toward defeat. He and his men had set out from Montreal in mid-June, sailing down Lake Champlain, then marching overland toward the Hudson. Giant trees felled by patriot militiamen slowed their progress to a crawl. An easy British triumph at Fort Ticonderoga in July was followed by two setbacks in August—the redcoats and Mohawks halted their march east after the bloody Battle at Oriskany, New York; and in a clash near Bennington, Vermont, American militiamen killed or captured over nine hundred of Burgoyne's troops, including a large number of German mercenaries.

6-4c Iroquois Confederacy Splinters

The August 1777 Battle at Oriskany revealed painful new divisions within the Six Nations of the Iroquois Confederacy, formally pledged to neutrality. The loyalist Mohawk bands led by **Molly and Joseph Brant** won over the Senecas and the Cayugas, all of whom contributed warriors to the British expedition. The Oneidas—committed to the American side—brought in the Tuscaroras before fragmenting into pro-British, pro-patriot, and neutral factions. At Oriskany, some Oneidas and Tuscaroras fought with patriot militiamen against their Mohawk brethren, shattering a three-hundred-year-old league of friendship.

Trenton New Jersey site of a battle where Continental forces took almost a thousand Hessian prisoners on December 26. The battle significantly boosted the flagging morale of Washington's troops, encouraging them to fight on.

Molly and Joseph Brant Mohawk leaders who supported the British.

A British View of the Continental Army

This cartoon, by the British satirist Matthew Darly, appeared in London print shops in August 1778. Six months earlier, France had entered the war on the American side, giving the rebels renewed hope of victory. Darly's image, entitled "A View in America, in 1778," mocks the state of the Continental Army. An officer, warmly dressed in a greatcoat and fitted with a ceremonial sash and sword of the sort that Congress used to establish the authority of the new fighting force, talks to a congressman robed in furs. The politician's eye wanders, seemingly blind to the suffering taking place on the other side of the scene: One soldier wearing a smart uniform mocks others who shiver in rags, without coats, while African American laborers huddle on the ground under blankets. A boy soldier holds a sign reading "Death or Liberty"; for him, death may loom closer than freedom.

Darly's view of the suffering of common soldiers in the American fighting forces was based in fact: Congress lacked sufficient funds to pay, clothe, and feed the Continental Army during the early stages of the war.

△ *A View in America, 1778*, by Matthew Darly

Library of Congress, Prints & Photographs Division, Reproduction number LC-US262-46659 (b&w film copy neg.)

CRITICAL THINKING

◻ How might such satires have served the British war effort?

◻ What details in the picture help the artist make his political point?

The collapse of Iroquois unity and the confederacy's abandonment of neutrality had devastating consequences. In 1778, British-allied warriors raided villages in western Pennsylvania and New York. To retaliate, Washington dispatched an expedition under General John Sullivan to burn Iroquois crops, orchards, and settlements the following summer. The advancing Americans torched dozens of towns and an estimated 160,000 bushels of corn. Some soldiers committed atrocities against the civilian population, mutilating bodies, desecrating graves, and raping Native women. An Onondaga chief later reported that Sullivan's troops had "put to death all the Women and Children, excepting some of the Young Women, whom they carried away for the use of their Soldiers & were afterwards put to death in a more shamefull manner." Sullivan's scorched-earth campaign forced many bands to seek food and shelter north of the Great Lakes. A large number of Iroquois followed Molly Brant's path into exile, leaving New York to settle permanently in Canada.

Saratoga Site of battles in September and October 1777 that marked a turning point in the American Revolution. The American victory at Saratoga convinced France that Americans could win the war, leading France to ally with the colonists.

6-4d Burgoyne's Surrender

Burgoyne's sluggish progress from Montreal had given American troops time to prepare for his arrival. After several skirmishes with American soldiers commanded by General Horatio Gates, Burgoyne was surrounded near **Saratoga**, New York. On October 17, 1777, he surrendered his entire force, more than six thousand men.

Burgoyne's defeat buoyed patriots and disheartened Britons. When the news reached London, Thomas Hutchinson wrote of "universal dejection" among loyalist exiles there. "Everybody in a gloom," he commented, "most of us expect to lay our bones here." The disaster prompted Lord North to authorize a peace commission to offer the Americans what they had requested in 1774—in effect, a return to the imperial system as it stood in 1763. But the proposal came too late: the patriots rejected the overture, and the peace commission sailed back to England empty-handed in mid-1778.

Most important, the American victory at Saratoga drew France formally into the conflict. Since 1763, the French had sought to avenge their defeat in the Seven Years' War. The American War gave them the opportunity. Even before Benjamin Franklin arrived in Paris in late 1776, France covertly supplied the revolutionaries with military necessities. Indeed, 90 percent of the gunpowder used by the Americans during the war's first two years came from France, transported via its Caribbean colony in Martinique.

6-4e Franco-American Alliance of 1778

Franklin worked tirelessly to strengthen ties between the two nations. He adopted a plain style of dress that played on the French image of Americans as virtuous farmers and made him conspicuous amid the luxury of the court of Louis XVI. His efforts culminated in February 1778, when the countries signed two treaties. In the Treaty of Amity and Commerce, France recognized American independence and established trading relations with the new nation. In the Treaty of Alliance, France and the United States pledged that neither would negotiate peace with the British without first consulting the other. France also abandoned any future claim to Canada and to North American territory east of the Mississippi River. In the years that followed, the most visible symbol of Franco-American cooperation was the Marquis de Lafayette, a young nobleman who volunteered for service with George Washington in 1777 and fought alongside American officers until the conflict ended.

The French alliance had two major benefits for the patriot cause. First, France began to aid the Americans openly, sending troops and warships in addition to arms, ammunition, clothing, and blankets. Second, the massing of French naval power on the patriots' behalf meant that Britain could no longer focus solely on the rebellious mainland colonies, for it had to fight France in the Caribbean and elsewhere. Spain's entry into the war as an ally of France (but not of the United States) in 1779, followed by Holland's in 1780, turned what had been a colonial rebellion into a global war. French, Spanish, Dutch, British, and American ships clashed in the West Indies, along the Atlantic coasts of North America and Africa, in India, the Mediterranean, and even in Britain's home waters. The French aided the Americans throughout the conflict, but in its latter half that assistance proved vital.

6-5 Battlefield and Home Front

▷ **What kinds of Americans served as militiamen, common soldiers, and Continental Army officers?**

▷ **Why was life in the army difficult and hard for enlisted men and officers?**

▷ **How did the war reshape the lives of men and women on the home front?**

As a series of military engagements, the American Revolution followed distinct regional and seasonal patterns. Beginning with Britain's early attempts to cut off the American insurgency at its New England roots, the shooting war remained in the northern and mid-Atlantic colonies through 1778. After France entered the conflict, Britain's attention shifted southward, and the colonies north of Pennsylvania saw little fighting. Yet the war also extended far beyond the battlefield; its insatiable demands for men and provisions, and the economic disruptions it caused, affected colonists across North America for eight long years. Roughly two hundred thousand men—nearly 40 percent of the free male population over the age of sixteen—served either in state militia units or in the Continental army over the course of the conflict. Their sacrifice and suffering changed their lives, and the lives of everyone in their households.

6-5a Militia Units

Only in the first months of the war was the revolutionaries' army manned primarily by the semi-mythical "citizen-soldier," the militiaman who swapped his plow for a musket. After a few months or at most a year, the early arrivals went home to their farms. They reenlisted briefly and only if the contending armies neared their farms and towns. In such militia units, elected officers and the soldiers who chose them reflected local status hierarchies, yet also retained a freedom and flexibility absent from the Continental army, composed of men in formally organized statewide units led by appointed officers.

6-5b Continental Army

The motley collection of former colonies that comprised the new United States could count only three entities of a national scope: the Congress, the navy, and the Continental army. Congress was able to mobilize a national fighting force so quickly in large part because its members drew on European—especially British—models for its structure, training, and tactics. As in Britain's military, the Continental army's officer corps was composed of gentlemen—men of property—who exercised strict control over the soldiers in their command. As in Britain, ordinary soldiers surrendered many of their liberties, including the right to trial by jury, when they joined the fight for American independence.

Continental soldiers were primarily young, single, or propertyless men. They enlisted for long periods or for the war's duration, and later expressed a variety of motivations for their choices. Some were ardent patriots. Pennsylvania's William Hutchinson, who signed up twice, recalled "being young and in love with the cause." But another soldier believed his prospects as an apprentice shoemaker were grim, and decided "to try my fortune by a Roving life" in the army. Some of these lower-status men saw the army as a chance to earn monetary bonuses or allotments of land after the war. As the fighting dragged on, such bounties grew. To meet their quotas, towns and states eagerly recruited everyone they could. Regiments from the middle states contained an especially large proportion of recent immigrants; nearly half of Pennsylvania soldiers were of Irish origin, and about 13 percent were German, some serving in German-speaking regiments.

Dunmore's proclamation led Congress in January 1776 to modify an earlier policy that had prohibited the enlistment of African Americans in the regular American army. Recruiters in northern states turned increasingly to enslaved men, often promising them freedom after the war. Southern states initially resisted the trend, but all except Georgia and South Carolina eventually enlisted black soldiers. Approximately five thousand African Americans served in the Continental army, commonly in racially integrated units.

△ This receipt, dated April 21, 1778, documents the value of the blankets given to two black patriot soldiers from Glastonbury. One bears the name Prince Sambo, almost certainly a slave's name. The other, Sampson Freeman, may have claimed freedom and renamed himself by fighting in the American ranks. Collection of the Smithsonian National Museum of African American History and Culture

They were assigned tasks that others shunned, such as burying the dead, foraging for food, and driving wagons. At any given time they comprised about 10 percent of the regular army, but they seldom served in militia units.

Also attached to the American forces were a number of women, the wives and widows of poor soldiers, who came to the army with their menfolk because they were too impoverished to survive alone. Such camp followers—estimated to be about 3 percent of the total number of troops—worked as cooks, nurses, and laundresses in return for rations and low wages.

6-5c Officer Corps

Drawn from different ranks of American society, officers in the Continental army lived according to different rules of conduct and compensation than did enlisted men. A colonel earned seven times as much as a common soldier, and a junior officer was paid one and one-half times as much. Officers were discouraged from fraternizing with enlisted men, and sometimes punished for doing so.

In their tight-knit ranks, Continental officers developed an intense sense of pride and commitment to the revolutionary cause. The hardships they endured and the difficulties

they overcame fostered an esprit de corps that outlasted the war. The realities of warfare were often dirty, messy, and corrupt, but the officers drew strength from a developing image of themselves as professionals who sacrificed personal gain for the good of the nation. Officers' wives, too, prided themselves on their and their husbands' service. Unlike poor women, they did not travel with the army but instead came for extended visits while the troops were in camp (usually during the winters). Martha Washington and other officers' wives, for example, lived at Valley Forge in the winter of 1777–1778. They brought with them food, clothing, and household furnishings to make their stay more comfortable, and they entertained each other and their menfolk at teas, dinners, and dances. In camp they created friendships later renewed in civilian life, when some of their husbands became the new nation's leaders.

6-5d Hardship and Disease

Ordinary soldiers endured more hardships than their officers, but life in the American army was difficult for everyone. Wages were low, and often the army could not meet the payroll. While in camp, soldiers occasionally hired themselves out as laborers to nearby farmers to augment their meager rations or earnings. Rations (a daily allotment of bread, meat, vegetables, milk, and beer) did not always appear, leaving men to forage for their own food. When conditions deteriorated, troops threatened mutiny (though only a few carried out that threat) or simply deserted. Punishments for desertion, theft, and assault were harsh; convicted soldiers were sentenced to hundreds of lashes, whereas officers were publicly humiliated, deprived of their commissions, and discharged in disgrace.

Disease—especially dysentery and, early in the war, smallpox—was a constant feature of camp life. Most native-born colonists had neither been exposed to smallpox nor inoculated against the disease, so soldiers and civilians were vulnerable when smallpox spread through the northern countryside beginning in early 1774. The disease ravaged residents of Boston during the British occupation, the troops attacking Quebec in 1775–1776, and the African Americans who fled to join Lord Dunmore (1775) and Lord Cornwallis (1781). Because most British soldiers had already survived smallpox (which was endemic in Europe), it did not pose as significant a threat to redcoat troops. In early 1777, Washington ordered that the entire regular army and all new recruits be inoculated. Some would die from the risky procedure, and survivors would be incapacitated for weeks. But those dramatic measures, coupled with the increasing numbers of foreign-born (and mostly immune) men who enlisted, helped to protect Continental soldiers later in the war, contributing significantly to the eventual American victory.

American soldiers and sailors unfortunate enough to be captured by the British endured great suffering, especially those held in makeshift prisons or on prison ships (known as hulks) in or near Manhattan. Because Britain refused to recognize the legitimacy of the American government,

◁ The horrors of the *Jersey* prison hulk survived in American memory for many years after the Revolution ended. This image of the interior of the ship, which depicts suffering American soldiers chained in filthy rags while a well-fed British regular stands guard with bayonet, was engraved in 1855, nearly eighty years after the war, as part of a book called *Life and Death on the Ocean: A Collection of Extraordinary Adventures*.

redcoat officers regarded the patriots as rebellious traitors rather than as prisoners of war. Fed meager rations and kept in crowded, unsanitary conditions, over half of these prisoners eventually died of disease. Particularly notorious was the hulk *Jersey*; survivors reported fighting over scraps of disgusting food, and each day having to remove the bodies of their dead comrades.

6-5e Home Front

Wartime disruptions affected the lives of all Americans. Both American and British soldiers plundered farms and houses, looking for food or salable items; they burned fence rails in their fires and took horses and oxen to transport their wagons. A farmer from Tiverton, Rhode Island, later recalled that most of the town's "beasts of the plow had been carried off by the enemy from the shores, or were removed back into the country out of their reach, or had been converted for food for the use of our own army." Moreover, troops carried disease wherever they went, including when they returned home.

Those living far from the lines of march also suffered from shortages of salt, soap, flour, and other necessities. New clothing was essentially unavailable—nor could people afford it. Severe inflation eroded the worth of every penny (see Figure 6.1). With export markets drastically curtailed, income fell dramatically. While revenues plummeted, the cost of free labor increased as farmers and artisans competed with the army for available hands. That the military campaign season overlapped with the labor-intensive growing season compounded these challenges.

Even such basic social patterns as gender roles were profoundly altered by the scale and duration of the war. More men were absent from their homes for more time than ever before in the colonies. Wives who previously had handled only the "indoor affairs" of their households found themselves responsible for "outdoor affairs" as well. As the wife of a Connecticut soldier later recalled, her husband "was out more or less" from 1777 to the end of the war, "so much so as to be unable to do anything on our farm. What was done, was done by myself." Most white women did not work in the fields themselves, but they supervised field hands and managed their families' finances. These new responsibilities added to the burdens of wives and mothers, but also gave some of them a sense of independence that increased their sense of connection to the public life of the new nation.

6-6 The War Moves South

▶ **Why did the British revise their military strategy?**

▶ **How was the British campaign in the South influenced by African American slaves and European powers?**

▶ **How did the island colonies of the West Indies affect the British campaign in the South?**

Shortly after shots rang out at Lexington, the royal governor of Georgia had warned Lord Dartmouth that the concentration of British troops around Boston weakened the other provinces. If legal governments were to recover their powers, he argued, a sizeable redcoat presence was "absolutely necessary in every Province." Such warnings went unheeded through the siege of Boston and the long campaigns in New York, New Jersey, and Pennsylvania. By the end of 1777, the British had won New York City and Philadelphia. But they had lost Burgoyne's army in the process. The Americans, meanwhile, had gained an ally with a navy nearly as powerful as Britain's own.

In the wake of the Saratoga disaster, British military leaders reassessed their strategy. With France (and soon Spain) fighting on the rebel side, the North American theater shrank in importance; defending the West Indies, and even the home islands, became priorities. Britain's attention shifted toward the southern colonies in large part to create a base of operations from which to sustain and protect its Caribbean dominions. After 1778, Britain continued the American war chiefly to serve the ends of empire in the West Indies and in Europe. Sir Henry Clinton, who replaced Howe as Britain's commander, later recalled that the ministry had then "relinquished all thoughts of reducing the rebellious colonies by force of arms" so that "the collected strength of the realm might be more at liberty to act against this new enemy," France.

6-6a South Carolina and the Caribbean

In June 1778, Clinton ordered the evacuation of Philadelphia in order to redeploy some five thousand troops to capture St. Lucia from the French. Britain took St. Lucia in December of that year, and the island became the key to the empire's operations in the Caribbean. Clinton also dispatched a small expedition to Georgia. Savannah and then Augusta fell easily into British hands, convincing Clinton that a southern strategy could succeed, and might even provide a base from which to attack the northern rebel colonies. In late 1779, Clinton sailed a large force down the coast from New York to besiege Charleston (see Map 6.2). The Americans trapped in the seaport held out for months, but on May 12, 1780, General Benjamin Lincoln was forced to surrender the patriots' entire southern army—5,500 men.

The redcoats quickly spread through South Carolina, establishing garrisons at key points in the interior. Hundreds of South Carolinians renounced their allegiance to the United States, proclaiming renewed loyalty to the Crown. Thousands of escaped slaves streamed into Charleston, ready to assist the British in exchange for the freedom Clinton promised them. Fleeing from their patriot masters individually and as families, they seriously disrupted planting and harvesting in the Carolinas and Georgia in 1780 and 1781.

As smallpox ravaged besieged Charleston, Clinton organized both black and white loyalist regiments, and the process of pacifying the south began. Because there were three sides in this phase of the conflict—the British army seeking to subdue the rebels, the Continental army seeking to win American independence, and over twenty thousand African Americans seeking freedom from bondage—the southern campaign evolved into what one scholar calls a "triagonal war." Throughout 1780–1781, the specter of slave rebellion, and the certainty of massive property loss from the escape of so many enslaved people, heightened tensions between loyalists and patriots, making the war in the South especially brutal.

To a greater degree than the northern phase of the Revolution, the entry of France, Spain, and Holland made the southern campaign a naval as well as a land war. American privateers had long infested Caribbean waters, seizing valuable cargoes bound to and from British islands. Now France's powerful navy picked off those islands one by one, including Grenada—second only to Jamaica in sugar production—and, in 1781, St. Christopher. The British captured the Dutch island of St. Eustatius in early 1781, but the victory did them little good. Indeed, it cost them dearly, for Admiral Sir George Rodney, determined to secure (and to plunder) the island, remained in St. Eustatius and neglected to pursue the French fleet to Virginia, where it would play a major role in the **Battle of Yorktown.**

On land, the British army established only partial control of the areas it seized in South Carolina and Georgia. The fall of Charleston only spurred the patriots to greater exertions in the region. Patriot women in four states formed the Ladies Association, which collected money to purchase shirts for needy soldiers. Recruiting efforts were revitalized. Patriot bands operated freely, and loyalists could not be adequately protected. Nevertheless, the war in South Carolina went badly for the patriots throughout most of 1780. At Camden in August, forces under **Lord Cornwallis,** the new British commander in the South, crushingly defeated a reorganized southern army led by Horatio Gates.

6-6b Greene and the Southern Campaign

After Gates's defeat at Camden, George Washington (who remained in the North to contain the British garrison at New York) appointed General Nathanael Greene to command the southern campaign. Greene was appalled by the conditions he found in South Carolina. His troops lacked clothing, blankets, and food. He told a friend that "a great part of this country is already laid waste and in the utmost danger of becoming a desert." He lamented that incessant guerrilla warfare had "so corrupted the principles of the people that they think of nothing but plundering one another."

In such dire circumstances, Greene moved cautiously, adopting a conciliatory policy toward the many Americans who had switched sides. He ordered his troops to treat captives fairly and not to loot loyalist property. To convince a war-weary populace that the patriots could bring stability to the region, he helped the shattered provincial

Battle of Yorktown The Battle at Yorktown, Virginia, (September 28–October 19, 1781) which resulted in the defeat of British military leader Lord Cornwallis and his surrender to George Washington.

Lord Cornwallis British general whose surrender at Yorktown in 1781 marked the last major engagement between the British and Continental armies.

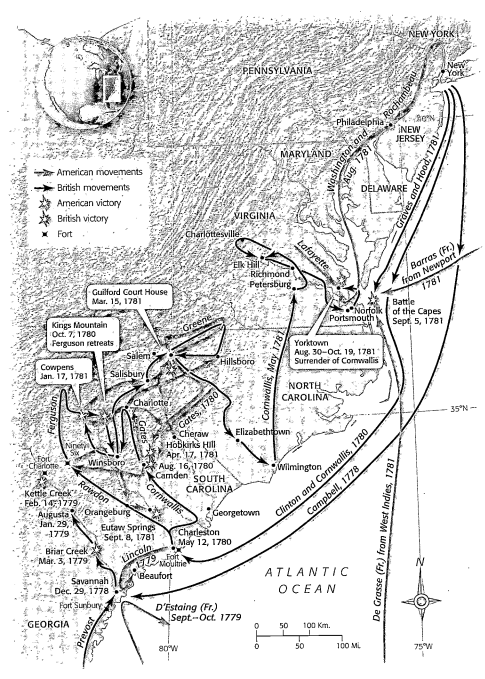

Map 6.2 The War in the South

The southern war—after the British invasion of Georgia in late 1778—was characterized by a series of British thrusts into the interior, leading to battles with American defenders in both North and South Carolina. Finally, after promising beginnings, Cornwallis's foray into Virginia ended with disaster at Yorktown in October 1781.

congresses of Georgia and South Carolina to reestablish civilian authority in the interior—a goal the British had failed to accomplish. Because he had so few regulars (only sixteen hundred when he took command), Greene had to rely on western volunteers. Because he could not afford to have frontier militia companies pinned down defending

their homes from Native attack, he pursued diplomacy aimed at keeping the Cherokee and the Catawba out of the war. Although the British army initially won some Native allies, Greene's careful maneuvers eventually proved successful. By war's end, only the Creeks remained allied with Great Britain.

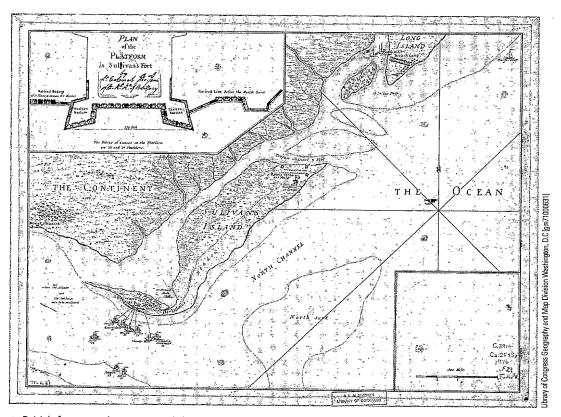

△ British forces early recognized the strategic importance of Charleston, South Carolina. This battle plan dates from the first attack on the southern port city, which took place in the summer of 1776. Continental troops successfully repulsed the British assault, and Charleston remained under rebel control until 1779, when the city fell to General Henry Clinton's besieging forces. During its long occupation thereafter, Charleston became a loyalist stronghold, filled with black as well as white refugees from the bloody fighting in the South.

Even before Greene took command in December 1780, the tide had begun to turn. At King's Mountain, in western North Carolina, a force from the backcountry defeated a large party of redcoats and loyalists that October. Then in January 1781, Greene's trusted aide Daniel Morgan brilliantly routed the British regiment Tarleton's Legion at nearby Cowpens. Greene himself confronted the main body of British troops under Lord Cornwallis at Guilford Court House, North Carolina, in March. Although Cornwallis controlled the field at the end of the day, much of his army had been destroyed. He had to retreat to Wilmington, on the coast, to await supplies and fresh troops dispatched from New York by sea. Meanwhile, Greene returned to South Carolina, where, in a series of swift strikes, he forced the redcoats to abandon their interior posts and retire to Charleston.

6-6c Surrender at Yorktown

Cornwallis headed north into Virginia, where he joined forces with a detachment of redcoats commanded by Benedict Arnold, a one-time patriot who had returned to the British fold. But instead of acting decisively with his new army of 7,200 men, Cornwallis withdrew to the peninsula between the York and James rivers. He fortified Yorktown and awaited

supplies and reinforcements from New York. The British commander Henry Clinton had dispatched 7,000 men and 25 battleships to relieve Cornwallis, explaining, "'Tis not a move of choice but of necessity. If Lord Cornwallis's army fails, I should have little hope of seeing British Dominion re-established in America" (Mackesy, p. 427). Events proved Clinton correct. Seizing the opportunity, Washington shipped more than seven thousand French and American troops south from New York. But it was French naval power that proved decisive. Admiral de Grasse's fleet arrived from the Caribbean just in time to defeat the Royal Navy vessels en route to relieve Cornwallis, and the British general found himself trapped. On October 19, 1781, Cornwallis surrendered. When news of the defeat reached London, Lord North's ministry fell, and negotiations for peace progressed rapidly.

Some thirty-five thousand British troops remained in America, and the king's forces continued to hold Halifax, New York City, Charleston, Savannah, and St. Augustine. But the catastrophe at Yorktown, coupled with losses in West Florida, Minorca, and India, and compounded by Spanish and French ships then besieging Gibraltar and menacing the English Channel, forced Britain to give up its thirteen rebel colonies for lost. In January 1782, Parliament voted to cease offensive operations in America and begin peace negotiations.

6-7 Uncertain Victories

▷ Why did the British attach so much importance to retaining Jamaica and other Caribbean colonies?

▷ What challenges did the United States face in negotiating a peace treaty?

The Battle of Yorktown marked the last engagement between the British and Continental armies, not the end of the Revolutionary War. Not until a year after news of Cornwallis's surrender reached Whitehall were preliminary peace terms settled; ratifying the **Treaty of Paris** took another nine months. In the long interim, sporadic guerilla warfare continued between loyalists and patriots from New York to Florida. In British-occupied New York, Charleston, and Savannah, some sixty thousand white and black loyalists awaited salvation. Meanwhile, the armies began the hard, slow work of withdrawing tens of thousands of British and Hessian troops and demobilizing tens of thousands of Continental soldiers and state militiamen, many of them wounded.

6-7a Saving Jamaica

Even after Yorktown, Britain remained reluctant to accept an independent United States. Indeed, George III threatened to relinquish the throne rather than recognize the new nation. "A separation from America would annihilate the rank in which the British empire stands among the European States," he wrote in January 1782. But that empire did not consist of thirteen rebel colonies alone. With the United States lost, British officials turned their full attention to the most valuable of all its American possessions: Jamaica. Jamaica produced two-fifths of Britain's sugar and nine-tenths of its rum. Its human capital—over 200,000 slaves—likewise added an enormous asset to the balance sheet of empire. Securing that prize had been a central British war aim since France entered the conflict. Through the autumn of 1781, while Cornwallis bumbled into Virginia, British strategists were consumed with the fate of Jamaica. From the perspective of the British Caribbean command, Yorktown was a disastrous distraction, allowing the French once again to mass their forces in the West Indies.

Treaty of Paris A treaty signed in 1783 when the British recognized the independence of the United States, established borders for the new nation, and agreed to withdraw all royal troops from the colonies.

△ Admiral Sir George Rodney's triumph over the French navy at the Battle of the Saintes in April 1782 preserved Britain's control of Jamaica, a cornerstone of the empire. The victory—a crucial success that stood out amidst the broader pattern of British losses in the American War—was celebrated with heroic sculptures and maritime paintings like this one, part of a series of images of the battle that Nicholas Pocock began in 1782.

Revolutionary Rhetoric

The United States was created in an event termed the American Revolution as early as 1776. Yet many historians today contend that it was not truly "revolutionary," if *revolution* means overturning an existing power structure. The nation won its independence and established a republic, radical events in the context of the eighteenth century. But with the exception of British officials, the same men who had led the colonies also led the new country. In sharp contrast, the nearly contemporary French Revolution witnessed the execution of the monarch and many aristocrats, and a significant redistribution of authority. So the legacy of the American Revolution appears ambiguous, at once radical and conservative.

Throughout the more than two hundred years since the "Revolution," groups holding widely varying political views have claimed to represent its true meaning. From far left to far right, Americans frequently declare that they are acting in the spirit of 1776. People protesting discriminatory policies against women and minorities invoke the "created equal" language of the Declaration of Independence. Left-wing organizations rail against concentrations of wealth and power in the hands of a few, again citing the Revolution's egalitarian thrust. Those protesting higher taxes often adopt the symbolism of the Boston Tea Party, as in the "tea party" movement that arose in the spring of 2009 to oppose Obama administration policies. "Party Like It's 1773," read a sign popular at their rallies. Right-wing militias arm themselves, preparing to defend their homes and families against a malevolent government, as they believe the minutemen did in

1775. Indeed, vigilante groups styling themselves "minutemen" patrol the United States–Mexico border to defend it against illegal aliens. The message of the Revolution can be invoked to support extralegal demonstrations of any description, from invasions of military bases by antiwar protesters to demonstrations outside abortion clinics by prolife advocates.

Just as Americans in the eighteenth century disagreed over the meaning of their struggle against the mother country, so the legacy of revolution remains contested in the twenty-first century, both for the nation thus created and for today's American people.

CRITICAL THINKING

▫ Which American revolutionary ideas have been most inspiring to contemporary liberals, and which to conservatives?

If the patriots' revolution ended in British defeat in Virginia in October 1781, Britain's American war ended in victory over the French at the Battle of the Saintes in April 1782. Admiral Sir George Rodney, whose decision to linger in St. Eustatius had contributed to the defeat in Yorktown, redeemed himself by capturing the French admiral and his Jamaica-bound convoy in the narrow passage between Dominica and Guadeloupe. The victory made Rodney an English national hero, and it helped Britain obtain favorable peace terms from France in the negotiations under way in Paris.

6-7b Treaty of Paris

Americans rejoiced when they learned of the signing of the preliminary peace treaty in November 1782. The American diplomats—Benjamin Franklin, John Jay, and John Adams—ignored Congress's instructions to let France take the lead and instead negotiated directly with Great Britain. Their instincts were sound: the French government was at least as much an enemy to Britain as a friend to the United States. French ministers worked behind the scenes to try to prevent the establishment of a strong, unified government in America. Spain's desire to claim the region between the Appalachian Mountains and the Mississippi River further complicated the negotiations. But though new to the world

stage, the American delegates proved adept at power politics, achieving their main goal: independence as a united nation. Weary of war, the new British government under Lord Shelburne made numerous concessions—so many, in fact, that Parliament forced Shelburne to resign shortly after peace terms were approved.

Signed on September 3, 1783, the Treaty of Paris granted unconditional independence to the United States of America. Generous boundaries delineated the new nation: to the north, approximately the present-day boundary with Canada; to the south, the 31st parallel (about the northern border of modern Florida); to the west, the Mississippi River. Florida, acquired by Britain in 1763, reverted to Spain (see Map 7.1). In ceding so much land to the United States, Britain ignored its Native American allies, sacrificing their territorial rights to the demands of European politics. British diplomats also poorly served loyalists and British merchants, who were disappointed in the peace terms.

Some provisions of the treaty rankled in the United States as well. Article Four, which allowed British merchants to recover prewar debts, and Article Five, which recommended that loyalists be allowed to recover their confiscated property, aroused considerable opposition in America. Sales of loyalists' confiscated land, houses, and possessions had helped to finance the war. Many of the purchasers were prominent patriots, and state officials hesitated to question the legitimacy of their property titles. State governments quickly passed laws denying British subjects the right to sue for recovery of debts or property in American courts, and town meetings decried the loyalists' homecoming. As residents of Norwalk, Connecticut, put it, few Americans wanted to permit the "Tory Villains" to return "while filial Tears are fresh upon our Cheeks and our Murdered Brethren scarcely cold in their Graves."

Tears were indeed plentiful. The war had been won at terrible cost. Over twenty-five thousand American soldiers had died of wounds and disease over the course of long conflict, the per capita equivalent of some 2.4 million deaths in today's United States. At least sixty thousand loyalists—the equivalent of more than 6 million people today—had fled. Years of guerrilla warfare and the escape of thousands of slaves shattered the southern economy. Everywhere, indebtedness soared, and few could afford to pay their taxes; local governments were crippled by lack of funds. It had taken thirteen rebel colonies eight years to complete the hard and violent work of demolishing a crucial part of Britain's empire. The work of building the new nation that would contain them was to last far longer.

Summary

The long war finally over, victorious Americans could contemplate their achievement with satisfaction and even awe. Having forged a working coalition among the disparate mainland colonies, they declared their membership in the family of nations and entered a successful alliance with France. An inexperienced army composed of militia and newly enlisted regulars had defeated the professional soldiers of the greatest military power in the world. They had won only a few battles—most notably, at Trenton, Saratoga, and Yorktown—but their army always survived to fight again, even after major losses at Manhattan and Charleston. Ultimately, the Americans wore down an enemy that had other parts of its empire to shore up.

In winning the war, the Americans reshaped the physical and mental landscapes in which they lived. They excluded from their new nation their loyalist neighbors who were unwilling to make a break with the mother country. They established republican governments at state and national levels. In the families of Continental army

soldiers in particular they began the process of creating new national loyalties. They laid claim to most of the territory east of the Mississippi River and south of the Great Lakes, thereby greatly expanding the land potentially open to their settlements and threatening Native dominance of the continent's interior. They had also begun, sometimes without recognizing it, the long national reckoning with slavery that would last nearly another century.

In achieving independence, Americans surmounted formidable challenges. But in the future they faced perhaps an even greater one: defining their nation and ensuring its survival in a world dominated by the bitter rivalries among Britain, France, and Spain, and threatened by divisions within the American people as well.

Suggestions for Further Reading

Emma Christopher, *A Merciless Place: The Fate of Britain's Convicts after the American Revolution* (2011)

Stephen Conway, *The British Isles and the War of American Independence* (2000)

Caroline Cox, *A Proper Sense of Honor: Service and Sacrifice in George Washington's Army* (2004)

Kathleen DuVal, *Independence Lost: Lives on the Edge of the American Revolution* (2015)

Edward G. Gray and Jane Kamensky, eds., *The Oxford Handbook of the American Revolution* (2012)

Maya Jasanoff, *Liberty's Exiles: American Loyalists in the Revolutionary World* (2011)

Jill Lepore, *The Whites of Their Eyes: The Tea Party's Revolution and the Battle over American History* (2010)

Piers Mackesy, *The War for America, 1775–1783* (1964)

Pauline Maier, *American Scripture: Making the Declaration of Independence* (1997)

Mary Beth Norton, *Liberty's Daughters: The Revolutionary Experience of American Women, 1750–1800* (2nd ed., 1996)

Andrew Jackson O'Shaughnessy, *The Men Who Lost America: British Leadership, the American Revolution, and the Fate of the Empire* (2013)

Robert G. Parkinson, *The Common Cause: Creating Race and Nation in the American Revolution* (2016).

Sophia Rosenfeld, *Common Sense: A Political History* (2011)

Alan Taylor, *American Revolutions: A Continental History, 1750–1804* (2016)

Forging a Nation, 1783–1800

The pullout began in March 1783, when news reached New York City that America and Britain had agreed upon preliminary terms of peace. Demilitarizing the occupied port posed a formidable challenge. Twenty thousand British troops had to be shipped to other corners of the empire, along with their cannons and mortars and guns. His Majesty's army sold its surplus, including 63,596 pairs of soldiers' boots. Every Wednesday and Sunday, the Wagon Office auctioned off the horses whose feed and transport the king's defeated cavalry could not afford.

Thirty-five thousand loyalist civilians also needed to find homes in a new world they had neither imagined nor embraced. As displaced patriots streamed back into the city, tensions flared. "Almost all those who have attempted to return to their homes have been exceedingly ill treated, many beaten, robbed of their money and clothing," lamented the British official in charge of the transfer. Ill treated or not, the patriots were home to stay. And so, like their counterparts in Savannah and Charleston, most of New York's loyalists would have to rebuild their shattered lives in exile. The fate of thousands of African American loyalists was especially insecure. A British commission met weekly in a tavern on Pearl Street to arbitrate the claims of people who had escaped slavery. Had they served the British cause and spent at least a year behind British lines, thus earning freedom by the terms of the treaty? Or would they be re-enslaved, recovered as lost property by their aggrieved owners?

Each Wednesday, the commissioners granted passage to the lucky ones whose names they recorded in a ledger called the "Book of Negroes." One of the first transport ships out, called *L'Abondance*, carried 132 free blacks to new lives in Nova Scotia. Among them was a man whom Lord Dunmore had

◁ This engraving of General George Washington's triumphant arrival in New York City was published in 1860. One of many popular versions of the scene, it offered an idealized image of American unity on the eve of the Civil War, when annual celebrations of New York's "Evacuation Day" would be absorbed by the new Union holiday of Thanksgiving. Library of Congress Prints and Photographs Division [LC-USZC4-524]

Chronology

1777	▦ Vermont becomes first jurisdiction to abolish slavery
1783	▪ British expelled from New York City
1784	▦ United States signs treaty with Iroquois at Fort Stanwix; Iroquois repudiate it two years later
1785	▦ Land Ordinance of 1785 provides for surveying and sale of national lands in Northwest Territory
1785–86	▦ United States negotiates treaties with Choctaws, Chickasaws, and Cherokees
1786	▧ Annapolis Convention discusses reforming government
1786–87	▦ Shays's Rebellion in western Massachusetts raises questions about future of the republic
1787	▪ Constitutional Convention drafts new form of government
1788	▪ Hamilton, Jay, and Madison urge ratification of the Constitution in *The Federalist* ▪ Constitution ratified
1789	▦ Washington inaugurated as first president ▪ Fall of the Bastille: French Revolution begins
1790	▪ Hamilton's *Report on the Public Credit* proposes national assumption of state debts
1791	▪ First ten amendments (Bill of Rights) ratified ▨ First national bank chartered ▦ Haitian Revolution begins

1793	▪ France declares war on Britain, Spain, and the Netherlands ▨ Washington proclaims American neutrality in Europe's war ▪ Democratic societies founded, the first grassroots political organizations
1794	▪ Whiskey Rebellion in western Pennsylvania protests taxation
1795	▨ Jay Treaty with Britain resolves issues remaining from the Revolution ▨ Pinckney's Treaty with Spain establishes southern boundary of the United States ▨ Treaty of Greenville with Miami Confederacy opens Ohio to settlement
1796	▨ First contested presidential election: Adams elected president, Jefferson vice president
1798	▨ XYZ Affair arouses American opinion against France ▪ Sedition Act penalizes dissent
1798–99	▪ Quasi-War with France ▪ Fries's Rebellion in Pennsylvania protests taxation
1800	▨ Gabriel's Rebellion threatens Virginia slave owners
1800–01	▨ Jefferson elected president by the House of Representatives after stalemate in electoral college

recruited from the workforce of a Virginia patriot when the war began. Harry Washington escaped Mount Vernon and never looked back, not even when his former owner assumed command of the Continental army. His exodus would take him from the Chesapeake to New York to a small settlement south of Halifax and eventually to the African American colony in Sierra Leone, whose capital the former slaves and their patrons named Freetown.

On November 25, 1783, months after *L'Abondance* spirited Harry Washington to lasting freedom, his onetime master—the commander-in-chief of the victorious American forces—rode into New York City in triumph. Sitting tall astride a tall gray charger, flanked by his officers and civilian leaders, General George Washington processed to the fort at the southern tip of Manhattan. At one o'clock, a cannon fired as the last British troops in the new United States climbed into longboats and rowed out to ships facing east, toward home.

Experience an interactive version of this story in MindTap®.

The evacuation of New York City marked one ending of the American Revolution. As the last British soldiers sailed out of New York harbor, Americans were left alone with the country whose independence they had won through eight years of bold and violent struggle against their erstwhile colonial parent. In the end, the transfer of power had been remarkably peaceful, noted one British officer who witnessed the evacuation. "These Americans are a curious original people," he quipped, "*they know how to govern themselves, but nobody else can govern them.*"

But *did* they know how to govern themselves? This "curious original people"—who were sovereign in the new American republic—now confronted urgent questions about their future: questions about liberty and property, about self-sacrifice and self-interest, about new allies and old enemies, about the states and the nation. How could Americans create and sustain that most fragile form of government, a virtuous republic? How would that republic take its place "among the powers of the earth," as the Declaration of Independence had put it? And how could the country's leaders foster consensus among a people so various in a nation so vast?

Fighting the British dissolved at least some of the boundaries that had long divided American colonists. But throughout the long civil war, Americans had remained stunningly diverse, even among the minority actively working for the patriot cause. Eastern planters held different priorities from western farmers. Native peoples battled backcountry settlers. Slaveholders found themselves at war with their bondspeople, and merchants contended with demands of poor laborers. Northern and southern interests, too, were increasingly distinct. *E Pluribus Unum*, the nation's new Great Seal proclaimed: "from many, one." Making one nation of many peoples—settling the Revolution—was the enormous task of the 1780s and 1790s. It remains unfinished still.

Nation-making involved formal politics and diplomacy, as the leading men of the United States set out to fashion a government from diverse polities and divergent republican ideals. The country's first such government, under the Articles of Confederation, proved too weak and decentralized. Political leaders tried another approach when they drafted the Constitution in 1787. Some historians have argued that the Articles of Confederation and the Constitution reflected opposing political philosophies, the Constitution representing an "aristocratic" counterrevolution against the more "democratic" Articles. The two documents are more accurately viewed as successive attempts to solve the same philosophical and practical problems. Neither succeeded in resolving those difficulties entirely.

Ratifying the Constitution provoked heated and sometimes violent contests in 1787 and 1788. Those battles between Federalists (supporters of the Constitution) and **Antifederalists** (its opponents) foreshadowed still deeper divisions over major questions confronting the republic: the relationship between national power and states' rights, the formulation of foreign policy, the future of Native territories encompassed within the borders of the United States, and the limits of dissent. Americans had not anticipated the acrimonious disagreements that roiled the 1790s, and could not fully accept the division of the nation's citizens into competing factions known as Federalists and Republicans (or Democratic–Republicans). In republics, they believed, consensus should prevail; the rise of factions signified corruption. Yet political leaders worked actively to galvanize supporters, thereby remaking the nation's political practice if not its theory. When the decade closed, Americans still had not come to terms with the implications of partisanship, as the election of 1800 vividly illustrated.

The hard work of settling the Revolution took place not only in the sphere of electoral politics and statecraft, but also in the realms of culture and ideas. In the early United States, novelists and playwrights, painters and architects, and educators at every level pursued explicitly moral goals. Women's education became newly important, for the mothers of the republic's "rising generation" were seen as responsible for ensuring the nation's future.

And then there were Thomas Jefferson's soaring words in the Declaration of Independence: "all men are created equal." Given that bold statement of principle, how could white republicans justify holding African Americans in perpetual bondage? During the war, thousands of enslaved men and women had answered that question by freeing themselves by any means necessary. Some white Americans, too, signed manumission papers, which freed particular slaves, or voted for state laws that abolished the institution of slavery. Others redoubled their defense of slavery, denying that blacks were "men" in the same sense as whites.

"We the People of the United States": in their name, and by their power, was the federal Constitution ratified. But who, precisely, were "the People," and how did various groups among them encounter the new nation? Some of the answers were clearer in 1800 than they had been in 1776. But as

Antifederalists So labeled by the Federalists, the Antifederalists were opposed to the Constitution because they feared it gave too much power to the central government and it did not contain a bill of rights.

Thomas Jefferson assumed the presidency, the long work of settling the Revolution had barely begun.

☐ *What challenges confronted the new nation's leaders at home and abroad during the 1780s and 1790s?*

☐ *What were the elements of the new national identity? How did poor farmers, women, Native peoples, and African Americans fit into that identity?*

☐ *What disputes divided the nation's citizens, and how did Americans react to those disputes?*

7-1 Trials of the Confederation

▶ **What domestic and international issues exposed the weaknesses of the Articles of Confederation?**

▶ **How did state governments relate to the national government under the Articles of Confederation?**

▶ **How did relations between Native American peoples and the United States evolve under the Articles of Confederation?**

In late 1777, the Second Continental Congress sent to the states the first blueprint of the national government, the Articles of Confederation. But not until 1781, when Maryland finally accepted the Articles, had the document finally been ratified. The delay signaled the fate of the national government in the ensuing years. The unicameral legislature, called the Second Continental Congress until 1781 and the Confederation Congress thereafter, proved unwieldy. Under the Articles, Congress was simultaneously a legislative body and a collective executive; there was no judiciary. It had no independent income and no authority to compel the states to accept its rulings. In the 1780s, the limitations of the Articles would become obvious—indeed, glaring.

7-1a Foreign Affairs

Because the Articles denied Congress the power to establish a national commercial policy, the realm of foreign trade exposed the new government's weaknesses. Immediately after the war, Britain, France, and Spain restricted America's trade with their colonies. Members of Congress watched helplessly as British manufactured goods flooded the United States while American produce could no longer be sold in the British West Indies. Although the United States reopened commerce with other European countries and started a

profitable trade with China in 1784, neither substituted for access to closer and larger markets.

The Spanish presence on the nation's southern and western borders caused other difficulties. Determined to check the republic's expansion, Spain in 1784 closed the Mississippi River to American navigation, thereby depriving the growing settlements west of the Appalachians of access to the Gulf of Mexico. The United States began negotiations with Spain in 1785, but the talks collapsed when Congress divided. Southerners and westerners insisted on navigation rights on the Mississippi, whereas northerners focused on winning commercial concessions in the West Indies. The impasse made some congressmen question the possibility of a national consensus on foreign affairs.

The refusal of state and local governments to comply with provisions of the Treaty of Paris relating to the payment of prewar debts and the confiscated property of loyalists gave Britain an excuse to maintain military posts on the Great Lakes. Furthermore, Congress's inability to convince states to implement the treaty disclosed its lack of power, even in an area—foreign affairs—in which the Articles gave it clear authority. "Will foreign nations be willing to undertake anything with us or for us," asked New York's Alexander Hamilton, "when they find that the nature of our governments will allow no dependence to be placed on our engagements?"

7-1b Order and Disorder in the West

Congressmen confronted other knotty problems beyond the Appalachians, where individual states continued to jockey over the vague western boundaries indicated by their colonial charters (see Map 7.1). Native American nations advanced their territorial rights as well. The United States assumed the Treaty of Paris had cleared its title to all land east of the Mississippi except the area still held by Spain. Still, recognizing that land cessions should be obtained from powerful tribes, Congress initiated negotiations with northern and southern Native peoples (see Map 7.2).

At Fort Stanwix, New York, in 1784, American diplomats negotiated a treaty with chiefs who claimed to represent the Iroquois; at Hopewell, South Carolina, in late 1785 and early 1786, they did the same with emissaries from the Choctaw, Chickasaw, and Cherokee nations. In 1786, the Iroquois repudiated the Fort Stanwix treaty, denying that the men who negotiated the pact had been authorized to speak for the Six Nations. The confederacy threatened new attacks on frontier settlements, but everyone knew the threat was empty; the flawed treaty stood by default. At intervals until the end of the decade, New York purchased large tracts of land from individual Iroquois nations. By 1790, the once-dominant confederacy was confined to a few scattered reservations.

In the South, too, the United States took the treaties as confirmation of its sovereignty. European Americans poured over the southern Appalachians, provoking the Creeks—who had not agreed to the Hopewell treaties—to defend their territory by declaring war. Only in 1790 did they come to terms with the United States.

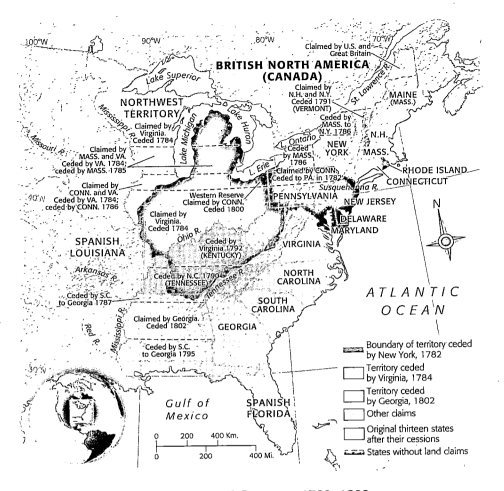

Map 7.1 Western Land Claims and Cessions, 1782–1802

After the United States achieved independence, states competed with one another for control of valuable lands to which their original charters granted them sometimes overlapping claims, largely ignoring the prior claims of Native American nations. That competition led to a series of compromises among the states or between individual states and the new nation, indicated on this map.

7-1c Ordinance of 1785

Western nations, such as the Shawnees, Chippewas, Ottawas, and Potawatomis, had begun to challenge Iroquois hegemony as early as the 1750s. After the collapse of Iroquois power in the late 1780s, they formed their own confederacy and demanded direct negotiations with the United States. At first, the American government ignored the western confederacy. Shortly after state land cessions were completed, Congress began to organize the Northwest Territory, bounded by the Mississippi River, the Great Lakes, and the Ohio River (see Map 7.1). Ordinances passed in 1784, 1785, and 1787 outlined the process through which the land would be governed and sold to settlers. The first of these laws, approved by Congress in April 1784, created procedures for settlers in the Northwest Territory to form governments and eventually organize new states that would join the federal union. To ensure orderly development, Congress in 1785 directed that

land in the Northwest Territory be surveyed into townships 6 miles square, each divided into thirty-six sections of 640 acres (one square mile). One dollar was the minimum price per acre; the minimum sale was one section. The resulting minimum outlay, $640, lay beyond the reach of small farmers, except for those veterans who received part of their army pay in land warrants. Proceeds from western land sales constituted the first independent revenues available to the national government.

7-1d Northwest Ordinance

The Northwest Ordinance of 1787 contained a bill of rights that guaranteed settlers in the territory freedom of religion and the right to jury trial, forbade cruel and unusual punishment, and prohibited slavery. Eventually, that prohibition became an important symbol for antislavery northerners, but at the time it had little effect. Some residents of the territory already held slaves,

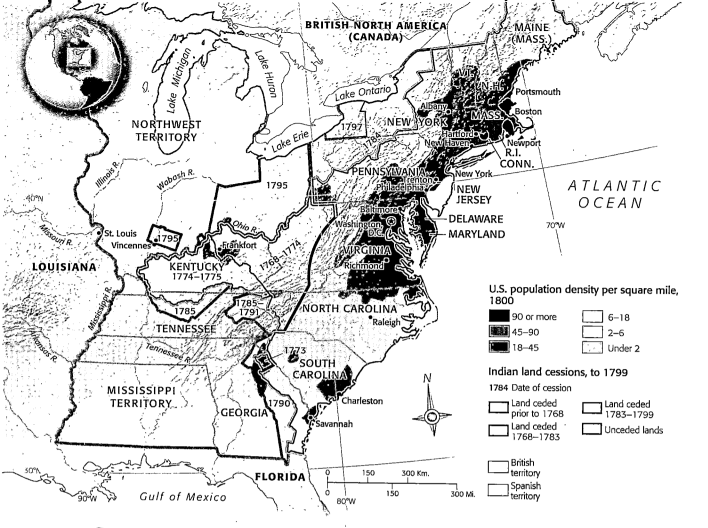

Map 7.2 Cession of Tribal Lands to the United States, 1775–1790

The land claims of the United States meant little as long as Native American nations still controlled vast territories within the new country's formal boundaries. A series of treaties in the 1780s and 1790s spelled the end of Native territorial sovereignty over some lands, which were opened to white settlement.

U.S. population density per square mile, 1800

- 90 or more
- 45–90
- 18–45
- 6–18
- 2–6
- Under 2

Indian land cessions, to 1799

1784 Date of cession

- Land ceded prior to 1768
- Land ceded 1768–1783
- Land ceded 1783–1799
- Unceded lands
- British territory
- Spanish territory

and Congress did not intend to seize their property. Moreover, the ordinance also contained a provision allowing slave owners to "lawfully reclaim" escaped slaves who took refuge in the territory—the first national fugitive slave law. Not until 1848 was enslavement abolished throughout the region, by then known as the Old Northwest. And by omission, Congress implied that slavery was legal in the territories south of the Ohio River.

The ordinance of 1787 also specified the process by which territorial residents could organize state governments and seek admission to the Union "on an equal footing with the original States," with the same rights held by citizens of the existing thirteen states. Having suffered under the rule of a colonial power, congressmen understood the importance of preparing the new nation's first "colony" for self-government.

Although the Northwest Ordinance is often viewed as one of the few lasting accomplishments of the Confederation Congress, its impact remained largely theoretical in 1787. Miamis, Shawnees, and Delawares in the region refused to acknowledge American sovereignty. They opposed the encroachment of the United States violently, attacking pioneers

who ventured too far north of the Ohio River. Not until after the Articles of Confederation were replaced with a new constitution could the United States muster sufficient force to implement the ordinance.

7-1e The First American Depression

The Revolution wrought sudden and permanent change in the American economy, and the Articles—with their severe limitations around matters of taxation and finance—were ill equipped to confront the transformation. During the war, trade between Europe (especially Britain) and North America all but ceased. Between 1777 and 1782, the United States imported and exported about one-tenth what it had before the outbreak of fighting. New England fishermen, merchants in the British-held port cities, farm wives in the backcountry, tobacco growers in the Chesapeake, rice and indigo planters in the Lower South: everyone felt the disruption. As vital sources of income and goods dried up, the plummeting value of the Continental dollar sharply diminished purchasing

△ A British cartoon ironically reflected Americans' hopes for postwar trade, hopes that were dashed after 1783. The Native woman symbolizing America sits on a pile of tobacco bales, near rice and indigo casks bound for Europe. The artist was satirizing the failed 1778 British peace commission and Britons' willingness to make concessions to the rebellious colonies, but his image captured Americans' belief in the importance of their produce.

power. After the peace, exporters of staple crops and importers of manufactured goods continued to suffer from restrictions that European powers imposed on American commerce.

Although recovery began by 1786, the war's effects proved hard to erase. Before the war broke out, per capita income in the rebel colonies had averaged roughly $2,130 (in today's dollars). In 1790, years after the war ended, per capita income averaged only $1,220. This drop of more than 40 percent nearly equaled the Americans' losses in the early years of the Great Depression. By 1805, average per capita income had rebounded to $1,830, but the recovery bypassed much of the countryside, especially in the Lower South.

The near-total cessation of foreign commerce during the war stimulated domestic manufacturing, and the postwar period witnessed the stirrings of American industrial development. The first American textile mill began production in Pawtucket, Rhode Island, in 1793. The country's export trade shifted from Europe and toward the West Indies, continuing a trend that began before the war. Foodstuffs shipped to the French and Dutch Caribbean colonies became America's largest single export, replacing tobacco (and thus accelerating the Chesapeake's conversion to grain production). South Carolina resumed importing slaves on a large scale, as planters sought to replace workers who fled during the war. Yet without British subsidies, American indigo could not compete with that produced in the Caribbean, and even rice planters struggled to find new markets.

7-2 From Crisis to the Constitution

▷ **How did Shays's Rebellion alter opinion about the Articles of Confederation?**

▷ **What issues divided the delegates at the Constitutional Convention?**

▷ **What were the respective positions of the Federalists and Antifederalists in the debates over the Constitution?**

Congress could not establish a uniform commercial policy or ensure compliance with the treaties it signed. Lacking the power to levy or collect taxes, it could not raise revenues needed to run the government. By the mid-1780s, Americans involved in overseas trade, western land speculation, foreign affairs, and finance had become acutely aware of the inadequacies of the Articles of Confederation.

7-2a Annapolis Convention

Recognizing the Confederation Congress's inability to deal with commercial matters, representatives of Virginia and Maryland met at George Washington's Mount Vernon plantation in March 1785 to negotiate an agreement about trade on the Potomac River. The meeting prompted an invitation to other states to discuss trade policy more broadly at a convention in Annapolis, Maryland. Although nine states named representatives to the gathering in September 1786, only five delegations attended—too few to have any significant impact. Those present issued a call for another convention, to be held in Philadelphia nine months later, "to devise such further provisions as shall . . . appear necessary to render the constitution of the federal government adequate to the exigencies of the Union."

At first, few other states responded. But the nation's economic problems also caused taxation woes. The states had run up huge debts to finance the war, issuing securities to pay soldiers, purchase supplies, and underwrite loans. During the hard times of the early 1780s, many veterans and other creditors sold those securities to speculators for pennies on the dollar. In 1785, Congress requisitioned still more taxes from the states to pay off foreign and domestic holders of national war bonds. When states tried to comply, they succeeded primarily in arousing popular protests. The most dramatic response came in Massachusetts, which levied heavy taxes to pay the securities (plus interest) at full price in specie before the end of the decade. Farmers faced with selling their land to pay the new taxes responded furiously. The actions of men from the state's western counties, many of them veterans from leading families, convinced doubters that reform was needed.

7-2b Shays's Rebellion

Daniel Shays, a former officer in the Continental army, assumed nominal leadership of the disgruntled westerners. On January 25, 1787, he led about fifteen hundred troops in an assault on the federal armory at Springfield. The militiamen mustered to defend the armory fired on their former comrades in arms, who suffered twenty-four casualties. Some (including Shays) fled the state; two were hanged; most paid fines and took oaths of allegiance to Massachusetts. The state legislature soon reduced the burden on landowners, easing tax collections and enacting new import duties instead.

Reprinted in newspapers throughout the United States, the words of the Shaysites reverberated around the new nation. Calling Massachusetts "tyrannical" and styling themselves "Regulators" (like backcountry Carolinians in the 1760s), they had linked their rebellion with the struggle for American independence, as political insurgents in the United States would do for decades to come.

7-2c Constitutional Convention

The words and actions of the Shaysites convinced many political leaders that only a much stronger federal government could solve the nation's problems. After most of the states had already appointed delegates, the Confederation Congress belatedly endorsed the proposed Philadelphia convention, "for the sole and express purpose of revising the Articles of Confederation." In mid-May 1787,

James Madison The Virginia congressman known as the "Father of the Constitution" and fourth president of the United States (1809–1817).

fifty-five men, representing all the states but Rhode Island, began to assemble in the Pennsylvania State House.

The vast majority of delegates to the Constitutional Convention were men of substantial property. Their ranks included merchants, planters, physicians, generals, governors, and especially lawyers—twenty-three had studied law. In an era when only a tiny handful of men had advanced education, more than half of them had attended college. The youngest delegate was twenty-six, the oldest—Benjamin Franklin—eighty-one. Like George Washington, whom they elected their presiding officer, most were in their vigorous middle years. All favored reform. Most wanted to give the national government new authority over taxation and foreign commerce. Yet they also sought to advance their states' divergent interests.

A dozen men did the bulk of the convention's work. Of those, **James Madison** of Virginia most fully deserves the title "Father of the Constitution." A Princeton graduate from western Virginia, he had served on the local Committee of Safety and was elected successively to the provincial convention, the state's lower and upper houses, and the Continental Congress (1780–1783). A promoter of the Annapolis Convention, he strongly supported further reform.

△ James Madison (1751–1836), the youthful scholar and skilled politician who shaped the Constitution. The American artist Charles Willson Peale painted this miniature portrait of Madison. Madison presented it to Kitty Floyd, a young woman to whom he proposed marriage in the spring of 1783. She would have worn it as a pin until she broke off the engagement several months later. Library of Congress Prints and Photographs Division [LC-USZC4-4097]

Madison carefully prepared for the Philadelphia meeting. Through his close friend Thomas Jefferson, he ordered more than two hundred books on history and government from Paris, analyzing their accounts of past republics. A month before the convention began, Madison summed up his research in a paper entitled "Vices of the Political System of the United States." What the government most needed, he argued, was "such a modification of the sovereignty as will render it sufficiently neutral between the different interests and factions." Rejecting the common assertion that republics had to be small to survive, Madison asserted that a large, diverse republic was less likely to succumb to the influence of a particular faction. No one set of interests would be able to control it, and political stability would result from compromises among contending parties.

7-2d Virginia and New Jersey Plans

The so-called **Virginia Plan**, introduced on May 29 by that state's governor, Edmund Randolph, embodied Madison's conception of national government. The plan provided for a two-house legislature with the lower house elected directly by the people and the upper house selected by the lower; representation in both houses proportional to property or population; an executive elected by Congress; a national judiciary; and congressional veto over state laws. The Virginia Plan gave Congress broad power to legislate "in all cases to which the separate states are incompetent."

Many delegates believed the Virginia Plan went too far in the direction of national consolidation. After two weeks of debate on Randolph's proposal, disaffected delegates—particularly those from small states—united under the leadership of William Paterson of New Jersey. On June 15, Paterson presented an alternative scheme, the **New Jersey Plan**. He proposed retaining a unicameral Congress in which each state had an equal vote, while giving Congress new powers of taxation and regulation. Although the convention initially rejected Paterson's position, he and his allies won a number of victories in the months that followed.

The delegates began their work by discussing the structure and functions of Congress. They readily agreed that the new government should have a two-house (bicameral) legislature. Further, in accordance with Americans' long-standing opposition to virtual representation, they concurred that "the people," however defined, should directly choose the members of at least one house. But they differed widely in their answers to three key questions: Should representation in both houses of Congress be proportional to population? How was representation in either house to be apportioned among the states? And, finally, how would the members of the two houses be elected?

The last issue proved easiest to resolve. To quote Pennsylvania's John Dickinson, the delegates deemed it "essential" that members of the lower branch of Congress be elected directly by the people and "expedient" that members of the upper house be chosen by state legislatures. This strategy had the virtue of placing the election of one house of Congress a step removed from the "lesser sort," whose judgment the wealthy convention delegates did not wholly trust.

The possibility of proportional representation in the Senate caused greater disagreement. Small states, through their spokesman Luther Martin of Maryland, argued for equal representation in the Senate. Such a scheme, they rightly supposed, would give them relatively more power at the national level. Large states, on the other hand, supported a proportional plan, which would allot them more votes in the upper house. For weeks, the convention deadlocked. A committee appointed to work out a compromise recommended equal representation in the Senate, coupled with a proviso that all appropriation bills originate in the lower house. Only the absence of several opponents of the compromise at the time of the vote averted a breakdown.

7-2e Slavery and the Constitution

The remaining critical question divided the nation along sectional lines rather than by size of state: how was representation in the lower house to be apportioned? Delegates concurred that a census should be conducted every ten years to determine the nation's population, and they agreed that Native peoples, who paid no taxes, should be excluded for purposes of representation. Delegates from states like Virginia and South Carolina, with large numbers of slaves, wanted to count inhabitants of African descent and those of European descent equally for the purposes of representation, though not for taxation and certainly not for the rights of citizenship. Delegates from states with few slaves wanted to count only free people. Slavery thus became inextricably linked to the foundation of the new government.

The convention resolved the dispute by using a formula developed by the Confederation Congress in 1783 to allocate financial assessments among states: three-fifths of slaves would be included in population totals. (The formula reflected delegates' judgment that slaves were less efficient producers of wealth than free people, not that they were three-fifths human and two-fifths property.) What came to be known as the "three-fifths compromise" on representation won unanimous approval. Only two delegates, Gouverneur Morris of New York and George Mason of Virginia, later spoke out against the institution of slavery.

The **three-fifths clause** not only assured southern voters congressional representation out of proportion

Virginia Plan A proposal calling for the establishment of a strong central government. It gave Congress virtually unrestricted rights of legislation and taxation, power to veto any state law, and authority to use military force against the states.

New Jersey Plan A proposal calling for a single-chamber congress in which each state had an equal vote, just as in the Articles, and strengthening the taxing and commercial powers of Congress.

three-fifths clause Allowed states to count three-fifths of their enslaved population for the purposes of congressional representation, giving large slaveholding states disproportionate power in congress and in the electoral college.

to the free populations of their states, but also granted them disproportionate influence on the selection of the president. In return for southerners' agreement that Congress could pass commercial regulations by a simple majority vote, New Englanders agreed that Congress could not end the importation of slaves for at least twenty years. Further, the fugitive slave clause (Article IV, Section 2) required all states to return runaways to their masters. By guaranteeing that the national government would aid any states threatened with "domestic violence," the Constitution promised aid in putting down future slave revolts, as well as incidents like Shays's Rebellion. Although the words *slave* and *slavery* never appear in the Constitution (the framers used such euphemisms as "other persons"), eleven of its eighty-four clauses concerned slavery in some fashion. All but one of those eleven protected slaveholders and the institution on which their wealth and power rested.

7-2f Congressional and Presidential Powers

Having compromised on the knotty, conjoined problems of slavery and representation, the delegates readily achieved consensus on other issues. All concurred that the national government needed the authority to tax and to regulate foreign and interstate commerce, but the delegates stopped short of giving Congress the nearly unlimited scope Randolph had proposed. Discarding the congressional veto contained in the Virginia Plan, the convention implied but did not explicitly authorize a national judicial veto of state laws. Delegates also drafted a long list of actions forbidden to states, including impairing contractual obligations—in other words, preventing the relief of debtors. Contrary to many state constitutions, they stipulated that religious tests could never be required of U.S. officeholders.

The convention placed primary responsibility for the conduct of foreign affairs in the hands of a new official, the president, who was also designated commander-in-chief of the armed forces. With the Senate's consent, the president could appoint judges and other federal officers. To select the president, delegates established the electoral college, whose members would be chosen in each state by legislatures or qualified voters. If a majority of electors failed to unite behind one candidate, the House of Representatives (voting as states, not as individuals) would choose the president, who was to serve for four years and be eligible for reelection.

The Constitution created a national government less powerful than Madison and Randolph's Virginia Plan had envisioned. It distributed political authority among executive, legislative, and judicial branches of the national government, and divided power between states and nation (a system known as *federalism*). The president could veto congressional legislation, but that veto could be overridden by two-thirds majorities in both houses. Treaties and major appointments required the Senate's consent. Congress could impeach the president and federal judges, but courts appeared to have the final say on interpreting the Constitution. Two-thirds of Congress and three-fourths of the states had to concur on amendments. These checks and balances would prevent the

government from becoming tyrannical, yet the elaborate system would sometimes prevent the government from acting decisively. And the line between state and national powers remained so blurry that the United States fought a civil war in the next century over that very issue.

The convention held its last session on September 17, 1787. Benjamin Franklin had written a speech calling for unity; because his voice had grown weak, another delegate read it for him. "I confess that there are several parts of this constitution which I do not at present approve," Franklin admitted. Yet he urged its acceptance "because I expect no better, and because I am not sure, that it is not the best." All but three of the 42 delegates still present then signed the Constitution. Only then was the document made public. The convention's proceedings had been entirely secret—and remained so until the delegates' private notes were published in the nineteenth century (see the appendix for the text of the Constitution).

Congress submitted the Constitution to the states in late September. The ratification clause provided for the new system to take effect once it was approved by special conventions in at least nine states, with delegates elected by qualified voters. Thus, the national Constitution, unlike the Articles of Confederation, would rest directly on popular authority.

7-2g Federalists and Antifederalists

As states began to elect delegates to their special conventions, newspapers and pamphlets vigorously defended or attacked the Philadelphia convention's decisions. Every newspaper in the country printed the full text of the Constitution, and most supported its adoption. It quickly became apparent, though, that the disputes in Philadelphia had been mild compared to divisions of opinion within the populace as a whole. Although most citizens concurred that the national government needed more power over taxation and commerce, some believed the proposed government held the potential for tyranny. The vigorous debate between the two sides was unprecedented, and frequently spilled into the streets.

Those supporting the proposed Constitution called themselves Federalists. They drew upon the tenets of classical republicanism, promoting a virtuous, self-sacrificing republic led by a manly aristocracy of talent. They argued that the separation of powers among legislative, executive, and judicial branches, and the division of powers between states and nation, would preclude tyranny. The liberties of the people would be guarded by men of the "better sort" whose only goal (said George Washington) was "to merit the approbation of good and virtuous men."

The Federalists termed those who opposed the Constitution Antifederalists, thus casting them in a negative light. Antifederalists recognized the need for a national source of revenue but feared a powerful central government. They saw the states as the chief protectors of individual rights against the rise of arbitrary power. Heirs of the Real Whig ideology of the late 1760s and early 1770s, Antifederalists stressed the need for constant popular vigilance to avert oppression. Indeed, some of those who had originally promulgated such ideas—Samuel Adams of Massachusetts, and Patrick Henry and Richard Henry Lee of Virginia—led the opposition to the Constitution. Older Americans, whose political opinions had been shaped prior to the Revolution, peopled the Antifederalist ranks. Joining them were small farmers determined to safeguard their property from excessive taxation, backcountry Baptists and Presbyterians, and ambitious, upwardly mobile men who would benefit from an economic and political system less tightly controlled than that the Constitution envisioned. Federalists denigrated such men as disorderly, licentious, and even "unmanly" because they would not follow the elites' lead in supporting the Constitution.

7-2h Bill of Rights

The Constitution's lack of specific guarantees to protect the rights of the people against the tyranny of a powerful central government troubled Antifederalists, who wanted the national governing document to incorporate a bill of rights, as did Britain's governing documents since the Glorious Revolution. Following the British model, most state constitutions had done so as well. *Letters of a Federal Farmer*, perhaps the most widely read Antifederalist pamphlet, listed the rights that should be enshrined: freedom of the press and religion, trial by jury, and protection from unreasonable searches. From Paris, Thomas Jefferson added his voice to the chorus. Replying to Madison's letter conveying a copy of the Constitution, Jefferson declared, "I like much the general idea" but not "the omission of a bill of rights. . . . A bill of rights is what the people are entitled to against every government on earth."

7-2i Ratification

As state conventions debated ratification, the lack of a bill of rights loomed ever larger as a flaw in the proposed government. Four of the first five states to ratify did so unanimously, but then Massachusetts, where Antifederalist forces benefited from the backlash against the state's treatment of the Shays rebels, ratified by only a slender majority (see Table 7.1). In June 1788, when New Hampshire ratified, the Constitution's requirement of nine states was satisfied. But New York and Virginia had not yet voted, and everyone realized the new framework could not succeed unless those powerful states accepted it.

Despite a valiant effort by Antifederalist Patrick Henry, pro-Constitution forces won by ten votes in the Virginia convention, which, like Massachusetts, recommended that a list of specific rights be added. In New York, James Madison, John Jay, and Alexander Hamilton, writing under the pseudonym "Publius," published *The Federalist*, a series of eighty-five essays explaining the theory behind the Constitution and masterfully answering its critics. Their reasoned arguments, coupled with Federalists' promise to add a bill of rights to the Constitution, helped win the battle there. On July 26, 1788, New York ratified the Constitution by just three votes. Although the last states—North Carolina and Rhode Island—did not join the Union for over a year, the new government was a reality.

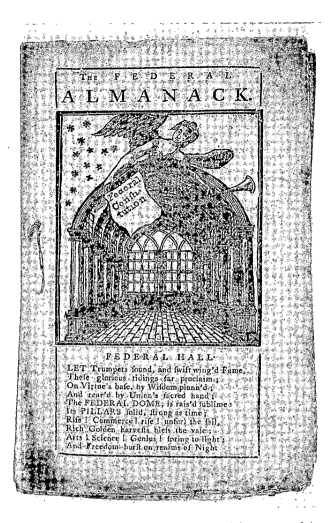

△ *The Federal Almanack* for 1789 trumpeted the virtues of the new Constitution. Not all Americans were so certain that the national government, here symbolized as an edifice supported by thirteen pillars, was as "solid, strong as time" as the printer proclaimed. Federal Almanac Weatherwise Boston (litho)/American School, (18th century)/AMERICAN ANTIQUARIAN SOCIETY/American Antiquarian Society, Worcester, Massachusetts, USA/Bridgeman Images

In many towns and cities, Americans celebrated ratification (somewhat prematurely) with parades on July 4, 1788, thus linking the Constitution to the Declaration of Independence. In carefully choreographed parades, marchers touted the unity of the new nation, seeking to drown out the dissent that had surfaced in recent years. Symbols expressing leaders' hopes for the industry and frugality of a virtuous public filled the Philadelphia celebration, planned by artist Charles Willson Peale. About five thousand people participated in the procession, which stretched for over a mile. Veterans trooped alongside farmers. Dozens of groups of tradesmen, including barbers, hatters, printers, cloth manufacturers, and clockmakers, sponsored elaborate floats. Lawyers, doctors, ministers, and congressmen followed the artisans. A final group of marchers symbolized the nation's future: students from the University of Pennsylvania and other schools carried a flag labeled "The Rising Generation."

Table 7.1 Ratification of the Constitution by State Conventions

State	Date	Vote
Delaware	December 7, 1787	30–0
Pennsylvania	December 12, 1787	46–23
New Jersey	December 18, 1787	38–0
Georgia	January 2, 1788	26–0
Connecticut	January 9, 1788	128–40
Massachusetts	February 6, 1788	187–168
Maryland	April 28, 1788	63–11
South Carolina	May 23, 1788	149–73
New Hampshire	June 21, 1788	57–47
Virginia	June 25, 1788	89–79
New York	July 26, 1788	30–27
North Carolina	November 21, 1789	194–77
Rhode Island	May 29, 1790	34–32

7-3 Promoting a Virtuous Citizenry

▶ How did Americans seek to infuse republican values in their society and culture?

▶ What role did education play in instilling republican values?

Citizens of the early United States believed they were embarking on an enterprise unprecedented in modern history, one that placed great moral burdens on the people. With pride in their new nation, they must replace the vices of monarchical Europe—luxury, decadence, and selfishness—with the sober virtues of republican America. They sought to embody republican principles not only in their governments but also in their society and culture, expecting painting, literature, drama, and architecture to promote national identity and virtue.

7-3a Virtue and the Arts

When the Revolution began, patriots toppled the gilded statue of George III that loomed over New York City's Bowling Green, melting the brass to make musket balls. Royalist icons had no place in the new republic. But what would American writers and artists erect in their places? Everywhere in the eighteenth-century world, artists struggled to find audiences and patronage for their work. Their task in the early United States was particularly fraught, for some republicans thought the fine arts signaled luxury and corruption, and questioned the very legitimacy of the enterprise.

Republican letters strove to edify. William Hill Brown's *The Power of Sympathy* (1789), the first novel published in the

United States, unfolded a story of seduction as a warning to "the Young Ladies of United Columbia," and promised to "Inspire the Female Mind with a Principle of Self Complacency." Mason Locke Weems intended his *Life of Washington* to "hold up his great Virtues . . . to the imitation of Our Youth." Published in 1800, shortly after George Washington's death, Weems's moralizing biography—with its invented tale of the boy who chopped down the cherry tree and could not tell a lie—soon became the era's most popular secular work.

Painters and architects, too, used their works to elevate republican taste. Two of the most prominent artists of the period, Gilbert Stuart and Charles Willson Peale, painted innumerable portraits of upstanding republican citizens. Stuart's portraits of George Washington—three painted from life, from which the artist made scores of copies, which in turn spawned countless engravings—came to represent the face of the young republic around the world. Stuart's own motives were commercial as well as patriotic. When he sailed to the United States in 1793 after nearly two decades in Britain,

George Washington, 1796 (oil on canvas)/Stuart, Gilbert (1755-1828)/MUSEUM OF FINE ARTS, BOSTON/Museum of Fine Arts, Boston, Massachusetts, USA/Bridgeman Images

△ During his second term as president, George Washington sat to the Rhode Island–born painter Gilbert Stuart three times in 1795 and 1796. The three sittings produced markedly different portraits, ranging from the formal full-length state portrait commissioned by the Marquis of Landsdowne to this ethereal unfinished bust, now known as the Athenaeum Washington, which became one of the most famous likenesses in the world even before it appeared on American currency. Copies of Stuart's portraits—painted as well as engraved—decorated homes throughout the early United States and surfaced as far away as Canton, China.

he told a friend, "I expect to make a fortune by Washington alone." Connecticut-born, London-trained painter John Trumbull's canvases depicted American milestones including Battle of Bunker Hill and the signing of the Declaration of Independence. Such portraits and historical scenes were intended to instill patriotic sentiments in their viewers, yet the artists rarely attracted public funding for their work, and struggled to make a living.

Architects likewise hoped to convey in their buildings a sense of the young republic's ideals. When the Virginia government asked Thomas Jefferson, then minister to France, for advice on the design of the state capitol in Richmond, Jefferson unhesitatingly recommended copying a Roman building, the Maison Carrée at Nîmes, an emblem of ancient republican simplicity. In Boston, Charles Bulfinch likewise designed his domed Massachusetts State House along classical lines.

Despite artists' efforts (or, some said, because of them), Americans began to detect signs of luxury and corruption by the mid-1780s. The resumption of European trade brought a return to imported fashions for both men and women. Elite families again attended balls and plays, threw parties, and played cards. Social clubs for young people multiplied. Especially alarming to fervent republicans like Samuel Adams was the establishment in 1783 of the Society of the Cincinnati, a hereditary association for Continental army officers and their firstborn male descendants. Although the organizers hoped to advance the notion of the citizen-soldier, opponents feared the group would become the nucleus of a native-born aristocracy.

7-3b Educational Reform

Americans' deep-seated concern for the future of the infant republic focused their attention on children, the "rising generation." Education had previously been seen as a private means to personal advancement, the concern of families. But if young people were to become useful citizens prepared for self-government, they would need a good education. In fact, the very survival of the nation depended on it. Inspired by such principles, some northern states began using tax money to support public elementary schools. In 1789, Massachusetts became one of the first states to require towns to offer their citizens free public elementary education.

To instruct their children adequately, mothers would have to be properly educated. Massachusetts insisted that town elementary schools teach girls as well as boys. Throughout the United States, private academies were founded to give teenage girls from well-to-do families an opportunity for advanced schooling. No one yet proposed opening colleges to women, but a few fortunate girls could study history, geography, rhetoric, and mathematics along with fancy needlework—the only artistic endeavor considered appropriate for ladies.

7-3c Judith Sargent Murray

Judith Sargent Murray of Gloucester, Massachusetts, became a leading theorist of women's education in the early republic.

△ Judith Sargent Stevens (later Murray), by John Singleton Copley, ca. 1769. The eventual author of essays advocating improvements in women's education sat for this portrait on the eve of her first marriage, some two decades before she began to publish her work. Her direct gaze and high forehead suggest both her intelligence and her seriousness of purpose.

In powerful essays published in the 1780s and 1790s, Murray argued that women and men had equal intellects but unequal schooling. If "an opportunity of acquiring knowledge hath been denied us," she declared, "the inferiority of our sex cannot fairly be deduced from thence." Boys and girls should be educated alike, Murray insisted, and girls should be taught to support themselves by their own labors: "Independence should be placed within their grasp." Murray's writings on female "independence" were part of a general rethinking of women's position that occurred in a climate of political upheaval. In 1798, Murray looked back on what she called "the happy revolution which the few past years have made" in women's "favour."

7-4 Building a Workable Government

▷ What challenges did Congress face in establishing a working government?

▷ How did Alexander Hamilton shape the United States' financial system?

▶ **Why did Alexander Hamilton's financial plan cause division in Congress?**

▶ **What was the significance of the Whiskey Rebellion?**

The first decade of government under the Constitution witnessed hesitant steps toward the creation of a United States that was more singular than plural. At first, consensus appeared possible. Only a few Antifederalists ran for office in the congressional elections held late in 1788; even fewer were elected. Thus, most members of the First U.S. Congress supported a strong national government. The drafters of the Constitution had deliberately left many key issues undecided, so the nationalists' domination of Congress meant that their views quickly prevailed.

7-4a First Congress

Congress faced four immediate tasks when it convened in April 1789: raising revenue, responding to calls for a bill of rights; setting up executive departments, and organizing the federal judiciary. The last duty was especially important. The Constitution established a Supreme Court but left it to Congress to decide whether to have other federal courts.

James Madison, representing Virginia in the House of Representatives, soon became as influential in Congress as he had been at the Constitutional Convention. During its first session, he persuaded Congress to adopt the Revenue Act of 1789, imposing a 5 percent tariff on certain imports. The First Congress thus quickly achieved what the Confederation Congress never had: an effective national tax law.

Madison also took the lead with respect to constitutional amendments. When introducing nineteen proposed amendments in June, he told his fellow representatives they needed to respond to the people's will as expressed in the state conventions, noting that North Carolina had vowed not to ratify the Constitution without a **Bill of Rights**. After lengthy, heated debates, Congress approved twelve amendments. The states ratified ten, which became part of the Constitution on December 15, 1791.

The First Amendment prohibited Congress from restricting freedom of religion, speech, the press, peaceable assembly, or petition. The next two amendments arose directly from the former colonists' fear of standing armies. Because a "well regulated Militia" was "necessary to the security of a free State," the Second Amendment guaranteed the right "to keep and bear arms." The Third Amendment limited the quartering of troops in private homes. The next five pertained to judicial procedures. The Fourth Amendment prohibited "unreasonable searches and seizures," the Fifth and Sixth established the rights of accused persons, the Seventh specified the conditions for jury trials in civil cases, and the Eighth forbade "cruel and unusual punishments." The Ninth and Tenth Amendments reserved to the people and the states other unspecified

Bill of Rights The first ten amendments of the Constitution, which guaranteed individual liberties.

Judiciary Act of 1789 Outlined the federal judiciary's jurisdiction and established the Supreme Court, as well as district and appellate courts.

rights and powers. In short, the amendments' authors made clear that, in listing some rights, they had not precluded the exercise of others.

7-4b Executive and Judiciary

Congress also considered the organization of the executive branch, preserving the three administrative departments established under the Articles of Confederation: War, Foreign Affairs (renamed State), and Treasury. Congress also instituted two lesser posts: the attorney general—the nation's official lawyer—and the postmaster general. Controversy arose over whether the president alone could dismiss officials whom he had appointed with the Senate's advice and consent. The House and Senate eventually agreed that he had such authority, making the heads of executive departments accountable solely to the president.

The First Congress's most far-reaching law, the **Judiciary Act of 1789**, defined the jurisdiction of the federal judiciary and established a six-member Supreme Court, thirteen district courts, and three appellate courts. Its most important provision, Section 25, allowed appeals from state to federal courts when cases raised certain constitutional questions. In the nineteenth century, judges and legislators committed to states' rights would challenge the constitutionality of Section 25.

During its first decade, the Supreme Court handled few cases of any importance, and several members resigned. (John Jay, the first chief justice, served only six years.) But in a significant 1796 decision, *Ware v. Hylton*, the Court for the first time declared a state law unconstitutional. The most important case of the decade, *Chisholm v. Georgia* (1793), established that states could be sued in federal courts by citizens of other states. Five years later, the Eleventh Amendment to the Constitution overturned that decision, which was unpopular with state governments.

7-4c Washington's First Steps

George Washington did not seek the presidency. In 1783, he resigned his army commission and retired to Mount Vernon, a soldier trading his sword for his plough, as the Roman statesman Cinncinatus had done. (Of course, Washington's hundreds of bondspeople actually wielded the ploughs at Mount Vernon.) Even after he retired from command, Americans never regarded Washington as just another private citizen. After the adoption of the new government, only George Washington was thought to have sufficient stature to serve as the republic's first president, an office largely designed with him in mind. The unanimous vote of the electoral college merely formalized that consensus. Symbolically, Washington donned a suit of homespun for the inaugural ceremony in April 1789.

Washington acted cautiously during his first months in office, knowing that whatever he did would set precedents for the future. His first major task was to choose the heads of the executive departments. For the War Department, he selected an old comrade in arms, Henry Knox of Massachusetts. His choice for the State Department was fellow Virginian

△ Alexander Hamilton, by James Sharpless, about 1796. This profile of Hamilton, painted near the end of Washington's presidency, shows the secretary of the treasury as he looked during the years of his first heated partisan battles with Thomas Jefferson and James Madison.

Thomas Jefferson, who had just returned to the United States from his post as minister to France. And for the crucial position of secretary of the treasury, the president chose the brilliant, intensely ambitious **Alexander Hamilton.**

7-4d Alexander Hamilton

The illegitimate son of a Scottish aristocrat, Hamilton—no relation to Dr. Alexander Hamilton, who toured the colonies in 1744 (see Chapter 4)—was born in the British West Indies in 1757. He spent his early years in poverty, but in 1773, financial support from friends allowed him to enroll at King's College (later Columbia University) in New York. Devoted to the patriot cause, Hamilton volunteered for service in the American army, where he came to Washington's attention. After the war, Hamilton practiced law in New York City and served as a delegate to the Annapolis Convention and later the Constitutional Convention. Although he exerted little influence at either gathering, his contributions to *The Federalist* in 1788 revealed him as one of the chief political thinkers in the republic.

Born in the Caribbean, Hamilton had no natal ties to any state; he neither sympathized with nor fully understood demands for local autonomy. In his dual role as treasury secretary and presidential adviser under Washington, Hamilton's primary loyalty lay with the nation. He never feared the exercise of centralized executive authority, and he favored close political and economic ties with Britain. Believing people to be motivated primarily by economic self-interest, his notion of republicanism placed little weight on self-sacrifice for the

common good. Those beliefs significantly influenced the way he tackled the monumental task before him: straightening out the new nation's tangled finances.

7-4e National and State Debts

Congress ordered the new secretary of the treasury to assess the public debt and submit recommendations for supporting the government's credit. Hamilton found that the country's remaining war debts fell into three categories: those owed to foreign governments and investors, mostly to France (about $11 million); those owed to merchants, former soldiers, holders of revolutionary bonds, and the like (about $27 million); and those owed by state governments (roughly $25 million).

Americans agreed that their new government could establish its credit only by repaying at full face value the obligations the nation had incurred while winning independence. But the state debts were another matter. Some states—notably, Virginia, Maryland, North Carolina, and Georgia—had largely paid off their war debts. They would oppose the national government's assumption of responsibility for other states' debts because their citizens would be taxed to pay such obligations. Massachusetts, Connecticut, and South Carolina, by contrast, still had sizable unpaid debts and would welcome a system of national assumption. The possible assumption of state debts also had political implications. Consolidating state debt in the hands of the national government would concentrate economic and political power at the national level, thus raising the specter of tyranny.

7-4f Hamilton's Financial Plan

Hamilton's first *Report on the Public Credit*, sent to Congress in January 1790, proposed that Congress assume outstanding state debts, combine them with national obligations, and issue securities covering both principal and accumulated unpaid interest. Hamilton thereby hoped to ensure that holders of the public debt—many of them wealthy merchants and speculators—had a significant financial stake in the new government's survival. The opposition coalesced around James Madison, who opposed the assumption of state debts for two reasons. First, his state of Virginia had already paid off most of its obligations, and second, he wanted to avoid rewarding wealthy speculators who had purchased state and national debt certificates at deep discounts from needy veterans and farmers.

Prompted in part by Madison, the House initially rejected the assumption of state debts. But the Senate adopted Hamilton's plan largely intact. A series of compromises followed, in which the assumption bill became linked to the other major controversial issue of that congressional session: the location of the permanent national capital. A southern site on the Potomac River (favored by Washington and close to Mount Vernon) was selected, and the first part of Hamilton's financial program became law in August 1790.

Alexander Hamilton First U.S. secretary of the treasury, under President George Washington.

Report on the Public Credit Hamilton's plan to ensure the creditworthiness of the United States by having Congress assume state debts.

7-4g First Bank of the United States

Four months later, Hamilton submitted to Congress a second report on public credit, recommending the creation of a national bank modeled on the Bank of England. The Bank of the United States was to be chartered for twenty years with $10 million of paid-in capital—$2 million from public funds, and the balance from private investors. The bank would collect and disburse moneys for the treasury, and its notes would circulate as the nation's currency. Most political leaders recognized that such an institution would remedy America's perpetual shortage of an acceptable medium of exchange. But another issue loomed large: did the Constitution give Congress the power to establish such a bank?

Madison answered that question with a resounding no; the Constitutional Convention had specifically rejected a clause authorizing Congress to issue corporate charters. Madison's contention disturbed President Washington, who decided to request other opinions before signing the bill into law. Edmund Randolph, the attorney general, and Thomas Jefferson, the secretary of state, agreed with Madison that the bank was unconstitutional. Washington asked Hamilton to reply to their verdict. In his *Defense of the Constitutionality of the Bank*, Hamilton argued forcefully that Congress could choose any means not specifically prohibited by the Constitution to achieve a constitutional end. Washington concurred, and the bill became law.

The Bank of the United States initially aroused heated opposition. But it proved successful, as did Hamilton's scheme for funding the national debt and assuming the states' debts. The new nation's securities became desirable investments at home and abroad. The resulting influx of capital, coupled with the high prices that American grain now commanded in European markets, eased farmers' debt burdens and contributed to a new prosperity in the 1790s.

Hamilton's *Report on Manufactures* (1791) outlined an ambitious plan to nurture the United States' infant industries, such as shoemaking and textile manufacturing. Hamilton argued that the nation could never be truly independent as long as it relied so heavily on Europe for manufactured goods, and he urged Congress to promote industrial development through limited use of protective tariffs. Many of Hamilton's ideas were implemented in later decades, but few congressmen in 1791 saw much merit in his proposals. Convinced that America's future lay in agriculture and the carrying (shipping) trade and that the mainstay of the republic was the yeoman farmer, Congress rejected the report.

The Granger Collection

△ The First Bank of the United States, constructed in the mid-1790s, as the building looked in Philadelphia in 1800. Its classical simplicity, meant to inspire confidence, concealed its contentious political origins.

Also controversial was another feature of Hamilton's financial program enacted in 1791: an excise tax on whiskey designed to provide additional income to the national government. The tax affected a relatively small number of westerners—the farmers who grew corn and the distillers who turned that corn into whiskey—and might also reduce the consumption of whiskey. (Eighteenth-century Americans consumed about twice as much alcohol per capita as Americans do today.) Moreover, Hamilton knew that western farmers and distillers tended to support Jefferson, and he saw the benefits of taxing them rather than the merchants who favored his own nationalist policies.

7-4h Whiskey Rebellion

News of the tax set off protests in the West, where residents were dissatisfied with the army's defense of their region from Native attack. To their minds, the same government that protected them inadequately was now proposing to tax them disproportionately. For two years, unrest continued on the frontiers of Pennsylvania, Maryland, and Virginia. Large groups of men drafted petitions protesting the tax, imitated crowd actions of the 1760s, and occasionally harassed tax collectors.

President Washington responded with restraint until July 1794, when western Pennsylvania farmers resisted two excisemen trying to collect the tax. On August 1, about seven thousand rebels convened to plot the destruction of Pittsburgh but decided not to face the heavy guns of the fort guarding the town. Washington then took decisive action to prevent a crisis reminiscent of Shays's Rebellion. On August 7, he called on the insurgents to disperse and summoned nearly thirteen thousand militiamen. Federal forces marched westward in October and November, led at times by Washington himself. The troops met no resistance and arrested only twenty suspects. Two men were convicted of treason; Washington pardoned both. The rebellion ended with little bloodshed.

The importance of the **Whiskey Rebellion** lay in the forceful message its suppression conveyed to the American people. The national government would not allow violent resistance to its laws. People dissatisfied with a given law should try to amend or repeal it, not take extralegal action as they had during the colonial era.

7-5 Building a Nation Among Nations

▷ **What domestic and international events contributed to rivalry between the Federalists and Republicans?**

▷ **How did George Washington respond to international developments during his terms as president?**

▷ **How did political culture operate in the 1790s?**

▷ **What were the domestic and international ramifications of the XYZ Affair?**

By 1794, some Americans were already beginning to seek change through electoral politics, even though traditional political theory regarded organized opposition—especially in a republic—as illegitimate. In a monarchy, formal opposition groups, commonly called factions, were expected. In a government of the people, by contrast, sustained factional disagreement was taken as a sign of corruption. Though widely held, such negative judgments did little to check partisan sentiment.

7-5a Republicans and Federalists

As early as 1792, Jefferson and Madison became convinced that Hamilton's policies, which favored wealthy commercial interests at the expense of agriculture, threatened the United States. Characterizing themselves as the true heirs of the Revolution, they charged Hamilton with plotting to subvert republican principles. To dramatize their point, Jefferson, Madison, and their followers in Congress began calling themselves Republicans. Hamilton accused Jefferson and Madison of the same offense: attempting to destroy the republic. To legitimize their claims and link themselves with the Constitution, Hamilton and his supporters called themselves Federalists. Newspapers aligned with each side fanned the flames of partisanship. Indeed, before parties fully coalesced, such newspapers served as the very foundation of political identity.

At first, President Washington tried to remain aloof from the dispute that divided his advisers. The growing controversy did help persuade him to promote unity by seeking office again in 1792. But after 1793, developments in Europe magnified the disagreements, as France (America's wartime ally) and Great Britain (America's essential trading partner) resumed the periodic hostilities that had originated centuries earlier.

7-5b French Revolution

In 1789, many American men and women welcomed the news of revolution in France. The French people's success in overthrowing an oppressive monarchy seemed to vindicate the United States' own revolution. Americans saw themselves as France's sister republic, the vanguard of a trend that would reshape the world. Dinners, public ceremonies, and balls celebrated the French revolutionaries; some began terming themselves "citizen" or, for women, "citesse," in the French manner.

But by 1793, the reports from France had grown alarming. Political leaders succeeded each other with bewildering rapidity. Executions mounted; the king himself was beheaded that January. Although many Americans, including Jefferson and Madison, retained sympathy for the revolution, others—Hamilton among them—began to cite France as a prime example of the perversion of republicanism into mob rule.

Whiskey Rebellion Tax protest by western farmers that turned violent. Washington's willingness to send troops in response demonstrated the increased power of the national government.

Newspapers of the Early Republic

In the 1790s newspapers did not attempt to present news objectively, and indeed, none of their readers expected them to do so. Instead, newspapers were linked to the rapidly expanding political factions of the new nation—the partisan groupings (not yet political parties in the modern sense) terming themselves *Federalists* and *Republicans*. The "official" paper of the Federalists was *The Gazette of*

the United States. (Colonial papers supported by individual governments too had been called *gazettes*—just as the *London Gazette* was tied to the English government.) Among the Republicans' many allied newspapers was *The New-York Journal, and Patriotic Register*. A reader comparing the front pages of any two issues could see at a glance the differences between them. *The Gazette of the United States* filled

its first page with sober news articles, whereas the face *The New-York Journal* presented to the world was consumed entirely with advertisements, some headed by intriguing design elements.

CRITICAL THINKING

◻ Which would appeal more directly to America's artisans and forward-thinking yeomen, and why?

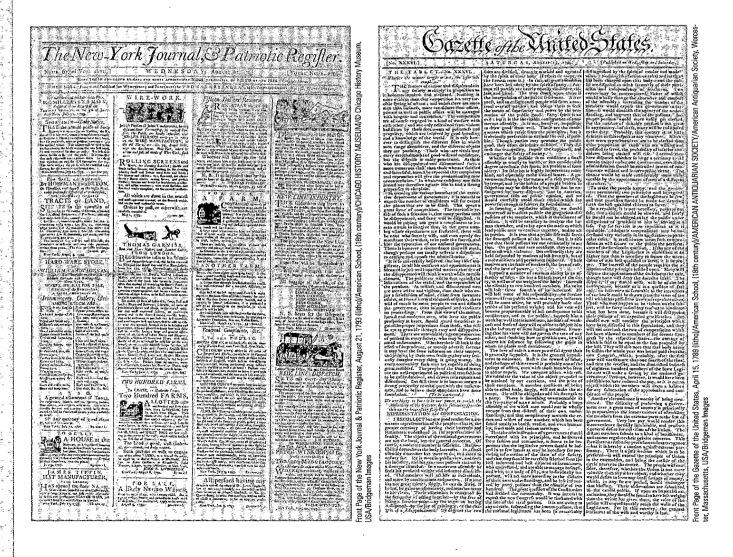

Debates within the United States intensified when republican France declared war on Austria in 1792, and then on Britain, Spain, and Holland the following year. That confronted the Americans with a dilemma. The 1778 Treaty of Alliance with France bound them to that nation "forever," and a mutual commitment to republicanism created ideological bonds as well. Yet the United States remained connected to Great Britain through their shared history and language, and through commerce. By the 1790s, Americans again purchased most of their manufactured goods from Great Britain. Indeed, because the revenues of the United States depended heavily on import tariffs, vigorous trade with the former mother country became vital to the nation's economic health.

The political and diplomatic climate grew even more complicated in April 1793, when Edmond Charles Genêt, the French government's minister to the United States, landed in Charleston, South Carolina, carrying instructions to renegotiate the alliance of 1778 for the new French government. Genêt found himself thronged by well-wishers when he disembarked at the Charleston docks. Some weeks later, Secretary of State Thomas Jefferson welcomed Genêt warmly in Philadelphia. But President Washington was cooler to the French diplomat. He and other Federalists questioned the continuing obligations of the United States to the ever more radical French revolutionary regime. Before receiving Genêt, Washington issued a proclamation stating that the United States would adopt "conduct friendly and impartial toward the belligerent powers" in the European war.

Federalist newspapers vociferously defended the neutrality proclamation, and partisan leaders organized rallies to praise the president's action. Republicans who favored assisting France reluctantly accepted the policy of neutrality, which had overwhelming popular support. But by July, Genêt's support for French privateers in the Caribbean had cost him the support even of Jefferson's allies, and Washington requested his recall to France.

7-5c Democratic Societies

Genêt's faction fell from power in Paris, and he subsequently sought political asylum in the United States. But his disappearance from the diplomatic scene did not diminish the impact of the French Revolution in America. Clubs called Democratic societies, formed by Americans sympathetic to the French Revolution, perpetuated the domestic divisions Genêt had helped to widen. More than forty such societies organized between 1793 and 1800. Their members cast themselves in the mold of the 1760s resistance movement, as defenders of fragile liberty from corrupt and self-serving Federalist rulers.

The rapid spread of citizens' groups outspokenly critical of the administration disturbed Hamilton and Washington. Federalist writers charged that the societies' true intention was "to involve the country in war, to assume the reins of government and tyrannize over the people." The counterattack climaxed in the fall of 1794 when Washington accused

the clubs of fomenting the Whiskey Rebellion. In retrospect, the administration's reaction seems disproportionately hostile. But as the first organized political dissenters in the United States, the Democratic societies alarmed officials who had not yet accepted the idea that one component of a free government was an organized loyal opposition.

7-5d Jay Treaty Debate

In 1794, George Washington dispatched Chief Justice John Jay to London to negotiate several unresolved questions in Anglo-American relations. The British had recently seized some American merchant ships trading in the French West Indies. The United States wanted to establish the principle of freedom of the seas and to assert its right, as a neutral nation, to unfettered trade with both combatants. Further, Great Britain still held posts in the American Northwest, thus violating the 1783 peace treaty. Settlers there believed the British responsible for renewed warfare with neighboring Native peoples, and they wanted that threat removed. Southern planters also wanted compensation for the slaves who left with the British army after the war.

Jay had little to offer the British in exchange for the concessions he sought. Britain agreed to evacuate the western forts and reduce restrictions on American trade to England and the Caribbean. The treaty established two arbitration commissions—one to deal with prewar debts Americans owed to British creditors and the other to hear claims for captured American merchant ships—but Britain adamantly refused to compensate slave owners for their lost human property. Under the circumstances, Jay had probably done the best he could. Nevertheless, most Americans, including the president, at first expressed dissatisfaction with the treaty.

The Senate debated the Jay Treaty in secret. Not until after its narrow ratification in June 1795 did the public learn its provisions in the pages of the leading Republican newspaper, Benjamin Franklin Bache's *Aurora*. Bache organized the protests that followed: publications and popular gatherings urging Washington to reject the treaty. Federalists countered with rallies and essays of their own, contending that Jay's treaty was preferable to no treaty at all. Displeased by the Republicans' organized opposition and convinced by pro-treaty arguments, Washington signed the pact in mid-August. Just one opportunity remained to prevent it from taking effect: Congress had to appropriate funds to carry out the treaty, and appropriation bills had to originate in the House of Representatives.

Hoping the opposition would dissipate, Washington delayed submitting the treaty to the House until March 1796. The treaty's congressional opponents initially commanded a majority, but pressure for appropriating the necessary funds built quickly. Federalists successfully linked the Jay Treaty with another, more popular pact that Thomas Pinckney of South Carolina had negotiated with Spain the previous year. Pinckney's Treaty gave the United States valuable navigation privileges on the Mississippi River and the right to land

and store goods at New Orleans tax-free. The Senate ratified it unanimously, and the overwhelming support it received helped to overcome opposition to the Jay Treaty. In late April, a divided House appropriated the money by a three-vote margin. All but two southerners opposed the treaty; all but three Federalists supported it.

Ironically, the Federalists' campaign to sway public opinion violated their fundamental philosophy of government. They believed ordinary people should defer to the judgment of elected leaders, yet in order to persuade the House to follow the president's lead, they actively engaged in grassroots politicking. Even Federalist women became involved by presenting patriotic banners to militia companies or by taking formal roles in July fourth celebrations. The Federalists won the battle, but in the long run they would lose the war, for Republicans ultimately proved far more effective in appealing to the citizenry at large.

To describe the growing partisanship in Congress and the nation is easier than to explain such fractures in the electorate. The terms used by Jefferson and Madison ("the people" versus "aristocrats") or by Hamilton and Washington ("true patriots" versus "subversive rabble") do not adequately describe the growing divisions. Simple economic differences between farmers and city folk do not provide the answer either, as more than 90 percent of Americans still lived in rural areas. Moreover, Jefferson's vision of a prosperous agrarian America rested on commercial farming, not rural self-sufficiency. Nor did the divisions in the 1790s simply repeat the ratification debates of 1787–1788. Even though most Antifederalists became Republicans, the party's leaders, Madison and Jefferson, had supported the Constitution.

Yet certain distinctions can be made. Republicans, especially strong in the southern and middle states, tended to be self-assured, confident, and optimistic. Southern planters, in control of their region and their bound labor force, foresaw a prosperous future fueled by continued westward expansion. Republicans employed democratic rhetoric to win the allegiance of small farmers in southern and mid-Atlantic states. Members of non-English ethnic groups found Republicans' message attractive. Artisans—like small farmers, fierce believers in household autonomy—joined the coalition. Republicans of all descriptions prized America's internal resources, remaining sympathetic to France but worrying less about the nation's place in the world than Federalists did.

By contrast, Federalists concentrated among the commercial interests of New England. They stressed the need for order, hierarchy, and obedience to political authority. Federalists, like their Republican opponents, realized that southern and middle-state interests would dominate western lands, so they had little incentive to focus on that potentially rich territory. Where Republicans faced West, Federalists faced East, toward London. In their eyes, the nation's internal and external enemies made alliance with Great Britain essential. Given the dangers posed to the nation by European warfare, Federalists' vision of international affairs may have been accurate, but it was also unappealing. Federalists offered voters little hope of a better future, and the Republicans prevailed in the end.

7-5e Washington's Farewell Address

After the treaty debate, wearied by the criticism to which he had been subjected, George Washington decided not to seek reelection. (Presidents had not yet been limited to two terms.) In September, Washington published his Farewell Address, most of which Hamilton wrote. The address outlined two principles that guided American foreign policy at least until the late 1940s: to maintain commercial but not political ties to other nations, and to reject permanent alliances. Washington also drew sharp distinctions between the United States and Europe, stressing America's uniqueness—its exceptionalism—and the need for independent action in foreign affairs, today called *unilateralism*.

Some interpret Washington's plea for an end to partisan strife as a call for politicians to consider the good of the whole nation. But in the context of the impending presidential election, the Farewell Address appears rather as an attack on the Republican opposition. Washington advocated unity behind the Federalist banner, which he viewed as the only proper stance. The Federalists (like the Republicans) continued to see themselves as the rightful heirs of the Revolution. Both sides perceived their opponents as illegitimate, unpatriotic troublemakers who sought to undermine revolutionary ideals. The Republican *Aurora* derided the address as empty words. Washington's administration had excelled at "the profession of republicanism, but the practice of monarchy and aristocracy," editor Bache wrote. Surely "the men of the revolution, who still feel its principles and its sympathies," would now follow a different and better course than the one the Federalists had charted.

7-5f Election of 1796

The two organized groups actively contending for office made the presidential **election of 1796** the first serious contest for the position. To succeed Washington, the Federalists in Congress put forward Vice President John Adams, with the diplomat Thomas Pinckney as his running mate. Congressional Republicans chose Thomas Jefferson as their presidential candidate; the lawyer, Revolutionary War veteran, and Republican politician Aaron Burr of New York agreed to stand for vice president. But the method of voting in the electoral college did not take into account the possibility of party slates. The Constitution's drafters had not foreseen the emergence of competing political organizations, so the document provided no way to express support for a ticket that included one candidate for president and another for vice president. The electors simply voted for two people. The man with the highest total became president; the second highest, vice president.

Election of 1796 Federalist John Adams won by three votes and, as the second-highest vote-getter in the electoral college, Thomas Jefferson became vice president.

△ This cartoon drawn during the XYZ Affair depicts the United States as a maiden being victimized by the five leaders of the French government's directorate. In the background, John Bull (England) watches from on high, while other European nations discuss the situation.

That procedure proved to be the Federalists' undoing. Adams won the presidency with 71 votes, but a number of Federalist electors failed to cast ballots for Pinckney. With 68 votes, the next highest total, Jefferson would become vice president. During the next four years, the new president and vice president, once allies and close friends, became bitter enemies.

7-5g XYZ Affair

As president, John Adams clung to an outdated notion discarded by George Washington as early as 1794: that the president should remain above politics. Thus, Adams kept Washington's cabinet intact, despite its key members' allegiance to his chief Federalist rival, Alexander Hamilton. Adams often adopted a passive posture, letting others (usually Hamilton) take the lead when the president should have acted decisively. But Adams's detachment from Hamilton's maneuverings did enable him to weather the greatest international crisis the republic had yet faced.

The Jay Treaty had improved America's relationship with Great Britain, but it provoked France to retaliate by seizing American vessels carrying British goods. In response, Congress authorized the building of ships and the stockpiling of weapons and ammunition. President Adams also sent three commissioners to Paris to negotiate a settlement. For months, the American commissioners sought talks with Talleyrand, the French foreign minister, but Talleyrand's agents demanded a bribe of $250,000

before negotiations could begin. The Americans retorted, "No, no; not a sixpence," and reported the incident in dispatches the president received in March 1798. Adams informed Congress and recommended further increases in military spending.

Convinced that Adams had deliberately sabotaged the negotiations, Republicans insisted that the dispatches be turned over to Congress. Adams complied, withholding only the names of the French agents, whom he labeled X, Y, and Z. The revelation that the Americans had been treated with contempt stimulated a wave of anti-French sentiment in the United States and became known as the **XYZ Affair.** One journalist's version of the commissioners' reply, "Millions for defense, but not a cent for tribute," became a national slogan. Congress formally abrogated the Treaty of Alliance and authorized American ships to commandeer French vessels.

7-5h Quasi-War with France

Thus began an undeclared war with France fought in Caribbean waters between warships of the U.S. Navy and French privateers. Although Americans initially suffered heavy losses, by early 1799 the U.S. Navy had established its superiority, easing the threat to America's vital Caribbean trade.

XYZ Affair French demand for bribes from American negotiators that triggered widespread anger in the United States and led to the ending of the American alliance with France.

The Republicans, who opposed war and continued to sympathize with France, could do little to stem the tide of anti-French feelings. Because Agent Y had boasted of the existence of a "French party in America," Federalists flatly accused Republicans of traitorous designs. John Adams wavered between denouncing the Republicans and acknowledging their right to oppose administration measures. His wife was less tolerant. "Those whom the French boast of as their Partizans," Abigail Adams declared, should be "adjudged traitors to their country."

7-5i Alien and Sedition Acts

Federalists saw an opportunity to deal a deathblow to their Republican opponents. Now that the country seemed to see the truth of what they had been saying ever since the Whiskey Rebellion in 1794—that Republicans were subversive foreign agents—Federalists would codify that belief. In 1798, the Federalist-controlled Congress adopted a set of four laws known as the **Alien and Sedition Acts**, intended to weaken the Republican faction.

Three of the acts targeted recently arrived immigrants, whom Federalists accurately suspected of sympathizing with Republicans. The Naturalization Act lengthened the residency period required for citizenship and ordered all resident aliens to register with the federal government. The two Alien Acts, though not immediately implemented, provided for the detention of enemy aliens during wartime and gave the president authority to deport any alien he deemed dangerous to the nation's security.

The fourth statute, the Sedition Act, sought to control both citizens and aliens. It outlawed conspiracies to prevent the enforcement of federal laws, setting the maximum punishment for such offenses at five years in prison and a $5,000 fine. The act also made writing, printing, or uttering "false, scandalous and malicious" statements "with intent to defame" the government or the president a crime punishable by as much as two years' imprisonment and a fine of $2,000. Today, a law punishing political speech would be unconstitutional. But in the eighteenth century, when organized opposition was suspect, many Americans supported such restrictions on free speech.

The Sedition Act led to fifteen indictments and ten guilty verdicts. Among those convicted were a congressman and former newspaper editor, Matthew Lyon of Vermont; and James Callender, a Scots immigrant and scandalmonger whose exposés forced Alexander Hamilton to acknowledge an extramarital affair. After turning his attention to President Adams, Callender was convicted, fined, and jailed for nine months. Energized rather than silenced by the persecution, growing numbers of Republican newspaper editors stepped up their relentless criticisms. One of the most outspoken, William Duane—successor to Bache as the *Aurora*'s editor—ignored a Sedition Act indictment, prosecutions in state and federal courts for other purported offenses, and even a vicious beating by Federalist thugs, to persist in partisan attacks. He and other Republicans created an informal network of newspapers that spread opposition ideas throughout the country.

Jefferson and Madison combated the acts in another way. Petitioning the Federalist-controlled Congress to repeal the laws would clearly fail, and Federalist judges refused to allow accused individuals to question the Sedition Act's constitutionality. Accordingly, Republican leaders turned to the only other forum available for formal protest: state legislatures. Carefully concealing their own roles, Jefferson and Madison drafted the **Virginia and Kentucky Resolutions**, which were introduced into those states' legislatures, respectively, in the fall of 1798. Because a compact among the states had created the Constitution, the resolutions contended, people speaking through their states had a legitimate right to judge the constitutionality of actions taken by the federal government. Both legislatures pronounced the Alien and Sedition Acts unconstitutional, thus advancing the doctrine later known as nullification.

Although no other state endorsed them, the Virginia and Kentucky Resolutions placed the opposition party squarely in the revolutionary tradition of resistance to tyrannical authority. Their theory of union inspired the Hartford Convention of 1814 and southern states' rights advocates in the 1830s and thereafter. Jefferson and Madison had identified a key constitutional issue: How far could states go in opposing the national government? How could conflicts between the two be resolved? These questions would not be definitively answered until the Civil War.

7-5j The Convention of 1800

Just as northern legislatures were rejecting the Virginia and Kentucky Resolutions, Federalists split over the course of action the United States should take toward France. Hamilton and his supporters called for a declaration legitimizing the undeclared naval war. Adams, though, received a number of private signals that the French government regretted its treatment of the American commissioners. In response, he dispatched William Vans Murray to Paris to negotiate with Napoleon Bonaparte, France's new leader. The United States wanted to receive compensation for ships the French had seized since 1793 and to abrogate the treaty of 1778. The Convention of 1800, which ended the Quasi-War, conceded only the latter point. Still, it freed the United States from its only permanent alliance, thus allowing the nation to follow the independent course George Washington had urged in his Farewell Address.

Alien and Sedition Acts A series of laws passed in 1798 that were intended to suppress dissent and block the rise of the Republican faction.

Virginia and Kentucky Resolutions A republican response to the Alien and Sedition Acts, the resolutions asserted the right of state legislatures to judge the constitutionality of federal laws.

7-6 The West in the New Nation

▷ How did the United States acquire additional lands in the 1790s?

▷ What was the national government's position toward Native peoples?

By 1800, the nation had added three states (Vermont, Kentucky, and Tennessee) to the original thirteen and more than 1 million people to the nearly 4 million counted by the 1790 census. The United States claimed sovereignty east of the Mississippi River and north of Spanish Florida. But the nation controlled the Northwest Territory only after considerable bloodshed, as American troops battled a powerful confederacy of eight Native American nations led by the Miamis.

7-6a War in the Northwest Territory

In 1789, General Arthur St. Clair, first governor of the Northwest Territory, failed to open more land to settlement through treaty negotiations with the western confederacy. Subsequently, Little Turtle, the confederacy's able war chief, defeated forces led by General Josiah Harmar (1790) and by St. Clair himself (1791) in battles near the border between modern Indiana and Ohio. In the United States' worst defeat in the entire history of the American frontier, more than six hundred of St. Clair's men died, and scores more were wounded.

The Miami Confederacy declared that peace could be achieved only if the United States recognized the Ohio River as its northwestern boundary. But the national government refused to relinquish its claims in the region. In August 1794, a newly invigorated army under the command of General Anthony Wayne, a Revolutionary War hero, attacked and defeated the confederacy at the Battle of Fallen Timbers, near present-day Toledo, Ohio (see Map 7.2). Eager to avoid a costly and prolonged frontier conflict between settlers whom the government regarded as "white savages" and Native leaders whom Wayne called "red gentlemen," the general reached agreement with the confederacy in August 1795.

The resulting Treaty of Greenville gave each side a portion of what it wanted. The United States gained the right to settle much of what was to become Ohio. In exchange, the indigenous peoples won an acknowledgment they had long sought: the United States formally accepted the principle of Native sovereignty, by virtue of residence, over all lands the Native peoples had not ceded. Never again would

△ The two chief antagonists at the Battle of Fallen Timbers and negotiators of the Treaty of Greenville (1795). On the left, Little Turtle, the leader of the Miami Confederacy; on the right, General Anthony Wayne. Little Turtle, in a copy of a portrait painted two years after the battle, appears to be wearing a miniature of Wayne on a bear-claw necklace.

△ In 1805, an unidentified artist painted Benjamin Hawkins, a trader and U.S. agent to the Creeks, near Macon, Georgia. Hawkins introduced European-style agriculture to the Creeks, who are shown here with vegetables from their fields. Throughout the eastern United States, Native peoples had to make similar adaptations of their traditional lifestyles in order to maintain their group identity.

the United States government claim that it had acquired Native American territory solely through negotiation with a European or North American country.

That same year, Pinckney's treaty with Spain established the 31st parallel as the boundary between the United States and Florida. Nevertheless, Spanish influence in the Old Southwest—where the Creeks, Cherokees, and other Native American nations continued to occupy much unceded territory—continued to raise questions about the loyalty of American settlers in the region. A Southwest Ordinance (1790) attempted to organize the territory; by permitting slavery, it made the region attractive to slaveholders.

7-6b "Civilizing" Native Peoples

Increasingly, even Native peoples who lived independent of federal authority came within the orbit of American influence. The nation's stated goal was to "civilize" them. "Instead of exterminating a part of the human race," Henry Knox contended in 1789, the government should "impart our knowledge of cultivation and the arts to the aboriginals of the country." To promote "a love for exclusive property"

among Native peoples, Knox proposed that the government give livestock and training in agriculture to people in native communities. Four years later, the Indian Trade and Intercourse Act of 1793 codified the secretary of war's proposals.

Knox's plan reflected federal officials' blindness to the realities of Native people's lives. Not only did it incorrectly posit that traditional commitment to communal notions of landowning could easily be overcome, it also ignored the centuries-old agricultural practices of eastern Native peoples. The policymakers focused only on Native American men: because they hunted, Native men were "savages" who had to be "civilized" by being taught to farm. That in these societies women traditionally raised the crops was irrelevant because, in the eyes of the officials, Native American women—like those of European descent—should properly confine themselves to child rearing, household chores, and home manufacturing.

Many indigenous nations responded cautiously to the "civilizing" plan. The Iroquois Confederacy had been devastated by the war; its people in the 1790s lived in what one historian has called "slums in the wilderness." Restricted to small reservations increasingly surrounded by Anglo-American farmlands, men could no longer hunt and often spent their days idle. Quaker missionaries started a demonstration farm among the Senecas, intending to teach men to plow, but they quickly learned that women showed greater interest in their message.

Iroquois men became more receptive to the reformers after the spring of 1799, when a Seneca named Handsome Lake experienced a remarkable series of visions. Like other Native prophets stretching back to Neolin in the 1760s, Handsome Lake preached that Native peoples should renounce alcohol, gambling, and other destructive European customs. Although he directed his followers to reorient men's and women's work assignments as the Quakers advocated, Handsome Lake aimed above all to preserve Iroquois culture. He recognized that, because men could no longer obtain meat through hunting, only by adopting the European sexual division of labor could the Iroquois retain their autonomy.

7-7 Created Equal?

▷ **What contradictions lay at the heart of the Declaration's assertion that "all men are created equal"?**

▷ **How did the battle of women's rights develop in the new nation?**

▷ **What divisions emerged over the question of slavery and the slave trade?**

The Constitution distinguished between "persons" and "citizens." All persons inhabiting the United States comprised, in some vague sense, *the people* who were sovereign in a republic. But only *citizens* voted; only citizens fully possessed the rights enumerated in the Constitution's first ten amendments. Slaves typically could not bear arms, for example. Women, like men, were entitled to "a speedy and public trial, by an impartial jury," but they could not themselves serve as jurors, let alone judges. The language of Jefferson's Declaration of Independence was far more sweeping: "all men are created equal." In eighteenth-century parlance, *all men* meant *all persons*; all *persons* had natural, "unalienable rights" including "life, liberty, and the pursuit of happiness." After independence, women, the enslaved, free people of color, and radical thinkers wrestled anew with the contradictions between such capacious notions of liberty and the laws and customs of the young United States.

7-7a Women and the Republic

"I long to hear that you have declared an independancy," wrote **Abigail Adams** to her husband John in March 1776, shortly after reading Paine's *Common Sense*. And "by the way," she continued, "in the new Code of Laws which I suppose it will be necessary for you to make I desire you would Remember the Ladies, and be more generous and favourable to them than your ancestors." She hoped that Congress

would "not put such unlimited power into the Hands of the Husbands," who traditionally held near-absolute authority over their wives' property and persons. "Remember all Men would be tyrants if they could," Adams noted. "If perticuliar care and attention is not paid to the Laidies [*sic*] we are determined to foment a Rebelion, and will not hold ourselves bound by any Laws in which we have no voice, or Representation."

Two weeks later, John Adams responded: "As to your extraordinary Code of Laws, I cannot but laugh." But the widening circle of rights talk was not so easily dismissed. Like many other disfranchised Americans in the age of revolution, Abigail Adams adapted the ideology patriots had developed to combat Parliament to serve purposes revolutionary leaders had never intended.

Abigail Adams did not ask for woman suffrage, but others did, and some male and female authors began to discuss and define the "rights of women" in general terms. Judith Sargent Murray, Thomas Paine, and James Otis all published essays on the topic, as did many transatlantic radicals. The Philadelphia physician Benjamin Rush, a wide-ranging reformer who argued against capital punishment and slavery, began agitating for women's access to education in 1787. Five years later, Britain's Mary Wollstonecraft inflamed readers throughout the English-speaking world with her tract entitled *A Vindication of the Rights of Woman*.

Nor was the battle for women's rights confined to the page. The drafters of the New Jersey state constitution in 1776 defined voters as "all free inhabitants"; subsequent state laws explicitly enfranchised female voters. For several decades, women who met the state's property qualifications—as well as free black landowners—regularly voted in New Jersey's elections. The anomaly was noted elsewhere; in 1800, one Boston newspaper reported, "Single Females in the State of New Jersey, possessed of a certain property, and having paid taxes, are entitled to vote at elections," and "many exercised this privilege." Had Massachusetts been "equally liberal," Abigail Adams quipped, she too would have cast her ballot. That women who could vote chose to do so was evidence of their altered perception of their place in the political life of the country.

Like their brothers, sons, and husbands, many elite and middling women engaged in nascent partisanship in the 1790s. A 1798 play entitled *Politicians; or, A State of Things*, satirized female characters named Mrs. Violent and Mrs. Turbulent. As political contests grew more openly combative, women's role in the public sphere came to seem more threatening—both to the republic and to womanhood itself. Increasingly, thinkers emphasized the differences between men and women rather than their shared humanity. After an election marred

Abigail Adams Wife of Revolutionary figure (and second U.S. President) John Adams. Influenced by the ideology of the Revolution, her letter to her husband is considered an early effort for greater rights for women.

△ Mary Wollstonecraft (1759–1797) was one of the most · famous thinkers of her day. Her 1792 treatise, *A Vindication of the Rights of Woman,* argued that the radical equality envisioned by the revolutionaries in France should be extended to relations between the sexes. *Vindication* became an international bestseller, with French, German, and American editions printed within the year. Engravings based on this portrait of Wollstonecraft by John Opie served as the frontispiece to later editions of her works, and circulated widely in the United States.

by drunken violence, New Jersey's state legislature concluded that the polls were no place for ladies and abolished female voting in 1807. Throughout the nation, as property qualifications for white male voters shrank, the presumed distinction between white men and everyone else grew. "We hear no longer of the *alarming,* and perhaps justly obnoxious din, of the 'rights of women,'" wrote one conservative female historian in 1832.

7-7b Emancipation and Manumission

On the eve of independence, people of African descent comprised nearly 20 percent of the American population (see Map 7.3). How did approximately seven hundred thousand enslaved and free blacks—persons but not necessarily citizens—fit into the developing nation? Well before the Constitution was ratified, the question engaged white and

black activists. In the late 1770s and early 1780s, enslaved men and women in New Hampshire, Connecticut, and Massachusetts petitioned their courts and legislatures for what some of them called "the sweets of freedom." "That liberty is a great thing we may know from our own feelings, and we may likewise judge so from the conduct of the white-people, in the late war," argued Jupiter Hammon, an enslaved New York writer. "I have hoped that God would open their eyes, when they were so much engaged for liberty, to think of the state of the poor blacks."

Such agitation catalyzed the gradual abolition of slavery in the North, a process now known as "the first emancipation." Vermont banned slavery in its 1777 constitution. Responding to lawsuits filed by enslaved men and women, Massachusetts courts ruled in 1783 that the state constitution prohibited slavery. Other states adopted gradual emancipation laws between 1780 (Pennsylvania) and 1804 (New Jersey). No southern state passed a general emancipation law, but the legislatures of Virginia (1782), Delaware (1787), and Maryland (1790 and 1796) altered statutes that restricted slave owners' ability to free their bondspeople.

7-7c Congress Debates Slavery

At the national level, too, the ideology and experience of Revolution transformed slavery from an unspoken assumption to an open question. In early 1790, three groups of Quakers submitted petitions to Congress calling for the abolition of slavery and the international slave trade. In the ensuing debates, the nation's political leaders directly addressed questions the Constitution had cloaked in euphemism. Southerners vigorously asserted that Congress should not even consider the petitions; had they imagined the federal government would interfere with slavery, they would never have ratified the Constitution. Insisting that slavery was integral to the Union and that abolition would cause more problems than it solved, such legislators developed a defense of slavery that forecast most of the arguments offered on the subject during the next seven decades. Congress accepted a committee report denying it the power to halt slave importations before 1808 or to emancipate slaves at any time, that authority "remaining with the several States alone." The precedent that Congress could not abolish slavery endured until the Civil War.

Revolutionary ideology thus had limited impact on the well-entrenched interests of large slaveholders. Only in the northern states—societies with slaves, not slave societies—did legislatures vote to abolish slavery. Even there, lawmakers' concern for the *property* rights of owners of human chattel—the Revolution, after all, was fought for property as well as for liberty—led them to favor gradual emancipation over immediate abolition. New York's law freed children born into slavery after July 4, 1799, but only after they reached their mid-twenties. And not until the

DEA PICTURE LIBRARY/Getty Images

late 1840s did Rhode Island and Connecticut abolish all vestiges of slavery. For decades, many African Americans in the North lived in an intermediate stage between slavery and freedom.

7-7d Growth of Free Black Population

Despite the slow progress of abolition, the number of free people of African descent grew dramatically after the Revolution. Wartime escapees from plantations, bondsmen who had served in the Continental army, and still others emancipated by their owners or by new state laws were now free. By 1790, nearly 60,000 free people of color lived in the United States; ten years later, they numbered more than 108,000, more than 10 percent of the African American population.

△ A sailor of African descent posed proudly for this portrait around 1800. The name of the artist remains unknown, but the sitter has been tentatively identified as Paul Slocum, the Massachusetts-born son of a West African freedman and a Wampanoag woman. Slocum later changed his name to Cuffee, after his father's Akan day name. As a boat builder and maritime trader, he amassed a fortune, becoming perhaps the wealthiest African American of the early nineteenth century. Subject to racial violence and discrimination, he founded a school, Cuffee's School, to educate black children, and became involved with the free black colony of Sierra Leone, in Africa.

Heritage Images/Hulton Fine Art Collection/Getty Images

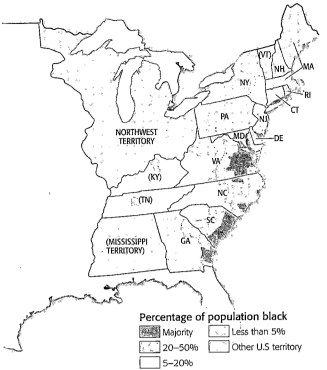

Percentage of population black

- Majority
- 20–50%
- 5–20%
- Less than 5%
- Other U.S territory

Map 7.3 African American Population, 1790: Proportion of Total Population

The first national census clearly indicated that the African American population was heavily concentrated in the coastal South. Although there were growing numbers of blacks in the backcountry—presumably taken there by migrating slave owners—most parts of the North and East had few African American residents. But slavery shaped the entire American economy in the early republic, and even in the mid-Atlantic and the North, its abolition took place gradually, sometimes over decades.

In the Chesapeake, manumissions were speeded by declining soil fertility and the shift from tobacco to grain production, as well as by the rising influence of Baptists and Methodists. Because grain cultivation was less labor intensive than tobacco growing, planters began to complain about "excess" slaves, and occasionally freed some of their less productive or more favored laborers. The enslaved also seized the opportunity to negotiate agreements allowing them to live and work independently until they could save enough to purchase themselves. The free black population of Virginia more than doubled in the two decades after 1790. By 1810, nearly one-quarter of Maryland's African American population lived outside of legal bondage.

7-7e Freedpeople's Lives

Freedpeople from rural areas often made their way to the port cities, especially Boston, Philadelphia, and the new boomtown of Baltimore. Women outnumbered men among the migrants, for they had better employment opportunities in the cities, especially in domestic service. Some freedmen also worked in domestic service, but larger numbers were employed as unskilled laborers and sailors. A few of the women and a sizable proportion of men (nearly one-third of those in Philadelphia in 1795) were skilled workers or retailers. Many cast off the surnames of former masters and chose names like Newman or Brown. As soon as possible they established independent two-parent families instead of continuing to live in their employers' households. They also began to occupy distinct neighborhoods, probably as a result of discrimination.

Emancipation did not bring equality. Even whites who recognized African Americans' right to freedom were unwilling to accept them as equals. Several states—including Delaware, Maryland, and South Carolina—adopted laws denying property-owning black men the vote. South Carolina forbade free blacks from testifying against whites in court. New Englanders used indenture contracts to control freed youths, who were also often barred from public schools. Freedmen found it difficult to purchase property and find good jobs. And though in many areas African Americans were accepted as members—even ministers—of evangelical churches, they were rarely allowed an equal voice in church affairs.

To survive and prosper, freedpeople came to rely on collective effort. In Charleston, mixed-race people formed the Brown Fellowship Society, which provided them insurance, financed a school, and helped to support orphans. In 1794, former slaves in Philadelphia and Baltimore, led by the African American clergyman Richard Allen, founded societies that eventually became the **African Methodist Episcopal (AME) Church.** AME congregations—along with African Baptist, African Episcopal, and African Presbyterian churches—became cultural centers of free black communities.

7-7f Development of Racist Theory

Their endeavors were all the more important because the post-revolutionary years witnessed the development of racist theory in the United States. European Americans had long regarded their slaves as inferior, but the most influential thinkers reasoned that bondspeople's seemingly debased character derived from their enslavement, rather than enslavement's being the consequence of inherited inferiority. In the Revolution's aftermath, though, slave owners became ever more defensive. To skirt the contradiction between slaveholding practice and the egalitarian implications of revolutionary theory, they redefined the theory, arguing that people of African descent were less than fully human and thus the principles of republican equality applied only to European Americans.

African Methodist Episcopal (AME) Church The first African American–led Protestant denomination.

A Philosophic Cock, 1804 (colour litho)/American School, (19th century)/AMERICAN ANTIQUARIAN SOCIETY/American Antiquarian Society, Worcester, Massachusetts, USA/Bridgeman Images

△ A Federalist political cartoon from the election 1804 satirizes Jefferson's pretensions as a *philosophe* in the French mode, and lampoons his relationship with the enslaved Sally Hemings. The engraving, entitled (in a deliberately dirty pun) "A Philosophic Cock," depicts the president as a brightly-plumed rooster, with a turbaned Hemings cowering beside him as a little brown hen.

Simultaneously, the concept of "race" began to be applied to groups defined by skin color. The rise of egalitarian thinking among European Americans at once downplayed status distinctions within their own group, and distinguished all "whites" from all others. (That distinction soon manifested itself in new state laws forbidding whites from marrying blacks or Native peoples.) Notions of "whiteness," "redness," and "blackness" developed alongside beliefs in European Americans' superiority.

The new racial thought had several intertwined elements. First came the assertion that, as Thomas Jefferson insisted in 1781, blacks were "inferior to the whites in the endowments both of body and mind." (He was less certain about Native people.) There followed the belief that those with black skin were inherently lazy and disorderly. Owners had often argued, conversely, that slaves made "natural" workers, but no one seemed to notice the contradiction. Third was the notion that blacks were sexually promiscuous, and that African American men lusted after European American women. The specter of sexual intercourse between black men

Haitian Refugees

Although many European Americans welcomed the news of the French Revolution in 1789, few expressed similar sentiments about the slave rebellion that broke out two years later in the French colony of St. Domingue (later Haiti). A large number of refugees soon flowed into the new United States from that nearby revolt, bringing with them consequences deemed undesirable by most political leaders. Less than a decade after winning independence, the new nation confronted its first immigration crisis.

Among the approximately 600,000 residents of St. Domingue in the early 1790s were about 100,000 free people, almost all of them slave owners; half were whites, the rest of mixed race. In the wake of the French Revolution, those free mixed-race people split the slaveholding population by seeking greater social and political equality. Slaves then seized the opportunity to revolt. By 1793, they had triumphed under the leadership of a former bondsman, Toussaint L'Ouverture. In 1804 they

finally ousted the French, establishing the republic of Haiti. Thousands of whites and free mixed-race people, accompanied by as many slaves as they could readily transport, sought asylum in the United States during those turbulent years.

Although willing to offer shelter to refugees, American political leaders nonetheless feared the consequences of their arrival. Southern plantation owners shuddered to think that slaves so familiar with ideas of freedom and equality would mingle with their own bondspeople. Many were uncomfortable with the arrival of numerous free people of color, even though the immigrants were part of the slaveholding class. Most southern states adopted laws forbidding the entry of Haitian slaves and free people of African descent, but the laws were difficult if not impossible to enforce, as was a later congressional act to the same effect. More than fifteen thousand refugees—white, black, and of mixed-race origins—flooded into the United States and Spanish Louisiana. Many ended up in Virginia (which did not

pass an exclusion law) or in the cities of Charleston, Savannah, and New Orleans.

In both New Orleans and Charleston, the influx of Haitians of mixed race gave rise to a heightened color consciousness that placed light-skinned people atop a hierarchy of people of color. After the United States purchased Louisiana in 1803, the number of free people of color in the territory almost doubled in three years, largely because of a final surge of immigration from the new Haitian republic. And, in Virginia, stories of the successful revolt helped to inspire local slaves in 1800 when they planned the action that has become known as Gabriel's Rebellion.

The Haitian refugees thus linked European Americans and African Americans to current events in the West Indies, indelibly affecting both groups of people.

CRITICAL THINKING

□ What threat did the free immigrant Haitian population present to American slavery defined by race?

◁ A free woman of color in Louisiana early in the nineteenth century, possibly one of the refugees from Haiti. Esteban Rodriguez Mir, named governor of Spanish Louisiana in 1782, ordered all slave and free black women to wear head wraps rather than hats—which were reserved for whites—but this woman and many others subverted his order by nominally complying, but nevertheless creating elaborate headdresses.

Courtesy of the Collections of the Louisiana State Museum

and white women haunted early American thought. The more common reverse circumstance—the sexual exploitation of enslaved women by their masters—generally aroused little concern, though Federalist newspaper editors did not hesitate to use Thomas Jefferson's long-standing relationship with Sally Hemings to inflame public opinion against him. "It is well known that the man, whom it delighteth the people to honor, keeps, and for many years has kept, as his concubine, one of his slaves. Her name is Sally," trumpeted the *Richmond Recorder* in September 1802.

African Americans did not allow developing racist notions to go unchallenged. Benjamin Banneker, a free black mathematical genius, disputed Thomas Jefferson's belief in Africans' intellectual inferiority. In 1791, Banneker sent Jefferson a copy of his latest almanac (which included his astronomical calculations) as an example of blacks' mental powers. Jefferson admitted Banneker's intelligence but regarded him as exceptional, and said he would need more evidence to change his mind about people of African descent.

7-7g A White Man's Republic

Though many men of African descent had served with honor in the Continental army, laws from the 1770s on linked male citizenship rights to "whiteness." Indeed, some historians argue that the subjugation of blacks, Native peoples, and women was a necessary precondition for theoretical equality among white men. Just as excluding women from the political realm reserved all power for men, so identifying common racial antagonists helped to foster white solidarity across class lines. After the Revolution, the division of American society between slave and free was transformed into a division between blacks—some of whom were free—and whites.

7-8 "Revolutions" at the End of the Century

▷ What did the "revolutions" at the end of the eighteenth century reveal about the government established in the United States?

▷ How did Fries's and Gabriel's Rebellion appropriate the language and experience of the Revolutionary Era?

Three events in the last two years of the eighteenth century can be deemed real or potential revolutions: Fries's Rebellion, Gabriel's Rebellion, and the election of Thomas Jefferson. Although they differed significantly, these events mirrored the tensions and uncertainties of the young republic. The Fries rebels resisted national authority to tax. Gabriel and his followers directly challenged the slave system so crucial to the Chesapeake economy. And the venomous, hard-fought

presidential election of 1800 exposed a flaw in the Constitution that would have to be corrected by amendment.

7-8a Fries's Rebellion

The tax resistance movement known by the name of one of its prominent leaders—Revolutionary War veteran John Fries—arose among German American farmers in Pennsylvania's Lehigh Valley in 1798–1799. To finance the Quasi-War against France, Congress taxed land, houses, and legal documents. German Americans, imbued with revolutionary ideals (nearly half were veterans), saw in the taxes a threat to

TOUSSAINT L'OUVERTURE.

△ This c. 1800 engraving depicts Toussaint L'Ouverture, leader of the movement for independence on the valuable sugar island of Saint Domingue, where slaves challenged French colonial rule in 1791. A decorated general on the Caribbean front of the French Revolution, L'Ouverture is shown as a hero in full military regalia. Newspapers in the United States followed his exploits closely; nearly 200 articles were printed about him during the year of Gabriel's rebellion. The uprising of the slaves of Saint Domingue—which became in 1804 the independent nation of Haiti—fascinated antislavery forces and terrified planters throughout the young United States.

Dissent During Wartime

The nation's first overseas conflict, the Quasi-War with France in 1798–1799, spawned its first attempt to suppress dissent. By criminalizing dissenting speech, the Sedition Act of 1798 tried to mute criticism of the war and President John Adams. Fifteen men were indicted and ten fined and jailed after being convicted under the statute's provisions.

Although Americans might assume that their right to free speech under the First Amendment, now more fully accepted than it was two centuries ago, protects dissenters during wartime, history suggests otherwise. Every conflict has stimulated efforts to suppress dissenters. During the Civil War, the Union jailed civilian Confederate sympathizers for long periods. During the First World War, a Sedition Act allowed the government to deport immigrant aliens who criticized the war effort, among them several outspoken Socialists and anarchists.

Moreover, angry neighbors subjected citizens who objected to government policies to a variety of formal and informal sanctions. World War II brought the silencing of those who had opposed American entry into the war. The consequences of antiwar protests in the Vietnam era still affect the nation today, for the American people remain divided over whether the proper course of action in the 1960s and 1970s was dissent from, or acquiescence to, government policy.

The USA PATRIOT Act, adopted after the terrorist attacks of September 11, 2001, removed long-standing restrictions on government surveillance of citizens, controversially granting access to library records. Criticism of the wars in Iraq and Afghanistan raised questions that arouse heated debate: Do newspapers that publish classified information or pictures of abused prisoners overstep the First Amendment? Can political figures censure the conduct

of the wars without being labeled unpatriotic?

Freedom of speech is never easy to maintain, and wartime conditions make it much more difficult. When the nation comes under attack, many argue that the time for dissent has ceased and that citizens should support the government. Others contend that, if American freedom is to mean anything, people must have the right to speak their mind at all times. Events in the United States since the 9/11 attacks suggest that this legacy remains contentious for the American people.

CRITICAL THINKING

◻ Over more than two centuries, the U.S. government has often passed laws to limit freedom of speech during times of national duress. What limitations on freedom of expression do Americans accept in the twenty-first century?

◻ How, besides enacting legislation, do we in the contemporary United States define the boundaries of acceptable political speech?

---

their liberties and livelihoods, as well as an echo of the hated Stamp Act of 1765. Asserting their right to resist unconstitutional laws, they raised liberty poles, petitioned Congress, and barred assessors from their homes.

When a federal judge ordered the arrest of twenty resisters, Fries led a troop of 120 militiamen to Bethlehem, where they surrounded a tavern temporarily housing the prisoners. President Adams described the militiamen's actions as acts of war. Fries and many of his neighbors were arrested and tried; he and two others were convicted of treason; thirty-two more of violating the Sedition Act. Although Fries and the other "traitors" were sentenced to hang, Adams pardoned them just two days before their scheduled execution. Despite clemency from a Federalist president, the region's residents became, and remained, Republican partisans.

7-8b Gabriel's Rebellion

Like their white compatriots in the Lehigh Valley and elsewhere, African Americans had witnessed the benefits of fighting collectively for freedom, a message reinforced by stunning news of the successful slave revolt in St. Domingue.

Gabriel, an enslaved Virginia blacksmith who planned the second end-of-the-century revolution, drew on both Haitian and American revolutionary experiences.

Gabriel first recruited to his cause other skilled African American artisans who lived, as he did, under minimal supervision. Next, he enlisted rural slaves. The rebels planned to attack Richmond on the night of August 30, 1800. They would set fire to the city, seize the capitol building, and capture the governor, James Monroe. At that point, Gabriel believed, other slaves and perhaps poor whites would join the movement.

The plan showed considerable political sophistication, but heavy rain forced a postponement. Several planters then learned of the plot and spread the alarm. Gabriel avoided arrest for weeks, but militia troops quickly apprehended and interrogated most of the rebellion's other leaders. Twenty-six rebels, including Gabriel himself, were hanged.

At his trial, one of Gabriel's followers made explicit the links that so frightened Chesapeake slaveholders. He told his judges that he, like George Washington, had "adventured my life in endeavouring to obtain the liberty of my country-men, and am a willing sacrifice in their cause." Southern state legislatures responded to such claims by passing increasingly severe laws regulating slavery, which soon became even more firmly entrenched as an economic institution and way of life in the region.

7-8c Election of 1800

The third end-of-the-century revolution was the election of Thomas Jefferson as president and a Congress dominated by Republicans after a decade of growing partisanship. Leading up to November 1800, Federalists and Republicans openly campaigned for congressional seats and maneuvered to control the outcome in the electoral college. Republicans again nominated Jefferson and Burr; Federalists named John Adams, with Charles Cotesworth Pinckney of South Carolina as vice president. The network of Republican newspapers forged in the fires of Sedition Act prosecutions vigorously promoted the Jeffersonian cause. When the votes were counted, Jefferson and Burr had tied with 73. Adams garnered 64 and Pinckney 63. Under the Constitution, the existing House of Representatives would decide the election; the newly elected Jeffersonians would not take office until the president did.

Voting in the House continued for six days. Through thirty-five ballots, Federalists supported Burr while Republicans held fast for Jefferson. Finally, James Bayard, a Federalist and Delaware's sole congressman, brokered a deal that gave the Virginian the presidency. The bitterly fought election prompted the adoption of the Twelfth Amendment, which provided that electors would thenceforth cast separate ballots for president and vice president.

Decades later, in a letter to then-president James Monroe, Jefferson looked back on his election as an accomplishment nearly as momentous as American independence. In an 1820 letter to then-president James Monroe, he linked "the revolution of 1776" to "that of 1800." Historians debate whether the so-called Revolution of 1800 deserves the name Jefferson later gave it. Many of the Republicans' promised reforms failed to materialize. The defeated Federalists retained and indeed strengthened their hold on the federal judiciary. But at the very least, Jefferson's inauguration—which marked the first peaceful transfer of power from one faction to another in a modern republic—ushered in a new era in American political culture, one in which republican theory and partisan practice could coexist. "We are all Republicans, we are all Federalists," the new president proclaimed in his first inaugural address.

Summary

During the 1780s, the republic's upheavals convinced many leaders that the United States needed a more powerful central government. Drafted in 1787, the Constitution created that stronger national framework. During heated debates over its ratification, the document's supporters—called Federalists—contended that their design was just as "republican" as the flawed Articles of Confederation had been. Those labeled Antifederalists argued otherwise, but ultimately lost the fight.

Inhabitants of the early United States faced changed lives as well as changed politics. Native peoples east of the Mississippi River found aspects of their cultures under assault. Enslaved African Americans faced increasingly restrictive laws in the southern colonies. In the North, freedom suits, manumissions, and gradual emancipation laws fostered a growing free black community. At the same time, a newly systematic and defensive pro-slavery argument emphasized race (rather than slave or free status) as the determinant of African Americans' standing in the nation. Imagined chiefly as mothers of the next generation and selfless contributors to the nation's welfare, white women played a limited role in the public life of the United States. Writers, artists, playwrights, and architects promoted feminine self-sacrifice and other such republican virtues.

The years between 1788 and 1800 established enduring precedents for Congress, the presidency, and the federal judiciary. Building on successful negotiations with Spain (Pinckney's Treaty), Britain (the Jay Treaty), and France (the Convention of 1800), the United States forged diplomatic independence. The French Revolution prompted vigorous debates over American foreign and domestic policy. In the 1790s, the United States saw the emergence of organized factionalism and grassroots politicking involving both men and women. In 1801, after more than a decade of struggle, the Jeffersonian view of an agrarian, decentralized republic prevailed over Alexander Hamilton's vision of a centralized economy and a strong national government.

Suggestions for Further Reading

Annette Gordon-Reed, *The Hemingses of Monticello: An American Family* (2008)

François Furstenberg, *When the United States Spoke French: Five Refugees Who Shaped a Nation* (2014)

Eliga Gould, *Among the Powers of the Earth: The American Revolution and the Making of a New World Empire* (2012)

Catherine O'Donnell Kaplan, *Men of Letters in the Early Republic: Cultivating Forums of Citizenship* (2008)

Pauline Maier, *Ratification: The People Debate the Constitution, 1787–1788* (2010)

Jeffrey L. Pasley, *"The Tyranny of Printers": Newspaper Politics in the Early American Republic* (2001)

Claudio Saunt, *West of the Revolution: An Uncommon History of 1776* (2014)

David Waldstreicher, *Slavery's Constitution: From Revolution to Ratification* (2009)

Caroline Winterer, *American Enlightenments: Pursuing Happiness in an Age of Reason* (2016)

Rosemarie Zagarri, *Revolutionary Backlash: Women and Politics in the Early American Republic* (2007)

MINDTAP
From Cengage

MindTap®is a fully online personalized learning experience built upon Cengage Learning content. MindTap® combines student learning tools—readings, multimedia, activities, and assessments—into a singular Learning Path that guides students through the course and helps students develop the critical thinking, analysis, and communication skills that are essential to academic and professional success.

Defining the Nation, 1801–1823

E ager to set himself apart from the allegedly aristocratic ways of his Federalist predecessors, President Thomas Jefferson displayed impatience, even disdain, for ceremony. But on his first New Year's Day in office, the third president eagerly awaited the ceremonial presentation of a much-heralded tribute to his commitment, in the words of one of the gift's bearers, to "defend Republicanism and baffle all the arts of Aristocracy." Crafted in Massachusetts, the belated inaugural gift had been nearly a month en route, traveling amid much fanfare for more than 400 miles by sleigh, boat, and wagon. Weighing more than twelve hundred pounds and measuring four feet in diameter, it bore the inscription "THE GREATEST CHEESE IN AMERICA—FOR THE GREATEST MAN IN AMERICA."

The idea for the "mammoth cheese," as it became known, had been born the previous July in a small farming community in western Massachusetts. The "Ladies" of Cheshire—a town as resolutely Jeffersonian-Republican as it was Baptist—had made the cheese from the milk of nine hundred cows as "a mark of the exalted esteem" in which the town's residents held the Republican president. As members of a religious minority in New England, where Congregationalists still dominated the pulpits and statehouses, the Cheshire Baptists had much to celebrate in the election of a president whose vision for the nation featured not just agrarianism but also separation of church and state. Their fiery pastor, John Leland, presented the cheese to the president and, two days later, preached the Sunday sermon in the House of Representatives, where at least one genteel listener dismissed his brand of evangelicalism as "horrid."

Federalist editors delighted in poking fun at the mammoth cheese—especially at those who had made it. Its semirotten, maggot-infested condition upon delivery symbolized, they said, the

◁ Federalists derided the Cheshire cheese as the "mammoth" cheese, after the mastodon (similar to the "woolly mammoth") unearthed by naturalist Charles Willson Peale in 1801. Here, workers search for fossils while a specially designed machine pumps water from an excavation pit. Partially funded by the Jefferson administration, Peale's expedition was considered a boondoggle by Federalists. New York Public Library/Science Source

Chronology

1801	▫ Marshall becomes chief justice
	▫ Jefferson inaugurated as president
1801–05	▫ United States defeats Barbary pirates
1803	▫ *Marbury v. Madison*
	▫ Louisiana Purchase
1804	▫ Jefferson reelected president, Clinton vice president
1804–06	▫ Lewis and Clark expedition
1805	▫ Tenskwatawa emerges as Shawnee leader
1807	▫ *Chesapeake* affair
	▫ Embargo Act
1808	▫ Congress bans slave importation
	▫ Madison elected president
1808–13	▫ Tenskwatawa and Tecumseh organize Native American resistance
1811	▫ National Road begun
1812	▫ Madison reelected president
1812–15	▫ War of 1812
1813	▫ Tecumseh's death
	▫ Boston Manufacturing Company starts textile mill in Waltham, Massachusetts
1814	▫ "The Star-Spangled Banner" is written
	▫ Treaty of Ghent
1814–15	▫ Hartford Convention
1815	▫ Battle of New Orleans
1817	▫ Regular steamboat travel begins on Mississippi
1817–25	▫ Erie Canal constructed
1819	▫ *McCulloch v. Maryland*
	▫ Adams-Onís Treaty
1819–early 1820s	▫ First major depression
1820–21	▫ Missouri Compromise
1822	▫ Colonization of Liberia begins (formally established in 1824)
1823	▫ Monroe Doctrine

nation under Republican rule. Its very existence, to say nothing of its size, resulted from the excesses of democracy, in which even women and backwoods preachers could play leading roles. The cheese, they scoffed, had been made of "*asses*' milk."

Yet the Federalists' derision of the mammoth cheese won them few new supporters and instead inspired additional showy expressions of democratic pride. In the following months, a Philadelphia baker sold "Mammoth Bread," while two butchers sent the president a "Mammoth veal." In Washington, a "Mammoth Eater" consumed forty-two eggs in ten minutes. Nor did the "mammoth" craze prove ephemeral: two years later, in 1804, a "mammoth loaf" was served—along with whiskey, hard cider, and wine—in the Capitol to a raucous crowd of Federalist-disparaging Republicans, including President Jefferson himself.

Experience an interactive version of this story in MindTap®.

Seemingly frivolous in retrospect, political symbolism and rivalries were deadly serious in the early republic, as attested to by those (most famously, Alexander Hamilton) who died in duels. People excluded from formal political participation often joined voting citizens in expressing ideal visions for the nation's future when they petitioned legislatures, marched in parades, engaged in heated tavern debates—and sent the president a mammoth cheese. Behind such symbolism lay serious political ideologies. Jeffersonians believed virtue derived from agricultural endeavors, and they thus celebrated the acquisition of the Louisiana Territory. Their efforts to expand their agriculturally based "empire of liberty" westward were resisted, however, by Native Americans and their European allies, and sometimes by Federalists, too. Not until the War of 1812 largely removed such resistance would the United States begin its nearly unbridled expansion across the continent. Although it resolved few of the issues that caused it, that war held profound consequences for American development. It secured the United States' sovereignty, opened much of the West to European Americans and their African American slaves, and helped spur revolutions in transportation and industry.

Although contemporary observers noted that the postwar nationalism heralded an "Era of Good Feelings," it soon became apparent that good feelings had limits. When economic boom turned to bust, the postwar bubble of nationalistic optimism and ostensible unity may not have popped, but it never again proved quite so buoyant. No issue proved more divisive than slavery's future in the West, as Missouri's petition for statehood revealed. Even as President Monroe tried to bolster the nation's international standing, the nation's internal tensions festered not far beneath the surface.

☐ *What characterized the two main competing visions for national development?*

☐ *How did America's relationship with Europe influence political and economic developments?*

☐ *In what ways did nonvoting Americans—most African Americans, women, and Native Americans—take part in defining the new nation?*

8-1 Political Visions

▶ **How did Democratic-Republicans seek to implement their political vision of the country after the election of Thomas Jefferson in 1800?**

▶ **How did the American political culture develop to encourage political activism and engagement?**

▶ **How did the Supreme Court develop as a branch of the federal government under Chief Justice John Marshall?**

In his inaugural address, Jefferson appealed to his opponents. Standing in the Senate chamber, the Capitol's only completed part, he addressed the electorate not as party members but as citizens with common beliefs: "We are all republicans, we are all federalists." Nearly a thousand people strained to hear his vision of a restored republicanism: "A wise and frugal government, which shall restrain men from injuring one another, which shall leave them free to regulate their pursuits of industry and improvement, and shall not take from the mouth of labor the bread it had earned. This is the sum of good government."

But outgoing president John Adams did not hear Jefferson's call for unity, having left Washington before dawn. He and Jefferson, once close friends, now disliked each other intensely. Despite the spirit of Jefferson's inaugural address, the Democratic-Republicans—as the Republicans of the 1790s now called themselves, after the Democratic societies of the 1790s—and the Federalists remained bitter opponents. These parties held different visions of how society and government should be organized. The Federalists advocated a strong national government with centralized authority to promote economic development. The Democratic-Republicans sought to restrain the national government, believing that

limited government would foster republican virtue, which derived from agricultural endeavors. Nearly two decades later, Jefferson would call his election "the revolution of 1800," which was "as real a revolution in the principles of our government as that of 1776 was in its form."

8-1a Separation of Church and State

When the Cheshire farmers sent Jefferson a mammoth cheese, they did so largely to express gratitude for his commitment to the separation of church and state. On the very day he received the overripe cheese, Jefferson reciprocated by penning a letter to the Baptist association in Danbury, Connecticut, proclaiming that the Constitution's First Amendment supported a "wall of separation between church and state." Jefferson's letter articulated a core component of his vision of limited government. The president declared that "religion is a matter which lies solely between Man & his God." It lay beyond the government's purview. New England Baptists hailed Jefferson as a hero, but New England Federalists believed their worst fears were confirmed. During the election of 1800, Federalists had waged a venomous campaign against Jefferson, incorrectly labeling him an atheist. Their rhetoric proved so effective that, after Jefferson's election, some New England women hid their Bibles in their gardens and wells to foil Democratic-Republicans allegedly bent on confiscating them. Jefferson's letter to the Danbury Baptists seemingly vindicated such hysteria.

8-1b Religious Revivals

Jefferson became president during a period of religious revivalism, particularly among Methodists and Baptists, whose democratic preaching—all humans, they said, were equal in God's eyes—encouraged a growing democratic political culture. The most famous revival was at Cane Ridge, Kentucky, in August 1801. One report estimated 25,000 people attended, including men and women, free and enslaved, at a time when Kentucky's largest city, Lexington, had fewer than two thousand inhabitants. The call to personal repentance and conversion invigorated southern Protestantism, giving churches an evangelical base. All revivalists, both in the South and the North, shared a belief in individual self-improvement, but northern revivalists also emphasized communal improvement, becoming missionaries for both individual salvation and social reform (see "Revivals and Reform," Section 10-7).

Emboldened by secular and religious ideologies about human equality, society's nonelites articulated their own political visions. Rather than simply taking stands in debates defined by social and political betters, they worked to reshape the debates. When the Cheshire Baptists sent their cheese to President Jefferson, for example, they pointedly informed the Virginia planter that it had been made "without a single slave to assist."

8-1c Political Mobilization

The revolution of 1800, which gave the Democratic-Republicans majorities in both houses of Congress in addition to the presidency, did not reflect a revolution in the electorate, which remained limited largely, but not exclusively, to property-holding men. The Constitution left the regulation of voting to the individual states. In no state but New Jersey could women vote even when meeting property qualifications, and in New Jersey that right was granted inadvertently and was revoked in 1807. In 1800, free black men meeting property qualifications could vote in all states but Delaware, Georgia, South Carolina, and Virginia, but local custom often kept them from exercising that right. Nonetheless, partisan politics captured nearly all Americans' imaginations, and politicians actively courted nonvoters along with voters. Most political mobilization took place locally, where partisans rallied popular support for candidates and their ideologies on militia training grounds, in taverns and churches, at court gatherings, and during holiday celebrations. Voters and nonvoters alike expressed their views by marching in parades, signing petitions, singing songs, and debating politically charged sermons. Perhaps most important, they devoured a growing print culture of pamphlets, broadsides (posters), almanacs, and—especially—newspapers.

8-1d The Partisan Press

Newspapers provided a forum for sustained political conversation. Read aloud in taverns, artisans' workshops, and homes, newspapers gave national importance to local events. Without newspaper publicity, Cheshire's mammoth cheese would have been little more than a massive hunk of curdled milk. With it, a cheese became worthy of presidential response. In 1800, the nation had 260 newspapers; by 1810, it had 396—virtually all of them unabashedly partisan.

The parties adopted official organs. Shortly after his election, Jefferson persuaded the *National Intelligencer* to move from Philadelphia to the new capital of Washington, where it became the Democratic-Republicans' voice. In 1801, Alexander Hamilton launched the *New York Evening Post* as the Federalist vehicle. It boosted Federalists while frequently calling Jefferson a liar and depicting him as the head of a slave harem. The party organs—published six or seven times a week, year in and year out—ensured that the growing American obsession with partisan politics extended beyond electoral campaigns.

8-1e Limited Government

Jefferson needed public servants as well as supporters. To bring into his administration men sharing his vision of individual liberty, an agrarian republic, and limited government, Jefferson refused to recognize appointments made by Adams in his presidency's last days and dismissed Federalist customs collectors. He awarded vacant treasury and judicial offices to Republicans. Federalists accused Jefferson of "hunting the Federalists like wild beasts" and abandoning the peaceful

△ Although most places limited the vote to property-owning white men, elections, such as this one in Philadelphia, drew multiracial crowds of men, women, and children.

Art Collection 3/Alamy

overtures of his inaugural address. Jeffersonians worked to make the government leaner. If Alexander Hamilton had viewed the national debt as the engine of economic growth, Jefferson deemed it the source of government corruption. Secretary of the Treasury Albert Gallatin cut the army budget in half and reduced the 1802 navy budget by two-thirds. He moved to reduce the national debt from $83 million to $57 million, hoping to retire it altogether by 1817. Austerity motivated Jefferson to close two of the nation's five diplomatic missions abroad, at The Hague and in Berlin. Jeffersonians attacked taxes as well as spending: the Democratic-Republican–controlled Congress oversaw the repeal of all internal taxes, including the despised whiskey tax of 1791.

The Democratic-Republicans also struck down Federalists' efforts to stiffen citizenship requirements and to restrict speech critical of the government. Jefferson declined to use the Alien and Sedition Acts of 1798 against his opponents, instead pardoning those already convicted of violating them. Congress let the Sedition Act expire in 1801 and the Alien Act in 1802, and repealed the Naturalization Act of 1798, which had required fourteen years of residency for citizenship. The 1802 act that replaced it, while stipulating the registration of aliens, required of would-be citizens only five years of residency, loyalty to the Constitution, and the forsaking of foreign allegiances and titles. The new act remained the basis of naturalized American citizenship into the twentieth century.

8-1f Judicial Politics

To many Democratic-Republicans, the judiciary represented a centralizing and undemocratic force, especially because judges were appointed, not elected, and served for life. Partisan Democratic-Republicans thus targeted opposition judges. At Jefferson's prompting, the House impeached (indicted) and the Senate convicted Federal District Judge John Pickering of New Hampshire. Allegedly deranged and alcoholic, Pickering made an easy mark. On the same day in 1803 that Pickering was ousted from office, the House impeached Supreme Court Justice Samuel Chase for judicial misconduct. A staunch Federalist, Chase had pushed for prosecutions under the Sedition Act, had actively campaigned for Adams in 1800, and had repeatedly denounced Jefferson's administration from the bench. But in the Senate, the Democratic-Republicans failed to muster the two-thirds majority necessary for conviction. The failure to remove Chase preserved the Court's independence and established the precedent that criminal actions, not political disagreements, justified removal from office.

8-1g The Marshall Court

Although Jefferson appointed three new Supreme Court justices during his two administrations, the Court remained a Federalist stronghold under the leadership of his distant cousin John Marshall. Marshall adopted some outward trappings of Republicanism—opting for a plain black gown over the more colorful academic robes of his fellow justices—but

adhered steadfastly to Federalist ideology. Even after the Democratic-Republicans achieved a majority of Court seats in 1811, Marshall remained extremely influential as chief justice. Under the Marshall Court (1801–1835), the Supreme Court consistently upheld federal supremacy over the states while protecting the interests of commerce and capital.

Marshall made the Court an equal branch of the government in practice as well as theory. Previously regarded lightly, judicial service became a coveted honor for ambitious and talented men. Marshall, moreover, strengthened the Court by having it speak with a more unified voice; rather than issuing a host of individual concurring judgments, the justices now issued joint majority opinions. Marshall became the voice of the majority: from 1801 through 1805, he wrote twenty-four of the Court's twenty-six decisions; through 1810, he wrote 85 percent of the opinions, including every important one.

8-1h Judicial Review

One of the most important involved Adams's midnight appointments. In his last hours in office, Adams had named Federalist William Marbury a justice of the peace in the District of Columbia. But Jefferson's secretary of state, James Madison, declined to certify the appointment, allowing the new president to appoint a Democratic-Republican instead. Marbury sued, requesting a writ of mandamus (a court order forcing the president to appoint him). *Marbury v. Madison* presented a political dilemma. If the Supreme Court ruled in Marbury's favor, the president probably would not comply with the writ, and the Court could not force him to do so. Yet by refusing to issue the writ, the Federalist-dominated bench would hand the Democratic-Republicans a victory.

To avoid both pitfalls, Marshall brilliantly recast the issue. Writing for the Court, he ruled that Marbury had a right to his appointment but that the Supreme Court could not compel Madison to honor the appointment because the Constitution did not grant the Court power to issue a writ of mandamus. In the absence of any specific mention in the Constitution, Marshall wrote, the section of the Judiciary Act of 1789 authorizing the Court to issue writs was unconstitutional. Thus, the Supreme Court denied itself the power to issue writs of mandamus but established its far greater power to judge the constitutionality of laws passed by Congress. In doing so, Marshall fashioned the theory of judicial review. Because the Constitution was "the supreme law of the land," Marshall wrote, any federal or state act contrary to the Constitution must be null and void. The Supreme Court, whose duty it was to uphold the law, would decide whether a legislative act contradicted the Constitution. "It is emphatically the province and duty of the judicial department," Marshall ruled, "to say what the law is." This power of the Supreme Court to determine the constitutionality of legislation and presidential acts permanently enhanced the independence of the judiciary and breathed life into the Constitution. "Marshall

Marbury v. Madison Case that established the Supreme Court's power to determine the constitutionality of laws.

found the Constitution paper and made it power," President James A. Garfield later observed.

8-1i Election of 1804 and Burr-Hamilton Animosity

In the first election after the Twelfth Amendment's ratification, Jefferson took no chances: he dropped Burr as his running mate and, in keeping with the already established convention of having a North-South balance on the ticket, chose George Clinton of New York. They swamped their opponents—South Carolinian Charles Cotesworth Pinckney and New Yorker Rufus King—in the electoral college by 162 votes to 14, carrying fifteen of the seventeen states. That 1804 election escalated the long-standing animosity between Burr and Hamilton, who supported Burr's rival in the New York gubernatorial election. When Hamilton called Burr a liar, Burr challenged Hamilton to a duel. Believing his honor was at stake, Hamilton accepted the challenge even though his son Philip had died in 1801 from dueling wounds. Because New York had outlawed dueling, the encounter took place across the Hudson River in New Jersey. Details of the duel itself remain hazy—did Hamilton withhold his fire, as he claimed he would?—but the outcome was clear: Hamilton died the following day, after being shot by Burr. In New York and New Jersey, prosecutors indicted Burr for murder.

Facing arrest if he returned to either state, and with his political career in ruins, Burr fled to the West. While historians disagree about his motives, the "Burr Conspiracy" was understood at the time to involve a scheme with Brigadier General James Wilkinson to create a new empire by using military force to acquire what is now Texas and by persuading already existing western territories to leave the United States and join the new empire. Brought to trial in the U.S. Circuit Court in Richmond for treason in 1807, Burr faced a prosecution aided by President Jefferson but presided over by Jefferson's political rival Chief Justice Marshall. (At the time, Supreme Court justices presided over circuit courts.) Prompted by Marshall to interpret treason narrowly, the jury acquitted Burr, who fled to Europe.

8-1j Nationalism and Culture

As statesmen bickered over how to realize the nation's potential, other Americans touted their own nationalist visions with paintbrushes and pens. Nearly three decades after the Constitution's ratification, painters continued to memorialize great birth scenes of American nationhood, such as the Declaration of Independence's signing, Revolutionary War battle scenes, and the Constitutional Convention. Four of John Trumbull's revolutionary scenes, commissioned in 1817, still hang in the rotunda of the Capitol building in Washington.

With architecture, Americans self-consciously constructed a new, independent nation. Designed by Major Pierre Charles

Eli Whitney Inventor of the cotton gin, which made cleaning of southern cotton faster and cheaper.

L'Enfant, a French-born engineer who served under George Washington during the Revolution, the city of Washington was meant to embody a "reciprocity of sight": Each of the government's three branches—the legislative, judicial, and executive—should keep an eye on one another at all times. But nationalism could be easier to envision than to construct. Beset by pragmatic difficulties, L'Enfant's plan took nearly a century to implement. A French visitor in 1851 noted that Washington had "streets without houses," "houses without streets," and was "striking proof of this truth, that one cannot create a great city at will." In Washington and elsewhere, wealthier Americans commissioned homes in the "federal" style, which imitated classical architecture in its economy of decoration and which made use of indigenous, rather than imported, building materials.

The era's best-selling book was Noah Webster's spelling book, which proposed making English more "republican." By some estimates, the book sold nearly 100 million copies by the end of the nineteenth century. Webster believed Americans should speak and spell like one another—they should bind together by speaking a national language—but unlike "King's English," their language should not require elite training to master. Words should be spelled as they sound—for example, "honor" should replace "honour." A shared language would unite an increasingly far-flung population.

8-2 Continental Expansion and Native American Resistance

▶ Why was American access to New Orleans and the Mississippi Valley important in the early nineteenth century?

▶ What did the Lewis and Clark expedition through the Louisiana Territory achieve?

▶ How did Native American peoples respond to American encroachment on their lands?

Little excited Jeffersonians' nationalistic imaginations more than the West and its seeming abundance of unoccupied land ripe for agrarian expansion. Federalists, though, often urged caution, fearing uncontrolled expansion would impede commercial development and federal oversight.

By 1800, hundreds of thousands of white Americans had settled in the rich Ohio River and Mississippi River valleys, intruding on Native peoples' lands. In the Northwest they raised foodstuffs, primarily wheat, and in the Southwest they cultivated cotton. At the time of the American Revolution, cotton production was profitable only for the Sea Island planters in South Carolina and Georgia, who grew the long-staple variety. Short-staple cotton, which grew readily in the interior and in all kinds of soil, was unmarketable because its sticky seeds could be removed only by hand. After a young New England inventor named **Eli Whitney** designed a cotton

△ Because Washington, DC, was designed to maintain a symbolic "reciprocity of sight" between the federal government's branches, the White House and Capitol had little but a dirt road separating them in 1826, when a British diplomat painted the young nation's capital city.

gin (short for "engine") in 1793, allowing one person to remove the same number of seeds that previously required fifty people working by hand, the cultivation of short-staple cotton spread rapidly westward into the fertile lands of Louisiana, Mississippi, Alabama, Arkansas, and Tennessee. By exponentially increasing the efficiency with which cotton fiber could be extracted from raw cotton, the cotton gin greatly increased the demand for slaves who seeded, tended, and harvested cotton fields.

Whatever crops they marketed, American settlers depended on free access to the Mississippi River and its Gulf port, New Orleans. "The Mississippi," wrote Secretary of State James Madison, "is to them [western settlers] everything. It is the Hudson, the Delaware, the Potomac and all navigable rivers of the Atlantic States formed into one stream." Whoever controlled the port of New Orleans had a hand on the American economy's throat.

8-2a New Orleans

Spain, which had acquired France's territory west of the Mississippi in the settlement of the Seven Years' War (1763), secretly transferred it back to France in 1800 and 1801. American officials learned of the transfer only in 1802, when Napoleon seemed poised to rebuild a French

empire in the New World. "Every eye in the United States is now focused on the affairs of Louisiana," Jefferson wrote to Robert R. Livingston, the American minister in Paris. American concerns intensified when Spanish officials, on the eve of ceding control to the French, violated Pinckney's treaty by denying Americans the privilege of storing their products (or exercising their "right of deposit") at New Orleans prior to transshipment to foreign markets. Western farmers and eastern merchants, who traded through New Orleans, thought a devious Napoleon had closed the port; they talked war.

To relieve the pressure for war and win western farmers' support, Jefferson urged Congress to authorize the call-up of eighty thousand militiamen but at the same time sent Virginia's Governor James Monroe to join Robert Livingston in France with instructions to buy the port of New Orleans and as much of the Mississippi valley as possible. Arriving in Paris in April 1803, Monroe learned with astonishment that France had already offered to sell all 827,000 square miles of Louisiana to the United States for a mere $15 million. With St. Domingue torn from French control by revolution and slave revolt, Napoleon gave up dreams of a New World empire and no longer needed Louisiana as its breadbasket. His more urgent need was for money to wage war against

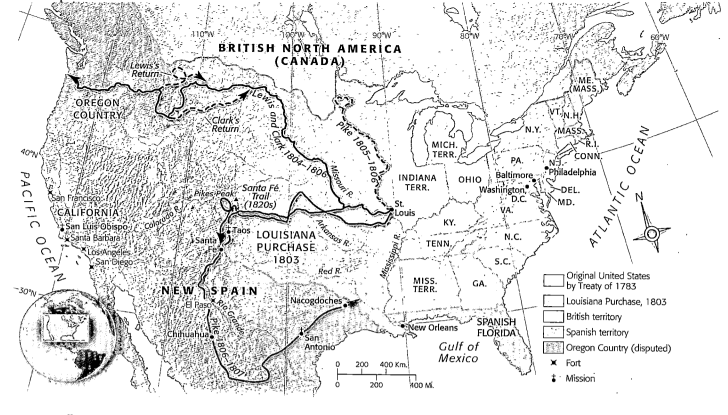

Map 8.1 Louisiana Purchase

The Louisiana Purchase (1803) doubled the area of the United States and opened the trans-Mississippi West for American settlement.

Britain. On April 30, Monroe and Livingston signed a treaty buying the vast territory, whose exact borders and land remained uncharted (see Map 8.1).

8-2b Louisiana Purchase

The **Louisiana Purchase** appealed to Americans with divergent ideas about how best to achieve national greatness and personal prosperity. The purchase ensured that the United States would control the Mississippi's mouth, giving peace of mind to western settlers who relied on the river to market their goods. It also inspired the commercial visions of those who imagined the United States as the nexus of international trade networks reaching between Europe and Asia. Louisiana promised to fulfill the dreams of easterners seeking cheap, fertile lands. Its vast expanse meant, too, that land could be set aside for Native peoples displaced by the incursion of white settlers and their black slaves, soothing the consciences of those white Americans who preferred to "civilize" rather than to exterminate the continent's first settlers. The purchase had its critics, though: some doubted its constitutionality (even Jefferson agonized over it); others worried that it belied the Democratic-Republicans' commitment to debt reduction; some New England Federalists complained that it undermined their commercial interests and threatened the sustainability of the republic by spreading the population beyond where it could be properly controlled.

Louisiana Purchase The U.S. purchase of the Louisiana Territory (the area from the Mississippi River to the Rocky Mountains) from France in 1803 for $15 million. The purchase virtually doubled the area of the United States.

Overall, though, the Louisiana Purchase was the most popular achievement of Jefferson's presidency.

Louisiana was not, however, the "vast wilderness" that some Federalists lamented and most Republicans coveted. When the United States acquired the territory, hundreds of thousands of people who had not been party to the agreement became American subjects. These included Native Americans from scores of nations who made their homes within the enormous territory, as well as people of European and African descent—or, often, a complex mixture of the two—who congregated primarily along the Gulf Coast. Around New Orleans, Louisiana's colonial heritage was reflected in its people: creoles of French and Spanish descent, slaves of African descent, free people of color, and Acadians, or Cajuns (descendants of French settlers in eastern Canada), as well as some Germans, Irish, and English. The 1810 census, the first taken after the purchase, reported that 97,000 non-Native Americans lived in the Louisiana Purchase area, of whom the great majority (77,000) lived in what is now the state of Louisiana. Not all these new Americans welcomed their new national identity. Although Jefferson imagined the West as an "empire of liberty," free people of color soon discovered their exclusion from the Louisiana Purchase treaty's provision that "the inhabitants of the ceded territory" would be accorded the rights of American citizenship. Denied the right to vote and serve on juries, New Orleans' people of color fought to retain their rights to form families and to bequeath as they pleased, and—with the help of sympathetic Anglos serving on juries, as justices, or as legislators—some of them succeeded.

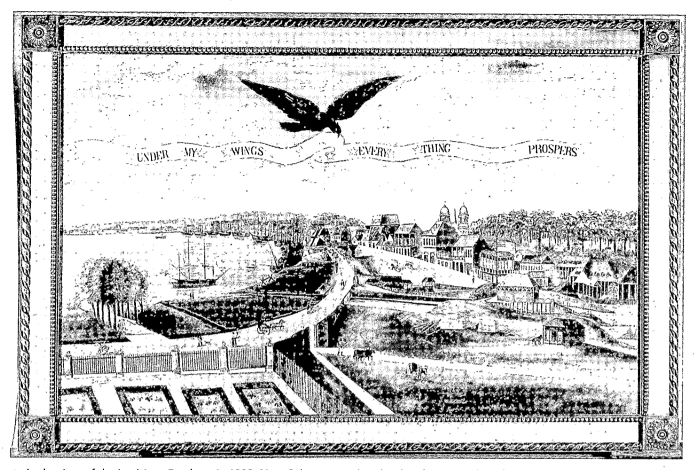

△ At the time of the Louisiana Purchase in 1803, New Orleans was already a bustling port, though boosters predicted an even brighter future under American "wings." View of New Orleans from the Plantation of Marigny, 1803 (oil on canvas), Woiseri, J. L. Bouquet de (fl.1797-1815) / © Chicago History Museum, USA / The Bridgeman Art Library

8-2c Lewis and Clark Expedition

Jefferson had a long-standing interest in the trans-Mississippi West, envisioning it as punctuated with volcanoes and mountains of pure salt, where llamas and mammoths roamed and Welshmen settled. He felt an urgent need to explore it, fearing that, if Americans did not claim it as their own, the British, who still claimed the northern reaches of the continent (in present-day Canada) and parts of the Pacific Northwest, surely would. He lost no time in launching a military-style mission that would chart the region's commercial possibilities—its water passages to the Pacific as well as its trading opportunities with Native peoples—while cataloging its geography, peoples, flora, and fauna.

The expedition, headed by Meriwether Lewis and William Clark, began in May 1804 and lasted for more than two years; it traveled up the Missouri River, across the Rockies, and then down the Columbia to the Pacific Ocean—and back. Along the way, the **Lewis and Clark expedition's** members "discovered" (as they saw it) dozens of previously unknown Native peoples, many of whom had long before discovered Europeans. Lewis and Clark found the Mandans and Hidatsas already well supplied with European

trade goods, such as knives, corduroy trousers, and rings. Although the Corps of Discovery, as the expedition came to be called, expected to find Native peoples and prepared for possible conflict, its goal was peaceable: to foster trade relations, win political allies, and take advantage of Native communities' knowledge of the landscape. Accordingly, Lewis and Clark brought with them twenty-one bags of gifts for Native American leaders, both to establish goodwill and to stimulate interest in trading for American manufactured goods. Most of the corps' interactions with Native peoples were cordial, but when the Native societies failed to be impressed by Lewis and Clark's gifts, tensions arose. After an encounter with the Lakota (or Sioux), Lewis denounced them as "the vilest miscreants of the savage race."

Although military in style, the Corps of Discovery proved unusually democratic in seating enlisted men on courts-martial and allowing Clark's black slave York as well as the expedition's female guide and translator **Sacagawea** to

Lewis and Clark expedition Expedition led by Meriwether Lewis and William Clark to explore the Louisiana Territory.

Sacagawea Female Native American guide who aided Lewis and Clark in exploring the Louisiana Territory.

△ Made by the Nootka people, this wicker hat was collected—either as a trade item or a gift—by Lewis and Clark during their expedition to the Columbia River.

for a constitutional amendment that would transport them west of the Mississippi into the newly acquired Louisiana Territory. He became personally involved in efforts to pressure the Chickasaws to sell their land, and in the event that legal methods for removing Native peoples should fail, he advocated trickery. Traders, he suggested, might run the "good and influential individuals" into debt, which they would have to repay "by a cessation of lands."

8-2d Divisions Among Native Peoples

Some Native American nations decided to deal with white intruders by adopting white customs as a means of survival and often agreeing to sell their lands and move west. These "accommodationists" (or "progressives") were opposed by "traditionalists," who urged adherence to Native ways and refused to relinquish their lands. Distinctions between accommodationists and traditionalists were not always so clear-cut, however, as the Seneca Handsome Lake had demonstrated just a few years before. (see "'Civilizing' Native Peoples," Section 7-6b)

In the early 1800s, two Shawnee brothers, Tenskwatawa (1775–1837) and **Tecumseh** (1768–1813), led a traditionalist revolt against American encroachment by fostering a pan-Native American federation that centered in the Old Northwest and reached into parts of the South. During

vote on where to locate winter quarters in 1805. But unlike the expedition's other members, neither York nor Sacagawea drew wages, and when York later demanded his freedom for his services, Clark repaid him instead with—in Clark's own words—"a severe trouncing."

Lewis and Clark failed to discover a Northwest Passage to the Pacific, and the route they mapped across the Rockies proved more perilous than practical, but their explorations contributed to nationalist visions of American expansion. Fossils and Native American artifacts collected during the expedition were displayed in Charles Willson Peale's museum at Independence Hall in Philadelphia, an institution emphasizing the uniqueness of America's geography and, especially, its republican experiment; in addition to housing natural and human "curiosities," Peale's museum displayed his own renowned portraits of Revolutionary heroes. Nationalists generally overlooked Native peoples' claims to American lands. Although Jefferson had more sympathy for Native Americans than did many of his contemporaries—he took interest in their cultures and believed Native Americans to be intellectually equal to whites—he nonetheless lobbied, unsuccessfully,

Tecumseh The Shawnee leader who sought to unite several tribes from Canada to Georgia against encroachment on their lands by American settlers; allied with the British in the War of 1812.

△ At his museum in Philadelphia, Charles Willson Peale displays some of the "natural curiosities" that many Americans believed contributed to the nation's uniqueness.

the two brothers' lifetimes, the Shawnees had lost most of their Ohio land; by the 1800s, they occupied only scattered sites in Ohio and in the Michigan and Louisiana territories. Despondent, Lalawethika—as Tenskwatawa had been called as a youth—had turned to a combination of European remedies (particularly whiskey) and Native American ones, becoming a shaman in 1804. But when European diseases ravaged his village, he despaired.

8-2e Tenskwatawa and Tecumseh

Lalawethika emerged from his own battle with illness in 1805 as a new man, renamed Tenskwatawa ("the Open Door") or—by whites—"the Prophet." Claiming to have died and been resurrected, he traveled widely in the Ohio River valley as a religious leader, attacking the decline of moral values among Native Americans, warning against whiskey, condemning intertribal battles, and stressing harmony and respect for elders. He urged Native peoples to return to the old ways and to abandon white ways: to hunt with bows and arrows, not guns; to stop wearing hats; and to give up bread for corn and beans. Tenskwatawa was building a religious movement that offered hope to the Shawnees, Potawatomis, and other displaced western Native communities.

By 1808, Tenskwatawa and his older brother Tecumseh talked less about spiritual renewal and more about resisting American aggression. They invited Native peoples from all nations to settle in pan-Native American towns in Indiana, first at Greenville (1806–1808) and then at Prophetstown (1808–1812), near modern-day Lafayette. The new towns

△ Sacagawea, a bilingual Shoshone, guides Meriwether Lewis (center) and William Clark, along the Missouri River in 1805.

challenged the treaty-making process by denying the claims of Native peoples who had been guaranteed the same land as part of the Treaty of Greenville of 1795 in exchange for enormous cessions. Younger Native Americans, in particular, flocked to Tecumseh, the more politically oriented of the two brothers.

Convinced that only a federation of Native peoples could stop the advance of white settlement, Tecumseh sought to unify northern and southern Native groups by preaching Native resistance across a wide swath of territory, ranging from Canada to Georgia. Among southern Native peoples, only one faction of the Creek nation welcomed him, but his efforts to spread his message southward nonetheless alarmed white settlers and government officials. In November 1811, while Tecumseh was in the South, Indiana governor William Henry Harrison moved against Tenskwatawa and his followers. During the Battle of Tippecanoe, the army burned their town; as they fled, the Native Americans exacted revenge on white settlers. "What other course is left for us to pursue," asked Harrison, "but to make a war of extirpation upon them?" With the stakes raised, Tecumseh entered a formal alliance with the British, who maintained forts in southern Ontario. This alliance in the West, combined with issues over American neutral rights on the high seas, were propelling the United States toward war with Britain.

8-3 The Nation in the Orbit of Europe

▷ How did "freedom of the seas" become a central international concern during Thomas Jefferson's presidency?

▷ How did the United States respond to threats to its sovereignty during Thomas Jefferson's presidency?

▷ What were the consequences of the end of the international slave trade?

▷ What political roles did women play in the early nineteenth century?

A decade earlier, in 1801, when Jefferson had sought to set a new course for the nation, he tried to put tensions with France to rest. "Peace, commerce, and honest friendship with all nations, entangling alliances with none," he had proclaimed in his first inaugural address. Yet, despite his wariness of foreign entanglements, the early republic's economy relied heavily on both fishing and the carrying trade, in which the American merchant marine transported commodities between nations. Merchants in Boston, Salem, and Philadelphia traded with China, sending cloth and metal to swap for furs with the Chinook people on the Oregon coast, and then sailing to China to trade for porcelain, tea, and silk. The slave trade lured American ships to Africa. America's commercial interests were clearly focused on the seas, and not long after Jefferson's first inaugural address, the United States was at war with Tripoli—a state along the Barbary Coast of North Africa—over a principle that would long be a cornerstone of American foreign policy: freedom of the seas. In other words, outside national territorial waters, the high seas should be open for free transit of all vessels.

8-3a International Entanglements

In 1801, the *bashaw* (pasha) of Tripoli declared war on the United States for its refusal to pay tribute for safe passage of its ships, sailors, and passengers through the Mediterranean. Jefferson deployed a naval squadron to protect American ships. After two years of stalemate, Jefferson declared a blockade of Tripoli, but when the American frigate *Philadelphia* ran aground in the harbor, its three hundred officers and sailors were imprisoned. Jefferson refused to ransom them, and a small American force accompanied by Arab, Greek, and African mercenaries marched from Egypt to the "shores of Tripoli" (memorialized to this day in the Marine Corps anthem) to seize the port of Derne. A treaty ended the war in 1805, but the United States continued to pay tribute to the three other Barbary states—Algiers, Morocco, and Tunis—until 1815. In the intervening years, the United States became embroiled in European conflicts.

At first, Jefferson managed to distance the nation from the turmoil in Europe in the wake of the French Revolution. After the Senate ratified the Jay Treaty in 1795, the United States and Great Britain appeared to reconcile their differences. Britain withdrew from its western forts on American soil (while still retaining those in Canada) and interfered less in American trade with France. Then, in May 1803, two weeks after Napoleon sold Louisiana to the United States, France was at war against Britain and, later, Britain's continental allies, Prussia, Austria, and Russia. The Napoleonic wars again trapped the United States between belligerents on the high seas. But at first the United States—as the world's largest neutral shipping carrier—actually benefited from the conflict, and American merchants gained control of most of the West Indian trade. After 1805, however, when Britain defeated the French and Spanish fleets at Trafalgar, Britain's Royal Navy tightened its control of the oceans. Two months later, Napoleon crushed the Russian and Austrian armies at Austerlitz. Stalemated, France and Britain launched a commercial war, blockading each other's trade. As a trading partner of both countries, the United States paid a high price.

8-3b Threats to American Sovereignty

One British tactic in particular threatened American sovereignty. To replenish their supply of sailors, British vessels stopped American ships and impressed (forcibly recruited) British deserters, British-born naturalized American seamen, and other sailors suspected of being British. Perhaps six to eight thousand Americans were impressed between 1803 and 1812. Moreover, alleged deserters—many of them

Embargo Act of 1807 Act that forbade exports from the United States to any country.

American citizens—faced British courts-martial. Americans saw the principle of "once a British subject, always a British subject" as a mockery of U.S. citizenship and an assault on their national sovereignty. Americans also resented the British interfering with their West Indian trade as well as their searching and seizing American vessels within U.S. territorial waters.

In April 1806, Congress responded with the Non-Importation Act, barring British manufactured goods from entering American ports. Because the act exempted most cloth and metal articles, it had little impact on British trade; instead, it warned the British what to expect if they continued to violate American neutral rights. In November, Jefferson suspended the act temporarily while William Pinkney, a Baltimore lawyer, joined James Monroe in London to negotiate a settlement. But the treaty they carried home violated Jefferson's instructions—it did not so much as mention impressment—and the president never submitted it to the Senate for ratification.

Anglo-American relations steadily deteriorated, coming to a head in June 1807 when the USS *Chesapeake*, sailing out of Norfolk for the Mediterranean, was stopped by the British frigate *Leopard*, whose officers demanded to search the ship for British deserters. Refused, the *Leopard* opened fire, killing three Americans and wounding eighteen others, including the captain. The British then seized four deserters, three of whom were Americans; one of them was hanged. The *Chesapeake* affair outraged Americans while also exposing American military weakness.

8-3c The Embargo of 1807

Had the United States been better prepared militarily, public indignation might have resulted in a declaration of war. Instead, Jefferson opted for what he called "peaceable coercion." In July, the president closed American waters to British warships and soon thereafter increased military and naval expenditures. In December 1807, Jefferson again put economic pressure on Great Britain by invoking the Non-Importation Act, followed eight days later by a new restriction, the **Embargo Act of 1807**. Jefferson and his congressional supporters saw the embargo, which forbade all exports from the United States to any country, as a short-term measure to avoid war by pressuring Britain and France to respect American rights and by preventing confrontation between American merchant vessels and European warships.

The embargo's biggest economic impact, however, fell on the United States. Exports declined by 80 percent in 1808, squeezing New England shippers and their workers as economic depression set in. Manufacturers, by contrast, received a boost, as the domestic market became theirs exclusively, and merchants began to shift their capital from shipping to manufacturing. In 1807, there were twenty cotton and woolen mills in New England; by 1813, there were more than two hundred. Meanwhile, merchants who were willing to engage in smuggling profited enormously.

△ *The Melee on Board the Chesapeake* (1813) portrays crew from the British frigate *Leopard* fighting to search the USS *Chesapeake* for British navy deserters. The sailors of the *Chesapeake* resisted, but the British overpowered them and seized four deserters, three of them American citizens. Americans were humiliated and angered by the British violation of American rights.

8-3d International Slave Trade

They had only to look at the vibrant slave trade to see how scarcity bred demand. With Jefferson's encouragement, Congress had voted in 1807 to abolish the international slave trade as of January 1, 1808—the earliest date permissible under the Constitution. South Carolina alone still allowed the legal importation of slaves, but most of the state's influential planters favored a ban on the trade, nervous (having seen what happened in St. Domingue) about adding to the black population of a state in which whites were already outnumbered. Congressional debate focused not on whether it was a good idea to abolish the trade, but on what should become of any Africans imported illegally after the ban took effect. The final bill provided that smuggled slaves would be sold in accordance with the laws of the state or territory in which they arrived. It underscored, in other words, that slaves (even illegal ones) were property. Had the bill not done so, threatened one Georgia congressman, the result might have

been "resistance to the authority of the Government," even civil war. Although the debate over the slave trade did not fall along strictly sectional (or regional) lines, sectional tensions never lay far beneath the surface in this era of heated partisan conflict.

In anticipation of the higher prices that their human property would fetch once the law took effect, traders temporarily withheld their slaves from the market in the months after the law's passage. During the last four months of 1807 alone, sixteen thousand African slaves arrived at Gadsden Wharf in Charleston, where they were detained by merchants eager to wait out the January 1 deadline. Although many of these slaves—hundreds, if not thousands—died in the cramped, disease-ridden holding "pens" before they could be sold, merchants calculated that the increased value of those who survived until the ban took effect would outweigh the losses. Not that January 1, 1808, brought an end to the international slave trade; a brisk—and profitable—illegal trade took over. As Justice Joseph Story noted in 1819, the slave trade "is still carried on with all the implacable ferocity and insatiable rapacity of former times. Avarice has grown more subtle in its evasions; and watches and seizes its prey with an appetite quickened rather than suppressed by its guilty vigils." In 1819, Congress passed a law authorizing the president to use force to intercept slave ships along the African coast, but even had the government been determined to enforce the law, the small American navy could not have halted the illicit trade in human beings.

8-3e Early Abolitionism and Colonization

The traffic in human beings helped galvanize early opposition to slavery, though African American abolitionists critiqued more than the slave trade itself; they also advocated slavery's immediate termination, assisted escaped slaves, and promoted legal equality for free blacks. From the

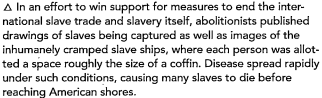

△ In an effort to win support for measures to end the international slave trade and slavery itself, abolitionists published drawings of slaves being captured as well as images of the inhumanely cramped slave ships, where each person was allotted a space roughly the size of a coffin. Disease spread rapidly under such conditions, causing many slaves to die before reaching American shores.

nation's earliest days—in places like Philadelphia, New York, Albany, Boston, and Nantucket—free blacks formed societies to petition legislatures, seek judicial redress, stage public marches, and, especially, publish tracts chronicling slavery's horrors. By 1830, the nation had fifty African American abolitionist societies.

In the years after the Revolution, white abolitionists had also formed antislavery organizations in places like Boston and, especially, Philadelphia, with its large population of Quakers, whose religious beliefs emphasized human equality. These early antislavery advocates pressed for an end to the international slave trade and for slavery's gradual abolition. Although they aided African Americans seeking freedom through judicial decisions, their assumptions about blacks' racial inferiority kept them from advocating for equal rights. Early white abolitionists tended to be wealthy, socially prominent men whose societies excluded women, African Americans, and less elite white men.

More often, elites supported the colonization movement, which crystallized in 1816 with the organization of the American Colonization Society. Its members planned to purchase and relocate American slaves, as well as free blacks, to Africa or the Caribbean. Among its supporters were Thomas Jefferson, James Madison, James Monroe, and Henry Clay, as well as many lesser-known men and women from the North and, especially, the Upper South. In 1822, the society founded Liberia, on Africa's west coast, and began a settlement for African Americans who were willing to go. The society had resettled nearly twelve thousand people in Liberia by 1860. (More followed in upcoming decades.) Some colonizationists aimed to strengthen slavery by ridding the South of troublesome slaves or to purge the North of African Americans altogether. Others hoped colonization would improve African Americans' conditions. Although some African Americans supported the movement, black abolitionists generally denounced it.

8-3f Election of 1808

Once congressional discussion of the international slave trade subsided, however, politicians focused their attention not on slavery but rather on the embargo, especially with the approach of the 1808 presidential election. Democratic-Republicans suffered from factional dissent and dissatisfaction in seaboard states hobbled by the trade restrictions. Although nine state legislatures passed resolutions urging Jefferson to run again, the president followed George Washington's lead in declining a third term. He supported James Madison, his secretary of state, as the Democratic-Republican standard-bearer. For the first time, however, the Democratic-Republican nomination was contested. Madison won the endorsement of the party's congressional caucus, but Virginia Democratic-Republicans put forth James Monroe, who later withdrew, and some easterners supported Vice President George Clinton. Madison and Clinton headed the ticket. Charles Cotesworth Pinckney and Rufus King again ran on the Federalist ticket, but with new vigor.

Emigration to Liberia

Even as European immigrants sought republican freedoms in the United States, Americans sought similar opportunities in Africa. For nearly thirteen thousand African Americans, the destination was Liberia—first a colony organized by the American Colonization Society (1822), then an independent nation (1847) along Africa's West Coast.

Excluded from the American Revolution's promises of equality, some African Americans advocated resettlement in the Caribbean, Canada, and, especially, Africa. In 1816, Paul Cuffee, an abolitionist and shipping merchant of African American and Native American descent, resettled nine African American families in Sierra Leone, a British colony established for freed slaves. After his death the following year, colonization efforts fell primarily to the newly organized American Colonization Society (ACS), whose membership included President James Monroe, Senator Henry Clay, and Supreme Court Justice Bushrod Washington (a nephew of George Washington). In 1824, the ACS formally established Liberia, to which it encouraged immigration of freeborn and recently freed African Americans.

The ACS's members held wide-ranging views; some saw slavery as a threat to American principles or prosperity, while others aimed primarily to deport free blacks, widely seen as a threat to slavery. Because ACS leaders called blacks "useless and pernicious" (Henry Clay) and reasoned that colonization would "secure the property of every master in the United States over his slaves" (John Randolph), many African Americans, including some who had endorsed Cuffee's efforts, denounced ACS-sponsored emigration.

But others seized what they saw as the best opportunity to secure their own freedom, one that might also allow them to help enlighten, as they saw it, native Africans. For many such emigrants, however, Liberia did not immediately prove a promised land. American transplants succumbed in large numbers to malaria, and when they attempted to wrestle land and power from indigenous populations, they met fierce resistance. Within a generation, though, the Americo-Liberians had established themselves as a social, economic, and political elite, subjecting the Native populations to the same sort of second-class citizenship that they had themselves experienced in the United States.

The Republic of Liberia declared its independence from the American Colonization Society in 1847, and today only about 5 percent of its population descends from original settlers. But the nation still bears many markers of its American heritage. Its constitution is modeled on the U.S. Constitution, its official language is English, its flag resembles the American stars-and-stripes design, its architecture has American vestiges, and the American dollar is accepted alongside the Liberian dollar. For the past three decades, the nation has suffered from violent political turmoil, at whose heart is the issue of who should rule: the descendants of the nineteenth-century Americo-Liberians or leaders of indigenous ethnic groups. Begun in the 1820s, African American emigration to Liberia forged a link with both immediate and enduring consequences.

CRITICAL THINKING

□ How is the political turmoil that exists in modern Liberia a by-product of the legacies of both racism and freedom in the United States?

◁ Eager to persuade readers of Liberia's success as a colony for former American slaves, colonizationists published images such as this one of the president's house in Monrovia, in which sparsely clad African natives are juxtaposed with genteel American transplants. Even as the image lauds the supposed superiority of African Americans to Africans, it implies that African Americans will themselves fare much better in Africa than they could in the United States.

Library of Congress/Getty Images

The younger Federalists made the most of the widespread disaffection with Democratic-Republican policy, especially the embargo. Pinckney received only 47 electoral votes to Madison's 122, but he carried all of New England except Vermont, won Delaware, and carried some electoral votes in two other states. Federalists also gained seats in Congress and captured the New York State legislature. Although the Federalist future looked promising, the transition from one Democratic-Republican administration to the next went smoothly.

8-3g Women and Politics

This transition was eased, in part, by the wives of elected and appointed officials in the new capital, who encouraged political and diplomatic negotiation. Such negotiations often took place in social settings, even private homes, where people with divergent interests could bridge their ideological divides through personal relationships. Women played crucial roles, fostering conversation, providing an ear or a voice for unofficial messages, and—in the case of international affairs—standing as surrogates for their nation. Elite women hosted events that muted domestic partisan rivalries, events at which Federalists and Democratic-Republicans could find common ground in civility, if not always in politics. Political wives' interactions among themselves served political purposes, too: when First Lady Dolley Madison visited congressmen's wives, she cultivated goodwill for her husband while collecting recipes that allowed her to serve regionally diverse cuisine at White House functions. Mrs. Madison hoped her menus would help keep simmering sectional tensions from reaching a boiling point.

But it was women's buying power that may have proved most influential in the era of the embargo. Recalling women's support of revolutionary-era boycotts, Jeffersonians appealed directly for women's support of their embargo. Sympathetic women responded by spurning imported fabric and making (or directing their slaves to make) homespun clothing for themselves and their families. Federalists, however, encouraged women to "keep commerce alive," and sympathetic women bought smuggled goods.

8-3h Failed Policies

Under the pressure of domestic opposition, the embargo eventually collapsed. In its place, the Non-Intercourse Act of 1809 reopened trade with all nations except Britain and France, and authorized the president to resume trade with those two nations once they respected American neutral rights. In June 1809, President Madison reopened trade with Britain after its minister to the United States offered assurances that Britain would repeal restrictions on American trade. But His Majesty's government in London repudiated the minister's assurances, leading Madison to revert to nonintercourse.

War Hawks Militant Republicans of the early nineteenth century who demanded more aggressive policies and who wanted war with Britain.

When the Non-Intercourse Act expired in 1810, Congress substituted Macon's Bill Number 2, reopening trade with both Great Britain and France but providing that, when either nation stopped violating American commercial rights, the president would suspend American commerce with the other. When Napoleon accepted the offer, Madison declared nonintercourse on Great Britain in 1811. Although the French continued to seize American ships, Britain became the main focus of American hostility because its Royal Navy dominated the seas.

In spring 1812, the British admiralty ordered its ships not to stop, search, or seize American warships, and in June Britain reopened the seas to American shipping. But before word of the change in British policy reached American shores, Congress declared war.

8-3i Mr. Madison's War

The vote was sharply divided. The House voted 79 to 49 for war; the Senate, 19 to 13. Democratic-Republicans favored war by a vote of 98 to 23; Federalists opposed it 39 to 0. Those who favored war, including President Madison, pointed to assaults on American sovereignty and honor: impressment, violation of neutral trading rights, and British alliances with Native peoples in the West. Others saw an opportunity to conquer and annex British Canada. Most militant were land-hungry southerners and westerners—the **"War Hawks"**—led by John C. Calhoun of South Carolina and first-term congressman and House Speaker Henry Clay of Kentucky. John Randolph of Virginia, an opponent of war, charged angrily, "Agrarian cupidity, not maritime rights, urges war!" He heard "but one word" in Congress: "Canada! Canada! Canada!" Most representatives from the coastal states, and especially from the Northeast, feared disruption to commerce and opposed what they called "Mr. Madison's War."

Initially, the Federalists benefited from antiwar sentiment. They joined renegade Democratic-Republicans in supporting New York City mayor DeWitt Clinton for president in the election of 1812. Clinton lost to President Madison by 128 to 89 electoral votes—a respectable showing against a wartime president—and the Federalists gained some congressional seats and carried many local elections. But the South and the West—areas that favored the war—remained solidly Democratic-Republican.

8-4 The War of 1812

▶ What challenges did the United States face in fighting the British during the War of 1812?

▶ How was the war in the South different from that in the North?

▶ What were the domestic and international consequences of the War of 1812?

Lasting from 1812 to 1815, the war unfolded in a series of scuffles and skirmishes (see Map 8.2) for which the U.S. armed forces, kept lean by Jeffersonian fiscal policies,

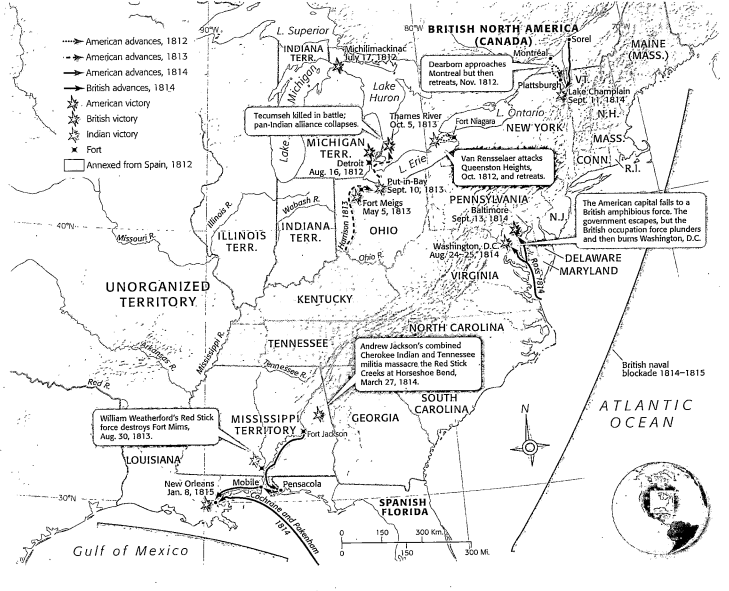

Map 8.2 Major Campaigns of the War of 1812

The land war centered on the U.S.–Canadian border, the Chesapeake Bay, and the Louisiana and Mississippi Territories.

Legend:
- ····▷ American advances, 1812
- ·▷ American advances, 1813
- ▷ American advances, 1814
- → British advances, 1814
- ⚔ American victory
- ⚔ British victory
- ⚔ Indian victory
- ✕ Fort
- ☐ Annexed from Spain, 1812

Map labels:
- Dearborn approaches Montreal but then retreats, Nov. 1812.
- Tecumseh killed in battle; pan-Indian alliance collapses.
- Van Rensselaer attacks Queenston Heights, Oct. 1812, and retreats.
- The American capital falls to a British amphibious force. The government escapes, but the British occupation force plunders and then burns Washington, D.C.
- Andrew Jackson's combined Cherokee Indian and Tennessee militia massacre the Red Stick Creeks at Horseshoe Bend, March 27, 1814.
- William Weatherford's Red Stick force destroys Fort Mims, Aug. 30, 1813.
- British naval blockade 1814–1815

---

were ill prepared. With few experienced army officers—the U.S. Military Academy at West Point, founded in 1802, had produced only eighty-nine regular officers—campaigns were executed poorly. Although the U.S. Navy had a corps of experienced officers, it proved no match for the Royal Navy.

Nor did the United States succeed at enlisting sufficient forces. The government's efforts to lure recruits—with sign-up bonuses, and promises of three months' pay and rights to purchase 160 acres of western land upon discharge—met with mixed success. At first, recruitment went well among westerners, who were motivated by civic spirit, desire for land, strong anti-Native American sentiment, and fears of Tecumseh's pan-Native American organization. But after word spread of delays in pay, as well as inadequate supplies and rations, recruitment dwindled. In New England, raising an army was even more difficult. Federalists discouraged enlistments, and even some New England

Democratic-Republicans declined to raise volunteer companies. Others promised their men that they would serve only in defensive roles, as in Maine, where they would guard the coastline. Militias in New England and New York often refused to fight outside their own states. Desperate for soldiers, New York offered freedom to slaves who enlisted, and compensation to their owners, and the U.S. Army made the same offer to slaves in the Old Northwest and in Canada. In Philadelphia, black leaders formed a "Black Brigade" to defend the city. But in the Deep South, fear of arming slaves kept them out of the military except in New Orleans, where a free black militia dated back to Spanish control of Louisiana. The British, on the other hand, recruited slaves by promising freedom in exchange for service. In the end, British forces—made up of British regulars, their Native allies, fugitive slaves, and Canadians, many of whom were loyalists who had fled during the American Revolution—outnumbered the Americans overall.

8-4a Invasion of Canada

Despite their recruitment problems, Americans expected to take Canada easily. Canada's population was sparse, its army small, and the Great Lakes inaccessible to the Royal Navy in the Atlantic. Americans hoped, too, that French Canadians might welcome U.S. forces.

American strategy aimed to split Canadian forces and isolate pro-British Native peoples, especially Tecumseh, whom the British had promised a Native American nation in the Great Lakes region. In July 1812, U.S. general William Hull, territorial governor of Michigan, marched his troops, who outnumbered those of the British and their allies, into Upper Canada (modern Ontario), hoping to conquer Montreal. But by abandoning Mackinac Island and Fort Dearborn, and by surrendering Fort Detroit, he left the entire Midwest exposed to the enemy. Captain Zachary Taylor provided the only bright spot, giving the Americans a land victory with his September 1812 defense of Fort Harrison in Indiana Territory. But by the winter of 1812–1813, the British controlled about half of the Old Northwest. The United States had no greater success on the Niagara Front, where New York borders Canada, in large part because New York militiamen refused to leave their state to join the invasion of Canada.

8-4b Naval Battles

Despite victories on the Atlantic by the USS *Constitution* (nicknamed "Old Ironsides" after its rout of HMS *Guerrière*), the USS *Wasp*, and the USS *United States*, the American navy—which began the war with just seventeen ships—could not match the powerful Royal Navy. The Royal Navy blockaded the Chesapeake and Delaware bays in December 1812, and by 1814 the blockade covered nearly all American ports along the Atlantic and Gulf coasts. After 1811, American trade overseas declined by nearly 90 percent, and the decline in revenue from customs duties threatened to bankrupt the federal government and prostrate New England.

The contest for control of the Great Lakes, the key to the war in the Northwest, evolved as a shipbuilding race. Under Master Commandant Oliver Hazard Perry and shipbuilder Noah Brown, the United States outbuilt the British on Lake Erie and defeated them at the bloody Battle of Put-in-Bay on September 10, 1813, gaining control of Lake Erie.

8-4c Burning Capitals

General William Henry Harrison then began what would be among the United States' most successful land campaigns. A ragged group of Kentucky militia volunteers, armed only with swords and knives, marched 20 to 30 miles a day to join Harrison's forces in Ohio. Now 4,500 strong, Harrison's forces attacked and took Detroit before crossing into Canada, where they razed the capital of York (now Toronto), looting and burning the Parliament building in April of 1813. Six months later, at the Battle of the Thames, also in Canada, they defeated British, Shawnee, and Chippewa forces. Among the dead was Tecumseh. After defeating Napoleon in Europe in April 1814, the British launched a land counteroffensive against the United States, concentrating on the Chesapeake Bay region. In retaliation for the burning of York—and to divert American troops from Lake Champlain, where the British planned a new offensive—royal troops occupied Washington, D.C., in August and set it ablaze, leaving the presidential mansion and parts of the city burning all night. Chaos ruled. The president and cabinet fled. Dolley Madison stayed long enough to oversee the removal of cabinet documents and, famously, to save a Gilbert Stuart portrait of George Washington.

The British intended the attack on Washington only as a diversion. The major battle occurred in September 1814 at Baltimore, where the Americans held firm. Francis Scott Key, detained on a British ship, watched the bombardment of Fort McHenry from Baltimore harbor and the next morning wrote the verses of "The Star-Spangled Banner" (which became the national anthem in 1931). Although the British inflicted heavy damage, they achieved little militarily; their offensive on Lake Champlain proved equally unsuccessful. The war had reached a stalemate.

8-4d War in the South

To the south, two wars were happening simultaneously. In what one historian calls "the other War of 1812" (or the Patriot War), a private army of Americans, with secret support from the Madison administration, tried to seize East Florida from Spain's control. What started as a settlers' rebellion along the Georgia-Florida border—in an effort to grab more land, strike at the Spaniards' Native American allies, and later to protest the Spaniards' arming of black soldiers (increasing white settlers' fears of slave rebellion)—turned into a war, with the Patriots receiving support from U.S. regular forces (land and naval) and Georgia militia units. Federalists condemned the invasion of a neutral territory, and the Senate refused twice (in 1812 and 1813) to support a military seizure of Florida. Politically embarrassed, Madison withdrew his support, and the movement collapsed in May 1814. Historians disagree about whether the Patriot War ultimately helped or hindered American efforts to win Florida from the Spanish.

In the war with Britain, the southern theater proved much more successful. The war's final campaign began with an American attack on the Red Stick Creeks along the Gulf of Mexico and on the British around New Orleans, and it ended with Americans gaining new territory for white settlement. The Red Sticks had responded to Tecumseh's call (his mother was a Creek) to resist U.S. expansion. Some had died in Indiana Territory, when General Harrison's troops routed Shawnee forces at Tippecanoe in 1811. In 1813, the Red Sticks attacked Fort Mims, about forty miles from Mobile, killing hundreds of white men, women, and children seeking

Selling War

The War of 1812 was not always a popular war, but in its aftermath many Americans trumpeted the war's successes. To the left, we see a recruitment poster from 1812, in which General William Henry Harrison seeks additional cavalrymen. Hampered in part by transportation difficulties, Harrison is unable to offer much—soldiers are even requested to supply their own bacon as well as their own horses—but he does promise that the expedition will be short, undoubtedly a concern to men eager to return to the fall harvest. To the right, we see a handkerchief made in 1815, after the Treaty of Ghent and the Battle of New Orleans; it features the United States' victories against the world's greatest naval power, Great Britain. Made with a decorative border, the kerchief may have been for display.

CRITICAL THINKING

□ What similar values do we see promoted in the two images, and what factors—such as their intended audiences, their purposes, and when they were created—might account for any differences between them?

△ Made in 1815 from cotton textiles—whose domestic production soared during the War of 1812, with trade cut off from Britain—this handkerchief helps promote American "liberty and independence."

Kerchief commemorating the victories of the War of 1812, c.1815 (cotton)/American School, (19th century)/NEW YORK HISTORICAL SOCIETY/© Collection of the New-York Historical Society, USA/Bridgeman Images

CIRCULAR.

ST. MARY's, September 20th, 1812.

SIR—As the force which I have collected at this place (of mounted men) is not sufficient to accomplish the object of the expedition, which it was proposed to set out from hence—You are hereby authorized to circulate through the country my wishes to be joined by any number of mounted men, (corps ready organized would be preferred) under the authority heretofore given by Gov. Meigs. Companies which may join me to serve for the expedition and which will furnish their own horses will have credit for a tour of duty, and the expedition is not expected to continue more than thirty days, and will, at any rate, not extend beyond forty.

        I am respectfully,
          your humble servant.
            WM H. HARRISON.

P. S. The men must bring on as much bacon as possible. Any one who will bring a spare horse, saddle and bridle, shall be allowed fifty cents per day for the use of them—The bearer is authorized to hire horses and give certificates which will be taken up and paid for by the Quarter Master.
                W—H HARRISO

Recruitment Poster for the War of 1812 (litho)/American School, (19th century)/CHICAGO HISTORY MUSEUM/© Chicago History Museum, USA/Bridgeman Images

△ With a tiny regular army, the United States often had to rely on short-term recruits to wage war on the British.

protection there. Looking for revenge, General Andrew Jackson of Tennessee rallied his militiamen as well as Native American opponents of the Red Sticks (including other Creeks favoring accommodation with whites) and crushed the Red Sticks at Horseshoe Bend (in present-day Alabama) in March 1814, leading to the Treaty of Fort Jackson, in which the Creeks ceded 23 million acres of their land, or about half of their holdings, and withdrew to the southern and western part of Mississippi Territory.

Jackson became a major general in the regular army and continued south toward the Gulf of Mexico, with his eye on New Orleans. After seizing Pensacola (in Spanish Florida) and then securing Mobile, Jackson's forces marched to New Orleans, where for three weeks they played a game of cat and mouse with the British soldiers. Finally, on January 8, 1815, the two forces met head-on. In fortified positions, Jackson's poorly trained army held its ground against two British frontal assaults. At day's end, more than two thousand British soldiers lay dead or wounded (a casualty rate of nearly one-third), while the Americans suffered only twenty-one casualties.

The Battle of New Orleans took place two weeks after the war's official conclusion: word had not yet reached America that British and United States diplomats had signed the **Treaty of Ghent** on December 24, 1814. Although militarily unnecessary, the Battle of New Orleans catapulted General Andrew Jackson to national political prominence, and the victory over a formidable foe inspired a sense of national pride.

Treaty of Ghent Treaty that ended the War of 1812, restoring the prewar status quo.

8-4e Treaty of Ghent

The Treaty of Ghent, negotiated between the British and Americans with no Native Americans present, essentially restored the prewar status quo. It provided for an end to hostilities with the British and with Native Americans, release of prisoners, restoration of conquered territory, and arbitration of boundary disputes. But the United States received no satisfaction on impressment, blockades, or other maritime rights for neutrals, and the British demands for territorial cessions from Maine to Minnesota went unmet. The British dropped their promise to Tecumseh of an independent Native American nation.

Why did the negotiators settle for so little? Napoleon's defeat allowed the United States to discard its prewar demands because peace in Europe made impressment and interference with American commerce moot issues. Similarly, war-weary Britain—its treasury nearly depleted—stopped pressing for military victory.

8-4f American Sovereignty Reasserted

Yet the War of 1812 had significant consequences for America's status in the world. It affirmed the independence

△ During the War of 1812, British forces and their Native American allies seized Fort Shelby in Wisconsin, renaming it Fort McKay. After the Treaty of Ghent (1814) restored the installation to American hands, British Captain W. Andrew Bulger bid farewell to his Native allies before withdrawing and burning the fort.

Hindisbacher, Peter/Wisconsin Historical Society, WHI-42292

of the American republic and ensured Canada's independence from the United States. Trade and territorial disputes with Great Britain continued, but they never again led to war. Americans strengthened their resolve to steer clear of European politics.

The return of peace allowed the United States to again focus on the Barbary Coast, where the *dey* (governor) of Algiers had taken advantage of the American preoccupation with British forces to declare his own war on the United States. In the Second Barbary War, U.S. forces captured and detained hundreds of Algerians while negotiating a treaty in the summer of 1815 that forever freed the United States from paying tributes for passage in the Mediterranean. The Second Barbary War reaffirmed America's sovereignty and its commitment to the principle of freedom of the seas.

8-4g Domestic Consequences

The War of 1812 had profound domestic consequences. The Federalists' hopes of returning to national prominence all but evaporated with the **Hartford Convention**, when delegates from New England—frustrated by the stalemated war and the shattered New England economy—met in Hartford, Connecticut, for three weeks in the winter of 1814–1815 to discuss revising the national compact or pulling out of the republic. Although moderates prevented a resolution of secession—a resolution to withdraw from the Union—the delegates condemned the war and the embargo while endorsing constitutional changes that would weaken the South's power vis-à-vis the North and make it harder to declare war. When news arrived in upcoming weeks of, first, Jackson's victory in New Orleans and, then, the Treaty of Ghent, the Hartford Convention made the Federalists look wrongheaded, even treasonous. Federalists survived in a handful of states until the 1820s, but the party faded from the national scene.

With Tecumseh's death, midwestern Native peoples lost their most powerful leader; with the withdrawal of the British, they lost their strongest ally. In the South, the Red Sticks had ceded vast tracts of fertile land. The war did not bring disaster to all Native Americans—some accommodationists, such as the Cherokees, temporarily flourished—but it effectively disarmed traditionalists bent on resisting American expansion. Although the Treaty of Ghent pledged the United States to end hostilities with Native peoples and to restore their prewar "possessions, rights, and privileges," Native groups could not make the United States adhere to the agreement.

For American farmers, the war opened vast tracts of formerly Native American land for cultivating cotton in the Old Southwest and wheat in the Old Northwest. For young industries, the war also ultimately proved a stimulant, as Americans could no longer rely on overseas imports of manufactured goods, particularly textiles. The War of 1812 thus fueled demand for raw cotton, and the newly acquired lands in the Southwest beckoned southerners, who migrated there with their slaves or with expectations of someday owning slaves. The war's conclusion accelerated three trends that would dominate U.S. history for upcoming decades: industrial takeoff, slavery's entrenchment, and westward expansion.

8-5 Early Industrialization

▷ **How was preindustrial labor organized?**

▷ **How did early industry begin to alter work routines and market relations?**

▷ **How was early industry in the North tied to slavery?**

As a result of the embargo and the War of 1812, the North underwent an accelerated industrial development even as the South became more dependent on cotton production (see Chapter 9). Although the two regions' economies followed different paths, however, they remained fundamentally interconnected.

8-5a Preindustrial Farms

Before the War of 1812, most American farmers practiced what is called mixed agriculture: they raised a variety of crops and livestock. Their goal was to procure what they called a "competence": everyday comforts and economic opportunities for their children. When they produced more than they needed, they traded the surplus with neighbors or sold it to local storekeepers. Such transactions often took place without money; farmers might trade eggs for shoes, or they might labor in their neighbor's fields in exchange for bales of hay.

Family members comprised the main source of farm labor, though some yeoman farmers, North and South, also relied on slaves or indentured servants. Work generally divided along gender lines. Men and boys worked in the fields, herded livestock, chopped firewood, fished, and hunted. Women and girls tended gardens, milked cows, spun and wove, processed and preserved food, prepared meals, washed clothes, and looked after infants and toddlers.

Farmers lent each other farm tools, harvested each other's fields, bartered goods, and raised their neighbors' barns and husked their corn. Little cash exchanged hands, in large part because money was in short supply. Still, farmers often kept elaborate accounts of their debts, whether in books (in New England) or in mental notes (in the South). Years might pass without debts repaid, and when they were, they were not always repaid directly. A farmer who owed a neighbor two days' labor might bring the local storekeeper his eggs, to be credited to the neighbor's account.

Many farmers engaged simultaneously in this local economy and in long-distance trade. In the local economy—where they exchanged goods with people

Hartford Convention
Federalist meeting that was perceived as disloyalty during time of war and began the downfall of the party.

whom they knew—a system of "just price" prevailed, in which neighbors calculated value in terms of how much labor was involved in producing a good or providing a service. When the same farmers engaged in long-distance trade—when they sold their goods to merchants who resold them to other merchants before the goods eventually traveled as far away as coastal cities or even Europe—they set prices based on what the market would bear. In the long-distance market, credit and debt were reckoned in monetary value.

8-5b Preindustrial Artisans

Farmers who lived near towns or villages often purchased crafted goods from local cobblers, saddlers, blacksmiths, gunsmiths, silversmiths, and tailors. Most artisans, though, lived in the nation's seaports, where master craftsmen (independent businessmen who owned their own shops and tools) oversaw workshops employing apprentices and journeymen. Although the vast majority of craftsmen, North and South, were white, free blacks were well represented in some cities' urban trades, such as tailoring and carpentry in Charleston, South Carolina. Teenage apprentices lived with their masters, who taught them a craft, lodged and fed them, and offered parental oversight in exchange for labor. The master's wife, assisted by her daughters, cooked, cleaned, and sewed for her husband's

workers. The relationship between a master craftsmen and his workers was often familial in nature, if not always harmonious. When the term of their apprenticeship expired, apprentices became journeymen who earned wages, usually hoping to one day open their own shops. The workplace had little division of labor or specialization. A tailor measured, designed, and sewed an entire suit; a cobbler did the same with shoes.

Men, women, and children worked long days on farms and in workshops, but the pace of work was generally uneven and unregimented. During busy periods, they worked from dawn to dusk; the pace of work slowed after the harvest or after a large order had been completed. Market and court days were as much about exchanging gossip and offering toasts as exchanging goods and watching justice unfold. Husking bees and barn raisings brought people together not only to shuck corn and raise buildings, but also to eat, drink, dance, and flirt. Busy periods did not stop artisans from punctuating the day with grog breaks or from reading the newspaper aloud; they might even close their shops to attend a political meeting. Nor did each workday adhere to a rigid schedule; journeymen often staggered in late on Monday mornings, if they showed up at all, after a long night of carousing on their day off. Although the master craftsman was the boss, his workers exerted a good deal of influence over the workplace.

△ Although separating flax fibers from their woody base could be arduous work, flax-scutching bees—much like corn-husking bees—brought together neighbors for frivolity as well as work.

National Gallery of Art, Washington, D.C. Gift of Edgar William and Bernice Chrysler Garbisch

8-5c Putting-Out and Early Factories

By the War of 1812, preindustrial habits were already changing, most noticeably in the Northeast, where early industry reorganized daily work routines and market relationships. Women and children had long made their family's clothing, hats, soap, and candles. In the late eighteenth and early nineteenth centuries, though, a "putting-out" system—similar to one existing in parts of western Europe—developed, particularly in Massachusetts, New Jersey, and Pennsylvania. Women and children continued to produce goods as they always had, but now did so in much greater quantities and for broader consumption. A merchant supplied them with raw materials, paid them a wage (usually a price for each piece they produced), and sold their wares in distant markets, pocketing the profit for himself. "Outwork," as it is sometimes called, appealed to women eager to earn cash, whether to secure some economic independence or to save money for land on which their children might establish their own farms. Particularly in New England—where population density, small farms, and tired soil constricted farming opportunities and thus created a surplus labor pool—the putting-out system provided cash with which to buy cheaper, more fertile western lands without requiring that family members seek employment away from home.

The earliest factories grew up in tandem with the putting-out system. When Samuel Slater helped set up the first American water-powered spinning mill in Rhode Island in 1790—using children to card and spin raw cotton into thread—he sent the spun thread to nearby farm families who wove it into cloth before sending it back to Slater, from whom they received a wage. Early shoe factories relied on a similar system: factory workers cut cowhide into uppers and bottoms that were sent to rural homes. There, women sewed the uppers while men lasted (or shaped) and pegged the bottoms, a process that also sometimes took place in small workshops. The change was subtle but significant: although the work remained familiar, women now operated their looms for wages and produced cloth for the market, not primarily for their families, while male cobblers made shoes for feet that would never walk into their shops or homes.

Despite their efforts to define themselves as a separate nation, Americans relied on British technology to bring together the many steps of textile manufacturing—carding (or disentangling) fibers, spinning yarn, and weaving cloth—under one factory roof. Slater, a British immigrant, had reconstructed from memory the complex machines he had used while working in a British cotton-spinning factory. But Slater's mill only carded and spun yarn; the yarn still needed

△ This contemporary painting shows the Boston Manufacturing Company's 1814 textile factory at Waltham, Massachusetts. All manufacturing processes were brought together under one roof, and the company built its first factories in rural New England to tap roaring rivers as a power source.

to be hand-woven into cloth, work often done by farm women seeking to earn cash. In 1810, Bostonian Francis Cabot Lowell, determined to introduce water-powered mechanical weaving in the United States, visited the British textile center of Manchester, where he toured factories, later sketching from memory what he had seen. In 1813, he and his business associates, calling themselves the Boston Manufacturing Company, brought together all phases of textile manufacturing under one roof in Waltham, Massachusetts. A decade later, the Boston Manufacturing Company established what it saw as a model industrial village—named for its now-deceased founder—along the banks of the Merrimack River. At Lowell, Massachusetts, there would be boardinghouses for workers, a healthy alternative to the tenements and slums of Manchester. American industrialists envisioned America industrializing without the poverty and degradation associated with European industrialization.

Early industrialization, primarily in the northern states, was inextricably linked to slavery. Much of the capital came from merchants who made their fortunes at least in part through the trade in African slaves, and two of the most prominent industries—textiles and shoes—expanded alongside a growing southern cotton economy. Southern cotton fed northern textile mills, and northern shoe factories sold their "Negro brogans" (work shoes) to southern planters. Even in the putting-out system, the connections to the slave South were strong: New England farm girls wove palm-leaf hats for merchants who sold them to southern planters for their slaves. Yet despite these connections, northerners and southerners often saw their economies as developing in fundamentally distinct ways.

8-6 Sectionalism and Nationalism

▷ **How did the federal government pursue a nationalist agenda to encourage domestic growth after the War of 1812?**

▷ **How did the North and South become more regionally distinct after the War of 1812?**

▷ **How did the United States seek to assert its position on the global stage after the War of 1812?**

Following the War of 1812, Madison and the Democratic-Republicans embraced a nationalist agenda, absorbing the Federalist idea that the federal government should encourage growth. In his December 1815 message to Congress, Madison recommended economic development and military expansion. His agenda, which Henry Clay later called the American System, included a national bank, improved transportation, and a protective tariff—a tax on imported goods that was designed to protect American manufacturers from foreign competition. Yet Madison did not stray entirely from his Jeffersonian roots; only a constitutional

amendment, he argued, could authorize the federal government to build local roads and canals. Instead, the bulk of internal improvements would fall to the states, which would, in turn, exacerbate regional patterns of economic development.

8-6a American System

Clay and other congressional leaders, such as Calhoun of South Carolina, believed the American System would ease sectional divides. The tariff would stimulate New England industry, whose manufactured goods would find markets in the South and West. At the same time, the South's and West's agricultural products—cotton and foodstuffs—would feed New England mills and their workers. Manufactured goods and agricultural products would move in all directions along roads and canals—what contemporaries called "internal improvements"—which tariff revenues would fund. A national bank would handle the transactions.

In the Madison administration's last year, the Democratic-Republican Congress enacted much of the nationalist program. In 1816, it chartered the Second Bank of the United States (the charter on the first bank had expired in 1811) to serve as a depository for federal funds and to issue currency, collect taxes, and pay the government's debts. The Second Bank of the United States would also oversee state and local banks, ensuring that their paper money had backing in specie (precious metals). Like its predecessor, the bank mixed public and private ownership; the government provided one-fifth of the bank's capital and appointed one-fifth of its directors.

Congress also passed a protective tariff to aid industries that flourished during the War of 1812 but that now were threatened by the resumption of overseas trade. The Tariff of 1816 levied taxes on imported woolens and cottons as well as on iron, leather, hats, paper, and sugar. Foreshadowing a growing trend, though, the tariff did more to divide than to unify the nation. New England as well as the western and Middle Atlantic states stood to benefit from it and thus applauded it, whereas many southerners objected that it raised the price of consumer goods while opening the possibility that Britain would retaliate with a tariff on cotton.

Some southerners did promote roads and canals to "bind the republic together," as Calhoun put it. However, on March 3, 1817, the day before leaving office, President Madison, citing constitutional scruples, stunned Congress by vetoing Calhoun's "Bonus Bill," which would have authorized federal funding for such public works.

8-6b Early Internal Improvements

Constitutional scruples aside, Federalists and Democratic-Republicans agreed that the nation's prosperity depended on improved transportation. For Federalists, roads and canals were necessary for commercial development; for Jeffersonians, they would spur western expansion and

The Metropolitan Museum of Art / Art Resource, NY

△ The young nation's dirt roads meant bumpy and dusty travel for goods as well as passengers, prompting calls for transportation innovations, such as canals and, later, railroads, to spur economic growth.

agrarian growth. In 1806, Congress had passed (and Jefferson had signed) a bill authorizing funding for the Cumberland Road (later, the National Road), running 130 miles between Cumberland, Maryland, and Wheeling, Virginia (now West Virginia). Construction began in 1811 and was completed in 1818. Two years later, Congress authorized a survey of the National Road to Columbus, Ohio, a project funded in 1825 and completed in 1833; the road would ultimately extend into Indiana.

After President Madison's veto of the Bonus Bill, though, most transportation initiatives received funding from states, private investors, or a combination of the two. Between 1817 and 1825, the State of New York constructed the **Erie Canal**, linking the Great Lakes to the Atlantic seaboard. Although southern states constructed modest canals, the South's trade depended on river-going steamboats after 1817, when steamboats began traveling regularly upriver on the Mississippi. With canals and steamboats, western agricultural products traveled to market much more quickly and inexpensively, fueling the nation's westward expansion. Unlike steamboats, though, canals expanded commercial networks into regions without natural waterways. Although the Mississippi provided the great commercial highway of

the early Republic, canals began to reorient midwestern commerce through the North.

8-6c Panic of 1819

Immediately following the War of 1812, the American economy had boomed. The international demand for (and price of) American commodities reached new heights. Poor weather in Europe led to crop failures, increasing demand for northern foodstuffs and southern cotton, which, in turn, touched off western land speculation. Speculators raced to buy large tracts of land at modest, government-established prices and then to resell it at a hefty profit to would-be settlers. Easy credit made this expansion possible. With loans and paper money, farmers and speculators bought land, while manufacturers established or enlarged enterprises.

Prosperity proved short-lived. Now recovered from war as well as weather, by the late 1810s Europeans could grow their own food, and Britain's new Corn Laws established a high tariff on imported foodstuffs, further lessening demand for American agricultural

Erie Canal Major canal that linked the Great Lakes to the Atlantic seaboard, opening the upper Midwest to wider development.

exports. Cotton prices fell in England. Wars in Latin America interfered with mining and reduced the supply of precious metals, leading European nations to hoard specie; in response, American banks furiously printed paper money and expanded credit even further. Fearful of inflation, the Second Bank of the United States, which had itself issued more loans than it could back in hard currency, demanded in 1819 that state banks repay loans in specie. State banks in turn called in the loans and mortgages they had made to individuals and companies. The falling prices of commodities meant that farmers could not pay their mortgages, and the decline of land values—from 50 to 75 percent in portions of the West—meant they could not meet their debts even by selling their farms. The nation's banking system collapsed. The 1819 financial panic reminded Americans all too starkly that they still lived within the economic orbit of Europe.

Hard times came to countryside and city alike. Foreclosures soared. Unemployment skyrocketed, even in older manufacturing areas that had focused on industries like iron making and tobacco processing. In Philadelphia, unemployment reached 75 percent. The contraction devastated workers and their families. As a Baltimore physician noted in 1819, working people felt hard times "a thousand fold more than the merchants." They could not build up savings during boom times to get them through the hard times; often, they could not make it through the winter without drawing on charity for food, clothing, and firewood.

The depression sent tremors throughout American society. Americans from all regions contemplated the virtues and hazards of rapid market expansion, disagreeing most intensely on where to place the blame for its shortcomings. Westerners blamed easterners; farmers and workers blamed bankers. Even as the nation's economy began to rebound in the early 1820s amid a flurry of internal improvement projects, no one could predict with confidence where—in what region, in what sector—the nation's economic and political fortunes would lie.

8-6d Missouri Compromise

Just as financial panic struck the nation in 1819, so, too, did political crisis. The issue was slavery's westward expansion. Although economic connections abounded between North and South, slavery had long been politically explosive. Since the drafting of the Constitution, Congress had tried to avoid the issue; the one exception had been debates over the international slave trade. In 1819, however, slavery once again burst onto the national political agenda when residents of the Missouri Territory—carved out of the Louisiana Territory—petitioned Congress for admission to the Union

Missouri Compromise
Attempt to end the debate over the number of slave and free states admitted to the Union by admitting Missouri as a slave state and Maine as a free state and banning slavery in the Louisiana Territory north of the 36°30′ latitude line.

with a constitution permitting slavery. At stake was more than the future of slavery in an individual state. Missouri's admission to the Union would give the slaveholding states a two-vote majority in the Senate, and what happened in Missouri would set a precedent for all the new western states created from the vast Louisiana Purchase. "This momentous question," wrote former president Thomas Jefferson, fearful for the life of the Union, "like a fire bell in the night, awakened and filled me with terror."

Following the Louisiana Purchase and especially after the end of the War of 1812, the American population had surged westward, leading five new states to join the Union: Louisiana (1812), Indiana (1816), Mississippi (1817), Illinois (1818), and Alabama (1819). Of these, Louisiana, Mississippi, and Alabama permitted slavery. Because Missouri was on the same latitude as free Illinois, Indiana, and Ohio (a state since 1803), its admission as a slave state would thrust slavery not just westward but also northward, as well as tilt the uneasy balance in the Senate.

For two and a half years the issue dominated Congress, with the fiery debate transcending the immediate issue of slavery in Missouri. When Representative James Tallmadge Jr. of New York proposed gradual emancipation in Missouri, some southerners accused the North of threatening to destroy the Union. "If you persist, the Union will be dissolved," Thomas W. Cobb of Georgia shouted at Tallmadge. Only "seas of blood" could extinguish the fire Tallmadge had ignited, warned Cobb. "Let it come," retorted Tallmadge. The House, which had a northern majority, passed the Tallmadge Amendment, but the Senate rejected it.

House Speaker Henry Clay—himself a western slaveholder—put forward a compromise in 1820. Maine, carved out of Massachusetts, would enter as a free state, followed by Missouri as a slave state, maintaining the balance between slave and free states, at twelve to twelve. In the rest of the Louisiana Territory north of Missouri's southern border of 36°30′, slavery would be prohibited forever (see Map 8.3).

The compromise carried but almost unraveled when Missouri submitted a constitution barring free blacks from entering the state, a provision that opponents contended would violate the federal constitutional provision that citizens of each state were "entitled to all privileges and immunities of citizens in the several States." Proponents countered that many states, North and South, already barred free blacks from entering. In 1821, Clay proposed a second compromise: Missouri would guarantee that none of its laws would discriminate against citizens of other states. (The compromise carried, but once admitted to the Union, Missouri twice adopted laws barring free blacks.) For more than three decades, the **Missouri Compromise** would govern congressional policy toward admitting new slave states. But the compromise masked rather than suppressed the simmering political conflict over slavery's westward expansion.

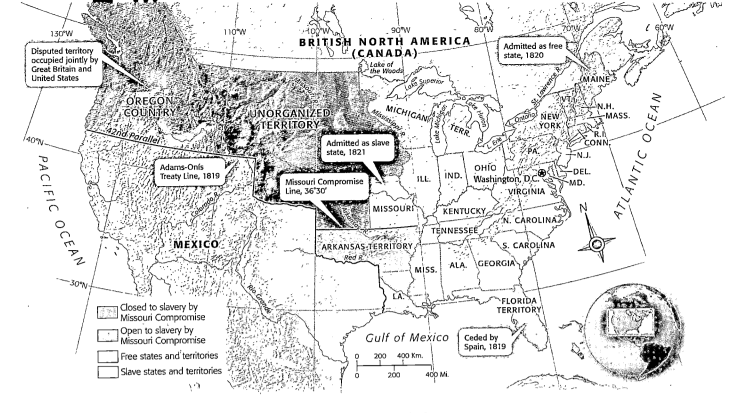

Map 8.3 Missouri Compromise and the State of the Union, 1820

The compromise worked out by House Speaker Henry Clay established a formula that avoided debate over whether new states would allow or prohibit slavery. In the process, it divided the United States into northern and southern regions.

8-6e The Era of Good Feelings

So, too, did the so-called "**Era of Good Feelings**," as a Boston newspaper dubbed the presidency of James Monroe, Madison's successor, which was marked by a lack of partisan political discord. Monroe was the last president to have attended the Constitutional Convention and the third Virginian elected president since 1801. A former senator and twice governor of Virginia, he had served under Madison as secretary of state and of war and had used his close association with Jefferson and Madison to attain the presidency. In 1816, he and his running mate, Daniel Tompkins, trounced the last Federalist presidential nominee, Rufus King, garnering all the electoral votes except those of the Federalist strongholds of Massachusetts, Connecticut, and Delaware. In office, Monroe continued Madison's domestic program, supporting tariffs and vetoing the Cumberland Road Bill (for repairs) in 1822.

Led by Federalist chief justice John Marshall, the Supreme Court became the bulwark of the nationalist agenda. In *McCulloch v. Maryland* (1819), the Court struck down a Maryland law taxing banks within the state that were not chartered by its legislature—a law aimed at hindering the Baltimore branch of the federally chartered Second Bank of the United States. The bank refused to pay the tax and sued. At issue was state versus federal jurisdiction. Writing for a unanimous Court, Marshall asserted the supremacy of the federal government over the states. "The Constitution and the laws thereof are supreme," he declared. "They control the constitution and laws of the respective states and cannot be

controlled by them." The Court ruled, too, that Congress had the power to charter banks under the Constitution's clause endowing it with the authority to pass "all laws which shall be necessary and proper for carrying into execution" the enumerated powers of government. The Marshall Court thus supported the Federalist view that the federal government could promote interstate commerce.

8-6f Government Promotion of Market Expansion

Later Supreme Court cases validated government promotion of economic development and encouraged business enterprise and risk taking. In *Gibbons v. Ogden* (1824), the Supreme Court overturned the New York law that had given Robert Fulton and Robert Livingston (and their successor, Aaron Ogden) a monopoly on the New York–New Jersey steamboat trade. Chief Justice Marshall ruled that the federal power to license new enterprises took precedence over New York's grant of monopoly rights and declared that Congress's power under the commerce clause of the Constitution extended to "every species of commercial intercourse," including transportation. The *Gibbons v. Ogden* ruling built on earlier Marshall Court decisions, such as those in *Dartmouth College v. Woodward* (1819), which

Era of Good Feelings Period of one-party politics during administration of James Monroe.

McCulloch v. Maryland Supreme Court decision that restated national supremacy over the states.

protected the sanctity of contracts against state interference, and *Fletcher v. Peck* (1810), which voided a Georgia law that violated individuals' rights to make contracts. Within two years of *Gibbons v. Ogden*, the number of steamboats operating in New York increased from six to forty-three. A later ruling under Chief Justice Roger Taney, *Charles River Bridge v. Warren Bridge* (1837), encouraged new enterprises and technologies by favoring competition over monopoly, and the public interest over implied privileges in old contracts.

Federal and state courts, in conjunction with state legislatures, encouraged the proliferation of corporations—organizations entitled to hold property and transact business as if they were individuals. Corporation owners, called shareholders, were granted limited liability, or freedom from personal responsibility for the company's debts beyond their original investment. Limited liability encouraged investors to back new business ventures.

The federal government assisted the development of a commercial economy in other ways. The U.S. Post Office fostered the circulation of information, a critical element of the market economy. The number of post offices grew from three thousand in 1815 to fourteen thousand in 1845. To promote individual creativity and economic growth, the government protected inventions through patent laws and domestic industries through tariffs on foreign imports.

8-6g Boundary Settlements

Monroe's secretary of state, John Quincy Adams, matched the Marshall Court in assertiveness and nationalism. Adams, the son of John and Abigail Adams, managed the nation's foreign policy from 1817 to 1825, pushing for expansion (through negotiations, not war), fishing rights for Americans in Atlantic waters, political distance from Europe, and peace. Under Adams's leadership, the United States settled points of conflict with both Britain and Spain. In 1817, the United States and Great Britain signed the Rush-Bagot Treaty limiting their naval forces to one ship each on Lake Champlain and Lake Ontario and to two ships each on Lakes Erie, Huron, and Superior. This first disarmament treaty of modern times demilitarized the border between the United States and Canada. Adams then pushed for the Convention of 1818, which fixed the U.S.–Canadian border from Lake of the Woods in Minnesota westward to the Rockies along the 49th parallel. When they could not agree on the boundary west of the Rockies, Britain and the United States settled on joint occupation of Oregon for ten years (renewed indefinitely in 1827).

Adams's negotiations resulted in the Adams-Onís Treaty, in which the United States gained Florida, already occupied by General Andrew Jackson under pretext of suppressing Seminole raids against American settlements across the border during the First Seminole War of 1817–1818. Although the

Monroe Doctrine Foreign policy statement that proclaimed that the American continents were not to be subjected to European colonization and demanded nonintervention by Europe in New World nations.

Louisiana Purchase had omitted reference to Spanish-ruled West Florida, the United States claimed the territory as far east as the Perdido River (the present-day Florida-Alabama border). During the War of 1812, the United States had seized Mobile and the remainder of West Florida, and after the war—with Spain preoccupied with its own domestic and colonial troubles—Adams had laid claim to East Florida. In 1819, Don Luís de Onís, the Spanish minister to the United States, agreed to cede Florida to the United States without payment if the United States renounced its dubious claims to northern Mexico (Texas) and assumed $5 million of claims by American citizens against Spain. The Adams-Onís (or Transcontinental) Treaty also defined the southwestern boundary of the Louisiana Purchase and set the line between Spanish Mexico and Oregon Country at the 42nd parallel.

8-6h Monroe Doctrine

John Quincy Adams's desire to insulate the United States and the Western Hemisphere from European conflict brought about his greatest achievement: the **Monroe Doctrine**. The immediate issue was recognition of new governments in Latin America. Between 1808 and 1822, the United Provinces of Río de la Plata (present-day northern Argentina, Paraguay, and Uruguay), Chile, Peru, Colombia, and Mexico all broke free from Spain (see Map 8.4). In 1822, shortly after the ratification of the Adams-Onís Treaty, the United States became the first nation outside Latin America to recognize the new states, including Mexico. But in Europe, reactionary regimes were ascending, and with France now occupying Spain to suppress a liberal rebellion, the United States feared that continental powers would attempt to return the new Latin American states to colonial rule. Having withdrawn from an alliance with continental nations, Britain proposed a joint declaration with the United States against European intervention in the Western Hemisphere. Adams rejected Britain's offer as just the kind of entanglement he sought to avoid, despite clear advantages to allying with the British and their powerful navy.

Monroe presented to Congress in December 1823 what became known as the Monroe Doctrine. His message announced that the American continents "are henceforth not to be considered subjects for future colonization by any European power." This principle addressed American anxiety not only about Latin America but also about Russian expansion beyond Alaska and its settlements in California. Monroe demanded nonintervention by Europe in the affairs of independent New World nations, and he pledged noninterference by the United States in European affairs, including those of Europe's existing New World colonies. Although Monroe's words carried no force—European nations stayed out of New World affairs because they feared the Royal Navy, not the United States' proclamations—they proved popular at home, tapping American nationalism as well as anti-British and anti-European feelings.

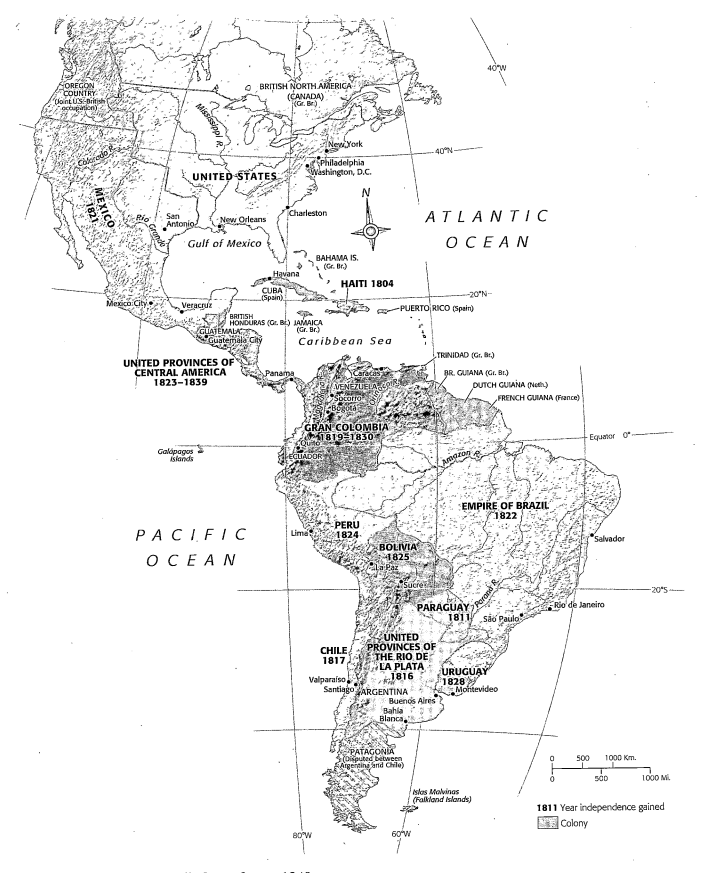

OREGON COUNTRY (Joint U.S.-British occupation)

Mississippi R.

Colorado R.

MEXICO 1821

UNITED STATES

Rio Grande

San Antonio

New Orleans

Gulf of Mexico

Mexico City

Veracruz

BRITISH NORTH AMERICA (CANADA) (Gr. Br.)

New York

Philadelphia

Washington, D.C.

Charleston

BAHAMA IS. (Gr. Br.)

Havana

HAITI 1804

CUBA (Spain)

PUERTO RICO (Spain)

ATLANTIC

OCEAN

N

40°W

40°N

20°N

BRITISH HONDURAS (Gr. Br.)

JAMAICA (Gr. Br.)

GUATEMALA

Guatemala City

Caribbean Sea

TRINIDAD (Gr. Br.)

UNITED PROVINCES OF CENTRAL AMERICA 1823–1839

Panama

Caracas

BR. GUIANA (Gr. Br.)

DUTCH GUIANA (Neth.)

FRENCH GUIANA (France)

VENEZUELA

Socorro

Bogotá

Orinoco R.

Magdalena R.

GRAN COLOMBIA 1819–1830

Quito

ECUADOR

Galápagos Islands

Amazon R.

Equator 0°

EMPIRE OF BRAZIL 1822

PERU 1824

Lima

Salvador

PACIFIC

OCEAN

BOLIVIA 1825

La Paz

Sucre

20°S

Rio de Janeiro

PARAGUAY 1811

Paraná R.

São Paulo

CHILE 1817

Valparaíso

Santiago

UNITED PROVINCES OF THE RIO DE LA PLATA 1816

URUGUAY 1828

Montevideo

ARGENTINA

Buenos Aires

Bahía Blanca

PATAGONIA (Disputed between Argentina and Chile)

Islas Malvinas (Falkland Islands)

80°W

60°W

| 0 | 500 | 1000 Km. |
| 0 | 500 | 1000 Mi. |

1811 Year independence gained

Colony

Map 8.4 Latin American Independence, 1840

With Central and South American colonies triumphing in their wars of independence against European colonial powers, President Monroe sought to enhance the United States' security by warning European nations against meddling in the region.

The Star-Spangled Banner

Like many contemporaries, Francis Scott Key—a Maryland lawyer, slaveowner, and amateur poet—opposed America's second war with Britain, denouncing it as a "lump of wickedness." But in September 1814, after American forces withstood the British navy's bombardment of Fort McHenry, in Baltimore Harbor, Key experienced a renewed sense of national pride, which he captured in four verses that spread quickly throughout the states. Cadenced to match a British tavern song, the patriotic slaveowner's poem famously hailed the United States as the "land of the free."

As "The Star-Spangled Banner"'s popularity grew in ensuing decades, politicians and activists, of various leanings, substituted their own lyrics. Pennsylvania temperance reformers sang, "Oh! Who has not seen, by the dawn's early light/Some poor bloated drunkard to his home weakly reeling/With blear eyes and red nose most revolting to sight." An anti-immigrant group called itself The Order of the Star-Spangled Banner, and a German translation of the song—"Das Star-Spangled Banner"—circulated. During the Civil War, the song rallied Unionists, while Confederates parodied it: "Oh! say has the star-spangled banner become/The flag of the Tory and Vile Northern scum?" Meanwhile, Confederate sympathizers in Maryland safeguarded the original star-spangled banner, the one spotted by Francis Scott Key atop Fort McHenry—the great symbol of the nation from which they hoped to separate but whose original values they cherished.

Union victory deepened northerners' attachment to Key's song, which became quasi-official when the Navy adopted it in 1889. Lobbyists, including many southerners, urged Congress to designate it the national anthem, but detractors voiced a variety of reservations: pragmatic (its difficult tune), emotional (its origins as a drinking song), and ideological (its militaristic tone and anti-British sentiments, problematic now that Britain was an ally). Finally, in 1931 Congress designated it the national anthem, and today it is routinely performed at sporting events, a practice that started during World War I and that became widespread by World War II.

During wartime, in particular, flags and anthems galvanize national pride and determination, but flags and anthems can also symbolize a nation's unfulfilled promises. At the 1968 Olympics in Mexico City, coinciding with the Black Power Movement, American medalists Tommie Smith and John Carlos raised their black-gloved fists and bowed their heads in protest when the anthem played. The U.S. Olympic Committee suspended them, but nearly fifty years later, President Obama welcomed Smith and Carlos at the White House, amid renewed protests from athletes at all levels—from professional to children's leagues—in response to fatal police shootings of unarmed African Americans. As "taking a knee" during the anthem spread, so did the practice's critics.

Over two centuries, "The Star-Spangled Banner" has fueled passionate patriotism even as it has been mired in irony and controversy. Yet by providing a touchstone for discussions of what it means to be an American, and what it should mean to be an American, "The Star-Spangled Banner" has proved an enduring and evolving legacy for a people and a nation.

CRITICAL THINKING

□ As early as the 1960s but more frequently now, in the wake of what has been deemed an epidemic of police shootings of unarmed African American men, Americans have used the singing of "The Star-Spangled Banner" as an opportunity to protest what they see as the unfulfilled promise of freedom and equality in the United States Critics suggest that such protests are unpatriotic. Are such protests patriotic or unpatriotic, or can they be both?

Yet even as the nation pursued a nationalist economic agenda and defined its position on the world stage, sectional tensions remained a persistent threat to the nation's proclaimed unity.

Summary

The partisanship of the 1790s, though alarming to the nation's political leaders, captured Americans' imaginations, making the early republic a period of pervasive and vigorous political engagement. Troubled by vicious partisanship, President Jefferson sought both to unify the nation and to solidify Democratic-Republican control of the government. With a vision of an agrarian nation that protected individual liberty, Jeffersonians promoted a limited national government—one that stayed out of religious affairs and spent little on military forces, diplomatic missions, and economic initiatives. The rival Federalists, who exerted most of their influence through the judiciary, declared federal supremacy over the states even as the judiciary affirmed its own supremacy over other branches of the government. Federalists hoped a strengthened federal government would promote commerce and industry.

Despite his belief in limited government, Jefferson considered the acquisition of the Louisiana Territory and the commissioning of the Corps of Discovery among his most significant presidential accomplishments. The enormous expanse of fertile lands fueled the Jeffersonian dream of an agrarian republic: Americans soon streamed into the Louisiana Territory. Even more would have done so had it not been for the Native peoples (and their British allies) who stood in their way and for poorly developed transportation routes.

Jefferson's vision rested, too, on American disentanglement from foreign affairs. But with its economy so focused on international shipping, the United States soon faced its greatest threats from abroad, not from partisan or sectional divisions. In its wars with the Barbary states, the United States sought to guard its commerce and ships on the high seas. The second war with Britain—the War of 1812—was fought for similar reasons but against a much more formidable power. Although a military stalemate, the war inspired a new sense of nationalism and launched a new era of American development.

The Treaty of Ghent reaffirmed American independence; thereafter, the nation was able to settle disputes with Great Britain at the bargaining table. The war also dealt a serious blow to Native peoples' resistance in the Midwest and Southwest. At the same time, embargoes and war accelerated the pace of American industrial growth. Because the Federalists' opposition to the war undermined their political credibility, their party all but disappeared from the national political scene by 1820. The absence of well-organized partisan conflict created what contemporaries called an "Era of Good Feelings."

Although overt tension was muted in the heady postwar years, competing visions of America's route to prosperity and greatness endured. Under Chief Justice John Marshall, the Supreme Court supported the Federalist agenda, issuing rulings that stimulated commerce and industry through economic nationalism. The Democratic-Republicans looked instead toward the South and West, the vast and fertile Louisiana Territory. Whether they supported agrarian or industrial development, almost all Americans could agree on the need for improved transportation, though most internal improvements took place in the North.

Internal improvements could not guarantee national prosperity or unity, and in 1819 the postwar economic boom came to a grinding halt even as congressmen predicted that dire consequences could result from the dispute over whether to admit Missouri as a slave state. Henry Clay's compromise removed the issue of slavery's expansion from political center stage, but—by addressing only those territories already owned by the United States—it did not permanently settle the issue.

During the first quarter of the nineteenth century, the United States vastly expanded its territorial reach, not just through the Louisiana Purchase but also with the acquisition of Florida. Fearful of European intentions to reassert influence in the Americas and emboldened by the nation's expanding boundaries, President Monroe proclaimed that the United States would not tolerate European intervention in American affairs. But even as its expanding boundaries strengthened the United States' international presence, that same territorial expansion would, in decades to come, threaten the nation's newfound political unity at home.

Suggestions for Further Reading

Stephen Aron, *American Confluence: The Missouri Frontier from Borderland to Border State* (2006)

Claude A. Clegg III, *The Price of Liberty: African Americans and the Making of Liberia* (2004)

David Edmunds, *Tecumseh and the Quest for Indian Leadership* (2006)

Richard S. Newman, *The Transformation of American Abolitionism: Fighting Slavery in the Early Republic* (2002)

Kent Newmyer, *John Marshall and the Heroic Age of the Supreme Court* (2001)

Jeffrey Ostler, *The Plains Sioux and U.S. Colonialism from Lewis and Clark to Wounded Knee* (2004)

Jeffrey Pasley, Andrew Robertson, and David Waldstreicher, eds., *Beyond the Founders: New Approaches to the Political History of the Early American Republic* (2004)

Alan Taylor, *The Civil War of 1812: American Citizens, British Subjects, Irish Rebels, and Indian Allies* (2010)

Gordon S. Wood, *Empire of Liberty: A History of the Early Republic, 1789–1815* (2009)

The Rise of the South, 1815–1860

The Thomas Jefferson died, as he had lived, in debt. Many Americans saw a providential hand at work when, on July 4, 1826, Jefferson and John Adams, rivals and founders of the American republic, died on the same day. But at Jefferson's home, Monticello, in Virginia, worldly anxiety abounded among the founder's white and black "families."

On January 15, 1827, a five-day estate sale took place at Monticello. Everything went up at auction, including paintings, furniture, and mementoes. Most expensive of all were "130 valuable negroes," described by Jefferson's grandson and executor, Thomas Jefferson Randolph, as "the most valuable for their number ever offered at one time in the state of Virginia." Large crowds gathered in frigid weather. Monticello's blacksmith, Joseph Fossett, watched his wife Edith and eight children sold at the auction to four different bidders.

Jefferson generally avoided separation of families and whipping except in rare cases. But he was intensely involved in the domestic lives and labor efficiency of his slaves, keeping production statistics on the young teenagers who worked in his nailery. After his wife, Martha (with whom he had two daughters), died in 1782, Jefferson also had at least six children, four of whom lived beyond infancy, with an enslaved woman whom he owned, Sally Hemings. Sally was the half-sister of Jefferson's wife, and part of a complex extended family of light-skinned Hemingses of Monticello.

Whole families of Jefferson's slaves were sold at the 1827 auction. Joseph Fossett, as promised by Jefferson, became free exactly one year after his master's death. Jefferson had already

◁ Peter Farley Fossett (1815–1901), born the son of Joseph and Edith Fossett, slaves owned by Thomas Jefferson. Joseph was head blacksmith and Edith head cook at Monticello. Peter had a stable family life in childhood until at age 10 when he was among Jefferson's 130 slaves sold at auction in 1827, including his mother and seven siblings. Peter lived 23 more years as a slave, obtaining his freedom and moving to Cincinnati to be near his parents in 1850. He became a successful caterer and an ordained Baptist minister, and in 1900 he returned to Monticello, was driven up the mountain by the son of the man who had taught him to read, and walked in the front door of the mansion. Thomas Jefferson Foundation at Monticello

Thomas Jefferson, President of the United States, author of the Declaration of Independence, slaveowner, three-quarter length portrait, seated at table. Library of Congress Prints and Photographs Division Washington, D.C. [LC-USZ62-8195]

Chronology

1810–20	An estimated 137,000 slaves are forced to move from the Upper South to Alabama, Mississippi, and other western regions
1822	Vesey's insurrection plot is discovered in South Carolina
1830s	Vast majority of African American slaves in America are native born
1830s–40s	Cotton trade grows into largest source of commercial wealth and America's leading export
1831	Turner leads a violent slave rebellion in Virginia
1832	Virginia holds the last debate in the South about the future of slavery; gradual abolition is voted down
	Publication of Dew's proslavery tract *Abolition of Negro Slavery*
1836	Arkansas gains admission to the Union as a slave state
1839	Mississippi's Married Women's Property Act gives married women some property rights
1845	Florida and Texas gain admission to the Union as slave states
	Publication of Douglass's *Narrative of the Life of Frederick Douglass, an American Slave, Written by Himself*
1850	Planters' share of agricultural wealth in the South is 90 to 95 percent
1850–60	Of some 300,000 slaves who migrate from the Upper to the Lower South, 60 to 70 percent go by outright sale
1857	Publication of Hinton R. Helper's *The Impending Crisis*, denouncing the slave system
	Publication of George Fitzhugh's *Southern Thought*, an aggressive defense of slavery
1860	There are 405,751 "mulattos" (biracial people) in the United States, accounting for 12.5 percent of the African American population
	Three-quarters of all southern white families own no slaves
	South produces largest cotton crop ever

earlier freed the four children he fathered with Sally Hemings: William Beverly Hemings, Harriet Hemings II, James Madison Hemings, and Thomas Eston Hemings. In 1822, Beverly and Harriet had left Monticello to pass as white people. Jefferson never freed Sally; Virginia law would have required him to attain, publicly, a dispensation from the state legislature in order to free her without removing her from the state. The Sage of Monticello wanted no more salacious publicity about his longtime house servant and mistress than had already occurred for many years. Sally died a slave, living in Charlottesville, Virginia, in 1835 at the age of sixty-two; she left numerous heirlooms for her children from her life with Jefferson: a pair of his eyeglasses, a shoe buckle, and an inkwell.

"Thank heaven the whole of this dreadful business is over," wrote Jefferson's granddaughter, Mary, when the auction had ended. She consoled herself that the vast majority of slaves had been sold within the state. She likened the "sad scene," though, to a "captured village in ancient times when all were sold as slaves." Monticello itself was sold in 1831. But across the South in the 1820s the "business" of slavery expansion and cotton production was hardly over at all.

Experience an interactive version of this story in MindTap®.

n 1815, the southern tier of states and territories, with fertile soil and a growing labor force of enslaved people to cultivate it, was poised for growth, prosperity, and power. New lands were settled, new states were peopled, and steadily the South emerged as the world's most extensive and vigorous commercial agricultural economy. The Old South's wealth came from export crops, land, and slaves, and its population was almost wholly rural. In the land where cotton became king, racial slavery affected not only economics but also values, customs, laws, class structure, and the region's relationship to the nation and the world. As slaves' bodies, labor, and lives came to be defined more and more as chattel, they struggled increasingly not only to survive but also to resist, sometimes overtly, but more often in daily life and cultural expression. By 1860, white southerners not only asserted the moral and economic benefits of slavery with a vigorous defense of the system, but also sought to sustain and advance their political power over the national government.

- How and why was the Old South a "slave society," with slavery permeating every class and group within it, free or unfree?

- How and why did white southerners come to see cotton as "king" of a global economy, and how did the cotton trade's international reach shape southern society from 1815 to 1860?

- How did African American slaves build and sustain a meaningful life and a sense of community amid the potential chaos and destruction of their circumstances?

- How would you weigh the comparative significance of the following central themes in the history of the Old South: class, race, migration, power, liberty, wealth?

9-1 The "Distinctive" South

▷ What did the North and South share in common in the early nineteenth century?

▷ How did the South's social development and structure differ from that of the North because of the institution of slavery?

▷ How did the southern proslavery argument evolve over the first half of the nineteenth century?

Not until the first half of the 1800s did the region of slaveholding states from the Chesapeake and Virginia to Missouri, and from Florida across to Texas, come to be designated as the South. Today, many still consider it America's most distinctive region. Historians have long examined how the Old South was like and unlike the rest of the nation. Because of its unique history, has the South, in the words of poet Allen Tate, always been "Uncle Sam's other province"? Or as southern writer W. J. Cash said in 1940, is the South "a tree with many age rings, with its limbs and trunk bent and twisted by all the winds of the years, but with its tap root in the Old South?" Analyzing just why the South seems more religious, more conservative, or more tragic than other regions of America has been an enduring practice in American culture and politics.

Certain American values, such as materialism, individualism, and faith in progress, have been associated with the North and values such as tradition, honor, and family loyalty,

with the South. The South, so the stereotype has it, was static, even "backward," and the North was dynamic in the decades leading up to the Civil War. There are many measures of just how different South was from North in the antebellum era. At the same time, there were many Souths: low-country rice and cotton regions with dense slave populations; mountainous regions of small farmers and subsistence agriculture; semitropical wetlands in the Southeast; **plantation** culture in the Cotton Belt and especially the Mississippi Valley; Texas grasslands; tobacco- and wheat-growing regions in Virginia and North Carolina; cities with bustling ports; and wilderness areas with only the rare homesteads of hillfolk.

9-1a South-North Similarity

The South was distinctive because of its commitment to slavery, but it also shared much in common with the rest of the nation. The geographic sizes of the South and the North were roughly the same. In 1815, white southerners shared with their fellow free citizens in the North a heritage of heroes and ideology from the era of the American Revolution and the War of 1812. With varying accents, southerners spoke the same language and worshiped the same Protestant God as northerners. Southerners lived under the same Constitution as northerners, and they shared a common mixture of nationalism and localism in their attitudes toward government. Down to the 1840s, northerners and southerners invoked with nearly equal frequency the doctrine of states' rights against federal authority. A sense of American mission inspired by the westward movement was as much a part of southern as of northern experience.

Indeed, some of the most eloquent visions of America as a land of yeomen—independent, self-sufficient farmers—expanding westward had come from a southerner, Thomas Jefferson. Jefferson believed that "virtue" rested in those who tilled the soil, that farmers made the best citizens. In 1804, Jefferson declared his "moral and physical preference of the agricultural over the manufacturing man." But as slavery and the plantation economy expanded (see Map 9.1), the South did not become a land of individual opportunity in the same manner as the North.

During the forty-five years before the Civil War, the South shared in the nation's economic booms and busts. Research has shown that, despite its enormous cruelties, slavery was a profitable labor system for planters. Southerners and northerners shared an expanding capitalist economy. As it grew, the slave-based economy reflected the rational choices of planters. More land and more slaves generally converted into more wealth. Slaveholders were good capitalists.

By the eve of the Civil War in 1860, the distribution of wealth and property in the two sections was almost identical: 50 percent of free adult males owned only 1 percent of real and personal property, and the richest 1 percent owned 27 percent of the wealth. One study comparing Texas and Wisconsin in 1850 shows that the richest 2 percent of families in

plantation Large landholding devoted to a cash crop such as cotton or tobacco.

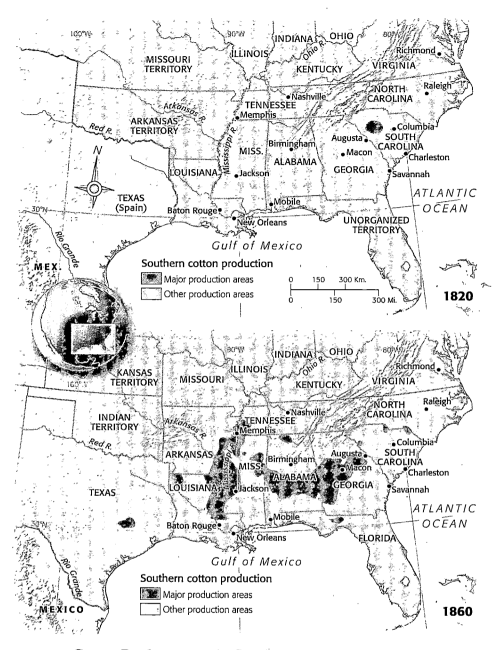

Map 9.1 Cotton Production in the South

These two maps reveal the rapid westward expansion of cotton production and its importance to the antebellum South.

each state owned 31 to 32 percent of the wealth. So both North and South had ruling classes, even if their wealth was invested in different kinds of property. Entrepreneurs in both sections, whether forging plantations out of Mississippi Delta land or shoe factories and textile mills in New England river towns, sought their fortunes in an expanding market economy.

9-1b South-North Dissimilarity

There were important differences between the North and the South. The South's climate and longer growing season gave it an unmistakably rural and agricultural destiny. Many great rivers provided rich soil and transportation routes to market. The South's people, white and black, developed an intense attachment to place, to the ways people were related to the land and to one another. The South developed as a biracial society of brutal inequality, where the liberty of one race depended directly on the enslavement of another. White wealth was built on highly valued black labor.

Cotton growers spread out over as large an area as possible to maximize production and income. As a result, population density in the South was low; by 1860, there were only 2.3 people per square mile in vast and largely unsettled Texas, 15.6 in Louisiana, and 18.0 in Georgia. By contrast, population density in the nonslaveholding states east of the Mississippi River was almost three times higher. The Northeast had an average of 65.4 people per square mile. Massachusetts had 153.1 people per square mile, and New York City compressed 86,400 people into each square mile. When, in the 1850s, young Frederick Law Olmsted of Connecticut, later renowned as a landscape architect, toured the South as a journalist, he traveled mostly on horseback along primitive trails. Between Columbus, Georgia, and Montgomery, Alabama, Olmsted found "a hilly wilderness, with a few dreary villages, and many isolated cotton farms." For one who would design Central Park in New York City, this was just too much ruralness.

Where people were scarce, it was difficult to finance and operate schools, churches, libraries, and even inns and restaurants. Similarly, the rural character of the South and the significance of the plantation as a self-sufficient social unit meant that the section put few resources into improving disease control and public health. Southerners were strongly committed to their churches, and some believed in the importance of universities, but all such institutions were far less developed than those in the North. Factories were rare because planters invested most of their capital in slaves. A few southerners did invest in iron or textiles on a small scale. But the largest southern "industry" was lumbering, and the largest factories used slave labor to make cigars. More decisively, the South was slower to develop a regional transportation network. Despite concerted efforts, the South had only 35 percent of the nation's railroad mileage in 1860.

The Old South never created its own banking and shipping capacity to any degree. If it had, its effort to be an international cartel might have succeeded longer. Most southern bank deposits were in the North, and southern cotton planters became ever more dependent on New York for shipping. As early as 1822, one-sixth of all southern cotton cleared for Liverpool or Le Havre from the port of New York and constituted two-fifths of all that city's exports. Many New York merchants and bankers developed deep interests in the fate of slavery and cotton prices. In a series of economic conventions held from 1837 to 1839, southern delegates debated the nature of foreign trade, dependence on northern importers and financiers, and other alleged threats to their commercial independence and security. But nothing, save rhetoric, came of these conventions; it was the last time southern planters would organize to break from their Yankee middlemen and shippers.

The South lagged far behind the North in nearly any measure of industrial growth. Its urban centers were mostly ports like New Orleans and Charleston, and to some extent Baltimore, which became crossroads of commerce and small-scale manufacturing. In the interior were small market towns dependent on agricultural trade—"urbanization without cities," as one historian has said. Slavery slowed urban growth. Likewise, because of a lack of manufacturing jobs, the South did not attract immigrants as readily as did the North. By 1860, only 13 percent of the nation's foreign-born population lived in the slave states.

Like most northerners, antebellum southerners were adherents to evangelical Christianity. Americans from all regions held in common a faith in a personal God and in conversion and piety as the means to salvation. But southern evangelicalism was distinct from its northern practice. In the South, Baptists and Methodists concentrated on personal rather than social improvement. By the 1830s in the North, evangelicalism was a major wellspring of reform movements (see "Revivals and Reform," Section 10-7); but in states where blacks were so numerous and unfree, and where the very social structure received increasingly aggressive attacks from abolitionists, religion, as one scholar has written, preached "a hands-off policy concerning slavery." Although slaves began to convert to Christianity in the early-nineteenth-century South, many southern whites feared a reform impulse that would foster what one historian has called an "interracial communion" in their churches. Moreover, those women who may have been reform minded were prevented from developing frequent associations with other reformers because of distance and sparse population.

The slave system made it inevitable that the interests and social structures of the North and the South would diverge after 1815. Because of its inherently conservative social structure, antebellum southern law restricted the authority of the courts, reinforcing a tradition of planter control. Penitentiaries tended to house only whites, as most blacks were under the authority of personal masters. Lawbreaking in the South tended to involve crimes of violence rather than crimes against property.

9-1c A Southern Worldview and the Proslavery Argument

Perhaps in no way was the South more distinctive than in its embrace of a particular worldview, a system of thought and meaning held especially by the planter class, but also influencing the entire society. Southerners' justifications for slavery were not so different from those of any other civilization trying to defend the institutions it inherits. But at the heart of the proslavery argument was a deep and abiding racism. The persistence of modern racism in all sections of the United States is all the more reason to comprehend antebellum southerners' rationalizations for human slavery.

In the wake of the American Revolution, the Enlightenment ideas of natural rights and equality did stimulate antislavery sentiment in the Upper South, produced a brief flurry of manumissions (the willful freeing of a slave by the owner), and led to considerable hope for gradual emancipation. In 1796, Virginian St. George Tucker argued that "slavery not only violates the laws of nature and of civil society, it also wounds the best forms of government." But confidence that the exercise of reason among gentlemen might end such a profitable system as slavery waned in the new nation. As slavery spread, southerners soon vigorously defended it. In 1816, George Bourne, a Presbyterian minister exiled from Virginia for his antislavery sermons and for expulsion of slaveholders

Library of Congress Prints and Photographs Division[LC-US2C4-5950]

△ *America, 1841*, lithograph and watercolor by Edward Williams Clay. An idealized portrayal of loyal and contented slaves, likely distributed by northern apologists for slavery. All is well on the plantation as well-dressed slaves dance and express their gratitude to their master and his perfect family. The text includes the old slave saying: "God bless you master! You feed and clothe us. When we are sick you nurse us, and when too old to work, you provide for us!" The master replies piously: "These poor creatures are a sacred legacy from my ancestors and while a dollar is left me, nothing shall be spared to increase their comfort and happiness."

from his church, charged that, whenever southerners were challenged on slavery, "they were fast choked, for they had a Negro stuck fast in their throats." After walking home with South Carolina statesman and proslavery advocate John C. Calhoun from an 1820 cabinet meeting, John Quincy Adams confided to his diary that too many southerners "writhe in agonies of fear at the very mention of human rights as applicable to men of color."

By the 1820s, white southerners went on the offensive, actively justifying slavery as a "**positive good**" and not merely a "necessary evil." They used the antiquity of slavery, as well as the Bible's many references to slaveholding, to foster a historical argument for bondage. Slavery, they deemed, was the natural status of blacks. Whites were the more intellectual race, and blacks the race more inherently physical and therefore destined for labor. Whites were the creators of civilizations, blacks the appointed hewers of wood and drawers of water. Proslavery writers did not mince words. In a

positive good Southern justification for slavery as beneficial to the larger society, both to white owners and their black slaves.

proslavery tract written in 1851, John Campbell confidently declared that "there is as much difference between the lowest tribe of negroes and the white Frenchman, Englishman, or American, as there is between the monkey and the negro."

Some southerners defended slavery in practical terms; they simply saw their slaves as economic necessities and symbols of their quest for prosperity. In 1845, James Henry Hammond of South Carolina argued that slaveholding was essentially a matter of property rights. Unwilling to "deal in abstractions" about the "right and wrong" of slavery, Hammond considered property sacred and protected by the Constitution, because slaves were legal property—end of argument. The deepest root of the proslavery argument was a hierarchical view of the social order as slavery's defenders believed God or nature had prescribed it. Southerners cherished tradition, duty, and honor, believing social change should come only in slow increments, if at all. As the Virginia legislature debated the gradual abolition of slavery in 1831–1832, in the wake of Nat Turner's rebellion, Thomas R. Dew, a slaveholder and professor of law and history at the College of William and Mary, contended that "that which is the growth of *ages* may require ages to remove." Dew's widely read work *Abolition of Negro Slavery* (1832) ushered in an outpouring of proslavery writing that would intensify over the next thirty years. Until Turner's bloody rebellion, Dew admitted, emancipation in the South had "never been seriously discussed." But as slavery expanded westward and fueled national prosperity, Dew cautioned southerners that any degree of gradual abolition threatened the whole region's "irremediable ruin." Dew declared black slavery part of the "order of nature," an indispensable part of the "deep and solid foundations of society" and the basis of the "well-ordered, well-established liberty" of white Americans. Dew's well-ordered society also included his conception of the proper division of men and women into separate spheres and functions.

Proslavery advocates held views very different from those of northern reformers on the concepts of freedom, progress, and equality. They turned natural-law doctrine to their favor, arguing that the natural state of humankind was inequality of ability and condition, not equality. A former U.S. senator in South Carolina, William Harper, charged in 1837 that Jefferson's famous dictum about equality in the Declaration of Independence was no more than a "sentimental phrase." "Is it not palpably nearer the truth to say that no man was ever born free," Harper argued, "and that no two men were ever born equal?" Proslavery writers believed that people were born to certain stations in life; they stressed dependence over autonomy and duty over rights as the human condition. As Virginia writer George Fitzhugh put it in 1854, "Men are not born entitled to equal rights. It would be far nearer the truth to say, that some were born with saddles on their backs, and others booted and spurred to ride them."

Many slaveholders believed their ownership of people bound them to a set of paternal obligations as guardians of a familial relationship between masters and slaves. Although contradicted by countless examples of slave resistance and escape, as well as by slave sales, planters needed to believe in the idea of the contented slave. The slaveholders who promoted their own freedom and pursued personal profits through the bondage of blacks had to justify themselves endlessly.

9-1d A Slave Society

Slavery and race affected everything in the Old South. Whites and blacks alike grew up, were socialized, married, reared children, worked, conceived of property, and honed their most basic habits of behavior under the influence of slavery. This was true of slaveholding and nonslaveholding whites as well as of blacks who were enslaved and free. Slavery shaped the social structure of the South, fueled almost anything meaningful in its economy, and came to dominate its politics. Rudolphe Lucien Desdunes, a Louisiana sugar planter, remembered growing up in a society where "slavery was the pivot around which everything revolved."

The South was interdependent with the North, the West, and even with Europe in a growing capitalist market system. To keep the cotton trade flowing, southerners relied on northern banks, on northern steamship companies working the great western rivers, and on northern merchants. But there were elements of this system that southerners increasingly rejected during the antebellum era, especially urbanism,

the wage labor system, a broadening right to vote, and any threat to their racial and class order.

In the antebellum era, as later, there were many Souths, but Americans have always been determined to define what one historian called the "Dixie difference." "The South is both American and something different," writes another historian, "at times a mirror or magnifier of national traits and at other times a counterculture." This was most acutely true in the decades before the Civil War.

Culturally, the South developed a proclivity to tell its own story. Its ruralness and its sense of tradition may have given southerners a special habit of telling tales. "Southerners . . . love a good tale," said Mississippi writer Eudora Welty. "They are born reciters, great memory retainers, diary keepers, letter exchangers, and letter savers, history tracers, and debaters, and—outstaying all the rest—great talkers." The South's story is both distinctive and national, and it begins in what we have come to call the Old South, a term only conceivable after the eviction of Native peoples from the region.

9-2 Southern Expansion, Native American Resistance and Removal

▷ **How did Native peoples respond to encroachments on their lands and southern expansion?**

▷ **How did state governments and the federal government treat Native peoples amid southern westward movement?**

Americans were a restless, moving people when the trans-Appalachian frontier opened in the wake of the War of 1812. Some 5 to 10 percent of the booming population moved each year, usually westward. In the first two decades of the century, they poured into the Ohio Valley; by the 1820s, after the death of the Shawnee chief Tecumseh and the collapse of the pan-Indian federation, they were migrating into the Mississippi River Valley and beyond. By 1850, two-thirds of Americans lived west of the Appalachians.

9-2a A Southern Westward Movement

As much as in any other region, this surging westward movement was a southern phenomenon. After 1820, the heart of cotton cultivation and the slave-based plantation system shifted from the coastal states to Alabama and the newly settled Mississippi Valley—Tennessee, Louisiana, Arkansas, and Mississippi. Southern slaveholders forced slaves to move with them to the newer areas of the South, and **yeoman** farmers followed, also hoping for new wealth through cheap land and the ownership of other people.

A wave of migration was evident everywhere in the Southeast. As early

yeoman Independent small farmer, usually nonslaveholding.

△ Delia, an enslaved woman on the Edgehill plantation near Columbia, South Carolina, photographed in 1850 by daguerreotypist Joseph Zealy for natural scientist Louis Agassiz. Delia was among seven people Agassiz had photographed nude in an effort to investigate the alleged inferior physiognomy of Africans and African Americans. Delia's tearful gaze haunts the tragic process by which the "racial sciences" tried to categorize and rank human beings in the service of proslavery arguments.

as 1817, Georgian Samuel McDonald observed a "disease prevalent" in his region. "The patient," he said, first exhibited a "great love" of talking about "the new country" to the west. Then he tried to "make sale of his stock" and "lastly . . . to sell his plantation." Once attacked by this "Alabama fever," most never recovered and were carried "off to the westward." That same year, a Charleston, South Carolina, newspaper reported with alarm that migration out of that state had already reached "unprecedented proportions." Indeed, almost half of the white people born in South Carolina after 1800 left the state, most for the Southwest. And by 1833, Tyrone Power, an Irish actor riding a stagecoach from Georgia into Alabama, encountered many "camps of immigrants" and found the roads "covered" by such pilgrims.

The way to wealth for seaboard planters in the South was to go west to grow cotton for the booming world markets, by purchasing ever more land and slaves. The population of Mississippi soared from 73,000 in 1820 to 607,000 in 1850, with African American slaves in the majority. Across the Mississippi River, the population of Arkansas went from 14,000 in 1820 to 210,000 in 1850. By 1835, the American immigrant population in Texas reached 35,000, including 3,000 slaves, outnumbering Mexicans two to one. Aggressive American settlers declared Texas's independence from Mexico in 1836, spurring further American immigration into the region. By 1845, "Texas fever" had boosted the Anglo population to 125,000. Statehood that year opened the floodgates to more immigrants from the east and to a confrontation with Mexico that would lead to war.

As the **cotton kingdom** grew to what southern political leaders dreamed would be national and world dominion, this westward migration, fueled at first by an optimistic nationalism, ultimately made migrant planters more sectional and more southern. In 1817, Congressman John C. Calhoun embraced national expansion as the means to "bind the Republic together," as he provided the process its unquestioned assumption: "Let us conquer space." In time, political dominance in the South migrated westward into the Cotton Belt as well. By the 1840s and 1850s, these energetic capitalist planters, ever mindful of world markets and fearful that their slave-based economy was under attack, sought to protect and expand their system. Increasingly, they saw themselves, as one historian has written, less as "landowners who happened to own slaves" than as "slaveholders who happened to own land."

cotton kingdom A broad swath of territory where cotton was a mainstay that stretched from South Carolina, Georgia, and northern Florida in the east through Alabama, Mississippi, central and western Tennessee, and Louisiana, and from there on to Arkansas and Texas.

Long in advance of all this expansion, however, other, older groups of Americans already occupied much of this land. Before 1830, large swaths of upper Georgia belonged to the Cherokee, and huge regions of Alabama and Mississippi were either Creek, Choctaw, or Chickasaw land. Native peoples were also on the move, but in forced migrations. The indigenous cultures of the eastern and southern woodlands had to be uprooted to make way for white expansion. For the vast majority of white Americans, Native Americans were in the way of their growing empire. Taking Native peoples' land, so the reasoning went, merely reflected the natural course of history: the "civilizers" had to displace the "children of the forest" in the name of progress. National leaders provided all the rhetoric and justification needed. "Nothing," said General Andrew Jackson as early as 1816, "can promote the welfare of the United States, and particularly the southwestern frontier so much as bringing into market . . . the whole of this fertile country." As president in 1830, Jackson spoke with certainty about why Native peoples must go. "What good man would prefer a country," he asked, "covered with forests and ranged by a few thousand savages to our extensive Republic, studded with cities, towns, and prosperous farms?"

9-2b American Indian Treaty Making

In theory, under the U.S. Constitution, the federal government recognized Native peoples' sovereignty and treated these groups as foreign nations. Indeed, the United States received Native American delegations with pomp and ceremony, exchanging gifts as tokens of friendship. Agreements between American Indian nations and the United States were signed, sealed, and ratified like other international treaties. In practice, however, swindle and fraud dominated the government's approach to treaty making and Native peoples' sovereignty. As the country expanded, new treaties replaced old ones, shrinking Native peoples' landholdings.

Although Native American resistance persisted against such pressure after the War of 1812, it only slowed the process. In the 1820s, Native peoples in the middle West, Ohio Valley, Mississippi Valley, and other parts of the cotton South ceded lands totaling 200 million acres for a pittance.

9-2c American Indian Accommodation

Increasingly, American Indian nations east of the Mississippi sought to survive through accommodation. In the first three decades of the century, the Choctaw, Creek, and Chickasaw peoples in the lower Mississippi became suppliers and traders in the nation's expanding market economy. Under treaty provisions, Native American commerce took place through trading posts and stores that provided Native peoples with supplies, and purchased or bartered Native-produced goods. The trading posts extended credit to chiefs, who increasingly fell into debt that they could pay off to the federal government only by selling their land.

By 1822, the Choctaw nation had sold 13 million acres but still carried a debt of $13,000. The Choctaw people struggled to adjust, increasing agricultural production and hunting, working as farmhands and craftsmen, and selling produce at market stalls in Natchez and New Orleans. As

The Amistad Case

In April 1839, a Spanish slave ship, *Tecora*, sailed from Lomboko, the region of West Africa that became Sierra Leone. On board were Mende people, captured and sold by their African enemies. In June, they arrived in Havana, Cuba, a Spanish colony. Two Spaniards purchased fifty-three of the Mende and set sail aboard *La Amistad* for their plantations elsewhere in Cuba. After three days at sea, the Africans revolted. Led by a man the Spaniards called Joseph Cinque, they killed the captain and seized control of the vessel. They ordered the two Spanish owners to take them back to Africa, but the slaveholders sailed east by day and north by night, trying to reach the shores of the American South. Far off course, *La Amistad* was seized by the USS *Washington* in Long Island Sound and brought ashore in Connecticut.

The "Amistad Africans" were soon a celebrated moral and legal cause for abolitionists and slaveholders, as well as in U.S.–Spanish relations. The Africans were imprisoned in New Haven, and a prolonged dispute ensued around many questions: Were they slaves and murderers, and the property of their Cuban owners, or were they free people exercising their natural rights? Were they Spanish property, seized on the high seas

in violation of a 1795 treaty? If a northern state could "free" captive Africans, what did it mean for enslaved African Americans in the South? Connecticut abolitionists immediately went to court, where a U.S. circuit court judge dismissed the charges of mutiny and murder but refused to release the Africans because their Spanish owners claimed them as property.

Meanwhile, the Mende were desperate to tell their own story. A Yale professor of ancient languages, Josiah Gibbs, visited the captives and learned their words for numbers. In New York, he walked up and down the docks repeating the Mende words until an African seaman, James Covey, responded. Covey journeyed to New Haven, conversed with the jubilant Africans, and soon their harrowing tale garnered sympathy all over Yankee New England.

In a new trial, the judge ruled that the Africans were illegally enslaved and ordered them returned to their homeland. Although slavery might be legal in Cuba, the slave trade between Africa and the Americas had been outlawed in a treaty between Spain and Great Britain. Spain's lawyers demanded the return of their "merchandise." In need of southern votes to win reelection, President Martin Van Buren supported the Spanish claims and advocated the Africans' return to a likely death in Cuba.

The administration appealed the case to the Supreme Court in February 1841. Arguing the abolitionists' case, former president John Quincy Adams famously pointed to a copy of the Declaration of Independence

on the wall of the court chambers, invoked the natural rights to life and liberty, and chastised the Van Buren administration for its "immense array of power . . . on the side of injustice." In a 7-to-1 decision, the Court ruled that the Africans were "free-born" with the right of self-defense, while remaining silent on slavery's legality in the United States.

Fund-raising and speaking tours featuring Cinque made the return voyage possible. On November 27, 1841, thirty-five survivors and five American missionaries embarked for Africa. They arrived in Sierra Leone on January 15, 1842, whereupon Cinque wrote a letter to the Amistad Committee. "I thank all 'merican people," he said. "I shall never forget 'merican people." But the international meanings of the Amistad case would endure. Sarah Magru, one of the child captives on *La Amistad*, stayed in America to attend Oberlin College and later returned to work at the Mende mission in Sierra Leone.

The Amistad case showed how intertwined slavery was with freedom, and the United States with the world. It poisoned diplomatic relations between America and Spain for a generation, and stimulated Christian mission work in Africa.

CRITICAL THINKING

☐ The *Amistad* case impacted Spanish-American diplomacy for a generation and led to wide-ranging change in Africa brought on by American missionary efforts. Why did the Supreme Court ruling declaring the *Amistad* captives free not impact the institution of slavery in the United States?

North Wind Picture Archives/Alamy

◁ Joseph Cinque, by Nathaniel Jocelyn, 1840. Cinque led the rebellion aboard *La Amistad*, a Spanish ship carrying captive Africans along the coast of Cuba in 1839. They commandeered the ship and sailed it north toward New England, where they were rescued off the coast of Connecticut. Cinque, celebrated as a great leader, sat for the painting while he and his people awaited trial. They were freed by a decision of the U.S. Supreme Court in 1841 and returned to their homeland in Sierra Leone in West Africa.

the United States expanded westward, white Americans promoted their assimilation, through education and conversion to Christianity, with renewed urgency. "Put into the hand of [Indian] children the primer and the hoe," the House Committee on Indian Affairs recommended in 1818, "and they will naturally, in time, take hold of the plough; and, as their minds become enlightened and expand, the Bible will be their book, and they will grow up in habits of morality and industry." In 1819, in response to missionary lobbying, Congress appropriated $10,000 annually for "civilization of the tribes adjoining the frontier settlements."

Within five years, thirty-two boarding schools enrolled Native American students. They substituted English for American Indian languages and taught agriculture alongside the Christian gospel. But this emphasis on agriculture and the value of private property did not deter settlers eyeing Native peoples' land. Wherever Native Americans lived, illegal settlers disrupted their lives. The federal government only halfheartedly enforced the integrity of treaties, as legitimate Native land rights gave way to the advance of white civilization.

Over time, however, Native Americans could not prevent the spread of the cotton economy that arose all around them. With loss of land came dependency. The Choctaw came to rely on white Americans not only for manufactured goods but even for food. Dependency, coupled with disease, facilitated removal of American Indian peoples to western lands. While the population of other groups increased rapidly, Native peoples' populations fell, some nations declining by 50 percent in only three decades. The French traveler and author Alexis de Tocqueville noticed the contrast. "Not only have these wild tribes receded, but they are destroyed," Tocqueville concluded, after personally observing the tragedy of forced removal in 1831, "and as they give way or perish, an immense and increasing people fill their place. There is no instance upon record of so prodigious a growth or so rapid a destruction." As many as 100,000 eastern and southern Native peoples were removed between 1820 and 1850; about 30,000 died in the process.

The wanderings of the Shawnee, the people of the Prophet and Tecumseh, illustrate the uprooting of Native peoples (see "Divisions Among American Indian Peoples," Section 8-2d and "Tenskwatawa and Tecumseh," Section 8-2e). After giving up 17 million acres in Ohio in a 1795 treaty, the Shawnee scattered to Indiana and eastern Missouri. After the War of 1812, some Shawnee sought protection from either the British in Canada or from Mexico. Yet another group moved to the Kansas territory in 1825. By 1854, Kansas was open to white settlement, and the Shawnee had to cede seven-eighths of their land, or 1.4 million acres.

Indian Removal Act Legislation authorizing Andrew Jackson to exchange public lands in the West for Native American territories in the East and appropriated federal funds to cover the expenses of removal.

Removal had a profound impact on all Shawnee. The men lost their traditional role as providers; their skills hunting woodland animals were useless on the prairies of Kansas. As grain became the tribe's dietary staple, Shawnee women played a greater role as providers, supplemented by government aid under treaty provisions. Remarkably, the Shawnee preserved their language and culture in the face of these devastating dislocations.

9-2d Indian Removal as Federal Policy

Much of the land of the southeastern tribes—Cherokee, Creek, Choctaw, Chickasaw, and Seminole—had remained intact after the War of 1812, and they had aggressively resisted white encroachment. In his last annual message to Congress in late 1824, President James Monroe proposed that all Native peoples be moved beyond the Mississippi River. Monroe described his proposal as an "honorable" one that would protect Native Americans' land from invasion and provide them with independence for "improvement and civilization." He believed force would be unnecessary.

But all four tribes unanimously rejected Monroe's proposition. Between 1789 and 1825, the four nations had negotiated thirty treaties with the United States, and they had reached their limit. Most wished to remain on what little was left of their ancestral land.

Pressure from Georgia had prompted Monroe's policy. In the 1820s, the state had accused the federal government of not fulfilling its 1802 promise to remove the Cherokee and Creek from northwestern Georgia in return for the state's renunciation of its claim to western lands. In 1826, under federal pressure, the Creek nation ceded all but a small strip of its Georgia acreage, but Georgians remained unmoved. Only the complete removal of the Georgia Creeks to the West could resolve the conflict between the state and the federal government. For the Creek, the outcome was devastating. In an ultimately unsuccessful attempt to hold fast to the remainder of their traditional lands, which were in Alabama, they radically altered their political structure. In 1829, at the expense of traditional village autonomy, they centralized tribal authority and forbade any chief from ceding land.

In 1830, after extensive debate and a narrow vote in both houses, Congress passed the **Indian Removal Act**, authorizing the president to negotiate treaties of removal with all tribes living east of the Mississippi. The bill, which provided federal funds for such relocations, would likely not have passed the House without the additional representation afforded slave states due to the three-fifths clause in the Constitution. Increasingly, slavery's expansion equated with political power and Native peoples' displacement in the South.

9-2e Cherokee

Adapting to American ways seemed no more successful than resistance in forestalling removal. No people met the challenge of assimilating to American standards more thoroughly than the Cherokee, whose traditional home centered on eastern Tennessee and northern Alabama and Georgia. Between 1819 and 1829, the tribe became economically self-sufficient and politically self-governing; during this Cherokee renaissance, the nearly fifteen thousand adult Cherokees came to think of themselves as a nation, not a collection of villages. In 1821 and 1822, Sequoyah, a self-educated Cherokee, devised an eighty-six-character phonetic alphabet that made possible a Cherokee-language Bible and a bilingual tribal newspaper, *Cherokee Phoenix* (1828). Between 1820 and 1823, the Cherokee created a formal government with a bicameral legislature, a court system, and a salaried bureaucracy. In 1827, they adopted a written constitution modeled after that of the United States. They transformed their economy from hunting, gathering, and subsistence agriculture to commodity trade based on barter, cash, and credit.

Cherokee land laws, however, differed from U.S. law. The nation collectively owned all Cherokee land and forbade land sales to outsiders. Nonetheless, economic change paralleled political adaptation. Many became individual farmers and slaveholders; by 1833, they held fifteen hundred black slaves, and over time Cherokee racial identity became very complex. Both before and after removal to the West, the designations of "mixed bloods" and "full bloods" were woven into the fabric of tribal society, and conflicts over membership as well as the legacy of Cherokee slaveholding still permeate the group today. But these Cherokee transformations failed to win respect or acceptance from white southerners. In the 1820s, Georgia pressed them to sell the 7,200 square miles of land they held in the state. Congress appropriated $30,000 in 1822 to buy the Cherokee land in Georgia, but the Cherokees resisted. Impatient with their refusals to negotiate cession, Georgia annulled the Cherokees' constitution, extended the state's sovereignty over them, prohibited the Cherokee National Council from meeting except to cede land, and ordered their lands seized. Then, the discovery of gold on Cherokee land in 1829 further whetted Georgia's appetite for Cherokee territory.

9-2f *Cherokee Nation v. Georgia*

Backed by sympathetic whites but not by President Andrew Jackson, the Cherokees under Chief John Ross turned to the federal courts to defend their treaty with the United States. Their legal strategy reflected their growing political sophistication. In *Cherokee Nation v. Georgia* (1831), Chief Justice John Marshall ruled that under the federal Constitution an American Indian tribe was neither a foreign nation nor a state and therefore had no standing in federal courts. American Indians' relationship with the United States was "marked," said Marshall, "by cardinal and peculiar distinctions which exist nowhere else." They were deemed "domestic, dependent nations." Legally, they were in but not of the United States.

Smithsonian American Art Museum/Art Resource, NY

△ *Kutteeotubbee*, a prominent southeastern Native American warrior, 1834.

Nonetheless, said Marshall, the American Indians had an unquestionable right to their lands; they could lose title only by voluntarily giving it up.

A year later, in *Worcester v. Georgia*, Marshall defined the Cherokee position more clearly. The Cherokee nation was, he declared, a distinct political community in which "the laws of Georgia can have no force" and into which Georgians could not enter without permission or treaty privilege. The Cherokee celebrated. *Phoenix* editor Elias Boudinot called the decision "glorious news." Jackson, however, whose reputation had been built as an Indian fighter, did his best to usurp the Court's action. Newspapers widely reported that Jackson had said, "John Marshall has made his decision: now let him enforce it." Keen to open up new lands for settlement, Jackson favored expelling the Cherokees.

Georgians, too, refused to comply; they would not tolerate a sovereign Cherokee nation within their borders, and they refused to hear the pleas of Native peoples to share their American dream. A Cherokee census indicated that they owned thirty-three grist mills, thirteen sawmills, one powder mill, sixty-nine blacksmith shops, two tanneries, 762 looms, 2,486 spinning wheels, 172 wagons, 2,923 plows, 7,683 horses, 22,531 cattle, 46,732 pigs, and 2,566 sheep. "You asked us to throw off the hunter and warrior state," declared the Cherokee leader, John Ridge, in 1832. "We did so—you asked us to form a republican government: We did so—adopting your own as a model. You asked us to cultivate the earth, and learn the mechanic arts: We did so. You asked us to learn to read: We did so. You asked us to cast away our idols, and worship your God: We did so." But neither the plow nor the Bible earned the Cherokees respect in the face of the economic, imperial, and racial quests of their fellow southerners (see Map 9.2).

9-2g Trail of Tears

The Choctaw went first; they made the forced journey from Mississippi and Alabama to the West in the winter of 1831 and 1832. Alexis de Tocqueville was visiting Memphis when they passed through: "The wounded, the sick, newborn babies, and the old men on the point of death . . . . I saw them embark to cross the great river," he wrote, "and the sight will never fade from my memory. Neither sob nor complaint rose from that silent assembly. Their afflictions were of long standing, and they felt them to be irremediable." Other tribes soon joined the forced march. The Creeks in Alabama resisted removal until 1836, when the army pushed them westward. A year later, the Chickasaw followed.

Having fought removal in the courts, the Cherokee were divided. Some believed that further resistance was hopeless and accepted removal as the only chance to preserve their civilization. The leaders of this minority agreed in 1835 to exchange their southern home for western land, in the Treaty of New Echota. Most, though, wanted to stand firm. John Ross, with petitions signed by fifteen thousand Cherokee, lobbied the Senate against ratification of the treaty. He lost. But when the time for evacuation came in 1838, most Cherokee refused to move. President Martin Van Buren sent federal troops to round them up. About twenty thousand Cherokee were evicted, held in detention camps, and marched under military escort to Indian Territory in present-day Oklahoma. Nearly one-quarter of them died of disease and exhaustion on what came to be known as the **Trail of Tears.**

Trail of Tears Forced migration in 1838 of the Cherokee people from their homelands in the southeast to what is now Oklahoma.

Map 9.2 Removal of Native Americans from the South, 1820–1840

Over a twenty-year period, the federal government and southern states forced Native Americans to exchange their traditional homes for western land. Some tribal groups remained in the South, but most settled in the alien western environment.

△ *The Trail of Tears, 1838.* The epic and tragic drama of Cherokee removal is here depicted in *The Trail of Tears, 1838.* Oil on canvas, 1942, by Robert Lindneux. Courtesy Granger, NYC. All rights reserved.

When the forced march to the West ended, Native peoples had traded about 100 million acres east of the Mississippi for 32 million acres west of the river plus $68 million. Only a few scattered remnants, among them the Seminoles in Florida and the Cherokees in the southern Appalachian Mountains, remained east of the Mississippi River.

Forced removal had a disastrous impact on the Cherokee and other displaced American Indian nations. In the West, they encountered an alien environment. Unable to live off the land, many became dependent on government payments for survival. Removal also brought new internal conflicts. The Cherokees in particular struggled over their tribal government. In 1839, followers of John Ross assassinated the leaders of the protreaty faction. Violence continued sporadically until a new treaty in 1846 imposed a temporary truce. In time, the Cherokee managed to reestablish their political institutions and a governing body in Tahlequah, in northeastern Oklahoma.

9-2h Seminole Wars

In Florida, a small band of Seminoles continued to resist. Some Seminole leaders agreed in the 1832 Treaty of Payne's Landing to relocate to the West within three years,

but others opposed the treaty, and some probably did not know it existed. A minority under Osceola, a charismatic leader, refused to vacate their homes and fought the pro-treaty group. When federal troops were sent to impose removal in 1835, Osceola waged a fierce guerrilla war against them.

The Florida Native peoples were a varied group that included many Creeks and people of mixed Native American and African American descent (mainly children of ex-slaves or descendants of fugitive slaves). The U.S. Army, however, considered them all Seminole, subject to removal. General Thomas Jesup believed that the fugitive slave population was the key to the war. "This, you may be assured, is a Negro, not an Indian war," he wrote a friend in 1836, "and if it be not speedily put down, the South will feel the effects of it on their slave population before the end of the next season."

Osceola was captured under a white flag of truce and died in an army prison in 1838, but the Seminole fought on under Chief Coacoochee (Wild Cat) and other leaders. In 1842, the United States abandoned the removal effort. Most of Osceola's followers agreed to move west to Indian Territory after another war in 1858, but some Seminoles remained in the Florida Everglades.

9-3 Social Pyramid in the Old South

▶ What were the socio-economic experiences of the groups that comprised the "social pyramid" of the Old South?

▶ What were the cultural experiences of the groups that comprised the "social pyramid" of the Old South?

▶ What tensions emerged among slaveholders and nonslaveholders in the Old South?

Native American lands were now open to restless and mobile white settlers. A large majority of white southern families (three-quarters in 1860) were yeoman farmers who owned their own land but did not own slaves. The social distance between poorer whites and the planter class could be great, although the line between slaveholder and nonslaveholder was fluid. Still greater was the distance between whites and blacks with free status. White yeomen, landless whites, and free blacks occupied the broad base of the social pyramid in the Old South.

9-3a Yeoman Farmers

Many of the white farmers pioneered the southern wilderness, moving into undeveloped regions or Native American land after removal. After the War of 1812, they moved in successive waves down the southern Appalachians into the Gulf lands or through the Cumberland Gap into Kentucky and Tennessee. In large sections of the South, especially inland from the coast and away from large rivers, small, self-sufficient farms were the norm. Lured by stories of good land, many men repeatedly uprooted their wives and children. So many shared the excitement over new lands that one North Carolinian wrote in alarm, "The Alabama Fever rages here with great violence . . . . I am apprehensive if it continues to spread as it has done, it will almost depopulate the country."

These farmers were individualistic and hardworking. Unlike their northern counterparts, their lives were not transformed by improvements in transportation. They could be independent thinkers as well, but their status as a numerical majority did not mean they set the political or economic direction of the larger society. Self-reliant and often isolated, absorbed in the work of their farms, they operated both apart from and within the slave-based staple-crop economy.

On the southern frontier, men cleared fields, built log cabins, and established farms while their wives labored in the household economy and patiently re-created the social ties—to relatives, neighbors, fellow churchgoers—that enriched everyone's experience. Women seldom shared the men's excitement about moving. They dreaded the isolation and loneliness of the frontier. "We have been [moving] all our lives," lamented one woman. "As soon as ever we get comfortably settled, it is time to be off to something new."

Some yeomen acquired large tracts of level land, purchased slaves, and became planters. They forged part of the new wealth of the cotton-boom states of Mississippi and Louisiana, where mobility into the slave-owning class was possible. Others clung to familiar mountainous areas or sought self-sufficiency because, as one frontiersman put it, they disliked "seeing the nose of my neighbor sticking out between the trees." As one historian has written, though they owned no slaves, yeomen were jealous of their independence, and "the household grounded their own claims to masterhood." Whatever the size of their property, they wanted control over their economic and domestic lives.

9-3b Yeoman Folk Culture

The yeomen enjoyed a folk culture based on family, church, and local region. Their speech patterns and inflections recalled their Scots-Irish and Irish backgrounds. They flocked to religious revivals called camp meetings, and in between they got together for house-raisings, logrolling, quilting bees, corn-shuckings, and hunting for both food and sport. Such occasions combined work with fun and fellowship, offering food and liquor in abundance.

A demanding round of work and family responsibilities shaped women's lives in the home. They worked in the fields to an extent that astonished travelers like Frederick Law Olmsted and British writer Frances Trollope, who believed yeomen had rendered their wives "slaves of the soil." Throughout the year, the care and preparation of food consumed much of women's time. Household tasks continued during frequent pregnancies and child care. Primary nursing and medical care also fell to mothers, who often relied on folk wisdom. Women, too, wanted to be masters of their household, the only space and power over which they could claim domain, although it came at the price of their health.

9-3c Yeomen's Livelihoods

Among the men, many aspired to wealth, eager to join the scramble for slaves and cotton profits. North Carolinian John F. Flintoff kept a diary of his struggle for success. At age eighteen in 1841, Flintoff went to Mississippi to seek his fortune. Like other aspiring yeomen, he worked as an overseer of slaves but often found it impossible to please his employers. At one point, he gave up and returned to North Carolina, where he married and lived for a while in his parents' house. But Flintoff was "impatient to get along in the world," so he tried Louisiana next and then Mississippi again.

Flintoff's health suffered in the Gulf region and, routinely, "first rate employment" alternated with "very low wages." Moreover, as a young man working on isolated plantations, Flintoff often felt lonely. Even at a revival meeting in 1844 he felt "little warm feeling." His employers found fault with his work, and in 1846 Flintoff concluded in despair that "managing negroes and large farms is soul destroying."

But a desire to succeed kept him going. At twenty-six, even before he owned any land, Flintoff bought his first slave, "a negro

Old Kentucky Home Life in the South, 1859 (oil on canvas)/Johnson, Eastman (1824-1906)/NEW YORK HISTORICAL SOCIETY/© Collection of the New-York Historical Society, USA/Bridgeman Images

△ *Old Kentucky Home Life in the South*, by Eastman Johnson, 1859, oil on canvas. Collection of the New-York Historical Society/ the Bridgeman Art Gallery.

boy 7 years old." Soon he had purchased two more children, the cheapest slaves available. Conscious of his status as a slave owner, Flintoff resented the low wages he was paid. In 1853, with nine young slaves and a growing family, Flintoff faced "the most unhappy time of my life." Fired by his uncle, he returned to North Carolina, sold some of his slaves, and purchased 124 acres with help from his in-laws. As he began to pay off his debts, he looked forward to freeing his wife from labor and possibly sending his sons to college. Although Flintoff demonstrated that a farmer could move in and out of the slaveholding class, he never achieved the cotton planter status that he desired.

Probably more typical of the southern yeoman was Ferdinand L. Steel, who as a young man moved from North Carolina to Tennessee to work as a river boatman but eventually took up farming in Mississippi. Steel and his family raised corn and wheat, though cotton was their cash product: they sold five or six bales a year to obtain money for sugar, coffee, salt, calico, gunpowder, and a few other store-bought goods.

Thus, Steel entered the market economy as a small farmer, but with mixed results. He picked his own cotton and complained that it was brutal work and not profitable. He felt like a serf in cotton's kingdom. When cotton prices fell, a small grower like Steel could be driven into debt and lose his farm.

Steel's life in Mississippi in the 1840s retained much of the flavor of the frontier, and he survived on a household economy. He made all the family's shoes; his wife and sister sewed dresses, shirts, and "pantaloons." The Steel women also rendered their own soap and spun and wove cotton into cloth; the men hunted game. Steel doctored his illnesses with boneset tea and other herbs. As the nation fell deeper into crisis over the future of free or slave labor, and as the planter class strove ever more aggressively to preserve its slave society, this independent farmer never came close to owning a slave.

The focus of Steel's life was family and religion. Family members prayed together daily, and he studied Scripture for

△ *North Carolina Emigrants: Poor White Folks*, oil on canvas, 1845, by James Henry Beard. This depicts a yeoman family, their belongings all on one hungry horse, as they migrate westward in search of new land and livelihood.

an hour after lunch. "My Faith increases, & I enjoy much of that peace which the world cannot give," he wrote in 1841. Seeking to prepare himself for Judgment Day, Steel borrowed histories, Latin and Greek grammars, and religious books from his church. Eventually, he became a traveling Methodist minister. "My life is one of toil," he reflected, "but blessed be God that it is as well with me as it is."

9-3d Landless Whites

Toil with even less security was the lot of two other groups of free southerners: landless whites and free blacks. A sizable minority of white southern workers—from 25 to 40 percent, depending on the state—were hired hands who owned no land and worked for others in the countryside and towns. Their property consisted of a few household items and some animals—usually pigs—that could feed themselves on the open range. The landless included some immigrants, especially Irish, who did heavy and dangerous work, such as building railroads and digging ditches.

In the countryside, white farm laborers struggled to purchase land in the face of low wages or, if they rented, unpredictable market prices for their crops. By scrimping

and finding odd jobs, some managed to climb into the ranks of yeomen. When James and Nancy Bennitt of North Carolina succeeded in their ten-year struggle to buy land, they decided to avoid the unstable market in cotton; thereafter they raised extra corn and wheat as sources of cash. People like the Bennitts were both participants in and victims of an economy dominated by cotton producers who relied on slave labor.

Herdsmen with pigs and other livestock had a desperate struggle to succeed. By 1860, as the South anticipated war to preserve its society, between 300,000 and 400,000 white people in the four states of Virginia, North and South Carolina, and Georgia—approximately one-fifth of the total white population—lived in genuine poverty. Their lives were harsh. An early antebellum traveler in central South Carolina described the white folk he encountered in the countryside: they "looked yellow, poor, and sickly. Some of them lived the most miserably I ever saw any poor people live."

9-3e Yeomen's Demands and White Class Relations

Class tensions emerged in the western, nonslaveholding parts of the seaboard states by the 1830s. There, yeoman farmers resented their underrepresentation in state legislatures and the corruption in local government. After vigorous debate, the reformers won many battles. Voters in the more recently settled states of the Old Southwest adopted white manhood suffrage and other electoral reforms, including popular election of governors, legislative apportionment based on white population only, and locally chosen county government. Slave owners with new wealth, however, were determined to hold the ultimate reins of power.

Given such tensions, it was perhaps remarkable that slaveholders and nonslaveholders did not experience more overt conflict. Historians have offered several explanations. One of the most important factors was race. The South's racial ideology stressed the superiority of all whites to blacks. Thus, slavery became the basis of equality among whites, and white privilege inflated the status of poor whites and gave them a common interest with the rich. At the same time, the dream of upward mobility blunted some class conflict.

Most important, before the Civil War many yeomen were able to pursue their independent lifestyle largely unhindered by slaveholding planters. They worked their farms, avoided debt, and marked progress for their families in rural habitats of their own making. Likewise, slaveholders pursued their goals quite independently of yeomen. Planters farmed for the market but also for themselves. Suppression of dissent also played an increasing role. After 1830, white southerners who criticized the slave system out of moral conviction or class resentment were intimidated, attacked, or rendered politically powerless in a society held together in part by white racial solidarity.

Still, there were signs of class conflict in the late antebellum period. As cotton lands filled up, nonslaveholders faced narrower economic prospects; meanwhile, wealthy planters enjoyed expanding profits. The risks of entering cotton production were becoming too great and the cost of slaves too high for many yeomen to rise in society. From 1830 to 1860, the percentage of white southern families holding slaves declined steadily, from 36 to 25 percent. Although slave owners were a distinct minority in the white population, planters' share of the South's agricultural wealth remained between 90 and 95 percent. This long-standing American dilemma of severe inequality of wealth, combined with white racial solidarity, finds one of its deepest roots in the Old South.

Anticipating possible secession, slave owners stood secure. In the 1850s, they occupied from 50 to 85 percent of the seats in state legislatures and a similarly high percentage of the South's congressional seats. And planters' interests controlled all the other major social institutions, such as churches and colleges.

9-3f Free Blacks

The nearly quarter-million free blacks in the South in 1860 also yearned for mobility. But their condition was generally worse than the yeoman's and often little better than the slave's. The free blacks of the Upper South were usually descendants of men and women manumitted by their owners

in the 1780s and 1790s. A remarkable number of slaveholders in Virginia and the Chesapeake region had freed their slaves because of religious principles and revolutionary ideals in the wake of American independence. Many free blacks also became free as fugitive slaves, especially by the 1830s, disappearing into the southern population; a few made their way northward. A small number of free blacks had purchased their own freedom.

White southerners were increasingly desperate to restrict this growing free black presence in their midst. "It seems the number of free Negroes," complained a Virginia slaveholder, "always exceeds the number of Negroes freed." Some free blacks worked in towns or cities, but most lived in rural areas and struggled to survive. They usually did not own land and had to labor in someone else's fields, often beside slaves. By law, free blacks could not own a gun, buy liquor, violate curfew, assemble except in church, testify in court, or (throughout the South after 1835) vote. Despite these obstacles, a minority bought land, and others found jobs as skilled craftsmen, especially in cities.

A few free blacks prospered and bought slaves. In 1830, there were 3,775 free black slaveholders in the South; 80 percent lived in the four states of Louisiana, South Carolina, Virginia, and Maryland, and approximately half of the total lived in the two cities of New Orleans and Charleston. Most of them purchased their own wives and children, whom they nevertheless could not free because laws required newly emancipated blacks to leave their state. In order to free family members whom they had purchased, hundreds of black slaveholders petitioned for exemption from the antimanumission laws passed in most southern states. At the same time, a few multiracial people in New Orleans were active slave traders in its booming market. The complex world of southern free blacks received new attention through Edward P. Jones's *The Known World*, a hugely successful novel published in 2003 about a Virginia family that rises from slavery to slave ownership. Although rare in the United States, the greed and the tragic quest for power that lay at the root of slavery could cross any racial or ethnic barrier.

9-3g Free Black Communities

In the Cotton Belt and Gulf regions, a large proportion of free blacks were of mixed race, the privileged offspring of wealthy white planters. Not all planters freed their mixed-race offspring, but those who did often recognized the moral obligation of giving their children a good education and financial backing. In a few cities like New Orleans, Charleston, and Mobile, extensive interracial sex, as well as migrations from the Caribbean, had produced a multiracial population that was recognized as a distinct class. Most multiracial people, however, experienced hardship. In the United States, "one drop" of black "blood" (any observable racial mixture to white people's eyes) made them black, and potentially enslaveable.

In many southern cities by the 1840s, free black communities formed, especially around an expanding number of churches. By the late 1850s, Baltimore had fifteen churches,

Louisville nine, and Nashville and St. Louis four each—most of them African Methodist Episcopal. Baltimore, from which **Frederick Douglass**, the slave, escaped in 1838 with his free-born fiancée, Anna Murray, developed an especially active free black society. In 1840, the city contained 17,967 free blacks and 3,199 slaves out of a total population of 102,313. Such a large assemblage of free people of color worked as all manner of menial laborer, from domestic servants to dockworkers and draymen, but they also suffered under a strict Black Code, denying any civil or political rights and restricting their movements.

9-4 The Planters' World

▶ **What were the social values of the planter class in the South?**

▶ **What was the relationship between slavery and global and domestic economy?**

▶ **What role did paternalism play in the relationships within the planter class?**

At the top of the southern social pyramid were slaveholding planters. Most lived in comfortable farmhouses, not on the opulent scale that legend suggests. The grand plantation mansions, with fabulous gardens and long rows of outlying slave quarters, are an enduring symbol of the Old South. But in 1850, 50 percent of southern slaveholders had fewer than five slaves; 72 percent had fewer than ten; 88 percent had fewer than twenty. Thus, the average slaveholder was not a wealthy aristocrat but an aspiring farmer.

9-4a The Newly Rich

Louisiana cotton planter Bennet Barrow, a newly rich planter of the 1840s, was preoccupied with moneymaking. He worried constantly over his cotton crop, filling his diary with weather reports and gloomy predictions of his yields. Yet Barrow also strove to appear above such worries. He hunted frequently and had a passion for racing horses and raising hounds. He could report the loss of a slave without feeling, but emotion broke through his laconic manner when illness afflicted his sporting animals. "Never was a person more unlucky than I am," he mourned. "My favorite pup never lives." His strongest feelings surfaced when his horse Jos Bell—equal to "the best Horse in the South"—"broke down running a mile ... ruined for Ever." The same day, the distraught Barrow gave his human property a "general Whipping." In 1841 diary entries, he worried about a rumored slave insurrection. He gave a "severe whipping" to several of his slaves when they disobediently killed a hog. And when a slave named Ginney Jerry "sherked" his cotton-picking duties and was rumored "about to run off," Barrow whipped him one day and the next, which he recorded matter-of-factly: "took my gun found him in the Bayou behind the Quarter, shot him in his thigh—etc. raining all around."

Frederick Douglass A former slave who was the leading black abolitionist during the antebellum period.

The richest planters used their wealth to model genteel sophistication. Extended visits, parties, and balls to which women wore the latest fashions provided opportunities for friendship, courtship, and display. Such parties were held during the Christmas holidays, but also on such occasions as molasses stewing, a bachelors' ball, a horse race, or the crowning of the May queen. These entertainments were especially important as diversions for plantation women, and at the same time they sustained a rigidly gendered society. Young women relished social events to break the monotony of their domestic lives. In 1826, a Virginia girl was ecstatic about the "week ... I was in Town. ... There were five beaux and as many belles in the house constantly," she declared, and all she and her companions did was "eat, visit, romp, and sleep."

Most of the planters in the cotton-boom states of Alabama and Mississippi were newly rich by the 1840s. As one historian put it, "a number of men mounted from log cabin to plantation mansion on a stairway of cotton bales, accumulating slaves as they climbed." They put their new wealth into cotton acreage and slaves even as they sought refinement and high social status.

William Faulkner immortalized the new wealthy planter in a fictional character, Thomas Sutpen, in his novel *Absalom, Absalom!* (1936). After a huge win at riverboat gambling, Sutpen arrives in a Mississippi county in the 1830s, buys a huge plantation he calls Sutpen's Hundred, and with his troop of slaves converts it into a wealthy enterprise. Sutpen marries a local woman, and although he is always viewed as a mysterious outsider by earlier residents of the county, he becomes a pillar of the slaveholding class, eventually an officer in the Confederate army. But Sutpen is a self-made man of indomitable will and slave-based wealth. Although his ambition is ultimately his undoing, one of the earliest lessons he learns about success in the South is that "you got to have land and niggers and a fine house."

The cotton boom in the Mississippi Valley created one-generation aristocrats. A nonfictional case in point is Greenwood Leflore, a Choctaw chieftain who owned a plantation in Mississippi with four hundred slaves. After selling his cotton on the world market, he spent $10,000 in France to furnish a single room of his mansion with handwoven carpets, furniture upholstered with gold leaf, tables and cabinets ornamented with tortoiseshell inlay, a variety of mirrors and paintings, and a clock and candelabra of brass and ebony.

9-4b Social Status and Planters' Values

Slave ownership was the main determinant of wealth in the South. Slaves were a commodity and an investment, much like gold; people bought them on speculation, hoping for a steady rise in their market value. Many slaveholders took out mortgages on their slaves and used them as collateral. Especially in the growing states, people who could not pay cash for slaves would ask the sellers to purchase the mortgage, just as banks give mortgages on houses today. The slaveholder would pay back the loan in installments with interest. Slaveholders and the people who lent them money put their faith in this "human collateral," believing it would increase in value. This was slaveholding capitalism as a growth industry. Hundreds of thousands of slaves were thus mortgaged, many several times and with full awareness of their masters' financial methods. In St. Landry's Parish, Louisiana, between 1833 and 1837, an eight-year-old slave boy named Jacques was mortgaged three times, sold twice, and converted into what one historian has called a "human cash machine and an investment vehicle" before the age of twelve.

Slavery's influence spread throughout the social system. The availability of slave labor tended to devalue free labor: where strenuous work under supervision was reserved for an enslaved race, few free people relished it. When Alexis de Tocqueville crossed from Ohio into Kentucky in his travels of 1831, he observed "the effect that slavery produces on society. On the right bank of the Ohio [River] everything is activity, industry; labor is honoured; there are no slaves. Pass to the left bank and the scene changes so suddenly that you think yourself on the other side of the world; the enterprising spirit is gone. There, work is not only painful; it is shameful." Tocqueville's own class impulses found a home in the South, however. There he found a "veritable aristocracy which . . . combines many prejudices with high sentiments and instincts."

The values of the aristocrat—lineage, privilege, pride, honor, and refinement of person and manner—commanded respect throughout the South. Many of those qualities were in short supply, however, in the recently settled portions of the cotton kingdom, where frontier values of courage and self-reliance ruled during the 1820s and 1830s. By the 1850s, a settled aristocratic group of planters did rule, however, in much of the Mississippi Valley. Indeed, by 1860 two-thirds of the millionaires in the United States were southern planters.

In this geographically mobile society, independence and codes of honor motivated both planter and frontier farmer alike. Instead of gradually disappearing, as it did in the North, the Code Duello, which required men to defend their honor through violence, lasted much longer in the South. In North Carolina in 1851, wealthy planter Samuel Fleming sought to settle disputes with lawyer William Waightstill Avery by "cowhiding" him on a public street. According to the code, Avery had two choices: to redeem his honor violently or to brand himself a coward through inaction. Three weeks later, he shot Fleming dead at point-blank range during a session of the Burke County Superior Court. A jury took only ten minutes to find Avery not guilty, and the spectators gave him a standing ovation.

In their pride, aristocratic planters expected not only to wield power but also to receive deference from poorer whites. But the sternly independent yeoman class resented infringements of their rights, and many belonged to evangelical faiths that exalted values of simplicity and condemned the planters' love of wealth.

9-4c King Cotton in a Global Economy

Planters always had their eyes on the international growth of the cotton markets. Cash crops such as cotton were for export; the planters' fate depended on world trade, especially with Europe. The American South so dominated the world's supply of cotton by the 1840s and 1850s that southern planters gained enormous confidence that the cotton boom was permanent and that the industrializing nations of England and France in particular would always bow to **King Cotton**.

American planters began producing cotton in the 1780s. Made possible in part by Eli Whitney's invention in 1793 of the cotton gin, a device for cleaning the short-staple variety of the crop that the British textile industry craved, American cotton production doubled in yield each decade after 1800 and provided three-fourths of the world's supply by the 1840s. Gins, which took on the scale of whole buildings with time, revolutionized cotton production and the investment of southern wealth in land and slaves. In the first decade of the nineteenth century in South Carolina alone, wrote one planter, cotton "trebled the price of land suitable to its growth" and "doubled" the annual income of growers. Southern staple crops were fully three-fifths of all American exports by 1850, and one of every seven workers in England depended on American cotton for his or her job. Indeed, cotton production made slaves the single most valuable financial asset in the United States—greater in dollar value than all of America's banks, railroads, and manufacturing combined. In 1860 dollars, the slaves' total value as property came to an estimated $3.5 billion. In early-twenty-first-century dollars, that would be approximately $75 billion.

"Cotton is King," the *Southern Cultivator* declared in 1859, "and wields an astonishing influence over the world's commerce." Until 1840, the cotton trade furnished much of the export capital to finance northern economic growth. After that date, however, the northern economy expanded without dependence on cotton profits. Free labor was in the long run more the engine of American capitalist growth than slave labor. Nevertheless, southern planters and politicians continued to boast of King Cotton's supremacy. "Our cotton is the most wonderful talisman in the world," announced a planter in 1853. "By its power we are transmuting whatever we choose into whatever we want." "No power on earth dares . . . to make war on cotton," James Hammond lectured the U.S. Senate in 1858; "Cotton is king."

9-4d Slavery and Capitalism

Historians have vigorously debated the relationship between slavery and capitalism in the Atlantic world. Slavery may not have caused the Industrial Revolution in the eighteenth and nineteenth centuries, one historian has written, but it "played an active role in its pattern and timing." Some historians once contended that American slavery was

King Cotton Term expressing the southern belief that the U.S. and British economies depended on cotton, making it "king."

pre-modern and pre-capitalist, but no longer. Although the debate can be ferocious over the extent and character of slavery's roots in capitalism, we no longer doubt that southern slaveholders were as intertwined in markets, investments, and the uses of credit and speculation as their northern industrializing counterparts. Especially with the westward movement of the domestic slave trade, slaveholders rationally organized the exploitation and sale of their human property on a huge scale for the production of commodities for a growing global market. Slaves were not only property, but moveable property in a system based on credit, debt, supply chains, and the reputations of both slave owners and slave traders. Slaves were virtually currency itself.

Cotton production, and therefore the productivity of slaves and the system they made possible, increased manifold in the forty years leading up to the Civil War. One historian has argued that such productivity was due to widespread "speed-ups" forced upon the enslaved and especially to increasing uses of "torture" to compel work. Other historians, however, have attributed the growth in cotton production over time to the use of hybrid seeds and other agricultural innovations that made the crop far more fruitful. Fewer than half of all slaves lived on cotton plantations by the late antebellum period; we must therefore be careful to paint pictures of slave experience and the capitalist system of American bondage with a broad brush. We must also be careful not to understand slavery and the southern or northern economies as products of impersonal economic forces alone. Systems do not commodify and sell people, people do. Slavery fueled capitalism and capitalism forged slavery. But ultimately the nation faced these issues as a deadly conflict in the only place it could—in political events and institutions, and at the ballot box.

9-4e Paternalism

Beyond cold economics, slaveholding men often embraced a paternalistic ideology that justified their dominance over both black slaves and white women. Instead of stressing the profitable aspects of commercial agriculture, they sometimes stressed their obligations, viewing themselves as custodians of the welfare of society in general, and of the black families they owned in particular. The paternalistic planter saw himself not as an oppressor but as the benevolent guardian of an inferior race.

Paul Carrington Cameron, North Carolina's largest slaveholder, exemplifies this mentality. After a period of sickness among his one thousand North Carolina slaves (he had hundreds more in Alabama and Mississippi), Cameron wrote, "I fear the Negroes have suffered much from the want of proper attention and kindness under this late distemper no love of lucre shall ever induce me to be cruel." On another occasion, he described to his sister the sense of responsibility he felt: "Do you remember a cold & frosty morning, during [our mother's] illness, when she said to me Paul my son the people ought to be shod' this is ever in my ears, whenever I see any ones shoes in bad order; and in my ears it will be, so long as I am master."

It was comforting to rich planters to see themselves in this way, and slaves—accommodating to the realities of power—encouraged their masters to think that their benevolence was appreciated. Paternalism also served as a defense against abolitionist criticism. Still, paternalism was often a matter of self-delusion, a means of avoiding some harsh dimensions of slave treatment. In reality, paternalism grew as a give-and-take relationship between masters and slaves, each extracting from the other what they desired—owners took labor from the bondsmen, while slaves, as best they could, obligated masters to provide them a measure of autonomy.

Charles Colcock Jones and his wife, Mary, were large slave owners on three Liberty County plantations south of Savannah, Georgia. A prominent Presbyterian minister and intellectual, trained in northeastern universities, Jones inherited and married into slaveholding. In the 1820s he and Mary thought slavery "one of the greatest curses," a terrible "wrong . . . unjust, contrary to nature and religion." Unable to imagine "total abolition" in the rice land of the low country, Jones sought a "middle way," believing slavery could be "reformed," that slaves, like whites, should be converted to evangelical Christianity.

In 1834 Jones published *Catechism for Colored Persons*, a manual for whites instructing slaves in Christian doctrine and obedience. But over time, his and Mary's theories about Christian reform of slavery fell to pieces. In 1857, desperately in debt and frustrated by sullen and runaway slaves, the Joneses resorted to what they claimed they would never do. They sold their longtime personal servants, Phoebe and Cassius, and their four children in the "least public" way possible at a Savannah slave market for $4,500. In long, wrenching letters the Joneses struggled with the morality of their decision, but congratulated themselves on selling Phoebe's family intact. They did not believe they had gotten the "best bargain," but Charles concluded: "Conscience is better than money."

Even Paul Cameron's benevolence vanished with changed circumstances. After the Civil War, he bristled at African Americans' efforts to be free and made sweeping economic decisions without regard for their welfare. Writing on Christmas Day 1865, Cameron showed little Christian charity (but a healthy profit motive) when he declared, "I am convinced that the people who gets rid of the free negro first will be the first to advance in improved agriculture. Have made no effort to retain any of mine." With that, he turned off his land nearly a thousand black people, rented his fields to several white farmers, and invested in industry.

Relations between men and women in the planter class were similarly defined by paternalism. The upper-class southern woman was raised and educated to be a wife, mother, and subordinate companion to men. South Carolina's Mary Boykin Chesnut wrote of her husband, "He is master of the house. To hear is to obey . . . . All the comfort of my life depends upon his being in a good humor." In a social system based on the coercion of an entire race, women found it very difficult to challenge society's rules on sexual or racial relations.

Planters' daughters usually attended one of the South's rapidly multiplying boarding schools. There, they formed friendships with other girls and received an education. Typically, the young woman had to choose a husband and commit herself for life to a man whom she generally had known for only a brief time. Young women were often alienated and emotionally unfulfilled. They had to follow the wishes of their family, especially their father. "It was for me best that I yielded to the wishes of papa," wrote a young North Carolinian in 1823. "I wonder when my best will cease to be painful and when I shall begin to enjoy life instead of enduring it."

Upon marriage, a planter-class woman ceded to her husband most of her legal rights, becoming part of his family. Most of the year she was isolated on a large plantation, where she had to oversee the cooking and preserving of food, manage the house, supervise care of the children, and attend sick slaves. All these realities were more rigid and confining on the frontier, where isolation was even greater. Women sought refuge in their extended family and associations with other women. Men on plantations could occasionally escape into the public realm—to town, business, or politics. Women could retreat from rural plantation culture only into kinship.

9-4f Marriage and Family Among Planters

It is not surprising that a perceptive young white woman sometimes approached marriage with anxiety. Women could hardly help viewing their wedding day, as one put it in 1832, as "the day to fix my fate." Lucy Breckinridge, a wealthy Virginia girl of twenty, lamented the autonomy she surrendered at the altar. In her diary, she recorded this unvarnished observation on marriage: "A woman's life after she is married, unless there is an immense amount of love, is nothing but suffering and hard work."

△ *Virginian Luxuries,* folk painting, artist unknown. Abby Aldrich Rockefeller Folk Art Museum, the Colonial Williamsburg Foundation.

Abby Aldrich Rockefeller Folk Art Museum, The Colonial Williamsburg Foundation. Museum Purchase.

Lucy loved young children but knew that childbearing often involved grief, poor health, and death. In 1840, the birth rate for white southern women in their childbearing years was almost 30 percent higher than the national average. The average southern white woman could expect to bear eight children in 1800; by 1860, the figure had decreased to only six, with one or more miscarriages likely. Complications of childbirth were a major cause of death, occurring twice as often in the hot, humid South as in the cooler and drier Northeast.

Sexual relations between planters and slaves were another source of problems that white women had to endure but were not supposed to notice. "Violations of the moral law ... made mulattos as common as blackberries," protested a woman in Georgia, but wives had to play "the ostrich game." "A magnate who runs a hideous black harem," wrote Mrs. Chesnut, ". . . poses as the model of all human virtues to these poor women whom God and the laws have given him." Such habits and dalliances, whatever the motives, such as at Jefferson's Monticello, produced a very large mixed-race population by the 1850s and a strained use of the term "family" across the South.

Southern men tolerated little discussion by women of the slavery issue. In the 1840s and 1850s, as abolitionist attacks on slavery increased, southern men published a barrage of articles stressing that women should restrict their concerns to the home. The *Southern Quarterly Review* declared, "The proper place for a woman is at home. One of her highest privileges, to be politically merged in the existence of her husband."

But some southern women were beginning to seek a larger role. A study of women in Petersburg, Virginia, a large tobacco-manufacturing town, revealed behavior that valued financial autonomy. Over several decades before 1860, the proportion of women who never married, or did not remarry after the death of a spouse, grew to exceed 33 percent. Likewise, the number of women who worked for wages, controlled their own property, and ran dressmaking businesses increased markedly.

9-5 Slave Life and Labor

▶ **What were the daily living conditions and work routines of slaves?**

▶ **How were slaves made to feel a sense of powerlessness in their lives?**

For African Americans, slavery was a burden that destroyed some people and forced others to develop modes of survival. Slaves knew a life of poverty, coercion, toil, and resentment. They provided the physical strength, and much of the know-how, to build an agricultural empire. But their daily lives embodied the nation's most basic contradiction: in the world's model republic, they were on the wrong side of a brutally unequal power relationship.

9-5a Slaves' Everyday Conditions

Although they generally had enough to eat, slaves' diet was monotonous and non-nutritious. Clothing, too, was plain, coarse, and inexpensive. Few slaves received more than one or two changes of clothing for hot and cold seasons, and one blanket each winter. Children of both sexes ran naked in hot weather and wore long cotton shirts in winter. Many slaves had to go without shoes until December, even as far north as Virginia. The bare feet of slaves were often symbolic of their status and one reason why, after freedom, many black parents were so concerned with providing their children with shoes. These conditions were generally better in cities, where slaves frequently lived in the same dwelling as their owners and were hired out to employers on a regular basis, enabling them to accumulate their own money.

Some of the richer plantations provided substantial houses, but the average slave lived in a crude, one-room cabin. The gravest drawback of slave cabins was not lack of comfort but an unhealthy environment. Each dwelling housed one or two entire families. Crowding and lack of sanitation fostered the spread of infection and such contagious diseases as typhoid fever, malaria, and dysentery. White plantation doctors were hired to care for sick slaves on a regular basis, but some "slave doctors" attained a degree of power in the quarters and with masters by practicing healing through herbalism and spiritualism.

9-5b Slave Work Routines

Hard work was the central fact of slaves' existence. The long hours and large work gangs that characterized Gulf Coast cotton districts operated almost like factories in the field. Overseers rang the morning bell before dawn, and black people of varying ages, tools in hand, walked toward the fields. Slaves who cultivated tobacco in the Upper South worked long hours picking the sticky, sometimes noxious, leaves under harsh discipline. And as one woman recalled when interviewed in the 1930s, "it was way after sundown 'fore they could stop that field work. Then they had to hustle to finish their night work [such as watering livestock or cleaning cotton] in time for supper, or go to bed without it."

Working "from sun to sun" became a norm in much of the South. As one planter put it, slaves were the best labor because "you could command them and make them do what was right." Profit took precedence over paternalism. Slave women did heavy fieldwork, even during pregnancy. Old people were kept busy caring for young children, doing light chores, or carding, ginning, and spinning cotton. The black abolitionist orator Frances Ellen Watkins captured the grinding economic reality of slavery in an 1857 speech, charging that slaveholders had "found out a fearful alchemy by which . . . blood can be transformed into gold. Instead of listening to the cry of agony, they listen to the ring of dollars and stoop down to pick up the coin."

task system Labor system in which each slave had a daily or weekly quota of tasks to complete.

By the 1830s, slave owners found that labor could be similarly motivated by the clock. Incentives had to be part of the labor regime. Planters like Charles Colcock Jones in the South Carolina and Georgia low country used a **task system** whereby slaves were assigned measured amounts of work to be performed in a given amount of time. So much cotton on a daily basis was to be picked from a designated field, so many rows hoed or plowed in a particular slave's specified section. When their tasks were finished, slaves' time was their own for working garden plots, tending hogs, even hiring out their own extra labor. From this experience and personal space, many slaves developed their own sense of property ownership. When the task system worked best, slaves and masters alike embraced it, fostering a degree of reciprocal trust.

Enslaved children were the future of the system and widely valued as potential labor. Of the 1860 population of 4 million slaves, fully half were under the age of sixteen. "A child raised every two years," wrote Thomas Jefferson, "is of more profit than the crop of the best laboring man." And in 1858, a slave owner writing in an agricultural magazine calculated that a slave girl he purchased in 1827 for $400 had borne three sons now worth $3,000 as his working field hands. Enslaved children gathered kindling, carried water to the fields, swept the yard, lifted cut sugar-cane stalks into carts, stacked wheat, chased birds away from sprouting rice plants, and labored at many levels of cotton and tobacco production. "Work," wrote one historian, "can be rightly called the thief who stole the childhood of youthful bond servants."

As enslaved children matured, they faced many psychological traumas. They faced a feeling of powerlessness as they became aware that their parents ultimately could not protect them. They had to muster strategies to fight internalizing what whites assumed was their inferiority. Thomas Jones, who grew up in North Carolina, remembered that his greatest struggle was with the sense of "suffering and shame" as he "was made to feel . . . degraded." Many former slaves resented foremost their denial of education. "There is one sin that slavery committed against me which I will never forgive," recollected the minister James Pennington. "It robbed me of my education." And for girls reaching maturity, the potential trauma of sexual abuse loomed over their lives.

9-5c Violence and Intimidation Against Slaves

Slaves could not demand much autonomy, of course, because the owner enjoyed a monopoly on force and violence. Whites throughout the South believed that slaves "can't be governed except with the whip." One South Carolinian frankly explained to a northern journalist that he whipped his slaves regularly, "say once a fortnight; . . . the fear of the lash kept them in good order." Evidence suggests that whippings were less frequent on small farms than on large plantations. But beatings symbolized authority to the master and tyranny to the slaves, who made them a benchmark for evaluating a master. In the words of former slaves, a good owner was one who did not "whip too much," whereas a bad owner "whipped till he's bloodied you and blistered you."

As these reports suggest, terrible abuses could and did occur. The master wielded virtually absolute authority on his plantation, and courts did not recognize the word of chattel slaves. Slaveholders rarely had to answer to the law or to the state. Yet physical cruelty may have been even more prevalent in other slaveholding parts of the New World than it was in the United States. In some of the sugar islands of the Caribbean in particular, treatment was so poor and death rates so high that the heavily male slave population shrank in size. In the United States, by contrast, the slave population experienced a steady natural increase, as births exceeded deaths and each generation grew larger.

The worst evil of American slavery was not its physical cruelty but the nature of slavery itself: coercion, belonging to another person, virtually no hope for mobility or change. Recalling their time in bondage, some former slaves emphasized the physical abuse, or the "bullwhip days," as one woman described her past. But memories of physical punishment focused on the tyranny of whipping as much as the pain. Delia Garlic made the essential point: "It's bad to belong to folks that own you soul an' body. I could tell you 'bout it all day, but even then you couldn't guess the awfulness of it." Thomas Lewis put it this way: "There was no such thing as being good to slaves. Many people were better than others, but a slave belonged to his master and there was no way to get out of it." To be a slave was to be the object of another person's will and material gain, to be owned, as the saying went, "from the cradle to the grave."

Most American slaves retained their mental independence and self-respect despite their bondage. Contrary to popular belief at the time, they were not loyal partners in their own oppression. They had to be subservient and speak honeyed words to their masters, but they talked and behaved quite differently among themselves. In *Narrative of the Life of Frederick Douglass, an American Slave, Written by Himself* (1845), Frederick Douglass wrote that most slaves, when asked about "their condition and the character of their masters, almost universally say they are contented, and that their masters are kind." Slaves did this, said Douglass, because they were governed by the maxim that "a still tongue makes a wise head," especially in the presence of unfamiliar people. Because they were "part of the human family," slaves often quarreled over who had the best master. But at the end of the day, Douglass remarked, when one had a bad master, he sought a better master; and when he had a better one, he wanted to "be his own master."

9-5d Slave-Master Relationships

Some former slaves remembered warm feelings between masters and slaves (they were sometimes related by blood), and some "special" bondsmen, such as highly skilled jockeys for planters who were great horsemen, enjoyed autonomy, privilege, and even fame. But the prevailing attitudes were distrust and antagonism. Slaves saw through acts of kindness. One woman said her mistress was "a mighty good somebody to belong to" but

only "'cause she was raisin' us to work for her." A man recalled that his owners took good care of their slaves, "and Grandma Maria say, 'Why shouldn't they—it was their money.'"

Slaves were alert to the thousand daily signs of their degraded status. One man recalled the general rule that slaves ate cornbread and owners ate biscuits. If blacks did get biscuits, "the flour that we made the biscuits out of was the third-grade sorts." A former slave recalled, "Us catch lots of 'possums," but "the white folks at [ate] 'em." If the owner took his slaves' garden produce to town and sold it for them, the slaves often suspected him of pocketing part of the profits.

Suspicion often grew into hatred. When a yellow fever epidemic struck in 1852, many slaves saw it as God's retribution. An elderly ex-slave named Minnie Fulkes cherished the conviction that God was going to punish white people for their cruelty to blacks. She described the whippings that her mother had to endure, and then she exclaimed, "Lord, Lord, I hate white people and the flood waters goin' to drown some more." On the plantation, of course, slaves had to keep such thoughts to themselves. Often they expressed one feeling to whites, another within their own household. In their daily lives, slaves created many ways to survive and to sustain their humanity in this world of repression.

9-6 Slave Culture and Resistance

▶ **What culture did slaves create amid the oppression of slavery?**

▶ **What role did religion play in the lives of slaves?**

▶ **What was the impact of slave resistance in the first half of the nineteenth century?**

A people is always "more than the sum of its brutalization," wrote African American novelist Ralph Ellison in 1967. What people create in the face of hard luck and oppression is what provides hope. The resource that enabled slaves to maintain such defiance was their culture: a body of beliefs, values, and practices born of their past and maintained in the present. As best they could, they built a community knitted together by stories, music, a religious worldview, leadership, the smells of their cooking, the sounds of their own voices, and the tapping of their feet. "The values expressed in folklore," wrote African American poet Sterling Brown, provided a "wellspring to which slaves . . . could return in times of doubt to be refreshed."

9-6a African Cultural Survival

Slave culture changed significantly after 1808, when Congress banned further importation of slaves and the generations born in Africa died out. For a few years, South Carolina illegally reopened the international slave trade, but by the 1830s, the vast majority of slaves in the South were native-born Americans. Many African Americans, in fact, can trace their American ancestry back further than most white Americans.

Yet African influences remained strong, despite lack of firsthand memory, especially in appearance and forms of expression. Some enslaved men plaited their hair into rows and fancy designs; enslaved women often wore their hair "in string"—tied in small bunches secured by a string or piece of cloth. A few men and many women wrapped their heads in kerchiefs of the styles and colors of West Africa. In burial practices, slaves used jars and other glass objects to decorate graves, following similar African traditions.

Music, religion, and folktales were parts of daily life for most slaves. Borrowing partly from their African background, as well as forging new American folkways, they developed what scholars have called a sacred worldview, which affected all aspects of work, leisure, and self-understanding. Slaves made musical instruments with carved motifs that resembled African stringed instruments. Their drumming and dancing followed African patterns that made whites marvel. One visitor to Georgia in the 1860s described a ritual dance of African origin: "A ring of singers is formed . . . . They then utter a kind of melodious chant, which gradually increases in strength, and in noise, until it fairly shakes the house, and it can be heard for a long distance." This observer of the "ring shout" also noted the agility of the dancers and the African call-and-response pattern in their chanting.

Many slaves continued to believe in spirit possession. Their belief resembled the African concept of the living dead—the idea that deceased relatives visit the earth for many years until the process of dying is complete. Slaves also practiced conjuration and quasi-magical root medicine. By the 1850s, the most notable conjurers and root doctors were reputed to live in South Carolina, Georgia, Louisiana, and other isolated coastal areas with high slave populations.

These cultural survivals provided slaves with a sense of a past. Such practices and beliefs were not static "Africanisms" or mere "retentions." They were cultural adaptations, living traditions re-formed in the Americas in response to new experience. African American slaves in the Old South were a people forged by two centuries of cultural mixture in the Atlantic world, and the South itself was a melding of many African and European cultural forces.

As they became African Americans, slaves also developed a sense of racial identity. In the colonial period, Africans had arrived in America from many different states and kingdoms, represented in distinctive languages, body markings, and traditions. Planters had used ethnic differences to create occupational hierarchies. By the early antebellum period, however, old ethnic identities gave way as American slaves increasingly saw themselves as a single group unified by race. Africans had arrived in the New World with virtually no concept of "race"; by the antebellum era, however, their descendants had learned through bitter experience that race was now the defining feature of their lives. They were a transplanted and transformed people.

9-6b Slaves' Religion and Music

As African culture gave way to a maturing African American culture, more and more slaves adopted Christianity. But they fashioned Christianity into an instrument of support and resistance. Theirs was a religion of justice and deliverance, quite unlike their masters' religious messages directed at them as a means of control. "You ought to have heard that preachin,'" said one man. "'Obey your master and mistress, don't steal chickens and eggs and meat,' but nary a word about havin' a soul to save." Slaves believed that Jesus cared about their souls and their plight. In their interpretations of biblical stories, as one historian has said, they were "literally willing themselves reborn." Just like their white owners or poorer whites in their region, blacks were drawn to revivalism, often attending the same Methodist camp meetings as their masters.

For slaves, Christianity was a religion of personal and group salvation. Devout men and women worshiped every day, "in the field or by the side of the road" or in special "prayer grounds" that afforded privacy. Some slaves held fervent secret prayer meetings that lasted far into the night. Many slaves nurtured an unshakable belief that God would enter history and end their bondage. They appropriated many of the Old Testament figures, such as Moses, and its greatest narratives, such as the Exodus story, to their own ends.

Slaves also adapted Christianity to African practices. In West African belief, devotees are possessed by a god so thoroughly that the god's own personality replaces the human personality. In the late antebellum era, Christian slaves experienced possession by the Protestant "Holy Spirit." The combination of shouting, singing, and dancing that seemed to overtake black worshipers formed the heart of their religious faith. "The old meeting house caught fire," recalled an ex-slave preacher. "The spirit was there . . . . God saw our need and came to us. I used to wonder what made people shout but now I don't. There is a joy on the inside and it wells up so strong that we can't keep still. It is fire in the bones. Any time that fire touches a man, he will jump." Out in brush arbors or in meetinghouses, slaves took in the presence of God, thrust their arms to heaven, made music with their feet, and sang away their woes. Many post-slavery black choirs could not perform properly without a good wooden floor to use as their "drum."

Rhythm and physical movement were crucial to slaves' religious experience. In black preachers' chanted sermons, which reached out to gather the sinner into a narrative of meanings and cadences along the way to conversion, an American tradition was born. The chanted sermon was both a message from Scripture and a patterned form that required audience response punctuated by "yes sirs!" and "amens!" But it was in song that the slaves left their most sublime gift to American culture.

Through the spirituals, slaves tried to impose order on the chaos of their lives. Many themes run through the lyrics of slave songs. Often referred to later as the "sorrow songs," they also anticipate imminent rebirth. Sadness could immediately give way to joy: "Did you ever stan' on a mountain, wash yo' hands in a cloud?" Rebirth was at the heart as well of the famous hymn "Oh, Freedom": "Oh, Oh,

△ Drawing by Lewis Miller of a *Lynchburg Negro Dance*, Lynchburg, Virginia, August 18, 1853. This work of art shows the slaves' use of elaborate costumes, string instruments, and "the bones"—folk percussion instruments of African origin, held between the fingers and used as clappers.

Freedom / Oh, Oh, Freedom over me— / But before I'll be a slave, / I'll be buried in my grave, / And go home to my Lord, / And Be Free!"

This tension and sudden change between sorrow and joy animates many songs: "Sometimes I feel like a motherless chile … / Sometimes I feel like an eagle in the air, / … Spread my wings and fly, fly, fly!" Many songs also express a sense of intimacy and closeness with God. Some songs display an unmistakable rebelliousness, such as the enduring "He said, and if I had my way / If I had my way, if I had my way, / I'd tear this building down!" And some spirituals reached for a collective sense of hope in the black community as a whole.

> O, gracious Lord! When shall it be,
> That we poor souls shall all be free;
> Lord, break them slavery powers—
> Will you go along with me?
> Lord break them slavery powers,
> Go sound the jubilee!

In many ways, African American slaves converted the Christian God to themselves. They sought an alternative world to live in—a home other than the one fate had given

them on earth. In a thousand variations of songs, they fashioned survival out of their own cultural imagination.

9-6c The Black Family in Slavery

African American slaves clung tenaciously to the personal relationships that gave meaning to life. Although American law did not recognize slave families, masters permitted them; in fact, slave owners *expected* slaves to form families and have children. As a result, even along the rapidly expanding edge of the cotton kingdom, there was a normal ratio of men to women, young to old. On some of the largest cotton plantations of South Carolina, when masters allowed their slaves increased autonomy through work on the task system, the property accumulation in livestock, tools, and garden produce thus fostered led to more stable and healthier families.

Following African kinship traditions, African Americans avoided marriage between cousins (commonplace among aristocratic slave owners). By naming their children after relatives of past generations, African Americans emphasized their family histories. Kinship networks and broadly extended families are what held life together in many slave communities.

For enslaved women, sexual abuse and rape by white masters were ever-present threats to themselves and their family life. By 1860, there were 405,751 biracial people in the United States, comprising 12.5 percent of the African American population. White planters were sometimes open with their sexual abuse of slave women, but not in the way they talked about it. As Mary Chesnut remarked, sex between slaveholding men and their slave women was "the thing we can't name." Buying slaves for sex was all too common at the New Orleans slave market. In what was called the "fancy trade" (a "fancy" was a young, attractive slave girl or woman), females were often sold for prices as much as 300 percent higher than the average.

Enslaved women had to negotiate this confused world of desire, threat, and shame. Harriet Jacobs, who spent much of her youth and early adult years dodging her owner's relentless sexual pursuit, described this circumstance as "the war of my life." In recollecting her desperate effort to protect her children and help them find a way north to freedom, Jacobs asked a haunting question that many enslaved women carried with them to their graves: "Why does the slave ever love? Why allow the tendrils of the heart to twine around objects which may at any moment be wrenched away by the hand of violence?"

9-6d The Domestic Slave Trade

Separation by violence from those they loved, sexual appropriation, and sale were what enslaved families most feared and hated. Many struggled for years to keep their children together and, after emancipation, to reestablish contact with loved ones lost by forced migration and sale. Between 1820 and 1860, an estimated 1 million slaves were moved into the region extending from western Georgia to eastern Texas. When the Union army registered thousands of black marriages in Mississippi and Louisiana in 1864 and 1865, fully 25 percent of the men over the age of forty reported that they had been forcibly separated from a previous wife. Thousands of black families were disrupted every year to serve the needs of the expanding cotton economy.

△ This photograph of five generations of an enslaved family, taken in Beaufort, South Carolina, in 1862, is silent but powerful testimony to the importance that enslaved African Americans placed on their ever-threatened family ties.

Library of Congress

Many antebellum white southerners made their living from the slave trade. A large slave trading firm such as Franklin & Armfield established its own credit system and a far-flung buying and distribution network from Richmond and Norfolk in Virginia, across Tennessee, and to the New Orleans market. They also owned their own ships for maritime transport of slaves, as well as jails for housing captives before their departures. The average time spent in a Norfolk jail for a slave awaiting transport in the Franklin & Armfield system was 117 days. Such firms ran businesses with full control over financing and supply chains of their objects of sale, all firmly within the law.

In South Carolina alone by the 1850s, there were more than one hundred slave-trading firms selling an annual average of approximately 6,500 slaves to southwestern states. Although southerners often denied it, vast numbers of slaves moved west by outright sale and not by migrating with their owners. A typical trader's advertisement read, "NEGROES WANTED. I am paying the highest cash prices for young and likely NEGROES, those having good front teeth and being otherwise sound." One estimate from 1858 indicated that slave sales in Richmond, Virginia, netted $4 million that year alone. A market guide to slave sales that same year in Richmond listed average prices for "likely ploughboys," ages twelve to fourteen, at $850 to $1,050; "extra number 1 fieldgirls" at $1,300 to $1,350; and "extra number 1 men" at $1,500.

Slave traders were practical, roving businessmen. They were sometimes considered degraded by white planters, but many slave owners did business with them. Market forces drove this commerce in humanity. At slave "pens" in cities like New Orleans, traders promoted "a large and commodious showroom ... prepared to accommodate over 200 Negroes for sale." Traders did their utmost to make their slaves appear young, healthy, and happy, cutting gray whiskers off men, using paddles as discipline so as not to scar their merchandise, and forcing people to dance and sing as buyers arrived for an auction. When transported to the southwestern markets, slaves were often chained together in "coffles," which made journeys of 500 miles or more on foot.

The complacent mixture of racism and business among traders is evident in their own language. "I refused a girl 20 year[s] old at 700 yesterday," one trader wrote to another in 1853. "If you think best to take her at 700 I can still get her. She is very badly whipped but good teeth." Some sales were transacted at owners' requests, often for tragically inhumane reasons. "Bought a cook yesterday that was to go out of state," wrote a trader; "she just made the people mad that was all." Some traders demonstrated how deeply slavery and racism were intertwined. "I have bought the boy Isaac for 1100," wrote a trader in 1854 to his partner. "I think him very prime .... He is a ... house servant ... first rate cook ... and splendid carriage driver. He is also a fine painter and varnisher and ... says he can make a fine panel door .... Also he performs well on the violin .... He is a genius and its strange to say I think he is smarter than I am."

Missouri Historical Museum

△ A bill of sale documents that this enslaved woman, Louisa, was owned by the young child whom she holds on her lap. In the future, Louisa's life would be subject to the child's wishes and decisions.

9-6e Strategies of Resistance

Slaves brought to their efforts at resistance the same common sense and determination that characterized their struggle to secure their family lives. The scales weighed heavily against overt revolution, and they knew it. But they seized opportunities to alter their work conditions. They sometimes slacked off when they were not being watched. Thus, owners complained that slaves "never would lay out their strength freely."

Daily discontent and desperation were also manifest in sabotage of equipment; in wanton carelessness about work; in theft of food, livestock, or crops; or in getting drunk on stolen liquor. Some slaves might just fall into recalcitrance. "I have a boy in my employ called Jim Archer," complained a Vicksburg, Mississippi, slaveholder in 1843. "Jim does not want to be under anyones control and says ... he wants to go home this summer." A woman named Ellen, hired as a cook in Tennessee in 1856, quietly put mercury poison into a roasted apple for her unsuspecting mistress. And some enslaved women resisted as best they could by trying to control their

A slave coffle marching across the USA, before the Civil War (coloured engraving)/American School, (19th century)/PETER NEWARK'S PICTURES/Private Collection/Bridgeman Images

△ A slave coffle on the march toward newly settled states of the Southwest.

own pregnancy, either by avoiding it or by seeking it as a way to improve their physical conditions.

Many individual slaves attempted to escape to the North, and some received assistance from the loose network known as the Underground Railroad (see "The Underground Railroad," Section 12-7d). But it was more common for slaves to escape temporarily to hide in the woods. Approximately 80 percent of fugitive slaves were male; women simply could not flee as readily because of their responsibility for children. Fear, disgruntlement over treatment, or family separation might motivate slaves to risk all in flight. Only a minority of those who tried such escapes ever made it to freedom in the North or Canada, but these fugitives made slavery a very insecure institution by the 1850s.

American slavery also produced some fearless revolutionaries. Gabriel's Rebellion involved as many as a thousand slaves when it was discovered in 1800, just before it would have exploded in Richmond, Virginia (see "Gabriel's Rebellion," Section 7-8b). According to controversial court testimony, a similar conspiracy existed in Charleston in 1822, led by a free black named Denmark Vesey. Born a slave in the Caribbean, Vesey won a lottery of $1,500 in 1799, bought his own freedom, and became a religious leader in the black community. According to one long-argued interpretation, Vesey was a heroic revolutionary

Nat Turner A slave who led a bloody rebellion in Southampton County, Virginia, in 1831.

determined to free his people or die trying. But in a recent challenge, historian Michael Johnson points out that the court testimony is the only reliable source on the alleged insurrection. Might the testimony reveal less of reality than of white South Carolina's fears of slave rebellion? The court, says Johnson, built its case on rumors and intimidated witnesses, and "conjured into being" an insurrection that was not about to occur in reality. Whatever the facts, when the arrests and trials were over, thirty-seven "conspirators" were executed, and more than three dozen others were banished from the state.

9-6f Nat Turner's Insurrection

The most famous rebel of all, **Nat Turner**, struck for freedom in Southampton County, Virginia, in 1831. The son of an African woman who passionately hated her enslavement, Nat Turner was a precocious child who learned to read when he was very young. Encouraged by his first owner to study the Bible, he enjoyed certain privileges but also endured hard work and changes of masters. His father successfully escaped to freedom.

Young Nat eventually became a preacher with a reputation for eloquence and mysticism. After nurturing his plan for several years, Turner led a band of rebels from farm to farm in the predawn darkness of August 22, 1831. The group severed limbs and crushed skulls with axes or killed their victims with guns. Before alarmed planters stopped them, Nat Turner and his followers had in forty-eight hours slaughtered sixty whites of both sexes and all ages. The rebellion was soon put down, and in retaliation whites killed slaves at random all over the region, including in adjoining states. Turner was eventually caught and then hanged. As many as two hundred African Americans, including innocent victims of marauding whites, lost their lives as a result of the rebellion.

Nat Turner remains one of the most haunting symbols in America's unresolved history with racial slavery and discrimination. While in jail awaiting execution, Turner was interviewed by a Virginia lawyer and slaveholder, Thomas R. Gray. Their intriguing creation, *The Confessions of Nat Turner*, became a best seller within a month of Turner's hanging. Turner told of his early childhood, his religious visions, his zeal to be free; Gray called the rebel a "gloomy fanatic," but in a manner that made him fascinating and produced one of the most remarkable documents in the annals of American slavery. In the wake of Turner's insurrection, many states passed stiffened legal codes against black education and religious practice.

Most important, in 1832 the state of Virginia, shocked to its core, held a full-scale legislative and public debate over gradual emancipation as a means of ridding itself of slavery and of blacks. The plan debated would not have freed any slaves until 1858, and it provided that eventually all blacks would be colonized outside Virginia. But when the House of Delegates voted, gradual abolition lost, 73 to 58. In the end, Virginia opted to do nothing except reinforce its own moral and economic defenses of slavery. It was the last time white southerners would debate any kind of emancipation until war forced their hand. And the United States itself, in its laws and institutions, fueled by the seemingly permanent, prosperous cotton South, remained a proslavery nation.

Imagining Nat Turner's Rebellion

Below is the title page from *The Confessions of Nat Turner*, by Thomas R. Gray, 1831. This document of nearly twenty pages was published by the lawyer, Gray, who recorded and likely refashioned Turner's lengthy statement during an interview in his jail cell before his execution. *The Confessions* became a widely sold and sensational documentation of Turner's identity and especially his motivations and methods during the rebellion. It portrayed Turner as a religious mystic and fanatic and allowed the broad public to imagine the mind of a religiously motivated slave rebel. Below and to the right is "Horrid Massacre in Virginia," 1831, woodcut. This composite of scenes depicts the slaughter of innocent women and children, as well as white men as both victims and resistants. The fear, confusion, and fierce retribution that dominated the aftermath of the Turner rebellion are on display here.

CRITICAL THINKING

- Why was Nat Turner's insurrection such a shock to the nation as well as to the South?
- What kind of impact did Nat Turner's rebellion have on the South's evolving defense of slavery in the coming decades?

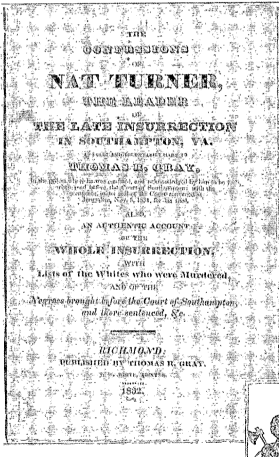

Everett Collection

Bible belonging to Nat Turner (photo)/SMITHSONIAN INSTITUTION/National Museum of African American History & Culture, Smithsonian Institution, USA/Bridgeman Images

The Library of Congress

Reparations for Slavery

How should the United States come to terms with 250 years of racial slavery? Is this period best forgotten as a terrible passage that African Americans as well as the country transcended over time? Or does the nation owe a long-overdue debt to black people for their oppression? In the wake of emancipation in 1865, and rooted in vague federal promises, many former slaves believed they were entitled to "forty acres and a mule," but for most these never materialized.

In 1897, Callie House, a poor mother of four who had been born in 1865 in a contraband camp for ex-slaves, organized the National Ex-Slave Pension and Bounty Association, modeled after the pension system established for soldiers. House traveled all over the South, recruiting 250,000 members at 10-cent dues. Her lobbying of the federal government for slave pensions failed; she was accused of mail fraud and imprisoned for one year in 1916.

More recently, a widespread debate over "reparations" for slavery has emerged. In the rewriting of slavery's history since the 1960s, Americans have learned a great deal about how slave labor created American wealth: how insurance companies insured slaves, how complicit the U.S. government was in slavery's defense and expansion, and how slaves built the U.S. Capitol while their owners received $5 a month for their labor.

The debate is fueled by a wealth of analogies: the reparations paid to Japanese Americans interned during World War II; the reparations paid to many Native American tribes for their stolen land; the reparations paid to thousands of Holocaust survivors and victims of forced labor; and a suit settled in 1999 that will pay an estimated $2 billion to some twenty thousand black farmers for discrimination practiced by the Agriculture Department in the early twentieth century.

On the other side, some argue that, because there are no living former slaves or slaveholders, reparations for slavery can never take the form of money. But in 2002, a lawsuit was filed against three major corporations that allegedly profited from slavery. Some city councils have passed resolutions forcing companies that do business in their jurisdictions to investigate their possible past complicity with slave trading or ownership, which has prompted some banks and other firms to establish scholarship programs for African Americans.

Critics argue that resources would be better spent "making sure black kids have a credible education" and rebuilding inner cities. And some now say that the new Smithsonian Museum of African American History and Culture on the Mall in Washington, DC is, as a living memorial, a kind of reparations. Yet advocates contend that, when "government participates in a crime against humanity," it is "obliged to make the victims whole." The movement for reparations has strong support in grassroots black communities, and the issue has become the subject of broad public debate. The legacy of slavery for a people and a nation is America's most traumatic test of how to reconcile its history with justice.

CRITICAL THINKING

- What are the arguments for and against reparations for slavery?
- If the United States did implement some form of "reparations," would it lead to improved or worsened race relations in the nation?

Summary

During the four decades before the Civil War, the South grew in land, wealth, and power along with the rest of the country. Although the southern states were deeply enmeshed in the nation's heritage and political economy, they also developed as a distinctive region, ideologically and economically, because of slavery. Far more than the North, the antebellum South was a biracial society; whites grew up directly influenced by black folkways and culture; and blacks, the vast majority of whom were slaves, became predominantly native-born Americans and the cobuilders with whites of a rural, agricultural society. From the Old South until modern times, white and black southerners have always shared a tragic mutual history, and many are blood relatives.

With the cotton boom, as well as state and federal policies of Indian Removal, the South grew into a huge slave society. The coercive influence of slavery affected virtually every element of southern life and politics, and increasingly produced a leadership determined to preserve a conservative, hierarchical social and racial order. Despite the white supremacy that united them, the democratic values of yeomen often clashed with the profit motives of aristocratic planters. The benevolent self-image and paternalistic ideology of slaveholders ultimately had to stand the test of the slaves' own judgments. African American slaves responded by fashioning over time a rich, expressive folk culture and a religion of personal and group deliverance. Their experiences could be profoundly different from one region and kind of labor to another. Some blacks were crushed by bondage; many others transcended it in an epic of survival and resistance.

By 1850, through their own wits and on the backs of African labor, white southerners had aggressively built one of the last profitable, expanding slave societies on earth. North of them and deeply intertwined with them in the same nation, economy, constitutional system, and history, a different kind of society had grown even faster—driven by industrialism and free labor. The clash of these two deeply connected—yet mutually fearful and divided—societies would soon explode in political storms over the nation's future.

Suggestions for Further Reading

Ira Berlin, *Generations of Captivity: A History of African American Slaves* (2003)

David Brion Davis, *Inhuman Bondage: The Rise and Fall of Slavery in the New World* (2006)

Erskine Clarke, *Dwelling Place: A Plantation Epic* (2005)

Steven Deyle, *Carry Me Back: The Domestic Slave Trade in American Life* (2005)

Annette Gordon-Reed, *The Hemingses of Monticello: An American Family* (2008)

Charles Joyner, *Down by the Riverside: A South Carolina Slave Community* (1984)

James D. Miller, *South by Southwest: Planter Emigration and Identity in the Slave South* (2002)

James Oakes, *Slavery and Freedom: An Interpretation of the Old South* (1991)

Michael O'Brien, *Conjectures of Order: Intellectual Life and the American South, 1810–1860*, 2 vols. (2004)

Seth Rockman, *Scraping By: Wage Labor, Slavery, and Survival in Early Baltimore* (2009)

Calvin Schermerhorn, *The Business of Slavery and the Rise of American Capitalism, 1815–1860* (2015)

Daniel H. Usner Jr., *American Indians in the Lower Mississippi Valley* (1998)

MindTap® is a fully online personalized learning experience built upon Cengage Learning content. MindTap® combines student learning tools—readings, multimedia, activities, and assessments—into a singular Learning Path that guides students through the course and helps students develop the critical thinking, analysis, and communication skills that are essential to academic and professional success.

The Restless North, 1815–1860

he four children, all under the age of ten, struggled to find their land legs. It was April 17, 1807, and they had spent the last twenty-five days on a stormy voyage from Scotland to New York. Their parents, Mary Ann and James Archbald, had left their ancestral homeland reluctantly, but envisioned a future in which their children would be beholden to no one—neither landlord nor employer. They had set sail in search of the Jeffersonian dream of republican independence.

The Archbalds bought a farm in central New York, along a tributary of the Hudson River, where they raised a large flock of sheep, grew hay and vegetables, skinned rabbits for their meat and fur—and then sold whatever food or fur the family did not need to feed or clothe itself. From the wool shorn by her husband and sons, Mary Ann and her daughters spun thread and wove cloth for their own use and for sale. They used the cash to pay their mortgage. Twenty-one years after leaving Scotland, Mary Ann, in anticipation of making their last payment, declared herself wealthy: "being out of debt is, in my estimation, being rich." By then, though, her sons were young adults and had their own visions of wealth. Theirs centered on water, not land.

Ten years earlier, on April 17, 1817—a decade to the day after the Archbalds had stepped onto American shores—the New York State legislature authorized construction of a canal that would connect Lake Erie to the Hudson River, and surveyors mapped a route that ran through the Archbalds' farm. The sons (one in his early twenties, the other a teenager) helped dig the canal, while Mary Ann and her daughters cooked and cleaned for the twenty Irish laborers whom the sons hired. Bitten by canal fever, the Archbald sons soon tried their hands at commercial speculation, borrowing

◁ Farm families transported their surplus produce and handicrafts to local marketplaces, where merchants purchased them for resale. American Scenes: Preparing for Market, published by N. Currier, 1856 (colour litho), Maurer, Louis (1832--1932) (after)/Private Collection/Peter Newark American Pictures/The Bridgeman Art Library

Chronology

1790s–1840s	Second Great Awakening
1820s	Model penitentiaries established
1820s–1840s	Utopian communities founded
1824	*Gibbons v. Ogden* prohibits steamboat monopolies
1825	Erie Canal completed
1826	American Society for Promotion of Temperance founded
1827	Construction begins on Baltimore and Ohio (B&O) Railroad
1830	First locomotive runs on B&O Railroad
	Joseph Smith organizes Mormon Church
1830s	Penny press emerges
1830s–1850s	Urban riots commonplace
1833	American Antislavery Society founded
1834	Women workers strike at Lowell
1837–42	Croton Aqueduct constructed
1839–43	Hard times spread unemployment and deflation
1840	Split in abolitionist movement; Liberty Party founded
1840s	Female mill workers' publications appear
1844	Federal government sponsors first telegraph line
	Lowell Female Reform Association formed
1845	Massive Irish immigration begins
1846	Smithsonian Institute founded
1848	American Association for the Advancement of Science established
1850s	Free-labor ideology spreads

money to buy wheat and lumber in western New York with the idea of reselling it at substantial profits to merchants in Albany and New York City. This was not the future Mary Ann had envisioned for her sons, and their ventures distressed, but did not surprise, her. As early as 1808, she had reached an unpleasant conclusion about her new home: "We are a nation of traders in spite of all Mr. Jefferson can say or do."

The United States may have already been a "nation of traders" as early as 1808, but in the years after the War of 1812, the market economy took off in ways few could have anticipated when the Archbald family decided to seek its independence in America. In the North, steamboats, canals, and then railroads remapped the young republic's geography and economy, setting off booms in westward migration, industry, commerce, and urban growth, and fueling optimism among commercially minded Americans.

Experience an interactive version of this story in MindTap®.

Although the transportation revolution would foster commercial exchange, technology alone could not make it happen. Even after the War of 1812, the United States' financial connections to Europe, particularly Britain, remained profound. When Europeans suffered hard times, so, too, did American merchants, manufacturers, farmers, workers—and their families. Particularly for those Americans who relied on wages for their livelihood, economic downturns often meant unemployment and destitution.

Economic downswings could shake even the most commercially committed northerners, as could other consequences of the economy's rapid expansion in the years after the War of 1812. Market expansion, some worried, threatened the nation's moral fiber if not properly controlled. It upset traditional patterns of family organization, and it relied heavily on unskilled workers—many of whom were immigrants and free African Americans—who at best seemed unfit for republican citizenship and at worst seemed threatening. The burgeoning cities spawned by market expansion seemed to bear out Thomas Jefferson's opinion that they were "pestilential to the morals, the health and the liberties of man." Like Jefferson, who also acknowledged that cities nourished the arts, commercially minded Americans could see cities as both exemplars of civilization and breeding grounds of depravity and conflict.

Anxious about the era's rapid changes, many Americans turned to evangelical religion, which in turn launched many of the era's myriad reform movements. Believing in the notion of human perfectibility, reformers worked to free individuals and society from sin. In the Northeast and Midwest, in particular, women and men organized to end the abuses of prostitution and alcohol, to improve conditions in prisons and asylums, and to establish public schools. Some embraced science as fervently as religion. Other reformers, instead of trying to fix society, established separate experimental communities that might model a new form of social relations. Opponents of slavery, meanwhile, worked within the existing system but sought to radically alter Americans' premises about the practical implications of the revolutionary declaration that "all men are created equal."

Only by maintaining a strong faith in improvement, progress, and upward mobility could these Americans remain hopeful that the nation's greatness lay with commercial expansion. They did so in part by articulating a free-labor ideology that at once rationalized the negative aspects of market expansion while promoting the northern labor system as superior to the South's.

▨ *What factors contributed to the commercialization of northern society, and why did they have less of an influence on the South?*

▨ *How did the daily lives—work, family, leisure—of northerners (rural and urban) change between 1815 and 1860?*

▨ *In what ways did reformers try to preserve existing American ideals, and in what ways did they try to change them?*

10-1 Or Was the North Distinctive?

▷ **What developments contributed to the divergence between the North and the South after the War of 1812?**

Historian James McPherson has proposed a new twist to the old question of southern distinctiveness: perhaps it was the *North*—New England, the Middle Atlantic, and the Old Northwest—that diverged from the norm. At the republic's birth, the North and South had much in common, with some similarities persisting for decades: slavery, religious heritage, an overwhelming proportion of the population engaged in agricultural pursuits, a small urban population. As late as the War of 1812, the regions were more similar than dissimilar. But all that started to change

with postwar economic development. Although often couched in nationalist terms, such development was undertaken mostly by state and local governments as well as private entrepreneurs, and it took place much more extensively and rapidly in the North. As the North embraced economic progress, it—rather than the South—diverged from the international norm. The North, writes McPherson, "hurtled forward eagerly toward a future that many Southerners found distasteful if not frightening." With its continual quest for improvement, the North—much more so than the South—embodied what Frenchman Alexis de Tocqueville, who toured the United States in 1831–1832, called the nation's "restless spirit."

While the South expanded as a slave society, the North changed rapidly and profoundly. It transformed, as one historian has put it, from a society with markets to a market society. In the colonial era, settlers lived in a society with markets, one in which they engaged in long-distance trade—selling their surpluses to merchants, who in turn sent raw materials to Europe, using the proceeds to purchase finished goods for resale—but in which most settlers remained self-sufficient. During and after the War of 1812, the North became more solidly a market society, one in which participation in long-distance commerce fundamentally altered individuals' aspirations and activities. With European trade largely halted during the war, entrepreneurs invested in domestic factories, setting off a series of changes in the organization of daily life. More men, women, and children began working for others in exchange for wages—rather than for themselves on a family farm—making the domestic demand for foodstuffs soar. The result was a transformation of agriculture itself. Farming became commercialized, with individual farmers abandoning self-sufficiency and specializing instead in crops that would yield cash on the market. With the cash that farmers earned when things went well, they now bought goods they had once made for themselves, such as cloth, candles, and soap as well as some luxuries. Unlike the typical southern yeoman, they were not self-reliant, and isolation was rare. In the North, market expansion altered, sometimes dramatically, virtually every aspect of life. Some historians see these rapid and pervasive changes as a market revolution.

10-2 The Transportation Revolution

▷ **What were the limitations of transportation methods prior to the War of 1812?**

▷ **How did transportation innovations developed after the War of 1812 shape American society?**

▷ **What regional connections were created because of transportation developments?**

To market goods at substantial distances from where they were produced, Americans needed internal improvements. Before the War of 1812, natural waterways provided the most readily available and cheapest transportation routes for people and goods, but with many limitations. Boatmen poled bateaux (cargo boats) down shallow rivers or floated flatboats down deep ones. Cargo generally moved downstream only, and most boats were broken up for lumber once they reached their destination. On portions of a few rivers, including the Mississippi and the Hudson, sailing ships could tack upstream under certain wind conditions, but upstream commerce was very limited.

10-2a Roads

Overland transport was limited, too. Roads, constructed during the colonial and revolutionary eras, often became obstructed by fallen trees, soaked by mud, or clouded in dust. To reduce mud and dust, turnpike companies built "corduroy" roads, whose tightly lined-up logs resembled ribbed cotton fabric. But the continual jolts caused nausea among passengers and discouraged merchants from shipping fragile wares. Land transportation was slow and expensive, demanding a good deal of human and animal power. In 1800, according to a report commissioned by the federal government, it cost as much to ship a ton of goods thirty miles into the country's interior as to ship the same goods from New York to England. The lack of cheap, quick transportation impeded westward expansion as well as industrial growth. When the Archbald family decided against moving to Ohio in 1810, Mary Ann Archbald explained, "It is at a great distance from markets."

After the American Revolution, some northern states chartered private stock companies to build turnpikes. These toll roads expanded commercial possibilities in southern New England and the Middle Atlantic, but during the War of 1812 the nation's paucity of roads in its more northerly and southerly reaches impeded the movement of troops and supplies, prompting renewed interest—in the name of defense—in building roads. Aside from the National Road (see "Early Internal Improvements," Section 8-6b), the financing fell on states and private investors, and generally the enthusiasm for building turnpikes greatly outpaced the money and manpower expended. Turnpike companies sometimes adopted improvements, such as laying hard surfaces made of crushed stone and gravel, but many of the newly built roads suffered from old problems. An urgent need arose not just for more, but also for better transportation.

10-2b Steamboats

The first major innovation was the steamboat. In 1807, Robert Fulton's *Clermont* traveled between New York and Albany on the Hudson River in thirty-two hours, demonstrating the feasibility of using steam engines to power boats. After the Supreme Court's ruling against steamboat monopolies in *Gibbons v. Ogden* (1824), steamboat companies flourished on eastern rivers and, to a lesser extent, on the Great Lakes. These boats carried more passengers than freight, transporting settlers to the Midwest, where they would grow grain and raise pigs that fed northeastern factory workers. Along western rivers like the Mississippi and the Ohio, steamboats played a more direct commercial role, carrying midwestern timber and grain and southern cotton to New Orleans,

Erie Canal Major canal that linked the Great Lakes to New York City, opening the upper Midwest to wider development.

where they were transferred to oceangoing vessels destined for northern and international ports. In the 1850s, steamboats began plying rivers as far west as California and Washington Territory. Privately owned and operated, steamboats became subject to federal regulations after frequent and deadly accidents in which boilers exploded, fires ignited, and boats collided.

To travel between Ohio and New Orleans by flatboat in 1815 took several months; in 1840, the same trip by steamboat took just ten days. But the steamboat did not supplant the flatboat. Rather, the number of flatboats traveling downstream to New Orleans more than doubled between 1816 and 1846. Now that flatboat crews could return upstream by steamboat rather than by foot, the greatest investment in flatboat travel—time—had been greatly reduced.

10-2c Canals

In the late eighteenth and early nineteenth centuries, private companies (sometimes with state subsidies) built small canals to transport goods and produce to and from interior locations previously accessible only by difficult-to-navigate rivers or by poorly maintained roads. These projects rarely reaped substantial profits, discouraging investment in other projects. In 1815, only three canals in the United States measured more than 2 miles long; the longest was 27 miles. After Madison's veto of the Bonus Bill (see "Sectionalism and Nationalism," Section 8-6) dashed commercially minded New Yorkers' hopes for a canal connecting Lake Erie to the port of New York, Governor DeWitt Clinton pushed for a state-sponsored initiative. What later became known as the **Erie Canal** was to run 363 miles between Buffalo and Albany, and was to be four feet deep. Skeptics derided it as "Clinton's Big Ditch."

But the optimists prevailed. Construction began—amid much symbolism and fanfare—on July 4, 1817. The canal, its promoters emphasized, would help fulfill the nation's revolutionary promise by demonstrating how American ingenuity and hard work could overcome any obstacle, including imposing natural ones, such as the combined ascent and descent of 680 feet between Buffalo and Albany. By so doing, it would help unify the nation and secure its commercial independence from Europe.

Over the next eight years, nearly nine thousand laborers felled forests, shoveled and piled dirt, picked at tree roots, blasted rock, heaved and hauled boulders, rechanneled streams, and molded the canal bed. Stonemasons and carpenters built aqueducts and locks. The work was dangerous, sometimes fatal, with workers succumbing to malaria, rattlesnake bites, gunpowder explosions, falls, and asphyxiation from collapsed canal beds.

The canal's promoters celebrated the waterway as the work of "republican free men," but few canal workers would have perceived their construction work as fulfilling Jefferson's notion of republican freedom. Unskilled laborers—including many immigrants and some convicts—greatly outnumbered artisans. Once completed, the Erie Canal relied on child labor: Boys led the horses who pulled the canal boats between the canal's eighty-three locks, while girls cooked and cleaned on the boats. When the canal froze shut in winter, many canal workers found themselves destitute, with neither employment nor shelter.

Once completed in 1825, the Erie Canal proved immediately successful. Horse-drawn boats, stacked with bushels of wheat, barrels of oats, and piles of logs, streamed eastward from Lake Erie and western New York. Tens of thousands of passengers—forty thousand in 1825 alone—traveled the waterway each year. The canal shortened the journey between Buffalo and New York City from twenty days to six and reduced freight charges by nearly 95 percent—thus securing New York City's position as the nation's preeminent port. Other states rushed to construct canals, and by 1840 canals crisscrossed the Northeast and Midwest, with mileage totaling 3,300. Southern states, with many easily navigable rivers, dug fewer canals. None of the new canals, North or South, enjoyed the Erie's financial success. As the high cost of construction combined with an economic contraction, investment slumped in the 1830s. Several midwestern states could not repay their canal loans, leading them to bankruptcy or near-bankruptcy. By midcentury, more miles were abandoned than built. The canal era had ended, though the Erie Canal (by then twice enlarged and rerouted) continued to prosper, remaining in commercial operation until the late twentieth century and even undergoing a minor resurgence today.

10-2d Railroads

The future belonged to railroads. Trains moved faster than canal boats and operated year-round. Railroads did not need to be built near natural sources of water, allowing them to connect remote locations to national and international markets. By 1860, the United States had 60,000 miles of track, most of it in the North. Railroads dramatically reduced the cost and the time involved in shipping goods, and excited the popular imagination.

The railroad era in the United States began in 1830 when Peter Cooper's locomotive, Tom Thumb, first steamed along 13 miles of Baltimore and Ohio Railroad track. In 1833, the nation's second railroad ran 136 miles from Charleston to Hamburg in South Carolina. Not until the 1850s, though, did railroads offer long-distance service at reasonable rates. Even then, the lack of a common standard for the width of track thwarted development of a national system. Pennsylvania and Ohio railroads, for example, had no fewer than seven different track widths. A journey from Philadelphia to Charleston involved eight different gauges, requiring passengers and freight to change trains seven times. Only at Bowling Green, Kentucky, did northern and southern railroads connect to one another. Although northerners and southerners alike raced to construct internal improvements, the nation's canals and railroads did little to unite the regions and promote nationalism, as the earliest proponents of government-sponsored internal improvements had hoped.

Northern governments and investors spent substantially more on internal improvements than did southerners.

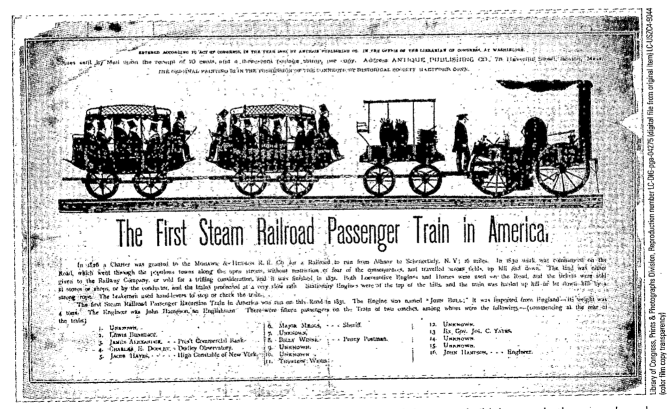

△ Railroads, introduced in the 1830s, soon surpassed canals. Easier, quicker, and cheaper to build than canals, they moved goods and people faster. The Mohawk & Hudson, pictured here, offered competition to the slower Erie Canal boats, yet its passenger cars (on the left) were styled after an even older technology: the stagecoach.

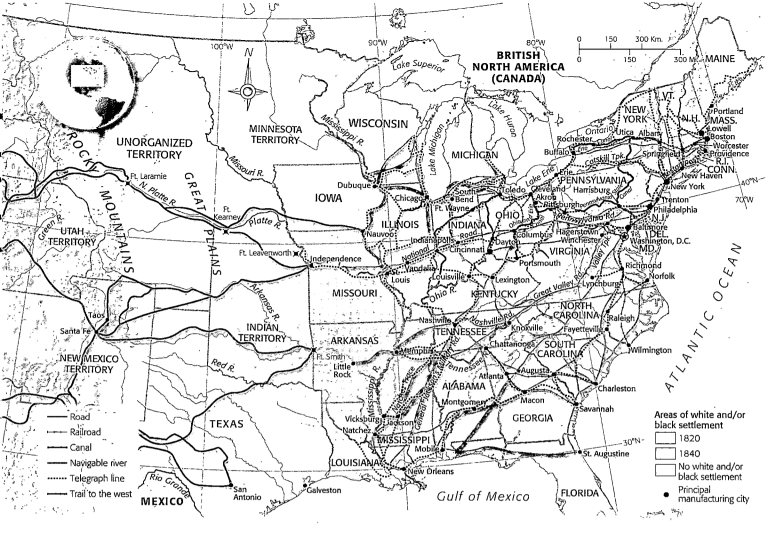

Map 10.1 Major Roads, Canals, and Railroads, 1850

A transportation network linked the seaboard to the interior. Settlers followed those routes westward, and they sent back grain, grain products, and cotton to the port cities.

Pennsylvania and New York together accounted for half of all state monies invested. Southern states did invest in railroads, but—with smaller free populations—they collected fewer taxes, leaving them with less to spend.

The North and South laid roughly the same amount of railroad track per person before the Civil War, but when measured in terms of overall mileage, the more populous North had a web of tracks that stretched considerably farther, forming an integrated system of local lines branching off major trunk lines. In the South, railroads remained local in nature, leaving southern travelers to patch together trips on railroads, stagecoaches, and boats. Neither people nor goods moved easily across the South, unless they traveled via steamboat or flatboat along the Mississippi River system—and even then, flooded banks disrupted passage for weeks at a time.

10-2e Regional Connections

Unlike southern investments in river improvements and steamboats, which disproportionately benefited planters whose lands bordered the region's riverbanks, the North's frenzy of canal and railroad building expanded transportation networks far into the hinterlands, proving not only more democratic but also more unifying. In 1815, nearly all the produce from the Old Northwest floated down the Mississippi to New Orleans, tying that region's fortunes to the South. By the 1850s, though, canals and railroads had strengthened the economic, cultural, and political links between the Old Northwest—particularly the more densely populated northern regions—and the Northeast (see Map 10.1).

Internal improvements hastened the population's westward migration. They eased the journey itself while also making western settlement more appealing by providing easy access to eastern markets and familiar comforts. News, visitors, and luxuries now traveled regularly to previously remote areas of the Northeast and Midwest. Delighted that the Erie Canal brought fresh seafood to central New York, hundreds of miles from the sea, Mary Archbald explained that "distance ... is reduced to nothing here."

Samuel F. B. Morse's invention of the telegraph in 1844 made the compression of distance and time even starker. News traveled almost instantaneously along telegraph wires. By 1852, the nation had more than 23,000 miles of telegraph lines, which enabled the birth of modern business practices involving the coordination of market conditions, production, and supply across great distances. Together, internal improvements and the telegraph allowed people in previously isolated areas to proclaim themselves—as did one western New Yorker—a "citizen of the world."

10-2f Ambivalence Toward Progress

Many northerners hailed internal improvements as symbols of progress. Northerners proclaimed that, by building canals and railroads, they had completed God's design for the North American continent. On a more practical level, canals and railroads allowed them to seek opportunities in the West.

But people who welcomed such opportunities could find much to lament. Mary Ann Archbald savored her fresh seafood dinners but regretted that her sons turned to speculation. Others decried the enormous numbers of Irish canal diggers and railroad track layers, whom they deemed depraved and inherently inferior. Still others worried that, by promoting urban growth, transportation innovations fostered social ills.

The degradation of the natural world proved worrisome, too. When streams were rerouted, swamps drained, and forests felled, natural habitats were disturbed, even ruined. Humans soon felt the consequences. Deprived of waterpower, mills no longer ran. Without forests to sustain them, wild animals—on which many rural people (Native American and European American) had relied for protein—sought homes elsewhere. Fishermen, too, found their sources of protein (and cash) dried up when natural waterways were dammed or rerouted to feed canals. If many northerners embraced progress, they also regretted its costs.

10-3 Factories and Industrialization

▶ How did the experience of work change with industrialization?

▶ What patterns of work and living were established in textile mills?

▶ How did factory workers seek to improve their workplace conditions and wages?

By dramatically lowering transportation costs, internal improvements made possible the Northeast's rapid manufacturing and commercial expansion. After canals and railroads opened the trans-Appalachian West for wide-scale settlement, western farmers supplied raw materials and foodstuffs for northeastern factories and their workers. They also created a larger domestic market for goods manufactured in the Northeast. With most of their time devoted to cultivating their land, western settlers preferred to buy rather than make cloth, shoes, and other goods.

10-3a Factory Work

In many industries, daily life changed dramatically. Much early industrialization involved processing raw materials—milling flour, turning hogs into packaged meat, sawing lumber—

and the pork-packing industry illustrates strikingly how specialization turned skilled craftsmen into laborers. Traditionally, each butcher carved an entire pig. Under the new industrial organization, each worker performed a particular task—such as cutting off the right front leg or scooping out the entrails—as the pig traveled down a "disassembly line."

Factory work, with its impersonal and regimented nature, contrasted sharply with the informal atmosphere of artisan shops and farm households. The bell, the steam whistle, or the clock governed work. In large factories, laborers never saw owners, working instead under paid supervisors, nor did they see the final product of their labor. Factory workers lost their sense of autonomy in the face of impersonal market forces. Competition from cheaper, less-skilled workers—particularly after European immigration soared in the 1840s—created job insecurity and few opportunities for advancement.

Machinery made mass production possible. Although initially Americans imported or copied British machines, they soon built their own. The **American System of Manufacturing**, as the British called it, produced interchangeable parts that did not require individual adjustment to fit. Eli Whitney, the cotton gin's inventor, promoted the idea of interchangeable parts in 1798, when he contracted with the federal government to make ten thousand rifles in twenty-eight months. In the 1820s, the United States Ordnance Department contracted with private firms to introduce machine-made interchangeable parts for firearms. The American System quickly produced the machine-tool industry—the manufacture of machines for the purpose of mass production. The new system permitted large-scale production at low costs, with items such as Waltham watches becoming inexpensive but high-quality household items.

10-3b Textile Mills

Mechanization was most dramatic in textiles, with production centered in New England, near water sources to power spinning machines and looms. After 1815, New England's rudimentary cotton mills developed into modern factories with mass-produced goods. Cotton cloth production rose from 4 million yards in 1817 to 323 million in 1840. Mechanization did not make workers obsolete; rather, it demanded more workers to monitor the machines. In the mid-1840s, the cotton mills employed approximately eighty thousand "operatives," more than half of them women. Mill owners employed a resident manager, thus separating ownership from management.

With labor scarce near the mills, managers recruited New England farm daughters, whom they paid wages and housed in dormitories and boardinghouses in what became known as the **Waltham** or **Lowell** plan of industrialization. People

American System of Manufacturing System of manufacturing that used interchangeable parts.

Waltham, Lowell Sites of early textile mills in New England, which were precursors to modern factories. Nearly 80 percent of the workers in Waltham, Lowell, and similar mills were young, unmarried women who sought economic opportunities and social independence in the mill towns.

Internal Improvements

On July 4, 1827, ninety-one-year-old Charles Carroll, the only surviving signer of the Declaration of Independence, shoveled the first spadeful of earth on the Baltimore and Ohio Railroad, the nation's first westward railroad. "I consider this moment the most important act of my life," he declared, "second only to my signing the Declaration of Independence, if even it be second to that." Internal improvements, he and many others believed, would cement the United States' economic independence by supplying the nation's growing industrial centers with food and raw materials, while transporting manufactured goods back to its far-flung rural population.

Although boosters championed the era's canals and railroads as the triumph of American republicanism, such transportation projects often depended on technology, funding, and labor from abroad. American engineers scrutinized canals and, later,

railroads in France, the Low Countries, and particularly England; one Erie Canal engineer spent nearly two years walking 2,000 miles alongside British canals. Railroad companies purchased locomotives from English manufacturers. Foreign investors, meanwhile, financed significant portions of projects heralded as symbols of American independence. In addition to borrowing know-how and money from abroad, Americans looked overseas for people to build their canals and railroads. Thousands of immigrants, mostly from Ireland, worked sunup to sundown blasting boulders, draining. malaria-filled swamps, picking at roots and rocks, and heaving dirt. After the Civil War, Chinese immigrants performed similarly arduous and dangerous tasks on the transcontinental railroad.

When completed, internal improvements allowed people, raw materials, and goods to move inexpensively and quickly across the continent, spurring the young nation's

growth—but also strengthening its ties to Europe. Eastward from the American heartland came cotton and grain, much of which was transferred to oceangoing vessels. The cotton fed European textile mills; the grain fed their workers. Thus, whenever economic conditions constricted in Europe, slowing textile production and leaving workers with smaller incomes with which to purchase food, reverberations could be felt on cotton and wheat farms across America.

Canals and railroads, hailed as great symbols of American independence, linked American farmers to an increasingly complex and volatile international economy.

CRITICAL THINKING

◻ At mid-century, the United States, particularly the northern part, was undergoing tremendous change in terms of transportation and industrialization. What domestic and international forces drove these changes?

Erie Canal, NY, 1831 (graphite, w/c and gouache on paper), Hill, John William (1812-79) / © Collection of the New-York Historical Society, USA / The Bridgeman Art Library

△ Workers repair a section of the Erie Canal, near Little Falls, in 1831. While hailed as a great achievement of human progress, the canal required frequent repairs, frustrating travelers, merchants, boat workers, and people living along its banks.

who made their living from farming often harbored suspicions of those who did not—particularly in the young United States, where an agrarian lifestyle was often associated with virtue itself—so some rural parents resisted sending their daughters to textile mills. To ease such concerns, mill managers offered paternalistic oversight; they enforced curfews, prohibited alcohol, and required church attendance.

Despite its restrictions, the Waltham system offered farm girls opportunities to socialize and to earn wages, which they used to help their families buy land or send a brother to college, to save for their own dowries or education, or to spend on personal items, such as fashionable clothing. Workers wrote literary pieces for the owner-subsidized *Lowell Offering* and attended educational lectures in the evenings. Still, most women imagined factory work as temporary, and factory conditions—the power looms' deafening roar, the long hours, the regimentation—made few change their minds. The average girl arrived at sixteen and stayed five years, usually leaving to get married, often to men they met in town rather than to farm boys at home.

Although the Waltham plan drew international attention for its novelty, more common was the Rhode Island (or Fall River) plan employed by Samuel Slater, among others. Mills hired entire families, lodging them in boardinghouses. Men often worked farm plots near the factories while their

△ Published between 1840 and 1845, the *Lowell Offering* showcased women mill workers' essays, stories, and letters.

wives and children worked in the mills, though as the system developed, men increasingly worked in the factories full time, directly supervising the labor of their wives and children in small, family-based work units.

10-3c Labor Protests

Mill life grew more difficult, especially during the depression of 1837 to 1843, when demand for cloth declined, causing most mills to run part time. To increase productivity, managers sped up machines and required each worker to operate more machines. In the race for profits, owners lengthened hours, cut wages, tightened discipline, and packed the boardinghouses.

Workers organized, accusing their bosses of treating them like wage slaves. In 1834, in reaction to a 25 percent wage cut, they unsuccessfully "turned out" (struck) against the Lowell mills. Two years later, when boardinghouse fees increased, they again turned out, unsuccessfully. With conditions worsening and strikes failing, workers resisted in new ways. In 1844, Massachusetts mill women formed the Lowell Female Reform Association and joined other workers in pressing, unsuccessfully, for state legislation mandating a ten-hour day—as opposed to the fourteen-hour days that some workers endured.

Women aired their complaints in worker-run newspapers: in 1842, the *Factory Girl* appeared in New Hampshire, the *Wampanoag, and Operatives' Journal* in Massachusetts. Two years later, mill workers founded the *Factory Girl's Garland* and the *Voice of Industry*, nicknamed "the factory girl's voice." Even the *Lowell Offering*, the owner-sponsored paper that was the pride of mill workers and managers alike, became embroiled in controversy when workers charged its editors with suppressing articles criticizing working conditions.

Worker turnover weakened organizational efforts. Few militant native-born mill workers stayed to fight the managers and owners, and gradually, fewer New England daughters entered the mills. In the 1850s, Irish immigrant women replaced them. Technological improvements made the work less skilled, enabling mills to hire inexperienced, lower-paid laborers. Male workers, too, protested changes wrought by the **market economy** and factories. But, unlike women, they could vote. Labor political parties first formed in Pennsylvania, New York, and Massachusetts in the 1820s, and then spread elsewhere; they advocated free public education and an end to imprisonment for debt, and opposed banks and monopolies. Some advocated free homesteads, a reminder that most early industrial workers still aspired to land ownership.

10-3d Labor Unions

The courts provided organized labor's greatest victory: protection from conspiracy laws. When journeyman shoemakers organized during the century's first decade, their employers accused them of criminal conspiracy. The cordwainers' (shoemakers') cases between 1806 and 1815 left labor organizations in an

market economy Newly developing commercial economy that depended on the long-distance exchange of goods and crops produced for sale rather than for personal consumption.

uncertain position. Although the courts acknowledged the journeymen's right to organize, judges viewed strikes as illegal until a Massachusetts case, **Commonwealth v. Hunt** (1842), ruled that Boston journeyman bootmakers could strike "in such manner as best to subserve their own interests," in the words of the state's chief justice Lemuel Shaw. Although the ruling applied to Massachusetts only, Shaw's national eminence extended the ruling's influence beyond the state's boundaries.

The first unions represented journeymen in printing, woodworking, shoemaking, and tailoring. Locally organized, they resembled medieval guilds, with members seeking protection against competition from inferior workmen by regulating apprenticeships and establishing minimum wages. Umbrella organizations composed of individual craft unions, like the National Trades' Union (1834), arose in several cities in the 1820s and 1830s. But the movement disintegrated amid wage reductions and unemployment in the hard times of 1839–1843.

Permanent labor organizations were difficult to sustain. Skilled craftsmen disdained less-skilled workers. Moreover, workers divided along ethnic, religious, racial, and gender lines.

10-4 Consumption and Commercialization

▶ What factors contributed to the emergence and development of the ready-made clothing industry in the first half of the nineteenth century?

▶ How did agricultural production and work change in the first half of the nineteenth century?

▶ What were the social and economic consequences of the emergence of commercial production?

By producing inexpensive cloth, New England mills spawned the ready-made clothing industry. Before the 1820s, women sewed most clothing at home, and some people purchased used clothing. Tailors and seamstresses made wealthy men's and women's clothing to order. By the 1820s and 1830s, much clothing was mass-produced for sale in retail clothing stores. The process often involved little more than the reorganization of work; tailors no longer performed every task involved in making an article of clothing, from measuring to finishing work. Standard sizes replaced measuring, and a division of labor took hold: one worker cut patterns all day, another sewed hems, another affixed buttons, still another attached collars. The sewing machine, invented in 1846 and widely available in the 1850s, accelerated the process. Although many farm families still made their own clothing, they bought clothes when they could afford to do so, freeing time for raising both crops and children.

Commonwealth v. Hunt An 1842 court case in which the Massachusetts Supreme Judicial Court ruled that labor unions were not illegal monopolies that restrained trade.

10-4a The Garment Industry

Market expansion created a demand for mass-produced clothing. Girls who left farms for factories no longer had time to sew clothes. Young immigrant men—often separated by thousands of miles from mothers and sisters—bought the crudely made, loose-fitting clothing. But the biggest market for ready-made clothes, at least initially, was in the cotton South. With the textile industry's success driving up the demand and price for raw cotton, planters bought ready-made shoes and clothes for slaves, in whose hands they would rather place a hoe than a needle and thread. Doing so made good economic sense.

Retailers often bought goods wholesale, though many manufactured shirts and trousers in their own factories. Lewis and Hanford of New York City boasted of cutting more than 100,000 garments in the winter of 1848–1849. The New York firm did business mostly in the South and owned a retail outlet in New Orleans. Paul Tulane, a New Orleans competitor, owned a New York factory that made goods for his Louisiana store. In the Midwest, Cincinnati became the center of the men's clothing industry. Nationally, though, New York remained the garment industry's capital.

The garment industry often took the form of what some historians call metropolitan industrialization, a form relying not on mechanization but on reorganization of labor, similar to the earlier putting-out system. Much production of ready-made clothing, for example, took place in tenements throughout New York City, where women spent hour after hour sewing on buttons for a piece of ready-made clothing, while others sewed hem after hem. In 1860, more than 16,000 women worked in New York's garment industry.

10-4b Specialization of Commerce

Commerce expanded with manufacturing. Commercial specialization transformed some traders in big cities, especially New York, into virtual merchant princes. After the Erie Canal opened, New York City became a stop on every major trade route from Europe, southern ports, and the West. New York traders were the intermediaries for southern cotton and western grain. Merchants in other cities played a similar role. Traders in turn sometimes invested their profits in factories, further stimulating urban manufacturing. Some cities specialized: Rochester became a milling center ("The Flour City"), and Cincinnati ("Porkopolis") became the first meatpacking center.

Merchants who engaged in complex commercial transactions required large office staffs, mostly all male. At the bottom of the hierarchy were messenger boys, often preteens, who delivered documents. Above them were copyists, who handcopied documents. Clerks processed documents and shipping papers and did translations. Above them were the bookkeeper and the confidential chief clerk. Those seeking employment in such an office, called a countinghouse, often studied under a writing master to acquire a "good hand." Most hoped to become partners, but their chances of success grew increasingly slim.

Commerce specialized more quickly in cities than in small towns, where merchants continued to exchange goods with local farm women—trading flour or pots and pans for eggs and other produce. Local craftsmen continued to sell their own finished goods, such as shoes and clothing. In some

△ Although many women in New York's garment industry worked in their tenements, others labored in factories, where regimentation and close supervision characterized the work day.

rural areas, particularly newly settled ones, peddlers acted as general merchants. But as transportation improved and towns grew, small-town merchants increasingly specialized.

10-4c Commercial Farming

Even amid the manufacturing and commercial booms, agriculture remained the northern economy's backbone. But the **transportation revolution** and market expansion transformed formerly semisubsistence farms into commercial enterprises, with families abandoning mixed agriculture for specialization in cash crops. By the 1820s, eastern farmers had cultivated nearly all the available land, and their small farms, often with uneven terrains, were ill suited for the labor-saving farm implements introduced in the 1830s, such as mechanical sowers, reapers, and threshers. Many northern farmers thus either moved west or quit farming for jobs in merchants' houses and factories.

Those farmers who remained, however, proved as adaptable on the farm as were their children working at water-powered looms or in countinghouses. In 1820, about one-third of all northern produce was intended for the market, but by 1850 the amount surpassed 50 percent. As farmers shifted toward specialization and market-oriented production, they often invested in additional land (buying the farms of neighbors who moved west), new farming equipment (such as improved

iron and steel plows), and new sources of labor (hired hands). Many New England and Middle Atlantic farm families faced steep competition from midwestern farmers after the opening of the Erie Canal, and began abandoning wheat and corn production. Instead, they raised livestock, especially cattle, and specialized in vegetable and fruit production. Much of what they produced ended up in the stomachs of the North's rapidly growing urban and manufacturing populations.

Farmers financed innovations through land sales and debts. Indeed, increasing land values, not the sale of agricultural products, promised the greatest profit. Farm families who owned their own land flourished, but it became harder to take up farming in the first place. The number of tenant farmers and hired hands increased, providing labor to drive commercial expansion. Farmers who had previously employed unpaid family members and enslaved workers now leased portions of their farms or hired paid labor to raise their livestock and crops.

10-4d Farm Women's Changing Labor

As the commercial economy expanded, rural women assumed additional responsibilities, increasing

transportation revolution
Innovations in the movement of people and goods—via canals, steamships, and railroads—that greatly increased the speed of travel even as they greatly decreased its cost.

their already substantial farm and domestic work. Some did outwork (see "Putting-Out and Early Factories," Section 8-5c). Many increased their production of eggs, dairy products, and garden produce for sale; others raised bees or silkworms.

With the New England textile mills producing more and more finished cloth, farm women and children often abandoned time-consuming spinning and weaving, bought factory-produced cloth, and dedicated the saved time to producing larger quantities of marketable products, such as butter and cheese. Some mixed-agriculture farms converted entirely to dairy production, with men taking over formerly female tasks. Canals and railroads carried cheese to eastern ports, where wholesalers sold it around the world, shipping it to California, England, and China. In 1844, Britain imported more than 5 million pounds of cheese from the United States.

10-4e Rural Communities

Although agricultural journals and societies exhorted farmers to manage their farms like time-efficient businesses, not all farmers abandoned the old practices of gathering at market, general stores, taverns, and church. They did not forgo barn raisings and husking bees, but by the 1830s there were fewer young people at such events to dance and flirt. Many young women had left for textile mills, and young men often worked as clerks or factory hands. Those who stayed behind were more likely to come dressed in store-bought clothing and to consume pies made with store-bought flour.

Even as they continued to swap labor and socialize with neighbors, farmers became more likely to reckon debts in dollars. They kept tighter accounts and watched national and international markets more closely. When financial panics hit, cash shortages almost halted business activity, casting many farmers further into debt, sometimes to the point of bankruptcy. Faced with the possibility of losing their land, farmers did what many would have considered unthinkable before: they called in debts with their neighbors, sometimes causing fissures in long-established relationships.

10-4f Cycles of Boom and Bust

The market economy's expansion led to cycles of boom and bust. Prosperity stimulated demand for finished goods, such as clothing and furniture. Increased demand in turn led not only to higher prices and still higher production, but also, because of business optimism and expectations of higher prices, to land speculation. Investment money was plentiful as Americans saved and foreign, mostly British, investors bought U.S. bonds and securities. Then production surpassed demand, causing prices and wages to fall; in response, land and stock values collapsed, and investment money flowed out of the United States. This boom-and-bust cycle influenced the entire country, but particularly the Northeast, where even the smallest localities became enmeshed in regional and national markets.

Panic of 1837 Financial crisis of international origins that led to bankruptcies, bank failures, and unemployment

Although the 1820s and 1830s were boom times, financial panic triggered a bust cycle in 1837, the year after the Second Bank of the United States closed. Economic contraction remained severe through 1843. Internal savings and foreign investments declined sharply. Many banks could not repay their depositors, and states, facing deficits because of the economy's decline, defaulted on their bonds. Because of the **Panic of 1837**, European, especially British, investors became suspicious of all U.S. loans and withdrew money from the United States.

Hard times had come. Philadelphia took on an eerie aura. "The streets seemed deserted," Sidney George Fisher observed in 1842. "The largest [merchant] houses are shut up and to rent, there is no business . . . no money, no confidence." New York countinghouses closed their doors. Former New York mayor Philip Hone later observed, "A deadly calm pervades this lately flourishing city. No goods are selling, no businesses stirring." The hungry formed lines in front of soup societies, and beggars crowded the sidewalks. Some workers looted. Crowds of laborers demanding their deposits gathered at closed banks. Sheriffs sold seized property at one-quarter of its former value. In smaller cities like Lynn, Massachusetts, shoemakers weathered hard times by fishing and tending gardens, while laborers became scavengers, digging for clams and harvesting dandelions. Once-prosperous businessmen—some victims of the market, others of their own recklessness—lost nearly everything, prompting Congress to pass the Federal Bankruptcy Law of 1841; by the time the law was repealed two years later, 41,000 bankrupts had sought protection under its provisions.

10-5 Families in Flux

▷ How did the emergence of the market economy contribute to changes in families and familial organization?

▷ What role did women play in the management of the home and in the family economy?

▷ How did the role of children in the family change in the first half of the nineteenth century?

Anxieties about economic fluctuations reverberated beyond factories and countinghouses into northern homes. Sweeping changes in the household economy, rural as well as urban, led to new family ideals. In the preindustrial era, the family had been primarily an economic unit; now it became a moral and cultural institution, though in reality few families could live up to the new ideal.

10-5a The "Ideal" Family

In the North, the market economy increasingly separated the home from the workplace, leading to a new middle-class ideal in which men functioned in the public sphere while women oversaw the private or domestic sphere. The home became, in theory, an emotional retreat from the competitive, selfish world of business, where men increasingly focused on their work, eager to prosper yet fearful of failure in the unpredictable market economy. At the home's center was a couple that married for love rather than for economic considerations. Men provided and protected,

York, Pennsylvania Family with Negro Servant, c.1828 (oil on panel), American School, (19th century)/Saint Louis Art Museum, Missouri, USA/Gift of Edgar William and Bernice Chrysler Garbisch/The Bridgeman Art Library

△ ·As they strove to live according to new domestic ideals, middle-class families often relied on African American or immigrant servants, who sacrificed time with their own children in order to care for their employers' children.

while women nurtured and guarded the family's morality, making sure that capitalism's excesses did not invade the private sphere. Childhood focused more on education than on work, and the definition of childhood itself expanded: children were to remain at home until their late teens or early twenties. This ideal became known as separate-sphere ideology, or sometimes the cult of domesticity or the cult of true womanhood. Although it rigidly separated the male and female spheres, this ideology gave new standing to domestic responsibilities. In her widely read *Treatise on Domestic Economy* (1841), Catharine Beecher approached housekeeping as a science even as she trumpeted mothers' role as their family's moral guardian. Although Beecher advocated the employment of young, single women as teachers, she believed that, once married, women belonged at home. She maintained that women's natural superiority as moral, nurturing caregivers made them especially suited for teaching (when single) and parenting (once married). Although Beecher saw the public sphere as a male domain, she insisted that the private sphere be elevated to the same status as the public.

10-5b Shrinking Families

These new domestic ideals depended on smaller families in which parents, particularly mothers, could offer children

greater attention, education, and financial help. With the market economy, parents could afford to have fewer children because children no longer played a vital economic role. Urban families produced fewer household goods, and commercial farmers, unlike self-sufficient ones, did not need large numbers of workers year-round, turning instead to hired laborers during peak work periods. Although smaller families resulted in part from first marriages' taking place at a later age—shortening the period of potential childbearing—they also resulted from planning, made easier when cheap rubber condoms became available in the 1850s. Some women chose, too, to end accidental pregnancies with abortion.

In 1800, American women bore seven or eight children; by 1860, five or six. This decline occurred even though many immigrants with large-family traditions were settling in the United States; thus, the birth rate among native-born women declined even more sharply. Although rural families remained larger than urban ones, birth rates among both groups declined comparably.

Yet even as birth rates fell, few northern women could fulfill the middle-class ideal of **separate spheres**. Most wage-earning women provided essential income for their families and could not stay home. They often saw domestic ideals as oppressive, as middle-class reformers mistook poverty for immorality, condemning working mothers for letting their children work or scavenge rather than attend school. Although most middle-class women stayed home, new standards of ·cleanliness and comfort proved time-consuming. These women's contributions to their families were generally assessed in moral terms, even though their economic contributions were significant. When they worked inside their homes, they provided, without remuneration, the labor for which wealthier women paid when they hired domestic servants to perform daily chores. Without servants, moreover, women could not devote themselves primarily to their children's upbringing, placing the ideals of the cult of domesticity beyond the reach of many middle-class families.

10-5c Women's Paid Labor

In working-class families, girls left home as early as age twelve to begin a lifetime of wage earning, with only short respites for bearing and rearing children. Unmarried girls and women worked primarily as domestic servants or in factories; married and widowed women worked as laundresses, seam- . stresses, and cooks. Some hawked food and wares on city streets; others did piecework at home, earning wages in the putting-out system; . and some became prostitutes. Few such occupations enabled women to support themselves or a family comfortably.

separate spheres Middle-class ideology that emerged with the market revolution and divided men's and women's roles into distinct and separate categories based on their perceived gender differences, abilities, and social functions. Men were assigned the public realm of business and politics, while women were assigned to the private world of home and family. In practice, however, few families adhered strictly, if at all, to this ideology.

Middle-class Americans sought to keep daughters closer to home, except for brief stints as mill girls or, especially, as teachers. In the 1830s, Catharine Beecher successfully campaigned for teacher-training schools for women. She argued in part for women's moral superiority and in part for their economic value; because these women would be single, she contended, they need not earn as much as their male counterparts, whom she presumed to be married, though not all were. Unmarried women earned about half the salary of male teachers. By 1850, school-teaching had become a woman's profession. Many women worked as teachers, usually for two to five years.

The proportion of single women in the population increased significantly in the nineteenth century. In the East, some single women would have preferred to marry but market and geographic expansion worked against them: more and more young men headed west in search of opportunity, leaving some eastern communities disproportionately female in makeup. Other women chose to remain independent, seeking opportunities opened by the market economy and urban expansion. Because women's work generally paid poorly, those who forswore marriage faced serious challenges, leaving many single women dependent on charitable or family assistance.

10-6 The Growth of Cities

▶ How did urban environments emerge and expand in the first half of the nineteenth century?

▶ What strains did urban development place on the city and its residents?

▶ How did ethnic and racial tensions manifest themselves in urban environments?

▶ What forms of culture emerged in urban environments?

To many contemporary observers, cities symbolized what market expansion had wrought—for better or for worse—on northern society. No period in American history saw more rapid urbanization than the years between 1820 and 1860. The percentage of people living in urban areas (defined as a place with a population of 2,500 or more) grew from just over 7 percent in 1820 to nearly 20 percent in 1860. Most of this growth took place in the Northeast and the Midwest. Although most northerners continued to live on farms or in small villages, the population of individual cities boomed. Many of those residents were temporary—soon moving on to another city or the countryside—and many came from foreign shores.

10-6a Urban Boom

Even as new cities sprang up, existing cities grew tremendously (see Map 10.2). In 1820, the United States had thirteen places with a population of ten thousand or more; in 1860, it had ninety-three. New York City, already the nation's largest city in 1820, saw its population grow from 123,706 people in that year to 813,669 in 1860—a growth factor of six and a half times. Philadelphia, the nation's second-largest city in both 1820 and 1860, saw the size of its population multiply ninefold during

that same forty-year period. In 1815, Rochester, New York, had a population of just 300 persons. By 1830, the Erie Canal had turned the sleepy agricultural town into a bustling manufacturing center; now the nation's twenty-fifth-largest city, its population was just over 9,000 and continued to multiply at fantastic rates. By 1860, it had more than 48,000 residents.

Cities expanded geographically as well. In 1825, Fourteenth Street was New York City's northern boundary. By 1860, 400,000 people lived above that divide, and Forty-second Street was the city's northern limit. Gone were the cow pastures, kitchen gardens, and orchards. Public transit made city expansion possible. Horse-drawn omnibuses appeared in New York in 1827, and the Harlem Railroad, completed in 1832, ran the length of Manhattan. By the 1850s, all big cities had horse-drawn streetcars, allowing wealthier residents who could afford the fare to settle on larger plots of land on the cities' outskirts.

10-6b Market-Related Development

The North urbanized more quickly than the South, but what was most striking about northern urbanization was where it took place. With only a few exceptions, southern cities were seaports, whereas the period between 1820 and 1860 saw the creation of many inland cities in the North—usually places that sprang to life with the creation of transportation lines or manufacturing establishments. The Boston Manufacturing Company, for example, selected the site for Lowell, Massachusetts, because of its proximity to the Merrimack River, whose rapidly flowing waters could power its textile mill. Incorporated in 1826, by the 1850s Lowell was the second-largest city in New England.

Northern cities developed elaborate systems of municipal services but lacked adequate taxing power to provide services for all. At best, they could tax property adjoining new sewers, paved streets, and water mains. New services and basic sanitation depended on residents' ability to pay. Another solution was to charter private companies to sell basic services, such as providing gas for lights. Baltimore first chartered a private gas company in 1816. By midcentury, every major city had done so. Private firms lacked the capital to build adequate water systems, though, and they laid pipe only in commercial and well-to-do residential areas, bypassing the poor. The task of supplying water ultimately fell on city governments.

10-6c Extremes of Wealth

Throughout the United States, wealth was concentrating with a relatively small number of people. By 1860, the top 5 percent of American families owned more than half of the nation's wealth, and the top 10 percent owned nearly three-quarters. In the South, the extremes of wealth were most apparent on rural plantations, but in the North, cities provided the starkest evidence of economic inequities.

Despite the optimistic forecasts of early textile manufacturers that American industrialization need not engender the poverty and degradation associated with European industrialization, America's industrial cities soon resembled European ones. A number of factors contributed to widespread poverty: poor wages, the inability of many workers to secure full-time

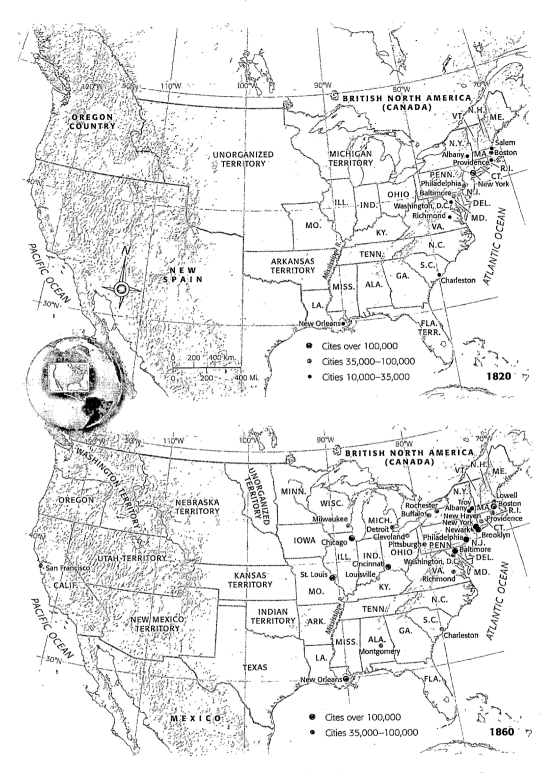

Map 10.2 Major American Cities in 1820 and 1860

The number of Americans who lived in cities increased rapidly between 1820 and 1860, and the number of large cities grew as well. In 1820, only New York City had a population exceeding 100,000; forty years later, eight more cities had surpassed that level.

△ Visible signs of urban poverty in the 1850s were the homeless and orphaned children, most of them immigrants, who wandered the streets of New York City. The Home for the Friendless Orphanage, at Twenty-ninth Street and Madison Avenue, provided shelter for some of the orphan girls.

employment, and the increasingly widespread employment of women and children, which drove down wages for everyone. Women and children, employers rationalized, did not need a living wage because they were—in the employers' way of thinking—dependent by nature and did not require a wage that allowed self-sufficiency. In reality, though, not all women or children had men to support them, nor were men's wages always adequate to support a family comfortably.

New York provides a striking example of the extremes of wealth accompanying industrialization. Where workers lived, conditions were crowded, unhealthy, and dangerous. Houses built for two families often held four; tenements built for six families held twelve. Some of those families took in lodgers

to pay the rent, adding to the unbearably crowded conditions that encouraged poorer New Yorkers to spend as much time as possible outdoors. But streets in poor neighborhoods were filthy. Excess sewage from outhouses drained into ditches, carrying urine and fecal matter into the streets. People piled garbage into gutters or dumped it in backyards or alleys. Pigs, geese, dogs, and vultures scavenged the streets, while enormous rats roamed under wooden sidewalks and through large buildings. Typhoid, dysentery, malaria, and tuberculosis thrived in such conditions, and epidemics of cholera struck in 1832, 1849, and again in 1866, claiming thousands of victims.

But within walking distance of poverty-stricken neighborhoods were lavish mansions, whose residents could escape

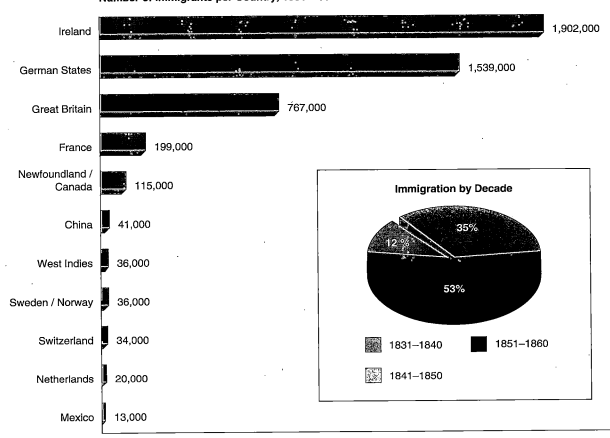

Number of Immigrants per Country, 1831–1860

Ireland	1,902,000
German States	1,539,000
Great Britain	767,000
France	199,000
Newfoundland / Canada	115,000
China	41,000
West Indies	36,000
Sweden / Norway	36,000
Switzerland	34,000
Netherlands	20,000
Mexico	13,000

Immigration by Decade

35%, 12%, 53%

1831–1840   1851–1860
1841–1850

Figure 10.1 Major Sources of Immigration to the United States, 1831–1860

Most immigrants came from two areas: Great Britain, of which Ireland was a part, and the German states. These two areas sent more immigrants between 1830 and 1860 than the inhabitants of the United States enumerated at the first census in 1790. By 1860, 15 percent of the white population was of foreign birth. *Data from Stephan Thernstrom, ed., Harvard Encyclopedia of American Ethnic Groups [Cambridge, Mass., and London: Harvard University Press, 1980], 1047.*

to country estates during the summer's brutal heat or during epidemics. Much of this wealth was inherited. For every John Jacob Astor, who became a millionaire in the western fur trade after beginning life in humble circumstances, ten others had inherited or married money. These rich New Yorkers were not idle, though; they worked at increasing their fortunes and power by investing in commerce and manufacturing.

Between the two extremes of wealth sat a distinct middle class, larger than the wealthy elite but substantially smaller than the working classes. They were businessmen, traders, and professionals, and the rapid turn toward industrialization and commercial specialization made them a much larger presence in northern cities than in southern ones. Middle-class families enjoyed new consumer items: wool carpeting, fine wallpaper, and rooms full of furniture replaced the bare floors, whitewashed walls, and relative sparseness of eighteenth-century homes. Houses were large, from four to six rooms. Middle-class children slept one to a bed, and by the 1840s and 1850s, middle-class families used indoor toilets that were mechanical, though not yet flushing. Middle-class families formed the backbone of urban clubs and societies,

filled the family pews in church, and sent their sons to college. They were as distinct from the world of John Jacob Astor as they were from the milieu of the working class and the poor.

10-6d Immigration

Many of the urban poor were immigrants. The 5 million immigrants who came to the United States between 1830 and 1860 outnumbered the country's entire population in 1790. The vast majority came from Europe, primarily Ireland and the German states (see Figure 10.1). During the peak period of pre–Civil War immigration (1847–1857), 3.3 million immigrants entered the United States, including 1.3 million Irish and 1.1 million Germans. By 1860, 15 percent of the white population was foreign born, with 90 percent of immigrants living in northern states. Not all planned to stay permanently, and many, like the Irish, saw themselves as exiles.

A combination of factors "pushed" Europeans from their homes and "pulled" them to the northern United States. In Ireland, the potato famine (1845–1850)—a period of widespread starvation caused by a diseased potato crop—drove millions from their homeland. Although economic conditions pushed most Germans as well, some were political refugees—liberals, freethinkers, socialists, communists, and anarchists—who fled after the abortive revolutions of 1848. Europeans' awareness of the United States grew as employers, states, and shipping companies promoted opportunities across the Atlantic. Often the message was stark: work and prosper in America, where everyone could aspire to be an independent farmer, or starve in Europe. Although boosters promised immigrants a land of milk and honey, many soon became disillusioned; hundreds of thousands returned home.

Many early immigrants lived or worked in rural areas. Like the Archbalds, a few settled immediately on farms and eventually bought land. Others, unable to afford even a modest down payment, worked as hired farmhands, canal diggers, or railroad track layers—often hoping to buy land later. Pádraig Cúndún was among the lucky. The Irishman used his earnings as a canal laborer to buy land in western New York, proclaiming proudly in 1834 that "I have a fine farm of land now, which I own outright. No one can demand rent from me. My family and I can eat our fill of bread and meat, butter and milk any day we like throughout the year, so I think being here is better than staying in Ireland, landless and powerless, without food or clothing." By the 1840s and 1850s—when the steady stream of immigration turned into a flood—the prospects of buying land became more remote.

By 1860, most immigrants settled in cities, often the port at which they arrived. The most destitute could not afford the fare to places farther inland. Others arrived with resources but fell victim to swindlers who preyed on newly arrived immigrants. Some liked the cities' ethnic flair. In 1855, 52 percent of New York's 623,000 inhabitants were immigrants, with 28 percent of the city's population from Ireland and 16 percent from the German states. Boston, another major entry port, took on a European tone; throughout the 1850s, the city was about 35 percent foreign born, of whom more than two-thirds were Irish.

Most of the new immigrants from Ireland were young, poor, rural, and Roman Catholic. Women worked as domestic servants or mill hands, while men labored in construction or transportation. Very few Germans settled in New England; most came with enough resources to head to the upper Mississippi and Ohio valleys, to states such as Ohio, Illinois, Wisconsin, and Missouri. Although some southern cities like Charleston and Savannah had significant numbers of Irish immigrants, the vast majority of European immigrants, many of whom arrived with aversions to slavery and to semitropical heat, settled in the Northeast or Midwest.

10-6e Ethnic Tensions

Tension—often resulting from anxieties over the era's economic changes—characterized the relationship between native-born Americans and immigrants, particularly Irish Catholics. Native-born workers blamed immigrants for scarce job opportunities and low wages. Middle-class whites blamed them for poverty and crime. As they saw it, immigrants' moral depravity—not poor wages—led to poverty.

Native-born Americans often associated the Irish with another group whom they deemed morally inferior: African Americans. White northerners often portrayed Irish immigrants as nonwhite, as African in appearance. But Irish and African Americans did not develop a sense of solidarity. Instead, some of the era's most virulent riots erupted between Irish immigrants and African Americans.

Closely related to racial stereotyping was anti-Catholicism, which became strident in the 1830s. In Boston, anti-Catholic riots occurred frequently. Nearby Charlestown, Massachusetts, saw a mob burn a convent in 1834. In Philadelphia, a crowd attacked priests and nuns and vandalized churches in 1844, and in Lawrence, Massachusetts, a mob leveled the Irish neighborhood in 1854. Anti-Catholic violence spread beyond urban areas—riots between native-born and Irish workers erupted along the nation's canals and railroads—but urban riots usually attracted more newspaper attention, fueling fears that cities were violent, depraved places.

German immigrants, at least the majority who were Protestants, mostly fared better. In part because Germans generally arrived with some resources and skills, Americans stereotyped them as hardworking, self-reliant, and intelligent. But non-Protestant Germans—Catholics and Jews (whom white Americans considered a separate race) frequently encountered hostility fed by racial and religious prejudice.

Immigrants often lived in ethnic enclaves. Intolerance between Protestants and Catholics ran both ways, and Irish Catholics tended to live in their own neighborhoods, where they established Catholic churches and schools. In larger cities, immigrants from the same German states clustered together. Immigrants set up social clubs and mutual-aid societies, such as the Hibernian Society and Sons of Erin (Irish), and B'nai B'rith (Jewish).

10-6f People of Color

African Americans also forged their own communities and culture. As late as the 1830s, significant numbers of them remained enslaved in New York and New Jersey, but the numbers of free African Americans grew steadily, and by 1860 nearly 250,000 (many of them refugees from southern slavery) lived in the urban North. Despite differences in status, occupation, wealth, education, and religion, African Americans often felt a sense of racial solidarity. **African Methodist Episcopal Churches** and preachers helped forge communities. Chapels and social halls functioned as town halls and school buildings. Ministers were political leaders, and their halls housed political forums, conventions, and protest meetings.

But white racism impinged on every aspect of northern African Americans' lives. Streetcars, hotels, restaurants, and theaters could turn away African Americans with no legal penalty. City laws barred African Americans from entering public buildings. Even where more liberal laws existed, popular attitudes often constrained African Americans' opportunities.

African Methodist Episcopal Churches First American denomination established by and for African Americans.

△ Domestic servants await their fate at a hiring office. Because servants resided with their employers, concerns about honesty often topped an employer's list of priorities for a suitable servant.

In Massachusetts, for example, African Americans enjoyed more legal rights than anywhere else, yet laws protecting civil and political rights could not make whites shop at black businesses. "Colored men in business in Massachusetts receive more respect, and less patronage than in any place I know of," proclaimed a prominent African American lawyer.

African Americans were excluded from factory and clerical jobs. Women worked as house servants, cooks, washerwomen, and child nurses. Most African American men worked as construction workers, porters, longshoremen, or day laborers—all jobs subject to frequent periods of unemployment. Others found employment in the lower-paying but more stable service industry, working as servants, waiters, cooks, barbers, and janitors. Many African American men became sailors and merchant seamen, as commercial sailing offered regular employment and opportunities for advancement, though not protection from racial taunts.

In the growing cities, African Americans turned service occupations into businesses, opening their own restaurants, taverns, hotels, barbershops, and employment agencies for domestic servants. Some became caterers. Others sold used clothing or were junk dealers or small-job contractors. A few became wealthy, invested in real estate, and loaned money. With professionals—ministers, teachers, physicians, dentists, lawyers, and newspaper editors—they formed a small but growing African American middle class.

In cities large and small, African Americans became targets of urban violence. White rioters clubbed and stoned African Americans, destroying their houses, churches, and businesses. Philadelphia experienced the most violence, with five major riots in the 1830s and 1840s, and major riots occurred in Providence and New York, where in July of 1834 many buildings were vandalized or destroyed during a three-day riot.

△ Born in Saint-Domingue and brought to New York as a slave in the early 1790s, Pierre Toussaint became a very successful hairdresser catering to the city's fashion-conscious, wealthy white women. After being freed, Toussaint bought his wife (Juliette, pictured on the right) and other relatives, established orphanages, and supported the city's Catholic church. (left) The New York Historical Society /Archive Photos/Getty Images (right) The New York Historical Society/Getty Images

10-6g Urban Culture

Living in cramped, squalid conditions, working-class families— white and black, immigrant and native-born—spent little time indoors. In the 1840s, a working-class youth culture developed on the Bowery, one of New York's entertainment strips. The lamp-lit promenade, lined with theaters, dance halls, and cafés, became an urban midway for the "Bowery boys and gals." The Bowery boys' greased hair, distinctive clothing, and swaggering gait frightened many middle-class New Yorkers, as did the Bowery girls' colorful costumes and ornate hats, which contrasted with genteel ladies' own modest veils and bonnets. Equally scandalous to an older generation were the middle-class clerks who succumbed to the city's temptations, most notably prostitution.

Gangs of garishly dressed young men and women— flaunting their sexuality, using foul language, sometimes speaking in foreign tongues, and drinking to excess—drove self-styled respectable citizenry to establish private clubs and associations. Some joined the Masonic order, which offered everything the bustling, chaotic city did not: an elaborate hierarchy, an older code of deference between ranks, harmony, and shared values. Although the Masons admitted men only, women organized their own associations, including literary clubs and benevolent societies.

Increasingly, urban recreation and sports became formal commodities. One had to buy a ticket to go to the theater, the circus, P. T. Barnum's American Museum in New York City, the racetrack, or the ballpark. Horse racing, walking races, and, in the 1850s, baseball attracted large urban male crowds.

Starting in 1831, enthusiasts could read the all-sports newspaper, *Spirit of the Times.* A group of Wall Street office workers formed the Knickerbocker Club in 1842 and in 1845 drew up rules for the game of baseball. By 1849, news of boxing was so much in demand that a round-by-round account of a Maryland boxing match was telegraphed throughout the East.

A theater was often the second public building constructed in a town, after a church. Large cities boasted two or more theaters catering to different classes. Some plays cut across class lines—Shakespeare was performed so often and appreciated so widely that even illiterate theatergoers knew his plays well— yet the same taste in plays did not soothe class tensions. In 1849, a dispute between an American and a British actor about how to properly stage Shakespeare's *Macbeth* escalated into a working-class riot at New York City's elitist Astor Place Opera House, which hosted the British actor. It was, as one observer explained, "the rich against the poor—the aristocracy against the people." As the disorder escalated, bringing thousands into the streets, militia fired into the working-class crowd, killing at least twenty-seven and injuring about 150.

In the 1840s, singing groups, theater troupes, and circuses traveled from city to city. Minstrel shows were particularly popular, featuring white men (often Irish) in burnt-cork makeup imitating African Americans in song, dance, and patter. In the early 1830s, Thomas D. Rice of New York became famous for his role as Jim Crow, an old southern slave. In ill-fitting patched clothing and torn shoes, the blackface Rice shuffled, danced, and sang. Minstrel performers told jokes mocking economic

△ On May 10, 1849, a working-class protest at the elitist Astor Place Theater in New York City led to a clash with state militia, resulting in at least 22 deaths and over 150 injuries.

and political elites, and evoked nostalgia for preindustrial work habits and morality, as supposedly embodied by carefree black men. At the same time, the antics of blackface actors encouraged a racist stereotyping of African Americans as sensual and lazy.

10-6h The Penny Press

Accounts of urban culture peppered the penny press, a new journalistic form that emerged in the 1830s, soon sweeping northern cities, particularly the ports of New York, Boston, Philadelphia, and Baltimore. Made possible by technological advances—the advent of the steam-powered press, improved methods for producing paper, and transportation innovations—the penny press (each newspaper cost one cent) contrasted fundamentally to the established six-cent newspapers. The older papers covered mostly commercial news and identified strongly with a political party; politicians themselves supplied much of the content, often reprinting their speeches. The penny press, by contrast, proclaimed political independence and dispersed paid reporters to cover local, national, and even international stories. Unlike six-cent newspapers, which relied primarily on mail subscriptions and contributions from political parties for their revenue, penny newspapers were sold by newsboys on the street, earned money by selling advertising, and circulated to a much larger and economically diverse readership. For the first time, working-class people could regularly buy newspapers.

Penny newspapers focused on daily life, what today would be called "human interest stories," giving individuals of one social class the opportunity to peer into the lives of different classes, ethnicities, and races. Working- and middle-class readers, for example, could read about high society—its balls, its horse racing, its excesses of various sorts. Wealthy and middle-class readers encountered stories about poorer neighborhoods—their crime, poverty, and insalubrious conditions. The penny press often sensationalized or slanted the news, and, in the process, influenced urban dwellers' views of one another, and of cities themselves.

10-6i Cities as Symbols of Progress

Many northerners saw cities—with their mixtures of people, rapid growth, municipal improvements, and violence—as symbolizing at once progress and decay. On the one hand, cities represented economic advancement; new ones grew at the crossroads of transportation and commerce. Cities nurtured churches, schools, civil governments, and museums—all signs of civilization and culture. As canals and railroads opened the West for mass settlement, many white northerners applauded the appearance of what they called "civilization"—church steeples, public buildings—in areas that had recently been what they called "savage wilderness," or territory controlled by Native Americans. One Methodist newspaper remarked in 1846 that the nation's rapid expansion westward would outpace "our means of moral and intellectual improvement." But the remedies, the editor noted, were evident: bring churches, schools, and moral reform societies to the West. "Cities, civilization, religion, mark our progress," he declared. To many nineteenth-century white Americans, cities represented the moral triumph of civilization over savagery and heathenism.

Yet some of the same Americans deplored the everyday character of the nation's largest cities, which they saw as havens of disease, poverty, crime, and vice. To many middle-class observers, disease and crime represented moral decline. They considered epidemics to be divine scourges, striking primarily those who were filthy, intemperate, and immoral. Theft and prostitution provided evidence of moral vice, and wealthy observers perceived these crimes not as by-products of poverty but as signs of individual failing. They pressed for laws against vagrancy and disturbing the peace, and pushed city officials to establish the nation's first police forces. Boston hired daytime policemen in 1838 to supplement its part-time night watchmen and constables, and New York formed its own police force, modeled on London's, in 1845.

How did northerners reconcile urban vice and depravity with their view of cities as symbols of progress? Middle-class reformers focused on purifying cities of disease and vice. If disease was a divine punishment, then Americans would have to become more godly. Middle-class reformers took to the streets and back alleys, trying to convince the urban working classes that life would improve if they gave up alcohol, worked even harder, and prayed frequently. This belief in hard work and virtuous habits became central to many northerners' ideas about progress.

10-7 Revivals and Reform

▷ How did religion influence the emergence of reform efforts in the first half of the nineteenth century?

▷ What role did women play in the reform movements?

▷ How were individual reform efforts in American society similar to one another?

Second Great Awakening Period of the religious revivals that swept the nation from the 1790s into the 1830s; these helped inspire northern reform movements.

Charles G. Finney A lawyer-turned-Presbyterian minister who conducted revivals in towns like Rochester along the Erie Canal, and who stressed individual responsibility for making moral decisions.

For many, those ideas were grounded in evangelical religion. During the late eighteenth and early nineteenth centuries, a series of religious revivals throughout the nation raised people's hopes for the Second Coming of the Christian messiah and the establishment of the Kingdom of God on earth. Sometimes called the **Second Great Awakening** for their resemblance to revivals of the Great Awakening of the eighteenth century, these revivals created communities of believers who resolved to combat sin in an effort to speed the millennium, or the thousand years of peace on earth that would accompany Christ's Second Coming. Some believed the United States had a special mission in God's design and a special role in eliminating evil. If sin and evil could be eliminated, individuals and society could be perfected, readying the earth for Christ's return.

Because it was not enough for an individual to embrace God and godliness, revivalists strove for large-scale conversions. Rural women, men, and children traveled long distances to camp meetings, where they listened to fiery sermons preached day and night from hastily constructed platforms and tents in forests or open fields. In cities, women in particular attended daily church services and prayer meetings, sometimes for months on end. Converts renounced personal sin, vowed to live sanctified lives, and committed themselves to helping others see the light.

10-7a Revivals

Northern revivalists emphasized social reform in a way that their southern counterparts did not. The most prominent northern preachers were Lyman Beecher, who made his base in New England before moving to Cincinnati, and **Charles G. Finney,** who traveled the canals and roads linking the Northeast to the Midwest. They, like many lesser-known preachers, argued that evil was avoidable, that Christians were not doomed by original sin, and that anyone could achieve salvation. In everyday language, Finney—a former lawyer who became a Presbyterian minister—preached that "God has made man a moral free agent." Finney's brand of revivalism transcended sects, class, and race. Revivalism thrived among Methodists and Baptists, whose denominational structures maximized democratic participation and drew ministers from ordinary folk.

Finney achieved his greatest successes in the area of western New York that had experienced rapid changes in transportation and industrialization—in what he called the "Burned-Over District" because of the region's intense evangelical fires. Rapid change raised fears of social disorder—family dissolution, drinking, swearing, and prostitution. Many individuals worried, too, whether their status would improve or decline in an economy cycling through booms and busts.

When northern revivalist preachers emphasized the importance of good works—good deeds and piety—they helped ignite many of the era's social reform movements, which began in the Burned-Over District and spread eastward to New England and the Middle Atlantic and westward to the upper Midwest. Evangelically inspired reform associations together constituted what historians call the "benevolent empire." While advocating for distinct causes, these associations shared a commitment to human perfectibility, and they often turned to the same wealthy men for financial resources and advice.

△ Often attracting worshippers in the thousands, revivalist meetings became known as "camp meetings" because the faithful camped out for days at a time to hear charismatic preachers, who offered sermons day and night.

10-7b Moral Reform

Those resources enabled them to make good use of the era's new technologies—steam presses and railroads—to spread the evangelical word. By mass-producing pamphlets and newspapers for distribution far into the country's interior, reformers spread their message throughout the Northeast and Midwest, strengthening cultural connections between regions increasingly tied together economically. With canals and railroads making travel easier, reformers could attend annual conventions and contact like-minded people personally, and local reform societies could host speakers from distant places. Most reform organizations, like political parties, sponsored weekly newspapers, creating a virtual community of reformers.

While industrialists and merchants provided financial resources for evangelical reform, their wives and daughters solicited new members and circulated petitions. Reforms sought to expand the cult of domesticity, which assigned women the role of moral guardianship of their families, into the public realm. Rather than simply providing moral guidance to their own children, women would establish reformatories for wayward youth or asylums for orphans. Participation in reform movements allowed women to exercise moral authority outside the household, giving them a new sense of influence. They might both improve people's lives and hasten

the millennium. Women also enjoyed the friendships and intellectual camaraderie with other women that participation in benevolent societies fostered.

Many female reformers had attended a female academy or seminary, where the curriculum included arts of "refinement"—music, dance, penmanship—but focused on science and literature. Based on the notion that women were men's intellectual equals, the curriculum was modeled on that of men's colleges, and by 1820, approximately the same number of men and women attended institutions of higher education. At the female academies and seminaries, and at the hundreds of reading circles and literary societies in which their alumnae participated, women honed their intellectual and persuasive skills, preparing themselves to influence public opinion even as many of them maintained substantial domestic responsibilities. A few of these women became prominent editors and writers, but most influenced society as educators and, especially, reformers.

The aftermath of an 1831 exposé of prostitution in New York City illustrates reformers' public influence. Even as female reformers organized a shelter for the city's prostitutes and tried to secure respectable employment for them, they publicized the names of brothel clients to shame the men contributing to the women's waywardness. The New York women organized themselves into the Female Moral Reform

Society, expanding their geographic scope and activities. By 1840, the society had 555 affiliated chapters across the nation. In the next few years, it entered the political sphere by lobbying successfully for criminal sanctions in New York State against men who seduced women into prostitution. If only prostitutes could be freed from the corrupting reach of the men who preyed on them, reformers believed, so-called "fallen women" might be morally uplifted.

10-7c Penitentiaries and Asylums

A similar belief in perfectibility led reformers to establish penitentiaries for criminals and delinquents that aimed not simply to punish, as jails did, but to transform criminals into productive members of society through disciplined regimens. Under the "Auburn system," prisoners worked together in the daytime but were isolated at night, while under the "Philadelphia system," utter silence and isolation prevailed day and night. Isolation and silence were meant to enable reflection and redemption—to provide opportunities for penitence—within individual prisoners. When Frenchman Alexis de Tocqueville came to America in 1831 to study its prisons, he noted that the Philadelphia system made him feel as if he "had traversed catacombs; there were a thousand living beings, and yet it was desert solitude."

Other reformers sought to improve treatment of the mentally ill, who were frequently imprisoned, often alongside criminals, and put in cages or dark dungeons, chained to walls, brutalized, or held in solitary confinement. **Dorothea Dix**, the movement's leader, exemplifies the early-nineteenth-century reformer who started with a religious belief in individual self-improvement and human perfectibility, and moved into social action by advocating collective responsibility. Investigating asylums, petitioning the Massachusetts legislature, and lobbying other states and Congress, Dix helped create a new public role for women. In response to Dix's efforts, twenty-eight of thirty-three states built public institutions for the mentally ill by 1860.

10-7d Temperance

Temperance reformers, who pushed for either partial or full abstinence from alcoholic beverages, likewise crossed into the political sphere. Drinking was widespread in the early nineteenth century, when men gathered in public houses and rural inns to drink whiskey, rum, and hard cider while they gossiped, talked politics, and played cards. Contracts were sealed, celebrations commemorated, and harvests toasted with liquor. "Respectable" women did not drink in public, but many tippled alcohol-based patent medicines promoted as cure-alls.

Evangelicals considered drinking sinful, and in many denominations, forsaking alcohol was part of conversion. Preachers condemned alcohol for violating the Sabbath—the only day workers had off, which some spent at the public house. Factory owners condemned alcohol for making workers unreliable. Civic leaders connected alcohol with crime. Middle-class reformers, often women, condemned it for squandering wages, diverting men from their family responsibilities, and fostering abusive behavior at home. In the early 1840s, thousands of ordinary women formed Martha Washington societies to protect families by reforming alcoholics, raising children as teetotalers, and spreading the temperance message. Abstinence from alcohol, reformers believed, would foster both religious perfectibility and secular progress.

As the temperance movement gained momentum, its goal shifted from moderation to voluntary abstinence and finally to prohibition. By the mid-1830s, five thousand state and local temperance societies touted teetotalism, and more than a million people had taken the pledge of abstinence, including several hundred thousand children who enlisted in the Cold Water Army. Per capita consumption of alcohol fell from five gallons per year in 1800 to below two gallons in the 1840s. The American Society for the Promotion of Temperance, organized in 1826 to promote pledges of abstinence, became a pressure group for legislation to end alcohol manufacture and sale. In 1851, Maine became the first state to ban alcohol except for medicinal purposes; by 1855, similar laws had been enacted throughout New England and in New York, Pennsylvania, and the Midwest.

The temperance campaign had a nativist—or anti-immigrant and anti-Catholic—strain to it. The Irish and Germans, complained the *American Protestant Magazine* in 1849, "bring the grog shops like the frogs of Egypt upon us." Along the nation's canals, reformers lamented the hundreds of taverns catering to the largely Irish workforce, and in the cities, they expressed outrage at the Sunday tradition of urban German families' gathering at beer gardens to eat and drink, to dance and sing, and sometimes to play cards. Some Catholics heeded the message, pledging abstinence and forming their own organizations, such as the St. Mary's Mutual Benevolent Total Abstinence Society in Boston.

But temperance spawned strong opposition, too. Many workers—Protestants as well as Catholics—rejected what they saw as reformers' efforts to impose middle-class values on people whose lives they did not understand, and they steadfastly defended their right to drink whatever they pleased. Workers agreed that poverty and crime were problems but believed that poor wages, not drinking habits, were responsible. Even some who abstained from alcohol opposed prohibition, believing that drinking should be a matter of self-control, not state coercion.

10-7e Public Schools

Protestants and Catholics often quarreled over education as well. Public education usually included religious education, but when teachers taught Protestant beliefs and used the King James version of the Bible, Catholics established their own schools, which taught Catholic doctrines. Some Protestants began

---

Dorothea Dix Leader of movement to improve conditions for the mentally ill.

temperance Abstinence from alcohol; the temperance movement advocated against using alcohol for nonmedicinal reasons.

Engaging Children

Hundreds of thousands of children joined the temperance movement, often by enlisting in the so-called Cold Water Army. Like adult temperance societies, the Cold Water Army advocated for complete abstinence from alcoholic beverages. On holidays such as George Washington's birthday and the Fourth of July, they marched at public gatherings, singing temperance songs and carrying banners and fans such as the one pictured at the right. Reverend Thomas P. Hunt, a Presbyterian minister, founded the Cold Water Army because he believed that by recruiting children, he stood a much greater chance of eradicating alcohol consumption than if he aimed his temperance efforts directly at adults.

CRITICAL THINKING

- What might have been Hunt's logic? Why might children have wanted to join a Cold Water Army?
- Do the images on the certificate and fan offer any clues? What were the benefits of participating in the movement?
- What were the implied consequences of failing to do so? Why might Hunt have chosen the term *army*, and what about that choice might have proved appealing to his young recruits?

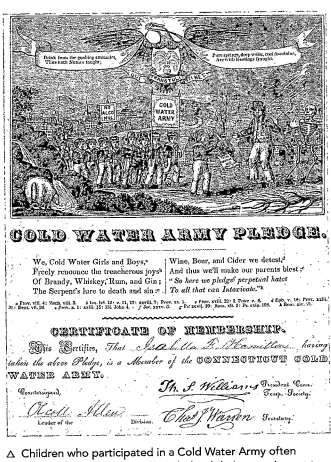

△ Children who participated in a Cold Water Army often received a certificate that acknowledged their commitment to the cause while reiterating the pledge they had taken. Cold Water Army Pledge (litho)/American School, (19th century)/NEW YORK HISTORICAL SOCIETY/© Collection of the New-York Historical Society, USA/Bridgeman Images

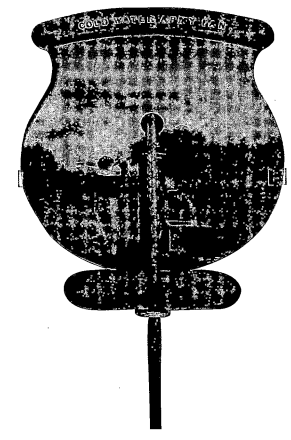

△ Children in Cold Water Army parades sometimes carried decorative fans, which they may have displayed in their homes as well, as reminders to themselves and their parents of temperance's virtues. Museum of American Political Life, University of Hartford

to fear that Catholics would never assimilate into American culture, and some charged Catholics with being exclusionists, plotting to undermine the republic and impose papal control. Yet even as these conflicts brewed, public education touched the lives of more Americans than did any other reform movement.

The movement's leader was **Horace Mann**, a Massachusetts lawyer and reformer from humble beginnings. Mann advocated free, tax-supported education to replace church schools and the private schools set up by untrained, itinerant young men. Universal education, Mann proposed, would end misery and crime, and would help Americanize immigrants. "If we do not prepare children to become good citizens," he argued, "if we do not develop their capacities, imbue their hearts with the love of truth and duty, and a reverence for all things sacred and holy, then our republic must go down to destruction."

During Mann's tenure as secretary of the Massachusetts Board of Education from 1837 to 1848, Massachusetts led the "common school" movement, establishing schools for training teachers (the "normal school," modeled on the French *école normale*, and the forerunner of teacher-training colleges); lengthening the school year; and raising teachers' salaries to make the profession more attractive. In keeping with the era's notions that women had special claims to morality and that they could be paid less because they were by nature dependents, Mann envisioned a system in which women would prepare future clerks, farmers, and workers with a practical curriculum that deemphasized classics in favor of geography, arithmetic, and science. Like other reform movements, educational reform rested on the notions of progress and perfectibility; given the proper guidance, individuals could educate themselves out of their material and moral circumstances.

Thanks in part to expanding public education in the North, by 1850 the vast majority of native-born white Americans were literate. Newspapers and magazines proliferated, and bookstores spread. Power printing presses and better transportation made possible wide distribution of books and periodicals. The religious press—of both traditional sects and revivalists—produced pamphlets, hymnals, Bibles, and religious newspapers. Secular newspapers and magazines—political organs, the penny press, and literary journals—also abounded from the 1830s on.

Fairmount Water Works, constructed between 1812 and 1815, Philadelphia took the lead in building municipal waterworks. After the devastating cholera epidemic of 1832, New York City planned its own massive waterworks: between 1837 and 1842, it built the 41-mile Croton Aqueduct, an elaborate system of iron pipes encased in brick masonry that brought water from upstate New York to Manhattan.

Science became increasingly important nationally, too, with the founding of institutions that still exist today. After James Smithson, a wealthy British scientist, left his estate to the United States government, Congress established the Smithsonian Institution (1846), which acquired and disseminated scientific knowledge. The Smithsonian's director was Joseph Henry, one of the nation's most talented scientists; his experiments in electromagnetism helped make possible both the telegraph and, later in the century, the telephone. In 1848, Henry helped found the American Association for the Advancement of Science to promote scientific collaboration and, thus, advancement. That Henry was a devoutly religious man did not deter him from seeking scientific knowledge. For many nineteenth-century Americans, particularly those in non-revivalist sects, religious devotion and scientific inquiry were compatible. They saw scientific discoveries as signs of progress, reassuring them that the millennium was approaching. God had created the natural world, they believed, and it was their Christian duty to perfect it in preparation for God's return.

10-8 Utopian Experiments

▷ **What did utopian communities seek to achieve in the first half of the nineteenth century?**

▷ **What were the features of the American Renaissance?**

Some idealists dreamed of an entirely new social order. They established dozens of utopian communities—ideal communities designed as models for broader society—based on either religious principles, a desire to resist what they deemed the market economy's excessive individualism, or both. Some groups, like the **Mormons**, arose during the Second Great Awakening, while others, like the Shakers, had originated in eighteenth-century Europe. Utopian communities attempted to recapture what they perceived as the past's more communal nature, even as they offered sometimes-radical departures from established practices of marriage and child rearing.

10-8a Mormons

No utopian experiment had a more lasting influence than the Church of Jesus Christ of Latter-day Saints, whose members were known as the Mormons. During the religious ferment of the 1820s in western New York, **Joseph Smith**, a young farmer, reported that an angel called Moroni had given him divinely engraved gold plates. Smith published his revelations as the *Book of Mormon* and organized a church in 1830. The next year, the community moved west to Ohio to build a "New Jerusalem" and await the Second Coming of Jesus.

Horace Mann First secretary of the newly created Massachusetts Board of Education who presided over sweeping reforms to transform schools into institutions that occupied most of a child's time and energy.

Mormons Members of the Church of Jesus Christ of Latter-day Saints, the first major religion founded in the United States; members were persecuted for many years.

Joseph Smith Founder of the Mormon Church.

10-7f Engineering and Science

Public education's emphasis on science reflected a broader tendency to look not just to moral reform but also to engineering and science to remedy the nation's problems. Not everyone blamed epidemics on immorality, for example; scientists and doctors saw unclean, stagnant water as the culprit. With its

The Museum of the City of New York / Art Resource, NY

△ The Croton Aqueduct, shown here near Harlem, New York, was an engineering marvel of its time. It brought fresh water to New York City.

After angry mobs drove the Mormons from Ohio, they settled in Missouri. Anti-Mormons charged that Mormonism was a scam by Joseph Smith, and feared Mormon economic and political power. In 1838, Missouri's governor charged Smith with fomenting insurrection and worked to indict him and other leaders for treason.

Smith and his followers left for Nauvoo, Illinois. The state legislature gave them a city charter making them self-governing and authorized a local militia. But again the Mormons met antagonism, especially after Smith introduced the practice of polygamy in 1841, allowing men to have several wives at once. The next year, Smith became mayor, and this consolidation of religious and political power, as well as Nauvoo's petition to the federal government to be a self-governing territory, further antagonized opponents, now including some former Mormons. In 1844, after Smith and his brother were charged with treason and jailed, and then murdered, the Mormons left Illinois to seek security in the western wilderness. Under the leadership of Brigham Young, they established a cooperative community in the Great Salt Lake Valley.

10-8b Shakers

The **Shakers**, the largest communal utopian experiment, reached their peak between 1820 and 1860, with six thousand members in twenty settlements in eight states. Shaker communities emphasized agriculture and handcrafts, selling their products beyond their own community; most became self-sufficient and profitable enterprises. The community's craft tradition contrasted with the new factory regime. But the Shakers were essentially a spiritual community. Founded in England in the early 1770s by Ann Lee, their name derived from their worship service, which included shaking their entire bodies, singing, dancing, and shouting. Ann Lee's children had died in infancy, and she saw their deaths as retribution for her sin of intercourse; thus, she advocated celibacy. After imprisonment in England in 1773–1774, she settled in America.

In religious practice and social relations, Shakers offered an alternative to the era's rapid changes. Shakers lived communally, with men and women in separate quarters; individual families were abolished. Men and women shared leadership equally. Many Shaker settlements became temporary refuges for orphans, widows, runaways, abused wives, and laid-off workers. Their settlements depended on new recruits,

Shakers Utopian sect that stressed celibacy and emphasized agriculture and handcrafts; became known for furniture designs long after the community itself ceased to exist.

not only because the practice of celibacy meant no reproduction, but also because some members left, unsuited to either communal living or the Shakers' spiritual message.

10-8c Oneidans, Owenites, and Fourierists

Other utopian communities joined in resisting the social changes accompanying industrialism. John Humphrey Noyes, a lawyer converted by Finney's revivals, established two perfectionist communities: first in Putney, Vermont, in 1840, and then—after being indicted for adultery—in Oneida, New York, in 1848. Noyes decried individualism, advocating instead communal property ownership, communal child rearing, and "complex marriage," in which all the community's men were married to all its women, but in which a woman could accept or reject a sexual proposition. The Oneida Colony forbade exclusive sexual relationships and required men to practice "male continence," or intercourse without ejaculation, in order to promote relationships built on more than sexual fulfillment. Pregnancies were to be planned; couples applied to Noyes for permission to have a child, or Noyes assigned two people to reproduce with each other. Robert Dale Owen's community in **New Harmony**, Indiana (1825–1828), also abolished private property and advocated communal child rearing. The Fourierists, named after French philosopher Charles Fourier, established more than two dozen communities in the Northeast and Midwest; these communities, too, resisted individualism and promoted equality between the sexes.

The most famous Fourier community was Brook Farm, in West Roxbury, Massachusetts, near Boston. Inspired by **transcendentalism**—the belief that the physical world is secondary to the spiritual realm, which human beings can reach not by custom and experience but only by intuition—Brook Farm's members rejected materialism. Their rural communalism combined spirituality, manual labor, intellectual life, and play. Originally founded in 1841 by the Unitarian minister George Ripley, Brook Farm attracted farmers, craftsmen, and writers, among them the novelist Nathaniel Hawthorne. Brook Farm residents contributed regularly to the *Dial*, the leading transcendentalist journal. Although Unitarians were not evangelicals, their largely middle- and upper-class followers had a long-standing "devotion to progress," as one of their most influential ministers put it. In 1845, Brook Farm's one hundred members organized themselves into phalanxes (working-living units), following a model suggested by Fourier. As rigid regimentation replaced individualism, membership dropped. A year after a disastrous fire in 1846, the experiment collapsed.

New Harmony A utopian community founded in Indiana by Robert Owen; it advocated communal property and child-rearing.

transcendentalism The belief that the physical world is secondary to the spiritual realm, which humans can reach only by intuition.

After visiting Brook Farm in 1843, transcendentalist Henry David Thoreau decided that organized utopian communities did not suit him: "As for these communities, I think I had rather keep bachelor's hall in hell than go to board in heaven." Two years later, Thoreau constructed his own one-man utopia in a small cabin along the shores of Walden Pond, in Massachusetts, where he meditated and wrote about nature, morality, spirituality, progress, society, and government.

10-8d American Renaissance

Thoreau joined a literary outpouring known today as the American Renaissance. Ralph Waldo Emerson, a pillar of the transcendental movement, was its prime inspiration. After quitting his Boston Unitarian ministry in 1832, followed by a two-year sojourn in Europe, Emerson returned to lecture and write, preaching individualism and self-reliance. Widely admired, he influenced Hawthorne, *Dial* editor Margaret Fuller, Herman Melville, and Thoreau, among many others. In philosophical intensity and moral idealism, the American Renaissance was both distinctively American and an outgrowth of the European romantic movement. It addressed universal themes using American settings and characters. Hawthorne, for instance, used Puritan New England as a backdrop, and Melville wrote of great spiritual quests as seafaring adventures.

Perhaps more than any other American Renaissance author, Thoreau emphasized individualism and its practical applications. In his 1849 essay on "Resistance to Civil Government" (known after his death as "Civil Disobedience"), Thoreau advocated individual resistance to a government engaged in immoral acts. Thoreau had already put into practice what he preached: In the midst of the War with Mexico (see Chapter 12, "Politics and the Fate of the Union, 1824–1859"), Thoreau refused to pay his taxes, believing they would aid an immoral war to expand slavery, and was briefly jailed. "I cannot for an instant recognize that political organization as my government which is the *slave's* government also," Thoreau wrote. Later, in defiance of federal law, Thoreau aided escaped slaves on their way to freedom.

10-9 Abolitionism

▷ How did evangelical abolitionism differ from its antislavery predecessors?

▷ What role did women and African Americans play in the abolitionist movement?

▷ What internal and external challenges did the abolitionist movement face?

Thoreau joined evangelical abolitionists in trying to eradicate slavery, which they deemed both an individual and a communal sin suffusing American society. Their efforts built on an earlier generation of antislavery activism among blacks and whites.

10-9a Evangelical Abolitionism

In the early 1830s, a new group of radical white abolitionists—most prominently, **William Lloyd Garrison**—rejected the gradual approaches of an earlier generation of white legal reformers and colonizationists (see "Early Abolitionism and Colonization," Section 8-3e). Instead, these overwhelmingly northern reformers demanded immediate, complete, and uncompensated emancipation. In the first issue of the abolitionist newspaper *The Liberator*, which he began publishing in 1831, Garrison declared, "I am in earnest—I will not equivocate—I will not excuse—I will not retreat a single inch—and *I will be heard.*" Two years later, he founded the American Antislavery Society, which became the era's largest abolitionist organization.

Immediatists, as they came to be called, believed slavery was an absolute sin needing urgent eradication. They were influenced by African American abolitionist societies and by evangelicals' notion that humans, not God, determined their own spiritual fate by deciding whether to choose good or evil. In that sense, all were equal before God's eyes. When all humans had chosen good over evil, the millennium would come. Slavery, however, denied enslaved men and women the ability to make such choices, the ability to act as what Finney called "moral free agents." For every day that slavery continued, the millennium was postponed.

Because the millennium depended on *all* hearts being won over to Christ, because it depended on the perfectibility of everyone, including slave owners, Garrison advocated "moral suasion." He and his followers hoped to bring about emancipation not through coercion, but by winning the hearts of slave owners as well as others who supported or tolerated slavery. Evangelical abolitionism depended, then, on large numbers of ministers and laypeople spreading the evangelical message all across the nation. Many of them joined local organizations affiliated with the American Antislavery Society.

10-9b The American Antislavery Society

By 1838, at its peak, the society reported 1,300 local affiliates and a membership of 250,000. Unlike earlier white abolitionist societies, the immediatist organizations welcomed men and women of all racial and class backgrounds. Lydia Maria Child, Maria Chapman, and Lucretia Mott served on its executive committee; Child edited its official paper, the *National Anti-Slavery Standard*, from 1841 to 1843, and Chapman coedited it from 1844 until 1848. The society sponsored black and female speakers, and women undertook most of the day-to-day conversion efforts. In rural and small-town northern and midwestern communities, women addressed mail, collected signatures, raised money, organized boycotts of textiles made from slave-grown cotton, and increased public awareness. With the "great postal campaign," launched in 1835, the society's membership flooded the mails with antislavery tracts. Women went door to door collecting signatures on antislavery petitions; by 1838, more than 130,000 petitions, each with numerous signatures, had been sent to Congress. Abolitionist-minded women met in "sewing circles," making clothes for escaped slaves while organizing future activities, such as antislavery fairs at which they sold goods—often items they had made themselves—whose proceeds they donated to antislavery causes. These fairs increased their cause's visibility and drew more Americans into direct contact with abolitionists and their ideas.

10-9c African American Abolitionists

Even as white abolitionist societies opened membership to African Americans and sponsored speaking tours by former slaves, African Americans continued their independent efforts to end slavery and to improve the status of free African Americans. Former slaves—most famously, Frederick Douglass, Henry Bibb, Harriet Tubman, and Sojourner Truth—dedicated their lives to ending slavery through their speeches, publications, and participation in a secret network known as the Underground Railroad, which spirited enslaved men, women, and children to freedom. By the thousands, less famous African Americans continued the work of the post-revolutionary generation and established their churches, founded moral reform societies, published newspapers, created schools and orphanages for African American children, and held conventions to consider tactics for improving African Americans' status within the free states.

Although genuine friendships emerged among white and black abolitionists, many white abolitionists treated blacks as inferiors, driving some African Americans to reject white antislavery organizations and to form their own. Others lacked the patience for the supposed immediatism of

△ Women played an activist role in reform, especially in abolitionism. A rare daguerreotype from August 1850 shows women and men, including Frederick Douglass, on the podium at an abolitionist rally in Cazenovia, New York.

The Art Archive /Art Resource, NY

William Lloyd Garrison
Founder of *The Liberator* and a controversial white advocate of abolition, he demanded an immediate end to slavery and embraced civil rights for blacks on par with those of whites.

William Lloyd Garrison; they did not object to moral suasion, but they sought even more immediate solutions, such as legislation, to African Americans' problems in both the South and the North. African American abolitionists nonetheless took heart in the immediatists' success at winning converts.

10-9d Opposition to Abolitionism

But that very success gave rise to a virulent, even violent, opposition, not only among southerners but also among northerners who recognized cotton's vital economic role, and who feared emancipation would prompt an enormous influx of freed slaves into their own region. Like many southerners, they questioned the institution's morality but not its practicality: they believed blacks to be inherently inferior and incapable of acquiring the attributes—virtue and diligence—required of freedom and citizenship. Some

northerners, too, objected to white women's involvement in abolitionism, believing that women's proper role lay within the home.

Opposition to abolitionism could become violent. In Boston, David Walker, a southern-born free black, died under mysterious circumstances in 1830, one year after advocating the violent overthrow of slavery in his *Appeal . . . to the Colored Citizens*. Among those northerners who most despised abolitionists were "gentlemen of property and standing"—a nineteenth-century term for commercial and political elites—who often had strong economic connections to the southern cotton economy and political connections to leading southerners. Northern gentlemen incited anti-abolitionist riots. In Utica, New York, in 1835 merchants and professionals broke up the state Anti-Slavery Convention, which had welcomed blacks and women. Mob violence peaked that year, with more than fifty riots aimed at

Destruction by Fire of Pennsylvania Hall,
On the night of the 17th May, 1838

△ Three days after its dedication in 1838, Pennsylvania Hall—an abolitionist center in Philadelphia—was burned to the ground by anti-abolitionist rioters.

The Burning of Pennsylvania Hall, 1838 (colour litho)/American School, (19th century)/LIBRARY COMPANY OF PHILADELPHIA/Library Company of Philadelphia, PA, USA/Bridgeman Images

P. T. Barnum's Publicity Stunts

Usually remembered for the Ringling Brothers and Barnum & Bailey Circus, P. T. Barnum (1810–1891) left another legacy: the publicity stunt. Using hoaxes and spectacles, Barnum's American Museum in New York City drew tens of millions of visitors between 1841 and 1868, making Barnum the era's second wealthiest American.

"I am indebted to the press . . . for almost every dollar that I possess," Barnum declared. Barnum first gained widespread publicity in 1835 with his traveling exhibition of Joice Heth, whom he claimed was the 161-year-old former slave of George Washington. When interest petered out, Barnum planted a rumor that she was a fake, a machine made of leather and bones.

The penny press reveled in the ensuing controversy, swelling admissions and earning Barnum enough to purchase the American Museum, whose "500,000 natural and artificial curiosities" he promoted through similar stunts. The "Feejee [Fiji] Mermaid," for example, caused a national stir, as scientists debated its authenticity. (It was a monkey's head sewn to a fish's body.) Barnum hosted promotional events, too, including the nation's first beauty pageant in 1854. Offensive to middle-class sensibilities, it flopped, but Barnum persevered with pageants featuring dogs, babies, and chickens. The baby show alone attracted 61,000 visitors. As Barnum wrote, "Without promotion, something terrible happens . . . Nothing!" Selling more than a million copies, Barnum's autobiography inspired generations of entrepreneurs.

Many of today's cultural icons began as promotional gimmicks, including the Miss America Pageant (1921), the Macy's Thanksgiving Day parade (1924), and the Goodyear blimp (1925). Since 1916, Nathan's has hosted an annual Fourth of July hot dog–eating contest, now attracting forty thousand live spectators and a national television audience; until recently, the event also included acts from the circus that bore Barnum's name until its closing in 2017. Nathan's rival, Oscar Mayer, launched its Wienermobile in 1936; seven hot dog–shaped cars now tour the country, with drivers selected from a nationally publicized competition. The *Guinness Book of World Records*, begun as an Irish beer company's promotional brochure, inspires pizza makers to attempt to make the world's largest pizza; ice-cream makers, to create the largest sundae; and billionaires to cross oceans in hot-air balloons sporting their conglomerate's logos. Even failed attempts generate publicity.

By staging stunts designed to garner free media exposure, today's entrepreneurs reveal the enduring legacy of P. T. Barnum, the self-proclaimed greatest showman on earth.

CRITICAL THINKING

◻ While the use of publicity stunts has become the norm in the entertainment industry and is used widely in the promotion of various products, it also has a legacy of use in American politics for good or ill. How has the advent of instant communication and (especially) social media altered the nature and influence of publicity stunts in our own era, compared to those of the 1840s–1860s?

Paul Fearn/Alamy

◁ In the 1840s, P.T. Barnum stirred controversy by exhibiting one of his most famous hoaxes, the "Feejee Mermaid," which he fabricated by sewing a monkey's head to a fish's body.

abolitionists or African Americans. In 1837, in Alton, Illinois, a mob murdered white abolitionist editor Elijah P. Lovejoy, and rioters sacked his printing office. The following year, rioters in Philadelphia hurled stones and insults at three thousand black and white women attending the Anti-Slavery Convention of American Women in the brand-new Pennsylvania Hall, a building constructed to house abolitionist meetings and an abolitionist bookstore. The following day, a mob burned the building to the ground, three days after its dedication.

10-9e Moral Suasion Versus Political Action

Such violence made some immediatists question whether moral suasion was a realistic tactic. Men like James G. Birney, the son of a Kentucky slave owner, embraced immediatism but believed abolition could be effected only in the male sphere of politics. Involving women violated the natural order of things and detracted from the ultimate goal: freedom for slaves. Thus, when William Lloyd Garrison, an ardent supporter of women's rights, endorsed Abby Kelly's appointment to the American Antislavery Society's business committee in 1840, he provoked an irreparable split in the abolitionist movement. Arthur Tappan and Theodore Weld led a dissident group that established the American and Foreign Anti-Slavery Society. That society in turn formed a new political party: the Liberty Party, which nominated Birney for president in 1840 and 1844.

Although committed to immediate abolitionism, the Liberty Party doubted the federal government's authority to abolish slavery where it already existed. States, not the federal government, had the jurisdiction to determine slavery's legality within their bounds. Where the federal government could act was in the western territories, and the party demanded that all new territories prohibit slavery. Some prominent black abolitionists, including Frederick Douglass, endorsed the party, whose leaders emphasized, too, the need to combat northern prejudice as a crucial step in allowing African Americans to achieve their full potential.

10-9f Free-Labor Ideology

Secular and religious beliefs in progress—and upward mobility—coalesced into the notion of free labor, the concept that, in a competitive marketplace, those who worked hard and lived virtuous lives could improve their status. Free-labor ideology appealed especially to manufacturers and merchants eager to believe that their own success emerged from hard work and moral virtue—and eager as well to encourage their factory hands and clerks to work hard and live virtuously, to remain optimistic despite current hardships. Many laborers initially rejected free-labor ideology, seeing it as a veiled attempt to tout industrial work habits, to rationalize poor wages, to denigrate Catholicism, and to quell worker protest. But by the 1850s, when the issue of slavery's expansion into the West returned to the political foreground, more and more northerners would embrace free-labor ideology and come to see slavery as antithetical to it. It was this way of thinking, perhaps more than anything else, that made the North distinctive.

Summary

During the first half of the nineteenth century, the North became rapidly enmeshed in a commercial culture. Northern states and capitalists invested heavily in internal improvements, which lay the groundwork for market expansion. Most northerners now turned either toward commercial farming or, in smaller numbers, toward industrial wage labor. Farmers gave up mixed agriculture and specialized in cash crops, while their children often went to work in factories or countinghouses.

To many northerners, the market economy symbolized progress, in which they found much to celebrate: easier access to cheap western lands, employment for surplus farm laborers, and the ready commercial availability of goods that had once been time-consuming to produce. At the same time, though, the market economy led to increased specialization, a less personal workplace, complex market relationships, more regimentation, a sharper divide between work and leisure, and a degradation of natural resources. Northerners' involvement in the market economy also tied them more directly to fluctuating national and international markets, and during economic downturns, many northern families experienced destitution.

With parents relying less directly on children's labor, northerners began producing smaller families. Even as working-class children continued to work as canal drivers and factory hands (or to scavenge urban streets), middle-class families created a sheltered model of childhood in which they tried to shield children from the perceived dangers of the world outside the family. Their mothers, in theory, became moral guardians of the household, keeping the home safe from the encroachment of the new economy's competitiveness and selfishness. Few women, though, had the luxury to devote themselves entirely to nurturing their children and husbands.

Immigrants and free African Americans performed much of the lowest-paying work in the expanding economy, and many native-born whites blamed them for the problems that accompanied the era's rapid economic changes. Anti-immigrant (especially anti-Catholic) and antiblack riots became commonplace. At the same time, immigrants and African Americans worked to form their own communities.

Cities came to symbolize for many Americans both the possibilities and the limits of market expansion. Urban areas were marked by extremes of wealth, and they fostered vibrant working-class cultures even as they encouraged poverty, crime, and mob violence. Driven by a belief in human perfectibility, many evangelicals, especially women, worked tirelessly to right the wrongs of American society. They hoped to trigger the millennium, the thousand years of earthly peace accompanying Christ's return. Reformers battled the evils of prostitution and alcohol, and they sought to reform criminals and delinquents, improve insane asylums, and establish public schools. Some rejected the possibility of reforming American society from within and instead joined experimental communities that modeled radical alternatives to the social and economic order. Abolitionists combined the reformers' and utopians' approaches; they worked to perfect American society from within but through radical means—the eradication of slavery. Drawing on both secular and religious ideals, middle-class northerners increasingly articulated an ideology of free labor, touting the possibility for upward mobility in a competitive marketplace. This ideology would become increasingly central to northern regional identity.

Suggestions for Further Reading

Jeanne Boydston, *Home and Work: Housework, Wages, and the Ideology of Labor in the Early Republic* (1990)

Nancy Cott, *The Bonds of Womanhood: "Women's Sphere" in New England, 1780–1835* (1977)

Daniel Walker Howe, *What Hath God Wrought: The Transformation of America, 1815–1848* (2007)

Mary Kelley, *Learning to Stand and Speak: Women, Education, and Public Life in America's Republic* (2006)

Bruce Laurie, *Artisans into Workers: Labor in Nineteenth-Century America* (1989)

Steven Mintz, *Moralists and Modernizers: America's Pre–Civil War Reformers* (1995)

Carol Sheriff, *The Artificial River: The Erie Canal and the Paradox of Progress, 1817–1862* (1996)

Christine Stansell, *City of Women: Sex and Class in New York, 1789–1860* (1986)

Melvyn Stokes and Stephen Conway, eds., *The Market Revolution in America: Social, Political, and Religious Expressions, 1800–1880* (1996)

George Rogers Taylor, *The Transportation Revolution, 1815–1860* (1951)

MINDTAP
From Cengage

MindTap® is a fully online personalized learning experience built upon Cengage Learning content. MindTap® combines student learning tools—readings, multimedia, activities, and assessments—into a singular Learning Path that guides students through the course and helps students develop the critical thinking, analysis, and communication skills that are essential to academic and professional success.

The Contested West, 1815–1860

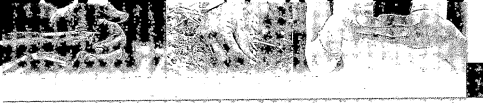

To eight-year-old Henry Clay Bruce, moving west was an adventure. In April 1844, the Virginia boy began a 1,500-mile, two-month trip to his new home in Missouri. Henry marveled at the newness of it all—beautiful natural terrain, impressive towns, different styles of dress. Nothing awed him more than the steamboat ride from Louisville to St. Louis; it felt like "a house floating on the water." Upon his arrival in Missouri, Henry was struck by how much the West differed from the East. The farms lay at much greater distances apart, and the countryside abounded with berries, wild fruits, game, and fish. But it was not paradise. Rattlesnakes, wolves, and vicious hogs roamed the countryside, keeping Henry and his playmates close to home.

Only one thing matched the wildlife's ferocity: Jack Perkinson, the owner of the plantation on which Henry now lived. For Henry was a slave boy who had been relocated, along with his mother and siblings, because his master decided to seek a new beginning in the West. Pettis Perkinson (Jack's brother and Henry's owner) and three other white Virginians had crammed their families, their slaves, and whatever belongings they could fit into three wagons—two for slaves, one for whites. Once in Missouri, Pettis resided with Jack Perkinson, who—according to Henry—readily yelled at and whipped his own slaves. Henry's first year in Missouri was as carefree as a slave child's life could be. The boy fished, hunted (with dogs, not guns), and gathered prairie chickens' eggs. But as his ninth birthday approached, Henry was hired out, first to a brickmaker, then to a tobacco factory. He worked sunup to sundown, and when he failed to satisfy his bosses, he was whipped.

Meanwhile, Pettis Perkinson, unenamored with Missouri, returned home to Virginia, only later summoning some of his slaves, including Henry, who returned "contrary to our will." A less

◁ Like Henry Clay Bruce, many emigrants in the 1840s traveled west by steamboat for part of their journey, making the rest of the trip on foot, horseback, wagon, canal boat, or—often—by some combination of means.
Joslyn Art Museum, Omaha, Nebraska

Chronology

1812	General Land Office established
1820	Price lowered on public lands
1821	Santa Fe Trail charted
	Mexico's independence
1823	Mexico allows Stephen Austin to settle U.S. citizens in Tejas
1824	Congressional General Survey Act
	Jedediah Smith's South Pass publicized
	Indian Office established
1825–32	*Empresario* contracts signed
1826	Fredonia rebellion fails
1830	Indian Removal Act (see Chapter 9)
1830–46	Comanche, Navajo, and Apache raiders devastate northern Mexican states
1832	Black Hawk War
1834	McCormick reaper patented
1836	Lone Star Republic founded
	U.S. Army Corps of Topographical Engineers established
1840–60	250,000 to 500,000 migrants travel overland
1841	Log Cabin Bill
	Texas annexed (see Chapter 12)
1846–48	War with Mexico (see Chapter 12)
1847	Mormons settle Great Salt Lake valley
1848	California gold discovered
1849–50s	Migrants stream into Great Plains and Far West
1849–1855	Border between United States and Mexico demarcated
1855	Ash Hollow Massacre
1857–58	Mormons and U.S. Army in armed conflict
1862	Homestead Act passed

rigorous work routine awaited the Perkinson slaves in Virginia, but that did not compensate for leaving loved ones behind in Missouri.

Soon Pettis Perkinson again grew weary of the tired, rocky soil on his Virginia farm, and with renewed determination to seek opportunity in the West, he moved to Mississippi, where his sister lived. But life on a cotton plantation suited neither Henry nor his master, who now decided—to his slaves' joy—to give Missouri a second chance.

Henry's master remained restless: two years after returning to Missouri, he decided to head for Texas. Henry, now in his late teens, and his brothers refused to go. Although livid, Pettis Perkinson abandoned his plans, apparently not wishing to contend with recalcitrant slaves. After being hired out several more times, Henry became the foreman on Perkinson's Missouri farm, where he remained until escaping during the Civil War to the free state of Kansas. Finally, Henry Clay Bruce found the opportunity and freedom that so many sought when they first headed westward.

Experience an interactive version of this story in MindTap®.

In 1820, about 20 percent of the nation's population lived west of the Appalachian Mountains. By 1860, nearly 50 percent did. Most white people and free blacks moved west because they—or their heads of household—believed better opportunities awaited them there. When easterners envisioned the West, they generally saw enormous tracts of fertile, uncultivated land. Or, beginning in the late 1840s, they imagined getting rich quick in the West's gold or silver mines. Some saw opportunities for lumbering or ranching or for selling goods or services to farmers, miners, lumbermen, and cattlemen.

For some white Americans, mostly from the South, the ability to own slaves in the West signaled the epitome of their own freedom. For others, from both the North and the South, slavery's westward expansion frustrated dreams for a new beginning in a region free from what they saw as slavery's degrading influence on white labor. Northerners, in particular, often set their sights on the Oregon Territory.

They believed the sacrifices brought about by an arduous transcontinental journey would be outweighed by the rewards: agricultural prosperity in a land free from blacks, enslaved and free.

Many of those heading west had no say in the matter. Men often made the decision without consulting their wives and children, and slaves' wishes received even less consideration. Nor did western settlers give much, if any, thought to how their migration would influence the Native peoples already living in the West—on lands they had occupied in some cases for generations and, in other cases, since being relocated by the U.S. government.

The federal government's involvement in westward expansion extended far beyond removing Native peoples. The government sponsored exploration, made laws regulating settlement and the establishment of territorial governments, surveyed and fixed prices on public lands, sold those lands, invested in transportation routes, and established a military presence (see Map. 11.1).

The Mexican government, too, played a role in Anglo-American settlement in the West—one it would later regret—by encouraging immigration to its northern borderlands in the 1820s. From the United States came settlers who vied with the region's other inhabitants—Native Americans, Hispanics, and people of mixed heritage—for land and other natural resources. A decade later, Texas, one of Mexico's northern provinces, declared its independence and sought annexation by the United States. Thus began an era of heightened tensions—not only between the United States and Mexico, but also within the United States as Texas's future became entangled with the thorny issue of slavery.

Human interactions in the West involved both cooperation and conflict. But with each passing decade, conflict—between expectations and reality, between people with different aspirations and worldviews—would increasingly define daily life.

▨ *How did conditions and tensions in the East influence western migration and settlement?*

▨ *How did public, private, and individual initiatives converge to shape the West's development?*

▨ *What motivated cooperation in the West, and what spurred conflict?*

11-1 The West in the American Imagination

▷ **What was the "West" to early-nineteenth-century Americans and emigrants?**

▷ **How did literature and art shape Americans' and Europeans' imaginations of the West?**

▷ **How did Euro-American artists portray Native peoples and their cultures?**

For historian Frederick Jackson Turner, writing in the late nineteenth century, it was the West, not the South or the North, that was distinctive. With its abundance of free land, the western frontier—what he saw as the "meeting point between savagery and civilization"—bred American democracy, shaped the American character, and made the United States exceptional among nations. Modern historians generally eschew the notion of American exceptionalism, stressing instead the deep and complex connections between the United States and the rest of the world. Although today's scholars also reject the racialist assumptions of Turner's definition of *frontier*, some see continued value in using the term to signify a meeting place of different cultures. Others see the West as fundamentally a place, not a process, though they disagree over what delineates it.

11-1a Defining the West

For early-nineteenth-century Americans of European descent, the West included anything west of the Appalachian Mountains. But it was, first and foremost, a place representing the future—a place offering economic and social betterment for themselves and their children. For many, betterment entailed landownership; the West's seeming abundance of land meant that anyone could hope to own a farm and achieve economic and political independence. Men who already owned land, like Pettis Perkinson, looked westward for cheaper, bigger, and more fertile landholdings. With the discovery of gold in California in 1848, the West became a place to strike it rich before returning home to live in increased comfort or even opulence.

Many people arrived in the West under the threat of force. These included enslaved men, women, and children whose owners moved them, often against their will, as well as Native peoples removed from their eastern homelands by the U.S. military under provisions of the Indian Removal Act of 1830.

To others, the very notion of the West would have been baffling. Emigrants from Mexico and Central or South America traveled north to get to what European Americans called the West. Chinese nationals traveled eastward to California. Many Native Americans simply considered the West home. Other Native peoples and French Canadians journeyed southward to the West. All these people, much like European Americans, arrived in the western portion of the North American continent because of a combination of factors pushing and pulling them.

11-1b Frontier Literature

For European Americans, Daniel Boone became the archetypical frontiersman, a man whose daring individualism opened the Eden-like West for virtuous and hard-working freedom lovers. Through biographies published by John Filson (1784) and by Timothy Flint (1833), Boone became a familiar figure in American and European households. The mythical Boone lived in the wilderness, became "natural" himself, and shrank from society, feeling compelled to relocate upon seeing smoke billowing from a neighboring cabin. He single-handedly overpowered bears and Indians. Even as he adopted wilderness ways, according to legend, Boone became the pathfinder for civilization. As a friend wrote, Boone "has been the instrument of opening the road to millions of the human family from the pressure of sterility and want, to a Land flowing with milk and honey." By borrowing biblical language—the land of milk and honey denoting the Promised Land, the idyllic place that God promised to the beleaguered Israelites—Boone's friend

suggested that Boone was Moses-like, leading his people to a land of abundance.

Such stories mythologized not only Boone, but the West itself. The Indian-fighting Boone, according to Flint's best-selling biography, had wrested for civilized society "the great west—the garden of the earth." Little matter that the real Boone regretted having killed Native peoples and often struggled to support his family. When Boone became the heroic model for James Fenimore Cooper's *Leatherstocking Tales* (1823–1841)—set on the frontier of western New York—he came to symbolize not only American adventure but also individualism and freedom.

With the invention of the steam press in the early 1830s, western adventure stories became cheap and widely read. Davy Crockett, another real-life figure turned into mythical hero, was featured in many of them. In real life, Crockett had first fought the Creeks under Andrew Jackson but later championed Native peoples' rights, rebuking the removal bill. After losing his life defending the Alamo mission during Texas's fight for

Map 11.1 Westward Expansion, 1800–1860

Through exploration, purchase, war, and treaty, the United States became a continental nation, stretching from the Atlantic to the Pacific.

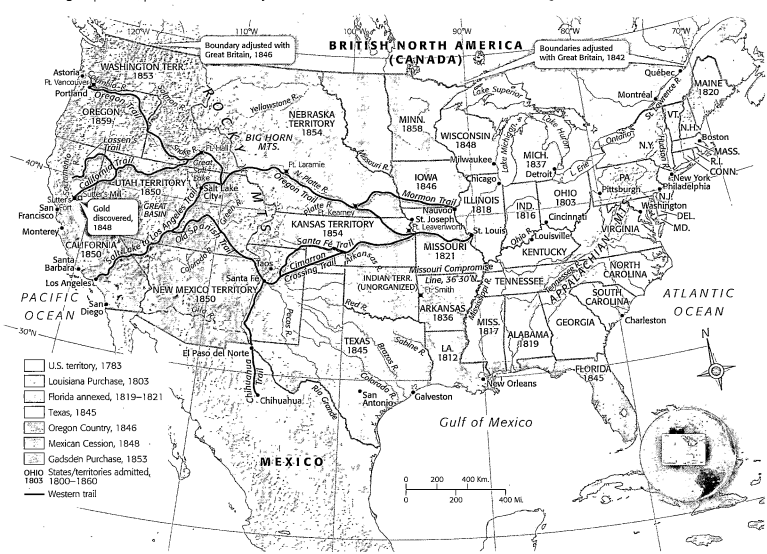

independence (1836), though, Crockett often appeared in stories portraying the West as violent, a place where one escaped civilized society and fought Indians and Mexicans. But even in this version of the western myth, the American West symbolized what white Americans saw as their nation's core value: freedom.

11-1c Western Art

Inspired partly by such literature, many easterners yearned to see the West and its Native peoples, and artists hastened to accommodate them. Yet the images they produced often revealed more about white Americans' ideals than about the West itself. In these portrayals, the West was sometimes an untamed wilderness inhabited by savages (noble or otherwise), and sometimes a cultivated garden, a land of milk and honey where the Jeffersonian agrarian dream was realized.

The first Anglo-American artists to travel west were Samuel Seymour and Titian Ramsay Peale, whom the federal government hired to accompany explorer Stephen H. Long on his 1820 expedition to the Rocky Mountains. They pioneered an influential art genre: facsimiles in government reports. Between 1840 and 1860, Congress published nearly sixty works on western exploration, featuring hundreds of lithographs and engravings of plants, animals, and people. Some reports became best sellers. The most popular was the twelve-volume Pacific Railway Survey (1855–1860), chronicling expeditions to explore four possible railroad routes. The government distributed more than 53,000 copies, helping easterners visualize for themselves the continent's western reaches.

Although government reports often faithfully reproduced original paintings, they sometimes made telling alterations. When Richard Kern accompanied explorer James H. Simpson in 1849 to the Southwest, for example, he painted a Navajo man in a submissive pose. The painting's reproduction for general distribution transformed the man's pose into a rebellious one. In other cases, the government reports transformed artists' depictions of Native American-occupied landscapes into empty terrain seemingly free for the taking.

Yet the original artwork did not necessarily offer an accurate view of the West either. Artists' own cultural assumptions colored their portrayals, and commercial artists produced what they thought the public craved. When **George Catlin** traveled west in the early 1830s, he may have genuinely hoped to paint what he saw as Native peoples' vanishing way of life. But he also aimed to attract a paying public of easterners to his exhibitions. Traveling and painting immediately following the Indian Removal Act of 1830, Catlin painted the West with a moral in mind: Native peoples came in two varieties—those who preserved their original, almost noble qualities, characterized by freedom and moderation, and those who, after coming in contact with whites, had become "dissolute." Native peoples, he implied, benefited from removal from white Americans' corrupting influence.

Western artwork became widely viewed as facsimiles appeared in magazines and books and even on banknotes. Such images nurtured easterners' curiosities and fantasies—and sometimes their itch to move westward.

Smithsonian American Art Museum, Washington, DC/Art Resource, NY

△ In one of his most famous portraits, George Catlin painted Wi-Jun-Jon, an Assiniboine man, both before and after he had mingled with white men. In the "before" stance, Wi-Jun-Jon is a dignified, peace-pipe-bearing warrior; in the "after" portrait, the "corrupted" Assiniboine has abandoned dignity for vanity and his peace pipe for a cigar.

11-1d Countering the Myths

But western realities often clashed with promoters' promises, and disappointed settlers sometimes tried to clarify matters for future migrants. From Philadelphia in the 1850s came a song parodying the familiar call of "to the West":

> At the west they told me there was wealth to be won,
> The forest to clear, was the work to be done;
> I tried it—couldn't do it—guv it up in despair,
> And just see if you'll ever again catch me there.
> The little snug farm I expected to buy,
> I quickly discovered was just all in my eye,
> I came back like a streak—you may go—but I'm bless'd
> If you'll ever again, sirs, catch me at the west.

Rebecca Burlend, an English immigrant in Illinois, encountered hardships aplenty—intemperate weather, difficult working conditions, swindlers—and with her son wrote an autobiographical account, *A True Picture of Emigration* (1848), alerting her countrymen to what awaited them in the American West. The Burlends had been lured to

George Catlin American painter who traveled throughout the West and produced numerous portraits of Native Americans that reflected his fascination with and beliefs about them.

Illinois by an Englishman's letters extolling "a land flowing with milk and honey." Burlend reckoned that he must have "gathered his honey rather from thorns than flowers." Her account sought not to discourage emigration but to substitute a realistic for a rosy description.

11-2 Expansion and Resistance in the Trans-Appalachian West

▶ How did individuals decide to move west?

▶ How did Native Americans respond to white settlement in the West?

▶ What were the realities of work in the West?

▶ How was the economy of the West linked to the East?

Americans had always been highly mobile, but never to the extent following the War of 1812, which weakened Native peoples' resistance and set off a flurry of transportation projects. In the 1820s and 1830s, settlers streamed west of the Appalachian Mountains into the Old Northwest and the Old Southwest. They traveled by foot, horseback, wagon, canal boat, steamboat, or—often—by some combination of means. Many people, like Pettis Perkinson and his slaves, moved several times, looking for better opportunities, and when opportunities failed to materialize, some returned home.

Both the Old Northwest and the Old Southwest saw population explosions during the early nineteenth century (see Map 11.2). But while the Old Southwest grew by an impressive 50 percent each decade, the Northwest's population grew exponentially. In 1790, the region's white population numbered just a few hundred people. By 1860, nearly 7 million people called the region home. Between 1810 and 1830, the population of Ohio more than quadrupled, while Indiana and Illinois grew fourteenfold and thirteenfold, respectively. Michigan's population multiplied by more than fifty times in the thirty years between 1820 and 1850. Migration rather than birth rates accounted for most of this growth, and once in the Old Northwest, people did not stay put. By the 1840s, more people left Ohio than moved into it. Geographic mobility, the search for more and better opportunities, and connections to the market economy defined the region that became known as the Midwest following the acquisition of U.S. territory farther west. This region came to symbolize, for many northerners, the heart of American values: freedom and upward mobility, both of which could be achieved (for white Americans and European immigrants) through hard work and virtuous behavior.

11-2a Deciding Where to Move

The decision to move west—and then to move again—could be difficult, even heartrending. Moving west meant leaving behind worn-out soil and settled areas with little land available for purchase, but it also meant leaving behind family, friends, and communities. One woman remembered how on the evening before her departure for the West, her entire family gathered together for the last time "looking as if we were all going to our graves the next morning." The journey promised to be arduous and expensive, as did the backbreaking labor of clearing new lands. The West was a land of opportunity but also of uncertainty. What if the soil proved less fertile than anticipated? What if neighbors—white as well as Native American—proved unfriendly, or worse? What if homesickness became unbearable?

Given all that western settlers risked, they tried to control as many variables as possible. Like Pettis Perkinson, people often relocated to communities where they had relatives or friends, and they often traveled with acquaintances from home. They moved to climates similar to those they left behind. Massachusetts farmers headed to western New York or Ohio, Virginians and North Carolinians went to Missouri, Georgians populated Mississippi and Texas, and Europeans—mostly Germans and Irish—headed to the Old Northwest in much larger numbers than to the Old Southwest. Migrants settled in ethnic communities or with people of similar religious values and affiliations. As a result, the Midwest was—in the words of two of its historians—"more like an ethnic and cultural checkerboard than the proverbial melting pot."

When westward-bound Americans fixed on particular destinations, their decisions often rested on slavery's status there. Some white southerners, tired of the planter elite's social and political power, sought homes in areas free from slavery—or at least where there were few plantations. Many others, though, went west to improve their chances of owning slaves, or of purchasing additional slaves. White northerners also resented elite slaveowners' economic and political power and hoped to distance themselves from slavery as well as from free blacks. One Bostonian captured the viewpoint of many white northerners who contemplated moving west: "As a great evil, I detest slavery, but what will you do with the blacks when it is abolished; they cant [sic] hold their own & if given a fair land would ruin it & relapse into African barbarism." Influenced by such sentiments, many midwestern states passed "black laws" in the 1850s prohibiting African Americans, free or enslaved, from living within their boundaries. (Oregon passed a similar law.) Ironically, many free blacks migrated west to free themselves from eastern prejudice. Enslaved men, women, and children moved west in enormous numbers in the years after 1815. Some traveled with their owners, either young couples whose parents had given them slaves as wedding gifts, or established planters who had headed west in search of more fertile soil. When white parents presented their westward-bound children with slaves, they often tore apart those slaves' own families, as spouses, children, parents, or siblings stayed behind. Many slaves moved west with slave traders, who manacled them to a chain connecting them to dozens of other slaves, "urged on by the whip," as one white observer described the slave coffle he encountered in a Mississippi swamp. Their first destination in

Map 11.2 Settlement in the Old Southwest and Old Northwest, 1820 and 1840

Removal of Native peoples and a growing transportation network opened up land to white and black settlers in the regions known as the Old Southwest and the Old Northwest, as the U.S. population grew from 9.6 million in 1820 to 17.1 million in 1840.

the West was the slave pen, often in New Orleans, where they were auctioned to the highest bidder, who became their new owner and took them farther west. Despite the hardships that slaves faced in the West, some took advantage of frontier conditions—tangled and vast forests, the comparative thinness of

law enforcement and slave patrol, and the proximity of Native American communities willing to harbor runaway slaves—to seize their freedom.

Between 1815 and 1860, few western migrants, white or black, settled on the Great Plains, a region reserved for

Native peoples until the 1850s, and relatively few easterners risked the overland journey to California and Oregon before the transcontinental railroad's completion in 1869. Although at first the Southwest seemed to hold the edge in attracting new white settlers, the Midwest—with its better-developed transportation routes, its more democratic access to economic markets, its smaller African American population, its smaller and cheaper average landholding, and its climatic similarity to New England and northern Europe—proved considerably more attractive in the decades after 1820. The Old Northwest's thriving transportation hubs also made good first stops for western migrants lacking cash to purchase land. They found work unloading canal boats, planting and harvesting wheat on nearby farms, grinding wheat into flour, or sawing trees into lumber—or, more often, cobbling together a combination of these seasonal jobs. The South offered fewer such opportunities. With the Old Northwest's population growing more quickly, white southerners worried increasingly about congressional representation and laws regarding slavery.

11-2b Indian Removal and Resistance

In both the Midwest and the Southwest, the expansion of white settlement depended on Native peoples' removal. Even as the U.S. Army escorted Native peoples from the Old Southwest, the federal government arranged treaties in which northeastern American Indian nations relinquished their land titles in exchange for lands west of the Mississippi River (see "Southern Expansion, Native American Resistance and Removal," Section 9-2). Between 1829 and 1851, the U.S. government and northern American Indian tribes signed eighty-six such treaties. Some northern Native peoples evaded removal, including the Miamis in Indiana, the Ottawas and Chippewas in the upper Midwest, and the Winnebagos in southern Wisconsin. In 1840, for example, Miami chiefs had acceded to pressure to exchange 500,000 acres in Indiana for equivalent acreage in Indian Country. Under the treaty's terms, their people had five years to move. When they did not, federal troops arrived to escort them. But about half of the Miami nation dodged the soldiers—and many of those who did trek to Indian Country later returned unauthorized. In Wisconsin, some Winnebagos similarly eluded removal or returned to Wisconsin after being escorted west by soldiers.

11-2c Black Hawk War

The Sauks (or "Sacs") and Fox fared much less well. In a series of treaties between 1804 and 1830, their leaders exchanged lands in northwestern Illinois and southwestern Wisconsin for lands across the Mississippi River in Iowa Territory. Black Hawk, a Sauk warrior who had sided with the British during the War of 1812, disputed the treaties' validity and vowed his people would return to their ancestral lands. "My reason teaches me that land cannot be sold,"

△ In 1834, Karl Bodmer painted a farm on the Illinois prairie, depicting the more permanent, if still modest, structures that farmers built after the initial urgency to clear fields for cultivation had subsided.

Joslyn Art Museum, Omaha, Nebraska

Black Hawk later recalled. "The Great Spirit gave it to his children to live upon, and cultivate, as far as is necessary for their subsistence ... Nothing can be sold but such things as can be carried away." In 1832, Black Hawk led a group of Sauk and Fox families to Illinois, causing panic among white settlers. The state's governor activated the militia, who were later joined by militia from surrounding states and territories as well as by U.S. Army regular soldiers. Over the next several months, hundreds of Sauk and Fox individuals and dozens of white settlers died under often gruesome circumstances in what is known as the Black Hawk War. As the Sauks and Fox tried to flee across the Mississippi River, American soldiers on a steamboat and on land fired indiscriminately. Those men, women, and children who survived the river crossing met gunfire on the western shore from Lakota (Sioux), their longtime enemies, now allied with the Americans.

Black Hawk survived to surrender, and U.S. officials undertook to impress on him and the uprising's other leaders the futility of resistance. After being imprisoned, then sent to Washington, D.C., along a route meant to underscore the United States' immense size and population, and then imprisoned again, the Sauk and Fox peoples were returned to their homes. The Black Hawk War marked the end of militant Native American uprisings in the Old Northwest, adding to the region's appeal to white settlers.

11-2d Selling the West

Land speculators, developers of "paper towns" (ones existing on paper only), steamboat companies, and manufacturers of farming implements all promoted the Midwest as a tranquil place of unbounded opportunity. Land proprietors emphasized the region's connections to eastern customs and markets. They knew that, when families uprooted themselves and headed west, they did not—the mythical Daniel Boone and Davy Crockett aside—seek to escape civilization. When Michael D. Row, the proprietor of Rowsburg in northern Ohio, sought to sell town lots in 1835, he emphasized that Rowsburg was in a "thickly settled" area, stood at the crossroads of public transportation leading in every direction, and had established mills and tanning yards.

Western settlement generally followed rather than preceded connections to national and international markets. Eastern farmers, looking to escape tired soil or tenancy, sought fertile lands for growing commercial crops. Labor-saving devices, such as Cyrus McCormick's reaper (1834) and John Deere's steel plow (1837), made the West more alluring. McCormick, a Virginia inventor, patented a horse-drawn reaper that allowed two men to harvest the same number of acres of wheat that previously required between four and six-teen men, depending on which handheld tool they wielded. Because the reaper's efficiency achieved its greatest payoffs on the prairies, where tracts of land were larger and flatter than in the Shenandoah Valley, McCormick relocated his factory to Chicago in 1847 and began a dogged campaign to sell his reaper—which at $100 was an expensive investment for the average farmer—and, along with it, the West itself.

Without John Deere's steel plow, which unlike wooden and iron plows could break through tough grass and roots and did not require constant cleaning, "breaking the plains" might not have been possible at all.

11-2e Clearing the Land

Most white migrants intended to farm. After locating a suitable land claim, they immediately constructed a rudimentary cabin if none already existed. Time did not permit more elaborate structures, for—contrary to McCormick reaper ads—few settlers found plowed fields awaiting them. First they had to clear the land.

For those settling in wooded areas, the quickest and easiest way to get crops in the ground was to girdle, or to cut deep notches with an ax around a tree's base, cutting off the flow of sap. A few weeks later, the trees would lose their leaves, which farmers burned for fertilizer. As soon as enough light came through, settlers planted corn—a durable and nutritious crop. Eventually the dead trees fell and were chopped for firewood and fences, leaving stumps whose removal was a backbreaking task. At the rate of five to ten acres a year, depending on a family's size, the average family needed ten years to fully clear a farm, assuming the family did not relocate sooner. Prairie land took less time. Throughout the 1850s, though, many farmers dismissed lands free of timber as equivalent to deserts, unfit for cultivation.

Whereas farming attracted families, lumbering and, later, mining appealed mostly to single young men. Lumbering involved long hours—sunup to sundown—and backbreaking labor; lumber workers not only felled trees, but hauled, hoisted, sawed, and stacked the wood. Although employers believed that married men constituted the most stable workforce, they did not want women encumbered by children in the camps. Instead, they looked for "good Families without children," whose wives would work as cooks or laundresses. As one Chicago mill owner informed his manager, "my Business will not warrant the payment of wages sufficient for any one to keep his wife as a Laidy [sic]." Few family men found lumbering to be attractive work.

By the 1840s, the nation's timber industry centered around the Great Lakes. As eastern forests became depleted, northeastern lumber companies and their laborers migrated to Wisconsin, Michigan, and Minnesota. Recently arrived Scandinavians and French Canadians also worked in the booming lumber industry, which provided construction materials for growing cities and wooden ties for expanding railroads. As the Great Lakes forests thinned, lumbermen moved again—some to the Gulf States' pine forests, some to Canada, and some to the Far West, where Mexicans in California and British in Canada had already established flourishing lumber industries. With the rapid growth of California's cities following the **Gold Rush of 1849**, timber's demand soared, drawing midwestern lumbermen farther west.

Gold Rush of 1849 After an American carpenter discovered gold in the foothills of California's Sierra Nevada range in 1848, Americans and people from around the world moved to California to look for gold.

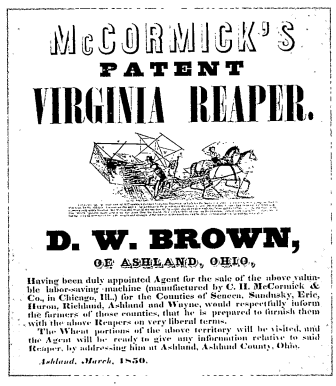

McCORMICK'S PATENT VIRGINIA REAPER.

D. W. BROWN,

OF ASHLAND, OHIO,

Having been duly appointed Agent for the sale of the above valuable labor-saving machine (manufactured by C. H. McCormick & Co., in Chicago, Ill.) for the Counties of Seneca, Sandusky, Erie, Huron, Richland, Ashland and Wayne, would respectfully inform the farmers of those counties, that he is prepared to furnish them with the above Reapers on very liberal terms.

The Wheat portions of the above territory will be visited, and the Agent will be ready to give any information relative to said Reaper, by addressing him at Ashland, Ashland County, Ohio.

Ashland, March, 1850.

△ The horse-drawn McCormick reaper made the harvesting of wheat far more efficient, increasing the allure of western prairie lands. McCormick's Patent Virginia Reaper Advert, 1850 (litho), American School, (19th century) /Private Collection/ Peter Newark American Pictures/ Bridgeman Images.

The Midwest's own cities nurtured the surrounding countryside's settlement. Steamboats turned river settlements like Louisville and Cincinnati into vibrant commercial centers, while Chicago, Detroit, and Cleveland grew up on the Great Lakes' banks. By the mid-nineteenth century, Chicago, with its railroads, stockyards, and grain elevators, dominated the region's economy; western farmers transported livestock and grain by rail to that city, where pigs became packed meat and grain became flour before being shipped east. The promise of future flour and future pigs gave rise to commodities markets. Some of the world's most sophisticated and speculative economic practices took place in Chicago.

11-3 The Federal Government and Westward Expansion

▶ What was the significance of early explorations and encounters in the West?

▶ What role did the federal government play in the exploration of and expansion into the West?

▶ Why did tensions emerge between the federal government and white settlers over the distribution of land?

Few white Americans considered settling in the West before the region had been explored, surveyed, secured, and "civilized," by which they meant not only the removal of Native populations but also the establishment of churches, businesses, and American legal structures. Although some individuals headed west in advance of European civilization, wide-scale settlement depended on the federal government's sponsorship.

11-3a The Fur Trade

No figure better represents the mythical westerner than the mountain man: the loner who wandered the mountains, trapping beaver, living off the land, casting off all semblance of civilization, and daring to go where no white person had ever trod. Fur trappers were, in fact, among the first white Americans in the trans-Appalachian West, but in reality, their lives bore faint resemblance to the myth. Although many had little contact with American society, they interacted regularly with the West's Native peoples. Fur trappers lived among Native peoples, became multilingual, and often married Native American women. Native women transformed animal carcasses into finished pelts, and they also smoothed trade relations between their husbands and their own Native communities. The offspring of such marriages—métis or mestizos (people of mixed Native American and European heritage)—often entered the fur trade and added to the West's cultural complexity.

The fur trade was an international business, with pelts from deep in the American interior finding their way to Europe and Asia. Until the 1820s, British companies dominated the trade, but American ventures prospered in the 1820s and 1830s. The American Fur Company made John Jacob Astor the nation's wealthiest man. While Astor lived lavishly in his New York City mansion, his business employed hundreds of trappers and traders who lived and worked among Native peoples in the Great Lakes and Pacific Northwest regions. From its base in Astoria on the Columbia River, just a few miles from the Pacific Ocean in present-day Oregon, the American Fur Company made millions by sending furs to China.

Even for the great majority of trappers who never made it to Astoria, the fur trade had an international dimension. Beginning in the 1820s, they came together annually for a "rendezvous"—a multiday gathering where they traded fur for guns, tobacco, and beads that they could later exchange with Native peoples. They also shared stories and alcohol, and gambled. Modeled on similar Native American gatherings that had occurred for generations, the rendezvous brought together Americans, Native peoples, Mexicans, and people of mixed heritage from all over the West—as far north as Canada and as far south as Mexico—in numbers that could reach up to one thousand. Rendezvous took place in remote mountain locations but were cosmopolitan affairs.

By 1840, when the final rendezvous took place, the American fur trade was fading. Beavers had been over-hunted and fashions had shifted, with silk supplanting

◁ In 1837, Alfred Jacob Miller, a noted painter of the American West, visited an annual rendezvous, where fur trappers and Native peoples exchanged goods and shared conviviality. Here, Miller portrays the fanfare with which he and his fellow travelers were greeted.

Gift of The Coe Foundation/Buffalo Bill Center of the West

beaver fur as the preferred material for hats. The traders' legacy includes setting a pattern of resource extraction and depletion (and boom and bust), introducing Native peoples to devastating diseases, and developing trails across the trans-Mississippi West.

11-3b Transcontinental Exploration

A desire for quicker and safer routes for transporting goods to trading posts drove much early exploration (see Map 11.3). William Becknell, an enterprising merchant, helped in 1821 to chart the **Santa Fe Trail** running between Missouri and Santa Fe, New Mexico, where it connected to the Chihuahua Trail running southward into Mexico, allowing American and Mexican merchants to develop a vibrant exchange of American manufactured goods for furs and other items. Fur trader Jedediah Smith rediscovered in 1824 the South Pass; this twenty-mile break in the Rocky Mountains in present-day Wyoming had previously been known only to Native Americans and a handful of fur trappers from the Pacific Fur Company who had passed through in 1812. The South Pass became the route followed by most overland travelers to California and Oregon. Less well-known traders, trappers, missionaries, and gold seekers, often assisted by Native American guides, also discovered traveling routes throughout the West, and some—most famously, mountain man Kit Carson—aided government expeditions.

Lewis and Clark's Corps of Discovery was only the first of many federally sponsored expeditions to chart the trans-Mississippi West. These expeditions often had diplomatic goals, aiming to establish cordial relations with Native groups with whom Americans might trade or enter military alliances. Some had scientific missions, charged with recording information about the region's Native inhabitants, flora, and fauna. But they were always also commercial in purpose. Just

as Lewis and Clark had hoped to find what proved to be an elusive Northwest Passage to the Pacific, so, too, did later explorers hope to locate land, water, and rail routes that would allow American businessmen and farmers to trade nationally and internationally.

In 1805, the U.S. Army dispatched Zebulon Pike to find the Mississippi River's source and a navigable route west. He was instructed to collect information on natural resources and Native peoples, and to foster diplomatic relationships with Native American leaders. Pike, like other explorers, was also instructed by government officials to identify and purchase Native peoples' lands suitable for military garrisons.

Although Pike failed to identify the Mississippi's source and had limited success in cultivating relationships and purchasing land, he nonetheless gathered important information. Shortly after returning from present-day Minnesota, he left for what are now Missouri, Nebraska, Kansas, and Colorado. After Pike and his men wandered into Spanish territory to the south, military officials held Pike captive for several months in Mexico, inadvertently giving him a tour of areas that he might not have otherwise explored. After his release, Pike wrote an account of his experiences describing a potential market in southwestern cities as well as bountiful furs and precious metals. The province of Tejas (Texas), with its fertile soil and rich grasslands, enchanted him. At the same time, Pike dismissed the other northern provinces of Mexico, whose boundaries stretched to the northern borders of present-day Nevada and Utah, as unsuitable for human habitation. Although nomadic Native peoples might sustain themselves there, he explained, the region was unfit for cultivation by civilized people.

Santa Fe Trail Trading route from St. Louis, Missouri, to Santa Fe, New Mexico, that enabled commerce to expand its reach farther west.

Map 11.3 Western Native Peoples and Routes of Exploration

Although western explorers believed they were discovering new routes and places, Native peoples had long lived in most of the areas through which explorers traveled.

Explorers' routes
➡ Pike, 1805
➡ Pike, 1806–1807
➡ Long, 1819–1820

Fremont
➡ 1842
➡ 1843
➡ 1845
➡ 1848
➡ 1854

UTE Major Indian tribe, 1850
—— U.S. boundaries, by 1854

Stephen Long, another army explorer, similarly declared in 1820 that the region comprising modern-day Oklahoma, Kansas, and Nebraska was "the Great American Desert," incapable of cultivation. Until the 1850s, when a transcontinental railroad was planned, this "desert" was reserved for Native peoples' settlement, and most army-sponsored exploration focused elsewhere. In 1838, Congress established the U.S. Army Corps of Topographical Engineers to systematically explore the West in advance of widespread settlement. As a second lieutenant in that corps, **John C. Frémont**

John C. Frémont Explorer who played a role in a California rebellion against Mexico; later a senator and presidential candidate and force in national politics.

undertook three expeditions to the region between the upper Mississippi and Missouri rivers, the Rockies, the Great Basin, Oregon, and California. He helped survey the Oregon Trail. With the assistance of his wife, Jessie Benton Frémont, Frémont published best-selling accounts of his explorations, earning him the nickname "The Pathfinder" and paving the way for a political career. The Corps of Topographical Engineers' most significant contributions came in the 1850s with its surveying of possible routes for a transcontinental railroad.

The federal government spent millions publicizing the results of its explorations, much more than it allotted for exploration itself. Westward migrants often carried two books with them: the Bible and Frémont's account of his army explorations.

11-3c A Military Presence

The army did more than explore. It also helped ready the West for settlement. With the General Survey Act of 1824, Congress empowered the military to chart transportation improvements deemed vital to the nation's military protection or commercial growth. In addition to working on federally funded projects, army engineers helped design state- and privately sponsored roads, canals, and railroads, and army soldiers cleared forests and lay roadbeds. A related bill, also in 1824, authorized the army to improve the Ohio and Mississippi rivers; a later amendment did the same for the Missouri.

By the 1850s, 90 percent of the U.S. military was stationed west of the Mississippi River. When Native peoples refused to relinquish their lands, the army escorted them westward; when they inflicted harm on whites or their property, the army waged war. The army sometimes destroyed the crops and buildings of white squatters refusing to vacate lands settled without legal title. But, primarily, the army assisted overland migration. Army forts on the periphery of Indian Country intimidated Native peoples, defended settlers and migrants from Native attacks, and supplied information and provisions. In theory, the army was also supposed to protect Native Americans by driving settlers off Native lands and enforcing laws prohibiting the sale of alcohol to Native peoples. Yet even when officers were disposed to enforce such policies, the army's small size relative to the territory it regulated made it virtually impossible to do so.

The Office of Indian Affairs handled the government's other interactions with Native peoples, including treaty negotiations, school management, and trade oversight. Created in 1824 as part of the War Department, the Indian Office cooperated with the military in removing Native peoples from lands that stood in the way of American expansion and in protecting those citizens who staked their future in the West. In 1849 the Indian Office became part of the newly established Department of the Interior and soon shifted its focus from removal to civilization, through a reservation system. Whereas some Native individuals accepted reservations as the best protection from white incursion, others rejected them, sometimes setting off deadly intratribal disagreements.

11-3d Public Lands

The federal government controlled vast tracts of land, procured either from the states' cessions of their western claims after the Revolution or through treaties with foreign powers, including American Indian nations. The General Land Office, established in 1812 as part of the Treasury Department, handled those lands' distribution. Its earliest policies, designed to raise revenue, divided western lands into 640-acre tracts to be sold at public auction at a minimum price of $2 an acre. These policies favored speculators over individual, cash-poor farmers. Speculators bought up millions of acres of land. Unable to afford federal lands, many settlers became squatters, prompting Congress

△ In this 1850 painting, George Caleb Bingham portrays squatters, or settlers who improved public lands before they went on sale, often in the hope that the government would later allow them to purchase the lands at low prices.

in 1820 to lower the price of land to $1.25 per acre and to make available tracts as small as 80 acres. Twelve years later, it began selling 40-acre tracts. Yet it demanded that the land be bought outright, and in a cash-poor society (particularly in the aftermath of the Panic of 1819), few would-be western settlers had enough cash to purchase government land. Because speculators sold land on credit, many small-time farmers bought from them instead, but at inflated prices.

Farmers pressed for a federal policy of preemption—that is, the right to settle on land without obtaining title, to improve it, and to buy it later at the minimum price ($1.25 an acre) established by law. Without such a law, farmers who had "squatted" on land—settled and improved it without legal title—risked losing it to speculators who could outbid them once the land became officially open for sale. One congressman explained the squatter's plight: "he would see his little home, on which he had toiled for years, where he hoped to rear his children and find a peaceful grave, pass into the hands of a rich moneyed company."

Although some states offered lands through preemption, and although Congress authorized preemption of federal lands in particular instances in the 1820s and 1830s, the first general preemption law, the so-called Log Cabin Bill, came in 1841, and even then, it applied only to surveyed land. The right of preemption extended to unsurveyed lands with the **Homestead Act of 1862**, which provided that land would

be provided free to any U.S. citizen (or foreigner who had declared the intention of becoming a citizen), provided he or she resided on it for five years and improved it. Alternatively, settlers could buy the land

Homestead Act of 1862
Passed in 1862, it embodied the Republican Party's ideal of "free soil, free labor, free men" by granting 160 acres of public land to settlers who resided on it for five years and improved it.

Gold in California

When James Marshall discovered gold in Sutter's Mill, California, in January 1848, word spread quickly—and quite literally around the world. Within a year, tens of thousands of adventurers from other countries rushed to California, making it the most cosmopolitan place in North America, and perhaps the entire world.

In an era before the telegraph crossed the oceans, the news traveled surprisingly fast. Mexicans heard first. Next, word spread to Chile, Peru, and throughout South America; then across the Pacific to Hawai'i, China, and Australia; and then to Europe—Ireland, France, and the German states. How did the news travel? Overland travelers brought the news south to Baja California and Sonora in Mexico. By spring 1849, some six thousand Mexicans were panning for gold around the newly established town of Sonora, California. Many of the Mexicans came north seasonally to seek gold, spreading news of California on every trip home.

Sailing ships brought news of California gold to Hawai'i. The newspaper *Honolulu Polynesian* announced it in the kingdom on June 24, 1848. "Honolulu has never before witnessed such an excitement as the gold fever has created," the *Polynesian* reported later that summer. Gold seekers and merchants sailed from Hawai'i to California, and their letters home recruited others. The constant traffic led to regular steamship service between Hawai'i and California as early as 1853.

A ship brought news of California gold discoveries to Valparaiso, Chile, in August 1848. More dramatically, a few weeks later, another sailing vessel landed with $2,500 in gold dust aboard. Although Chilean newspapers initially ignored the discovery, people in Chile's cities talked feverishly about gold. By November, newspapers reported rumors of California's overnight riches. Before year's end, two thousand Chileans had left for California, and many Chilean merchants opened branch stores in San Francisco.

Word of gold and California reached Australia in December 1848. Gold seekers quickly made travel arrangements, and by 1850 every ship in Sydney Harbour was destined for California. News had already reached China in mid-1848. A San Francisco merchant headed for the gold fields, Chum Ming, had written a cousin about his hopes for wealth. Four months later, the cousin arrived in San Francisco—with fellow villagers. Widespread poverty and gold's allure prompted many other Chinese to follow. By the mid-1850s, one in five gold miners was Chinese.

Californians, new and old, foreign and native-born, expressed amazement at the ethnic variety. One described it as "the most curious Babel of a place imaginable." In 1850, the new state of California had nearly 40 percent foreign-born inhabitants, the majority non-European. Through word of mouth, rumor, letters home, and newspaper reports, the discovery of gold in 1848 linked California to millions of ordinary people around the globe.

CRITICAL THINKING

◻ Reading this feature and section 11-2f on the Gold Rush, evaluate the extent to which the influx of immigrants from countries around the world as well as the arrival of Americans from the East unsettled patterns of migration that had existed up until this point. How did California's gold rush change life there for newcomers, existing residents, and Native peoples?

◁ This 1855 Frank Marryat drawing of a San Francisco saloon dramatizes the international nature of the California gold rush. Like theater performers, the patrons of the saloon dress their parts as Yankees, Mexicans, Asians, and South Americans.

The Art Archive at Art Resource, NY

outright at $1.25 an acre after six months of residency, an arrangement that allowed them to use the land as collateral for loans to purchase additional land, farming supplies, or machinery. By the time of the Homestead Act, though, much of the remaining federal land was arid, and 160 acres was not always enough for an independent farm. Most of the best land, moreover, ended up in speculators' hands.

11-4 The Southwestern Borderlands

▷ What was life like for Hispanics and Native peoples prior to settlement by white Americans?

▷ How did white settlement and expansion in the Southwest and Texas influence Native peoples?

▷ How did the relationship between Mexico and Americans evolve amid efforts to obtain Texas independence?

Along the Louisiana Territory's southwestern border lay vast provinces controlled mostly by the Comanches and other Native American groups but claimed first by Spain and then—after 1821—by the newly independent nation of Mexico (see Map 11.4). **New Mexico**, with its bustling commercial centers of Albuquerque and Santa Fe, remained under Mexican federal control until the United States conquered the territory during its War with Mexico. Texas, by contrast, had a much more attenuated relationship with the Mexican government; in 1824, it became an autonomous state (Coahuila y Tejas), giving it substantially more political independence from federal authorities than New Mexico enjoyed. This situation fostered Texas's struggle for national independence and then annexation to the United States, which in turn returned the divisive issue of slavery to the forefront of American political debate (see Chapter 12).

11-4a Southwestern Slavery

By the time Anglo-Americans became interested in Mexico's northern reaches, slavery in the Southwest was centuries old. Yet as practiced by indigenous peoples—Comanches, Apaches, Kiowas, Navajos, Utes, and Pueblos—and by Spaniards, slavery differed from the chattel slavery of Africans and African Americans in the American South. Southwestern slavery was no less violent, but it centered on capturing women and children, who were then assimilated into their captors' communities, where they provided labor and status while fostering economic and diplomatic exchanges with the communities from which they had been captured.

This system of "captives and cousins," as one scholar terms it, was built on racial mixing—a practice anathema to most white Americans. As white slaveholders from the Southeast pushed their way into Mexican territory during the 1820s and 1830s, they often justified their conquest in racial

terms. Even the region's Hispanic settlers, they reasoned, had been rendered lazy and barbarous by racial intermixing and were thus destined to be supplanted, whether peaceably or otherwise.

11-4b The New Mexican Frontier

When Mexico gained independence from Spain in 1821, the Hispanic population of New Mexico outnumbered the indigenous Pueblo peoples by three to one. There were 28,000 Hispanics, including people born in Spain and, especially, *criollos*, people born in New Spain to parents of Spanish descent. Whether Spanish, Native American, criollo, or mestizo, most New Mexicans engaged in irrigated agriculture. To the north of Santa Fe, they farmed small plots, but to the south, larger farms and ranches predominated. Rancheros' wealth came from selling their wool and corn in distant markets, and from relying on unpaid laborers: farmhands, often their own relatives, bound to the rancheros by debt. United by a threat from the province's raiding Native groups—Apaches, Utes, Navajos, and Comanches—Hispanics, Pueblos, and mestizos sometimes united in common defense. But relations among Hispanics and the sedentary Pueblos were not always peaceful. Their numerical superiority allowed Hispanics to seize many of the Pueblos' villages and lands in the rich northern river valleys of an otherwise arid region.

The Santa Fe Trail caused a commercial explosion in New Mexico, doubling the value of imports in just two years. Whereas the Spanish had tried to keep foreigners out, the Mexican government offered enormous land grants to Anglo-American and French entrepreneurs, sometimes in partnership with the region's Hispanic residents, hoping they would develop the region's industry and agriculture, and strengthen commercial ties with the United States.

Although commercial ties did strengthen, very few Americans settled permanently in New Mexico during the 1820s and 1830s. Most of the best lands had already been taken by Native peoples and Hispanics. And Americans in search of cheap, fertile land did not need to travel that far west; they could find what they were looking for in Texas.

11-4c The Texas Frontier

That they would do so, however, was not evident at the time of Mexican independence. Unlike in New Mexico, indigenous peoples remained the dominant group in Texas in 1821, though the population also included Hispanics, Anglos, mestizos, and immigrant Native Americans. Of the thirty thousand indigenous people, most were Comanches, but there were also Coahuiltecans, Tonkawas, Karankawas, Apaches, Caddos, and Wichitas. Texas was part of what one historian has called the Comanche Empire, an enormous territory spreading from northern Mexico to Louisiana that the Comanches dominated through a combination of kinship ties, trade, diplomacy, and violence. People of European heritage were a relatively

New Mexico Former Spanish colony in the upper Rio Grande Valley that became part of Mexico after 1821.

Map 11.4 Mexico's Far North

What is now considered the American Southwest was made up of the northern provinces of Mexico until the United States conquered the territory during the Mexican War (1846–1848).

small presence in Texas in 1821. Hispanic peoples had been there since the 1500s, establishing missions and presidios, but by 1820, they numbered only two thousand. Most raised livestock on ranches, while others made their living from trading with Native peoples. Living so distant from the Spanish colonial capital in Mexico City, they formed a distinctive identity, seeing themselves as **Tejanos** (or Texans) rather than as Spaniards. Many intermarried with Native peoples.

After the War of 1812, Anglo-Americans had begun entering Texas, where they sought furs, silver, or adventure. They traded manufactured goods—such as guns, ammunition, and kettles—for animal hides, horses, and mules; soon they largely supplanted the Tejanos as Native peoples' trading partners. Although

Tejanos Native Texans of Mexican descent.

some Anglos settled in Texas, often living among Native peoples, most simply traveled the Santa Fe and Chihuahua trails without settling. They were deterred in part by the region's violence.

11-4d The Comanche Empire

As Native Americans competed with one another for resources, the southwestern borderlands experienced intermittent but often brutal violence. Mounted on horses, the Comanches hunted bison, took captives, and stole horses, livestock, and crops from their enemies, among whom were the Pawnees, Arapahos, Cheyennes, and Osage. Other, smaller Native groups, such as the Wichitas and Caddos, mostly farmed, growing enough corn, beans, squash, and

Smithsonian American Art Museum, Washington, DC/Art Resource, NY

△ The Comanche controlled a vast empire along the Louisiana Territory's southwestern with Mexico. Here, in a George Catlin painting from 1834, Comanche women dress robes and dry meat.

pumpkin to feed themselves and to trade with the more mobile Comanches. When crops failed, farmers often turned to bison hunting as well, sometimes causing conflict with the Comanches.

Tensions increased around the time of Mexican independence, when another ten thousand Native Americans began migrating into the region. From the Old Northwest came Shawnees and Kickapoos—former members of Tecumseh's confederacy—who after their defeat during the War of 1812 had headed north to Canada before heading back southward into Kansas, Indian Territory, and then Texas. From the Old Southwest came Cherokees, Creeks, Choctaws, Chickasaws, and Seminoles, some with African American slaves. Native newcomers often clashed with indigenous Native peoples, with whom they vied for land and animals. The conflict was cultural, too: some Native American immigrants, having adopted Anglo clothing and racial ideologies, dismissed as "savage" the indigenous Native peoples who hunted buffalo, wore skins, and did not value land as a commodity.

Because such violence threatened the viability of southeastern Native peoples' removal and disrupted trade, the U.S. government brokered a treaty in 1835: the Comanches agreed to allow immigrants onto their lands in exchange for trade opportunities. Before long, trade boomed. Native American immigrants swapped agricultural products and manufactured goods, such as rifles and ammunition, for the Comanches' meats, robes, and horses. The Comanches also traded human captives, seized in Texas or northern Mexico. That same year, the Comanches ended more than a century of war with the Osages. As peace returned, so too did American traders, who now built permanent trading posts. Meanwhile, the U.S. government's Indian removal continued apace, fueling Americans' commitment to cotton cultivation and expansionism. Mexican officials feared for the region's future.

11-4e American *Empresarios*

More than a decade earlier, before Mexican independence, the Spanish had worried about the security of Texas, which they saw as a buffer between hostile Native peoples, particularly Comanches, and the United States. Their solution was to populate the region. Thus when Moses Austin, a miner and

Paintings and Cultural Impressions

Although few people of Spanish descent settled in Texas, those who did developed a distinctive and proud cultural identity. Calling themselves Tejanos, they adapted their inherited culture—music, dances, and cuisine—to their new surroundings. In the painting below of an 1844 celebration in San Antonio, French-born painter Theodore Gentilz captures the mixture of cultural carryovers and frontier adaptations.

CRITICAL THINKING

◻ Which elements of the scene seem reminiscent of life in Spain or in the colonial capital of Mexico City?

◻ Which elements seem to be adaptations to life along a cultural frontier and political borderland?

◻ Which elements of the painting seem to celebrate Tejano culture, and which, if any, seem critical of it?

◻ If you were using this painting as a source of information about Tejano culture and its influence on contemporary music and dance, what else would you want to know about the artist and the scene he has captured?

bpk, Berlin/Art Resource, NY

◁ Although the musician in Gentilz's painting is playing the fiddle, other artistic depictions record the widespread use of the guitar, which helped give rise to the corridor, a folk ballad whose legacy is still apparent in today's country and western music.

Daughters of the Republic of Texas Library

△ Theodore Gentilz arrived in Texas in the 1840s and soon began portraying the region's culture with his paintbrush. Here, Tejano settlers perform the fandango, a Spanish dance.

trader from Missouri, approached Spanish authorities in December 1820 about settling Americans in Texas, they were willing to make a deal, finalized the following month, as long as Austin brought with him Americans willing to assimilate into Texas society. In exchange for promising to bring three hundred Catholic families—and no slaves—Austin would receive an enormous land grant of approximately two hundred thousand acres along the Brazos River. Before Austin could act, though, he died, and Mexico won its independence from Spain in September 1821.

Austin's son, Stephen, pursued his father's scheme, pressing the new Mexican government to honor the grant, which it did in 1823, provided that the younger Austin renounce his American citizenship and become a Mexican national. Recruiting families proved challenging, however, because of fears of Native peoples' attacks. When Mexican officials expressed frustration at Austin's slow progress in settling the area, he complained, "the Situation I am placed in near the frontiers of two Nations, and surrounded on every side by hostile Indians and exposed to their attacks . . . vexatious pilfering and robbing . . . renders my task particularly laborious." But by 1825, Stephen Austin had settled three hundred families (1,357 white people) and, despite the promise of no slaves, 443 "contract laborers" of African descent. With contracts that ran for ninety-nine years, these African Americans were essentially slaves. Still, faced with the urgency of peopling the region, the Mexican government signed three more contracts granting Austin land in exchange for his bringing nine hundred additional families.

Generally satisfied with the Austin experiment, in 1824 Mexico passed a Colonization Law providing land and tax incentives to future foreign settlers and leaving the details of colonization to the individual Mexican states. Coahuila y Texas specified that the head of a family could have either 177 acres (if just farming), 4,251 acres (if just grazing), or 4,428 acres (if both farming and grazing). The land was cheap, and—unlike land in the United States—could be paid for in installments over six years, with no money due until the fourth year. To be eligible, foreigners had to be upstanding Christians with "good habits," and they had to establish permanent residency. As an incentive for these new settlers to assimilate into Mexican society, the Coahuila y Texas government provided additional land to those who married Mexican women.

Most U.S. citizens who settled in Mexico did so under the auspices of an *empresario*, or immigration agent, who took responsibility for selecting "moral" colonists, distributing lands, and enforcing regulations. In exchange, he received nearly 25,000 acres of grazing land and 1,000 acres of farming land for every hundred families that he settled. Between 1825 and 1832, approximately twenty-four empresario contracts (seventeen of which went to foreigners, mostly Anglo-Americans) had been signed, with the empresarios agreeing to bring eight thousand families total. The

land grants were so vast that together they covered almost all of present-day Texas.

During the 1820s, Anglo-Americans emigrated, with their slaves, to Texas, motivated by a combination of push and pull factors. Some felt pushed by the hard times following the Panic of 1819; at the same time, they were drawn by cheap land and, especially, generous credit terms. Despite Mexican efforts to encourage assimilation, these Americans tended to settle in separate communities and to interact little with the Tejanos. Even more troubling to the Mexican government, the Anglo-Americans outnumbered the Tejanos two to one. Authorities worried that the transplanted Americans would try to make Texas part of the United States.

11-4f Texas Politics

In 1826, their fears seemed to materialize when an empresario named Haden Edwards called for an independent Texas, the "Fredonia Republic." Other empresarios, reasoning that they had more to gain than to lose from peaceful relations with the Mexican government, resisted Edwards's secessionist movement. Austin even sent militia to help quash the rebellion. Although the Fredonia revolt failed, Mexican authorities dreaded what it might foreshadow.

The answer to the secessionist threat, Mexican authorities thought, was to weaken the American presence in Texas. In 1830, they terminated legal immigration from the United States while simultaneously encouraging immigration from Europe and other parts of Mexico in order to dilute the American influence. They prohibited American slaves from entering Texas, a provision that brought Texas in line with the rest of Mexico—where slavery had been outlawed the previous year—and that was meant to repel American slaveholders. Yet these laws did little to discourage Americans and their slaves from coming; soon they controlled most of the Texas coastline and its border with the United States. Mexican authorities repealed the anti-immigration law in 1833, reasoning that it discouraged upstanding settlers but did nothing to stem the influx of undesirable settlers. By 1835, the non-Native population of Texas was nearly thirty thousand, with Americans outnumbering Tejanos seven to one.

White Texans divided into two main factions. There were those, like Stephen Austin, who favored staying in Mexico but demanding more autonomy, the legalization of slavery, and free trade with the United States. Others pushed for secession from Mexico and asked to be annexed to the United States. In 1835, the secessionists overtook a Mexican military installation charged with collecting taxes at Galveston Bay. Austin advocated a peaceful resolution to the crisis, but Mexican authorities nonetheless considered him suspicious and jailed him for eighteen months, an act that helped convert him to the independence cause. But it would be Sam Houston and Davy Crockett—newly arrived Americans—who would lead the movement.

△ Like George Allen, many Texas settlers relied on slave labor to work their fields and maintain their households.

11-4g The Lone Star Republic

With discontent increasing throughout Mexico, Mexican president **General Antonio Lopez de Santa Anna** declared himself dictator and marched his army toward Texas. Fearing Santa Anna would free their slaves, and citing similarities between their own cause and that of the American colonies in the 1770s, Texans staged an armed rebellion. After initial defeats at the Alamo mission in San Antonio and at Goliad in March 1836, the Texans easily triumphed by year's end. They declared themselves the Lone Star Republic and elected **Sam Houston** as president. Their constitution legalized slavery and banned free blacks from living within Texas.

Texas then faced the challenge of nation building, which to its leaders involved Indian removal. When Native peoples refused to leave, Mirabeau Lamar, the nation's second president, mobilized the Texas Rangers—mounted nonuniformed militia—to drive them out through terror. Sanctioned by the Texas government, but sometimes acting on their own, the Rangers raided Native peoples' villages, where they robbed, raped, and murdered. Although some Texas officials tried to negotiate with the Native peoples and Tejanos, it was what one historian has called "ethnic cleansing" that cleared the land of its Native settlers to make room for white Americans and their African American slaves. Before long, the surviving Comanches would face starvation and depopulation—weakened by European disease, drought, and overhunting. First, though, they would ravage the northern Mexico countryside and its inhabits, inadvertently paving the way for American conquest.

General Antonio Lopez de Santa Anna Mexican president and dictator whose actions led Texans to revolt.

Sam Houston Military and political leader of Texas during and after the Texas Revolution.

11-4h "War of a Thousand Deserts"

Since the early 1830s, Mexico's ten northern states had been wracked by raiding warfare perpetrated by Native peoples of the Plains—Comanches, Navajos, and Apaches. Even as the Comanches negotiated with Texans and agreed to peace with the Cheyenne and Arapaho to their north, they intensified their raids into Mexico, sending raiders on horseback to seize bounties of horses, goods, and human captives that they then traded throughout the Plains, bringing them and their families status and wealth. When Mexicans resisted their attacks by killing Comanches or their Kiowa allies, the Comanches escalated their violence, ravishing the countryside and its inhabitants in what one historian has deemed vengeance killings, those in which the victims often bore no individual responsibility for the Comanches' deaths. When additional Comanches fell in the course of avenging a killing, then another round of revenge killing ensued, in what became an ongoing, vicious cycle. The raiders devastated Mexican settlements, where once-thriving farms became man-made "deserts," as Mexico's minister of war called them. Passing through one abandoned village in 1846, a British traveler noted that "a dreary stillness reigned over the whole place, unbroken by any sound, save the croaking of a bullfrog in the spring."

Smithsonian American Art Museum, Washington, DC/Art Resource, NY

△ Native peoples of the Plains, including the Apaches portrayed here, frequently and brutally raided the northern provinces of Mexico beginning in the 1830s, leading to a cycle of vengeance killings that devastated the region and made it more vulnerable to invasion by the U.S. army during the War with Mexico in the mid-1840s.

With the Mexican government's concerns trained more directly on threats from the United States and France, individual Mexican states pursued their own responses to the raids, and in the process they often turned against one another, with Mexicans killing other Mexicans. The resulting carnage, with Mexicans falling at one another's hands and at the hands of Native peoples, gave fodder to proponents of **manifest destiny** in the United States—those who believed that racially superior (white) Americans were destined to spread their culture westward to regions inhabited by inferior races (Native Americans and Mexicans). Using the rationale of manifest destiny, the United States would justify its war with Mexico from 1846 to 1848 (see "The War with Mexico and Its Consequences," Section 12-6). When American soldiers marched to Mexico's capital with seeming ease, they did so because they traversed huge swaths of Mexican territory that had been devastated or deserted by fifteen years of Native American raiding.

11-4i Wartime Losses and Profits

After annexing Texas in 1845, the United States, seeking to further expand its territorial reach, waged war against Mexico. In the borderlands, as in Mexico itself, civilians—Native peoples, Tejanos, Californios, and Mexicans—got caught in the fray. Some lost their lives, and many more, precariously caught between the two sides, suffered wartime depredations. If they aided the Mexicans,

manifest destiny Coined by editor John L. O'Sullivan, it was the belief that the United States was endowed by God with a mission to spread its republican government and brand of freedom and Christianity to less fortunate and uncivilized peoples; it also justified U.S. territorial expansion.

the U.S. Army destroyed their homes; if they refused aid to the Mexicans, then the Mexicans destroyed their homes. A U.S. Army report in 1847 acknowledged that its "wild volunteers . . . committed . . . all sorts of atrocities on the persons and property of Mexicans." Many civilians fled. Even once the war ended in the borderlands, violence did not stop. From 1847 to 1848, Texas Rangers slaughtered Native peoples. "They think that the death of an Indian is a fair offsett [sic] to the loss of a horse," wrote one Anglo-American.

Yet some civilians profited from the war. Farmers sold provisions and mules to the armies, peddlers sold alcohol and food to soldiers, and others set up gambling and prostitution businesses near army camps. Still, tension generally characterized the relationship between civilians and soldiers, largely because of the American soldiers' attitude of racial superiority.

11-5 Cultural Frontiers in the Far West

▷ How did religion shape the culture of the Far West?

▷ What was the nature of emigrant interactions with Native peoples along the overland migration routes?

▷ What actions did the federal government take to ease westward migration and commerce?

▷ What impact did European American migration and settlement have on Native Americans in the Far West?

▷ How did the discovery of mineral wealth transform the society and economy of California?

Even before the United States seized tremendous amounts of new territory during the war with Mexico, some Americans took the gamble of a lifetime and moved to the Far West, often to places—such as California and Utah—that Mexico controlled. Some sought religious freedom or to convert others to Christianity, but most wanted fertile farmland. Whatever their reasons for moving west, they often encountered people from different cultures. Such encounters sometimes led to cooperation, but more often to tension or open conflict.

11-5a Western Missionaries

Catholic missionaries maintained a strong presence in the Far West. In the Spanish missions, priests treated Native peoples as "spiritual children," introducing them to Catholic sacraments; holding them to a rigid system of prayer, sexual conduct, and work; and treating them as legal minors. When they failed to live up to priests' or soldiers' expectations, they were subject to corporal punishment. When they ran away, they were forcibly returned. With no political voice and few other choices, Native peoples often responded to abusive practices with armed uprisings, in the process helping to weaken the mission system itself.

A Mexican law secularized the California missions in 1833, removing them from ecclesiastical control and using them primarily to organize Indian labor. Some Native peoples stayed at the missions, while others left to farm their own land or to find employment elsewhere, but for almost all,

secularization brought enhanced personal freedom despite persistent limitations to their legal rights.

Even after the missions' secularization, Catholic missionaries—Americans, Europeans, and Native converts—continued ministering to immigrants, working to convert other Native peoples, and encouraging specifically Roman Catholic colonies. Missionaries founded schools and colleges, introduced medical services, and even aided in railroad explorations.

In the Pacific Northwest, Catholics vied directly with Protestants for Native peoples' souls. Although evangelicals focused on the Midwest, a few hoped to bring Christianity to the Native peoples of the Far West. Under the auspices of the American Board of Commissioners for Foreign Missions, two missionary couples—generally credited as being the first white migrants along the Oregon Trail—traveled to the Pacific Northwest in 1836. Narcissa and Marcus Whitman built a meetinghouse for the Cayuse in Waiilatpu, near present-day Walla Walla, Washington, while Eliza and Henry Spalding worked to convert the Nez Percé at Lapwai, in what is now Idaho. The Whitmans did little to endear themselves to the Cayuses, whom Narcissa deemed "insolent, proud domineering arrogant and ferocious"; their dark skin, she concluded, was fitting of their "heathenism." The Cayuse, in turn, saw the Whitmans as "very severe and hard," and none converted. The Whitmans redirected their efforts toward the ever-increasing stream of white migrants flowing into Oregon beginning in the 1840s.

These migrants' arrival escalated tensions with the Cayuses, and when a devastating measles epidemic struck in 1847, the Cayuses saw it as a calculated assault. They retaliated by murdering the Whitmans and at least ten other missionaries. After the Whitmans' violent deaths, the Spaldings abandoned their own, more successful mission; blamed Catholics for inciting the massacre; and became farmers in Oregon, not returning to Lapwai for another fifteen years.

11-5b Mormons

The Mormons, who had been persecuted in Missouri and Illinois, sought religious sanctuary in the West. In 1847, Brigham Young led them to their "Promised Land" in the Great Salt Lake valley, still under Mexican control but soon to become part of the unorganized U.S. territory of Utah. As non-Mormons began to settle in Utah, Brigham Young tried to dilute their influence by attracting new Mormon settlers to what he called the state of Deseret. In 1849, Young and his associates established the Perpetual Emigration Fund, which sponsored "handcart companies" of poor migrants, particularly from Europe, who pushed all their belongings to Utah in small handcarts.

The Mormons' arrival in the Great Basin complicated the region's already complex relations among Native peoples. The Utes, for example, had long traded in stolen goods and captured people, particularly Paiutes. After Mormons tried to curtail the slave trade, Ute slavers tortured their Paiute captives, particularly children, calculating that Mormons would buy them. The ploy

△ This rare stereocard shows an emigrant train, including two women and possibly a child, dwarfed by the natural landscape in Strawberry Valley, California, in the 1860s.

often worked; when it did not, Ute slavers sometimes killed the children, in one case dangling them by their feet and thrashing them against stones. The purchased children often worked as servants in Mormon homes, which encouraged their distraught families, eager for proximity to their children, to settle near Mormon villages. Although the Mormons tried to bring the Paiutes into their religious fold, they—much like Catholic missionaries in California—treated adult Native Americans as children, causing friction, even violence, when the Paiutes sought to secure their autonomy. Sharing the Utes as a common enemy, the Mormons and Paiutes nonetheless formed an uneasy alliance in the early 1850s.

With their slave trade threatened and their economy in shambles, the Utes attacked Mormon and Paiute settlements to steal livestock and horses for resale, and then to vandalize their crops and property in an effort to drive away the Mormons. War erupted in 1853, and although an uneasy truce was reached in 1854, tensions continued between the Mormons and their Native neighbors.

And between Mormons and their white neighbors. Although Mormons prospered from providing services, such as ferries, and supplies to tens of thousands of California-bound settlers and miners passing by their settlements, Young discouraged "gentiles" (his term for non-Mormons) from settling in Deseret and advocated boycotts of gentile businesses. When in 1852 the Mormons openly sanctioned polygamy, which some followers had practiced for more than a decade, anti-Mormon sentiment increased throughout the nation. After some young Mormons vandalized federal offices in Utah, President James Buchanan—hoping to divert Americans' attention from the increasingly divisive slavery issue—dispatched 2,500 federal troops in June 1857 to suppress an alleged Mormon rebellion.

Anxious over their own safety, a group of Mormons joined some Paiutes in attacking a passing wagon train of non-Mormon migrants. Approximately 120 men, women, and children died in the so-called Mountain Meadows Massacre in September 1857. In the next two years, the U.S. Army and the Mormons engaged in armed conflict, resulting in much property destruction but no fatalities. As the Mormons' relationships with their neighbors and passersby indicate, western violence often emerged from complex interactions and alliances that did not simply pit Native communities against newcomers.

11-5c Oregon and California Trails

Nor were all encounters between natives and newcomers violent. From 1840 until 1860, between 250,000 and 500,000 people, including many children, walked across much of the continent, a trek that took seven months on average. Although they traveled armed for conflict, most of their encounters with Native peoples were peaceful, if tense.

The overland journeys began at one of the so-called jumping-off points—towns such as Independence, St. Joseph, and Westport Landing—along the Missouri River, where migrants bought supplies for the 2,000-mile trip still ahead of them. After cramming supplies into wagons already overflowing with household possessions, they set out either in organized wagon trains or on their own. While miners frequently traveled alone or in groups of fortune-seeking young men, farmers—including many women migrating only at their husbands' insistence—often traveled with relatives, neighbors, fellow church members, and other acquaintances.

They timed their departures to be late enough that they could find forage grass for their oxen and livestock, but not so late that they would encounter the treacherous snows that came early to the Rockies and the Sierra Nevada. Not all were successful. From 1846 to 1847, the Donner Party took a wrong turn, got caught in a blizzard, and resorted to cannibalism. More fortunate overland migrants trudged alongside their wagons, beginning their days well before dawn, pausing only for a short midday break, and walking until late afternoon. They covered on average fifteen miles a day, in weather ranging from freezing cold to blistering heat. In wagon trains composed of families, men generally tended livestock during the day, while women—after an energy-draining day on the trail—set up camp, prepared meals, and tended small children. Many women gave birth on the trail, where an always-difficult experience could become excruciating. "Her sufferings were so great," one woman wrote about her sister. "It all seems like a jumble of jolting wagon, crying baby, dust, sagebrush and the never ceasing pain." Even under normal circumstances, trail life was exhausting, both physically and emotionally. Overlanders worried about attack by Native peoples, getting lost, running out of provisions or water, and losing loved ones, who would have to be buried along the trail, in graves never again to be visited. But for most adults, trail life did not prove particularly dangerous, with Native attacks rare and death rates approximating those of society at large. Children, though, had a greater risk than adults of being crushed by wagon wheels or drowning during river crossings.

Native peoples were usually peaceful, if cautious. Particularly during the trails' early days, Native peoples provided food and information or ferried migrants across rivers; in exchange, migrants offered wool blankets, knives, metal pots, tobacco, ornamental beads, and other items in short supply in Native societies. When exchanges went wrong—when one of the parties misunderstood the other's cultural practices or tried to swindle the other—relationships grew tense, not just between the particular persons involved, but between Native peoples and migrants more generally. Native peoples grew suspicious of all white people, just as migrants failed to distinguish between different native bands or tribes.

A persistent aggravation among migrants was the theft of livestock, which they usually blamed on Native peoples even though white thieves stole livestock, too. Native peoples who took livestock often did so when whites failed to offer gifts in exchange for grazing rights. One such incident, the so-called Mormon Cow Incident (or the Grattan Massacre), resulted in human bloodshed, forever altering relationships along the Oregon Trail.

In August 1854, a Lakota in present-day Wyoming slaughtered a cow that had strayed from a nearby Mormon camp. When Lakota leaders offered compensation, U.S. Army Lieutenant John Grattan, intent on making a point, refused the offer. Tempers flared, Grattan ordered his men to shoot, and after a Lakota chief fell dead, the Lakotas returned the fire, killing Grattan, all twenty-nine of his men, and a French interpreter. In retaliation, the following year General William Harney led six hundred soldiers to a village near Ash Hollow, where migrants and Native peoples had traded peaceably for many years. When the Lakota leaders refused to surrender any of their people to Harney, the general ordered his men to fire. Thirty minutes later, eighty-five Lakotas lay dead, with more wounded, and seventy women and children had been taken prisoner. The event disrupted peaceful exchange along the trail and laid the groundwork for nearly two decades of warfare between the Lakotas and the U.S. Army.

11-5d Treaties with Native Peoples

Even as the U.S. Army became embroiled in armed conflict, the Indian Office worked to negotiate treaties to keep Native peoples—and their intertribal conflicts—from interfering with western migration and commerce. The **Fort Laramie Treaty of 1851** (or the Horse Creek Council Treaty) was signed by the United States and eight northern Plains tribes—the Lakotas, Cheyennes, Arapahos, Crows, Assiniboines, Gros-Ventres, Mandans, and Arikaras—who occupied the Platte River valley through which the three great overland routes westward—the Oregon, California, and Mormon Trails—all passed. Two years later, in 1853, the United States signed a treaty with three southwestern nations, the Comanches, Kiowas, and Apaches, who lived in the vicinity of the Sante Fe Trail. Under the terms of both treaties, these Native groups agreed to maintain peace among themselves, to recognize government-delineated tribal boundaries, to allow the United States to construct roads and forts within those boundaries, to refrain from depredations against western migrants, and to issue restitution for any depredations nonetheless committed. In return, they

Fort Laramie Treaty of 1851 Also known as the Horse Creek Treaty; a treaty between the United States and eight northern Plains tribes in which the Native Americans agreed to maintain intertribal peace, accepted the U.S.-defined territorial regions for each tribe, and allowed the United States to construct roads. In exchange, they received annual payouts of provisions and agricultural necessities.

Interior of Fort Laramie, 1858–60 (w/c on paper), Miller, Alfred Jacob (1810–74) / Walters Art Museum, Baltimore, USA / Bridgeman Images

△ Established in 1834 in eastern Wyoming, Fort Laramie—pictured here three years later by Alfred Jacob Miller— served as a fur-trading site, where Native peoples and trappers of European or mixed heritage came together not only to exchange goods but also to socialize. In 1849, as interactions between Native peoples and overland migrants to Oregon grew increasingly tense, the U.S. Army took over the fort, now designed to protect overland emigrants.

would receive annual allotments from the U.S. government for ten years, to be paid with provisions, domestic animals, and agricultural implements. These allotments could be renewed for another five years at the discretion of the president of the United States.

But these treaties often meant different things to their American Indian signatories and to the U.S. officials who brokered them. Contrary to U.S. expectations, Native American chiefs did not see such treaties as perpetually binding. Government officials, meanwhile, promised allotments but did little to ensure their timely arrival, often leaving Native peoples starving and freezing. The treaties did not end intertribal warfare, nor did they fully secure the overlanders' safety. But they did represent the U.S. government's efforts to promote expansion and to protect those citizens who caught the western fever.

11-5e Ecological Consequences of Cultural Contact

Armed conflict took relatively few lives compared to cholera, smallpox, and other maladies. The trails' jumping-off points, where migrants camped in close quarters while preparing for their journeys, bred disease, which migrants inadvertently carried to the Native peoples with whom they traded. Fearful of infection, Native peoples and migrants increasingly shied away from trading.

The disappearance of the buffalo (American bison) from the trails' environs further inflamed tensions. The buffalo not only provided protein to Native peoples of the Plains; they also held great spiritual significance. Many Native Americans blamed the migrants for the buffalo's disappearance, even though most overlanders never laid eyes on a buffalo. By the

△ The vibrant trade in buffalo hides prompted both Native Americans and whites to overhunt the American bison, leading to near extinction for the animal by the latter part of the nineteenth century.

time the overland migration reached its peak in the late 1840s and 1850s, the herds had already been overhunted, in part by Native Americans eager to trade their hides. As traffic increased along the trail, the surviving buffalo scattered to where the grass was safe from the voracious appetites, and trampling feet, of the overlanders' livestock. But on those rare occasions when wagon trains did stumble upon bison herds, men rushed to fulfill their frontier fantasies—nurtured by the literature they had read—and shot the animals; such buffalo chases provided diversions from the trail's drudgery. Overlanders hunted other animals for sport, too, leaving behind rotting carcasses of antelopes, wolves, bears, and birds—animals that held spiritual significance for many Native Americans.

Overland migrants also sparked prairie fires. Native peoples had long used fire to clear farmland, to stimulate the growth of grasslands, and to create barren zones that would discourage bison from roaming into a rival nation's territory. But now emigrants—accustomed to stoves, not open fires—accidentally started fires that raged across the prairies, killing animals and the vegetation on which they survived. On rarer occasions, Native peoples started fires in the hope of capturing the migrants' fleeing livestock. Stories about intentionally lit fires exaggerated their extent, but they, too, contributed to increasing hostility between the two groups.

11-5f Gold Rush

Nowhere did migrants intrude more deeply on Native American life than near the California gold strikes. In January 1848, James Wilson Marshall discovered gold on John Sutter's property along a shallow tributary to the American River near present-day Sacramento, California. During the next year, tens of thousands of "forty-niners" rushed to California, where they practiced what is called placer mining, panning and dredging for gold in the hope of instant riches.

Some did indeed make fortunes. Peter Brown, a black man from Ste. Genevieve, Missouri, wrote his wife in 1851 that "California is the best country in the world to make money. It is also the best place for black folks on the globe." But not

The Mexican-United States Border

Under the Treaty of Guadalupe Hidalgo (1848), ending the United States' war with Mexico, Mexico ceded modern-day California, Arizona, and New Mexico, and parts of Utah, Nevada, and Colorado. The task of delimiting the new border, including adjustments made in a subsequent treaty, fell to the Joint United States and Mexican Boundary Commission, whose crew of more than one hundred men labored through rugged terrain, climactic extremes, and Native American raids. Where the boundary strayed from natural features and human settlements, as it often did along its western end, the Commission demarcated it with scattered, often-improvised markers, in one instance erecting just seven markers along a 140-mile stretch. Completing its field work between 1849 and 1855, the Commission created the nearly 2,000-mile border that exists today.

The border's contested nature manifested itself immediately, as Native peoples recognized neither Mexico's nor the United States' sovereignty in the region. In 1882, Mexico and the United States agreed to reciprocal border crossings, allowing the U.S. Army to defeat the powerful Chiricahua Apaches four years later. Only then did the United States begin restricting border crossings, with efforts focused on Chinese, not Mexican, nationals. In 1897, President McKinley established a sixty-foot-wide clearance through Nogales, a town on the Arizona-Mexico border; the government stripped the area of homes and businesses to improve surveillance of cattle rustlers and drug smugglers, and to ease tariff collection and immigration controls. Four years later, President Teddy Roosevelt extended McKinley's "reservation strip" into New Mexico, Arizona, and California, foreshadowing increasing division of binational communities. Yet in 1904, only eighteen U.S. immigration inspectors patrolled the 550-mile border dividing Mexico from Arizona and New Mexico, and fences built in the early twentieth century restricted cattle, not people.

With the Mexican Revolution (1910–1920), the two governments agreed to construct more substantial fences. Mexico aimed to block smuggled military supplies; the United States, to staunch the influx of refugees from wartime devastation. With the Great Depression, pressure to control immigration increased alongside U.S. workers' fear of job competition. When labor surpluses turned into shortages during World War II, the United States implemented its Bracero (guestworker) program, but many employers preferred undocumented workers, whose susceptibility to deportation led to lower wages and poorer working conditions. To protect the Bracero program, the United States deported undocumented Mexicans; in 1954 alone, the Border Patrol reported more than one million deportations. Later initiatives focused more on erecting barriers and increasing patrols. In 2006, the Secure Fence Act mandated 700 miles of fencing, designed to "reform" immigration while enhancing national security post-9/11. The extremely expensive project remains unfinished, though during the 2016 election Donald J. Trump promised to "build a wall" to stop illegal Mexican immigration. If built, such a wall would entail formidable fiscal and logistical challenges. "Often," according to the U.S. Border Patrol's official website, "the border is a barely discernible line in uninhabited deserts, canyons, or mountains."

In the mid-nineteenth century, while trekking through those deserts, canyons, and mountains, the Boundary Commissioners never imagined that their scattered and makeshift markers would be replaced with fences and walls, reinforced with aerial surveillance and electronic sensors. Yet by demarcating a border governed by neither natural nor human geography, they created a legacy for a people and a nation.

CRITICAL THINKING

▢ Consider the legacy of "a border governed by neither natural nor human geography" from a scattering of random markers to the promise made in 2016 by then-candidate Donald Trump to "build a wall" along the border, a feat with both logistical and financial complexities. What other solutions might there be to the "problem" of the Mexican/U.S. border?

---

everyone reveled in the gold strikes. John Sutter complained that gold "destroyed" his milling and tanning businesses, as his Native American and Mormon workers left him for the mines and vandals stole his property. Most forty-niners never found enough gold to pay their expenses. "The stories you hear frequently in the States," one gold seeker wrote home, "are the most extravagant lies imaginable—the mines are a humbug." With their dreams dashed—and too poor or embarrassed to return home—many forty-niners took wage-paying jobs with large mining companies that used dangerous machinery to cut deep into the earth's surface to reach mineral veins.

The discovery of gold changed the face of California (see Map 11.5). As a remote Mexican province, California had a chain of small settlements surrounded by military forts (presidios) and missions. It was inhabited mostly by Native peoples, along with a small number of Mexican rancheros, who raised cattle and sheep on enormous landholdings worked by coerced Native American laborers. As word spread of gold strikes, new

Map 11.5 The California Gold Rush

Gold was discovered at Sutter's Mill in 1848, sparking the California gold rush that took place mostly along the western foothills of the Sierra Nevada Mountains.

migrants—from South America, Asia, Australia, and Europe—rushed to California. Although a California Supreme Court ruling—*People v. Hall* (1854)—made it virtually impossible to prevent violence against Chinese immigrants, Chinese citizens continued to seek their fortunes in California; by 1859, approximately 35,000 of them worked in the goldfields.

With so many hungry gold miners to feed, California experienced an agricultural boom. Although the immediate vicinity of mines became barren, when hydraulic mining washed away surface soil to expose buried lodes, California agriculture thrived overall, with wheat becoming the preferred crop: it required minimal investment, was easily planted, and had a relatively short growing season. In contrast to the Midwest's and Oregon's family farms, though, California's large-scale wheat farming depended on bonded Native American laborers.

11-5g Mining Settlements

Mining brought a commercial and industrial boom, too, as enterprising merchants rushed to supply, feed, and clothe the new settlers. Among them was Levi Strauss, a German Jewish immigrant, whose tough mining pants found a ready market among the prospectors. Because men greatly outnumbered

women, women's skills (and company) were in great demand. Even as men set up all-male households and performed tasks that bent prevailing notions of gender propriety, women received high fees for cooking, laundering, and sewing. Women also ran boardinghouses, hotels, and brothels.

Cities sprang up. In 1848, San Francisco had been a small mission settlement of about 1,000 Mexicans, Anglos, soldiers, friars, and Native Americans. With the gold rush, it became an instant city, ballooning to 35,000 people in 1850. It was the West Coast gateway to the interior, and ships bringing people and supplies jammed the harbor. A French visitor in that year wrote, "At San Francisco, where fifteen months ago one found only a half-dozen large cabins, one finds today a stock exchange, a theater, churches of all Christian cults, and a large number of quite beautiful homes."

Yet as the Anglo-American, European, Hispanic, Asian, and African American populations swelled, the Native American population experienced devastation. Although California was admitted into the Union as a free state in 1850, its legislature soon passed "An Act for the Government and Protection of Indians" that essentially legalized Native peoples' enslavement. The practice of using enslaved Native Americans in the mines between 1849 and 1851 ended only when newly arrived miners brutally attacked the Native American workers, believing they degraded white labor and gave an unfair advantage to established miners. Those slaves who survived the violence were sent to work instead as field workers and house servants. Between 1821 and 1860, the Native American population of California fell from 200,000 to 30,000, as Native peoples died from disease, starvation, and violence. Because masters separated male and female workers, even Native Americans who survived failed to reproduce in large numbers.

Summary

Encouraged by literary and artistic images of the frontier, easterners often viewed the West as a place of natural abundance, where hardworking individuals could seek security, freedom, and perhaps even fortune. By the millions they poured into the Old Southwest and Old Northwest in the early decades of the nineteenth century. Although the federal government promoted westward expansion—in the form of support for transportation improvements, surveying, cheap land, and protection from Native peoples—western migrants did not make the decision to head west lightly. Nor did they always find what they were looking for. Some returned home, some moved to new locations, and some—too poor or too embarrassed—stayed in the West, where they reluctantly abandoned their dreams of economic independence. Others found what they were looking for in the West, though often the road to success proved much slower and more circuitous than they had anticipated.

Not everyone who went west did so voluntarily, nor did everyone in the West think of it as an expanding region. African American slaves were moved westward by their owners or slave traders in enormous numbers in the years between 1820 and 1860. Native Americans saw their lands and their livelihoods constrict, and their environments so altered that their economic and spiritual lives were threatened. Some Native peoples responded to the white incursion through accommodation and peaceful overtures; others resisted, sometimes forcefully. If their first strategy failed, then they tried another. But the sheer force of numbers favored whites. For Native Americans in Texas and California, white incursions brought devastation, yet not before the Comanches and their allies had ravaged farming settlements along the borderland between Mexico and the United States, paving the way for the U.S. Army to invade its southern neighbor with little resistance. That war, lasting from 1846 to 1848, would bring to the brink of collapse the system of political rivalries that had emerged during the 1829–1837 presidency of a frontier Indian fighter and slave owner: Andrew Jackson.

Suggestions for Further Reading

Gary Clayton Anderson, *The Conquest of Texas: Ethnic Cleansing in the Promised Land, 1820–1875* (2005)

Stuart Banner, *How the Indians Lost Their Land: Law and Power on the Frontier* (2005)

Ned Blackhawk, *Violence over the Land: Indians and Empires in the Early American West* (2006)

Andrew R. L. Cayton and Peter S. Onuf, *The Midwest and the Nation: Rethinking the History of an American Region* (1990)

William Cronon, *Nature's Metropolis: Chicago and the Great West* (1991)

Brian DeLay, *War of a Thousand Deserts: Indian Raids and the U.S.-Mexican War* (2008)

Pekka Hämäläinen, *The Comanche Empire* (2008)

Robert V. Hine and John Mack Faragher, *The American West: A New Interpretive History* (2000)

Albert L. Hurtado, *Indian Survival on the California Frontier* (1998)

Anne F. Hyde, *Empires, Nations & Families: A History of the North American West, 1800–1860* (2011)

Susan L. Johnson, *Roaring Camp: The Social World of the California Gold Rush* (2000)

Andrés Reséndez, *Changing National Identities at the Frontier: Texas and New Mexico, 1800–1850* (2005)

Rachel St. John, *Line in the Sand: A History of the Western U.S.-Mexico Border* (2011)

Michael L. Tate, *Indians and Emigrants: Encounters on the Overland Trails* (2006)

MINDTAP
From Cengage

Politics and the Fate of the Union, 1824–1859

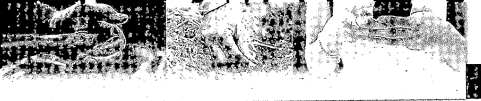

n *Uncle Tom's Cabin* (1852), Harriet Beecher Stowe created countless scenes and characters remembered through the ages, but none more than this: "A thousand lives seemed to be concentrated in that one moment to Eliza. Her room opened by a side door to the river. She caught her child and sprang down the steps toward it. The trader caught a full glimpse of her just as she was disappearing down the bank." No scene in American literature has been more often depicted in the visual arts than the young slave Eliza, child in arms, escaping across the Ohio River, after her owner had just sold the infant to a slave trader. Never has a work of popular literature so caught the roiling tide of politics. "Nerved with strength such as God gives only to the desperate," continued Stowe, "with one wild cry and flying leap, she [Eliza] vaulted clear over the turbid current . . . on to the raft of ice beyond. . . . With wild cries and desperate energy she leaped to another. . . . Her shoes are gone—her stockings cut from her feet—while blood marked every step; but she . . . felt nothing, till dimly, as in a dream, she saw the Ohio side, and a man helping her up the bank."

As the United States slowly collapsed into disunion, millions of Americans either loved or hated *Uncle Tom's Cabin*; many of the book's characters and episodes entered household, as well as public, conversation. The daughter and sister of some of the nation's most prominent preachers and theologians, Harriet Stowe (she married a pious theology professor, Calvin Stowe) was

◁ *Eliza Crossing the Ice Flows of the Ohio River*, depicting one of the most famous scenes in American literature, illustration from *Uncle Tom's Cabin*, engraved by Charles Bour. Private collection, the John Bridgeman Library.

Chronology

1824	No electoral college majority in presidential election
1825	House of Representatives elects Adams president
1828	Tariff of Abominations
	Jackson elected president
1830s–40s	Democratic-Whig competition gels in second party system
1831	Antimasons hold first national political convention
1832	Jackson vetoes rechartering Second Bank of the United States
	Jackson reelected president
1832–33	Nullification Crisis
1836	Specie Circular
	Van Buren elected president
1837	Financial panic ends boom of the 1830s
1839–43	Hard times spread unemployment and deflation
1840	Whigs win presidency under Harrison
1841	Tyler assumes presidency after Harrison's death
1845	Texas annexed
	"Manifest destiny" term coined
1846	War with Mexico begins
	Oregon Treaty negotiated
	Wilmot Proviso inflames sectional divisions
1847	Cass proposes idea of popular sovereignty
1848	Treaty of Guadalupe Hidalgo gives United States new territory in the Southwest
	Free-Soil Party formed
	Taylor elected president
	Gold discovered in California, which later applies for admission to Union as free state
	Seneca Falls Woman's Rights Convention
1850	Compromise of 1850 passes, containing controversial Fugitive Slave Act
1852	Stowe publishes *Uncle Tom's Cabin*
	Pierce elected president
1854	"Appeal of the Independent Democrats" published
	Kansas-Nebraska Act approved, igniting controversy
	Republican Party formed
	Fugitive Burns returned to slavery in Virginia
1856	Bleeding Kansas troubles nation
	Brooks attacks Sumner in Senate chamber
	Buchanan elected president, but Republican Frémont wins most northern states
1857	*Dred Scott v. Sanford* endorses white southern views on black citizenship and slavery in territories
	Economic panic and widespread unemployment begin
1858	Kansas voters reject Lecompton Constitution
	Lincoln-Douglas debates
	Douglas contends popular sovereignty prevails over *Dred Scott* decision in territories
1859	Brown raids Harpers Ferry

a little-known writer and mother of seven children when she began to conceive her classic. Serialized in a Washington, D.C., newspaper, the *National Era*, in 1851, and published as a book in 1852, the sentimental but highly charged political novel captured the agonies of slave families broken apart and sold, and

now ever more endangered by the Fugitive Slave Act of 1850. Stowe ingeniously indicted the institution of slavery more than any individuals, while spreading the blame widely. The most evil slaveholder (Simon Legree) is a transplanted New Englander, and in Miss Ophelia, a Vermont woman whose visit to a southern plantation reveals her squeamishness about blacks, we see northern racism fully exposed. The story's most humane slaveholder, St. Clair, is southern bred, but almost too good for this corrupt world, and dies before he can reform it. In Eliza, Little Eva, Topsy, and Uncle Tom himself, a Christ-like figure whom the story ultimately ushers toward unforgettable martyrdom, the nation and the world vicariously experienced not only slavery's inhumanity, but its destruction of the human soul itself, as it also threatened the life of the republic.

No book had ever exposed so effectively the nation's gravest problem—slavery and its hold on America's institutions and collective psyche. Although it can seem romantic and sugar-coated to modern readers, *Uncle Tom's Cabin* was the nineteenth century's best seller. By mid-1853, the book had sold over 1 million copies. A publishing sensation in England, too, the book was soon translated into numerous foreign languages, and recreated for the dramatic stage and performed nonstop well into the twentieth century.

The popularity of *Uncle Tom's Cabin* alarmed anxious white southerners, prompting a forceful defense of slavery's morality. Nearly twenty anti–Uncle Tom novels were published in the 1850s, providing a cultural counterpart to the heightened ideological defense of slavery in the realm of politics. Southern writers defended slavery as more humane than northern wage labor, blamed slave trading on the "outside interference" of Yankee speculators, and attacked Stowe for breaking gender conventions as a woman engaging in such a public critique of the South's integrity. In stories such as J. W. Page's *Uncle Robin in His Cabin and Tom Without One in Boston*, fiendish abolitionists induced slaves to run away, leaving them to all but starve in northern cities. In these novels, masters are benevolent and slaves loyal as they perform roles dictated by nature and God. One narrator made clear blacks' destiny: "Africans hate civilization, and are never happier . . . than when allowed to live in the abandonment, nakedness, and filth their instincts crave." Many of the novels let slaves philosophize on slavery's behalf. In *Aunt Phillis's Cabin*, Phillis accompanies her owners on a visit to the North, where wicked abolitionists encourage her to escape. "I want none of your help," she declares; she refuses to "steal" herself, longing instead for her southern "home." Yet another slave character speaks for all proslavery philosophers: "The Declaration of 'Dependence may do . . . for white folks . . . but isn't worth a chaw of backer to a nigger . . . . I don't b'leeve it was ever 'tended for them."

Experience an interactive version of this story in MindTap®.

n *Uncle Tom's Cabin,* Stowe had thrown down a feminist, abolitionist, Christian thunderbolt into the national debate over slavery's future. Although potentially explosive, that debate had been largely submerged in the political system dominated, beginning in the 1830s, by the Jacksonian Democrats and the Whigs.

Despite this, the Democrats and **Whigs** took distinct positions on many salient issues. With certain exceptions, such as removing Native peoples from ancestral lands, Democrats emphasized small government, whereas Whigs advocated an activist federal government to promote economic development and maintain social order. Democrats championed the nation's agricultural expansion into the West, while Whigs urged industrial and commercial growth in the East, fostered through their "American System" of high protective tariffs, centralized banking, and federally funded internal improvements. Together, Whigs and Democrats forged the second party system, characterized by strong organizations in both North and South, intense loyalty, and religious and ethnic voting patterns.

Sectional conflict resurfaced after the annexation of Texas in 1845. From 1846 to 1848, the United States went to war against Mexico, unleashing the problem of slavery's expansion as never before. As part of the Compromise of 1850, a new fugitive slave law sent thousands of free and fugitive blacks fleeing into Canada, and prompted Mrs. Stowe to

Uncle Tom's Cabin Harriet Beecher Stowe's best-selling 1852 novel that aroused widespread northern sympathy for slaves (especially fugitives) and widespread southern anger.

Whigs Formerly called the National Republicans; a major political party in the 1830s.

write her controversial novel. By 1855, open warfare exploded in Kansas Territory between proslavery and antislavery settlers. On the U.S. Senate floor, a southern representative beat a northern senator senseless in 1856. The following year, the Supreme Court issued a dramatic decision about slavery's constitutionality, as well as the status of African American citizenship—to the delight of most white southerners and the anger of many northerners. And by 1858, violence brewed under the surface of the country; abolitionist John Brown was planning a raid into Virginia to start a slave rebellion.

The political culture of the American republic was disintegrating. As the 1850s advanced, slavery pulled Americans, North and South, into a maelstrom of dispute that its best statesmen could not subdue. The old nationwide political parties fractured, and a realignment that reinforced a virulent sectionalism took their place.

A feeling grew in both North and South that America's future was at stake—the character of its economy, its definition of constitutional liberty, and its racial self-definition. In 1855, the famous black leader Frederick Douglass spoke for the enslaved when he wrote that "the thought of only being a creature of the *present* and the *past*, troubled me, and I longed to have a *future*—a future with hope in it." In those words, Douglass spoke as well to the entire nation's central dilemma.

■ What were the main issues dividing Democrats and Whigs?

■ After 1845, how and why did westward expansion become so intertwined with the future of slavery and freedom?

■ During the 1850s, why did Americans (voters and nonvoters alike) care so deeply about electoral politics?

12-1 Jacksonianism and Party Politics

▶ How did the American political culture become more democratic in the 1820s and 1830s?

▶ What impact did the elections of 1824 and 1828 have on the country's political parties?

▶ What were the defining characteristics of Jacksonian Democrats?

Throughout the 1820s and 1830s, politicians reframed their political visions to appeal to an increasingly broad-based

electorate. Hotly contested elections helped make politics the great nineteenth-century American pastime, drawing the interest and participation of voters and nonvoters alike. Voter turnout skyrocketed, and elections really mattered in the expanding republic. But intense interest also fueled bitter, even deadly, rivalries.

12-1a Expanding Political Participation

Property restrictions for voters, which states began abandoning during the 1810s, remained in only seven of twenty-six states by 1840. Some states even allowed foreign nationals who had officially declared their intention of becoming American citizens to vote. The net effect was a sharply higher number of votes cast in presidential elections. Between 1824 and 1828, that number increased threefold, from 360,000 to over 1.1 million. In 1840, 2.4 million men cast votes. The proportion of eligible voters who cast ballots also grew, from about 27 percent in 1824 to more than 80 percent in 1840.

At the same time, the method of choosing presidential electors became more democratic. Previously, a caucus of party leaders had done so in most states, but by 1824 eighteen out of twenty-four states chose electors by popular vote, compared to just five of sixteen in 1800. Politicians thus appealed directly to voters, and the election of 1824 saw the end of the congressional caucus, when House and Senate members of the same political party came together to select their candidate.

12-1b Election of 1824

As a result, five candidates, all of whom identified as Democratic-Republicans, entered the presidential campaign of 1824. The poorly attended Republican caucus chose William H. Crawford of Georgia, secretary of the treasury, as its presidential candidate. But other Democratic-Republicans boycotted the caucus as undemocratic, ending Congress's role in nominating presidential candidates. Instead, state legislatures nominated candidates, offering the expanded electorate a slate of sectional candidates. John Quincy Adams drew support from New England, while westerners backed House Speaker Henry Clay of Kentucky. Some southerners at first supported Secretary of War John C. Calhoun, who later dropped his bid for the presidency and ran for the vice presidency instead. The Tennessee legislature nominated Andrew Jackson, a military hero with unknown political views.

Among the four candidates remaining in the race until the election, Jackson led in both electoral and popular votes, but no candidate received an electoral college majority. Adams finished second; Crawford and Clay trailed far behind. Under the Constitution, the House of Representatives, voting by state delegation, one vote to a state, would select the next president from among the three leaders in electoral votes. Clay, with the fewest votes, was dropped, and the three others courted his support, hoping he would influence his electors to vote for them. Crawford, disabled from a stroke suffered before the election, never received serious consideration. Clay dramatically backed Adams, who won with thirteen of the twenty-four state delegations and thus became president (see Map 12.1). Adams named Clay to the cabinet position of secretary of state, the traditional stepping-stone to the presidency.

Angry Jacksonians denounced the election's outcome as a "corrupt bargain," claiming Adams had stolen the election by offering Clay a cabinet position in exchange for his votes. Jackson's bitterness fueled his later emphasis on the people's will. The Republican Party split. The Adams wing emerged as the National Republicans, and the Jacksonians became the **Democrats**; as an insurgent political force, they immediately began planning for 1828.

As president, Adams proposed a strong nationalist policy incorporating Henry Clay's American System, a program of protective tariffs, a national bank, and internal improvements. Adams believed the federal government's active role should extend to education, science, and the arts, and he proposed a national university in Washington, D.C. Brilliant as

△ Presidential candidate Andrew Jackson is portrayed on a trinket or sewing box in 1832. This is an example both of how campaigns entered popular culture and of the active role of women, excluded from voting, in politics.

a diplomat and secretary of state, Adams fared less well as chief executive. He underestimated the lingering effects of the Panic of 1819 and the resulting staunch opposition to national banks and tariffs.

12-1c Election of 1828

The 1828 election pitted Adams against Jackson in a rowdy campaign. Nicknamed "Old Hickory" after the toughest of American hardwood, Jackson was a rough-and-tumble, ambitious man. Born in South Carolina in 1767, he rose from humble beginnings to become a wealthy Tennessee planter and slaveholder. After leading the Tennessee militia campaign to remove Creeks from the Alabama and Georgia frontier, Jackson burst onto the national scene in 1815 as the hero of the Battle of New Orleans; in 1818, he enhanced his glory in an expedition against Seminoles in Spanish Florida. Jackson served as a congressman from Tennessee, then as the first territorial governor of Florida, and then returned to Washington as a senator from Tennessee, before running for president in 1824.

Both voters and nonvoters displayed enthusiasm

Democrats Members of the party that emerged from Jefferson's Republican Party as one of the two dominant parties in the second party system.

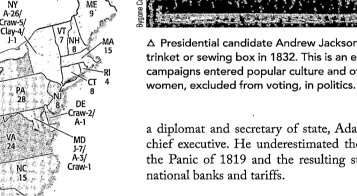

1824

Candidate	Electoral Vote		Popular Vote	
Jackson	99	38%	153,544	43.1%
J. Q. Adams	84	32%	108,740	30.5%
Crawford	41	16%	46,618	13.1%
Clay	37	14%	47,136	13.2%
Territories, unsettled, etc.				

Map 12.1 Presidential Election, 1824

Andrew Jackson led in both electoral and popular votes but failed to win a majority of electoral college votes. The House elected John Quincy Adams president.

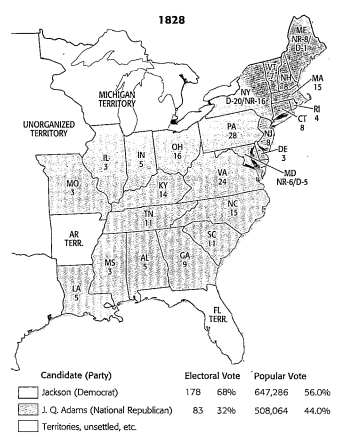

1828

Candidate (Party)	Electoral Vote		Popular Vote	
Jackson (Democrat)	178	68%	647,286	56.0%
J. Q. Adams (National Republican)	83	32%	508,064	44.0%
Territories, unsettled, etc.				

Map 12.2 Presidential Election, 1828

In 1828, Andrew Jackson swept the presidential election, avenging his defeat in 1824.

for Jackson with badges, medals, and other campaign paraphernalia, mass-produced for the first time. In an intensely personal contest, Jackson's supporters accused Adams of stealing the 1824 election and, when he was envoy to Russia, of having secured prostitutes for the czar. Adams supporters countered with reports that Jackson's wife, Rachel, had married Jackson before divorcing her first husband, making her an adulterer and a bigamist. In 1806 Jackson, attempting to defend Rachel's integrity, had killed a man during a duel, and the cry of "murderer!" was revived in the election. Such elements of this campaign were harbingers of many modern elections to come.

Although Adams kept all but one of the states (New York) he had won in 1824, his opposition now unified behind a single candidate, and Jackson swamped him, polling 56 percent of the popular vote and winning in the electoral college by 178 to 83 votes (see Map 12.2). Jacksonians believed the people's will had finally prevailed. Through a lavishly financed coalition of state parties, political leaders, and newspaper editors, a popular movement had elected the president. The Democrats became the nation's first well-organized national party.

spoils system Practice of rewarding political supporters with public office.

12-1d Democrats

The Democrats represented a wide range of views but shared a fundamental commitment to the Jeffersonian concept of an agrarian society. They viewed a strong central government as antithetical to individual liberty, and they condemned government intervention in the economy as favoring the rich at the expense of the artisan and the ordinary farmer. When it came to westward expansion, though, Jacksonians called for federal intervention, with Jackson initiating removal of Native peoples despite protests from northeastern reformers.

Like Jefferson, Jackson strengthened the government's executive branch even as he advocated limited government. In combining the roles of party leader and chief of state, he centralized power in the White House. He relied on political friends, his "Kitchen Cabinet," for advice, rarely consulting his official cabinet. Jackson commanded enormous loyalty and rewarded his followers handsomely. Rotating officeholders, Jackson claimed, made government more responsive to the public will, and he appointed loyal Democrats to office, a practice his critics called the **spoils system**, in which the victor gives power and place to his supporters, valuing loyalty above all else. Although not the first president to do so—Jefferson had replaced many of John Adams's appointees—Jackson's own outcry against corrupt bargains made him an easy target for inflammatory charges of hypocrisy.

12-1e King Andrew

Opponents mocked Jackson as "King Andrew I," charging him with abuse of power by ignoring the Supreme Court's ruling on Cherokee rights, by sidestepping his cabinet, and by replacing officeholders with his own political cronies. They rejected his claim of restoring republican virtue and accused him of recklessly destroying the economy.

Perhaps nothing rankled Jackson's critics more than his frequent use of the veto, which he employed to promote his vision of a limited government. In 1830, he vetoed the Maysville Road bill, which would have funded construction of a sixty-mile turnpike from Maysville to Lexington, Kentucky. Constitutionally, he insisted, states and not the federal government bore responsibility for funding internal improvements confined to a single state. The veto undermined Henry Clay's American System, personally embarrassed Clay because the project was in his home district, and drew lines of stark difference between the two parties.

From George Washington to John Quincy Adams, the first six presidents had vetoed nine bills; Jackson alone vetoed twelve. Previous presidents believed vetoes were justified only on constitutional grounds, but Jackson considered policy disagreements legitimate grounds as well. He made the veto an effective weapon for controlling Congress, which had to weigh the possibility of a presidential veto as it deliberated.

12-2 Federalism at Issue: The Nullification and Bank Controversies

▷ What did the Nullification Crisis reveal about the relationship between state versus federal power?

▷ What role did violence play in American politics in the 1820s and 1830s?

▷ How did Andrew Jackson use presidential power in the dispute over the Second Bank of the United States?

Soon after the Maysville Road veto, Jackson directly faced the question of state versus federal power. The slave South feared federal power, and no state more so than South Carolina, where the planter class was the strongest and slavery the most concentrated. Southerners also resented protectionist tariffs, one of the foundations of Clay's American System, which in 1824 and 1828 bolstered manufacturers by imposing import duties on foreign cloth and iron. In protecting northern factories, the tariff raised the costs of manufactured goods to southerners, who quickly labeled the high tariff of 1828 the **Tariff of Abominations**.

12-2a Nullification

South Carolina's political leaders rejected the 1828 tariff, invoking the doctrine of nullification, maintaining that a state had the right to overrule, or nullify, federal legislation. Nullification drew from the idea expressed in the Virginia and Kentucky Resolutions of 1798—that the states, representing the people, have a right to judge the constitutionality of federal actions. Jackson's vice president, John C. Calhoun of South Carolina, argued in his unsigned *Exposition and Protest* that, in any disagreement between the federal government and a state, a special state convention—like the conventions called to ratify the Constitution—should decide the conflict by either nullifying or affirming the federal law. Only the power of nullification, Calhoun asserted, could protect the minority against the majority's tyranny.

As Jackson's running mate in 1828, Calhoun had avoided endorsing nullification and thus embarrassing the Democratic ticket; he also hoped to win Jackson's support as the Democratic presidential heir apparent. Thus, in early 1830, Calhoun presided silently over the Senate and its packed galleries when Senator Daniel Webster of Massachusetts and Senator Robert Y. Hayne of South Carolina debated states' rights. The debate started over a resolution to restrict western land sales, soon turned to the tariff, and from there focused on the nature of the Union, with nullification a subtext. Hayne charged the North with threatening to bring disunity. For two days, Webster eloquently defended New England and the republic. Although debating Hayne, he aimed his remarks at Calhoun. At the debate's climax, Webster invoked two powerful images. One was the outcome of nullification: "states

dissevered, discordant, belligerent; on a land rent with civil feuds, or drenched . . . in fraternal blood!" The other was a patriotic vision of a great nation flourishing under the motto "Liberty and Union, now and forever, one and inseparable."

Though sympathetic to states' rights and distrustful of the federal government, Jackson rejected the idea of state sovereignty. He strongly believed sovereignty rested with the people. Believing deeply in the Union, he shared Webster's dread of nullification. Soon after the Webster-Hayne debate, the president made his position clear at a Jefferson Day dinner with the toast "Our Federal Union, it must be preserved." Vice President Calhoun, when his turn came, toasted "The Federal Union—next to our liberty the most dear," revealing his adherence to states' rights. Calhoun and Jackson grew apart, and Jackson looked to the secretary of state, Martin Van Buren, not Calhoun, as his successor.

Tension resumed in 1832 when Congress passed a new tariff, reducing some duties but retaining high taxes on imported iron, cottons, and woolens. Although a majority of southern representatives supported the new tariff, South Carolinians did not, insisting that the constitutional right to control their own destiny had been sacrificed to northern industrialists' demands. They feared the act could set a precedent for congressional legislation on slavery. In November 1832, a South Carolina state convention nullified both the 1828 and the 1832 tariffs, declaring it unlawful for federal officials to collect duties in the state. Differing visions of states' rights and the practice of federalism would remain an eternal conflict in American political life. Both Jackson and Calhoun were slaveholders with differing conceptions of how best to protect it within or outside the Union.

12-2b The Force Bill

Jackson soon issued a proclamation opposing nullification. He moved troops to federal forts in South Carolina and prepared U.S. marshals to collect the duties. At Jackson's request, Congress passed the Force Bill, authorizing the president to call up troops but also offering a way to avoid force by collecting duties before foreign ships reached Charleston's harbor. Jackson also extended an olive branch by recommending tariff reductions.

Calhoun resigned as vice president and soon won election to the U.S. Senate, where he worked with Henry Clay to draw up the compromise Tariff of 1833. Quickly passed by Congress and signed by the president, the new tariff lengthened the list of duty-free items and reduced duties over nine years. Satisfied, South Carolina's convention repealed its nullification law. In a final salvo, it also nullified Jackson's Force Bill. Jackson ignored the gesture.

Nullification offered a genuine debate on the nature and principles of the republic. Each side believed it was upholding the Constitution and opposing subversion of republican values. South Carolina's leaders opposed the tyranny of the federal government and manufacturing interests, while long term, they

Tariff of Abominations
Protective tariff of 1828 that infuriated southerners and spawned the Nullification Crisis.

also sought to protect slavery. Jackson fought the tyranny of South Carolina, whose refusal to bow to federal authority threatened to split the republic. Neither side won a clear victory, though both claimed to have done so. It took another crisis, over a central bank, to define the powers of the federal government more clearly.

12-2c Second Bank of the United States

At stake was survival of the Second Bank of the United States, whose twenty-year charter would expire in 1836. The bank served as a depository for federal funds and provided credit for businesses. Its notes circulated as currency throughout the country; they could be readily exchanged for gold, and the federal government accepted them as payment in all transactions. Through its twenty-five branch offices, the Second Bank acted as a clearinghouse for state banks, refusing to accept bank notes of any local bank lacking sufficient gold reserves. Most state banks resented the central bank's police role. Moreover, state banks could not compete equally with the Second Bank, which had greater reserves.

Many state governments regarded the national bank as unresponsive to local needs, and many western settlers and urban workers remembered bitterly the bank's conservative credit policies during the Panic of 1819. As a private, profit-making institution, its policies reflected the interest of its owners, especially its powerful president, Nicholas Biddle. An eastern patrician, Biddle symbolized all that westerners feared about the bank, and all that eastern workers despised about the commercial elite.

12-2d Political Violence

Controversy over the Second Bank inflamed long-standing political animosities, igniting street violence. Elections often involved fraud, and with no secret ballot, political parties employed operatives to intimidate voters. New York City was home to the most powerful political machine, the Democrats' Tammany Hall, and in New York's mayoral election of 1834, the first in which the mayor was elected by popular vote, this combination of machine politics and the bank controversy's exacerbation of tensions nationwide led to mayhem.

Three days of rioting began when Democratic operatives attacked Whig headquarters in the sixth ward. After beating some Whigs unconscious, the Democrats turned their ire on the police, injuring eight of them severely; even the mayor suffered wounds. Vowing revenge, more than five hundred Whigs stole weapons from the armory, but before they could use them, the state militia restored order.

A few months later, an election-day riot in Philadelphia left two dead and five buildings burned to the ground. Although these two riots stood out for their proportions and intensity, voter intimidation and fraud—initiated by both Democrats and Whigs—characterized the second party system.

12-2e Antimasonry

Violence was a catalyst for the formation of the Antimason Party, which formed in upstate New York in the mid-1820s as a grassroots movement against Freemasonry, a secret male fraternity that attracted middle- and upper-class men prominent in commerce and civic affairs. Opponents of Masonry claimed the fraternity to be unrepublican; Masons colluded to bestow business and political favors on each other, and—in the incident that sparked the organized Antimasonry movement—Masons had obstructed justice in the investigation of the 1826 disappearance and presumed murder of a disgruntled former member who had written an exposé of the society. Evangelicals denounced Masonry, claiming its members neglected their families for alcohol and ribald entertainment.

Antimasonry, rooted in the deep American fear of concentrated power and conspiracy, soon developed into a vibrant political movement in the Northeast and parts of the Midwest. In the 1828 presidential election, the Antimasons opposed Jackson, himself a Mason. With their confidence bolstered by strong showings in gubernatorial elections in 1830, the Antimasons held the first national political convention in Baltimore in 1831, nominating William Wirt of Maryland for president and Amos Ellmaker of Pennsylvania for vice president.

12-2f Election of 1832

Following the Antimasons' lead, the Democrats and National Republicans held their own conventions. The Democrats reaffirmed the choice of Jackson, who had already been nominated by state legislatures, for president and nominated Martin Van Buren of New York for vice president. (In the election, however, South Carolina's electors would break from the rest of the party and support John Floyd and Henry Lee of Virginia; as Virginia's governor, Floyd had supported nullification, making him popular in the South Carolina legislature, which chose its state electors.) The National Republican convention selected Clay and John Sergeant of Pennsylvania. The Bank of the United States became the election's main issue. Jacksonians denounced it as a vehicle for special privilege and economic power, while the Republicans supported it as a pillar of their plan for economic nationalism. The bank's charter was valid until 1836, but as part of his campaign strategy, Clay persuaded Biddle to ask Congress to approve an early rechartering. If Jackson signed the rechartering bill, then Clay could attack the president's inconsistency on the issue. If he vetoed it, then—Clay reasoned—the voters would give Clay the nod. The plan backfired. The president vetoed the bill and issued a pointed veto message appealing to voters who feared that the era's rapid economic development spread its advantages undemocratically. Jackson acknowledged that prosperity could never be evenly dispersed, but he took a strong stand against special interests that tried to use the government to their own advantage. "It is to be regretted," he wrote, "that the rich and powerful too often bend the acts of government to their selfish purposes." The message proved powerful and successful. Jackson won 54 percent of the popular vote to Clay's 37 percent, and he captured 76 percent of the electoral college. Although the Antimasons won just one state, Vermont, they nonetheless helped galvanize the anti-Jackson opposition.

12-2g Jackson's Second Term

After a sweeping victory, Jackson began in 1833 to dismantle the Second Bank and to deposit federal funds in state-chartered banks (termed "pet banks" by critics). When its federal charter expired in 1836, it became just another Pennsylvania-chartered private bank, closing five years later. As Congress allowed the Second Bank to die, it passed the Deposit Act of 1836, authorizing the secretary of the treasury to designate one bank in each state and territory to provide services formerly performed by the Bank of the United States. The act also provided that the bulk of the federal surplus—income derived from the sale of public lands to speculators, who bought large quantities of land to resell at a profit—be distributed to the states as interest-free loans (or "deposits") beginning in 1837. (The loans were understood to be forgiven and, in fact, they were never repaid.) Eager to use the money for state-funded internal improvements, Democrats joined Whigs in supporting the measure overwhelmingly. Fearing that the act would fuel speculation, promote inflation, and thus undermine farmers' interests, Jackson opposed it. Because support was strong enough to override a veto, Jackson signed the bill but first insisted on a provision prohibiting state banks from issuing or accepting small-denomination paper money. Jackson hoped that by encouraging the use of coins, the provision would prevent unscrupulous businessmen from defrauding workers by paying them in devalued paper bills.

12-2h Specie Circular

The president then ordered treasury secretary Levi Woodbury to issue the Specie Circular, which provided that, after August 1836, only settlers could use paper money to buy land; speculators would have to use specie (gold or silver). The policy proved disastrous, significantly reducing public land sales, which in turn reduced the federal government's surplus and its loans to the states. Meanwhile, a banking crisis emerged. Fearful that bank notes would lose value, people sought to redeem them for specie, creating a shortage that forced the banks to suspend payment. Jackson's opponents were irate. Now "King Andrew" had used presidential powers to defy legislative will, and with disastrous consequences. In the waning days of Jackson's administration, Congress repealed the circular, but the president pocket-vetoed the bill by holding it unsigned until Congress adjourned. Finally, in May 1838, after Jackson had left office, a joint resolution of Congress overturned the circular.

△ Whigs, who named themselves after the loyal opposition in Britain, delighted in portraying Andrew Jackson as a power-hungry leader eager to turn a republic into a monarchy.

12-3 The Second Party System

▷ What were the main differences between the Democrats and Whigs?

▷ How did economic challenges influence electoral politics in the 1830s?

▷ What factors influenced Americans in choosing their political affiliation?

In the 1830s, opponents of the Democrats, including remnants of the National Republican and Antimason parties, joined together to become the Whig Party. Resentful of Jackson's domination of Congress, the Whigs borrowed the name of the eighteenth-century British party that opposed the Hanoverian monarchs' tyranny. They, too, were the loyal opposition. From 1834 through the 1840s, the Whigs and the Democrats competed on nearly equal footing, and each drew supporters from all regions. The era's political competition—the second party system—thrived on intense ideological rivalry.

12-3a Democrats and Whigs

The two parties held very different visions of the route to national prosperity. For Democrats, the West's fertile and abundant lands were essential for creating a society in which white men could establish independent livelihoods and receive equal rights, freed from the undue influence of established slaveholders or urban elites. Whigs were more suspicious of rapid westward expansion, though they welcomed the commercial opportunities it might bring. Instead, they pushed for industrial and commercial development within the nation's current boundaries. Henry Clay, a leading Whig, explained that it "is much more important that we unite, harmonize, and improve what we have than attempt to acquire more."

The Whigs' vision of economic expansion demanded an activist government, while Democrats reaffirmed the Jeffersonian principle of limited government. Whigs supported corporate charters, a national bank, and paper currency; Democrats opposed all three. Whigs generally professed a strong belief in progress and perfectibility, and they favored social reforms, including public schools, prison and asylum reform, and temperance. Jacksonians criticized reform associations for undermining the people's will by giving undue influence to political minorities; Whigs countered they served the common good. Nor did Whigs object to helping special interests if doing so promoted the general welfare. The chartering of corporations, they argued, expanded economic opportunity for everyone, laborers and farmers alike. Democrats distrusted concentrated economic power as well as moral and economic coercion. Whigs stressed a "harmony of interests" among all classes and interests while Democrats saw society as divided into the "haves" and the "have nots." Whigs feared the "excesses of democracy" and preferred to see society ruled from the top down; they touted self-improvement and thought that society's wealthy and powerful had risen by their own merits. Democrats embraced a motto of "equal rights," alleging that the wealthy and powerful had often benefited from special favors.

12-3b Political Coalitions

But religion and ethnicity, as much as class, influenced party affiliation. The Whigs' support for energetic government and moral reform appealed to evangelical Protestants. In many locales, the membership rolls of reform societies overlapped those of the party. Indeed, Whigs practiced a kind of political revivalism. Their rallies resembled camp meetings; their speeches employed pulpit rhetoric; their programs embodied reformers' perfectionist beliefs.

By appealing to evangelicals, Whigs alienated members of other faiths. The evangelicals' ideal Christian state had no room for nonevangelical Protestants, Catholics, Mormons, or religious freethinkers. Those groups opposed Sabbath laws and temperance legislation in particular, and state interference in moral and religious questions in general. In fact, they preferred to keep religion and politics separate. As a result, more than 95 percent of Irish Catholics, 90 percent of Reformed Dutch, and 80 percent of German Catholics voted Democratic.

The parties' platforms thus attracted what might seem to be odd coalitions of voters. Democrats' promises to open additional lands for settlement—and to remove the Native peoples on those lands—attracted yeoman farmers, wage earners, frontier slave owners, and immigrants. The Whigs' preference for a slower, controlled settlement of western lands attracted groups as diverse as African American New Englanders and well-settled slave owners, especially in the Upper South; the former hoped Whig policies would undercut slavery itself, and the latter wanted to protect their investments in land and slaves from cheap western competition. With such broad coalitions of voters, room existed within each party for a wide spectrum of beliefs, particularly in relation to slavery.

Yet slavery also had a long history of being politically divisive, leading some politicians to take extreme measures to remove it from national political debate. In response to the American Antislavery Society's petitioning campaign, the House of Representatives in 1836 adopted what abolitionists labeled the "gag rule," which automatically tabled abolitionist petitions, effectively preventing debate on them. Former president John Quincy Adams, now a representative from Massachusetts, dramatically defended the right to petition and took to the floor many times to decry the gag rule, which was ultimately repealed in 1844.

12-3c Election of 1836

Vice President Martin Van Buren, handpicked by Jackson, headed the Democratic ticket in the 1836 presidential election. A career politician, Van Buren had built a political machine—the Albany Regency—in New York and joined Jackson's cabinet in 1829, first as secretary of state and then as American minister to Great Britain.

Because the Whigs in 1836 had not yet coalesced into a national party, they entered three sectional candidates: Daniel Webster (from New England), Hugh White (from the South), and William Henry Harrison (from the West). By splintering the vote, they hoped to throw the election into the House of Representatives. Van Buren, however, comfortably captured the electoral college even though he had only a 25,000-vote edge out of a total of 1.5 million votes cast. No vice presidential candidate received a majority of electoral votes, and for the only time in American history, the Senate decided a vice presidential race, selecting Democratic candidate Richard M. Johnson of Kentucky.

12-3d Van Buren and Hard Times

Just weeks after Van Buren took office, the American credit system collapsed. With banks refusing to redeem paper currency with gold in response to the Specie Circular, a downward economic spiral curtailed bank loans and strangled business confidence. After a brief recovery, hard times persisted from 1839 until 1843.

Van Buren followed Jackson's hard-money, antibank policies, proposing the Independent Treasury Bill, which became law in 1840 but which was repealed in 1841 when Whigs regained congressional control. The independent treasury—so named for its independence from both the Bank of the United States and British capital—created regional treasury branches that accepted and dispersed only gold and silver coin; they did not accept paper currency or checks drawn on state banks, and thus accelerated deflation.

The issue of the government's role in economic development sharply divided the parties. Whigs favored new banks, more paper currency, and readily available corporate and bank charters. Democrats favored eliminating paper currency altogether. Increasingly, the Democrats became distrustful even of state banks; by the mid-1840s, a majority favored eliminating all bank corporations.

12-3e William Henry Harrison and the Election of 1840

With the nation gripped by hard times, the Whigs confidently approached the election of 1840 with a simple strategy: maintain loyal supporters and court independents by blaming hard times on the Democrats. The Whigs rallied behind a military hero, General William Henry Harrison, conqueror of the Shawnees at Tippecanoe Creek in 1811. The Democrats renominated President Van Buren, and the newly formed Liberty Party ran James Birney on its antislavery, free-soil platform.

Harrison, or "Old Tippecanoe," and his running mate, John Tyler of Virginia, ran a "log cabin and hard cider" campaign—a people's crusade—against the aristocratic president in "the Palace." Although descended from a Virginia plantation family, Harrison presented himself as an ordinary farmer. While party hacks blamed Democrats for hard times, Harrison remained silent, earning the nickname "General Mum." Whigs wooed voters with huge rallies, parades, songs, posters, campaign mementos, and a party newspaper, *The Log Cabin*.

They appealed to voters as well as nonvoters, including women, who attended their rallies and speeches, and women actively promoted the Whig cause; one Virginia woman, for example, published two pamphlets backing Harrison's candidacy. In a huge turnout, 80 percent of eligible voters cast ballots. Narrowly winning the popular vote, Harrison swept the electoral college, 234 to 60. The Whigs had beaten the Jacksonians at their own game.

Franklin D. Roosevelt Library

△ Even as the Whigs opposed the Democrats, they adopted many of the Democrats' campaign techniques, appealing to the common man with their "log cabin and cider" campaign of 1840. The band in this street scene is riding a wagon decorated with a log-cabin painting. The campaign's excitement appealed to nonvoters as well as voters, and 80 percent of eligible voters cast ballots.

12-4 Women's Rights

▷ **What were the origins of the women's rights movement?**

▷ **How did women's legal status change in the first half of the nineteenth century?**

▷ **What were the connections between the women's rights movement and the abolitionist movement?**

Although women participated in electoral campaigns, states denied them the right to vote, along with other rights afforded male citizens. Some radical reformers, such as Fanny Wright, had long decried such inequality, but the movement for women's rights did not pick up steam until the religious revivalism and reform movements of the 1830s (see "Revivals and Reform," Section 10-7). While revivals emphasized human equality, reform movements brought middle-class women into the public sphere:

By the 1840s, female abolitionists took the lead in demanding women's legal and political rights. Committed

Smithsonian American Art Museum, Washington, DC/Art Resource, NY

△ This 1861 painting captures the notion of manifest destiny, in which European Americans displace Native Americans in a divinely ordained mission to spread "civilization" into the West.

to the general notion of human equality, they were especially frustrated by their subordinated status within the abolitionist movement itself. Dismayed that female abolitionists were denied seats in the main hall at the first World Anti-Slavery Convention in London in 1840, Lucretia Mott and Elizabeth Cady Stanton joined together eight years later to help organize the first American women's rights convention. Other early women's rights activists included **Angelina and Sarah Grimké,** sisters who were born into a South Carolina slaveholding family and who became abolitionists in the North, where critics attacked them for speaking to audiences that included men. Lesser-known women also developed their political consciousness from abolitionist activities. After Congress voted to automatically table antislavery petitions with the "gag rule" of 1836, women defended their right to petition, employed more demanding language, and began offering specific legislative advice. Some thought the next step was obvious: full citizenship rights for women.

Angelina and Sarah Grimké
Southern-born sisters who were powerful antislavery speakers; later leaders of the women's rights movement.

12-4a Legal Rights

After independence, American states carried over traditional English marriage law, giving husbands absolute control over the family. Husbands owned their wives' personal property and whatever their wives or their children produced or earned. Fathers were their children's legal guardians and could deny their daughters' choice of husband, though by 1800 few did.

Married women made modest legal gains beginning in the 1830s. Arkansas in 1835 passed the first married women's property law, and by 1860 sixteen states allowed women— single, married, or divorced—to own and convey property. When a wife inherited property, it was hers, not her husband's, though money earned or acquired in other ways still belonged to her husband. Women could also write wills. Wealthy Americans, South and North, favored such laws, hoping to protect family fortunes during periods of economic boom and bust; a woman's property was safe from her husband's creditors. In the 1830s, states also liberalized divorce laws, adding cruelty and desertion as grounds for divorce, but divorce remained rare.

12-4b Political Rights

The organized movement to secure women's political rights was launched in July 1848, when abolitionists Elizabeth Cady Stanton, Lucretia Mott, Mary Ann McClintock, Martha Wright, and Jane Hunt organized the first Woman's Rights

Convention at **Seneca Falls**, New York. The three hundred women and men in attendance demanded women's social and economic equality, with some advocating political equality, too. They protested women's legal disabilities and social restrictions, such as exclusion from many occupations. Their Declaration of Sentiments, modeled on the Declaration of Independence, broadcast the injustices suffered by women: "All men and women are created equal," the declaration proclaimed. The similar premises of abolitionism and women's rights led many reformers, including former slaves like Sojourner Truth, to work simultaneously for both movements in the 1850s. Even among those supporting the movement's general aims, though, the question of female suffrage became divisive. Abolitionists William Lloyd Garrison and Frederick Douglass supported women's right to vote, but most men actively opposed it. At Seneca Falls, the resolution on woman suffrage passed only after Douglass, one of only a few men to take an active role at the convention, passionately endorsed it, but some participants still refused to sign. In 1851, **Elizabeth Cady Stanton** joined with **Susan B. Anthony,** a temperance advocate, to become the most vocal and persistent activists for woman suffrage. They won relatively few converts, but they continued to gather many critics even as other national issues eclipsed women's rights.

12-5 The Politics of Territorial Expansion

▷ **What developments fueled westward expansion?**

▷ **What role did the federal government play in territorial acquisition?**

▷ **How were westward expansion and territorial acquisition issues in party politics?**

Fiscal policy and westward expansion dominated national politics. Immediately after taking office in 1841, President Harrison convened Congress in special session to pass the Whig program: repeal of the independent treasury system and adoption of a new national bank and a higher protective tariff. But the sixty-eight-year-old Harrison caught pneumonia and died within a month of his inauguration. His vice president, John Tyler, who had left the Democratic Party to protest Jackson's nullification proclamation, now became the first vice president to succeed to the presidency. The Constitution did not stipulate what should happen, but Tyler quickly took full possession of executive powers, setting a crucial precedent that would not be codified in the Constitution until 1967 with the Twenty-fifth Amendment's ratification.

12-5a President Tyler

In office, Tyler became more a Democrat than a Whig. He repeatedly vetoed Clay's protective tariffs, internal improvements, and bills to revive the Bank of the United States. Two days after Tyler's second veto of a bank bill, the entire cabinet resigned, with the exception of Secretary of State Webster, who would soon step down, but not until completing treaty negotiations with Britain over the eastern end of the Canadian-U.S. boundary. Tyler became a president without a party, and the Whigs lost the presidency without losing an election. Disgusted Whigs referred to Tyler as "His Accidency."

Like Jackson, Tyler expanded presidential powers and emphasized westward expansion. His expansionist vision contained Whig elements, though: he eyed commercial markets in Hawai'i and China. During his presidency, the United States negotiated its first treaties with China, and Tyler expanded the Monroe Doctrine to include Hawai'i (or the Sandwich Islands, as they had been named by the English explorer James Cook). Tyler was a Virginia slaveholder; his vision for the nation's path to greatness fixed mostly on Texas and westward expansion.

12-5b Texas and "Manifest Destiny"

Soon after establishing the Lone Star Republic in 1836, Sam Houston approached American authorities to propose annexation as a state. But a new slave state would upset the balance of slave and free states in the Senate, a balance maintained since before the Missouri Compromise. Neither Whigs nor Democrats, wary of causing sectional divisions within their ranks, were inclined to confront the issue. In the 1830s, Democratic presidents Andrew Jackson and Martin Van Buren—one a strong proponent of slavery, the other a mild opponent—sidestepped the issue. But by the mid-1840s—with cotton cultivation expanding rapidly—some Democratic politicians equated the annexation of Texas with the nation's manifest destiny.

The belief that American expansion westward and southward was inevitable, just, and divinely ordained dated to the nation's founding but was first labeled "manifest destiny" in 1845, amid the debate over Texas annexation, by John L. O'Sullivan, editor of the *United States Magazine and Democratic Review.* O'Sullivan claimed that Texas annexation would be "the fulfillment of our manifest destiny to overspread the continent allotted by Providence for the free development of our yearly multiplying millions." The nation's destiny, he and others believed, was to encompass the continent. Manifest destiny implied that Americans had a God-given right, perhaps even an obligation, to expand their republican and Christian institutions to less fortunate and less civilized peoples. Manifest destiny provided a political and ideological rationale for territorial expansion.

Implicit in the idea of manifest destiny was the belief that Native Americans and Hispanics, much like people of African descent, were inferior peoples best controlled or conquered. White racial theorists believed that, unlike white people, Native peoples and blacks were not capable of self-improvement. Nor, according to these racial theorists, were Hispanics, because intermarriage with Native Americans had left

Seneca Falls Town in New York which hosted a women's rights convention in 1848.

Elizabeth Cady Stanton, Susan B. Anthony Vocal advocates of women's suffrage.

them incapable of improvement. Many white Americans believed that in their conquest of the West they were implementing God's will.

Not all white Americans subscribed to such views, however. During debates over Texas annexation, transcendentalist William Ellery Channing argued that the United States should expand its empire by example, not conquest: It should "assume the role of sublime moral empire, with a mission to diffuse freedom by manifesting its fruits, not to plunder, crush, and destroy."

In June 1846, impatient expansionists, including John C. Frémont, staged an armed rebellion against Mexican authorities and declared California an independent republic. Because the U.S. military soon conquered California in its War with Mexico, the "Bear Flag Rebellion"—so named for the symbol on the revolutionaries' flag—was short-lived but further inflamed racial tensions in California.

12-5c "Fifty-Four Forty or Fight"

To the north, Britain and the United States had jointly occupied the disputed Oregon Territory since 1818. Beginning with John Quincy Adams's administration, the United States had tried to fix the boundary at the forty-ninth parallel, but Britain was determined to maintain access to Puget Sound and the Columbia River. As migrants streamed into Oregon in the early 1840s, expansionists demanded the entire Oregon Country for the United States, up to its northernmost border at latitude 54° 40'. Soon "fifty-four forty or fight" became their rallying cry.

President Tyler wanted both Oregon and Texas, but was obsessed with Texas. He argued that there was little to fear from slavery's expansion, for it would spread the nation's black population more thinly, causing the institution's gradual demise. But when word leaked out that Secretary of State John Calhoun had written to the British minister in Washington to justify Texas annexation as a way of protecting slavery—"a political institution essential to the peace, safety, and prosperity of those States in which it exists"—the Senate rejected annexation in 1844 by a vote of 35 to 16.

12-5d Polk and the Election of 1844

Worried southern Democrats persuaded their party's 1844 convention to adopt a rule requiring that the presidential nominee receive two-thirds of the convention votes, effectively giving the southern states a veto and allowing them to block the nomination of Martin Van Buren, an opponent of annexation. Instead, the party ran "Young Hickory," House Speaker **James K. Polk,** an avid expansionist and slaveholding cotton planter from Tennessee. The Democratic platform

James K. Polk Eleventh president of the United States (1845–1849); supporter of immediate annexation of Texas who wanted to gain California and Oregon for the United States as well.

called for occupation of the entire Oregon Territory and annexation of Texas. The Whigs, who ran Henry Clay, argued that the Democrats' belligerent nationalism would trigger war with Great Britain or Mexico or both. Clay favored expansion through negotiation, whereas many northern Whigs opposed annexation altogether, fearful it would add slave states and strain relations with vital trading partners.

Polk won the election by 170 electoral votes to 105, though with a margin of just 38,000 out of 2.7 million votes cast. Polk won New York's 36 electoral votes by just 5,000 popular votes. Abolitionist James G. Birney, the Liberty Party candidate, had drawn almost 16,000 votes from Clay by running on a Free-Soil platform. Without Birney, Clay might have won New York, giving him an edge of 141 to 134 in the electoral college. Abolitionist forces thus unwittingly helped elect a slaveholder as president, and some antislavery Whigs, such as Abraham Lincoln, never forgave the abolitionists for helping defeat Clay.

12-5e Annexation of Texas

Interpreting Polk's victory as a mandate for annexation, President Tyler proposed that Texas be admitted by joint resolution of Congress. The usual method of annexation, by treaty negotiation, required a two-thirds majority in the Senate—which annexationists did not have because of opposition to slavery's expansion. Joint resolution required only a simple majority in each house. On March 1, 1845, the resolution passed the House by 120 to 98 and the Senate by 27 to 25. Three days before leaving office, Tyler signed the measure. Mexico, which had never recognized Texas independence, immediately broke relations with the United States. In October, the citizens of Texas ratified annexation, and Texas joined the Union, with a constitution permitting slavery. The nation was on the brink of war with Mexico. That conflict—like none other before it—would lay bare the inextricable relationships among westward expansion, slavery, and sectional discord.

12-6 The War with Mexico and Its Consequences

▶ **What actions and decisions drew the United States into war with Mexico?**

▶ **How did Americans respond to the war with Mexico?**

▶ **How did the Wilmot Proviso and the election of 1848 change the debate on the issue of slavery?**

The annexation of Texas did not necessarily make war with Mexico inevitable, but through a series of calculated decisions, President Polk triggered the conflict. During the annexation process, Polk urged Texans to seize all land to the Rio Grande and claim the river as their southern and western border. Mexico held that the Nueces River was the border; hence, the stage was set for conflict. Polk wanted Mexico's territory all the way to the Pacific, and all of Oregon Country as well. He and his expansionist cabinet achieved their goals, largely unaware of the price in domestic harmony that expansion would exact.

12-6a Oregon

During the 1844 campaign, Polk's supporters had threatened war with Great Britain to gain all of Oregon. As president, however, Polk turned first to diplomacy. Not wanting to fight Mexico and Great Britain simultaneously, he tried to avoid bloodshed in the Northwest, where America and Britain had since 1819 jointly occupied disputed territory. In 1846, the Oregon Treaty gave the United States all of present-day Oregon, Washington, and Idaho, and parts of Wyoming and Montana (see Map 12.3). Thus, a new era of land acquisition and conquest had begun under the eleventh president of the United States, the sixth to be a slaveholder and one who, through an agent, secretly bought and sold slaves from the White House.

12-6b "Mr. Polk's War"

Toward Mexico, Polk was particularly aggressive. In early 1846, he ordered American troops under "Old Rough and

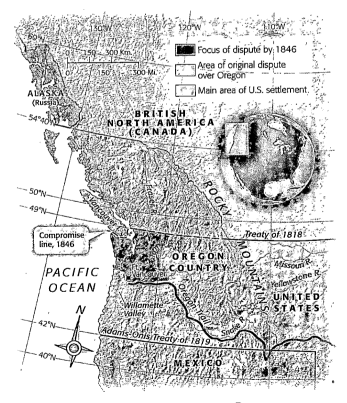

Map 12.3 American Expansion in Oregon

The slogan of Polk's supporters had been "fifty-four forty or fight," but negotiation of a boundary at the forty-ninth parallel avoided the danger of war with Great Britain.

Ready," General Zachary Taylor, to march south and defend the contested border of the Rio Grande across from the town of Matamoros, Mexico (see Map 12.4). Polk especially desired California as the prize in his expansionist strategy, and he attempted to buy from Mexico a huge tract of land extending to the Pacific. When that effort failed, Polk waited for war. Negotiations between troops on the Rio Grande were awkwardly conducted in French because no American officer spoke Spanish and no Mexican spoke English. After a three-week standoff, the tense situation came to a head. On April 24, 1846, Mexican troops ambushed a U.S. cavalry unit on the north side of the river; eleven Americans were killed, and sixty-three were taken captive. On April 26, Taylor sent a dispatch overland to Washington, D.C., which took two weeks to arrive, announcing, "Hostilities may now be considered as commenced."

Polk now drafted a message to Congress: Mexico "passed the boundary of the United States, has invaded our territory and shed American blood on American soil." In the bill accompanying the war message, Polk deceptively declared that "war exists by the act of Mexico itself" and summoned the nation to arms. On May 12, the Senate voted 40 to 2 (with numerous abstentions) for war, reaffirming the House's similarly lopsided vote of 174-14. Some antislavery Whigs in Congress had tried to oppose the war, but they were barely allowed to speak. Because Polk withheld key facts, the full reality of what had happened on the distant Rio Grande was not known. But the theory and practice of manifest destiny had launched the United States into its first major war on foreign territory.

12-6c Foreign War and the Popular Imagination

The idea of war unleashed great public celebrations. Huge crowds gathered in southern cities, such as Richmond and Louisville, to voice support for the war effort. Twenty thousand Philadelphians and even more New Yorkers rallied in the same spirit. After news came of General Taylor's first two battlefield victories at Palo Alto and Resaca de la Palma, volunteers swarmed recruiting stations. From his home in Lansingburgh, New York, writer Herman Melville remarked that "the people here are all in a state of delirium. . . . A military ardor pervades all ranks. . . . Nothing is talked of but the Halls of the Montezumas." Publishers rushed books about Mexican geography into print; "Palo Alto" hats and root beer went on sale. And new daily newspapers, now printed on rotary presses, boosted their sales by giving the war a romantic appeal.

Here was an adventurous war of conquest in a far-off, exotic land. Here was the fulfillment of an Anglo-Saxon–Christian destiny to expand and possess the North American continent and to take civilization to the "semi-Indian" Mexicans. For many, racism fueled the expansionist spirit. In 1846, an Illinois newspaper justified the war on the basis that Mexicans were "reptiles in the path of progressive democracy." For those who read newspapers, the War with Mexico became the first national

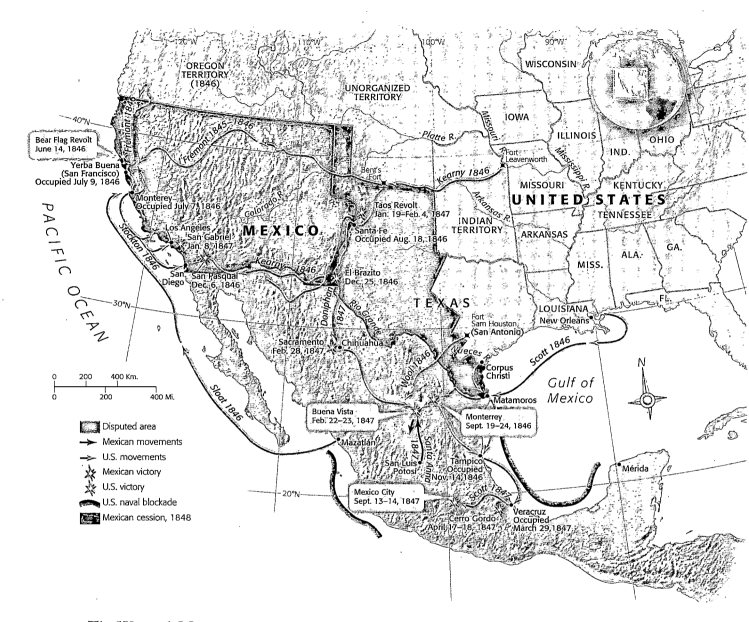

Map 12.4 The War with Mexico

This map shows the territory disputed between the United States and Mexico. After U.S. gains in northeastern Mexico, in New Mexico, and in California, General Winfield Scott captured Mexico City in the decisive campaign of the war.

event experienced with immediacy. War correspondents reported the battles south of the border. From Veracruz on the Gulf Coast of Mexico, ships carried news dispatches to New Orleans, whose nine daily newspapers ran a faster steamer out to meet them. With stories set in type before they even reached shore, riders carried the news to the North. By war's end, news traveled by telegraph in only three days from New Orleans to Washington, D.C., as war fueled the communication revolution.

The war spawned an outpouring of poetry, song, drama, travel literature, and lithographs that captured the popular imagination and glorified the conflict. New lyrics to the tune of "Yankee Doodle" proclaimed: "They attacked our men upon

our land / and crossed our river too sir / now show them all with sword in hand / what yankee boys can do sir." Most of the war-inspired flowering of the popular arts was patriotic. But not everyone cheered. Abolitionist James Russell Lowell considered the war a "national crime committed in behoof of slavery, our common sin." Ralph Waldo Emerson confided to his journals in 1847, "The United States will conquer Mexico, but it will be as the man swallows arsenic, which brings him down in turn. Mexico will poison us." Even proslavery spokesman John C. Calhoun saw the perils of expansionism. Mexico, he said, was "the forbidden fruit; the penalty of eating it would be to subject our institutions to political death."

12-6d Conquest

The U.S. troops proved unruly and undisciplined, and their politically ambitious commanders quarreled among themselves. Nevertheless, early in the war, U.S. forces made significant gains. In May 1846, Polk ordered Colonel Stephen Kearny and a small detachment to invade the remote and thinly populated provinces of New Mexico and California. General Zachary Taylor's forces attacked and occupied Monterrey, which surrendered in September, securing northeastern Mexico (see Map 12.4).

New Mexico proved more difficult to subdue, however. In January 1847, in Taos, northwest of Santa Fe, Hispanics and Native Americans led by Pablo Montoya and Tomas Romero rebelled against the Americans and killed numerous government officials. In what came to be known as the Taos Revolt, some 500 Mexican and Native American insurgents laid siege to a mill in Arroyo Hondo, outside Taos. The U.S. command acted swiftly to suppress the revolt with 300 heavily armed troops. The growing band of insurgents eventually retreated to Taos Pueblo and held out in a thick-walled church. With cannon, the U.S. Army succeeded in killing some 150 and capturing 400 of the rebels. Approximately 28 insurgent leaders were hanged in the Taos plaza, ending the bloody resistance to U.S. occupation of lands still claimed by Mexican and Native peoples.

Before the end of 1846, American forces had also established dominion over California. General Winfield Scott then carried the war to the enemy's heartland. Landing at Veracruz, he led fourteen thousand men toward Mexico City. This daring invasion proved the war's decisive campaign. Scott's men, outnumbered and threatened by yellow fever, encountered a series of formidable Mexican defenses, but engineers repeatedly discovered flanking routes around their foes. After a series of hard-fought battles, U.S. troops captured the Mexican capital.

12-6e Treaty of Guadalupe Hidalgo

Representatives of both countries signed the **Treaty of Guadalupe Hidalgo** in February 1848. The United States gained California and New Mexico (including present-day Nevada, Utah, and Arizona, and parts of Colorado and Wyoming), and recognition of the Rio Grande as the southern boundary of Texas. In return, the American government agreed to settle the $3.2 million in claims of its citizens (mostly Texans) against Mexico and to pay Mexico a mere $15 million.

The war's costs included the lives of thirteen thousand Americans (mostly from disease) and, according to some estimates, fifty thousand Mexicans. Moreover, enmity between Mexico and the United States endured into the twenty-first century. The domestic cost to the United States was even higher. Public opinion was sharply divided. Southwesterners were enthusiastic about the war, as were most southern planters; New Englanders strenuously opposed it. Whigs in Congress charged that Polk, a Democrat, had "provoked" an unnecessary war and "usurped the power of Congress." The aged John Quincy Adams denounced the war, and an Illinois Whig named Abraham Lincoln called Polk's justifications the "half insane mumbling of a fever-dream." Abolitionists and a small minority of antislavery Whigs charged that the war was a plot to extend slavery.

12-6f "Slave Power Conspiracy"

These charges fed northern fear of the "Slave Power." Abolitionists had long warned of a slaveholding oligarchy that intended to dominate the nation through its hold on federal power. Slaveholders had gained control of the South by suppressing dissent. They had forced the gag rule on Congress in 1836 and threatened northern liberties. To many white northerners, even those who saw nothing wrong with slavery, it was the battle over free speech that first made the idea of a Slave Power credible. The War with Mexico deepened such fears.

Northern opinion on slavery's expansion began to shift, but the war's impact on southern opinion was even more dramatic. At first, some southern Whigs attacked the Democratic president for causing the war, and few southern congressmen saw slavery as the paramount issue. Many whites, North and South, feared that large land seizures would bring thousands of nonwhite Mexicans into the United States and upset the racial order. An Indiana politician did not want "any mixed races in our Union, nor men of any color except white, unless they be slaves." And the *Charleston* (South Carolina) *Mercury* asked if the nation expected "to melt into our population eight millions of men, at war with us by race, by language, by religion, manners and laws." Yet, despite their racism and such numerical exaggerations, many statesmen soon saw other prospects in the outcomes of a war of conquest in the Southwest.

12-6g Wilmot Proviso

In August 1846, David Wilmot, a Pennsylvania Democrat, proposed an amendment, or proviso, to a military appropriations bill: that "neither slavery nor involuntary servitude shall ever exist" in any territory gained from Mexico. Although the proviso never passed both houses of Congress, its repeated introduction by northerners transformed the debate over the expansion of slavery. Southerners suddenly circled their wagons to protect the future of a slave society. Alexander H. Stephens, until recently "no defender of slavery," now declared that slavery was based on the Bible and above moral criticism, and John C. Calhoun took an aggressive stand. The territories, Calhoun insisted, belonged to all the

Treaty of Guadalupe Hidalgo Agreement that ended the U.S. War with Mexico, in which Mexico ceded vast amounts of its territory and was forced to recognize the Rio Grande as Texas's southern boundary.

Table 12.1 New Political Parties

Party	Period of Influence	Area of Influence	Outcome
Liberty Party	1839–1848	North	Merged with other antislavery groups to form Free-Soil Party
Free-Soil Party	1848–1854	North	Merged with Republican Party
Know-Nothings (American Party)	1853–1856	Nationwide	Disappeared, freeing most to join Republican Party
Republican Party	1854–present	North (later nationwide)	Became rival of Democratic Party and won presidency in 1860

states, and the federal government could not limit the spread of slavery there. Southern slaveholders had a constitutional right rooted in the Fifth Amendment, Calhoun claimed, to take their slaves (as property) anywhere in the territories.

This position, often called "state sovereignty," which quickly became a test of orthodoxy among southern politicians, was a radical reversal of history. In 1787, the Confederation Congress had discouraged if not fully excluded slavery from the Northwest Territory; Article IV of the U.S. Constitution had authorized Congress to make "all needful rules and regulations" for the territories; and the Missouri Compromise had barred slavery from most of the Louisiana Purchase. Now, however, southern leaders demanded future guarantees for slavery.

In the North, the **Wilmot Proviso** became a rallying cry for abolitionists. Eventually the legislatures of fourteen northern states endorsed it—and not because all of its supporters were abolitionists. David Wilmot, significantly, was neither an abolitionist nor an antislavery Whig. He denied having any "squeamish sensitiveness upon the subject of slavery" or "morbid sympathy for the slave." Instead, he sought to defend "the rights of white freemen" and to obtain California "for free white labor."

As Wilmot demonstrated, it was possible to be both a racist and an opponent of slavery. The vast majority of white northerners were not active abolitionists, and their desire to keep the West free from slavery was often matched by their desire to keep blacks from settling there. Fear of the Slave Power was thus building a potent antislavery movement that united abolitionists and antiblack voters. At stake was an abiding version of the American Dream: the free individual's access to social mobility through acquisition of land in the West. This sacred ideal of free labor, and its dread of concentrated power, fueled a new political persuasion.

Wilmot Proviso A proposed amendment to an 1846 military appropriations bill that would have prohibited slavery in territories acquired from Mexico; though it never passed, it transformed the national debate over slavery.

Free-Soil Party A political party that sprang from and represented the movement to prevent slavery in the western territories.

Slave labor, thousands of northerners had come to believe, would degrade the honest toil of free men and render them unemployable.

12-6h The Election of 1848 and Popular Sovereignty

The divisive slavery question now infested national politics. After Polk renounced a second term as president, the Democrats nominated Senator Lewis Cass of Michigan for president and General William Butler of Kentucky for vice president. Cass, a party loyalist who had served in Jackson's cabinet, had devised in 1847 the idea of "popular sovereignty"—letting residents in the western territories decide the slavery question for themselves. His party's platform declared that Congress lacked the power to interfere with slavery's expansion. The Whigs nominated General Zachary Taylor, a southern slaveholder and war hero; Congressman Millard Fillmore of New York was his running mate. The Whig convention similarly refused to assert that Congress had power over slavery in the territories.

But the issue could not be avoided. Many southern Democrats distrusted Cass and eventually voted for Taylor because he was a slaveholder. Among northerners, concern over slavery led to the formation of a new party. New York Democrats committed to the Wilmot Proviso rebelled against Cass and nominated former president Martin Van Buren. Antislavery Whigs and former supporters of the Liberty Party then joined them to organize the **Free-Soil Party**, with Van Buren as its candidate (see Table 12.1). This party, which sought to restrict slavery expansion to any western territories and whose slogan was "Free Soil, Free Speech, Free Labor, and Free Men," won almost 300,000 northern votes. For a new third party to win 10 percent of the national vote was unprecedented. Taylor polled 1.4 million votes to Cass's 1.2 million and won the White House, but the results were more ominous than decisive.

American politics had split along sectional lines as never before. Religious denominations, too, severed into northern and southern wings. As the 1850s dawned, the legacies of the War with Mexico threatened the nature of the Union itself.

The Mexican War in Popular Imagination

The War with Mexico was the first American foreign conflict to be covered by the press with actual correspondents and the first to stimulate the creation of widespread promotional popular art and commemorative objects. General Zachary Taylor, the American commander in Mexico, became the hero of the war, and in its wake, was elected president in 1848 in a campaign that featured countless forms of this art.

CRITICAL THINKING

▢ Why was the War with Mexico the first American foreign war to be covered by journalists and so widely depicted in political and military art?

▢ Do you think the artistic depictions of the War with Mexico increased or decreased the popularity of the war?

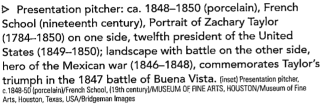

▷ Presentation pitcher: ca. 1848–1850 (porcelain), French School (nineteenth century), Portrait of Zachary Taylor (1784–1850) on one side, twelfth president of the United States (1849–1850); landscape with battle on the other side, hero of the Mexican war (1846–1848), commemorates Taylor's triumph in the 1847 battle of Buena Vista. (inset) Presentation pitcher, c.1848-50 (porcelain)/French School, (19th century)/MUSEUM OF FINE ARTS, HOUSTON/Museum of Fine Arts, Houston, Texas, USA/Bridgeman Images

General Zachary Taylor at the Battle of Buena Vista in 1847 (oil on canvas)/Powell, William Henry (1823-79)/CHICAGO HISTORY MUSEUM/© Chicago History Museum, USA/Bridgeman Images

△ Painting, General Zachary Taylor in command at the Battle of Buena Vista, in Mexico, 1847, oil on canvas, by William Henry Powell (1823–1879).

12-7 1850: Compromise or Armistice?

▶ Why was the debate over slavery in newly acquired territories so contentious?

▶ How did northerners respond to the Fugitive Slave Law?

▷ How did Franklin Pierce's election contribute to increased conflicts over slavery?

The new decade's first sectional battle involved California. More than eighty thousand Americans flooded into California during the gold rush of 1849. With Congress unable to agree on a formula to govern the territories, President Taylor urged these settlers to apply directly for admission to the Union. They promptly did so, proposing a state constitution that did not permit slavery. Because California's admission as a free state would upset the Senate's sectional balance of power (the ratio of slave to free states was fifteen to fifteen), southern politicians wanted to postpone admission and make California a slave territory, or at least extend the Missouri Compromise line west to the Pacific.

12-7a Debate Over Slavery in the Territories

Henry Clay, the venerable Whig leader, sensed that the Union was in peril. Twice before—in 1820 and 1833—Clay, the "Great Pacificator," had taken the lead in shaping sectional compromise; now he struggled again to preserve the nation. To hushed Senate galleries, Clay presented a series of compromise measures in the winter of 1850. At one point, he held up what he claimed was a piece of George Washington's coffin as a means of inspiring unity. Over the weeks that followed, he and Senator Stephen A. Douglas of Illinois steered their compromise package through debate and amendment.

The problems to be solved were numerous and difficult. Would California, or part of it, become a free state? How should the territory acquired from Mexico be organized? Texas, which allowed slavery, claimed large portions of the new land as far west as Santa Fe. Southerners complained that fugitive slaves were not returned as the Constitution required, and northerners objected to slave auctions held in the nation's capital. Most troublesome of all, however, was the status of slavery in the territories.

Clay and Douglas hoped to avoid a specific formula, and in the idea of popular sovereignty they discovered what one historian called a "charm of ambiguity." Ultimately Congress would have to approve statehood for a territory, but "in the meantime," said Lewis Cass, it should allow the people living there "to regulate their own concerns in their own way."

Those simple words proved all but unenforceable. When could settlers prohibit slavery? To avoid dissension within their party, northern and southern Democrats explained Cass's statement to their constituents in two incompatible ways. Southerners claimed that neither Congress nor a territorial legislature could bar slavery. Only late in the territorial process, when settlers were ready to draft a state constitution, could they take that step, thus allowing time for slavery to take root. Northerners, however, insisted that Americans living in a territory were entitled to local self-government and thus could outlaw slavery at any time.

The cause of compromise gained a powerful supporter when Senator Daniel Webster committed his prestige and eloquence to Clay's bill. "I wish to speak today," Webster declaimed on March 7 in a scene of high drama, "not as a Massachusetts man, nor as a Northern man, but as an American. I speak today for the preservation of the Union." Abandoning his earlier support for the Wilmot Proviso, Webster urged northerners not to "taunt or reproach" the South with antislavery measures. To southern firebrands, he issued a warning that disunion inevitably would cause violence and destruction. For his efforts at compromise, Webster was condemned by many former abolitionist friends in New England who accused him of going over to the "devil."

Only three days earlier, with equal drama, Calhoun had been carried from his sickbed to deliver a speech opposing the compromise. As Calhoun was unable to stand and speak, Senator James Mason of Virginia read his address for him. Grizzled and dying, the South's intellectual defender warned .that the "cords which bind these states" were "already greatly weakened." Calhoun did not address the specific measures in the bill; he predicted disunion if southern demands were not met, thereby frightening some into support of compromise.

With Clay sick and absent from Washington, Douglas reintroduced the compromise measures one at a time. Although there was no majority for compromise, Douglas shrewdly realized that different majorities might be created for the separate measures. Because southerners favored some bills and northerners the rest, a small majority for compromise could be achieved on each distinct issue, and for now, the strategy worked.

12-7b Compromise of 1850

The compromise had five essential measures:

1. California became a free state.
2. The Texas boundary was set at its present limits, and the United States paid Texas $10 million in compensation for the loss of New Mexico Territory (see Map 12.5).
3. The territories of New Mexico and Utah were organized on a basis of popular sovereignty.
4. The fugitive slave law was strengthened.
5. The slave trade was abolished in the District of Columbia.

Jubilation greeted passage of the compromise; crowds in Washington and other cities celebrated the happy news. "On one glorious night," records one modern historian, "the word went abroad that it was the duty of every patriot to get drunk. Before the next morning many a citizen had proved his patriotism."

In reality, there was less cause for celebration than people hoped. At best, the Compromise of 1850 was an artful evasion. As one historian has argued, the legislation was more an "armistice," delaying greater conflict, than a compromise. Douglas had found a way to pass the five proposals without convincing northerners and southerners to agree on fundamentals; narrow majorities emerged as

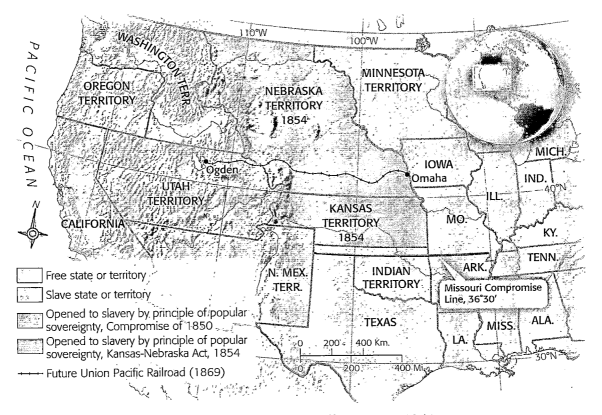

Map 12.5 The Kansas-Nebraska Act and Slavery Expansion, 1854

The vote on the Kansas-Nebraska Act in the House of Representatives (see also Table 12.2) demonstrates the sectionalization of American politics due to the slavery question.

Congressmen and Senators voted on the measures one by one. The compromise bought time for the nation, but it did not provide a real settlement of the territorial questions.

Furthermore, the compromise had two basic flaws. The first concerned the ambiguity of popular sovereignty. Southerners insisted there would be no prohibition of slavery during the territorial stage, and northerners declared that settlers could bar slavery whenever they wished. The compromise even allowed for the appeal of a territorial legislature's action to the Supreme Court. One

Table 12.2 The Vote on the Kansas-Nebraska Act

The vote was 113 to 100 in favor.

Party	Aye	Nay
Northern Democrats	44	42
Southern Democrats	57	2
Northern Whigs	0	45
Southern Whigs	12	7
Northern Free-Soilers	0	4

witty politician remarked that the legislators had enacted a lawsuit instead of a law.

12-7c Fugitive Slave Act

The second flaw lay in the **Fugitive Slave Act,** which gave new—and controversial—protection to slavery. The law empowered slave owners to make a legal claim in their own states that a person owing them "service" or "labor" had become a fugitive. That claim would then serve as legal proof of a person's slave status, even in free states and territories. Specially appointed federal commissioners adjudicated the identity of the alleged fugitives, and those commissioners were paid fees that favored slaveholders: $10 if they found the person to be a fugitive, and $5 if they judged that he or she was not. The law also made it a felony to harbor fugitives, and required that citizens, even in free states and territories, could be summoned to hunt fugitives.

Abolitionist newspapers quickly attacked the Fugitive Slave Act as a violation of fundamental American rights. Why were alleged

Fugitive Slave Act Part of the Compromise of 1850, this controversial measure gave additional powers to slave owners to recapture slaves and angered northerners by requiring their complicity in the return of fugitive slaves.

fugitives denied a trial by jury? Why were they given no chance to present evidence or cross-examine witnesses? Why did the law give authorities a financial incentive to send suspected fugitives into bondage, and why would northerners now be arrested if they harbored runaways? The "free" states, moreover, were no longer a safe haven for black folk, whatever their origins; an estimated twenty thousand fled to Canada in the wake of the Fugitive Slave Act.

Between 1850 and 1854, protests and violent resistance to slave catchers occurred in dozens of northern towns. Sometimes a captured fugitive was broken out of jail or from the clutches of slave agents by abolitionists, as in the 1851 Boston case of Shadrach Minkins, who was spirited by a series of wagons and trains across Massachusetts, up through Vermont, to Montreal, Canada. Also in 1851, a fugitive named Jerry McHenry was freed by an abolitionist mob in Syracuse, New York, and hurried to Canadian freedom. That same year as well, the small black community in Lancaster County, Pennsylvania, took up arms to defend four escaped slaves from a federal posse charged with re-enslaving them. At this "Christiana riot," the fugitives shot and killed Edward Gorsuch, the Maryland slave owner who sought the return of his "property." Amid increasing border warfare over fugitive slaves, a headline reporting the Christiana affair screamed, "Civil War, The First Blow Struck!"

Many abolitionists became convinced by their experience of resisting the Fugitive Slave Act that violence was a legitimate means of opposing slavery. In an 1854 column entitled "Is It Right and Wise to Kill a Kidnapper?," Frederick Douglass said that the only way to make the fugitive slave law "dead letter" was to make a "few dead slave catchers." Into this new and volatile mixture of violence, lawbreaking, and sectional as well as racial fear, Harriet Beecher Stowe's *Uncle Tom's Cabin* became a literary sensation.

12-7d The Underground Railroad

In reality, by the 1850s slaveholders were especially disturbed over what was widely called the **Underground Railroad**. This loose, illegal network of civil disobedience, spiriting runaways to freedom, had never been very organized, with the possible exception of routes from the eastern shore of Maryland through Delaware to New York City. Thousands of slaves did escape by these routes, but largely through their own wits and courage, and through the assistance of blacks in some northern cities. Lewis Hayden in Boston, David Ruggles in New York, William Still in Philadelphia, John Parker in Ripley, Ohio, and Jacob Gibbs in Washington, D.C., were some of the many black abolitionists who assisted fugitive slaves. Moreover, William Howard Gay, editor of a major antislavery newspaper, provided an effective sanctuary and escape means to many fugitives through New York.

Famously, Harriet Tubman, herself an escapee in 1848, returned to her native Maryland and to

Underground Railroad A loosely organized route by which fugitive slaves escaped to freedom in the northern United States and Canada.

△ Portrait photograph of Harriet Tubman (1823–1913, Ohio History Connection, 1887, by H. G. Smith, Smith Studio, Boston, MA). This will be the image used on the new U.S. twenty dollar bill.

Ohio History Connection

Virginia at least a dozen times, and through clandestine measures helped possibly as many as three hundred slaves, some of them her own family members, to freedom. Maryland planters were so outraged that they offered a $40,000 reward (nearly $1,200,000 today) for her capture.

In Ohio, numerous white abolitionists, often Quakers, joined with blacks as agents of slave liberation at various points along the river border between slavery and freedom. The Underground Railroad also had numerous maritime routes, as coastal slaves escaped aboard ships out of Virginia or the Carolinas, or from New Orleans, and ended up in northern port cities, the Caribbean, or England. Many fugitive slaves from the Lower South and Texas escaped to Mexico, which had abolished slavery in 1829. Some slaves escaped by joining the Seminole communities in Florida, where they joined forces against the U.S. Army in the Seminole Wars of 1835–1842 and 1855–1858.

This constant, dangerous flow of humanity was a testament to human courage and the will for freedom. Although it never reached the scale believed by some angry slaveholders and claimed today by some northern towns that harbored runaways in safe houses and hideaways, the Underground Railroad applied pressure to the institution of slavery and provided slaves with a focus for hope.

12-7e Election of 1852 and the Collapse of Compromise

The 1852 election gave southern leaders hope that slavery would be secure under the new presidential administration. Franklin Pierce, a Democrat from New Hampshire, won an easy victory over the Whig nominee, General Winfield Scott. Because Scott's views on the compromise had been unknown and the Free-Soil candidate, John P. Hale of New Hampshire, had openly rejected it, Pierce's victory suggested widespread support for the compromise.

The Whig Party was weak, however, and by 1852 sectional discord had rendered it all but dead. President Pierce's embrace of the compromise appalled many northerners. His vigorous enforcement of the Fugitive Slave Act provoked outrage and fear of the Slave Power, especially in the case of the fugitive slave Anthony Burns, who had fled Virginia by stowing away on a ship in 1852. In Boston, thinking he was safe in a city known for abolitionism, Burns began a new life. But in 1854, federal marshals found and placed him under guard in Boston's courthouse. An interracial crowd of abolitionists attacked the courthouse, killing a jailer in an unsuccessful attempt to free Burns, whose case attracted nationwide attention.

Pierce moved decisively to enforce the Fugitive Slave Act. He telegraphed local officials to "incur any expense to insure the execution of the law" and sent marines, cavalry, and artillery to Boston. U.S. troops marched Burns to Boston harbor through streets that his supporters had draped in black and hung with American flags at half-mast. At a cost of $100,000, a single black man was returned to slavery through the power of federal law.

The national will to sustain slavery was now tested at every turn. This demonstration of federal support for slavery radicalized opinion, even among many conservatives. Textile manufacturer Amos A. Lawrence observed that "we went to bed one night old fashioned, conservative, Compromise Union Whigs & waked up stark mad Abolitionists." Juries refused to convict the abolitionists who had stormed the Boston courthouse, and New England states passed personal-liberty laws that absolved local judges from enforcing the Fugitive Slave Act, in effect nullifying federal authority. What northerners now saw as evidence of a dominating Slave Power, outraged slaveholders saw as the legal defense of their rights.

Pierce confronted sectional conflict at every turn. His proposal for a transcontinental railroad derailed when congressmen fought over its location, North or South. His attempts to acquire foreign territory stirred more trouble. An annexation treaty with Hawai'i failed because southern senators would not vote for another free state, and efforts to acquire slaveholding Cuba through the Ostend Manifesto angered northerners. Written after a meeting among the U.S. foreign ministers to Britain, France, and Spain, the document advocated conquest of Cuba if it could not be "purchased." The ministers predicted that Cuba "would be Africanized and become a second St. Domingo, with all its attendant horrors to the white race." Antislavery advocates once again saw schemes of the Slave Power as political division and social fear deepened.

12-8 Slavery Expansion and Collapse of the Party System

▷ **What were the consequences of the passage of the Kansas-Nebraska Act?**

▷ **What was the ideological foundation of the Republican Party?**

▷ **How did southern Democrats respond to the dissolution of the Whig Party?**

▷ **Why did violence erupt in Kansas and on the floor of the U.S. Senate?**

An even greater controversy over slavery expansion began in a surprising way. Stephen A. Douglas, one of the architects of the Compromise of 1850, introduced a bill to establish the Kansas and Nebraska Territories. Talented and ambitious for the presidency, Douglas was known for compromise, not sectional quarreling. But he did not view slavery as a fundamental problem, and he was willing to risk some controversy to win economic benefits for Illinois, his home state. A transcontinental railroad would encourage settlement of the Great Plains and stimulate the Illinois economy. Thus, with these goals in mind, Douglas inflamed sectional passions to new levels.

12-8a The Kansas-Nebraska Act

The **Kansas-Nebraska Act** exposed the conflicting interpretations of popular sovereignty. Douglas's bill left "all questions pertaining to slavery in the Territories . . . to the people residing therein." Northerners and southerners, however, still disagreed violently over what territorial settlers could constitutionally do. Moreover, the Kansas and Nebraska Territories lay within the Louisiana Purchase, and the Missouri Compromise of 1820 prohibited slavery in all that land from latitude 36° 30′ north to the Canadian border. If popular sovereignty were to mean anything in Kansas and Nebraska, it had to mean that the Missouri Compromise was no longer in effect and that settlers could establish slavery there.

Southern congressmen, anxious to establish slaveholders' right to take slaves into any territory, pressed Douglas to concede this point. They demanded an explicit repeal of the 36° 30′ limitation as the price of their support. During a carriage ride with Senator Archibald Dixon of Kentucky, Douglas debated the point at length. Finally, he made an impulsive decision: "By God, Sir, you are right. I will incorporate it in my bill, though I know it will raise a hell of a storm."

Perhaps Douglas underestimated the storm because he believed that conditions of climate and soil would keep slavery out of Kansas and Nebraska. Nevertheless, his bill threw open to slavery land from which it had been prohibited for thirty-four years. Opposition from Free-Soilers and antislavery forces was immediate and enduring; many considered this turn of events a betrayal of a sacred trust. The struggle in Congress lasted three and a half months. Douglas won the support of President Pierce and eventually prevailed: the bill became law in

Kansas-Nebraska Act Repealed the Missouri Compromise and inflamed sectional disputes around the expansion of slavery in the territories. The act left the decision of whether to allow slavery in the new territories of Kansas and Nebraska up to voters residing there (popular sovereignty).

May 1854 by a vote that demonstrated the dangerous sectionalization of American politics (see Map 12.5 and Table 12.2).

But the storm was just beginning. Northern fears of slavery's influence deepened. Opposition to the Fugitive Slave Act grew dramatically; between 1855 and 1859, Connecticut, Rhode Island, Massachusetts, Michigan, Maine, Ohio, and Wisconsin passed personal-liberty laws. These laws enraged southern leaders by providing counsel for alleged fugitives and requiring trial by jury. More important was the devastating impact of the Kansas-Nebraska Act on political parties. The weakened Whig Party broke apart into northern and southern wings that could no longer cooperate nationally. The Democrats survived, but their support in the North fell drastically in the 1854 elections. Northern Democrats lost sixty-six of their ninety-one congressional seats and lost control of all but two free-state legislatures.

12-8b Birth of the Republican Party

The beneficiary of northern voters' wrath was a new political party. During debate on the Kansas-Nebraska Act, six congressmen had published an "Appeal of the Independent Democrats." Joshua Giddings, Salmon Chase, and Charles Sumner—the principal authors of this protest—attacked Douglas's legislation as a "gross violation of a sacred pledge" (the Missouri Compromise) and a "criminal betrayal of precious rights" that would make free territory a "dreary region of despotism." Their appeal tapped a reservoir of deep concerns in the North, cogently expressed by Abraham Lincoln of Illinois.

Lincoln did not personally condemn southerners—"They are just what we would be in their situation"—but exposed the meaning of the Kansas-Nebraska Act. Lincoln argued that the founders, from love of liberty, had banned slavery from the Northwest Territory, kept the word *slavery* out of the Constitution, and treated it overall as a "cancer" on the republic. Rather than encouraging liberty, the Kansas-Nebraska Act put slavery "on the high road to extension and perpetuity," and that constituted a "moral wrong and injustice." America's future, Lincoln warned, was being mortgaged to slavery and all its influences.

Thousands of ordinary white northerners agreed. During the summer and fall of 1854, antislavery Whigs and Democrats, Free-Soilers, and other reformers throughout the Old Northwest met to form the new Republican Party, a coalition dedicated to keeping slavery out of the territories. The influence of the Republicans rapidly spread to the East, and they won a stunning victory in the 1854 elections. In their first appearance on the ballot, Republicans captured a majority of northern House seats. Antislavery sentiment had created a new party and caused roughly a quarter of northern Democrats to desert their party.

For the first time, too, a sectional party had gained significant power in the

political system. Now the Whigs were gone, and only the Democrats struggled to maintain national membership. The Republicans absorbed the Free-Soil Party and grew rapidly in the North. Indeed, the emergence of the Republican coalition of antislavery interests is the most rapid transformation in party allegiance and voter behavior in American history.

12-8c Know-Nothings

Republicans also drew into their coalition a fast-growing nativist movement that called itself the American Party, or **Know-Nothings** (because its first members kept their purposes secret, answering, "I know nothing" to all questions). This group exploited fear of foreigners and Catholics. Between 1848 and 1860, nearly 3.5 million immigrants entered the United States—proportionally the heaviest inflow of foreigners ever in American history. Democrats courted the votes of these new citizens, but many native-born Anglo-Saxon Protestants believed that Irish and German Catholics would owe primary allegiance to the pope in Rome and not to the American nation.

In 1854, anti-immigrant fears gave the Know-Nothings spectacular success in some northern states. They triumphed

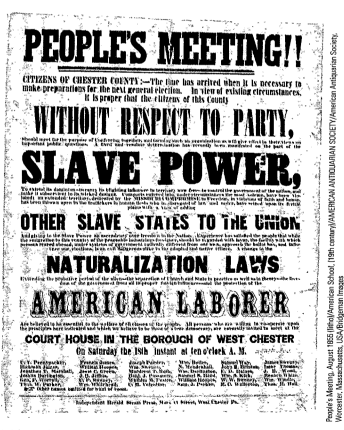

△ Throughout the North, the Kansas-Nebraska Act kindled fires of alarm over the Slave Power's "determination to extend its dominion" and "control the government of the nation." Public meetings like the one announced here, held in West Chester, Pennsylvania, aided the new Republican Party.

Know-Nothings Anti-Catholic and anti-immigrant party whose influence peaked in the mid-1850s.

especially in Massachusetts, electing 11 congressmen, a governor, all state officers, all state senators, and all but 2 of 378 state representatives. The temperance movement also gained new strength early in the 1850s with its promises to stamp out the evils associated with liquor and immigrants (a particularly anti-Irish campaign). In this context, the Know-Nothings strove to reinforce Protestant morality and to restrict voting and office holding to the native born. As the Whig Party faded from the scene, the Know-Nothings temporarily filled the void, inaugurating a long tradition of cycles of nativism in party politics. But like the Whigs, the Know-Nothings could not keep their northern and southern wings together on the issue of slavery's expansion, and they dissolved after 1856. The growing Republican coalition wooed the nativists with temperance ordinances and laws postponing suffrage for naturalized citizens (see Table 12.1).

12-8d Party Realignment and the Republicans' Appeal

With nearly half of the old electorate up for grabs, the demise of the Whig Party ensured a major political realignment. The remaining parties appealed to various segments of the electorate on such issues as immigration, temperance, homestead bills, the tariff, and internal improvements. The Republicans appealed strongly to those interested in the economic development of the West. Commercial agriculture was booming in the Old Northwest, but residents of that region desired more canals, roads, and river and harbor improvements. Because credit was scarce, a homestead program—the idea that western land should be free to individuals who would farm it and make a home on it—attracted many voters. The Republicans seized on these political desires.

Partisan ideological appeals characterized the realigned political system. As Republicans preached, "Free Soil, Free Labor, Free Men," they captured a self-image of many northerners. These phrases resonated with traditional ideals of equality, liberty, and opportunity under self-government—the heritage of republicanism. Invoking that heritage also undercut charges that the Republican Party was radical and abolitionist.

The northern economy was booming, and thousands of migrants had moved west to establish productive farms and growing communities. Midwesterners multiplied their yields by using new machines, such as mechanical reapers. Railroads were carrying their crops to urban markets. And industry was beginning to perform wonders of production, making available goods that only recently had been beyond the reach of the average person.

12-8e Republican Ideology

The key to progress appeared, to many people, to be free labor—the dignity of work and the incentive of opportunity. Any hardworking and virtuous man, it was thought, could improve his condition and achieve economic independence. Republicans argued that the South, with little industry and slave labor, remained backward.

Traditional republicanism hailed the virtuous common man as the backbone of the country. In Abraham Lincoln, a man of humble origins who had become a successful lawyer and political leader, Republicans had a symbol of that tradition. They portrayed their party as the guardian of economic opportunity, giving individuals a chance to work, acquire land, and attain success. In the words of an Iowa Republican, the United States was thriving because its "door is thrown open to all, and even the poorest and humblest in the land, may, by industry and application, gain a position which will entitle him to the respect … of his fellow-men."

At stake in the crises of the 1850s were thus two competing definitions of "liberty": southern planters' claims to protection of their liberty in the possession and transport of their slaves anywhere in the land, and northern workers' and farmers' claims to protection of their liberty to seek a new start on free land, unimpeded by a system that defined labor as slave and black.

Opposition to slavery's extension had brought the Republicans into being, but they carefully broadened their appeal. Their coalition ideology consisted of many elements: resentment of southern political power, devotion to unionism, antislavery convictions based on free-labor arguments, moral revulsion to slavery, and racial prejudice. As *New York Tribune* editor Horace Greeley wrote in 1856, "It is beaten into my bones that the American people are not yet anti-slavery." Four years later, Greeley again observed that "an Anti-Slavery man *per se* cannot be elected." But, he added, "a Tariff, River-and-Harbor, Pacific Railroad, Free Homestead man, may succeed although he is Anti-Slavery."

12-8f Southern Democrats

In the South, the disintegration of the Whig Party had left many southerners at loose ends politically; they included a good number of wealthy planters, smaller slaveholders, and urban businessmen. In the increasingly tense atmosphere of sectional crisis, these people were highly susceptible to strong states' rights positions and the defense of slavery. The security of their own communities seemed at stake, and in the 1850s, most formerly Whig slaveholders converted to the Democratic Party.

Since Andrew Jackson's day, however, nonslaveholding yeomen had been the heart of the Democratic Party. Democratic politicians, though often slave owners themselves, lauded the common man and argued that their policies advanced his interests. According to the southern version of republicanism, white citizens in a slave society enjoyed liberty and social equality because black people were enslaved. As Jefferson Davis put it in 1851, in other societies distinctions were drawn "by property, between the rich and the poor." But in the South, slavery elevated every white person's status and allowed the nonslaveholder to "stand upon the broad level of equality with the rich man." To retain the support of ordinary whites, southern Democrats appealed to racism, warning starkly of the main issue: "shall negroes govern white men, or white men govern negroes?"

Southern leaders also portrayed sectional controversies as matters of injustice and insult to the South's honor and prestige. The rights of all southern whites were in jeopardy, they argued, because antislavery and Free-Soil forces threatened an institution protected in the Constitution. The stable, well-ordered South was the true defender of constitutional principles; the rapidly changing North, their destroyer.

Racial fears and traditional political loyalties helped keep the volatile political alliance between yeoman farmers and planters largely intact through the 1850s. Across class lines, white southerners joined together in the interest of community security against what they perceived as the Republican Party's capacity to cause slave unrest in their midst. In the South, no viable party emerged to replace the Whigs, and as in the North, political realignment sharpened sectional identities.

Political leaders of both sections used race in their arguments about opportunity, but northerners and southerners saw different futures. The *Montgomery* (Alabama) *Mail* warned southern whites in 1860 that the Republicans intended "to free the negroes and force amalgamation between them and the children of the poor men of the South. The rich will be able to keep out of the way of the contamination." Republicans warned northern workers that, if slavery entered the territories, the great reservoir of opportunity for ordinary citizens would be poisoned.

12-8g Bleeding Kansas

The Kansas-Nebraska Act spawned hatred and violence as land-hungry partisans in the sectional struggle clashed repeatedly in Kansas Territory. Abolitionists and religious groups sent in armed Free-Soil settlers; southerners sent in their reinforcements to establish slavery and prevent "northern hordes" from stealing Kansas. Conflicts led to vicious bloodshed, and soon the whole nation was talking about "Bleeding Kansas."

During elections for a territorial legislature in 1855, thousands of proslavery Missourians—known as Border Ruffians—invaded the polls and won a large but fraudulent majority for proslavery candidates. They murdered and intimidated free-state settlers. At one rally of such ruffians with other southerners, flags flapped in the breeze with the mottoes "Southern Rights," "Supremacy of the White Race," and "Alabama for Kansas." The resulting legislature legalized slavery, and in response Free-Soilers held an unauthorized convention at which they created their own government and constitution. Kansas was a tinderbox. By the spring of 1856, newspapers screamed for violence. "In a fight, let our motto be War to the knife, and knife to the hilt," demanded the proslavery *Squatter Sovereign.* Slavery's advocates taunted their adversaries as cowards and likened "abolitionists" to "infidels" worthy only of "total extermination."

In May, a proslavery posse sent to arrest the Free-Soil leaders sacked the Kansas town of Lawrence, killing several people and destroying a hotel with cannon shot. In revenge, John Brown, a radical abolitionist with a band of followers, murdered five proslavery settlers living along Pottawatomie Creek. The victims were taken in the dark of night from the clutches of their families, their heads and limbs hacked to pieces by heavy broadswords, their bodies heaved into dead brush. Brown himself did not wield the swords, but he did fire a single shot into the head of one senseless foe to ensure his death. Soon, armed bands of guerrillas roamed the territory, battling over land claims as well as slavery.

These passions brought violence to the U.S. Senate in May 1856, when Charles Sumner of Massachusetts denounced "the Crime against Kansas." Radical in his anti-slavery views, Sumner bitterly assailed the president, the South, and Senator Andrew P. Butler of South Carolina. Soon thereafter, Butler's cousin, Representative Preston Brooks, approached Sumner at the latter's Senate desk, raised his cane, announced the defense of his kin's honor, and mercilessly beat Sumner on the head. The senator collapsed, bleeding, on the floor while unsympathetic colleagues watched.

Shocked northerners recoiled from what they saw as another case of wanton southern violence and an assault on free speech. William Cullen Bryant, editor of the *New York Evening Post,* asked, "Has it come to this, that we must speak with bated breath in the presence of our southern masters?" As if in reply, the *Richmond Enquirer* denounced "vulgar Abolitionists in the Senate" who "have been suffered to run too long without collars. They must be lashed into submission." Popular opinion in Massachusetts strongly supported Sumner; South Carolina voters reelected Brooks and sent him dozens of commemorative canes.

12-8h Election of 1856

The election of 1856 showed how extreme such polarization had become. For Republicans, "Bleeding Sumner" and "Bleeding Kansas" had become rallying cries. When Democrats met to select a nominee, they shied away from prominent leaders whose views on the territorial question invited controversy. Instead, they chose James Buchanan of Pennsylvania, whose chief virtue was that for the past four years he had been ambassador to Britain, uninvolved in territorial controversies. Superior party organization helped Buchanan win 1.8 million votes and the election, but he owed his victory to southern support. Hence, he was tagged with the label "a northern man with southern principles."

Eleven of sixteen free states voted against Buchanan, and Democrats did not regain ascendancy in those states for decades. The Republican candidate, John C. Frémont, famous as a western explorer, won those eleven free states and 1.3 million votes; Republicans had become the dominant party in the North after only two years of existence. The Know-Nothing

William Walker and Filibustering

Between 1848 and 1861, the United States was officially at peace with foreign nations. But that did not stop private citizens, sometimes with the support of politicians and businessmen, from launching adventurous attempts to take over foreign lands, especially in Mexico, Central America, and the Caribbean. The 1850s was the heyday of "filibustering," defined in this era as private military expeditions designed to destabilize or conquer foreign lands in the name of manifest destiny, commerce, the spread of slavery and white supremacy, or masculine daring.

At least a dozen filibustering schemes emerged in this era of expansion and sectional crises, all of them illegal and often opposed by American presidents as blatant violations of the Neutrality Act of 1818 that outlawed the attempted overthrow of foreign "dominions." Such laws did not stop some senators, railroad and shipping entrepreneurs, and especially self-styled soldier of fortune William Walker from flaunting the law and seeking the "Southern dream" of a Latin American empire. The law also did not stop several American presidents from engaging in numerous more official attempts to annex Cuba in these years.

Born in Tennessee, Walker traveled and studied in Europe as the 1848 revolutions rocked that continent. After a short stint editing a newspaper in New Orleans, he moved to California, practiced law, and courted conflict by fighting at least three duels. After an ill-fated but determined attempt in 1853 to create by force an American "colony" in Sonora and the Baja peninsula in Mexico, Walker turned his sights to Nicaragua, already of great interest to thousands of Americans using its isthmus as the fastest route to the California gold fields.

With a small army of mercenaries, Walker invaded Nicaragua in 1856, exploited its ongoing civil war, seized its government, declared himself president, and reintroduced slavery into a society that had banned it. Defeated by a coalition of Nicaraguans and British in 1857, Walker returned to the United States and launched a fund-raising and speaking campaign on which he was often treated as a romantic hero. On his return to Nicaragua, he was arrested by a U.S. Navy squadron, brought once again to American soil, tried, and acquitted.

In 1860, Walker published an account of his exploits, *War in Nicaragua*. His wide fame was due in part to his swashbuckling character; some saw him as a pirate serving the "Slave Power Conspiracy," and others as the "grey-eyed man of destiny" advancing the causes of slavery and American hegemony. Walker became more aggressively proslavery in Nicaragua when he desperately needed southern political support to supply his plots. On Walker's third return to Central America in 1860 to pursue his insatiable dream of fame and power, he was arrested by a British captain who turned him over to Honduran authorities, who promptly executed him by firing squad. These filibustering adventures fired the imagination of manifest destiny and were merely small precursors of a larger Latin American exploitation and conquest by the United States in the century to follow. Walker's legend, both heroic and notorious, lives on today in Central America, as well as in two American movies, *Burn* (1969), starring Marlon Brando, and *Walker* (1987), starring Ed Harris. Filibusters were links to the world that gave the United States a difficult legacy to overcome with its neighbors from Cuba to Hawai'i.

CRITICAL THINKING

□ Although Walker and others' attempts to overthrow foreign dominions in the first half of the nineteenth century were illegal, how are they reflective of larger ideas and beliefs about American exceptionalism?

Library of Congress Prints and Photographs Division[LC-USZC4-10802]

◁ Portrait of William Walker, Tennessee-born filibusterer, a self-styled soldier of fortune who attempted to create his own empire in Nicaragua, where he reinstituted slavery. To some, especially white southerners, he was a romantic hero, but to others, especially northerners and the U.S. government, he was a notorious villain and arch proponent of the worst aspects of manifest destiny.

candidate, Millard Fillmore, won almost 1 million votes, but this election was that party's last hurrah. The coming battle would pit a sectional Republican Party against an increasingly divided Democratic Party. With huge voter turnouts, as high as 75 to 80 percent in many states, Americans were about to learn that elections really matter.

12-9 Slavery and the Nation's Future

▶ How did abolitionists and the Republican Party respond to the Supreme Court's decision in *Dred Scott v. Sanford*?

▶ Why did the Democratic Party become fractured in the wake of *Dred Scott v. Sanford*?

▶ Why did John Brown's position on slavery and his actions anger white southerners?

For years, the issue of slavery in the territories had convulsed Congress, and Congress had tried to settle the issue with vague formulas. In 1857, the Supreme Court entered the fray, took up this emotionally charged subject, and attempted to silence controversy with a definitive verdict.

12-9a *Dred Scott* Case

A Missouri slave named Dred Scott and his wife, Harriet Robinson Scott, had sued for their freedom. Scott based his claim on the fact that his former owner, an army surgeon, had taken him for several years into Illinois, a free state, and to Fort Snelling in the Minnesota Territory, from which slavery had been barred by the Missouri Compromise. Scott first won and then lost his case as it moved on appeal through the state courts into the federal system and, finally, after eleven years, to the Supreme Court.

The impetus for the lawsuit likely came as much from Harriet as from Dred Scott. They were legally married at Fort Snelling (free territory) in 1836 when Dred was forty and Harriet seventeen. She had already lived as a slave on free soil for at least five years and had given birth to four children, also born on free soil: two sons who died in infancy and two daughters, Eliza and Lizzie, who lived. In all likelihood, the quest to achieve "freedom papers" through a lawsuit—begun in 1846 as two separate cases, one in his name and one in hers—came as much from Harriet's desire to sustain her family and protect her two teenage daughters from potential sale and sexual abuse as from the aging and sickly Dred. Indeed, her legal case for freedom may have been even stronger than Dred's, but their lawyers subsumed her case into his during the long appeal process.

Normally, Supreme Court justices were reluctant to inject themselves into major political issues. An 1851 decision had declared that state courts determined the status of blacks who lived within their jurisdictions. The Supreme Court had only

△ Frank Leslie's *Illustrated Newspaper*, June 27, 1857. Dred Scott and his wife, Harriet, below, and their two children, Eliza and Lizzie, above. Such dignified pictures and informative articles provided Americans broadly with images of the otherwise mysterious Dred Scott and his family in the landmark Supreme Court case.

to follow this precedent to avoid ruling on substantive, and very controversial, issues: Was a black person like Dred Scott a citizen of the United States and thus eligible to sue in federal court? Had residence in a free state or territory made him free? Did Congress have the power to prohibit or promote slavery in a territory?

After hesitation, the Supreme Court agreed to hear *Dred Scott v. Sanford* and decided to rule on the Missouri Compromise after all. Two northern justices indicated they would dissent from the assigned opinion and argue for Scott's freedom and the constitutionality of the Missouri Compromise. Their decision emboldened southerners on the Court, who were growing eager to declare the 1820 geographical restriction on slavery unconstitutional. Southern sympathizers in Washington were pressing for a proslavery verdict, and several justices felt they should simply try to resolve sectional strife once and for all.

In March 1857, Chief Justice Roger B. Taney of Maryland delivered the majority opinion of a divided Court (the vote was 7 to 2). Taney declared that Scott was not a citizen of either the United States or Missouri, that residence in free territory did not make Scott free, and that Congress had no power to bar slavery from any territory. The decision not only overturned a sectional compromise that had been honored for thirty-seven years, it also invalidated the basic ideas of the Wilmot Proviso and popular sovereignty.

The Slave Power seemed to have won a major constitutional victory. African Americans were especially dismayed, for Taney's decision asserted that the founders had never intended for black people to be citizens. At the nation's founding, the chief justice wrote, blacks had been regarded "as beings of an inferior order" with "no rights which the white man was bound to respect." Taney was mistaken, however. African Americans had been citizens in several of the original states and had in fact voted.

Nevertheless, the ruling seemed to shut the door permanently on black hopes for justice. After 1857, African Americans lived in the land of the **Dred Scott** **decision**. In northern black communities, rage and despair prevailed. Many who were still fugitive slaves sought refuge in Canada; others considered emigration to the Caribbean or even to Africa. Mary Ann Shadd Cary, who was free and the leader of an emigration movement to Canada, advised her fellow blacks, "Your national ship is rotten and sinking, why not leave it?" Another black abolitionist said that the *Dred Scott* decision had made slavery "the supreme law of the land and all descendants of the African race denationalized." In this state of social dislocation and fear, blacks contemplated whether they had any future in the United States.

Northern whites who rejected the decision's content were suspicious of the circumstances that had produced it. Five of the nine justices were southerners; three of the northern justices actively dissented or refused to concur in parts of the decision. The only northerner who supported Taney's opinion, Justice Robert Grier of Pennsylvania, was known to be close to President Buchanan. A storm of angry reaction broke in the North. The decision seemed to confirm every charge against the aggressive Slave Power. "There is such a thing as the slave power," warned the *Cincinnati Daily Commercial.* "It has marched over and annihilated the boundaries of the states. We are now one great homogenous slaveholding community." The *Cincinnati Freeman* asked, "What security have the Germans and the Irish that their children will not, within a hundred years, be reduced to slavery in this land of their adoption?" Poet James Russell Lowell expressed the racial and economic anxieties of poor northern whites when he had his Yankee character Ezekiel Biglow say, in the language of the day,

> Wy, it's just ez clear ez figgers,
> Clear ez one an' one make two,
> Chaps thet make black slaves o' niggers,
> Want to make wite slaves o' you.

12-9b Abraham Lincoln and the Slave Power

Republican politicians used these fears to strengthen their antislavery coalition. Abraham Lincoln stressed that the territorial question affected every citizen. "The whole nation," he had declared as early as 1854, "is interested that the best use shall be made of these Territories. We want them for homes of free white people. This they cannot be, to any considerable extent, if slavery shall be planted within them." The territories must be reserved, he insisted, "as an outlet for free white people everywhere" so that immigrants could come to America and "find new homes and better their condition in life."

More important, Lincoln warned of slavery's increasing control over the nation. The founders had created a government dedicated to freedom, Lincoln insisted. Admittedly they had recognized slavery's existence, but the public mind, he argued in the "House Divided" speech of 1858, by which he launched his campaign against Stephen Douglas for the U.S. Senate from Illinois, had always rested in the belief that slavery would die either naturally or by legislation. The next step in the unfolding Slave Power conspiracy, Lincoln alleged, would be a Supreme Court decision "declaring that the Constitution does not permit a State to exclude slavery from its limits.... We shall lie down pleasantly, dreaming that the people of Missouri are on the verge of making their State free; and we shall awake to the reality instead, that the Supreme Court has made Illinois a slave State." This charge was not hyperbole, for lawsuits soon challenged state laws that freed slaves brought within their borders. Countless northerners heeded Lincoln's warnings, as events convinced them that slaveholders were intent on making slavery a national institution. Southerners, fatefully, never forgot Lincoln's use of the direct words "ultimate extinction."

They also never forgot the epic Lincoln-Douglas debates, staged before massive crowds in September-October, 1858. Both candidates crisscrossed Illinois, with Lincoln traveling 4,350 miles and delivering some 63 major speeches, and Douglas logging over 5,000 miles and speaking 130 times. These two talented candidates, one tall and lean, the other short and stocky, squared off over the great issues dividing the country: the westward expansion of slavery, the meaning of abolitionism, the character of federal power over property in slaves, whether the Declaration of Independence had signaled some kind of racial equality, and ultimately the future existence of the American republic. Tens of thousands of people attended these outdoor events, arriving by foot, by wagon, on trains, and accompanied by brass bands. Perhaps never before or since have Americans demonstrated such an appetite for democratic engagement. "The prairies

---

Dred Scott decision
Controversial 1857 Supreme Court decision that stated that no black Americans, whether enslaved or free, were U.S. citizens. It also declared that the Missouri Compromise had been unconstitutional because Congress lacked the authority to ban slavery in the territories.

are on fire," wrote an eastern journalist. "It is astonishing how deep an interest in politics this people takes."

As Lincoln showed in these debates, politically, Republicans were now locked in conflict with the *Dred Scott* decision. By endorsing the South's doctrine of state sovereignty, the Court had in effect declared that the central position of the Republican Party—no extension of slavery—was unconstitutional. Republicans could only repudiate the decision, appealing to a "higher law," or hope to change the personnel of the Court.

12-9c The Lecompton Constitution and Disharmony Among Democrats

For northern Democrats like Stephen Douglas, the Court's decision posed an awful dilemma. Northern voters were alarmed by the prospect that the territories would be opened to slavery. To retain their support, Douglas had to find some way to reassure these voters. Yet given his presidential

ambitions, Douglas could not afford to alienate southern Democrats.

Douglas chose to stand by his principle of popular sovereignty, even if the result angered southerners. In December 1857, Kansans voted on a proslavery constitution that had been drafted at Lecompton. Believing the election to be rigged, most "free staters"—those who opposed legalizing slavery—boycotted the election, giving the proslavery constitution an overwhelming victory. The free staters, who controlled the territorial legislature, quickly called for a new referendum in January; this time, the proslavery forces boycotted, resulting in an overwhelming defeat of the constitution. Although evidence suggests that most Kansans opposed slavery, President Buchanan tried to force the Lecompton Constitution through Congress in an effort to hastily organize the territory.

Never had the Slave Power's influence over the government seemed more blatant; the Buchanan administration and southerners demanded a proslavery outcome, contrary to the majority will in Kansas. Breaking with the administration,

△ Abraham Lincoln (right) and Stephen A. Douglas (left), 1860. The formal studio photographs depict each man in a stance he might have assumed in the famous debates of 1858 as they squared off for the U.S. Senate election in Illinois.

Douglas threw his weight against the Lecompton Constitution. But his action infuriated southern Democrats. After the *Dred Scott* decision, southerners like Senator Albert G. Brown of Mississippi believed slavery was protected in the territories: "The Constitution as expounded by the Supreme Court awards it. We demand it; we mean to have it." Increasingly, though, many southerners believed their sectional rights and slavery would be safe only in a separate nation. And northern Democrats, led by Douglas, found it harder to support the territorial protection for slavery that southern Democrats insisted was theirs as a constitutional right. Thus, in North and South, the issue of slavery in the territories continued to destroy moderation and promote militancy. (After numerous additional votes on its constitution, Kansas would ultimately enter the Union in 1861 as a free state.)

12-9d John Brown's Raid on Harpers Ferry

Soon after the Congressional showdown on the Lecompton Constitution, the entire nation's focus would be drawn to a new dimension of the slavery question—armed rebellion, led by the abolitionist who had killed proslavery settlers along Pottawatomie Creek in "Bleeding Kansas." Born in Connecticut in 1800, John Brown had been raised by staunchly religious antislavery parents. Between 1820 and 1855, he engaged in some twenty business ventures, including farming, nearly all of them failures. But Brown had a distinctive vision of abolitionism. He relied on an Old Testament conception of justice—"an eye for an eye"—and he had a puritanical obsession with the wickedness of others, especially southern slave owners. Brown believed that slavery was an "unjustifiable" state of war conducted by one group of people against another. He also believed violence in a righteous cause was a holy act, even a rite of purification for those who engaged in it. To Brown, the destruction of slavery in America required revolutionary ideology and revolutionary acts.

On October 16, 1859, Brown led a band of eighteen whites and blacks in an attack on the federal arsenal at Harpers Ferry, Virginia. Hoping to trigger a slave rebellion, Brown failed miserably and was quickly captured. In a celebrated trial in November and a widely publicized execution in December, in Charles Town, Virginia, Brown became one of the most enduring martyrs, as well as villains, of American history. His attempted insurrection struck fear into the South.

Then it became known that Brown had received financial backing from several prominent abolitionists. When such northern intellectuals as Ralph Waldo Emerson and Henry David Thoreau praised Brown as a holy warrior who "would make the gallows as glorious as the cross," white southerners' outrage intensified. The white South almost universally interpreted Brown's attack at Harpers Ferry as an act of midnight terrorism, as the fulfillment of their long-stated dread of "abolition emissaries" who would infiltrate the region to incite slave rebellion.

Perhaps most telling of all was the fact that the pivotal election of 1860 was less than a year away when Brown went so eagerly to the gallows, handing a note to his jailer with the

The Metropolitan Museum of Art. Image source: Art Resource, NY

△ *The Last Moments of John Brown*, depicting Brown's mythical kissing of the black child while leaving the jail for his journey to the gallows, by Thomas Hovenden, oil on canvas, 1882. Metropolitan Museum of Art, New York, Art Resource New York.

famous prediction "I John Brown am now quite certain that the crimes of this guilty land will never be purged away, but with blood." Most troubling to white southerners, perhaps, was their awareness that, though Republican politicians condemned Brown's crimes, they did so in a way that deflected attention onto the still-greater crime of slavery. After eighty-four years of growth from its birth in a revolution against monarchy and empire, the American republic now faced its most dire test of existence—whether the expansion of freedom or slavery would define its future. As both hero and villain on the two sides of the slavery question, John Brown had driven a stake into the American Union.

Summary

During the 1820s, politicians reshaped public discourse to broaden their appeal to an expanding electorate of white men, helping give birth to the second party system with its heated rivalry between the Democrats and Whigs. The two parties competed almost equally in the 1830s and 1840s for voter loyalty by building strong organizations that vied in national and local elections often characterized by fraud, and sometimes by violence. Both parties favored economic development but by different means: the Whigs advocated centralized government initiative to spur commercial growth, whereas

Coalition Politics

In a democracy, constituencies with diverse interests often form coalition parties in the hope of winning elections. Although the Jacksonian Democrats and Whigs in the 1830s and 1840s demonstrated their sharp differences over the nature of government, banking, reform, and expansion, each party's constituents held a wide range of beliefs, particularly regarding slavery. From the Mexican War into the 1850s, when significant third parties (the Free-Soilers and nativists) threatened the two-party system, and with the ultimate triumph of the Republicans in forging a new antislavery alliance that destroyed the second party system, the antebellum era provided a lasting model of coalition politics and realignment.

The most potent and rapidly successful third-party movement in American history was the Republican Party, founded in 1854 in the wake of the Kansas-Nebraska Act and its potential opening of the entire American West to slavery. Never before or since has a coalition of politicians and voters from previously long-standing parties and persuasions coalesced so successfully around a cluster of interests aimed at a single goal—in this case, stopping slavery's spread.

So many northern Democrats bolted to the Republicans that by the 1856 election, they formed perhaps 25 percent of the new party's vote. Northern Whigs, with their historic advocacy of activist government and social reform, also joined the Republicans. Radical abolitionists who had entered politics through the old Liberty or Free-Soil parties now found leadership positions among the exclusively northern Republicans.

This antislavery coalition forged numerous divergent outlooks into a new worldview: resentment of southern society and political power; an aggressive antislavery stance based on the free-labor argument and a celebration of the wage earner and small farmer; devotion to the Union against increasing southern threats of disunion; moral revulsion to slavery as inhumane and a threat to the country's future; a racist urge to keep the West open for white immigrant laborers and free of black competition; and finally, commitment to the northern social order as the model of progress, capitalist enterprise, and social mobility. Such a multipart ideology coalesced against the common foe of the "Slave Power Conspiracy,"

an alleged southern oligarchy of concentrated power determined to control the nation's future.

Whether in the diverse alliances of rural and urban reformers that formed the Populist and Progressive movements of the late nineteenth and early twentieth centuries; the mixture of urban working classes, labor unions, rural southern whites, African Americans, and artists and intellectuals that formed the New Deal coalition that reshaped America from the Great Depression to the 1970s; the Obama coalition of 2008–2016 that combined racial minorities, women, and young voters; or the modern conservative counterrevolution, with its antigovernment determination to dismantle the New Deal's social contract, all such coalitions have drawn upon this enduring legacy of pre–Civil War American politics. In the wake of the stunning election of Donald Trump in 2016, we may find new coalitions forming or dissolving.

CRITICAL THINKING

- Does the election of Donald Trump represent the rise of a new coalition?
- If so, what causes are driving this political realignment?

Democrats advocated limited government and sought agricultural expansion. Andrew Jackson did not hesitate, however, to use presidential authority, leading his opponents to dub him "King Andrew." The controversies over the Second Bank of the United States and nullification exposed different interpretations of the nation's founding principles and intensified political rivalries. Although women participated in political campaigns, activists for women's legal and political equality won few supporters. Instead, the nation focused its attention on economic development and westward expansion.

Long submerged, political debate over slavery was forced into the open after the annexation of Texas led to the War with Mexico, during which the United States acquired massive amounts of new land. The Compromise of 1850 attempted to settle the dispute but only added fuel to the fires of sectional contention, leading to the fateful Kansas–Nebraska Act of

1854, which tore asunder the political party system and gave birth to a genuine antislavery coalition. With Bleeding Kansas and the *Dred Scott* decision, by 1857 Americans North and South faced clear and dangerous choices about the future of labor and the meaning of liberty in an ambitious and expanding society. And finally, by 1859, when radical abolitionist John Brown attacked Harpers Ferry to foment a slave insurrection, southerners and northerners came to see each other in conspiratorial terms. Meanwhile, African Americans, slave and free, fled from slave catchers in unprecedented numbers and grew to expect violent if uncertain resolutions to their dreams of freedom in America. No one knew the future, but all knew the issues and conflicts were real.

Throughout the 1840s and 1850s, many able leaders had worked to avert the outcome of disunion. As late as 1858, even Jefferson Davis had declared, "This great country will continue united." But within two years he found himself in the midst of a movement for disunion in order to preserve his section's slave society and their definition of states' rights.

During the 1850s, every southern victory in territorial expansion increased fear of the Slave Power, and each new expression of Free-Soil sentiment prompted slaveholders to harden their demands. In the profoundest sense, slavery was the root of the conflict. As a people and a nation, Americans had reached the most fateful turning point in their history. Answers would now come from a completely polarized election, disunion, and the battlefield.

Suggestions for Further Reading

Edward L. Ayers and Carolyn R. Martin, eds., *America on the Eve of the Civil War* (2010)

Donald B. Cole, *Vindicating Andrew Jackson: The 1828 Election and the Rise of the Two-Party System* (2009)

Marc Egnal, *Clash of Extremes: The Economic Origins of the Civil War* (2009)

Nicole Etcheson, *Bleeding Kansas: Contested Liberty in the Civil War Era* (2004)

Don E. Fehrenbacher, *The Slaveholding Republic: An Account of the United States Government's Relations to Slavery* (2001)

Joan D. Hedrick, *Harriet Beecher Stowe: A Life* (1994)

Daniel Walker Howe, *What Hath God Wrought: The Transformation of America, 1815–1848* (2007)

Robert W. Johannsen, *To the Halls of the Montezumas: The Mexican War and the American Imagination* (1985)

Lynn Hudson Parsons, *The Birth of Modern Politics: Andrew Jackson, John Quincy Adams, and the Election of 1828* (2009)

Richard H. Sewell, *Ballots for Freedom: Antislavery Politics Before the Civil War* (1976)

Elizabeth R. Varon, *Disunion! The Coming of the American Civil War, 1789–1859* (2008)

Harry L. Watson, *Liberty and Power: The Politics of Jacksonian America* (2006)

Susan Zaeske, *Signatures of Citizenship: Petitioning, Antislavery, and Women's Political Identity* (2003)

MINDTAP
From Cengage

MindTap® is a fully online personalized learning experience built upon Cengage Learning content. MindTap® combines student learning tools—readings, multimedia, activities, and assessments—into a singular Learning Path that guides students through the course and helps students develop the critical thinking, analysis, and communication skills that are essential to academic and professional success.

Transforming Fire: The Civil War, 1860–1865

S lave prisons, known as slave pens, were the dark and ugly crossroads of American history. To see, hear, and smell one was to understand why the Civil War happened. Wallace Turnage, a seventeen-year-old slave from a cotton plantation in Pickens County, Alabama, entered wartime Mobile in December 1862 through the slave traders' yard; he would leave Mobile from that same yard a year and eight months later.

Turnage was born in 1846 on a remote tobacco farm near Snow Hill, North Carolina. In mid-1860, as the nation teetered on the brink of disunion, he was sold to a Richmond, Virginia, slave trader named Hector Davis. Turnage worked in Davis's three-story slave jail, organizing daily auctions until he was sold for $1,000 in early 1861 to a cotton planter from Pickens County, Alabama. Frequently whipped and longing for escape, the desperate teenager tried four times over the next two years to escape to Mississippi, seeking the lines of the Union armies. Although he remained at large for months, he was captured each time and returned to his owner in southeastern Alabama.

In frustration, his owner took Turnage to the Mobile slave traders' yard, where the youth was sold for $2,000 to a wealthy merchant in the port city. During 1864, as Union admiral David Farragut prepared his fleet for an assault on Mobile Bay and the city came under siege, its

◁ A fugitive slave chased by dogs and slave catchers, a 19th century illustration. The escaped slave, or "runaway," was one of the most oft-depicted visual images of American slavery.

slaves were enlisted to build elaborate trenchworks. Meanwhile, Turnage labored at all manner of urban tasks for his new owner's family, including driving their carriage on errands.

One day in early August, Turnage crashed the old carriage on a Mobile street. In anger, his owner took him to the slave pen and hired the jailer to administer thirty lashes in the special "whipping house." Stripped naked, his hands tied in ropes, Turnage was hoisted up on a hook on the wall. At the end of the gruesome ritual, his owner instructed Wallace to walk home. Instead, Turnage "took courage," as he wrote in his postwar narrative, "prayed faithfully," and walked steadfastly southwest, right through the Confederate encampment and trenchworks. The soldiers took the bloodied and tattered black teenager for simply one among the hundreds of slaves who did camp labor.

For the next three weeks, Turnage crawled and waded for twenty-five miles through the snake-infested swamps of the Foul River estuary, down the west edge of Mobile Bay. Nearly starved and narrowly escaping Confederate patrols, Turnage made it all the way to Cedar Point, where he could look out at the forbidding mouth of Mobile Bay to Dauphin Island, now occupied by Union forces. Alligators swam in their wallows nearby, delta grass swayed waist high in the hot breezes, and the laughing gulls squawked around him as Turnage hid from Confederate lookouts in a swampy den. He remembered his choices starkly: "It was death to go back and it was death to stay there and freedom was before me; it could only be death to go forward if I was caught and freedom if I escaped."

Turnage barely survived a desperate attempt to ride a log out into the ocean and narrowly made it back to shore. Then, one day at the water's edge, he noticed an old rowboat that had rolled in with the tide. The veteran fugitive now took a "piece of board" and began to row out into the bay. As a squall with "water like a hill coming" at him nearly swamped him, he suddenly "heard the crash of oars and behold there was eight Yankees in a boat." Following the rhythm of the oars, Turnage jumped into the Union gunboat. For a stunning few moments, he remembered, the oarsmen in blue "were struck with silence" as they contemplated the frail young black man crouched in front of them. Turnage turned

his head and looked back at Confederate soldiers on the shore and measured the distance of his bravery at sea. Then he took his first breaths of freedom.

Experience an interactive version of this story in MindTap®.

The Civil War brought astonishing changes to individuals everywhere in the North and South. It obliterated the normal patterns of life. Millions of men were swept away into training camps and regiments. Armies numbering in the hundreds of thousands marched over the South, devastating the countryside. Families struggled to survive without their men; businesses tried to cope with the loss of workers. Women on both sides took on extra responsibilities in the home and moved into new jobs in the workforce, including the ranks of nurses and hospital workers. No sphere of life went untouched.

But southern soldiers and their families also experienced what few other groups of Americans have—utter defeat. For most of them, wealth changed to poverty and hope to despair as countless southern farms were ruined. Late in the war, many southerners yearned only for an end to inflation, to shortages, to the escape of their slaves, and to the death that visited nearly every family. Even the South's slaves, who eventually placed great hope in the war, did not always encounter sympathetic liberators such as those who took Turnage from his drowning boat, fed and clothed him in a tent, and took him before a Union general, where the freedman was given two choices: join a black regiment or become a camp servant for a white officer. For the remainder of the war, Turnage cooked for a Maryland captain.

In the North, farm boys and mechanics from all regions would be asked for heretofore unimagined sacrifices. The conflict ensured vast government expenditures and lucrative federal contracts. *Harper's Monthly* reported that an eminent financier expected a long and prosperous war. "The battle of Bull Run," predicted the financier, "makes the fortune of every man in Wall Street who is not a natural idiot."

Change was most drastic in the South, where secessionists had launched a conservative revolution for their section's national independence. Born of states' rights doctrine, the Confederacy now had to be transformed into a centralized nation to fight a vast war. Southern whites had feared that a peacetime government of Republicans would interfere with slavery and ruin plantation life. Instead, their own actions led to a war that turned southern society upside down and imperiled the very existence of slavery.

The war created social strains in both North and South. Disaffection was strongest, though, in the Confederacy, where poverty and class resentment threatened the South from within as federal armies assailed it from without. In the North, dissent against the rising powers of the federal government also flourished, and antiwar sentiment occasionally erupted into violence.

Ultimately, the Civil War forced on the nation a social and political revolution regarding race. Its greatest effect was to compel leaders and citizens to finally face the great question of slavery. And blacks themselves embraced what was for them the most fundamental turning point in their experience as Americans.

- *How and why did the Civil War bring social transformations to both South and North?*

- *How did the war to preserve the Union or for southern independence become the war to free the slaves?*

- *By 1865, when Americans on all sides searched for the meaning of the war they had just fought, what might some of their answers have been?*

13-1 Election of 1860 and Secession Crisis

▷ **How did slavery affect the election of 1860 and the immediate aftermath of the election?**

▷ **What were the varying positions on secession in the South after the election of 1860?**

▷ **How did Abraham Lincoln address the dilemma regarding Fort Sumter?**

Many Americans believed the election of 1860 would decide the fate of the Union. The Democratic Party was the only party that was truly national in scope. "One after another," wrote a Mississippi editor, "the links which have bound the North and South together, have been severed . . . [but] the Democratic party looms gradually up . . . and waves the olive branch over the troubled waters of politics." But, fatefully, at its 1860 convention in Charleston, South Carolina, the Democratic Party split.

Stephen Douglas wanted his party's presidential nomination, but he could not afford to alienate northern voters by accepting the southern position on the territories. Southern Democrats, however, insisted on recognition of their rights—as the *Dred Scott* decision had defined them—and they moved to block Douglas's nomination. When Douglas obtained a majority for his version of the platform, delegates from the Deep South walked out of the convention. After efforts at compromise failed, the Democrats presented two nominees: Douglas for the northern wing, and Vice President John C. Breckinridge of Kentucky for the southern.

The Republicans nominated Abraham Lincoln at a rousing convention in Chicago. The choice of Lincoln reflected the growing power of the Midwest, and he was perceived as more moderate on slavery than the early front-runner, Senator William H. Seward of New York. A Constitutional Union Party, formed to preserve the nation but strong only in the Upper South, nominated John Bell of Tennessee.

Bell's only issue in the ensuing campaign was the urgency of preserving the Union; Constitutional Unionists hoped to appeal to history and sentiment to hold the country together. Douglas desperately sought to unite his northern and southern supporters, but the slavery question and the Breckinridge candidacy had permanently divided the party. Although Lincoln and the Republicans denied any intent to interfere with slavery in the states where it existed, they stood firm against the extension of slavery into the territories.

But the election of 1860 was sectional in character, and the only one in American history in which the losers refused to accept the result. Lincoln won, but Douglas, Breckinridge, and Bell together received a majority of the votes. Douglas had broad-based support but won few states. Breckinridge carried nine southern states, all in the Deep South. Bell won pluralities in Virginia, Kentucky, and Tennessee. Lincoln prevailed in the North, but in the four slave states that ultimately remained loyal to the Union (Missouri, Kentucky, Maryland, and Delaware—the border states) he gained only a plurality, not a majority (see Table 13.1). Lincoln's victory was won in the electoral college. He polled only 40 percent of the total vote and was not even on the ballot in ten slave states.

Opposition to slavery's extension was the core issue for Lincoln and the Republican Party. Meanwhile, in the South, proslavery advocates and secessionists whipped up public opinion and demanded that state conventions assemble to consider secession.

Lincoln made the crucial decision not to soften his party's position on the territories. He wrote of the necessity of maintaining the bond of faith between voter and candidate and of declining to set "the minority over the majority." Although many conservative Republicans—eastern businessmen and former Whigs who did not feel strongly about slavery—hoped for a compromise, the original and most committed Republicans—old

Jefferson Davis President of the Confederacy.

Table 13.1 Presidential Vote in 1860

Lincoln (Republican)*	Carried all northern states and all electoral votes except 3 in New Jersey
Breckinridge (Southern Democrat)	Carried all slave states except Virginia, Kentucky, Tennessee, Missouri
Bell (Constitutional Union)	Carried Virginia, Kentucky, Tennessee
Douglas (Northern Democrat)	Carried only Missouri

*Lincoln received only 26,000 votes in the entire South and was not even on the ballot in ten slave states. Breckinridge was not on the ballot in three northern states.

Free-Soilers and antislavery Whigs—held the line on slavery expansion.

In the winter of 1860–1861, numerous compromise proposals were floated in Washington, including resurrecting the Missouri Compromise line, 36°30', and even initiating a "plural presidency," with one president from each section. When Lincoln ruled out concessions on the territorial issue, these peacemaking efforts, based largely on old or discredited ideas, collapsed.

13-1a Secession and the Confederate States of America

Meanwhile, on December 20, 1860, South Carolina passed an ordinance of secession amid jubilation and cheering. By reclaiming its "independence," South Carolina raised the stakes in the sectional confrontation. No longer was secession an unthinkable step; the Union was broken. Secessionists now argued that other states should follow South Carolina and that those who favored compromise could make a better deal outside the Union than in it. Moderates from regions with fewer slaves and more diversified economies than the cotton belt (such as upstate Georgia, as opposed to the southern tier of the state), fearing economic chaos and arguing for "resistance short of secession," still felt deep affection for the Union and had family ties in the North; secession was by no means inevitable or widely popular in Upper South states like Virginia or Tennessee.

Southern extremists soon got their way in the Deep South. Overwhelming their opposition, they called separate state conventions and passed secession ordinances in Mississippi, Florida, Alabama, Georgia, Louisiana, and Texas. By February 1861, these states had joined South Carolina to form a new government in Montgomery, Alabama: a revolutionary movement now called the Confederate States of America. The delegates at Montgomery chose **Jefferson Davis** of Mississippi as their president.

This apparent unanimity of action was deceiving. Confused and dissatisfied with the alternatives, many southerners—perhaps even 40 percent of those in the Deep South—opposed immediate secession. In some state conventions, the secession vote was close and decided by overrepresentation of plantation districts. In Georgia, where more than three in five voters were nonslaveholders, the secession convention voted 166–130 to secede after a bitterly divided debate. Four states in the Upper South where wheat production and commercial ties to the North had grown steadily in the 1850s—Virginia, North Carolina, Tennessee, and Arkansas—flatly rejected secession and did not join the Confederacy until after fighting had begun. In Augusta County, Virginia, in the Shenandoah Valley, where one-fifth of households held slaves, the majority steadfastly sought alternatives to secession until after Fort Sumter. In the border states, popular sentiment was deeply divided; minorities in Kentucky and Missouri tried to secede, but these slave states ultimately came under Union control, along with Maryland and Delaware (see Map 13.1).

Such misgivings were not surprising. Secession posed enormous challenges for southerners. Analysis of election returns from 1860 and 1861 indicates that slaveholders and nonslaveholders were beginning to part company politically. Heavily slaveholding counties strongly supported secession. But nonslaveholding areas that had favored Breckinridge in the presidential election proved far less willing to support secession: economic interests and fear of war on their own soil provided a potent, negative reaction to abstractions such as "state rights."

As for why the Deep South bolted, we need look no further than the speeches and writings of the secession commissioners sent out by the seven seceded states to try to convince the other slave states to join them. Repeatedly, they stressed independence as the only way to preserve white racial security and the slave system against the hostile Republicans. Upon "slavery," said the Alabama commissioner, Stephen Hale, to the Kentucky legislature, rested "not only the wealth and prosperity of the southern people, but their very existence as a political community." Only secession, Hale contended, could sustain the "heaven-ordained superiority of the white over the black race." This combination of economic interests and beliefs fueled the tragedy about to happen. Southern states seceded from the Union to preserve slavery and white supremacy.

13-1b Fort Sumter and Outbreak of War

President Lincoln's dilemma on Inauguration Day in March 1861 was unprecedented—how to maintain the authority of the federal government without provoking war. Proceeding

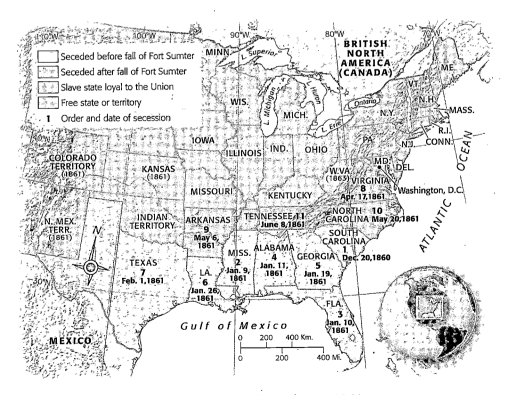

Map 13.1 The Divided Nation—Slave and Free Areas, 1861

After fighting began, the Upper South joined the Deep South in the Confederacy. The nation's pattern of division corresponded to the distribution of slavery and the percentage of black people in the population.

△ Photograph of interior of Fort Sumter, in Charleston Harbor, April 14, 1861, the day Major Robert Anderson and his troops surrendered and the Civil War began.

cautiously, he sought only to hold onto forts in the states that had left the Union, reasoning that in this way he could assert federal sovereignty while waiting for a restoration. But Jefferson Davis, who could not claim to lead a sovereign nation if the Confederate ports were under foreign (that is, U.S.) control, was unwilling to be so patient. A collision soon came.

It arrived in the early morning hours of April 12, 1861, at **Fort Sumter** in Charleston harbor. A federal garrison there ran low on food, and Lincoln notified the South Carolinians that he was sending a ship to resupply the fort. For the Montgomery government, the alternatives were to attack the fort or to acquiesce to Lincoln's authority. After the Confederate cabinet met, the secretary of war ordered local commanders to obtain a surrender or attack the fort. After two days of heavy bombardment, the federal garrison finally surrendered. No one died in battle, though an accident during postbattle ceremonies killed two Union soldiers. Confederates permitted the U.S. troops to sail away on unarmed vessels while Charlestonians celebrated wildly. The Civil War—the bloodiest war in America's history—had begun.

13-1c Causation

Fort Sumter Federal fort in Charleston harbor, South Carolina where the first shots of the Civil War were fired when the Union attempted to resupply troops.

Historians have long debated the immediate and long-term roots of the Civil War. Some have interpreted it as an "irrepressible conflict," the clash of two civilizations on divergent trajectories of history. Another group saw the war as "needless," the result of a "blundering generation" of irrational politicians and activists who trumped up an avoidable conflict. But the issues dividing Americans in 1861 were fundamental to the future of the republic. The logic of Republican ideology tended in the direction of abolishing slavery. The logic of southern arguments led to establishing slavery potentially everywhere.

Republicans were devoted to promoting the North's free-labor economy, burgeoning in the Great Lakes region through homesteading, internal improvements, and protective tariffs. The lords of the cotton kingdom, owners of more than $3 billion in slave property and the largest single asset in the American economy, were determined to protect and expand their "way of life." Small investors in land and large investors in slaves were on a collision course. Both sides had watched for more than thirty years the consequences of British emancipation in the Caribbean and had reached different conclusions about its meaning. Indeed, the American antislavery movement had been emboldened by emancipation in the British empire.

Lincoln put these facts succinctly. In a postelection letter to his old congressional colleague, Alexander Stephens of Georgia, soon to be vice president of the Confederacy, Lincoln offered assurance that Republicans would not attack slavery in the states where it existed. But Lincoln continued, "You think slavery is right and ought to be expanded; while we think it is wrong and ought to be restricted. That I suppose is the rub."

As a matter of *interests* and *morality*, disunion and war came because of the great political struggle over slavery. Without slavery, there would have been no war. Many Americans still hold to a belief that the war was about states' rights, the theory and practice of the proper relationship of state to federal authority. But the significance of states' rights, then as now, is always in the cause in which it is employed. Americans still debate this question because its implications never seem to subside in the present.

13-2 America Goes to War, 1861–1862

▷ What were the respective strategies of the Union and Confederacy in fighting the war?

▷ How did the war in the West differ from that in Virginia during the first year of the war?

▷ What were the Confederate objectives in bringing the war to Maryland and Kentucky?

Few Americans understood what they were getting into when the war began. The onset of hostilities sparked patriotic sentiments, optimistic speeches, and joyous ceremonies in both North and South. Northern communities raised companies of volunteers eager to save the Union and sent them off with fanfare. In the South, confident recruits boasted of whipping the Yankees and returning home before Christmas. Southern women sewed dashing uniforms for men who would soon be lucky to wear drab gray or butternut homespun. Americans went to war in 1861 with decidedly romantic notions of what they would experience.

13-2a First Battle of Bull Run

Through the spring of 1861, both sides scrambled to organize and train their undisciplined armies. On July 21, 1861, the first battle took place outside Manassas Junction, Virginia, near a stream called **Bull Run**. General Irvin McDowell and thirty thousand Union troops attacked General P. G. T. Beauregard's 22,000 southerners (see Map 13.3). As raw recruits struggled amid the confusion of their first battle, federal forces began to gain ground. Then they ran into a line of Virginia troops under General Thomas Jackson. "There is Jackson standing like a stone wall," shouted one Confederate. "Stonewall" Jackson's line held, and the arrival of nine thousand Confederate reinforcements by train won the day for the South. Union troops fled back to Washington, observed by shocked northern congressmen and spectators who had watched the battle; a few sightseers were actually captured for their folly.

The unexpected rout at Bull Run gave northerners their first hint of the nature of the war to come. Although the United States enjoyed an enormous advantage in resources, victory would not be easy. Pro-Union feeling was growing in western Virginia, and loyalties were divided in the four border slave states—Missouri, Kentucky, Maryland,

and Delaware. But the rest of the Upper South—the states of North Carolina, Virginia, Tennessee, and Arkansas—joined the Confederacy in the wake of the attack on Fort Sumter. Moved by an outpouring of regional loyalty, half a million southerners volunteered to fight—so many that the Confederate government could hardly arm them all. The United States therefore undertook a massive mobilization of troops around Washington, D.C.

Lincoln gave command of the army to General **George B. McClellan**, an officer who proved better at organization and training than at fighting. McClellan put his growing army into camp and devoted the fall and winter of 1861 to readying a formidable force of nearly two hundred thousand men whose mission would be to take Richmond, established as the Confederate capital by July 1861. "The vast preparation of the enemy," wrote one southern soldier, produced a "feeling of despondency" in the South for the first time. But southern morale remained high early in the war.

13-2b Grand Strategy

While McClellan prepared, the Union began to implement other parts of its overall strategy, which called for a blockade of southern ports and eventual capture of the Mississippi River. Like a constricting snake, this **"Anaconda plan"** would strangle the Confederacy (see Map 13.2). At first, the Union navy had too few ships to patrol 3,550 miles of coastline and block the Confederacy's avenues of supply. Gradually, however, the navy increased the blockade's effectiveness, though it never stopped southern commerce completely.

The Confederate strategy was essentially defensive. A defensive posture was not only consistent with the South's claim of independence, but also reasonable in light of the North's advantage in resources (see Figure 13.1). But Jefferson Davis called the southern strategy an "offensive defensive," taking advantage of opportunities to attack and using its interior lines of transportation to concentrate troops at crucial points. In its war aims, the Confederacy did not need to conquer the North; the Union effort, however, as time would tell, required conquest of the South.

Strategic thinking on both sides slighted the importance of the West, that vast expanse of territory between Virginia and the Mississippi River and beyond. Guerrilla warfare broke out in 1861 in the politically divided state of Missouri, and key locations along the Mississippi and other major western rivers would prove crucial prizes in the North's eventual victory. Beyond the Mississippi River, the Confederacy hoped to gain an advantage by negotiating treaties with the Creeks, Choctaws,

Bull Run The location of the first major land battle in the Civil War.

George B. McClellan Union general very popular with troops who proved better at organization and training than at fighting.

"Anaconda plan" Called for the Union to blockade southern ports, capture the Mississippi River, and, like a snake, strangle the Confederacy.

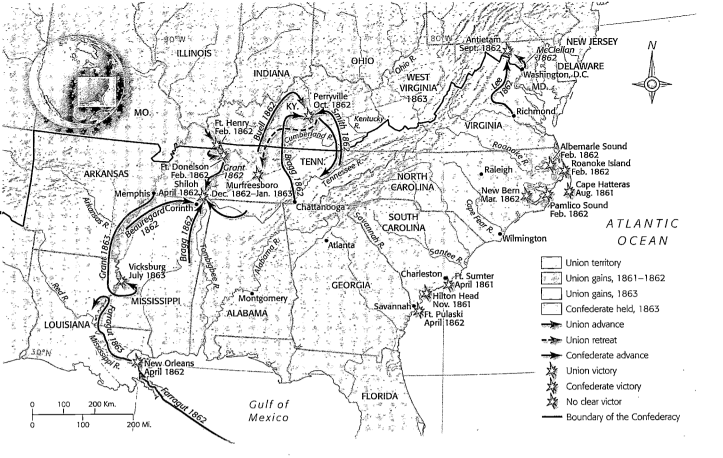

Map 13.2 The War in the West

An overview of the Union's successful campaigns in the West and its seizure of the key points on the Mississippi River, as well as along the Atlantic coast in 1862 and 1863. These actions were decisive in paving the way for ultimate northern victory.

Chickasaws, Cherokees, Seminoles, and smaller groups of Native peoples on the Plains. At the same time, the Republican U.S. Congress carved the West into territories in anticipation of state making. For most Native Americans west of the Mississippi, the Civil War marked the beginning of nearly three decades of offensive warfare against them, an enveloping strategy of conquest, relocation, and slaughter. Meanwhile, Native Americans would fight on both sides in the Civil War, and in some cases (especially the Cherokee) they would have their own deep struggles over emancipation of their own slaves.

13-2c Union Naval Campaign

The last half of 1861 brought no major land battles, but the North made gains by sea. Late in the summer, Union naval forces captured Cape Hatteras and then Hilton Head, one of the Sea Islands off Port Royal, South Carolina. A few months later, similar operations secured vital coastal points in North Carolina as well as Fort Pulaski, which defended Savannah. Federal naval operations established significant beachheads along the Confederate coastline (see Map 13.2).

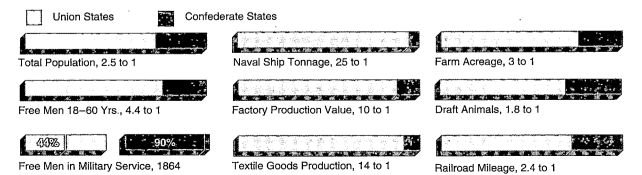

Figure 13.1 Comparative Resources, Union and Confederate States, 1861

The North had vastly superior resources. Although the North's advantages in manpower and industrial capacity proved very important, the South still had to be conquered, its society and its will crushed. Source: The Times Atlas of World History

The coastal victories off South Carolina foreshadowed a revolution in slave society. At the federal gunboats' approach, planters abandoned their land and fled. For a while, Confederate cavalry tried to round up slaves and move them to the interior as well. But thousands of slaves greeted what they hoped to be freedom with rejoicing and broke the hated cotton gins. Some entered their masters' homes and took clothing and furniture, which they conspicuously displayed. A growing stream of fugitive slaves poured into Union lines. Unwilling at first to wage a war against slavery, the federal government did not acknowledge the slaves' freedom—though it began to use their labor in the Union cause. This swelling tide of emancipated slaves, defined by many Union officers as "contraband" of war (confiscated enemy property), forced first a bitter debate within the Union army and government over how to treat the freedmen, and then a forthright attempt to harness their labor and military power.

The coastal incursions worried southerners, but the spring of 1862 brought even stronger evidence of the war's gravity. In March, two ironclad ships—the USS *Monitor* (a Union warship) and the CSS *Virginia* (a Confederate warship built on the hull of the Union steam frigate USS *Merrimack*, which had been burned and abandoned by Union forces when they evacuated Norfolk)—fought each other for the first time off the coast of Virginia. Their battle, though indecisive, ushered in a new era in naval design. In April, Union ships commanded by Admiral David Farragut smashed through log booms blocking the Mississippi River and fought their way upstream to capture New Orleans. The city at the mouth of the Mississippi, the South's greatest seaport and slave-trading center, was now in federal hands.

13-2d War in the Far West

Farther west, three full Confederate regiments were organized, mostly of Cherokees, from Indian Territory, but a Union victory at Elkhorn Tavern, Arkansas, shattered southern control of the region. Thereafter, Confederate operations in Indian Territory amounted to little more than guerrilla raids.

In the westernmost campaign of the war, from February to May 1862, some three thousand Confederate and four thousand Union forces fought for control of New Mexico Territory. The military significance of the New Mexico campaign was limited, but the Confederate invasion had grander aims: access to the trade riches of the Santa Fe Trail and possession of gold mines in Colorado and California. If the campaign had succeeded, the Confederacy would have been much stronger with a western empire. But Colorado and New Mexico Unionists fought for their region, and in a series of battles at Glorieta Pass, twenty miles east of Santa Fe, on March 26 through 28, they blocked the Confederate invasion. By May 1, Confederate forces straggled down the Rio Grande River back into Texas, ending their effort to take New Mexico.

△ Monument to fallen soldiers, near Water Oaks Pond, Shiloh National Battlefield Park, near Pittsburg Landing, TN.

13-2e Grant's Tennessee Campaign and the Battle of Shiloh

Meanwhile, in February 1862, land and river forces in northern Tennessee won significant victories for the Union. A Union commander named **Ulysses S. Grant** saw the strategic importance of Fort Henry and Fort Donelson, the Confederate outposts guarding the Tennessee and Cumberland rivers. If federal troops could capture these forts, Grant realized, they would open two prime routes into the heartland of the Confederacy. In just ten days, he seized the forts—completely cutting off the Confederates and demanding "unconditional surrender" of Fort Donelson. A path into Tennessee, Alabama, and Mississippi now lay open before the Union army. Grant's achievement of such a surrender from his former West Point classmate, Confederate commander Simon Bolivar Buckner, inspired northern public opinion.

Grant moved on into southern Tennessee and the first of the war's shockingly bloody encounters, the **Battle of Shiloh** (see Map 13.2). On April 6, Confederate general Albert Sidney Johnston caught federal troops with their backs to the water awaiting reinforcements along the Tennessee River. The Confederates attacked early in the morning and inflicted heavy damage all day. Close to victory, General Johnston was shot from his horse and killed. Southern forces almost achieved a breakthrough, but Union reinforcements arrived that night. The next day, the tide of battle turned and, after ten hours of terrible combat, Grant's men forced the Confederates to withdraw.

Neither side won a decisive victory at Shiloh, yet the losses were staggering, and the Confederates were forced to retreat into northern Mississippi.

"Ulysses S. Grant Union general who, in 1864, became Commanding General of the United States Army.

Battle of Shiloh The bloodiest battle in American history to that date (April 6–7, 1862)

Northern troops lost thirteen thousand men (killed, wounded, or captured) out of sixty-three thousand; southerners sacrificed eleven thousand out of forty thousand. Total casualties in this single battle exceeded those in all three of America's previous wars combined. Now both sides were beginning to sense the true nature of the war. "I saw an open field," Grant recalled, "over which Confederates had made repeated charges . . . so covered with dead that it would have been possible to walk across the clearing, in any direction, stepping on dead bodies, without a foot touching the ground." Shiloh utterly changed Grant's thinking about the war. He had hoped that southerners would soon be "heartily tired" of the conflict. After Shiloh, "I gave up all idea of saving the Union except by complete conquest." Memories of the Shiloh battlefield, and many others to come, would haunt the soldiers who survived for the rest of their lives. Herman Melville's "Shiloh, A Requiem" captures the pathos of that spring day when armies learned the truth about war:

> Skimming lightly, wheeling still,
> The swallows fly low
> Over the field in clouded days,
> The forest-field of Shiloh—
> Over the field where April rain
> Solaced the parched ones stretched in pain
> Through the pause of night
> That followed the Sunday fight
> Around the church of Shiloh—
> The church so lone, the log-built one,
> That echoed to many a parting groan
> And natural prayer
> Of dying foemen mingled there—
> Foemen at morn, but friends at eve—
> Fame or country least their care:
> (What like a bullet can undeceive!)
> But now they lie low,
> While over them the swallows skim,
> And all is hushed at Shiloh.

13-2f McClellan and the Peninsula Campaign

On the Virginia front, President Lincoln had a different problem. General McClellan was slow to move. Only thirty-six, McClellan had already achieved notable success as an army officer and railroad president. Habitually overestimating the size of enemy forces, he called repeatedly for reinforcements and ignored Lincoln's directions to advance. McClellan advocated war of limited aims that would lead to a quick reunion. He intended neither disruption of slavery nor war on noncombatants. Finally, the cautious, even insubordinate, McClellan chose to move by a water route, sailing his troops down the Chesapeake, landing them on the peninsula between the York and James rivers, and advancing on Richmond from the east (see Map 13.3).

Robert E. Lee Confederate general who, in 1862, commanded the Army of Northern Virginia. In 1865 he became general-in-chief of the Confederate army.

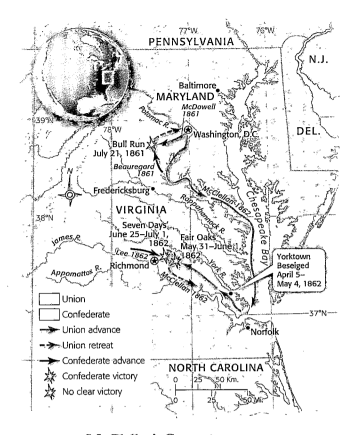

Map 13.3 McClellan's Campaign

This map shows the water route chosen by McClellan to threaten Richmond during the Peninsula Campaign.

After a bloody but indecisive battle at Fair Oaks on May 31 through June 1, the federal armies moved to within seven miles of the Confederate capital. They could see the spires on Richmond churches. The Confederate commanding general, Joseph E. Johnston, was badly wounded at Fair Oaks, and President Jefferson Davis placed his chief military adviser, **Robert E. Lee**, in command. The fifty-five-year-old Lee was an aristocratic Virginian, a lifelong military officer, and a decorated veteran of the War with Mexico. Although he initially opposed secession, Lee loyally gave his allegiance to his state and became a staunch Confederate nationalist. He soon foiled McClellan's legions.

First, Lee sent Stonewall Jackson's corps of seventeen thousand northwest into the Shenandoah Valley behind Union forces, where they threatened Washington, D.C., and with rapid-strike mobility drew some federal troops away from Richmond to protect their own capital. Further, in mid-June, in an extraordinary four-day ride around the entire Union army, Confederate cavalry under J. E. B. Stuart, a self-styled Virginia cavalier with red cape and plumed hat, confirmed the exposed position of a major portion of McClellan's army north of the rain-swollen Chickahominy River. Then, in a series of engagements known as the Seven Days Battles, from June 26 through July 1, Lee struck at McClellan's army. Lee never managed to close his pincers around the retreating Union forces, but the daring move of taking the majority of his army northeast and attacking the Union right flank, while leaving only a small force to defend Richmond, forced McClellan (who always believed he was outnumbered) to retreat toward the James River.

During the sustained fighting of the Seven Days, the Union forces suffered 20,614 casualties and the Confederates, 15,849. After repeated rebel assaults against entrenched positions on high ground at Malvern Hill had been beaten back, an officer concluded, "It was not war, it was murder." By August 3, McClellan withdrew his army back to the Potomac and the environs of Washington. Richmond remained safe for almost two more years.

13-2g Confederate Offensive in Maryland and Kentucky

Buoyed by these results, Jefferson Davis conceived an ambitious plan to turn the tide of the war and gain recognition of the Confederacy by European nations. He ordered a general offensive, sending Lee north into Maryland and Generals Kirby Smith and Braxton Bragg into Kentucky. Calling on residents of Maryland and Kentucky, still slave states, to make a separate peace with his government, Davis also invited northwestern states like Indiana, which sent much of their trade down the Mississippi to New Orleans, to leave the Union. This was a coordinated effort to take the war to the North and to try to force both a military and a political turning point.

The plan was promising (it almost worked), but in the end the offensive failed. Lee's forces achieved a striking success at the Second battle of Bull Run, August 29 through 30, just southwest of Washington, D.C. On the same killing fields along Bull Run Creek where federal troops had been defeated the previous summer, an entire Union army was sent in retreat back into the federal capital. Thousands of wounded occupied schools and churches, and two thousand suffered on cots in the rotunda of the U.S. Capitol.

But in the bloodiest day of the entire war, September 17, 1862, McClellan turned Lee back from Sharpsburg, Maryland. In this **Battle of Antietam,** five thousand men died, and another eighteen thousand were wounded in the course of eight horrible hours. Lee was lucky to escape destruction, for McClellan had intercepted a lost battle order, wrapped around cigars for each Confederate corps commander and inadvertently dropped by a courier. But McClellan moved slowly, failed to use

Battle of Antietam First major battle on northern soil.

◁ Photograph of "Sunken Road," Antietam battlefield, taken shortly after the battle, September, 1862, often called "the Harvest of Battle."

Library of Congress Prints and Photographs Division Washington, D.C.[LC-DIG-ppmsca-07751]

his larger forces in simultaneous attacks, and allowed Lee's stricken army to retreat to safety across the Potomac. In the wake of Antietam, Lincoln, after long frustration, removed McClellan from command.

In Kentucky, Generals Smith and Bragg secured Lexington and Frankfort, but their effort to force the Yankees back to the Ohio River was stopped at the Battle of Perryville on October 8. Bragg's army retreated back into Tennessee, where—from December 31, 1862, to January 2, 1863—they fought an indecisive but much bloodier battle at Murfreesboro. Casualties exceeded even those of Shiloh, and many lives were sacrificed on a bitter winter landscape.

Confederate leaders marshaled all their strength for a breakthrough but failed. Outnumbered and disadvantaged in resources, the South could not continue the offensive. Profoundly disappointed, Davis admitted to a committee of Confederate representatives that southerners were entering "the darkest and most dangerous period we have yet had."

But 1862 also brought painful lessons to the North. Confederate general J. E. B. Stuart executed a daring cavalry raid into Pennsylvania in October. Then, on December 13, Union general Ambrose Burnside, now in command of the Army of the Potomac, unwisely ordered his soldiers to attack Lee's army, which held fortified positions on high ground at Fredericksburg, Virginia. Lee's men performed so efficiently in killing northerners that Lee was moved to say, "It is well that war is so terrible. We should grow too fond of it." Burnside's repeated assaults up Marye's Heights shocked even the opponents. "The Federals had fallen like the steady dripping of rain from the eaves of a house," remarked Confederate general James Longstreet. And a Union officer observed of the carnage of thirteen hundred dead and ninety-six hundred wounded Union soldiers, "The whole plain was covered with men, prostrate and dropping. . . . I had never before seen fighting like that . . . the next brigade coming up in succession would do its duty, and melt like snow coming down on warm ground." The scale of carnage now challenged people on both sides to search deeply for the meaning of such a war. At the front, some soldiers lost their sense of humanity in the face of the challenge. In the wake of Antietam's death toll, one Union burial crew, exhausted and perhaps inebriated, threw fifty-eight Confederate bodies down the well of a local farmer.

13-3 War Transforms the South

▶ How did the Confederacy manage to create a functioning federal government while fighting an all-out war?

▶ How did the war affect Southern civilian populations?

▶ How did wartime needs reveal inequities in the Confederacy?

The war caused tremendous disruptions in civilian life and altered southern society beyond all expectations. One of the first traditions to fall was the southern preference for local and limited government. States' rights had been a formative ideology for the Confederacy, but state governments were weak operations. To withstand the massive power of the North, the South needed to centralize; like the colonial revolutionaries, southerners faced a choice of joining together or dying separately.

13-3a The Confederacy and Centralization

Jefferson Davis moved promptly to bring all arms, supplies, and troops under centralized control. But by early 1862, the scope and duration of the conflict required something more. Tens of thousands of Confederate soldiers had volunteered for just one year's service, planning to return home in the spring to plant their crops. More recruits were needed constantly to keep southern armies in the field. However, as one official admitted, "the spirit of volunteering had died out." Finally, faced with a critical shortage of troops, in April 1862 the Confederate government enacted the first national conscription (draft) law in American history. Thus, the war forced unprecedented change on states that had seceded out of fear of change.

Davis adopted a firm leadership role toward the Confederate Congress, which raised taxes and later passed a tax-in-kind—paid in farm products. Nearly forty-five hundred agents dispersed to collect the tax. Where opposition arose, the government suspended the writ of habeas corpus (which prevented individuals from being held without trial) and imposed martial law. Despite Davis's unyielding stance, this tax system proved inadequate as well as unpopular for the South's war effort.

Davis further exhorted state governments to require farmers to switch from cash crops to food crops. But the army remained short of food and labor. The War Department resorted to impressing slaves to work on fortifications, and after 1861 the government relied heavily on confiscation of food to feed the troops. Officers swooped down on farms in the line of march and carted away grain, meat, wagons, and draft animals. Such raids caused increased hardship and resentment for women managing farms in the absence of husbands and sons.

Soon, the Confederate administration in Richmond gained virtually complete control over the southern economy. The Confederate Congress also gave the central government a great deal of control of the railroads. A large bureaucracy sprang up to administer these operations: over seventy thousand civilians staffed the Confederate administration. By war's end, the southern bureaucracy, a "big government" by any measure, was larger in proportion to population than its northern counterpart.

13-3b Confederate Nationalism

Historians have long argued over whether the Confederacy itself was a "rebellion," a "revolution," or the creation of a genuine "nation." Whatever label we apply, Confederates created a culture and an ideology of nationalism. Southerners immediately tried to forge their own national symbols and identity. In flags, songs, language, seals, school readers, and other national characteristics, Confederates created their own story.

In its conservative crusade to preserve states' rights, the social order, and racial slavery, southerners believed the Confederacy was the true legacy of the American Revolution—a bulwark against centralized power. In this view, southern "liberty" was no less a holy cause than that of the patriots of 1776. To southerners, theirs was a continuing revolution against the excesses of Yankee democracy, and George Washington (a Virginian) on horseback formed the center of the official seal of the Confederacy.

Also central to Confederate nationalism was a refurbished defense of slavery as a benign, protective institution. In wartime schoolbooks, children were instructed in the divinely inspired, paternalistic character of slavery. And the idea of the "faithful slave" was key to southerners' nationalist cause. A poem popular among whites captured an old slave's rejection of the Emancipation Proclamation:

> Now, Massa, dis is berry fine, dese words
> You've spoke to me,
> No doubt you mean it kindly, but ole Dinah
> Won't be free . . .
> Ole Massa's berry good to me—and though I am
> His slave,
> He treats me like I'se kin to him—and I would
> Rather have
> A home in Massa's cabin, and eat his black
> Bread too,
> Dan leave ole Massa's children and go and
> Lib wid you.

In the face of defeat and devastation, this and other forms of Confederate nationalism collapsed in the final year of the war. But much of the spirit and substance of Confederate nationalism would revive in the postwar period in a new racial ideology of the Lost Cause.

13-3c Southern Cities and Industry

Clerks and subordinate officials crowded the towns and cities where Confederate departments set up their offices. The sudden urban migration that resulted overwhelmed the housing supply and stimulated new construction. The pressure was especially great in Richmond, whose population increased 250 percent. Mobile's population jumped from 29,000 to 41,000; Atlanta, too, began to grow; and 10,000 people poured into war-related industries in little Selma, Alabama.

As the Union blockade disrupted imports of manufactured products, the traditionally agricultural South forged new industries. Many planters shared Davis's hope that industrialization would bring "deliverance, full and unrestricted, from all commercial dependence" on the North or the world. Indeed, beginning almost from scratch, the Confederacy achieved tremendous feats of industrial development. Chief of Ordnance Josiah Gorgas increased the capacity of Richmond's Tredegar Iron Works and other factories to the point that by 1865, his Ordnance Bureau was supplying all Confederate small arms and ammunition. Meanwhile, the government constructed new railroad lines and ironworks, and much of the labor consisted of slaves relocated from farms and plantations.

13-3d Changing Roles of Women

White women, restricted to narrow roles in antebellum society, gained substantial new responsibilities in wartime. The wives and mothers of soldiers now headed households and performed men's work, including raising crops and tending animals. Women in nonslaveholding families cultivated fields themselves, while wealthier women suddenly had to perform as overseers and manage field work. In the cities, white women—who had been largely excluded from the labor force—found a limited number of respectable paying jobs, often in the Confederate bureaucracy, where some found clerks' jobs as "government girls." And female schoolteachers appeared in the South for the first time.

Women experienced both confidence and agony from their new responsibilities. Among them was Janie Smith, a young North Carolinian. Raised in a rural area by prosperous parents, she now faced grim realities as the war reached her farm and troops turned her home into a hospital. "It makes me shudder when I think of the awful sights I witnessed that morning," she wrote to a friend. "Ambulance after ambulance drove up with our wounded. . . . Under every shed and tree, the tables were carried for amputating the limbs. . . . The blood lay in puddles in the grove; the groans of the dying . . . were horrible." But Janie Smith learned to cope with crisis. She ended her account with the proud words, "I can dress amputated limbs now and do most anything in the way of nursing wounded soldiers."

Patriotic sacrifice appealed to some women, but others resented their new burdens. A Texas woman who had struggled to discipline slaves pronounced herself "sick of trying to do a man's business." Others grew angry over shortages, scornful of the war itself, and demanded that their men return to help provide for their families.

13-3e Human Suffering, Hoarding, and Inflation

For millions of ordinary southerners, the war brought privation and suffering. Mass poverty descended for the first time on a large minority of the white population. Many yeoman families had lost their breadwinners to the army. As a South Carolina newspaper put it, "The duties of war have called away from home the sole supports of many, many families. . . . Help must be given, or the poor will suffer." Women on their own sought help from relatives, neighbors, friends, anyone. Sometimes they pleaded their case to the Confederate government. "In the name of humanity," begged one woman, "discharge my husband he is not able to do your government much good and he might do his children some

△ Five Texans in the Confederate cavalry sitting for a formal photograph. Four have the "lone star" on their hats. Like thousands of others, these men posed to send their image to the folks back home, but also perhaps as an act of comradeship at the war front.

good . . . my poor children have no home nor no Father." To the extent that the South eventually lost the will to fight in the face of defeat, women played a role in demanding an end to the war.

The South was in many places so sparsely populated that the conscription of one skilled craftsman could wreak hardship on the people of an entire county. Often, they begged in unison for the exemption or discharge of the local miller, or the neighborhood tanner or wheelwright. Physicians were also in short supply. Most serious, however, was the loss of a blacksmith. As a petition from Alabama explained, "Our Section of County [is] left entirely Destitute of any man that is able to keep in order any kind of Farming Tules."

The blockade of Confederate shipping created shortages of important supplies—salt, sugar, coffee, nails—and speculation and hoarding made the shortages worse. Greedy businessmen cornered the supply of some commodities; prosperous citizens stocked up on food. The *Richmond Enquirer* criticized a planter who purchased so many wagonloads of supplies that his "lawn and paths looked like a wharf covered with a ship's loads."

Inflation raged out of control, fueled by the Confederate government's heavy borrowing and inadequate taxes, until prices had increased almost 7,000 percent. Inflation particularly imperiled urban dwellers without their own sources of food. As early as 1862, newspapers reported that "want and starvation are staring thousands in the face," and troubled officials predicted that "women and children are bound to come to suffering if not starvation." A rudimentary relief program organized by the Confederacy failed to meet the need.

13-3f Inequities of the Confederate Draft

As their fortunes declined, people of once-modest means looked around and found abundant evidence that all classes were not sacrificing equally. The Confederate government enacted policies that decidedly favored the upper class. Until the last year of the war, for example, prosperous southerners could avoid military service by hiring substitutes. Prices for substitutes skyrocketed until it cost a man $5,000 or $6,000 to send someone to the front in his place. Well over fifty thousand upper-class southerners purchased such substitutes. Mary Boykin Chesnut knew of one young aristocrat who "spent a fortune in substitutes.... He is at the end of his row now, for all able-bodied men are ordered to the front. I hear he is going as some general's courier."

Anger at such discrimination exploded in October 1862, when the Confederate Congress exempted from military duty anyone who was supervising at least twenty slaves. "Never did a law meet with more universal odium," observed one representative. "Its influence upon the poor is most calamitous." Protests poured in from every corner of the Confederacy, and North Carolina's legislators formally condemned the law. Its defenders argued, however, that the exemption preserved order and aided food production.

This "twenty Negro" law is indicative of the racial fears many Confederates felt as the war threatened to overturn southern society. But it also fueled desertion and stimulated new levels of overt Unionism in nonslaveholding regions of the South. In Jones County, Mississippi, an area of piney woods and few slaves or plantations, Newt Knight, a Confederate soldier, led a band of renegades who took over the county, declared their allegiance to the Union, and called their district the "Free State of Jones." They held out for the remainder of the war as an interracial enclave of independent Union sympathizers.

The bitterness of letters to Confederate officials suggests the depth of the dissension and class anger. "If I and my little children suffer [and] die while there Father is in service," threatened one woman, "I invoke God Almighty that our blood rest upon the South." War magnified existing social tensions in the Confederacy, and created a few new ones.

13-4 Wartime Northern Economy and Society

▷ What was the nature of the partnership between the Union government and businesses?

▷ How did the war affect labor relations and expectations?

▷ What role did women play in the Union war effort, on homefronts and warfronts?

With the onset of war, a tidal wave of change rolled over the North as well. Factories and citizens' associations geared up to support the war, and the federal government and its executive branch gained new powers. The energies of an industrializing society were harnessed to serve the cause of the Union. Idealism and greed flourished together, and the northern economy proved its awesome productivity.

13-4a Northern Business, Industry, and Agriculture

At first, the war was a shock to business. Northern firms lost their southern markets, and many companies had to change their products and find new customers. Southern debts became uncollectible, jeopardizing not only northern

merchants but also many western banks. Farm families struggled with a shortage of labor caused by army enlistments. A few enterprises never pulled out of the tailspin caused by the war. Cotton mills lacked cotton; construction declined; and shoe manufacturers sold few of the cheap shoes that planters had bought for their slaves. Those manufacturers that provided all manner of slave clothing and farm implements for the South had to diversify into other products.

Certain entrepreneurs, such as wool producers, benefited from shortages of competing products, and soaring demand for war-related goods swept some businesses to new success. To feed the hungry war machine, the federal government pumped unprecedented sums into the economy. The Treasury issued $3.2 billion in bonds and paper money called "greenbacks," and the War Department spent over $360 million in revenues from new taxes, including the nation's first income tax.

War-related spending revived business in many northern states. In 1863, a merchants' magazine examined the effects of the war in Massachusetts: "Seldom, if ever, has the business of Massachusetts been more active or profitable than during the past year.... In every department of labor the government has been, directly or indirectly, the chief employer and paymaster." Government contracts saved Massachusetts shoe manufacturers, as well as many firms in other states, from ruin.

The northern economy also grew because of a complementary relationship between agriculture and industry. Mechanization of agriculture had begun before the war. Wartime recruitment and conscription, however, gave western farmers an added incentive to purchase laborsaving machinery. The boom in the sale of agricultural tools was tremendous. Cyrus and William McCormick built an industrial empire in Chicago from the sale of their reapers. Between 1862 and 1864, the manufacture of mowers and reapers doubled to 70,000 yearly; by war's end, 375,000 reapers were in use, triple the number in 1861. Thus, northern farm families whose breadwinners went to war did not suffer as much as did their counterparts in the South. "We have seen," one magazine observed, "a stout matron whose sons are in the army, cutting hay with her team ... and she cut seven acres with ease in a day, riding leisurely upon her cutter." Northern farms, generally not ravaged by foraging armies and devastation, thrived during wartime.

13-4b The Quartermaster and Military-Government Mobilization

This government-business marriage emerged from a greatly empowered Quartermaster Department, which as a bureaucracy grew to be the single largest employer in the United States, issuing thousands of manufacturing contracts to hundreds of firms. The 100,000 civilian employees of the Quartermaster Department labored throughout a network of procurement centers, especially in the cities of Washington, D.C., Philadelphia, New York, Cincinnati, and St. Louis.

A portion of Secretary of War Edwin M. Stanton's list of the weapons supplies alone needed by the Ordnance Department indicates the scope of the demand for government

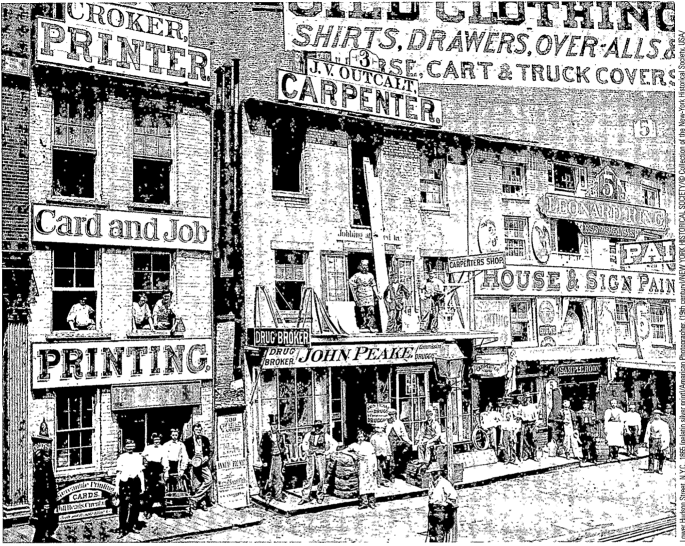

△ Despite initial problems, the task of supplying a vast war machine kept the northern economy humming. This photograph shows businesses on the west side of Hudson Street in New York City in 1865.

and business cooperation: "7,892 cannon, 11,787 artillery carriages, 4,022,130 small-arms, . . . 1,022,176,474 cartridges for small-arms, 1,220,555,435 percussion caps, . . . 26,440,054 pounds of gunpowder, . . . and 90,416,295 pounds of lead." In an unprecedented military mobilization, the government also purchased huge quantities of uniforms, boots, food, camp equipment, saddles, horses, ships, and other necessities. By 1865, the government had purchased some 640,000 horses and 300,000 mules at a cost well over $100 million.

Two-thirds of all U.S. war spending went to supply the forces in the field and, to command that process, President Lincoln appointed the talented West Point–trained engineer Montgomery Meigs. Meigs, whose experience included overseeing the building of the Capitol dome, insisted on issuing government contracts only with competitive bidding. He spent $1.8 billion of the public's money to wage the war, a figure larger than all previous U.S. government

expenditures since independence combined. His efforts, argued one historian, made the Union army "the best fed, most lavishly supplied army that had ever existed." Many historians consider Meigs the "unsung hero of Northern victory," a claim hard to deny, although he benefited from his corps of Quartermaster officers, who won the war one contract at a time. The success of such military mobilization left an indelible mark on American political-economic history and provided perhaps the oldest root of the modern American military-industrial state.

Nothing illustrated the wartime partnership between business and government better than the work of Jay Cooke, a wealthy New York financier. Cooke threw himself into the marketing of government bonds to finance the war effort. With imagination and energy, he convinced both large investors and ordinary citizens to invest enormous sums, in the process earning hefty commissions for himself. But the financier's profit served the Union cause, as the interests of capitalism and government successfully merged in American history's first era of "big government."

13-4c Northern Workers' Militancy

Northern industrial and urban workers did not fare as well as many of the companies for which they labored. After the initial slump, jobs became plentiful, but inflation ate up much of a worker's paycheck. The price of coffee had tripled; rice and sugar had doubled; and clothing, fuel, and rent had all climbed. Between 1860 and 1864, consumer prices rose at least 76 percent, while daily wages rose only 42 percent. Workers' families consequently suffered a substantial decline in their standard of living.

As their real wages shrank, industrial workers lost job security. To increase production, some employers replaced workers with laborsaving machines. Other employers urged the government to promote immigration to secure cheap labor. Workers responded by forming unions and sometimes by striking. Skilled craftsmen organized to combat the loss of their jobs and status to machines; women and unskilled workers, who were excluded by the craftsmen, formed their own unions. Indeed, thirteen occupational groups—including tailors, coal miners, and railway engineers—formed national unions during the Civil War, and the number of strikes climbed steadily.

Employers reacted with hostility to this new labor independence. Manufacturers viewed labor activism as a threat to their freedom of action and accordingly formed statewide or craft-based associations to cooperate and pool information. These employers shared blacklists of union members and required new workers to sign "yellow dog" contracts (promises not to join a union). To put down strikes, they hired strikebreakers, and sometimes used federal troops to break the unions' will.

Labor militancy, however, prevented employers neither from making profits nor from profiteering on government contracts. Unscrupulous businessmen took advantage of the suddenly immense demand for army supplies by selling clothing and blankets made of "shoddy"—wool fibers reclaimed from rags or worn cloth. Shoddy goods often came apart in the rain; most of the shoes purchased in the early months of the war were worthless. Contractors sold inferior guns for double the usual price and passed off tainted meat as good. Corruption was so widespread that it led to a yearlong investigation by the House of Representatives.

13-4d Economic Nationalism and Government-Business Partnership

Legitimate enterprises also made healthy profits. The output of woolen mills increased so dramatically that dividends in the industry nearly tripled. Some cotton mills made record profits on what they sold, even though they reduced their output. Brokerage houses worked until midnight and earned unheard-of commissions. Railroads carried immense quantities of freight and passengers, increasing their business to the point that railroad stocks skyrocketed in value.

Railroads were also a leading beneficiary of government largesse. With southern representatives absent from Congress, the northern route of the transcontinental railroad quickly prevailed. In 1862 and 1864, Congress chartered two corporations—the Union Pacific Railroad and the Central Pacific Railroad—and assisted them financially in connecting Omaha, Nebraska, with Sacramento, California. For each mile of track laid, the railroads received a loan of from $16,000 to $48,000 in government bonds plus 20 square miles of land along a free 400-foot-wide right of way. Overall, the two corporations gained approximately 20 million acres of land and nearly $60 million in loans. Railroad owners never decried government involvement in the economy.

Other businessmen benefited handsomely from the **Morrill Land Grant** Act (1862). To promote public education in agriculture, engineering, and military science, Congress granted each state thirty thousand acres of federal land for each of its congressional districts. The law eventually fostered sixty-nine colleges and universities as it also enriched a few prominent speculators. At the same time, the Homestead Act of 1862 offered cheap, and sometimes free, land to people who would settle the West and improve their property.

Before the war, adequate national banking, taxation, and currency did not exist. Banks operating under state charters issued no fewer than seven thousand different kinds of notes. During the war, Congress and the Treasury Department established a national banking system empowered to issue national bank notes and, by 1865, most state banks were forced by a prohibitive tax to join the national system. This process created sounder currency but also inflexibility in the money supply and an eastern-oriented financial structure that, later in the century, pushed farmers in need of credit and cash to revolt.

Republican economic policies expanded the scope of government and bonded people to the nation as never before. Yet ostentation coexisted with idealism. In the excitement of wartime moneymaking, an eagerness to display one's wealth flourished in the largest cities. *Harper's Monthly* reported that "the suddenly enriched contractors, speculators, and stock-jobbers ... are spending money with a profusion never before witnessed in our country. ... The men button their waistcoats with diamonds ... and the women powder their hair with gold and silver dust." The *New York Herald* summarized that city's atmosphere: "This war has entirely changed the American character. ... The individual who makes the most money—no matter how—and spends the most—no matter for what—is considered the greatest man."

13-4e The Union Cause

In thousands of self-governing towns and communities, northern citizens felt a personal connection to representative government. Secession threatened to destroy their system, and northerners rallied to its defense. In the first two years of the war, northern morale remained

Morrill Land Grant Act Law in which Congress granted land to states to establish colleges focusing on agriculture, engineering, and military science.

△ Union women's volunteer defense unit, ca. 1864. The soldiers' caps and muskets make this a rare image of women's lives on the home front during the Civil War.

remarkably high for a cause that today may seem abstract—the Union—but at the time meant the preservation of a social and political order that people cherished.

Secular and church leaders supported the cause, and even ministers who preferred to separate politics and pulpit denounced "the iniquity of causeless rebellion." Abolitionists campaigned to turn the war into a crusade against slavery. Free black communities and churches, both black and white, responded to the needs of slaves who flocked to the Union lines, sending clothing, ministers, and teachers to aid the freedpeople. Indeed, northern blacks gave wholehearted support to the war, volunteering by the thousands at first, despite the initial rejection they received from the Lincoln administration.

Thus, northern society embraced strangely contradictory tendencies. Materialism and greed flourished alongside idealism, religious conviction, and self-sacrifice. In decades to come, Americans would commemorate and build monuments to soldiers' sacrifice and idealism, not to opportunism and sometimes not even to the causes for which they fought, which provided a way of forgetting the deeper

U.S. Sanitary Commission Civilian organization in the North, staffed by large numbers of women, that was a major source of medical and nutritional aid for soldiers.

Clara Barton Nurse who worked for the Sanitary Commission and later founded the Red Cross.

nature of the conflict. But almost no one on the Northern side ever forgot the preservation of the Union, even as the larger society struggled mightily to face the legacies of emancipation and the beginnings of black equality.

13-4f Northern Women on Home Front and Battlefront

Northern women, like their southern counterparts, took on new roles. Those who stayed home organized over ten thousand soldiers' aid societies, rolled bandages, and raised $3 million to aid injured troops. Women were instrumental in pressing for the first trained ambulance corps in the Union army, and they formed the backbone of the **U.S. Sanitary Commission,** a civilian agency officially recognized by the War Department in 1861. The Sanitary Commission provided crucial nutritional and medical aid to soldiers. Although most of its officers were men, the bulk of the volunteers who ran its seven thousand auxiliaries were women. Women organized elaborate "Sanitary Fairs" to raise money and awareness for soldiers' health and hygiene.

Approximately thirty-two hundred women also served as nurses in frontline hospitals. Yet women had to fight for a chance to serve at all; the professionalization of medicine since the Revolution had created a medical system dominated by men, and many male physicians did not want women's aid. Even **Clara Barton,** famous for her persistence in working

△ Nurse Anne Bell tending to wounded soldiers in a federal hospital, Nashville, Tennessee, ca. 1863. The distant gaze of the man on the left and the grateful gaze of the one on the right realistically represent the agonies of military hospitals.

in the worst hospitals at the front, was ousted from her post in 1863. But along with Barton, women such as the stern Dorothea Dix, well known for her efforts to reform asylums for the insane, and an Illinois widow, Mary Ann Bickerdyke, who served tirelessly in Sherman's army in the West, established a heroic tradition for Civil War nurses. They also advanced the professionalization of nursing, as several schools of nursing were established in northern cities during or after the war.

Women also wrote popular fiction about the war. In sentimental war poetry, short stories, and novels, and in printed war songs that reached thousands of readers, women produced a commercial literature in illustrated weeklies, monthly periodicals, and special "story papers." In many stories, female characters seek recognition for their loyalty and service to the Union, while others probe the suffering and death of loved ones at the front. One female writer, Louisa May Alcott, arrived at her job as a nurse in Washington, D.C., just after the horrific Union defeat at Fredericksburg, in December 1862. She later immortalized her experience in *Hospital Sketches* (1863), a popular book in which she described shattered men, "riddled with shot and shell," who had "borne suffering for which we have no name." Alcott provided northern readers a clear-eyed view of the hospitals in which so many of their loved ones agonized and perished.

At its heart, in what one historian has called a "feminized war literature," women writers explored the relationship between individual and national needs, between home and "the cause." And by 1863, many women found the liberation of slaves an inspiring subject, as did Julia Ward Howe in her immortal "Battle Hymn of the Republic":

> As He died to make men holy
> Let us die to make men free.

13-4g Walt Whitman's War

The poet **Walt Whitman** also left a record of his experiences as a volunteer nurse in Washington, D.C. As he dressed wounds and tried to comfort suffering and lonely men, Whitman found "the marrow of the tragedy concentrated in those Army Hospitals." But despite "indescribably horrid wounds," he also found inspiration in such suffering and a deepening faith in American democracy. Whitman celebrated the "incredible dauntlessness" and sacrifice of the common soldier who fought for the Union. As

Walt Whitman Well-known poet and author of *Leaves of Grass*; Whitman wrote about his experiences as a nurse and his renewed faith in democracy.

he had written in the preface to his great work *Leaves of Grass* (1855), "The genius of the United States is not best or most in its executives or legislatures, but always most in the common people." Whitman worked this idealization of the common man into his poetry, which also explored homoerotic themes and rejected the lofty meter and rhyme of European verse to strive for a "genuineness" that would appeal to the masses.

In "The Wound Dresser," Whitman meditated unforgettably on the deaths he had witnessed on both sides:

> On, on I go, (open doors of time! open hospital doors!)
> The crush'd head I dress, (poor crazed hand tear not the bandage away,)
> The neck of the cavalry-man with the bullet through and through I examine,
> Hard the breathing rattles, quite glazed already the eye, yet life struggles hard, (Come sweet death! be persuaded O beautiful death! In mercy come quickly.)

Whitman mused for millions in the war who suffered the death of a husband, brother, father, or friend. Indeed, the scale of death in this war shocked many Americans into believing that the conflict had to be for purposes larger than themselves.

13-5 The Advent of Emancipation

▷ What was the relationship between Abraham Lincoln's personal views of, and official acts on, slavery?

▷ What competing views and policies emerged within the Union government on the issue of slavery?

▷ How was the Emancipation Proclamation both a legal and a moral document?

▷ How did African Americans seek to enact their own emancipation and advancement in society?

Despite the sense of loyalty to cause that animated soldiers and civilians on both sides, the governments of the United States and the Confederacy lacked clarity about the purpose of the war. Throughout the first several months of the struggle, both Davis and Lincoln studiously avoided references to slavery. Davis realized that emphasis on the issue could increase class conflict in the South. To avoid identifying the Confederacy only with the interests of slaveholders, he articulated a broader, traditional ideology. Davis told southerners they were fighting for constitutional liberty: northerners had betrayed the founders' legacy, and southerners had seceded to preserve it. As long as Lincoln also avoided making slavery an issue, Davis's strategy seemed to work.

Lincoln had his own reasons for avoiding slavery. It was crucial at first not to antagonize the Union's border slave states, whose loyalty was tenuous. Also, for many months

Lincoln hoped that a pro-Union majority would assert itself in the South. It might be possible, he thought, to coax the South back into the Union and stop the fighting, short of what he later called "the result so fundamental and astounding"—emancipation. Raising the slavery issue would severely undermine both goals. Powerful political considerations also dictated Lincoln's reticence. The Republican Party was a young and unwieldy coalition. Some Republicans burned with moral outrage over slavery; others were frankly racist, dedicated to protecting free whites from the Slave Power and the competition of cheap slave labor. No Republican, or even northern, consensus on what to do about slavery existed early in the war.

13-5a Lincoln and Emancipation

The president's hesitancy ran counter to some of his personal feelings. Lincoln's compassion, humility, and moral anguish during the war were evident in his speeches and writings. But as a politician, Lincoln distinguished between his own moral convictions and his official acts. His political positions were studied and complex, calculated for maximum advantage.

Many black people attacked Lincoln furiously during the first year of the war for his refusal to convert the struggle into an "abolition war." When Lincoln countermanded General John C. Frémont's order of liberation for slaves owned by disloyal masters in Missouri in September 1861, the *Anglo-African* declared that the president, by his actions, "hurls back into the hell of slavery thousands . . . rightfully set free." As late as July 1862, Frederick Douglass condemned Lincoln as a "miserable tool of traitors and rebels," and characterized administration policy as reconstruction of "the old union on the old and corrupting basis of compromise, by which slavery shall retain all the power that it ever had." Douglass wanted the old Union destroyed and a new one created in the crucible of a war that would destroy slavery and rewrite the Constitution in the name of human equality. To the black leader's own amazement, within a year, just such a profound result began to take place.

Lincoln first broached the subject of slavery in a substantive way in March 1862, when he proposed that the states consider emancipation on their own. He asked Congress to promise aid to any state that decided to emancipate, appealing especially to border state representatives. What Lincoln proposed was gradual emancipation, with compensation for slaveholders and colonization of the freed slaves outside the United States. To a delegation of free blacks in August 1862, in perhaps his worst racial moment, he explained that "it is better for us both . . . to be separated."

Until well into 1864, Lincoln's administration promoted schemes to colonize black people in Central America or the Caribbean. Lincoln saw colonization as one option among others in dealing with the impending freedom of America's 4 million slaves. He was as yet unconvinced that America had any prospect as a biracial society, and he desperately feared that white northerners might not support a war for black freedom. Led by Frederick Douglass, black abolitionists vehemently opposed these machinations by the Lincoln administration.

△ A group of "contrabands" (liberated slaves), photographed at Cumberland Landing, Virginia, May 14, 1862, at a sensitive point in the war when their legal status was still not fully determined. The faces and generations of the women, men, and children represent the human drama of emancipation.

Other politicians had much greater plans for a struggle against slavery. A group of Republicans in Congress, known as the **Radical Republicans** and led by men such as George Julian, Charles Sumner, and Thaddeus Stevens, dedicated themselves to a war for emancipation. They were instrumental in creating a special House–Senate committee on the conduct of the war, which investigated Union reverses, sought to make the war effort more efficient, and prodded the president to take stronger measures against slavery.

13-5b Confiscation Acts

In August 1861, at the Radicals' instigation, Congress passed its first confiscation act. Designed to punish the Confederates, the law confiscated all property used for "insurrectionary purposes." Thus, if the South used slaves in a hostile action, those slaves were seized and liberated as "contraband" of war. A second confiscation act (July 1862) went much further: it confiscated the property of anyone who supported the rebellion, even those who merely resided in the South and paid Confederate taxes. Their slaves were declared "forever free of their servitude." These acts stemmed from the logic that, in order to crush the southern rebellion, the government had to use extraordinary powers.

Although he signed the second confiscation act, Lincoln refused to adopt that view in the summer of 1862; he stood by his proposal of voluntary gradual emancipation by the states. His stance provoked a public protest from Horace Greeley, editor of the powerful *New York Tribune*. In an open letter to the president entitled "The Prayer of Twenty Millions,"

Greeley pleaded with Lincoln to "execute the laws" and declared, "On the face of this wide earth, Mr. President, there is not one . . . intelligent champion of the Union cause who does not feel that all attempts to put down the Rebellion and at the same time uphold its inciting cause are preposterous and futile." Lincoln's reply was an explicit statement of his calculated approach to the question. He disagreed, he said, with all those who would make slavery the paramount issue of the war. "I would save the Union," announced Lincoln. "If I could save the Union without freeing any slave I would do it, and if I could save it by freeing all the slaves I would do it; and if I could save it by freeing some and leaving others alone I would also do that. What I do about slavery, and the colored race, I do because I believe it helps to save the Union." Lincoln closed with a personal disclaimer: "I have here stated my purpose according to my view of official duty; and I intend no modification of my oft-expressed personal wish that all men everywhere could be free."

When he wrote those words, Lincoln had already decided to boldly issue a presidential **Emancipation Proclamation.** He was waiting, however, for a Union victory so that it would not appear to be an act of desperation. Yet the

> **Radical Republicans** A group of Republicans who assailed President Lincoln early in the war for failing to make emancipation a war goal and, later, for making it too easy for defeated rebel states to return to the Union.
>
> **Emancipation Proclamation** Lincoln's decree freeing all slaves in Confederate-held territories. It exempted border slave states that remained within the Union.

letter to Greeley represents Lincoln's concern with conditioning public opinion as best he could for the coming social revolution, and he needed to delicately consider international opinion as well.

13-5c Emancipation Proclamations

On September 22, 1862, shortly after Union success at the Battle of Antietam, Lincoln issued the first part of his two-part proclamation. Invoking his powers as commander-in-chief of the armed forces, he announced that on January 1, 1863, he would emancipate the slaves in the states "in rebellion." Lincoln made plain that he would judge a state to be in rebellion in January if it lacked legitimate representatives in the U.S. Congress. Thus, his September 1862 proclamation was less a declaration of the right of slaves to be free than a threat to southerners: unless they put down their arms and returned to Congress, they would lose their slaves. "Knowing the value that was set on the slaves by the rebels," said Garrison Frazier, a black Georgia minister, "the President thought that his proclamation would stimulate them to lay down their arms . . . and their not doing so has now made the freedom of the slaves a part of the war." Lincoln had little expectation that southerners would give up their effort, but he was determined to make them reply.

In the fateful January 1, 1863, proclamation, Lincoln declared that "all persons held as slaves" in areas in rebellion "shall be then, thenceforward, and forever free." But he excepted (as areas in rebellion) every Confederate county or city that had fallen under Union control. Those areas, he declared, "are, for the present, left precisely as if this proclamation were not issued." Nor did Lincoln liberate slaves in the border slave states that remained in the Union. "The President has purposely made the proclamation inoperative in all places where . . . the slaves [are] accessible," charged the anti-administration *New York World.* "He has proclaimed emancipation only where he has notoriously no power to execute it." Partisanship aside, even Secretary of State Seward said sarcastically, "We show our sympathy with slavery by emancipating slaves where we cannot reach them and holding them in bondage where we can set them free."

But Lincoln was worried about the constitutionality of his acts, and he anticipated that after the war southerners might sue in court for restoration of their "property." Making the liberation of the slaves "a fit and necessary war measure" raised a variety of legal questions: How long did a war measure remain in force? Did it expire with the suppression of a rebellion? The proclamation did little to clarify the status or citizenship of the freed slaves, although it did open the possibility of military service for blacks. How, indeed, would this change the character and purpose of the war? Just what kind of revolution would it launch?

Thus the Emancipation Proclamation was legally an ambiguous document. But as a moral and political document it had great meaning. Because the proclamation defined the war as a war against slavery, congressional Radicals could applaud it. Yet at the same time, it protected Lincoln's position with conservatives, leaving him room to retreat if he chose and forcing no immediate changes on the border slave states. It was a delicate balancing act, but one from which there was no turning back.

Most important, though, thousands of slaves had already reached Union lines in various sections of the South. They had "voted with their feet" for emancipation, as many said, well before the proclamation. And now, every advance of federal forces into slave society was a liberating step.

Across the North and in Union-occupied sections of the South, black people and their white allies celebrated the Emancipation Proclamation with unprecedented fervor. Full of praise songs, these celebrations demonstrated that, whatever the fine print of the proclamation, black folks knew they had lived to see a new day. At a large "contraband camp" in Washington, D.C., some six hundred black men, women, and children gathered at the superintendent's headquarters on New Year's Eve and sang through the night. In chorus after chorus of "Go Down, Moses" they announced the magnitude of their painful but beautiful exodus. One newly supplied verse concluded with "Go down, Abraham, away down in Dixie's land, tell Jeff Davis to let my people go!"

13-5d African American Recruits

The need for men soon convinced the administration to recruit northern and southern blacks for the Union army. By the spring of 1863, African American troops were answering the call of a dozen or more black recruiters barnstorming the cities and towns of the North. Lincoln came to see black soldiers as "the great available and yet unavailed of force for restoring the Union."

African American leaders hoped that military service would secure equal rights for their people. Once the black soldier had fought for the Union, wrote Frederick Douglass, "there is no power on earth which can deny that he has earned the right of citizenship in the United States." If black soldiers turned the tide, asked another man, "would the nation refuse us our rights?"

In June 1864, with thousands of black former slaves in blue uniforms, Lincoln gave his support to a constitutional ban on slavery. On the eve of the Republican national convention, Lincoln called on the party to "put into the platform as the keystone, the amendment of the Constitution abolishing and prohibiting slavery forever." The party promptly called for the **Thirteenth Amendment.** Republican delegates probably would have adopted such a plank without his urging, but Lincoln demonstrated his commitment by lobbying Congress for quick approval of the measure. The proposed amendment passed in early 1865 and was sent to the states for ratification. The war to save the Union had also become the war to free the slaves.

13-5e Who Freed the Slaves?

It has long been debated whether Abraham Lincoln deserved the label (one he never claimed for himself) of "Great Emancipator." Was Lincoln ultimately a reluctant emancipator,

---

Thirteenth Amendment
Ratified in December 1865, it permanently abolished slavery in all U.S. territories.

following rather than leading Congress and public opinion? Or did Lincoln give essential presidential leadership to the most transformative and sensitive aspect of the war by going slow on emancipation but, once moving, never backpedaling on black freedom? Once he had realized the total character of the war and decided to prosecute it to the unconditional surrender of the Confederates, Lincoln made the destruction of slavery central to the war's purpose.

Others have argued, however, that the slaves themselves are the central story in the achievement of their own freedom. When they were in proximity to the war zones or had opportunities as traveling laborers, slaves fled for their freedom by the thousands. Some worked as camp laborers for the Union armies, and eventually more than 180,000 black men served in the Union army and navy. Sometimes freedom came as a combination of confusion, fear, and joy in the rural hinterlands of the South. Some found freedom as individuals in 1861, and some not until 1865, as members of trains of refugees trekking great distances to reach contraband camps. And tragically, war always causes disease among large numbers of displaced people; thousands of freedmen died from exposure and illness in their quest for liberation.

However freedom came to individuals, emancipation was a historical confluence of two essential forces: one, a policy directed by and dependent on the military authority of the president in his effort to win the war; and the other, the will and courage necessary for acts of self-emancipation. Wallace Turnage's escape in Mobile Bay in 1864 demonstrates that emancipation could result from both a slave's own extraordinary heroism and the liberating actions of the Union forces. Most African Americans comprehended their freedom as both given and taken, but also as their human right. "I now dreaded the gun and handcuffs . . . no more," remembered Turnage of his liberation. "Nor the blowing of horns and running of hounds, nor the threats of death from rebels' authority." He was free in body and mind. "I could now speak my opinion," Turnage concluded, "to men of all grades and colors."

13-5f A Confederate Plan of Emancipation

Before the war was over, the Confederacy, too, addressed the issue of emancipation. Late in the war, Jefferson Davis himself was willing to sacrifice slavery to achieve independence. He proposed that the Confederate government purchase forty thousand slaves to work for the army as laborers, with a promise of freedom at the end of their service. Soon Davis upgraded the idea, calling for the recruitment and arming of slaves as soldiers, who likewise would gain their freedom at war's end. The wives and children of these soldiers, he made plain, must also receive freedom from the states. Davis and his advisers envisioned an "intermediate" status for ex-slaves of "serfage or peonage." Thus, at the bitter end, a few southerners were willing to sacrifice some of the racial, if not class, destiny for which they had launched their revolution.

Bitter debate over Davis's plan resounded through the Confederacy. When the Confederate Congress finally approved slave enlistments in March 1865, owners had to comply only on a "voluntary" basis. In sheer desperation for manpower, General Lee also supported the idea of slave soldiers. Against the reality all around them of slaves fleeing to Union lines, some southern leaders mistakenly hoped that they could still count on the "loyalty" of the South's bondsmen. Most Confederate slaveholders and editors vehemently opposed the enlistment plan; those who did support it acknowledged that the war had already freed some portion of the slave population. Their aim was to fight to a stalemate, achieve independence, and control the postwar racial order through their limited wartime emancipation schemes. It was too late. As a Mississippi planter wrote to his state's governor, the plan seemed "like a drowning man catching at straws."

By contrast, Lincoln's Emancipation Proclamation stimulated a vital infusion of forces into the Union armies. As both policy and process, emancipation had profound practical and moral implications for the new nation to be born out of the war.

13-6 The Soldiers' War

▶ **What motivated soldiers to fight in the Union army?**

▶ **What were the characteristics of camp life and combat for soldiers?**

▶ **How did the recruitment of African American soldiers change race relations in the Union army?**

The intricacies of policymaking and social revolutions were often far from the minds of most ordinary soldiers. Military service completely altered their lives. Enlistment took young men from their homes and submerged them in large organizations whose military discipline ignored their individuality. Army life meant tedium, physical hardship, and separation from loved ones. Yet the military experience had powerful attractions as well.

13-6a Ordinary Soldiers and Ideology

Most common soldiers, according to recent studies, were also committed to the ideological purposes of the war on both sides and not merely pawns caught up in a struggle they did not comprehend. The thousands of soldiers' letters, as well as regimental newspapers, indicate a deep awareness, if varying degrees of resolve, about slavery as the principal reason for the war.

The old idea that Civil War soldiers fought largely because of unit cohesion and the devotion of the men next to them is no longer an adequate explanation of why so many endured so much hardship for so long. Comradeship, duty, and honor were all powerful motivators for the men of the line. So were "union," "home," "the government," "freedom," "flag," "liberty," and "states' rights." But multitudes of literate soldiers left testimony of how much they saw slavery at the heart of the matter. In typical phrasing, members of the Thirteenth Wisconsin Infantry declared the conflict "a war of, by and for Slavery . . . as plain as the noon day sun." And their foes in Morgan's Confederate Brigade from Virginia agreed with different intentions: "any man who pretends to believe that this is not a war for the emancipation of the blacks . . . is either a fool or a liar."

13-6b Hospitals and Camp Life

The soldiers' lot was often misery. They benefited from certain new products, such as canned condensed milk, but blankets, clothing, and arms were often of poor quality. Hospitals were badly managed at first. Rules of hygiene in large camps were scarcely enforced; latrines were poorly made or carelessly used. One investigation turned up "an area of over three acres, encircling the camp as a broad belt, on which is deposited an almost perfect layer of human excrement." Water supplies were unsafe and typhoid epidemics common. About 57,000 men died from dysentery and diarrhea; in fact, 224,000 Union troops died from disease or accidents, far more than the 110,100 who died as a result of battle. Confederate troops were less well supplied, especially in the latter part of the war. Still, an extensive network of hospitals, aided by many white female volunteers and black female slaves, sprang up to aid the sick and wounded.

On both sides, troops quickly learned that soldiering was far from glorious. "The dirt of a camp life knocks all its poetry into a cocked hat," wrote a North Carolina volunteer in 1862. One year later, he marveled at his earlier innocence. Fighting had taught him "the realities of a soldier's life. We had no tents after the 6th of August, but slept on the ground, in the woods or open fields. . . . I learned to eat fat bacon raw, and to like it. . . . Without time to wash our clothes or our persons . . . the whole army became lousy more or less with body lice."

Few had seen violent death before, but war soon exposed them to the blasted bodies of their friends and comrades. "Any one who goes over a battlefield after a battle," wrote one Confederate, "never cares to go over another. . . . It is a sad sight to see the dead and if possible more sad to see the wounded—shot in every possible way you can imagine." Many men died gallantly; there were innumerable striking displays of courage. But often soldiers gave up their lives in mass sacrifice, in tactics that made little sense.

Still, Civil War soldiers developed deep commitments to each other and to their task. As campaigns dragged on, many soldiers grew determined to see the struggle through. "We now, like true Soldiers go determined not to yield one inch," wrote a New York corporal. When at last the war was over, "it seemed like breaking up a family to separate," one man observed. Another admitted, "We shook hands all around, and laughed and seemed to make merry, while our hearts were heavy and our eyes ready to shed tears."

13-6c The Rifled Musket

Advances in technology made the Civil War particularly deadly. By far the most important were the rifle and the "minie ball." Bullets fired from a smoothbore musket tumbled and wobbled as they flew through the air, and thus were not accurate at distances over eighty yards. Cutting spiraled grooves inside the barrel gave the projectile a spin and much greater accuracy, but rifles remained difficult to load and use until Frenchman Claude Minie and American James Burton developed a new kind of bullet. Civil War bullets were lead slugs with a cavity at the bottom that expanded on firing so that the bullet "took" the rifling and flew accurately. With these bullets, rifles were deadly at four hundred yards.

This meant, of course, that soldiers assaulting a position defended by riflemen were in greater peril than ever before; the defense thus gained a significant advantage. While artillery now fired from a safe distance, there was no substitute for the infantry assault or the popular turning movements aimed at an enemy's flank. Thus, advancing soldiers had to expose themselves repeatedly to accurate rifle fire. Because medical knowledge was rudimentary, even minor wounds often led to amputation and death through infection. Never before in Europe or America had such massive forces pummeled each other with weapons of such destructive power. As losses mounted, many citizens wondered at what Union soldier (and future Supreme Court justice) Oliver Wendell Holmes Jr. called "the butcher's bill."

13-6d The Black Soldier's Fight for Manhood

At the outset of the war, most white soldiers wanted nothing to do with black people and regarded them as inferior. "I never came out here for to free the black devils," wrote one soldier, and another objected to fighting beside African Americans because "[w]e are a too superior race for that." For many, acceptance of black troops grew only because they could do heavy labor and "stop Bullets as well as white people." A popular song celebrated "Sambo's Right to Be Kilt" as the only justification for black enlistments.

But among some, a change occurred. While recruiting black troops in Virginia in late 1864, Massachusetts soldier Charles Brewster sometimes denigrated the very men he sought to enlist. But he was delighted at the sight of a black cavalry unit because it made the local "secesh" furious, and he praised black soldiers who "fought nobly" and filled hospitals with "their wounded and mangled bodies." White officers who volunteered to lead segregated black units only to gain promotion found that experience altered their opinions. After just one month with black troops, a white captain informed his wife, "I have a more elevated opinion of their abilities than I ever had before. I know that many of them are vastly the superiors of those . . . who would condemn them all to a life of brutal degradation." One general reported that his "colored regiments" possessed "remarkable aptitude for military training."

Black troops created this change through their own dedication. They had a mission to destroy slavery and demonstrate their equality. "When Rebellion is crushed," wrote a black volunteer from Connecticut, "who will be more proud than I to say, I was one of the first of the despised race to leave the free North with a rifle on my shoulder, and give the lie to the old story that the black man will not fight." Corporal James Henry Gooding of Massachusetts's black Fifty-fourth Regiment explained that his unit intended "to live down all prejudice against its color, by a determination to do well in any position it is put." After an engagement, he was proud that "a regiment of white men gave us three cheers as we were passing them" because "it shows that we did our duty as men should."

Black Soldiers in the Civil War

The image below is of the storming of Fort Wagner in July 1863 by the Fifty-fourth Massachusetts regiment, in Charleston, South Carolina, by Chicago printmakers Kurtz and Allison. Kurtz and Allison issued vivid and colorful chromolithographs in the 1880s, celebrating the military valor of African Americans. This scene depicts the most famous combat action of black troops in the Civil War; the Fifty-fourth was the first northern-recruited black unit, and their bravery and sacrifice served as a measure of African American devotion to the Union cause. At left is the Robert Gould Shaw memorial commemorating the Fifty-fourth Massachusetts Regiment.

CRITICAL THINKING

□ Why was this regiment such a symbolic test case for the military ability and political meaning of black soldiers in the Civil War?

□ Why did black men have to die on battlefields for many Americans in the Civil War era to consider them fully men and citizens?

STORMING FORT WAGNER.

Library of Congress Prints and Photographs Division[LC-DIG-pga-01949]

Jerry L. Thompson / Art Resource, NY

△ The image is of the storming of Fort Wagner in July 1863 by the Fifty-fourth Massachusetts regiment, in Charleston, South Carolina, by Chicago printmakers Kurtz and Allison. Kurtz and Allison issued vivid and colorful chromolithographs in the 1880s, celebrating the military valor of African Americans. This scene depicts the most famous combat action of black troops in the Civil War; the Fifty-fourth was the first northern-recruited black unit, and their bravery and sacrifice served as a measure of African American devotion to the Union cause.

△ Robert Gould Shaw Memorial, Boston Common, by Augustus Saint Gaudens, unveiled in 1897, and considered his Civil War masterpiece. Depicts the march of the Fifty-fourth Massachusetts black regiment when then departed for war in May, 1863.

Through such experience under fire, the blacks and whites of the Fifty-fourth Massachusetts forged deep bonds. Just before the regiment launched its costly assault on Fort Wagner in Charleston harbor, in July 1863, a black soldier called out to abolitionist Colonel Robert Gould Shaw, who would perish that day, "Colonel, I will stay by you till I die." "And he kept his word," noted a survivor of the attack. "He has never been seen since." Indeed, the heroic assault on Fort Wagner was celebrated for demonstrating the valor of black men. This bloody chapter in the history of American racism proved many things, not least of which was that black men had to die in battle to be acknowledged as men.

Such valor emerged despite persistent discrimination. The Union government paid white privates $13 per month plus a clothing allowance of $3.50, whereas black privates earned only $10 per month less $3 for clothing. Outraged by this injustice, several regiments refused to accept any pay whatsoever, and Congress eventually remedied the inequity. In this instance at least, the majority of legislators agreed with a white private that black troops had "proved their title to manhood on many a bloody field fighting freedom's battles."

13-7 1863: The Tide of Battle Turns

▶ Why were Vicksburg and Gettysburg significant defeats for the Confederacy, and therefore turning points in the war?

▶ Despite major Union victories during 1863, why or how could the Confederacy still have won the war in their terms during the following year?

The fighting in the spring and summer of 1863 did not settle the war, but it began to suggest the outcome as it provided bloody turning-points. The campaigns began in a deceptively positive way for Confederates, as Lee's army performed brilliantly in battles in central Virginia.

13-7a Battle of Chancellorsville

For once, a large Civil War army was not slow and cumbersome, but executed tactics with speed and precision. On May 2 and 3, west of Fredericksburg, Virginia, some 130,000 members of the Union Army of the Potomac bore down on fewer than 60,000 Confederates. Boldly, Lee and Stonewall Jackson divided their forces, ordering 30,000 men under Jackson on a daylong march westward to prepare a flank attack.

This classic turning movement was carried out in the face of great numerical disadvantage. Arriving at their position late in the afternoon, Jackson's seasoned "foot cavalry" found unprepared Union troops laughing, smoking, and playing cards. The Union soldiers had no idea they were under

Vicksburg Union victory that gave the North complete control of the Mississippi River.

Gettysburg Union victory that halted the Confederate invasion of Pennsylvania; turning point in the war in the East.

attack until frightened deer and rabbits bounded out of the forest, followed by gray-clad troops. The Confederate attack drove the entire right side of the Union army back in confusion. Eager to press his advantage, Jackson rode forward with a few officers to study the ground. As they returned at twilight, southern troops mistook them for federals and fired, fatally wounding their commander. The next day, Union forces left in defeat. Chancellorsville was a remarkable southern victory, but costly because of the loss of Stonewall Jackson, who would forever remain a legend in Confederate memory.

13-7b Siege of Vicksburg

July brought crushing defeats for the Confederacy in two critical battles that severely damaged Confederate hopes for independence. One of these battles occurred at **Vicksburg**, Mississippi. Vicksburg was a vital western citadel, the last major fortification on the Mississippi River in southern hands (see Map 13.2). After months of searching through swamps and bayous, General Ulysses S. Grant found an advantageous approach to the city. He laid siege to Vicksburg in May, bottling up the defending army of General John Pemberton. If Vicksburg fell, Union forces would control the river, cutting the Confederacy in two and gaining an open path into its interior. To stave off such a result, Jefferson Davis gave command of all other forces in the area to General Joseph E. Johnston and beseeched him to go to Pemberton's aid. Meanwhile, at a council of war in Richmond, General Robert E. Lee proposed a Confederate invasion of the North. Although such an offensive would not relieve Vicksburg directly, it could stun and dismay the North and, if successful, possibly even lead to peace. By invading the North a second time, Lee hoped to take the war out of war-weary Virginia, garner civilian support in Maryland, win a major victory on northern soil, threaten major cities, and thereby force a Union capitulation on his terms.

As Lee's emboldened army advanced through western Maryland and into Pennsylvania, Confederate prospects to the south along the Mississippi darkened. Davis repeatedly wired General Johnston, urging him to concentrate his forces and attack Grant's army. Johnston, however, did little, telegraphing back: "I consider saving Vicksburg hopeless." Grant's men, meanwhile, were supplying themselves from the abundant crops of the Mississippi River valley and could continue their siege indefinitely.

13-7c Battle of Gettysburg

In such circumstances, the fall of Vicksburg was inevitable, and on July 4, 1863, its commander surrendered. The same day, the other battle, which had been raging for three days, concluded at **Gettysburg**, Pennsylvania (see Map 13.4). On July 1, Confederate forces hunting for a supply of shoes had collided with part of the Union army. Heavy fighting on the second day over two steep hills left federal forces in possession

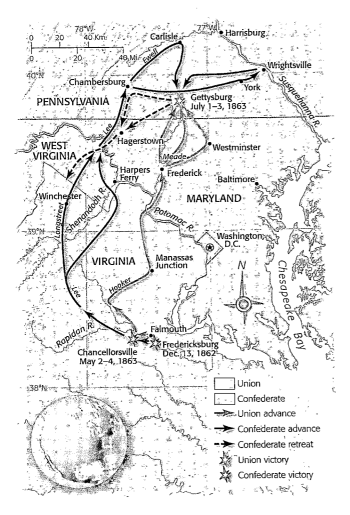

Map 13.4 Battle of Gettysburg

In the war's greatest battle, fought around a small market town in southern Pennsylvania, Lee's invasion of the North was repulsed. Union forces had the advantage of the high ground, shorter lines, and superior numbers. The casualties for the two armies—dead, wounded, and missing—exceeded 50,000 men.

of high ground along Cemetery Ridge, running more than a mile south of the town. There, they enjoyed the protection of a stone wall and a clear view of their foe across almost a mile of open field.

Undaunted, Lee believed his reinforced troops could break the Union line and, on July 3, he ordered a direct assault. Full of foreboding, General James Longstreet warned Lee that "no 15,000 men ever arrayed for battle can take that position." But Lee stuck to his plan. Virginians under General George E. Pickett and North Carolinians under General James Pettigrew methodically marched up the slope in a doomed assault known as Pickett's Charge. For a moment, a few hundred Confederates breached the enemy's line, but most fell in heavy slaughter. On July 4, Lee had to withdraw, having suffered almost 4,000 dead and about 24,000 missing

and wounded. The Confederate general reported to President Davis that "I am alone to blame" and offered to resign. Davis replied that to find a more capable commander was "an impossibility." The Confederacy had reached what many consider its "high-water mark" on that ridge at Gettysburg.

Southern troops displayed unforgettable courage and dedication at Gettysburg, and under General George G. Meade, the Union army, which suffered 23,000 casualties (nearly one-quarter of the force), exhibited the same bravery in stopping the Confederate invasion. But the results there and at Vicksburg were disastrous for the South. The Confederacy was split in two; west of the Mississippi, General E. Kirby Smith had to operate on his own, virtually independent of Richmond. Moreover, the heartland of Louisiana, Tennessee, and Mississippi lay exposed to invasion. Far to the north, Lee's defeat spelled the end of major southern offensive actions. By refusing to give up, and by wearing down northern morale while fighting defensively, the South might yet win, but its prospects were darker than before.

13-8 Disunity: South, North, and West

▷ **How did internal stresses and external pressures contribute to disaffection and defeat in the Confederacy?**

▷ **How did the Confederacy disintegrate internally over the course of the war?**

▷ **How did Northerners demonstrate their disaffection with the government and opposition to the war?**

▷ **What was the significance of the election of 1864?**

Both northern and southern governments waged the final two years of the war in the face of increasing opposition at home. Dissatisfactions that had surfaced earlier grew more intense and sometimes violent. The gigantic costs of a civil war that neither side seemed able to win fed the unrest. But protest also arose from fundamental stresses in the social structures of North and South.

13-8a Union Occupation Zones

Wherever Union forces invaded, they imposed a military occupation consisting roughly of three zones: garrisoned towns, with large numbers of troops in control of civilian and economic life; the Confederate frontier, areas still under southern control but also with some federal military penetration; and "no man's land," the land between the two armies, beyond Confederate authority and under frequent Union patrols.

As many as one hundred southern towns were garrisoned during the war, causing severe disruption to the social landscape. Large regions of Tennessee, Virginia, Louisiana, Mississippi, and Georgia fell under this pattern of occupation and suffered food shortages, crop and property destruction, disease, roadway banditry, guerrilla warfare, summary executions, and the random flow of escaped slaves. After two years of occupation, a southern white woman wrote to a kinsman about their native Clarksville, Tennessee. "You would scarcely know the place," she lamented, "it is nothing but a dirty hole filled . . . with niggers and Yankees."

13-8b Disintegration of Confederate Unity

Vastly disadvantaged in industrial capacity, natural resources, and labor, southerners felt the cost of the war more directly and more painfully than northerners. But even more fundamental were the Confederacy's internal problems; the southern class system threatened the Confederate cause.

One ominous development was the planters' increasing opposition to their own government. Along with new taxation, Confederate military authorities also impressed slaves to build fortifications. And when Union forces advanced on plantation areas, Confederate commanders burned stores of cotton that lay in the enemy's path. Many planters bitterly complained about such interference with their interests.

The Confederate constitution had granted substantial powers to the central government, especially in time of war. But many planters took the position articulated by R. B. Rhett, editor of the *Charleston Mercury*, that the Confederate constitution "leaves the States untouched in their Sovereignty, and commits to the Confederate Government only a few simple objects, and a few simple powers to enforce them." Governor Joseph E. Brown of Georgia took a similar states' rights position, occasionally prohibiting supplies and that state's soldiers from leaving its borders.

Years of opposition to the federal government within the Union had frozen southerners in a defensive posture. Now they erected the barrier of states' rights as a defense against change, hiding behind it while their capacity for creative statesmanship atrophied. As secession revolutionized their world and hard war took so many lives, some could never fully commit to the cause.

Confused and embittered planters struck out at Jefferson Davis. Conscription, thundered Governor Brown, was "subversive of [Georgia's] sovereignty, and at war with all the principles for the support of which Georgia entered into this revolution." Searching for ways to frustrate the law, Brown ordered local enrollment officials not to cooperate with the Confederacy. The *Charleston Mercury* told readers that "conscription . . . is . . . the very embodiment of Lincolnism, which our gallant armies are today fighting." In a gesture of stubborn selfishness, Robert Toombs of Georgia, a former U.S. senator, refused to switch from cotton to food crops, defying the wishes of the government, the newspapers, and his neighbors' petitions.

13-8c Food Riots in Southern Cities

Meanwhile, for ordinary southerners, the dire predictions of hunger and suffering were becoming a reality. Food riots occurred in the spring of 1863 in Atlanta, Macon, Columbus, and Augusta, Georgia, and in Salisbury and High Point, North Carolina. On April 2, a crowd assembled in Richmond to demand relief. A passerby, noticing the excitement, asked a young girl, "Is there some celebration?" "We celebrate our right to live," replied the girl. "We are starving. As soon as enough of us get together we are going to the bakeries and each of us will take a loaf of bread." Soon they did just that, sparking a riot that Davis ordered quelled at gunpoint.

Throughout the rural South, ordinary people resisted more quietly—by refusing to cooperate with conscription, tax collection, and impressments of food. "In all the States impressments are evaded by every means which ingenuity can suggest, and in some openly resisted," wrote a commissary officer. Farmers who did provide food for the army refused to accept payment in certificates of credit or government bonds, as required by law. Conscription officers increasingly found no one to draft. "The disposition to avoid military service is general," observed one of Georgia's senators in 1864. In some areas, tax agents were killed in the line of duty.

Jefferson Davis was ill equipped to deal with such discontent. Austere and private by nature, he failed to communicate with the masses. His class perspective also distanced him from the sufferings of the common people. While his social circle in Richmond dined on duck and oysters, ordinary southerners recovered salt from the drippings on their smokehouse floors and went hungry.

13-8d Desertions from the Confederate Army

Such discontent was certain to affect the Confederate armies. "What man is there that would stay in the army and no that his family is sufring at home?" an angry citizen wrote anonymously to the secretary of war. Worried about their loved ones and resentful of what they saw as a rich man's war, large numbers of men did indeed leave the armies. Their friends and neighbors gave them support. Mary Chesnut observed a man being dragged back to the army as his wife looked on. "Desert agin, Jake!" she cried openly. "You desert agin, quick as you kin. Come back to your wife and children."

Desertion did not become a serious problem for the Confederacy until mid-1862, and stiffer policing solved the problem that year. But from 1863 on, the number of men on duty fell rapidly. By mid-1863, John A. Campbell, the South's assistant secretary of war, wondered whether "so general a habit" as desertion could be considered a crime. Campbell estimated that 40,000 to 50,000 troops were absent without leave and that 100,000 were evading duty in some way. Furloughs, amnesty proclamations, and appeals to return had little effect; by November 1863, Secretary of War James Seddon admitted that one-third of the army could not be accounted for.

The defeats at Gettysburg and Vicksburg dealt a heavy blow to Confederate morale. When the news reached Josiah Gorgas, the genius of Confederate ordnance operations, he confided to his diary, "Today absolute ruin seems our portion. The Confederacy totters to its destruction." In desperation, President Davis and several state governors resorted to threats and racial scare tactics to drive southern whites to further sacrifice. Defeat, Davis warned, would mean "extermination of yourselves, your wives, and children." Governor Charles Clark of Mississippi predicted "elevation of the black race to a position of equality—aye, of superiority, that will make them your masters and rulers." Confederate leaders knew they were facing an apocalyptic revolution in the world as they had known it.

From this point on, the internal disintegration of the Confederacy quickened. Confederate leaders began to realize they were losing the support of the common people. It is, indeed, remarkable how long and how effectively the Confederacy sustained a military effort in the face of such internal division.

13-8e Antiwar Sentiment, South and North

In North Carolina, a peace movement grew under the leadership of William W. Holden, a popular Democratic politician and editor. He and his followers convened over one hundred public meetings in support of peace negotiations, which took place during the summer of 1863. In Georgia early in 1864, Governor Brown and Alexander H. Stephens, vice president of the Confederacy, led a similar effort. Ultimately, however, these movements came to naught. The lack of a two-party system threw into question the legitimacy of any criticism of the government; even Holden and Brown could not entirely escape the taint of dishonor and disloyalty.

The results of the 1863 congressional elections strengthened dissent in the Confederacy. Everywhere, secessionists and supporters of the administration lost seats to men not identified with the government. In the last years of the war, Davis's support in the Confederate Congress dwindled. Some newspaper editors and a core of courageous, determined soldiers, especially in Lee's Army of Northern Virginia, kept the Confederacy alive in spite of disintegrating popular support.

By 1864, much of the opposition to the war had moved entirely outside the political sphere. Southerners were simply giving up the struggle. Deserters dominated some whole towns and counties. Active dissent was particularly common in upland and mountain regions, where support for the Union had always been genuine. "The condition of things in the mountain districts of North Carolina, South Carolina, Georgia, and Alabama," admitted Assistant Secretary of War Campbell, "menaces the existence of the Confederacy as fatally as either of the armies of the United States."

Opposition to the war, though less severe, existed in the North as well. Alarm intensified over the growing centralization of government and, by 1863, war weariness was widespread. Resentment of the draft sparked protest, especially among poor citizens, and the Union army, too, struggled with a troubling desertion rate. But the Union was so much richer than the South in human resources that none of these problems ever threatened the effectiveness of the government.

Moreover, Lincoln possessed a talent that Davis lacked: he knew how to stay in touch with the ordinary citizen. Through public letters to newspapers and private ones to soldiers' families, he reached the common people. The battlefield

carnage, the tortuous political problems, and the ceaseless criticism weighed heavily on him, but his administration never lost control of the federal war effort.

13-8f Peace Democrats

Much of the wartime protest in the North was political in origin. The Democratic Party fought to regain power by blaming Lincoln for the war's death toll, the expansion of federal powers, inflation and the high tariff, and the emancipation of blacks. Appealing to tradition, its leaders called for an end to the war and reunion on the basis of "the Constitution as it is and the Union as it was." The Democrats denounced conscription and martial law and defended states' rights. They charged repeatedly that Republican policies were designed to flood the North with blacks, threatening white men's privileges. In the 1862 congressional elections, the Democrats made a strong comeback, with peace Democrats wielding influence in New York State and majorities in the legislatures of Illinois and Indiana.

Led by outspoken men like Representative Clement L. Vallandigham of Ohio, the peace Democrats became highly visible. Vallandigham criticized Lincoln as a "dictator" who had suspended the writ of habeas corpus without congressional authority, arrested thousands of innocent citizens, and shut down opposition newspapers (which was true). He condemned both conscription and emancipation, and urged voters to use their power at the polls to depose "King Abraham." Vallandigham stayed carefully within legal bounds, but his attacks seemed so damaging to the war effort that military authorities arrested him for treason. Lincoln wisely decided against punishment—and martyr's status—for the Ohioan and exiled him to the Confederacy. Vallandigham eventually returned to the North through Canada.

Some antiwar Democrats did encourage draft resistance, discourage enlistment, sabotage communications, and generally plot to aid the Confederacy. Likening such groups to a poisonous snake, Republicans sometimes branded them—and by extension the peace Democrats—as **"Copperheads"**. Although some Confederate agents were active in the North and Canada, they never genuinely threatened the Union war effort and their suppression remains a vexing legal legacy.

13-8g New York City Draft Riots

More violent opposition to the government arose from ordinary citizens facing the draft, which became law in 1863. Although many soldiers risked their lives willingly out of a desire to preserve the Union or extend freedom, others openly sought to avoid service.

The urban poor and immigrants in strongly Democratic areas were especially hostile to conscription. Federal enrolling officers made up the lists of eligibles, a procedure open to personal favoritism and

"Copperheads" Poisonous snakes; also the Republican nickname for antiwar northern Democrats. Some were pacifists, while others were activists who encouraged draft resistance, sabotage, and efforts to aid the Confederacy.

prejudice. The North's poor viewed the system as discriminatory, and many immigrants suspected (wrongly, on the whole) that they were called in disproportionate numbers. (Approximately 200,000 men born in Germany and 150,000 born in Ireland served in the Union army.)

As a result, there were scores of disturbances. Enrolling officers received rough treatment in many parts of the North, and riots occurred in New Jersey, Ohio, Indiana, Pennsylvania, Illinois, and Wisconsin. By far the most serious outbreak of violence occurred in New York City in July 1863. The war was unpopular in that Democratic stronghold, and racial, ethnic, and class tensions ran high. Shippers had recently broken a longshoremen's strike by hiring black strikebreakers to work under police protection. Working-class New Yorkers feared an inflow of black labor from the South and regarded blacks as the cause of the war. Poor Irish workers resented being forced to serve in the place of others who could afford to avoid the draft by paying a substitute.

Military police officers came under attack first, and then mobs crying, "Down with the rich" looted wealthy homes and stores. But blacks became the special target. The mob rampaged through African American neighborhoods, beating and murdering people in the streets, and burning an orphan asylum. At least seventy-four people died in the violence, which raged out of control for three days. Only the dispatch of army units directly from Gettysburg ended this tragic episode of racism and class resentment.

13-8h War Against Native Americans in the Far West

East and West, over race, land, and culture, America was a deeply divided country. A civil war of another kind raged on the Great Plains and in the Southwest. By 1864, U.S. troops under the command of Colonel John Chivington waged full-scale war against the Sioux, Arapaho, and Cheyenne in order to eradicate Native peoples' title to all of eastern Colorado. Native American chiefs sought peace, but American commanders had orders to "burn villages and kill Cheyennes whenever and wherever found." A Cheyenne chief, Lean Bear, was shot from his horse as he rode toward U.S. troops, holding in his hand papers given him by President Lincoln during a visit to Washington, D.C. Another chief, Black Kettle, was told by the U.S. command that, by moving his people to Sand Creek, Colorado, they would find a safe haven. But on

THE RIOTS IN NEW YORK : DESTRUCTION OF THE COLOURED ORPHAN ASYLUM.

△ A contemporary wood engraving of the destruction of the Colored Orphan Asylum during the New York City draft riots, July 13–16, 1863.

November 29, 1864, 700 cavalrymen, many drunk, attacked the Cheyenne village. With most of the men absent hunting, the slaughter included 105 Cheyenne women and children and 28 men. American soldiers scalped and mutilated their victims, carrying women's body parts on their saddles or hats back to Denver. The Sand Creek Massacre, and the retaliation against white ranches and stagecoaches by Native peoples in 1865, would live in western historical memory forever.

In New Mexico and Arizona Territories, an authoritarian and brutal commander, General James Carleton, waged war on the Apaches and the Navajos. Both tribes had engaged for generations in raiding the Pueblo and Hispanic peoples of the region to maintain their security and economy. During the Civil War years, Anglo-American farms also became Indian targets. In 1863, the New Mexico Volunteers, commanded in the field by former mountain man Kit Carson, defeated the Mescalero Apaches and forced them onto a reservation at Bosque Redondo in the Pecos River valley.

But the Navajos, who lived in a vast region of canyons and high deserts, resisted. In a "scorched earth" campaign, Carson destroyed the Navajos' livestock, orchards, and crops. On the run, starving and demoralized, the Navajos began to surrender for food in January 1864. Three-quarters of the twelve thousand Navajos were rounded up and forced to march 400 miles (the "Long Walk") to the Bosque Redondo Reservation, suffering malnutrition and death along the way. When General William T. Sherman visited the reservation in 1868, he found the Navajos "sunk into a condition of absolute poverty and despair." Permitted to return to a fraction of their homelands later that year, the Navajos carried with them searing memories of the federal government's ruthless policies of both removal and eradication of Native peoples. The Civil War was thus a harbinger of the more sweeping Indian Wars in the West to follow in the 1870s and 1880s.

13-8i Election of 1864

Back east, war weariness reached a peak in the summer of 1864, when the Democratic Party nominated the popular general George B. McClellan for president and inserted a peace plank into its platform. The plank, written by Vallandigham, called for an armistice and spoke vaguely about preserving the Union. The Democrats made racist appeals to white insecurity, calling Lincoln "Abe the nigger-lover" and "Abe the widow-maker." Lincoln concluded that it was "exceedingly probable that this Administration will not be reelected." No incumbent president had been reelected since 1832, and no nation had ever held a general election in the midst of all-out civil war. Some Republicans worked to dump Lincoln from their ticket in favor of either Salmon P. Chase or John C. Frémont, although little came of either effort. The Republican Party, declaring itself for "unconditional surrender" of the Confederacy and a constitutional amendment abolishing slavery, had to contend with the horrible casualty lists and the battlefield stalemate of the summer of 1864.

The fortunes of war soon changed the electoral situation. With the fall of Atlanta and Union victories in the Shenandoah Valley by early September, Lincoln's prospects rose. Decisive in the election was that eighteen states allowed troops to vote at the front; Lincoln won an extraordinary 78 percent of the soldier vote. In taking 55 percent of the total popular vote, Lincoln's reelection—a referendum on the war and emancipation—had a devastating impact on southern morale. Without such a political outcome in 1864, a Union military victory and a redefined nation might never have been possible.

13-9 1864–1865: The Final Test of Wills

▷ What role did foreign diplomacy play in the direction of the war?

▷ How did Ulysses S. Grant and William T. Sherman institute "total war" in the South in the last year of the war?

▷ What were the human and financial costs of the Civil War?

During the final year of the war, the Confederates could still have won their version of victory if military stalemate and northern antiwar sentiment had forced a negotiated settlement. But events and northern determination prevailed, as Americans endured the bloodiest nightmare in their history.

13-9a Northern Diplomatic Strategy

The North's long-term diplomatic strategy succeeded in 1864. From the outset, the North had pursued one paramount goal: to prevent recognition of the Confederacy by European nations. Foreign recognition would belie Lincoln's claim that the United States was fighting an illegal rebellion and would open the way to the financial and military aid that could ensure Confederate independence. Both England and France stood to benefit from a divided and weakened America. Thus, to achieve their goal, Lincoln and Secretary of State Seward needed to avoid both serious military defeats and controversies with the European powers.

Aware that the textile industry employed one-fifth of the British population directly or indirectly, southerners banked on British recognition of the Confederacy. But at the beginning of the war, British mills had a 50 percent surplus of cotton on hand, and they later found new sources of supply in India, Egypt, and Brazil. And throughout the war, some southern cotton continued to reach Europe, despite the Confederacy's embargo on cotton production, an ill-fated policy aimed at securing British support. The British government flirted with recognition of the Confederacy but awaited battlefield demonstrations of southern success. France, though sympathetic to the South, was unwilling to act independently of Britain. Confederate agents managed to purchase valuable arms and supplies in Europe and obtained loans from European financiers, but they never achieved a diplomatic breakthrough.

More than once, the Union strategy nearly broke down. An acute crisis occurred in 1861 when the overzealous commander of an American frigate stopped the British steamer *Trent* and removed two Confederate ambassadors, James Mason and John Slidell, sailing to Britain. When they were imprisoned in Boston, northerners cheered, but the British interpreted the capture as a violation of freedom of the seas and demanded the prisoners' release. Lincoln and Seward waited until northern public opinion cooled and then released the two southerners. The incident strained U.S.-British relations.

Then the sale to the Confederacy of warships constructed in England sparked vigorous protest from U.S. ambassador Charles Francis Adams. A few English-built ships, notably the *Alabama,* reached open water to serve the South. Over a period of twenty-two months, without entering a southern port (because of the Union blockade), the *Alabama* destroyed or captured more than sixty U.S. ships, leaving a bitter legal legacy to be settled in the postwar period.

13-9b Battlefield Stalemate and a Union Strategy for Victory

On the battlefield, northern victory was far from won in 1864. General Nathaniel Banks's Red River campaign, designed to capture more of Louisiana and Texas, fell apart, and the capture of Mobile Bay in August did not cause the fall of Mobile. Union general William Tecumseh Sherman commented that the North had to "keep the war South until they are not only ruined, exhausted, but humbled in pride and spirit." Sherman soon brought total war to the southern heartland. On the eastern front during the winter of 1863–1864, the two armies in Virginia settled into a stalemate awaiting yet another spring offensive by the North.

Military authorities throughout history have agreed that deep invasion is very risky: the farther an army penetrates enemy territory, the more vulnerable are its own communications and supply lines. Moreover, observed the Prussian expert Karl von Clausewitz, if the invader encounters a "truly national" resistance, his troops will be "everywhere exposed to attacks by an insurgent population." The South's vast size and a determined resistance could yet make a northern victory elusive.

General Grant, by now in command of all the federal armies, decided to test southern will with a strategic innovation of his own: raids on a massive scale. Less tied to tradition and textbook maneuver than most other Union commanders, Grant proposed to use armies to destroy Confederate railroads, thus ruining the enemy's transportation and economy. Abandoning their lines of support, Union troops would live off the land while laying waste all resources useful to the military and to the civilian population of the Confederacy. After General George H. Thomas's troops won the Battle of Chattanooga in November 1863, the heartland of Georgia lay open. Grant entrusted General Sherman with one hundred thousand men for an invasion deep into the South, toward the rail center of Atlanta.

△ ▷ Both General Grant (left) and General Lee (right) were West Point graduates and had served in the U.S. Army during the War with Mexico. Their bloody battles against each other in 1864 stirred northern revulsion to the war even as they brought its end in sight.

National Archives

The Civil War in Britain

So engaged was the British public with America's disunion and war that an unemployed weaver, John Ward, frequently trekked many miles from Britain's Low Moor to Clitheroe just to read newspaper accounts of the strife.

Because of the direct reliance of the British textile industry on southern cotton (cut off by the war) as well as the many ideological and familial ties between the two nations, the American war was significant in Britain's economy and domestic politics. The British aristocracy and most cotton mill owners were solidly pro-Confederate and proslavery, whereas a combination of clergymen, shopkeepers, artisans, and radical politicians worked for the causes of Union and emancipation. Most British workers saw their future at stake in a war for slave emancipation. "Freedom" to the huge British working class (who could not vote) meant basic political and civil rights as well as the bread and butter of secure jobs in an industrializing economy, now damaged by a "cotton famine" that threw millhands out of work.

English aristocrats saw Americans as untutored, wayward cousins and took satisfaction in America's troubles. Conservatives believed in the superiority of the British system of government and looked askance at America's leveling tendencies. And some aristocratic British Liberals also saw Americans through their class bias and sympathized with the Confederacy's demand for "order" and independence. English racism also intensified in these years, exemplified by the popularity of minstrelsy and the employment of science in the service of racial theory. Their views on race had also been hardened by their own recent experience in the Indian Rebellion of 1857–1859, a revolt against British control characterized by acts of extreme cruelty on both sides, in which at least 800,000 people (mostly Indians) are thought to have died.

The intensity of the British propaganda war over the American conflict is evident in the methods of their debate: public meetings organized by both sides were huge affairs, with cheering and jeering, competing banners, carts and floats, orators and resolutions. In a press war, the British argued over when rebellion is justified, whether secession was right or legal, whether slavery was at the heart of the conflict, and especially over the democratic image of America itself. This bitter debate about America's trial became a test of reform in Britain: those eager for a broadened franchise and increased democracy were pro-Union, and those who preferred to preserve Britain's class-ridden political system favored the Confederacy.

The nature of the internal British debate was no better symbolized than by the dozens of African Americans who served as pro-Union agents in England. The most popular was William Andrew Jackson, Confederate president Jefferson Davis's former coachman, who had escaped from Richmond in September 1862. Jackson's articulate presence at British public meetings countered pro-Confederate arguments that the war was not about slavery.

In the end, the British government did not recognize the Confederacy and, by 1864, English cotton lords had found new sources of the crop in Egypt and India. But in this link between America and its English roots at its time of greatest travail, we can see that the Civil War was a transformation of international significance.

CRITICAL THINKING

☐ How was the debate over the American Civil War in England illustrative of the importance of the United States' economy to the global economy?

The Granger Collection, NYC

◁ Some southern leaders pronounced that cotton was king and would bring Britain to their cause. This British cartoon shows King Cotton brought down in chains by the American eagle, anticipating the cotton famine to follow and the intense debate in Great Britain over the nature and meaning of the American Civil War.

13-9c Fall of Atlanta

Jefferson Davis countered by positioning the army of General Joseph E. Johnston in Sherman's path. Davis hoped that southern resolve would lead to the political defeat of Lincoln and the election of a president who would sue for peace. When General Johnston slowly but steadily fell back toward Atlanta, Davis grew anxious and sought assurances that Atlanta would be held. From a purely military point of view, Johnston maneuvered skillfully. But when Johnston fell silent and continued to retreat, Davis replaced him with the one-legged General John Hood, who knew his job was to fight. "Our all depends on that army at Atlanta," wrote Mary Chesnut. "If that fails us, the game is up."

For southern morale, the game *was* up. Hood attacked but was beaten, and Sherman's army occupied Atlanta on September 2, 1864. The victory buoyed northern spirits and all but ensured Lincoln's reelection. A government clerk in Richmond wrote, "Our fondly-cherished visions of peace have vanished like a mirage of the desert." Davis exhorted southerners to fight on and win new victories before the federal elections, but he had to admit that "two-thirds of our men are absent . . . without leave." In a desperate diversion, Hood's army marched north to cut Sherman's supply lines and force him to withdraw, but Sherman began to march sixty thousand of his marauding men straight to the sea, destroying Confederate resources as he went (see Map 13.5).

13-9d Sherman's March to the Sea

Sherman's army was an unusually formidable force, composed almost entirely of battle-tested veterans and officers who had risen through the ranks from the midwestern states. Before the march began, army doctors weeded out any men who were weak or sick. Weathered, bearded, and tough, the remaining veterans were determined, as one put it, "to Conquer this Rebelien or Die." They believed "the South are to blame for this war" and were ready to make the South pay. Although many harbored racist attitudes, most had come to support emancipation because, as one said, "Slavery stands in the way of putting down the rebellion." Confederate General Johnston later commented, "There has been no such army since the days of Julius Caesar."

As Sherman's men moved across Georgia, they cut a path 50 to 60 miles wide and more than 200 miles long. The totality of the destruction later prompted many historians to deem this the first modern "total war." A Georgia woman described the "Burnt Country" this way: "The fields were trampled down and the road was lined with carcasses of horses, hogs, and cattle that the invaders, unable either to consume or

Map 13.5 Sherman's March to the Sea

The Deep South proved a decisive theater at the end of the war. From Chattanooga, Union forces drove into Georgia, capturing Atlanta. Following the fall of Atlanta, General Sherman embarked on his march of destruction through Georgia to the coast and then northward through the Carolinas.

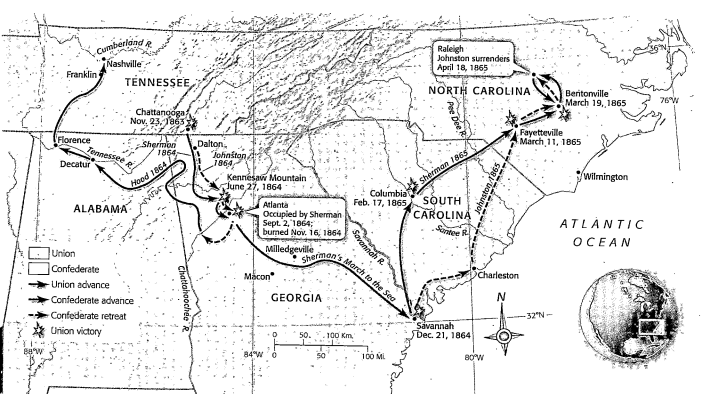

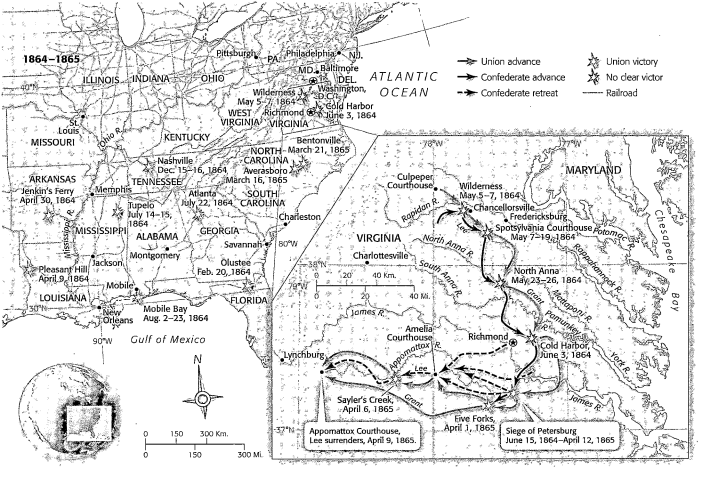

Map 13.6 The War in Virginia

At great cost, Grant hammered away at Lee's army until the weakened southern forces finally surrendered at Appomattox Court House.

to carry with them, had wantonly shot down to starve our people. . . . The stench in some places was unbearable." Such devastation diminished the South's material resources and sapped its will to resist.

After reaching Savannah in December, Sherman marched his armies north into the Carolinas. To his soldiers, South Carolina was "the root of secession." They burned and destroyed as they marched, encountering little resistance. The opposing army of General Johnston was small, but Sherman's men should have been prime targets for guerrilla raids and harassing attacks by local defense units. The absence of both led South Carolina's James Chesnut Jr. (a politician and the husband of Mary Chesnut) to write that his state "was shamefully and unnecessarily lost. . . . We had time, opportunity and means to destroy him. But there was wholly wanting the energy and ability required." Southerners had lost the will to continue the struggle.

Sherman's march drew additional human resources to the Union cause. In Georgia alone, nearly twenty thousand slaves gladly embraced emancipation and followed the marauding Union troops. Others remained on the plantations to await the end of the war because of either an ingrained wariness of whites or negative experiences with federal soldiers. The destruction of food harmed slaves as

well as white rebels, and many blacks lost livestock, crops, and other valuables to their liberators. In fact, the brutality of Sherman's troops shocked some liberated slaves. "I've seen them cut the hams off of a live pig or ox and go off leavin' the animal groanin,'" recalled one man. "The master had 'em kilt then, but it was awful."

13-9e Virginia's Bloody Soil

It was awful, too, in Virginia, where the path to victory proved protracted and ghastly. Throughout the spring and summer of 1864, intent on capturing Richmond, Grant hurled his troops at Lee's army and suffered appalling losses: almost eighteen thousand casualties in the Battle of the Wilderness, where skeletons poked out of the shallow graves dug one year before after the Battle of Chancellorsville; more than eight thousand at Spotsylvania; and twelve thousand in the space of a few hours at Cold Harbor (see Map 13.6).

Before the assault at Cold Harbor (which Grant later admitted was a grave mistake), Union troops pinned scraps of paper bearing their names and addresses to their backs, certain they would be mowed down as they rushed Lee's trenches. In four weeks in May and June, Grant lost as many men as were enrolled in Lee's entire army. From early May until July, when Union forces had marched and fought all the way from forests west of Fredericksburg to Petersburg, south of Richmond, which they besieged, the two armies engaged each other nearly every day. The war had reached a horribly modern scale. Wagon trains carrying thousands of Union wounded crawled back toward Washington. "It was as if war," wrote historian Bruce Catton, "the great clumsy machine for maiming people, had at last been perfected. Instead of turning out its grist spasmodically, with long waits between each delivery, it was at last able to produce every day, without any gaps at all."

Undaunted, Grant kept up the pressure, saying, "I propose to fight it out along this line if it takes all summer." Although costly, and testing northern morale to its limits, these battles prepared the way for eventual victory: Lee's army shrank until offensive action was no longer possible, while Grant's army kept replenishing its forces with new recruits. The siege of Petersburg, with the armies facing each other in miles of trenches, lasted throughout the winter of 1864–1865.

13-9f Surrender at Appomattox

The end finally came in the spring of 1865. Grant kept battering Lee, who tried but failed to break through the Union line. With the numerical superiority of Grant's army now greater than two to one, Confederate defeat was inevitable. On April 2, Lee abandoned Richmond and Petersburg. On April 9, hemmed in by Union troops, short of rations, and with fewer than thirty thousand men left, he surrendered at Appomattox Court House. Grant treated his rival with respect and paroled the defeated troops, allowing cavalrymen to keep their horses and take them home. The war was over at last. Within weeks, Confederate forces under Johnston surrendered to Sherman in North Carolina, and Davis, who had fled Richmond but wanted the war to continue, was captured in Georgia. The North rejoiced, and most southerners fell into despair, expecting waves of punishment. In the profound relief and stillness of the surrender field at Appomattox, no one could know the harrowing tasks of healing and justice that lay ahead.

With Lee's surrender, Lincoln knew the Union had been preserved, yet he lived to see but a few days of war's aftermath. On the evening of Good Friday, April 14, he accompanied his wife to Ford's Theatre in Washington to enjoy a popular comedy. There John Wilkes Booth, an embittered southern sympathizer, shot the president in the head at point-blank range. Lincoln died the next day. Twelve days later, troops tracked down and killed Booth. The Union had lost its wartime leader, and millions publicly mourned the martyred chief executive along the route of the funeral train that took his body home to Illinois. Relief at the war's end mingled hauntingly with a renewed sense of loss and anxiety about the future. Millions never forgot where they were and how they felt at the news of Lincoln's assassination.

13-9g Financial Tally

Property damage and financial costs were enormous, though difficult to tally. U.S. loans and taxes during the conflict totaled almost $3 billion, and interest on the war debt was $2.8 billion. The Confederacy borrowed over $2 billion but lost far more in the destruction of homes, crops, livestock, and other property. In southern war zones, the landscape was desolated. Over wide regions, fences and crops were destroyed; houses, barns, and bridges burned; and fields abandoned and left to erode. Union troops had looted factories and put two-thirds of the South's railroad system out of service.

Estimates of the total cost of the war exceed $20 billion—five times the total expenditures of the federal government from its creation until 1861. By 1865, the federal government's spending had soared to twenty times the prewar level and accounted for over 26 percent of the gross national product. Many of these changes were more or less permanent, as wartime measures left the government more deeply involved in manufacturing, banking, and transportation.

13-9h Death Toll and Its Impact

The human costs of the Civil War were especially staggering. The total number of military casualties on both sides far exceeded 1 million—a frightful toll for a nation of 31 million people. Using microdata samples from the 1850, 1860, 1870, and 1880 censuses, a recent study has markedly raised the former official count of 620,000 dead in the Civil War to approximately 750,000. Scholarship also shows that we have never been able to carefully account for civilian casualties in the war, nor for the possibly one in four freedpeople who died in the process of achieving their own freedom. These startling numbers demonstrate that more people died in the Civil War than in all other American wars combined until Vietnam. Not all died on the battlefield: 30,218 northerners died in southern prisons, and 25,976 Confederates died in Union prisons.

The scale and the anonymous nature of death overwhelmed American culture and led to the establishment of national cemeteries, where the large majority of the fallen were buried without identification. This prompted desperate efforts by families to find their loved ones, usually in vain. In a Christian culture believing in the "good death," where the deceased is surrounded by family and a clear narrative of the final hours could be remembered, mass death and dismembered bodies strewn on war-ravaged landscapes violated the values of a religious and romantic age. On the private level, countless Americans, soldiers and family members alike, never psychologically recovered or found true consolation from the war's personal loss. The age's earlier belief that suffering was always purposeful underwent fundamental shock. The desperate urge to memorialize individual soldiers in this war, writes historian Drew Faust, stemmed from "the anguish of wives, parents, siblings, and

△ The ruins of Charleston, South Carolina, late spring 1865. The city fell and was evacuated on February 18, 1865. Union gunboats and siege cannons had bombarded Charleston during the final year of the war, leaving much of the beautiful neoclassical architecture of that city, where secession had begun four years earlier, in devastation. An African American regiment accepted the formal surrender of the city.

children who found undocumented, unconfirmed, and unrecognizable loss intolerable." For some, the magnitude of death meant living could never be the same.

These unprecedented losses flowed from fundamental strife over the nature of the Union and the liberty of black people. Both sides saw vital interests in the struggle but lost control of its scope. As Julia Ward Howe wrote in her famous "Battle Hymn of the Republic," they had heard "the trumpet that shall never call retreat." And so the war took its horrifying toll.

Abraham Lincoln's Second Inaugural Address

Historian Don Fehrenbacher wrote that "some of Lincoln's words have acquired transcendent meaning as contributions to the permanent literary treasure of the nation." How is this so with the short oration Lincoln delivered from the north portico of the Capitol on March 4, 1865? Why have so many book titles been drawn from its text?

In a 701-word prose poem at the occasion of his second inauguration, Lincoln chose not to celebrate the Union armies' impending victory, nor his own at the polls. Instead, he probed the tragedy at the heart of the Civil War and interpreted its ultimate meanings. The prosaic first paragraph acknowledges wide understanding of the "progress of our arms" over four years of war. In the second paragraph, Lincoln entwines North and South in a mutual fate, but suggests responsibility for which side "would make war," and which side "would accept war," and leaves it to posterity: "And the war came."

Then, the speech transforms and Lincoln boldly offers a theological-historical explanation of the war that still resonates today in how Americans interpret this crucial turning point in their history. Evenhandedly, but forcefully, Lincoln declares that "all knew . . . somehow" slavery was the "cause" of the conflict. Both sides appealed to the "same God" to favor their cause. But quoting Matthew 18:7, he warned that the "Almighty has his own purposes," and though "offences" will always come from human frailty, "woe to that man by whom the offence cometh!" Wary of judging, but unrestrained, Lincoln called it "strange that any men should dare to ask a just God's assistance in ringing their bread from the sweat of other men's faces." Lincoln did not claim to utterly know God's will, but he imagined slavery as an "offence" that came "in the providence of God," and brought "this mighty scourge of war" as its awful price.

Suddenly, in rhetoric so unusual for presidential inaugurals, Lincoln assumed the prophet's mantle: "Yet if God wills that it [the war] continue, until all the wealth piled by the bond-man's two hundred and fifty years of unrequited toil shall be sunk, and until every drop of blood drawn by the lash, shall be paid by another drawn with the sword, as was said three thousand years ago, so still it must be said 'the judgments of the Lord are true and righteous altogether.'"

Famously, Lincoln ended with a single-sentence paragraph where he declared "malice toward none . . . charity for all" the healing balm for the "nation's wounds." But in that third paragraph—less popular or savored in modern memory—Lincoln transcended time and place and delivered what Frederick Douglass would call a "sacred effort" to explain what the Civil War was really about. Whether Lincoln was the nation's healer or its war-maker who would demand any sacrifice to restore the Union and destroy slavery has always animated the endless study of his personal story. The legacy of the Civil War, and Lincoln's place in it, are forever enmeshed in how we interpret this oratorical masterpiece.

CRITICAL THINKING

- In Lincoln's third paragraph of the address, he asserts that "all knew... somehow" slavery was the "cause" of the conflict, yet in a 2011 CNN poll 42 percent of Americans said that slavery was not the cause of the war. How should we interpret the disparity between how Civil War–era Americans and modern Americans understand the causes of the war?

Summary

The Civil War altered American society forever. The first great legacy of the war in the lives of its survivors was, therefore, death itself. Although precise figures on enlistments are unavailable, it appears that 700,000 to 800,000 men served in the Confederate armies. Far more, possibly 2.3 million, served in the Union armies. All of these men were taken from home, family, and personal goals; their lives, if they survived, were disrupted in ways that were never repaired. During the war, in both North and South, women, too, took on new roles as they struggled to manage the hardships of the home front, to grieve, and to support the war effort.

Industrialization and economic enterprises grew exponentially in tandem with the war. Ordinary citizens found that their futures were increasingly tied to huge organizations. The character and extent of government power, too, changed markedly. Under Republican leadership, the federal government expanded its power not only to preserve the Union but also to extend freedom. A social revolution and government authority emancipated the slaves. A republic desperately divided against itself had survived, but in new constitutional forms yet to take shape during Reconstruction.

It was unclear at the end of the war how or whether the nation would use its power to protect the rights of the former slaves. Secession was dead, but whether Americans would continue to embrace a centralized nationalism remained to be seen. The war ended decisively after tremendous sacrifice, but it left many unanswered questions: How would white southerners, embittered and impoverished, respond to efforts to reconstruct the nation? How would the country care for the maimed, the orphans, the farming women without men to work their land, and all the dead who had to be found and properly buried? What would be the place of black men and women in American life? How would Americans struggle over the memory of this, their most divisive experience in the decades ahead?

In the West, two civil wars had raged: one between Union and Confederate forces and the other resulting in a conquest of southwestern Native peoples by U.S. troops and land-hungry settlers. On the diplomatic front, the Union government had delicately managed to keep Great Britain and other foreign powers out of the war. Dissent flourished in both North and South, playing a crucial role in the ultimate collapse of the Confederacy.

In the Civil War, Americans had undergone an epic of destruction and survival—a transformation like nothing else in their history. White southerners had experienced defeat that few other Americans would ever face. Blacks were moving proudly but anxiously through great hardship from slavery to freedom. White northerners were, by and large, self-conscious victors in a massive war for the nation's existence and for new definitions of freedom. The war, with all of its drama, sacrifice, and social and political change, would leave a compelling memory in American hearts and minds for generations.

Suggestions for Further Reading

Stephen V. Ash, *When the Yankees Came: Conflict and Chaos in the Occupied South* (1995)

Edward L. Ayers, *In the Presence of Mine Enemies: War in the Heart of America, 1859–1863* (2002)

Ira Berlin et al., eds., *Freedom: A Documentary History of Emancipation, 1861–1867,* 3 vols. (1979–1982)

David W. Blight, *Race and Reunion: The Civil War in American Memory* (2001)

Alice Fahs, *The Imagined Civil War: Popular Literature of the North and South* (2001)

Drew G. Faust, *This Republic of Suffering: Death and the American Civil War* (2008)

Gary W. Gallagher, *The Confederate War* (1997)

J. David Hacker, "A Census-Based Count of the Civil War Dead," *Civil War History,* (Dec. 2011).

Chandra Manning, *What This Cruel War Was Over: Soldiers, Slavery, and the Civil War* (2007)

James M. McPherson, *Battle Cry of Freedom: The Civil War Era* (1987)

Philip S. Paludan, *"A People's Contest": The Union and the Civil War* (1989)

Mark R. Wilson, *The Business of Civil War: Military Mobilization and the State, 1861–1865* (2006)

MindTap® is a fully online personalized learning experience built upon Cengage Learning content. MindTap® combines student learning tools—readings, multimedia, activities, and assessments—into a singular Learning Path that guides students through the course and helps students develop the critical thinking, analysis, and communication skills that are essential to academic and professional success.

MINDTAP
From Cengage

Reconstruction: An Unfinished Revolution, 1865–1877

he lower half of the city of Charleston, South Carolina, the seedbed of secession, lay in ruin when most of the white population evacuated on February 18, 1865. A bombardment by Union batteries and gunboats around Charleston harbor had already destroyed many of the lovely, neoclassical townhomes of the low-country planters. Then, as the city was abandoned, fires broke out everywhere, ignited in bales of cotton left in huge stockpiles in public squares. To many observers, the flames were the funeral pyres of a dying civilization.

Among the first Union troops to enter Charleston was the Twenty-first U.S. Colored Regiment, which received the surrender of the city from its mayor. For black Charlestonians, most of whom were former slaves, this was a time of celebration. In symbolic ceremonies, they proclaimed their freedom and announced their rebirth. Whatever the postwar order would bring, the freedpeople of Charleston converted Confederate ruin into a vision of Reconstruction based on Union victory and black liberation.

Still, in Charleston as elsewhere, death demanded attention. During the final year of the war, the Confederates had converted the planters' Race Course, a horse-racing track, and its famed Washington Jockey Club, into a prison. Union soldiers were kept in terrible conditions in the interior of the track, without shelter. The 257 who died there of exposure and disease were buried in a mass grave behind the grandstand. After the fall of the city, Charleston's black people organized to create a proper burial ground for the Union dead. During April,

◁ Photograph of the grandstand and clubhouse of the Washington Jockey Club and Race Course, Charleston, SC, site of Confederate prison and burial ground of more than 260 Union soldiers, as well as the first commemoration of Decoration Day, May 1, 1865. Library of Congress, Prints & Photographs Division [LC-DIG-stereo-1s02451]

Chronology

1865	▪ Johnson begins rapid and lenient Reconstruction
	▪ White southern governments pass restrictive black codes
	▪ Congress refuses to seat southern representatives
	▪ Thirteenth Amendment ratified, abolishing slavery
1866	▪ Congress passes Civil Rights Act and renewal of Freedmen's Bureau over Johnson's veto
	▪ Congress approves Fourteenth Amendment
	▪ In *Ex parte Milligan*, the Supreme Court reasserts its influence
1867	▪ Congress passes First Reconstruction Act and Tenure of Office Act
	▪ Constitutional conventions called in southern states
1868	▪ House impeaches and Senate acquits Johnson
	▪ Most southern states readmitted to Union under Radical plan
	▪ Fourteenth Amendment ratified
	▪ Grant elected president
1869	▪ Congress approves Fifteenth Amendment (ratified in 1870)
	▪ Sharecropping takes hold across a cash-poor southern economy
1871	▪ Congress passes second Enforcement Act and Ku Klux Klan Act
	▪ Treaty with England settles *Alabama* claims
1872	▪ Amnesty Act frees almost all remaining Confederates from restrictions on holding office
	▪ Grant reelected
1873	▪ Slaughter-House cases limit power of Fourteenth Amendment
	▪ Panic of 1873 leads to widespread unemployment and labor strife
1874	▪ Democrats win majority in House of Representatives
1875	▪ Several Grant appointees indicted for corruption
	▪ Congress passes weak Civil Rights Act
	▪ Democratic Party increases control of southern states with white supremacy campaigns
1876	▪ *U.S. v. Cruikshank* further weakens Fourteenth Amendment
	▪ Presidential election disputed
1877	▪ Congress elects Hayes president

more than twenty black workmen reinterred the dead in marked graves and built a high fence around the cemetery. On the archway over the cemetery's entrance they painted the inscription "Martyrs of the Race Course."

And then they planned an extraordinary ceremony. On the morning of May 1, 1865, a procession of ten thousand people marched around the planters' Race Course, led by three thousand children carrying armloads of roses and singing "John Brown's Body." The children were followed by black women with baskets of flowers and wreaths, and then by black men. The parade concluded with members

of black and white Union regiments, along with white missionaries and teachers led by James Redpath, the supervisor of freedmen's schools in the region. All who could fit assembled at the gravesite; five black ministers read from scripture, and a black children's choir sang "America," "We'll Rally 'Round the Flag," "The Star-Spangled Banner," and Negro spirituals. When the ceremony ended, the huge crowd retired to the Race Course for speeches, picnics, and military festivities.

Experience an interactive version of this story in MindTap®.

The war was over in Charleston, and "Decoration Day"—now Memorial Day, the day to remember the war dead and decorate their graves with flowers—had been founded by African Americans and their allies. Black people—by their labor, their words, their songs, and their marching feet on the old planters' Race Course—had created an American tradition. In their vision, they were creating the Independence Day of a Second American Revolution.

Reconstruction would bring revolutionary circumstances, but revolutions can also go backward. The Civil War and its aftermath wrought unprecedented changes in American society, law, and politics, but the underlying realities of economic power, racism, and judicial conservatism limited Reconstruction's revolutionary potential. As never before, the nation had to determine the nature of federal-state relations, whether confiscated land could be redistributed, and how to bring justice to both freedpeople and aggrieved white southerners whose property and lives had been devastated. Americans were about to try to redefine citizenship, fundamental civil and political rights, and equality before law against unrelenting opposition. A disunited country faced the harrowing challenge of psychological healing from a bloody and fratricidal war. How they would negotiate the tangled relationship between healing and justice would determine the fate of Reconstruction.

Nowhere was the turmoil of Reconstruction more evident than in national politics. Lincoln's successor, Andrew Johnson, fought bitterly with Congress over the shaping of Reconstruction policies. Although a southerner, Johnson had always been a foe of the South's wealthy planters, and his first acts as president suggested that he would be tough on "traitors." Before the end of 1865, however, Johnson's policies changed direction, and he became the protector of white southern interests.

Johnson imagined a lenient and rapid "restoration" of the South to the Union rather than the fundamental "reconstruction" that Republican congressmen favored. Between 1866 and 1868, the president and the Republican leadership in Congress engaged in a bitter power struggle over how to put the United States back together again. Before the struggle ceased, Congress had impeached the president, enfranchised freedmen, and given them a role in reconstructing the South. The nation also adopted the Fourteenth and Fifteenth Amendments, ushering in equal protection of the law, a definition of birthright citizenship, and universal manhood suffrage into the Constitution.

By 1868–1869, the Ku Klux Klan employed extensive violence and terror to thwart Reconstruction and undermine black freedom. As white Democrats in the South took control of state governments in the 1870s, they encountered little opposition from the North. Moreover, the wartime industrial boom had created new opportunities and priorities. The West, with its seemingly limitless potential and its wars against Native peoples, drew American resources and consciousness like never before. Americans moved in huge numbers and sought new "homes" in the trans-Mississippi West and the homes of Native Americans were displaced or destroyed. Political corruption became a nationwide scandal, and bribery a way of doing business.

Thus, Reconstruction became a revolution eclipsed. The white South's desire to reclaim control of its states and of race relations overwhelmed the national interest in stopping it. But Reconstruction left enduring legacies from which the nation has benefited and with which it has struggled ever since. In every succeeding racial or constitutional reckoning, we often return to Reconstruction as a means of understanding ourselves anew.

- Should the Reconstruction era be considered the Second American Revolution? By what criteria should we make such a judgment?

- What were the origins and meanings of the Fourteenth Amendment in the 1860s? What is its significance today?

- Reconstruction is judged to have "ended" in 1877. Over the course of the 1870s, what caused its end?

14-1 Wartime Reconstruction

▷ **What were the features of Abraham Lincoln's vision for Reconstruction?**

▷ **Why did Abraham Lincoln and Congress differ over Reconstruction policy?**

▷ **How did the creation and operation of the Freedman's Bureau signify a new expansive role for the federal government in society?**

Civil wars leave immense challenges of healing, justice, and physical rebuilding. Anticipating that process, reconstruction of the Union was an issue as early as 1863, well before the war ended. Many key questions loomed on the horizon when and if the North succeeded on the battlefield: How would the nation be restored? How would southern states and leaders be treated—as errant brothers or as traitors? How would a devastated southern economy be revived? What was the constitutional basis for readmission of states to the Union, and where, if anywhere, could American statesmen look for precedence or guidance? As winners of the war, could radical Republicans take their emancipation and human equality agenda abroad and spread it to foreign lands? More specifically, four vexing problems compelled early thinking and would haunt the Reconstruction era throughout. One, who would rule in the South once it was defeated? Two, who would rule in the federal government—Congress or the president? Three, what were the dimensions of black freedom, and what rights under law would the freedmen enjoy? And four, would Reconstruction be a preservation of the old republic or a second Revolution, a reinvention of a new republic?

14-1a Lincoln's 10 Percent Plan

Abraham Lincoln had never been antisouthern, though he had become the leader of an antislavery war. He lost three brothers-in-law, killed in the war on the Confederate side. His worst fear was that the war would collapse at the end into guerrilla warfare across the South, with surviving bands of Confederates carrying on resistance. Lincoln insisted that his generals give lenient terms to southern soldiers once they surrendered. In his Second Inaugural Address, delivered only a month before his assassination, Lincoln promised "malice toward none; with charity for all," as Americans strove to "bind up the nation's wounds."

Lincoln planned early for a swift and moderate Reconstruction process. In his "Proclamation of Amnesty and Reconstruction," issued in December 1863, he proposed to replace majority rule with "loyal rule" as a means of reconstructing southern state governments. He proposed pardons to all ex-Confederates except the highest-ranking military and civilian officers. Then, as soon as 10 percent of the voting population in the 1860 general election in a given state had taken an oath to the United States and established a government, the new state would be recognized. Lincoln did not consult Congress in these plans, and "loyal" assemblies (known as "Lincoln governments") were created in Louisiana, Tennessee, and Arkansas in 1864, states largely occupied by Union troops. These governments were weak and dependent on northern armies for survival.

14-1b Congress and the Wade-Davis Bill

Congress responded with great hostility to Lincoln's moves to readmit southern states in what seemed such a premature manner. Many Radical Republicans, strong proponents of emancipation and of aggressive prosecution of the war against the South, considered the 10 percent plan a "mere mockery" of democracy. Led by Thaddeus Stevens of Pennsylvania in the House and Charles Sumner of Massachusetts

Thirteenth Amendment The constitutional amendment that abolished slavery; passed by Congress in 1865.

in the Senate, congressional Republicans locked horns with Lincoln and proposed a longer and harsher approach to Reconstruction. Stevens advocated a "conquered provinces" theory, arguing that southerners had organized as a foreign nation to make war on the United States and, by secession, had destroyed their status as states. They therefore must be treated as "conquered foreign lands" and returned to the status of "unorganized territories" before any process of readmission could be entertained by Congress.

In July 1864, the Wade-Davis bill, named for its sponsors, Senator Benjamin Wade of Ohio and Congressman Henry W. Davis of Maryland, emerged from Congress with three specific conditions for southern readmission.

1. It demanded a "majority" of white male citizens participate in the creation of a new government.
2. To vote or be a delegate to constitutional conventions, men had to take an "iron-clad" oath (declaring that they had never aided the Confederate war effort).
3. All officers above the rank of lieutenant and all civil officials in the Confederacy would be disfranchised and deemed "not a citizen of the United States."

The Confederate states were to be defined as "conquered enemies," said Davis, and the process of readmission was to be harsh and slow. Lincoln, ever the adroit politician, pocket-vetoed the bill and issued a conciliatory proclamation of his own, announcing that he would not be inflexibly committed to any "one plan" of Reconstruction.

This exchange came during Grant's bloody campaign against Lee in Virginia, when the outcome of the war and Lincoln's reelection were still in doubt. On August 5, Radical Republicans issued the "Wade-Davis Manifesto" to newspapers. An unprecedented attack on a sitting president by members of his own party, it accused Lincoln of usurpation of presidential powers and disgraceful leniency toward an eventually conquered South. What emerged in 1864–1865 was a clear debate and a potential constitutional crisis. Lincoln saw Reconstruction as a means of weakening the Confederacy and winning the war; the Radicals saw it as a longer-term transformation of the political and racial order of the country.

14-1c Thirteenth Amendment

In early 1865, Congress and Lincoln joined in two important measures that recognized slavery's centrality to the war. On January 31, with strong administration backing, Congress passed the **Thirteenth Amendment**, which had two provisions: first, it abolished involuntary servitude everywhere in the United States; second, it declared that Congress shall have the power to enforce this outcome by "appropriate legislation." When the measure passed by 119 to 56, a mere two votes more than the necessary two-thirds, rejoicing broke out in Congress. A Republican recorded in his diary, "Members joined in the shouting and kept it up for some minutes. Some embraced one another, others wept like children. I have felt ever since the vote, as if I were in a new country."

But the Thirteenth Amendment had emerged from a long congressional debate and considerable petitioning and public advocacy. One of the first and most remarkable petitions for a constitutional amendment abolishing slavery was submitted early in 1864 by Elizabeth Cady Stanton, Susan B. Anthony, and the Women's Loyal National League. Women throughout the Union accumulated thousands of signatures, even venturing into staunchly pro-Confederate regions of Kentucky and Missouri to secure supporters. It was a long road from the Emancipation Proclamation to the Thirteenth Amendment—through treacherous constitutional theory about individual "property rights," a bedrock of belief that the sacred document ought never to be altered, and partisan politics. There had not been a Constitutional amendment since 1789, when the Twelfth Amendment established what we today call the Electoral College. But the logic of winning the war by crushing slavery, and of securing a new beginning under law for the nation that so many had died to save, won the day.

14-1d Freedmen's Bureau

Potentially as significant, on March 3, 1865, Congress created the Bureau of Refugees, Freedmen, and Abandoned Lands—the Freedmen's Bureau, an unprecedented agency of social uplift necessitated by the ravages of the war. Americans had never engaged in federal aid to citizens on such a scale. With thousands of refugees, white and black, displaced in the South, the government continued what private freedmen's aid societies had started as early as 1862. In the mere four years of its existence, the Freedmen's Bureau supplied food and medical services, built several thousand schools and some colleges, negotiated several hundred thousand employment contracts between freedpeople and their former masters, and tried to manage confiscated land.

Throughout its existence—it lasted until 1872, when Congress refused to approve renewal legislation—the Bureau remained controversial within the South, where whites generally hated it, and within the federal government, where politicians divided over its constitutionality. Some bureau agents were devoted to freedmen's rights, whereas others were opportunists who exploited the chaos of the postwar South. The war had forced into the open an eternal question of republics: what are the social welfare obligations of the state toward its people, and what do people owe their governments in return? Apart from their conquest and displacement of eastern Native peoples, Americans were relatively inexperienced at the Freedmen's Bureau's task—social reform through military occupation. They were also unaccustomed to the sheer reality that *government* possessed the only resources and institutions capable of confronting the social and economic chaos wrought by the war. Military occupation of significant parts of the South lasted into the late 1860s, but Americans had little experience with this kind of federal power.

14-1e Ruins and Enmity

In 1865, due to the devastation of the war, America was now a land with ruins. Like the countries of Europe, it now seemed an older, more historic landscape. Physically, politically, and spiritually, it had torn itself asunder. Some of its cities lay in rubble, large stretches of the southern countryside were depopulated and defoliated, and thousands of people, white and black, were refugees. Some of this would in time seem romantic to northern travelers in the postwar South.

Thousands of yeoman farmer-soldiers, some paroled by surrenders, walked home too late in the season to plant a crop in a collapsed economy. Many white refugees faced genuine starvation. Of the approximately 18,300,000 rations distributed across the South in the first three years of the Freedmen's Bureau, 5,230,000 went to whites. In early 1866, in a proud agricultural society, the legislature of South Carolina issued $300,000 in state bonds to purchase corn for the destitute.

In October 1865, just after a five-month imprisonment in Boston, former Confederate vice president Alexander H. Stephens rode a slow train southward. In Virginia, he found "the desolation of the country . . . was horrible to behold." When Stephens reached northern Georgia, his native state, his shock ran over: "War has left a terrible impression. . . . Fences gone, fields all a-waste, houses burnt." A northern journalist visiting Richmond that same fall observed a city "mourning for her sins . . . in dust and ashes." The "burnt district" was a "bed of cinders . . . broken and blackened walls, impassable streets deluged with debris." Above all, every northern traveler encountered a wall of hatred among white southerners for their conquerors. An innkeeper in North Carolina told a journalist that Yankees had killed his sons in the war, burned his house, and stolen his slaves. "They left me one inestimable privilege," he said, "to hate 'em. I git up at half-past four in the morning, and sit up 'til twelve at night, to hate 'em."

14-2 The Meanings of Freedom

▷ How did African Americans respond to and explore their new freedom after the war?

▷ What challenges did freedpeople face in obtaining land?

▷ How did education for freedpeople develop after the war?

▷ How did sharecropping affect freedpeople's desire to be economically independent?

Black southerners entered into life after slavery with hope and circumspection. A Texas man recalled his father telling him, even before the war was over, "Our forever was going to be spent living among the Southerners, after they got licked." Freed men and women tried to gain as much as they could from their new circumstances. Often the changes they valued the most were personal—alterations in location, employer, or living arrangements.

14-2a The Feel of Freedom

For America's former slaves, Reconstruction had one paramount meaning: a chance to explore freedom. A southern white woman admitted in her diary that the black people "showed a natural and exultant joy at being free." Former slaves remembered singing far into the night after federal troops, who confirmed rumors of their emancipation, reached their plantations. The slaves on a Texas plantation shouted for joy, their leader proclaiming, "We is free—no more whippings and beatings." A few people gave in to the natural desire to do what had been impossible before. One angry grandmother dropped her hoe and ran to confront her mistress. "I'm free!" she yelled. "Yes, I'm free! Ain't got to work for you no more! You can't put me in your pocket now!" Another man recalled that he and others "started on the move," either to search for family members or just to exercise the human right of mobility.

Many freed men and women reacted more cautiously and shrewdly, taking care to test the boundaries of their new condition. "After the war was over," explained one man, "we was afraid to move. Just like terrapins or turtles after emancipation. Just stick our heads out to see how the land lay." As slaves, they had learned to expect hostility from white people, and they did not presume it would instantly disappear. Life in freedom might still be a matter of what was possible, not what was right. Many freedpeople evaluated potential employers with shrewd caution. "Most all the Negroes that had good owners stayed with 'em, but the others left. Some of 'em come back and some didn't," explained one man. After considerable wandering in search of better circumstances, a majority of blacks eventually settled as agricultural workers back on their former farms or plantations. They often relocated their houses and did their utmost to control the conditions of their labor.

14-2b Reunion of African American Families

Throughout the South, former slaves devoted themselves to reuniting their families, separated during slavery by sale or hardship, and during the war by dislocation and the emancipation process. With only shreds of information to guide them, thousands of freedpeople embarked on odysseys in search of a husband, wife, child, or parent. By relying on the black community for help and information, and by placing ads that continued to appear in black newspapers such as the *Christian Recorder*, a national journal published by the African Methodist Episcopal Church, well into the 1880s, some succeeded in their quest, while others searched in vain.

Husbands and wives who had belonged to different masters established homes together for the first time, and, as they had tried under slavery, parents asserted the right to raise their own children. A mother bristled when her old master claimed a right to whip her children. She informed him that "he warn't goin' to brush none of her chilluns no more." The

freed men and women were too much at risk to act recklessly, but, as one man put it, they were tired of punishment and "sure didn't take no more foolishness off of white folks."

14-2c African Americans' Search for Independence

Many black people wanted to minimize contact with whites because, as Reverend Garrison Frazier told General Sherman in January 1865, "There is a prejudice against us ... that will take years to get over." To avoid contact with overbearing whites who were used to supervising them, blacks abandoned the slave quarters and fanned out to distant corners of the land they worked. "After the war my stepfather come," recalled Annie Young, "and got my mother and we moved out in the piney woods." Others described moving "across the creek" or building a "saplin house . . . back in the woods." Some rural dwellers established small, all-black settlements that still exist along the back roads of the South.

Even once-privileged slaves desired such independence and social separation. One man turned down his master's offer of the overseer's house and moved instead to a shack in "Freetown." He also declined to let the former owner grind his grain for free because it "make him feel like a free man to pay for things just like anyone else."

14-2d Freedpeople's Desire for Land

In addition to a fair employer, what freed men and women most wanted was the ownership of land. Land represented self-sufficiency and a chance to gain compensation for generations of bondage. General Sherman's special Field Order Number 15, issued in February 1865, set aside 400,000 acres of land in the Sea Islands region for the exclusive settlement of freedpeople. Hope swelled among ex-slaves as forty-acre plots, mules, and "possessary titles" were promised to them. But President Johnson ordered them removed in October and the land returned to its original owners under army enforcement. A northern observer noted that slaves freed in the Sea Islands of South Carolina and Georgia made "plain, straightforward" inquiries as they settled on new land. They wanted to be sure the land "would be theirs after they had improved it." Everywhere, black people young and old thirsted for homes of their own.

But most members of both political parties opposed genuine land redistribution to the freedmen. Even northern reformers who had administered the Sea Islands during the war showed little sympathy for black aspirations. The former Sea Island slaves wanted to establish small, self-sufficient farms. Northern soldiers, officials, and missionaries of both races brought education and aid to the freedmen but also insisted that they grow cotton for the competitive market.

"The Yankees preach nothing but cotton, cotton!" complained one Sea Island black. "We wants land," wrote another, but tax officials "make the lots too big, and cut we out." Indeed, the U.S. government eventually sold thousands of acres in the Sea Islands, 90 percent of which went to wealthy investors from the North. At a protest against evictions from a contraband camp in Virginia in 1866, freedman Bayley Wyatt made black desires and claims clear: "We has a right to the land where we are located. For why? I tell you. Our wives, our children, our husbands, has been sold over and over again to purchase the lands we now locates upon; for that reason we have a divine right to the land."

14-2e Freed Men and Women Embrace Education

Ex-slaves everywhere reached out for education. Black people of all ages hungered for the knowledge in books that had been permitted only to white people. With freedom, they started schools and filled classrooms both day and night. On log seats and dirt floors, freed men and women studied their letters in old almanacs and in discarded dictionaries. Young children brought infants to school with them, and adults attended at night or after "the crops were laid by." Many a teacher had "to make herself heard over three other classes reciting in concert" in a small room. The desire to escape slavery's ignorance was so great that, despite their poverty, many blacks paid tuition, typically $1 or $1.50 a month. These small amounts constituted major portions of a person's agricultural wages and added up to more than $1 million by 1870.

The federal government and northern reformers of both races assisted this pursuit of education. In its brief life, the Freedmen's Bureau founded over four thousand schools, and idealistic men and women from the North established others funded by private philanthropy. The Yankee schoolmarm—dedicated, selfless, and religious—became an agent of progress in many southern communities. Thus did African Americans seek a break from their past through learning. More than 600,000 were enrolled in elementary school by 1877. In a rural agricultural society recovering from wartime devastation, this was a stunning achievement.

Black people and their white allies also saw the need for colleges and universities. The American Missionary Association founded seven colleges, including Fisk University and Atlanta University, between 1866 and 1869. The Freedmen's Bureau helped to establish Howard University in Washington, D.C., and northern religious groups, such as the Methodists, Baptists, and Congregationalists, supported dozens of seminaries and teachers' colleges.

During Reconstruction, African American leaders often were highly educated individuals; many were from the prewar elite of free people of color. Francis Cardozo, who held various offices in South Carolina, had attended universities in Scotland and England. P. B. S. Pinchback, who became lieutenant governor of Louisiana, was the son of a planter who had sent him to school in Cincinnati. Both of the two black senators from Mississippi, Blanche K. Bruce and Hiram Revels, possessed privileged educations. Bruce was the son of a planter who had provided tutoring at home; Revels was the son of free black North Carolinians who had sent him to Knox College in Illinois.

14-2f Growth of Black Churches

Freed from the restrictions and regulations of slavery, African Americans could build their own institutions as they saw fit. The secret churches of slavery came into the open; in countless communities throughout the South, ex-slaves "started a brush arbor." A brush arbor was merely "a sort of . . . shelter with leaves for a roof," but the freed men and women worshipped in it enthusiastically. "Preachin' and shouting sometimes lasted all day," they recalled, for the opportunity to worship together freely meant "glorious times."

Within a few years, independent branches of the Methodist and Baptist denominations had attracted the great majority of black Christians in the South. By 1877, in South Carolina alone, the African Methodist Episcopal (AME) Church had a thousand ministers, 44,000 members, and its own school of theology, while the AME Zion Church had 45,000 members. In the rapid growth of churches, some of which became the wealthiest and most autonomous institutions in black life, the freedpeople demonstrated their most secure claim on freedom.

Photo by Rudolf Eickemeyer. Division of Culture & the Arts, National Museum of American History, Behring Center, Smithsonian Institution.

△ African Americans of all ages eagerly pursued the opportunity to gain an education in freedom. This young woman in Mt. Meigs, Alabama, is helping her mother learn to read.

◁ Churches became a center of African American life, both social and political, during and after Reconstruction. Churches large and small, like this one in Georgia became the first black-owned institutions for the postfreedom generation.

Library of Congress, Prints & Photographs Division, Reproduction number LC-US262-114267 (b&w film copy neg.)

14-2g Rise of the Sharecropping System

The desire to gain as much independence as possible also shaped the former slaves' economic arrangements. Since most of them lacked money to buy land, they preferred the next best thing: renting the land they worked. But the South had a cash-poor economy with few sources of credit, and few whites would consider renting land to blacks. Most blacks had no means to get cash before the harvest, so other alternatives had to be tried.

Black farmers and white landowners therefore turned to **sharecropping,** a system in which farmers kept part of their crop and gave the rest to the landowner while living on his property. The landlord or a merchant "furnished" food and supplies, such as draft animals and seed, and he received payment from the crop. White landowners and black farmers bargained with one another; sharecroppers would hold out, or move and try to switch employers from one year to another. As the system matured during the 1870s and 1880s, most sharecroppers worked "on halves"—half for the owner and half for themselves.

sharecropping The system of tenant farming that replaced slavery; freedpeople "worked on halves," giving half of their crop to the landowner and taking half to market. The system left most freedpeople mired in debt with no social or geographic mobility.

The sharecropping system, which materialized as early as 1868 in parts of the South, originated as a desirable compromise between former slaves and landowners. It eased landowners' problems with cash and credit, and provided them a permanent, dependent labor force; blacks accepted it because it gave them freedom from daily supervision. In some districts women could leave field work, or even bargain for themselves to do less physical labor. Instead of working in the hated gangs under a white overseer, as in slavery, they farmed their own plots of land in family groups. But sharecropping later proved to be a disaster. Owners and merchants developed a monopoly of control over the agricultural economy, as sharecroppers found themselves mired in ever-increasing debt.

The fundamental problem, however, was that southern farmers as a whole still concentrated on cotton. In freedom, black women often chose to stay away from the fields and cotton picking to concentrate on domestic chores. Given the diminishing incentives of the system, they placed greater value on independent choices about gender roles and family organization than on reaching higher levels of production. The South did recover its prewar share of British cotton purchases, but cotton prices began a long decline, as world demand fell off.

Thus, southern agriculture slipped deeper and deeper into depression. Black sharecroppers struggled under a growing burden of debt that bound them to landowners and to "furnishing" merchants almost as oppressively as slavery had bound them to their masters. Many white farmers became debtors, too, gradually lost their land, and joined the ranks of sharecroppers. By the end of Reconstruction, over one-third of all southern farms were worked by sharecropping tenants, white and black.

Sharecropping: Enslaved to Debt

Sharecropping became an oppressive system in the postwar South. A new labor structure that began as a compromise between freedpeople who wanted independence and landowners who wanted a stable workforce evolved into a method of working on "halves," where tenants owed endless debts to the furnishing merchants, who owned plantation stores like this one, photographed in Mississippi in 1868. Merchants recorded in ledger books the debts that few sharecroppers were able to repay.

CRITICAL THINKING

◻ Why did both former slaves and former slave owners initially find sharecropping an agreeable, if difficult, new labor arrangement?

◻ What were the short- and long-term consequences of the sharecropping system for the freedpeople and for the southern economy?

◁ This Mississippi plantation store, shown in 1868, is a typical example of the new institution of the furnishing merchant and its power over postslavery agriculture in the South.

The Amistad Center of Art & Culture

◁ African Americans stand beside a log cabin home in Savannah, GA, c. 1867–1890.

Library of Congress, Prints & Photographs Division [LC-DIG-ppmsca-39591]

14-3 Johnson's Reconstruction Plan

▷ **How did Andrew Johnson's political beliefs and personal background shape his views of former Confederates and freedpeople?**

▷ **What Reconstruction policies did Johnson enact?**

▷ **How did Johnson's Reconstruction policies affect freedpeople?**

When Reconstruction began under President Andrew Johnson, many expected his policies to be harsh. Throughout his career in Tennessee, he had criticized the wealthy planters and championed the small farmers. When an assassin's bullet thrust Johnson into the presidency, many former slave owners shared the dismay of a North Carolina woman who wrote, "Think of Andy Johnson [as] the president! What will become of us—'the aristocrats of the South' as we are termed?" Northern Radicals also had reason to believe that Johnson would deal sternly with the South. When one of them suggested the exile or execution of ten or twelve leading rebels to set an example, Johnson replied, "How are you going to pick out so small a number? . . . Treason is a crime; and crime must be punished."

14-3a Andrew Johnson of Tennessee

Like his martyred predecessor, Johnson followed a path in antebellum politics from obscurity to power. With no formal education, he became a tailor's apprentice. But from 1829, while in his early twenties, he held nearly every office in Tennessee politics: alderman, state representative, congressman, two terms as governor, and U.S. senator by 1857. Although elected as a southern Democrat, Johnson was the only senator from a seceded state who refused to follow his state out of the Union. Lincoln appointed him war governor of Tennessee in 1862; hence his symbolic place on the ticket in the president's bid for reelection in 1864.

Although a Unionist, Johnson's political beliefs made him an old Jacksonian Democrat. And as they said in the mountainous region of east Tennessee, where Johnson established a reputation as a stump speaker, "Old Andy never went back on his raisin'." Johnson was also an ardent states' rightist. Before the war, he had supported tax-funded public schools and homestead legislation, fashioning himself as a champion of the common man. Although he vehemently opposed secession, Johnson advocated limited government. He shared none of the Radicals' expansive conception of federal power. His philosophy toward Reconstruction may be summed up in the slogan he adopted: "The Constitution as it is, and the Union as it was."

Through most of 1865, Johnson alone controlled Reconstruction policy, for Congress recessed shortly before he became president and did not reconvene until December. In the following eight months, Johnson formed new state governments in the South by using his power to grant pardons. He advanced Lincoln's leniency by extending even easier terms to former Confederates.

14-3b Johnson's Racial Views

Johnson had owned house slaves, although he had never been a planter. He accepted emancipation as a result of the war, but he did not favor black civil and political rights. Johnson believed that black suffrage could never be imposed on a southern state by the federal government, and that set him on a collision course with the Radicals. When it came to race, Johnson was a thoroughgoing white supremacist. He held what one politician called "unconquerable prejudices against the African race." In perhaps the most blatantly racist official statement ever delivered by an American president, Johnson declared in his annual message of 1867 that blacks possessed "less capacity for government than any other race of people. No independent government of any form has ever been successful in their hands; . . . wherever they have been left to their own devices they have shown a constant tendency to relapse into barbarism."

Such racial views had an enduring effect on Johnson's policies. Where whites were concerned, however, Johnson seemed to be pursuing changes in class relations. He proposed rules that would keep the wealthy planter class at least temporarily out of power.

△ Combative and inflexible, President Andrew Johnson contributed greatly to the failure of his own Reconstruction program.

14-3c Johnson's Pardon Policy

White southerners were required to swear an oath of loyalty as a condition of gaining amnesty or pardon, but Johnson barred several categories of people from taking the oath: former federal officials, high-ranking Confederate officers, and political leaders or graduates of West Point or Annapolis who joined the Confederacy. To this list, Johnson added another important group: all ex-Confederates whose taxable property was worth more than $20,000. These individuals had to apply personally to the president for pardon and restoration of their political rights. The president, it seemed, meant to take revenge on the old planter elite.

Johnson appointed provisional governors, who began the Reconstruction process by calling state constitutional conventions. The delegates chosen for these conventions had to draft new constitutions that eliminated slavery and invalidated secession. After ratification of these constitutions, new governments could be elected, and the states would be restored to the Union with full congressional representation. But only those southerners who had taken the oath of amnesty and had been eligible to vote on the day the state seceded could participate in this process. Thus unpardoned whites and former slaves were not eligible.

14-3d Presidential Reconstruction

If Johnson intended to strip former aristocrats of their power, he did not hold to his plan. The old white leadership proved resilient and influential; prominent Confederates won elections and turned up in various appointive offices. Then Johnson started pardoning planters and leading rebels. He hired additional clerks to prepare the necessary documents and then began to issue pardons to large categories of people. By September 1865, hundreds were issued in a single day. These pardons, plus the rapid return of planters' abandoned lands, restored the old elite to power and quickly gave Johnson an image as the South's champion.

Why did Johnson allow the planters to regain power? He was determined to achieve a rapid Reconstruction in order to deny the Radicals any opportunity for the more thorough racial and political changes they desired in the South. And Johnson needed southern support in the 1866 elections; hence, he declared Reconstruction complete only eight months after Appomattox. Thus, in December 1865, many Confederate congressmen traveled to Washington to claim seats in the U.S. Congress. Even Alexander Stephens, vice president of the Confederacy, returned to Capitol Hill as a senator-elect from Georgia.

The election of such prominent rebels troubled many northerners. Some of the state conventions were slow to repudiate secession; others admitted only grudgingly that slavery was dead and wrote new laws to show it.

14-3e Black Codes

To define the status of freed men and women and control their labor, some legislatures merely revised large sections of the slave codes by substituting the word *freedmen* for *slaves*.

The new black codes compelled former slaves to carry passes, observe a curfew, live in housing provided by a landowner, and give up hope of entering many desirable occupations. Stiff vagrancy laws and restrictive labor contracts bound freedpeople to plantations, and "anti-enticement" laws punished anyone who tried to lure these workers to other employment. State-supported schools and orphanages excluded blacks entirely.

It seemed to some northerners that the South was intent on returning African Americans to servility and that Johnson's Reconstruction policy held no one responsible for the terrible war. But memories of the war—not yet even a year over—were still raw and would dominate political behavior for several elections to come. Thus, the Republican majority in Congress decided to call a halt to the results of Johnson's plan. On reconvening, the House and Senate considered the credentials of the newly elected southern representatives and decided not to admit them. Instead, they bluntly challenged the president's authority and established a joint committee to study and investigate a new direction for Reconstruction.

14-4 The Congressional Reconstruction Plan

- ▷ **What political divisions existed in Congress?**
- ▷ **How did the relationship between the president and Congress evolve in the postwar period?**
- ▷ **What was the significance of the Fourteenth and Fifteenth Amendments?**
- ▷ **How did Congress re-incorporate former Confederate states into the Union?**

Northern congressmen were hardly unified, but they did not doubt their right to shape Reconstruction policy. The Constitution mentioned neither secession nor reunion, but it gave Congress the primary role in the admission of states. Moreover, the Constitution declared that the United States shall guarantee to each state a "republican form of government." This provision, legislators believed, gave them the authority to devise policies for Reconstruction.

They soon faced other grave constitutional questions. What, for example, had rebellion done to the relationship between southern states and the Union? Lincoln had always believed secession impossible—the Confederate states had engaged in an "insurrection" within the Union in his view. Congressmen who favored vigorous Reconstruction measures argued that the war had broken the Union and that the South was subject to the victor's will. Moderate congressmen held that the states had forfeited their rights through rebellion and thus had come under congressional supervision.

14-4a The Radicals

These theories mirrored the diversity of Congress itself. Northern Democrats, weakened by their opposition to the war in its final year, denounced any idea of racial equality and supported Johnson's policies. Conservative Republicans, despite their party loyalty, favored a limited federal role in Reconstruction. The Radical Republicans, led by Thaddeus Stevens, Charles Sumner, and George Julian, wanted to transform the South. Although a minority in their party, they had the advantage of clearly defined goals. They believed it was essential to democratize the South, establish public education, and ensure the rights of the freedpeople. They favored black suffrage, supported some land confiscation and redistribution, and were willing to exclude the South from the Union for several years if necessary to achieve their goals.

Born of the war and its outcome, the Radicals brought a new civic vision to American life; they wanted to create an activist federal government and the beginnings of racial equality. A large group of moderate Republicans, led by Lyman Trumbull, opposed Johnson's leniency but wanted to restrain the Radicals. Trumbull and the moderates were, however, committed to federalizing the enforcement of civil, if not political, rights for the freedmen.

One overwhelming political reality faced all four groups: the 1866 elections. Ironically, Johnson and the Democrats sabotaged the possibility of a conservative coalition. They refused to cooperate with moderate Republicans and insisted that Reconstruction was over, that the new state governments were legitimate, and that southern representatives should be admitted to Congress. Among the Republicans, the Radicals' influence grew in proportion to Johnson's intransigence and outright provocation. It is an old story in American politics: when compromise or coalition fails, more radical visions will fill the void. Sometimes this leads to great social change, but other times to crisis and disaster.

14-4b Congress Versus Johnson

Trying to work with Johnson, Republicans believed a compromise had been reached in the spring of 1866. Under its terms, Johnson would agree to two modifications of his program: extension of the Freedmen's Bureau for another year and passage of a civil rights bill to counteract the black codes. This bill would force southern courts to practice equality under the ultimate scrutiny of the federal judiciary. Its provisions applied to public, not private, acts of discrimination. The Civil Rights Bill of 1866 was the first statutory definition of the rights of American citizens and is still on the books today.

Johnson destroyed the compromise, however, by vetoing both bills (they later became law when Congress overrode the president's veto). Denouncing any change in his program, the president condemned Congress's action and revealed his own racism. Because the Civil Rights Bill defined U.S. citizens as native-born persons who were taxed, Johnson claimed it discriminated against "large numbers of intelligent, worthy, and patriotic

Fourteenth Amendment
Defined U.S. citizens as anyone born or naturalized in the United States, barred states from interfering with citizens' constitutional rights, and stated for the first time that voters must be male.

△ Photograph of Thaddeus Stevens, Republican Congressman and staunch abolitionist from Pennsylvania, and leader of the "radicals" during the creation of Reconstruction policies, 1866–68.

foreigners . . . in favor of the negro." Anticipating arguments used by modern conservatives, the bill, he said, operated "in favor of the colored and against the white race."

All hope of presidential-congressional cooperation was now dead. In 1866, newspapers reported daily violations of black peoples' rights in the South and carried alarming accounts of anti-black violence—notably in Memphis and New Orleans, where police aided brutal mobs in their attacks. In Memphis, forty blacks were killed and twelve schools burned by white mobs, and in New Orleans, the toll was thirty-four African Americans dead and two hundred wounded. Such violence convinced Republicans, and the northern public, that more needed to be done. A new Republican plan took the form of the **Fourteenth Amendment** to the Constitution.

14-4c Fourteenth Amendment

Of the five sections of the Fourteenth Amendment, the first would have the greatest legal significance in later years. Written by John Bingham of Ohio, it conferred citizenship on "all persons born or naturalized in the United States" and prohibited states from abridging their constitutional "privileges and immunities" (see the Appendix for the Constitution and all amendments). It also barred any state from taking a person's life, liberty, or property "without due process of law" and from denying "equal protection of the laws." These resounding phrases have become powerful guarantees of African

Americans' civil rights—indeed, of the rights of all citizens, except for Native Americans, who were not granted citizenship rights until 1924.

Nearly universal agreement emerged among Republicans on the amendment's second and third sections. The fourth declared the Confederate debt null and void, and guaranteed the war debt of the United States. Northerners rejected the notion of paying taxes to reimburse those who had financed a rebellion, and business groups agreed on the necessity of upholding the credit of the U.S. government, an element of the Fourteenth Amendment that was invoked in bitter debates between congressional Republicans and the Obama administration over raising the federal "debt ceiling" in 2011 and again in 2013. The second and third sections barred Confederate leaders from holding state and federal office. Only Congress, by a two-thirds vote of each house, could remove the penalty. The amendment thus guaranteed a degree of punishment for the leaders of the Confederacy.

The second section of the amendment also dealt with representation and embodied the compromises that produced the document. Northerners disagreed about whether black people should have the right to vote. As a citizen of Indiana wrote to a southern relative, "[a]lthough there is a great deal [of] profession among us for the relief of the darkey yet I think much of it is far from being cincere. I guess we want to compell you to do right by them while we are not willing ourselves to do so." Those arched words are indicative not only of how revolutionary Reconstruction had become, but also of how far the public will, North and South, lagged behind the enactments that became new constitutional cornerstones. Many northern states still maintained black disfranchisement laws during Reconstruction.

Emancipation finally ended the three-fifths clause for the purpose of counting blacks, which would increase southern representation. Thus, the postwar South stood to gain power in Congress, and if white southerners did not allow black southerners to vote, former secessionists would derive the political benefit from emancipation. That was more irony than most northerners could bear. So Republicans determined that, if a southern state did not grant black men the vote, their representation would be reduced proportionally. If they did enfranchise black men, their representation would be increased proportionally. This compromise avoided a direct enactment of black suffrage but would deliver future black southern voters to the Republican Party.

The Fourteenth Amendment specified for the first time that voters were "male" and ignored female citizens, black and white. For this reason, it provoked a strong reaction from the women's rights movement. Advocates of women's equality had worked with abolitionists for decades, often subordinating their cause to that of the slaves. During the drafting of the Fourteenth Amendment, however, female activists demanded to be heard. Prominent leaders, such as Elizabeth Cady Stanton and Susan B. Anthony, ended their alliance with abolitionists and fought for women,

while others remained committed to the idea that it was "the Negro's hour." Thus, the amendment infused new life into the women's rights movement and caused considerable strife among old allies.

14-4d The South's and Johnson's Defiance

In 1866, however, the major question in Reconstruction politics was how the public would respond to the congressional initiative. Johnson did his best to block the Fourteenth Amendment in both North and South. Condemning Congress for its refusal to seat southern representatives, the president urged state legislatures in the South to vote against ratification. Every southern legislature, except Tennessee's, rejected the amendment by a wide margin.

To present his case to northerners, Johnson organized a National Union Convention and took to the stump himself. In an age when active personal campaigning was rare for a president, Johnson boarded a special train for a "swing around the circle" that carried his message into the Northeast, the Midwest, and then back to Washington. In city after city, he criticized the Republicans in a ranting, undignified style. Increasingly, audiences rejected his views, hooting and jeering at him. In this whistle-stop tour, Johnson began to hand out American flags with thirty-six rather than twenty-five stars, declaring the Union already restored. At many towns, he likened himself to a "persecuted" Jesus who might now be martyred "upon the cross" for his magnanimity toward the South. And, repeatedly, he labeled the Radicals "traitors" for their efforts to take over Reconstruction.

The elections of 1866 were a resounding victory, though, for Republicans in Congress. Radicals and moderates whom Johnson had denounced won reelection by large margins, and the Republican majority grew to two-thirds of both houses of Congress. The North had spoken clearly: Johnson's official policies of states' rights and white supremacy were prematurely giving the advantage to former rebels and traitors. Thus, Republican congressional leaders won a mandate to pursue their Reconstruction plan.

But Johnson and southern intransigence had brought the plan to an impasse. Nothing could be accomplished as long as the "Johnson governments" existed and the southern electorate remained exclusively white. Republicans resolved to form new state governments in the South and enfranchise the freedmen.

14-4e Reconstruction Acts of 1867–1868

After some embittered debate in which Republicans and the remaining Democrats in Congress argued over the meaning and memory of the Civil War itself, the First Reconstruction Act passed in March 1867. This plan, under which the southern states were actually readmitted to the Union, incorporated only a part of the Radical program. Union generals, commanding small garrisons of troops and charged with supervising elections, assumed control in five military districts in the South (see Map 14.1). Confederate leaders designated in the Fourteenth Amendment were barred from voting until

Map 14.1 The Reconstruction Act of 1867

This map shows the five military districts established when Congress passed the Reconstruction Act of 1867. As the dates within each state indicate, conservative Democratic forces quickly regained control of government in four southern states. So-called Radical Reconstruction was curtailed in most of the others as factions within the weakened Republican Party began to cooperate with conservative Democrats.

new state constitutions were ratified. The act guaranteed freedmen the right to vote in elections as well as serve in state constitutional conventions and in subsequent elections. In addition, each southern state was required to ratify the Fourteenth Amendment, to approve its new constitution by majority vote, and to submit it to Congress for acceptance (see Table 14.1).

Thus, African Americans gained an opportunity to fight for a better life through the political process, and ex-Confederates were given what they interpreted as a bitter pill to swallow in order to return to the Union. The Second, Third, and Fourth Reconstruction Acts, passed between March 1867 and March 1868, provided the details of operation for voter registration boards, the adoption of constitutions, and the administration of "good faith" oaths on the part of white southerners.

14-4f Failure of Land Redistribution

In the words of one historian, the Radicals succeeded in "clipping Johnson's wings." But they had hoped Congress could do much more. Thaddeus Stevens, for example, argued that economic opportunity was essential to the freedmen. "If we do not furnish them with homesteads from forfeited and rebel property," Stevens declared, "and hedge them around with protective laws . . . we had better left them in bondage." Stevens therefore drew up a plan for extensive confiscation and redistribution of land, but it was never realized. Some historians see this as the great lost opportunity of Reconstruction.

Racial fears among whites and an American obsession with the sanctity of private property made land redistribution unpopular. Northerners were accustomed to a limited role for government, and the business community staunchly opposed any interference with private-property rights, even for former Confederates. Thus, black farmers were forced to seek work in a hostile environment in which landowners opposed their acquisition of land.

14-4g Constitutional Crisis

Congress's quarrels with Andrew Johnson grew still worse. To restrict Johnson's influence and safeguard its plan, Congress passed a number of controversial laws. First, it limited Johnson's power over the army by requiring the president to issue military orders through the General of the Army, Ulysses S. Grant, who could not be dismissed without the Senate's consent. Then Congress passed the Tenure of Office Act, which gave the Senate power to approve changes in the president's cabinet. Designed to protect Secretary of War Stanton, who sympathized with the Radicals, this law violated the tradition that a president controlled appointments to his own cabinet.

All of these measures, as well as each of the Reconstruction Acts, were passed by a two-thirds override of presidential vetoes. The situation led some to believe that the federal government had reached a stage of "congressional tyranny" and others to conclude that Johnson had become an obstacle to the legitimate will of the people in reconstructing the nation on a just and permanent basis.

Table 14.1 Plans for Reconstruction Compared

	Johnson's Plan	Radicals' Plan	Fourteenth Amendment	Reconstruction Act of 1867
Voting	Whites only; high-ranking Confederate leaders must seek pardons	Give vote to black males	Southern whites may decide but can lose representation if they deny black suffrage	Black men gain vote; whites barred from office by Fourteenth Amendment cannot vote while new state governments are being formed
Office holding	Many prominent Confederates regain power	Only loyal white and black males eligible	Confederate leaders barred until Congress votes amnesty	Fourteenth Amendment in effect
Time out of Union	Brief	Several years; until South is thoroughly democratized	Brief	3–5 years after war
Other change in southern society	Little; gain of power by yeomen not realized; emancipation grudgingly accepted, but no black civil or political rights	Expand education; confiscate land and provide farms for freedmen; expansion of activist federal government	Probably slight, depending on enforcement	Considerable, depending on action of new state governments

Johnson took several belligerent steps of his own. He issued orders to military commanders in the South, limiting their powers and increasing the powers of the civil governments he had created in 1865. Then he removed military officers who were conscientiously enforcing Congress's new law, preferring commanders who allowed disqualified Confederates to vote. Finally, he tried to remove Secretary of War Stanton. With that attempt, the confrontation reached its climax.

14-4h Impeachment of President Johnson

Impeachment is a political procedure provided for in the Constitution as a remedy for crimes or serious abuses of power by presidents, federal judges, and other high government officials. Those impeached (politically indicted) in the House are then tried in the Senate. Historically, this power has generally not been used as a means to investigate and judge the private lives of presidents, although in recent times it was used in this manner in the case of President Bill Clinton.

Twice in 1867, the House Judiciary Committee had considered impeachment of Johnson, rejecting the idea once and then recommending it by only a 5-to-4 vote. That recommendation was decisively defeated by the House. After Johnson tried to remove Stanton, however, a third attempt to impeach the president carried easily in early 1868. The indictment concentrated on his violation of the Tenure of Office Act, though many modern scholars regard his efforts to obstruct enforcement of the Reconstruction Act of 1867 as a far more serious offense.

Johnson's trial in the Senate lasted more than three months. The prosecution, led by Radicals, attempted to prove that Johnson was guilty of "high crimes and misdemeanors."

But they also argued that the trial was a means to judge Johnson's performance, not a judicial determination of guilt or innocence. The Senate ultimately rejected such reasoning, which could have made removal from office a political weapon against any chief executive who disagreed with Congress. Although a majority of senators voted to convict Johnson, the prosecution fell one vote short of the necessary two-thirds majority. Johnson remained in office, politically weakened and with less than a year left in his term. Some Republicans backed away from impeachment because they had their eyes on the 1868 election and did not want to hurt their prospects of regaining the White House.

14-4i Election of 1868

In the 1868 presidential election, Ulysses S. Grant, running as a Republican, defeated Horatio Seymour, a New York Democrat. Grant was not a Radical, but his platform supported **Congressional Reconstruction** and endorsed black suffrage in the South. (Significantly, Republicans stopped short of endorsing black suffrage in the North.) The Democrats, meanwhile, vigorously denounced Reconstruction and preached white supremacy. Indeed, in the 1868 election, the Democrats conducted the most openly racist campaign to that point in American history. Both sides waved the "bloody shirt," accusing each other as the villains of the war's sacrifices. By associating themselves

Impeachment Process to remove a president from office; attempted but failed in the case of Andrew Johnson.

Congressional Reconstruction The process by which the Republican-controlled Congress sought to make the Reconstruction of the ex-Confederate states longer, harsher, and under greater congressional control.

△ *His First Vote*, 1868, by Thomas Waterman Wood, oil on canvas, invoking the power and significance of black male suffrage during Reconstruction.

with rebellion and with Johnson's repudiated program, the Democrats went down to defeat in all but eight states, though the popular vote was fairly close. Participating in their first presidential election ever on a wide scale, African Americans decisively voted en masse for General Grant.

In office, Grant acted as an administrator of Reconstruction but not as its enthusiastic advocate. He vacillated in his dealings with the southern states, sometimes defending Republican regimes and sometimes currying favor with Democrats. On occasion, Grant called out federal troops to stop violence or enforce acts of Congress. But he never imposed a true military occupation on the South. Rapid demobilization had reduced a federal army of more than 1 million to 57,000 within a year of the surrender at Appomattox. Thereafter, the number of troops in the South continued to fall,

Fifteenth Amendment
Prohibited states from denying the vote to any citizen on account of "race, color, or previous condition of servitude."

until in 1874 there were only 4,000 in the southern states outside Texas. The later legend of "military rule," so important to southern claims of victimization during Reconstruction, was steeped in myth.

14-4j Fifteenth Amendment

In 1869, the Radicals pushed through the **Fifteenth Amendment**, the final major measure in the constitutional revolution of Reconstruction. This measure forbade states to deny the right to vote "on account of race, color, or previous condition of servitude." Such wording did not guarantee the right to vote. It deliberately left states free to restrict suffrage on other grounds so that northern states could continue to deny suffrage to women and certain groups of men—Chinese immigrants, illiterate men, and those too poor to pay poll taxes.

Although several states outside the South refused to ratify, three-fourths of the states approved the measure, and the Fifteenth Amendment became law in 1870. It, too, had been a political compromise, and though African Americans rejoiced all across the land at its enactment, it left open the possibility for states to create countless qualification tests to obstruct voting in the future.

With passage of the Fifteenth Amendment, many Americans, especially supportive northerners, considered Reconstruction essentially completed. "Let us have done with Reconstruction," pleaded the *New York Tribune* in April 1870. "The country is tired and sick of it . . . . Let us have Peace!" But some northerners, like abolitionist Wendell Phillips, worried. "Our day," he warned, "is fast slipping away. Once let public thought float off from the great issue of the war, and it will take . . . more than a generation to bring it back again."

14-5 Politics and Reconstruction in the South

▷ **How did white Southerners resist the end of slavery and Reconstruction?**

▷ **How did Republican governments rule in the South?**

▷ **What was the relationship between African Americans and whites inside and outside of the Republican Party?**

▷ **How did white Southern conservatives seek to discredit Republican governments in the South?**

From the start, Reconstruction encountered the resistance of white southerners. In the black codes and in private attitudes, many whites stubbornly opposed emancipation, and the former planter class proved especially unbending because of its tremendous financial loss in slaves. In 1866, a Georgia newspaper frankly observed that "most of the white citizens believe that the institution of slavery was right, and . . . they will believe that the condition, which comes nearest to slavery, that can now be established will be the best." And for many poor whites who had never owned slaves and yet had sacrificed enormously in the war, destitution, plummeting

His First Vote, 1868, 1868 [oil on panel]/Wood, Thomas Waterman (1823–1903)/CHRISTIES IMAGES/Private Collection/Bridgeman Images

agricultural prices, disease, and the uncertainties of a grow-ing urban industrialization drove them off land, toward cities, and into hatred of the very idea of black equality.

14-5a White Resistance

Fearing loss of control over their slaves, some planters attempted to postpone freedom by denying or misrepresent-ing events. Former slaves reported that their owners "didn't tell them it was freedom" or "wouldn't let [them] go." Agents of the Freedmen's Bureau reported that "the old system of slavery [is] working with even more rigor than formerly at a few miles distant from any point where U.S. troops are stationed." To hold onto their workers, some landowners claimed control over black children and used guardianship and apprentice laws to bind black families to the plantation.

Whites also blocked blacks from acquiring land. A few planters divided up plots among their slaves, but most con-demned the idea of making blacks landowners. A Georgia woman whose family was known for its support of religious education for slaves was outraged that two property owners planned to "rent their lands to the Negroes!" Such action was, she declared, "injurious to the best interest of the community."

Adamant resistance by whites soon manifested itself in other ways, including violence. In one North Carolina town, a local magistrate clubbed a black man on a public street, and in several states bands of "Regulators" terrorized blacks who displayed any independence. Amid their defeat, many plant-ers believed, as a South Carolinian put it, that blacks "can't be

△ Black Southerners attempting to vote are halted by White Leaguers in this engraving by J. H. Wares. The black man doffing his cap holds a "Republican ticket" but it will not get him to the ballot box, guarded by the election judge with a loaded pistol.

governed except with the whip." And after President Johnson encouraged the South to resist congressional Reconstruction, many white conservatives worked hard to capture the new state governments.

14-5b Black Voters and the Southern Republican Party

Enthusiastically, black men voted Republican. Most agreed with one man who felt he should "stick to the end with the party that freed me." Illiteracy did not prohibit blacks (or uneducated whites) from making intelligent choices. Although Mississippi's William Henry could read only "a little," he testified that he and his friends had no difficulty selecting the Republican ballot. "We stood around and watched," he explained. "We saw D. Sledge vote; he owned half the county. We knowed he voted Democratic so we voted the other ticket so it would be Republican." Women, who could not vote, encouraged their husbands and sons, and preachers exhorted their congregations to use the franchise. Zeal for voting spread through entire black communities.

Thanks to a large black turnout and the restrictions on prominent Confederates, a new southern Republican Party came to power in the constitutional conventions of 1868–1870. Republican delegates consisted of a sizable contingent of blacks (265 out of the total of just over 1,000 delegates throughout the South), some northerners who had moved to the South, and native southern whites who favored change. The new constitutions drafted by this Republican coalition were more democratic than anything previously adopted in the history of the South. They eliminated property qualifica-tions for voting and holding office, and they turned many appointed offices into elective posts. They provided for public schools and institutions to care for the mentally ill, the blind, the deaf, the destitute, and the orphaned.

The conventions broadened women's rights in prop-erty holding and divorce. Usually, the goal was not to make women equal with men but to provide relief to thousands of suffering debtors. In white families left poverty-stricken by the war and weighed down by debt, it was usually the husband who had contracted the debts. Thus, giving women legal control over their own property provided some protec-tion to their families.

14-5c Triumph of Republican Governments

Under these new constitutions, the southern states elected Republican-controlled governments. For the first time, the ranks of state legislators in 1868 included black southern-ers. Contrary to what white southerners would later claim, the Republican state governments did not disfranchise ex-Confederates as a group. James Lynch, a leading black poli-tician from Mississippi, explained why African Americans shunned the "folly" of disfranchising whites. Unlike north-erners who "can leave when it becomes too uncomfortable," landless former slaves "must be in friendly relations with the great body of the whites in the state. Otherwise . . . peace can be maintained only by a standing army." Despised and lacking material or social power, southern Republicans strove for acceptance, legitimacy, and safe ways to gain a foothold in a depressed economy.

Far from being vindictive toward the race that had enslaved them, most black southerners treated leading rebels with generosity and appealed to white southerners to adopt a spirit of fairness. In this way, the South's Republican Party condemned itself to defeat if white voters would not cooperate. Within a few years, most of the fledgling Republican parties in the southern states would be struggling for survival against violent white hostility. Utter obstruction, the politics of fear, and violence has sometimes worked as a means to power in America. But for a time, some propertied whites accepted congressional Reconstruction as a reality.

14-5d Industrialization and Mill Towns

Reflecting northern ideals and southern necessity, the Reconstruction governments enthusiastically promoted industry. Accordingly, Reconstruction legislatures encouraged investment with loans, subsidies, and short-term exemptions from taxation. The southern railroad system was rebuilt and expanded, and coal and iron mining made possible Birmingham's steel plants. Between 1860 and 1880, the number of manufacturing establishments in the South nearly doubled.

This emphasis on business enterprise, however, produced higher state debts and taxes, drew money away from schools and other programs, and multiplied possibilities for corruption in state legislatures. The alliance between business and government took firm hold, often at the expense of the needs of common farmers and laborers. It also locked Republicans into a conservative strategy and doomed their chances with poorer whites.

Poverty remained the lot of vast numbers of southern whites. On a daily basis during the Reconstruction years, they had to subordinate politics to the struggle for livelihood. The war had caused a massive onetime loss of income-producing wealth, such as livestock, and a steep decline in land values. In many regions, the old planter class still ruled the best land and access to credit or markets.

As many poor whites and blacks found farming less tenable, they moved to cities and new mill towns. Industrialization did not sweep the South as it did the North, but it certainly laid deep roots. Attracting textile mills to southern towns became a competitive crusade. "Next to God," shouted a North Carolina evangelist, "what this town needs is a cotton mill!" In 1860, the South counted some 10,000 mill workers; by 1880, the number grew to 16,741 and, by the end of the century, to 97,559. Thus, poor southerners began the multigenerational journey from farmer to urban wage earner.

14-5e Republicans and Racial Equality

Policies appealing to African American voters rarely went beyond equality before the law. In fact, the whites who controlled the southern Republican Party were reluctant to allow blacks a share of offices proportionate to their electoral strength. Aware of their weakness, black leaders did not push very far for revolutionary economic or social change. In every

The Queen of Industry, Or, The New South.

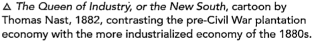

△ *The Queen of Industry, or the New South*, cartoon by Thomas Nast, 1882, contrasting the pre-Civil War plantation economy with the more industrialized economy of the 1880s.

southern state, they led efforts to establish public schools, although they did not press for integrated facilities. In 1870, South Carolina passed the first comprehensive school law in the South. By 1875, in a major achievement for a Reconstruction government, 50 percent of black school-age children in that state were enrolled in school, and approximately one-third of the three thousand teachers were black.

Some African American politicians did fight for civil rights and integration. Many were from cities such as New Orleans or Mobile, where large populations of light-skinned free black people had existed before the war. Their experience in such communities had made them sensitive to issues of status, and they spoke out for open and equal public accommodations. Laws requiring equal accommodations won passage, but they often went unenforced.

The vexing questions of land reform and enforcement of racial equality, however, all but overwhelmed the Republican governments. Land reform largely failed because in most states whites were in the majority, and former slave owners controlled the best land and other sources of economic power. Economic progress was uppermost in the minds of most freedpeople. Black southerners needed land, and much land did fall into state hands for nonpayment of taxes. Such land was offered for sale in small lots. But most freedmen had too little cash to bid against investors or speculators. South Carolina established a land commission, but it could help only those with money to buy. Widespread redistribution of land had to arise from Congress, which never supported such action.

14-5f Myth of "Negro Rule"

Within a few years, white hostility to congressional Reconstruction began to dominate. Some conservatives had always wanted to fight Reconstruction through pressure and racist propaganda. They put economic and social pressure on black people: one black Republican reported that "my neighbors will not employ me, nor sell me a farthing's worth of anything." Charging that the South had been turned over to ignorant blacks, conservatives deplored "black domination," which became a rallying cry for a return to white supremacy.

Such attacks were inflammatory propaganda and part of the growing myth of "Negro rule," which would serve as a central theme in battles over the memory of Reconstruction. African Americans participated in politics but hardly dominated or controlled events. They were a majority in only two out of ten state constitutional writing conventions (transplanted northerners were a majority in one). In the state legislatures, only in the lower house in South Carolina did black legislators ever constitute a majority. Sixteen black men won seats in Congress before Reconstruction was over, but none was ever elected governor. Only eighteen served in a high state office, such as lieutenant governor, treasurer, superintendent of education, or secretary of state.

In all, some four hundred black men served in political office during the Reconstruction era, a signal achievement by any standard. Although they never dominated the process, they established a rich tradition of government service and civic activism. Elected officials, such as Robert Smalls in South Carolina, labored tirelessly for cheaper land prices, better health care, access to schools, and the enforcement of civil rights for black people. For too long, the black politicians of Reconstruction were the forgotten heroes of this seedtime of America's long civil rights movement.

14-5g Carpetbaggers and Scalawags

Conservatives also assailed the allies of black Republicans. Their propaganda denounced whites from the North as **"carpetbaggers,"** greedy crooks planning to pour stolen tax revenues into their sturdy luggage made of carpet material. Immigrants from the North, who held the largest share of Republican offices, were all tarred with this rhetorical brush.

In fact, most northerners who settled in the South had come seeking business opportunities, as schoolteachers, or to find a warmer climate; most never entered politics. Those who did enter politics generally wanted to democratize the South and to introduce northern ways, such as industry and public education. Carpetbaggers' ideals were tested by hard times and ostracism by white southerners.

Carpetbaggers' real actions never matched the sensational stereotypes, although by the mid-1870s even some

△ *The Carpetbagger*, American lithograph song sheet music cover, ca. 1869. Emanating from the heyday of anti-carpetbagger propaganda, the figure seems to be part Uncle Sam and part scheming scoundrel with his bagful of Yankee notions, both religious and secular.

northerners who soured on Reconstruction or despaired over southern violence endorsed the images. Thomas Wentworth Higginson, a Union officer and commander of an African American regiment during the Civil War, suggested that any Yankee politician who remained in the South by 1874 was, more likely than not, a "mean man," a "scoundrel," and "like Shakespeare's Shylock." And that same year, the African American editors of the *Christian Recorder* distanced themselves from carpetbaggers. The "corrupt political vampires who rob and cheat and prey upon the prejudices of our people" and "feed upon the political carcass of a prostrate state," the paper insisted, were not black folks' allies. The white southern counterrevolutionaries seemed to be winning the propaganda war.

Conservatives also invented the term **scalawag** to discredit any native white southerner who cooperated with the Republicans.

"carpetbaggers" Derogatory nickname southerners gave to northerners who moved south after the Civil War, perceiving them as greedy opportunists who hoped to cash in on the South's plight.

scalawag Term used by conservative southerners to describe other white southerners who were perceived as aiding or benefiting from Reconstruction.

A substantial number of southerners did so, including some wealthy and prominent men. Most scalawags, however, were yeoman farmers, men from mountain areas and nonslaveholding districts who had been Unionists under the Confederacy. They saw that they could benefit from the education and opportunities promoted by Republicans. Sometimes banding together with freedmen, they pursued common class interests and hoped to make headway against the power of long-dominant planters. In the long run, however, the hope of such black-white coalitions floundered in the quicksand of racism.

14-5h Tax Policy and Corruption as Political Wedges

Taxation was a major problem for the Reconstruction governments. Republicans wanted to repair the war's destruction, stimulate industry, and support such new ventures as public schools. But the Civil War had destroyed much of the South's tax base. One category of valuable property—slaves—had disappeared entirely. And hundreds of thousands of citizens had lost much of the rest of their property—money, livestock, fences, and buildings—to the war. Thus, an increase in taxes (sales, excise, and property) was necessary even to maintain traditional services. Inevitably, Republican tax policies aroused strong opposition.

Corruption was another serious charge leveled against the Republicans. Unfortunately, it was often true. Many carpetbaggers and black politicians engaged in fraudulent schemes, sold their votes, or padded expenses, taking part in what scholars recognize was a nationwide surge of corruption in an age ruled by "spoilsmen." Corruption carried no

△ Ku Klux Klan "Worse Than Slavery," an 1874 cartoon by Thomas Nast showing "White Leaguers" and the Klan combining in violence against blacks. The Granger Collection New York

party label, but the Democrats successfully pinned the blame on unqualified blacks and greedy carpetbaggers among southern Republicans.

14-5i Ku Klux Klan

All these problems hurt the Republicans, whose leaders also allowed factionalism along racial and class lines to undermine party unity. But in many southern states, the deathblow came through violence. The Ku Klux Klan (its members altered the Greek word for "circle," *kuklos*), a secret veterans' club that began in Tennessee in 1866, spread through the South, and rapidly evolved into a terrorist organization. Violence against African Americans occurred from the first days of Reconstruction but became far more organized and purposeful after 1867. Klansmen sought to frustrate Reconstruction and keep the freedmen in subjection. Nighttime harassment, whippings, beatings, rapes, and murders became common, as terrorism dominated some counties and regions.

Although the Klan tormented black people who stood up for their rights as laborers or individuals, its main purpose was political. Lawless night riders made active Republicans the target of their attacks. Leading white and black Republicans were killed in several states. After freedmen who worked for a South Carolina scalawag started voting, terrorists visited the plantation and, in the words of one victim, "whipped every . . . [black] man they could lay their hands on." Klansmen also attacked Union League clubs—Republican organizations that mobilized the black vote—and schoolteachers who were aiding the freedmen.

Klan violence was not a spontaneous outburst of racism; very specific social forces shaped and directed it. In North Carolina, for example, Alamance and Caswell counties were the sites of the worst Klan violence. Slim Republican majorities there rested on cooperation between black voters and white yeomen, particularly those whose Unionism or discontent with the Confederacy had turned them against local Democratic officials. Together, these black and white Republicans had ousted officials long entrenched in power. The wealthy and powerful men in Alamance and Caswell who had lost their accustomed political control were the Klan's county officers and local chieftains. They organized a deliberate campaign of terror, recruiting members and planning atrocities.

Klan violence injured and ultimately destroyed Republicans across the South. One of every ten black leaders who had been delegates to the 1867–1868 state constitutional conventions was attacked, seven fatally. In one judicial district of North Carolina, the Ku Klux Klan was responsible for twelve murders, over seven hundred beatings, and other acts of violence, including rape and arson. A single attack on Alabama Republicans in the town of Eutaw left four blacks dead and fifty-four wounded. In South Carolina, five hundred masked Klansmen lynched eight black prisoners at the Union County jail, and in nearby York County, the Klan committed at least eleven murders and hundreds of whippings. According to historian Eric Foner, the Klan "made it

virtually impossible for Republicans to campaign or vote in large parts of Georgia."

Thus, a combination of difficult fiscal problems, Republican mistakes, racial hostility, and terror brought down the Republican regimes. In most southern states, Radical Reconstruction lasted only a few years (see Map 14.1). The most enduring failure of Reconstruction, however, was not political; it was social and economic.

14-6 Retreat from Reconstruction

▷ **How did the federal government respond to white conservative resistance to Reconstruction?**

▷ **What developments inside and outside of the South contributed to declining support for federal Reconstruction policies?**

▷ **How did relations between various ethnic and racial groups in the West contribute to additional conflict over race in the post-war period?**

▷ **What was the impact of the Supreme Court's rulings, particularly related to the Fourteenth Amendment?**

▷ **How was the disputed election of 1876 resolved?**

During the 1870s, northerners increasingly lost the political will to sustain Reconstruction in the South as a vast economic and social transformation occurred in their own region as well as in the West. Radical Republicans like Albion Tourgée, a former Union soldier who moved to North Carolina and was elected a judge, condemned Congress's timidity. Turning the freedman out on his own without protection, said Tourgée, constituted "cheap philanthropy." Indeed, many African Americans believed that, during Reconstruction, the North "threw all the Negroes on the world without any way of getting along." As the North underwent its own transformations and lost interest in the South's dilemmas, Reconstruction collapsed.

14-6a Political Implications of Klan Terrorism

In one southern state after another, Democrats regained control, and they threatened to defeat Republicans in the North as well. Whites in the old Confederacy referred to this decline of Reconstruction as "southern redemption," and during the 1870s, "redeemer" Democrats claimed to be the saviors of the South from alleged "black domination" and "carpetbag rule." And for one of only a few times in American history, violence and terror emerged as tactics in normal politics.

In 1870 and 1871, the violent campaigns of the Ku Klux Klan forced Congress to pass two **Enforcement Acts** and an anti-Klan law. These laws

Enforcement Acts Laws that sought to protect black voters, made violations of civil and political rights a federal offense, and sought to end Ku Klux Klan violence.

made actions by individuals against the civil and political rights of others a federal criminal offense for the first time. They also provided for election supervisors and permitted martial law and suspension of the writ of habeas corpus to combat murders, beatings, and threats by the Klan. Federal prosecutors used the laws rather selectively. In 1872 and 1873, Mississippi and the Carolinas saw many prosecutions; but in other states where violence flourished, the laws were virtually ignored. Southern juries sometimes refused to convict Klansmen; out of a total of 3,310 cases, only 1,143 ended in convictions. Although many Klansmen (roughly 2,000 in South Carolina alone) fled their state to avoid prosecution, and the Klan officially disbanded, the threat of violence did not end. Paramilitary organizations known as Rifle Clubs and Red Shirts often took the Klan's place.

Klan terrorism openly defied Congress, yet even on this issue there were ominous signs that the North's commitment to racial justice was fading. Some conservative but influential Republicans opposed the anti-Klan laws. Rejecting other Republicans' arguments that the Thirteenth, Fourteenth, and Fifteenth Amendments had made the federal government the protector of the rights of citizens, these dissenters echoed an old Democratic charge that Congress was infringing on states' rights. Senator Lyman Trumbull of Illinois, who had been a key author of the Thirteenth Amendment, declared that the states remained "the depositories of the rights of the individual." If Congress could punish crimes like assault or murder, he asked, "what is the need of the State governments?" For years, Democrats had complained of "centralization and consolidation"; now some Republicans seemed to agree with them. This opposition foreshadowed a more general revolt within Republican ranks in 1872.

14-6b Industrial Expansion and Reconstruction in the North

Both immigration and industrialization surged in the North. Between 1865 and 1873, 3 million immigrants entered the country, most settling in the industrial cities of the North and West. Within only eight years, postwar industrial production increased by 75 percent. For the first time, nonagricultural workers outnumbered farmers, and wage earners outnumbered independent craftsmen. And by 1873, only Britain's industrial output was greater than that of the United States. Government financial policies did much to bring about this rapid growth. Low taxes on investment and high tariffs on manufactured goods aided the growth of a new class of powerful industrialists, especially railroad entrepreneurs.

Railroads became the symbol of and the stimulus for the American age of capital. From 1865 to 1873, 35,000 miles of new track were laid, a total exceeding the entire national rail network of 1860. Railroad building fueled the banking industry and made Wall Street the center of American capitalism. Eastern railroad magnates, such as Thomas Scott of the Pennsylvania Railroad, the largest corporation

of its time, created economic empires with the assistance of huge government subsidies of cash and land. Railroad corporations also bought up mining operations, granaries, and lumber companies. In Congress and in every state legislature, big business now employed lobbyists to curry favor with government. Corruption ran rampant; some congressmen and legislators were paid annual retainers by major companies. Indeed, the transcontinental railroads helped Americans imagine how to conquer vast spaces, as well as conceive of time in new ways. The railroads brought modernity to the United States like almost nothing else; but they also taught the nation sordid lessons about the perils of monopoly and corruption, and by the late nineteenth century railroad entrepreneurs were the most hated men in the West. Moreover, in this laissez-faire world without rules, many railroads were overbuilt and thereby endangered the economy.

This soaring capitalist–politician alliance led as well to an intensified struggle between labor and capital. As captains of industry amassed unprecedented fortunes in an age with no income tax, gross economic inequality polarized American society. The workforce, worried a prominent Massachusetts business leader, was in a "transition state . . . living in boarding houses" and becoming a "permanent factory population." In Cincinnati, three large factories employed as many workers as the city's thousands of small shops. In New York or Philadelphia, workers increasingly lived in dark, unhealthy tenement housing. Thousands would list themselves on the census as "common laborer" or "general jobber." Many of the free-labor maxims of the Republican Party were now under great duress. Did the individual work ethic guarantee social mobility in America or erode, under the pressure of profit making, into a world of unsafe factories, child labor, and declining wages? In 1868, the Republicans managed to pass an eight-hour workday bill in Congress that applied to federal workers. The "labor question" now preoccupied northerners far more than the "southern" or the "freedmen" question (see Chapter 16).

Then, the Panic of 1873 ushered in more than five years of economic contraction. Three million people lost their jobs as class attitudes diverged, especially in large cities. Debtors and the unemployed sought easy-money policies to spur economic expansion (workers and farmers desperately needed cash). Businessmen, disturbed by the widespread strikes and industrial violence that accompanied the panic, fiercely defended property rights and demanded "sound money" policies as they sought to crush labor unions. The chasm between farmers and workers on the one hand, and wealthy industrialists on the other, grew ever wider.

14-6c Liberal Republican Revolt

Disenchanted with Reconstruction, a largely northern group calling itself the Liberal Republicans bolted the party in 1872 and nominated Horace Greeley, the famous editor of the

New York Tribune, for president. The Liberal Republicans were a varied group, including foes of corruption and advocates of a lower tariff. Normally such disparate elements would not cooperate with one another, but two popular and widespread attitudes united them: distaste for federal intervention in the South and an elitist desire to let market forces and the "best men" determine policy.

The Democrats also gave their nomination to Greeley in 1872. The combination was not enough to defeat Grant, who won reelection, but it reinforced Grant's desire to avoid confrontation with white southerners. Greeley's campaign for North–South reunion, for "clasping hands across the bloody chasm," was a bit premature to win at the polls but was a harbinger of the future in American politics. Organized Blue-Gray fraternalism (gatherings of Union and Confederate veterans) began as early as 1874. Grant continued to use military force sparingly and in 1875 refused a desperate request from the governor of Mississippi for troops to quell racial and political terrorism in that state.

Dissatisfaction with Grant's administration grew during his second term. Strong-willed but politically naive, Grant made a series of poor appointments. His secretary of war, his private secretary, and officials in the treasury department and navy were involved in bribery or tax-cheating scandals. Instead of exposing the corruption, Grant defended the culprits. In 1874, as Grant's popularity and his party's prestige declined, the Democrats recaptured the House of Representatives, signaling the end of the Radical Republican vision of Reconstruction. "Republican Party Struck by Lightning," read a Buffalo newspaper headline. And "Busted! The Republican Machine Gone to Smash!" said the *Louisville Courier-Journal* gleefully. Of thirty-five states holding legislative elections, twenty-three were won by Democrats.

14-6d General Amnesty

Such a political turnaround in Congress weakened legislative resolve on southern issues. Congress had already lifted the political disabilities of the Fourteenth Amendment from many former Confederates. In 1872, it had adopted a sweeping Amnesty Act, which pardoned most of the remaining rebels and left only five hundred barred from political office holding. In 1875, Congress passed a **Civil Rights Act**, partly as a tribute to the recently deceased Charles Sumner, purporting to guarantee black people equal accommodations in public places, such as inns and theaters, but the bill was watered down and contained no effective provisions for enforcement. (The Supreme Court later struck down this law.)

Democrats regained control of four state governments before 1872 and a total of eight by the end of January 1876 (see Map 14.1). In the North, Democrats successfully stressed the failure and scandals of Reconstruction governments. As opinion shifted, many Republicans sensed that their constituents were tiring of southern issues and the racial legacies of the war. Sectional reconciliation now seemed crucial for commerce. The nation was expanding westward rapidly, and the South was a new frontier for investment.

14-6e The West, Race, and Reconstruction

Nowhere did the new complexity and violence of American race relations play out so vividly as in the West. As the Fourteenth Amendment and other enactments granted to blacks the beginnings of citizenship, other nonwhite peoples faced continued persecution. Across the West, the federal government pursued a policy of containment against Native Americans. In California, where white farmers and ranchers often forced Native peoples into captive labor, some civilians practiced a more violent form of "Indian hunting." By 1880, thirty years of such violence left an estimated 4,500 Californian Native people dead at the hands of white settlers. Some historians have considered this policy a regional genocide.

In Texas and the Southwest, the rhetoric of national expansion still deemed Mexicans and other mixed-race Hispanics to be debased, "lazy," and incapable of self-government. And in California and other states of the Far West, thousands of Chinese immigrants became the victims of brutal violence. Few whites had objected to the Chinese who did the dangerous work of building railroads through the Rocky Mountains. But when the Chinese began to compete for urban, industrial jobs, great conflict emerged. Anti-coolie clubs appeared in California in the 1870s, seeking laws against Chinese labor, fanning the flames of racism, and organizing vigilante attacks on Chinese workers and the factories that employed them. Western politicians sought white votes by pandering to prejudice, and in 1879 the new California constitution denied the vote to Chinese immigrants.

If we view America from coast to coast, and not merely on the North–South axis, the Civil War and Reconstruction years both dismantled racial slavery and fostered a volatile new racial complexity, especially in the West. During the same age when early anthropologists employed elaborate theories of "scientific" racism to determine a hierarchy of racial types, the West was a vast region of racial mixing and conflict. Some African Americans, despite generations of mixture with Native Americans, asserted that they were more like whites than the nomadic, "uncivilized" Native Americans, while others, like the Creek freedmen of Indian Territory, sought Native identities. In Texas, whites, Native peoples, blacks, and Hispanics had mixed for decades, and by the 1870s forced reconsideration in law and custom of who was white and who was not.

During Reconstruction, America was undergoing what one historian has called a reconstruction of the very idea of *race* itself. As it did so, tumbling into some of the darkest years of American race relations, the turbulence of the expanding

Civil Rights Act An act that was designed to desegregate public places, but that lacked enforcement provisions.

◁ Anti-Chinese cartoon, "Every Dog (No Distinction of Color) Has His Day." The imagery here links Native Americans, African Americans, and Chinese immigrants in the same racist and xenophobic fear.

The Granger Collection, NYC

West reinforced the new nationalism and the reconciliation of North and South based on a resurgent white supremacy.

14-6f Foreign Expansion

Following the Civil War, pressure for expansion reemerged, and in 1867 Secretary of State William H. Seward arranged a vast addition of territory to the national domain through the purchase of Alaska from Russia (see Chapter 19). Opponents ridiculed Seward's $7.2 million venture, calling Alaska "Frigidia," "the Polar Bear Garden," and "Walrussia." But Seward convinced important congressmen of Alaska's economic potential, and other lawmakers favored the dawning of friendship with Russia.

Also in 1867, the United States took control of the Midway Islands, a thousand miles northwest of Hawai'i. And in 1870, President Grant tried unsuccessfully to annex the Dominican Republic. Leaders of American foreign policy, including some former abolitionists, believed that the new United States, re-founded by the war and emancipation, should export its values of antislavery and equality to

the world, especially in the Caribbean. This brand of liberal imperialism mixed with the pursuit of commerce and naval coaling stations, animated American expansion for the rest of the century.

Seward and his successor, Hamilton Fish, also resolved troubling Civil War grievances against Great Britain. Through diplomacy they arranged a financial settlement of claims on Britain for damage done by the *Alabama* and other cruisers built in England and sold to the Confederacy. They recognized that sectional reconciliation in Reconstruction America would serve new foreign ambitions.

14-6g Judicial Retreat from Reconstruction

Meanwhile, the Supreme Court played a major part in the northern retreat from Reconstruction. During the Civil War, the Court had been cautious and inactive. Reaction to the *Dred Scott* decision (1857) had been so vehement, and the Union's wartime emergency so great, that the Court had avoided interference with government actions. The justices breathed a collective sigh of relief, for example, when legal

The "Back to Africa" Movement

In the wake of the Civil War, and especially after the despairing end of Reconstruction, some African Americans sought to leave the South for the American West or North, but also to relocate to Africa. Liberia had been founded in the 1820s by the white-led American Colonization Society (ACS), an organization dedicated to relocating blacks "back" in Africa. Some eleven thousand African Americans had emigrated voluntarily to Liberia by 1860, with largely disastrous results. Many died of disease, and others felt disoriented in the strange new land and ultimately returned to the United States.

Reconstruction reinvigorated the emigration impulse, especially in cotton-growing districts where blacks had achieved political power before 1870 but were crushed by violence and intimidation in the following decade. When blacks felt confident in their future, the idea of leaving America fell quiet; but when threatened or under assault, whole black communities dreamed of a place where they could become an independent "race," a "people," or a "nation" as their appeals often announced. Often that dream, more imagined than realized, lay in West Africa. Before the Civil War, most blacks had denounced the ACS for its racism and its hostility to their sense of American birthright. But letters of

inquiry flooded into the organization's headquarters after 1875. Wherever blacks felt the reversal of the promise of emancipation the keenest, they formed local groups such as the Liberia Exodus Association of Pinesville, Florida; or the Liberian Exodus Arkansas Colony; and many others.

At emigration conventions, and especially in churches, blacks penned letters to the ACS asking for maps or any information about a new African homeland. Some local organizers would announce eighty or a hundred recruits "widawake for Liberia," although such enthusiasm rarely converted into an Atlantic voyage. The impulse was genuine, however. "We wants to be a People," wrote the leader of a Mississippi emigration committee; "we can't be it heare and find that we ar compel to leve this Cuntry." Henry Adams, a former Louisiana slave, Union soldier, and itinerant emigration organizer, advocated Liberia, but also supported "Kansas fever" with both biblical and natural rights arguments. "God . . . has a place and a land for all his people," he wrote in 1879. "It is not that we think the soil climate or temperature" elsewhere is "more congenial to us— but it is the idea that pervades our breast 'that at last we will be free,' free from oppression, free from tyranny,

free from bulldozing, murderous southern whites."

By the 1890s, Henry McNeal Turner, a freeborn former Georgia Reconstruction politician, and now bishop of the African Methodist Episcopal Church, made three trips to Africa and vigorously campaigned through press and pulpit for blacks to "Christianize" and "civilize" Africa. Two shiploads of African Americans sailed to Liberia, although most returned disillusioned or ill. Turner's plan of "Africa for the Africans" was as much a religious vision as an emigration system, but like all such efforts then and since, it reflected the despair of racial conditions in America more than realities in Africa. The numbers do not tell the tale of the depth of the impulse in this link to the world: in 1879–1880, approximately 25,000 southern blacks moved to Kansas, whereas from 1865 to 1900, just under 4,000 emigrated to West Africa.

CRITICAL THINKING

☐ While there were certainly practical reasons some African Americans did not want to emigrate to West Africa, what other reasons might compel an African American person to prefer to remain in the United States, and perhaps even in the South, despite the unfulfilled promises of freedom and equality?

◁ Departure of African American emigrants to Liberia aboard the *Laurada*, Savannah, Georgia, March 1896. The large crowd bidding farewell to the much smaller group aboard the ship may indicate both the fascination with and the ambivalence about this issue among blacks in the South.

Library of Congress/Getty Images

technicalities prevented them from reviewing the case of Clement Vallandigham, a Democratic opponent of Lincoln's war effort who had been convicted by a military tribunal of aiding the enemy. But in 1866, a similar case, *Ex parte Milligan*, reached the Court.

Lambdin P. Milligan of Indiana had plotted to free Confederate prisoners of war and overthrow state governments. For these acts, a military court sentenced Milligan, a civilian, to death. Milligan challenged the authority of the military tribunal, claiming he had a right to a civil trial. Reasserting its authority, the Supreme Court declared that military trials were illegal when civil courts were open and functioning.

In the 1870s, the Court successfully renewed its challenge to Congress's actions when it narrowed the meaning and effectiveness of the Fourteenth Amendment. The *Slaughter-House* cases (1873) began in 1869, when the Louisiana legislature granted one company a monopoly on the slaughtering of livestock in New Orleans. Rival butchers in the city promptly sued. Their attorney, former Supreme Court Justice John A. Campbell, argued that Louisiana had violated the rights of some of its citizens in favor of others. The Fourteenth Amendment, Campbell contended, had revolutionized the constitutional system by bringing individual rights under federal protection, safeguarding them from state interference.

But in the *Slaughter-House* decision, the Supreme Court dealt a stunning blow to the scope of the Fourteenth Amendment. The Court declared state citizenship and national citizenship separate. National citizenship involved only matters such as the right to travel freely from state to state, and only such narrow rights, held the Court, were protected by the Fourteenth Amendment.

The Supreme Court also concluded that the butchers who sued had not been deprived of their rights or property in violation of the due-process clause of the amendment. Shrinking from a role as "perpetual censor" for civil rights, the Court's majority declared that the framers of the recent amendments had not intended to "destroy" the federal system, in which the states exercised "powers for domestic and local government, including the regulation of civil rights." Thus, the justices severely limited the amendment's potential for securing and protecting the rights of black citizens—its original intent.

The next day, the Court decided *Bradwell v. Illinois*, a case in which Myra Bradwell, a female attorney, had been denied the right to practice law in Illinois because she was a married woman, and hence not considered a free agent. Pointing to the Fourteenth Amendment, Bradwell's attorneys contended the state had unconstitutionally abridged her "privileges and immunities" as a citizen. The Supreme Court rejected her claim, declaring a woman's "paramount destiny ... to fulfill the noble and benign offices of wife and mother."

In 1876, the Court weakened the Reconstruction-era amendments even further by emasculating the enforcement clause of the Fourteenth Amendment and revealing deficiencies inherent in the Fifteenth Amendment. In *U.S. v. Cruikshank*, the Court overruled the conviction under the 1870 Enforcement Act of Louisiana whites who had attacked a meeting of blacks and conspired to deprive them of their rights. The justices ruled that the Fourteenth Amendment did not give the federal government power to act against these whites, who had murdered possibly as many as one hundred blacks. The duty of protecting citizens' equal rights, the Court said, "rests alone with the States." Such judicial conservatism as well as states' rights doctrine, practiced by justices who had all been appointed by Republican presidents Lincoln and Grant, left a profound imprint down through the next century, blunting the revolutionary potential in the Civil War amendments.

14-6h Disputed Election of 1876 and Compromise of 1877

As the 1876 elections approached, Americans increasingly focused on economic issues. The North was no longer willing to pursue the goals of Reconstruction. The results of a disputed presidential election confirmed this fact. Samuel J. Tilden, the Democratic governor of New York, ran strongly in the South and needed only one more electoral vote to triumph over Rutherford B. Hayes, the Republican nominee. Nineteen electoral votes from Louisiana, South Carolina, and Florida (the only southern states not yet under Democratic rule) were disputed; both Democrats and Republicans claimed to have won in those states despite fraud committed by their opponents (see Map 14.2).

To resolve this unprecedented situation, Congress established a fifteen-member electoral commission. Membership on the commission was to be balanced between Democrats and Republicans. Because the Republicans held the majority in Congress, they prevailed, 8 to 7, on every attempt to count the returns, with commission members voting along strict party lines. Hayes would become president if Congress accepted the commission's findings.

Congressional acceptance was not certain. Democrats controlled the House and could filibuster to block action on the vote. Many citizens worried that the nation would slip once again into civil war, as some southerners vowed, "Tilden or Fight!" The crisis was resolved when Democrats acquiesced in the election of Hayes based on a "deal" cut in a Washington hotel between Hayes's supporters and southerners who wanted federal aid to railroads, internal improvements, federal patronage, and removal of troops from southern states. Northern and southern Democrats simply decided not to contest the election of a Republican who was not going to continue Reconstruction policies in the South. Thus, Hayes became president, inaugurated privately inside the White House to avoid any threat of violence. Southerners relished their promises of economic aid, and Reconstruction was unmistakably over. Tilden had won the popular vote, but

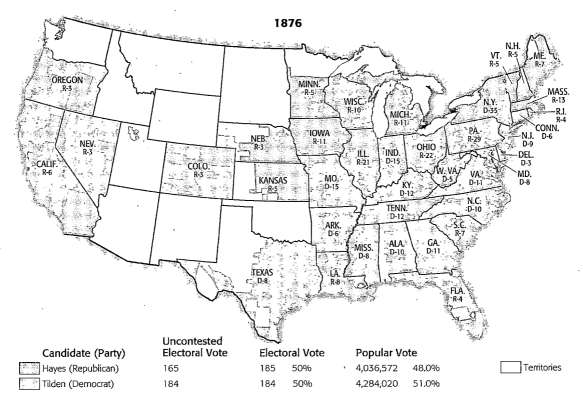

1876

Candidate (Party)	Uncontested Electoral Vote	Electoral Vote		Popular Vote		
Hayes (Republican)	165	185	50%	4,036,572	48.0%	☐ Territories
Tilden (Democrat)	184	184	50%	4,284,020	51.0%	

Map 14.2 Presidential Election of 1876 and the Compromise of 1877

In 1876, a combination of solid southern support and Democratic gains in the North gave Samuel Tilden the majority of popular votes, but Rutherford B. Hayes won the disputed election in the electoral college, after a deal satisfied Democratic wishes for an end to Reconstruction.

narrowly, not winning the Electoral College, the first of four such times in American history when the presidential winner did not win the most votes, a constitutional anomaly that still mystifies much of the world.

Southern Democrats rejoiced, but African Americans grieved over the betrayal of their hopes for equality. The Civil War had brought emancipation, and Reconstruction had guaranteed their rights under law. But events and attitudes in larger white America were foreboding. In a Fourth of July speech in Washington, D.C., in 1875, Frederick Douglass anticipated this predicament. He reflected anxiously on the American centennial to be celebrated the following year. The nation, Douglass feared, would "lift to the sky its million voices in one grand Centennial hosanna of peace and good will to all the white race . . . from gulf to lakes and from sea to sea." Douglass looked back on fifteen years of unparalleled change for his people and worried about the hold of white supremacy on America's historical memory: "If war among the whites brought peace and liberty to the blacks, what will peace among the whites bring?" Douglass's question would echo down through American political culture for decades.

Summary

Reconstruction left a contradictory record. It was an era of tragic aspirations and failures, but also of unprecedented legal, political, and social change. The Union victory brought about an increase in federal power, stronger nationalism, sweeping federal intervention in the southern states, and landmark amendments to the Constitution. It also sparked a revolution in how people would see the role of the state in their lives, often resulting in positive modes of dependence on government heretofore unimagined. But northern commitment to make these changes endure eroded, and the revolution remained unfinished. The mystic sense of promise for new lives and liberties among the freedpeople, demonstrated in that first Decoration Day in Charleston, was tarnished although not dead by 1877.

The North embraced emancipation, black suffrage, and constitutional alterations strengthening the central government. But it did so to defeat the rebellion and secure the peace. As the pressure of these crises declined, Americans, especially in the North, retreated from Reconstruction. The American people and the courts maintained a preference for

The Lost Cause

All major wars and their aftermath compel a struggle over their memory. Sometimes losers prevail over winners in contests to shape historical memory. After the Civil War, white southerners and their northern allies constructed a "Lost Cause" tradition, a potent and racially exclusive version of the war and Reconstruction that persists in American culture today.

The Lost Cause emerged among ex-Confederates as a mourning ritual and a psychological response to the trauma of defeat. But with time it also took root in selective reinterpretations of the war's causes; in southern resistance to Reconstruction; in doctrines of white supremacy; and in a nostalgic popular culture enjoyed and promoted by northerners and southerners alike. Lost Cause advocates—from high-ranking officers to common soldiers writing reminiscences to women leading memorial associations—argued that the war had never been about slavery, that the Confederates had only lost to Yankee numbers and resources, and that the nation should reconcile by equally honoring both southern and northern sacrifice. In the industrial, urban, multiethnic America of the emerging twentieth century, an Old South of benevolent masters and faithful slaves, of Robert E. Lee

portrayed as America's truest Christian soldier, provided a sentimentalized road to reunion.

From 1865 to the 1880s, this Confederate legend had been forged by wartime participants determined to vindicate the Confederacy. By the 1890s, however, Lost Cause culture emerged especially with the United Daughters of the Confederacy. Elite southern white women built monuments, lobbied congressmen, delivered lectures, ran essay contests for schoolchildren, and strove to control the content of history textbooks, all in the service of an exalted South. Above all, Lost Causers advocated a story not at all about loss, but about what one historian has called a "victory narrative." This new victory was the nation's triumph over the racial revolution and constitutional transformations of Reconstruction. In his 1881 memoir, Jefferson Davis argued that slavery "was in no wise the cause of the conflict" and that slaves had been "contented with their lot." He also declared the Lost Cause not lost: "Well may we rejoice in the regained possession of self-government. . . . This is the great victory . . . a total noninterference by the Federal government in the domestic affairs of the States."

These stories and images reverberated in the very heartbeat of Jim Crow America, and they endure in modern tastes for Civil War memorabilia, such as the epic *Gone with the Wind*, the 2003 film *Gods and Generals*, and uses of the Confederate flag to oppose civil rights and represent southern identity. And the Confederate state rights tradition has been employed by some states and advocacy groups to suppress the voting rights of certain minority groups, to resist federal environmental policy, national health care reform, and the presidency of Barack Obama. Confederate mythology also inspired a horrendous mass murder by a young white supremacist in the Emanuel AME church in Charleston, South Carolina in June, 2015.

CRITICAL THINKING

□ The Lost Cause mythology emerged originally as part of southern whites' mourning for those who died in the war and for the loss of the war. Over time, it transformed the nation's historical memory of the antebellum South, slavery, the war, and Reconstruction, quite literally whitewashing the past. Many modern proponents of the Lost Cause claim that their purpose is "heritage, not hate." Is it possible for the Lost Cause to be solely about heritage?

state authority and a distrust of federal power. The ideology of free labor dictated that property should be respected and that individuals should be self-reliant. Racism endured and transformed into the even more virulent forms of Klan terror and theories of black degeneration. Concern for the human rights of African Americans and other reforms frequently had less appeal than moneymaking in an individualistic, industrializing society.

New challenges began to overwhelm the aims of Reconstruction. How would the country develop its immense resources in an increasingly interconnected national economy? Could farmers, industrial workers, immigrants, and

capitalists coexist? Industrialization not only promised prosperity but also wrought increased exploitation of labor. Moreover, industry increased the nation's power and laid the foundation for an enlarged American role in international affairs.

In the wake of the Civil War, Americans faced two profound tasks—the achievement of healing and the dispensing of justice. Both had to occur, but they never developed in historical balance. Making sectional reunion compatible with black freedom and equality overwhelmed the imagination in American political culture, and the nation still faced much of this dilemma more than a century later.

Suggestions for Further Reading

David W. Blight, *Race and Reunion: The Civil War in American Memory* (2001)

Gregory P. Downs, *Declarations of Dependence: The Long Reconstruction of Popular Politics in the South, 1861–1908* (2011)

W. E. B. Du Bois, *Black Reconstruction in America* (1935)

Eric Foner, *Reconstruction: America's Unfinished Revolution, 1863–1877* (1988)

William Gillette, *Retreat from Reconstruction, 1869–1879* (1980)

Gerald Jaynes, *Branches Without Roots: The Genesis of the Black Working Class in the American South, 1862–1882* (1986)

George Rable, *But There Was No Peace* (1984)

Heather Cox Richardson, *West from Appomattox: The Reconstruction of America after the Civil War* (2007)

Elliot West, "Reconstructing Race," *Western Historical Quarterly* (Spring 2003)

Richard White, *Railroaded: The Transcontinentals and the Making of Modern America* (2011)

Richard White, *The Republic for Which It Stands: The United States During Reconstruction and the Gilded Age* (2017)

MINDTAP
From Cengage

MindTap® is a fully online personalized learning experience built upon Cengage Learning content. MindTap® combines student learning tools—readings, multimedia, activities, and assessments—into a singular Learning Path that guides students through the course and helps students develop the critical thinking, analysis, and communication skills that are essential to academic and professional success.

The Ecology of the West and South, 1865–1900

Surrounded by eastern Arkansas lowlands that flooded every year, Nannie Stillwell Jackson kept a diary of her life as a farmwife in late-nineteenth-century America. Her everyday routine of tedious work and heartwarming generosity represented the human ecology—the interaction between people and their environment—that ordinary individuals experienced as they coped with challenges that they faced.

Nannie was headstrong and compassionate. She had to be. Her husband, ten years younger than herself—both she and he had been widowed and this was their second marriage—drank, stayed out late, and often disliked her independence. One Saturday in 1890, for example, Nannie went to town and bought a pair of stockings, then later wrote in her diary, ". . . Mr. Jackson got mad because I bought what I did today but I can't help it if he did." She also participated in a supporting network of neighboring farm women, who exchanged visits, food, clothing, meals, and aid almost daily. On August 6, 1890, for example, Nannie wrote, ". . . Aunt Mary Williams she brought me a nice mess of squash for dinner. Caroline Coalman is sick & sent Rosa to me to send her a piece of beef I sent her a bucket full of cold victuals . . ." Nature was both Nannie's ally and enemy. She often sent her teenage daughter to bring "water from the bayou to wash with," but she also complained "no rain yet & we do need rain so bad." And water-born typhoid fever killed several of her neighbors.

The humdrum events of Nannie's life occurred innumerable times in the American West and South as people worked hard with each other and with—sometimes against—the environment. Though much of this life was timeless, the human ecology of these regions was changing. In the part of the South where Nannie Jackson lived, the Missouri Pacific Railroad was nearby, and she had access to the outside world and its goods, such as the store-bought stockings she brought home, much to her husband's displeasure. During her lifetime, a "New South" emerged, built upon railroads, factories, and

◁ This Montana farm woman resembled Nannie Jackson in her hard work taking care of her farm. And like Nannie, she probably had gone to a nearby town to purchase the clothes she wore while milking her cows. Montana Historical Society

Chronology

1862	▣ Homestead Act grants free land to citizens who live on and improve the land
	▣ Morrill Land Grant Act gives states public land to sell in order to finance agricultural and industrial colleges
1864	▣ Chivington's militia massacres Black Kettle's Cheyennes at Sand Creek
1869	▣ First transcontinental railroad completed
1872	▣ Yellowstone becomes first national park
1876	▣ Custer's federal troops attack Lakotas and Cheyenne at Little Big Horn, Montana; suffer major defeat
1877	▣ Nez Percé Indians under Young Joseph surrender to U.S. troops
1878	▣ Timber and Stone Act allows citizens to buy timberland cheaply but also enables large companies to acquire huge tracts of forest land
1879	▣ Carlisle School for Indians established in Pennsylvania
1880	▣ Cigarette-making machine invented
1881–82	▣ Chinese Exclusion Acts prohibit Chinese immigration to the United States
1883	▣ National time zones established
1884	▣ U.S. Supreme Court first denies Indians as wards under government protection
1887	▣ Dawes Severalty Act ends communal ownership of Indian lands and grants land allotments to individual Native families; "California Plan" advances irrigation
1887–88	▣ Devastating winter on Plains destroys countless livestock and forces farmers into economic hardship
1889	▣ Asa Candler buys and develops Coca-Cola Company
1890	▣ Final suppression of Plains Indians by U.S. Army at Wounded Knee
	▣ Census Bureau announces closing of the frontier
	▣ Yosemite National Park established
1892	▣ John Muir helps found Sierra Club
1902	▣ Newlands Reclamation Act passed

cities. Farther west, population grew at a furious pace as new migrants streamed in to develop the land and extract its wealth.

Experience an interactive version of this story in MindTap®.

Throughout the nation's history, the region known as the "South" had a relatively stable definition. It encompassed most of the states and territories beneath the 39th parallel westward to the Mississippi River and sometimes including Oklahoma and Texas. The meaning of the "West," however, changed. In the eighteenth century, the West encompassed the entire area beyond the Appalachian Mountains. As the result of settlement of the Midwest following the Civil War, the West came to be defined by the land between the Mississippi River and the Pacific Ocean, including the plains between the Mississippi and the Rocky Mountains, the Rockies themselves, and the mountains and valleys of the Far West.

Before migrants arrived, much of the West was not empty. It was occupied by long-time indigenous inhabitants, whose human ecology of communities working with natural resources operated in quite different ways from those that became common once others occupied the region. On the Plains, for example, the Pawnees planted crops in springtime, left their fields in summer to hunt buffalo, then returned for harvesting. They sometimes battled with nearby Cheyenne and Arapahoe peoples, who wanted hunting grounds and crops for their own purposes. In what now is the American Southwest, including Southern California, Native peoples shared the land and sometimes integrated with descendants of Spanish colonists. All these peoples survived by developing and using natural resources in limited ways, and they had at most only occasional access to outside markets. After the Civil War, however, white Americans flooded into the West, overwhelming Native and Hispanic communities. Between 1870 and 1890, the white population living in the region swelled from 7 million to nearly 17 million.

As newcomers built communities in the West and South in the late nineteenth century, however, they exploited the environment for profit far more extensively than did Native peoples. They excavated the earth to remove minerals, felled forests for timber to construct and heat homes, pierced the countryside with railroads to carry goods and link markets, and dammed rivers and plowed soil with machines to grow crops. Their goal was not mere survival; it included buying and selling in regional, national, and international markets. Nannie Jackson partook of only a tiny portion of this change when she went to town to buy stockings, but it surrounded her nonetheless. The abundance of exploitable land and raw materials of these regions filled Americans with faith that anyone eager and persistent enough could succeed and that faith fueled the new human ecology. But the confidence also rested on a belief that white people were somehow superior, and individual ambition often asserted itself at the expense of minority people and the environment. As new settlers transformed the landscape in both the West and South, the triumph of their market economies transformed the nation. Both optimism and discrimination, hope and hardship, were parts of the new human ecology.

□ *How did the interaction between people and the environment shape the physical landscapes of the West and South?*

□ *Describe the societal and technological changes the revolutionized lives of farmers in the West and South.*

□ *How did the U.S. government's relations with Native Americans change over time throughout the late nineteenth century?*

15-1 The Transformation of Native Cultures

▷ **How did Native American peoples simultaneously depend upon and shape their surrounding environment?**

▷ **Why did Native American economic systems weaken in the late nineteenth century?**

▷ **What policies did the U.S. government pursue in relationship to Native American peoples?**

▷ **How did Native American peoples resist encroachment by settlers and the U.S. government?**

Indigenous peoples settled the West long before other Americans migrated there. Neither passive nor powerless in the face of nature, these Native peoples had been shaping their environment—for better and for worse—for centuries. Nevertheless, almost all Native peoples' economic systems weakened in the late nineteenth century. Several factors explain why and how these declines happened.

15-1a Subsistence Cultures

Among Native peoples, ecologies varied. Some Native peoples inhabited permanent settlements; others lived in a series of temporary camps. Seldom completely isolated, most were

both participants and recipients in a flow of goods, culture, language, and disease carried by bands that migrated from one region to another. Regardless of their type of community, all Native peoples based their economies to differing degrees on four activities: 1) crop growing; 2) livestock raising; 3) hunting, fishing, and gathering; and 4) trading and raiding. Corn was the most common crop; sheep and horses, acquired from Spanish colonizers and from enemies, were the livestock; and buffalo (American bison) and salmon were the primary prey of hunting and fishing. Native peoples raided one another for food, tools, and horses, which in turn they used in trading with other Native groups and with whites. They also attacked to avenge wrongs and to oust competitors from hunting grounds. To achieve their standards of living, Native peoples tried to balance their economic systems. When a buffalo hunt failed, they subsisted on crops. When crops failed, they could still hunt buffalo and steal food and horses in a raid or trade livestock and furs for necessities.

For indigenous peoples on the Plains, whether nomads, such as the Lakotas ("Sioux"), or village dwellers, such as the Pawnees, everyday life focused on buffalo. They cooked and preserved buffalo meat; fashioned hides into clothing, moccasins, and blankets; used sinew for thread and bowstrings; and carved tools from bones and horns. Buffalo were so valuable that Pawnees and Lakotas often fought over access to herds. Plains communities also depended on horses, which they used for hunting, and as symbols of wealth. To provide food for their herds, **Plains Indians** altered the environment by periodically setting fire to tall-grass prairies. The fires burned away dead plants, facilitating growth of new grass in the spring so that horses could feed all summer.

In the Southwest, Native peoples led varying lifestyles, depending upon the environment. For example, among the O'odham of southeastern Arizona and northwest Mexico, whose name translates into "The People" to distinguish themselves from "others," some groups grew irrigated crops in the region's few river valleys while those who inhabited mountainous and desert territories followed more of a hunter-gatherer existence. Once foreigners arrived, The People traded for what was useful—tools, cloth, tobacco, livestock—and aided in raids against the Apache, who were enemies of O'odham. (Significantly, the Apache called themselves Nnee, which also means "The People.") The Navaho (or Dine', also meaning "The People") were herders, whose sheep, goats, and horses provided food, transportation, and status.

What buffalo were to Plains communities and sheep were to the ecology of southwestern natives, salmon were to Native peoples of the Northwest. Before the mid-nineteenth century, the Columbia River and its tributaries supported the densest population of Native peoples in North America, all of whom fished for salmon in the summer and stored dried fish for the winter. To harvest fish, the Clatsops, Klamath, and S'Klallams developed technologies of stream diversion, platform

Plains Indians Diverse Native American societies inhabiting the region from the Dakotas to Texas.

Library of Congress Prints and Photographs Division Washington, D.C. [LC-DIG-ppmsca-39873]

△ Outfitted in elaborate attire, including a headdress with buffalo horns, metal armbands, and an animal hide shirt decorated with metal medallions, Cloud Man was a member of the Assisisboine people of the Northern Great Plains. His father was French and his mother Native American, but Cloud Man served as chief of his band and always identified himself as Native American.

construction over the water, and special baskets to catch fish from the platforms. Like native societies of other regions, many of these Indians traded for horses, buffalo robes, beads, cloth, and knives.

15-1b Slaughter of Buffalo

On the Plains and in parts of the Southwest, indigenous ecologies began to dissolve after 1850, when white migrants entered and competed with Native peoples for access to and control over natural resources. Perceiving buffalo and indigenous peoples as hindrances to their ambitions, whites endeavored to eliminate both. Huge herds of buffalo sometimes blocked trains from moving, so railroads made concerted efforts to remove them permanently. When the U.S. Army failed to enforce treaties that reserved hunting grounds for exclusive use by Native peoples, railroads sponsored buffalo hunts in which eastern sportsmen shot at the bulky targets from slow-moving trains, killing thousands. Some hunters collected from $1 to $3 each for hides that were sent east for use mainly as belts to drive industrial machinery; others did not even stop to pick up their kill.

Unbeknownst to both Native peoples and white migrants, however, a complex combination of circumstances had already doomed the buffalo before the slaughter of the late 1800s. Native peoples contributed to the depletion of the herds by increasing their kills, especially to trade hides with whites and other Native communities. Also, a period of dry years in the 1840s and 1850s had forced Native peoples such as the Lakota to set up camps in river basins, where they competed with buffalo for space and water. As a result, the buffalo were pushed out of nourishing grazing territory and faced threats of starvation. When whites arrived on the Plains, they, too, sought to settle in river basins, further depriving buffalo from nutritious grasslands. At the same time, lethal animal diseases, such as anthrax and brucellosis, brought in by white-owned livestock, decimated buffalo already weakened by malnutrition and drought. Increasing numbers of horses, oxen, and sheep, owned by white newcomers as well as by some Native peoples, also upset the buffalo's grazing patterns by devouring vital grass supplies. In sum, human and ecological shocks created vulnerability among the buffalo, to which mass killing only struck the final blow. By the 1880s only a few hundred of the 25 million buffalo estimated on the Plains in 1820 remained.

15-1c Decline of Salmon

In the Northwest, the basic wild source of Native peoples' food supply, salmon, suffered a fate similar to that of the buffalo, but for different reasons. White commercial fishermen and canneries moved into the Columbia and Willamette River valleys during the 1860s and 1870s. When commercial fishermen harvested increasing numbers of salmon running upriver to spawn before laying their eggs, the fish supply was not replenished. By the 1880s whites had greatly diminished salmon runs on the Columbia, and by the early 1900s, construction of dams on the river and its tributaries further impeded the salmon's ability to reproduce. The U.S. government protected Native peoples' fishing rights, but not the supply of fish on the river. Hatcheries helped restore some of this supply, but dams built to provide power, combined with overfishing and pollution, diminished salmon stocks.

15-1d Influence of Young White Men

Buffalo slaughter and salmon reduction undermined western native subsistence, but a unique mix of human demography contributed as well. For most of the nineteenth century, white populations that migrated into western lands inhabited by indigenous peoples were overwhelmingly young and male. In 1870 white men outnumbered white women by three to two in California, two to one in Colorado, and two to one in Dakota Territory. By 1900, preponderances of men remained throughout these places. Most of these males were unmarried and in their twenties and thirties, the stage of life when they were most prone to violent behavior. In other words, the whites with whom Native peoples were most likely to come into contact first were traders, trappers, soldiers, prospectors, and cowboys—almost all of whom owned guns and had few qualms about using them against animals and humans who got in their way.

Moreover, these men subscribed to prevailing attitudes that Native peoples were primitive, lazy, devious, and cruel. Such contempt made exploiting and killing Native peoples all the easier, and whites often justified violence against Native peoples by claiming preemptive defense against threats to life and property. When Native bands raided white settlements, they sometimes mutilated bodies, burned buildings, and kidnapped women, acts that were embellished in campfire stories, pamphlets, and popular fiction—all of which reinforced images of Native peoples as savages. Inside the bachelor society of saloons and cabins, white men boasted of exploits in Indian fighting and showed off trophies of scalps and other body parts taken from victims.

Native warriors, too, were young, armed, and prone to violence. Valuing bravery and vengeance, they boasted of fighting white interlopers. But indigenous communities contrasted with those of whites in that they contained excesses of women, the elderly, and children, making Native bands less mobile and therefore vulnerable to attack. They also were susceptible to bad habits of bachelor white society. Native men copied white males' behavior of bingeing on cheap whiskey and indulging in prostitution. The syphilis and gonorrhea that Native men contracted from Native women infected by white men killed many and reduced Native peoples' ability to reproduce, a consequence that their populations, already declining from smallpox and other diseases spread by whites, could not afford. Thus age and gender structures of the white frontier population, combined with attitudes of racial contempt, created a further threat to western Native peoples' existence.

15-1e Government Policy and Treaties

U.S. government policy reinforced efforts to remove Native peoples from the path of white ambitions, but the cultural organization of indigenous groups caused confusion. North American Native peoples were constituted not so much into tribes, as whites believed, as into countless bands and confederacies that shifted in composition. In the West, some two hundred languages and dialects separated these groups, making it difficult for indigenous groups to unite against white invaders. Although a language group could be defined as a tribe, separate bands and clans within each group had their own leaders, and seldom did a chief hold widespread power. Moreover, bands often spent more time battling among themselves than with white settlers.

Nevertheless, the government needed some way of categorizing Native peoples so as to fashion a policy toward them. It did so by imputing more meaning to tribal organization than was warranted. After 1795, American officials considered Indian tribes to be separate nations with which they could make treaties that ensured peace and defined boundaries between Native and white lands. This was a faulty assumption because chiefs who agreed to a treaty did not always speak for all members of a band and the group would not necessarily abide by an agreement. Moreover, white settlers seldom accepted treaties as guarantees of natives' land rights. On the Plains, whites assumed that they could settle wherever they wished, and they rarely hesitated to commandeer choice farmland along river valleys. In the Northwest, whites considered treaties protecting Native peoples' fishing rights on the Columbia River to be nuisances and ousted Native peoples from the best locations so that they could use mechanical devices to harvest fish. As white migrants pressed into indigenous territories, treaties made one week were violated the next.

15-1f Reservation Policy

Prior to the 1880s, the federal government tried to force western indigenous peoples onto reservations, where, it was thought, Native peoples could be "civilized." Reservations usually consisted of those areas of a group's previous territory that were least desirable to whites. When assigning Native groups to such parcels, the government promised protection from white encroachment and agreed to provide food, clothing, and other necessities.

Reservation policy helped make way for the market economy. In early years of contact in the West, trade had benefited both Native peoples and whites and had taken place on a nearly equal footing, much as it had between eastern Native peoples and whites in the preceding century. Native peoples acquired clothing, guns, and horses from whites in return for furs, hides, jewelry, and, sometimes, military assistance against enemy Native groups. In the West, however, whites' needs and economic power grew disproportionate to Native peoples' needs and power. Native peoples became more dependent, and whites increasingly dictated what was to be traded and on what terms. For example, white traders persuaded Navajo weavers in the Southwest to produce heavy rugs, which the Native groups rarely could use but appealed to eastern customers, and to adopt new designs and colors to boost sales. Meanwhile, by focusing on commercial production, Navajos raised fewer crops and were forced to buy food because the market economy undermined their subsistence agriculture. Soon they were selling land and labor to whites as well, and their dependency made it easier to force them onto reservations.

Reservation policy had degrading consequences. First, Native communities had no say over their own affairs on reservations. Supreme Court decisions in 1884 and 1886 defined them as wards (like helpless children under government protection) and denied them the right to become U.S. citizens. Thus they were unprotected by the Fourteenth and Fifteenth Amendments, which had extended the privileges and legal protections of citizenship to African Americans. Second, pressure from white farmers, miners, and herders who continually sought Native lands made it difficult for the government to preserve reservations intact. Third, the government ignored Native peoples' history, even combining on the same reservation Indian bands that habitually had warred against each other. Rather than serving as civilizing communities, reservations weakened every aspect of Native life, except the resolve to survive.

15-1g Native Resistance

Not all Native peoples succumbed to market forces and reservation restrictions. Apache bands long had raided white settlements in the Southwest and continued their insurgence even after most of their people had been forced onto reservations. Their raiding ended only after the last of their leaders, the Chiricahua chief Geronimo, was captured in 1886. Pawnees in the Midwest resisted disadvantageous deals that white traders tried to impose on them. In the Northwest, Nez Percé Indians defied being forced onto a reservation in Idaho by fleeing in 1877. They successfully eluded U.S. troops and the military's Crow and Cheyenne scouts over 1,800 miles of rugged terrain, but when they reached Montana, their leader, Young Joseph, decided that they could not escape, and he ended the flight. Sent to a reservation, Joseph repeatedly petitioned the government to return his peoples' ancestral lands, but his appeals went unheeded.

As they had done earlier in the East, whites responded to western Native peoples' defiance with military aggression. The attitude of many resembled that of an Arizona journalist who wrote, "Extermination is our only hope, and the sooner the better." In 1860, for example, Navajos, reacting to U.S. military pressure, carried out a destructive raid on Fort Defiance in Arizona Territory. In reprisal, the army eventually attacked and starved the Navajo into submission, destroying their fields, houses, and livestock, and in 1863–1864 forced them on a "Long Walk" from their homelands to a reservation at Bosque Redondo in New Mexico. Also in 1864, in order to eliminate Native peoples who blocked white ambitions in the Sand Creek region of Colorado, a militia commanded by Methodist minister John Chivington attacked a Cheyenne band led by Black Kettle, killing almost every warrior. In 1879, 4,000 U.S. soldiers forced surrender from Utes who already had given up most of their ancestral territory in western Colorado but were resisting further concessions.

The most publicized battle occurred in June 1876, when 2,500 Lakotas and Cheyennes led by Chiefs Rain-in-the-Face, Sitting Bull, and Crazy Horse surrounded and annihilated 256 government troops led by Colonel George A. Custer near Little Big Horn River in southern Montana. Although Native peoples consistently demonstrated military skill in such battles, shortages of supplies and relentless pursuit by U.S. soldiers, including African American units of Union Army veterans called Buffalo Soldiers (so named by the Cheyennes and Comanches they fought), eventually overwhelmed armed Native groups' resistance. Indigenous people were not so much conquered in battle as they were harassed and starved into submission.

15-1h Reform of Indian Policy

In the 1870s and 1880s, reformers and government officials sought more purposely than in the past to "civilize" and "uplift" Native peoples through landholding and education. This meant changing Native identities and outlawing customs deemed to be "savage and barbarous." In this regard, the United States copied imperialist policies of other nations, such as the French, who banned native religious ceremonies in their Pacific island colonies, and the British, who jailed Native African religious leaders. The American government determined to persuade indigenous peoples to abandon their

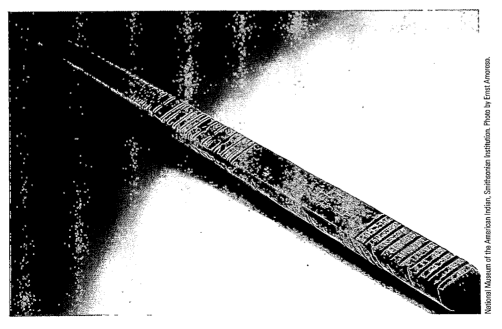

◁ The O'odham people kept track of historical events by carving scratches, dots, and notches year by year into wooden rods or cactus ribs. The "calendar sticks" were made by one man who functioned as a historian and who would retell the stories symbolized by his carvings. Markings of different colors served to remind the calendar stick recorder of details about an event.

National Museum of the American Indian, Smithsonian Institution. Photo by Ernst Amoroso.

traditional cultures and adopt American values of ambition, thrift, and materialism.

At the same time, other groups argued for sympathetic—and sometimes patronizing—treatment. Reform treatises, such as George Manypenny's *Our Indian Wards* (1880) and Helen Hunt Jackson's *A Century of Dishonor* (1881), plus unfavorable comparison with Canada's management of Indian affairs aroused American humanitarianism. Canada had granted Native peoples the rights of British subjects and proceeded more slowly than the United States in efforts to acculturate Native peoples. A high rate of intermarriage between Canadian Native peoples and Canadian whites also promoted smoother relations.

In the United States, the most active reform organizations were the Women's National Indian Association (WNIA) and the Indian Rights Association (IRA). The WNIA sought to use women's domestic qualities of nurture and compassion to help people in need and urged gradual assimilation. The IRA, which was more influential but numbered few Native Americans among its members, advocated citizenship and landholding by individual Native families. Most reformers believed Native Americans were culturally inferior to whites and assumed Native peoples could succeed economically only if they embraced middle-class values of diligence and education.

Reformers particularly deplored Native communities' sexual division of labor. Native women seemed to do all the work—tending crops, raising children, cooking, making tools and clothes—while being servile to men, who hunted but were otherwise idle. Ignoring the fact that white men sometimes mistreated white women, groups such as the WNIA and IRA wanted Native men to bear more responsibilities, treat women more respectfully, and resemble male heads of white middle-class households. But when Native men and women adopted this model of white society, in which women were supposed to be submissive and private, Native women lost much of the economic independence and power over daily life that they once had.

15-1i Zitkala-Sa

Some exceptional Native Americans managed to use white-controlled education to their advantage. Zitkala-Sa (Red Bird) was a Yankton Sioux born on Pine Ridge reservation in South Dakota in 1876. At age twelve, she was sent to a Quaker boarding school in Indiana and later attended Earlham College and the Boston Conservatory of Music. She became an accomplished orator and violinist, but her major contribution was her writing on behalf of her people's needs and the preservation of their cultures. In 1901 Zitkala-Sa published *Old Indian Legends*, in which she translated Sioux oral tradition into stories. She wrote other pieces for *Harper's* and *Atlantic Monthly*, and served in various capacities on the Standing Rock and Ute reservations. In 1902 Zitkala-Sa married a mixed-race army captain who had taken the name Ray Bonnin, and she became known as Gertrude Bonnin. Subsequently, she was elected the first

full-blooded Native American secretary of the Society of American Indians and served as editor of *American Indian Magazine*, all the while advocating for Indian rights.

15-1j Dawes Severalty Act

In 1887 Congress reversed its reservation policy and passed the **Dawes Severalty Act**. The act, supported by reformers, authorized dissolution of community-owned Native American property and granted land allotments to individual native families. A family head received 160 acres; each child under eighteen received 40 acres. The government held that land in trust for twenty-five years, so families could not sell their allotments. The law also awarded citizenship to all who accepted allotments (an act of Congress in 1906 delayed citizenship for those who had not yet taken their allotment). It also entitled the government to sell unallocated land to whites.

Indian policy, as implemented by the Interior Department, now assumed two main features, both of which aimed at assimilating Native peoples into white American culture. First and foremost, as required by the Dawes Act, the government distributed reservation land to families in the belief that property ownership would create productive citizens and integrate indigenous peoples into the larger society. As one official stated, the goal was to "weaken and destroy tribal relations and individualize them by giving each a separate home and having them subsist by industry." Second, officials believed that Native peoples would abandon their "barbaric" habits more quickly if their children were educated in boarding schools away from the reservations.

The Dawes Act represented a Euro-American and Christian worldview, an earnest but narrow belief that a society of landholding families headed by men was the most desired model. Government agents and reformers were joined by educators who viewed schools as tools to create a patriotic, industrious citizenry. Using the model of Hampton Institute, founded in Virginia in 1869 to educate newly freed slaves, educators helped establish the Carlisle School in Pennsylvania in 1879, which served as the flagship of the government's school system for Native Americans. In keeping with Euro-American custom, the boarding schools imposed white-defined sex roles: boys were taught farming and carpentry, and girls learned sewing, cleaning, and cooking.

15-1k Ghost Dance

In 1890 the government made one final show of force. With active resistance having been suppressed, some Lakotas and other groups turned to **Ghost Dance** religious movement as a spiritual means of preserving native cultures. Inspired by a

Dawes Severalty Act U.S. Dawes Severalty Act law designed to "civilize" Indians by dividing up and distributing communal tribal lands to individuals.

Ghost Dance Ritual where Ghost Dance Sioux dancers moved in a circle, accelerating until they reached a trancelike state and experienced visions of the future where white society would vanish from Native American lands.

Attempts to Make Native Americans Look and Act Like "Americans"

Government officials believed that they could "civilize" indigenous children in boarding schools by not only educating them to act like white people but also by making them look like white people. Thus the boys in the photograph on the left were given baseball uniforms and the girl on the right was made to wear a dress and carry a purse and umbrella, all of which were foreign to Native peoples. These images convey information about how indigenous peoples were treated, but they also suggest attitudes of the photographer and the artist who made the images.

CRITICAL THINKING

□ What messages about "civilizing" Native peoples did the person who photographed the baseball team and the artist who drew the picture of the girl reuniting with her people want the viewer to receive?

△ In an attempt to inculcate "American" customs into its Native students, the Fort Spokane Indian School in Spokane, Washington, created a baseball team for the young men who boarded there.

University of Washington Libraries, Special Collections NA4117

△ In an 1884 edition, *Frank Leslie's Weekly*, one of the most popular illustrated news and fiction publications of the late nineteenth and early twentieth centuries, depicted an "Americanized" Native girl dressed as a proper young lady returning from the Carlisle boarding school to visit her home at the Pine Ridge Agency in South Dakota.

Library of Congress Prints and Photographs Division [LC-USZ62-100543]

Paiute prophet named Wovoka, the Ghost Dance consisted of movement in a circle until dancers reached a trancelike state and envisioned dead ancestors who, dancers believed, heralded a day when buffalo would return and all elements of white civilization, including guns and whiskey, would be buried. The ritual expressed this messianic vision in several days of dancing and meditation.

Ghost Dancers forswore violence but appeared threatening when they donned sacred shirts that they believed would repel the white man's bullets. As the religion spread, government agents became alarmed about the possibility of renewed native uprisings. Charging that the cult was anti-Christian, the army began arresting Ghost Dancers. Late in 1890, the government sent the Seventh Cavalry, Custer's old regiment, to detain Lakota moving toward Pine Ridge, South Dakota. Although the Lakotas were starving and seeking shelter, the army assumed they were armed for revolt. Overtaking the band at a creek called **Wounded Knee**, the troops massacred an estimated three hundred men, women, and children in the snow.

15-1l The Losing of the West

American Indian wars and the Dawes Act effectively accomplished what whites wanted and Native peoples feared: they reduced Native peoples' independence and dissolved their human ecology. Speculators induced indigenous peoples to sell newly acquired property, in spite of federal safeguards against such practices. Between 1887 and the 1930s, Native peoples' landholdings dwindled from 138 million acres to 52 million. Land-grabbing whites were particularly cruel to Ojibwas in the northern plains. In 1906 Minnesota Senator Moses E. Clapp attached to an Indian appropriations bill a rider declaring that mixed-blood adults on the White Earth reservation were "competent" (meaning educated in white ways) enough to sell their land without having to observe the twenty-five-year waiting period stipulated in the Dawes Act. When the bill became law, speculators duped many Ojibwas into signing away their property in return for counterfeit money and worthless merchandise. The Ojibwas lost more than half their original holdings, and economic ruin overtook them.

Government policy had other injurious effects on Native peoples' ways of life. The boarding-school program enrolled thousands of children and tried to teach them that their inherited customs were inferior, but most schoolchildren returned to reservations demoralized rather than ready to assimilate into white society. Polingaysi Qoyawayma, a Hopi woman forced to take the Christian name Elizabeth Q. White, recalled after four years spent at the Sherman Institute in Riverside, California, "As a Hopi, I was misunderstood by the white man; as a convert of the missionaries, I was looked upon with suspicion by the Hopi people."

Ultimately, political and ecological crises overwhelmed western indigenous groups. White violence and military superiority alone did not defeat them. Their economic systems had started to break down before military campaigns

occurred. Buffalo extinction, enemy raids, and disease combined to hobble subsistence culture to the point where Native Americans had no alternative but to yield their lands to market-oriented whites. Believing their culture to be superior, whites determined to transform Native peoples into successful farmers by teaching them the value of private property, educating them in American ideals, and eradicating their "backward" languages, lifestyles, and religions. Although Native peoples tried to retain their culture and adapt to the demands they faced, by the end of the century they had lost control of the land and were under increasing pressure to shed their group identity. The West was won at their expense, and to this day they remain casualties of an aggressive age.

15-2 The Extraction of Natural Resources

▷ **What methods were used to extract natural resources in the West?**

▷ **What role did the Government play in the economic development of the West?**

▷ **What role did racial groups and race play in the development of the West?**

In contrast to indigenous peoples, who used natural resources to meet subsistence needs and small-scale trading, most whites who migrated to the West and Great Plains in the late nineteenth century were driven by the desire for material success. To their eyes, the vast stretches of territory promised untapped sources of wealth that could bring about a better life (see Map 15.1). Extraction of these resources advanced settlement and created new markets at home and abroad; it also fueled revolutions in transportation, agriculture, and industry that swept across the United States. This ecological relationship between nature and humans also gave rise to wasteful practices and fed habits of racial and sexual oppression.

15-2a Mining

In the mid-1800s, prospectors began to comb western terrain for gold, silver, copper, and other minerals. The mining frontier advanced rapidly, drawing thousands of people, mostly men, to Nevada, Idaho, Montana, Utah, and Colorado. California, where a gold rush helped populate a thriving state by 1850, furnished many of the miners, who traveled to nearby states in search of riches. Others seeking mineral riches followed traditional routes, moving from the East and Midwest to western mining regions.

Wounded Knee South Dakota site of a bloody clash between Sioux Indians and whites. Within minutes, white troops—mistakenly assuming the starving Sioux were armed for revolt—slaughtered three hundred people, including seven infants.

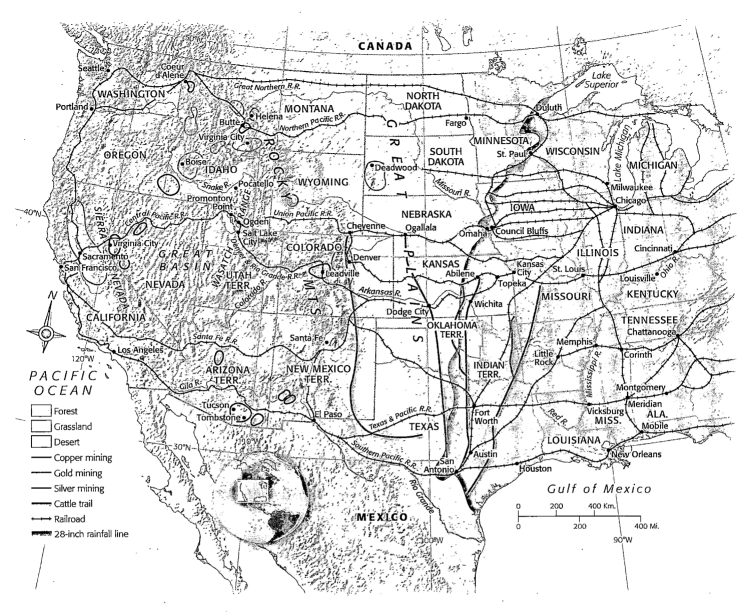

Map 15.1 The Development and Natural Resources of the West

By 1890, mining, lumbering, and cattle ranching had penetrated many areas west of the Mississippi River, and railroad construction had linked together the western economy. These activities, along with the spread of mechanized agriculture, altered both the economy and the people who were involved in them.

Prospectors tended to be restless optimists, willing to climb mountains and trek across deserts in search of a telltale glint of precious metal. They lived outdoors, shot animals for food, and financed their explorations by convincing merchants to advance credit for equipment in return for a share of the as-yet-undiscovered lode. Unlucky prospectors whose credit ran out took jobs and saved up for another search.

Digging up and transporting minerals was extremely expensive, so prospectors who did discover veins of metal seldom mined them. Instead, they sold their claims to large mining syndicates, such as the Anaconda Copper Company. Financed by eastern capital, these companies brought in engineers, heavy machinery, railroad lines, and work crews. Workers and businesses to serve the mining operations also settled cities and helped boost populations in places such as El Paso and Tucson. In doing so, they made western mining

corporate, just like eastern manufacturing. Though discoveries of gold and silver sparked national publicity, mining companies usually exploited less romantic but usually more-lucrative bonanzas of lead, zinc, tin, quartz, and copper.

15-2b Lumbering and Oil Drilling

Unlike mining, cutting trees to supply demands for construction and heating materials required vast tracts of forest land to be profitable. Because timber supplies in the upper Midwest and South had been depleted by earlier logging, lumber corporations moved into forests of the Northwest, where they felled trees, used horses and oxen to drag them to a nearby river, then floated the logs downstream to sawmills to be cut into boards. Large companies often grabbed millions of western acres under the Timber and Stone Act, passed by Congress in 1878 to stimulate settlement in California, Nevada,

The Australian Frontier

America's frontier West was not unique. Australia, founded like the United States as a European colony, had a frontier society that resembled the American West in several ways, especially in its mining development, its folk society, and its treatment of racial minorities. Australia experienced a gold rush in 1851, just two years after the United States did, and large-scale mining companies quickly moved into its western regions to extract mineral deposits. In 1897 future U.S. president Herbert Hoover, who at that time was a twenty-two-year-old geology graduate, went to work in Australia and began his successful career as a mining engineer.

Promise of mineral wealth lured thousands of immigrants to Australia in the late nineteenth century. Many of the newcomers arrived from China, and, as in the United States, these immigrants, most of them men, encountered abusive treatment. Anti-Chinese riots erupted in ports in New South Wales in 1861 and 1873, and beginning in 1854, the Australian government passed several laws restricting Chinese immigration. When the country became an independent British federation in 1901, one of its first acts applied a strict literacy test that virtually terminated Chinese immigration for over fifty years.

As in the American West, the Australian frontier bred folk heroes who came to symbolize white masculinity. In a society where men vastly outnumbered women, Australians glorified the tough, aggressive individual who displayed self-reliance and quick judgment that made the Australian backcountry man as idealized as the American cowboy. Similarly, Australian outlaws (called "bushrangers") such as Ned Kelly, an infamous bandit who was hanged in 1880, achieved the same notoriety as Americans Jesse James and Billy the Kid.

Although Australians celebrated white men who brought a spirit of personal liberty and opportunism to a new country, they also considered indigenous peoples, whom they called "Aborigines," as savages needing to be conquered and civilized. Christian missionaries viewed aborigines as lost in pagan darkness and tried to convert them. In 1869 the government of Victoria Province passed an Aborigine Protection Act that, like United States' policy toward Native Americans, encouraged removal of indigenous children from their families so they could learn European customs in schools run by whites. Australian natives adapted in their own ways. They formed cricket teams, and those with light skin sometimes hid their identity by telling census takers they were white. In the end, though, assimilation did not work, and Australians resorted to reservations as a means of "protecting" Native peoples, just as Americans isolated Native peoples on reserved land. Like the Americans, white Australians could not find a place for indigenous peoples in a land of opportunity.

△ Much like the American counterpart, the Australian frontier involved mining operations and was populated by indigenous peoples. Here, the "Aborigines," as the natives were called, are using track to bring down ore extracted from a hill.

CRITICAL THINKING

◻ How can white attitudes toward natural resources in both the United States and Australia explain treatment of indigenous peoples in both places?

◻ Can attitudes toward Asian immigrants in both places also be explained in this manner? Why or why not?

◁ After gold was discovered along the Klondike River in northwest Canada in 1896, tens of thousands of eager Americans flocked to the area, leaving jobs and families in hopes of striking it rich. These jubilant miners found a gold nugget, but most were not so lucky. The gold rush subsided by the end of the century as the remoteness of the area, difficulties in prospecting without heavy machinery, and discoveries of gold elsewhere in Canada forced most prospectors to give up their quest.

Hulton Archive/Getty Images

Oregon, and Washington. The law allowed private citizens to buy, at a low price, 160-acre plots "unfit for cultivation" and "valuable chiefly for timber." Lumber companies hired seamen from waterfront boarding houses to register claims to timberland and then transfer those claims to the company owners. By 1900, private citizens had bought over 3.5 million acres, but most of that land belonged to corporations.

While mining corporations were excavating western mineral deposits and lumber corporations were cutting down Northwest timberlands, oil companies were beginning to drill wells in the Southwest. In 1900, most of the nation's petroleum still came from the Appalachians and Midwest, but rich oil reserves had been discovered in Southern California and eastern Texas, creating not only new wealth but also boosting boom cities, such as Los Angeles and Houston. Although oil and kerosene were still used mostly for lubrication and lighting, oil discovered in the Southwest soon became a vital source of fuel for autos and other machines.

15-2c Water and Irrigation

Glittering gold, tall trees, and gushing oil shaped popular images of the West, but water gave it life. If western lands promised wealth from mining, cutting, and drilling, their agricultural potential promised more—but only if settlers could find a way to bring water to the arid soil. Western economic development is the story of how public and private interests used technology and organization to utilize the region's sometimes scarce water resources to make the land agriculturally productive. Just as control of land was central to western ecology, so, too, was control of water.

For centuries, Native Americans irrigated southwestern fields to sustain their subsistence farming. When the

Spanish arrived, they began tapping the Rio Grande River to irrigate farms in southwest Texas and New Mexico. Later they channeled water to California mission communities of San Diego and Los Angeles. The first Americans of European ancestry to practice extensive irrigation were the Mormons. After arriving in Utah in 1847, they diverted streams and rivers into networks of canals, whose water enabled them to farm the hard-baked soil. By 1890 Utah boasted over 263,000 irrigated acres supporting more than 200,000 people.

15-2d Rights to Water

Efforts at land reclamation through irrigation in Colorado and California sparked conflict over rights to precious streams that flowed through the West. Americans inherited the English common-law principle of riparian rights, which held that only those who owned land along a river's banks could appropriate from the water's flow. The stream itself, according to riparianism, belonged to God; those who lived near it could take water for normal needs but were not to diminish the river. According to business owners, this principle, intended to protect nature, discouraged economic development because it prohibited property owners from damming or diverting water for large-scale economic development.

Americans who settled the West rejected riparianism in favor of prior appropriation, which awarded a river's water to the first person who claimed it. Westerners, taking cues in part from eastern Americans who had diverted waterways to power mills and factories, asserted that water, like timber, minerals, and other natural resources, existed to serve human needs and advance profits. They argued that anyone intending a "reasonable" or "beneficial" (economically productive) use of river water should have the right to appropriation, and the courts generally agreed.

15-2e Government Supervision of Water Rights

Under appropriation, someone who dammed and diverted water often reduced the flow of water downstream. People disadvantaged by such action could protect their interests either by suing those who deprived them of water or by establishing a public authority to regulate water usage. Thus in 1879 the state of Colorado created several regional water divisions throughout the state, each with a commissioner to regulate water rights. In 1890 Wyoming enlarged the concept of government control with a constitutional provision declaring that the state's rivers were public property subject to supervision.

Destined to become the most productive agricultural state, California devised a dramatic response to the problem of water rights, sometimes called the California Solution. In the 1860s, a few individuals controlled huge tracts of land in the fertile Sacramento and San Joaquin River valleys, which they used for speculating in real estate, raising cattle, and growing wheat. But around the edges of the wheat fields lay unoccupied lands that could profitably support vegetable and fruit farming if irrigated properly.

Unlike western states that had favored appropriation rights over riparian rights, California maintained a mixed legal system that upheld riparianism while allowing for some appropriation. This system disadvantaged irrigators and prompted them to seek to change state law. In 1887 the legislature passed a bill permitting farmers to organize into districts that would construct and operate irrigation projects. An irrigation district could use its authority to purchase water rights, seize private property to build irrigation canals, and finance projects through taxation or by issuing bonds. As a result of this legislation, California became the nation's leader in irrigated acreage, with more than 1 million irrigated acres by 1890, making the state's fruit and vegetable agriculture the most profitable in the country.

15-2f Newlands Reclamation Act

Although state-supervised irrigation stimulated farming, the federal government still owned most western land in the 1890s, ranging from 64 percent of California to 96 percent of Nevada. Prodded by land-hungry developers, state governments wanted the federal government to transfer to them at least part of public domain lands. States claimed that they could make these lands profitable through reclamation—providing them with irrigated water. Congress generally refused such transfers because of the controversies they raised. If one state sponsored irrigation to develop its own land, who would regulate waterways that flowed through more than one state? If, for example, California assumed control of the Truckee River, which flowed westward out of Lake Tahoe on the California-Nevada border, how would Nevadans be assured that California would allow

them sufficient water? Only the federal government, it seemed, had the power to regulate interstate water development.

In 1902, after years of debate, Congress passed the **Newlands Reclamation Act**. Named for the bill's sponsor, Nevada's Democratic congressman Francis Newlands, the law allowed the federal government to sell western public lands to individuals in parcels not to exceed 160 acres and to use proceeds from such sales to finance irrigation projects. The Newlands Act provided for control of water but did not address conservation, even though three-fourths of the water used in open-ditch irrigation, the most common form, was lost to evaporation. Thus the Newlands Reclamation Act fell squarely within the tradition of development of nature for human profit. It represented a decision by the federal government to aid the agricultural and general economic expansion of the West.

15-2g Complex Communities

As the West developed, it became a rich multiracial society, including not only Native Americans and white migrants but also Mexicans, African Americans, and Asians, all involved in community building. A crescent of territory, a borderland stretching from western Texas through New Mexico and Arizona to Northern California, but also including Mexico, supported ranchers and sheepherders, descendants of the Spanish who had originally claimed the land from the natives. In New Mexico, Spaniards intermarried with Native peoples to form a *mestizo* population of small farmers and ranchers. All along the Southwest frontier, Mexican immigrants moved into American territory to find work. Some returned to Mexico seasonally; others stayed. Although the Treaty of Guadalupe Hidalgo (1848) had guaranteed property rights to Hispanics, "Anglo" (the Mexican name for a white American) miners, speculators, and railroads used fraud and other means to obtain much of Hispanic landholdings. As a result, many Mexicanos moved to cities such as San Antonio and Tucson, and became wage laborers.

Before the Chinese Exclusion Act of 1882 prohibited the immigration of Chinese laborers, some 200,000 Chinese—mostly young, single males—entered the United States and built communities in California, Oregon, and Washington. Many came with five-year contracts to work on railroad construction, then return home, presumably with resources for a better life. They also labored in the fields. By the 1870s, Chinese people composed half of California's agricultural work force. The state's farms and citrus groves demanded a huge migrant work force to harvest the crops, and Chinese laborers moved from one ripening crop to another, working as pickers and packers. In cities such as San Francisco, they labored in textile and cigar factories and lived in large, densely-packed boarding houses. Few married because Chinese women were scarce.

Like Chinese and Mexicans, Japanese and European immigrants, especially Irish, moved from place to place as they worked on railroads and in mining

Newlands Reclamation Act Federal legislation that authorized the U.S. government to sell western public lands to finance dams and irrigation projects in the West.

and agricultural communities. The region consequently developed its own migrant economy, with workers traveling across a large geographical area as they took short-term jobs in mining, farming, and railroad construction.

African Americans tended to be more settled, many of them "exodusters" or former slaves who had fled the South and built all-black towns, mostly in Kansas. Nicodemus, Kansas, for example, was founded in 1877 by black migrants from Lexington, Kentucky, and grew to 600 residents within two years. Early experiences were challenging, but eventually the town boasted newspapers, shops, churches, a hotel, and a bank. When attempts to obtain railroad connections failed, however, the town declined, and many of its businesses moved across the Solomon River to the town of Bogue, where a Union Pacific Railroad camp was located. Other black migrants, encouraged by editors and land speculators, went to Oklahoma Territory. In the 1890s and early 1900s, African American settlers founded thirty-two all-black communities in Oklahoma, and the territory boasted several successful black farmers.

15-2h Western Women

Although unmarried men numerically dominated the western natural-resource frontier, many communities contained populations of white women who had come for the same reason as men: to make their fortune. But in the West as elsewhere, women's independence was limited; they usually accompanied a husband or father and seldom prospected themselves. Even so, many women used their labor as a resource and earned money by cooking and laundering, and in some cases providing sexual services for miners in houses of prostitution. In the Northwest, they worked in canneries, cleaning and salting the fish that their husbands caught. Mexicano women took jobs in cities as laundresses and seamstresses.

A number of white women helped to bolster family and community life as members of the home mission movement. Protestant missions had long sponsored benevolent activities abroad, such as in China, and had aided the settlement of Oregon in the 1830s and 1840s. But in the mid-nineteenth century, some women broke away from male-dominated missionary organizations. Using the slogan "Woman's work for women," they exerted moral authority in the West by establishing their own missionary societies and aiding women—unmarried mothers, Mormons, Native Americans, and Chinese—who they believed had fallen prey to men or who had not yet accepted principles of Christian virtue.

15-2i Significance of Race

To control labor and social relations within this human ecological complex, white settlers made race an important distinguishing characteristic within a hierarchy that included numerous categories. At the top were those descended from white Europeans, but this group had many subranks, with Anglo-Saxons

"exodusters" Freed people who migrated from the South to the North and Midwest for better opportunities.

first, followed by less valued white groups, such as Celts, Turks, Slavs, Hebrews, and many more. Below whites were people considered (by whites) as nonwhite and inferior: Native Americans, Mexicans (both Mexican Americans, who had originally inhabited western lands, and Mexican immigrants), "Mongolians" (a term applied to Chinese), and "Negroes." In applying these categories, whites imposed racial distinctions on people who, with the possible exception of African Americans, had never before considered themselves to be a "race." Whites using these categories ascribed demeaning characteristics to all others, judging them to be permanently inferior. In 1878, for example, a federal judge in California ruled that Chinese could not become U.S. citizens because they were not "white persons."

Racial and ethnic minorities in western communities occupied the bottom segment of a two-tiered labor system. Whites dominated the top tier of managerial and skilled labor positions, while Irish, Chinese, Mexican, and African Americans generally held unskilled positions. All non-Anglo groups encountered prejudice, especially as dominant whites tried to reserve for themselves whatever riches the West might yield. Anti-Chinese violence erupted during hard times. For example, when the Union Pacific Railroad tried to replace white workers with lower-waged Chinese in Rock Springs, Wyoming, in 1885, unemployed whites invaded and burned down the Chinese part of town, killing twenty-eight. Mexicans, many of whom had been the original owners of the land in California and elsewhere, saw their property claims ignored or stolen by white miners and farmers.

The multiracial quality of western communities, however, also included a cross-racial dimension. Because so many white male migrants were single, intermarriages, or at least cohabitation, with Mexican and Native American women were common. Such unions were acceptable for white men, but not for white women, especially where Asian immigrants were involved. Most miscegenation laws passed by western legislatures were intended to prevent Chinese and Japanese men from marrying white women.

15-2j Conservation Movement

As whites were wresting ownership of the land from Native American and Mexican inhabitants, questions arose over who should control the nation's animal, mineral, and timber resources. Much of the undeveloped territory west of the Mississippi was in the public domain, and some people believed that the federal government, as its owner, should limit its exploitation. Others, however, believed that their own and the nation's prosperity depended on unlimited utilization of the land and its contents.

Questions about natural resources caught Americans between a desire for progress and a fear of spoiling nature. After the Civil War, people eager to protect the natural landscape began to organize a conservation movement. Sports hunters, concerned about depletion of wildlife, opposed mass commercial hunting and lobbied state legislatures to pass hunting regulations. Artists and tourists in 1864 persuaded

Congress to preserve the beautiful Yosemite Valley by granting it to the state of California, which reserved it for public use. Then, in 1872, Congress designated the Yellowstone River region in Wyoming as the first national park. And in 1891 conservationists, led by naturalist John Muir, pressured Congress to authorize President Benjamin Harrison to create forest reserves—public lands protected from private timber cutters.

Such policies met with strong objections from lumber companies and railroads. Despite Muir's activism and efforts by the Sierra Club (which Muir helped found in 1892) and by such corporations as the Southern Pacific Railroad, which supported rational resource development, opposition was loudest in the West, where people remained eager to take advantage of nature's bounty. Ironically, however, by prohibiting trespass in areas such as Yosemite and Yellowstone, conservation policy deprived Native Americans and white settlers of the wildlife, water, and firewood that they had previously taken from federal lands.

15-2k Admission of New States

Development of mining and forest regions, as well as of farms and cities, brought western territories to the economic and population threshold of statehood (see Map 15.2). In 1889 Republicans seeking to solidify control of Congress passed an omnibus bill granting statehood to North Dakota, South Dakota, Washington, and Montana, where Republican politicians dominated. Wyoming and Idaho, both of which allowed

women to vote in state elections, were admitted the following year. Congress denied statehood to Utah until 1896, wanting assurances from the Mormons, who constituted a majority of the territory's population and controlled its government, that they would prohibit polygamy.

Western states' varied communities fostered a "go-getter" optimism that distinguished the American spirit. The lawlessness and hedonism of places such as Deadwood, in Dakota Territory, and Tombstone, in Arizona Territory, gave the region notoriety and romance. Legends, only partly true, arose about characters whose lives both typified and magnified western experience.

15-2l Western Folk Heroes

Arizona's mining towns, with their free-flowing cash and loose law enforcement, attracted gamblers, thieves, and opportunists whose names came to stand for the Wild West. Near Tombstone, the infamous Clanton family and their partner Johnny Ringo engaged in smuggling and cattle rustling. Inside the town, the Earp brothers—Wyatt, Jim, Morgan, Virgil, and Warren—and their friends William ("Bat") Masterson and John Henry ("Doc") Holliday operated on both sides of the law as gunmen, gamblers, and politicians. A feud between the Clantons and Earps climaxed on October 26, 1881, in a shootout at the O.K. Corral, where three members of the Clanton group were killed and Holliday and Morgan Earp were wounded. These characters and their exploits provided material for future novels, movies, and television programs.

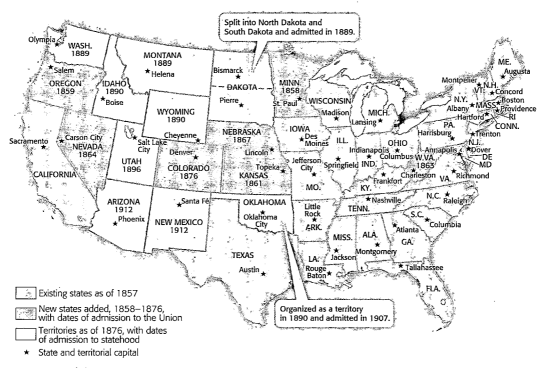

Map 15.2 The United States, 1876–1912

A wave of admissions between 1889 and 1912 brought remaining territories to statehood and marked the final creation of new states until Alaska and Hawai'i were admitted in the 1950s.

Writers Mark Twain, Bret Harte, and others captured the flavor of western life, and characters such as Buffalo Bill, Annie Oakley, and Wild Bill Hickok became western folk heroes. But violence and eccentricity were not widely common. Most miners and lumbermen worked long hours, often for corporations rather than as rugged individuals, and had little time, energy, or money for gambling, carousing, or gunfights. Women worked as long or longer as teachers, laundresses, storekeepers, and housewives. Only a few were sharpshooters or dance-hall queens. For most, western life was a matter of adapting and surviving.

15-3 The Age of Railroad Expansion

▷ **How did railroad construction contribute to changes in social organization?**

Between 1865 and 1890, railroad construction boomed, as total track grew from 35,000 to 200,000 miles, mostly from construction west of the Mississippi River (see Map 15.1). By 1900 the United States contained one-third of all railroad track in the world. A diverse mix of workers made up construction crews. The Central Pacific, built eastward from San Francisco, employed thousands of Chinese; the Union Pacific, extending westward from Omaha, Nebraska, used mainly Irish labor. Workers lived in shacks and tents that they dismantled, loaded on flatcars, and relocated each day.

Railroad expansion had powerful economic effects. After 1880, when steel rails replaced iron rails, railroads helped to boost the nation's steel industry to international leadership. Railroads also spawned related industries, including coal mining (for fuel), passenger- and freight-car manufacture, and depot construction. Influential and essential, railroads gave important impetus to western urbanization. With their ability to transport large loads of people and freight, lines such as the Union Pacific and the Southern Pacific accelerated the growth of western hubs, such as Chicago, Omaha, Kansas City, Cheyenne, Los Angeles, Portland, and Seattle.

15-3a Railroad Subsidies

Unlike European countries, where railroads were state-owned, American railroads were privately owned and managed. Yet, American railroads accomplished their massive construction feats with help from some of the largest government subsidies in American history. Promoters argued that because railroads were a public benefit, the government should grant them land from the public domain, which they could then sell to finance construction. During the Civil War, Congress, dominated by business-minded Republicans, was sympathetic, as it had been when it aided steamboat companies earlier in the century. As a result,

Library of Congress

△ The rim of the horseshoe in this advertisement depicts reasons why railroad travel was better than other forms: one could avoid crowds of immigrants on steamships, move faster than a canal boat being towed by a mule, and be safe from bandits holding up a stagecoach. At the bottom of the poster are two depictions of luxurious dining and relaxed travel in a chair car that a railroad offered.

the federal government granted railroad corporations over 180 million acres, mostly for interstate routes. These grants usually consisted of a right-of-way, plus alternate sections of land in a strip 20 to 80 miles wide along the right-of-way. Railroads funded construction by using these lands as security for bonds—loans from investors—or by selling parcels for cash. States and localities heaped on further subsidies. State legislators, many of whom had financial interests in a railroad's success, granted some 50 million acres. Cities and towns also assisted, usually by offering loans or by purchasing railroad bonds or stocks.

Government subsidies had mixed effects. Although capitalists often opposed government involvement in the economic affairs of private businesses, railroads nevertheless readily accepted public aid and pressured governments into meeting their needs. The Southern Pacific, for example, threatened to bypass Los Angeles unless the city paid a bonus and built a depot. Without government help, few railroads could have prospered sufficiently to attract private investment, yet such aid was not always salutary. During the 1880s, the policy of generosity haunted communities whose zeal had prompted them to commit too much to railroads that were never built or that defaulted on loans. Some laborers and farmers fought subsidies, arguing that companies such as the Southern Pacific would become too powerful. Many communities boomed, however, because they had linked their fortunes to the iron horse. Moreover, railroads helped attract investment into the West and drew farmers into the market economy.

15-3b Standard Gauge, Standard Time

Railroad construction brought about important technological and organizational reforms. By the late 1880s, almost all lines had adopted standard-gauge rails so that tracks built by different companies could connect with one another. Air brakes, automatic car couplers, and other devices made rail transportation safer and more efficient. The need for gradings, tunnels, and bridges spurred the growth of the American engineering profession. Organizational advances included systems for coordinating passenger and freight schedules. Railroads also, however, reinforced racial segregation by separating black from white passengers on railroad cars and in stations.

Rail transportation altered conceptions of time and space. First, as they surmounted physical barriers by bridging rivers and tunneling through mountains, railroads transformed space into time. Instead of expressing distance between places in miles, people began to refer to the amount of time it took to travel from one place to another. Second, railroad scheduling required nationwide standardization of time so that shippers could be certain about when a train would depart or arrive. Before railroads, local clocks struck noon when the sun was directly overhead, and people set clocks and watches accordingly. But because the sun was not overhead at exactly the same moment everywhere, time varied from place to place. Boston's clocks, for instance, differed from those in New York by almost twelve minutes. To impose regularity, railroads created their own time zones. In 1883, without authority from Congress, the nation's railroads agreed to establish four standard time zones for the country. Most communities adjusted accordingly, and railroad time became national time.

15-4 Farming the Plains

▷ **What environmental, social, and economic challenges did settlers face in the West?**

▷ **How did settlers adapt to life and farming in the West?**

▷ **How did ranching evolve over the course of the nineteenth century?**

While California emerged as the nation's highest-yielding agricultural state, extraordinary ecological development occurred in the Great Plains. There, farming in the late 1800s exemplified two important achievements: the transformation by people of arid, windswept prairies into arable land that would feed the nation, and the transformation of agriculture into big business by means of mechanization, long-distance transportation, and scientific cultivation. These feats did not come easily. The region's climate and terrain presented formidable challenges, and overcoming them did not guarantee success. Irrigation and mechanized agriculture enabled farmers to feed the nation's burgeoning population and turned the United States into the world's breadbasket, but the experience also scarred the lives of countless people who made that accomplishment possible.

15-4a Settlement of the Plains

During the 1870s and 1880s, more acres were put under cultivation in states such as Kansas, Nebraska, and Texas than in the entire nation during the previous 250 years. The number of farms tripled between 1860 and 1910, as hundreds of thousands of hopeful migrants streamed into the Plains region. The Homestead Act of 1862 and other measures to encourage western settlement offered cheap or free plots to people who would reside on and improve their property. Railroads that had received land subsidies were especially active in recruiting settlers, advertising cheap land, arranging credit, offering reduced fares, and promising instant success. Railroad agents—often former immigrants—traveled to Denmark, Sweden, Germany, and other European nations to encourage immigration, and greeted newcomers at eastern ports.

Most families who occupied western farmlands migrated because opportunities there seemed to promise a second chance, a better existence than their previous one. Railroad expansion gave farmers in remote regions a way to ship crops to market, and construction of grain elevators eased problems of storage. As a result of worldwide as well as national population growth, demand for farm products burgeoned, and the prospects for commercial agriculture—growing crops for profit and shipment to distant, including international, markets—became more favorable than ever.

15-4b Hardship on the Plains

Farm life, however, was much harder than advertisements and railroad agents insinuated. Migrants often encountered scarcities of essentials that they had once taken for granted, and they had to adapt to the environment. Barren prairies contained insufficient lumber for housing and fuel, so pioneer families built houses of sod and burned buffalo dung for heat. Water for cooking and cleaning was sometimes scarce also. Machinery for drilling wells was expensive, as were windmills for drawing water to the surface.

Weather was even more forbidding than the terrain. The climate between the Missouri River and the Rocky Mountains divides along a line running from Minnesota southwest through Oklahoma, then south, bisecting Texas. West of this line, annual rainfall averages less than twenty-eight inches,

Library of Congress

◁ Three adults and a child are posing alongside a road and in front of a sod house with their horse team in the background. Much of the farm frontier was virtually treeless, dry, and dusty. This family at least had enough resources to afford a relatively "high-toned" house and a windmill to bring up scarce water.

not enough for most crops, and even scant life-giving rain was never certain (see Map 15.3). Heartened by adequate water one year, farmers gagged on dust and broke plows on hardened soil the next.

Weather seldom followed predictable cycles. Weeks of summer heat and parching winds suddenly gave way to violent storms that washed away crops and property. Frigid winter blizzards piled up mountainous snowdrifts that halted outdoor movement and froze livestock. During the winter of 1887–87, it snowed almost constantly on the Plains, prompting one farmer to observe that it "seemed as if all the world's ice from time's beginning had come on a wind that howled and screamed with the fury of demons." In springtime, melting snow swelled streams, and floods threatened millions of acres. In fall, a week without rain turned dry grasslands into tinder, and the slightest spark could ignite a raging prairie fire. Severe drought in Texas between 1884 and 1886 drove many farmers off the land, and a more widespread drought in 1886 struck areas as diverse as Dakota, Wyoming, and California.

Nature could be cruel even under good conditions. Weather that was favorable for crops also benefitted breeding insects. Worms and flying pests ravaged fields. In the 1870s and 1880s, grasshopper swarms ate up entire farms. Heralded only by the din of buzzing wings, a mile-long cloud of insects would smother the land and devour everything: plants, tree bark, and clothing. As one farmer lamented, the "hoppers left behind nothing but the mortgage."

15-4c Social Isolation

Settlers also had to cope with social isolation. In New England and Europe, farmers lived in villages and traveled daily to and from nearby fields. This pattern of community life was rare in the expanses of the Plains—and in the Far West and South as well—where peculiarities of land division compelled rural dwellers to live apart from each other. Because most farm plots

were rectangular—usually encompassing 160 acres—at most four families could live near one another, but only if they built homes around their shared four-corner intersection. In practice, households usually lived back from their boundary lines, and at least a half-mile separated farmhouses. Women were especially isolated, confined by domestic chores to the household. Like Nannie Jackson, they visited and exchanged food and services with neighbor women when they could and occasionally went to town, but, as one writer observed, a farm woman's life was "a weary, monotonous round of cooking and washing and mending."

Letters that Ed Donnell, a young Nebraska homesteader, wrote to his family in Missouri reveal how time and circumstances could dull optimism. In the fall of 1885, Donnell rejoiced to his mother, "I like Nebr first rate. . . . I have saw a pretty tuff time a part of the time since I have been out here, but I started out to get a home and I was determined to win or die in the attempt. . . . Have got a good crop of corn, a floor in my house and got it ceiled overhead." Already, though, Donnell was lonely. He went on, "There is lots of other bachelors here but I am the only one I know who doesn't have kinfolks living handy. . . . You wanted to know when I was going to get married. Just as quick as I can get money ahead to get a cow."

A year and a half later, Donnell's dreams were dissolving and, still a bachelor, he was beginning to look for a second chance elsewhere. He wrote to his brother, "The rats eat my sod stable down. . . . I may sell out this summer, ... If I sell I am going west and grow up with the country." By fall, conditions had worsened. Donnell lamented, "We have been having wet weather for 3 weeks. . . . My health has been so poor this summer and the wind and the sun hurts my head so. I think if I can sell I will . . . move to town for I can get $40 a month working in a grist mill and I would not be exposed to the weather." Donnell's doubts and hardships, shared by thousands of people, fed the cityward migration of farm folk that fueled late-nineteenth-century

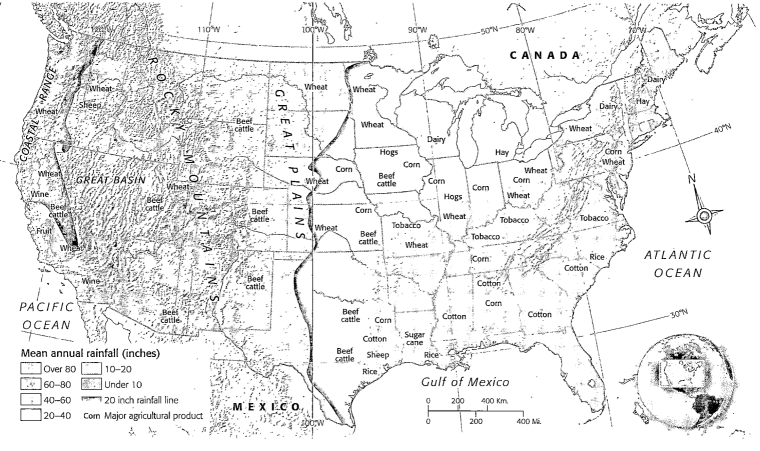

Mean annual rainfall (inches)
- Over 80
- 60–80
- 40–60
- 20–40
- 10–20
- Under 10
- 20 inch rainfall line
- Corn Major agricultural product

Map 15.3 Agricultural Regions of the United States, 1890

In the Pacific Northwest and east of the twenty-eight-inch-rainfall line, farmers could grow a greater variety of crops. Territory west of the line was either too mountainous or too arid to support agriculture without irrigation. The grasslands that once fed buffalo herds could now feed beef cattle.

urban growth (see "Growth of the Modern American City," Section 16-4).

15-4d Mail-Order Companies and Rural Free Delivery

Farm families survived by sheer resolve and by organizing churches and clubs where they could socialize a few times a month. By 1900 two developments had brought rural settlers

who lived east of the rainfall line into closer contact with modern consumer society. First, mail-order companies, such as Montgomery Ward (founded 1872) and Sears, Roebuck (founded 1893), made new products attainable through catalog sales. Emphasizing personal attention to customers, Ward and Sears received letters that often reported family news and sought advice on needs from gifts to childcare. A Washington man wrote to Mr. Ward, "As you advertise everything for sale that a

◁ Farm women sometimes relieved their isolation by getting together and creating a quilt. Note the different age groups represented in this activity and the animal trophy hanging conspicuously above them.

person wants, I thought I would write you, as I am in need of a wife, and see what you could do for me." Another reported, "I suppose you wonder why we haven't ordered anything from you since the fall. The cow kicked my arm and broke it and besides my wife was sick, and there was the doctor bill. But now, thank God, that is paid, and we are all well again, and we have a fine new baby boy, and please send plush bonnet number 29d8077."

Second, in 1896, after farmers petitioned Congress for extension of the postal service, the government made Rural Free Delivery (RFD) widely available. Farmers previously had to go to town to pick up mail. Now they could receive letters, newspapers, and catalogs in a roadside mailbox nearly every day. In 1913 the postal service inaugurated parcel post, which enabled people to receive packages, such as orders from Ward and Sears, more cheaply.

15-4e Mechanization of Agriculture

As with industrial production (see "Technology and the Triumph of Industrialism," Section 16-1), the late-nineteenth-century agricultural revolution was driven by expanded use of machinery. When the Civil War drew men away from farms in the upper Mississippi River Valley to fight in the army, women and older men who remained behind began using mechanical implements to grow crops to satisfy demand for food and take advantage of high grain prices. After the war, high demand encouraged farmers to continue utilizing machines, and inventors developed new implements to facilitate planting and harvesting. Seeders, combines, binders, reapers, and rotary plows, carried westward by railroads, facilitated grain-growing on the Plains and in California. Technology also aided dairy and poultry farming. The centrifugal cream separator, patented in 1879, sped the process of skimming cream from milk, and a mechanized incubator, invented in 1885, made chicken-raising more profitable.

For centuries, the acreage of grain a farmer planted was limited by the amount that could be harvested by hand. Machines significantly increased productivity. Before mechanization, a farmer working alone could harvest about 7.5 acres of wheat. Using an automatic binder that cut and bundled the grain, a farmer could harvest 135 acres. Machines dramatically reduced the time and cost of farming other crops as well.

15-4f Legislative and Scientific Aids

Meanwhile, Congress and scientists worked to improve existing crops and develop new ones. The 1862 Morrill Land Grant Act gave each state federal lands to sell in order to finance agricultural research at educational institutions. The act prompted establishment of public universities in Wisconsin, Illinois, Minnesota, California, and other states. A second Morrill Act in 1890 aided more schools, including several all-black colleges. The Hatch Act of 1887 provided for agricultural experiment stations in every state, further encouraging the advancement of agricultural science and technology.

Science also enabled farmers to use the soil more efficiently. Researchers developed dry farming, a technique of plowing and harrowing that minimized evaporation of precious moisture. Botanists perfected varieties of "hard" wheat whose seeds could withstand northern winters, and millers invented a process for grinding the tougher wheat kernels into flour. Agriculturists adapted new varieties of wheat from Russia and rice from Asia. Horticulturist Luther Burbank developed new food plants and flowers at a garden laboratory in Sebastopol, California. George Washington Carver, son of black slaves who became a chemist and taught at Alabama's Tuskegee Institute, created hundreds of products from peanuts, soybeans, and sweet potatoes. Other scientists devised means of combating plant and animal diseases. Just as in mining and manufacturing, science and technology provided American farming with means for expanding productivity in the market economy (see Table 15.1).

15-4g The Ranching Frontier

When commercial farming overspread the West, it ran headlong into one of the region's most romantic industries—ranching. Beginning in the sixteenth century, Spanish landholders raised cattle commercially in Mexico and what would become the American Southwest. They employed indigenous peoples and Mexicans as cowboys, known as *vaqueros*, who tended herds and rounded up cattle to be branded and slaughtered. Anglo ranchers moving into Texas and California in the early nineteenth century hired *vaqueros*, who in turn taught skills in roping, branding, and horse training to white and African American cowboys.

Table 15.1 Summary: Government Land Policy

Railroad land grants (1850–1871)	Granted 181 million acres to railroads to encourage construction and development
Homestead Act (1862)	Gave 80 million acres to settlers to encourage settlement
Morrill Act (1862)	Granted 11 million acres to states to sell to fund public agricultural colleges
Other grants	Granted 129 million acres to states to sell for other educational and related purposes
Dawes Act (1887)	Allotted some reservation lands to individual Native Americans to promote private property and weaken tribal values among Native groups and offered remaining reservation lands for sale to whites (by 1906, some 75 million acres had been acquired by whites)
Various laws	Permitted direct sales of 100 million acres by the Land Office

Source: Goldfield, David; Abbott, Carl; Anderson, Virginia Dejohn; Argersinger, Jo Ann; Argersinger, Peter H.; Barney, William L.; and Weir, Robert M., The American Journey, Volume II, 3rd ed., © 2004. Reproduced by permission of Pearson Education, Inc., Upper Saddle River, New Jersey.

△ This lithograph, drawn from a photo in 1878, displays the transition from old means of farming, using horses and wagons, to new machines, such as the steam-powered wheat thresher depicted on this Dakota Territory farm.

By the 1860s, cattle ranching became increasingly profitable, as population growth boosted demand for beef and railroads simplified transportation of food. By 1870 drovers were herding thousands of Texas cattle on long drives northward to Kansas, Missouri, and Wyoming (see Map 15.1). At the northern terminus, the cattle were sold to northern feed lots or loaded onto trains bound for Chicago and St. Louis for slaughter and distribution to national and international markets.

The long drive gave rise to images of bellowing cattle, buckskin-clad cowboys, and smoky campfires under starry skies, but the process was not very efficient. Trekking 1,000 miles or more for two to three months made cattle sinewy and tough. Herds traveling through Native peoples' territories and farmers' fields were sometimes shot at and later prohibited from such trespass by state laws. Ranchers adjusted by raising herds nearer to railroad routes. When cattlemen discovered that crossing Texas longhorns with heavier Hereford and Angus breeds produced animals better able to survive harsh winters, cattle raising expanded northward, and proliferating herds in Kansas, Nebraska, Colorado, Wyoming, Montana, and Dakota crowded out already declining buffalo populations. Profits were considerable. A rancher could purchase a calf for $5, let it feed on grasslands for a few years, recapture it in a roundup, and sell it at a market price of $40 or $45.

15-4h The Open Range

Cattle raisers needed vast pastures to graze their herds while spending as little as possible on land acquisition. Thus they often bought a few acres bordering a stream and turned their herds loose on adjacent public domain that no one wanted because it lacked water access. By this method, called open-range ranching, a cattleman could utilize thousands of acres by owning only a hundred or so. Neighboring ranchers often formed associations

and allowed herds to graze together. Owners identified their cattle by burning a brand into each animal's hide. Each ranch had its own unique brand—a shorthand method for labeling movable property. But as more profit-seeking ranchers flowed into the Plains, cattle began to overrun the range, and other groups challenged ranchers over use of the land.

In California and New Mexico, sheepherders also grazed herds on public land, sparking territorial clashes. Ranchers complained that sheep ruined grassland by eating down to the roots and that cattle refused to graze where sheep had been. Occasionally ranchers and sheepherders resorted to armed conflict rather than settle disagreements in court, where a judge might discover that both were using public land illegally.

More importantly, however, the advancing farming frontier was generating new demands for acreage. Devising a way to mark property resulted in an unheralded but significant change in land management. The problem was fencing. Lacking sufficient timber and stone for fencing, western settlers could not easily define and protect their property. Tensions flared when farmers accused cattlemen of allowing their herds to trespass on cropland and when herders in turn charged that farmers should fence their property against grazing animals. Ranchers and farmers alike lacked an economical means of enclosing herds and fields.

15-4i Barbed Wire

The solution was barbed wire. Patented in 1873 by Joseph Glidden, a DeKalb, Illinois, farmer, this fencing consisted of twisted wire strands that held sharp wire barbs in place at regular intervals. Mass produced by the Washburn and Moen Manufacturing Company of Worcester, Massachusetts— 80.5 million pounds in 1880 alone—barbed wire provided a cheap and durable means of enclosure. It benefited homesteaders by enabling them to protect their property from grazing cattle. It also ended open-range ranching and made roundups unnecessary, because it enabled ranchers to enclose their herds. In addition, the development of the round silo for storing hay without it spoiling enabled cattle raisers to feed their herds without grazing them on vast stretches of land.

15-4k Ranching as Big Business

By 1890 big businesses were taking over the cattle industry and applying scientific methods of breeding and feeding. Corporations also used technology to squeeze larger returns out of meat-packing. Like buffalo, all parts of a cow had uses. Only about half of it consisted of salable meat. Larger profits came from by-products: hides for leather, bones for fertilizer, hooves for glue, and fat for candles and soap. But cattle processing also had harmful environmental impact. What meatpackers could not sell they dumped into rivers and streams. By the late nineteenth century, the stench from the Chicago River, which flowed past the city's mammoth processing plants, made nearby residents sick.

Open-range ranching made beef a staple of the American diet and created a few fortunes, but it could not survive the rush of history. During the 1880s, overgrazing destroyed grass supplies on the Plains, and the brutal winter of 1886–1887 killed 90 percent of some herds and drove small ranchers out of business. By 1890, large-scale ranchers owned or leased the land they used, though some illegal fencing persisted. Cowboys formed labor organizations and participated in strikes for higher pay. The myth of the cowboy's freedom and individualism lived on, but ranching, like mining and farming, quickly became a corporate business.

15-5 The South After Reconstruction

▷ How did new forms of organizing agricultural labor and ranching practices impact white and black Southerners?

▷ How did the Southern industrial economy develop after Reconstruction?

▷ How was the South both "new" and "old" by 1890?

While the Great Plains and West were being transformed, the South developed its own human ecologies, involving resource exploitation, market economies, and land control. During and after Reconstruction, important shifts in the nature of agriculture swept the South. Between 1860 and 1880, the total number of farms in southern states more than doubled, from 450,000 to 1.1 million. The number of landowners, however, did not increase, because a growing proportion of southern farmers rented, rather than owned, their land. Meanwhile, average farm size actually decreased, from 347 to 156 acres. One-third of farmers counted in the 1880 federal census were sharecroppers and tenants; the proportion increased to two-thirds by 1920.

Ravaged by the Civil War, southern agriculture recovered slowly. Rather than diversify, farmers concentrated on growing cotton even more single-mindedly than before the war

in an attempt to recover a share of national and international markets. The effort did not work out well. High prices for seed and implements, declining prices for crops, taxes, and, most of all, debt trapped many white southerners in poverty. Conditions were even worse for African Americans, who endured brutal racism along with economic hardship.

15-5a Sharecropping and Tenant Farming in the South

Southern agriculture, unlike that of the Midwest, did not benefit much from mechanization. Tobacco and cotton, the principal southern crops, required constant hoeing and weeding by hand. Tobacco needed careful harvesting, because the leaves matured at different rates and the stems were too fragile for machines. Also, mechanical devices were not precise enough to pick cotton. Thus, southern agriculture remained labor-intensive, and laborlords who had once utilized slaves were replaced by landlords, who employed sharecroppers and tenant farmers.

Sharecropping and tenant farming—meaning that farmers rented their land rather than owned it—entangled millions of black and white southerners in webs of debt and humiliation, weighed down by the crop lien. Most farmers, too poor to have ready cash, borrowed in order to buy necessities such as seed, tools, and food. They could offer as collateral only what they could grow. A farmer helpless without supplies dealt with a "furnishing merchant," who would exchange provisions for a "lien," or legal claim, on the farmer's forthcoming crop. After the crop was harvested and brought to market, the merchant claimed the portion of the crop that would repay the loan. All too often, however, the debt exceeded the crop's value. The farmer could pay off only part of the loan but still needed supplies for the coming year. The only way to obtain these necessities was to sink deeper into debt by reborrowing and giving the merchant a lien on the next year's crop.

Merchants frequently exploited farmers' powerlessness by inflating prices and charging excessive interest on the advances farmers received. Suppose, for example, that a cash-poor farmer needed a 20-cent bag of seed or a 20-cent piece of cloth. The furnishing merchant would sell the item on credit but would boost the price to 28 cents. At year's end, that 28-cent loan would have accumulated interest of 50 percent, raising the farmer's debt to 42 cents—more than double the item's original cost. The farmer, having pledged more than his crop's worth against scores of such debts, fell behind in payments and never recovered. If he fell too far behind, he and his family could be evicted.

In the southern backcountry, which in antebellum times had been characterized by small, family-owned farms, few slaves, and diversified agriculture, economic changes compounded crop-lien problems. New spending habits illustrate these changes. In 1884 Jephta Dickson, who farmed land in the northern Georgia hills, bought $55.90 worth of flour, potatoes, peas, meat, and corn from merchants. Before the Civil War, farmers like Dickson grew almost all the food they needed and such expenditures would have been rare. But after the war, Dickson and others like him shifted to commercial farming; in the South that meant cotton rather than diversified agriculture. This specialization came about for two reasons: constant

△ In the post-Reconstruction South, cotton remained central to the economy. Here, African American workers are sorting and baling the cotton for shipment, all under the watchful eye of a white supervisor.

debt forced farmers to grow crops that would bring in cash, and railroads enabled them to transport cotton to market more easily than before. As backcountry yeomen devoted more acres to cotton, they produced less of what they needed on a daily basis and found themselves at the mercy of merchants.

15-5b Closing the Southern Range

At the same time, many small black and white farmers who occupied settlements in the back-country suffered from laws that essentially closed the southern range—lands owned by the federal government but used freely by southern herders. This change resulted from the same commercialization of agriculture affecting farming in the West and Midwest. Before the 1870s, southern farmers, like western open-range ranchers, had let their livestock roam freely to search for food and water. By custom, farmers who wished to protect their crops would build fences to keep out foraging livestock. But as commercial agriculture reached the back-country, large landowners and merchants induced county and state governments to require the fencing-in of animals rather than crops. These laws hurt poor farmers who had little land, requiring them to use more of their acreage for pasture. Such laws undermined the cooperative customs that yeomen cherished and that people like Nannie Jackson practiced by forcing them to close themselves off from neighbors.

Poor whites in the rural South, facing economic hardship, also feared that newly enfranchised blacks would challenge whatever political and social superiority (real and imagined) they enjoyed. Wealthy white landowners and merchants fanned these fears, using racism to divide whites and blacks and to distract poor whites from protesting their economic subjugation.

15-5c Leading Industries

Southern agriculture had a close relationship with its two leading industries: cotton and tobacco. In the 1870s, textile mills began to appear in the old Cotton Belt. Powered by the region's abundant rivers, manned cheaply by whites eager to escape hardship on the land, and aided by low taxes and northern capital investment, such factories multiplied. By 1900, the South had four hundred mills with a total of 4 million spindles, and was on the verge of eclipsing New England in textile manufacturing supremacy. Proximity to raw materials and cheap labor also aided the tobacco industry, and the invention in 1880 of a cigarette-making machine enhanced the marketability of tobacco.

◁ Cigarette factories were among the few southern industries that employed African American workers. Here, a workforce of men are pressing and storing tobacco leaves in a Richmond, Virginia, tobacco company in 1899.

National Parks

The idea of embodying greatness in the natural splendor of national parks has been a uniquely American contribution to world culture. Initially, however, Congress did not recognize this possibility, even when in 1872 it created Yellowstone National Park to preserve its untouched beauty. No funds were appropriated for the park's protection and the government lacked sensitivity to the park's needs. For example, the area contained one of the country's few remaining buffalo herds, but poaching reduced the herd to just twenty-two animals. In 1886, however, the Secretary of the Interior requested and was granted cavalry soldiers to supervise the park; originally meant to be temporary, they stayed until 1922.

Slowly, Congress created other parks, including Yosemite and Sequoia in California in 1890 and sites in Oregon, Utah, Arizona, Montana, and Colorado between 1902 and 1915. From the beginning, conflicts arose between those who, like naturalist John Muir and the Sierra Club, wished to preserve parks in as pristine a quality as possible, and those, such as Senator William A. Clark of Montana, who wanted to lease the land to private businesses for logging, mining, railroads, and tourism. (Clark, who bribed and bullied his way

to power, was labeled by Mark Twain as "as rotten a human being as can be found under the flag.") To regularize park management, Congress in 1916 created the National Park Service (NPS) with the mission to conserve natural and historic territory while at the same time providing for their enjoyment by present and future generations. Stephen Mather, appointed head of the service, took his job of preservation seriously but also allowed hotel construction in parks for the comfort of visitors.

At first, all national parks were located in the West, but after 1920 the Park Service began establishing southern sites, beginning with the Great Smokies in Tennessee and North Carolina and Shenandoah in Virginia. A major turning point occurred in 1933 when President Franklin Roosevelt transferred supervision of all national monuments and historic sites to the NPS, giving the NPS jurisdiction over the Statue of Liberty and Civil War battlefields as well as Yosemite. A few years later, NPS began administering national seashores, and from the 1960s onward urban sites such as Golden Gate National Recreation Area near San Francisco and the Jean Lafitte area at New Orleans were included.

Success created problems for many sites because the American public was loving them to death. By 1950, 30 million people visited national parks annually. Roads fell into disrepair, campgrounds became dilapidated, and litter piled up. Moreover, those eager for the economic development of parklands continued to lobby for permission to expand roads, and build hotels, gas stations, and restaurants. In 1964, Congress passed a bill providing funds for future parkland acquisition, but achieving a balance between preserving natural beauty and allowing the public to enjoy it firsthand remains controversial. Today, there are almost 400 national park units, encompassing more than 84 million acres. They stand as a legacy from the past, and their status as national treasures poses challenges to the future.

CRITICAL THINKING

- With almost 400 national park units, encompassing more than 84 million acres, does the United States have enough such spaces?
- What should be the criteria for whether or not new areas should be designated as national parks?
- When should development and other economic interests take precedence?

Cigarette factories, located in cities, employed both black and white workers (though in segregated sections of the factories). Textile mills, concentrated in small towns, developed a separate labor system that employed women and children from poor white families and paid 50 cents a day for twelve or more hours of work. Such wages were barely half of those paid to northern workers. Many companies built villages around their mills, where they controlled housing, stores, schools, and churches. Inside these towns, companies banned criticism of the management and squelched attempts at union organization. Mill families soon found that factory jobs changed their status very little: the company store and the mill owner dominated their everyday lives.

Other industries utilizing nature were launched under the sponsorship of northern and European capital. Between 1890 and 1900, northern syndicates moved into pine forests of the Gulf States, boosting lumber production by 500 percent. During the 1880s, northern investors developed southern iron

deposits into steel manufacturing, much of it in the boom city of Birmingham, Alabama. What was to become the most famous southern product, Coca-Cola, was first formulated by Dr. John Pemberton, an Atlanta pharmacist, who in 1889 sold his recipe to another Atlantean, Asa Candler, who made a fortune marketing the drink nationally. Coal mining and railroad construction also expanded rapidly, though, as was the case with other southern industries, New York and London financiers dominated the boards of directors.

15-5d The New South

Regardless of outside influence, the new economy prompted local boosters to herald the emergence of a New South ready to compete with economies of the West and North by challenging the old economic order that had been dominated by the planter class. Believing that the South should put military defeat of the Civil War behind them—though never forgetting the heroism of Confederate soldiers—businessmen advocated emulating northern industrialism. Henry Grady, editor of the *Atlanta Constitution* and the voice of southern progress, proclaimed, "We have sowed towns and cities in the place of theories, and put business in place of politics. We have challenged your spinners in Massachusetts and your iron-makers in Pennsylvania. . . . We have fallen in love with work."

Yet in 1900 the South was as rural as it had been in 1860. Staple-crop agriculture remained central to its ecology, and white supremacy permeated its social and political relations. Furthermore, the South attracted few immigrants because of its low wages and except for only a few places, such as the city of New Orleans, did not benefit much from the energizing influence of foreign cultures. A New South would emerge, but not until after a world war and a massive African American exodus had shaken up old habits and attitudes.

Summary

The complex interactions between people and their environments transformed the West, the South, and the nation. In the West, indigenous people had used, and sometimes abused, the land to support subsistence cultures that included trade and war as well as hunting and farming. Living mostly in small groups, they depended on delicate resources, such as buffalo herds and salmon runs. When they came into contact with commerce-minded, migratory European Americans, their resistance to the market economy, diseases, and violence that whites brought into the West failed. The result was that the story of the American West became the story of the invaders, not that of the Native peoples.

Mexicans, Chinese, African Americans, and Anglos entered into a reciprocal relationship between human activities and the nonhuman world, with results that they had not always anticipated. Miners, timber cutters, farmers, and builders extracted raw minerals to supply eastern factories, used irrigation and machines to bring forth agricultural abundance from the land, filled pastures with cattle and sheep to expand food sources, and constructed railroads to tie the nation together. In doing so, they transformed half of the nation's territory within a few decades. But the environment also exerted its power over humans, through its climate, its insects and parasites, and its impenetrable hazards and barriers to human movement and agriculture.

The West's settlers, moreover, employed violence and greed that sustained discrimination within a multiracial society; left many farmers feeling cheated and betrayed; provoked contests over use of water and pastures; and sacrificed environmental

balance for market profits. The region's raw materials and agricultural products raised living standards and hastened industrial progress, but not without human and environmental costs.

Longer-settled, the South experienced its own set of changes. The end of slavery left African Americans still tied to the land as tenant farmers and sharecroppers and still subject to various forms of discrimination, while white farmers, landholders as well as tenants, found themselves at increasing disadvantage in expanding markets. To achieve sectional independence, some southerners tried to promote industrialization. Their efforts partially succeeded, but by 1900 many southern industries remained mere subsidiaries of northern firms. Moreover, southern planters, shippers, and manufacturers depended heavily on northern banks to finance their operations. Equally important, low wages and stunted opportunities discouraged potential migrants and immigrants who might have brought needed labor, skills, and capital. Thus although the South did grow economically in some ways, it remained a dependent region in the national economy. People of all sorts now belonged to one nation, indivisible, but sectional differences continued to make the nation increasingly diverse.

Suggestions for Further Reading

Edward Ayers, *The Promise of the New South: Life After Reconstruction* (1992)

William Cronon, *Nature's Metropolis: Chicago and the Great West* (1991)

Robert V. Hine and John Mack Faragher, *The American West: A New Interpretive History* (2000)

Andrew C. Isenberg, *The Destruction of the Bison: An Environmental History* (2000)

Karl Jacoby, *Shadows at Dawn: A Borderlands Massacre and the Violence of History* (2009)

Patricia Nelson Limerick, *Something in the Soil: Legacies and Reckoning in the New West* (2000)

Robert McMath, Jr., *The Populist Vanguard: A History of the Southern Farmers' Alliance* (1975)

Eugene P. Moehring, *Urbanism and Empire in the Far West, 1840–1890* (2004)

Robert M. Utley, *The Indian Frontier of the American West, 1846–1890* (1984)

Richard White, *"It's Your Misfortune and None of My Own": A New History of the American West* (1991)

Donald Worster, *A Passion for Nature: The Life of John Muir* (2008)

Building Factories, Building Cities, 1877–1920

A s immigrants sailed into the New York harbor in the late nineteenth and early twentieth centuries, the first landmass they saw was Coney Island, a peninsula jutting out from Brooklyn. By this time, its easy access from New York City by carriage road and ferry lines, plus its beaches, parks, and other attractions had made Coney Island the largest entertainment resort in the world. A 300-foot tower, with an elevator to the top, was moved there after the 1876 World's Fair in Philadelphia. Electric arc lamps lighted the beaches for nighttime swimming. Racetracks and theaters attracted thousands of tourists. By 1904, the resort boasted three fantasy-filled amusement parks with the alluring names of Steeplechase, Luna, and Dreamland. Rides, such as the world's first roller coaster plus "A Trip to the Moon" (on a vehicle with flapping wings) and "Hell Gate" (a boat ride on swirling waters), dazzled visitors. Before it burned down in 1896, there was even a hotel shaped like an elephant that included guest rooms, a candy store, and a cigar shop. As one excited observer wrote of Coney Island, "... not to have seen it is not to have seen your own country."

Experience an interactive version of this story in MindTap®.

◁ Between 1884 and 1896, Coney Island featured an "Elephantine Colossus," at which visitors could stay overnight. According to an official description, each leg of the wooden behemoth was 60 feet high; its ears were 40 feet wide; and the trunk measured 72 feet. The forelegs housed a diorama and a cigar store, and the hind legs contained staircases leading to 31 hotel rooms, including "a main hall head room, 2 side body rooms, 2 thigh rooms, 2 shoulder rooms, 2 cheek rooms, 1 throat room, 1 stomach room, 4 hoof rooms, 6 leg rooms, 2 side rooms, and 2 hip rooms." Library of Congress Prints and Photographs Division Washington, D.C. [LC-USZ62-102887]

Chronology

1869	■ Knights of Labor founded
1873–78	■ Economy declines
1876	■ National League of Professional Baseball Clubs founded
1877	■ Widespread railroad strikes protest wage cuts
1878	■ Edison Electric Light Company founded
1880s	■ "New" immigrants from eastern and southern Europe begin to arrive in large numbers
1882	■ Standard Oil Trust founded
1883	■ Pulitzer buys New York World, creating major publication for yellow journalism
1886	■ Haymarket riot in Chicago protests police brutality against labor demonstrations
	■ American Federation of Labor (AFL) founded
1890	■ Sherman Anti-Trust Act outlaws "combinations in restraint of trade"
1892	■ Homestead (Pennsylvania) steelworkers strike against Carnegie Steel Company

1893–97	■ Economic depression causes high unemployment and business failures
1895	■ U.S. v. E. C. Knight Co. limits Congress's power to regulate manufacturing
1896	■ Holden v. Harcy upholds law regulating miners' working hours
1900–10	■ Immigration reaches peak
1905	■ Lochner v. New York overturns law limiting bakery workers' working hours and limits labor protection law
	■ Intercollegiate Athletic Association, forerunner of National Intercollegiate Athletic Association (NCAA), is formed, restructuring rules of football
1908	■ Muller v. Oregon upholds law limiting women to ten-hour workday
	■ First Ford Model T built
1911	■ Triangle Shirtwaist Company fire in New York City leaves 146 workers dead
1913	■ Ford begins moving assembly-line production
1920	■ Majority (51.4 percent) of Americans live in cities

Coney Island blended the ingredients of the modern American nation. Steel structures, inventions, electricity, consumer goods, and commercial amusement all combined to serve new needs and demands of a people ready to work but also eager to play in a burgeoning city. Everything at Coney Island was not permanent. A fire started by a carelessly thrown cigarette destroyed almost all of Steeplechase Park in 1907, and a combination of flammable materials and electric malfunction caused a huge fire that burned down Dreamland in 1911. But no one could deny that much about the way people lived was new and improved.

The industrialization that made Coney Island possible was a complex process whose chief feature was production of goods by new technology. In the mid-nineteenth century, an industrial revolution swept through parts of the United States, and the mechanization that characterized it powered a second round in the late 1800s. By that time, the United

States had become the world's most productive industrial nation, as well as the largest producer of raw materials and food (see Map 16.1). Four themes characterized American industrialization. First, inventors and manufacturers harnessed technology to serve production in ways never before imagined. Second, to increase production and maximize use of technology, factory owners divided work routines into repetitive tasks and organized them according to dictates of the clock, turning workers who once had thought of themselves as producers into employees. Third, a new consumer society took shape as goods such as canned foods and machine-made clothing became common. Fourth, in their quest for growth and profits, corporation owners amassed great power through new forms of corporate organization.

At the same time, technological advances and industrialization helped make cities a fact of national life. *Urbanization* is the process whereby cities and their areas expand

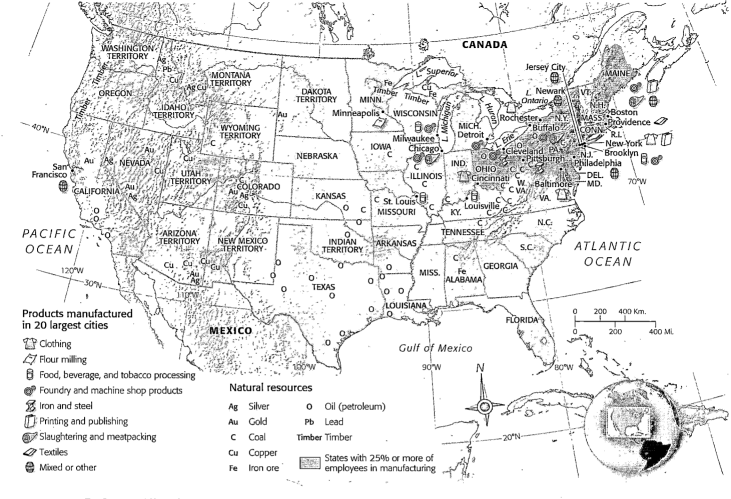

Map 16.1 Industrial Production, 1919

By the early twentieth century, each state could boast at least one kind of industrial production. Although the value of goods produced was still highest in the Northeast, states such as Minnesota and California had impressive dollar values of outputs. *Source: Data from the U.S. Bureau of the Census, Fourteenth Census of the United States, 1920, Vol. IX, Manufacturing (Washington, D.C.: US Government Printing Office, 1921).*

more rapidly than do their surrounding environments. This process accelerated after the Civil War and by 1920 a milestone of urbanization was passed: that year's census showed that, for the first time, a majority of Americans (51.4 percent) lived in cities. City dwellers both propelled industrialization by furnishing its workforces and benefited from it by consuming its goods and services, such as those offered at Coney Island. The many migrants and immigrants to cities utilized their economic and political opportunities to free themselves from uncertainties of the past. But poverty and discrimination also haunted many urban dwellers, combining the era's opportunities with the persistence of poverty and inequality. The ways that people built cities and adjusted to the industrial environment shaped modern American society.

▨ *How did mechanization affect the lives of average workers and the makeup of the labor force?*

▨ *What were the most important factors contributing to the urban growth of the period 1877–1920?*

▨ *How did immigrants adjust to and reshape their adopted homeland?*

16-1 Technology and the Triumph of Industrialism

▷ **How did technology contribute to the process of industrialization?**

▷ **How was electricity harnessed to produce goods?**

▷ **How did technology impact Americans in their day-to-day lives?**

While some people chased natural resource opportunities in the West and South, others employed a spirit of inventiveness to drive the new industrialization. Between 1860 and 1930, the U.S. Patent Office, created by the Constitution to "promote the Progress of science and the useful Arts," granted 1.5 million patents for new inventions; it granted only 36,000 between 1790 and 1860. Inventions often sprang from a marriage between technology and business organization. The harnessing of electricity, internal combustion, steelmaking, and chemistry illustrate how the marriage worked.

16-1a Birth of the Electrical Industry

Thomas Edison, America's most celebrated inventor, opened an "invention factory" in Menlo Park, New Jersey, in 1876. There, his application of electricity to light, sound, and images, plus his system for delivering electric power, brought new products to the nation and laid the foundation for how Americans live today. His most notable invention, created after tedious experimentation, was the incandescent light bulb. But also, his Edison Electric Light Company (founded in 1878) devised a system of power generation that provided electricity conveniently to manifold customers. Acting as his own publicist, Edison marketed his ideas by demonstrating how electric lighting could transform night into day. Such illumination not only lit homes and offices but enhanced the appeal of Coney Island parks and advertising signs.

Other entrepreneurs adapted electricity for countless purposes. George Westinghouse, for example, showed how alternating current could transmit electricity over long distances. Granville T. Woods, an African American engineer sometimes called "the black Edison," patented thirty-five devices vital to electronics and communications. Financiers Henry Villard and J. P. Morgan bought patents from inventors such as Woods, merged equipment manufacturing companies into the General Electric Company, and established research laboratories in which scientists created electrical products for practical use.

16-1b Henry Ford and the Automobile Industry

Meanwhile, the gas-powered internal combustion engine, developed in Germany, inspired one of America's most visionary manufacturers, **Henry Ford**. Originally an electrical engineer, Ford adapted the internal combustion engine to propel a vehicle. Though another inventor had already done the same thing, Ford applied organizational genius to the invention and spawned a massive industry, predicting in 1909, "I am going to democratize the automobile. When I'm through, everybody will be able to afford one, and about everyone will have one." Ford set about mass-producing identical cars on assembly lines that divided the manufacturing process into single tasks repeatedly performed by workers using the same specialized

Thomas Edison Inventor and founder of the first industrial research laboratory.

Henry Ford Founder of the Ford Motor Company and pioneer of modern assembly lines used in mass production.

Andrew Carnegie Scottish immigrant who built an enormous steel company and became a renowned philanthropist.

machines. By 1914, the Ford Motor Company outside of Detroit was producing 248,000 cars per year, and auto manufacturing spawned new industries in steel, oil, rubber, and glass, each of which utilized precision machines to standardize production and applied electricity to power assembly lines. A new Ford cost $490, still unaffordable to workers who earned at best $2 a day. To enable his employees to afford a car, as well as reduce labor turnover and head off unionization, Ford began a Five-Dollar-Day pay plan that combined wages and profit sharing.

In the 1850s, British engineer Henry Bessemer developed a process for producing steel, the strong, durable metal needed for many new products, from molten iron. In America, Scottish immigrant **Andrew Carnegie** recognized the benefits of the Bessemer process and in the 1870s built steelmaking plants near Pittsburgh that eventually furnished materials for rails and bridges, as well as barbed wire, tubing, and household appliances. In 1892, Carnegie combined his assets into the Carnegie Steel Company and by 1900 controlled 60 percent of the country's steel business. In 1901, he retired, selling his holdings to a group led by J. P. Morgan, who formed the huge U.S. Steel Corporation.

Industrial chemistry was pioneered by French immigrant E. I. du Pont, who manufactured gunpowder in Delaware in the early 1890s. In 1902, three du Pont cousins took over the company and expanded production into fertilizer, dyes, and other chemical products. In 1911, du Pont research labs adapted cellulose to the production of consumer goods such as photographic film, textile fibers, and plastics. The company also developed new methods of management and recordkeeping, all leading to higher profits.

16-1c Technology and Southern Industry

In the South, new industries developed around natural resources. The tobacco crop inspired North Carolinian James B. Duke to create a machine for making cigarettes. He began mass production in 1885. Like Edison and Ford, Duke used marketing and advertising to attract customers. By 1900, his American Tobacco Company was a global business with sales in England and Japan as well as the United States. Also, electric-powered cotton looms and a cheap labor force enabled the southern textile industry to surpass water-powered New England mills and attract investors. Many textile companies built villages around their mills and controlled housing, stores, schools, and churches. Northern capitalists also invested in southern iron and steel manufacturing, especially in the boom city of Birmingham, Alabama. And between 1890 and 1900, northern lumber syndicates moved into pine forests of the Gulf States, boosting wood production and prompting the relocation of furniture and paper production from North to South.

16-1d Technology and Everyday Life

In all regions, machines and technology altered everyday life. Telephones and typewriters made face-to-face communications less important and facilitated correspondence. Electric sewing machines made mass-produced clothing in standardized sizes available to almost everyone and gave homemakers more convenient ways of creating and mending clothing. Manufacturers

△ Tobacco production was one southern industry that traditionally hired African American laborers. This scene from a Richmond tobacco factory around 1880 shows women and children preparing leaves for curing by tearing off the stems.

of "ready-to-wear" garments emphasized comfort, using less fabric for women's clothes and creating lighter-weight, yet durable suits for middle-class men and cheaper denim overalls for workingmen. Eating habits also changed. Refrigeration enabled preservation and shipment of fresh meat, produce, and dairy products; canning preserved foods such as tomatoes, fish, and milk that otherwise would have spoiled easily. Dietary reformers William K. Kellogg and Charles W. Post mass-produced new breakfast foods such as cornflakes and Grape-Nuts, and the discovery of vitamins heightened interest in food's health. Low-income families still consumed cheap dishes such as corn mush and hog fatback that were heavy in starches and carbohydrates, but increased availability and variety of processed foods meant that American workers never suffered the severe malnutrition that plagued other developing nations.

New technology even affected personal hygiene. Flush toilets, invented in England, reached American shores in the 1880s. More rapidly than Europeans, middle-class Americans combined a desire for cleanliness with an urge for convenience and began installing modern toilets in their urban houses,

making the bathroom a place of utmost privacy. At the same time, brothers Edward and Clarence Scott applied a new process for producing white tissue in rolls, providing Americans a form of toilet tissue more convenient than the rough paper they previously used. All these developments in communications, clothing, food, and plumbing contributed to a democratization of convenience that accompanied mass production and consumerism.

16-2 Big Business and Its Critics

▷ What structures of organization contributed to the expansion and consolidation of businesses in the late nineteenth and early twentieth century?

▷ What competing views of big business emerged in the late nineteenth and early twentieth century?

▷ How did state governments and the federal government seek to regulate big business?

Library of Congress Prints and Photographs Division Washington, D.C. [LC-DIG-ppmsca-05944]

△ As mass-produced brand-name products became more common, companies used visual images to advertise them. Artwork such as this ad for Ivory Soap captured attention more effectively than the written word.

All was not rosy for business, however. New technologies required large capital investments, and the more manufacturers produced, the more they needed to sell. To expand, businesses borrowed from banks and sought higher profits to repay loans and reward stockholders. This spiraling process strangled small firms that could not keep pace and caused uncertainty in transportation and banking. Optimism could vanish at the hint that a large debtor was about to fail. Economic downturns occurred with painful regularity—in 1871, 1884, and 1893—as overproduction, underconsumption, and unregulated banking strained the system, causing business owners to seek ways to create stability.

John D. Rockefeller Creator of Standard Oil and master of the use of pools and trusts to monopolize an industry.

horizontal integration Business strategy in which a holding company would seek to control all aspects of the industry in which it functioned, fusing related businesses together under one management.

Corporations proved to be the best instruments for industrial expansion. These were companies that raised capital by selling shares to stockholders who received a portion of company profits without personal risk because laws limited their liability for company debts to the amount of their own investments. Firms such as General Electric and the American Tobacco Corporation won judicial safeguards in 1886 when Chief Justice Morrison R. Waite of the Supreme Court accepted the contention by business interests that corporations, like ordinary individuals, are protected by laws preventing government from depriving them of property rights without due process of law, an opinion that has lasted to the present day. During the 1880s, a number of corporations in the same industry made agreements, called *pools*, to share markets and profits. But these arrangements often broke down because they lacked dependable enforcement.

16-2a Trusts and Holding Companies

Trusts soon came to dominate a few industries. These were large corporations formed to enable one company to control an industry by luring or forcing stockholders of smaller companies in that industry to yield control of their stock "in trust" to the larger company's board of trustees. This method enabled a company such as **John D. Rockefeller**'s Standard Oil to achieve domination by combining with, or *vertically integrating*, other oil refineries. In 1898, New Jersey adopted laws allowing companies chartered there to own stock in other states, facilitating creation of holding companies, which merged the buildings, equipment, inventory, and cash of several firms under single management. Using this **horizontal integration**, holding companies could dominate all aspects of an industry, including raw-material extraction, manufacture, and distribution. For example, Gustavus Swift's Chicago meat-processing operation controlled livestock, slaughterhouses, refrigerator cars, and marketing.

Trusts and holding companies provided solutions to big corporations' search for orderly profits. Between 1889 and 1903, some three hundred of these combinations formed, including American Sugar Refining Company and U.S. Rubber Company. A new species of businessman, the financier, aided the process by creating a holding company through stock sales and bank loans, then persuading firms to sell out to him. The practice often put small companies out of business and made huge fortunes for shrewd bankers such as J. P. Morgan and Jacob Schiff.

Growth of corporations turned stock and bond exchanges into hubs of activity. In 1869, only 145 industrial corporations traded on the New York Stock Exchange; by 1914, 511 did. Impressed by the safety and opportunity of the American economy, foreign investors poured huge sums into American companies. Banks and insurance companies also invested in railroads and industrial enterprises. As one journal proclaimed, "Nearly the whole country (including the typical widow and orphan) is interested in the stock market."

16-2b Social Darwinism

Business leaders involved in the formation of large corporations often justified their actions by invoking **Social Darwinism**, a theory developed by British philosopher Herbert Spencer. This philosophy loosely grafted Charles Darwin's theory of survival of the fittest onto laissez-faire, the doctrine that government should not interfere in private economic matters. Social Darwinists reasoned that in a free-market economy, wealth would naturally flow to those most capable of creating it. To them, acquisition of wealth thus was a sacred and deserved right. As one proponent argued, "If we do not have survival of the fittest, we have only one possible alternative, and that is survival of the unfittest."

Like western entrepreneurs who lauded individual effort while seeking government assistance for their railroads and timber companies, corporation heads praised private initiative while seeking public assistance. They denounced legislation that regulated work hours and factory conditions as interference with natural economic laws, but they lobbied forcefully for subsidies, tax relief, and tariffs that they said encouraged business growth.

16-2c Dissenting Voices

Critics charged that new forms of big business were unnatural because they stifled opportunity and fostered greed. Farmers, workers, and intellectuals feared that corporations were creating monopolies—domination of an economic activity by one powerful company—and that companies such as Standard Oil crushed small businesses, fixed prices, and corrupted politicians.

By the mid-1880s, a few intellectuals began to challenge Social Darwinism and laissez-faire. For example, sociologist Lester Ward, in his book *Dynamic Sociology* (1883), argued that human control of nature, not natural law, accounted for civilization's advance. A system that guaranteed survival only to the fittest, he wrote, was wasteful and brutal. Instead, cooperative activity fostered by government intervention was more just. Economists Richard Ely and Edward Bemis agreed that natural forces should be harnessed for the public good, and they denounced laissez-faire.

At the same time, visionaries such as Henry George and Edward Bellamy questioned why the United States had so many poor people while a few became fabulously wealthy. George, a printer alarmed by the poverty of working people like himself, came to believe that inequality stemmed from the ability of property owners to profit from rising land values and the rents they charged. To prevent profiteering, George proposed to replace all taxes with a "single tax" on the rise in property values caused by increased market demand. George's scheme, presented in *Progress and Poverty* (1879), had great popular appeal and influenced subsequent reformers.

Unlike George, who accepted private ownership, Edward Bellamy believed competitive capitalism promoted waste. Instead, he proposed a state in which government owned the means of production. Bellamy outlined his dream in *Looking Backward* (1888), a novel that depicted Boston in the year 2000

△ A cartoon protesting John D. Rockefeller's power over the oil and railroad industries shows him wearing a golden crown and regal robe, and standing on an oil storage tank labeled "Standard Oil." The huge crown is topped with a dollar sign and made of oil tanks and railroad cars four railroad companies owned by Rockefeller: Lehigh Valley R.R., St. Paul R.R., Jersey Central R.R., and Reading Rail Road.

as a peaceful community where everyone had a job and a "principle of fraternal cooperation" replaced vicious competition and monopoly. Bellamy's vision, called "Nationalism," sparked formation of Nationalist clubs across the country and kindled efforts for political reform and government ownership of railroads and utilities.

16-2d Antitrust Legislation

Plans by George and Bellamy did not succeed, but several states took steps to prohibit monopolies and regulate business. By 1900, twenty-seven states had laws forbidding pools and

Social Darwinism Extended Charles Darwin's theory of "survival of the fittest" to the free-market system, arguing that competition would weed out weaker firms and allow stronger, fitter firms to thrive.

fifteen outlawed trusts. Most were agricultural states in the South and West whose politicians were responding to anti-monopolistic pressure from farmers (see "Agrarian Unrest and Populism," Section 17-5). But states lacked the staff and judicial support for effective attacks on big business, and corporations found ways to evade restrictions. Only national legislation, it seemed, could work.

Congress moved hesitantly but in 1890 passed the Sherman Anti-Trust Act that made illegal "every contract, combination in the form of trust or otherwise, or conspiracy in the restraint of trade." Those convicted of violating the law could receive fines and jail terms and victims could sue for triple damages. However, the law, under influence from pro-business eastern senators, was left purposefully vague. It did not clearly define "restraint of trade" and left interpretation of its provisions to the courts, which at the time were allies of business. When in 1895 the federal government prosecuted the Sugar Trust for owning 98 percent of the nation's sugar-refining capacity, eight of nine Supreme Court justices ruled in *U.S. v. E. C. Knight Co.* that control of sugar manufacturing did not necessarily mean control of trade. And because the Knight Company's manufacturing took place entirely within Pennsylvania, its business could not be considered as interstate commerce. Between 1890 and 1900, the federal government prosecuted only eighteen cases under the Sherman Anti-Trust Act, most of them against railroads. Ironically, the act equipped the government with a tool for breaking up labor unions, which, when they went on strike, were deemed in restraint of trade.

16-3 Mechanization and the Changing Status of Labor

▶ How did new means of organizing labor change the experience for workers in industry?

▶ How did laborers seek to advocate for their own interests in the workplace environment?

▶ How effective were unions in representing the interests of industrial workers?

Technology made possible higher profits for factory owners at lower costs. Workers faced less rewarding results. Skilled crafts such as cabinetmaking and metalworking survived, but as mechanized assembly lines made large-scale production more economical, owners invested in machines, hired fewer workers, and paid lower wages. Profitability relied as much on efficient methods of production as on the machines in use. Where previously workers controlled the methods and timing of production, by the 1890s, engineers and managers with expert knowledge were assuming this responsibility, using planning and standardization to reduce the need for human skills and judgment.

16-3a Frederick W. Taylor

The most influential advocate of efficiency was Frederick W. Taylor. As engineer for a Pennsylvania steel company in the 1880s, Taylor concluded that the best way a company could reduce costs and increase profits was to study "how quickly the various kinds of work . . . ought to be done." The "ought" in Taylor's scheme signified more output at lower costs, usually by eliminating workers. The "how quickly" meant that time and money were equivalent. He called his system "scientific management," which he later outlined in his book, *Principles of Scientific Management* (1911). In 1898, Taylor took a stopwatch to Bethlehem Steel Company to apply his principles. After observing workers shoveling iron ore, he designed fifteen kinds of shovels and prescribed proper motions for their use, enabling the plant to reduce a crew of 600 men to 140. Soon other companies began implementing Taylor's theories. Taylor had little respect for ordinary laborers, calling steelworkers "stupid" and "rarely able to comprehend the science of handling pig iron." Only managers, he argued, could understand and enforce his principles.

16-3b Workers Become Employees

Workers increasingly came to fear that they were becoming another kind of interchangeable part in an industrial machine. No longer able to consider themselves producers, who like farmers and craftsmen were paid according to the quality of what they produced, industrial workers instead were becoming employees, wage earners who worked not on their own but when someone hired them and paid them for time spent on the job. Mass production standardized manufacturing so that tasks were regulated by the clock, and carefully supervised. As a Massachusetts factory hand testified in 1879, "during working hours the men are not allowed to speak to each other, though working close together, on pain of discharge. Men are hired to watch and patrol the shop." Such work was dangerous as well as tedious. The slightest mistake on high-speed machinery could be serious, if not fatal, and accidents occurred often, killing hundreds of thousands each year. For those with mangled limbs, infections, and chronic illnesses, there was no insurance to replace lost income, and families stricken by such misfortune suffered acutely.

Workers attempted to retain autonomy and self-respect in the face of employers' ever-increasing power. Artisans such as glassworkers and printers fought to preserve traditional customs, such as appointing a fellow worker to read a newspaper aloud while they labored. Immigrants working in factories tried to persuade foremen to hire their relatives and friends. Off the job, workers gathered in saloons and parks for relaxation, drinking, and holiday celebrations, ignoring employers' attempts to control their social lives.

16-3c Women and Children in the Workforce

Employers cut labor costs another way by hiring women and children and paying them low wages. Between 1880 and 1900, numbers of employed women soared from 2.6 million to

8.6 million. As Figure 16.1 shows, the proportion of women working in domestic service (maids, cooks, laundresses), the most common and lowest paid form of female employment, dropped as clerical jobs (typists, filing clerks, and store clerks) expanded. Inventions such as the typewriter and cash register simplified clerical tasks, and employers replaced males with lower-paid females. By 1920, women filled nearly half of all clerical jobs; they held only 4 percent of them in 1880. Although poorly paid, women were attracted to sales and secretarial positions because of the respectability and pleasant surroundings compared with factory and domestic work. Nevertheless, for women lacking skills and education, jobs at low pay were the only choice. In manufacturing, women usually held menial positions in textile mills and food-processing plants that paid as little as $1.56 a week for seventy hours of work. (Unskilled men received $7 to $10 for a similar workweek.)

Although most children who worked toiled on their parents' farms, they too entered new occupations. In 1890, more than 18 percent of all children between ages ten and

fifteen held paying jobs. Mechanization in textile and shoe production created light tasks such as running errands and helping machine operators, which children could handle at a fraction of adult wages. In the South, textile mill owners induced sharecroppers, who desperately needed extra income, to bind their children over to factories at miserably low wages. Several states, especially in the Northeast, passed laws limiting ages and hours of child laborers. But large firms evaded regulations, which applied only to companies operating solely within a state's borders, exempting those involved in interstate commerce. Also, parents needing income from child labor lied about their children's ages, and employers seldom asked. Children also contributed to family needs by engaging in informal street trades, such as peddling newspapers, shining shoes, and scavenging for discarded wood, coal, and furniture.

16-3d Freedom of Contract

To justify their treatment of employees, employers said laborers had "freedom of contract," meaning that workers operated

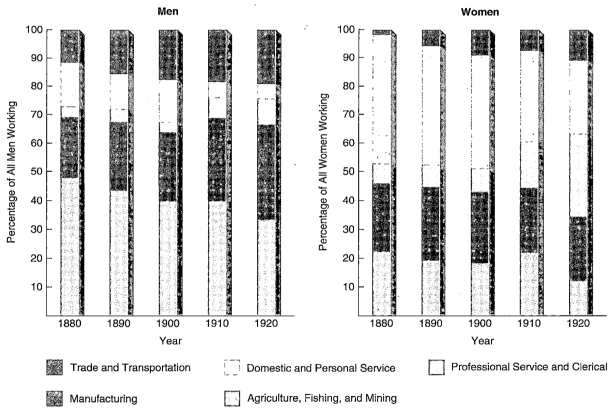

Figure 16.1 Distribution of Occupational Categories Among Employed Men and Women, 1880–1920

The changing lengths of the bar segments of each part of this graph represent trends in male and female employment. Over the forty years covered by this graph, the agriculture, fishing, and mining segment for men and the domestic service segment for women declined the most, whereas notable increases occurred in manufacturing for men and professional services (especially store clerks and teachers) for women. *Source: U.S. Bureau of the Census, Census of the United States, 1880, 1890, 1900, 1910, 1920 (Washington, D.C.: U.S. Government Printing Office).*

in a free market in which they sold their labor. By this principle, a worker who did not like the wages and hours being offered was free to decline a job and seek better conditions from another employer. In practice, however, employers used supply and demand to set wages as low as laborers would accept, forcing those needing work to take whatever they could get. When some states tried to improve working conditions through regulatory legislation, business interests enlisted courts, including the Supreme Court of the United States, to oppose such measures. Though the Court in *Holden v. Hardy* (1891) did uphold a law restricting miners' working hours because an overly long workday increased the threat of injury, it voided a law limiting bakery workers to a sixty-hour week and ten-hour day (*Lochner v. New York*, 1905), reasoning that baking was not dangerous enough to prevent workers from selling their labor freely.

In one case, *Muller v. Oregon* (1908), the Supreme Court made an exception for women. It concluded that a law regulating hours of female laundry workers was constitutional because a woman's well-being as bearer of children was "an object of public interest . . ." The case represented a victory for reform groups such as the Consumers' League, which wanted to safeguard women from exploitation. As a result of the *Muller* decision, however, labor laws effectively prevented women from being hired for physically demanding jobs such as printing and transportation, further confining women to low-paying, dead-end occupations.

Workers adjusted to mechanization as best they could. Some adapted to assembly lines and time clocks. Others resisted. Individuals challenged the system by ignoring management's rules or quitting. Still others, disgruntled over low wages and anxious to restore independence and better conditions, joined unions and went out on strikes (see Table 16.1).

16-3e Railroad Strikes of 1877

In 1877, a crisis in the railroad industry caused by four years of wage cuts, layoffs, and increased workloads climaxed with a series of violent strikes in which workers attacked railroad property from Pennsylvania and West Virginia to Texas and California. State militia, organized and commanded by employers, broke up picket lines and fired upon strikers, and railroads hired strikebreakers to replace union men. The worst violence occurred in Pittsburgh, where in July 1877, troopers attacked demonstrators, killing ten and wounding many more. After over a month of fighting in which more were killed and much property was destroyed, President Rutherford B. Hayes sent in federal soldiers—the first significant use of the army to quell labor unrest.

16-3f Knights of Labor

Railroadmen struck in their own interest, but about the same time an organization called the Knights of Labor tried to organize a broad base of laborers. Aided by Terrence Powderly, a machinist and mayor of Scranton, Pennsylvania, who was elected grand master in 1879, the Knights built a membership of 730,000 by 1886. In contrast to most

Jay Gould Captain of industry and owner of the Union Pacific Railroad.

Table 16.1 American Living Standards, 1890–1910

	1890	1910
Income and Earnings		
Annual income		
Clerical worker	$848	$1,156
Public schoolteacher	256	492
Industrial worker	486	630
Farm laborer	233	336
Hourly wage		
Soft-coal miner	0.18[a]	0.21
Ironworker	0.17[a]	0.23
Shoe worker	0.14[a]	0.19
Paper worker	0.12[a]	0.17
Labor Statistics		
Number of people in labor force	28.5 million	41.7 million[b]
Average workweek in manufacturing	60 hours	51 hours

[a]1892
[b]1920

craft unions, Knights welcomed unskilled and semiskilled workers, including women, African Americans, and immigrants (but not Chinese). The organization tried to bypass conflict between labor and management by establishing a cooperative society in which workers, not capitalists, owned factories, mines, and railroads. This ideal was difficult to achieve because employers held economic leverage and could outcompete laborers who might try to operate their own businesses. Powderly discouraged Knights members from going on strike, arguing that the goal of a cooperative society was more important than conflict and that workers too often lost strikes. Some Knights, however, chose militant action. In 1886, they struck against railroads in the Southwest. When owner **Jay Gould** refused to negotiate, the strike spread and violence increased. Powderly tried to negotiate, but Gould refused and the Knights gave in. Thereafter membership in the Knights dwindled, although its cooperative vision inspired the Populist movement of the 1890s (see "Agrarian Unrest and Populism," Section 17-5).

The same year that Knights struck against railroads, unionized and nonunionized workers staged strikes in favor of an eight-hour workday. On May 1, 1886, in Chicago, one hundred thousand workers massed for a huge demonstration. Two days later, fearing that anarchists in the crowd were fomenting antigovernment violence, Chicago police mobilized at the McCormick reaper plant and broke up a battle between unionists and strikebreakers, killing two

Impact of the 1911 Triangle Shirtwaist Fire

On March 25, 1911, the worst factory fire in U.S. history occurred at the Triangle Shirtwaist Company, which occupied the top three floors of a building in New York City. Fed by piles of combustible fabric, the fire spread quickly, killing 146 of the 500 young women, mostly Jewish immigrants, employed in the factory. Many of the victims were burned to death because they were locked inside workrooms by their employer; others plunged from windows. These images show two ways the public received news of the tragedy: through friends and relatives who came to identify and claim the bodies of victims, and through a critical cartoon.

CRITICAL THINKING

- Which of these images seems more powerful and likely to inspire reform?
- How do mass tragedies get communicated to the public today?
- What limitations in communications existed in 1911?

▲ Many of the victims of the Triangle Shirtwaist fire of 1911 were lined up in coffins, and their bodies were identified by relatives arriving at a makeshift morgue.

Bettmann/Getty Images

The Granger Collection, NYC

▲ John French Sloan, an artist with radical leanings, drew this cartoon in the wake of the Triangle fire. Eager to assert that profit-minded capitalists were responsible for unnecessary deaths, Sloan used stark images to convey his message.

and wounding others. On May 4, demonstrators gathered at Haymarket Square near downtown Chicago to protest police brutality. As police approached, a bomb exploded, killing seven and injuring sixty-seven. In reaction, authorities arrested several anarchists, eight of whom were convicted of the bombing though evidence of their guilt was weak. Four were executed, one committed suicide in jail, and three received pardons from Governor John Altgeld in 1893. The presence of foreign-born anarchists and socialists at the Haymarket violence created fear among civic leaders that labor turmoil threatened social order. In response, governments strengthened police forces, and employer associations circulated blacklists of union activists whom they would not employ and began hiring private detectives to protect company property.

16-3g American Federation of Labor

The **American Federation of Labor (AFL)**, an alliance of craft unions, emerged from the 1886 upheavals as the major workers' organization. Led by English-born **Samuel Gompers**, former head of the Cigar Makers Union, the AFL avoided the Knights' idealistic goals in favor of concrete issues of higher wages, shorter hours, and the right to bargain collectively. A pragmatist rather than a radical, Gompers and the AFL accepted capitalism and worked to improve conditions within it.

The union avoided party politics, adhering instead to Gompers's policy of supporting labor's friends and opposing its enemies regardless of party. AFL membership grew from 140,000 in 1886 to 1 million in 1901 and 2.5 million in 1917, when it consisted of 111 national unions.

Organized by craft rather than by workplace, the AFL rebuffed unskilled laborers and excluded women. Male unionists insisted that women would depress wages and should stay at home because, as one put it, "Woman is not qualified for the conditions of wage labor.... The mental and physical makeup of woman is in revolt against wage service. She is competing with the man who is her father or husband or is to become her husband." Most unions also excluded immigrants and African Americans, fearing job competition from men who might work for less pay. Long-held prejudices

were reinforced when blacks and immigrants, eager for any work they could get, accepted jobs as strikebreakers to replace striking native whites.

16-3h Homestead and Pullman Strikes

The AFL and entire labor movement suffered setbacks in the early 1890s when once again violence stirred public fears. In July 1892, the AFL-affiliated Amalgamated Association of Iron and Steelworkers launched the **Homestead Strike** against Homestead Steel in Pennsylvania over pay cuts. Henry Frick, president of Carnegie Steel Company, Homestead's owner, hired three hundred guards from the Pinkerton Detective Agency to protect the factory, but angry strikers attacked the guards, sending them into retreat. State troopers intervened and, after five months, the strikers gave up.

In 1894, employees at the Pullman Palace Car Company, maker of railroad passenger cars, walked out over exploitive policies at the company town near Chicago. The owner, George Pullman, controlled nearly everything in the so-called model town of twelve thousand: land, buildings, school, bank, and rents. Pullman refused to negotiate with workers, and when he cut wages without reducing rents, the American Railway Union, led by charismatic **Eugene Debs**, went on strike. Pullman closed the factory and the union retaliated by refusing to handle all Pullman cars attached to any train. The railroad owners' association enlisted aid from the federal government and Debs was arrested for defying a court injunction against the strike. President Grover Cleveland ordered federal troops to Chicago, ostensibly to protect rail-carried mail, but in reality to crush the strike. The union ended the walkout and Debs received a six-month prison sentence.

16-3i Labor Violence in the West

In the West, unionized mine workers, led by the Western Federation of Miners (WFM), engaged in violent strikes during the 1890s. In 1894, fighting erupted in Cripple Creek, Colorado, when mine owners increased work hours without increasing pay. The governor called in state militia after two weeks of battles, and the owners agreed to restore the eight-hour workday. In Idaho, federal troops intervened three times in strikes by miners. In 1905, former Idaho governor Frank Steuenberg was assassinated and speculation arose that the WFM was exacting revenge for when Steuenberg imposed martial law during a strike in 1899. After the assassination, authorities arrested WFM activist William "Big Bill" Haywood, a brawny, one-eyed radical, and tried him for murder in 1907. He was acquitted after his famous defense attorney, Clarence Darrow, proved that a key witness was being paid by the mine owners.

In 1905, radical laborers formed the **Industrial Workers of the World (IWW)**. Unlike the AFL, but like the Knights of Labor, the IWW tried to unite unskilled workers under the motto, "An injury to one is an injury to all." Embracing violent tactics and the rhetoric of class conflict and socialism, the

American Federation of Labor (AFL) Skilled craft unions united under leadership of Samuel Gompers.

Samuel Gompers AFL leader who focused on practical goals like improved wages, hours, and working conditions.

Homestead Strike Worker walkout after wage cuts at a Carnegie Steel plant in 1892; officials responded to the strike by shutting down the plant.

Eugene Debs Indiana labor leader who organized workers in the Pullman Strike of 1893; would be the Socialist Party of America's presidential candidate five times between 1900 and 1920.

Industrial Workers of the World (IWW) Radical labor organization that sought to unionize all workers; nicknamed Wobblies, the IWW embraced socialism and led mass strikes of mine workers in Nevada and Minnesota and timber workers in Louisiana, Texas, and the Northwest.

"Wobblies," as IWW members were known, believed workers should seize and run the nation's industries. Their leaders, including Haywood, Mary "Mother" Jones, a coalfield organizer; Elizabeth Gurley Flynn, a fiery orator; Italian radical Carlo Tresca; and songwriter Joe Hill, headed strife-torn strikes in steel towns, textile communities, and lumber camps. The union attracted much publicity but collapsed during the First World War when federal prosecutors sent many of its leaders to prison and local police harassed IWW activities.

16-3j Women Unionists

Though generally excluded from unions, some female workers organized and battled employers as strenuously as men did. In 1909, male and female members of the International Ladies Gárment Workers' Union, consisting mostly of Jewish immigrant shirtwaist workers, staged a strike known as "Uprising of the 20,000" in New York City. Women also were prominent in the 1912 "Bread and Roses" strike against textile owners in Lawrence, Massachusetts, and their Telephone Operators' Department of the International Brotherhood of Electrical Workers sponsored a strike over wage issues that paralyzed the New England Bell telephone system in 1919. Without aid from male electrical workers, the telephone operators nevertheless won concessions of higher wages and the right to bargain collectively.

The Women's Trade Union League (WTUL), founded in 1903, played a key role in representing laboring women. Patterned after a British women's league, WTUL sought legislation to establish shorter hours and better working conditions, supported strikes, sponsored educational activities, and campaigned for women's suffrage. At first, sympathetic middle-class women held most WTUL offices, but after 1910 control shifted to working-class leaders such as Agnes Nestor, a glove maker, and Rose Schneiderman, a capmaker. By inspiring working women to press for rights and by training leaders, WTUL provided a vital link between labor and the women's movement into the 1920s.

16-3k The Nonunionized Workforce

The high-profile activities of organized labor obscure the fact that the vast majority of American wage workers in these years did not belong to unions. In 1877, less than a million workers were unionized; by 1920, union membership had grown to 5 million but accounted for only 13 percent of the total labor force. For many, getting and keeping a job took priority over bargaining for higher pay and shorter hours. Few companies employed a full workforce year-round; they hired during peak seasons and laid off employees during slack times. Moreover, union organizers took no interest in unskilled laborers and intentionally excluded women, African Americans, and immigrants.

The men, women, and children who were not unionized coped with pressures of the industrial age as best they could. They joined societies such as the Polish Roman Catholic Union, African American Colored Brotherhood, and Jewish B'nai B'rith, which for small fees provided services such as life insurance, sickness benefits, and burial costs. For these Americans as well as for those in unions, the machine age had mixed results. Though wages generally rose between 1877 and 1914, boosting purchasing power and consumerism, hourly pay averaged around 20 cents for skilled work and 10 cents for unskilled. And even as wages rose, living costs rose faster. Those two dimensions of industrialism—work and lifestyle—displayed their most dramatic effects in cities.

◁ In 1919, telephone operators, mostly female, went on strike and shut down phone service throughout New England. The male-dominated leadership of the International Brotherhood of Electrical Workers, to which the operators belonged, opposed the strike, but the women refused to back down and eventually achieved several of their demands against the New England Telephone Company.

George Rinhart/Getty Images

16-4 Growth of the Modern American City

▷ How did transportation developments and population growth alter the urban landscape in the late nineteenth and early twentieth century?

▷ How did immigrants adapt to American society and retain features of their ethnic cultures?

▷ What systemic problems emerged in cities in the late nineteenth and early twentieth century?

▷ How did political machines and urban reformers seek to solve the systemic problems of city life?

Though their initial functions had been as centers for trade, cities became the arenas for industrial development in the late nineteenth century. As hubs for labor, transportation, communications, and consumption, cities supplied everything factories needed. Most cities housed a variety of manufacturing enterprises, but product specialization was common. Mass-produced clothing concentrated in New York City, the shoe industry in Philadelphia, food processing in Minneapolis, meat processing in Chicago, fish canning in Seattle, steelmaking in Pittsburgh and Birmingham, and oil refining in Houston and Los Angeles. Such activities increased cities' magnetic attraction for people and capital.

16-4a Mechanization of Mass Transportation

As cities grew, the compact landscape of earlier eras, where residences mingled among shops and factories, burst open as settlement sprawled beyond original boundaries. No longer did walking distance determine a city's size. Instead, cities separated into distinct districts: working- and middle-class neighborhoods, commercial strips, downtown, and suburbs. Two forces created this new arrangement: One, mass transportation, propelled people and enterprises outward; the other, economic change, drew human and material resources inward.

By the 1870s, horse-drawn vehicles began sharing city streets with motor-driven conveyances that moved riders faster and farther. Commuter railroads and cable cars came first, followed by electric-powered streetcars. In a few cities, such as New York and Chicago, companies raised track onto trestles, enabling "elevated" trains to move above jammed streets. In others, such as Boston and New York, underground subways avoided traffic congestion. Also, electric interurban railways, linking neighboring cities in the Midwest and West, furthered urban development.

These forms of mass transit launched urban dwellers into outlying neighborhoods and created a commuting public. The development mainly benefited the middle class. Working-class families, who needed every cent, found streetcar fares, usually five cents a ride, too high. But those with means could move to single-family bungalows in tree-lined, outlying neighborhoods and travel to the central city for work, shopping, and entertainment. Mass transit also altered commercial patterns. When consumers moved outward, shops, banks, and

restaurants followed, locating at trolley-line intersections and creating secondary business districts. Meanwhile, the urban core became a work zone, where tall buildings loomed over streets clogged with people, horses, and vehicles.

16-4b Population Growth

Between 1870 and 1920, the number of Americans living in cities increased from 10 million to 54 million, and the number of places with more than 100,000 people swelled from fifteen to sixty-four. Several cities grew big in a hurry. Chicago, with 109,000 people in 1860, swelled to 2.2 million by 1910. Pittsburgh had just 49,000 in 1860; by 1910, it housed 534,000. Cities in the South also grew, just not as explosively. Baltimore and New Orleans, the region's largest places in 1860 with 212,000 and 169,000, respectively, remained the largest in 1910, with 558,000 and 339,000.

Urban growth derived mainly from two sources. One was annexation of nearby territory, such as when Chicago tripled its area by adding three surrounding towns in 1889 and when New York City (Manhattan) merged with Brooklyn, Staten Island, and part of Queens in 1898, doubling from 1.5 million to 3 million people. Most communities agreed to be annexed

△ Tall buildings, streetcars, offices, and shop characterized the new downtown of cities. The aptly-named Market Street of San Francisco resembled main streets in many other cities.

Library of Congress, Prints & Photographs Division, Reproduction number LC-DIG-ppmsca-39502 (digital file from original item)

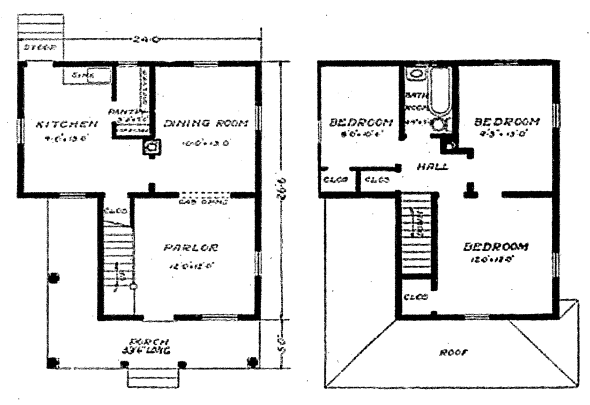

FIRST FLOOR PLAN   SECOND FLOOR PLAN

△ Along with mass-produced consumer goods, such as clothing and household items, Sears, Roebuck and Company marketed architectural plans for middle-class housing. The "tiny house design," published in one of the company's catalogs, illustrates the layout and finished look of the kind of housing built on urban outskirts in the early twentieth century.

because they could take advantage of the schools, water, and fire protection that could be obtained from the nearby city.

More importantly, in-migration from the countryside and abroad contributed to urban population growth. As debt and crop prices worsened, many rural dwellers fled to big cities such as Chicago and San Francisco, and smaller places such as Indianapolis and Nashville. Both men and women, especially young adults, were attracted by the independence that city life offered. Rural African Americans felt the additional pressures of discrimination that drove them cityward. By 1900, thirty-two cities, mostly in the South but in the North also, had more than ten thousand black residents. Because few factories would employ African Americans, most found jobs in the service sector—cleaning, cooking, and driving—usually at very low wages. But such jobs were usually better than tenant farming.

16-4c New Foreign Immigrants

More newcomers were immigrants from a foreign country. They were part of a global movement resulting from population pressures, land redistribution, religious persecution, and industrialization that induced millions of families and individuals to leave Europe and Asia for Canada, Australia, Brazil, Argentina, and the United States. Migration has always characterized human history, but in the late nineteenth century advances in communications and transportation spread news of opportunities and made travel cheaper and safer. Before 1880, most immigrants had come from northern and western Europe—England, Ireland, and Germany. After 1880, a second wave from eastern and southern Europe, plus immigrants from Canada, Mexico, and Japan, joined the first groups (see Map 16.2).

Map 16.2 Sources of European-Born Population, 1900 and 1920

In just a few decades, the proportion of European immigrants to the United States who came from northern and western Europe decreased (Ireland and Germany) or remained relatively stable (England and Scandinavia), while the proportion from eastern and southern Europe increased dramatically. *Source: Data from U.S. Census Bureau, "Historical Census Statistics on the Foreign-Born Population of the United States: 1850–1990," February 1999, http://www.census.gov/population (accessed February 12, 2000).*

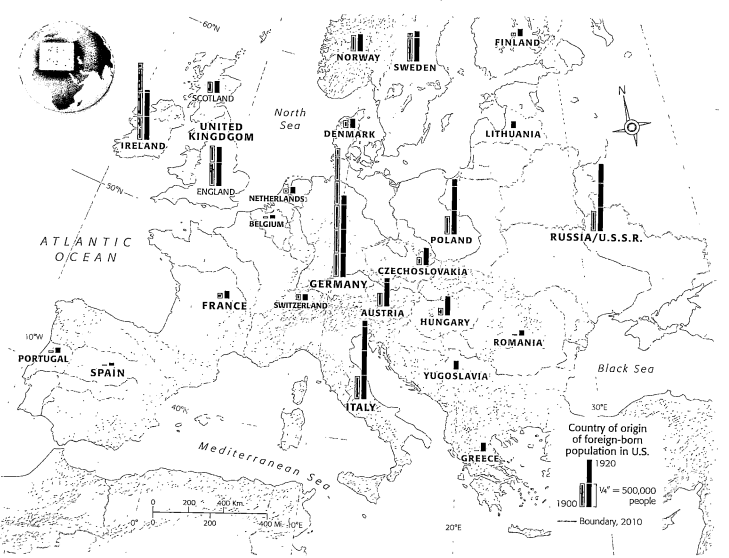

Between 1900 and 1910, two-thirds of immigrants came from Italy, Austria-Hungary, and Russia, and by 1910 arrivals from Mexico outnumbered those from Ireland. Some wanted only to make enough money to return home and live in greater security. Still, most of the 26 million arriving between 1870 and 1920 remained and settled in cities, where they helped to reshape American culture.

Many long-settled Americans feared those they called "new immigrants," whose customs, Catholic and Jewish faiths, unfamiliar languages, low-skill occupations, and poverty made them seem more alien than previous newcomers. Yet old and new immigrants resembled each other in their strategies for coping. The majority of both groups hailed from societies that made family the focus of life, and they sustained family bonds after reaching America. New arrivals often received aid from relatives who had already immigrated, and family members pooled resources to help them adapt.

16-4d Geographical and Social Mobility

Once they arrived in a city, newcomers seldom stayed put. Each year, millions of families packed up and moved, some to another neighborhood, others to a new town or the countryside. Migration was a means by which people tried to escape from poor housing and employment and move to a place where they hoped conditions and jobs would be better. Women migrated within and between cities, but they usually went with fathers and husbands whose economic standing defined their class. For African Americans, Native Americans, Mexican Americans, and Asian Americans, opportunities were scarcer. Assigned to low-paying occupations by prejudice, they made fewer gains.

Few individuals became rich from these moves, but many traveled the road from poverty to moderate success. Advances through work were available mostly to white males. Thousands of businesses were needed to serve burgeoning urban populations, and growing corporations were hiring new personnel. An aspiring merchant could open a saloon or shop for a few hundred dollars, and knowledge of accounting could qualify one for clerical jobs with higher income than manual labor. In fast-growing cities such as Atlanta and Los Angeles, approximately one in five white manual workers rose to white-collar or owner positions within ten years. In older cities, upward rates were slightly lower, perhaps one in six. Some men chose the security of a steady job over the risk of starting a business or the stigma of an unmanly clerical job. A Sicilian who lived in Bridgeport, Connecticut, observed, "The people that come here they afraid to get in business because they don't know how that business goes. In Italy these people don't know much about things because most of them work on farms or in a trade." Many, particularly unskilled workers, did not improve their status. They could not maintain Old World occupations and were forced to accept low-paying jobs and frustrated hopes. Still, the possibilities for upward mobility

seemed to temper people's dissatisfactions. Although gaps between rich and poor widened and discrimination dashed hopes, expanding urban economies created enough opportunities for those in between.

16-4e Cultural Retention

Despite the constant movement that made them turbulent places, cities contained collections of functioning subcommunities where people, most of whom had migrated from somewhere else, coped with daily challenges. Rather than yield completely to pressures to assimilate, migrants and immigrants interacted with their environment in a way that enabled them to retain their identity while also altering their outlook and the society in which they lived. Where the English language was a struggle, where clocks regulated their day, and where housing and employment were uncertain, immigrants first anchored their lives to

Photo by Lewis W. Hine/George Eastman House/Getty Images

△ Male immigrants and an immigration official are looking through a wire fence at an Italian immigrant woman and her daughter who have recently arrived at the immigrant inspection station at Ellis Island, outside of New York City. The main port of entry for European immigrants after 1892, Ellis Island stands in the shadow of the Statue of Liberty.

what they knew best: their culture. Old World customs persisted in districts of Italians from the same province, Japanese from the same island, and Jews from the same Russian *shtetl*. Newcomers created aid organizations known in their homelands, such as Japanese *ken* societies that sponsored holiday celebrations and relief services and Chinese loan associations called *whey*, that helped members start businesses. Southern Italians transferred the *padrone* system, whereby for a payoff a boss found them jobs. Newcomers practiced religion as they always had, married within their group, and pursued long-standing feuds with people from rival villages.

16-4f Urban Borderlands

In large cities, such as Chicago and Philadelphia, immigrants initially clustered in inner-city neighborhoods where jobs and cheap housing were available. These districts often were multi-ethnic "urban borderlands," where diverse people and lifestyles coexisted. Even in districts identified with a specific group, such as "Little Italy" or "Greektown," rapid mobility constantly undermined stability as former inhabitants dispersed to other neighborhoods and new residents moved in. Often, an area's institutions such as bakeries, butcher shops, and churches, usually operated by and for one ethnic group and accessible by mass transportation, gave a neighborhood its identity more than the people who lived there.

For first- and second-generation immigrants, their neighborhoods acted as havens until they were ready to leave the borderlands for other districts where neighbors were of the same class but not necessarily the same nationality. Discrimination persisted as Jews were excluded from certain neighborhoods and Italians found it hard to break into political positions. But prejudice was rarely systematic for Europeans. For African Americans, Asians, and Mexicans, however, borderlands kept a more persistent and homogeneous character, largely due to discrimination.

16-4g Racial Segregation and Violence

By the late nineteenth century, racial bias forced African Americans into highly segregated ghettos. In cities such as Chicago, Cleveland, and Detroit, two-thirds or more of the black population was confined to only 10 percent of total residential area. Within their neighborhoods, blacks, like other urban dwellers, nurtured institutions such as churches, newspapers, and clubs that helped them cope with city life. Branches of Baptist and African Methodist Episcopal (AME) Protestantism were especially active in aiding members. In virtually all cities, religious associations dominated African American communities and fostered cooperation across class lines.

Often, the only way African Americans could relieve pressures of crowding in ghettos was to expand residential borders into surrounding, previously white neighborhoods, a process that resulted in harassment and attacks by white residents whose intolerance intensified from fears that property values would decline if they had black neighbors. Competition between blacks and whites for housing, jobs, and political influence in the North and South sparked incidents of racial violence. In Atlanta in 1906, newspaper accounts alleging attacks by black men against white women provoked whites into an outburst of shooting that left twelve blacks dead and several injured. An influx of black strikebreakers into East St. Louis, Illinois, in 1917 heightened racial tensions. When some blacks fired back at a car from which they believed shots had been fired at their homes, they mistakenly killed two policemen. The next day, whites retaliated. The riot ended only after nine whites and thirty-nine blacks had been killed and three hundred buildings destroyed.

Though Chinese and Japanese immigrants usually preferred to live apart from Anglos and maintain their own business and social institutions in San Francisco, Seattle, Los Angeles, and New York, Anglos made every effort to keep them separate. In San Francisco, Denis Kearney, an Irish immigrant labor leader, blamed the Chinese for job competition and white unemployment in the 1870s. Promoting the slogan, "The Chinese must go," Kearney and his followers tried to prevent employers from hiring Chinese, often resorting to violence. In 1880, San Francisco banned Chinese laundries, which were social centers for immigrants, from locating in white neighborhoods, justifying the ban by saying they were fire hazards. In 1882, the U.S. Congress passed the Chinese Exclusion Act, suspending the immigration of Chinese laborers, and in 1892 the Geary Act extended previous restrictions and required Chinese Americans to carry certificates of residence. Japanese suffered similar restrictions, prevented by law from becoming citizens.

16-4h Mexican Barrios

In southwestern cities such as Los Angeles, Tucson, Albuquerque, and San Antonio, Mexicans had been the original inhabitants, Anglos the newcomers. But as Anglo arrivals increased, they pushed Mexicans into isolated residential and commercial districts called *barrios*. These areas tended to be located away from multi-ethnic borderlands housing European immigrants. To a considerable extent, then, racial and ethnic bias made urban experiences of African Americans, Asians, and Mexicans unique and hindered their opportunities to remake their lives.

Virtually everywhere newcomers lived, immigrant culture mingled with existing realities. Although many foreigners identified themselves by their village or regional birthplace, native-born Americans simplified by categorizing them by nationality. Thus people born in County Cork and County Limerick were all called Irish. Those from Calabria and Campobasso became Italians. At the same time, the diversity of American cities prompted foreigners to modify their attitudes and habits. They could not avoid contact with people different from themselves on the streets and in workplaces. They learned the English language, used locally grown foods for traditional meals, fashioned mass-produced clothing into Old World styles, and went to American doctors while still practicing folk medicine. Music especially revealed adaptation. Polish polka bands blended American and homeland folk music; Mexican ballads reflected new themes about hardship in the United States.

16-4i Religious Diversity

The influx of multiple immigrants transformed the United States into a religiously diverse nation. Newcomers from Italy, Polish lands, and Slovakia joined Irish and Germans to increase Catholic populations significantly in cities such as Buffalo, Cleveland, and Milwaukee. Catholic Mexicans constituted over half the population of El Paso, and New York City came to house one of the largest Jewish populations in the world. By 1920, Buddhism was well established among Japanese immigrants on the West Coast and in Hawai'i. As they coped with new conditions, Catholics and Jews tried to adjust their faiths to their environments by adopting English in services and altering traditional rituals. Changes were not complete, however. Catholic immigrant parishes pressured bishops into appointing priests of the same ethnicity as parishioners, and Orthodox Jews retained Old World customs such as separating men and women inside synagogues. An exchange of cultural patterns occurred when Catholics and Jews married co-religionists of different nationality groups—an Italian marrying a Pole, for example, kept religious identity strong while blending ethnic identities.

Each of the major migrant groups that peopled cities—native-born whites, foreigners, and native-born blacks—created the pluralism of modern American culture. The nation's broad diversity prevented domination by a single racial or ethnic majority and nurtured rich cultural variety: American folk literature, Italian and Mexican cuisine, Yiddish theater, African American music and dance, and much more. Newcomers changed their environment as much as it changed them.

Though rich in varied cultures, central sections of cities often were places challenged by crowding, poverty, crime, and disease. People coped as best they could, and technology, private enterprise, and government achieved some remarkable advances. But many problems evaded permanent solution.

16-4j Housing

Population growth created scarcity of adequate housing. Those with low incomes adapted to high rents and short supply by sharing space, resulting in homes and apartments intended for one family being occupied by two or three families plus boarders. The result was unprecedented crowding. In 1890, New York City's immigrant-packed Lower East Side averaged 702 people per acre, one of the highest population densities in the world. Inside tenements and row houses in New York, Philadelphia, and New Orleans spaces were cramped and interior rooms lacked light and fresh air. States such as New York passed regulations to establish ventilation and safety codes for new tenement buildings, but such measures could not remedy ills of existing buildings.

Eventually, technology and science brought about important changes in home life. Improved furnaces, electric lighting, and indoor plumbing created more comfort for middle-class households and, later, for most others. These advances occurred as a result of private enterprise; landlords and humanitarians alike opposed government financing of better housing, fearing that such a step would undermine profits. The major government-sponsored improvements occurred outside of buildings, where publicly financed street paving, modernized firefighting equipment, and electric street lighting made cities safer.

16-4k Poverty and Crime

Poverty, however, continued to burden many urbanites. Employment, especially for unskilled workers, fluctuated with business cycles, causing low-income families to live on the margins of survival. Since colonial days, an attitude that anyone could escape poverty through hard work and clean living had prevailed in American culture. According to this reasoning, poor people were morally weak and aiding them would encourage dependence on public support. Only those incapable of supporting themselves—orphans, people with disabilities, and widows—deserved relief. Close observance of the urban poor, however, prompted reformers such as Jacob Riis, a New York journalist, to conclude that people's environment contributed to hardship and that society ought to shoulder greater responsibility for improving conditions. Riis's series of articles, combined into a book, *How the Other Half Lives* (1890), alerted readers to the deplorable conditions of slum housing. Other reformers advocated public efforts to improve housing, education, and job opportunities to help the poor help themselves. Others, however, clung to the tenet that in a society of abundance, poverty relief could be tolerated but never encouraged. As one charity worker observed, relief "should be surrounded by circumstances that shall . . . repel everyone . . . from accepting it."

Crime and violence increased at an alarming rate in American cities in contrast to falling rates in other industrializing nations such as England and Germany. The American murder rate, for example, rose from 25 per million people in 1881 to 107 per million in 1898. Though police forces were becoming more professionalized, law enforcement was complicated because various urban groups differed in their views of how laws should be enforced. Ethnic and racial minorities were more likely to be arrested than those with economic or political influence. Also, while moralists clamored for crackdowns on drinking and gambling, those who enjoyed a drink or a card game favored personal freedom to indulge in these activities. Nativists were quick to blame immigrants for urban

△ Inner-city dwellers used not only indoor space as efficiently as possible, but also what little outdoor space was available to them. Scores of families living in this cramped block of six-story tenements in New York strung clotheslines behind the buildings. Notice that there is virtually no space between buildings—only rooms at the front and back received daylight and fresh air.

crime, but urban lawlessness probably did not exceed that of mining camps and southern plantations, and the lawbreaking population included native-born offenders as well as foreigners.

16-4l Water Purity and Waste Disposal

Finding sources of pure water and a way to dispose of waste also challenged city dwellers. Old methods of sinking wells for water and dumping human and industrial waste into rivers and streams could no longer suffice. By the 1880s, doctors began to accept the theory that microorganisms caused disease, prompting new concerns over purity of water sources, where germs were believed to breed. Most cities replaced private water companies with more copious public supplies, but sewers, flush toilets, and factory waste created noxious pollution and sometimes disease. By 1900, for example, the Passaic River in New Jersey, once a popular recreation site, had been ruined by discharge from cities along its banks. Improvements came slowly as states passed laws prohibiting disposing of raw sewage into rivers, and a few cities began to filter their water and use chemicals to treat sewage. Though death rates from tuberculosis remained high, public regulation of water and food purity helped control diseases such as cholera, typhoid fever, and diphtheria.

Trash, however, was a growing problem. Experts in 1900 estimated that every New Yorker annually generated 160 pounds of garbage (food), 1,200 pounds of ashes (from stoves and furnaces), and 105 pounds of rubbish (other discarded items). Europeans of that era produced half as much trash. Factories created tons of solid waste (scrap metal, wood), and each of the 3.5 million horses in American cities daily dumped 20 pounds of manure and a gallon of urine on the streets. All this refuse created health and safety hazards. At the urging of women's groups, some cities hired engineers to address the dilemma. One such engineer, George Waring, Jr., designed efficient systems for sewage disposal and street cleaning in Memphis and New York. As a result of such efforts, cities became cleaner, but the trash problem continues to nag urban communities to the present.

16-4m Political Machines

The necessity for health and safety protection, schools, parks, and more strained the resources of growing cities. Most urban governments were complex entities, with power shared among a mayor, city council, and numerous boards and agencies. Philadelphia at one time had thirty different boards to administer health, poverty relief, public works, and more. Moreover, state laws usually limited a city's ability to levy taxes to fund its needs. Out of this complex system of urban

△ This scene, captured by a Philadelphia photographer in order to record the extent of trash that was littering city streets and sidewalks, illustrates the problems of disposal confronting inner-city, immigrant neighborhoods and the necessity for some form of public service to remove the refuse. Seemingly oblivious to the debris, the residents pose for the photographer.

management arose **political machines**, organizations whose goals were to obtain and retain power. Machine politicians used fraud and bribery to further their ends. But they also provided relief and service to those who voted for them. By meeting people's needs, machine politicians accomplished things that others had been unable or unwilling to attempt.

Most big cities were run by political machines at one time or another and for varying lengths of time. The most notable machines existed in New York, Philadelphia, and Chicago, but they also arose in places as varied as Cincinnati, Memphis, Kansas City, New Orleans, and San Francisco. These organizations bred leaders, called **bosses**, who built power bases among immigrant working classes. Bosses understood people's problems from firsthand experience and dealt with people on a personal basis. Martin Lomasney, a Boston boss, once remarked, "There's got to be in every ward somebody that any bloke can come to—no matter what he's done—and get help. Help, you understand, none of your law and justice, but help." To bosses, politics was a full-time profession. They attended weddings and wakes, sponsored picnics, and held open house in saloons where neighborhood folk could speak directly to them. In return for jobs, food, and intervention when someone got arrested, people gave machine politicians the votes that kept them in power.

To finance their activities, bosses used political influence to control the awarding of public contracts and streetcar and utility franchises. In return, recipients of city business and jobs were expected to repay the machine with a portion of their profits or salaries. Critics called this process graft; bosses called it gratitude. Though waste and corruption were often involved, bosses could boast major achievements. Aided by a new generation of professional engineers, machine-led governments constructed much of the new urban infrastructure—public buildings, sewer systems, schools, and streetcar lines—and expanded services such as firefighting, police, and public health.

Machines were rarely neutral or fair, however. Racial minorities and new immigrant groups such as Italians and Poles received only token favors and jobs, if any. Bribes and kickbacks made machine projects costly. Unable to raise enough revenue from taxes and fees, bosses financed

political machines Organizations that emerged in urban, often working-class and immigrant neighborhoods. They solicited votes for particular candidates and promised jobs and other services to supporters; putting their candidates in office gave them power over local government.

Bosses Headed political machines; often of similar background to constituents, these popular local figures exchanged votes for money, support, and other favors.

expansion with loans in the form of municipal bonds. As a result, public debts soared. Also, payoffs from gambling and illegal liquor traffic were important sources of machine revenues. But bosses likely were no guiltier of greed and discrimination than were those businessmen who exploited workers, spoiled the environment, and manipulated government in pursuit of profits. Sometimes humane, sometimes criminal, bosses acted as brokers between sectors of urban society and an uncertain world.

16-4n Civic and Social Reform

Reacting to ways bosses exercised power and disturbed by mounting costs and corruption in government, reformers tried to unseat machines. One group, mostly middle- and upper-class types called civic reformers, sought to replace machine politics with government run according to business principles of economy and efficiency. They advocated for structural changes such as tighter control of budgets, city manager and commission forms of government, and nonpartisan elections. In several places reform campaigns managed to oust machines, and a few reform mayors, such as Hazen Pingree of Detroit and Tom Johnson of Cleveland, worked not only for governmental change but to provide jobs and better housing for poor people. But most civic reformers only wanted to economize and root out dishonesty; they seldom held office for very long.

Beyond politics and government, another group, social reformers, undertook efforts to investigate and solve everyday problems. Mostly middle class, this group pressed government for building codes to ensure safer tenements, improved public and vocational schools to better prepare immigrants for citizenship, and medical care for those unable to afford it. Often led by women such as **Jane Addams** and **Florence Kelley,** social reformers also promoted safer food, public playgrounds, and school nurses. Environmental reformers, such as those in the City Beautiful movement, sought to improve cities' built environments. Inspired by the World's Columbian Exposition of 1893, a dazzling fair built on Chicago's South Side, architects and planners urged construction of civic centers, parks, and boulevards that would make cities economically efficient as well as more attractive. Many plans, however, were only dreams. Neither government nor private businesses could finance large-scale projects, and planners disagreed among themselves over whether beautification would really solve urban problems.

Regardless of their focus, urban reformers wanted to save cities, not abandon them. They believed they could improve urban society by fostering cooperation among all citizens. They often failed, however, to understand a city's diversity and that different people had conflicting goals. To civic reformers, appointing government workers on the basis of civil service exams rather than party loyalty meant progress, but to working-class men, jobs given for party loyalty were what counted. Moral reformers believed that restricting the sale of alcoholic beverages would prevent husbands from squandering wages and ruining their health, but immigrants saw such crusades as interference in their private lives. Planners envisioned boulevards and buildings as modern necessities, but such structures often displaced the poor. Well-meaning humanitarians tried to change the ways immigrant mothers shopped, cooked, and raised children without regard for mothers' inability to afford new products of the consumer economy. Thus urban reform merged idealism with insensitivity.

16-5 Family Life and Individual Life

▶ **How did the makeup of a household and family alter in the late nineteenth and early twentieth century?**

▶ **What role did family play in the lives of the inhabitants of cities?**

For the majority of urban dwellers, family, not government, was the most crucial institution. But increasingly, new institutions—schools, ethnic clubs, unions—competed with the family to provide education and security. Still, the family unit retained its fundamental role as a cushion in a harsh, uncertain world.

Throughout modern western history, most people have lived in two overlapping social units: household and family. A household is a grouping of related and/or unrelated people who share the same residence. A family is a group related by kinship, some of whom live together. Until recently, when the number of single people living alone has increased markedly, most American households (75 percent or more) have consisted of nuclear families—usually a married couple with or without children. About 15 to 20 percent of households have consisted of extended families—usually a nuclear family plus one or more adult relatives. This pattern held relatively consistent among various ethnic, racial, and socioeconomic groups.

Several factors explain this pattern. Because immigrants tended to be young, the population as a whole was young. In 1880, the median age of the American population was under twenty-one, and by 1920 it was still only twenty-five. (Median age at present is thirty-seven.) Moreover, death rates among people aged forty-five to sixty-four were double what they are today, and the proportion of the population aged sixty-five and older was just 4 percent in 1900; it is 14.5 percent today. Thus in the late nineteenth and early twentieth century, fewer children than today had living grandparents, and three-generation households of children, parents, and grandparents were rare.

Jane Addams Social worker, pioneer of the settlement house movement, and founder of Chicago's Hull House, which provided education, training, and social activities for immigrants and the poor.

Florence Kelley Settlement house worker who became the chief factory inspector for Illinois in 1893.

Falling birth rates reduced family sizes. In 1880, there were 40 live births per 1,000 people; by 1900 the rate had dropped to 32; and by 1920 it was 28. Several factors explain this pattern. First, the United States was becoming an urban nation, and birth rates are historically lower in cities than in rural areas. Second, as nutrition and medical care improved, infant mortality fell and families did not have to bear as many children to ensure that some would survive. Third, awareness that smaller families meant improved quality of life for each surviving child influenced parents' decisions to limit family size so that three or four children instead of five or six became the norm. Birth-control technology—diaphragms and condoms—had existed for centuries, but in this era new materials such as vulcanized rubber made devices more convenient and dependable.

16-5a Family as a Resource

Young adults who left home to work altered household composition, especially in cities, as many became boarders in homes and lodging houses. For people on the move, boarding was a transitional stage before setting up their own household. It also allowed families with spare space to obtain extra income by renting rooms to boarders. Families also took in widowed parents or unmarried adult siblings.

At a time when welfare agencies were rare, the family was the resource to which people turned in times of need. Relatives often resided near each other and aided one another with child care, meals, advice, and consolation. As one family member recalled, "After two days my brother took me to the shop he was working in and his boss saw me and he gave me the job." But obligations of kinship were not always welcome. Immigrant parents pressured daughters to stay at home to help with housework and child care, stifling opportunities for education and independence. Tensions also erupted when immigrant parents and their American-born children clashed over the abandonment of Old World ways or the amount of wages employed children should contribute to the household. Nevertheless, kinship helped people cope with the stresses of urban-industrial society.

16-5b The Unmarried

Although marriage rates were high, large numbers of city dwellers were unmarried, mainly because young people postponed marriage until their late twenties. In 1890 almost 42 percent of adult men and 37 percent of adult women were single, almost twice as high as in 1960 (though lower than today). About half lived with parents, but others inhabited rented rooms. Mostly young, they developed a subculture that patronized dance halls, saloons, cafes, and organizations such as the YMCA and YWCA.

Some unmarried people were part of homosexual populations that gathered in large cities such as New York, San Francisco, and Boston. Though numbers are difficult to estimate, gay men patronized their own clubs, restaurants, coffeehouses, and theaters. A number of same-sex couples,

especially women, formed lasting relationships, sometimes called "Boston marriages." People in this subculture were categorized more by how they acted—men acting like women, women acting like men—than by who their sexual partners were. The term "homosexual" was not used. Men who dressed and acted like women were called "fairies." Gay women remained largely hidden, and a visible lesbian subculture was rare until the 1920s.

16-5c Stages of Life

Before the late nineteenth century, stages of life were less distinct than they are today. Childhood, for instance, had been regarded as a period during which youngsters prepared for adulthood by gradually assuming adult responsibilities. Subdivisions of youth—toddlers, schoolchildren, teenagers—were not recognized. Because married couples had more children over a longer time span, active parenthood occupied most of adult life. Children who cared for younger siblings might begin parenting responsibilities before reaching adulthood. Older people often did not retire; they worked until they were physically incapable.

In the late nineteenth century, demographic and social changes altered these patterns. Decreasing birth rates shortened the period of parenting, so more middle-aged couples experienced an "empty nest" once their children grew up and left home. Longer life expectancy and a tendency by employers to force aged workers to retire separated the old from the young. As states passed compulsory school attendance laws and established graded schools in the 1870s and 1880s, children spent more time with others of the same age than with older or younger people. Childhood and adolescence became distinct stages, and peers rather than family influenced youngsters' behavior more than previously. People's roles in school, in the family, on the job, and in the community came to be determined by age more than any other characteristic.

By 1900, new agencies were assuming tasks formerly performed by families. Schools made education a community responsibility. Employment agencies, political machines, and labor unions became responsible for getting people jobs and for job security. Age-based peer groups exerted influence over people's values and sociability. Yet kinship remained a dependable though not always appreciated institution. Family togetherness became especially visible at holiday celebrations. Thanksgiving, Christmas, and Easter were times for family reunions and child-centered activities. Birthdays, too, took on new festive qualities as milestones for measuring age-related norms and life stages. In 1914, President Woodrow Wilson proclaimed the second Sunday in May as Mother's Day, capping a six-year campaign by schoolteacher Anna Jarvis, who believed children were neglecting their mothers. Ethnic, religious, and racial groups adapted celebrations to their cultures, preparing special foods and engaging in special ceremonies. For many, holidays served as testimony to the vitality of family life.

16-6 New Leisure and Mass Culture

▷ What commercial activities emerged for amusement and leisure in the urban environments?

▷ How did sports and new forms of communication contribute to the creation of a mass culture?

▷ How did new forms of amusement and entertainment provide opportunities for minority groups in American society?

On December 2, 1889, as laborers paraded through Worcester, Massachusetts, seeking shorter working hours, a group of carpenters hoisted a banner proclaiming, "Eight Hours for Work, Eight Hours for Rest, Eight Hours for What We Will." That last phrase expressed claim to a new segment of daily life: leisure.

16-6a Increase in Leisure Time

By the late 1800s, technology had become truly time-saving. Machines and assembly lines cut average workweeks from sixty-six hours in 1860 to sixty in 1890 and forty-seven in 1920, giving workers shorter workdays and freer weekends. White-collar employees spent eight to ten hours a day on the job and often worked only half a day or not at all on weekends. Many Americans now had time for a variety of diversions, and entrepreneurs profited from their new leisure time.

Amusement became a new commercial activity. Production of games, toys, and musical instruments expanded. Improvements in cardboard production aided increased popularity of board games from manufacturers such as Milton Bradley and Parker Brothers. Significantly, the content of board games shifted from moral lessons to topics involving transportation, finance, and sports. Also, by the 1890s, middle-class families were buying mass-produced pianos and sheet music that made singing a popular home entertainment. The vanguard of new leisure pursuits, however, was sports. Formerly a fashionable indulgence of elites, organized sports became a favorite pastime of all classes.

16-6b Baseball

Baseball ruled as the most popular sport. Derived from older bat, ball, and base-circling games, baseball was formalized in 1845 by the Knickerbocker Club of New York City. By 1860 at least fifty baseball clubs existed, and youths played informal games on vacant city lots and rural fields across the nation. In 1866, the Cincinnati Red Stockings became the first fully professional baseball club, compiling a perfect 65–0 record playing local teams across the country. The founding of the National League of Professional Baseball Clubs in 1876 gave the sport a stable business structure, though as early as 1867, a "color line" excluded black players from major professional teams. In 1903 the National League and competing American League (formed in 1901) began a World Series between

their championship teams. The Boston Americans (later, Red Sox) defeated the Pittsburgh Pirates five games to three.

16-6c Croquet and Cycling

Croquet and cycling were popular pastimes attracting men and women alike. Played on lawns, sometimes with lighted wickets for nighttime competition, croquet encouraged socializing. Cycling was as popular as baseball, especially after 1885, when the cumbersome velocipede, with its huge front wheel and tall seat, gave way to safety bicycles with pneumatic tires and wheels of identical size. By 1900, Americans owned 10 million bicycles, and cycling clubs lobbied governments to build more paved roads. Cycle races brought international fame to professional riders such as Major Taylor, an African American. Also, bicycles helped free women from constraints of Victorian fashion. In order to ride safety bicycles, women had to wear divided skirts and simple undergarments. As the 1900 census proclaimed, "Few articles . . . have created so great a revolution in social conditions as the bicycle."

16-6d Football

American football, as an intercollegiate competition, attracted players and spectators wealthy enough to have access to higher education. By the late nineteenth century, however, the game was appealing to a wider audience. While the Princeton-Yale game drew fifty thousand spectators, informal games were played in yards and playgrounds throughout the country.

College football's violence and "tramp athletes"—nonstudents hired to help teams win—sparked a national scandal, climaxing in 1905 when 18 players died from game-related injuries and more than 150 were seriously injured. President Theodore Roosevelt, an advocate of athletics, convened a White House conference to discuss ways of eliminating brutality and foul play. The gathering founded the Intercollegiate Athletic Association (renamed the National Collegiate Athletic Association, or NCAA, in 1910) to police college sports. In 1906, the association altered football rules to make the game less violent by outlawing the "flying wedge," extending from five to ten yards the distance needed to make a first down, legalizing the forward pass, and tightening player eligibility.

As more women enrolled in college, they participated in sports such as rowing, track, swimming, archery, and baseball. Eventually, they made basketball their most popular intercollegiate sport. Basketball was invented in 1891 as a winter sport for men, but Senda Berenson of Smith College drafted special women's rules in 1899, limiting dribbling and running and encouraging passing.

16-6e Show Business

American show business matured in these years, becoming a mode of entertainment created by and for ordinary people. New theatrical performances offered audiences escape into

Japanese Baseball

Baseball, the "national pastime," was one new leisure-time pursuit that Americans took into different parts of the world. The Shanghai Base Ball Club was founded by Americans in China in 1863, but few Chinese paid much attention to the sport, largely because the Imperial Court denounced the game as spiritually corrupting. However, when Horace Wilson, an American teacher, taught baseball to his Japanese students in 1873, the game received an enthusiastic reception as a reinforcement of traditional virtues. In fact, baseball quickly became so much a part of Japanese culture that one Japanese writer commented, "Baseball is perfect for us. If the Americans hadn't invented it, we probably would have."

During the 1870s, scores of Japanese high schools and colleges sponsored organized baseball, and in 1883 Hiroshi Hiraoka, a railroad engineer who had studied in Boston, founded the first official local team, the Shimbashi Athletic Club Athletics. Fans displayed wild devotion to this and similar teams as they developed over the next several years.

Before Americans introduced baseball to Japan, the Japanese had no team sports and no predilection for recreational athletics. Once they learned about baseball, they found that the idea of a team sport fit their culture very well. But the Japanese had difficulty applying the American concept of leisure to the game. For them, baseball was serious business, involving hard and often brutal training. Practices at Ichiko, one of Japan's top high school baseball teams in the late nineteenth century, were dubbed "Bloody Urine" because many players passed blood after a day of drilling. There was a spiritual quality as well, linked to Buddhist values. According to one Japanese coach, "The purpose of [baseball] training is not health but the forging of the soul, and a strong soul is only born from strong practice. . . . Student baseball must be the baseball of self-discipline, or trying to attain the truth, just as in Zen Buddhism." This attitude prompted the Japanese to consider baseball a new method for pursuing the spirit of Bushido, the way of the samurai.

When Americans played baseball in Japan, the Japanese found them to be strong and talented but lacking in discipline and respect. Americans insulted the Japanese by refusing to remove their hats and bow when they stepped up to bat. An international dispute occurred in 1891 when William Imbrie, an American professor at Tokyo's Meijo University, arrived late for a game. Finding the gate locked, he climbed over the fence in order to enter the field. The fence, however, had sacred meaning, and Japanese fans attacked Imbrie for his sacrilege. Imbrie suffered facial injuries, prompting the American embassy to lodge a formal complaint. Americans assumed that their game would encourage Japanese to become like westerners, but the Japanese transformed the American pastime into an expression of team spirit, discipline, and nationalism that was uniquely Japanese.

CRITICAL THINKING

- The Japanese made baseball "their own" after Americans introduced it to their country. How are baseball and other professional sports today more like Japanese baseball than they are like their ancestral forms in the U.S.?
- How do we account for that change?

◁ Replete with bats, gloves, and uniforms, this Japanese baseball team of 1890 very much resembles its American counterpart of that era. The Japanese adopted baseball soon after Americans became involved in their country but also added their cultural qualities to the game.

Transcendental Graphics/Archive Photos/Getty Images

adventure, melodrama, and comedy. Plots were simple, heroes and villains recognizable. For urban people unfamiliar with other times and places, productions made the Wild West and Old South come alive through dramas of Buffalo Bill, Davy Crockett, and the Civil War. Musical comedies entertained with songs, humor, and dance. Folksy comedy and catchy tunes were performed by popular performers such as **George M. Cohan**. A singer and dancer born into an Irish family, Cohan drew on patriotism and traditional values in songs such as "The Yankee Doodle Boy" and "You're a Grand Old Flag."

By 1900, vaudeville was the most popular mass entertainment because it offered something for everyone. Shows, whose acts followed a fixed schedule just like trains and factory production, featured jugglers, magicians, acrobats, comedians, singers, dancers, and animal acts. Shrewd entrepreneurs made vaudeville a big business. The famous producer Florenz Ziegfeld packaged shows in a stylish format—the Ziegfeld Follies—and created a new form of femininity, the Ziegfeld Girl, whose graceful dancing and alluring costumes suggested a haunting sexuality.

16-6f Opportunities for Women and Minorities

Show business provided new opportunities for female, African American, and immigrant performers, but at the cost of stereotyping and exploitation. Comic opera diva Lillian Russell, vaudeville comedienne-singer Fanny Brice, and burlesque queen Eva Tanguay attracted loyal fans and handsome fees. In contrast to the demure Victorian female, they conveyed images of pluck and creativity. Tanguay exuded something both shocking and confident when she sang, "It's All Been Done Before But Not the Way I Do It." But lesser female performers were often exploited by male promoters and theater owners, who wanted to profit by titillating the public with scantily clad women onstage.

Before the 1890s, the chief form of commercial entertainment employing African Americans was the **minstrel show**. Vaudeville gave black artists new opportunities but reinforced demeaning social attitudes. Pandering to prejudices of white audiences, composers and white singers degraded blacks in songs such as "You May Be a Hawaiian on Old Broadway, But You're Just Another Nigger to Me." Black performers such as Bert Williams, a talented comedian and dancer who had graduated from high school at a time when most whites did not, achieved success by wearing blackface makeup and playing stereotypical roles of a smiling fool and dandy, living their lives tormented by the humiliation they had to suffer.

George M. Cohan Singer, dancer, and songwriter who drew on patriotic and traditional values in songs.

minstrel show Early stage show in which white men wore blackface makeup and played to the prejudices of white audiences by offering demeaning and caricatured portrayals of African Americans in songs, dances, and skits.

△ Eva Tanguay was one of the most popular and highly-paid vaudeville entertainers of her era. She began performing in the 1890s, shown here, and her career lasted until the 1930s. An energetic singer who billed herself as "the girl who made vaudeville famous," Tanguay dressed in elaborate costumes and sang suggestive songs, many of which were written just for her and epitomized her carefree style.

Immigrants occupied the core of American popular entertainment. Vaudeville in particular used ethnic humor and exaggerated dialects in skits and songs. Performers reinforced ethnic stereotypes, but such distortions were more self-conscious and sympathetic than those involving blacks. Ethnic comedy often satirized everyday difficulties that immigrants faced. A typical scene featuring Italians, for example, highlighted a character's uncertain grasp of English, which caused him to confuse *diploma* with *the plumber* and *pallbearer* with *polar bear*. Such scenes allowed audiences to laugh with, rather than at, foibles of the human condition.

16-6g Movies

Shortly after 1900, live entertainment began to yield to motion pictures. Perfected by Thomas Edison in the 1880s, movies began as slot-machine peep shows in arcades and billiard parlors. Eventually, images were projected onto a screen so that large audiences could view them, and a new medium was born. Producers, many of them from Jewish immigrant backgrounds, discovered that a film could tell a dramatic story that catered to viewers' desires. Using themes of patriotism and working-class life, early filmmakers helped shift American culture away from straitlaced Victorian values to a more cosmopolitan outlook. And as new technology enabled movie lengths to expand from minutes to hours, producers presented social messages as well as intense drama. For example, *The Birth of a Nation* (1915), directed by D. W. Griffith, was a stunning epic about the Civil War and Reconstruction. But it also fanned racial prejudice by depicting African Americans as threats to white moral values. The National Association for the Advancement of Colored People (NAACP), formed in 1909, led organized protests against it. But the film's pioneering techniques—close-ups, fade-outs, and battle scenes—heightened its appeal.

By mass-producing sound and images, technology made entertainment an important consumer industry. The still camera, modernized by George Eastman, enabled ordinary people to record and preserve family memories. The phonograph, another Edison invention, brought musical performances into the home. News also became a consumer product. Using high-speed printing presses, cheap paper, and revenues from advertisements, shrewd publishers created a much-desired medium. Increased leisure time and high literacy rates nurtured a fascination with the sensational, and from the 1880s onward, popular urban newspapers increasingly whetted that appetite.

16-6h Yellow Journalism

Joseph Pulitzer, a Hungarian immigrant who bought the *New York World* in 1883, pioneered a new branch of journalism by filling *World* pages with stories of disasters, crimes, and scandals under screaming headlines set in large bold type. Pulitzer also popularized comics, and the yellow ink they were printed in brought about the term "yellow journalism" as a synonym for sensationalism. In one year, the *World's* circulation rose from 20,000 to 100,000, and by the late 1890s it reached 1 million. Soon other publishers, such as William Randolph Hearst, who bought the *New York Journal* in 1895 and started a newspaper empire, adopted Pulitzer's techniques. Pulitzer, Hearst, and their rivals boosted circulations further by presenting sports and women's news in separate sections. Also, popular magazines, such as *Saturday Evening Post* and *Ladies Home Journal*, increased their circulation with human-interest stories, photographs, and eye-catching ads.

Other forms of communication also expanded, aided by technology. In 1891, there was less than one telephone for every hundred people in the United States; by 1901 the number had doubled, and by 1921 it had swelled to 12.6. In 1900, Americans used 4 billion postage stamps; in 1922, they bought 14.3 billion. The term *community*

took on new dimensions, as people used the media, mail, and telephone to extend their horizons far beyond their immediate locality. More than ever before, people in different parts of the country knew about and discussed the same news event, whether it was a sensational murder, sex scandal, or the fortunes of an entertainer or athlete. American was becoming a mass society where the same products, same technology, and same information dominated everyday life.

To some extent, the new amusements allowed ethnic and social groups to share common experiences. Amusement parks such as at Coney Island, ball fields, vaudeville shows, movies, and feature sections of newspapers and magazines were nonsectarian and apolitical. Yet different groups consumed them to suit their own needs. Immigrants, for example, used parks and amusement areas as sites for special ethnic gatherings. To the dismay of natives who hoped that public recreation and holidays would assimilate newcomers and teach them habits of restraint, immigrants converted picnics and Fourth of July celebrations into occasions for boisterous festivity. Young working-class men and women resisted parents' and moralizers' warnings and frequented dance halls, where they explored forms of courtship and sexual behavior free from adult oversight. And children often used streets, alleys, and rooftops to create their own recreation rather than participate in adult-supervised games in parks and playgrounds. Thus, as the American people learned to play, their leisure—like their work and politics—expressed, and was shaped by, the pluralistic forces that thrived in the new urban-industrial society.

Summary

Industrialization, propelled by machines and inventions, and urbanization, enriched by waves of newly arrived people and their diverse cultures, altered the United States and its human ecology in dramatic ways in the late nineteenth and early twentieth century. Industrial growth converted the country from a debtor, agricultural nation into a manufacturing, financial, and exporting power. Immigrants and their offspring outnumbered the native born in many cities, and the industrial economy depended on these new workers and consumers. And the era's new technologies, whether on assembly lines or in homes, also made cities safer and daily life more comfortable.

But in industry, massive size and aggressive consolidation of businesses engulfed the individual, changing the nature of work from a singular activity undertaken by skilled producers to mass production undertaken by wage earners. Laborers fought to retain control of their work and organized unions to advance their cause. Urban life, for its part, brought forward its own challenges, especially to newcomers, of finding adequate housing, a decent job, and a safe environment. In urban communities, politics and reform

Technology of Recorded Sound

Today's widespread markets for downloaded music come from a combination of technology, chemistry, and human resourcefulness that came together in the late nineteenth century. In 1877, even before he invented the light bulb, Thomas Edison devised a way to preserve and reproduce his own voice by storing it on indentations made in tinfoil. At first, Edison intended his "speaking machine" to help businesses store dictated messages and replace undependable secretaries. But in 1878 he was stirred by a rivalry with Alexander Graham Bell, inventor of the telephone, who also was working on a device that reproduced sounds, to invent a phonograph that played recorded music. By the 1890s, entrepreneurs were charging audiences admission to hear recorded sounds from these machines.

By 1901, companies such as the Columbia Phonograph Company and Victor Talking Machine Company began to produce machines that played music recorded on cylinders molded and hardened from a chemical wax compound more durable than the metal cylinders that Edison had used. Over the next ten years, various inventors improved the phonograph so that it played back sound from a

stylus (needle) vibrating in grooves of a shellac disc. These developments increased the playing time of records from two minutes to four.

Phonograph records then replaced sheet music as the most popular medium of popular music, but soon another technological wonder—radio—rose to prominence and helped boost record sales. The popularity of the radio could not have been possible without another feat of electronic acoustic technology—the microphone. The microphone achieved better sound quality over previously used megaphones by picking up sound from a performance and turning it into electrical currents that were transmitted via wire from the microphone to a radio station, which then broadcast the sound. As phonograph prices declined and sound quality improved, more records became available.

The invention in 1938 of the idler wheel, which enabled a phonograph turntable to spin a disk at the speed necessary for the stylus to pick up the sound accurately, brought an important advance. Shortly thereafter, more significant inventions in sound recording, such as the magnetic tape recorder, allowed for more manipulation of

sound in the recording studio than ever before. Tape and slower-speed turntables lengthened play time, and in 1963 Philips, a Dutch electronics firm, introduced the compact audiocassette. Two decades later, Philips joined with the Japanese corporation Sony to adapt digital laser discs, which an American had invented to store video images, to record music by transforming sound into sequences of numbers. The compact disc (CD) was born, and from there it was a short step for the Apple Computer Company to create the iPod, which housed CD-quality music on an internal hard drive. And more recently, online music sites have used compressed file sizes and marketed music for digital audio players, and downloaded music has replaced records, tapes, and discs, and has become a multi-billion-dollar industry.

CRITICAL THINKING

☐ As digital music downloads have begun to dominate all other forms of musical recording, the music industry has struggled to keep up in terms of artists' royalties and rights. This struggle is symptomatic of a larger problem regarding copyright and the dissemination of information digitally. What should the government's role be in regulating copyright and the web?

took on new meanings, and family life reflected both change and continuity.

An uneven distribution of power and wealth characterized the era. Corporations consolidated to control resources and make profits more certain. Workers and their allies had numbers and ideas but lacked influence, believing businesses were profiting at their expense. And the urban society that materialized when native inventiveness met the traditions of European, African, and Asian cultures seldom functioned smoothly, yet cities managed to thrive because of, rather than in spite of, their diverse fragments. When the desire to hold on to one's culture met with the need to fit in, often the results were compound identifications: Irish American, Italian American, Polish American, and the like.

By 1920, the foundation of the country's urban-industrial structure had been laid, climaxing an era of extraordinary dynamism.

Suggestions for Further Reading

John Bodnar, *The Transplanted: A History of Immigrants in Urban America* (1985)

Howard P. Chudacoff, *How Old Are You: Age Consciousness in American Culture* (1989)

Howard P. Chudacoff and Judith E. Smith, *The Evolution of American Urban Society*, 8th ed. (2014)

Steven J. Diner, *A Very Different Age: Americans of the Progressive Era* (1998)

Nancy Foner and George M. Frederickson, eds., *Not Just Black and White: Historical and Contemporary Perspectives on Immigration, Race, and Ethnicity in the United States* (2004)

Kenneth T. Jackson, *The Crabgrass Frontier: The Suburbanization of the United States* (1985)

Matthew Frye Jacobson, *Whiteness of a Different Color: European Immigrants and the Alchemy of Race* (1998)

John F. Kasson, *Amusing the Million: Coney Island at the Turn of the Century* (1978)

Alice Kessler-Harris, *Out to Work: A History of Wage-Earning Women in the United States* (2003)

T. J. Jackson Lears and Richard W. Fox, eds., *The Culture of Consumption: Critical Essays in American History, 1880–1980* (1983)

Robyn Muncy, *Creating a Female Dominion in American Reform, 1890–1935* (1991)

Kathy Peiss, *Cheap Amusements: Working Women and Leisure in Turn-of-the-Century New York* (1986)

MINDTAP
From Cengage

MindTap® is a fully online personalized learning experience built upon Cengage Learning content. MindTap® combines student learning tools—readings, multimedia, activities, and assessments—into a singular Learning Path that guides students through the course and helps students develop the critical thinking, analysis, and communication skills that are essential to academic and professional success.

Gilded Age Politics, 1877–1900

W illiam Graham Sumner did not think much of people who were lazy, immoral, or criminal. He once observed, with regard to these people, "it would have been better for society and would have involved no pain to them, if they had never been born." Sumner, who distanced himself from those whom he considered objectional types, traveled several roads to success. Born in New Jersey, he was raised in Hartford, Connecticut, the son of a railroad employee and wife who both had immigrated from England. In spite of his family's modest means, Sumner was able to attend and graduate from Yale College (later Yale University) in 1863, after which he studied in Germany and England, then was ordained an Episcopal priest in 1869. But society and economics, rather than theology, were his real passions. So in 1872 he left his post at the Church of the Redeemer in Morristown, New Jersey, and accepted a professorship in political and social science at Yale, where he remained until retiring in 1909. Yale proved to be a good place for William's sister Alice as well as himself. In 1888, Alice fell in love with and married Yale's new football coach, Walter Camp, who shortly thereafter became one of the most influential powers in college sports.

Professor Sumner was a staunch believer in individual liberty and a champion of laissez-faire, the ideology that government involvement in private affairs should be kept to a minimum. He wrote numerous books and articles on these topics and has been credited among those who adapted Charles Darwin's theory of the survival of the fittest to social and economic relations. In an essay published in 1887, Sumner expressed his views on laissez-faire by asserting that the American people had "reached the point where individualism is possible" and that "legislative and administrative interference" should be resisted. Otherwise, he concluded, "whenever we try to get paternalized (meaning controlled by government) we only succeed in getting policed."

Experience an interactive version of this story in MindTap®.

◁ Politics in the late nineteenth century was an important community activity. In an age before movies, television, and shopping malls, forceful orators performed amidst lights, flags, streamers, and fireworks with speeches that sometimes lasted for hours. Granger, NYC — All rights reserved.

ith his coarse opinions on individualism and people whom he deemed "unfit," Sumner can be seen as an icon of the age of the nation's rampant economic expansion. The traumatic Civil War and its aftermath plus the rise of large corporations between 1877 and 1900 influenced politics and government as much as they shaped everyday life. It was an era characterized by greed, special interest, and political exclusion. The obsession with corporation and individual profits prompted Mark Twain and his novelist friend Charles Dudley Warner to pen a novel titled *The Gilded Age 1874* that satirized America as a nation shiny and golden on the outside but in reality decadent and money-grubbing. Ever since, historians have used the expression "Gilded Age" to characterize the late nineteenth century.

At first glance, the Gilded Age may appear as the era in which laissez-faire, the doctrine that Sumner so passionately espoused, was triumphant. Corporations seemed to expand unfettered and government spending, especially on social programs, was kept to a minimum. The U.S. Congress was preoccupied with matters designed to aid business, and in a series of influential decisions, the Supreme Court limited the ability of government to control corporations.

Such a view, however, would miss some of the most vital developments of the era, developments that expanded government power at federal, state, and local levels far more than people at the time realized. Though certain groups resisted the imposition of government authority, others welcomed and actively sought it. Reformers could claim several accomplishments. In spite of partisan and regional rivalries, Congress achieved legislative landmarks in railroad regulation, tariff and currency reform, creation of the civil service, and other important issues. The presidency was occupied by honest, respectable men who, though not as exceptional as Washington, Jefferson, or Lincoln, asserted their authority and independence from Congress. And, state and local governments expanded their police power—the authority to protect the health, safety, and morals of their citizens. Nevertheless, past injustices continued, as exclusion prevented the majority of Americans—including women, African Americans, Native Americans, uneducated whites, and unnaturalized immigrants—from voting and from access to the tools of democracy.

From the 1870s to the 1890s, a stable party system and balance of power among geographic sections kept politics in a delicate equilibrium. Then, in the 1890s, rural discontent rumbled through the West and South, and a deep economic depression bared flaws in the industrial system. A presidential campaign in 1896 stirred the American people as they had not been stirred for a generation. Old parties split, a new party system arose, sectional unity dissolved, and fundamental disputes about the nation's future climaxed. The nation emerged from the turbulent 1890s with new economic configurations and new political alignments.

- ◻ *What were the functions of government in the Gilded Age, and how did they change?*

- ◻ *How did policies of exclusion and discrimination make their mark on the political culture of the age?*

- ◻ *How did the economic climate give rise to the Populist movement?*

17-1 The Nature of Party Politics

▷ How did the public relate to party politics in the late nineteenth century?

▷ What was the relationship between and within the major political parties of the late nineteenth century?

At no other time in the nation's history was public interest in elections more avid than between 1870 and 1896. Consistently, around 80 percent of eligible voters (white and black males in the North and West, somewhat lower rates among mostly white males in the South) cast ballots in local, state, and national elections—a rate 20 to 30 percent higher than today's. Politics served as a form of recreation, more popular than baseball or circuses. Actual voting provided only the final step in a process that included parades, picnics, and speeches. As one observer remarked, "What the theatre is to the French, or the bull fight . . . to the Spanish . . . [election campaigns] are to our people."

17-1a Cultural–Political Alignments

In contrast to the present, when many voters consider themselves independents, in the Gilded Age party loyalty was vigorous and emotional. With some exceptions, people who opposed government interference in matters of personal liberty identified with the Democratic Party; those who believed government could be an agent of reform identified with the Republican Party. There was also a geographic dimension to these divisions. Northern Republicans tried to capitalize on bitter memories of the Civil War by "waving the bloody shirt" at northern and southern Democrats. As one Republican orator scolded in 1876, "Every man that tried to destroy this nation was a Democrat. . . . Soldiers, every scar you have on your heroic bodies was given you by a Democrat." Democrats

in the North tended to address urban and economic issues, but southern Democratic candidates waved a different bloody shirt, calling Republicans traitors to white supremacy and states' rights.

Issues of the era made politics a personal as well as a community activity. In an age before media celebrities occupied public attention, people formed emotional loyalties to individual politicians, loyalties that often overlooked crassness and corruption. James G. Blaine—Maine's flamboyant and powerful Republican congressman, senator, presidential aspirant, and two-time secretary of state—typified this appeal. Followers called him the "Plumed Knight," composed songs and organized parades in his honor, and sat mesmerized by his long speeches, while disregarding his corrupt alliances with businessmen and his animosities toward laborers and farmers.

Political allegiances were so evenly divided that no party gained dominance nationally for any sustained period of time. Between 1877 and 1897, Republicans held the presidency for three terms, Democrats for two. Rarely did the same party control both the presidency and Congress simultaneously. From 1876 through 1892, presidential elections were extremely close. The outcome often hinged on votes in a few populous northern states—Connecticut, New York, New Jersey, Ohio, Indiana, and Illinois. Both parties tried to gain advantages by nominating presidential and vice presidential candidates from these states (and by committing vote fraud on their candidates' behalf).

17-1b Party Factions

Internal quarrels split both the Republican and Democratic parties. Among Republicans, New York's Senator Roscoe Conkling led one faction, known as "Stalwarts." A physical fitness devotee labeled "the finest torso in public life," Conkling worked the spoils system to win government jobs for his supporters. Stalwarts' rivals were the "Half Breeds," led by James G. Blaine, who pursued influence as blatantly as Conkling did. On the sidelines stood more idealistic Republicans, or "**Mugwumps**" (supposedly an Algonquian term meaning "important person"). Mugwumps, such as Missouri Republican Senator Carl Schurz, scorned the political roguishness that tainted his party's leaders and believed that only righteous, educated men like themselves should govern. Republican allies of big business wanted gold to be the standard for currency, whereas those from western mining regions favored silver. Democrats also subdivided into interest groups: white supremacist southerners; working-class advocates; immigrant-stock supporters of urban political machines; business-oriented advocates of low tariffs and the gold standard; and debtor-oriented advocates of free silver. Like Republicans, Democrats avidly pursued the spoils of office.

In many states, one party usually dominated, and a few men typically held dictatorial sway. Often the state "boss" was a senator who doled out jobs and parlayed his clout into national influence.

"Mugwumps" Term used for idealistic Republican reformers.

(Until ratification of the Seventeenth Amendment to the Constitution in 1913, state legislatures elected U.S. senators.) Besides Conkling and Blaine, senatorial powers included Thomas C. Platt of New York, Nelson W. Aldrich of Rhode Island, Mark A. Hanna of Ohio, and Matthew S. Quay of Pennsylvania. These men exercised power brazenly. Quay once responded to an inquiry about using secret information from a Senate investigation to profit from an investment in the American Sugar Refining Company by pronouncing, "I do not feel that there is anything in my connection with the Senate to interfere with my buying or selling stock when I please, and I propose to do so in the future."

17-2 The Activism of Government

▶ **How did government at all levels become more active in people's everyday lives?**

▶ **How did government seek to intervene in the operation of railroad businesses?**

▶ **What political divisions emerged over the development of economic policy in the late nineteenth century?**

In spite of all the numerous divisions, government at every level came to play a much greater role in people's lives than ever before. Most of what governing bodies did for people was to pass laws and establish mechanisms intended to safeguard health and safety. These efforts evolved at state and local levels largely from the constitutional provision of "police power," meaning the authority, within certain limits, to regulate and enforce order to ensure the general welfare of the population.

17-2a Uses of Police Power

From the earliest days of the Republic, state and local governments intervened in people's lives to protect safety and morals. There were restrictions on where citizens could construct buildings (for fire protection), where they could dispose of waste, at what age they could marry, quarantines to prevent the spread of disease, and more. By the time of the Gilded Age, these laws and regulations extended into every corner of society. There were laws making it criminal to mistreat animals and children; laws providing for the purity of foods and medicines; laws establishing minimum requirements for professionals such as doctors, teachers, and ship captains; and laws to ensure the legitimacy of banks and insurance companies. Other laws required the licensing of, and sometimes prohibition of, liquor sales, prizefighting, and obscene literature; laws regulated rates and operations of streetcars and railroads; laws limited the working hours of women and

---

Interstate Commerce Act An 1887 law that established the Interstate Commerce Commission, the nation's first regulatory agency, to investigate railroad rate-making and discriminatory rate practices.

---

children; and laws mandated racial segregation. Though many of these measures met with some objection, representatives in state legislatures and city councils passed these laws with broad consent of the people they governed. Moreover, courts generally upheld them.

17-2b Due Process

When the exercise of police power was challenged, protestors asserted that governments were interfering with a person's or company's right to use of private property. This right was lodged in the clause of the Fifth Amendment to the Constitution that stated that no person could "be deprived of life, liberty, or property, without due process of law; nor shall private property be taken for public use without just compensation." The restriction originally applied to actions by the federal government, but Section 1 of the Fourteenth Amendment—in what is called the "due process clause"—extended the limitation to state governments as well.

The matter of railroad rates provides an example of how business interests tried to use due process as a protection against state and federal government regulation. As rail networks spread, so did competition. In their quest for customers, railroads reduced rates to outmaneuver rivals, but rate wars hurt profits, and inconsistent freight charges angered shippers and farmers. On noncompetitive routes, railroads often boosted charges as high as possible to compensate for unprofitably low rates on competitive routes, making pricing disproportionate to distance. Per mile charges for short-distance shipments served by only one line could exceed charges on long-distance shipments served by competing lines. Railroads also played favorites, reducing rates to large shippers and offering free passenger passes to preferred customers and politicians.

17-2c Railroad Regulation

Such favoritism stirred farmers, small merchants, and reform politicians to demand rate regulation to protect the welfare of all shippers. Their efforts succeeded first at the state level. By 1880, fourteen states had established commissions to limit freight and storage charges of state-chartered lines. Using lobbyists and pressure tactics, railroads fought these measures, arguing that the due process clause of the Fourteenth Amendment guaranteed them freedom to use their property without state government restraint. But in 1877, in *Munn v. Illinois,* the U.S. Supreme Court, using police power as a basis, upheld the principle of state regulation, declaring that grain warehouses owned by railroads acted in the public interest and therefore must submit to regulation for "the common good."

State legislatures, however, could not regulate commerce that crossed state lines, a limitation affirmed by the Supreme Court in the *Wabash* case of 1886, in which the Court declared that only Congress could limit rates involving interstate commerce. Reformers thereupon demanded action by the federal government. With support from businessmen who believed that they, like farmers, suffered from discriminatory rates, Congress passed the **Interstate Commerce Act** in 1887. The law prohibited rebates and rate discrimination and created the

△ The patronage system—the practice of rewarding political supporters with jobs and favors—reached such an extent during the Gilded Age that critics likened it to the stock exchange, where traders clamored to be heard. President James A. Garfield is shown on a pedestal in the center of this cartoon surrounded by pleading job seekers while on the left, Senator Thomas C. Platt, Republican leader from New York State, is handcuffed to a man handing "orders from the boss" to Vice President Chester A. Arthur. The Pendleton Civil Service Act of 1883 was intended to replace patronage by making federal appointments based on merit rather than on political connections.

Interstate Commerce Commission (ICC), the nation's first regulatory agency, to investigate railroad rate-making, issue cease and desist orders against illegal practices, and seek court aid to enforce compliance. The legislation's weak provisions for enforcement, however, left railroads room for evasion, and federal judges reversed course and diminished both state and ICC powers. In the *Maximum Freight Rate* case (1897), for example, the Supreme Court evoked the due process provision, ruling that regulation interfered with a railroad's right to a "fair return" from its property. Even so, the principle of regulation, though weakened by a standoff between police power and due process, remained in force.

17-2d Veterans' Pensions

In addition to railroad regulation, issues of pensions, patronage abuses, tariffs, and currency provoked heated debates and partisan discord, but Congress nevertheless managed to pass significant legislation. From the end of the Civil War into the 1880s, Congress spent much time discussing soldiers' pensions. The **Grand Army of the Republic**, an organization of Union army veterans, allied with the Republican Party and cajoled the government into providing pensions for former northern soldiers and their widows. These grants were deserved but costly. Union troops had been poorly paid, and thousands of wives had been widowed. Although the North spent $2 billion to fight the Civil War, pensions to veterans ultimately cost

$8 billion, one of the largest welfare commitments the federal government has ever made. By 1900 soldiers' pensions accounted for roughly 40 percent of the federal budget. Soldiers who had fought for the Confederate cause, however, received none of this money, though some southern states funded small pensions and built old-age homes for ex-soldiers.

17-2e Civil Service Reform

Few politicians dared oppose pensions, but some attempted to dismantle the spoils system. During the Civil War, the federal government had expanded considerably, and the practice of awarding government jobs—spoils—to political supporters regardless of their qualifications flourished after the war. As the postal service, diplomatic corps, and other government agencies expanded, so did the public payroll. Between 1865 and 1891, the number of federal employees tripled, from 53,000 to 166,000. (There are about 2.1 million today.) Elected officials scrambled to control these jobs as a means to benefit themselves, their constituents, and their party. In return for comparatively short hours and high pay, appointees to federal positions pledged votes and a portion of their earnings to those who had caused them to be hired.

Grand Army of the Republic (GAR) A social and political lobbying organization of northern Civil War veterans that convinced Congress to provide $8 billion in pensions for former Union soldiers and widows.

◁ Federal economic policies such as tariffs sparked heated debates between businesses and their allies in Congress on one side and those who believed these policies benefited only special interests. This cartoon, clearly opposing the McKinley Tariff, depicts Uncle Sam, the symbol for America, bound up and held captive by the tariff and its raucous Senate supporters.

The Granger Collection, NYC

Shocked by such corruption, especially after revelations of scandals during the presidential administration of Ulysses S. Grant, some reformers began advocating appointments and promotions based on merit—civil service—rather than on political connections. Support for change accelerated in 1881 when a distraught job seeker assassinated President James Garfield. The **Pendleton Civil Service Act**, passed by Congress in 1882 and signed by President Chester Arthur in 1883, created the Civil Service Commission to oversee competitive examinations for government positions. The act gave the commission jurisdiction over only 10 percent of federal jobs, but the president could expand the list. Because the Constitution barred Congress from interfering in state affairs, civil service at state and local levels developed in a haphazard manner. Nevertheless, the Pendleton Act marked a beginning and provided a model for further reform.

17-2f Tariff Policy

Veterans' pensions and civil service reform were not the main issues of the Gilded Age, however. Rather, economic policy dominated congressional debates. The issue of tariffs carried strong political implications. From 1789 onward, Congress had created tariffs, which levied duties (taxes) on imported goods, to protect American manufactures and agricultural products from foreign competition. But tariffs quickly became a tool by which special interests could enhance their profits. By the 1880s these interests had succeeded in obtaining tariffs on more than four thousand items. A few economists and farmers argued for free trade (no tariffs), but most politicians insisted that tariffs were a necessary form of government assistance to support American industry and preserve jobs.

Pendleton Civil Service Act Attempt to end the spoils system; created the Civil Service Commission to oversee competitive exams for government jobs.

To support economic growth, the Republican Party put protective tariffs at the core of its political agenda. Democrats complained that tariffs made prices artificially high by discouraging importation of less-expensive goods, hurting farmers whose crops were not protected and consumers wanting to buy manufactured goods. For example, a yard of flannel produced in England might cost 10 cents, but an 8-cent-per-yard import duty raised the price to 18 cents. An American manufacturer of a similar yard of flannel, also costing 10 cents, could charge 17 cents, underselling foreign competition by 1 cent yet still pocketing a 7-cent profit.

During the Gilded Age, revenues from tariffs and other levies created a surplus in the federal treasury. Most Republicans liked the idea that the government was earning more than it spent and hoped to keep the surplus as a reserve or to spend it on projects such as harbor improvements, which would aid commerce. Democrats, however, asserted that the federal government should not be a profit-making operation. They acknowledged a need for protection of some manufactured goods and raw materials, but they favored lower tariff duties to encourage foreign trade and to reduce the treasury surplus.

Manufacturers and their congressional allies firmly controlled tariff policy. The Republican-sponsored McKinley Tariff of 1890 boosted already-high rates by 4 percent. When House Democrats, supported by President Grover Cleveland, passed a bill to trim tariffs in 1894, Senate Republicans, aided by southern Democrats eager to protect their region's infant textile and steel industries, added six hundred amendments restoring most cuts (the Wilson-Gorman Tariff). In 1897, the Dingley Tariff raised rates further. Attacks on duties, though unsuccessful, made tariffs a symbol of privileged business in the public mind and a continuing target for reformers.

17-2g Monetary Policy

Debates over monetary policy inflamed even stronger emotions than tariffs did because they represented conflict between haves and have-nots. When increased industrial and agricultural production caused prices to fall after the Civil War, debtors (have-nots) and creditors (haves) had opposing reactions. Farmers suffered because the prices they received for crops were dropping, but because high demand for a relatively limited supply of money in circulation raised interest rates on loans, it was costly for them to borrow funds to pay off mortgages and other debts. They favored the coinage of silver to increase the amount of currency in circulation, which in turn would reduce interest rates, making their debts less burdensome. Small businessmen, also in need of loans, agreed with farmers. Large merchants, manufacturers, and bankers favored a limited, more stable money supply backed only by gold. They feared the value of currency not backed by gold would fluctuate and that the resulting uncertainty would threaten investors' confidence in the U.S. economy. Arguments over the quantity and quality of money also reflected sectional cleavages: western silver-mining areas and agricultural regions of the South and West against the more conservative industrial Northeast.

Before the 1870s, the federal government had bought both gold and silver to back its paper money (dollars), setting a ratio that made a gold dollar worth sixteen times more than a silver dollar. In theory, a person holding a specific sum of dollar bills could exchange (redeem) them for one ounce of gold or sixteen ounces of silver. Discovery of gold in the West, however, increased the gold supply and lowered its market price relative to that of silver. Consequently, silver dollars disappeared from circulation—because of their inflated value relative to gold, owners hoarded them—and in 1873 a congressional act stopped the coinage of silver dollars. Through this action the United States unofficially adopted the gold standard, meaning that its currency was backed chiefly by gold.

But within a few years, new mines in the West began to flood the market with silver, and its price dropped. Because gold now became relatively less plentiful than silver and therefore worth *more* than sixteen times the value of silver, it became worthwhile for people to spend rather than hoard silver dollars. Silver producers wanted the government to resume buying silver at the old sixteen-to-one ratio, because they then could sell silver to the government above its market price. Debtors, hurt by the economic hard times of 1873–1878, saw silver as a means of expanding the currency supply, so they joined silver producers to press for resumption of silver coinage at the old sixteen-to-one ratio.

With both political parties split into silver and gold factions, Congress first tried to compromise. The Bland-Allison Act (1878) authorized the U.S. Treasury to buy between $2 million and $4 million worth of silver each month, and the **Sherman Silver Purchase Act** (1890) increased the government's monthly silver purchase by specifying weight (4.5 million ounces) rather than dollars. Neither measure satisfied the different interest groups. Creditors wanted the

government to stop buying silver, whereas for debtors, the legislation failed to expand the money supply satisfactorily and still left the impression that the government favored creditors' interests. The issue would become even more emotional during the presidential election of 1896 (see "Silver Crusade and the Election of 1896," page 516).

17-2h Legislative Accomplishments

Members of Congress dealt with issues such as railroad regulation, civil service, and tariff policy under difficult conditions. Senators and representatives earned small salaries and usually had the financial burden of maintaining two residences: one in their home district and one in Washington. Most members of Congress had no private office space, only a desk. They worked long hours responding to constituents' requests, wrote their own speeches, and paid for staff out of their own pocket. Yet, though corruption and greed tainted several, most politicians were principled and dedicated. They managed to deal with important issues and pass significant legislation that increased the power of the federal government.

17-3 Presidential Initiative

▶ **How did party politics between the Democrats and Republicans unfold in the Gilded Age?**

▶ **How did Gilded Age presidents use executive power to influence the development of legislation?**

Operating under the cloud of Andrew Johnson's impeachment, Ulysses S. Grant's scandals, and doubts about the legitimacy of the 1876 election (see "Retreat from Reconstruction," Section 14-6), American presidents between 1877 and 1900 moved gingerly to restore authority to their office. Proper and honest, Presidents Rutherford Hayes (1877–1881), James Garfield (1881), Chester Arthur (1881–1885), Grover Cleveland (1885–1889 and 1893–1897), Benjamin Harrison (1889–1893), and William McKinley (1897–1901) tried to be legislative as well as administrative leaders. Like other politicians, they used symbols. Hayes served lemonade at the White House to emphasize that he, unlike his predecessor, Grant, was no hard drinker. McKinley set aside his cigar in public so photographers would not catch him setting a bad example for youth. More important, each president made cautious attempts to initiate legislation and use vetoes to guide national policy.

17-3a Hayes, Garfield, and Arthur

Rutherford B. Hayes had been a Union general and an Ohio congressman and governor before his disputed election to the presidency, an event that prompted opponents to label him "Rutherfraud." Although Republicans expected him to serve business interests, Hayes played a quiet role as conciliator. He emphasized national harmony over sectional rivalry and opposed

Sherman Silver Purchase Act Law that instructed the treasury to buy, at current market prices, 4.5 million ounces of silver monthly.

The Spectacle of Gilded Age Politics

During the Gilded Age, political events, especially presidential elections, provided opportunity for elaborate spectacle, and politicians occupied the limelight as major celebrities. A presidential campaign functioned as a public festival at a time when mass entertainments such as movies and sports did not exist to offer people outlets for their emotions. Campaigns often included parades, fireworks, and marching bands. This image, an artist's rendering, presents evidence of how people of the era might have expressed themselves politically.

CRITICAL THINKING

□ How did Gilded Age presidents use executive power to influence the development of legislation?

□ What similarities to modern-day campaign events and symbols does this image represent? In what ways is it different?

□ Did politics and campaigning in the Gilded Age play a different role in the nation's culture than they do at present?

FUN FOR THE POLITICIANS, BUT ROUGH ON THE BUSINESS MAN.

△ Though business interests generally prevailed in the Gilded Age, various interest groups supported regulation. In this cartoon, a businessman is being tossed around by a "Silverite" (the man in the red shirt who is supporting free silver), a Republican (the bearded man in the frock coat), a Populist (the man in overalls), and a Democrat (the man in the checked suit).

racial violence. He tried to overhaul the spoils system by appointing civil service reformer Carl Schurz to his cabinet and by battling New York's patronage king, Senator Conkling. (He fired Conkling's protégé, Chester A. Arthur, from the post of New York customs house collector.) Though averse to using government power to aid the oppressed, Hayes believed society should not ignore the needs of the American Chinese and Native peoples, and after retiring from the presidency he worked to aid former slaves.

When Hayes declined to run for reelection in 1880, Republicans nominated another Ohio congressman and Civil War hero, James A. Garfield, who defeated Democrat Winfield Scott Hancock, also a Civil War hero, by only forty thousand votes out of 9 million cast. By winning the pivotal states of New York and Indiana, however, Garfield carried the electoral college by a comfortable margin, 214 to 155.

Solemn and cautious, Garfield tried to secure an independent position among party potentates. He hoped to reduce the tariff and develop economic relations with Latin America, and he pleased civil service reformers by rebuffing Conkling's patronage demands. But his chance to make lasting contributions ended in July 1881 when Charles Guiteau shot him in a Washington railroad station. Garfield lingered for seventy-nine days with a bullet in his spine that his inept doctor tried unsuccessfully to remove, but he succumbed to infection, heart ailments, and pneumonia and died September 19.

Garfield's successor was Vice President Chester A. Arthur, the New York Stalwart whom Hayes had fired. Republicans had nominated Arthur for vice president only to help Garfield win New York State's electoral votes. Although his elevation to the presidency made reformers shudder, Arthur became a dignified and temperate executive. He signed the Pendleton Civil Service Act, urged Congress to modify outdated tariff rates, and supported federal regulation of railroads. He wielded the veto aggressively, killing bills that excessively benefited railroads and corporations. Arthur wanted to run for president in 1884 but Republicans nominated James G. Blaine instead.

To oppose Blaine, Democrats picked New York's governor, Grover Cleveland, a bachelor who admitted during the campaign that he had fathered an out-of-wedlock son. The election reflected the nastiness of partisanship. Alluding to Cleveland's son, Republicans chided him with catcalls of "Ma! Ma! Where's my pa?" to which Democrats replied, "Gone to the White House, Ha! Ha! Ha!" Distaste for Blaine prompted some Mugwump Republicans to desert their party for Cleveland. On Election Day, Cleveland beat Blaine by only 29,000 popular votes; his tiny margin of 1,149 votes in New York gave him that state's 36 electoral votes, enough for a 219-to-182 victory in the electoral college. Cleveland may have won New York thanks to last-minute remarks of a Protestant minister, who equated Democrats with "rum, Romanism, and rebellion." Democrats eagerly publicized the slur among New York's large Irish Catholic population, urging voters to protest by supporting Cleveland.

17-3b Cleveland and Harrison

Cleveland, the first Democratic president since James Buchanan (1857–1861), tried to exert vigorous leadership. He expanded civil service, vetoed private pension bills, and urged Congress to cut tariff duties. When advisers warned that his actions might weaken his chances for reelection, the president retorted, "What is the use of being elected or reelected, unless you stand for something?" But Senate protectionists killed tariff reform passed by the House, and when Democrats renominated Cleveland for president in 1888, businessmen in the party convinced him to moderate his attacks on high tariffs.

Republicans in 1888 nominated Benjamin Harrison, former senator from Indiana and grandson of President William Henry Harrison (1841). During the campaign, some Republicans manipulated a British diplomat into stating that Cleveland's reelection would be good for England. Irish Democrats, who hated England's colonial rule over Ireland, took offense, as intended, and turned against Cleveland. Perhaps more beneficial to Harrison were the bribery and multiple voting that helped him win Indiana by 2,300 votes and New York by 14,000. (Democrats also indulged in fraud, but Republicans proved more successful at it.) Those states' electoral votes ensured Harrison's victory. Although Cleveland outpolled Harrison by 90,000 popular votes, Harrison carried the electoral college by 233 to 168.

The first president since 1875 whose party had majorities in both houses of Congress, Harrison used various methods, ranging from threats of vetoes to informal dinners and consultations with politicians, to influence the course of legislation. Partly in response, the Congress of 1889–1891 passed 517 bills, 200 more than the average passed by Congresses between 1875 and 1889. Harrison showed support for civil service by appointing reformer Theodore Roosevelt as civil service commissioner, but neither the president nor Congress could resist pressures from special interests, especially those waving the bloody shirt. Harrison signed the Dependents' Pension Act of 1890, which provided pensions for Union veterans who had suffered war-related disabilities and granted aid to their widows and children. The bill doubled the number of welfare recipients from 490,000 to 966,000.

The Pension Act and other appropriations pushed the 1890 federal budget past $1 billion for the first time in the nation's history. Democrats blamed the "Billion-Dollar Congress" on spendthrift Republicans. Voters reacted by unseating seventy-eight Republicans in the congressional elections of 1890. Seeking to capitalize on voter unrest, Democrats nominated Grover Cleveland to run against Harrison in 1892. This time Cleveland attracted large contributions from business and beat Harrison by 370,000 popular votes (3 percent of the total), easily winning the electoral vote.

In office again, Cleveland addressed problems of currency, tariffs, and labor unrest, but his actions reflected political weakness. During his campaign Cleveland had promised sweeping tariff reform, but he made little effort to line up support in the Senate, where protectionists undercut efforts to reduce rates. And he bowed to requests from railroad interests and sent federal troops to put down the Pullman strike of 1894. In spite of Cleveland's attempts to take initiative, major events—particularly economic downturn and agrarian ferment—pushed the nation in a different direction.

17-4 Discrimination and Disfranchisement

▶ **What forms of social and legal discrimination did African Americans face in the Gilded Age?**

▶ **How did African Americans respond to and challenge discrimination?**

▶ **How were women active in society and politics in the Gilded Age?**

Although speechmakers often spoke of freedom and opportunity during the Gilded Age, policies of discrimination and exclusion continued to haunt more than half of the nation's people. Just as during Reconstruction, issues of race shaped politics in the South, where white farmers and workers, facing economic insecurity, feared that newly enfranchised African American men would challenge whatever political and social superiority (real and imagined) they enjoyed. Wealthy landowners and merchants fanned these fears, using them to divide the races and to distract poor whites from protesting their own economic subjugation. Even some white feminists, such as Susan B. Anthony, opposed voting and other rights for African Americans on grounds that white women deserved such rights before black men did.

In the North, custom more than law limited opportunities of black people. Discrimination in housing, employment, and access to facilities such as parks, hotels, and department stores kept African Americans separate. Whites always were concerned that blacks should remain "in their place."Whether it was the wages they earned, the return they received for their crops, or the prices they paid for goods, African Americans felt the sting of their imposed inferiority.

17-4a Violence Against African Americans

The abolition of slavery altered the legal status of African Americans, but it did not markedly improve their economic opportunities. In 1880, the South was home to the vast majority of African Americans, and 90 percent of them depended for a living on farming or personal and domestic service—the same occupations they had held as slaves. Discrimination was rampant. Some communities considered themselves "sundown towns," where only whites were allowed on the streets at night. The New South, moreover, proved to be as violent as the Old South. Between 1889 and 1909, more than seventeen hundred African Americans were lynched in the South. About a quarter of **lynching** victims were accused of assault—rarely proved—on a white woman. Most of those lynched, however, had simply said something or acted in a way that made insecure whites feel disrespected, or they had succeeded in business or taken a job that made whites feel inferior.

African Americans did not suffer such violence silently. Their most notable activist at this time was **Ida B. Wells**, a Memphis, Tennessee, schoolteacher. In 1884 Wells was forcibly removed from a railroad car when she refused to surrender her seat to a white man. The incident sparked her career as a tireless spokesperson against white supremacy and violence. In 1889 Wells became partner of a Memphis newspaper, the *Free Speech and*

lynching Vigilante hanging of those accused of crimes; used primarily against African Americans.

Ida B. Wells African American journalist and activist who mounted a national antilynching campaign.

Headlight, in which she published attacks against injustice. When three black Memphis grocers were lynched in 1892 after defending themselves against whites who had attacked them, Wells wrote an editorial urging local blacks to migrate to the West. She subsequently toured England and Europe, giving speeches and writing articles drumming up opposition to lynching and discrimination. Unable to return to hostile Memphis, she moved to Chicago, where she became a powerful advocate for racial justice.

17-4b Disfranchisement

In northern communities, whites sometimes made it uncomfortable for people of color to vote and hold office, but it was mainly in the South that white leaders instituted official measures of political discrimination. Despite threats and intimidation against them in the wake of Reconstruction's demise, blacks still formed the backbone of the southern Republican Party and won numerous elective positions. In North Carolina, for example, eleven African Americans served in the state senate and forty-three in the house between 1877 and 1890. Situations like these were unacceptable to many whites, and racist politicians reacted by depriving blacks of their right to vote. Beginning with Florida and Tennessee in 1889 and eventually in every southern state, governments levied taxes of $1 to $2 on all citizens wishing to vote. These poll taxes proved prohibitive to most blacks, who were so poor and deeply in debt that they rarely had cash for any purpose. Other schemes disfranchised African Americans who could not read.

Disfranchisement was also accomplished in other devious ways. The Supreme Court determined in *U.S. v. Reese* (1876) that Congress had no control over local and state elections other than the explicit provisions of the Fifteenth Amendment, which prohibits states from denying the vote "on account of race, color, or previous condition of servitude."

◁ Lynching could mean other than simple hanging. In 1893, a mob estimated at 10,000 gathered in Paris, Texas, to watch the torture and killing of an African American man believed to have assaulted and murdered a four-year-old white girl. This photo was taken just as Henry Smith, the alleged assailant, was tortured fifty times by red-hot iron brands, then doused with kerosene and set on fire. After the gruesome event, the vengeful crowd burned down the scaffold.

Library of Congress Prints and Photographs Division, LC-USZ62-68958

State legislators found ways to exclude black voters without mentioning race, color, or servitude. For instance, an 1890 state constitutional convention established the "Mississippi Plan," requiring prospective voters to pay a poll tax eight months before each election, present the tax receipt at election time, and prove that they could read and interpret the state constitution. South Carolina, Virginia, and Texas established similar provisions. Registration officials applied stiffer standards to blacks than to whites, even declaring black college graduates ineligible on grounds of illiteracy. In 1898 Louisiana enacted the first "grandfather clause," which established literacy and property qualifications for voting but exempted sons and grandsons of those eligible to vote before 1867—a year in which no blacks could vote in Louisiana. Other southern states initiated similar measures.

Such restrictions proved effective. In South Carolina, for example, 70 percent of eligible blacks voted in the 1880 election; by 1896, the rate dropped to 11 percent. By the 1900s, African Americans had effectively lost political rights in the South. More importantly, because voting is often considered a common right of citizenship, disfranchisement stripped African American men of their social standing as U.S. citizens. Disfranchisement also affected poor whites, few of whom could meet poll tax, property, and literacy requirements. Consequently, the total number of eligible voters in Mississippi shrank from 257,000 in 1876 to 77,000 in 1892.

17-4c Legal Segregation

Discrimination also stiffened in areas beyond voting, as existing customs of racial separation expanded. In all regions of the country, segregation by custom was common, as whites in power sought to keep racial minorities isolated by refusing them service and access. But in a series of cases during the 1870s, the Supreme Court opened the door to laws that strengthened racial discrimination by ruling that the Fourteenth Amendment protected citizens' rights only against infringement by state governments, not over what individuals, private businesses, or local governments might do. These rulings climaxed in 1883 when, in the *Civil Rights* cases, the Court struck down the 1875 Civil Rights Act, which prohibited segregation in facilities such as streetcars, theaters, and parks. Again, the Court declared that the federal government could not regulate private behavior in matters of race relations. Thus railroads, such as the Chesapeake & Ohio Railroad, which had forced Ida B. Wells out of her seat, could legally maintain discriminatory policies.

The Supreme Court also upheld legal segregation on a "separate but equal" basis in the case of *Plessy v. Ferguson* (1896). This case began in 1892 when a New Orleans organization of African Americans chose Homer Plessy, a fair-skinned, French-speaking Creole who was only one-eighth black (but still considered a "Negro" by Louisiana law), as a volunteer to violate a state law requiring "equal but separate accommodations" by sitting in a whites-only railroad car. As expected, Plessy was arrested. His lawyer appealed the conviction on grounds that the law violated Plessy's right to "life,

liberty," and property" under the Fourteenth Amendment, and the case reached the U.S. Supreme Court in 1896. The Court disappointed Plessy's supporters by affirming that a state law providing for separate facilities for the races was reasonable because it preserved "public peace and good order"—police power operating to the disadvantage of one group. Writing for the Court, Associate Justice Billings Brown asserted that legislation could not alter prejudice. "If the two races are to meet upon terms of social equality," he wrote, "it must be the result of . . . a voluntary consent of individuals." Thus, believed the Court, a law separating the races did not necessarily "destroy the legal equality of the races." Although the ruling did not specify the phrase "separate but equal," it legalized separate facilities for black and white people. In 1899 the Court applied the separate but equal doctrine to schools in *Cummins v. County Board of Education*, permitting school segregation until *Brown v. Board of Education* overturned the decision in 1954.

Segregation laws—known as Jim Crow laws—multiplied throughout the South, confronting African Americans with daily reminders of inferior status. State and local statutes, most of which were passed in the 1890s, restricted blacks to the rear of streetcars, to separate public drinking fountains and toilets, and to separate sections of hospitals and cemeteries. A Birmingham, Alabama, ordinance required that the races be "distinctly separated . . . by well defined physical barriers" in "any room, hall, theatre, picture house, auditorium, yard, court, ballpark, or other indoor or outdoor place." Mobile, Alabama, passed a curfew requiring blacks to be off the streets by 10 p.m., and Atlanta mandated separate Bibles for the swearing in of black witnesses in court. Jim Crow laws thus were products of active governments, but their goal was to restrict rather than expand liberty.

17-4d African American Activism

African American women and men challenged injustice in several ways. Some organized boycotts of segregated streetcars and discriminatory businesses; others promoted "Negro enterprise." In 1898, for example, Atlanta University professor John Hope called on blacks to become their own employers and supported formation of Negro Business Men's Leagues. A number of blacks used higher education as a means of elevating their status. In all-black teachers' colleges, young men and women sought to expand opportunities for themselves and all African Americans. Education could have presented a way to foster interracial cooperation. But the white supremacy that Jim Crow laws reflected taught southern blacks that they would have to negotiate in a biracial, rather than an interracial, society.

While disfranchisement diminished the public lives of African American men, who in contrast to women had previously been able to vote, African American women used traditional domestic roles as mothers, educators, and moral guardians to uplift the race and seek

Plessy v. Ferguson Supreme Court ruling validating legal segregation; legalized separate facilities for blacks and whites as long as they were equal.

Courtesy of Heritage Hall, Livingstone College, Salisbury, North Carolina

△ Livingstone College in North Carolina was one of several institutions of higher learning established by and for African Americans in the late nineteenth century. With a curriculum that emphasized training for educational and religious work in the South and in Africa, these colleges were coeducational, operating on the belief that both men and women could have public roles.

better services for black communities. Their efforts signified political activity that was more subtle than voting—though they also did fight for the vote. They successfully lobbied southern governments for cleaner city streets, better public health, expanded charity services, and vocational education. In these efforts, black women found ways to join with white women in campaigns to negotiate with the white male power structure to achieve their goals. In many instances, however, white women sympathized with white men in support of racial exclusion.

17-4e Women's Suffrage

Though some women acquiesced to their inferior status, others challenged male power structures by seeking the right to vote. Some, such as Frances Willard, chose indirect tactics. Willard believed that religious faith would empower women, and she advocated what she called "home politics," a combination of women's traditional roles with an urge to improve society. From 1879 until her death in 1898, Willard served as president of the Woman's Christian Temperance Union (WCTU), the nation's largest female organization. She traveled the country making speeches and encouraged women who joined the WCTU to sign a pledge to abstain from alcohol as a first step toward protecting home and family from the evils of drink. But Willard also believed the WCTU could best do the Lord's work of improving society if women could vote. Thus, at its 1884 convention, the WCTU passed a resolution deploring the "disenfranchisement of 12 million people who are citizens." The 12 million, however, did not

include people of color. Willard confined black WCTU members to segregated branches and accused African Americans, who she said "multiply like the locusts of Egypt," of causing the defeat of temperance laws in the South. Ida Wells, for her part, criticized Willard for not speaking out against lynching and for making racial statements that led to white violence.

The direct crusade for suffrage was conducted by two organizations, the National Woman Suffrage Association (NWSA) and the American Woman Suffrage Association (AWSA). The NWSA, led by Elizabeth Cady Stanton and Susan B. Anthony, advocated women's rights in courts and workplaces as well as at the ballot box. The two women, both veterans of the women's rights movement of the 1840s, did not always agree. Anthony was less radical, believing that the NWSA should accommodate moderate suffragists. Stanton disdained religiosity and supported birth control, liberalized divorce laws, and property rights for women. She once wrote, "I would rather live under a government of man alone with religious liberty than under a mixed government without it." Nevertheless, Anthony and Stanton remained friends and worked tirelessly on behalf of their cause.

The AWSA, led by former abolitionist Lucy Stone, focused more narrowly on suffrage. Consisting of female and male moderate advocates of free suffrage, the AWSA worked especially at the state level. Personality conflicts, more than ideology, separated the NWSA and AWSA. But in the late 1880s, Stone proposed that the two groups overcome their differences, and they merged in 1890 to form the National American Woman Suffrage Association, with Stanton as its first president.

Congress failed to heed appeals for women's suffrage. Anthony's argument for a constitutional amendment giving women the vote received little support. On the few occasions when the Senate discussed a bill to create the amendment, senators voted it down, claiming that suffrage would interfere with women's family obligations. Moreover, the women's suffrage campaign was tainted by racial intolerance. Many movement leaders espoused the superiority of whites and accommodated racial prejudices of both the North and South in order to retain support from organization members. AWSA and NWSA membership was all white and mostly middle class. African Americans who joined the WCTU did

so within a separate Department of Colored Temperance. Also, leaders such as Anthony and Stanton resented that the Fifteenth Amendment enfranchised black men but not women. Such suffragists believed that "educated" white women should vote and that "illiterate" blacks, both men and women, should not have such a privilege.

Women did win partial victories. Between 1870 and 1910, eleven states, mostly in the West, gave women limited voting rights. By 1890 nineteen states allowed women to vote on school issues, and three granted suffrage on tax and bond issues. The right to vote in national elections awaited a later generation, but the efforts of leaders such as Wells, Anthony, and Stone proved that women did not have to vote to be politically active. And although their campaigns succeeded only slightly, they helped train a corps of female leaders in political organizing and public speaking.

17-5 Agrarian Unrest and Populism

▶ **How did farmers and rural populations respond to economic hardships and inequality?**

▶ **How did agrarian activism become politicized during the Gilded Age?**

▶ **How successful were farmers and rural populations in addressing economic hardships and inequality?**

While ending voting exclusion and racial segregation had no major successes, economic inequality sparked a mass movement that would shake American society. Despite rapid industrialization and urbanization in the Gilded Age, the United States remained an agrarian nation. In 1890, 64 percent of the total population lived in rural areas, where they suffered economic hardship and were primed for protest. The expression of farmers' discontent—a mixture of strident rhetoric, nostalgic dreams, and hardheaded egalitarianism—began in Grange organizations in the early 1870s. It accelerated when Farmers' Alliances formed in the late 1870s and spread across the South and Great Plains in the 1880s. The Alliance movement flourished chiefly in areas where debt, weather, and insects demoralized struggling farmers. Once under way, the agrarian rebellion inspired visions of a cooperative, democratic society.

17-5a Hardship in the Midwest and West

In the Midwest, as growers cultivated more land, as mechanization boosted productivity, and as foreign competition increased, supplies of agricultural products exceeded national and worldwide demand. Consequently, prices for staple crops dropped steadily. A bushel of wheat selling for $1.45 in 1866 brought only 80 cents in the mid-1880s and 49 cents by the mid-1890s. Meanwhile, transportation and storage fees remained high. Expenses for seed, fertilizer, manufactured goods, taxes, and mortgage interest trapped many farm families in stressful and sometimes desperate

Library of Congress, Prints & Photographs Division, Reproduction number LC-USZ61-790 (b&w film copy neg.)

△ Frances Willard, shown here, became the second and best-known president of the national Woman's Christian Temperance Union (WCTU), founded in 1874. Beyond promoting abstinence from drinking alcohol, Willard and the WCTU were involved in other reforms, including women's suffrage. In 1893, Willard took her crusade worldwide and became the first president of the International Council of Women.

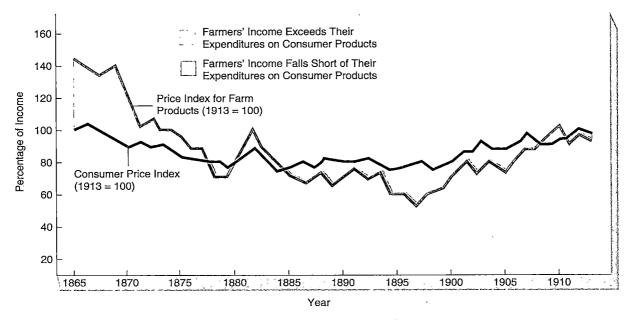

Figure 17.1 Consumer Prices and Farm Product Prices, 1865–1913

Until the late 1870s, in spite of falling farm prices, farmers were able to receive more income from their crops than they spent on consumer goods. But beginning in the mid-1880s, consumer prices leveled off and then rose, while prices for farm products continued to drop. As a result, farmers found it increasingly difficult to afford consumer goods, a problem that plagued them well into the twentieth century.

circumstances. In order to buy necessities and pay bills, farmers had to produce more. But the spiral wound ever more tightly: the more farmers produced, the lower crop prices dropped (see Figure 17.1).

The West suffered from special hardships. In Colorado, absentee capitalists seized control of access to transportation and water, and concentration of technology in the hands of large mining companies pushed out small firms. Charges of monopolistic behavior by railroads echoed among farmers, miners, and ranchers in Wyoming and Montana. In California, Washington, and Oregon, wheat and fruit growers found that railroads' control of transportation and storage rates blocked opportunities for higher incomes.

17-5b Grange Movement

Even before they felt the full impact of these developments, farmers began to organize. With aid from Oliver H. Kelley, a Bureau of Agriculture employee who wanted to elevate the status of farming, farmers in almost every state during the 1860s and 1870s founded chapters of the National Grange of the Patrons of Husbandry, or the Grange, dedicated to improving economic and social conditions. By 1875 the Grange had twenty thousand branches and a million members. Like voluntary organizations throughout the country, Granges wrote constitutions, elected officers, and required

Greenback Labor Party Advocated expanding the money supply through the government printing of money not backed by gold.

membership oaths. Strongest in the Midwest and South, Granges sponsored meetings and educational events to relieve the loneliness of rural life. Family oriented, Granges welcomed women's participation.

As membership flourished, Granges turned to economic and political action. Many members joined the **Greenback Labor Party,** formed in 1876 to advocate expanding the money supply by keeping "greenbacks"—paper money created by the government during the Civil War to help pay costs—in circulation. Grange branches formed cooperative associations to buy supplies and to market crops and livestock. In a few instances, Grangers ran farm implement factories and insurance companies. Most enterprises failed, however, because farmers lacked capital for large-scale buying and because competition from large manufacturers and dealers undercut them. For example, the mail-order firm Montgomery Ward could furnish rural customers with cheaper products more conveniently than could Granges.

Granges achieved some political successes in the late 1870s. They convinced states to establish agricultural colleges, elected sympathetic legislators, and pressed state legislatures for laws to regulate transportation and storage rates. But these ventures faltered when the U.S. Supreme Court denied states the power to regulate railroad rates (*Wabash* case, 1886). Granges disavowed party politics and thus would not challenge the power of business interests within the two major parties. Their attempts at economic and political influence declined, and today Granges exist mainly as social and service organizations.

MPI/Archive Photos/Getty Images

△ The Grange aimed not only to aid farmers but also to oppose oppressive policies against farmers by railroads. This cartoon, titled "Grange Awakening the Sleepers," depicts a farmer warning people complacently sleeping under railroad tracks that a train, with cars labeled "Consolidation Train, extortion, and bribery," is about to run them over.

17-5c The White Hats

In the Southwest, migration of English-speaking ranchers into pastureland used communally by Mexican farmers sparked resistance that sometimes turned violent. In the late 1880s, a group calling itself *Las Gorras Blancas*, or White Hats, struggled to control grazing areas that their ancestors had once held. In protest against Anglo intrusions, they burned buildings, destroyed fences, and threatened the town of Las Vegas in New Mexico territory. Sounding like the Grangers and Knights of Labor before them and the Populists after them, the White Hats proclaimed in 1889, "Our purpose is to protect the rights and interest of the people in general and especially those of the helpless classes." Their cause, however, could not halt Anglos from legally buying and using public land, and by 1900 many Mexicans had given up farm owning to work as agricultural laborers or migrate to cities.

17-5d Farmers' Alliances

By 1890, rural activism shifted to the Farmers' Alliances, two networks of organizations—one in the Great Plains, one in the South—that constituted a new mass movement. (The West had small Alliance groups, but they tended to be more closely linked to labor radicals and antimonopoly organizations.) The first Alliances arose in Texas, where hard-pressed farmers rallied against crop liens, merchants, and railroads in particular, and against money power in general. Using traveling

lecturers to recruit members, Alliance leaders expanded the movement into other southern states. By 1889 the southern Alliance boasted 2 million members, and a separate Colored Farmers' National Alliance claimed 1 million black members. A similar movement arose in the Plains, which in the late 1880s organized 2 million members in Kansas, Nebraska, and the Dakotas. Like Granges, Farmers' Alliances tried to foster community spirit. Women participated actively in Alliance activities, and members of the Knights of Labor were invited to join the "struggle against monopolistic oppression."

The Alliance remedy for economic woes combined a culture of generosity with government assistance. To bypass corporate power and control markets, Alliances, like the Grange, proposed that farmers form cooperatives, in which as a unified group they would sell crops and livestock, and buy supplies and manufactured goods. By pooling resources, Alliances reasoned, farmers could exert more economic pressure than they could individually, and they could share the benefits of their hard work rather than compete against each other.

To relieve the most serious rural problem, shortages of cash and credit, Alliances proposed a system of government aid called a *subtreasury*. The plan had two parts. One called for the federal government to construct warehouses where farmers could store nonperishable crops while awaiting higher market prices; during the wait, the government would loan farmers U.S. Treasury notes amounting to 80 percent of the market price that the stored crops would bring. Farmers could use these notes to pay debts and make purchases. Once the stored crops were sold, farmers would repay the loans plus small interest and storage fees. This provision would enable farmers to avoid the exploitative crop lien system.

Under the subtreasury plan's second part, the government would provide low-interest loans to farmers who wanted to buy land. These loans, along with the treasury notes loaned to farmers who temporarily stored crops in government warehouses, would inject cash into the economy and encourage the kind of inflation that advocates hoped would raise crop prices without raising other prices. If the government subsidized business through tariffs and land grants, reasoned Alliance members, it should help farmers earn a decent living, too.

17-5e Problems in Achieving Alliance Unity

If Farmers' Alliances had been able to unite politically, they could have wielded formidable power; but racial and sectional differences, plus personality clashes, thwarted early attempts at merging. Racial barriers weakened Alliance voter strength because southern white Democrats had succeeded in creating restrictions that prevented African Americans from voting. In addition, raw racism blocked acceptance of blacks by white Alliances. Some southern leaders, such as Georgia's Senator Tom Watson, tried to unite black and white farmers, realizing that both races suffered from similar burdens. But white farmers could not drop their prejudices. Many considered African Americans an inferior people and took comfort in the belief that there always would be people worse off than they were. At an 1889 meeting in St. Louis, white southerners rejected uniting with northern Alliances because such a merger would have ended their whites-only membership rules.

Differences on regional issues also prevented unity. Northern Alliances declined to unite with southerners, fearing domination by more politically experienced southern leaders. Northern farmers also favored protective tariffs to keep out foreign grain, whereas white southerners wanted low tariffs to curb costs of imported manufactured goods. Northern and southern Alliances agreed on some issues, however; both favored government regulation of railroads, equitable taxation, currency reform, ending election fraud that perpetuated special interests in office, and prohibition of landownership by foreign investors.

17-5f Rise of Populism

In spite of their divisions, growing membership and rising confidence drew Alliances into politics. By 1890, farmers had elected several officeholders sympathetic to their cause, especially in the South, where Alliance allies won four governorships, eight state legislatures, forty-four seats in the House of Representatives, and three in the Senate. In the Midwest, Alliance candidates running on third-party tickets, such as the Greenback Party, won victories in Kansas, Nebraska, and the Dakotas. During the summer of 1890, the Kansas Alliance held a "convention of the people" and nominated candidates who swept the state's fall elections. Formation of this People's, or Populist, Party gave a title to Alliance political activism. (Populism, derived from *populus*, the Latin word for "people," is the political doctrine that asserts the rights and powers of common people in their struggle against privileged elites.) Election successes in 1890 energized efforts to unite Alliance groups into a single **Populist Party**. By 1892, southern Alliance members decided to leave the Democratic Party and join northern counterparts in summoning a People's Party convention to draft a platform and nominate a presidential candidate. The gathering met in Omaha, Nebraska, on July 4.

The new party's platform was a sweeping reform document, reflecting goals of moral regeneration, political democracy, and antimonopolism. Its preamble charged that the nation had been "brought to the verge of moral, political, and material ruin. Corruption dominates the ballot box, the legislatures, the Congress, and . . . even the [courts]." Charging that inequality (between white classes) threatened to splinter society, the platform declared, "The fruits of the toil of millions are boldly stolen to build up colossal fortunes for a few,"

and that "wealth belongs to him that creates it." The document addressed three central sources of rural unrest: transportation, land, and money. Frustrated with

weak state and federal regulation, Populists demanded government ownership of railroad and telegraph lines. They urged the federal government to reclaim all land owned for speculative purposes by railroads and foreigners. The monetary plank called on the government to expand the currency by making more money available for farm loans and by restoring unlimited coinage of silver. Other planks advocated a graduated income tax, direct election of U.S. senators, and a shorter workday. As its presidential candidate, the party nominated James B. Weaver of Iowa, a former Union general and supporter of an expanded money supply, who already had run for the presidency as the Greenback Party's candidate in 1880.

17-5g Populist Spokespeople

The Populist campaign featured dynamic personalities and rousing rhetoric. The Kansas plains rumbled with speeches by Mary Lease, who could allegedly "set a crowd hooting and harrahing at her will," and by "Sockless Jerry" Simpson, an unschooled but canny rural reformer who got his nickname after he ridiculed silk-stockinged wealthy people, causing a reporter to muse that Simpson probably never wore stockings. The South produced equally dynamic leaders, such as Georgia's Tom Watson and North Carolina's Leonidas Polk. Colorado's governor, Davis "Bloody Bridles" Waite, attacked mine owners, and Texas governor James Hogg battled railroads and other corporations. (Governor Hogg also saddled his daughter with the awkward name of Ima.) Minnesota's Ignatius Donnelly, pseudoscientist and writer of apocalyptic novels, became chief visionary of the northern plains and penned the Omaha platform's thunderous language. The campaign also attracted opportunists, such as the one-eyed, sharp-tongued South Carolina senator "Pitchfork Ben" Tillman, who exploited agrarian resentments for their own political ends.

In the 1892 presidential election, Populist candidate James Weaver garnered 8 percent of the popular vote, majorities in four states, and twenty-two electoral votes. Not since 1856 had a third party done so well in its first national effort. Nevertheless, the party had little national impact. The election had been successful for Populists only in the West. The vote-rich Northeast ignored Weaver, and Alabama was the only southern state that gave Populists as much as one-third of its votes.

Still, Populism gave rural dwellers faith in a future of cooperation and democracy. Although Populists were flawed egalitarians—they mistrusted blacks and foreigners—they sought change in order to fulfill their version of American ideals. Amid hardship and desperation, millions of people came to believe that a cooperative democracy in which government would ensure equal opportunity could overcome corporate power. A banner draped above the stage at the Omaha convention captured the movement's spirit: "We do not ask for sympathy or pity. We ask for justice." With this goal, Populists looked ahead to the presidential election of 1896 with hope.

Populist Party "People's Party" that raised an agrarian-based, third-party challenge to the Republicans and Democrats and advocated for the rights of the common man.

Russian Populism

Before American Populism arose late in the 1890s, a different form of populism took shape in another largely rural country: Russia. Whereas American Populism emerged from the Alliance organizations of farmers, Russian populism was the creation of intellectuals who wanted to educate peasants to agitate for social and economic freedom.

Propelled by reforms imposed by Czar Alexander II, Russian society had begun to modernize in the mid-nineteenth century. Government administration and the judiciary were reorganized, town governments were given control of taxation, and education became more widespread. Perhaps most importantly, in 1861 Alexander signed an Edict of Emancipation, freeing Russian serfs (slaves attached to specific lands) and granting them compensation to buy land from their landlords. The reforms were slow to take hold, however, prompting some young, educated Russians, called nihilists because they opposed the czar and feudalism, to press for more radical reforms, including socialism. The reformers became known as *narodniki*, or populists, from *narod*, the Russian term for "peasant."

Narodniki envisioned a society of self-governing village communes, somewhat like the cooperatives proposed by American Farmers' Alliances, and in the 1870s they visited Russian villages and attempted to educate peasants to their ideas. One of their leaders, Peter Lavrov, believed that intellectuals needed to bridge the gap between themselves and ordinary people, and help the masses improve their lives. This message, however, included a more radical tone than the American Populists' campaign for democracy, because Russian populists believed that only a revolutionary uprising against the czar could realize their goals. When Alexander instituted repressive policies against the narodniki in the late 1870s, many of them turned to terrorism, a move that resulted in the assassination of Alexander II in 1881.

Russian populism failed in different ways than American Populism. Russian peasants were not receptive to intervention from educated young people, and many peasants, still tied to tradition, could not abandon loyalty to the czar. Arrests and imprisonments after Alexander's assassination discouraged populists' efforts, and the movement declined. Nevertheless, just as many aims of American Populists were adopted by other reformers after the turn of the century, the ideas of Russian populism became the cornerstone of the Russian Revolution of 1917 and of Soviet social and political ideology that followed.

CRITICAL THINKING

▢ American populism did not turn toward socialism the way that Russian populism did. What factors explain this significant difference despite the many similarities between American and Russian populism?

◁ Russian peasants, like American tenant farmers and owners of small landholdings, suffered from poverty and pressures of the expanded market economy. The plight of struggling Russian farm families stirred up empathy from young populist intellectuals, who adopted radical solutions that did not capture as much political fervor among farmers as American Populism did.

Bettmann/Getty Images

Kean Collection/Getty Images

△ The son of an Irish immigrant, Ignatius Donnelly was a Republican politician from Minnesota who wrote the rousing preamble to the Populist Party's platform presented at the party's historic convention in Omaha in 1892. Outside of politics, Donnelly published works asserting that there once was a continent named Atlantis that had been destroyed before the Great Flood of the Bible, and he argued that Shakespeare's plays had actually been written by Francis Bacon.

17-6 The Depression and Protests of the 1890s

▷ **What were the characteristics of the economic depression of the 1890s?**

▷ **How did the federal government respond to the economic depression of the 1890s?**

▷ **How was the country's economic and industrial system challenged in the 1890s?**

Before that election took place, economic crisis engulfed the nation. In 1893, shortly before Grover Cleveland's second presidency began, the Philadelphia & Reading Railroad, once a thriving and profitable line, went bankrupt. Like other railroads, it had borrowed heavily to lay track and build stations and bridges. But overexpansion cut into profits, and the company was unable to pay its debts. The same problem beset manufacturers. For example, output at McCormick farm machinery factories was nine times greater in 1893 than in 1879, but revenues only tripled. To compensate, the company bought more equipment and squeezed more work out of fewer laborers. This strategy, however, increased debt and unemployment. Jobless workers found themselves in the same plight as employers: they could not pay their bills. Banks

suffered, too, when their customers defaulted. The failure of the National Cordage Company in May 1893 sparked a chain reaction of business and bank closings. By year's end, five hundred banks and sixteen hundred businesses had failed. An adviser warned President Cleveland, "We are on the eve of a very dark night." He was right. Between 1893 and 1897, the nation suffered a staggering economic depression.

Personal hardship followed business collapse; nearly 20 percent of the labor force was jobless for a significant time during the depression. Falling demand caused prices to drop between 1892 and 1895, but layoffs and wage cuts more than offset declining living costs. Many people could not afford basic necessities. The New York police estimated that twenty thousand homeless and jobless people roamed the city's streets. Surveying the impact on Boston, Henry Adams wrote, "Men died like flies under the strain, and Boston grew suddenly old, haggard, and thin."

17-6a Continuing Currency Problems

As the depression deepened, so did the currency dilemma. The Sherman Silver Purchase Act of 1890 had committed the government to using treasury notes (silver certificates) to buy 4.5 million ounces of silver each month. Recipients could redeem these certificates for gold, at the ratio of one ounce of gold for every sixteen ounces of silver. But a western mining boom made silver more plentiful, causing its market value relative to gold to fall and prompting holders of silver certificates and greenback currency issued during the Civil War to cash in their notes in exchange for more valuable gold. As a result, the nation's gold reserves dwindled, falling below $100 million in early 1893.

The $100 million level had psychological importance. If investors believed that the country's gold reserves were disappearing, they would lose confidence in America's economic stability and refrain from investing. British capitalists, for example, owned $4 billion in American stocks and bonds. If dollars were to depreciate because there was too little gold to back them up, the British would stop investing in American economic growth. In fact, the lower the gold reserve dropped, the more people rushed to redeem their money—to get gold before it disappeared. Panic spread, causing more bankruptcies and unemployment.

Vowing to protect the gold reserves, President Cleveland called a special session of Congress to repeal the Sherman Silver Purchase Act. Repeal passed in late 1893, but the run on gold continued. In early 1895, reserves fell to $41 million. In desperation, Cleveland accepted an offer from a banking syndicate led by financier J. P. Morgan to sell the government 3.5 million ounces of gold in return for $65 million worth of federal bonds. When the bankers resold the bonds to the public, they made a $2 million profit. Cleveland claimed he had saved the reserves, but discontented farmers, workers, silver miners, and even some of Cleveland's Democratic allies saw only humiliation in the president's deal with big businessmen. "When Judas betrayed Christ," charged Senator Tillman, "his heart was not blacker than this scoundrel, Cleveland, in betraying the [Democratic Party]."

Few people knew what the president was privately enduring. At about the time Cleveland called Congress into special session, doctors discovered a tumor on his palate that required immediate removal. Fearful that publicity of his illness would hasten the run on gold, and intent on preventing Vice President Adlai E. Stevenson, a silver supporter, from gaining influence, Cleveland kept his condition a secret. He announced that he was going sailing, and doctors removed his cancer while the yacht floated outside New York City. Outfitted with a rubber jaw, Cleveland resumed a full schedule five days later, hiding terrible pain to dispel rumors that he was seriously ill. He eventually recovered, but those who knew of his surgery believed it had sapped his vitality.

The deal between Cleveland and Morgan did not end the depression. After improving slightly in 1895, the economy plunged again. Farm income, declining since 1887, slid further; factories closed; banks that remained open restricted withdrawals. The tight money supply depressed housing construction, drying up jobs and discouraging immigration. Cities encouraged citizens to cultivate "potato patches" on vacant land to help alleviate food shortages. Each night, urban police stations filled up with homeless persons with no place to stay.

17-6b Consequences of Depression

The depression ultimately ran its course. In the late 1890s, gold discoveries in Alaska, good harvests, and industrial revival brought relief. But the downturn hastened the crumbling of the old economic system and emergence of a new one. The American economy had expanded well beyond local and sectional bases; the fate of a large business in one part of the country now had repercussions elsewhere. When farmers fell into debt and lost purchasing power, their depressed condition in turn weakened railroads, farm implement manufacturers, and banks. Moreover, the trend toward corporate consolidation that characterized the new business system had tempted many companies to expand too rapidly. When the bubble burst in 1893, their reckless debts dragged them down, and they pulled other industries with them.

At the same time, a new global marketplace was emerging, forcing American farmers to contend not only with discriminatory transportation rates and falling crop prices at home, but also to compete with Canadian and Russian wheat growers, Argentine cattle ranchers, Indian and Egyptian cotton manufacturers, and Australian wool producers. More than ever before, the condition of one country's economy affected the economies of other countries. In addition, the glutted domestic market persuaded American businessmen to seek new markets abroad (see Chapter 19).

17-6c Depression-Era Protests

The depression exposed fundamental tensions in the industrial system. Technological and organizational changes had been widening the gap between employees and employers

for half a century, prompting discord. An era of labor protest began with the railroad strikes of 1877. The vehemence of those strikes, and the support they drew from working-class people, raised fears that the United States would experience a popular uprising like the one in France in 1871, which had briefly overturned the government and introduced communist principles. The Haymarket riot of 1886, the prolonged strike at the Carnegie Homestead Steel plant in 1892, and the extensive labor violence among western miners heightened anxieties (see "Mechanization and the Changing Status of Labor," Section 16-3). To many middle- and upper-class people, it seemed as if worker protests portended an economic and political explosion. In 1894, the year the economy plunged into depression, there were more than thirteen hundred strikes and countless riots. Contrary to accusations of business leaders, few protesters were immigrant anarchists or communists come to sabotage American democracy. Rather, the disaffected included thousands of patriotic Americans who believed that in a democracy, their voices should be heard.

17-6d Socialists

Small numbers of socialists did participate in these confrontations. Some socialists believed that workers should control factories and businesses; others supported government ownership. All socialists, however, opposed capitalism. Their ideas derived from the writings of Karl Marx (1818–1883), the German philosopher and father of communism, who contended that whoever controls the means of production determines how well people live. Marx wrote that industrial capitalism generates profits by paying workers less than the value of their labor and that mechanization and mass production alienate workers from their labor. Thus, Marx contended, capitalists and laborers engage in an inescapable conflict over how much workers should benefit from their efforts. According to Marx, only by abolishing the return on capital—profits—could labor receive its true value, an outcome possible only if workers owned the means of production. Marx predicted that workers worldwide would become so discontented that they would revolt and seize factories, farms, banks, and transportation lines. This revolution would establish a socialist order of justice and equality. Marx's vision appealed to some workers, including many who did not consider themselves socialists, because it promised independence and security. It appealed to some intellectuals as well, because it promised to end class conflict and crass materialism.

In America, socialists disagreed over how to achieve Marx's vision. Much of the movement was influenced by immigrants, first from Germany but also by Russian Jews, Italians, Hungarians, and Poles. Although American socialism splintered into small groups, one of its main factions was the Socialist Labor Party, led by Daniel DeLeon, a fiery editor and lawyer born in Curaçao and educated in Germany, who criticized American labor organizations like the AFL as too conservative. Yet, as he and other socialists argued points of doctrine, they ignored everyday needs and thus failed to attract the mass of laborers. Nor could they rebut clergy and business leaders who celebrated opportunity, self-improvement, social mobility, and consumerism. Most workers hoped that they or their children would benefit through education and acquisition of property or by becoming their own boss; they thus sought individual advancement rather than the betterment of all.

17-6e Eugene V. Debs

As the nineteenth century closed, a new leader invigorated American socialism. Indiana-born Eugene V. Debs headed the American Railway Union, which had carried out the 1894 strike against the Pullman Company. Jailed for defying an injunction against striking rail workers, Debs read Marx's works in prison. Once released, he flirted briefly with Populism, then became leading spokesman for American socialism, combining visionary Marxism with Populist antimonopolism. Debs captivated audiences with passionate eloquence and indignant attacks on the free-enterprise system. "Many of you think you are competing," he would lecture. "Against whom? Against Rockefeller? About as I would if I had a wheelbarrow and competed with the Santa Fe [railroad] from here to Kansas City." By 1900 the group soon to be called the Socialist Party of America was uniting around Debs. It would make its presence felt more forcefully in the new century.

17-6f Coxey's Army

In 1894, not Debs but rather a quiet businessman named Jacob Coxey, a Civil War veteran and small business owner from Massillon, Ohio, captured public attention with his act of protest. Coxey had a vision. He was convinced that, to aid debtors, the federal government should issue $500 million of "legal tender" paper money and make low-interest loans to local governments, which would in turn use the funds to pay unemployed men to build roads and other public works. He planned to publicize his scheme by leading a march from Massillon to Washington, D.C., gathering a "petition in boots" of unemployed workers along the way. To emphasize his sincerity, Coxey named his newborn son Legal Tender and proposed that his teenage daughter lead the procession on a white horse.

Coxey's Army, about two hundred strong, left in March 1894. Hiking across Ohio into Pennsylvania, the marchers received food and housing in depressed industrial towns and rural villages and attracted additional recruits. Elsewhere, a dozen similar processions from places such as Seattle, San Francisco, and Los Angeles also began the trek eastward. Sore feet prompted some marchers to commandeer trains, but most marches were peaceful and law abiding.

Coxey's band, now of five hundred, including women and children, entered Washington, D.C., on April 30. The next day, the group, armed with "war clubs of peace," advanced to the Capitol. When Coxey and a few others vaulted a wall surrounding the grounds, mounted police moved in and routed the demonstrators. Coxey tried to speak from the Capitol steps, but police dragged him away. As arrests and clubbings

continued, Coxey's dream of a demonstration of four hundred thousand jobless workers dissolved. Like the strikes, the first people's march on Washington yielded to police muscle.

Unlike socialists, who wished to replace the capitalist system, Coxey's troops merely wanted more jobs and better living standards. Today, in an age of union contracts, regulation of business, and government-sponsored unemployment relief, their goals do not appear radical. The brutal reactions of officials, however, reveal how threatening dissenters like Coxey and Debs seemed to defenders of the existing social order.

17-7 Silver Crusade and the Election of 1896

▶ **What were the main issues during the election of 1896?**

▶ **What was the state of the political party system during the election of 1896?**

▶ **How did the election of 1896 impact the Populist Party?**

Amid the tumult of social protest and economic depression, it appeared that the presidential election of 1896 would be pivotal. Debates over money and power were climaxing, Democrats and Republicans continued their battle over control of Congress and the presidency, and Populists stood at the center of a political whirlwind. The key question was whether voters would abandon old party loyalties for the Populist Party.

17-7a Free Silver

The Populist crusade against "money power" settled on the issue of silver, which many people saw as a simple solution to the nation's complex ills. To them, coinage of silver symbolized an end to special privileges for the rich and return of government to the people, because it would increase the amount of cash in circulation, reduce interest rates, and lift struggling families out of debt. Populists made free coinage of silver their political battle cry.

As the 1896 election approached, Populists had to decide how to translate their few previous electoral victories into broader success. Should they join with sympathetic factions of one of the major parties, risking a loss of identity? Or should they remain an independent third party and settle for minor wins at best? Except in mining areas of the Rocky Mountain states, where coinage of silver had strong support, Republicans were unlikely allies because their support for the gold standard and big business orientation represented what Populists opposed.

In the North and West, alliance with Democrats was more plausible. There, the Democratic Party retained vestiges of antimonopoly ideology and sympathy for a looser currency system, though "gold Democrats," such as President Cleveland and Senator David Hill of New York, held powerful

◁ Walking at the head of his informal "Commonweal Army" of protesters, Jacob Coxey marches toward Washington, D.C., in 1894. His troops, which included men on foot, on bicycles, and on horseback and his daughter riding a white horse, wanted the federal government to provide jobs to those made jobless by the depression of the 1890s.

Library of Congress Prints and Photographs Division Washington| LC-USZ62-98526|

influence. Populists assumed they shared common interests with Democratic urban workers, whom they believed suffered the same oppression that beset farmers. In the South, Alliances had supported a few Democratic candidates, but the failure of these candidates to carry out their promises once in office caused southern farmers to feel betrayed. Whichever option they chose, fusion (alliance with Democrats) or independence, Populists ensured that the election campaign of 1896 would be the most issue oriented since 1860.

17-7b Nomination of McKinley

As they prepared to nominate their presidential candidate, both major parties were divided. Republicans were guided by Ohio industrialist Marcus A. Hanna, who for a year had been maneuvering to win the nomination for Ohio's governor, William McKinley. By the time the party convened in St. Louis, Hanna had corralled enough delegates to succeed. "He had advertised McKinley," quipped Theodore Roosevelt, "as if he were a patent medicine." The Republicans' only distress occurred when they adopted a platform supporting the gold standard, rejecting a prosilver stance proposed by Colorado senator Henry M. Teller. Teller, who had been among the party's founders forty years earlier, walked out of the convention in tears, taking a small group of silver Republicans with him.

At the Democratic convention, prosilver delegates wearing silver badges and waving silver banners paraded through the Chicago Amphitheatre. Observing their tumultuous demonstrations, one delegate wrote, "For the first time I can understand the scenes of the French Revolution!" A *New York World* reporter remarked, "all the silverites need is a Moses." They found one in **William Jennings Bryan**.

17-7c William Jennings Bryan

Bryan arrived at the Democratic convention as a member of a contested Nebraska delegation. A former congressman whose support for coinage of silver had annoyed President Cleveland, Bryan found the depression's impact on midwestern farmers distressing. Shortly after the convention seated Bryan and his colleagues instead of a competing faction that supported the gold standard, Bryan joined the party's resolutions committee and helped write a platform calling for unlimited coinage of silver. When the committee presented the platform to the full convention, Bryan rose to speak on its behalf. His now-famous closing words ignited the delegates.

> Having behind us the producing masses of this nation and the world, supported by the commercial interests, the laboring interests, and the toilers everywhere, we will answer [the wealthy classes'] demand for a gold standard by saying to them: You shall not press down upon the brow of labor this crown of thorns, you shall not crucify mankind upon a cross of gold.

The speech could not have been better timed. Delegates who backed Bryan for president now began gathering support. It took five ballots to win the nomination, but the magnetic "Boy Orator" proved irresistible. In accepting the silverite goals of southerners and westerners and repudiating Cleveland's policies, the Democratic

William Jennings Bryan Orator, anti-imperialist, champion of farm interests, and three-time Democratic presidential candidate.

△ During the 1896 presidential campaign, Republicans depicted their candidate, William McKinley, as holding the key to prosperity for both the working man and the white-collar laborer, shown here raising their hats to the candidate. Republicans successfully made this economic theme—rather than the silver crusade of McKinley's unsuccessful opponent, William Jennings Bryan—the difference in the election's outcome.

△ William Jennings Bryan (1860–1925) posed for this photograph in 1896, when he first ran for president at the age of thirty-six. Bryan's emotional speeches turned agrarian unrest and the issue of free silver into a moral crusade.

Party became more attractive to discontented farmers. But, like the Republicans, it, too, alienated a minority wing. Some gold Democrats withdrew and nominated their own candidate.

Bryan's nomination presented the Populist Party meeting in St. Louis with a dilemma. Should Populists join Democrats in support of Bryan, or should they nominate their own candidate? Tom Watson, who opposed fusion with Democrats, warned, "the Democratic idea of fusion [is] that we play Jonah while they play whale." Others reasoned that supporting a separate candidate would split the anti-McKinley vote and guarantee a Republican victory. In the end, the convention compromised, first naming Watson as its vice-presidential nominee to preserve party identity (Democrats had nominated Maine shipping magnate

Arthur Sewall for vice president) and then nominating Bryan for president.

The campaign, as Kansas journalist William Allen White observed, "took the form of religious frenzy . . . as the crusaders of the revolution rode home, praising the people's will as though it were God's will and cursing wealth for its iniquity." Bryan preached that "every great economic question is in reality a great moral question." Republicans countered Bryan's attacks on privilege by predicting chaos if he won. While Bryan raced around the country giving twenty speeches a day, Hanna invited thousands of people to McKinley's home in Canton, Ohio, where the candidate plied them with homilies on moderation and prosperity, promising something for everyone. In an appeal to working-class voters, Republicans stressed the new jobs that a protective tariff would create.

17-7d Election Results

The election results revealed that the political standoff had ended. McKinley, symbol of urban and corporate ascendancy, beat Bryan by 600,000 popular votes and won in the electoral college by 271 to 176 (see Map 17.1). It was the most lop-sided presidential election since 1872.

Bryan had worked hard to rally the nation, but obsession with silver prevented Populists from building the urban-rural coalition that would have solidified their appeal. The silver issue diverted voters from focusing on broader reforms of cooperation and government aid that

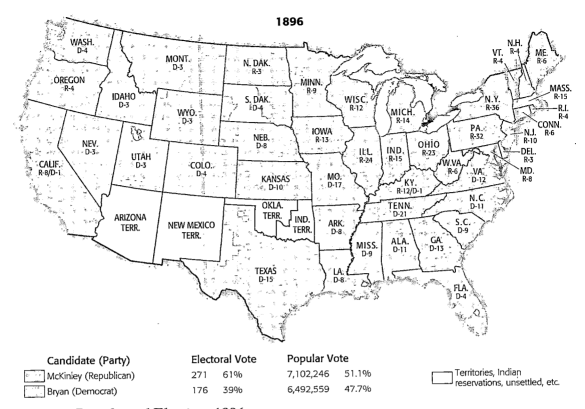

1896

Candidate (Party)	Electoral Vote		Popular Vote	
McKinley (Republican)	271	61%	7,102,246	51.1%
Bryan (Democrat)	176	39%	6,492,559	47.7%

Territories, Indian reservations, unsettled, etc.

Map 17.1 Presidential Election, 1896

William Jennings Bryan had strong voter support in the South and West, but the numerically superior industrial states, plus California, created majorities for William McKinley.

the Alliance movement and Omaha platform had proposed. Urban workers, who might have benefited from Populist goals, feared that silver coinage would shrink the value of their wages. Labor leaders, such as the AFL's Samuel Gompers, though partly sympathetic, would not commit themselves fully because they viewed farmers as businessmen, not workers. And socialists like Daniel DeLeon denounced Populists as "retrograde" because they, unlike socialists, believed in free enterprise. Thus the Populist crusade collapsed. Although Populists and fusion candidates won a few state and congressional elections, the Bryan-Watson ticket of the Populist Party polled only 222,600 votes nationwide.

17-7e The McKinley Presidency

As president, McKinley reinforced his support of business by signing the Gold Standard Act (1900), requiring that all paper money be backed by gold. A seasoned and personable politician, McKinley was best known for crafting protective tariffs; as a congressman, he had guided passage of record-high tariff rates in 1890. He accordingly supported the Dingley Tariff of 1897, which raised duties even higher. A believer in opening markets abroad to sustain profits

at home, McKinley encouraged imperialistic ventures in Latin America and the Pacific. Domestic tensions subsided as prosperity returned. Better times and victory in the Spanish-American War enabled him to beat Bryan again in 1900.

Summary

Though buffeted by special interests and lingering consequences of the Civil War, Gilded Age politicians succeeded in making many modest, and some major, accomplishments. Guided by well-meaning, generally competent people, much of what occurred in city halls, statehouses, the halls of Congress, and the White House prepared the nation for the twentieth century. Laws encouraging economic growth with some principles of regulation, measures expanding government agencies while reducing crass patronage, and federal intervention in trade and currency issues all evolved during the 1870s and 1880s, to the distress of Social Darwinists such as William Graham Sumner. Principles of police power clashed with those of due process, but many laws that were passed set the stage for the expanded government activism after the turn of the century.

Interpreting a Fairy Tale

The Wizard of Oz, released in 1939 and one of the most popular movies of all time, began as a work of juvenile literature penned by journalist L. Frank Baum in 1900. Originally titled *The Wonderful Wizard of Oz,* the story used memorable characters to create a fun-filled and adventurous quest.

Although children have viewed the tale and film as a fantasy, adults have been tempted to seek hidden meanings. In 1964 one scholar, Henry M. Littlefield, published an article in which he asserted that Baum really intended to write a Populist parable illustrating the conditions of overburdened farmers and laborers. The characters in *The Wonderful Wizard of Oz,* Littlefield opined, supported his theory. Dorothy symbolized the well-intentioned common person; the Scarecrow, the struggling farmer; the Tin Man, the industrial worker. Hoping for a better life, these friends, along with the Cowardly Lion (William Jennings Bryan with a loud roar but little power), followed a yellow brick road (the gold standard) that led nowhere. The Emerald City that they find is presided over by a wizard, who rules from behind a screen. A typical politician, the wizard tries to be all

things to all people, but Dorothy reveals him as a fraud. Dorothy is able to leave this muddled society and return to her simple Kansas farm family of Aunt Em and Uncle Henry by using her magical silver slippers (representing coinage of silver, though the movie made them red).

Subsequent theorists identified additional symbols, such as Oz being the abbreviation for ounces (oz.), the chief measurement of gold: The Wicked Witch of the East—who, Baum wrote, kept the little people (Munchkins) "in bondage, . . . making them slaves for her night and day"—could be seen as representing the force of industrial capitalism. Baum's story, viewed in film by most Americans, became a tool for explaining Populism to students, and by the 1970s its apparent message had strong appeal to critics of "the Establishment."

But then investigators began to take another look and offer different conclusions. In 1983 historian William R. Leach asserted that Baum's tale actually was a celebration of urban consumer culture. Its language exalted the opulence of Emerald City, which to Leach resembled the "White City" of the Chicago World's Fair of 1893, and

Dorothy's upbeat nature symbolized the optimism of the industrial era. Moreover, Baum's career supported this new interpretation. Before he was a writer, he had designed display windows and was involved in theater—activities that gave him an appreciation of modern urban life.

Rather than confusion, the real legacy of *The Wonderful Wizard of Oz* has been its ability to provoke differing interpretations. What matters is that Baum's turn-of-the-century fairy tale, the first truly American work of this sort, has bequeathed to the present so many fascinating images about the diversity and contradictions of American culture.

CRITICAL THINKING

- The legacy of *The Wonderful Wizard of Oz* lies in its ability to reveal the diversity and contradictions of American culture during the Populist era. Consider what message *The Wonderful Wizard of Oz* might have for Americans of today in light of the vast cultural and political divides within our nation revealed by the election of 2016. Based on your reading of this chapter, how do you interpret *The Wizard of Oz?*
- What are the merits and flaws in each of the interpretations presented here?

Nevertheless, the United States remained a nation of inconsistencies. Those who supported disfranchisement of African Americans and continued legal and social discrimination against women and racial minorities still dominated politics in the South, and extralegal inequities against these groups remained common in the North. People in power, often representing special-interest groups, could not tolerate radical views like those expressed by socialists, Coxey, or Populists, but many of the ideas raised by these groups continued to find supporters as the new century dawned.

The 1896 election realigned national politics. The Republican Party, founded in the 1850s amid a crusade against slavery and benefiting from northern victory in the Civil War, became the majority party by emphasizing government aid to business, expanding its social base among the urban middle class, and playing down its moralism. The Democratic Party miscalculated on the silver issue but held its support in the

South and inside urban political machines. At the national level, however, loyalties lacked the potency they once had. Suspicion of party politics increased, and voter participation rates declined. Populists tried to energize a third-party movement, but their success was fleeting. A new kind of politics was brewing, one in which technical experts and scientific organization would attempt to supplant the backroom deals and favoritism that had characterized the previous age.

Though the silver issue faded, many Populist goals eventually were incorporated by the major parties, including regulation of railroads, banks, and utilities; shorter workdays; a variant of the subtreasury plan; a graduated income tax; and direct election of senators. These reforms succeeded because a variety of groups united behind them. Immigration, urbanization, and industrialization had transformed the United States into a pluralistic nation in which compromise among interest groups had become a political fact of life. As the Gilded Age ended, business was still ascendant, and large segments of the population were still excluded from political and economic opportunity. But the winds of dissent and reform had begun to blow more strongly.

Suggestions for Further Reading

Edward L. Ayers, *The Promise of the New South: Life After Reconstruction* (1992)

Jean Baker, *Sisters: The Lives of America's Suffragists* (2005)

Ruth Bordin, *Frances Willard: A Biography (1986)*

Charles C. Calhoun, *Conceiving a New Republic* (2006)

Glenda Elizabeth Gilmore, *Gender and Jim Crow: Women and the Politics of White Supremacy in North Carolina, 1896–1920* (1996)

Steven Hahn, *A Nation Under Our Feet: Black Political Struggles in the Rural South, from Slavery to the Great Migration* (2003)

Michael Kazin, *A Godly Hero: The Life of William Jennings Bryan* (2006)

Jean V. Matthews, *The Rise of the New Woman: The Women's Movement in America, 1875–1930* (2003)

Robert C. McMath, *American Populism* (1993)

Nick Salvatore, *Eugene V. Debs: Citizen and Socialist* (1992)

MINDTAP
From Cengage

MindTap® is a fully online personalized learning experience built upon Cengage Learning content. MindTap® combines student learning tools—readings, multimedia, activities, and assessments—into a singular Learning Path that guides students through the course and helps students develop the critical thinking, analysis, and communication skills that are essential to academic and professional success.

The Progressive Era, 1895–1920

W hat Ben Lindsey saw made him furious. As a young Colorado lawyer in the 1890s, he was asked by a judge to defend two boys, about twelve years old, accused of burglary. The boys had already been imprisoned for sixty days without a trial and did not understand what the word *burglary* meant, let alone how the justice system worked. When Lindsey visited the youngsters in jail, he found them playing poker with two older cellmates, one a safecracker and the other a horse thief. Lindsey asked the warden how many other boys were in the jail. "Oh, quite a number" was the answer. Outraged that "good-natured" children were housed with hardened criminals, Lindsey later wrote, "Here were two boys, neither of them serious enemies of society, who were about to be convicted of burglary and have felony records for the rest of their lives. . . . I had made up my mind to smash the system that meant so much injustice to youth."

In 1901, Lindsey ran for county judge and began a long career "smashing the system" and advocating for the welfare of children. He spoke and wrote extensively about protecting juveniles from hard-hearted criminal prosecution, exploitive labor practices, and burdens of poverty. He and his wife, Henrietta, worked to promote a separate juvenile court system and aid to families whose children might be at risk of becoming lawbreakers. They wrote reform laws that were adopted by many states and foreign countries. The Lindseys' efforts to abolish injustice showed both genuine compassion and middle-class bias, and they occupied part of a broader movement aimed at finding solutions to the social and economic problems of modern American society.

◁ Judge Ben Lindsey (1869–1943) of Denver was a Progressive reformer who worked for children's legal protection. Like many reformers of his era, Lindsey had an earnest faith in the ability of humankind to build a better world. The Library of Congress

Chronology

1895	Booker T. Washington gives Atlanta Compromise speech
	National Association of Colored Women founded
1898	*Holden v. Hardy* upholds limits on miners' working hours
1901	McKinley assassinated; T. Roosevelt assumes presidency
1904	*Northern Securities* case dissolves railroad trust
1905	*Lochner v. New York* removes limits on bakers' working hours
1906	Hepburn Act tightens ICC control over railroads
	Meat Inspection Act passed
	Pure Food and Drug Act Passed
1908	*Muller v. Oregon* upholds limits on women's working hours
1909	NAACP founded
1910	Mann-Elkins Act reinforces ICC powers
	White Slave Traffic Act (Mann Act) prohibits transportation of women for "immoral purposes"
	Taft fires Pinchot
1911	Society of American Indians founded
1913	Sixteenth Amendment ratified, legalizing income tax
	Seventeenth Amendment ratified, providing for direct election of senators
	Underwood Tariff institutes income tax
	Federal Reserve Act establishes central banking system
1914	Federal Trade Commission created to investigate unfair trade practices
	Clayton Anti-Trust Act outlaws monopolistic business practices
1919	Eighteenth Amendment ratified, establishing prohibition of alcoholic beverages
1920	Nineteenth Amendment ratified, giving women the vote in federal elections

During the 1890s, economic depression, labor violence, political upheaval, and foreign entanglements shook the nation. Technology had fulfilled many promises, but numerous Americans continued to suffer from poverty and injustice. Some critics regarded industrialists as monsters who controlled markets and prices for the sole purpose of maximizing profits. Others believed government was corroded by bosses who enriched themselves through abuse of power. Still others felt that members of the new middle class overlooked the needs of the laboring classes. Tensions created by urbanization and industrialization seemed to be fragmenting society into conflicting interest groups.

Experience an interactive version of this story in MindTap®.

B y 1900, the previous decade's political tumult had calmed, and economic depression subsided. The nation emerged victorious from a war against Spain (see Chapter 19), and an era of new political leaders, including a new brand of president, was dawning. A sense of renewal served both to intensify anxiety over continuing problems and to raise hopes that somehow those problems could be fixed so that democracy could be reconciled with capitalism.

From these circumstances emerged a complex and many-sided reform campaign. By the 1910s, reformers of various sorts were calling themselves Progressives; in 1912, they formed a political party by that name to embody their principles. Historians have uniformly used the term *Progressivism* to refer to the era's spirit, while disagreeing over its meaning and over who actually was a Progressive. Nonetheless, the era between 1895 and 1920 included a series of movements, each aiming in one way or another to renovate or restore American society, values, and institutions with hope that a better future lay ahead.

The reform impulse had many sources. Industrial capitalism had created awesome technology, unprecedented productivity, and a cornucopia of consumer goods. But it also brought harmful overproduction, domineering monopolies, labor strife, and destruction of natural resources. Burgeoning cities facilitated the amassing and distribution of goods, services, and cultural amenities; they also bred poverty, disease, and crime. The influx of immigrants and rise of a new class of managers and professionals reconfigured the social order. And the depression of the 1890s forced leading citizens to realize what working people already knew: the promise of American life was not being kept; equality of opportunity was elusive.

These problems galvanized members of both the middle and working classes to work toward change, though in differing ways. Middle-class reformers organized their ideas and actions around three goals. First, they sought to end abuses of power. Attacks on monopoly and corruption were not new; Jacksonian reformers of the 1830s and 1840s, as well as Populists of the 1890s, belonged to the same tradition. Progressives, however, broadened the offensive. Trust-busting, consumers' rights, and good government became compelling political issues. Second, Progressives such as Ben Lindsey wished to supplant corrupt power with humane institutions, such as schools, courts, and medical clinics. Though eager to protect individual rights, they asserted that society had the responsibility and power to improve individual lives, and they believed that government, acting for society at large, must intervene to protect the common good and elevate public interest above self-interest. Their revolt against fixed categories of thought challenged entrenched views on women's roles, race relations, education, legal and scientific thought, and morality. Third, Progressives wanted to enlist experts who would apply their special knowledge to end wasteful competition and promote social and economic order. Science and the scientific method—planning, control, predictability—were their central values. Just as corporations applied scientific management techniques to achieve economic efficiency, Progressives advocated expertise and planning to achieve social and political efficiency.

Another kind of reform arose from the everyday needs and problems of industrial working classes. Reformers representing this group sometimes allied with others interested in social welfare and sometimes worked on their own to promote greater public responsibility for the health, safety, and security of families and workers at risk in the new urban industrial world.

Befitting their name, Progressives had faith in the ability of humankind to create a better world. They voiced such phrases as "humanity's universal growth" and "the upward spiral of human development." Rising incomes, new educational opportunities, and increased availability of goods and services created an aura of confidence that social improvement would follow. Judge Lindsey expressed the Progressive creed when he wrote, "In the end the people

are bound to do the right thing, no matter how much they fail at times."

- ▢ *What were the major characteristics of Progressivism?*

- ▢ *In what ways did Progressive reform succeed, and in what ways did it fail?*

- ▢ *How did women and racial minorities challenge previous ways of thinking about American society?*

18-1 The Varied Progressive Impulse

▷ **How did politics become more oriented toward social issues in the Progressive Era?**

▷ **What role did the upper, middle, and working class play in the Progressive Era?**

▷ **How did religion influence the reformist impulse of the Progressive Era?**

▷ **How was Progressivism similar and different in the South and West from other regions?**

Progressive reformers addressed vexing issues that had surfaced in the previous half-century, but they did so in a new political climate. After the heated election of 1896, party loyalties eroded and voter turnout declined. (As before, only adult males could vote, and some states still retained property qualifications for participation in some elections. Others used poll taxes and literacy tests to deny the voting privilege to nonwhite and poor white males.) In northern states, voter participation in presidential elections dropped from 80 percent of the eligible electorate in the 1880s to under 60 percent by 1912. In southern states, it fell below 30 percent. Parties, it seemed, were losing sway over the ways that the people viewed politics. At the same time, new interest groups—which championed their own special causes—gained influence, making Progressive reform issue-oriented rather than influenced by party ideologies.

18-1a National Associations and Foreign Influences

Many formerly local organizations that had formed around specific interests and issues became nationwide after 1890. These organizations included professional associations, such as the American Bar Association; women's organizations, such as the National American Woman Suffrage Association; problem-oriented groups, such as the National Consumers League; civic-minded clubs, such as the National Municipal

League; and minority group associations, such as the National Negro Business League and the Society of American Indians. Because they usually acted outside established parties, such groups made politics more fragmented and issue focused than in earlier eras.

American reformers also adopted foreign ideas. Some reform plans were introduced by Americans who had encountered them while studying in England, France, and Germany; others, by foreigners visiting the United States. (Europeans also learned from Americans, but the balance of the idea flow tilted toward the United States.) Americans copied from England such schemes as the settlement house, in which reformers went to live among and aid the urban poor, and workers' compensation for victims of industrial accidents. Ideas about city planning were imported from Germany. Other reforms, such as old-age insurance, subsidized workers' housing, and rural reconstruction, also originated abroad.

Issues and methods of implementation distinguished Progressive reform from the preceding Populist movement. Although goals of the rural-based Populists—moral regeneration, political democracy, and antimonopolism—continued after the movement faded, the Progressive quest for social justice, educational and legal reform, and government streamlining had a largely urban quality. Utilizing advances in mail, telephone, and telegraph communications, urban reformers could exchange information and coordinate efforts across the nation more easily than could rural reformers.

18-1b The New Middle Class and Muckrakers

Progressive goals—ending abuse of power, protecting the welfare of all people, reforming institutions, and promoting social efficiency—existed at all levels of society. But a new middle class of men and women in professions of law, medicine, engineering, social service, religion, teaching, and business formed an important reform vanguard. Offended by corruption and immorality in business, government, and human relations, these people were determined to apply the rational techniques that they had learned in their professions to problems of the larger society. They also believed they could create a unified nation by "Americanizing" immigrants and Native peoples—meaning educating them to conform to middle-class customs and ideals.

Indignation over abuses of power motivated many middle-class reformers. Their views were voiced by journalists whom Theodore Roosevelt dubbed "**muckrakers**" (after a character in the Puritan allegory *Pilgrim's Progress*, who, rather than looking heavenward at beauty, looked downward and raked the muck on the floor to expose evil). Muckrakers fed public tastes for scandal and sensation by exposing social, economic, and political wrongs. Their investigative articles in *McClure's*, *Cosmopolitan*, and other popular magazines attacked adulterated foods, fraudulent insurance, prostitution, and political corruption. Lincoln Steffens's articles in *McClure's*, later

muckrakers Journalists who wrote articles exposing urban political corruption and corporate wrongdoing.

published as *The Shame of the Cities* (1904), epitomized muckraking style. Steffens hoped his exposés of bosses' misrule in various cities would inspire outrage and, ultimately, reform. Other celebrated muckraking works included Upton Sinclair's *The Jungle* (1906), a novel that disclosed outrages of the meatpacking industry; Ida M. Tarbell's disparaging history of Standard Oil (first published in *McClure's*, 1902–1904); Burton J. Hendrick's *Story of Life Insurance* (1907); and David Graham Phillips's *Treason of the Senate* (1906).

To remedy corrupt politics, these Progressives advocated nonpartisan elections to prevent the fraud and bribery bred by party loyalties. To make officeholders more responsible, they urged adoption of the initiative, which permitted voters to propose new laws; the referendum, which enabled voters to accept or reject a law; and the recall, which allowed voters to remove offending officials and judges from office. The goal, like that of the business consolidation movement, was efficiency: middle-class Progressives would reclaim government by replacing the boss system with accountable managers chosen by a responsible electorate.

18-1c Upper-Class Reformers

The Progressive spirit also stirred some male business leaders and wealthy women. Executives like Alexander Cassatt of the Pennsylvania Railroad supported some—but not excessive—government regulation and political restructuring to protect their interests from more radical reformers. Others, like E. A. Filene, founder of a Boston department store, and Tom Johnson, a Cleveland streetcar magnate, were humanitarians who worked unselfishly for social justice. Business-dominated organizations like the Municipal Voters League and U.S. Chamber of Commerce thought that running schools, hospitals, and local government like efficient businesses would help stabilize society. Elite women led and gave financial support to organizations like the Young Women's Christian Association (YWCA), which aided unmarried workingwomen, and to settlement houses.

18-1d Settlement Houses

Young, educated middle-class women and men tried to bridge the gap between social classes that industrialism seemed to have opened by leaving their comfortable surroundings and living in inner-city outposts called settlement houses, an idea adopted from England. Residents envisioned the settlement house as a place where people could learn from each other and mutually mitigate modern problems through education, art, and reform. Between 1886 and 1910, over four hundred settlements were established, mostly in big cities, and they sponsored a variety of activities ranging from English language classes, kindergartens and nurseries, health clinics, vocational training, and playgrounds to art exhibits and amateur theater. As firsthand observers of urban poverty and poor housing, settlement house workers focused considerable energy on improving living conditions and marched at the vanguard of Progressivism. They backed housing and labor reform, offered meeting space to unions, and served as

Toynbee Hall, London

The settlement house movement, one of the Progressive Era's most idealized undertakings, owed most of its existence to Toynbee Hall in London, England. During the late nineteenth century, British middle-class university graduates began to feel uneasy about the failure of industrialization to provide adequate living conditions for the urban working class. Inspired by new curricula of social research, they sought to apply their knowledge to real situations. With this in mind, in 1884, Anglican clergyman Samuel Barnett and his wife Henrietta founded a residence in the London slums, where college students could live among working people and help them overcome their poverty. The Barnetts named the settlement Toynbee Hall after a friend, historian Arnold Toynbee (uncle of a famous historian of the same name), who had died the previous year. Their goal, as well as that of those who joined them, was to combine a religious mission to serve others with a scientific way of allaying class conflict by working with and learning from the masses through education and social welfare programs.

London and the nearby universities of Oxford and Cambridge at this time were destinations for young, idealistic Americans seeking to broaden their education and find a place for themselves in the modern world. The experiment at Toynbee Hall attracted them and several took up temporary residence there, then returned with motivation to establish similar reform centers in their own cities. Practically every founder of a settlement house established in American cities during the Progressive Era had been directly influenced by Toynbee Hall. Jane Addams, cofounder of Chicago's Hull House in 1889, visited Toynbee Hall in 1887 and called Hull House a "Toynbee Hall experiment." Vida Scudder, a Smith College graduate, undertook graduate studies at Oxford, and, influenced by Toynbee Hall, founded settlements in New York and Boston. Everett Wheeler visited Toynbee Hall in 1889 and established East Side House in New York in 1891. In 1893, George Hodges opened Kingsley House in Pittsburgh after spending a summer studying settlements in England. All these and more adopted the Toynbee philosophy "to bring men and women of education in to closer relations with the laboring classes for their mutual benefit."

American settlements diverged from their British model in a few respects. More women participated in American settlements than in British, mainly because many were graduates of new women's colleges established in the United States between the 1870s and 1890s. Also, because American settlement residents often were paid from funds raised from outside donors, they exhibited more of a sense of professionalism than their British counterparts, who normally were unpaid volunteers. And in the growing ethnic and racial diversity of the United States, which was less extensive in Great Britain, American settlements also adopted more explicit goals of assimilation.

CRITICAL THINKING

▢ Despite many differences between them, American and English settlement houses both represent an attempt by well-meaning members of the upper and middle classes to impose reform on the working classes. What kinds of problems might these efforts have caused among the working classes even as they tried to resolve other problems?

◁ Founded in 1884 and located in a working-class district in East London, the settlement of Toynbee Hall attracted graduates from Oxford and Cambridge Universities who wished to live among impoverished industrial laborers, learn from them, and improve their conditions. The effort inspired young American social reformers to launch similar projects in American cities.

TOYNBEE HALL Commercial Street Whitechapel London E.

school nurses, juvenile probation officers, and teachers. They also worked in reform political campaigns.

Though several men helped initiate the settlement movement, the most influential participants were women. Jane Addams, Ellen Gates Starr, and Florence Kelley of Chicago's Hull House settlement, Lillian Wald of New York's Henry Street settlement, and Vida Scudder of Boston's Denison House were among many strong-minded leaders who not only broadened traditional roles of female service but also used settlement work as a springboard to larger roles in reform. Kelley's investigations into the exploitation of child labor prompted Illinois governor John Altgeld to appoint her state factory inspector; she later founded the National Consumers League. Wald helped make nursing a respected profession and cofounded the NAACP. And Addams had broad political influence, and her efforts on behalf of world peace garnered her the Nobel Peace Prize in 1931.

18-1e Working-Class Reformers

Vital elements of what became modern American liberalism derived from working-class urban experiences. By 1900, many urban workers were pressing for government intervention to ensure job safety and security. They advocated such bread-and-butter reforms as safe factories, shorter workdays, workers' compensation, protection of child and women laborers, better housing, and a more equitable tax structure. Politicians like Senator Robert F. Wagner of New York and Governor Edward F. Dunne of Illinois worked to alleviate hardships that resulted from urban-industrial growth. They trained in the trenches of machine politics, and their constituents were the same people who supported political bosses, supposedly the enemies of reform. Yet bossism was not necessarily incompatible with humanitarianism. When "Big Tim" Sullivan, an influential boss in New York's Tammany Hall machine, was asked why he supported shorter workdays for women, he explained, "I had seen me sister go out to work when she was only fourteen and I know we ought to help these gals by giving 'em a law which will prevent 'em from being broken down while they're still young." Those who represented working-class interests did not subscribe to all reforms. As protectors of individual liberty, they opposed schemes such as prohibition, Sunday closing laws, civil service, and nonpartisan elections, which conflicted with their constituents' interests. On the other hand, they joined with other reformers to pass laws aiding labor and promoting social welfare.

18-1f The Social Gospel

Much of Progressive reform rested on religious underpinnings from which arose new thoughts about how to fortify social relations with moral principles. In particular, a movement known as the **Social Gospel**, led by Protestant ministers Walter Rauschenbusch, Washington Gladden, and

Social Gospel Movement launched in the 1870s that stressed that true Christianity commits men and women to fight social injustice wherever it exists.

Charles Sheldon, would counter cutthroat capitalism by interjecting Christian churches into worldly matters, such as arbitrating industrial harmony and improving the conditions of the poor. Believing that service to fellow humans provided the way to securing individual salvation and creating God's kingdom on earth, Social Gospelers actively participated in social reform and governed their lives by asking, "What would Jesus do?"

Others took more secular pathways. Those who believed in service to all people tried to assimilate immigrants and Native peoples by expanding their educational, economic, and cultural opportunities. At times, well-intentioned humanitarians undermined their efforts by imposing their own values on people of different cultures. Working-class Catholic and Jewish immigrants, for example, sometimes rejected the Protestant creed and Americanization efforts of Social Gospelers and resented middle-class reformers' interference in their prerogative to raise children according to their own beliefs.

18-1g Socialists

Some people felt disillusioned and wanted to create a different society altogether. A blend of immigrant intellectuals, industrial workers, former Populists, and women's rights activists, they turned to socialism. Taking a cue from European counterparts—especially in Germany, England, and France, where the government sponsored such socialist goals as low-cost housing, workers' compensation, old-age pensions, public ownership of municipal services, and labor reform—they advocated that the United States adopt similar measures. By 1912, the Socialist Party of America, founded in 1901, claimed 150,000 members, and the socialist newspaper *Appeal to Reason* achieved the largest circulation—700,000 subscribers—of any weekly newspaper in the country.

In politics, socialists united behind Eugene V. Debs, the American Railway Union organizer who drew nearly 100,000 votes as Socialist Party candidate in the 1900 presidential election. A spellbinding orator who appealed to urban immigrants and western farmers alike, Debs won 400,000 votes in 1904 and polled 900,000 in 1912, at the pinnacle of his and his party's career. Although Debs and other Socialist Party leaders, such as Victor Berger of Wisconsin, the first socialist to be elected to the U.S. Congress, and New York labor lawyer Morris Hillquit, did not always agree on tactics, they made compelling overtures to reform-minded people.

Ultimately, American socialism had difficulty sustaining widespread acceptance. Some Progressives joined the Socialist Party, but most reformers favored capitalism too much to want it overthrown. Municipal ownership of public utilities represented their limit of drastic change. In Wisconsin, where Progressivism was most advanced, reformers refused to join forces with Berger's more radical group. In California, Progressives temporarily allied with conservatives to prevent socialists from gaining power in Los Angeles. Although some AFL unions supported socialist goals and candidates, many other unions opposed a reform like unemployment insurance

△ Although their objectives sometimes differed from those of middle-class Progressive reformers, socialists also became a more active force in the early twentieth century. Socialist parades on May Day, like this one in 1910, were meant to express the solidarity of all working people.

because it would increase taxes. Moreover, private real estate interests opposed government intervention in housing, and manufacturers tried to suppress socialist activity by blacklisting militant laborers.

18-1h Southern and Western Progressivism

In some ways, Progressive reform in the South resembled that in other regions. Essentially urban and middle class in nature, it included the same goals of business regulation, factory safety, pure food and drug legislation, and moral reform as existed in the North. The South pioneered some political reforms; the direct primary originated in North Carolina; the city commission plan arose in Galveston, Texas; and the city manager plan began in Staunton, Virginia. Progressive governors, such as Braxton Bragg Comer of Alabama and Hoke Smith of Georgia, introduced business regulation, educational expansion, and other reforms that duplicated actions taken by their northern counterparts.

In the West, several politicians championed humanitarianism and regulation, putting the region at the forefront of campaigns to expand functions of federal and state governments. Nevada's Progressive Senator Francis Newlands advocated national planning and federal control of water resources. California governor Hiram Johnson fought for direct primaries, regulation of child and women's labor, workers' compensation, a pure food and drug act, and educational reform. Montana's Senator Thomas J. Walsh fought against corruption and for woman suffrage.

Southern and western women, white and black, made notable contributions to Progressive causes, just as they did in the North and East. In western states, women could vote on state and local matters and thus participated directly in political reform. But the more effective women's reform efforts in both regions took place outside politics, and their projects remained racially distinct. White women crusaded against child labor, founded social service organizations, and challenged unfair wage rates. African American women, using a nonpolitical guise as homemakers and religious leaders—roles that whites found more acceptable than political activism—served their communities by advocating for cleaner streets, better education, and health reforms.

18-1i Opponents of Progressivism

It would be a mistake to assume that a Progressive spirit captivated all of American society between 1895 and 1920. Large numbers of people, heavily represented in Congress, disliked government interference in economic affairs and found no fault with existing power structures. Defenders of free enterprise opposed regulatory measures out of fear that government programs undermined the initiative and competition that they believed were basic to a free-market system. "Old-guard" Republicans, such as Senator Nelson W. Aldrich of Rhode Island and House Speaker Joseph Cannon of Illinois, championed this ideology. Outside Washington, D.C., tycoons like J. P. Morgan and John D. Rockefeller insisted that progress would result only from maintaining the profit incentive and an unfettered economy.

Moreover, prominent Progressives were not "progressive" in every respect. Their attempts to Americanize immigrants reflected bigotry as well as naiveté. As governor,

Hiram Johnson promoted discrimination against Japanese Americans, and whether Progressive or not, most southern governors, such as Smith, Comer, Charles B. Aycock of North Carolina, and James K. Vardaman of Mississippi, rested their power on appeals to white supremacy. In the South, the disfranchisement of African Americans through poll taxes, literacy requirements, and other means meant that electoral reforms benefitted only whites—and then only white men with enough cash and schooling to satisfy voting prerequisites. Settlement houses in northern cities kept blacks and whites apart in separate programs and buildings.

Progressive reformers generally occupied the center of the ideological spectrum. Moderate, socially aware, sometimes contradictory, they believed on one hand that laissez-faire was obsolete and on the other that a radical departure from free enterprise was dangerous. Like Thomas Jefferson, they expressed faith in the conscience and will of the people; like Alexander Hamilton, they desired strong central government to act in the interest of conscience. Their goals were both idealistic and realistic. As minister-reformer Walter Rauschenbusch wrote, "We shall demand perfection and never expect to get it."

18-2 Government and Legislative Reform

▷ How did government become more active in society during the Progressive Era?

▷ What steps were taken by reformers to make government more efficient?

▷ How did reformers address concerns about matters of social and individual morality?

Mistrust of tyranny had traditionally prompted Americans to believe that democratic government should be small, interfere in private affairs only in unique circumstances, and withdraw when balance had been restored. But in the late 1800s, this laissez-faire viewpoint weakened when problems resulting from economic change seemed to overwhelm individual effort. Corporations pursued government aid and protection for their enterprises. Discontented farmers sought government regulation of railroads and other monopolistic businesses. And city dwellers, accustomed to favors performed by political machines, came to expect government to act on their behalf. Before 1900, state governments had been concerned largely with railroads and economic growth; the federal government had focused primarily on tariffs and the currency. But after 1900, issues of regulation, both economic and social, demanded attention. More than in the past, public opinion, roused by muckraking media, influenced change.

18-2a Restructuring Government

Middle-class Progressive reformers rejected the laissez-faire principle of government. Increasingly aware that a simple, inflexible government was inadequate in a complex industrial age, they reasoned that public authority needed to counteract inefficiency and exploitation. But before activists could effectively use such power, they would have to reclaim government from politicians—whose venality, they believed, had soiled the democratic system. Thus, eliminating corruption from government was one central thrust of Progressive activity.

Prior to the Progressive Era, reformers had attacked dishonesty in city governments through such reforms as civil service, nonpartisan elections, and close scrutiny of public expenditures. After 1900, campaigns to make cities run more efficiently resulted in city-manager and commission forms of government, in which urban officials were chosen for professional expertise rather than for political connections. But reforming city administration was not sufficient to realize the improvements reformers sought, and they turned to state and federal governments for help.

At the state level, faith in a reform-minded executive prompted Progressives to support a number of skillful and charismatic governors. Perhaps the most dynamic of these governors was Wisconsin's Robert M. La Follette. A small-town lawyer, La Follette rose through the state Republican Party to become governor in 1900. In office, he initiated a multipronged reform program, including direct primaries, more equitable taxes, and regulation of railroads. He also appointed commissions staffed by experts, who supplied him with data that he used in speeches to arouse support for his policies. After three terms as governor, La Follette became a U.S. senator and carried his ideals into national politics. "Fighting Bob" displayed a rare ability to approach reform scientifically while still exciting people with moving rhetoric. His goal, he proclaimed, was "not to 'smash' corporations, but to drive them out of politics, and then to treat them exactly the same as other people are treated."

Crusades against corrupt politics made the system more democratic. By 1916, all but three states had direct primaries, and many had adopted the initiative, referendum, and recall. Political reformers achieved a major goal in 1913 with adoption of the Seventeenth Amendment to the Constitution, which provided for direct election of U.S. senators, replacing election by state legislatures. Such measures, however, did not always achieve desired ends. Party bosses, better organized and more experienced than reformers, were still able to control elections, and special-interest groups spent large sums to influence voting. Moreover, courts usually aided entrenched power rather than reining it in.

18-2b Labor Reform

State laws resulting from Progressive efforts to improve labor conditions had more effect than did political reforms because middle-class and working-class reformers agreed on the need for them. Prodded by middle-class/working-class coalitions, many states enacted factory inspection laws, and by 1916 nearly two-thirds of states required compensation for victims of industrial accidents. The same

◁ Robert M. La Follette (1855–1925) was one of the most dynamic of Progressive politicians. As governor of Wisconsin, he sponsored a program of political reform and business regulation known as the Wisconsin Plan. In 1906, he entered the U.S. Senate and continued to champion Progressive reform. The National Progressive Republican League, which La Follette founded in 1911, became the core of the Progressive Party.

Library of Congress Prints and Photographs Division Washington, D.C.[LC-US262-58275]

alliance induced some legislatures to grant aid to low-income mothers with dependent children. Under pressure from the National Child Labor Committee, nearly every state set a minimum age for employment (varying from twelve to sixteen) and limited hours that employers could make children work. Labor laws did not work perfectly, however. They seldom provided for the close inspection of factories that enforcement required. And families that needed extra income evaded child labor restrictions by falsifying their children's ages to employers.

Several middle- and working-class groups also united behind measures that restricted working hours for women and that aided retirees. After 1908, when the Supreme Court, in *Muller v. Oregon*, upheld Oregon's law prohibiting laundries from making female employees work more than ten hours a day, more states passed laws protecting female workers. Meanwhile, in 1914, efforts of the American Association for Old Age Security made progress when Arizona established old-age pensions. Judges struck down the law, but demand for pensions continued, and in the 1920s many states enacted laws to provide for needy elderly people.

18-2c Prohibition

Protecting women and children brought together reform coalitions. But when an issue involved regulating behavior such as drinking habits and sexual conduct, class differences emerged, especially when reformers used morality and social

control as bases for their agenda. For example, the **Anti-Saloon League,** formed in 1893, intensified the long-standing campaign against drunkenness and its costs to society. This organization allied with the Woman's Christian Temperance Union (founded in 1874) to publicize alcoholism's role in causing health problems and family distress. The league was especially successful in shifting attention from the immorality of drunkenness to using law enforcement to break the alleged link between the drinking that saloons encouraged and the accidents, poverty, and poor productivity that resulted. Against the wishes of many working-class people who valued individual freedom to drink where and when they wanted, the war on saloons prompted many states and localities to restrict liquor consumption. By 1900, one-fourth of the nation's population lived in "dry" communities that prohibited the sale of liquor.

Nevertheless, consumption of alcohol increased as a result of the influx of immigrants whose cultures included social drinking, convincing prohibitionists that a nationwide ban was the best solution. They enlisted support from such notables as Supreme Court Justice Louis D. Brandeis and former president William Howard Taft, and in 1918 Congress passed the

Anti-Saloon League Advocacy group founded in 1893 that sought to ban alcohol by publicizing its harmful effects on families and individuals and its link to accidents and health problems.

Eighteenth Amendment (ratified in 1919 and implemented in 1920), outlawing the manufacture, sale, and transportation of intoxicating liquors. Not all prohibitionists were Progressive reformers, and not all Progressives were prohibitionists. Nevertheless, the Eighteenth Amendment represents an expression of the Progressive goal to protect family and workplace through reform legislation.

18-2d Controlling Prostitution

Moral outrage erupted when muckraking journalists charged that international gangs were kidnapping young white women and forcing them into prostitution, a practice called "white slavery." Accusations were exaggerated, but they alarmed some moralists who falsely perceived a link between immigration and prostitution, and who feared that prostitutes were producing genetically inferior children. (These moralists seldom expressed the same concern for African American women.) Although some women voluntarily entered "the profession" because it offered much higher income than other forms of work and other women occasionally performed sexual favors in return for gifts, those fearful about the social consequences of prostitution prodded governments to investigate and pass corrective legislation. The Chicago Vice Commission, for example, undertook a "scientific" survey of dance halls and illicit sex, and published its findings as *The Social Evil in Chicago* in 1911. The report concluded that poverty, gullibility, and desperation drove women into prostitution. Such investigations publicized rising numbers of prostitutes but failed to prove that criminal organizations deliberately lured women into "the trade."

Reformers nonetheless believed they could attack prostitution by punishing both those who promoted it and those who practiced it. In 1910, Congress passed the White Slave Traffic Act (Mann Act), prohibiting interstate and international transportation of a woman for immoral purposes. By 1915, nearly every state had outlawed brothels and solicitation of sex. Such laws ostensibly protected young women from exploitation, but in reality they failed to address the more serious problem of sexual violence that women suffered at the hands of family members, presumed friends, and employers.

Like prohibition, the Mann Act reflected sentiment that government could improve behavior by restricting it. Middle-class reformers believed that the source of evil was neither original sin nor human nature but the social environment. If evil was created by human will, it followed that sin could be eradicated by human effort. The new working classes, however, resented such meddling as unwarranted attempts to control them. Thus, when Chicagoans voted on a referendum to make their city dry shortly before the Eighteenth Amendment was passed, three-fourths of the city's immigrant voters opposed it, and the measure went down to defeat.

Eighteenth Amendment
Amendment to the Constitution that established national prohibition of alcohol.

18-3 New Ideas in Social Institutions

▷ What reforms were made in institutions of education in the Progressive Era?

▷ How did scientific principles impact the fields of the law and social sciences?

▷ How did Social Darwinism influence societal views of immigrants and persons of color?

In addition to legislative paths, Progressive reform opened new vistas in the ways social institutions were organized. Reformers' preoccupation with efficiency and scientific management infiltrated realms of education, law, religion, and social science. Darwin's theory of evolution had challenged traditional beliefs in a God-created world, immigration had created complex social diversity, and technology had made old habits of production obsolete. Thoughtful people in several professions grappled with how to respond to this new era yet preserve what was best from the past.

18-3a John Dewey and Progressive Education

Changing attitudes about childhood and increases in school attendance altered approaches to education. As late as 1870, when families needed children at home to do farmwork, Americans attended school for an average of only a few months a year for only four years. By 1900, however, the urban-industrial economy and its expanding middle class helped to create a more widespread appreciation of childhood as a special life stage requiring that youngsters be sheltered from society's dangers and promoting their physical and emotional growth. Those concerned about children's development believed that youngsters required forms of education and activity appropriate to a child's biological and cultural development.

Educators argued that expanded schooling, especially for swelling populations of immigrant and migrant children, produced responsible citizens and workers. Consequently, in the 1870s and 1880s, states passed laws that required children to attend school to age fourteen. Meanwhile, the number of public high schools grew from five hundred in 1870 to ten thousand in 1910. By 1900, educational reformers, such as psychologist G. Stanley Hall and philosopher John Dewey, asserted that to prepare children for a modern world, personal development should be the focus of the curriculum and that the school be the center of the community.

Progressive education, based on Dewey's *The School and Society* (1899) and *Democracy and Education* (1916), was a uniquely American phenomenon. Dewey believed that children should be taught to use intelligence and ingenuity as instruments for controlling their environments. From kindergarten through high school, Dewey argued, children needed to learn through direct experience, not by rote memorization. Dewey and his wife, Alice, put these ideas into practice in their own Laboratory School, located at the University of Chicago.

18-3b Growth of Colleges and Universities

A more practical curriculum also became the driving principle behind reform in higher education. Previously, the purpose of American colleges and universities had resembled that of their European counterparts: to train a select few for careers in law, medicine, and religion. But in the late 1800s, institutions of higher learning multiplied as states established public universities using federal funds from the Morrill Acts of 1862 and 1890. The number of private institutions also expanded. Between 1870 and 1910, the total number of BA degrees granted by American colleges and universities grew from 9,400 to 37,200. Curricula broadened as educators sought to keep pace with technological and social changes. Harvard University, under President Charles W. Eliot, pioneered in substituting electives for required courses and experimenting with new teaching methods. The University of Wisconsin and other state universities achieved distinction in new areas of study, such as political science, economics, and sociology. Many schools, private and public, considered athletics vital to a student's growth, and men's intercollegiate sports became a permanent feature of student life and source of school pride.

Southern states, in keeping with separate but equal policies, created segregated colleges for blacks in addition to institutions for whites. Aided by land grant funds, such schools as Alabama Agricultural and Mechanical University (A&M), South Carolina State University, and the A&M College for the Colored Race (North Carolina) opened their doors. "Separate" was a more accurate description of these institutions than "equal" as African Americans continued to suffer from inferior educational opportunities. Nevertheless, African American men and women found intellectual stimulation in all-black colleges and used education to promote the advancement of their race.

As higher education expanded, so did female enrollments. Between 1890 and 1910, the number of women attending colleges and universities swelled from 56,000 to 140,000. Of these, 106,000 attended coeducational institutions (mostly state universities); the rest enrolled in women's colleges, such as Wellesley and Barnard. By 1920, 283,000 women attended college, accounting for 47 percent of total enrollment. But discrimination lingered in admissions and curriculum policies. Women were encouraged (indeed, they usually sought) to take home economics and education courses rather than science and mathematics, and most medical schools refused to admit women or imposed stringent quotas. Separate women's medical schools, such as the Women's Medical College of Philadelphia and Women's Medical College of Chicago, trained female physicians, but most of these schools were absorbed or put out of business by larger institutions dominated by men.

American educators justifiably congratulated themselves for increasing enrollments and making instruction more meaningful. By 1920, 78 percent of children between ages five and seventeen were enrolled in public schools; another 8 percent attended private and parochial schools. These figures represented a huge increase over 1870 attendance rates. There were 600,000 college and graduate students in 1920, compared with only 52,000 in 1870. Yet few people

△ These members of the University of Michigan's Class of 1892 represent the student body of a publicly funded college in the late nineteenth century. With their varied curricula, inclusion of women, and increasing enrollments, such schools transformed American higher education in the Progressive Era.

looked beyond the numbers to assess how well schools were doing their job. Critical analysis seldom tested the faith that schools could promote equality as well as personal growth and responsible citizenship.

18-3c Progressive Legal Thought

The legal profession also embraced new emphases on experience and scientific principles. Harvard law professor Roscoe Pound and Oliver Wendell Holmes Jr., associate justice of the Supreme Court (1902–1932), led an attack on traditional views of law as universal and unchanging. "The life of the law," wrote Holmes, sounding like Dewey, "has not been logic; it has been experience." The opinion that law should reflect society's needs challenged the practice of invoking inflexible legal precedents that often obstructed social legislation. Louis D. Brandeis, a lawyer who later joined Holmes on the Supreme Court, insisted that judges' opinions be based on scientifically gathered information about social realities. Using this approach, Brandeis collected extensive data on harmful effects of long working hours to convince the Supreme Court, in *Muller v. Oregon,* to uphold Oregon's ten-hour limit on women's workday.

New legal thinking provoked some resistance. Judges loyal to laissez-faire economics and strict interpretation of the Constitution overturned laws that Progressives thought necessary for effective reform. Thus, despite Holmes's forceful dissent, in 1905 the Supreme Court, in *Lochner v. New York,* revoked a state law limiting bakers' working hours. In this and similar cases, the Court's majority argued that the Fourteenth Amendment protected an individual's right to make employment contracts without government interference. Judges also weakened federal regulations by invoking the Tenth Amendment, which prohibited the federal government from interfering in matters reserved to the states.

Courts did uphold some regulatory measures, particularly those intended to safeguard life and limb. A string of decisions, beginning with *Holden v. Hardy* (1898), in which the Supreme Court sustained a Utah law regulating working hours for miners, confirmed the use of state police power to protect health, safety, and morals. Judges also affirmed federal police power and Congress's authority over interstate commerce by upholding legislation, such as the Pure Food and Drug Act, the Meat Inspection Act, and the Mann Act. In these instances citizens' welfare took precedence over the Fourteenth and Tenth Amendments.

But the concept of general welfare often conflicted with the principle of equal rights when majorities imposed their will on minorities. Even if one agreed that laws should address society's needs, whose needs should prevail? The United States was (and remains) a mixed nation where interests of gender, race, religion, and ethnicity often conflict. Thus outcries resulted when a native-born Protestant majority imposed Bible reading in public schools (offending Catholics and Jews), required businesses to close on Sundays, limited women's rights, restricted religious practices of Mormons and other groups, prohibited interracial marriage, and enforced

racial segregation. Justice Holmes asserted that laws should be made for "people of fundamentally differing views," but fitting such laws to a nation of so many different interest groups sparked debates that continue to this day.

18-3d Social Science

Social science—the study of society and its institutions—experienced changes similar to those affecting education and law. In economics, scholars used statistics to argue that laws governing economic relationships were not timeless. Instead, they claimed, theory should reflect prevailing social conditions. Economist Richard T. Ely, for example, argued that poverty and impersonality resulting from industrialization required intervention by "the united efforts of Church, state, and science." A new breed of sociologists led by Lester Ward, Albion Small, and Edward A. Ross agreed, adding that citizens should work to cure social ills rather than passively wait for problems to solve themselves.

Meanwhile, historians Frederick Jackson Turner, Charles A. Beard, and Vernon L. Parrington examined the past to explain present American society. Beard, like other Progressives, believed that the Constitution was a flexible document amenable to growth and change, not a sacred code imposed by wise forefathers. His *Economic Interpretation of the Constitution* (1913) argued that a group of merchants and business-oriented lawyers created the Constitution to defend private property. If the Constitution had served special interests in one age, he argued, it could be changed to serve broader interests in another age.

Public health organizations such as the National Consumers League (NCL) joined physicians and social scientists to bring about some of the most far-reaching Progressive reforms. Founded by Florence Kelley in 1899, the NCL pursued protection of female and child laborers and elimination of health hazards in the marketplace. After aiding in the success of *Muller v. Oregon,* the organization supported reform lawyers Louis Brandeis and Felix Frankfurter in court cases to protect women workers. Local NCL branches united with women's clubs to advance consumer protection measures, such as the licensing of food vendors and inspection of dairies. They also urged city governments to fund neighborhood clinics that provided health education and medical care to the poor.

18-3e Eugenics

The Social Gospel served as a response to Social Darwinism, the application of natural selection and survival of the fittest to human interactions. But another movement that flourished during the Progressive Era, eugenics, sought to apply Darwinian principles to society in a more intrusive way. The brainchild of Francis Galton, an English statistician and cousin of Charles Darwin, eugenics rested on the belief that human character and habits could be inherited. If good traits could be inherited, so could unwanted traits, such as criminality and mental illness. Just as some Progressives believed that society had an obligation to intervene and erase poverty and injustice, eugenicists believed that society had an obligation to prevent the reproduction of those thought to be mentally defective and criminally inclined by preventing them from marrying and, in extreme cases, sterilizing them. Such ideas targeted immigrants and people of color. Though supported by such American notables as Alexander Graham Bell, Margaret Sanger, and **W. E. B. Du Bois**, eugenics was discredited, especially after it became a linchpin of Nazi racial policies, but modern genetic engineering has evolved from some of the eugenics legacy.

Some reformers saw immigration restriction as an acceptable way of controlling the composition of American society. A leading restrictionist was Madison Grant, whose *The Passing of the Great Race* (1916) strongly bolstered theories that immigrants from southern and eastern Europe threatened to weaken American society because they were inferior mentally and morally to earlier Nordic immigrants. Such ideas prompted many people, including some Progressives, to conclude that new laws should curtail the influx of Poles, Italians, Jews, and other eastern and southern Europeans, as well as Asians. Efforts to limit immigration reached fruition in the 1920s, when restrictive legislation drastically closed the door to "new" immigrants.

Thus, a new breed of men and women pressed for political reform and institutional change in the two decades before the First World War. Concerned middle-class professionals, confident that new ways of thinking and planning could bring about progress, and representatives of working classes, who experienced social problems firsthand, helped broaden government's role to meet the needs of a mature industrial society. But their questioning of prevailing assumptions also unsettled conventional attitudes toward race and gender.

18-4 Challenges to Racial and Sex Discrimination

▷ **What were the competing views among African Americans regarding assimilation to new environments?**

▷ **How did Native Americans address questions of identity in the Progressive Era?**

▷ **How did the views and actions of the women's movement shift after 1910?**

White male reformers of the Progressive Era dealt primarily with issues of politics and institutions, and in so doing often ignored issues directly affecting former slaves, nonwhite immigrants, American Indians, and women. Yet activists within these groups caught the Progressive spirit, challenged entrenched customs, and made strides toward their own advancement. Their efforts, however, posed a dilemma. Should women and nonwhites aim to imitate white men, with white men's values as well as their rights? Or was there something unique about racial and sexual cultures that they should preserve at the risk of sacrificing broader gains? Both

groups fluctuated between attraction to and rejection of the culture that excluded them.

18-4a Continued Discrimination for African Americans

In 1900, nine-tenths of African Americans lived in the South, where repressive Jim Crow laws had multiplied in the 1880s and 1890s (see "Discrimination and Disfranchisement," Section 17-4). Denied legal and voting rights, and officially segregated in almost all walks of life, southern blacks faced constant exclusion as well as relentless violence from lynching and countless acts of intimidation. In 1910, only 8,000 out of 970,000 high-school-age blacks were enrolled in southern high schools. In response, many African Americans moved northward in the 1880s, accelerating their migration after 1900. The conditions they found in places like Chicago, Cleveland, and Detroit represented relative improvement over rural sharecropping, but they still confronted job discrimination, inferior schools, and segregated housing.

African American leaders differed sharply over how—and whether—to pursue assimilation in their new environments. In the wake of emancipation, ex-slave Frederick Douglass urged "ultimate assimilation through self-assertion, and on no other terms." Others favored separation from white society and supported emigration to Africa or the establishment of all-black communities in Oklahoma Territory and Kansas. Others advocated militancy, believing, as Lewis H. Douglass, Frederick Douglass's son, wrote in the wake of a vicious attack on African Americans in Atlanta in 1906, "Our people must die to be saved and in dying must take as many along with them as it is possible to do with the aid of firearms and all other weapons."

18-4b Booker T. Washington and Self-Help

Most black people could neither escape nor conquer white society. They sought other routes to economic and social improvement. Self-help, a strategy articulated by educator **Booker T. Washington**, offered one popular alternative. Born into slavery in Virginia in 1856, Washington obtained an education and in 1881 founded Tuskegee Institute, an all-black vocational school, in Alabama. There he developed a philosophy that blacks' best hope for assimilation lay in at least temporarily accommodating to whites. Rather than fighting for political rights, Washington counseled African Americans to work hard, acquire property, and prove they were worthy of respect. Washington voiced his views in a speech at the Atlanta Exposition in 1895. "Dignify and glorify common labor," he

W. E. B. Du Bois African American educator and activist who demanded full racial equality, including the same educational opportunities open to whites, and called on black people to resist all forms of racism.

Booker T. Washington Leading African American activist of the late nineteenth century who advocated education and accommodation with white society as the best strategy for racial advancement.

urged, in what became known as the Atlanta Compromise. "Agitation of questions of racial equality is the extremest folly." Envisioning a society where blacks and whites would remain apart but share similar goals, Washington observed that "in all things that are purely social we can be as separate as the fingers, yet one as the hand in all matters essential to mutual progress."

Whites welcomed Washington's accommodation policy because it advised patience and reminded black people to stay in their place. Because he said what they wanted to hear, white businesspeople, reformers, and politicians chose to regard Washington as representing all African Americans. Although Washington endorsed a separate-but-equal policy, he projected a subtle racial pride that would find more direct expression in black nationalism in the twentieth century, when some African Americans would advocate control of their own businesses and schools. Washington never argued that blacks were inferior; rather, he asserted that they could enhance their dignity through self-improvement.

Some blacks, however, concluded that Washington endorsed second-class citizenship. His southern-based philosophy did not appeal to educated northern African Americans like newspaper editors William Monroe Trotter in Boston and T. Thomas Fortune in New York. In 1905, a group of "anti-Bookerites" convened near Niagara Falls and pledged militant pursuit of such rights as unrestricted voting, economic opportunity, integration, and equality before the law. Representing the Niagara movement was W. E. B. Du Bois, an outspoken critic of the Atlanta Compromise.

18-4c W. E. B. Du Bois and the "Talented Tenth"

A New Englander and the first African American to receive a PhD from Harvard, Du Bois was both a Progressive and a member of the black elite. He first studied at all-black Fisk University, then in Germany, where he learned about scientific investigation. While a faculty member at Atlanta University, Du Bois compiled fact-filled sociological studies of black urban life and wrote poetically in support of civil rights. He treated Washington politely but could not accept accommodation. "The way for a people to gain their reasonable rights," Du Bois asserted, "is not by voluntarily throwing them away." Instead, blacks must agitate for what was rightfully theirs. Du Bois believed that an intellectual vanguard of cultured, educated blacks, the "Talented Tenth," should lead in the pursuit of racial equality. In 1909, he joined white liberals who also were discontented with Washington's accommodationism to form the **National Association for the Advancement of Colored People (NAACP).** The organization aimed to end racial discrimination, eradicate lynching, and obtain voting rights

National Association for the Advancement of Colored People (NAACP) Organization that called for sustained activism, including legal challenges, to achieve political equality for black people and full integration into American life.

through legal redress in the courts. By 1914, the NAACP had fifty branch offices and six thousand members.

Within the NAACP and in other ways, African Americans struggled with questions about their place in white society. Du Bois voiced this dilemma poignantly, admitting that "one ever feels his twoness—an American, a Negro, two souls, two thoughts, two unreconciled strivings, two warring ideals in one dark body." Somehow blacks had to reconcile that two-ness by combining racial pride with national identity. As Du Bois wrote in 1903, a black "would not Africanize America, for America has too much to teach the world and Africa. He would not bleach his Negro soul in a flood of white Americanism, for he knows that Negro blood has a message for the world. He simply wishes to make it possible for a man to be both a Negro and an American." That simple wish would haunt the nation for decades to come.

18-4d Society of American Indians

The dilemma of identity also vexed American Indians, but had an added tribal dimension. Since the 1880s, most Native American reformers had belonged to white-led organizations. In 1911, however, some middle-class Native Americans formed their own association, the Society of American Indians (SAI), to work for better education, civil rights, and health care. Under leadership of prominent professionals, who called themselves "Red Progressives," the SAI sought to promote unity among all Native peoples and, like white Progressives, invested faith in inevitable progress. To this end, the society advocated an annual "American Indian Days" to cultivate pride and offset images of savage peoples promulgated in Wild West shows.

The SAI's emphasis on racial pride, however, was squeezed between pressures for assimilation on one side and tribal allegiance on the other. Its small membership did not fully represent the diverse and unconnected Native American groups, and its attempt to establish a unifying governing body fizzled. Some tribal governments no longer existed to select representatives, and most SAI members simply promoted their self-interest. At the same time, the goal of achieving acceptance in white society proved elusive. Individual hard work was not enough to overcome prejudice and condescension, and attempts to redress grievances through legal action faltered for lack of funds. Ultimately, the SAI offered little to poverty-stricken Native Americans on reservations and elsewhere, who seldom knew that the organization even existed. Torn by internal disputes, the association folded in the early 1920s.

18-4e "The Woman Movement"

Challenges to established social assumptions also raised questions of identity among women. The ensuing quandaries resembled those faced by racial minorities: What tactics should women use to achieve rights? What should be women's role in society? Should they try to achieve equality within a male-dominated society? Or should they assert particular female virtues to create a new place for themselves within society?

Heavyweight Boxing Champion Jack Johnson as Race Hero

It is probable that more African Americans in the 1910s paid attention to Jack Johnson than they did to either Booker T. Washington or W. E. B. Du Bois. In 1908, Jackson became the first black heavyweight champion of the world by knocking out Tommy Burns. Immediately, white boxing fans began searching for a "Great White Hope" to recapture the title, and in 1910, former champion James J. Jeffries came out of retirement to fight Johnson, boasting that he would "demonstrate that a white man is king of them all." But after fifteen rounds of

pummeling from Johnson, Jeffries gave up. African Americans around the nation celebrated their hero's victory, and in some places race riots erupted as angry whites attacked jubilant revelers. Racist reaction was particularly venomous because Johnson refused to accept white standards for the way a black man should behave. He courted and married white women, flaunted his taste for fast cars and fancy clothing, and dealt with opponents and reporters with a pompous attitude. In 1915, Johnson, then thirty-seven years old, lost his title to Jess Willard in Cuba. The fight took

place outside the country because in 1913 Johnson had been convicted of violating the Mann Act for allegedly transporting Belle Schreiber, a white prostitute, across state lines for "immoral purposes." Sentenced to a year in jail, Johnson fled the country, but he returned in 1920 to serve his sentence.

CRITICAL THINKING

▫ How do these three images reveal racial attitudes, both black and white, toward Jack Johnson?

▫ What messages do they convey to the viewer?

Library of Congress, Prints & Photographs Division, Reproduction number LC-DIG-ppmsca-31941 (digital file from original photo)LC-USZ62-28040 (b&w film copy neg.)

△ Jack Johnson, posing with his white wife, Etta.

Bettmann/Getty Images

△ Jack Johnson successfully defends his championship against Jim Jeffries.

Library of Congress, Prints & Photographs Division, Reproduction number LC-USZ62-130087 (b&w film copy neg.)

△ A crowd rushes to see their popular hero, Jack Johnson.

The answers that women found involved a subtle but important shift in their politics. Before 1910, crusaders for women's rights referred to themselves as "the woman movement." This label applied to middle-class women who strove to move beyond the household into higher education and paid professions. Like African American and Native American leaders, women argued that legal and voting rights were indispensable to such moves. They based their claims on the theory that women's special, even superior, traits as guardians of family and morality would humanize society. Settlement house founder Jane Addams, for example, endorsed woman suffrage by asking, "If women have in any sense been responsible for the gentler side of life which softens and blurs some of its harsher conditions, may not they have a duty to perform in our American cities?"

18-4f "Social Housekeeping"

Because female activists were generally barred from holding public office (except in a few western states), they asserted traditional female responsibilities for home and family as the rationale for reforming society through an enterprise that historians have called "social housekeeping." Rather than advocate reforms like trust-busting and direct primaries, female reformers formed organizations and worked collectively for factory inspection, regulation of children's and women's labor, improved housing, and consumer protection.

Such efforts were not confined to white women. Mostly excluded from white women's organizations, African American women had their own associations, including the Colored Women's Federation, which sought, among other goals, to establish a training school for "colored girls." Founded in 1895, the National Association of Colored Women was the nation's first African American social service organization; it concentrated on establishing nurseries, kindergartens, and retirement homes. Black women also developed reform organizations within Black Baptist and African Methodist Episcopal churches.

18-4g Feminism

Around 1910, some of those concerned with women's place in society began using the term *feminism* to represent their ideas. Whereas the woman movement spoke generally of duty and moral purity, feminists emphasized rights and self-development as key to economic and sexual independence. Charlotte Perkins Gilman, a major figure in the movement, denounced Victorian notions of womanhood and articulated feminist goals in her numerous writings. Her book *Women and Economics* (1898), for example, declared that domesticity and female innocence were obsolete, and attacked men's monopoly on economic opportunity. Arguing that paid employees should handle domestic chores, such as cooking, cleaning, and childcare, Gilman asserted that modern women must have access to jobs in industry and the professions.

18-4h Margaret Sanger's Crusade

Feminists also supported a single standard of behavior for men and women, and several feminists joined the birth control movement led by Margaret Sanger. A former visiting nurse who believed in a woman's right to sexual pleasure and to determine when to have a child, Sanger helped reverse state and federal laws that had banned publication and distribution of information about sex and contraception. Her speeches and actions aroused opposition from those who saw birth control as a threat to family and morality. Ironically, while she advocated greater reproductive freedom for women, her beliefs had a darker side; she also was a eugenicist who perceived birth control as a means of limiting the numbers of children born to "inferior" immigrant and nonwhite mothers. Regardless, Sanger persevered and in 1921 formed the American Birth Control League, enlisting physicians and social workers to convince judges to allow distribution of birth control information. Most states still prohibited the sale of contraceptives, but Sanger succeeded in introducing the issue into public debate.

18-4i Women's Suffrage

A new generation of Progressive feminists, represented by Harriot Stanton Blatch, daughter of nineteenth-century suffragist Elizabeth Cady Stanton, carried on women's battle for the vote. Blatch had broad experience in suffrage activities, having accompanied her mother on speaking tours, and participated in the British women's suffrage movement. In America, Blatch linked voting rights to the improvement of women's working conditions. She joined the Women's Trade Union League and founded the Equality League of Self Supporting Women in 1907. Declaring that every woman worked, whether she performed paid labor or unpaid housework, Blatch believed that all women's efforts contributed to society's betterment. In her view, achievement rather than wealth and refinement was the best criterion for public status. Thus, women should exercise the vote, not to enhance the power of elites, but to promote and protect women's economic roles.

△ The rise of the settlement house movement provided young middle-class women with opportunities to aid inner-city working-class neighborhoods and formed the basis of the social work profession. In this photograph, a settlement worker is teaching neighborhood girls how to knit.

By the early twentieth century, suffragists had achieved some successes. Nine states, all in the West, allowed women to vote in state and local elections by 1912, and women continued to press for national suffrage (see Map 18.1). Their tactics ranged from letter writing and publications of the National American Woman Suffrage Association, led by **Carrie Chapman Catt**, to spirited meetings and militant marches of the National Woman's Party, led by Alice Paul and Harriot Stanton Blatch. All these activities heightened public awareness. More decisive, however, was women's service during the First World War as factory laborers, medical volunteers, and municipal workers. By convincing legislators that women could successfully shoulder public responsibilities, women's wartime contributions gave final impetus to passage of the national suffrage amendment (the Nineteenth Amendment) in 1920.

In spite of these accomplishments, the activities of women's organizations, feminists, and suffragists failed to create an interest group united or powerful enough to overcome men's political, economic, and social power. During the Progressive Era, the efforts of leaders like Blatch, Paul, and Catt helped clarify issues that concerned women and finally won women the right to vote, but that victory was only a step, not a conclusion. Discrimination in employment, education, and law continued to shadow women for decades to come. As feminist Crystal Eastman observed in the aftermath of the suffrage crusade: "Men are saying perhaps, 'Thank God, this everlasting women's fight is over!' But women, if I know them, are saying, 'Now at last we can begin.'... Now they can say what they are really after, in common with all the rest of the struggling world, is freedom."

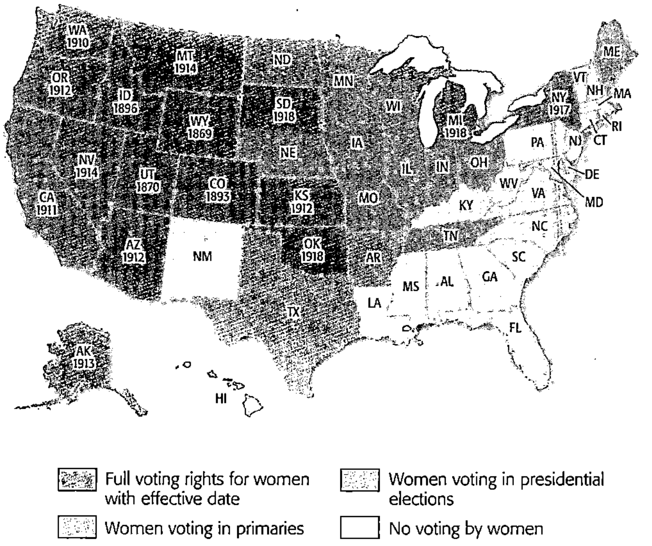

Map 18.1 Woman Suffrage Before 1920

Before Congress passed and the states ratified the Nineteenth Amendment, woman suffrage already existed, but mainly in the West. Several midwestern states allowed women to vote only in presidential elections, but legislatures in the South and the Northeast generally refused such rights until forced to do so by constitutional amendment.

18-5 Theodore Roosevelt and Revival of the Presidency

▶ How did Roosevelt employ the power of the federal government in the affairs of business and industry?

▶ What role did the federal government play in the use and regulation of the environment?

▶ What divisions emerged in the Republican Party after the election of William Howard Taft?

▶ How did New Nationalism differ from New Freedom?

The Progressive Era's theme of reform in politics, institutions, and social relations drew attention to government, especially the federal government, as the foremost agent of change. Although the federal government had notable accomplishments during the preceding Gilded Age, its role had been mainly to support rather than control economic expansion, as when it transferred western public lands and resources to private ownership. Then, in September 1901, the political climate suddenly shifted. The assassination of President William McKinley by anarchist Leon Czolgosz vaulted **Theodore Roosevelt**, the young vice president (he was forty-two), into the White House. As governor of New York, Roosevelt had angered state Republican bosses by showing sympathy for regulatory legislation, so they rid themselves of him by pushing him into national politics. Little did they anticipate that they provided the stepping-stone for the nation's most forceful president since Abraham Lincoln, one who imbued the office with much of its twentieth-century character.

18-5a Theodore Roosevelt

As a youth, Roosevelt suffered from asthma and nearsightedness. Driven throughout his life by an obsession to overcome his physical limitations, he exerted what he and his contemporaries called "manliness," meaning a zest for action and display of courage in a "strenuous life." In his teens, he became a marksman and horseman, and as a college student competed on Harvard's boxing and wrestling teams. In the 1880s, he went to live on a Dakota ranch, where he roped cattle and brawled with cowboys. Descended from a Dutch aristocratic family, Roosevelt had wealth to indulge in such pursuits. But he also inherited a sense of civic responsibility that guided him into a career in public service. He served three terms in the New York legislature, sat on the federal Civil Service Commission, served as New York City's police commissioner, was assistant secretary of the navy, and won election as governor of New York. In these offices Roosevelt earned a reputation as a combative, politically crafty leader. In 1898, he thrust himself into the

Carrie Chapman Catt President of the National American Woman Suffrage Association in the early twentieth century.

Theodore Roosevelt Youthful successor to slain president William McKinley in 1901; twenty-sixth president of the United States, 1901–1909; promoted an agenda of progressive reform.

△ Looking eager for battle in his neatly-pressed new uniform from the elite haberdasher Brooks Brothers, Theodore Roosevelt served as a colonel in the U.S. Volunteers and joined the U.S. Army's campaign to oust Spain from Cuba in 1898. His bravado helped propel his political career into the governorship of New York and vice presidency of the United States.

Spanish-American War by organizing a volunteer cavalry brigade, called the Rough Riders, to fight in Cuba. Although his dramatic act had little impact on the war's outcome, it excited public imagination and made him a media hero.

Roosevelt carried his youthful exuberance into the White House. (A British diplomat once quipped, "You must always remember that the president is about six.") Considering himself a Progressive, he concurred with his allies that a small, uninvolved government would not suffice in the industrial era. Instead, economic progress necessitated a government powerful enough to guide national affairs. "A simple and poor society," he observed, "can exist as a democracy on the basis of sheer individualism. But a rich and complex society cannot so exist." Especially in economic matters, Roosevelt wanted government to act as an umpire, deciding when big business was good and when it was bad. But his brash patriotism and dislike of qualities that he considered effeminate also recalled earlier eras of unbridled expansion, when raw power prevailed in social and economic affairs.

Hepburn Act Legislation that strengthened regulatory powers of the Interstate Commerce Commission, particularly over railroads, and later other businesses and industries.

18-5b Regulation of Trusts

The federal regulation of business that has continued to the present began with Roosevelt's presidency. Roosevelt turned attention first to massive trusts created in previous decades by corporate consolidation. Although labeled a "trustbuster," Roosevelt actually considered business consolidation an efficient means to achieve material progress, but he distinguished between good and bad trusts; bad ones were those that unfairly manipulated markets. Thus, he instructed the Justice Department to use antitrust laws to prosecute railroad, meatpacking, and oil trusts, which he believed exploited the public. Roosevelt's policy triumphed in 1904 when the Supreme Court, convinced by the government's arguments, ordered the breakup of Northern Securities Company, the huge railroad combination created by J. P. Morgan. Roosevelt chose, however, not to attack other trusts, such as U.S. Steel, another of Morgan's creations.

When prosecution of Northern Securities began, Morgan reportedly collared Roosevelt and offered, "If we have done anything wrong, send your man to my man and they can fix it up." The president refused but was more sympathetic to cooperation between business and government than his rebuff might suggest. Rather than prosecute at every turn, he urged the Bureau of Corporations (part of the newly created Department of Labor and Commerce) to assist companies in merging and expanding. Through investigation and consultation, the administration cajoled businesses to regulate themselves; corporations often cooperated because government regulation helped them operate more efficiently and reduced overproduction.

Roosevelt also supported regulatory legislation, especially after his resounding victory in the presidential election of 1904, in which he won votes from Progressives and businesspeople alike. After a year of wrangling with railroads and their political allies, Roosevelt persuaded Congress to pass the **Hepburn Act** (1906), which strengthened the Interstate Commerce Commission (ICC) by giving it authority to inspect railroad financial records and set "just and reasonable" freight rates and extending that authority over ferries, express companies, storage facilities, and oil pipelines. The Hepburn Act still allowed courts to overturn ICC decisions, but in a break from previous laws, it required shippers to prove they were not in violation of regulations, rather than making the government demonstrate violations.

18-5c Pure Food and Drug Laws

Knowing that the political process made it difficult to achieve full business regulation, Roosevelt showed willingness to compromise on legislation to ensure the purity of food and drugs. For decades, reformers had been urging government regulation of processed meat and patent medicines. Public outrage at fraud and adulteration flared in 1906 when Upton Sinclair published *The Jungle,* a fictionalized exposé of Chicago meatpacking plants. Sinclair, a socialist whose objective was to improve working conditions, shocked public sensibilities with vivid descriptions. He wrote in one passage:

> There would be meat stored in great piles in rooms; and the water from the leaky roofs would drip over it, and thousands of rats would race about on it. It was too dark in these storage places to see well, but a man could run his hand over these piles of meat and sweep off handfuls of dried dung of rats. These rats were a nuisance, and the packers would put poisoned bread out for them; they would die, and then rats, bread, and meat would go into the hoppers together.

After reading the novel, Roosevelt ordered an investigation. Finding Sinclair's descriptions accurate, he supported the Meat Inspection Act, which, after considerable political maneuvering, passed Congress in 1906. Like the Hepburn Act, this law reinforced the principle of government regulation, requiring that government agents monitor the quality of processed meat. But as part of a compromise with meatpackers and their congressional allies, the bill provided that the government, rather than the meatpackers, had to finance inspections, and meatpackers could appeal adverse decisions in court. Nor were companies required to provide date-of-processing information on canned meats. Most large meatpackers welcomed the legislation anyway because it restored foreign confidence in American meat products.

The Pure Food and Drug Act (1906) not only prohibited dangerously adulterated foods but also addressed abuses in the patent medicine industry. Makers of tonics and pills had long been making undue claims about their products' effects and liberally using alcohol and narcotics as ingredients. Ads in popular publications, like one for a "Brain Stimulator and Nerve Tonic" in the Sears, Roebuck catalogue, made wildly exaggerated claims. Although the law did not ban such products, it required that labels list the ingredients—a goal consistent with Progressive confidence that if people knew the facts, they would make wiser purchases.

Roosevelt's approach to labor resembled his compromises with business over matters of regulation. When the United Mine Workers struck against Pennsylvania coal mine owners in 1902 over an eight-hour workday and higher pay, the president urged arbitration between the conflicting parties. Owners, however, refused to recognize the union or to discuss grievances. As winter approached and nationwide fuel shortages threatened, Roosevelt roused public opinion. He threatened to use federal troops to reopen the mines, thus forcing management to accept arbitration of the dispute by a special commission. The commission decided in favor of higher wages and reduced hours and required management to deal with grievance committees elected by the miners. But in a compromise with management, it did not mandate recognition of the union. The decision, according to Roosevelt, provided a "square deal" for all. The settlement also embodied Roosevelt's belief that the president or his representatives should determine which labor demands were legitimate and which were not. In Roosevelt's mind, there were good and

△ Makers of unregulated patent medicines advertised their products' exorbitant abilities to cure almost any ailment and remedy any unwanted physical condition. Loring's Fat-Ten-U tablets and Loring's Corpula were two such products. The Pure Food and Drug Act of 1906 did not ban these items but tried to prevent manufacturers from making unsubstantiated claims.

bad labor organizations (socialists, for example, were bad), just as there were good and bad business combinations.

18-5d Race Relations

Although he angered southern congressmen by inviting Booker T. Washington to the White House to discuss racial matters, Roosevelt believed in white superiority and was neutral toward blacks only when it helped him politically. An incident in 1906 illustrates this belief. That year, the army transferred a battalion of African American soldiers from Nebraska to Brownsville, Texas. Anglo and Mexican residents resented their presence and banned them from parks and businesses. They also protested unsuccessfully to Washington. On August 14, a battle between blacks and whites broke out, and a white man was killed. Brownsville residents blamed the soldiers, but when army investigators asked the troops to identify who had participated in the riot, none of the soldiers cooperated. As a result, Roosevelt discharged 167 black soldiers without a hearing or trial, and prevented them from receiving their pay and pensions even though there was no evidence against them. Black leaders were outraged. Roosevelt, hoping that African Americans would support Republican candidates in the 1906 elections, had stalled before doing anything. But after the elections, he signed the discharge papers and offered no support when a bill was introduced in the Senate to allow the soldiers to reenlist.

18-5e Conservation

Roosevelt combined the Progressive impulse for efficiency with his love for the outdoors to make lasting contributions to resource conservation. Government involvement in this endeavor, especially the establishment of national parks, had begun in the late nineteenth century. Roosevelt advanced the movement by favoring *conservation* over *preservation*. He not only exercised presidential power to protect such natural wonders as the Olympic Peninsula in Washington and the Grand Canyon in Arizona, as well as such human marvels as the native cliff dwellings in Colorado and Arizona, by declaring them national monuments; he also backed a policy of "wise use" of forests, waterways, and other resources to conserve them for future generations. Previously, the government had transferred ownership and control of natural resources on federal land to the states and private interests. Roosevelt, however, believed the most efficient way to use and conserve resources would be for the federal government to retain management over lands that remained in the public domain.

Roosevelt used federal authority over resources in several ways. He created five national parks and fifty-one national bird reservations, and protected waterpower sites from sale to private interests. He also supported the Newlands Reclamation Act of 1902, which controlled sale of irrigated federal land in the West (see "Newlands Reclamation Act," Section 15-2f), and in 1908 brought the nation's governors to the White House to discuss the efficient use of resources. During his presidency, Roosevelt tripled the number and acreage of national forests and backed conservationist Gifford Pinchot in creating the U.S. Forest Service.

18-5f Gifford Pinchot

As chief forester of the United States and principal advocate of "wise use" policy, Pinchot promoted scientific management of the nation's woodlands. He obtained Roosevelt's support for transferring management of the national forests from the Interior Department to his bureau in the Agriculture Department, arguing that forests were crops grown on "tree farms." Under his guidance, the Forest Service charged fees for grazing livestock within national forests, supervised bidding for the cutting of timber, and hired university-trained foresters as federal employees.

Pinchot and Roosevelt did not seek to lock up— preserve—resources permanently; rather, they wanted to guarantee—conserve—their efficient use and make those who profited from using public lands pay the government for that privilege. Although antigovernment, pro-development attitudes still prevailed in the West, many of those involved in natural resource development welcomed such a policy because, like regulation of food and drugs, it enabled them to manage their operations more effectively, such as when Roosevelt and Pinchot encouraged lumber companies to engage in reforestation. As a result of new federal policies, the West and its resources fell under the Progressive spell of expert management.

18-5g Panic of 1907

In 1907, economic crisis forced Roosevelt to compromise his principles and work more closely with big business. That year, a financial panic caused by reckless speculation forced some New York banks to close in order to prevent frightened depositors from withdrawing money. J. P. Morgan helped stem the panic by persuading financiers to stop dumping stocks. In return for Morgan's aid, Roosevelt approved a deal allowing U.S. Steel to absorb the Tennessee Iron and Coal Company— a deal at odds with Roosevelt's trust-busting aims.

But during his last year in office, Roosevelt retreated from the Republican Party's traditional friendliness to big business. He lashed out at "malefactors of great wealth" and supported stronger business regulation and heavier taxation of the rich. Having promised that he would not seek reelection, Roosevelt backed his friend, Secretary of War **William Howard Taft**, for the Republican nomination in 1908, hoping that Taft would continue his initiatives. Democrats nominated William Jennings Bryan for the third time, but the "Great Commoner" lost again. Aided by Roosevelt, who still enjoyed great popularity, Taft won by 1.25 million popular votes and a 2-to-1 margin in the electoral college.

18-5h Taft Administration

Early in 1909, Roosevelt traveled to Africa to shoot game, leaving Taft to face political problems that Roosevelt had managed to postpone. Foremost was the tariff; rates had risen to excessive levels. Honoring Taft's pledge to cut tariffs, the House passed a bill sponsored by New York representative Sereno E. Payne that provided for numerous reductions. Protectionists in the Senate prepared, as in the past, to amend the bill and revise rates upward. But Senate Progressives, led by La Follette, attacked the tariff for benefiting special interests, trapping Taft between reformers who claimed to be preserving Roosevelt's antitrust campaign and protectionists who still dominated the Republican Party. In the end, Senator Aldrich restored most cuts the Payne bill had made, and Taft—who believed the bill had some positive provisions and understood that extreme cuts

William Howard Taft Roosevelt's handpicked successor for president (1909–1913); later served as chief justice of the U.S. Supreme Court.

were not politically possible—signed what became known as the Payne-Aldrich Tariff (1909). In Progressives' eyes, Taft had failed the test of filling Roosevelt's shoes.

Progressive and conservative wings of the Republican Party openly split. Soon after the tariff controversy, a group of insurgents in the House, led by Nebraska's George Norris, challenged Speaker "Uncle Joe" Cannon of Illinois, whose power over committee assignments and the scheduling of debates could make or break a piece of legislation. Taft first supported, then abandoned, the insurgents, who nevertheless managed to liberalize procedures by enlarging the influential Rules Committee and removing selection of its members from Cannon's control. In 1910, Taft also angered conservationists by firing Gifford Pinchot, who had protested Secretary of the Interior Richard A. Ballinger's plans to aid private development by selling Alaskan coal lands and reducing federal supervision of western waterpower sites.

In reality, Taft was as sympathetic to reform as Roosevelt was. He prosecuted more trusts than Roosevelt; expanded national forest reserves; signed the Mann-Elkins Act (1910), which bolstered regulatory powers of the ICC; and supported such labor reforms as shorter work hours and mine safety legislation. The Sixteenth Amendment, which legalized the federal income tax as a permanent source of federal revenue, and the Seventeenth Amendment, which provided for direct election of U.S. senators, were initiated during Taft's presidency (and ratified in 1913). Like Roosevelt, Taft compromised with big business, but unlike Roosevelt, he lacked the ability to rouse the public with spirited rhetoric. Roosevelt had expanded presidential power and infused the presidency with vitality. "I believe in a strong executive," he once asserted. "I believe in power." Taft, by contrast, believed in the restraint of law. He had been a successful lawyer and judge, and returned to the bench as chief justice of the United States between 1921 and 1930. His caution and unwillingness to offend disappointed those accustomed to Roosevelt's magnetism.

18-5i Candidates in 1912

In 1910, when Roosevelt returned from Africa, he found his party torn and tormented. Reformers, angered by Taft's apparent insensitivity to their causes, formed the National Progressive Republican League and rallied behind Robert La Follette for president in 1912, though many hoped Roosevelt would run. Another wing of the party remained loyal to Taft. Disappointed by Taft's performance (particularly his firing of Pinchot), Roosevelt began to speak out. He filled speeches with references to "the welfare of the people" and stronger regulation of business. When La Follette became ill early in 1912, Roosevelt, proclaiming himself fit as a "bull moose," threw his hat into the ring for the Republican presidential nomination.

Taft's supporters controlled the Republican convention and nominated him for a second term. In protest, Roosevelt's supporters bolted the convention to form a third party—the Progressive, or Bull Moose, Party—and nominated the fifty-three-year-old former president. Meanwhile, Democrats took forty-six ballots to select their candidate, New Jersey's

Progressive governor **Woodrow Wilson**. Socialists, by now an organized and growing party, again nominated Eugene V. Debs. The ensuing campaign exposed voters to the most thorough debate on the nature of American democracy since 1896.

18-5j New Nationalism Versus New Freedom

Central to Theodore Roosevelt's campaign as Progressive Party nominee was a scheme called the "New Nationalism," a term coined by reform editor Herbert Croly. The New Nationalism envisioned an era of national unity in which government would coordinate and regulate economic activity. Echoing his statements made in the last years of his presidency, Roosevelt asserted that he would establish regulatory commissions of experts who would protect citizens' interests and ensure wise use of economic power. "The effort at prohibiting all combinations has substantially failed," he claimed. "The way out lies . . . in completely controlling them."

Wilson offered a more idealistic proposal, the "New Freedom," based on ideas of Progressive lawyer Louis Brandeis. Wilson argued that concentrated economic power threatened individual liberty and that monopolies should be broken up so that the marketplace could become genuinely open. But he would not restore laissez-faire. Like Roosevelt, Wilson would enhance government authority to protect and regulate. "Freedom today," he declared, "is something more than being let alone. Without the watchful . . . resolute interference of the government, there can be no fair play between individuals and such powerful institutions as the trust." Wilson stopped short, however, of advocating the cooperation between business and government inherent in Roosevelt's New Nationalism.

Roosevelt and Wilson stood closer together than their rhetoric implied. Despite his faith in experts as regulators, Roosevelt's belief in individual freedom was as strong as Wilson's. And Wilson was not completely hostile to concentrated economic power. Both men supported equality of opportunity (chiefly for white males), conservation of natural resources, fair wages, and social betterment. Neither would hesitate to expand government intervention through strong personal leadership and bureaucratic reform.

Amid passionate moral pronouncements from Roosevelt and Wilson, as well as a hard-hitting critique from Debs and a low-key defense of conservatism from Taft, the popular vote was inconclusive. The victorious Wilson won just 42 percent, though he did capture 435 out of 531 electoral votes (see Map 18.2). Roosevelt received 27 percent of the popular vote. Taft finished third, polling 23 percent and only 8 electoral votes. Debs won 6 percent but no electoral votes. One major outcome was evident, however; three-quarters of the electorate supported some alternative to the view of restrained government that Taft represented. Thus, Wilson could proclaim on Inauguration Day in 1913, "The Nation has been deeply stirred by a solemn passion. . . . The feelings with which we face this new age

Woodrow Wilson Democratic president whose election in 1912 ushered in a second wave of progressive reforms on the national level; served as president until 1921.

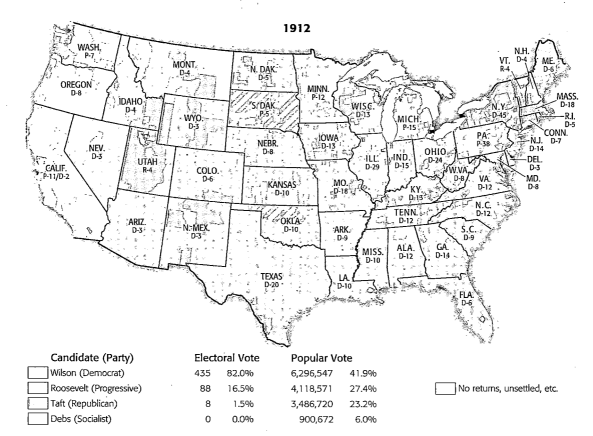

1912

Candidate (Party)	Electoral Vote		Popular Vote	
Wilson (Democrat)	435	82.0%	6,296,547	41.9%
Roosevelt (Progressive)	88	16.5%	4,118,571	27.4%
Taft (Republican)	8	1.5%	3,486,720	23.2%
Debs (Socialist)	0	0.0%	900,672	6.0%

No returns, unsettled, etc.

Map 18.2 Presidential Election, 1912

Although he had only a minority of the popular votes, Woodrow Wilson captured so many states that he achieved an easy victory in the electoral college.

of right and opportunity sweep across our heartstrings like some air out of God's own presence, where justice and mercy are reconciled and the judge and the brother are one."

18-6 Woodrow Wilson and Extension of Progressive Reform

▷ How did Woodrow Wilson's personality differ from that of Theodore Roosevelt?

▷ What economic regularity policies and reforms did Woodrow Wilson implement?

▷ What was Woodrow Wilson's position on race?

18-6a Woodrow Wilson

The public fondly called Roosevelt "Teddy" and "TR," but Thomas Woodrow Wilson was too aloof to be nicknamed "Woody" or "WW." Born in Virginia in 1856 and raised in the South, Wilson was the son of a Presbyterian minister. He earned a BA degree at Princeton, studied law at the University

of Virginia, received a PhD from Johns Hopkins University, and became a professor of history, jurisprudence, and political economy before returning to Princeton, where he served as the university's president from 1902 to 1910. Between 1885 and 1908, he published several respected books on American history and government.

Wilson's manner and attitudes reflected his background. On one hand, he was a superb orator who could inspire loyalty from white people with religious imagery and eloquent expressions of American ideals. But he harbored strong disdain for African Americans; he wrote that southern slaves had been treated "indulgently," belittled blacks who held office during Reconstruction, opposed admitting blacks to Princeton, and had no misgivings about Jim Crow laws. At Princeton, he upset tradition with curricular reforms and battles against the university's aristocratic elements, and he earned enough of a reputation as a reformer so that in 1910 New Jersey's Democrats, eager for respectability, nominated him for governor. After winning the election, Wilson repudiated the party bosses and promoted Progressive legislation. A poor administrator, he often lost his temper and stubbornly refused to compromise. His accomplishments nevertheless attracted national attention and won him the Democratic nomination for president in 1912.

18-6b Wilson's Policy on Business Regulation

As president, Wilson found it necessary to blend New Freedom competition with New Nationalism regulation; in so doing, he set the direction of future federal economic policy. Corporate consolidation had made restoration of open competition impossible. Wilson could only try to prevent abuses by expanding government's regulatory powers. He thus supported congressional passage in 1914 of the Clayton Anti-Trust Act and a bill creating the **Federal Trade Commission (FTC)**. The Clayton Act corrected deficiencies of the Sherman Anti-Trust Act of 1890 by outlawing such practices as price discrimination (lowering prices in some regions but not in others) and interlocking directorates (management of two or more competing companies by the same executives). The act also aided labor by exempting unions from its anti-combination provision, thereby making peaceful strikes, boycotts, and picketing less vulnerable to government interference. The FTC could investigate companies and issue cease and desist orders against unfair practices. Accused companies could appeal FTC orders in court; nevertheless, the FTC represented another step toward consumer protection.

Also under Wilson, the Federal Reserve Act (1913) established the nation's first central banking system since 1836. To break the power that syndicates like that of J. P. Morgan held over the money supply, the act created twelve district banks to hold reserves of member banks throughout the nation. The district banks, supervised by the Federal Reserve Board, would lend money to member banks at low interest, called the discount rate. By adjusting this rate (and thus the amount a member bank could afford to borrow), district banks could increase or decrease the supply of money in circulation. In other words, in response to the nation's economic needs, the Federal Reserve Board could loosen or tighten credit, making interest rates fairer, especially for small borrowers.

18-6c Tariff and Tax Reform

Wilson and Congress attempted to restore trade competition and aid consumers with the Underwood Tariff of 1913. By reducing or eliminating certain tariff rates, the Underwood Tariff encouraged importation of cheaper foreign materials and manufactured goods. To replace revenues lost because of tariff reductions, the act levied a graduated income tax on U.S. residents—an option made possible when the Sixteenth Amendment, which empowered Congress to create such a tax, was ratified earlier that year. The tax was tame by today's standards. Incomes under $4,000 ($98,000 in current dollars) were exempt; thus, almost all factory workers and most farmers escaped taxation. Individuals and corporations earning between $4,000 and $20,000 had to pay a 1 percent tax; thereafter rates rose to a maximum of 6 percent on earnings over $500,000.

The outbreak of the First World War (see Chapter 20) and approaching presidential election campaign prompted Wilson to support stronger reforms in 1916. To aid farmers, he backed the Federal Farm Loan Act. This measure created twelve federally supported banks (not to be confused with Federal Reserve banks), which could lend money at moderate interest

△ Woodrow Wilson on the left, looking stiff and formal, stands with William Howard Taft, looking more at ease, outside the White House at Wilson's inauguration in March of 1917.

to farmers who belonged to credit institutions—a diluted version of the subtreasury plan that Populists had proposed a generation earlier (see "Farmers' Alliances," Section 17-5d). To forestall railroad strikes that might disrupt transportation at a time of national emergency, Wilson also pushed passage of the Adamson Act, which mandated eight-hour workdays and time-and-a-half overtime pay for railroad laborers. He pleased Progressives by appointing Brandeis, the "people's advocate," to the Supreme Court, though an anti-Semitic backlash almost blocked Senate approval of the Court's first Jewish justice. In addition, Wilson backed laws that regulated child labor and provided workers' compensation for federal employees who suffered work-related injuries or illness.

Amid his reforms, however, Wilson never overcame his racism. He fired several black federal officials, and his administration preserved racial separation in Washington, D.C. restrooms, restaurants, and government buildings. Wilson responded to protesting blacks that "segregation is not a humiliation but a benefit, and ought to be so regarded by you gentlemen." When the pathbreaking but inflammatory film about the Civil War and Reconstruction *The Birth of a Nation* was released in 1915, Wilson allowed a showing at the White House, though he subsequently prohibited it during the First World War.

Federal Trade Commission (FTC) Agency formed in 1914 to ensure fair trade practices.

Margaret Sanger, Planned Parenthood, and the Birth Control Controversy

Some reforms of the Progressive Era illustrate how earnest intentions to help can become tangled in divisive issues of morality. Such is the legacy of birth control advocate Margaret Sanger. In 1912, Sanger began writing a column on sex education in the *New York Call* entitled "What Every Girl Should Know." Almost immediately, moralists accused her of producing obscene literature because she publicly discussed venereal disease and contraception. The issue of limiting family size, however, became her passion, and she began counseling poor women on New York's Lower East Side about how to avoid the pain of frequent childbirth, miscarriage, and bungled abortion. In 1914, Sanger published the first issue of *The Woman Rebel*, a monthly newspaper that advocated a woman's right to practice birth control. Indicted for distributing obscenity through the mails, she fled to England. There she joined a set of radicals and gave speeches on behalf of family planning and a woman's need to enjoy sexual fulfillment without fear of pregnancy.

Returning to the United States, Sanger opened the country's first birth control clinic in Brooklyn in 1916. She was arrested, but when a court exempted physicians from a law prohibiting dissemination of contraceptive information, she set up a doctor-run clinic in 1923. Staffed by female doctors and social workers, the Birth Control Clinical Research Bureau acted as a model for other clinics. Sanger also organized the American Birth Control League (1921) and tried to win support from medical and social reformers, including some from the eugenics movement, for legalized

birth control. Eventually, her radical views caused her to fall out with some of her allies, and she resigned from the American Birth Control League in 1928.

The movement continued, however, and in 1938 the American Birth Control League and the Birth Control Clinical Research Bureau merged to form the Birth Control Federation of America, renamed the Planned Parenthood Federation of America (PPFA) in 1942. The organization's name defined its mission to strengthen the family and stabilize society with the help of governmental support, rather than to focus more directly on the feminist issue of whether or not a woman should have the right of voluntary motherhood. Throughout the 1940s, the PPFA emphasized family planning through making contraceptives more accessible. In 1970, it began receiving funds under a federal program to provide family-planning services.

In the 1960s, the emergence of new feminist agitation for women's rights and rising concerns about overpopulation moved issues of birth control and abortion into an arena of passionate controversy. Although the PPFA had initially dissociated itself from abortion as a means of family planning, the debate between a woman's "choice" and a fetus's "right to life" drew the organization into the fray, especially after 1973, when the Supreme Court validated women's right to an abortion in *Roe v. Wade*. The national PPFA and its local branches have fought legislative and court attempts to make abortions illegal ever since; most recently, in another landmark case in 2016, the Supreme Court overturned a Texas law that had restricted women's access to

clinics that provided abortions. In 1989, the PPFA helped organize a women's march on Washington for equality and abortion rights, but at the same time, some Latino and African American groups attacked the PPFA's stance, charging that legalized abortion was a kind of eugenics program meant to reduce births among nonwhite races.

Because of the PPFA's involvement in abortion politics, several of its clinics have been targets of picketing and even violence by those who believe abortion to be immoral. Also, debates have raged over whether government funding for Planned Parenthood clinics should be eliminated because the money might directly or indirectly be used to fund abortions. The PPFA now operates nearly nine hundred health centers providing medical services and education nationwide to more than 5 million women, most of whom are poor, and has fulfilled Margaret Sanger's dream of legalized contraception and family planning. But as with other reforms dealing with issues of morality and individual rights, birth control has left a legacy to a people and a nation of disagreement over whose rights and whose morality should prevail.

CRITICAL THINKING

- Should a person's health care decisions belong exclusively to that person or should the government play a role?
- If the government should play a role, how do we determine when the government should intervene in matters of a citizen's health?
- Consider this debate in terms of abortion rights; the use of alcohol, drugs, or tobacco; obesity, and medically-assisted suicide.

18-6d Election of 1916

In selecting a candidate to oppose Wilson in the presidential election of 1916, Republicans snubbed Theodore Roosevelt in favor of Charles Evans Hughes, Supreme Court justice and former reform governor of New York. Aware of public anxiety over the world war raging in Europe since 1914, Wilson ran on

a platform of neutrality, using the slogan "He Kept Us Out of War." Hughes advocated military preparedness, but Wilson's peace platform resonated with voters. The election was close. Wilson received 9.1 million votes to Hughes's 8.5 million and barely won in the electoral college, 277 to 254. The Socialist Party candidate, newspaperman Allan Benson, drew only

600,000 votes, down from 901,000 in 1912, largely because Wilson's reforms had won over some socialists and because the ailing Eugene Debs was no longer the party's standard-bearer.

During Wilson's second term, U.S. involvement in the First World War increased government regulation of the economy. Mobilization and war, he believed, required government-directed coordination of production and cooperation between the public and private sectors. The War Industries Board exemplified this cooperation: private businesses regulated by the board submitted to its control on condition that their profit motives would continue to be satisfied. After the war, Wilson's administration dropped most cooperative and regulatory measures, including farm price supports, guarantees of collective bargaining, and high taxes. This retreat from regulation, prompted in part by the election of a Republican Congress in 1918, stimulated a new era of business ascendancy in the 1920s.

Summary

By 1920, a quarter-century of reform had wrought momentous changes in the ways government, the economy, and society operated. In their efforts to end abuses of power, reform institutions, and apply scientific and efficient planning and management, Progressives established the principle of public intervention to ensure fairness, health, and safety. As well, concern over poverty and injustice reached new heights.

Multiple and sometimes contradictory goals characterized the era. By no means was there a single Progressive movement. Programs on the national level ranged from Roosevelt's faith in big government as a coordinator of big business to Wilson's promise to dissolve economic concentrations and legislate open competition. At state and local levels, reformers pursued causes as varied as neighborhood improvement, government reorganization, public ownership of utilities, and betterment of working conditions. National associations coordinated efforts on specific issues, but reformers with different goals often worked at cross-purposes, sometimes expanding rights but at other times restricting liberty. Women and African Americans developed a new consciousness about identity, and although women made some inroads into public life, both groups still found themselves in confined social positions and lacking white male support for their quest for dignity and recognition.

In spite of their successes, the failure of many Progressive initiatives indicates the strength of the opposition as well as weaknesses within reform movements themselves. As issues such as Americanization, eugenics, prohibition, education, and moral uplift illustrate, social reform often meant social control—attempting to impose one group's values on all of society and to regulate behavior of immigrant and nonwhite racial groups. In political matters, courts asserted constitutional and liberty-of-contract doctrines in undercutting key Progressive legislation, notably the federal law prohibiting child labor. In states and cities, adoption of the initiative, referendum, and recall did not encourage greater participation in government as had been hoped; those mechanisms either were seldom used or became tools of special interests. Federal regulatory agencies lacked enough resources for thorough investigation and enforcement; they had to depend on information from the very companies they policed. Progressives thus failed in many respects to redistribute power. In 1920, as in 1900, government remained under the influence of business, a situation that many people in power considered quite satisfactory.

Yet the reform movements that characterized the Progressive Era reshaped the national outlook. Trust-busting, however faulty, made industrialists more sensitive to public opinion, and insurgents in Congress partially diluted the power of dictatorial politicians. Progressive legislation equipped government with tools to protect consumers against price fixing and dangerous products. Social reformers relieved some ills of urban and industrial life. And perhaps most important, Progressives challenged old ways of thinking. Although the questions they raised about the quality of American life remained unresolved, Progressives made the nation acutely aware of its principles and promises.

Suggestions for Further Reading

Nancy F. Cott, *The Grounding of Modern Feminism* (1987)

Steven J. Diner, *A Very Different Age: Americans of the Progressive Era* (1998)

Laurie Collier Hillstrom, *The Muckrakers and the Progressive Era* (2010)

Hugh D. Hindman, *Child Labor: An American History* (2002)

Alice Kessler-Harris, *Out to Work: A History of Wage-Earning Women in the United States*, 20th anniversary ed. (2003)

Michael McGerr, *A Fierce Discontent: The Rise and Fall of the Progressive Movement in America, 1870–1920* (2003)

Sidney Milkis and Jerome Mileur, eds., *Progressivism and the New Democracy* (1999)

Patricia A. Schecter, *Ida B. Wells and American Reform, 1880–1930* (2001)

David Tyack, *Seeking Common Ground: Public Schools in a Diverse Society* (2003)

Robert H. Wiebe, *The Search for Order, 1877–1920* (1967)

The Quest for Empire, 1865–1914

"D evil!" they shouted at Lottie Moon. "Foreign devil!" The Southern Baptist missionary, half a world away from home, braced herself against the cries of the Chinese "rabble" whom she had been determined to convert to Christianity. On that day in the 1880s, she walked "steadily and persistently" through the throng of hecklers, silently vowing to win their acceptance and then their souls.

Born in 1840 in Virginia and educated at what is now Hollins College, Charlotte Diggs Moon volunteered in 1873 for "woman's work" in northern China. There she taught and proselytized, largely among women and children, because women seldom preached to men and men were forbidden to preach to women. This compassionate, pious, and courageous single woman, "putting love into action," worked in China until her death in 1912.

In the 1870s and 1880s, Lottie Moon (Mu Ladi, or 幕拉第) made bold and sometimes dangerous evangelizing trips to isolated Chinese hamlets. "O! The torture of human eyes upon you; scanning every feature, every look, every gesture!" Curious peasant women pinched her, pulled on her skirts, and purred, "How white her hand is!" They peppered her with questions: "How old are you?" "Where do you get money to live on?" Speaking in Chinese, Lottie held high a picture book of Jesus Christ's birth and crucifixion, drawing the crowd's attention to the "foreign doctrine" that she hoped would displace Confucianism, Buddhism, and Taoism.

In the 1890s, a "storm of persecution" directed against foreigners swept China. Because missionaries were upending traditional ways and authority, they became hated targets. One missionary conceded that, in "believing Jesus," girls and women alarmed men who worried that "disobedient wives and daughters" would no longer "worship the idols when told." In the village of Shaling in early 1890, Lottie Moon's Christian converts were beaten and the "foreign devils" ordered to move out. Fearing for her life, she

◁ The missionary Lottie Moon (1840–1912) in 1901 with English-language students in Japan, during her refuge from the Boxer Rebellion in China. Virginia Baptist Historical Society

Chronology

1861–69	Seward sets expansionist course
1867	United States acquires Alaska and Midway
1876	Pro-U.S. Díaz begins thirty-four-year rule in Mexico
1878	United States gains naval rights in Samoa
1885	Strong's *Our Country* celebrates Anglo-Saxon destiny of dominance
1887	United States gains naval rights to Pearl Harbor, Hawai'i
	McKinley Tariff hurts Hawaiian sugar exports
1893	Economic crisis leads to business failures and mass unemployment
	Pro-U.S. interests stage successful coup against Queen Lili'uokalani of Hawai'i
1895	Cuban revolution against Spain begins
	Japan defeats China in war, annexes Korea and Formosa (Taiwan)
1898	United States formally annexes Hawai'i
	U.S. battleship *Maine* blows up in Havana harbor
	United States defeats Spain in Spanish-American War

1899	Treaty of Paris enlarges U.S. empire
	United Fruit Company forms and becomes influential in Central America
	Philippine Insurrection breaks out, led by Emilio Aguinaldo
1901	McKinley assassinated; Theodore Roosevelt becomes president
1903	Panama grants canal rights to United States
	Platt Amendment subjugates Cuba
1904	Roosevelt Corollary declares United States a hemispheric "police power"
1905	Portsmouth Conference ends Russo-Japanese War
1906	San Francisco School Board segregates Asian schoolchildren
	United States invades Cuba to quell revolt
1907	"Great White Fleet" makes world tour
1910	Mexican revolution threatens U.S. interests
1914	U.S. troops invade Mexico
	First World War begins
	Panama Canal opens

had to flee. For several months in 1900, during the violent Boxer Rebellion, she had to leave China altogether, as a multinational force (including U.S. troops) intervened to save foreign missionaries, diplomats, and merchants.

Lottie Moon and thousands of other missionaries managed to convert to Christianity only a very small minority of the Chinese people. Although she, like other missionaries, probably never shed the Western view that she represented a superior religion and culture, she seldom wavered in her affection for the Chinese people and in her devotion to the foreign missionary project—in her "rejoicing to suffer." In frequent letters and articles directed to a U.S. audience, she lobbied to recruit "a band of ardent, enthusiastic, and experienced Christian women," to stir up "a mighty wave of enthusiasm for

Woman's Work for Woman." To this day, the Lottie Moon Christmas Offering in Southern Baptist churches raises millions of dollars for missions abroad.

Like so many other Americans who went overseas in the late nineteenth and early twentieth centuries, Lottie Moon helped spread American culture and influence abroad. In this complex process, other peoples sometimes adopted and sometimes rejected American ways. At the same time, American participants in this cultural expansion and the cultural collisions it generated became transformed. Lottie Moon, for example, strove to understand the Chinese people and to learn their language. She assumed their dress and abandoned such derogatory phrases as "heathen Chinese" and "great unwashed." She reminded other, less sensitive missionaries that the Chinese rightfully took pride in their own ancient history and thus had no reason to "gape in astonishment at Western civilization."

Lottie Moon also changed—again, in her own words—from "a timid self-distrustful girl into a brave self-reliant woman." As she questioned the Chinese confinement of women, most conspicuous in arranged marriages, foot binding, and sexual segregation, she advanced women's rights. She understood that she could not convert Chinese women unless they had the freedom to listen to her appeals. Bucking the gender ideology of the times, she also uneasily rose to challenge the male domination of America's religious missions. When the Southern Baptist Foreign Mission Board denied female missionaries the right to vote in meetings, she resigned in protest. The board soon reversed itself.

In later decades, critics labeled the activities of Lottie Moon and other missionaries "cultural imperialism," accusing them of seeking to subvert indigenous traditions and of sparking destructive cultural clashes. Defenders of missionary work, on the other hand, have celebrated their efforts to break down cultural barriers and to bring the world's peoples closer together. Either way, Lottie Moon's story illustrates how Americans in the late nineteenth century interacted with the world in diverse ways, how through their experiences the categories "domestic" and "foreign" came to intersect, and how they expanded abroad not only to seek land, trade, investments, and strategic bases, but also to promote American culture, including the Christian faith.

Experience an interactive version of this story in MindTap®.

B etween the Civil War and the First World War, an expansionist United States joined the ranks of the great world powers. Before the Civil War, Americans had repeatedly extended the frontier: they bought Louisiana; annexed Florida, Oregon, and Texas; pushed Native Americans out of the path of white migration westward; seized California and other western areas from Mexico; and acquired southern parts of present-day Arizona and New Mexico from Mexico (the Gadsden Purchase). Americans had also developed a lucrative foreign trade with most of the world and promoted American culture wherever they traveled. They rekindled their expansionist course after the Civil War, building, managing, and protecting an overseas empire.

It was an age of empire. By the 1870s, most of Europe's powers were carving up Africa and large parts of Asia and Oceania for themselves. By 1900 the powers had conquered more than 10 million square miles (one-fifth of the earth's land) and 150 million people. As the century turned, France, Russia, and Germany were spending heavily on modern steel navies, challenging an overextended Great Britain. In Asia, meanwhile, a rapidly modernizing Japan expanded at the expense of both China and Russia.

Engineering advances altered the world's political geography through the Suez Canal (1869), the British Trans-Indian railroad (1870), and the Russian Trans-Siberian Railway (1904), while steamships, machine guns, telegraphs, and malaria drugs greatly facilitated the imperialists' task. Simultaneously, the optimistic spirit that had characterized

European political discourse in the 1850s and 1860s gave way to a brooding pessimism and a sense of impending warfare informed by notions of racial conflict and survival of the fittest.

This transformation of world politics did not escape notice by perceptive Americans. Some argued that the United States risked being "left behind" if it failed to join the scramble for territory and markets. Republican senator Henry Cabot Lodge of Massachusetts, claiming that the "great nations" were seizing "the waste areas of the world," advised that "the United States must not fall out of the line of march" because "civilization and the advancement of the [Anglo-Saxon] race" were at stake. Such thinking helped fuel Americans' desire in the years after the Civil War to exert their influence beyond the continental United States, to reach for more space, more land, more markets, more cultural penetration, and more power.

By 1900, the United States had emerged as a great power with particular clout in Latin America, especially as Spain declined and Britain disengaged from the Western Hemisphere. In the Pacific, the new U.S. empire included Hawai'i, American Samoa, and the Philippines. Theodore Roosevelt, who in the 1890s was a leading spokesman for the imperialist cause, would, as president in the decade that followed, seek to consolidate this newfound power.

Most Americans applauded expansionism—the outward movement of goods, ships, dollars, people, and ideas—as a traditional feature of their nation's history. But many became uneasy whenever expansionism gave way to imperialism—the imposition of control over other peoples, undermining their sovereignty and usurping their freedom to make their own decisions. Abroad, native nationalists, commercial competitors, and other imperial nations tried to block the spread of U.S. influence.

▣ What accounts for the increased importance of foreign policy concerns in American politics in the closing years of the nineteenth century?

▣ What key arguments were made by American anti-imperialists?

▣ How did late-nineteenth-century imperialism transform the United States?

19-1 Imperial Dreams

▷ Why did the United States take a more active role in international affairs and foreign policy in the late nineteenth century?

▷ What methods did expansionists seek to use to spread American influence abroad?

▷ What intellectual developments contributed to American activism abroad?

Foreign policy assumed a new importance for Americans in the closing years of the nineteenth century. For much of the Gilded Age, they had been preoccupied by internal matters, such as industrialization, the construction of the railroads, and the settlement of the West. Over time, however, increasing numbers of political and business leaders began to look outward, and to advocate a more activist approach to world affairs. The motives of these expansionists were complex and varied, but all of them emphasized the supposed benefits of such an approach to the country's domestic health.

That proponents of overseas expansion stressed the benefits that would accrue at home should come as no surprise, for foreign policy has always sprung from the domestic setting of a nation—its needs and moods, its ideology and culture. The leaders who guided America's expansionist foreign relations were the same ones who guided the economic development of the machine age, forged the transcontinental railroad, built the nation's bustling cities and giant corporations, and shaped a mass culture. They unabashedly espoused the idea that the United States was an exceptional nation, so different from and superior to others because of its Anglo-Saxon heritage and its God-favored and prosperous history.

Exceptionalism was but one in an intertwined set of ideas that figured prominently in the American march toward empire. Nationalism, capitalism, Social Darwinism, and a paternalistic attitude toward foreigners influenced American

leaders as well. "They are children and we are men in these deep matters of government," future president Woodrow Wilson announced in 1898. The very words he chose reveal the gender and age bias of American attitudes. Where these attitudes intersected with foreign cultures, there came not only adoption but rejection, not only imitation but conflict, as Lottie Moon learned.

19-1a Foreign Policy Elite

It would take time for most Americans to grasp the changes under way. "The people" may influence domestic policy directly, but the making of foreign policy is usually dominated by what scholars have labeled the "foreign policy elite"— opinion leaders in politics, journalism, business, agriculture, religion, education, and the military. In the post–Civil War era, this small group, whom Secretary of State Walter Q. Gresham called "the thoughtful men of the country," expressed the opinions that counted. Better read and better traveled than most Americans, more cosmopolitan in outlook, and politically active, they believed that U.S. prosperity and security depended on the exertion of U.S. influence abroad. Increasingly in the late nineteenth century, and especially in the 1890s, the expansionist-minded elite urged both formal and informal imperialism. Ambitious and clannish, the imperialists often met in Washington, D.C., at the homes of historian Henry Adams and of writer and diplomat John Hay (who became secretary of state in 1898) or at the Metropolitan Club. They talked about building a bigger navy and digging a canal across Panama, Central America, or Mexico; establishing colonies; and selling surpluses abroad. Theodore Roosevelt, appointed assistant secretary of the navy in 1897, was among them; so were Senator Henry Cabot Lodge, who joined the Foreign Relations Committee in 1896, and corporate lawyer Elihu Root, who later would serve as both secretary of war and secretary of state. Such well-positioned luminaries kept up the drumbeat for empire.

These American leaders believed that selling, buying, and investing in foreign marketplaces were important to the United States. Why? One reason was profits from foreign sales. "It is my dream," declared the governor of Georgia in 1878, to see "in every valley . . . a cotton factory to convert the raw material of the neighborhood into fabrics which shall warm the limbs of Japanese and Chinese." Fear also helped make the case for foreign trade, as foreign commerce might serve as a safety valve to relieve overproduction, unemployment, economic depression, and the social tension that arose from them. The nation's farms and factories produced more than Americans could consume, all the more so during the 1890s depression. Surpluses had to be exported, the economist David A. Wells warned, or "we are certain to be smothered in our own grease." Economic ties also permitted political influence to be exerted abroad and helped spread the American way of life, especially capitalism, creating a world more hospitable to Americans. In an era when the most powerful nations in the world were also the greatest traders, vigorous foreign economic expansion symbolized national stature.

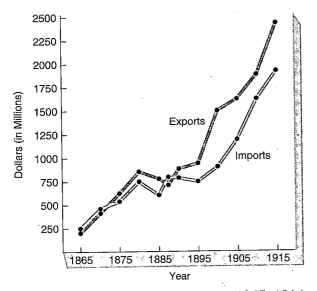

Figure 19.1 U.S. Trade Expansion, 1865–1914

This figure illustrates two key characteristics of U.S. foreign trade: first, that the United States began in the 1870s to enjoy a favorable balance of trade (exporting more than it imported), and second, that U.S. exports expanded tremendously, making the United States one of the world's economic giants. Adapted from Thomas G. Paterson, J. Garry Clifford, and Kenneth J. Hagan, *American Foreign Relations: A History,* 5th ed. Copyright 2000 by Houghton Mifflin Company.

19-1b Foreign Trade Expansion

Although most business leaders remained focused on the domestic marketplace, foreign trade figured prominently in the tremendous economic growth of the United States after the Civil War. Foreign commerce in turn stimulated the building of a larger protective navy, the professionalization of the foreign service, calls for more colonies, and a more interventionist foreign policy. In 1865, U.S. exports totaled $234 million; by 1900, they had climbed to $1.5 billion (see Figure 19.1). By 1914, at the outbreak of the First World War, exports had reached $2.5 billion, prompting some Europeans to protest an American "invasion" of goods. In 1874, the United States reversed its historically unfavorable balance of trade (importing more than it exported) and began to enjoy a long-term favorable balance (exporting more than it imported)—though the balance of payments remained in the red. Most of America's products went to Britain, continental Europe, and Canada, but increasing amounts flowed to new markets in Latin America and Asia. Meanwhile, direct American investments abroad reached $3.5 billion by 1914, placing the United States among the top four investor countries.

Agricultural goods accounted for about three-fourths of total exports in 1870 and about two-thirds in 1900, with grain, cotton, meat, and dairy products topping the export list that year. More than half of the annual cotton crop was exported each year. Midwestern farmers transported their crops by railroad to seaboard cities and then on to foreign markets. Farmers' livelihoods thus became tied to world market conditions and the outcomes of foreign wars. Wisconsin cheesemakers shipped to Britain; the Swift and Armour meat companies exported refrigerated beef to Europe. To sell American grain abroad, James J. Hill of the Great Northern Railroad distributed wheat cookbooks translated into several Asian languages.

In 1913, when the United States outranked both Great Britain and Germany in manufacturing production, manufactured goods led U.S. exports for the first time. Substantial proportions of America's steel, copper, and petroleum were sold abroad, making many workers in those industries dependent on American exports. George Westinghouse marketed his air brakes in Europe; almost as many Singer sewing machines were exported as were sold at home; and Cyrus McCormick's "reaper kings" harvested the wheat of Russian fields (see Figure 19.2).

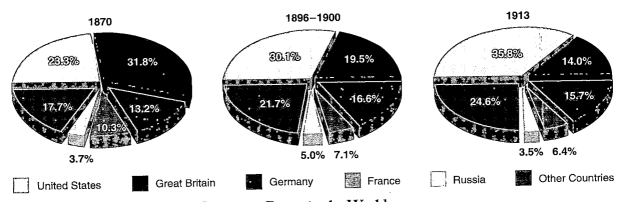

Figure 19.2 The Rise of U.S. Economic Power in the World

These pie charts showing percentage shares of world manufacturing production for the major nations of the world demonstrate that the United States came to surpass Great Britain in this significant economic measurement of power. Adapted from Aaron L Friedberg, *The Weary Titan,* Princeton University Press, 1989 paperback edition. Reprinted by permission of Princeton University Press.

Messages in Advertising

The American march toward empire was also reflected in advertising. On the front and back covers of this 1901 promotional booklet, the Singer Sewing Machine Company is marketing not only its product but the idea that a sewing machine can unite nations.

The image that emerges of the United States is that of peacemaker and unifier.

CRITICAL THINKING

□ In the 1892 Singer sewing machine advertisement card, the Zulu people are sewing American-style clothes. What message is being sent here, do you think?

□ How does it compare to the recent advertising campaigns by firms such as Starbucks, Nike, and Subaru that push the product in question only indirectly and instead show people around the world connecting despite their differences?

△ This Singer advertisement from 1892 shows people in national costumes using treadle machines.

△ Singer sewing machine advertisement card, showing six people from Zululand (South Africa) with a Singer sewing machine.

19-1c Race Thinking and the Male Ethos

In promoting the expansion of U.S. influence overseas, many officials championed a nationalism based on notions of American supremacy. Some, echoing the articulations of European imperialists (who had their own conceptions of national supremacy), found justification for expansionism in racist theories then permeating Western thought and politics. For decades, the Western scientific establishment had classified humankind by race, and students of physical anthropology drew on phrenology and physiognomy—the analysis of skull size and shape, and the comparison of facial features—to produce a hierarchy of superior and inferior races. One well-known French researcher, for example, claimed that blacks represented a "female race" and "like the woman, the black is deprived of political and scientific intelligence; he has never created a great state . . . he has never accomplished anything in industrial mechanics. But on the other hand he has great virtues of sentiment. Like women he also likes jewelry, dancing, and singing."

The language of U.S. leaders was also weighted with words like *manliness* and *weakling*. Congressman Augustus P. Gardner, son-in-law of Senator Lodge and Spanish-American War veteran, extolled the "arena of lust and blood, where true men are to be found." The warrior and president Theodore Roosevelt viewed people of color (or "darkeys," as he called them) as effeminate weaklings who lacked the ability to govern themselves and could not cope with world politics. Americans regularly debased Latin Americans as half-breeds needing close supervision, distressed damsels begging for manly rescue, or children requiring tutelage. The gendered imagery prevalent in U.S. foreign relations joined race thinking to place women, people of color, and nations weaker than the United States in the low ranks of the hierarchy of power and, hence, in a necessarily dependent status justifying U.S. dominance.

Reverend Josiah Strong's popular and influential *Our Country* (1885) celebrated an Anglo-Saxon race destined to lead others. "As America goes, so goes the world," he declared. A few years later, he wrote that "to be a Christian and an Anglo-Saxon and an American . . . is to stand at the very mountaintop of privilege." Social Darwinists saw Americans as a superior people certain to overcome all competition. Secretary of State Thomas F. Bayard (1885–1889) applauded the "overflow of our population and capital" into Mexico to "saturate those regions with Americanism." But, he added, "we do not want them" until "they are fit."

Race thinking—popularized in magazine photos and cartoons, world's fairs, postcards, school textbooks, museums, and political orations—reinforced notions of American greatness, influenced the way U.S. leaders dealt with other peoples, and obviated the need to think about the subtle textures of other societies. The magazine *National Geographic*, which published its first issue in 1888, chronicled with photographs America's new overseas involvements in Asia and the Pacific. Even when smiling faces predominated in these shots, the image portrayed was that of strange, exotic, premodern peoples who had not become "Western." Fairs also put so-called uncivilized people of color on display in the "freak" or "midway" section. Dog-eating Filipinos aroused particular comment at the 1904 St. Louis World's Fair. Such racism downgraded diplomacy and justified domination and war because self-proclaimed superiors do not negotiate with people ranked as inferiors.

The same thinking permeated attitudes toward immigrants, whose entry into the United States was first restricted in these years. Although the Burlingame Treaty (1868) had provided for free immigration between the United States and China, riots against Chinese immigrants erupted again and again in the American West—in Los Angeles (1871), San Francisco (1877), Denver (1880), and Seattle (1886). A new treaty in 1880 permitted Congress to suspend Chinese immigration to the United States, and it did so two years later. A violent incident occurred in Rock Springs, Wyoming, in 1885, when white coal miners and railway workers rioted and massacred at least twenty-five Chinese.

In 1906, the San Francisco School Board, reflecting the anti-Asian bias of many West Coast Americans, ordered the segregation of all Chinese, Koreans, and Japanese in special schools. Tokyo protested the discrimination against its citizens. The following year, President Roosevelt quieted the crisis by striking a "gentleman's agreement" with Tokyo restricting the inflow of Japanese immigrants; San Francisco then rescinded its segregation order. Relations with Tokyo were jolted again in 1913 when the California legislature denied Japanese residents the right to own property in the state.

19-1d The "Civilizing" Impulse

With a mixture of self-interest and idealism typical of American thinking on foreign policy, expansionists believed that empire benefited both Americans and those who came under their control. When the United States intervened in other lands or lectured weaker states, Americans claimed that in remaking foreign societies they were extending liberty and prosperity to less-fortunate people. William Howard Taft, as civil governor of the Philippines (1901–1904), described the United States' mission in its new colony as lifting Filipinos up "to a point of civilization" that will make them "call the name of the United States blessed." Later, after becoming secretary of war (1904–1908), Taft said about the Chinese that "the more civilized they become . . . the wealthier they become, and the better market they become for us." "The world is to be Christianized and civilized," declared Reverend Josiah Strong. "And what is the process of civilizing but the creating of more and higher wants."

Missionaries dispatched to Africa and Asia, like Lottie Moon, helped spur the transfer of American culture and power abroad—"the peaceful conquest of the world," as Reverend Frederick Gates put it. One organization, the Student Volunteers for Foreign Missions, began in the 1880s on college campuses and by 1914 had placed some 6,000 missionaries abroad. In 1915 a total of 10,000 American

National Geographic

On a winter day in early 1888, thirty-three members of the elite Cosmos Club in Washington, D.C., convened around a mahogany table to consider "the advisability of organizing a society for the increase and diffusion of geographical knowledge." The result was the National Geographic Society, destined to become the largest nonprofit scientific and educational institution in the world.

At the heart of the enterprise would be a magazine designed to win broad support for the society. *National Geographic Magazine* (later simply *National Geographic*) appeared for the first time in October 1888. Early issues were brief, technical, and visually bland, and sales lagged. In 1898, however, Alexander Graham Bell became president of the society and made two key changes: he shifted emphasis from newsstand sales to society membership, reasoning correctly that armchair travelers would flock to join a distinguished fellowship, and he appointed a talented new editor, Gilbert H. Grosvenor, age twenty-three. Grosvenor commissioned articles of general interest and, in an unprecedented move, filled eleven pages of one issue with photographs.

These and other early photos showed people stiffly posed in their native costumes, displayed as anthropological specimens. But they caused a sensation. By 1908, pictures occupied 50 percent of the magazine's space. In 1910, the first color photographs appeared, in a twenty-four-page spread on Korea and China—at that time the largest collection of color photographs ever published in a single issue of any magazine. In later years, *National Geographic* would have several other photographic firsts, including the first natural-color photos of Arctic life and the undersea world.

The society also used membership dues to sponsor expeditions, such as the 1909 journey to the North Pole by Robert Peary and Matthew Henson and, later, Jacques Cousteau's many oceanic explorations and Jane Goodall's up-close observations of wild chimpanzees. The tales of these adventures then appeared in the magazine's pages, along with stunning photographs. By the end of Grosvenor's tenure as editor, in 1954, circulation had grown to more than 2 million.

Grosvenor's winning formula included less-admirable elements. His editors pressured photographers to provide "pictures of pretty girls" to the point at which, as one photographer recalled, "hundreds of bare-breasted women, all from poorer countries, were published at a time of booming subscription rates." Editors also developed a well-earned reputation for avoiding controversial issues and presenting a rosy view of the world. An article about Berlin published just before the start of World War II, for example, contained no criticism of the Nazi regime and no mention of its persecution of Jews. Recent years have seen the magazine take on more newsworthy items—AIDS, stem cell research, Hurricane Katrina, global warming—but in measured, generally nonpolitical tones.

Throughout, the society has continued to expand its reach, moving into the production of books, atlases, globes, and television documentaries. Targeting overseas readers, the society in 1995 launched a Japanese-language edition and subsequently added twenty-five other foreign editions. *National Geographic*, after a century of linking Americans to faraway places, now went in the other direction, connecting readers in many of those locales to the United States.

CRITICAL THINKING

- How was National Geographic a reflection of American imperialism?
- Does it continue to be so today?

◁ In 1916, as the National Geographic Society neared the end of its third decade, members gathered for this photo on the Society's front steps. On the front right is inventor Alexander Graham Bell. On the right two rows above, in the fur collar, is Gilbert H. Grosvenor.

△ Cartoonists sometimes mocked the proselytizing efforts of U.S. and European missionaries. This illustration, from 1895, shows two missionaries, one British and one American, with bags of money and their respective militaries behind them, preaching to a Chinese man. The caption reads: "According to the ideas of our missionary maniacs, the Chinaman must be converted, even if it takes the whole military and naval forces of the two greatest nations of the world to do it." Note the labels on the guns.

missionaries worked overseas. In China by 1915, more than 2,500 American Protestant missionaries—most of them female—labored to preach the gospel, teach school, and administer medical care.

19-2 Ambitions and Strategies

▷ What early actions did the national government take to advance American interests abroad?

▷ What institutions and structures were established to help the United States expand its influence abroad?

The U.S. empire grew gradually, sometimes haltingly, as American leaders defined guiding principles and built institutions to support overseas ambitions. William H. Seward, one of its chief architects, argued relentlessly for extension of the American frontier as senator from New York (1849–1861) and secretary of state (1861–1869). "There is not in the history of the Roman Empire an ambition for aggrandizement so marked as that which characterizes the American people," he once said. Seward envisioned a large, coordinated U.S. empire encompassing Canada, the Caribbean, Cuba, Central America, Mexico, Hawai'i, Iceland, Greenland, and the Pacific islands. This empire would be built not by war but by a natural process of gravitation toward the United States. Commerce would hurry the process, as would a canal across Central America, a

transcontinental American railroad to link up with Asian markets, and a telegraph system to speed communications.

19-2a Seward's Quest for Empire

Most of Seward's grandiose plans did not reach fruition in his own day. In 1867, for example, he signed a treaty with Denmark to buy the Danish West Indies (Virgin Islands), but his domestic political foes in the Senate and a hurricane that wrecked St. Thomas scuttled his effort. The Virgin Islanders, who had voted for annexation, had to wait until 1917 for official U.S. status. Also doomed to failure was Seward's scheme with unscrupulous Dominican Republic leaders to gain a Caribbean naval base at Samana Bay. The stench of corruption rising over this unsavory dealmaking wafted into the Ulysses S. Grant administration and foiled Grant's initiative in 1870 to buy the entire island nation. The Senate rejected annexation.

Anti-imperialism, not just politics, blocked Seward. Opponents of the empire argued that the country already had enough unsettled land and that creating a showcase of democracy and prosperity at home would best persuade other peoples to adopt American institutions and principles. Some anti-imperialists, sharing the racism of the times, opposed the annexation of territory populated by dark-skinned people.

Seward did enjoy some successes. In 1866, citing the Monroe Doctrine (see "Monroe Doctrine," Section 8-6h), he sent troops to the border with Mexico and demanded

OUR NEW SENATORS.

SECRETARY SEWARD—"*My dear Mr. Kamskatca, you really must dine with me. I have some of the very finest tallow candles and the loveliest train oil you ever tasted, and my whale's blubber is exquisite—and pray bring your friend Mr. Seal along with you. The President will be one of the party.*"

△ Humorists had a field day with the U.S. acquisition of Alaska. This cartoon, titled "Our New Senators," shows Secretary of State William H. Seward and President Andrew Johnson welcoming the representatives of the new territory to Washington.

that France abandon its puppet regime there. Also facing angry Mexican nationalists, Napoleon III abandoned the Maximilian monarchy that he had installed by force three years earlier. In 1867, Seward paid Russia $7.2 million for the 591,000 square miles of Alaska—land twice the size of Texas. Some critics lampooned "Seward's Icebox," but the secretary of state extolled the Russian territory's rich natural resources, and the Senate voted overwhelmingly for the treaty. That same year, Seward laid claim to the Midway Islands (two small islands and a coral atoll northwest of Hawai'i, so named because they are nearly halfway between North America and Asia) in the Pacific Ocean.

19-2b International Communications

Seward realized his dream of a world knit together by a giant communications system. In 1866, through the persevering efforts of financier Cyrus Field, an underwater transatlantic cable linked European and American telegraph networks. Backed by J. P. Morgan's capital, communications pioneer James A. Scrymser strung telegraph lines to Latin America, entering Chile in 1890. In 1903, a submarine cable reached across the Pacific to the Philippines; three years later, it extended to Japan and China. Information about markets, crises, and

Alfred Thayer Mahan U.S. Navy captain and author of *The Influence of Sea Power upon History* (1890) and an advocate of a stronger navy and imperialism.

war flowed steadily and quickly. Wire telegraphy—like radio (wireless telegraphy) later—shrank the globe. Drawn closer to one another through improved communications and transportation, nations found that faraway events had more and more impact on their prosperity and security.

More and more, American diplomats found that they could enter negotiations with their European counterparts on roughly equal terms—a sure sign that the United States had arrived on the international stage. Washington officials, for example, successfully confronted European powers in a contest over Samoa, a group of beautiful South Pacific islands located four thousand miles from San Francisco on the trade route to Australia. In 1878, the United States gained exclusive rights to a coaling station at Samoa's coveted port of Pago Pago (pronounced "Pango Pango"). Eyeing the same prize, Britain and Germany began to cultivate ties with Samoan leaders. Year by year, tensions grew as the powers dispatched warships to Samoa and aggravated factionalism among Samoa's chiefs. War seemed possible. At the eleventh hour, however, Britain, Germany, and the United States met in Berlin in 1889 and, without consulting the Samoans, devised a three-part protectorate that limited Samoa's independence. Ten years later, the three powers partitioned Samoa: the United States received Pago Pago through annexation of part of the islands (now called American Samoa and administered by the U.S. Department of the Interior); Germany took what is today independent Western Samoa; and Britain, for renouncing its claims to Samoa, obtained the Gilbert Islands and the Solomon Islands.

19-2c Alfred T. Mahan and Navalism

With eyes on all parts of the world, even on Africa, where U.S. interests were minimal, ardent expansionists embraced navalism—the campaign to build an imperial navy. Calling attention to the naval buildup by the European powers, notably Germany, they argued for a bigger, modernized navy, adding the "blue water" command of the seas to its traditional role of "brown water" coastline defense and riverine operations. Captain **Alfred Thayer Mahan** became a major popularizer for this "New Navy." Because foreign trade was vital to the United States, he argued, the nation required an efficient navy to protect its shipping; in turn, a navy required colonies for bases. "Whether they will or no," Mahan wrote, "Americans must now begin to look outward. The growing production of the country demands it." Mahan's lectures at the Naval War College in Newport, Rhode Island, where he served as president, were published as *The Influence of Sea Power upon History* (1890). This book sat on every serious expansionist's shelf, and foreign leaders read it too. Theodore Roosevelt and Henry Cabot Lodge eagerly consulted Mahan, sharing his belief in the links among trade, navy, and colonies, and his growing alarm over "the aggressive military spirit" of Germany.

Not do be outdone, Congress in 1883 moved toward naval authorization by authorizing construction of the first steel-hulled warships. American factories went to work to produce steam engines, high-velocity shells, powerful guns, and precision instruments. The navy shifted from sail power to steam and from wood construction to steel. Often named for states and cities to kindle patriotism and local support for naval expansion, New Navy ships, such as the *Maine, Oregon,* and *Boston,* thrust the United States into naval prominence, especially during crises in the 1890s.

19-3 Crises in the 1890s: Hawai'i, Venezuela, and Cuba

▷ **How did American business and government actions serve to undermine the Native government in Hawai'i?**

▷ **How did Great Britain and the United States address a boundary dispute in Venezuela?**

▷ **How were the interests of Cubans and Americans intertwined with one another in the late nineteenth century?**

▷ **What developments drew the United States into war with Spain over Cuba?**

In the depression-plagued 1890s, crises in Hawai'i and Cuba gave expansionist Americans opportunities to act on their zealous arguments for what Senator Lodge called a "large policy." Belief that the frontier at home had closed accentuated the expansionist case. In 1893, historian Frederick Jackson Turner postulated that an ever-expanding continental frontier had shaped the American character. That "frontier has gone," Turner pronounced, "and with its going has closed the first period of American history." He did not explicitly say that a new frontier had to be found overseas in order to sustain the U.S. way of life, but he did claim that "American energy will continually demand a wider field for its exercise."

19-3a Annexation of Hawai'i

Hawai'i, the Pacific Ocean archipelago of eight major islands located two thousand miles from the West Coast of the United States, emerged as a new frontier for Americans. The Hawaiian Islands had long commanded American attention—commercial, missionary religious, naval, and diplomatic. Wide-eyed U.S. expansionists envisioned ships sailing from the eastern seaboard through a Central American canal to Hawai'i and then on to the fabled China market. By 1881, Secretary of State James Blaine had already declared the Hawaiian Islands "essentially a part of the American system." By 1890, Americans owned about three-quarters of Hawai'i's wealth and subordinated its economy to that of the United States through sugar exports that entered the U.S. marketplace duty free.

In Hawai'i's multiracial society, Chinese and Japanese nationals far outnumbered Americans, who represented a mere 2.1 percent of the population. Prominent Americans on the islands—lawyers, businessmen, and sugar planters, many

of them the sons of missionaries—organized secret clubs and military units to contest the royal government. In 1887, they forced the king to accept a constitution that granted foreigners the right to vote and shifted decision-making authority from the monarchy to the legislature. The same year, Hawai'i granted the United States naval rights to Pearl Harbor. Many Native Hawai'ians (53 percent of the population in 1890) believed that the *haole* (foreigners)—especially Americans—were taking their country from them.

The McKinley Tariff of 1890 created an economic crisis for Hawai'i that further undermined the Native government. The tariff eliminated the duty-free status of Hawaiian sugar exports in the United States. Suffering declining sugar prices and profits, the American island elite pressed for annexation of the islands by the United States so that their sugar would be classified as domestic rather than foreign. When Princess Lili'uokalani assumed the throne in 1891, she sought to roll back the political power of the *haole.* The next year, the white oligarchy—questioning her moral rectitude, fearing Hawaiian nationalism, and reeling from the McKinley Tariff—formed the subversive Annexation Club.

The annexationists struck in January 1893 in collusion with John L. Stevens, the chief American diplomat in Hawai'i, who dispatched troops from the USS *Boston* to occupy Honolulu. The queen, arrested and confined, surrendered. However, rather than yield to the new provisional regime, headed by Sanford B. Dole, son of missionaries and a prominent attorney, she relinquished authority to the U.S. government. Up went the American flag. "The Hawaiian pear is now fully ripe and this is the golden hour to pluck it," a triumphant Stevens informed Washington. Against the queen's protests as well as those of Japan, President Benjamin Harrison hurriedly sent an annexation treaty to the Senate.

Sensing foul play, incoming president Grover Cleveland ordered an investigation, which confirmed a conspiracy by the economic elite in league with Stevens and noted that most Hawai'ians opposed annexation. Down came the American flag. But when Hawai'i gained renewed attention as a strategic and commercial way station to Asia and the Philippines during the Spanish-American War, President William McKinley maneuvered annexation through Congress on July 7, 1898, by means of a majority vote (the Newlands Resolution) rather than by a treaty, which would have required a two-thirds count. Under the Organic Act of June 1900, the people of Hawai'i became U.S. citizens with the right to vote in local elections and to send a nonvoting delegate to Congress. Statehood for Hawai'i came in 1959.

19-3b Venezuelan Boundary Dispute

The Venezuelan crisis of 1895 also saw the United States in an expansive mood. For decades Venezuela and Great Britain had quarreled over the border between Venezuela and British Guiana. The disputed territory contained rich gold deposits and the mouth of the Orinoco River, a commercial gateway to northern South America. Venezuela asked for U.S. help. President Cleveland decided that the "mean and hoggish" British had to be warned away. In July 1895, Secretary of State Richard Olney brashly lectured the British that the Monroe Doctrine prohibited European powers from denying self-government to nations in the Western Hemisphere. He aimed his spread-eagle words at an international audience, proclaiming the United States "a civilized state" whose "fiat is law" in the Americas. The United States, he declared, is "master of the situation and practically invulnerable as against any or all other powers." The British, seeking international friends to counter intensifying competition from Germany, quietly retreated from the crisis. In 1896, an Anglo-American arbitration board divided the disputed territory between Britain and Venezuela. The Venezuelans were barely consulted. Thus, the United States displayed a trait common to imperialists: disregard for the rights and sensibilities of small nations.

△ Queen Lili'uokalani (1838–1917), ousted from her throne in 1893 by wealthy revolutionaries, vigorously protested the U.S. annexation of Hawai'i in 1898. In her autobiography and diary, as well as in interviews, she defended Hawaiian nationalism and emphasized that American officials in 1893 had conspired with Sanford B. Dole and others to overthrow the Native monarchy.

In 1895 came another crisis forced by U.S. policy, this one in Cuba. From 1868 to 1878, the Cubans had battled Spain for their independence. Slavery was abolished but independence denied. While the Cuban economy suffered depression, repressive Spanish rule continued. Insurgents committed to *Cuba libre* waited for another chance, and José Martí, one of the heroes of Cuban history, collected money, arms, and men in the United States.

19-3c Revolution in Cuba

American financial support of the Cuban cause was but one of the many ways the lives of Americans and Cubans intersected. Their cultures, for example, melded. Cubans of all classes had settled in Baltimore, New York, Boston, and Philadelphia. Prominent Cubans on the island had sent their children to schools in the United States. When Cuban expatriates returned home, many came in American clothes, spoke English, had American names, played baseball, and had jettisoned Catholicism for Protestant denominations. Struggling with competing identities, Cubans admired American culture but resented U.S. economic hegemony (predominance).

The Cuban and U.S. economies were also intertwined. American investments of $50 million, mostly in sugar plantations, dominated the Caribbean island. More than 90 percent of Cuba's sugar was exported to the United States, and most island imports came from the United States. Havana's famed cigar factories relocated to Key West and Tampa to evade protectionist U.S. tariff laws. Martí, however, feared that "economic union means political union," for "the nation that buys, commands" and "the nation that sells, serves." Watch out, he warned, for a U.S. "conquering policy" that reduced Latin American countries to "dependencies."

Martí's fears were prophetic. In 1894, the Wilson-Gorman Tariff imposed a duty on Cuban sugar, which had been entering the United States duty free under the McKinley Tariff. The Cuban economy, highly dependent on exports, plunged into deep crisis, hastening the island's revolution against Spain and its further incorporation into "the American system."

In 1895, from American soil, Martí launched a revolution against Spain that mounted in human and material costs. Rebels burned sugar cane fields and razed mills, conducting an economic war and using guerrilla tactics to avoid head-on clashes with Spanish soldiers. "It is necessary to burn the hive to disperse the swarm," explained insurgent leader Máximo Gómez. U.S. investments went up in smoke, and Cuban-American trade dwindled. To separate the insurgents from their supporters among the Cuban people, Spanish general Valeriano Weyler instituted a policy of "reconcentration." Some three hundred thousand Cubans were herded into fortified towns and camps, where hunger, starvation, and disease led to tens of thousands of deaths. As reports of atrocity and destruction became headline news in the American yellow press, Americans increasingly sympathized with the insurrectionists. In late 1897, a new government in Madrid modified reconcentration and promised some autonomy for Cuba, but the insurgents continued to gain ground.

19-3d Sinking of the *Maine*

President.William McKinley had come to office as an imperialist who advocated foreign bases for the New Navy, the export of surplus production, and U.S. supremacy in the Western Hemisphere. Vexed by the turmoil in Cuba, he came to believe that Spain should give up its colony. At one point, he explored the purchase of Cuba by the United States for $300 million. Events in early 1898 caused McKinley to lose faith in Madrid's ability to bring peace to Cuba. In January, when antireform pro-Spanish loyalists and army personnel rioted in Havana, Washington ordered the battleship *Maine* to Havana harbor to demonstrate U.S. concern and to protect American citizens.

On February 15, an explosion ripped the *Maine*, killing 266 of 354 American officers and crew. Just a week earlier, William Randolph Hearst's inflammatory *New York Journal* had published a stolen private letter written by the Spanish minister in Washington, Enrique Dupuy de Lôme, who belittled McKinley as "weak and a bidder for the admiration of the crowd" and suggested that Spain would fight on. Congress soon complied unanimously with McKinley's request for $50 million in defense funds. The naval board investigating the *Maine* disaster then reported that a mine had caused the explosion. Vengeful Americans blamed Spain. (Later, official and unofficial studies attributed the sinking to an accidental internal explosion, most likely caused by spontaneous combustion of inadequately ventilated coal bunkers.)

19-3e McKinley's Ultimatum and War Decision

The impact of these events narrowed McKinley's diplomatic options. Though reluctant to go to war, he decided to send Spain an ultimatum. In late March, the United States insisted that Spain accept an armistice, end reconcentration altogether, and designate McKinley as arbiter. Madrid made concessions. It abolished reconcentration and rejected, then accepted, an armistice. The weary president hesitated, but he would no longer tolerate chronic disorder just ninety miles off the U.S. coast. On April 11, McKinley asked Congress for authorization to use force "to secure a full and final termination of hostilities between . . . Spain and . . . Cuba, and to secure in the island the establishment of a stable government, capable of maintaining order." American intervention, he said, meant "hostile constraint upon both the parties to the contest."

McKinley listed the reasons for war: the "cause of humanity"; the protection of American life and property; the "very serious injury to the commerce, trade, and business of our people"; and, referring to the destruction of the *Maine*, the "constant menace to our peace." At the end of his message, McKinley mentioned Spain's recent concessions but made little of them. He did not mention another possible motivation: de Lôme's depiction of him as "weak," a charge also leveled by Assistant Secretary of the Navy Theodore Roosevelt. On April 19, Congress declared Cuba free and independent and directed the president to use force to remove Spanish authority from the island. The legislators also passed the Teller Amendment, which disclaimed any U.S. intention to annex Cuba or control the island except to ensure its "pacification" (by which they meant the suppression of any actively hostile elements of the population). McKinley beat back a congressional amendment to recognize the rebel government.

◁ This 1899 print shows "the dream of the anti-expansionist," as Admiral George Dewey and General Elwell S. Otis, along with a sailor and a soldier, come ashore in the Philippines to offer their weapons and the U.S flag in surrender to Emilio Aguinaldo and a ragged but haughty group of Filipinos.

Believing that the Cubans were not ready for self-government, he argued that they needed a period of American tutoring.

19-4 The Spanish-American War and the Debate over Empire

▷ What motivated Americans to support and participate in war with Spain?

▷ What characteristics defined the debate over empire between anti-imperialists and imperialists?

Diplomacy had failed. By the time the Spanish concessions were on the table, events had already pushed the antagonists to the brink. Washington might have been more patient, and Madrid might have faced the fact that its once-grand empire had disintegrated. Still, prospects for compromise appeared dim because the advancing Cuban insurgents would settle for nothing less than full independence, and no Spanish government could have given up and remained in office. Nor did the United States welcome a truly independent Cuban government that might attempt to reduce U.S. interests. As historian Louis A. Perez Jr. has argued, McKinley's decision for war may have been "directed as much against Cuban independence as it was against Spanish sovereignty." Thus came a war some have titled (clumsily, but accurately) the "Spanish-American-Cuban-Filipino War" so as to represent all the major participants and identify where the war was fought and whose interests were most at stake.

19-4a Motives for War

The motives of Americans who favored war were mixed and complex. McKinley's April message expressed a humanitarian impulse to stop the bloodletting, a concern for commerce and property, and the psychological need to end the nightmarish anxiety once and for all. Republican politicians advised McKinley that their party would lose the upcoming congressional elections unless he solved the Cuba question. Many businesspeople, who had been hesitant before the crisis of early 1898, joined many farmers in the belief that ejecting Spain from Cuba would open new markets for surplus production.

Inveterate imperialists saw the war as an opportunity to fulfill expansionist dreams, while conservatives, alarmed by Populism and violent labor strikes, welcomed war as a national unifier. One senator commented that "internal discord" was disappearing in the "fervent heat of patriotism." Sensationalism also figured in the march to war, with the yellow press exaggerating stories of Spanish misdeeds. Theodore Roosevelt and others too young to remember the bloody Civil War looked on war as adventure and used masculine rhetoric to trumpet the call to arms.

More than 263,000 regulars and volunteers served in the army and another 25,000 in the navy during the war. Most of them never left the United States. The typical volunteer was young (early twenties), white, unmarried, native born, and working class. Many were southerners, a fact that helped the cause of reconciliation following the bitter divisions of the Civil War era. Deaths numbered 5,462—but only 379 in combat. The rest fell to yellow fever and typhoid, and most died in the United States, especially in camps in Tennessee, Virginia, and Florida, where in July and August a typhoid epidemic devastated the ranks. About 10,000 African American troops, assigned to segregated regiments, found no relief from racism and Jim Crow, even though black troops played a key role in the victorious battle for Santiago de Cuba. For all, food quality, sanitary conditions, and medical care were bad. Still, Roosevelt could hardly contain himself. Although his Rough Riders, a motley unit of Ivy Leaguers and cowboys, proved undisciplined and often ineffective, they nonetheless received good press largely because of Roosevelt's self-serving publicity efforts.

19-4b Dewey in the Philippines

To the surprise of most Americans, the first war news actually came from faraway Asia, from the Spanish colony of the Philippine Islands. Here, too, Madrid faced a rebellion from Filipinos seeking independence. On May 1, 1898, Commodore George Dewey's New Navy ship *Olympia* led an American squadron into Manila Bay and wrecked the outgunned Spanish fleet. Dewey and his sailors had been on alert in Hong Kong since February, when he received orders from imperial-minded Washington to attack the islands if war broke out. Manila ranked with Pearl Harbor and Pago Pago as a choice

△ Like soldiers in all wars at all times, those in the Spanish-American War were keen to communicate with loved ones at home. Here two unidentified American soldiers write letters before taking part in the Siege of Santiago de Cuba.

The Granger Collection, NYC

△ On July 1, 1898, U.S. troops stormed Spanish positions on San Juan Hill near Santiago, Cuba. Both sides suffered heavy casualties. A *Harper's* magazine correspondent reported a "ghastly" scene of hundreds killed and thousands wounded. The American painter William Glackens (1870–1938) put to canvas what he saw. Because Santiago surrendered on July 17, propelling the United States to victory in the war, and because Rough Rider Theodore Roosevelt fought at San Juan Hill and later gave a self-congratulatory account of the experience, the human toll has often gone unnoticed.

harbor, and the Philippines sat significantly on the way to China and its potentially huge market.

Facing Americans and rebels in both Cuba and the Philippines, Spanish resistance collapsed rapidly. U.S. ships blockaded Cuban ports to prevent Spain from resupplying its army, which suffered hunger and disease because Cuban insurgents had cut off supplies from the countryside. American troops saw their first ground-war action on June 22, the day several thousand of them landed near Santiago de Cuba and laid siege to the city. On July 3, U.S. warships sank the Spanish Caribbean squadron in Santiago harbor. American forces then assaulted the Spanish colony of Puerto Rico to obtain another Caribbean base for the navy and a strategic site to help protect a Central American canal. Losing on all fronts, Madrid sued for peace.

19-4c Treaty of Paris

On August 12, Spain and the United States signed an armistice to end the war. In Paris, in December 1898, American and Spanish negotiators agreed on the peace terms: independence for Cuba from Spain; cession of the Philippines, Puerto Rico, and the Pacific island of Guam to the United States; and American payment of $20 million to Spain for the territories. The U.S. empire now stretched deep into Asia, and the annexation of Wake Island (1898), Hawai'i (1898), and Samoa (1899) gave American traders, missionaries, and naval promoters other stepping-stones to China.

During the war with Spain, the *Washington Post* detected "a new appetite, a yearning to show our strength.... The taste of empire is in the mouth of the people." But as the nation debated the Treaty of Paris, anti-imperialists such as author Mark Twain, Nebraska politician William Jennings Bryan, intellectual William Graham Sumner, reformer Jane Addams, industrialist Andrew Carnegie, and Senator George Hoar of

◁ In this color illustration from 1899 we see the armored cruiser *USS Brooklyn*, under Commodore Winfield Scott Schley, which participated in the Battle of Santiago Bay on July 3, 1898. Later, in December 1899, the Brooklyn became the flagship of the Asiatic Squadron at Manila Bay, Philippines.

Massachusetts argued vigorously against annexation of the Philippines. They were disturbed that a war to free Cuba had led to empire, and they stimulated a momentous debate over the fundamental course in American foreign policy.

19-4d Anti-Imperialist Arguments

Imperial control could be imposed either formally (by military occupation, annexation, or colonialism) or informally (by economic domination, political manipulation, or the threat of intervention). Anti-imperialist ire focused mostly on the formal kind of imperial control, involving an overseas territorial empire comprised of people of color living far from the mainland. Some critics appealed to principle, citing the Declaration of Independence and the Constitution: the conquest of people against their wills violated the right of self-determination. Philosopher William James charged that the United States was throwing away its special place among nations; it was, he warned, about to "puke up its heritage."

Other anti-imperialists feared that the American character was being corrupted by imperialist zeal. Jane Addams, seeing children play war games in the streets of Chicago, pointed out that they were not freeing Cubans but rather slaying Spaniards. Hoping to build a distinct foreign policy constituency out of networks of women's clubs and organizations, prominent women like Addams championed peace and an end to imperial conquest.

Some anti-imperialists protested that the United States was practicing a double standard—"offering liberty to the Cubans with one hand, cramming liberty down the throats of the Filipinos with the other, but with both feet planted upon the neck of the negro," as an African American politician from Massachusetts put it. Still other anti-imperialists warned that annexing people of color would undermine Anglo-Saxon purity and supremacy at home.

For Samuel Gompers and other anti-imperialist labor leaders, the issue was jobs: they worried that what Gompers called the "half-breeds and semi-barbaric people" of the new colonies would undercut American labor. Might not the new colonials be imported as cheap contract labor to drive down the wages of American workers? Would not exploitation of the weak abroad become contagious and lead to further exploitation of the weak at home? Would not an overseas empire drain interest and resources from pressing domestic problems, delaying reform?

The anti-imperialists entered the debate with many handicaps and never launched an effective campaign. Although they organized the Anti-Imperialist League in November 1898, they differed so profoundly on domestic issues that they found it difficult to speak with one voice on a foreign-policy question. They also appeared inconsistent: Gompers favored the war but not the postwar annexations; Carnegie would accept colonies if they were not acquired by force; Hoar voted for annexation of Hawai'i but not of the Philippines; Bryan backed the Treaty of Paris but only, he said, to hurry the process

Emilio Aguinaldo Nationalist leader of Filipino war against American occupation.

toward Philippine independence. Finally, possession of the Philippines was an established fact, very hard to undo.

19-4e Imperialist Arguments

The imperialists answered their critics with appeals to patriotism, destiny, and commerce. They sketched a scenario of American greatness: merchant ships plying the waters to boundless Asian markets; naval vessels cruising the Pacific to protect U.S. interests; missionaries uplifting inferior peoples. It was America's duty, they insisted, quoting a then-popular Rudyard Kipling poem, to "take up the white man's burden." Furthermore, Filipino insurgents were beginning to resist U.S. rule, and it seemed cowardly to pull out under fire. Germany and Japan, two powerful international competitors, were nosing around the Philippines, apparently ready to seize them if the United States' grip loosened. National honor dictated that Americans keep what they had shed blood to take. Republican Senator Albert Beveridge of Indiana asked, "Shall [history] say that, called by events to captain and command the proudest, ablest, purest race of history in history's noblest work, we declined that great commission?"

In February 1899, by a 57-to-27 vote (just one more than the necessary two-thirds majority), the Senate passed the Treaty of Paris, ending the war with Spain. Most Republicans voted yes and most Democrats no. An amendment promising independence as soon as the Filipinos formed a stable government lost by the slimmest margin possible: the tie-breaking ballot of the vice president. Democratic presidential candidate Bryan carried the anti-imperialist case into the election of 1900, warning that repudiation of self-government in the Philippines would weaken the principle at home. But the victorious McKinley refused to apologize for American imperialism, asserting that his policies had served the nation's interests.

19-5 Asian Encounters: War in the Philippines, Diplomacy in China

▶ **What methods did Americans and Filipinos use against one another in the Philippine Insurrection?**

▶ **How did the United States seek to protect its commercial interests in China?**

As McKinley knew, however, the Philippine crisis was far from over. He said he intended to "uplift and civilize" the Filipinos, but they denied that they needed U.S. help. **Emilio Aguinaldo**, the Philippine nationalist leader who had been battling the Spanish for years, believed that American officials had promised independence for his country. But after the victory over Spain, U.S. officers ordered Aguinaldo out of Manila and isolated him from decisions affecting his nation. In early 1899, feeling betrayed by the Treaty of Paris, he proclaimed an independent Philippine Republic and took up arms. U.S. officials responded with force.

19-5a Philippine Insurrection and Pacification

In a war fought viciously by both sides, American soldiers burned crops and villages and tortured captives, while Filipino forces staged hit-and-run ambushes that were often brutally effective. Like guerrillas in many later wars, they would strike suddenly and ferociously, and then melt into the jungle or friendly villages. Americans spoke of the "savage" Filipino; one soldier declared that the Philippines "won't be pacified until the niggers [Filipinos] are killed off like the Indians." U.S. troops introduced a variant of the Spanish reconcentration policy—in the province of Batangas, for instance, U.S. troops forced residents to live in designated zones in an effort to separate the insurgents from local supporters. Disaster followed. Poor sanitation, starvation, and malaria and cholera killed several thousand people. Outside the secure areas, Americans destroyed food supplies to starve out the rebels. At least one-quarter of the population of Batangas died or fled.

Before the Philippine Insurrection was suppressed in 1902, some 20,000 Filipinos had died in combat, and as many as 600,000 had succumbed to starvation and disease. More than 4,000 Americans lay dead. Resistance to U.S. rule, however, did not disappear. The fiercely independent, vehemently anti-Christian, and often violent Muslim Filipinos of Moro Province refused to knuckle under. The U.S. military ordered them to submit or be exterminated. In 1906, the Moros finally met defeat; 600 of them, including many women and children, were slaughtered at the Battle of Bud Dajo. As General Leonard Wood, the Moro provincial governor, wrote the president, "Work of this kind has its disagreeable side."

U.S. officials, with a stern military hand, soon tried to Americanize the Philippines. Architect Daniel Burnham, leader of the City Beautiful movement, planned modern Manila. U.S. authorities instituted a new educational system, with English as the main language of instruction. Thousands of young American educators, many of them motivated by idealism, were recruited to teach in the new schools. The Philippine economy grew while it was an American satellite, and a sedition act silenced critics of U.S. authority by sending them to prison. In 1916, the Jones Act vaguely promised independence once the Philippines established a "stable government." The United States finally ended its rule in 1946 during an intense period of decolonization after the Second World War.

19-5b China and the Open Door Policy

In China, McKinley opted for an approach that emphasized negotiations, with greater success. Outsiders had been pecking away at China since the 1840s, but the Japanese onslaught intensified the international scramble. Taking advantage of the Qing (Manchu) dynasty's weakness, the major imperial powers carved out spheres of influence (regions over which the outside powers claimed political control and exclusive commercial privileges): Germany in Shandong, Russia in Manchuria, France in Yunnan and Hainan, Britain in Kowloon and Hong Kong. Then, in 1895, the same year as the outbreak of the Cuban revolution, Japan claimed victory over China in a short war and assumed control of Formosa and Korea as well as parts of China proper (see Map 19.1). American religious and business leaders petitioned Washington to halt the dismemberment of China before they were closed out.

Secretary of State John Hay knew the United States could not force the imperial powers out of China, but he was determined to protect American commerce and missionaries like Lottie Moon. He knew that missionaries had become targets of Chinese nationalist anger and that American oil and textile companies had been disappointed in the results of their investments in the country. Thus, in September 1899, Hay sent the nations with spheres of influence in China a note asking them to respect the principle of equal trade opportunity—an **Open Door**. The recipients sent evasive replies, privately complaining that the United States was seeking, for free, the trade rights in China that they had gained at considerable military and administrative cost.

The next year, a Chinese secret society called the Boxers (so named in the Western press because some members were martial artists) incited riots that killed foreigners, including missionaries, and laid siege to the foreign legations in Beijing. The **Boxer Rebellion**, as it came to be known, sought ultimately to expel all foreigners from China. The United States, applauded by American merchants and missionaries alike, joined the other imperial powers in sending troops to lift the siege. Hay also sent a second Open Door note in July, which instructed other nations to preserve China's territorial integrity and to honor "equal and impartial trade." Hay's protests notwithstanding, China continued for years to be fertile soil for foreign exploitation, especially by the Japanese.

Although Hay's foray into Asian politics settled little, the Open Door policy became a cornerstone of U.S. diplomacy. The "open door" had actually been a long-standing American principle, for as a trading nation the United States opposed barriers to international commerce and demanded equal access to foreign markets. After 1900, however, when the United States began to emerge as the premier world trader, the Open Door policy became an instrument first to pry open markets and then to dominate them, not just in China but throughout the world. The Open Door also developed as an ideology with several tenets: first, that America's domestic well-being required exports; second, that foreign trade would suffer interruption unless the United States intervened abroad to implant American principles and keep markets open; and third, that the closing of any area to American products, citizens, or ideas threatened the survival of the United States itself.

Open Door Foreign policy proposed by U.S. Secretary of State John Hay, in which he asked the major European powers to ensure trading rights in China by opening the ports in their spheres of influence to all countries.

Boxer Rebellion Chinese insurgency against Christians and foreigners, defeated by an international force.

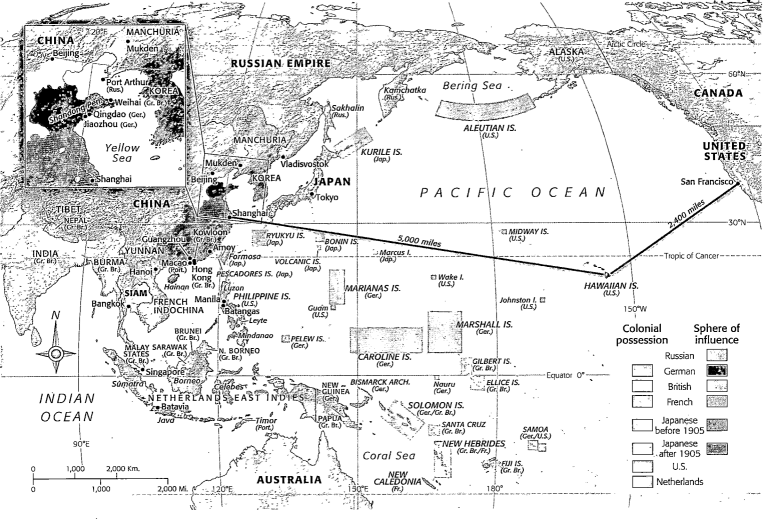

Map 19.1 Imperialism in Asia: Turn of the Century

China and the Pacific region had become imperialist hunting grounds by the turn of the century. The European powers and Japan controlled more areas than the United States, which nonetheless participated in the imperial race by annexing the Philippines, Wake, Guam, Hawai'i, and Samoa; announcing the Open Door policy; and expanding trade. As the spheres of influence in China demonstrate, that besieged nation succumbed to outsiders despite the Open Door policy.

19-6 TR's World

▷ **What ideas guided Theodore Roosevelt in his views of U.S. foreign policy?**

▷ **How did Roosevelt use presidential power and authority on the international stage?**

▷ **How did Latin American countries respond to the expansion of American influence?**

▷ **What actions did the United States take to stem European threats to its hegemony?**

Theodore Roosevelt played an important role in shaping U.S. foreign policy in the McKinley administration. As assistant secretary of the navy (1897–1898), as a Spanish-American War hero, and then as vice president in McKinley's second term, Roosevelt worked tirelessly to make the United States a key member of the great power club. He had long had a fascination with power and its uses. He also relished hunting and killing. After an argument with a girlfriend in his youth, he vented his anger by shooting a neighbor's dog. When he killed his first buffalo in the West, he danced crazily around the carcass as his Indian guide watched in amazement. Roosevelt justified the slaughtering of American Indians, if necessary, and took his Rough Riders to Cuba, desperate to get in on the fighting. He was not disappointed. "Did I tell you," he wrote Henry Cabot Lodge afterward, "that I killed a Spaniard with my own hands?"

Like many other Americans of his day, Roosevelt took for granted the superiority of Protestant Anglo-American culture, and he believed in the importance of using American power to shape world affairs (a conviction he summarized by citing the West African proverb "Speak softly and carry a big stick, and you will go far"). In TR's world, there were "civilized" and "uncivilized" nations; the former, primarily white and Anglo-Saxon or Teutonic, had a right and a duty to intervene in the affairs of the latter (generally nonwhite, Latin, or Slavic, and therefore "backward") to preserve order and stability. If violent means had to be used to accomplish this task, so be it.

19-6a Presidential Authority

Roosevelt's love of the good fight caused many to rue his ascension to the presidency after McKinley's assassination in September 1901. But there was more to this "cowboy" than mere bluster; he was also an astute analyst of foreign policy and world affairs. TR understood that American power, though growing year by year, remained limited, and that in many parts of the world the United States would have to rely on diplomacy and nonmilitary means to achieve satisfactory outcomes. It would have to work in concert with other powers.

Roosevelt sought to centralize foreign policy in the White House. The president had to take charge of foreign relations, he believed, in the same way he took the lead in formulating domestic priorities of reorganization and reform. Congress was too large and unwieldy. As for public opinion, it was, Roosevelt said, "the voice of the devil, or what is still worse, the voice of the fool." This conviction that the executive branch should be supreme in foreign policy was to be shared by most presidents who followed TR in office, down to the present day.

With this bald assertion of presidential and national power, Roosevelt stepped onto the international stage. His first efforts were focused on Latin America, where U.S. economic and strategic interests and power towered (see Map 19.2), and on Europe, where repeated political and military disputes persuaded Americans to develop friendlier relations with Great Britain while avoiding entrapment in the continent's troubles, many of which Americans blamed on Germany.

As U.S. economic interests expanded in Latin America, so did U.S. political influence. Exports to Latin America, which exceeded $50 million in the 1870s, had risen to more than $120 million when Roosevelt became president in 1901, and then reached $300 million in 1914. Investments by U.S. citizens in Latin America climbed to a commanding $1.26 billion in 1914. In 1899, two large banana importers had merged to form the United Fruit Company. United Fruit owned much of the land in Central America (more than a million acres in 1913), as well as the railroad and steamship lines, and the firm became an influential economic and political force in the region. The company worked to eradicate yellow fever and malaria at the same time it manipulated Central American politics, partly by bankrolling favored officeholders.

Map 19.2 U.S. Hegemony in the Caribbean and Latin America

Through many interventions, territorial acquisitions, and robust economic expansion, the United States became the predominant power in Latin America in the early twentieth century. The United States often backed up the Roosevelt Corollary's declaration of a "police power" by dispatching troops to Caribbean nations, where they met nationalist opposition.

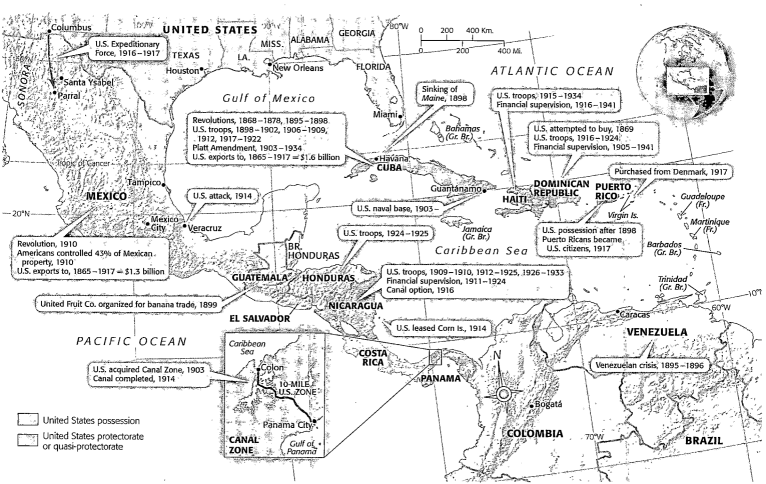

19-6b Cuba and the Platt Amendment

After the destructive war in Cuba, U.S. citizens and corporations continued to dominate the island's economy, controlling the sugar, mining, tobacco, and utilities industries, and most of the rural lands. Private U.S. investments in Cuba grew from $50 million before the revolution to $220 million by 1913, and U.S. exports to the island rose from $26 million in 1900 to $196 million in 1917. The Teller Amendment outlawed the annexation of Cuba, but officials in Washington soon used the document's call for "pacification" to justify U.S. control. American troops remained there until 1902.

Favoring the "better classes," U.S. authorities restricted voting rights largely to propertied Cuban males, excluding two-thirds of adult men and all women. American officials also forced the Cubans to append to their constitution a frank avowal of U.S. hegemony known as the **Platt Amendment.** This statement prohibited Cuba from making a treaty with another nation that might impair its independence; in practice, this meant that all treaties had to have U.S. approval. Most important, another Platt Amendment provision granted the United States "the right to intervene" to preserve the island's independence and to maintain domestic order. The amendment also required Cuba to lease a naval base to the United States (at Guantánamo Bay, still under U.S. jurisdiction today). Formalized in a 1903 treaty, the amendment governed Cuban-American relations until 1934. "There is, of course, little or no independence left Cuba under the Platt Amendment," General Wood, military governor of the island until 1902, told President Roosevelt.

The Cubans, like the Filipinos, chafed under U.S. mastery. Widespread demonstrations protested the Platt Amendment, and a rebellion against the Cuban government in 1906 prompted Roosevelt to order another invasion of Cuba. The marines stayed until 1909, returned briefly in 1912, and occupied the island again from 1917 to 1922. All the while, U.S. officials helped to develop a transportation system, expand the public school system, found a national army, and increase sugar production. When Dr. Walter Reed's experiments, based on the theory of the Cuban physician Carlos Juan Finlay, proved that mosquitoes transmitted yellow fever, sanitary engineers controlled the insect and eradicated the disease.

Platt Amendment Added to Cuba's constitution of 1903 under American pressure, it gave the United States the right to intervene if Cuban independence or internal order were threatened, and granted a naval base to the United States at Guantánamo Bay.

Panama Canal Major waterway that traverses the Isthmus of Panama in Central America, connecting the Atlantic and Pacific oceans. Built by the United States for $352 million; construction began in 1906 and was completed in 1914.

Puerto Rico, the Caribbean island taken as a spoil of war in the Treaty of Paris, also developed under U.S. tutelage. Although no Puerto Rican sat at the negotiating table for that treaty, the Puerto Rican elite at first welcomed the United States as an improvement over Spain. But disillusionment soon set in. The condescending U.S. military governor, General Guy V. Henry, regarded Puerto Ricans as naughty, ill-educated children who needed "kindergarten instruction in controlling themselves without allowing them too much liberty." Some residents warned against the "Yankee peril"; others applauded the "Yankee model" and futilely anticipated statehood.

19-6c Panama Canal

Panama, meanwhile, became the site of a bold U.S. expansionist venture. In 1869, the world had marveled at the completion of the Suez Canal, a waterway in northeast Africa that greatly facilitated travel between the Indian Ocean and Mediterranean Sea, and enhanced the power of the British empire. Surely that feat could be duplicated in the Western Hemisphere, possibly in Panama, a province of Colombia. One expansionist, U.S. Navy Captain Robert W. Shufeldt, predicted that a new canal would convert "the Gulf of Mexico into an American lake." Business interests joined politicians, diplomats, and navy officers in insisting that the United States control such an interoceanic canal.

To construct such a canal, however, the United States had to overcome daunting obstacles. The Clayton-Bulwer Treaty with Britain (1850) had provided for joint control of a canal. The British, recognizing their diminishing influence in the region and cultivating friendship with the United States as a counterweight to Germany, stepped aside in the Hay-Pauncefote Treaty (1901) to permit a solely U.S.-run canal. When Colombia hesitated to meet Washington's terms, Roosevelt encouraged Panamanian rebels to declare independence and ordered American warships to the isthmus to back them.

In 1903, the new Panama awarded the United States a canal zone and long-term rights to its control. The treaty also guaranteed Panama its independence. (In 1922, the United States paid Colombia $25 million in "conscience money" but did not apologize.) The completion of the **Panama Canal** in 1914 marked a major technological achievement. During the canal's first year of operation, more than one thousand merchant ships squeezed through its locks.

19-6d Roosevelt Corollary

As for the rest of the Caribbean, Theodore Roosevelt resisted challenges to U.S. hegemony. Worried that Latin American nations' defaults on debts owed to European banks were provoking European intervention (England, Germany, and Italy sent warships to Venezuela in 1902), the president in 1904 issued the Roosevelt Corollary to the Monroe Doctrine. He warned Latin Americans to stabilize their politics and finances. "Chronic wrongdoing," the corollary lectured, might require "intervention by some civilized nation," and "in flagrant cases of such wrongdoing or impotence," the United States would have to assume the role of "an international police power." Laced with presumptions of superiority, Roosevelt's declaration provided the rationale for frequent U.S. interventions in Latin America.

From 1900 to 1917, U.S. presidents ordered American troops to Cuba, Panama, Nicaragua, the Dominican Republic, Mexico, and Haiti to quell civil wars, thwart challenges to U.S. influence, gain ports and bases, and forestall European meddling (see Map 19.2). U.S. authorities

△ In a suit and hat, President Theodore Roosevelt occupies the controls of a ninety-five-ton power shovel at a Panama Canal worksite. Roosevelt's November 1906 trip to inspect the massive project was the first time a sitting president left the United States.

ran elections, trained national guards that became politically powerful, and renegotiated foreign debts, shifting them to U.S. banks. They also took over customs houses to control tariff revenues and government budgets (as in the Dominican Republic, from 1905 to 1941).

19-6e U.S.-Mexican Relations

U.S. officials focused particular attention on Mexico, where longtime dictator Porfirio Díaz (1876–1910) aggressively recruited foreign investors through tax incentives and land grants. American capitalists came to own Mexico's railroads and mines and invested heavily in petroleum and banking. By the early 1890s, the United States dominated Mexico's foreign trade. By 1910, Americans controlled 43 percent of Mexican property and produced more than half of the country's oil; in the state of Sonora, 186 of 208 mining companies were American owned. The Mexican revolutionaries who ousted Díaz in 1910, like nationalists elsewhere in Latin America, set out to reclaim their nation's sovereignty by ending their economic dependency on the United States.

The revolution descended into a bloody civil war with strong anti-Yankee overtones, and the Mexican government intended to nationalize extensive American-owned properties. Washington leaders worked to thwart this aim, with President Woodrow Wilson twice ordering troops onto Mexican soil: once in 1914, at Veracruz, to avenge a slight to the U.S. uniform and flag and to overthrow the nationalistic government of President Victoriano Huerta; and again in 1916, in northern Mexico, where General John J. "Black Jack" Pershing spent months pursuing Pancho Villa after the Mexican rebel had

raided an American border town. Having failed to capture Villa and facing another nationalistic government led by Venustiano Carranza, U.S. forces departed in January 1917.

As the United States reaffirmed the Monroe Doctrine against European expansion in the hemisphere and demonstrated the power to enforce it, European nations reluctantly honored U.S. hegemony in Latin America. In turn, the United States held to its tradition of standing outside European embroilments. The balance of power in Europe was precarious, and seldom did an American president involve the United States directly. Theodore Roosevelt did help settle a Franco-German clash over Morocco by mediating a settlement at Algeciras, Spain (1906). But the president drew American criticism for entangling the United States in a European problem. Americans endorsed the ultimately futile Hague peace conferences (1899 and 1907) and negotiated various arbitration treaties, but on the whole stayed outside the European arena, except to profit from extensive trade with it.

19-6f Peacemaking in East Asia

In East Asia, though, both Roosevelt and his successor, William Howard Taft, took an activist approach. Both sought to preserve the Open Door and to contain Japan's

△ Francisco "Pancho" Villa presented himself as a selfless Mexican patriot. Americans living along the border thought otherwise, particularly after Villa's forces murdered more than 30 U.S. civilians. American troops pursued Villa more than 300 miles into Mexico but never caught him.

Guantánamo Bay

Four hundred miles from Miami, near the southeastern corner of Cuba, sits U.S. Naval Base Guantánamo Bay. It is the oldest American base outside the United States, and the only one located in a country with which Washington does not have a fully open political and economic relationship. The United States has occupied the base for more than a century, since the aftermath of the Spanish-American War, leasing it from Cuba for $4,085 per year (originally, $2,000 in gold coins).

From an early point, Cuban leaders expressed dissatisfaction with the deal, and in the aftermath of Fidel Castro's communist takeover in 1959, Guantánamo was a source of constant tension between the two countries. Castro called the 45-square-mile base "a dagger pointed at Cuba's heart" and over the years he pointedly refused to cash the rent checks. He did cash the very first check, though, and Washington has used that fact to argue that his government accepts the terms of the lease.

Since late 2001, "Gitmo," as the base is known to U.S. service members, has contained a detainment camp for persons alleged to be militant combatants captured in Afghanistan and, later, Iraq and elsewhere. The first group of twenty detainees arrived in January 2002, after a twenty-hour flight from Afghanistan. By the end of 2005, the number exceeded five hundred, from more than forty countries. The George W. Bush administration called the detainees "unlawful enemy combatants" rather than "prisoners of war" but promised early on to abide by the Geneva accords governing prisoners of war. But soon there were allegations of abuse and complaints that holding detainees without trial, charges, or any prospect of release was cruel and unlawful. Some detainees committed suicide. For many critics, the camp became an international symbol of American heavy-handedness, and even some administration allies said that the controversy surrounding the camp was severely hurting America's image abroad.

In June 2006, the U.S. Supreme Court ruled that President Bush had overstepped his power in setting up the procedures for the Guantánamo detainees without specific authority from Congress. The Court further said that the procedures violated both the Uniform Code of Military Justice and the Geneva accords. In January 2009, President Barack Obama signed an executive order closing the detention center within one year, but strong opposition (even from some Democrats) as well as complications concerning detainee trials and resettlements ensured that the deadline would not be met. When Obama left office eight years later, the center remained in operation.

CRITICAL THINKING

- The question for a people and a nation thus remained: how would the United States balance its security needs with its commitment to due process and the rule of law?

---

rising power in the region. Many race-minded Japanese interpreted the U.S. advance into the Pacific as an attempt by whites to gain ascendancy over Asians. Japanese leaders nonetheless urged their citizens to go to America to study it as a model for industrializing and achieving world power. Although some Americans proudly proclaimed the Japanese the "Yankees of the East," the United States gradually had to make concessions to Japan to protect the vulnerable Philippines and to sustain the Open Door policy. Japan continued to plant interests in China and then smashed the Russians in the Russo-Japanese War (1904–1905). President Roosevelt mediated the negotiations at the Portsmouth Conference in New Hampshire and won the Nobel Peace Prize for this effort to preserve a balance of power in Asia and shrink Japan's "big head."

In 1905, in the Taft-Katsura Agreement, the United States conceded Japanese hegemony over Korea in return for Japan's pledge not to undermine the U.S. position in the Philippines. Three years later, in the Root-Takahira Agreement, Washington recognized Japan's interests in Manchuria, whereas Japan again pledged the security of the Pacific possessions held by the United States and endorsed the Open Door in China. Roosevelt also built up American

naval power to deter the Japanese; in late 1907, he sent on a world tour the navy's "Great White Fleet" (so named because the ships were painted white for the voyage). Duly impressed, the Japanese began to build a bigger navy of their own.

19-6g Dollar Diplomacy

President Taft, for his part, thought he might counter Japanese advances in Asia through dollar diplomacy—the use of private funds to serve American diplomatic goals and garner profits for American financiers—and at the same time bring reform to less-developed countries. In this case, Taft induced American bankers to join an international consortium to build a railway in China. Taft's venture, however, seemed only to embolden Japan to solidify and extend its holdings in China, where internal discord continued after the nationalist revolution of 1911 overthrew the Qing dynasty.

In 1914, when the First World War broke out in Europe, Japan seized Shandong and some Pacific islands from the Germans. In 1915, Japan issued its Twenty-One Demands, virtually insisting on hegemony over all of China. The Chinese door was being slammed shut, but the United States lacked adequate countervailing power in Asia to block Japan's imperial thrusts. A new president, Woodrow Wilson, worried about how the "white race" could blunt the rise of "the yellow race."

19-6h Anglo-American Rapprochement

British officials in London shared this concern, though their attention was focused primarily on rising tensions in Europe. A special feature of American-European relations in the TR-Taft years was the flowering of an Anglo-American cooperation that had been growing throughout the late nineteenth century. One outcome of the intense German-British rivalry and the rise of the United States to world power was London's quest for friendship with Washington. Already prepared by racial ideas of Anglo-Saxon kinship, a common language, and respect for representative government and private-property rights, Americans appreciated British support in the 1898 war and the Hay-Pauncefote Treaty, and London's virtual endorsement of the Roosevelt Corollary and withdrawal of British warships from the Caribbean. As Mark Twain said of the two imperialist powers, "We are kin in sin."

British-American trade and U.S. investment in Britain also secured ties. By 1914, more than 140 American companies operated in Britain, including H. J. Heinz's processed foods and F. W. Woolworth's "penny markets." Many Britons decried an Americanization of British culture. One journalist complained that a Briton "wakes in the morning at the sound of an American alarm clock; rises from his New England sheets, and shaves with . . . a Yankee safety razor. He . . . slips his Waterbury watch into his pocket [and] catches an electric train made in New York. . . . At his office . . . he sits on a Nebraskan swivel chair, before a Michigan roll-top desk." Such exaggerated fears and the always prickly character of the Anglo-American relationship, however, gave way to cooperation in world affairs, most evident in 1917 when the United States threw its weapons and soldiers into the First World War on the British side against Germany.

Summary

In the years from the Civil War to the First World War, expansionism and imperialism elevated the United States to world power status. By 1914, Americans held extensive economic, strategic, and political interests in a world made smaller by modern technology. The victory over Spain in 1898 was but the most dramatic moment in the long process. The outward reach of U.S. foreign policy from Seward to Wilson sparked opposition from domestic critics, other imperialist nations,

and foreign nationalists, but expansionists prevailed, and the trend toward empire endured.

From Asia to Latin America, economic and strategic needs and ideology motivated and justified expansion and empire. The belief that the United States needed foreign markets to absorb surplus production in order to save the domestic economy joined missionary zeal in reforming other societies through the promotion of American products and culture. Notions of racial and male supremacy and appeals to national greatness also fed the appetite for foreign adventure and commitments. The greatly augmented navy became a primary means for satisfying American ideas and wants.

Revealing the great diversity of America's intersection with the world, missionaries like Moon in China, generals like Wood in Cuba, companies like Singer in Africa and Heinz in Britain, and politicians like Taft in the Philippines carried American ways, ideas, guns, and goods abroad to a mixed reception. The conspicuous declarations of Olney, Hay, Roosevelt, and other leaders became the guiding texts for U.S. principles and behavior in world affairs. A world power with far-flung interests to protect, the United States had to face a tough test of its self-proclaimed greatness and reconsider its political isolation from Europe when a world war broke out in August 1914.

Suggestions for Further Reading

Gail Bederman, *Manliness and Civilization: A Cultural History of Gender and Race in the United States, 1880–1917* (1995)

Julian Go, *American Empire and the Politics of Meaning: Elite Political Cultures in the Philippines and Puerto Rico* (2008)

Kristin L. Hoganson, *Fighting for American Manhood: How Gender Politics Provoked the Spanish–American and Philippine–American Wars* (1998)

Michael H. Hunt, *Ideology and U.S. Foreign Policy* (1987)

Paul A. Kramer, *The Blood of Government: Race, Empire, the United States, and the Philippines* (2006)

Walter LaFeber, *The American Search for Opportunity, 1865–1913* (2015)

Brian M. Linn, *The Philippine War, 1899–1902* (2000)

Eric T. Love, *Race over Empire: Racism and U.S. Imperialism, 1865–1900* (2004)

John Offner, *An Unwanted War: The Diplomacy of the United States and Spain over Cuba, 1895–1898* (1992)

Louis A. Perez Jr., *The War of 1898: The United States and Cuba in History and Historiography* (1998)

MINDTAP
From Cengage

Americans in the Great War, 1914–1920

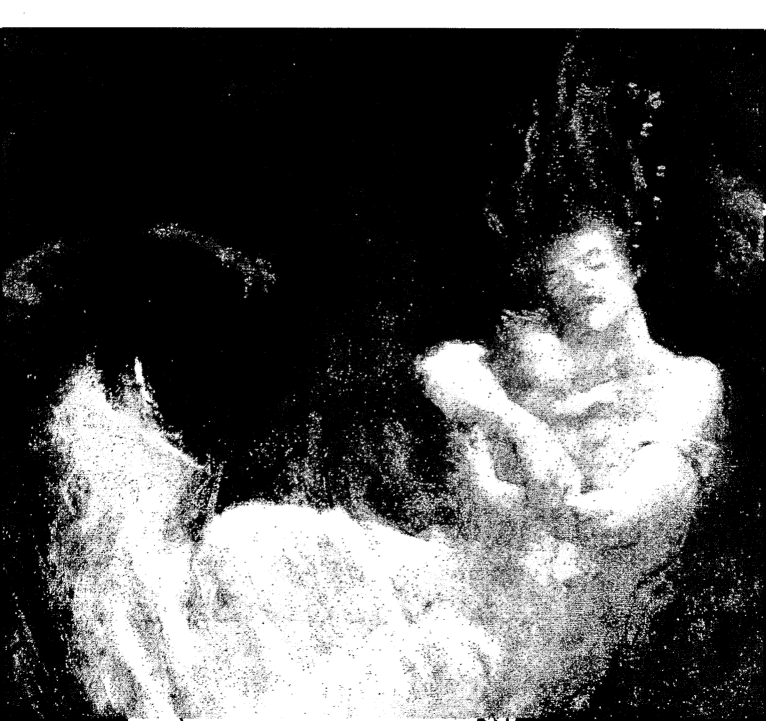

O n May 7, 1915, Secretary of State William Jennings Bryan was having lunch with several cabinet members at the Shoreham Hotel in Washington when he received a bulletin: the luxurious British ocean liner *Lusitania* had been sunk, apparently by a German submarine. He rushed to his office, and at 3:06 pm came the confirmation from London: "THE LUSITANIA WAS TORPEDOED OFF THE IRISH COAST AND SANK IN HALF AN HOUR. NO NEWS YET OF PASSENGERS." In fact, 1,198 people had perished, including 128 Americans. The giant vessel had taken, not half an hour, but just eighteen minutes to go down. Bryan was deeply distraught but not altogether surprised. The European powers were at war, and he had feared precisely this kind of calamity. Britain had imposed a naval blockade on Germany, and the Germans had responded by launching submarine warfare against Allied shipping. Berlin authorities had proclaimed the North Atlantic a danger zone, and German submarines had already sunk numerous British and Allied ships. As a passenger liner, the *Lusitania* was supposed to be spared, but German officials had placed notices in U.S. newspapers warning that Americans who traveled on British or Allied ships did so at their own risk; passenger liners suspected of carrying munitions or other contraband were subject to attack. For weeks, Bryan had urged President Woodrow Wilson to stop Americans from booking passage on British ships; Wilson had refused.

That evening, Bryan mused to his wife, "I wonder if that ship carried munitions of war. . . . If she did carry them, it puts a different face on the whole matter! England has been using our citizens to protect her ammunition!" The *Lusitania*, it soon emerged, *was* carrying munitions, and Bryan set about urging a restrained U.S. response. Desperate to keep the United States

◁ This poster by Fred Spear, published in Boston not long after the *Lusitania* sinking, captured the anger Americans felt at the loss of 128 of their fellow citizens, among them women and children. Nearly two years before U.S. entry into the war, posters like this one urged Americans to enlist as preparation for the day when they must surely confront the German enemy. Library of Congress Prints and Photographs Division[LC-USZC4-1129]

Chronology

1914	▣ First World War begins in Europe
1915	▣ Germans sink RMS *Lusitania* off coast of Ireland
1916	▣ After torpedoing the *Sussex*, Germany pledges not to attack merchant ships without warning
	▣ National Defense Act expands military
1917	▣ Germany declares unrestricted submarine warfare
	▣ Russian Revolution ousts the czar; Bolsheviks later take power
	▣ United States enters First World War
	▣ Selective Service Act creates draft
	▣ Espionage Act limits First Amendment rights
	▣ Race riot breaks out in East St. Louis, Illinois
1918	▣ Wilson announces Fourteen Points for new world order
	▣ Sedition Act further limits free speech
	▣ U.S. troops at Château-Thierry help blunt German offensive
	▣ U.S. troops intervene in Russia against Bolsheviks
	▣ Spanish flu pandemic kills 20 million worldwide
	▣ Armistice ends First World War
1919	▣ Paris Peace Conference punishes Germany and launches League of Nations
	▣ May Day bombings help instigate Red Scare
	▣ American Legion organizes for veterans' benefits and antiradicalism
	▣ Wilson suffers stroke after speaking tour
	▣ Senate rejects Treaty of Versailles and U.S. membership in League of Nations
	▣ *Schenck v. U.S.* upholds Espionage Act
1920	▣ Palmer Raids round up suspected radicals

out of the war, he urged Wilson to couple his condemnation of the German action with an equally tough note to Britain protesting its blockade and to ban Americans from traveling on belligerent ships. Wilson hesitated. Others, including former president Theodore Roosevelt, called the sinking "an act of piracy" and pressed for war. Wilson did not want war, but neither did he accept Bryan's argument that the British and German violations should be treated the same. He sent a strong protest note to Berlin, calling on the German government to end its submarine warfare.

For the next several weeks, as Bryan continued to press his case, he sensed his growing isolation within the administration. When in early June Wilson made it clear that he would not ban Americans from travel on belligerent ships and that he intended to send a second protest note to Germany, Bryan resigned. Privately, Wilson called Bryan a "strange man" who suffered from a "singular sort of moral blindness."

The division between the president and his secretary of state reflected divisions within the American populace over Europe's war. The split could be seen in the reaction to Bryan's resignation. Eastern newspapers charged him with "unspeakable treachery" and of stabbing the country in the back. But in the Midwest and South, Bryan was accorded respect, and he won praise from pacifists and German American groups for his "act of courage." A few weeks later, speaking to a capacity crowd of fifteen thousand at Madison Square Garden (another fifty thousand had been turned away), Bryan was loudly applauded when he warned against "war with any of the belligerent nations." Although many Americans felt, like President Wilson, that honor was more important than peace, others joined Bryan in thinking that some sacrifice of neutral rights was reasonable if the country could thereby stay out of the fighting. The debate would continue up until U.S. entry into the war in 1917, and the tensions would still ripple thereafter.

Experience an interactive version of this story in MindTap®.

Like most Americans, Bryan had been stunned by the outbreak of the Great War (as it quickly became known) in 1914. For years, the United States had participated in the international competition for colonies, markets, and weapons supremacy. But full-scale war seemed unthinkable. The new machine guns, howitzers, submarines, and dreadnoughts were such awesome death engines that leaders surely would not use them. When they did, lamented one social reformer, "civilization is all gone, and barbarism comes."

For almost three years, President Wilson kept America out of the war. During this time, he sought to protect U.S. trade interests and improve the nation's military posture while also lecturing the belligerents to rediscover their humanity and to respect international law. But American property, lives, and neutrality fell victim to British and German naval warfare. When, two years after the *Lusitania* went down, the president finally asked Congress for a declaration of war, he did so with his characteristic crusading zeal. America entered the battle not just to win the war but to reform the postwar world: to "make the world safe for democracy."

A year and a half later, the Great War would be over. It exacted a terrible cost on Europe, for a whole generation of young men was cut down—some 10 million soldiers perished. Europeans looked at their gigantic cemeteries and could scarcely believe what had happened. They experienced an acute spiritual loss in the destruction of ideals, confidence, and goodwill. Economically, too, the damage was immense. Most portentous of all for the future of the twentieth century, the Great War toppled four empires of the Old World—the German, Austro-Hungarian, Russian, and Ottoman Turkish—and left two others, the British and French, drastically weakened.

For the United States, the human and material cost was comparatively small, yet Americans could rightly claim to have helped tip the scales in favor of the Allies with their infusion of war materiel and troops as well as their extension of loans and food supplies. The war years also witnessed a massive international transfer of wealth from Europe across the Atlantic, as the United States went from being the world's largest debtor nation to being its largest creditor nation. The conflict marked the United States' coming of age as a world power. In these and other respects, the Great War was a great triumph for Americans.

In other ways, though, World War I was a difficult, painful experience. It accentuated and intensified social divisions. Racial tensions accompanied the northward migration of southern blacks, and pacifists and German Americans were harassed. The federal government, eager to stimulate

patriotism, trampled on civil liberties to silence critics. And following a communist revolution in Russia, a Red Scare in America repressed radicals and tarnished America's reputation as a democratic society. Although reformers continued after the armistice to devote themselves to issues like prohibition and woman suffrage, the war experience helped splinter the Progressive movement. Jane Addams sadly remarked that "the spirit of fighting burns away all those impulses . . . which foster the will to justice."

Abroad, Americans who had marched to battle as if on a crusade grew disillusioned with the peace process. They recoiled from the spectacle of the victors squabbling over the spoils, and they chided Wilson for failing to deliver the "peace without victory" that he had promised. As in the 1790s, the 1840s, and the 1890s, Americans once again engaged in a searching national debate about the fundamentals of their foreign policy. After negotiating the Treaty of Versailles at Paris following World War I, the president urged U.S. membership in the new League of Nations, which he promoted as a vehicle for reforming world politics. The Senate rejected his appeal (the League nonetheless organized without U.S. membership) because many Americans feared that the League might threaten U.S. interests and entangle Americans in Europe's problems.

- *Why did the United States try to remain neutral and then enter the European war in 1917?*

- *How was American society changed by the war?*

- *What were the main elements of Woodrow Wilson's postwar vision, and why did he fail to realize them?*

20-1 Precarious Neutrality

▷ **Why was it difficult for Americans to remain neutral when war broke out in Europe in August 1914?**

▷ **What was "Wilsonianism"?**

▷ **How was American neutrality undermined by the actions of the Allies and Central Powers?**

The war that erupted in August 1914 grew from years of European competition over trade, colonies, allies, and armaments. Two powerful alliance systems had formed: the Triple Alliance of Germany, Austria-Hungary, and Italy, and the Triple Entente of Britain, France, and Russia. All had imperial holdings and ambitions for more, but Germany seemed particularly bold, as it rivaled Great Britain for world leadership. Many Americans saw Germany as a threat to U.S. interests in the Western Hemisphere and viewed Germans as an excessively militaristic people who embraced autocracy and spurned democracy.

20-1a Outbreak of the First World War

Strategists said that Europe enjoyed a balance of power, but crises in the Balkan countries of southeastern Europe triggered a chain of events that shattered the "balance." Slavic nationalists sought to enlarge Serbia, an independent Slavic nation, by annexing regions such as Bosnia, then a province of the Austro-Hungarian Empire (see Map 20.1). On June 28, 1914, Archduke Franz Ferdinand, heir to the Austro-Hungarian throne, was assassinated by Gavrilo Princip, a Serbian nationalist, while on a state visit to Sarajevo, the capital of Bosnia. Alarmed by the prospect of an engorged Serbia on

its border, Austria-Hungary consulted its Triple Alliance partner Germany, which urged toughness. When Serbia called on its Slavic friend Russia for help, Russia in turn looked for backing from its ally France. In late July, Austria-Hungary declared war against Serbia. Russia then began to mobilize its armies.

Germany—having goaded Austria-Hungary toward war and believing war inevitable—struck first, declaring war against Russia on August 1 and against France two days later. Britain hesitated, but when German forces slashed into neutral Belgium to get at France, London declared war against Germany on August 4. Eventually, Turkey (the Ottoman Empire) joined Germany and Austria-Hungary as the Central Powers, and Italy (switching sides) and Japan teamed up with Britain, France, and Russia as the Allies. Japan took advantage of the European war to seize Shandong, Germany's area of influence in China.

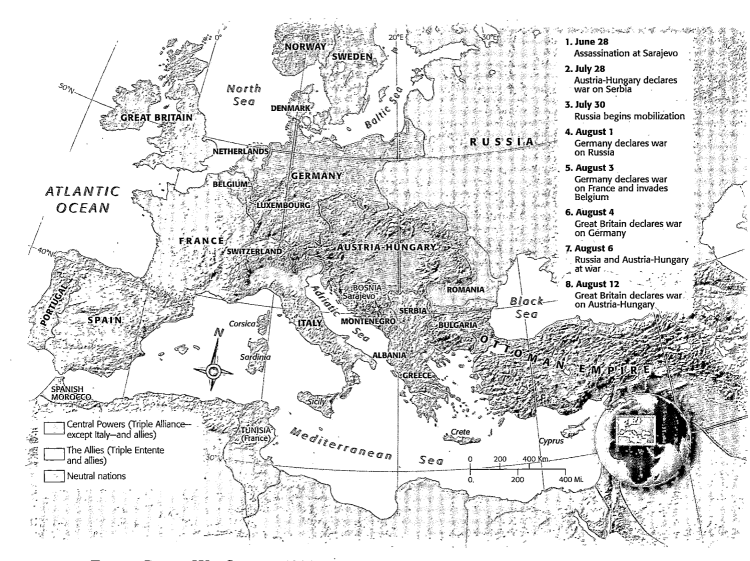

1. June 28
Assassination at Sarajevo

2. July 28
Austria-Hungary declares war on Serbia

3. July 30
Russia begins mobilization

4. August 1
Germany declares war on Russia

5. August 3
Germany declares war on France and invades Belgium

6. August 4
Great Britain declares war on Germany

7. August 6
Russia and Austria-Hungary at war

8. August 12
Great Britain declares war on Austria-Hungary

Central Powers (Triple Alliance—except Italy—and allies)

The Allies (Triple Entente and allies)

Neutral nations

Map 20.1 Europe Goes to War, Summer 1914

Bound by alliances and stirred by turmoil in the Balkans, where Serbs repeatedly upended peace, the nations of Europe descended into war in the summer of 1914. Step by step, a Balkan crisis escalated into the "Great War."

President Wilson at first sought to distance America from the conflagration by issuing a proclamation of neutrality—the traditional U.S. policy toward European wars. He also asked Americans to refrain from taking sides, to exhibit "the dignity of self-control." In private, the president said, "We definitely have to be neutral, since otherwise our mixed populations would wage war on each other." The United States, he fervently hoped, would stand apart as a sane, civilized nation in a deranged international system.

20-1b Taking Sides

Wilson's lofty appeal for American neutrality and unity at home collided with several realities. First, ethnic groups in the United States did take sides. Many German Americans and anti-British Irish Americans (Ireland was then trying to break free from British rule) cheered for the Central Powers. Americans of British and French ancestry, and others with roots in Allied nations, tended to champion the Allied cause. Germany's attack on Belgium confirmed in many people's minds that Germany had become the archetype of unbridled militarism.

The pro-Allied sympathies of Wilson's administration also weakened the U.S. neutrality proclamation. Honoring Anglo-American rapprochement, Wilson shared the conviction with British leaders that a German victory would destroy free enterprise and government by law. If Germany won the war, he prophesied, "it would change the course of our civilization and make the United States a military nation." Several of Wilson's chief advisers and diplomats—his assistant, Colonel Edward House; ambassador to London Walter Hines Page; and Robert Lansing, a counselor in the State Department who later became secretary of state—held similar anti-German views, which often translated into pro-Allied policies.

U.S. economic links with the Allies also rendered neutrality difficult, if not impossible. England had long been one of the nation's best customers. Now the British flooded America with new orders, especially for arms. Sales to the Allies helped pull the American economy out of its recession. Between 1914 and 1916, American exports to England and France grew 365 percent, from $753 million to $2.75 billion. In the same period, however, largely because of Britain's naval blockade, exports to Germany dropped by more than 90 percent, from $345 million to only $29 million. Loans to Britain and France from private American banks—totaling $2.3 billion during the neutrality period—financed much of U.S. trade with the Allies. Germany received only $27 million in the same period. The Wilson administration, which at first frowned on these transactions, came to see them as necessary to the economic health of the United States.

From Germany's perspective, the links between the American economy and the Allies meant that the United States had become the Allied arsenal and bank. Americans, however, faced a dilemma: cutting their economic ties with Britain would constitute a nonneutral act in favor of Germany. Under international law, Britain—which controlled the seas—could buy both contraband (war-related

goods) and noncontraband from neutrals. It was Germany's responsibility, not America's, to stop such trade in ways that international law prescribed—that is, by an effective blockade of the enemy's territory, by the seizure of contraband from neutral (American) ships, or by the confiscation of goods from belligerent (British) ships. Germans, of course, judged the huge U.S. trade with the Allies an act of nonneutrality that had to be stopped.

20-1c Wilsonianism

The president and his aides believed, finally, that Wilsonian principles stood a better chance of international acceptance if Britain, rather than the Central Powers, sat astride the postwar world. "Wilsonianism," the cluster of ideas that Wilson espoused, consisted of traditional American principles (such as democracy and the Open Door) and a conviction that the United States was a beacon of freedom to the world. Only the United States could lead the convulsed world into a new, peaceful era of unobstructed commerce, free-market capitalism, democratic politics, and open diplomacy. American Progressivism, it seemed, was to be projected onto the world.

"America had the infinite privilege of fulfilling her destiny and saving the world," Wilson claimed. Empires had to be dismantled to honor the principle of self-determination. Armaments had to be reduced. Critics charged that Wilson often violated his own credos in his eagerness to force them on others—as his military interventions in Mexico in 1914, Haiti in 1915, and the Dominican Republic in 1916 testified. All agreed, though, that such ideals served American commercial purposes; in this way idealism and self-interest were married.

To say that American neutrality was never a real possibility given ethnic loyalties, economic ties, and Wilsonian preferences is not to say that Wilson sought to enter the war. He emphatically wanted to keep the United States out. Time and again, he tried to mediate the crisis to prevent one power from crushing another. In early 1917, the president remarked that "we are the only one of the great white nations that is free from war today, and it would be a crime against civilization for us to go in." But go in the United States finally did. Why?

20-1d Violation of Neutral Rights

The short answer is that Americans got caught in the Allied–Central Power crossfire. British naval policy aimed to sever neutral trade with Germany in order to cripple the German economy. The British, "ruling the waves and waiving the rules," declared a blockade of water entrances to Germany and mined the North Sea. They also harassed neutral shipping by seizing cargoes and defining a broad list of contraband (including foodstuffs) that they prohibited neutrals from shipping to Germany. American commerce with Germany dwindled rapidly. Furthermore, to counter German submarines, the British flouted international law by arming their merchant ships and flying neutral (sometimes American) flags. Wilson frequently protested British violations of neutral rights, pointing out that neutrals had the right to sell and ship noncontraband goods to belligerents without interference. But London often deftly defused Washington's criticism by paying for confiscated cargoes, and German provocations made British behavior appear less offensive by comparison.

Unable to win the war on land and determined to lift the blockade and halt American-Allied commerce, Germany looked for victory at sea by using submarines. In February 1915, Berlin declared a war zone around the British Isles, warned neutral vessels to stay out so as not to be attacked by mistake, and advised passengers from neutral nations to stay off Allied ships. President Wilson informed Germany that the United States would hold it to "strict accountability" for any losses of American life and property.

Wilson was interpreting international law in the strictest possible sense. The law that an attacker had to warn a passenger or merchant ship before attacking, so that passengers and crew could disembark safely into lifeboats, predated the submarine. The Germans thought the slender, frail, and sluggish *Unterseebooten* (U-boats) should not be expected to surface to warn ships, for surfacing would cancel out the U-boats' advantage of surprise and leave them vulnerable to attack. Berlin protested that Wilson was denying it the one weapon that could break the British economic stranglehold, disrupt the Allies' substantial connection with U.S. producers and bankers, and win the war. To all concerned—British, Germans, and Americans—naval warfare became a matter of life and death.

20-2 The Decision for War

▶ Why did peace advocates oppose American involvement in World War I?

▶ What developments drew the United States into the war?

Ultimately, it was the war at sea that doomed the prospects for U.S. neutrality. In the early months of 1915, German U-boats sank ship after ship, most notably the British liner *Lusitania* on May 7. Of 159 Americans on board, 128 died. In mid-August, after a lull following Germany's promise to refrain from attacking passenger liners, another British vessel, the *Arabic*, was sunk off Ireland. Three Americans died. The Germans quickly pledged that an unarmed passenger ship would never again be attacked without warning. But the sinking of the *Arabic* fueled debate over American passengers on belligerent vessels. Echoing Bryan's plea from the previous spring (see the chapter-opening vignette), critics asked: why not require Americans to sail on American craft? From August 1914 to March 1917, after all, only 3 Americans died on an American ship (the tanker *Gulflight*, sunk by a German U-boat in May 1915), whereas about 190 were killed on belligerent ships.

20-2a Peace Advocates

In March 1916, a U-boat attack on the *Sussex*, a French vessel crossing the English Channel, took the United States a

△ Initially underestimated as a weapon, the German U-boat proved to be frighteningly effective against Allied ships. At the beginning of the war, Germany had about twenty operational submarines in its High Seas Fleet, but officials moved swiftly to speed up production. This 1914 German poster showing U-boats choking off supplies to Britain celebrates German submarine production.

step closer to war. Four Americans were injured on that ship, which the U-boat commander mistook for a minelayer. Stop the marauding submarines, Wilson lectured Berlin, or the United States would sever diplomatic relations. Again the Germans retreated, pledging not to attack merchant vessels without warning. At about the same time, U.S. relations with Britain soured. The British crushing of the Easter Rebellion in Ireland and further British restriction of U.S. trade with the Central Powers aroused American anger.

As the United States became more entangled in the Great War, many Americans urged Wilson to keep the nation out. In early 1915, Jane Addams, Carrie Chapman Catt, and other suffragists helped found the Woman's Peace Party, the U.S. section of the Women's International League for Peace and Freedom. "The mother half of humanity," claimed women peace advocates, had a special role as "the guardians of life." Later that same year, some pacifist Progressives—including

Oswald Garrison Villard, Paul Kellogg, and Lillian Wald—organized an antiwar coalition, the American Union Against Militarism. Businessman Andrew Carnegie, who in 1910 had established the Carnegie Endowment for International Peace, helped finance peace groups. So did Henry Ford, who in late 1915 traveled on a "peace ship" to Europe to propagandize for a negotiated settlement. Socialists like Eugene Debs added their voices to the peace movement.

Antiwar advocates emphasized several points: that war drained a nation of its youth, resources, and reform impulse; that it fostered repression at home; that it violated Christian morality; and that wartime business barons reaped huge profits at the expense of the people. Militarism and conscription, Addams pointed out, were what millions of immigrants had left behind in Europe. Were they now—in the United States—to be forced into the decadent system they had escaped? Although the peace movement was splintered—some wanted to keep the United States out of the conflict but did not endorse the pacifists' claim that intervention could never be justified—it carried political and intellectual weight that Wilson could not ignore, and it articulated several ideas that he shared. In fact, he campaigned on a peace platform in the 1916 presidential election. After his triumph, Wilson futilely labored once again to bring the belligerents to the conference table. In early 1917, he advised them to temper their acquisitive war aims, appealing for "peace without victory."

20-2b Unrestricted Submarine Warfare

In Germany, Wilson's overture went unheeded. Since August 1916, leaders in Berlin had debated whether to resume the unrestricted U-boat campaign. Opponents feared a break with the United States, but proponents claimed there was no choice. Only through an all-out attack on Britain's supply shipping, they argued, could Germany win the war before the British blockade and trench warfare in France had exhausted Germany's ability to keep fighting. If the U-boats could sink 600,000 tons of Allied shipping per month, the German admiralty estimated, Britain would be brought to the brink of starvation. True, the United States might enter the war, but that was a risk worth taking. Victory might be achieved before U.S. troops could be ferried across the Atlantic in sizable numbers. It proved a winning argument. In early February 1917, Germany launched unrestricted submarine warfare. All warships and merchant vessels—belligerent or neutral—would be attacked if sighted in the declared war zone. Wilson quickly broke diplomatic relations with Berlin.

This German challenge to American neutral rights and economic interests was soon followed by a German threat to U.S. security. In late February, British intelligence intercepted and passed to American officials a telegram addressed to the German minister in Mexico from German foreign secretary Arthur Zimmermann. Its message: if Mexico joined a military alliance against the United States, Germany would help Mexico recover the territories it had lost in 1848, including several western states. Zimmermann hoped to "set new

enemies on America's neck—enemies which give them plenty to take care of over there."

The Zimmermann telegram stiffened Wilson's resolve. Even though Mexico City rejected Germany's offer, the Wilson administration judged Zimmermann's telegram "a conspiracy against this country." Mexico still might let German agents use Mexican soil to propagandize against the United States, if not sabotage American properties. The prospect of a German-Mexican collaboration helped turn the tide of opinion in the American Southwest, where antiwar sentiment had been strong.

Soon afterward, Wilson asked Congress for "armed neutrality" to defend American lives and commerce. He requested authority to arm American merchant ships and to "employ any other instrumentalities or methods that may be necessary." In the midst of the debate, Wilson released Zimmermann's telegram to the press. Americans were outraged. Still, antiwar senators Robert M. La Follette and George Norris, among others, saw the armed-ship bill as a blank check for the president to move the country to war, and they filibustered it to death. Wilson proceeded to arm America's commercial vessels anyway. The action came too late to prevent the sinking of several American ships. War cries echoed across the nation. In late March, an agonized Wilson called Congress into special session.

20-2c War Message and War Declaration

On April 2, 1917, the president stepped before a hushed Congress. Solemnly, he accused the Germans of "warfare against mankind." Passionately and eloquently, Wilson enumerated U.S. grievances: Germany's violation of freedom of the seas, disruption of commerce, interference with Mexico, and breach of human rights by killing innocent Americans. The "Prussian autocracy" had to be punished by "the democracies." Russia was now among the latter, he was pleased to report, because the Russian Revolution had ousted the czar just weeks before. Congress declared war against Germany on April 6 by a vote of 373 to 50 in the House and 82 to 6 in the Senate. (This vote was for war against Germany only; a declaration of war against Austria-Hungary came several months later, on December 7.) Montana's Jeannette Rankin, the first woman ever to sit in Congress, cast a ringing no vote. "Peace is a woman's job," she declared, "because men have a natural fear of being classed as cowards if they oppose war" and because mothers should protect their children from death-dealing weapons.

For principle, for morality, for honor, for commerce, for security, for reform—for all of these reasons, Wilson took the United States into the Great War. The submarine was certainly the culprit that drew a reluctant president and nation into the maelstrom. Yet critics did not attribute the U.S. descent into war to the U-boat alone. They emphasized Wilson's rigid definition of international law, which did not accommodate the submarine's tactics. They faulted his contention that Americans should be entitled to travel anywhere, even on a belligerent ship loaded with

△ Jeannette Rankin (1880–1973) of Montana was the first woman to sit in the House of Representatives (elected in 1916) and the only member of Congress to vote against U.S. entry into both world wars (in 1917 and 1941). A lifelong pacifist, she would later lead a march in Washington, D.C.—at age eighty-seven—against U.S. participation in the Vietnam War. Here she is addressing a rally in Union Square, New York City, September 1924.

20-3 Winning the War

▶ What actions did the federal government take to prepare for and prosecute the war?

▶ How did the nature of combat impact soldiers?

▶ How did Woodrow Wilson's vision for world affairs clash with that of Vladimir Lenin?

Even before the U.S. declaration of war, the Wilson administration—encouraged by such groups as the National Security League and the Navy League, and by mounting public outrage against Germany's submarine warfare—had been strengthening the military under the banner of "preparedness." When the pacifist song "I Didn't Raise My Boy to Be a Soldier" became popular, preparedness proponents retorted, "I Didn't Raise My Boy to Be a Coward." The National Defense Act of 1916 provided for increases in the army and National Guard and for summer training camps modeled on the one in Plattsburgh, New York, where a slice of America's social and economic elite had trained in 1915 as "citizen-soldiers." The Navy Act of 1916 started the largest naval expansion in American history.

20-3a The Draft and the Soldier

To raise an army after the declaration of war, Congress in May 1917 passed the **Selective Service Act**, requiring all males between the ages of twenty-one and thirty (later changed to eighteen and forty-five) to register. National service, proponents believed, would not only prepare the nation for battle but also instill patriotism and respect for order, democracy, and personal sacrifice. Critics feared it would lead to the militarization of American life.

On June 5, 1917, more than 9.5 million men signed up for the "great national lottery." By war's end, 24 million men had been registered by local draft boards. Of this number, 4.8 million had served in the armed forces, 2 million of that number in France. Among them were hundreds of thousands who had volunteered before December 1917, when the government prohibited enlistment because the military judged voluntarism too inefficient (many volunteers were more useful in civilian factories than in the army) and too competitive (enlistees got to choose the service they wanted, thus setting off recruiting wars). Millions of laborers received deferments from military duty because they worked in war industries or had dependents.

The typical soldier was a draftee in his early to midtwenties, white, single, American born, and poorly educated (most had not attended high school, and perhaps 30 percent could not read or write). Tens of thousands of women enlisted in the army Nurse Corps, served as "hello girls" (volunteer bilingual telephone operators) in the army Signal Corps, and became clerks in the navy and Marine Corps. On college campuses, 150,000 students joined the Student Army Training Corps or similar navy and marine units. At officer training camps, the army turned out "ninety-day wonders."

FPG/Archive Photos/Getty Images

contraband. They criticized his policies as nonneutral. But they lost the debate. Most Americans came to accept Wilson's view that the Germans had to be checked to ensure an open, orderly world in which U.S. principles and interests would be safe.

America went to war to reform world politics, not to destroy Germany. By early 1917, the president concluded that the United States would not be able to claim a seat at the postwar peace conference unless it became a combatant. At the peace conference, President Wilson intended to promote the principles he thought essential to a stable world order, to advance democracy and the Open Door, and to outlaw revolution and aggression. He tried to preserve part of his country's status as a neutral by designating the United States an "Associated" power rather than a full-fledged Allied nation, but this was akin to a hope of being only partly pregnant.

Selective Service Act Law that required all men between twenty-one and thirty (later expanded to eighteen through forty-five) to register with local draft boards.

Some 400,000 African Americans also served in the military. Although many southern politicians feared arming blacks, the army drafted them into segregated units, where they were assigned to menial labor and endured crude abuse and miserable conditions. Ultimately, more than 40,000 African Americans would see combat in Europe, however, and several black units served with distinction in various divisions of the French army. The all-black 369th Infantry Regiment, for example, spent more time in the trenches—191 days—and received more medals than any other American outfit. The French government awarded the entire regiment the Croix de Guerre.

Although French officers had their share of racial prejudice and often treated the soldiers from their own African colonies poorly, black Americans serving with the French reported a degree of respect and cooperation generally lacking in the U.S. Army. They also spoke of getting a much warmer reception from French civilians than they were used to in the United States. The irony was not lost on African American leaders, such as W. E. B. Du Bois. Du Bois had endorsed the support of the National Association for the Advancement of Colored People (NAACP) for the war and echoed its call for blacks to volunteer for the fight so that they might help make the world safe for democracy and help blur the color lines at home.

But not everyone eligible for military service was eager to sign up. Approximately 3 million men evaded draft registration. Some were arrested, and others fled to Mexico or Canada, but most stayed at home and were never discovered. Another 338,000 men who had registered and been summoned by their draft boards failed to show up for induction. According to arrest records, most of these "deserters" and the more numerous "evaders" were lower-income agricultural and industrial laborers. Some simply felt overwhelmed by the government bureaucracy and stayed away; others were members of minority or ethnic groups who felt alienated. Although nearly 65,000 draftees initially applied for conscientious-objector status (refusing to bear arms for religious or pacifist reasons), some changed their minds or, like so many others, failed preinduction examinations. Quakers and Mennonites were numerous among the 4,000 inductees actually classified as conscientious objectors (COs). They did not have it easy. General Leonard Wood called COs "enemies of the Republic," and the military harassed them. COs who refused noncombat service, such as in the medical corps, faced imprisonment.

20-3b Trench Warfare

The U.S. troops who shipped out to France would do their fighting under American command. General **John J. Pershing**, head of the **American Expeditionary Forces (AEF)**, insisted that his "sturdy rookies" remain a separate, independent army. He was not about to turn over his "doughboys" (so termed, according to one theory, because the large buttons on American uniforms in the 1860s resembled a deep-fried bread of that name) to Allied commanders, who had become wedded to unimaginative and deadly trench warfare,

△ Some fifteen thousand Native Americans served in the military in World War I. Most of them were enlistees who sought escape from restrictive Indian schools and lives of poverty, opportunities to develop new skills, and chances to prove their patriotism. This photo shows Fred Fast Horse, a Rosebud Sioux, as he recuperates in a New York hospital after suffering injury and paralysis during the Meuse-Argonne campaign of fall 1918. Unlike African Americans, Native Americans were not assigned to segregated units during the war. Native Americans participated in all major battles against German forces and suffered a high casualty rate in large part because they served as scouts, messengers, and snipers.

producing a military stalemate and ghastly casualties on the western front. Since the fall of 1914, zigzag trenches fronted by barbed wire and mines stretched across France. Between the muddy, stinking trenches lay "no man's land," denuded by artillery fire. When ordered out, soldiers would charge enemy trenches. If machine gun fire did not greet them, poison gas might.

First used by the Germans in April 1915, chlorine gas stimulated overproduction of fluid in the lungs, leading to death by drowning. One British officer tending to troops who had been gassed reported that "quite 200 men passed through my hands. . . . Some died with me, others on the way down . . . I had to argue with many of them as to whether they were dead or not." Gas in a variety of forms (mustard and phosgene, in addition to chlorine) would continue in use throughout the war, sometimes blistering, sometimes incapacitating, often killing.

The extent of the dying in the trench warfare is hard to comprehend.

John J. Pershing Commander of American Expeditionary Forces that fought in Europe.

American Expeditionary Forces U.S. soldiers who fought in Europe during World War I.

At the Battle of the Somme in 1916, the British (who suffered nearly 60,000 casualties on the opening day) and French suffered 600,000 dead or wounded to earn only 125 square miles; the Germans lost 400,000 men. At Verdun that same year, 336,000 Germans perished, and at Passchendaele in 1917 more than 370,000 British men died to gain about 40 miles of mud and barbed wire. Ambassador Page grew sickened by what Europe had become—"a bankrupt slaughter-house inhabited by unmated women."

20-3c Shell Shock

The first American units landed in France on June 26, 1917, marched in a Fourth of July parade in Paris, and then moved by train toward the front. They soon learned about the horrors caused by advanced weaponry. Some suffered shell shock, a form of mental illness also known as war psychosis. Symptoms included a fixed, empty stare; violent tremors; paralyzed limbs; listlessness; jabbering and screaming; and haunting dreams. The illness could strike anyone; even those soldiers who appeared most manly and courageous cracked after days of incessant shelling and inescapable human carnage. "There was a limit to human endurance," one lieutenant explained. Providing some relief were Red Cross canteens, staffed by women volunteers, which gave soldiers way stations in a strange land and offered haircuts, food, and recreation. Some ten thousand Red Cross nurses also cared for the young warriors, while the American Library Association distributed 10 million books and magazines.

In Paris, where forty large houses of prostitution thrived, it became commonplace to hear that the British were drunkards, the French were whoremongers, and the Americans were both. Venereal disease became a serious problem. French Prime Minister Georges Clemenceau offered licensed, inspected prostitutes in "special houses" to the American army. When the generous Gallic offer reached Washington, Secretary of War Newton Baker gasped, "For God's sake . . . don't show this to the President or he'll stop the war." By war's end, about 15 percent of America's soldiers had contracted venereal disease, costing the army $50 million and 7 million days of active duty. Periodic inspections, chemical prophylactic treatments, and the threat of court-martial for infected soldiers kept the problem from being even greater.

20-3d American Units in France

The experience of being in Europe enlarged what for many American draftees had been a circumscribed world. Soldiers filled their diaries and letters with descriptions of the local customs and "ancient" architecture, and noted how the grimy and war-torn French countryside bore little resemblance to the groomed landscapes they had seen in paintings. Some felt both admiration for the spirit of endurance they saw in the populace and irritation that the locals were not more grateful for the Americans' arrival. "Life in France for the American soldier meant marching in the dirt and mud, living in cellars in filth, being wet and cold and fighting," the chief of staff of the Fourth Division remarked. "He had come to help France in the hour of distress and he was glad he came but these French people did not seem to appreciate him at all."

◁ A U.S. soldier of Company K, 110th Infantry Regiment, receives aid during fighting at Verennes, France.

National Archives

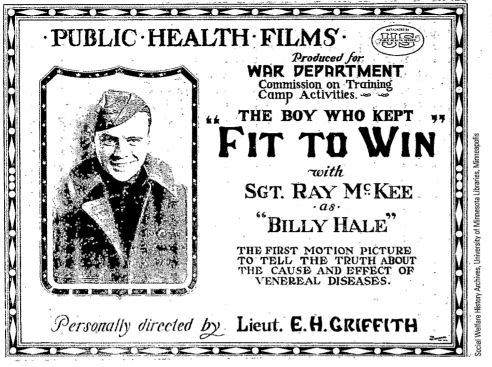

◁ During the First World War, the War Department promoted a film to combat sexually transmitted diseases. After the war, the New York State Board of Censors declared the film obscene.

The influx of American men and materiel—and the morale blow they delivered to the Central Powers—decided the outcome of the First World War. With both sides exhausted, the Americans tipped the balance toward the Allies. It took time, though, for the weight of the American military machine to make itself felt. From an early point, the U.S. Navy battled submarines and escorted troop carriers, and pilots in the U.S. Air Service, flying mostly British and French aircraft, saw limited action, mostly against German ground troops and transport. American "aces" like Eddie Rickenbacker took on their German counterparts in aerial "dogfights" and became heroes, as much in France as in their own country. But only ground troops could make a decisive difference, and American units actually did not engage in much combat until after the lull in the fighting during the harsh winter of 1917–1918.

20-3e The Bolshevik Revolution

By then, the military and diplomatic situation had changed dramatically because of an event that was arguably the most important political development of the twentieth century: the Bolshevik Revolution in Russia. In November 1917, the liberal-democratic government of Aleksander Kerensky, which had led the country since the czar's abdication early in the year, was overthrown by radical socialists led by Vladimir Ilyich Ulyanov, better known by the alias Lenin. Lenin seized power vowing to change world politics and end imperial rivalries on terms that challenged Woodrow Wilson's. Lenin saw the war as signaling the impending end of capitalism and looked for a global revolution, carried out by workers, that would sweep away the

"imperialist order." For Western leaders, the prospect of Bolshevik-style revolutions spreading worldwide was too frightening to contemplate. The ascendancy of the world's laboring classes working in unity would destroy governments everywhere.

In the weeks following their takeover, the Bolsheviks attempted to embarrass the capitalist governments and incite world revolution by publishing several secret agreements among the Allies for dividing up the colonies and other territories of the Central Powers in the event of an Allied victory. Veteran watchers of world affairs found nothing particularly shocking in the documents, and Wilson had known of them, but the disclosures belied the noble rhetoric of Allied war aims. Wilson confided to Colonel House that he really wanted to tell the Bolsheviks to "go to hell," but he accepted the colonel's argument that he would have to address Lenin's claims that there was little to distinguish the two warring sides and that socialism represented the future.

20-3f Fourteen Points

The result was the **Fourteen Points**, unveiled in January 1918, in which Wilson reaffirmed America's commitment to an international system governed by laws and renounced territorial gains as a legitimate war aim. The first five points called for diplomacy "in the public view," freedom of the seas, lower tariffs, reductions in armaments, and the decolonization of empires. The next eight points

Fourteen Points President Wilson's program for world peace; presented to Congress in a 1918 speech, in the midst of World War I.

specified the evacuation of foreign troops from Russia, Belgium, and France, and appealed for self-determination for nationalities in Europe, such as the Poles. For Wilson, the fourteenth point was the most important—the mechanism for achieving all the others: "a general association of nations" or League of Nations.

Wilson's appeal did not impress Lenin, who called for an immediate end to the fighting, the eradication of colonialism, and self-determination for all peoples. Lenin also made a separate peace with Germany—the Treaty of Brest-Litovsk, signed on March 3, 1918. The deal erased centuries of Russian expansion, as Poland, Finland, and the Baltic states were taken from Russia and Ukraine was granted independence. One of Lenin's motives was to allow Russian troops loyal to the Bolsheviks to return home to fight anti-Bolshevik forces, who had launched a civil war to oust the new government.

The emerging feud between Lenin and Wilson contained the seeds of the superpower confrontation that would dominate the international system after 1945. Both men rejected the old diplomacy, which they claimed had created the conditions for the current war; both insisted on the need for a new world order. Although each professed adherence to democratic principles, they defined democracy differently. For Lenin, it meant workers everywhere seizing control from the owners of capital and establishing worker-led governments. For Wilson, it meant independent governments operating within capitalist systems and according to republican political practices.

20-3g Americans in Battle

In March 1918, with German troops released from the Russian front and transferred to France, the Germans launched a major offensive. By May, they had pushed to within fifty miles of Paris. Late that month, troops of the U.S. First Division helped blunt the German advance at Cantigny (see Map 20.2). In June, the Third Division and French forces held positions along the Marne River at Château-Thierry, and the Second Division soon attacked the Germans in the Belleau Wood. American soldiers won the battle after three weeks of fighting, but thousands died or were wounded after they made almost sacrificial frontal assaults against German machine guns.

Allied victory in the Second Battle of the Marne in July 1918 stemmed all German advances. In September, French and American forces took St. Mihiel in a ferocious battle in which American gunners fired 100,000 rounds of phosgene gas shells. Then the Allies began their massive Meuse-Argonne offensive. More than 1 million Americans joined British and French troops in weeks of fierce combat; some 26,000 Americans died before the Allies claimed the Argonne Forest on October 10. For Germany—its ground and submarine war stymied, its troops and cities mutinous, its allies Turkey and Austria dropping out, its kaiser

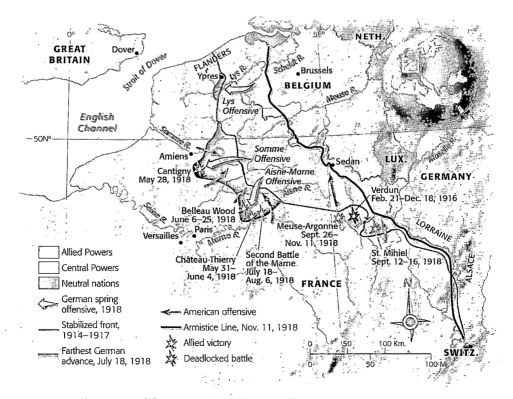

Map 20.2 American Troops at the Western Front, 1918

America's 2 million troops in France met German forces head-on, ensuring the defeat of the Central Powers in 1918.

The Influenza Pandemic of 1918

In the summer and fall of 1918, as World War I neared its end, a terrible plague swept the earth. It was a massive outbreak of influenza, and it would kill more than twice as many as the Great War itself—somewhere between 25 million and 40 million people. In the United States, 675,000 people died.

The first cases were identified in midwestern military camps in early March. Soldiers complained of flulike symptoms—headache, sore throat, fever—and many did not recover. At Fort Riley, Kansas, 48 men died. But with the war effort in full swing, few in government or the press took notice. Soldiers shipped out to Europe in large numbers (84,000 in March), some unknowingly carrying the virus in their lungs. The illness appeared on the western front in April. By the end of June, an estimated 8 million Spaniards were infected, thereby giving the disease its name, the Spanish flu.

In August, after a midsummer lull, a second, deadlier form of influenza began spreading. This time, the epidemic erupted simultaneously in three cities on three continents: Freetown, Sierra Leone, in Africa; Brest, France, the port of entry for many American soldiers; and Boston, Massachusetts. In September, the disease swept down the East Coast

to New York, Philadelphia, and beyond. That month, 12,000 Americans died.

It was a flu like no other. People could be healthy at the start of the weekend and dead by the end of it. Some experienced a rapid accumulation of fluid in the lungs and would quite literally drown. Others died more slowly, of secondary infections with bacterial pneumonia. Mortality rates were highest for twenty- to twenty-nine-year-olds—the same group dying in huge numbers in the trenches.

In October, the epidemic hit full force. It spread to Japan, India, Africa, and Latin America. In the United States, 200,000 perished. There was a nationwide shortage of caskets and gravediggers, and funerals were limited to fifteen minutes. Bodies were left in gutters or on front porches, to be picked up by trucks that drove the streets. Stores were forbidden to hold sales; schools and cinemas closed. Army surgeon general Victor Vaughan made a frightening calculation: "If the epidemic continues its mathematical rate of acceleration, civilization could easily disappear from the face of the earth within a few weeks."

Then, suddenly, in November, for reasons still unclear, the epidemic

eased, though the dying continued into 1919. In England and Wales, the final toll was 200,000. Samoa lost a quarter of its population, while in India the epidemic may have claimed a staggering 20 million. It was, in historian Roy Porter's words, "the greatest single demographic shock mankind has ever experienced."

World War I had helped spread the disease, but so had technological improvements that in previous decades facilitated global travel. The world was a smaller, more intimate place, often for good but sometimes for ill. Americans, accustomed to thinking that two great oceans could isolate them, were reminded that they were immutably linked to the rest of humankind.

CRITICAL THINKING

- World War I and the Spanish flu pandemic challenged many Americans' belief that the United States was protected by the vastness of the Atlantic and Pacific Oceans on either side of the continent. Even so, many Americans still assume a level of isolation. Does that assumption continue to color American foreign policy?
- What other events in the twentieth and twenty-first centuries have challenged the assumption of continental isolation?

PhotoQuest/Getty Images

◁ The rapid spread of the influenza pandemic required the construction of emergency hospitals in numerous locales, such as this one in Brookline, Massachusetts, pictured in October 1918.

abdicated, and facing the prospect of endless American troop reinforcements—peace became imperative. The Germans accepted a punishing armistice that took effect on the morning of November 11, 1918, at the eleventh hour of the eleventh day of the eleventh month.

20-3h Casualties

The cost of the war is impossible to compute, but the scale is clear enough: the belligerents counted 10 million soldiers and 6.6 million civilians dead and 21.3 million people wounded. Fifty-three thousand American soldiers died in battle, and another 62,000 died from disease. Many of the latter died from the virulent strain of influenza that ravaged the world in late 1918 and would ultimately claim more victims than the Great War itself. The economic damage was colossal as well, helping to account for the widespread starvation Europe experienced in the winter of 1918–1919. Economic output on the continent dwindled, and transport over any distance was in some countries virtually nonexistent. "We are at the dead season of our fortunes," wrote one British observer. "Never in the lifetime of men now living has the universal element in the soul of man burnt so dimly."

Casualties of the conflagration, the German, Austro-Hungarian, Ottoman, and Russian empires were no more. For a time, it appeared the Bolshevik Revolution might spread westward, as communist uprisings shook Germany and parts of central Europe. Even before the armistice, revolutionaries temporarily took power in the German cities of Bremen, Hamburg, and Lübeck. In Hungary, a revolutionary government actually held power for several months, while Austria was racked by left-wing demonstrations. In Moscow, meanwhile, the new Soviet state sought to consolidate its power. "We are sitting upon an open powder magazine," Colonel House worried, "and some day a spark may ignite it."

20-4 Mobilizing the Home Front

▷ What role did the federal government play in mobilizing the economy during World War I?

▷ What impact did wartime production needs have on workers?

▷ How did minority groups respond to wartime mobilization?

"It is not an army that we must shape and train for war," declared President Wilson, "it is a nation." The United States was a belligerent for only nineteen months, but the war had a tremendous impact at home. The federal government moved swiftly to expand its power over the economy to meet war needs and intervened in American life as never before. The vastly enlarged Washington bureaucracy

managed the economy, labor force, military, public opinion, and more. Federal expenditures increased tremendously as the government spent more than $760 million a month from April 1917 to August 1919. As tax revenues lagged behind, the administration resorted to deficit spending (see Figure 20.1). The total cost of the war was difficult to calculate because future generations would have to pay veterans' benefits and interest on loans. To Progressives of the New Nationalist persuasion, the wartime expansion and centralization of government power were welcome. To others, these changes seemed excessive, leading to concentrated, hence dangerous, federal power.

20-4a Business-Government Cooperation

The federal government and private business became partners during the war. So-called dollar-a-year executives flocked to the nation's capital from major companies, retaining their corporate salaries while serving in official

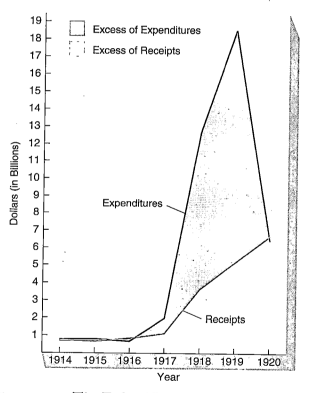
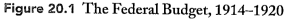

Figure 20.1 The Federal Budget, 1914–1920

During the First World War, the federal government spent more money than it received from increased taxes. It borrowed from banks or sold bonds through Liberty Loan drives. To meet the mounting costs of the war, in other words, the federal government had to resort to deficit spending. Expenditures topped receipts by more than $13 billion in 1919. Given this wartime fiscal pattern, moreover, the U.S. federal debt rose from $1 billion in 1914 to $25 billion in 1919. *Source: U.S. Department of Commerce, Historical Statistics of the United States: Colonial Times to 1957 (Washington, D.C.: Bureau of the Census, 1960), p. 711.*

administrative and consulting capacities. But evidence of self-interested businesspeople cashing in on the national interest aroused public protest. The head of the aluminum advisory committee, for example, was also president of the largest aluminum company. The assorted committees were disbanded in July 1917 in favor of a single manager, the **War Industries Board (WIB)**. But the federal government continued to work closely with business through trade associations, which grew significantly to two thousand by 1920. The government also suspended antitrust laws and signed cost-plus contracts, which guaranteed companies a healthy profit and a means to pay higher wages to head off labor strikes. Competitive bidding was virtually abandoned. Under such wartime practices, big business grew bigger.

Hundreds of new government agencies, staffed primarily by businesspeople, placed controls on the economy in order to shift the nation's resources to the Allies, the AEF, and war-related production. The Food Administration, led by engineer and investor Herbert Hoover, launched voluntary programs to increase production and conserve food—Americans were urged to grow "victory gardens" and to eat meatless and wheatless meals—but it also set prices and regulated distribution. The Railroad Administration took over the railway industry. The Fuel Administration controlled coal supplies and rationed gasoline. When strikes threatened the telephone and telegraph companies, the federal government seized and ran them.

The largest of the superagencies was the War Industries Board (WIB), headed by financier Bernard Baruch. At one point, this Wall Streeter told Henry Ford frankly that he would dispatch the military to seize his plants if the automaker did not accept WIB limits on car production. Ford relented. Although the WIB seemed all-powerful, in reality it had to conciliate competing interest groups and compromise with the business executives whose advice it so valued. Designed as a clearinghouse for coordinating the national economy, the WIB made purchases, allocated supplies, and fixed prices at levels that business requested. The WIB also ordered the standardization of goods to save materials and streamline production. The varieties of automobile tires, for example, were reduced from 287 to 3.

20-4b Economic Performance

The performance of the mobilized economy was mixed, but it delivered enough men and material to France to ensure the defeat of the Central Powers. About one-quarter of all American production was diverted to war needs. As farmers enjoyed boom years of higher prices, they put more acreage into production and mechanized as never before. From 1915 to 1920, the number of tractors in American fields jumped tenfold. Gross farm income for the period from 1914 to 1919 increased more than 230 percent. Although manufacturing output leveled off in 1918, some industries realized substantial growth because of wartime demand. Steel reached a peak

production of 45 million tons in 1917, twice the prewar figure. As U.S. soldiers popularized American brands in Europe, tobacconists profited from a huge increase in cigarette sales: from 26 billion cigarettes in 1916 to 48 billion in 1918. Overall, the gross national product in 1920 stood 237 percent higher than in 1914.

The rush to complete massive assignments caused mistakes to be made. Weapons deliveries fell short of demand; the bloated bureaucracy of the War Shipping Board failed to build enough ships. In the severe winter of 1917–1918, millions of Americans could not get coal. Coal companies held back on production to raise prices; railroads did not have enough coal cars; and harbors froze, closing out coal barges. People died from pneumonia and freezing. A Brooklyn man went out in the morning to forage for coal and returned to find his two-month-old daughter frozen to death in her crib.

To help pay its wartime bills, the government dramatically increased taxes. The Revenue Act in 1916 started the process by raising the surtax on high incomes and corporate profits, imposing a federal tax on large estates, and significantly increasing the tax on munitions manufacturers. Still, the government financed only one-third of the war through taxes. The other two-thirds came from loans, including Liberty bonds sold to the American people through aggressive campaigns. The War Revenue Act of 1917 provided for a more steeply graduated personal income tax; a corporate income tax; an excess profits tax; and increased excise taxes on alcoholic beverages, tobacco, and luxury items.

Although these taxes did curb excessive corporate profiteering, there were loopholes. Sometimes companies inflated costs to conceal profits or paid high salaries and bonuses to their executives. Four officers of Bethlehem Steel, for example, divided bonuses of $2.3 million in 1917 and $2.1 million the next year. Corporate net earnings for 1913 totaled $4 billion; in 1917, they reached $7 billion; and in 1918, after the tax bite and the war's end, they still stood at $4.5 billion. Profits and patriotism went hand in hand in America's war experience.

20-4c Labor Shortage

For American workers, the full-employment wartime economy increased earnings and gave many of them time-and-a-half pay for overtime work. With the higher cost of living, however, workers saw minimal improvement in their economic standing. Turnover rates were high as workers switched jobs for higher pay and better conditions. Some employers sought to overcome labor shortages by expanding welfare and social programs, and by establishing personnel departments—"specialized human nature engineers to keep its human machinery frictionless," General Electric explained.

War Industries Board (WIB)
Government agency established to coordinate military purchasing, ensure production efficiency, and provide weapons and supplies to the military.

Eating to Win

The war effort mobilized Americans as never before and also demanded that they make sacrifices. Herbert Hoover's Food Administration used colorful posters to persuade Americans to change their eating habits. The poster below uses bold type and a man standing over a fallen German soldier to send a patriotic message to eat less and save food for the troops. The poster at right has a 1940s Uncle Sam as teacher with a book promoting City and Farm Gardens and asking folks to learn more. The poster below and to the right uses religion (and guilt) to motivate the public.

CRITICAL THINKING

- Which poster do you find most effective, and why?
- How are Americans persuaded today to change their eating habits?

△ In this colorful 1917 poster, Uncle Sam, posing as a teacher, says, "Garden to cut food costs." The poster offers a free Department of Agriculture "bulletin on gardening—it's food for thought."

△ Hispanic artist Francis Luis Mora used strong graphics for his 1918 poster showing a man standing over a fallen German soldier.

△ This 1917 poster showing a bounty of fall harvest fruits and vegetables—"This is what God gives us"—uses richly detailed illustration and colorful red type to get attention and ask the question, "What are you giving so that others may live?"

To meet the labor crisis, the Department of Labor's U.S. Employment Service matched laborers with job vacancies, especially attracting workers from the South and Midwest to war industries in the East. The department also temporarily relaxed the literacy test and head tax provisions of immigration law to attract farm labor, miners, and railroad workers from Mexico. Because the labor crisis also generated a housing crisis as workers crammed into cities, the U.S. Housing Corporation and Emergency Fleet Corporation, following the British example, built row houses in Newport News, Virginia, and Eddystone, Pennsylvania.

The tight wartime labor market had another consequence: new work opportunities for women. In Connecticut, a special motion picture, *Mr. and Mrs. Hines of Stamford Do Their Bit*, appealed to housewives' patriotism, urging them to take factory jobs. Although the total number of women in the workforce increased slightly, the real story was that many changed jobs, sometimes moving into formerly male domains. Some white women left domestic service for factories, shifted from clerking in department stores to stenography and typing, or departed textile mills for employment in firearms plants. At least 20 percent of all workers in the wartime electrical machinery, airplane, and food industries were women. Some one hundred thousand women worked in the railroad industry. As white women took advantage of these new opportunities, black women took some of their places in domestic service and in textile factories. For the first time, department stores employed black women as elevator operators and cafeteria waitresses. Most working women were single and remained concentrated in sex-segregated occupations, serving as typists, nurses, teachers, and domestic servants.

Women also participated in the war effort in other ways. As volunteers, they made clothing for refugees and soldiers, served at Red Cross facilities, and taught French to nurses. Some drove ambulances in the war zone. Many worked for the Women's Committee of the Council of National Defense, whose leaders included Ida Tarbell and Carrie Chapman Catt. A vast network of state, county, and town volunteer organizations, the council publicized government mobilization programs, encouraged home gardens, sponsored drives to sell Liberty bonds, and continued the push for social welfare reforms. This patriotic work won praise from men and improved the prospects for passage of the Nineteenth Amendment granting woman suffrage. "We have made partners of women in this war," Wilson said as he endorsed woman suffrage in 1918. "Shall we admit them only to a partnership of suffering and sacrifice ... and not to a partnership of privilege and right?"

Among African Americans, war mobilization wrought significant change as southern blacks undertook a great migration to northern cities to work in railroad yards, packinghouses, steel mills, shipyards, and coal mines. Between 1910 and 1920, Cleveland's black population swelled by more than 300 percent, Detroit's by more than 600 percent, and Chicago's by 150 percent. Much of the increase occurred between 1916 and 1919. All told, about a half-million African Americans

△ Stella Young (1896–1989), a Canadian-born woman from Chelsea, Massachusetts, became widely known as the "Doughnut Girl" because of her service during the First World War with the American branch of the Salvation Army, an international organization devoted to social work. She arrived in France in March 1918 and worked in emergency canteens near the battlefront, providing U.S. troops with coffee, cocoa, sandwiches, doughnuts, pie, and fruit. Stella Young became famous when a picture of her wearing a khaki uniform and a "doughboy" steel helmet was widely circulated as a postcard. This piece of sheet music was even written about her, and her postcard image was used to create the cover. She served again in World War II. Chelsea named a city square in her honor in 1968.

uprooted themselves to move to the North. Families sometimes pooled savings to send one member; others sold their household goods to pay for the journey. Most of the migrants were males—young (in their early twenties), unmarried, and skilled or semiskilled. Wartime jobs in the North provided an escape from low wages, sharecropping, tenancy, crop liens, debt peonage, lynchings, and political disfranchisement. To a friend back in Mississippi, one African American wrote: "I just begin to feel like a man.... I don't have to humble to no one. I have registered. Will vote the next election."

20-4d National War Labor Board

To keep factories running smoothly, Wilson instituted the National War Labor Board (NWLB) in early 1918. The NWLB discouraged strikes and lockouts and urged management to negotiate with existing unions. In July, after the Western Union Company fired eight hundred union members for trying to organize the firm's workers and then defied an NWLB request to reinstate the employees, the president nationalized the telegraph lines and put the laborers back to work. That month, too, the NWLB directed General Electric to raise wages and stop discriminating against metal trades union members in Schenectady, New York. On the other hand, in September the NWLB ordered striking Bridgeport, Connecticut, machinists back to munitions factories, threatening to revoke their draft exemptions (granted earlier because they worked in an "essential" industry).

Many labor leaders hoped the war would offer opportunities for recognition and better pay through partnership with government. Samuel Gompers threw the AFL's loyalty to the Wilson administration, promising to deter strikes. He and other moderate labor leaders accepted appointments to federal agencies. The antiwar Socialist Party blasted the AFL for becoming a "fifth wheel on [the] capitalist war chariot," but union membership climbed from roughly 2.5 million in 1916 to more than 4 million in 1919.

The AFL, however, could not curb strikes by the radical Industrial Workers of the World (IWW, also known as "Wobblies") or rebellious AFL locals, especially those controlled by labor activists and socialists. In the nineteen war months, more than six thousand strikes expressed workers' demands for a "living wage" and improved working conditions (many called for an eight-hour workday). Exploiting Wilsonian wartime rhetoric, workers and their unions also sought to create "industrial democracy," a more representative workplace with a role for labor in determining job categories and content, and with workplace representation through shop committees. By 1920, in defiance of the national AFL, labor parties had sprung up in twenty-three states.

20-5 Civil Liberties Under Challenge

▶ How did the federal government seek to win and maintain public support for the war?

▶ What actions were taken by governmental and other actors to try to quash wartime dissent?

Gompers's backing of the call to arms meant a great deal to Wilson and his advisers, and they noted with satisfaction that most newspapers, religious leaders, and public officials were similarly supportive. They were less certain, however, about the attitudes of ordinary Americans. "Woe be to the man that seeks to stand in our way in this day of high resolution," the president

Committee on Public Information (CPI) Wartime propaganda agency, headed by journalist George Creel. While claiming merely to combat rumors with facts, the Creel committee in reality publicized the government's version of events and discredited all who questioned that version.

warned. An official and unofficial campaign soon began to silence dissenters who questioned Wilson's decision for war or who protested the draft. In the end, the Wilson administration compiled one of the worst civil liberties records in American history.

The targets of governmental and quasi-vigilante repression were the hundreds of thousands of Americans and aliens who refused to support the war: pacifists from all walks of life, conscientious objectors, socialists, radical labor groups, the debt-ridden tenant farmers of Oklahoma who staged the Green Corn Rebellion against the draft, the Non-Partisan League, reformers like Robert La Follette and Jane Addams, and countless others. In the wartime process of debating the question of the right to speak freely in a democracy, the concept of "civil liberties" emerged for the first time in American history as a major public policy issue (see "Legacy for a People and a Nation," at the end of this chapter).

20-5a The Committee on Public Information

The centerpiece of the administration's campaign to win support for the war was the **Committee on Public Information (CPI)**, formed in April 1917 and headed by Progressive journalist George Creel. Employing some of the nation's most talented writers and scholars, the CPI used propaganda to shape and mobilize public opinion. Pamphlets and films demonized the Germans, and CPI "Four-Minute Men" spoke at movie theaters, schools, and churches to pump up a patriotic mood. Encouraged by the CPI to promote American participation in the war, film companies and their trade association, the National Association of the Motion Picture Industry, produced documentaries, newsreels, and anti-German movies, such as *The Kaiser, the Beast of Berlin* (1918), and *To Hell with the Kaiser* (1918).

The committee also urged the press to practice "self-censorship" and encouraged people to spy on their neighbors. Ultrapatriotic groups, such as the Sedition Slammers and the American Defense Society, used vigilantism. A German-American miner in Illinois was wrapped in a flag and lynched. In Hilger, Montana, citizens burned history texts that mentioned Germany. By the end of the war, sixteen states had banned the teaching of the German language. To avoid trouble, the Kaiser-Kuhn grocery in St. Louis changed its name to Pioneer Grocery. Germantown, Nebraska, became Garland, and the townspeople in Berlin, Iowa, henceforth hailed from Lincoln. The German shepherd became the Alsatian shepherd.

Because towns had Liberty Loan quotas to fill, they sometimes bullied "slackers" into purchasing bonds. Nativist advocates of "100 percent Americanism" exploited the emotional atmosphere to exhort immigrants to throw off their Old World cultures. Companies offered English language and naturalization classes in their factories and refused jobs and promotions to those who did not make adequate strides toward learning English. Even labor's drive for compulsory health insurance, which before the

◁ A member of the Eighth Regiment of the Illinois National Guard with his family, circa 1918. Originally organized as a volunteer regiment during the Spanish-American War in 1898, the Eighth Regiment achieved its greatest fame during World War I. The only regiment to be entirely commanded by African Americans and headquartered at the only black armory in the United States, the "Fighting Eighth" served with distinction in France, with 143 of its members losing their lives.

Chicago History Museum/Getty Images

war had gained advocates in several states, including New York and California, became victimized by the poisoned war atmosphere. Many physicians and insurance companies had for years denounced health insurance as "socialistic"; after the United States entered the war, they discredited it as "Made in Germany."

Even institutions that had long prided themselves on tolerance became contaminated by the spirit of coercion. Wellesley College economics professor Emily Greene Balch was fired for her pacifist views (she won the Nobel Peace Prize in 1946). Three Columbia University students were apprehended in mid-1917 for circulating an antiwar petition. Columbia also fired Professor J. M. Cattell, a distinguished psychologist, for his antiwar stand. His colleague Charles Beard, a historian with a prowar perspective, resigned in protest, stating, "If we have to suppress everything we don't like to hear, this country is resting on a pretty wobbly basis." In a number of states, local school boards dismissed teachers who questioned the war.

20-5b Espionage and Sedition Acts

The Wilson administration also guided through an obliging Congress the **Espionage Act** (1917) and the Sedition Act (1918). The first statute forbade "false statements" designed to impede the draft or promote military insubordination, and it banned from the mails materials considered treasonous. The Sedition Act made it unlawful to obstruct the sale of war bonds and to use "disloyal, profane, scurrilous, or abusive" language to describe the government, the Constitution, the flag, or the military uniform. These

loosely worded laws gave the government wide latitude to crack down on critics. More than two thousand people were prosecuted under the acts, and many others were intimidated into silence.

Progressives and conservatives alike used the war emergency to throttle the Industrial Workers of the World and the Socialist Party. Government agents raided IWW meetings, and the army marched into western mining and lumber regions to put down IWW strikes. By the end of the war, most of the union's leaders were in jail. In summer 1918, with a government stenographer present, Socialist Party leader Eugene V. Debs delivered a spirited oration extolling socialism and freedom of speech—including the freedom to criticize the Wilson administration for taking America into the war. Federal agents arrested him, and he was sentenced to ten years in prison. He remained incarcerated until late 1921, when he received a pardon.

The Supreme Court endorsed such convictions. In *Schenck v. U.S.* (1919), the Court unanimously upheld the conviction of a Socialist Party member who had mailed pamphlets urging resistance to the draft. In time of war, Justice Oliver Wendell Holmes wrote, the First Amendment could be restricted: "Free speech would not protect a man falsely shouting 'fire' in a theater and causing panic." If, according to Holmes, words "are of such a nature as to create a clear and present danger that they will bring about the substantial evils that Congress has a right to prevent," free speech could be limited.

Espionage Act Law that set fines and prison sentences for a variety of loosely defined antiwar activities.

DON'T TALK

THE WEB
IS SPUN
FOR YOU
WITH
INVISIBLE
THREADS

KEEP OUT OF IT

HELP TO DESTROY IT

STOP = THINK

ASK YOURSELF IF WHAT
YOU WERE ABOUT TO SAY
MIGHT HELP THE ENEMY

SPIES ARE LISTENING

△ Through its concerted propaganda effort, the Committee on Public Information helped sell to the American people U.S. participation in the First World War. In this 1917 poster, the committee also warned against German spies, perhaps even German American spies, who might pick up secrets from unsuspecting citizens.

20-6 Red Scare, Red Summer

▶ What were the main characteristics of the Red Scare?

▶ Why did labor unions and immigrants stir up concern in postwar American society?

▶ Why did racial violence emerge in postwar American society?

The line between wartime suppression of dissent and the postwar Red Scare is not easily drawn. In the name of patriotism, both harassed suspected internal enemies and deprived them of their constitutional rights; both had government sanction. Together, they stabbed at the Bill of Rights and wounded radicalism in America. Yet in at least two respects, the phenomena were different. Whereas in wartime the main fear had been of subversion, after the armistice it was revolution; and whereas in 1917 the target had often been German Americans, in 1919 it was frequently organized labor. The Russian Revolution and the communist uprisings elsewhere in Europe alarmed many Americans, and the fears grew when in 1919 the Soviet

leadership announced the formation of the Communist International (or Comintern), whose purpose was to export revolution throughout the world. Terrified conservatives responded by looking for pro-Bolshevik sympathizers (or "Reds," from the red flag used by communists) in the United States, especially in immigrant groups and labor unions.

20-6a Labor Strikes

Labor union leaders emerged out of the war determined to secure higher wages for workers to meet rising prices and to retain wartime bargaining rights. Employers instead rescinded benefits they had been forced to grant to labor during the war, including recognition of unions. The result was a rash of labor strikes in 1919, which sparked the Red Scare. All told, more than 3,300 strikes involving 4 million laborers jolted the nation that year, including the Seattle general strike in January. On May 1, a day of celebration for workers around the world, bombs were sent through the mails to prominent Americans. Most of the devices were intercepted and dismantled, but police never captured the conspirators. Most people assumed, not unreasonably, that anarchists and others bent on the destruction of the American way of life were responsible.

Unrest in the steel industry in September stirred more ominous fears. Many steelworkers worked twelve hours a day, seven days a week, and lived in squalid housing. They looked to local steel unions, organized by the National Committee for Organizing Iron and Steel Workers, to help them improve their lives. When postwar unemployment in the industry climbed and the U.S. Steel Corporation refused to meet with committee representatives, some 350,000 workers walked off the job, demanding the right to collective bargaining, a shorter workday, and a living wage. The steel barons hired strikebreakers and sent agents to club strikers. Worried about both the 1919 strikes and Bolshevism, President Wilson warned against "the poison of disorder" and the "poison of revolt." But in the case of steel, the companies won; the strike collapsed in early 1920.

One of the leaders of the steel strike was William Z. Foster, a former IWW member and militant labor organizer who later joined the Communist Party. His presence in a labor movement seeking bread-and-butter goals permitted political and business leaders to dismiss the steel strike as a foreign threat orchestrated by American radicals. There was in fact no conspiracy, and the American left was badly splintered. Two defectors from the Socialist Party, John Reed and Benjamin Gitlow, founded the Communist Labor Party in 1919. The rival Communist Party of the United States of America, composed largely of immigrants, was launched the same year. Neither party commanded many followers—their combined membership probably did not exceed seventy thousand—and in 1919 the harassed Socialist Party could muster no more than thirty thousand members.

20-6b American Legion

Although divisiveness among radicals actually signified weakness, both Progressives and conservatives interpreted the advent of the new parties as strengthening the radical menace. That is certainly how the American Legion saw the question. Organized in May 1919 to lobby for veterans' benefits, the Legion soon preached an antiradicalism that fueled the Red Scare. By 1920, 843,000 Legion members, mostly middle and upper class, had become stalwarts of an impassioned Americanism that demanded conformity.

Wilson's attorney general, A. Mitchell Palmer, also insisted that Americans think alike. A Progressive reformer, Quaker, and ambitious politician, Palmer appointed J. Edgar Hoover to head the Radical Division of the Department of Justice. The zealous Hoover compiled index cards bearing the names of allegedly radical individuals and organizations. During 1919, agents jailed IWW members, and Palmer saw to it that 249 alien radicals, including the outspoken anarchist Emma Goldman, were deported to Russia.

Again, state and local governments took their cue from the Wilson administration. States passed peacetime sedition acts under which hundreds of people were arrested. Vigilante groups and mobs flourished once again, their numbers swelled by returning veterans. In November 1919, in Centralia, Washington, American Legionnaires broke from a parade to storm the IWW hall. Several were wounded. A number of Wobblies were soon arrested, and one of them, an ex-soldier, was taken from jail by a mob, then beaten, castrated, and shot. The New York State legislature expelled five duly elected Socialist Party members in early 1920.

20-6c Palmer Raids

The Red Scare reached a climax in January 1920 in the Palmer Raids. J. Edgar Hoover planned and directed the operation; government agents in thirty-three cities broke into meeting halls and homes without search warrants. More than four thousand people were jailed and denied counsel. In Boston, some four hundred people were kept in detainment on bitterly cold Deer Island; two died of pneumonia, one leaped to his death, and another went insane. Because of court rulings and the courageous efforts of Assistant Secretary of Labor Louis Post, who deliberately held up paperwork, most of the arrestees were released, although in 1920–1921 nearly six hundred aliens were deported.

Palmer's disregard for elementary civil liberties drew criticism, with many charging that his tactics violated the Constitution. Many of the arrested "communists" had committed no crimes. When Palmer called for a peacetime sedition act, he alarmed both liberal and conservative leaders. His dire prediction that pro-Soviet radicals would incite violence on May Day 1920 proved mistaken—not a single disturbance occurred anywhere in the country. Palmer, who had taken to calling himself the "Fighting Quaker," was jeered as the "Quaking Fighter."

20-6d Racial Unrest

Palmer also blamed communists for the racial violence that gripped the nation in these years. Here again, the charge was baseless. African Americans realized well before the end of

the war that their participation did little to change discriminatory white attitudes. Segregation remained social custom. The Ku Klux Klan was reviving, and racist films like D.W. Griffith's *The Birth of a Nation* (1915) fed prejudice with its celebration of the Klan and its demeaning depiction of blacks. Lynching statistics exposed the wide gap between wartime declarations of humanity and the American practice of inhumanity at home: between 1914 and 1920, 382 blacks were lynched, some of them in military uniform.

Northern whites who resented "the Negro invasion" vented their anger in riots, as in East St. Louis, Illinois, in July 1917. The next month, in Houston, where African American soldiers faced white harassment and refused to obey segregation laws, whites and blacks exchanged gunfire. Seventeen whites and two African Americans died, and the army sentenced thirteen black soldiers to death and forty-one to life imprisonment for mutiny. During the bloody "Red Summer" of 1919 (so named by black author James Weldon Johnson for the blood that was spilled), race riots rocked two dozen cities and towns. The worst violence occurred in Chicago, a favorite destination for migrating blacks. In the very hot days of July 1919, a black youth swimming at a segregated white beach was hit by a thrown rock and drowned. Rumors spread, tempers flared, and soon blacks and whites were battling each other. Stabbings, burnings, and shootings went on for days until state police restored some calm. Thirty-eight people died, twenty-three African Americans and fifteen whites.

By the time of this tragedy, a disillusioned W. E. B. Du Bois had already concluded that black support for the war had not diminished whites' adherence to inequality and segregation. That spring he vowed a struggle: "We return. We return from fighting. We return fighting." Or as poet Claude McKay put it after the Chicago riot in a poem he titled "If We Must Die,"

> Like men we'll face the murderous cowardly pack.
> Pressed to the wall, dying, but fighting back.

20-6e Black Militancy

The exhortations of Du Bois and McKay reflected a newfound militancy among black veterans and in the growing black communities of the North. Editorials in African American newspapers subjected white politicians, including the president, to increasingly harsh criticism and at the same time implored readers to embrace their own prowess and beauty: "The black man is a power of great potentiality upon whom consciousness of his own strength is about to dawn." The NAACP stepped up its campaign for civil rights and equality, vowing in 1919 to publicize the terrors of the lynch law and to seek legislation to stop "Judge Lynch." Other blacks, doubting the potential for equality, turned instead to a charismatic Jamaican immigrant named Marcus Garvey (see "Marcus Garvey," Section 21-4a), who called on African Americans to abandon their hopes for integration and to seek a separate black nation.

△ An African American is confronted by state militia members during the race riots in Chicago in 1919. The troops were called in after Mayor Bill Thompson determined that the city police could not restore order.

The crackdown on laborers and radicals, and the resurgence of racism in 1919, dashed wartime hopes. Although the passage of the **Nineteenth Amendment** in 1920, guaranteeing women the right to vote, showed that reform could happen, it was the exception to the rule. Unemployment, inflation, racial conflict, labor upheaval, a campaign against free speech—all inspired disillusionment in the immediate postwar years.

20-7 The Defeat of Peace

▷ **What actions did Woodrow Wilson seek to take to deter radicalism abroad?**

▷ **What provisions did Wilson seek to include in a peace treaty?**

▷ **Why did Wilson fail to achieve his main goals and objectives in the peace treaty?**

President Wilson seemed more focused on confronting the threat of radicalism abroad than at home. Throughout the final months of the war, he fretted about the Soviet takeover in Russia, and he watched with apprehension the communist uprisings in various parts of central Europe. Months earlier, in mid-1918, Wilson had revealed his ardent anti-Bolshevism

Nineteenth Amendment
Amendment to the Constitution that granted women the right to vote.

when he ordered five thousand American troops to northern Russia and ten thousand more to Siberia, where they joined other Allied contingents in fighting what was now a Russian civil war. They fought on the side of the "Whites" (various counterrevolutionary forces) against the "Reds" (the Bolsheviks). Wilson did not consult Congress. He said the military expeditions would guard Allied supplies and Russian railroads from German seizure and would also rescue a group of Czechs who wished to return home to fight the Germans.

Worried that the Japanese were building influence in Siberia and closing the Open Door, Wilson also hoped to deter Japan from further advances in Asia. Mostly, though, he wanted to smash the infant Bolshevik government, a challenge to his new world order. Thus, he backed an economic blockade of Russia, sent arms to anti-Bolshevik forces, and refused to recognize Lenin's government. The United States also secretly passed military information to anti-Bolshevik forces and used food relief to shore up opponents of the Soviets in the Baltic region. Later, at the Paris Peace Conference, representatives of the new Soviet government were denied a seat. U.S. troops did not leave Russia until spring 1920, after the Bolsheviks had demonstrated their staying power. The actions by Wilson and other Allied leaders in 1918–1920 generated powerful feelings of resentment and suspicion among many Russians.

Wilson faced a monumental task in securing a postwar settlement. When he departed for the Paris Peace Conference in December 1918, he faced obstacles erected by his political enemies, by the Allies, and by himself. Some observers suggested that a cocky Wilson underestimated his task. During the 1918 congressional elections, Wilson committed the blunder of suggesting that patriotism required the election of a Democratic Congress; Republicans had a field day blasting the president for questioning their love of country. The GOP gained control of both houses, and Wilson aggravated his political problems by not naming a senator to his advisory American Peace Commission. He also refused to take any prominent Republicans with him to Paris or to consult with the Senate Foreign Relations Committee before the conference. It did not help that the president denounced his critics as "blind and little provincial people."

Wilson was greeted with huge and adoring crowds in Paris, London, and Rome. Behind closed doors, however, the leaders of these countries—Georges Clemenceau of France, David Lloyd George of Britain, and Vittorio Orlando of Italy (with Wilson, the Big Four)—became formidable adversaries. Clemenceau mused, "God gave man the Ten Commandments, and he broke every one. Wilson has given us Fourteen Points. We shall see." After four years of horrible war, the Allies were not about to be cheated out of the fruits of victory. Wilson could wax lyrical about a "peace without victory," but the late-arriving Americans had not suffered the way the peoples of France and Great Britain had suffered. Germany would have to pay, and pay big, for the calamity it had caused.

20-7a Paris Peace Conference

At the conference, held at the ornate palace of Versailles, the Big Four tried to work out an agreement, mostly behind closed doors. Critics quickly pointed out that Wilson had immediately abandoned the first of his Fourteen Points: diplomacy "in the public view." The victors demanded that Germany (which had not been invited to the proceedings) pay a huge reparations bill. Wilson instead called for a small indemnity, fearing that a resentful and economically hobbled Germany might turn to Bolshevism or disrupt the postwar community in some other way. Unable to moderate the Allied position, the president reluctantly gave way, agreeing to a clause blaming the war on the Germans and to the creation of a commission to determine the amount of reparations (later set at $33 billion). Wilson acknowledged that the peace terms were "hard," but he also came to believe that "the German people must be made to hate war."

As for the breaking up of empires and the principle of self-determination, Wilson could deliver on only some of his goals. To the crushing disappointment of much of the world's nonwhite majority, the imperial system emerged largely unscathed, as the conferees created a League-administered "mandate" system that placed former German and Turkish colonies under the control of other imperial nations. Japan gained authority over Germany's colonies in the Pacific, while France and Britain obtained parts of the Middle East—the French obtained what became Lebanon and Syria, while the British received the three former Ottoman provinces that became Iraq. Britain also secured Palestine, on the condition that it uphold its wartime promise to promote "the establishment in Palestine of a national home for the Jewish

people" without prejudice to "the civil and religious rights of existing non-Jewish communities"—the so-called Balfour Declaration of 1917.

In other arrangements, Japan replaced Germany as the imperial overlord of China's Shandong Peninsula, and France was permitted occupation rights in Germany's Rhineland. Elsewhere in Europe, Wilson's prescriptions fared better. Out of Austria-Hungary and Russia came the newly independent states of Austria, Hungary, Yugoslavia, Czechoslovakia, and Poland. Wilson and his colleagues also built a *cordon sanitaire* (buffer zone) of new westward-looking nations (Finland, Estonia, Latvia, and Lithuania) around Russia, to quarantine the Bolshevik contagion (see Map 20.3).

20-7b League of Nations and Article 10

Wilson worked hardest on the charter for the **League of Nations**, the centerpiece of his plans for the postwar world. He envisioned the League as having power over all disputes among states, including those that did not arise from the peace agreement; as such, it could transform international relations. Even so, the great powers would have a preponderant say: the organization would have an influential council of five permanent members and elected delegates from smaller states, an assembly of all members, and a World Court.

Wilson identified Article 10 as the "kingpin" of the League covenant: "The Members of the League undertake to respect and preserve as against external aggression the territorial integrity and existing political independence of all Members of the League. In case of any such aggression or in case of any threat or danger of such aggression the Council shall advise upon the means by which this obligation shall be fulfilled." This collective-security provision, along with the entire League charter, became part of the peace treaty because Wilson insisted there could be no future peace with Germany without a league to oversee it.

German representatives at first refused to sign the punitive treaty but submitted in June 1919. They gave up 13 percent of Germany's territory, 10 percent of its population, all of its colonies, and a huge portion of its national wealth. Many people wondered how the League could function in the poisoned postwar atmosphere of humiliation and revenge. But Wilson waxed euphoric: "The stage is set, the destiny disclosed. It has come about by no plan of our conceiving, but by the hand of God."

20-7c Critics of the Treaty

Critics in the United States were not so sure. In March 1919, thirty-nine senators (enough to deny the treaty the necessary two-thirds vote) had signed a petition stating that the League's structure did not adequately protect U.S. interests. Wilson denounced his critics as "pygmy" minds, but he persuaded the peace conference to exempt the Monroe Doctrine and domestic matters from League jurisdiction. Having made these concessions to senatorial advice, Wilson

League of Nations An international deliberative body, viewed as necessary to keep the peace; it was rejected by the U.S. Senate, and the United States never joined.

Map 20.3 Europe Transformed by War and Peace

After President Wilson and the other conferees at the Paris Peace Conference negotiated the Treaty of Versailles, empires were broken up. In eastern Europe in particular, new nations emerged.

Legend:
- Boundaries of German, Russian, and Austro-Hungarian Empires in 1914
- Areas lost by Austro-Hungarian Empire
- Areas lost by Russian Empire
- Areas lost by German Empire
- Areas lost by Bulgaria
- Demilitarized Zones
- Boundaries of 1926

would budge no more. Compromises with other nations had been necessary to keep the conference going, he insisted, and the League would rectify wrongs. Could his critics not see that membership in the League would give the United States "leadership in the world"?

By summer, criticism intensified: Wilson had bastardized his own principles. He had conceded Shandong to Japan. He had personally killed a provision affirming the racial equality of all peoples. The treaty did not mention freedom of the seas, and tariffs were not reduced. Reparations on Germany promised to be punishing. Senator La Follette and other critics on the left protested that the League would perpetuate empire. Conservative critics feared that the League would limit American freedom of action in world affairs, stymie U.S. expansion, and intrude on domestic questions. And Article 10 raised serious questions: Would the United States be *obligated*

to use armed force to ensure collective security? And what about colonial rebellions, such as in Ireland or India? Would the League feel compelled to crush them? "Were a League of Nations in existence in the days when George Washington fought and won," an Irish American editor wrote, "we would still be an English colony."

Henry Cabot Lodge of Massachusetts led the Senate opposition to the League. A Harvard-educated PhD and partisan Republican who also had an intense personal dislike of Wilson, Lodge packed the Foreign Relations Committee with critics and prolonged public hearings. He introduced several reservations to the treaty, the most important of which held that Congress had to approve any obligation under Article 10.

In September 1919, Wilson embarked on a speaking tour of the United States. Growing more exhausted every day, he dismissed his antagonists as "contemptible quitters." Provoked by Irish American and German American hecklers, he lashed out in Red Scare terms: "Any man who carries a hyphen about him carries a dagger which he is ready to plunge into the vitals of the Republic." While doubts about Article 10 multiplied, Wilson tried to highlight neglected features of the League charter—such as the arbitration of disputes and an international conference to abolish child labor. In Colorado, a day after delivering another passionate speech, the president awoke to nausea and uncontrollable facial twitching. "I just feel as if I am going to pieces," he said. A few days later, he suffered a massive stroke that paralyzed his left side. He became peevish and even more stubborn, increasingly unable to conduct presidential business. More and more, his wife, Edith, had to select issues for his attention and delegate other matters to his cabinet heads. Advised to placate Lodge and other "Reservationist" senatorial critics so the Versailles treaty would have a chance of being approved by Congress, Wilson rejected "dishonorable compromise." From Senate Democrats he demanded utter loyalty—a vote against all reservations.

20-7d Senate Rejection of the Treaty and League

Twice in November the Senate rejected the Treaty of Versailles and thus U.S. membership in the League. In the first vote, Democrats joined sixteen "Irreconcilables," mostly Republicans who opposed any treaty whatsoever, to defeat the treaty with reservations (39 for and 55 against). In the second vote, Republicans and Irreconcilables turned down the treaty without reservations (38 for and 53 against). In March 1920, the Senate again voted; this time, a majority (49 for and 35 against) favored the treaty with reservations, but the tally fell short of the two-thirds needed. Had Wilson permitted Democrats to compromise—to accept reservations—he could have achieved his fervent goal of membership in the League, which, despite the U.S. absence, came into being.

At the core of the debate lay a basic issue in American foreign policy: whether the United States would endorse collective security or continue to travel the more solitary path articulated in George Washington's Farewell Address and in the Monroe Doctrine. In a world dominated by imperialist states unwilling to subordinate their strategic ambitions to an international organization, Americans preferred their traditional nonalignment and freedom of choice over binding commitments to collective action. That is why so many of Wilson's critics targeted Article 10. Wilson countered that this argument amounted to embracing the status quo—the European imperialist states are selfish, so the United States should be, too. Acceptance of Article 10 and membership in the League promised something better, he believed, for the United States and for the world; it promised collective security in place of the frail protection of alliances and the instability of a balance of power.

Library of Congress

△ In October 1919, President Woodrow Wilson (1856–1924) receives assistance after his massive stroke, which made it difficult for him to maintain his train of thought and manage government affairs. Historians continue to debate the influence of Wilson's poor health on the president's losing battle for U.S. membership in the League of Nations.

20-7e An Unsafe World

In the end, World War I did not make the world safe for democracy. Wilson failed to create a new world order through reform. Still, the United States emerged from the First World

Freedom of Speech and the ACLU

Although freedom of speech is enshrined in the U.S. Constitution, for more than a century after the nation's founding the concept had little standing in American jurisprudence. Before World War I, those with radical views often met with harsh treatment for exercising what today would be termed their freedom of speech. During the war, however, the Wilson administration's suppression of dissidents led some Americans to reformulate the traditional definition of allowable speech. Two key figures in this movement were Roger Baldwin, a conscientious objector, and woman suffrage activist Crystal Eastman. Baldwin and Eastman were among the first to advance the idea that the content of political speech could be separated from the identity of the speaker and that patriotic Americans could—indeed should—defend the right of others to express political beliefs abhorrent to their own. After working during the war to defend the rights of conscientious objectors, Baldwin and Eastman—joined by activists such as Jane Addams, Helen Keller, and Norman Thomas—formed the American Civil Liberties Union (ACLU).

Since 1920, the ACLU—which today has some three hundred thousand members in three hundred chapters nationwide—has aimed to protect the basic civil liberties of all Americans and to extend them to those to whom they have traditionally been denied. The organization has been involved in almost every major civil liberties case contested in U.S. courts, among them the John Scopes "monkey trial" (1925), concerning the teaching of evolution at a Tennessee school, and the landmark *Brown v. Board of Education* case (1954), which ended federal tolerance of racial segregation. More recently, the ACLU was involved in a 1997 case in which the Supreme Court decided that the 1996 Communications Act banning "indecent speech" violated First Amendment rights.

Conservatives have long criticized the ACLU for its opposition to official prayers in public schools and its support of the legality of abortion, as well as for what they see as its selectivity in deciding whose freedom of speech to defend. Backers of the organization counter that it has also defended those on the right, such as Oliver North, a key figure in the Iran-Contra scandal of the 1980s.

Either way, the principle of free speech is today broadly accepted by Americans, so much so that even ACLU bashers take it for granted. Membership rose sharply after the terrorist attacks on September 11, 2001, due to concern among some people that government policies have eroded privacy and legal protections, not only for Americans but also for foreign detainees at the Guantánamo Bay detention facility. Ironically, the Wilson administration's crackdown on dissent produced an expanded commitment to freedom of speech for a people and a nation.

CRITICAL THINKING

- The ACLU has traditionally fought to protect American civil liberties, perhaps most notably our freedom of speech. Has social media allowed for an increase in "hate speech"?
- If so, should that type of speech still fall under the protection of the ACLU's efforts?

War an even greater world power. By 1920, the United States had become the world's leading economic power, producing 40 percent of its coal, 70 percent of its petroleum, and half of its pig iron. It also rose to first rank in world trade. American companies took advantage of the war to nudge the Germans and British out of foreign markets, especially in Latin America. Meanwhile, the United States shifted from a debtor to a creditor nation, becoming the world's leading banker.

After the disappointment of Versailles, appeals for arms control accelerated, and the peace movement revitalized. At the same time, the military became better armed and more professional. The Reserve Officers Training Corps (ROTC) became permanent; military "colleges" provided upper-echelon training; and the Army Industrial College, founded in 1924, pursued business-military cooperation in the area of logistics and planning. The National Research Council, created in 1916 with government money and Carnegie and Rockefeller funds, continued after the war as an alliance of scientists and businesspeople engaged in research relating to national defense. Tanks, quick-firing guns, armor-piercing explosives, and oxygen masks for high-altitude-flying pilots were just some of the technological advances that emerged from the First World War.

The international system born in these years was unstable and fragmented. Espousing decolonization and taking to heart the Wilsonian principle of self-determination, nationalist leaders active during the First World War, such as Ho Chi Minh of Indochina and Mohandas K. Gandhi of India, vowed to achieve independence for their peoples. Communism became a disruptive force in world politics, and the Soviets bore a grudge against those invaders who had tried to thwart their revolution. The new states in central and eastern Europe proved weak, dependent on outsiders for security. Germans bitterly resented the harsh peace settlement, and German war debts and reparations problems dogged international order for many years (Germany finally finished making reparations payments in 2010). As it entered the 1920s, the international system that Woodrow Wilson had vowed to reform was fraught with unresolved problems.

Summary

At the close of the First World War, historian Albert Bushnell Hart observed that "it is easy to see that the United States is a new country." Actually, America came out of the war an unsettled mix of the old and the new. The war years marked the emergence of the United States as a world power, and Americans could take justifiable pride in the contribution they had made to the Allied victory. At the same time, the war exposed deep divisions among Americans: white versus black, nativist versus immigrant, capital versus labor, men versus women, radical versus Progressive and conservative, pacifist versus interventionist, nationalist versus internationalist. It is little wonder that Americans—having experienced race riots, labor strikes, disputes over civil liberties, and the League fight—wanted to escape into what President Warren G. Harding called "normalcy."

During the war, the federal government intervened in the economy and influenced people's everyday lives as never before. Centralization of control in Washington, D.C., and mobilization of the home front served as models for the future. Although the Wilson administration shunned reconstruction or reconversion plans (war housing projects, for example, were sold to private investors) and quickly dismantled the many government agencies, the World War I experience of the activist state served as guidance for 1930s reformers battling the Great Depression (see Chapter 22). The partnership of government and business in managing the wartime economy advanced the development of a mass society through the standardization of products and the promotion of efficiency. Wilsonian wartime policies also nourished the concentration of corporate ownership through the suspension of antitrust laws. Business power dominated the next decade. American labor, by contrast, entered lean years, although new labor management practices, including corporate welfare programs, survived.

Although the disillusionment evident after Versailles did not cause the United States to adopt a policy of isolationist withdrawal (see Chapter 22), skepticism about America's ability to right wrongs abroad marked the postwar American mood. The war was grimy and ugly, far less glorious than Wilson's lofty rhetoric had suggested. People recoiled from photographs of shell-shocked faces and bodies dangling from barbed wire. American soldiers, tired of idealism, craved the latest baseball scores and their regular jobs. Those Progressives who had believed that entry into the war would deliver the millennium later marveled at their naïveté. Many lost their enthusiasm for crusades, and many others turned away in disgust from the bickering of the victors. Some felt betrayed. Journalist William Allen White angrily wrote to a friend that the Allies "have—those damned vultures—taken the heart out of the peace, taken the joy out of the great enterprise of the war, and have made it a sordid malicious miserable thing like all the other wars in the world."

By 1920, Woodrow Wilson's idealism seemed to many Americans to be a spent force, both at home and abroad. Aware of their country's newfound status as a leading world power, they were unsure what this reality meant for the nation, or for their individual lives. With a mixed legacy from the Great War, and a sense of uneasiness, the country entered the new era of the 1920s.

Suggestions for Further Reading

John Milton Cooper Jr., *Breaking the Heart of the World: Woodrow Wilson and the Fight for the League of Nations* (2001)

Alan Dawley, *Changing the World: American Progressives in War and Revolution, 1914–1924* (2003)

David S. Foglesong, *America's Secret War Against Bolshevism* (1995)

Michael Kazin, *A Godly Hero: The Life of William Jennings Bryan* (2006)

Jennifer D. Keene, *Doughboys, the Great War, and the Remaking of America* (2001)

David M. Kennedy, *Over Here: The Home Front in the First World War* (1980)

Thomas J. Knock, *To End All Wars: Woodrow Wilson and the Quest for a New World Order* (1992)

Margaret MacMillan, *Paris 1919: Six Months That Changed the World* (2002)

Michael S. Neiberg, *The Path to War: How the First World War Created Modern America* (2016)

David R. Woodward, *The American Army and the First World War* (2014)

MINDTAP From Cengage

MindTap® is a fully online personalized learning experience built upon Cengage Learning content. MindTap® combines student learning tools—readings, multimedia, activities, and assessments—into a singular Learning Path that guides students through the course and helps students develop the critical thinking, analysis, and communication skills that are essential to academic and professional success.

The New Era, 1920–1929

B eth and Robert Gordon did not seem to be compatible marriage partners. Beth was frumpy and demanding; Robert liked to party. One evening at a nightclub, he met Sally Clark, who liked to party, too. They danced close together, and when Robert came home, Beth smelled perfume on his suit. The spouses argued, and shortly they divorced. It was not long, however, before Robert found that Sally's appeal had worn off; he missed Beth's intellect and wisdom. Meanwhile, Beth concluded that she needed to change her dowdy image. She bought new clothes and makeup, turning herself into a glamorous beauty. By coincidence, Beth and Robert visited the same summer resort and rekindled their romance. When Robert was injured in an accident, Beth took him home and nursed him back to health, much to Sally's disappointment. In the end, Beth and Robert remarried, and Sally accepted her loss of Robert philosophically, concluding with the wry remark "The only good thing about marriage, anyway, is the alimony."

The experiences of Beth, Robert, and Sally make up the plot of the 1920 motion picture *Why Change Your Wife?*—one of dozens of films directed by Cecil B. DeMille. DeMille succeeded by giving audiences what they wanted to see and what they fantasized about doing. Beth, Robert, and Sally dressed stylishly, went out dancing, listened to phonograph records, rode in cars, and visited resorts. Although DeMille's films and others of the 1920s usually ended by reinforcing marriage, ruling out premarital sex, and supporting the work ethic, they also exuded a new morality. Female lead characters were not mothers tied to the home; both males and females shed old-style values for the pursuit of luxury, fun, and sexual freedom, just as the actors and actresses themselves, such as Gloria

◁ Dressed in stylish fashions and indulging in some flirtatious banter, Thomas Meighan and Gloria Swanson, stars of Cecil B. DeMille's romantic comedy *Why Change Your Wife?* represent ways that movies and movie personalities gave the public images, sometimes accurate but often exaggerated, of new social mores in the 1920s. Everett Collection

Chronology

1920
- Volstead Act implements prohibition (Eighteenth Amendment)
- Nineteenth Amendment ratified, legalizing vote for women in federal elections
- Harding elected president
- KDKA transmits first commercial radio broadcast

1920–21
- Postwar deflation and depression

1921
- Federal Highway Act funds national highway system
- Emergency Quota Act establishes immigration quotas
- Sacco and Vanzetti convicted
- Sheppard-Towner Act allots funds to states to set up maternity and pediatric clinics
- Washington Conference limits naval arms

1922
- Economic recovery raises standards of living
- *Coronado Coal Company v. United Mine Workers* rules that strikes may be illegal actions in restraint of trade
- *Bailey v. Drexel Furniture Company* voids restrictions on child labor
- Federal government ends strikes by railroad shop workers and miners
- Fordney-McCumber Tariff raises rates on imports

1923
- Harding dies; Coolidge assumes presidency
- *Adkins v. Children's Hospital* overturns a minimum wage law affecting women

1923–24
- Government scandals (Teapot Dome) exposed

1924
- Snyder Act grants citizenship to all Indians not previously citizens
- National Origins Act revises immigration quotas
- Coolidge elected president

1925
- Scopes trial highlights battle between religious fundamentalists and modernists

1927
- Lindbergh pilots solo transatlantic flight
- *The Jazz Singer*, first movie with sound, released

1928
- Stock market soars
- Kellogg-Briand Pact outlaws war
- Hoover elected president

1929
- Stock market crashes; Great Depression begins

Swanson and Thomas Meighan, the stars of *Why Change Your Wife?* did in their off-screen lives. Just like the characters they played, the actors were icons for America's new mass culture. In this way, *Why Change Your Wife?* was a harbinger, though an inexact one, of a new era.

Experience an interactive version of this story in MindTap®.

During the 1920s, consumerism flourished, represented by the products, entertainment, and leisure that film characters and the stars who played them enjoyed. Although poverty beset small farmers, workers in declining industries, and nonwhites everywhere, most other people enjoyed a high standard of living relative to that of previous generations. Spurred by advertising and installment buying, Americans eagerly acquired radios, automobiles, real estate, and stocks. Changes in work habits, family responsibilities, and health care fostered new uses of time and new attitudes about behavior, including encouragements to "think young." Winds of change also stirred up waves of resistance from those who held tight to traditional beliefs, and cultural divisions roiled politics.

As in the Gilded Age, the federal government nurtured a favorable climate for business. In contrast to the Progressive Era, crusades for change at the national level cooled. Yet state and local governments, extending the reach of public authority, undertook important reforms. Endeavors for reform also extended into international affairs, as both the federal government and private organizations searched for ways to secure world peace and prevent the horrors that had occurred in the First World War. Though many Americans now regarded themselves as isolationists, meaning they wanted no part of Europe's political squabbles, military alliances, or the League of Nations, the nation remained active in global affairs, as government and business leaders worked to facilitate American prosperity and security.

An unseen storm lurked on the horizon, however. The glitter of consumer culture that dominated DeMille's films and their audiences' everyday lives blinded Americans to rising debt and uneven prosperity. Just before the decade closed, a devastating depression brought the era to a brutal close.

- *How did developments in technology stimulate social change and influence foreign policy during the 1920s?*

▣ *What were the benefits and costs of consumerism, and how did people deal with challenges to old-time values?*

◻ *What caused the stock market crash and the ensuing deep depression that signaled the end of the era?*

21-1 Economic Expansion

▷ **What factors contributed to the recovery and expansion of the American economy after World War I?**

▷ **How did the development of the American economy become globally oriented after World War I?**

▷ **How did the federal government help businesses thrive in the 1920s?**

The 1920s began with a jolting economic decline. Shortly after the First World War ended, industrial output dropped as wartime orders dried up. As European agriculture recovered from war, American exports diminished and farm incomes plunged. In the West, railroads and the mining industry suffered. As demobilized soldiers flooded the workforce, unemployment, around 2 percent in 1919, passed 12 percent in 1921. Layoffs spread through New England as textile companies abandoned outdated factories for the convenient raw materials and cheap labor of the South. As a consequence of these patterns, consumer spending dwindled, causing more contraction and joblessness.

21-1a Business Triumphant

Aided by electric energy, a recovery began in 1922 and continued unevenly until 1929. Electric motors enabled manufacturers to replace steam engines and produce goods more cheaply and efficiently. Using new metal alloys, such as aluminum, and synthetic materials, such as rayon, producers could turn out an expanded array of consumer goods, including refrigerators, toasters, vacuum cleaners, and clothing. In addition, most urban households now had electric service, enabling them to utilize new appliances. The expanding economy gave Americans more spending money for these products, as well as for restaurants, beauty salons, and movie theaters. More important, installment, or time-payment, plans ("A dollar down and a dollar forever," one critic quipped) drove the new consumerism. Of 3.5 million automobiles sold in 1923, 80 percent were bought on credit. By the late 1920s, the United States produced nearly half of the world's industrial goods and ranked first among exporters.

Economic expansion brought a continuation of the corporate consolidation that had created trusts and holding companies in the late nineteenth century. Although Progressive Era trust-busting had achieved some regulation of big business, it had not eliminated oligopoly, the control of an entire industry by one or a few large firms. Now, sprawling companies such as U.S. Steel and General Electric dominated basic industries, and oligopolies dominated much of marketing, distribution, and finance as well.

21-1b Languishing Agriculture

The picture was different in farming. Pressed into competition with growers in other countries and trying to increase productivity by investing in machines, such as harvesters and tractors, American farmers found themselves steeped in hardship. Irrigation and mechanization had created "factories in the fields," making large-scale farming so efficient that fewer farmers could produce more crops than ever before. As a result, crop prices plunged, big agribusinesses took over, and small landholders and tenants could not make a living. Shortly after the end of the First World War, for example, the price that farmers could get for cotton dropped by two-thirds and that for livestock fell by half. Incomes of small farmers (but not agribusinesses) plummeted, and debts rose.

21-1c Economic Expansion Abroad

Flush with industrial expansion at home, business and government leaders attempted to use American prosperity to create economic stability at home and profits abroad. The First World War had left Europe in shambles. Between 1914 and 1924, Europe suffered tens of millions of casualties from world war, civil war, massacres, the influenza epidemic, and famine. Germany and France both lost 10 percent of their workers. Crops, livestock, factories, trains, bridges—little was spared. The American Relief Administration and private charities delivered food to needy people, including Russians wracked by famine in 1921 and 1922.

These efforts accompanied a move to strengthen America's prominence in the international economy. Because of World War I, the United States became a creditor nation and the financial capital of the world (see Figure 21.1). From 1914 to 1930, private investment abroad grew fivefold, to more than $17 billion. For example, General Electric invested heavily in Germany, and U.S. firms began to challenge British control of oil in the Middle East. Also, American know-how became an export product. Germans marveled at Henry Ford's economic success and industrial techniques ("Fordismus"), buying out translations of his autobiography, *My Life and Work* (1922). Further advertising the American capitalist model were the Phelps-Stokes Fund, exporting to black Africa Booker T. Washington's Tuskegee philosophy of education, and the Rockefeller Foundation, battling diseases in Latin America and Africa, supporting colleges to train doctors in Lebanon and China, and funding medical research and nurses' training in Europe.

21-1d Investments in Latin America

American companies focused especially on Latin America, where they began to exploit Venezuela's rich petroleum resources, where the United Fruit Company became a huge landowner, and where Pam American Airways first developed

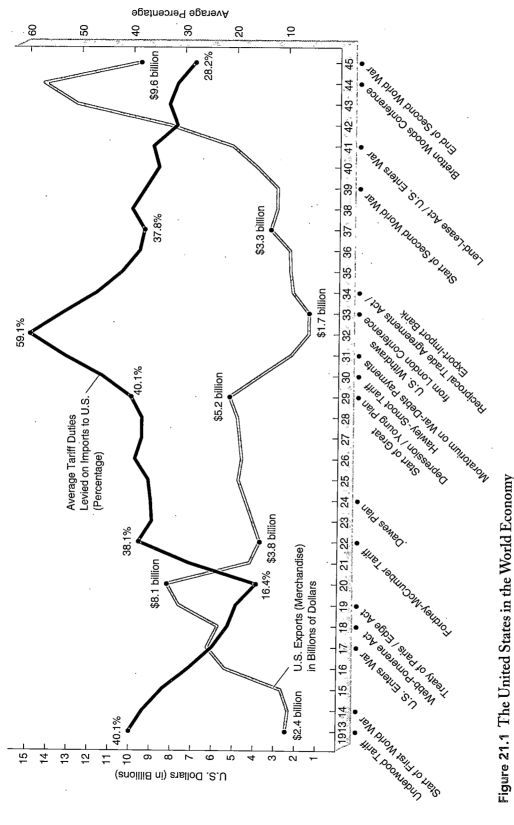

Figure 21.1 The United States in the World Economy

In the 1920s and 1930s, global depression and war scuttled the United States' hope for a stable economic order. This graph suggests, moreover, that high American tariffs meant lower exports, further impeding world trade. The Reciprocal Trade Agreements program initiated in the early 1930s was designed to ease tariff wars with other nations. *Source: U.S. Bureau of the Census, Historical Statistics of the United States, Colonial Times to 1970 (Washington, D.C., 1975).*

Margaret Mead and *Coming of Age in Samoa*

In 1925, Margaret Mead, age twenty-four, journeyed to the South Pacific where for nine months she lived among and studied natives who inhabited the island territory of American Samoa. Having just earned a masters degree from Columbia University, where she had studied with Franz Boas and Ruth Benedict,

two of the country's most noted anthropologists, Meade set out to investigate whether a supposed "primitive" people might have their own highly developed culture that was not inferior to that of Americans and Europeans but only different. What she observed and later wrote about in her best-selling book, *Coming of Age in Samoa* (1928), shocked the nation, not only exposing Americans to manners and ethical standards much different from their own but also making Americans reconsider how they were raising their own children.

In Samoa, Mead focused her attention primarily on adolescent girls with the object of finding out how their experiences differed from those of American teenagers. She wanted to consider whether those experiences could teach anything to Americans and whether, as she wrote, "societies could be changed by changing the way children were brought up." Based on interviews of and psychological tests on 68 girls from three villages, Mead concluded that because of relaxed and more open attitudes toward sex in Samoan culture, adolescence there was a much less stressful stage of life than it was among American girls, who were pressured to conform to a particular kind of sexual behavior. Samoan children were allowed to observe, even experience, nudity, masturbation, intercourse, and homosexuality without adult-imposed judgments about whether such acts were shameful. As a result,

Mead concluded, Samoans had less stormy adolescence because of Samoan culture—what anthropologists and psychologists would call "nurture"—rather than because they biologically were teenagers (what would be called "nature").

Mead's book had considerable impact, not just because it exposed Americans to much different customs, some of which were deemed scandalous, but also because it included a critique of American culture in which, according to Mead, children were "denied all firsthand knowledge of birth and love and death, harried by a society which will not let adolescents grow up at their own pace, imprisoned in the small, fragile, nuclear family from which there is no escape and in which there is little security." At the time, and later, critics accused Mead of being too gullible and admiring in her dealings with Samoans, and that "nature" had more importance than she would admit. Though the "nature vs. nurture" argument remains unresolved today, Mead's descriptions and the influence of her work on the field of anthropology have had lasting effect.

CRITICAL THINKING

◻ Although Margaret Mead's study of Samoan adolescence was widely criticized by those who argued that she had failed to view Samoan culture with an objective eye, how did deeply ingrained American ideas about gender likely influence many Americans' refusal to accept her findings as valid?

△ Posing in 1925 with two young Samoan women, Margaret Mead, who was just twenty-four years old at the time of this photograph, captured world attention three years later with publication of her study *Coming of Age in Samoa*. The book, based on Mead's observations of Samoan culture, caused controversy by concluding that adolescence was not a stressful time for Samoan girls because the native culture was more open about sexuality than American culture. Some critics complained that Mead romanticized Samoan life, but others found her findings revealing about American ways of raising children.

Manuscript Division, Library of Congress

air service. By 1929, direct American investment in the region totaled $3.5 billion and U.S. exports dominated trade. Country after country experienced repercussions from American economic and political decisions. For example, the price that Americans set for Chilean copper determined the health of Chile's economy. North American oil executives bribed Venezuelan politicians for tax breaks.

Latin American nationalists protested that their resources were being drained away as profits for U.S. companies. A distinguished Argentine writer, Manuel Ugarte, asserted that the United States had become a new Rome, annexing wealth rather than territory, and that unapologetic Americans wrongly believed they were bringing only material improvements and blessings of liberty to Latin American neighbors. Criticism mounted as years passed. In 1928, at the Havana Inter-American conference, U.S. officials unsuccessfully tried to kill a resolution stating that "no state has a right to intervene in the internal affairs of another." Two years later, a Chilean newspaper warned that the American "Colossus" had "financial might" without "equal in history" and that its aim was "Americas for the Americans—of the North."

21-1e Associations and "New Lobbying"

Business and professional organizations that had arisen around 1900 also expanded in the 1920s. Retailers and manufacturers formed trade associations to swap information and coordinate planning. Farm bureaus promoted scientific agriculture and tried to stabilize markets for agricultural products. Lawyers, engineers, and doctors expanded their professional societies. In a complex society where government was playing an increasingly influential role, hundreds of organizations sought to convince federal and state legislators to support their interests through "new lobbying." One Washington, D.C., observer contended that "lobbyists were so thick they were constantly falling over one another."

Government policies helped business thrive, and legislators depended on lobbyists' expertise in making decisions. Prodded by lobbyists, Congress cut taxes on corporations and wealthy individuals in 1921 and passed the Fordney-McCumber Tariff (1922) to raise tariff rates. Presidents Warren G. Harding, Calvin Coolidge, and Herbert Hoover appointed cabinet officers who were favorable toward business. Regulatory agencies, such as the Federal Trade Commission and the Interstate Commerce Commission, monitored company activities but, under the influence of lobbyists, cooperated with corporations more than they regulated them.

The Supreme Court, led by Chief Justice William Howard Taft, the former president whom Harding nominated to the Court in 1921, protected business and private property as aggressively as in the Gilded Age and abandoned its Progressive Era antitrust stance. Key decisions sheltered business from government regulation and hindered organized labor's ability to achieve its ends through strikes and legislation. In *Coronado Coal Company v. United Mine Workers* (1922), Taft ruled that a striking union, like a trust, could

be prosecuted for illegal restraint of trade, yet in *Maple Floor Association v. U.S.* (1929), the Court decided that trade associations that distributed anti-union information were not acting in restraint of trade. The Court also voided the federal law restricting child labor (*Bailey v. Drexel Furniture Company*, 1922) because it infringed on state power, and it overturned a minimum wage law affecting women because it infringed on liberty of contract (*Adkins v. Children's Hospital*, 1923).

21-1f Setbacks for Organized Labor

Organized labor suffered other setbacks during the 1920s. Fearful of communism allegedly being brought into the country by radical immigrants, public opinion turned against workers who disrupted everyday life with strikes. Perpetuating tactics used during the Red Scare of 1919, the Harding administration in 1922 obtained a court injunction to quash a strike by 400,000 railroad shop workers. The same year, the Justice Department helped end a nationwide strike by 650,000 miners. Courts at both the state and federal levels issued injunctions to prevent strikes and permitted businesses to sue unions for damages suffered because of labor actions.

Meanwhile, corporations fought unions directly. To prevent labor organization, employers imposed "yellow-dog contracts" that, as a condition of employment, compelled an employee to agree not to join a union. Companies also countered the appeal of unions by offering pensions, profit sharing, and company-sponsored picnics and sporting events—a policy known as "welfare capitalism." State legislators aided employers by prohibiting closed shops (workplaces where unions required that all employees be members of their labor organization) and permitting open shops (in which employers could hire nonunion employees). As a result of court action, welfare capitalism, and ineffective leadership, union membership fell from 5.1 million in 1920 to 3.6 million in 1929.

21-2 Government, Politics, and Reform

▶ **How were women politically active in the postwar period?**

▶ **How did the national government demonstrate "goodwill" toward businesses during the presidencies of Warren G. Harding and Calvin Coolidge?**

▶ **How were efforts to achieve international peace advanced at the social and political levels in the 1920s?**

During the 1920s, politics reflected a shift away from the activism of the Progressive Era, yet certain continuities remained, and women, enfranchised nationally by the Nineteenth Amendment, brought new influence to national and international affairs. A series of Republican presidents reinforced economic expansion by reinforcing

Theodore Roosevelt's notion of government-business cooperation, but they saw government as a compliant coordinator rather than the active manager Roosevelt had advocated. At the same time, the government extended reform programs at home and embarked on new efforts for peace and disarmament abroad.

21-2a Women and Politics

Though they had achieved suffrage through the Nineteenth Amendment, ratified in 1920, politically active women remained excluded from local and national power structures. But like business associations, women's voluntary organizations used tactics that advanced pressure-group politics. Whether the issue was birth control, world peace, education, American Indian affairs, or opposition to lynching, women in these associations lobbied for legislation to support their causes. For example, the League of Women Voters reorganized out of the National Woman Suffrage Association, encouraged women to run for office, and actively lobbied for laws to improve conditions for employed women, the mentally ill, and the poor.

In 1921, action by women's groups persuaded Congress to pass the **Sheppard-Towner Act**, which allotted funds to states to create maternity and pediatric clinics as means to reduce infant mortality. (The measure ended in 1929 when Congress, pressured by the American Medical Association, which believed the act was socialistic and threatened a doctor's professional prerogatives, canceled funding.) The Cable Act of 1923 reversed the law under which an American woman who married a foreigner lost her U.S. citizenship and had to assume her husband's citizenship. At the state level, women achieved rights such as the ability to serve as jurors.

Internal divisions, however, complicated women's tasks in achieving their goals. Members of the National Association of Colored Women, for example, fought for the rights of minority women and men without support from white women's groups. Some organizations, such as the National Woman's Party, pressed for a constitutional amendment to ensure women's equality with men under the law. But such activity alienated the National Consumers League, the Women's Trade Union League, the League of Women Voters, and other groups that supported special protective legislation to limit hours and improve conditions for employed women.

21-2b American Indian Affairs

Disturbed by the federal government's generally apathetic American Indian policy, reform organizations such as the Indian Rights Association, the Indian Defense Association, and the General Federation of Women's Clubs worked to obtain justice and social services, including better education and return of tribal lands. But because most Americans perceived American Indians as no longer a threat to whites' ambitions, they expected them to assimilate like other minorities. Such an assumption overlooked important problems. Severalty, the federal policy created by the Dawes Act of 1887 that allotted land to individuals rather than to tribes, had failed to make American Indians self-supporting. Native American farmers had to suffer poor soil, unavailable irrigation, and scarce medical care. Deeply attached to their land, they showed little inclination to move to cities. Whites still hoped to convert native peoples into "productive" citizens, but in a way that ignored indigenous cultures. Reformers were especially critical of Native American women, who refused to adopt middle-class homemaking habits and balked at sending their children to boarding schools.

Meanwhile, the federal government struggled to clarify American Indians' citizenship status. The Dawes Act had conferred citizenship on all Native Americans who accepted land allotments, but not on those who remained on reservations. Also, the government retained control over Native Americans that it did not exercise over others. For example, because of alleged drunkenness on reservations, federal law banned the sale of liquor to American Indians even before ratification of prohibition. After several court challenges, Congress finally passed an Indian Citizenship Act (Snyder Act) in 1924, granting full citizenship to all Native Americans who previously had not received it in hopes that American Indians would help each other to assimilate.

21-2c Presidency of Warren Harding

A symbol of the federal government's goodwill toward business was President **Warren G. Harding**, elected in 1920 over Democratic nominee and Ohio Governor James M. Cox, whose running mate was New York Governor Franklin D. Roosevelt (Teddy's cousin). Garnering 16 million popular votes to Cox's 9 million, Harding won the most lopsided victory in a presidential election to that date. (The total vote in the 1920 presidential election was 36 percent higher than in 1916, reflecting participation of women voters for the first time.) A small-town newspaperman and senator from Ohio who relished jokes and poker, Harding seemed suited to a nation recovering from world war and domestic hard times.

Harding also benefited from voter disillusionment with the League of Nations and the collective world security system envisioned by Woodrow Wilson and previously rejected by the Senate (see "Senate Rejection of the Treaty and League," Section 20-7d). The League proved feeble as a peacemaker, not just because the United States refused to join, but also because League members failed to utilize it to settle important disputes. In due course, however, American officials participated discreetly in League meetings on public health, prostitution, drug and arms trafficking, counterfeiting of currency, and other international issues. American jurists served on the Permanent Court of International Justice, and the Rockefeller Foundation donated $100,000 a year to support League work in public health.

Sheppard-Towner Act Sought to reduce infant mortality by providing matching funds to states to create prenatal and child health clinics. It was repealed in 1929.

Warren G. Harding The twenty-ninth president of the United States (1921–1923).

21-2d Scandals of the Harding Administration

Once in office, Harding gave primary attention to economic matters, and he appointed some capable assistants who helped promote business growth, notably Secretary of State Charles Evans Hughes, Secretary of Commerce Herbert Hoover, Secretary of the Treasury Andrew Mellon, and Secretary of Agriculture Henry C. Wallace. But Harding had personal weaknesses, and these soon took a toll on his presidency. As a senator, he had an extramarital liaison with the wife of an Ohio merchant. In 1917, he began a relationship with Nan Britton, who was thirty-one years his junior and who had been obsessed with Harding since her girlhood. A daughter was born from the affair in 1919, and Britton revealed the secret in a book, *The President's Daughter*, published in 1927. Unlike Grover Cleveland, Harding never acknowledged his illegitimate offspring.

Of more consequence than his sexual escapades, Harding appointed cronies who saw office holding as an invitation to personal gain. Charles Forbes, head of the Veterans Bureau, went to federal prison, convicted of fraud and bribery in connection with government contracts. Attorney General Harry Daugherty resigned after being implicated in a kickback scheme involving bootleggers of illegal liquor; he escaped prosecution by refusing to testify against himself. Most notoriously, a congressional inquiry in 1923–1924 revealed that Secretary of the Interior Albert Fall had accepted bribes to lease government

Teapot Dome scandal Scandal that rocked the Harding administration after Harding's secretary of the interior was found guilty of secretly leasing government oil reserves to two oilmen in exchange for a bribe.

Calvin Coolidge The thirtieth president of the United States (1923–1929); took office after the death of President Warren Harding in 1923.

property to private oil companies. For his role in the affair—called the **Teapot Dome scandal** after a Wyoming oil reserve that he handed to the Mammoth Oil Company—Fall was fined $100,000 and spent a year in jail, the first cabinet member ever to be so disgraced.

By mid-1923, Harding had become disillusioned. Amid rumors of mismanagement and crime, he told a journalist, "My God, this is a hell of a job. I have no trouble with my enemies. . . . But my friends, my God-damned friends . . . they're the ones that keep me walking the floor nights." On a speaking tour that summer, Harding became ill and died in San Francisco on August 2. Although his death preceded revelation of the Teapot Dome scandal, some people speculated that, to avoid impeachment, Harding committed suicide or was poisoned by his wife. Most evidence, however, points to death from natural causes, probably heart disease. Regardless, Harding was widely mourned.

21-2e Coolidge Prosperity

Vice President **Calvin Coolidge**, who now became president, was far less outgoing than his predecessor. Journalists nicknamed him "Silent Cal," and one quipped that Coolidge could say nothing in five languages. As governor of Massachusetts, Coolidge attracted national attention in 1919 when he used the National Guard to end a strike by Boston policemen, an action that won him business support and the vice presidential nomination in 1920. Coolidge's presidency coincided with and assisted business prosperity. Respectful of private enterprise and aided by treasury secretary Andrew Mellon, Coolidge's administration reduced federal debt, lowered income tax rates (especially for the wealthy), and began construction of a national highway system. But Coolidge refused to apply government power to assist struggling farmers. Responding to farmers'

◁ President Calvin Coolidge felt comfortable among leaders of big business. He is shown here autographing a bucket for Henry Ford, with Harvey Firestone (from the Firestone Tire Company) on Ford's right, Thomas Edison on Coolidge's immediate left, Russell Firestone (Harvey's son) standing, and the president's father, Col. John Coolidge, seated next to Edison.

Library of Congress Prints and Photographs Division [LC-US262-14793]

complaints of falling prices, Congress twice passed bills to establish government-backed price supports for staple crops (the McNary-Haugen bills of 1927 and 1928). Resembling the subtreasury scheme that Farmers' Alliances had advocated in the 1890s, these bills proposed to establish a system whereby the government would buy surplus farm products and either hold them until prices rose or sell them abroad. Farmers argued that they deserved as much government protection as manufacturers got. Coolidge, however, vetoed the measures both times as improper government interference in the market economy.

"Coolidge prosperity" was the decisive issue in the 1924 presidential election. Both major parties ran candidates who favored private initiative over government intervention. Republicans nominated Coolidge with little dissent. At their national convention, Democrats first debated whether to denounce the revived Ku Klux Klan, voting 546 to 543 against condemnation. They then endured 103 ballots, deadlocked between southern prohibitionists, who supported former treasury secretary William G. McAdoo, and antiprohibition easterners, who backed New York's governor, Alfred E. Smith. They finally compromised on John W. Davis, a New York corporate lawyer. Remnants of the Progressive movement formed a new Progressive Party and nominated Robert M. La Follette, the aging Wisconsin reformer. The new party stressed previous reform issues: public ownership of railroads and power plants, conservation of natural resources, aid to farmers, rights for organized labor, and regulation of business. The electorate, however, endorsed Coolidge prosperity. Coolidge beat Davis by 15.7 million to 8.4 million popular votes, and 382 to 136 electoral votes. La Follette finished third, receiving 4.8 million popular votes and 13 electoral votes.

In Congress and the presidency, the urgency for political and economic reform that had moved the generation of Progressive reformers faded in the 1920s. Much reform, however, occurred at state and local levels. Following initiatives begun before the First World War, thirty-four states instituted or expanded workers' compensation laws and public welfare programs in the 1920s. In cities, social workers strove for better housing and poverty relief. By 1926, every major city and many smaller ones had planning and zoning commissions to harness physical growth to the common good. As a result of their efforts, a new generation of reformers who later influenced national affairs acquired valuable experience in statehouses, city halls, and universities.

21-2f The Search for Lasting Peace

The Progressive quest for justice and humanity combined with a desire to prevent future world wars to energize a widespread peace movement in the United States. Societies such as the Fellowship of Reconciliation and the National Council for Prevention of War worked to keep alive Woodrow Wilson's dream for a world body to preserve peace. Women peace advocates, blocked by male leaders from influence in these groups, formed their own organization. Carrie Chapman

Catt's moderate National Conference on the Cure and Cause of War formed in 1924, and the more radical U.S. section of the Women's International League for Peace and Freedom (WILPF), organized in 1915 under leadership from Jane Addams and Emily Greene Balch, became the largest women's peace group. When Addams won the Nobel Peace Prize in 1921, she donated the money to the League of Nations.

Most peace groups worked to prevent war from becoming a means of solving international disputes, but they differed over strategies to ensure world order. Some urged cooperation with the League of Nations and World Court. Others championed such causes as the arbitration of disputes, disarmament, the outlawing of war, and neutrality by noncombatants during armed conflict. The WILPF called for an end to U.S. economic imperialism and military intervention

War Is a Crime Against Humanity

Gassed; Near Dnn-sur-Meuse, in the Woods, France

To you who are filled with horror at the sufferings of war-ridden mankind;

To you who remember that <u>ten million men</u> were slaughtered in the last war;

To you who have the courage to face the reality of <u>war,</u> stripped of its sentimental <u>"glory"</u>;

We make this appeal:—

Eight years since the signing of the Armistice! And peace is still hard beset by preparations for war. In another war men, women and children would be more wantonly, more cruelly massacred, by death rays, gas, disease germs, and machines more fiendish than those used in the last war. Those whom you love must share in its universal destruction.

<u>Can You Afford Not To Give Your Utmost To Cleanse The World Of This Black Plague Of Needless Death and Suffering?</u>

Send your contribution to an uncompromising Peace organization

THE WOMEN'S PEACE UNION
39 Pearl Street, New York

Schwimmer-Lloyd Collection, Frieda Langer Lazarus Papers. The New York Public Library. Astor, Lenox and Tilden Foundations/ Art Resource, NY

△ The Women's Peace Union (WPU) distributed this flier in the 1920s to remind Americans of the human costs of the First World War. One of many peace societies active in the interwar years, the WPU lobbied for a constitutional amendment requiring a national referendum on a declaration of war. In the 1930s, Representative Louis Ludlow (Democrat from Indiana) worked to pass such a measure in Congress, but he failed.

in Latin America to protect business interests. The Women's Peace Union, organized in 1921, lobbied for a constitutional amendment to require a national referendum on a declaration of war. Quakers, YMCA officials, and Social Gospel clergy in 1917 created the American Friends Service Committee to promote alternatives to warmaking. In all, peace seekers believed that their reform activities could and must deliver a world without war.

21-2g Washington Naval Conference and Kellogg-Briand Pact

In this climate, peace advocates convinced President Harding to convene the **Washington Naval Conference** of November 1921–February 1922. Delegates from Great Britain, France, Japan, Italy, China, Portugal, Belgium, and the Netherlands joined a U.S. team led by Secretary of State Charles Evans Hughes to discuss limits on naval armaments. Britain, the United States, and Japan were facing a naval arms race whose huge military spending endangered economic recovery. American leaders also worried that an expansionist Japan, with the world's third-largest navy, would overtake the United States, ranked second behind Britain.

Hughes opened the conference with a stunning announcement: he proposed to achieve real disarmament by offering to scrap thirty major U.S. ships, totaling 846,000 tons. He then turned to the shocked British and Japanese delegations and urged them to do away with smaller amounts. The final limit, Hughes declared, should be 500,000 tons each for the Americans and British, 300,000 tons for the Japanese, and 175,000 tons each for the French and Italians—a ratio of 5:3:1.75. These totals were ratified in the Five-Power Treaty, which also set a ten-year moratorium on construction of battleships and aircraft carriers. The governments also pledged not to build new fortifications in their Pacific possessions (such as the Philippines).

Next, the conferees in Washington passed the Nine-Power Treaty, reaffirming the Open Door in China and recognizing Chinese sovereignty. Finally, in the Four-Power Treaty, the United States, Britain, France, and Japan agreed to respect one another's Pacific possessions. The three treaties did not limit submarines, destroyers, or carriers, nor did they provide enforcement powers. Still, the conference was a major accomplishment for Hughes. He achieved genuine arms limitations and at the same time improved America's strategic position vis-à-vis Japan in the Pacific.

Peace advocates also applauded the Locarno Pact of 1925, a set of agreements among European nations that sought to reduce tensions between Germany and France, and the Kellogg-Briand Pact of 1928. The latter document, named for U.S. secretary of state Frank B. Kellogg and French premier Aristide Briand, pledged sixty-two

Washington Naval Conference Multinational conference led by U.S. Secretary of State Hughes to address the problem of the United States, Great Britain, and Japan edging toward a dangerous (and costly) naval arms race.

nations to "condemn recourse to war for the solution of international controversies, and renounce it as an instrument of national policy." The accord passed the U.S. Senate 85–1, but many lawmakers considered it little more than a statement of moral preference because it lacked enforcement provisions. Nevertheless, the agreement reflected popular aversion to war, and it stimulated further discussions of keeping the peace.

21-3 A Consumer Society

▷ **How did the development of the automobile alter individual lives and American society?**

▷ **How did radio and advertising encourage consumption in American society?**

The consumerism depicted in *Why Change Your Wife?* and that expanded American influence abroad reflected important economic changes affecting the people and the nation. Between 1919 and 1929, the gross national product—the total value of goods and services produced in the United States—swelled by 40 percent. Wages and salaries also grew (though not as drastically), while the cost of living remained relatively stable. People had more purchasing power, and they spent as Americans had never spent (see Table 21.1).

Table 21.1 Consumerism in the 1920s

1900	
2 bicycles	$ 70.00
Wringer and washboard	5.00
Brushes and brooms	5.00
Sewing machine (mechanical)	25.00
TOTAL	$ 105.00

1928	
Automobile	$ 700.00
Radio	75.00
Phonograph	50.00
Washing machine	150.00
Vacuum cleaner	50.00
Sewing machine (electric)	60.00
Other electrical equipment	25.00
Telephone (per year)	35.00
TOTAL	$ 1,145.00

Source: From an article in Survey Magazine in 1928 reprinted in *Another Part of the Twenties,* by Paul Carter. Copyright 1977 by Columbia University Press. Reprinted with permission of the publisher.

Technology's benefits reached more households than ever before. New products and services were available to more than just the rich, especially to people living in cities. By 1929, two-thirds of all Americans lived in dwellings that had electricity, compared with one-sixth in 1912. Indoor plumbing became more common in private residences, and canned foods and ready-made clothes were more affordable. In 1929, one-fourth of all families owned electric vacuum cleaners and one-fifth had toasters. Many could afford these goods plus radios, cosmetics, and movie tickets because more than one family member earned wages or because the breadwinner took a second job.

21-3a Effects of the Automobile

The automobile stood as vanguard of the era's material wonders. During the 1920s, automobile registrations soared from 8 million to 23 million, and by 1929 one in every five Americans had a car. Mass production and competition made autos affordable even to some working-class families. A Ford Model T cost less than $300, and a Chevrolet sold for $700 by 1926—when factory workers earned about $1,300 a year and clerical workers about $2,300. Used cars cost less. At those prices, people could consider the car a necessity rather than a luxury. "There is no such thing as a 'pleasure automobile,'" proclaimed one newspaper ad in 1925. "You might as well talk of 'pleasure fresh air,' or of 'pleasure beef steak.' . . . The automobile increases length of life, increases happiness, represents above all other achievements the progress and the civilization of our age."

Automobiles altered American life as railroads had seventy-five years earlier. Owners acquired a new "riding habit" and abandoned crowded, slow trolleys. Streets became cleaner as autos replaced horse-drawn carriages. Female drivers achieved newfound independence, taking touring trips with friends, conquering muddy roads, and making repairs when their vehicles broke down. Families created "homes on wheels," packing food and camping equipment to "get away from it all." By 1927, most autos were enclosed (they previously had open tops), offering young people new private space for courtship and sex. A vast choice of models (108 automobile manufacturers in 1923) and colors allowed owners to express personal tastes.

Americans' passion for driving necessitated extensive road construction and abundant fuel supplies. Since the late 1800s, farmers and bicyclists had been lobbying for improved roads. After the First World War, motorists joined the campaign, and in the 1920s government aid made "automobility" truly feasible. In 1921, Congress passed the Federal Highway Act, providing funds for state roads, and in 1923 the Bureau of Public Roads planned a national highway system. Roadbuilding in turn inspired such technological developments as mechanized graders and concrete mixers. The oil-refining industry, which produced gasoline, became vast and powerful. In 1920, the United States produced about 65 percent of the world's oil. Automobiles also forced public officials to pay attention to safety and traffic control. General Electric Company produced the first timed stop-and-go traffic light in 1924.

◁ Automobiles supposedly gave women new independence and skills as well as new mobility. Though it is unlikely that a woman dressed in furs and high heels, such as the woman posing in this photograph, would have changed a flat tire, the automobile nevertheless did give middle-class women exposure to and knowledge about a new technology with all its complexity and potential problems.

H. Armstrong Roberts/Getty Images

21-3b Advertising and Radio

Advertising, an essential component of consumerism, acquired new prominence. By 1929, more money was spent on advertising goods and services than on all types of formal education. Blending psychological theory with practical cynicism, advertising theorists confidently asserted that any person's tastes could be manipulated, and marketers developed new techniques to achieve their ends. For example, cosmetics manufacturers like Max Factor, Helena Rubenstein, and African American entrepreneur Madame C. J. Walker used movie stars and beauty advice in magazines to induce women to buy their products. Other advertisers hired baseball star Babe Ruth and football's Red Grange to endorse food and sporting goods.

Radio became a powerful advertising and entertainment agent. By 1929, 10 million families owned radios, and Americans spent $850 million a year on radio equipment. In the early 1920s, Congress decided that broadcasting should be a private enterprise, not a tax-supported public service as in Great Britain. As a result, American radio programming consisted mainly of entertainment rather than educational content because drama. music, and comedy attracted larger audiences and higher profits from advertisers. Station KDKA in Pittsburgh, owned by Westinghouse Electric Company, pioneered commercial radio in 1920, broadcasting results of the 1920 presidential election. Then, in 1922, an AT&T-run station in New York City broadcast recurring advertisements—"commercials"—for a real estate developer. Other stations began airing commercials; by the end of 1922, there were 508 such stations. In 1929, the National Broadcasting Company began assembling a network of stations and soon was charging advertisers $10,000 (equivalent to about $121,000 today) to sponsor an hour-long show.

21-3c Export of American Consumerism

While radio and advertising expanded consumerism at home, America's economic prominence stimulated interest in its products abroad. Though some foreigners warned against American economic domination, others eagerly accepted the products. Coca-Cola opened a bottling plant in Essen, Germany. Ford built an automobile assembly factory in Cologne, and General Motors built one for trucks near Berlin. German writer Hans Joachim claimed that cultural adoption might promote a peaceful, democratic world because "our interest in elevators, radio towers, and jazz was . . . an attitude that wanted to convert the flame thrower into a vacuum cleaner."

Products such as automobiles and radios helped create a new American people. As a result of its mass marketing and standardized programming, radio had the effect of blurring ethnic boundaries and creating—at least in one way—a homogeneous culture. And the automobile served as a social equalizer, prompting some observers to believe that it might calm social unrest among different ethnic groups. As one writer wrote in 1924, "It is hard to convince Steve Popovich, or Antonio Branca, or plain John Smith that he is being ground into the dust by Capital when at will he may drive the same highways, view the same country, and get as much enjoyment from his trip as the modern Midas."

◁ Even more than movies and books, radio reached corners of American society that previously had not been exposed to new popular culture. Note the elaborate equipment, such as headphones and large antenna, needed by this farmer in order to receive a radio signal in the 1920s.

Library of Congress Prints and Photographs Division[LC-USZ62-60682]

21-4 Cities, Migrants, and Suburbs

▷ What factors contributed to the expansion of urban areas in the 1920s?

▷ How did the racial and ethnic demographic makeup of urban areas change in the 1920s?

▷ Why did suburban growth occur in the 1920s?

Consumerism signified not merely an economically mature nation but also an urbanized one. The 1920 federal census revealed that, for the first time, a majority of Americans lived in urban areas (places with 2,500 or more people); the city had become the focus of national experience. In addition to growth in metropolises like Chicago and New York, manufacturing and services helped propel expansion in dozens of regional centers. Industries like steel, oil, and auto production energized Birmingham, Houston, and Detroit; services and retail trades boosted Seattle, Atlanta, and Minneapolis. Explosive growth also occurred in warm-climate cities—notably Miami and San Diego—where promises of comfort and profit attracted thousands of real estate speculators.

As cities grew, the agrarian way of life waned. During the 1920s, 6 million Americans left farms for the city. Young people who felt stifled when they compared their existence with the flashy openness of urban life moved to regional centers like Kansas City and Indianapolis or to the West. Between 1920 and 1930, California's population increased 67 percent, and California became a highly urbanized state while retaining its status as a leader in agricultural production. Meanwhile, streams of rural southerners moved to western industrial cities or rode railroads northward to Chicago and Cleveland.

21-4a African American Migration

African Americans, continuing their Great Migration that had begun in 1910, made up a sizable portion of people on the move. Pushed from cotton farming by a boll weevil plague and lured by industrial jobs, 1.5 million blacks migrated, doubling African American populations of New York, Chicago, Detroit, and Houston. Black communities also enlarged in Los Angeles, San Francisco, and San Diego. In these cities, they found work just as exploitive as that in the South—menial labor as janitors, longshoremen, and domestic servants. But the move northward included psychological release because a parcel of freedom was available in New York and Chicago that did not exist in Charleston or Atlanta. In the North, a black person did not always have to act subordinately to a white. As one migrant wrote back home, "I . . . am living well. . . . I can ride in the [streetcar] anywhere I can get a seat."

Forced by low wages and discrimination to seek the cheapest housing, African American newcomers squeezed into ghettos such as Chicago's South Side, New York's Harlem, and Los Angeles's Central Avenue. On the West Coast, however, black homeownership rates were higher than in other regions. Many took advantage of Los Angeles's "bungalow boom," in which they could purchase a small, one-story house for as little as $900. But unlike white migrants, who were free to move away from the inner city when they could afford to, blacks everywhere found better neighborhoods closed to them. They could either crowd further into already densely populated black neighborhoods or spill into nearby white neighborhoods, a process that sparked resistance and violence. Fears of such "invasion" prompted neighborhood associations to adopt restrictive covenants, whereby white homeowners pledged not to sell or rent property to blacks.

21-4b Marcus Garvey

In response to discrimination, threats, and violence, thousands of urban African Americans joined movements that glorified racial independence. The most influential of these black nationalist groups was the Universal Negro Improvement Association (UNIA), headquartered in New York City's Harlem area and led by **Marcus Garvey**, a Jamaican immigrant who believed blacks should separate from corrupt white society. Proclaiming, "I am the equal of any white man," and appealing for pride in African heritage, Garvey spread his message with mass meetings and parades. Unlike the NAACP, which had been formed by elite African American and white liberals, the UNIA was comprised exclusively of blacks, most of whom occupied lower rungs of the economic hierarchy.

Garvey promoted economic independence by encouraging black-owned businesses that would manufacture and sell products to black consumers, and his proposed Phillis Wheatley Hotel (named after a notable African American poet) would enable any black person to make a reservation. His newspaper, *Negro World*, preached black pride, and he founded the Black Star steamship line to transport manufactured goods and raw materials to black businesses in North America, the Caribbean, and Africa. In an era when whites were pouring money into stock market speculation, thousands of hopeful blacks invested their dollars in the Black Star Line.

The UNIA declined in the mid-1920s after mismanagement plagued Garvey's plans. In 1923, Garvey was imprisoned for mail fraud involving the bankrupt Black Star Line and then deported to Jamaica in 1927 for trying to sell stock by advertising a ship that his company did not own. His prosecution, however, was politically motivated. Middle-class black leaders, such as W.E.B. Du Bois, and several clergymen opposed the UNIA, fearing that its extremism would undermine their efforts and influence. Beginning in 1919, the U.S. Bureau of Investigation (BOI), forerunner to the FBI, had been monitoring Garvey's radical activities by infiltrating the UNIA, and the BOI's deputy head, J. Edgar Hoover, proclaimed Garvey to be one of the most dangerous blacks in America. Du Bois also became incensed when word leaked

Marcus Garvey Charismatic black leader who promoted racial pride and independence and believed blacks should separate from white society.

out in 1922 that Garvey had met secretly with leaders of the Ku Klux Klan, who supported Garvey's idea of enabling blacks to move to Africa. Nevertheless, for several years the UNIA attracted a large following (contemporaries estimated 500,000; Garvey claimed 6 million), and Garvey's speeches instilled in many African Americans a heightened sense of racial pride.

21-4c Newcomers from Mexico and Puerto Rico

The newest immigrants came from Mexico and Puerto Rico, where, as in rural North America, declining fortunes pushed people off the land. In parts of California and the Southwest, Mexicans had been among the original inhabitants and Anglo-Europeans were the immigrants. But by the twentieth century, Anglos had settled and taken control of many communities and businesses. During the 1910s, Anglo farmers' associations encouraged immigration from Mexico in order to obtain a source of cheap workers; by the 1920s, Mexican migrants constituted three-fourths of farm labor in the American West. Growers treated these laborers as slaves, paying them extremely low wages. Resembling other immigrant groups, Mexican newcomers lacked resources and skills, and men outnumbered women. Although some achieved middle-class status as shopkeepers and professionals, most crowded into low-rent districts in growing cities like Denver, San Antonio, Los Angeles, and Tucson, where they suffered poor sanitation, poor police protection, and poor schools. Both rural and urban Mexicans moved back and forth between their homeland and the United States, seeking jobs and creating a way of life that Mexicans called *sin fronteras*—without borders.

The 1920s also witnessed an influx of Puerto Ricans to the mainland. Puerto Rico had been a U.S. possession since 1898, and its natives were granted U.S. citizenship in 1916. When a shift in the island's economy from sugar to coffee production created a labor surplus, Puerto Ricans left for New York and other cities, attracted by employers seeking cheap labor. In the cities, they created *barrios* (communities) and found jobs in factories, restaurants, and domestic service. Puerto Ricans developed businesses—*bodegas* (grocery stores), cafes, boardinghouses—and social organizations to help them adapt to American society. As with Mexicans, educated Puerto Rican elites—doctors, lawyers, business owners—became community leaders.

21-4d Suburbanization

As urbanization peaked, suburban growth accelerated. Though towns had sprouted around major cities since the nation's earliest years, prosperity and automobile transportation in the 1920s made suburbs more accessible to those wishing to leave urban neighborhoods. Between 1920 and 1930, suburbs of Chicago (such as Oak Park and Evanston), Cleveland (Shaker Heights), and Los Angeles (Burbank and Inglewood) grew five to ten times faster than did nearby central cities. They sparked an outburst of home construction; Los Angeles builders alone erected 250,000 homes for auto-owning suburbanites. Although some suburbs, such as Highland Park (near Detroit) and East Chicago, were industrial satellites, most were middle- and upper-class bedroom communities.

Suburbanites wanted to escape big-city crime, grime, and taxes, and they fought to preserve control over their police, schools, and water and gas services. Consequently, suburbs increasingly resisted annexation to core cities. Particularly in the Northeast and Midwest, suburbs' fierce independence choked off expansion by the central cities and prevented them from access to the resources and tax bases of wealthier suburban residents. Suburban expansion had other costs, too, as automobiles and the dispersal of population spread the environmental problems of city life—trash, pollution, noise—across the entire metropolitan area.

◁ Over half a million Mexicans immigrated to the United States during the 1920s. Many of them traveled in families and worked together in the fields and orchards of California and other western states. This family is shown pitting apricots in Los Angeles County in 1924.

Expansion of Suburbs in the 1920s

An outburst of housing and highway construction made possible the rapid growth of suburbs in the 1920s. The Chicago suburb of Niles Center, ultimately called the Village of Skokie, was incorporated in 1888. Aided by the service of commuter railroads, the village began to grow in the early 1900s, and in 1913 the first permanently paved road in Cook County was built there. After 1920, a real estate boom began, and by the mid-1920s the village had its own water, sewer, and street lighting services, along with many more paved roads. Wealthy Chicagoans such as utilities and railroad investor Samuel Insull built lavish homes in Niles Center, and soon commercial and office buildings sprang up along its major thoroughfares. Population grew so rapidly that the community boasted that it was "The World's Largest Village." The Great Depression halted the boom in 1929, but significant growth resumed after the Second World War.

CRITICAL THINKING

□ How do you think daily life changed as a result of the growth of suburbs?

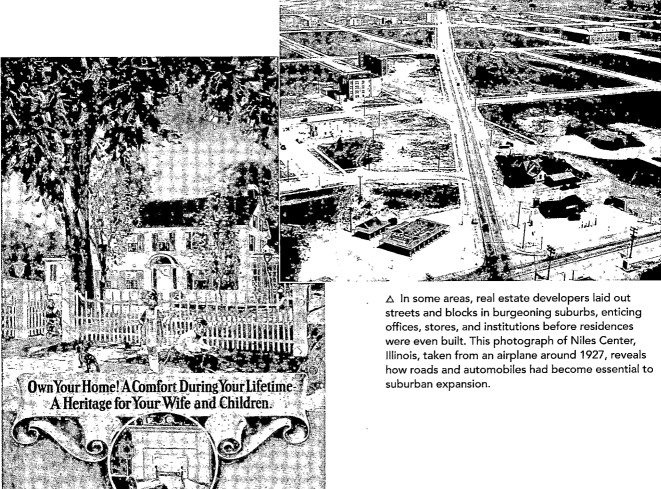

David Pollack/Getty Images

Provided by the Skokie Historical Society

Own Your Home! A Comfort During Your Lifetime
A Heritage for Your Wife and Children.

25

△ In some areas, real estate developers laid out streets and blocks in burgeoning suburbs, enticing offices, stores, and institutions before residences were even built. This photograph of Niles Center, Illinois, taken from an airplane around 1927, reveals how roads and automobiles had become essential to suburban expansion.

△ During the 1920s, the ideal of a "home of one's own" became a motivating factor for buying a house in the suburbs. The ideal included not only a spacious cottage but also a grassy yard, white picket fence, shade trees, and an environment where children could play in safety.

Together, cities and suburbs fostered the mass culture that gave the decade its character. Most consumers who jammed shops, movie houses, and sporting arenas and who embraced fads like crossword puzzles and miniature golf lived in or around cities. In these places, people defied older morals by patronizing speakeasies (illegal saloons during prohibition), wearing outlandish clothes, and dancing to jazz. Yet the ideal of small-town society survived. While millions thronged cityward, Americans reminisced about the simplicity of a world gone by, however mythical that world might have been. This was the dilemma the modern nation faced: how does one anchor oneself in a world of rampant materialism and rapid social change?

21-5 New Rhythms of Everyday Life

▷ How did Americans experience changes in the allocation of time to work, family, and leisure in the 1920s?

▷ What new social values and behaviors emerged in the 1920s?

▷ How did views of gender and sexuality shift in the 1920s?

Amid expanded consumerism, American people experienced new patterns of everyday life. One new pattern involved uses of time. People increasingly split their day into distinct time-based compartments: work, family, and leisure. For many, time on the job shrank as mechanization and resulting higher productivity enabled employers to shorten the workweek for many industrial laborers from six days to five and a half. White-collar employees often worked a forty-hour week, enjoyed the weekend off, and received paid vacations as a job benefit.

Family time is harder to measure, but certain trends emerged. Family size decreased between 1920 and 1930 as birth control became more widely practiced. Among American women who married in the 1870s and 1880s, over half who survived to age fifty had five or more children; of their counterparts who married in the 1920s, however, just 20 percent had five or more children. Lower birth rates and longer life expectancy meant that adults were devoting a smaller portion of their lives to raising children and having more time for nonfamily activities. Meanwhile, divorce rates rose. In 1920, there was 1 divorce for every 7.5 marriages; by 1929, the national ratio was 1 in 6, and in many cities it was 2 in 7.

21-5a Household Management

At home, housewives still toiled long hours cleaning, cooking, and raising children, but machines now lightened some tasks and enabled women to use time differently than their forebears had. Especially in middle-class households, electric irons and washing machines simplified some chores. Gas- and oil-powered central heating and hot water heaters

eliminated the hauling of wood, coal, and water, the upkeep of a kitchen fire, and the removal of ashes.

Even as technology and economic change simplified some tasks, they also created new demands on a mother's time. The pool of those who could help housewives with cleaning, cooking, and childcare shrank because daughters stayed in school longer, and alternative forms of employment caused a shortage of domestic servants. In addition, the availability of washing machines, hot water, vacuum cleaners, and commercial soap put greater pressure on housewives to keep everything clean. Advertisers of these products tried to make women feel guilty for not devoting enough attention to cleaning the home. No longer a producer of food and clothing as her ancestors had been, a mother instead became the chief shopper, responsible for making sure her family spent money wisely. And the automobile made the wife chief chauffeur. One survey found that urban housewives spent on average seven and one-half hours per week driving to shop and transport children.

21-5b Health and Life Expectancy

Emphasis on nutrition added a scientific dimension to housewives' responsibilities. With the discovery of vitamins between 1915 and 1930, nutritionists began advocating consumption of certain foods to promote health. Producers of milk, canned fruits and vegetables, and other foods exploited the vitamin craze with claims about benefits that were hard to dispute because little was known about these invisible, tasteless ingredients. Welch's Grape Juice, for example, avoided mentioning the excess sugars in its product when it advertised that it was "Rich in Health Values" and "the laxative properties you cannot do without." Even chocolate candy manufacturers plugged their bars as vitamin packed.

Better diets and improved hygiene made Americans generally healthier. Life expectancy at birth increased from fifty-four to sixty years between 1920 and 1930, and infant mortality decreased by two-thirds. Public sanitation and research in bacteriology combined to reduce risks of life-threatening diseases such as tuberculosis and diphtheria. Medical progress did not benefit all groups equally; race and class mattered in health trends as they did in everything else. Infant mortality rates were 50 to 100 percent higher among nonwhites than among whites, and tuberculosis in *barrios* and inner-city slums remained alarmingly common. Moreover, fatalities from automobile accidents rose 150 percent, and deaths from heart disease and cancer—ailments of old age—increased 15 percent. Nevertheless, Americans in general were living longer: the total population over age sixty-five grew 35 percent between 1920 and 1930, while other age groups increased only 15 percent.

21-5c Older Americans and Retirement

As numbers of elderly increased, their worsening economic status stirred interest in pensions and other forms of old-age assistance. Industrialism put premiums on youth and agility, pushing older people into poverty from forced retirement and reduced income. Recognizing the needs of aging citizens, most European countries established state-supported pension systems in the early 1900s. Many Americans, however, believed that individuals should prepare for old age by saving in their youth; pensions, they felt, smacked of socialism. As late as 1923, the Pennsylvania Chamber of Commerce labeled old-age assistance "un-American and socialistic . . . an entering wedge of communistic propaganda."

Yet conditions were alarming. Most inmates in state poorhouses were older people, and almost one-third of Americans age sixty-five and older depended financially on someone else. Few employers, including the federal government, provided for retired employees. Noting that the government fed retired horses until they died, one postal worker complained, "For the purpose of drawing a pension, it would have been better had I been a horse than a human being." Resistance finally broke at the state level in the 1920s. Led by physician Isaac Max Rubinow and journalist Abraham Epstein, reformers persuaded voluntary associations, labor unions, and legislators to endorse old-age assistance through pensions, insurance, and retirement homes. By 1933, almost every state provided at least minimal support to needy elderly people, and a path had been opened for a national program of old-age insurance—social security.

21-5d Social Values

As Americans encountered new ways to use their time, altered behaviors and values were inevitable. Aided by new fabrics and chemical dyes, clothes became a means of self-expression as women and men wore more casual and gaily colored styles than their parents would have considered. The line between acceptable and inappropriate behavior blurred as smoking, drinking, and frankness about sex became fashionable. Birth control gained a large following in respectable circles. Newspapers, magazines, motion pictures (such as *Why Change Your Wife?*), and popular songs (such as "I Don't Care") made certain that Americans did not suffer from "sex starvation."

A typical movie ad promised "brilliant men, beautiful jazz babies, champagne baths, midnight revels, petting parties in the purple dawn, all ending in one terrific smashing climax that makes you gasp."

Other trends weakened inherited customs. Because restrictive child labor laws and compulsory attendance rules kept children in school longer than ever before, peer groups rather than parents played an influential role in socializing youngsters. In earlier eras, different age groups had often shared the same activities: children interacted with adults in fields and kitchens, and young apprentices toiled in workshops beside older journeymen and craftsmen. Now, graded school classes, sports, and clubs constantly brought together children of the same age, separating them from the company and influence of adults.

Furthermore, the ways that young people interacted with each other underwent fundamental changes. Between 1890 and the mid-1920s, ritualized middle- and upper-class courtship, consisting of men formally "calling" on women and of chaperoned social engagements, faded in favor of unsupervised "dating," in which a man "asked out" a woman and spent money on her. Unmarried young people, living in cities away from family restraints, eagerly went on dates to new commercial amusements, such as movies and nightclubs, and automobiles made dating even more extensive. A woman's job seldom provided sufficient income for her to afford these entertainments, but she could enjoy them if a man escorted and "treated" her. Companionship, romance, and, at times, sexual exploitation accompanied the practice, especially when a woman was expected to give sexual favors in return for being treated. A date thus ironically weakened a woman's prerogative at the same time that it expanded her opportunities. Under the courtship system, a woman had control over who could "call" on her. But once she entered a system in which a man's money enabled her to fulfill her desire for entertainment and independence, she might find herself faced with difficult moral choices.

◁ Department stores provided women with new responsibilities for handling money. When a customer paid the sales clerk for a purchase on the store's display floor and needed change and a receipt, the clerk would send the money by pneumatic (vacuum) tubes to another floor (here, the basement) where a cashier would make the change and send it back to the sales clerk who would then hand it to the customer. Previously, store owners would trust only men to make the change, but by the 1920s women were deemed responsible enough to make the transaction.

Underwood Archives/Getty Images

21-5e Women in the Workforce

The practice of dating burgeoned because, after the First World War, women streamed into the labor force. By 1930, 10.8 million women held paying jobs, an increase of 2 million since war's end (see Figure 21.2). The sex segregation that had long characterized workplaces persisted; most women took work that men seldom sought. Thus, more than 1 million women held jobs as teachers and nurses. In the clerical category, some 2.2 million women were typists, bookkeepers, and filing clerks, a tenfold increase since 1920. Another 736,000 were store clerks, and growing numbers could be found in the personal service category as waitresses and hairdressers. Wherever women were employed, their wages seldom exceeded half of those paid to men for similar work. Even though the vast majority of married women did not hold paying jobs (only 12 percent were employed in 1930), married women as a proportion of the workforce rose by 30 percent during the 1920s, and the number of employed married women swelled from 1.9 million to 3.1 million. These figures omit countless widowed, divorced, and abandoned women who held jobs and who, like married women, often had children to support.

The proportion of racial and ethnic minority women in paid labor was double that of white women. Often they entered the workforce because their husbands were unemployed or underemployed. The majority of employed African American women held domestic jobs doing cooking, cleaning, and laundry. The few who had manufacturing jobs, such as in cigarette factories and meatpacking plants, performed the least desirable, lowest-paying tasks. Some opportunities opened for educated black women in social work, teaching, and nursing, but these women also faced discrimination and low incomes. More than white mothers, employed black mothers called on a family network of grandmothers and aunts to help with child care. Economic necessity also drew other minority women into the labor force. Mexican women worked as domestic servants, operatives in garment factories, and agricultural laborers. Next to black women, Japanese American women were the most likely to hold paying jobs. They toiled as field hands and domestics, jobs in which they encountered racial bias and low pay.

21-5f Alternative Images of Femininity

Employed or not, women remade the image of femininity. In contrast to the heavy, floor-length dresses and long hair of previous generations, the short skirts and bobbed hair of the 1920s "flapper" symbolized independence and sexual freedom. Although few women lived the flapper life, the look became fashionable among office workers and store clerks as well as college students. As Cecil B. DeMille's movies showed, chaste models of female behavior were eclipsed by movie temptresses, such as Clara Bow, known as the "'It' Girl," and Gloria Swanson, notorious for torrid love affairs on and off the screen. Many women asserted social equality with men. One observer described "the new woman" as intriguingly independent.

> She takes a man's point of view as her mother never could. ... She will never make you a hatband or knit you a necktie, but she'll drive you from the station ... in her own little sports car. She'll don knickers and go skiing with you, ... she'll dive as well as you, perhaps better, she'll dance as long as you care to, and she'll take everything you say the way you mean it.

21-5g Gay and Lesbian Culture

The era's openness regarding sexuality also enabled the underground homosexual culture to surface a little more than in previous eras. In nontraditional city neighborhoods, such as New York's Greenwich Village and Harlem, cheap rents

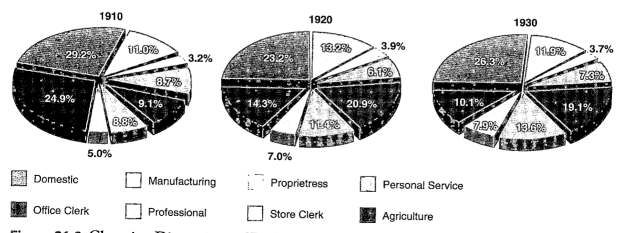

1910 — 29.2% 11.0% 3.2% 8.7% 24.9% 9.1% 8.8% 5.0%

1920 — 23.2% 13.2% 3.9% 6.1% 14.3% 20.9% 11.4% 7.0%

1930 — 26.3% 11.9% 3.7% 7.3% 10.1% 19.1% 7.9% 13.6%

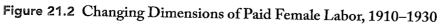

■ Domestic   □ Manufacturing   □ Proprietress   □ Personal Service

■ Office Clerk   □ Professional   □ Store Clerk   ■ Agriculture

Figure 21.2 Changing Dimensions of Paid Female Labor, 1910–1930

These charts reveal the extraordinary growth in clerical and professional occupations among employed women and the accompanying decline in agricultural labor in the early twentieth century. Notice that manufacturing employment peaked in 1920 and that domestic service fluctuated as white immigrant women began to move out of these jobs and were replaced by women of color.

and a tolerance for alternate lifestyles attracted gay men and lesbians, who patronized dance halls, speakeasies, cafes, and other gathering places. Establishments that catered to a gay clientele remained targets for police raids, however, demonstrating that gays and lesbians could not expect acceptance from the rest of society.

These trends represented a break with the more restrained culture of the nineteenth century. But social change rarely proceeds smoothly. As the decade wore on, various groups mobilized to defend older values.

21-6 Lines of Defense

▷ **How was the pluralism of American society challenged socially and politically in the 1920s?**

▷ **What were the key characteristics of the anti-immigrant sentiment in the 1920s?**

▷ **How did Protestant Christianity respond to the shift in social values and behavior in modern society?**

Early in 1920, the leader of a newly formed organization, using a tactic adopted by modern businesses, hired two public relations experts to recruit members. Edward Clarke and Elizabeth Tyler canvassed communities in the South, Southwest, and Midwest, where they found countless people eager to pay a $10 membership fee and $6 for a white uniform. Clarke and Tyler pocketed $2.50 from each membership they sold. Their success helped build the organization to 5 million members and four thousand chapters by 1923.

21-6a Ku Klux Klan

No ordinary civic club, this was the Ku Klux Klan (KKK), a revived version of the hooded order that terrorized southern communities after the Civil War. Reconstituted in 1915 by William J. Simmons, an Atlanta, Georgia, evangelist and insurance salesman, the Klan adopted the hoods, intimidating tactics, and mystical terminology of its forerunner (its leader was the Imperial Wizard; its book of rituals, the Kloran). But the new Klan had broader objectives than the old. It fanned outward from the Deep South and for a time wielded political power in places as diverse as Oregon, where Portland's mayor was a Klan member, and Indiana, where Klansmen held the governorship and several seats in the legislature. Its membership included men from the urban middle class who were fearful of losing social and economic gains achieved from postwar prosperity and nervous about immigration and a new youth culture that seemed to be eluding family control. It also included a women's adjunct, Women of the Ku Klux Klan, boasting an estimated half-million members.

One phrase summed up Klan goals: "Native, white, Protestant supremacy." Native meant no immigration, no "mongrelization" of American culture. According to Imperial Wizard Hiram Wesley Evans, white supremacy was a matter of survival. "The world," he warned, "has been so made so that each race must fight for its life, must conquer, accept

slavery, or die. The Klansman believes the whites will not become slaves, and he does not intend to die before his time." Evans praised Protestantism for promoting "unhampered individual development," and accused the Catholic Church of discouraging assimilation and enslaving people to priests and a foreign pope.

Using threatening assemblies, violence, and economic pressure, the new Klan menaced many communities. Klansmen meted out vigilante justice to suspected bootleggers, wife beaters, and adulterers; forced schools to stop teaching the theory of evolution; campaigned against Catholic and Jewish political candidates; urged members not to buy from merchants who did not share their views; and fueled racial tensions against Mexicans in Texas border cities, immigrants in northern cities, and African Americans everywhere. Although men firmly controlled Klan activities, women not only promoted native white Protestantism but also, with male approval, worked for moral reform and enforcement of prohibition. Because the KKK vowed to protect the "virtue" of women, housewives and other women sometimes appealed to the Klan for help in punishing abusive, unfaithful, or irresponsible husbands and fathers when legal authorities would not intervene. Rather than an arrest and trial, the Klan's method of justice was flogging.

By 1925, however, the Invisible Empire was weakening, as scandal undermined its moral base. Most notably, in 1925 Indiana grand dragon David Stephenson was convicted of second-degree murder after he kidnapped and raped a woman who later died either from taking poison or from infection caused by bites on her body. More generally, the Klan's negative, exclusive brand of patriotism and purity could not compete in a pluralistic society.

The KKK had no monopoly on bigotry; intolerance pervaded American society. Nativists had urged an end to open immigration since the 1880s. They charged that Catholic and Jewish immigrants clogged city slums and stubbornly embraced alien religious and political beliefs. Fear of immigrant radicals also fueled a dramatic trial in 1921, when two Italian anarchists, **Nicola Sacco and Bartolomeo Vanzetti**, were convicted of murdering a paymaster and guard in Braintree, Massachusetts. Evidence for their guilt was flimsy, but Judge Webster Thayer openly sided with the prosecution, privately calling the defendants "anarchistic bastards."

21-6b Immigration Quotas

Guided by such sentiments, the movement to restrict immigration gathered support. Labor leaders charged that alien workers depressed wages and caused unemployment of native-born men. Business executives, who formerly had opposed restrictions because they desired cheap immigrant laborers, changed their minds, having realized that they could keep wages low by

Nicola Sacco and Bartolomeo Vanzetti Italian immigrants found guilty of a Massachusetts murder and sentenced to death. Sacco and Vanzetti were also anarchists and much of their murder trial focused on their radicalism.

mechanizing. Even some humanitarian reformers supported restriction as a means of reducing poverty and easing assimilation. Drawing support from such groups, Congress reversed previous policy and, in the Emergency Quota Act of 1921, set yearly immigration allocations for each nationality. Reflecting preference for Anglo-Saxon Protestant immigrants and prejudice against Catholics and Jews from southern and eastern Europe, Congress stipulated that annual immigration of a given nationality could not exceed 3 percent of the number of immigrants from that nation residing in the United States in 1910. The act thereby discriminated against immigrants from southern and eastern Europe, whose numbers were small in 1910 relative to those from northern Europe.

In 1924, Congress replaced the Quota Act with the **National Origins Act**.

National Origins Act of 1924 Restricted annual immigration from any foreign country to 2 percent of that nationality residing in the United States in 1890 (but barred Asians); also limited total annual immigration to 150,000.

This law limited annual immigration to 150,000 people and set quotas at 2 percent of each nationality residing in the United States in 1890, except for Asians, who were banned completely (Chinese immigration had been banned since 1882 by the Chinese Exclusion Act). The National Origins Act further restricted southern and eastern Europeans because even fewer of those groups lived in the United States in 1890 than in 1910. The law did, however, allow foreign-born wives and children of U.S. citizens to enter as nonquota immigrants. In 1927, a revised National Origins Act apportioned new quotas to begin in 1929. It retained the annual limit of 150,000 but redefined quotas to be distributed among European countries in proportion to the "national-origins" (country of birth or descent) of American inhabitants in 1920. People coming from the Western Hemisphere did not fall under the quotas (except for those whom the Labor Department defined as potential paupers), and soon they became the largest immigrant groups (see Figure 21.3).

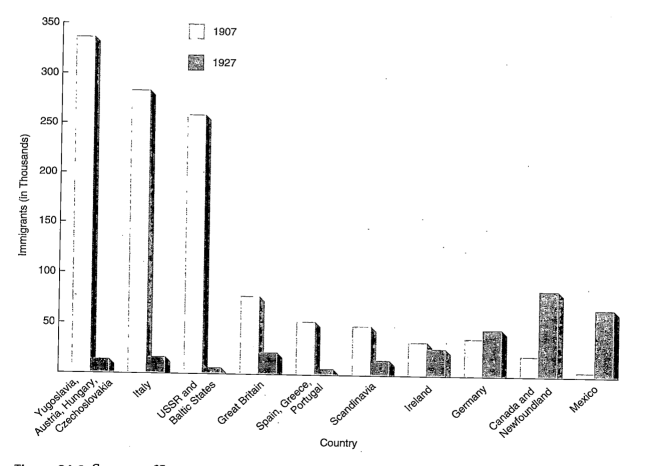

Figure 21.3 Sources of Immigration, 1907 and 1927

Immigration peaked in 1907 and 1908, when newcomers from southern and eastern Europe poured into the United States. After immigration restriction laws were passed in the 1920s, the greatest number of immigrants came from the Western Hemisphere (Canada and Mexico), which was exempted from the quotas, and the number coming from eastern and southern Europe shrank.

21-6c Fundamentalism and the Scopes Trial

Whereas nativists tried to establish ethnic and racial purity, the pursuit of spiritual purity stirred religious fundamentalists. Millions of Americans sought certainty and salvation by following Protestant evangelical denominations that interpreted the Bible literally. Resolutely believing that God's miracles created the world and its living creatures, they condemned the theory of evolution as heresy and argued that wherever fundamentalists constituted a majority of a community, as they did in many places, they should be able to determine what would be taught in schools. Their enemies were "modernists," who used reasoning from social sciences, such as psychology and anthropology, to interpret behavior. To modernists, God was important to the study of culture and history, but science was responsible for advancing knowledge.

In 1925, Christian **fundamentalism** clashed with modernism in a celebrated case in Dayton, Tennessee, that came to be known as the **Scopes Trial**. Early that year, the state legislature passed a law forbidding public school instructors to teach the theory that humans had evolved from lower forms of life rather than descended from Adam and Eve. Shortly thereafter, high-school teacher John Thomas Scopes volunteered to serve in a test case and was arrested for violating the law. Scopes's trial that summer became a headline event. William Jennings Bryan, former secretary of state and three-time presidential candidate, argued for the prosecution, and a team of civil liberties lawyers headed by noted defense attorney Clarence Darrow represented Scopes. News correspondents crowded into the small town, and radio stations broadcast the trial.

Although Scopes was convicted—clearly he had broken the law—modernists claimed victory. The testimony, they believed, showed fundamentalism to be illogical. The trial's climax occurred when Bryan took the witness stand as an expert on the Bible. Responding to Darrow's probing, Bryan asserted that Eve really had been created from Adam's rib, that the Tower of Babel was responsible for the diversity of languages, and that Jonah had been swallowed by a big fish. Spectators in Dayton cheered Bryan for his declarations, but the liberal press mocked him and his allies. Nevertheless, fundamentalism continued to expand. For example, the evangelical Southern Baptist Convention became the fastest-growing Protestant sect, and, along with other fundamentalist groups, pressured school boards to stop teaching about evolution. Advocates for what they believed to be basic values of family and conduct, these churches created an independent subculture, with their own schools, camps, radio ministries, and missionary societies.

21-6d Religious Revivalism

Religious fervor spread wherever people struggling with economic insecurity became nervous about modernism's attack on old-time religion. Countless urban and rural Pentecostal churches attracted blacks and whites swayed by their pageantry and depiction of a personal Savior. Using modern advertising techniques and elaborately staged broadcasts on radio, magnetic "revivalist" preachers—such as the flamboyant Aimee Semple McPherson, whose radio broadcasts drew hundreds of thousands of listeners and who built the nation's first "megachurch"; former baseball player Billy Sunday, who preached to large crowds as on his nationwide travels; and Father Divine, an African American who amassed an interracial following from his base on Long Island—stirred revivalist fervor.

Revivalism represented only one means of sustaining old-fashioned values and finding comfort in a fast-moving consumer society. Millions who did not belong to the KKK firmly believed that nonwhites and immigrants were inferior people who imperiled national welfare. Clergy and teachers of all faiths condemned dancing, new dress styles, and sex in movies and parked cars. Many urban dwellers supported prohibition, believing that eliminating the temptation of drink would help win the battle against poverty, vice, and corruption. Yet even while mourning a lost past, most Americans sincerely sought some kind of balance as they tried to adjust to the modern order in one way or another. Few refrained from listening to the radio and seeing movies like *Why Change Your Wife?*—activities that proved less corrupting than critics feared. More than ever, Americans sought fellowship in civic organizations such as Rotary, Elks, and women's clubs. Perhaps most important, more people were finding release in recreation and new uses of leisure time.

21-7 The Age of Play

▷ What form of entertainment and leisure did Americans engage in during the 1920s?

▷ What role did "heroes" play in American society in the 1920s?

▷ What cultural expressions were created and nurtured by African Americans in the 1920s?

Americans in the 1920s embraced commercial entertainment as never before. In 1919, they spent $2.5 billion on leisure activities; by 1929, such expenditures topped $4.3 billion, a figure not again equaled until after the Second World War. Spectator amusements—movies, music, and sports—accounted for 21 percent of the 1929 total; the rest involved participatory recreation such as games, hobbies, and travel. Entrepreneurs responded to an appetite for fads and spectacles. Early in the 1920s, mahjong, a Chinese tile game, was the craze. In the mid-1920s, devotees popularized crossword puzzles, printed in mass-circulation newspapers and magazines. Next, fun seekers adopted miniature golf. By 1930, the nation boasted thirty thousand miniature golf courses featuring tiny castles, windmills, and waterfalls. Dances like the

fundamentalism Twentieth-century movement within Protestantism that taught literal interpretation of the Bible.

Scopes Trial Trial that took place after high school teacher John Scopes challenged a Tennessee law that banned teaching the theory of evolution in public schools.

Charleston won fans throughout the country, aided by live and recorded music and the growing popularity of jazz.

21-7a Movies and Sports

In addition to indulging actively, Americans were avid spectators, particularly of movies and sports. In total capital investment, motion pictures became one of the nation's leading industries. Nearly every community had at least one theater, whether a hundred-seat, small-town establishment or a big-city "picture palace" with ornate lobbies and two thousand cushioned seats. In 1922, movies attracted 40 million viewers weekly; by 1929, the number neared 100 million—at a time when the nation's population was 120 million and total weekly church attendance was 60 million. New technology increased movies' appeal. Between 1922 and 1927, the Technicolor Corporation developed a means of producing movies in color. This process, along with the introduction of sound in *The Jazz Singer* in 1927, made movies even more exciting and realistic.

Responding to tastes of mass audiences, the movie industry produced escapist entertainment. Although DeMille's romantic comedies like *Why Change Your Wife?* explored worldly themes, his most popular films—*The Ten Commandments* (1923) and *The King of Kings* (1927)—were biblical. Lurid dramas like *Souls for Sale* (1923) and *A Woman*

Who Sinned (1924) also drew big audiences, as did slapstick comedies starring Harold Lloyd and Charlie Chaplin. Movie content was tame by current standards. In 1927, producers, bowing to pressure from legislators and religious leaders, instituted self-censorship, forbidding nudity, rough language, and plots that did not end with justice and morality triumphant. Movies also reproduced social prejudices. Although white actresses and actors played roles as glamour queens and action heroes, what few black actors there were had to take roles as maids and butlers.

Spectator sports also boomed as each year millions packed stadiums and ballparks. In an age when technology and mass production had robbed experiences and objects of their uniqueness, sports provided the unpredictability and drama that people craved. Newspapers and radio magnified this tension, feeding sports news to eager readers and glorifying events with such dramatic narrative that sports promoters did not need to buy advertising space.

Baseball's drawn-out suspense, diverse plays, and potential for keeping statistics attracted a huge following. After the "Black Sox scandal" of 1919, when eight members of the Chicago White Sox were banned from the game for allegedly throwing the World Series to the Cincinnati Reds (even though a jury acquitted them), baseball regained respectability by transforming itself. Discovering that home

National Baseball Hall of Fame, Cooperstown, N.Y.

△ Excluded from playing in white-dominated professional baseball, African Americans organized their own teams and leagues. The Indianapolis ABCs, named after the American Brewing Company, was one of the more successful teams in the Negro National League during the 1920s and featured some of the best black baseball players of the era, including Oscar Charleston, Elwood "Bingo" DeMoss, and "Cannonball" Dick Redding.

runs excited fans, the leagues redesigned the ball so that batters more easily could hit home runs. Game attendance skyrocketed. A record 300,000 people attended the six-game 1921 World Series between the New York Giants and New York Yankees. Millions gathered regularly to watch local teams, and even more listened to professional games on the radio. Although African American ballplayers were prohibited from playing in the major leagues, they formed their own teams, and in 1920 the first successful Negro League was founded, consisting of eight teams from places such as Chicago, Kansas City, and Indianapolis.

21-7b Sports Heroes

Sports, movies, and the news created a galaxy of heroes. As technology and mass society made the individual less significant, people clung to heroic personalities as a means of identifying with the unique. Athletes like Bill Tilden in tennis, Gertrude Ederle in swimming (in 1926, she became the first woman to swim across the English Channel), and Bobby Jones in golf had national and international reputations. The power and action of boxing, football, and baseball produced the most popular sports heroes. Heavyweight champion Jack Dempsey attracted the first of several million-dollar gates in his fight with Frenchman Georges Carpentier in 1921. Harold "Red" Grange, running back for the University of Illinois football team, thrilled fans and sportswriters (who called him "The Galloping Ghost") with his speed and agility.

Baseball's foremost hero was George Herman "Babe" Ruth, who began his career as a pitcher but found he could use his prodigious strength to better advantage hitting home runs. Ruth hit twenty-nine homers in 1919, fifty-four in 1920 (the year the Boston Red Sox sold him to the New York Yankees), fifty-nine in 1921, and sixty in 1927—each year a record. His talent and boyish grin endeared him to millions. Known for overindulgence in food, drink, and sex, he charmed fans into forgiving his excesses by appearing at public events and visiting hospitalized children.

21-7c Movie Stars and Public Heroes

Americans also fulfilled a yearning for romance and adventure through movie idols. The films and personal lives of Douglas Fairbanks, Gloria Swanson, and Charlie Chaplin were discussed in parlors and pool halls across the country. One of the decade's most adored movie personalities was Italian-born Rudolph Valentino, whose looks and suave manner made women swoon and men imitate his pomaded hairdo and slick sideburns. Valentino's image exploited the era's sexual liberalism and flirtation with wickedness. In his most famous film, Valentino played a passionate sheik who carried away beautiful women to his tent, combining the roles of abductor and seducer. When he died at thirty-one of complications from ulcers and appendicitis, the press turned his funeral into a public extravaganza. Mourners lined up for a mile to file past his coffin.

◁ Named the "Spirit of St. Louis" to honor the St. Louis businessmen who financed Lindbergh's flight, the plane was a custom-built single-engine, single-seat monoplane built in San Diego, California, for a total cost of $10,580—$2,000 of which was paid by Lindbergh himself from his earnings as an air mail pilot. The plane is shown here arriving in Boston and being thronged by spectators and soldiers, some of them mounted, during Lindbergh's triumphant tour of the United States after his historic flight.

Bettmann/Getty Images

The era's most celebrated hero, however, was **Charles A. Lindbergh**, an intrepid aviator who in May 1927 flew a plane solo from New York to Paris. The flight seized the attention of millions, as newspaper and telegraph reports followed Lindbergh's progress. After the pilot landed successfully, President Coolidge dispatched a warship to bring "Lucky Lindy" back home. Celebrants sent Lindbergh 55,000 telegrams and some 3 million to 4 million people celebrated him in a triumphant homecoming parade. Among countless prizes, Lindbergh received the Distinguished Flying Cross and the Congressional Medal of Honor. Promoters offered him millions of dollars to tour the world and $700,000 for a movie contract. Through it all, Lindbergh, nicknamed "The Lone Eagle," remained dignified, even aloof. Although his flight and its aftermath symbolized the new combination of technology and mass culture of the 1920s, Lindbergh himself epitomized individual achievement, self-reliance, and courage—old-fashioned values that attracted public respect amid the media frenzy.

21-7d Prohibition

In their quest for fun and self-expression, some Americans became lawbreakers by refusing to give up drinking. The Eighteenth Amendment (1919), which prohibited the manufacture, sale, and transportation of alcoholic beverages, and the federal law that implemented it (the Volstead Act of 1920) worked well at first. Per capita consumption of liquor dropped, as did arrests for drunkenness, and the price of illegal booze exceeded what average workers could afford. But federal and state authorities for the most part refrained from enforcing the new law. In 1922, Congress gave the Prohibition Bureau only three thousand employees and less than $7 million for nationwide enforcement, and by 1927 most state budgets omitted funds to enforce prohibition.

After 1925, the so-called noble experiment faltered as thousands of people made their own wine and gin illegally, and bootleg importers along the country's borders and shorelines easily evaded the few patrols that attempted to intercept them. Moreover, drinking, like gambling and prostitution, was a business with willing customers, and criminal organizations capitalized on public demand. The most notorious of such mobs belonged to Al Capone, a burly thug who seized control of illegal liquor, gambling, and prostitution in Chicago, maintaining power over politicians and the vice business through intimidation, bribery, and violence. Other mobsters, such as Charles "Lucky" Luciano (born Salvatore Lucania) and Arnold "the Brain" Rothstein, also netted huge incomes from the illegal production and sale of alcoholic beverages. Capone contended, in a statement revealing of the era, "Prohibition is a business. All I do is supply a public demand." Americans wanted their liquor and beer, and until 1931, when a federal court convicted and imprisoned him for income tax evasion (the only charge for which authorities could obtain hard evidence), Capone supplied them. Reflecting on contradictions inherent in prohibition,

Charles A. Lindbergh Popular aviator who flew solo across the Atlantic in his small single-engine plane, the *Spirit of St. Louis*, in May 1927.

columnist Walter Lippmann wrote in 1931, "The high level of lawlessness is maintained by the fact that Americans desire to do so many things which they also desire to prohibit."

At the same time that consumerism inspired Americans to do "so many things," the era's hardships and crassness spawned unease, and intellectuals like Lippmann were quick to point to persisting hypocrisies. Serious authors and artists felt at odds with society, and their rejection of materialism and conformity was both biting and bitter. In protest, several writers from the so-called Lost Generation, including novelist Ernest Hemingway and poets Ezra Pound and T. S. Eliot, abandoned the United States for Europe. Others, like novelists William Faulkner, Sinclair Lewis, and Edith Wharton remained in America but, like the expatriates, expressed disillusionment with the materialism that they witnessed.

21-7e Harlem Renaissance

Discontent quite different from that of white authors characterized a new generation of African American artists. Middle class, educated, and proud of their African heritage, black writers rejected white culture and exalted the militantly assertive "New Negro." Most of them lived in New York's Harlem; in this "Negro Mecca," intellectuals and artists, aided by a few white patrons, celebrated black culture during what became known as the Harlem Renaissance.

The 1921 musical comedy *Shuffle Along* is often credited with launching the Harlem Renaissance. The show featured talented black artists, such as lyricist Noble Sissle; composer Eubie Blake; and singers Florence Mills, Josephine Baker, and Mabel Mercer. The Harlem Renaissance also showcased several gifted writers, among them poets Langston Hughes, Countee Cullen, and Claude McKay; novelists Zora Neale Hurston, Jessie Fauset, and Jean Toomer; and essayist Alain Locke. The movement also included painter Aaron Douglas and sculptress Augusta Savage. Black writers from other parts of the country also flourished during the decade. They included novelist Sutton E. Griggs of Houston and Memphis and journalist and historian Drusilla Dunjee Houston from Oklahoma.

These artists and intellectuals grappled with notions of identity. Though cherishing their African heritage and the folk culture of the slave South, they realized that blacks had to come to terms with themselves as free American people. Thus, Alain Locke urged that the New Negro should become "a collaborator and participant in American civilization." But Langston Hughes wrote, "We younger Negro artists who create now intend to express our individual dark-skinned selves without fear or shame. If white people are pleased, we are glad. If they are not, it doesn't matter. We know we are beautiful."

21-7f Jazz

The Jazz Age, as the 1920s is sometimes called, owes its name to the music of black culture. Evolving from African and African American folk music, early jazz communicated exuberance, humor, and autonomy that black people seldom experienced in their public and political lives. With its emotional rhythms

△ African American blues and jazz music fueled much of the cultural outburst of the 1920s and gave opportunities to both male and female talent. This photograph, taken at the Sunset Café in Chicago in 1922, features singer and actor Clarence Muse on the floor with blues singers Mary Stafford and Frankie "Half-Pint" Jaxon behind him, performing with the Carroll Dickerson Band.

and improvisation, jazz blurred the distinction between composer and performer and created intimacy between performer and audience. Jazz arose in New Orleans (where it replaced African American ragtime music), and as African Americans moved northward and westward after slavery, their music traveled with them. Centers of jazz formed in Kansas City, Chicago, and San Diego. Urban dance halls and nightclubs, some of which included interracial audiences, featured gifted jazz performers like trumpeter Louis Armstrong, trombonist Kid Ory, and blues singer Bessie Smith. They and others enjoyed wide fame thanks to phonograph records and radio. Music recorded by black artists and aimed at black consumers (sometimes called "race records") gave African Americans a place in commercial culture. More important, jazz endowed the nation with its own distinctive art form.

In many ways, the 1920s were the most creative years the nation had yet experienced. Painters such as Georgia O'Keeffe and John Marin forged a uniquely American style of visual art. Composer Henry Cowell pioneered electronic music, and Aaron Copland built orchestral works around native folk motifs. George Gershwin blended jazz rhythms, classical forms, and folk melodies in serious works (*Rhapsody in Blue*, 1924, and *Piano Concerto in F*, 1925), musical dramas (*Funny Face*, 1927), and hit tunes such as "The Man I Love."

At the beginning of the decade, essayist Harold Stearns complained that "the most . . . pathetic fact in the social life of America today is emotional and aesthetic starvation." By 1929, that contention had been disproved.

21-8 The Election of 1928 and End of the New Era

▷ **How did Herbert Hoover and Al Smith represent the changing nature of American society in the 1920s?**

▷ **What domestic and international factors contributed to the stock market crash and the economic depression that followed?**

Intellectuals' uneasiness about materialism seldom altered the confident rhetoric of politics. Herbert Hoover voiced that confidence when he accepted the Republican nomination for president in 1928. "We in America today," Hoover boasted, "are nearer to the final triumph over poverty than ever before in the history of any land. . . . We have not yet reached the goal, but, given a chance to go forward with the policies of the last eight years, we shall soon, with the help of God, be in sight of the day when poverty will be banished from this nation."

21-8a Herbert Hoover

Hoover was an apt Republican candidate (Coolidge chose not to seek reelection) because he fused the traditional value of individual hard work with modern emphasis on corporate action. A Quaker from Iowa, orphaned at age ten, Hoover worked his way through Stanford University and became a wealthy mining engineer. During and after the First World War, he distinguished himself as U.S. food administrator and head of food relief for Europe.

As secretary of commerce under Presidents Harding and Coolidge, Hoover promoted "associationalism." Recognizing the extent to which nationwide associations dominated commerce and industry, Hoover wanted to stimulate a cooperative, associational relationship between business and government. He took every opportunity to make the Commerce Department a center for the promotion of business, encouraging the formation of trade associations, holding conferences, and issuing reports, all aimed at improving productivity and profits. His active leadership prompted one observer to quip that Hoover was "Secretary of Commerce and assistant secretary of everything else."

21-8b Al Smith

As their candidate, Democrats in 1928 chose New York's governor Alfred E. Smith, whose background contrasted with Hoover's. Hoover had rural, native-born, Protestant, and business roots and had never previously run for public office. Smith was an urbane, gregarious politician of Irish stock with a career embedded in New York City's Tammany Hall political machine. His relish for the give-and-take of city streets is apparent in his response to a heckler during the campaign. When the heckler shouted, "Tell them all you know, Al. It won't take long!" Smith unflinchingly retorted, "I'll tell them all we both know, and it won't take any longer!"

Smith was the first Roman Catholic to run for president on a major party ticket. His religion enhanced his appeal among urban ethnics (including women), who were voting in increasing numbers, but anti-Catholic sentiments lost him southern and rural votes. Smith had compiled a strong record on Progressive reform and civil rights during his governorship, but his campaign failed to build a coalition of farmers and city dwellers because he stressed issues unlikely to unite these groups, particularly his opposition to prohibition.

Hoover, who emphasized national prosperity under Republican administrations, won the popular vote by 21 million to 15 million and the electoral vote by 444 to 87. Smith's candidacy nevertheless had beneficial effects on the Democratic Party. By luring millions of foreign-stock voters to the polls, he carried the nation's twelve largest cities, which formerly had given majorities to Republican presidential candidates. For the next forty years, the Democratic Party solidified this urban base, which in conjunction with its traditional strength in the South made the party a formidable force in national elections.

21-8c Hoover's Administration

At his inaugural, Hoover proclaimed a New Day, "bright with hope." His cabinet, composed mostly of businessmen committed to the existing order, included six millionaires. To the lower ranks of government, Hoover appointed young professionals who agreed with him that a scientific approach could solve national problems. If Hoover was optimistic, so were the people who voted for him. There was widespread belief among them that success resulted from individual effort and that unemployment and poverty signaled personal weakness. Prevailing opinion also held that fluctuations of the business cycle were natural and therefore not to be tampered with by government.

21-8d Stock Market Crash

This trust dissolved on October 24, 1929, known as Black Thursday, when stock market prices suddenly plunged, wiping out $10 billion in value (worth over $100 billion today). Panic selling set in. Prices of many stocks hit record lows; some sellers could find no buyers. Stunned crowds gathered outside the frantic New York Stock Exchange. At noon, leading bankers met at the headquarters of J. P. Morgan and Company. To restore faith, they put up $20 million and ceremoniously began buying stocks. The mood brightened, and some stocks rallied. The bankers, it seemed, had saved the day.

But as news of Black Thursday spread, frightened investors decided to sell stocks rather than risk further losses. On Black Tuesday, October 29, with so many people trying to sell, prices plummeted again. Hoover, who had never approved of what he called "the fever of speculation," assured Americans that "the crisis will be over in sixty days." Three months later, he still believed that "the worst is over without a doubt." He shared the popular assumptions that the stock market's ills could be quarantined and that the economy was strong enough to endure until the market righted itself. Instead, the crash ultimately helped to unleash a devastating worldwide depression.

In hindsight, it is evident that the Depression began long before the stock market crash. Prosperity in the 1920s was not as widespread as optimists believed. Agriculture had been languishing for decades, and many areas, especially in the South, had been excluded from the bounty of consumer society. Racial minorities suffered from economic as well as social discrimination in both urban and rural settings. Industries such as mining and textiles failed to sustain profits throughout most of the decade, and even the high-flying automotive and household goods industries stagnated after 1926. The fever of speculation that concerned Hoover included rash investments in California and Florida real estate, as well as in the stock market, and masked much of what was unhealthy in the national economy.

21-8e Declining Demand

More generally, the economic weakness that underlay the Great Depression had several interrelated causes. One was declining demand. Since mid-1928, demand for new housing had faltered, leading to declining sales of building materials and unemployment among construction workers. Growth

△ As the stock market tumbled on October 24, 1929, a crowd of concerned investors gathered outside the New York Stock Exchange on Wall Street, unprepared for an unprecedented economic decline that would send the country into a tailspin for the next decade.

industries, such as automobiles and electric appliances, had been able to expand as long as consumers bought their products. Expansion, however, could not continue unabated. When demand leveled off, factory owners had to cut production and pare workforces. Retailers had amassed large inventories that were going unsold and, in turn, they started ordering less from manufacturers. Farm prices continued to sag, leaving farmers with less income to purchase new machinery and goods. As wages and employment fell, families could not afford things they needed and wanted. Thus, by 1929, a sizable population of underconsumers was causing serious repercussions.

Underconsumption also resulted from widening divisions in income distribution. As the rich grew richer, middle- and lower-income Americans made modest gains at best. Although average per capita disposable income (income after taxes) rose about 9 percent between 1920 and 1929, income of the wealthiest 1 percent rose 75 percent, accounting for most of the general increase. Much of this money went for stock market speculation, not consumer goods.

21-8f Corporate Debt and Stock Market Speculation

Furthermore, in their eagerness to boost profits, many businesses overloaded themselves with debt. To obtain loans, they misrepresented their assets in ways that hid their inability to repay if forced to do so. Such practices, overlooked by lending agencies, put the nation's banking system on a precarious footing. When one part of the edifice collapsed, the entire structure crumbled.

Risky stock market speculation also precipitated the Depression. Individuals and corporations bought millions of stock shares on margin, meaning that they invested by placing a down payment of only a fraction of a stock's actual price and then used stocks they had bought, but not fully paid for, as collateral for more stock purchases. When stock prices stopped rising, investors tried to minimize losses by selling holdings they had bought on margin. But numerous investors selling at the same time caused prices to plunge. As stock values crumbled, brokers demanded full payment for stocks bought on margin. Investors attempted to comply by withdrawing savings from banks or selling stocks for whatever they could get. Cash-short bankers pressured businesses to pay back their loans, tightening the vise further. The more obligations went unmet, the more the system tottered. Inevitably, banks and investment companies collapsed.

21-8g Economic Troubles Abroad; Federal Failure at Home

International economic conditions also contributed to the Depression. During the First World War and postwar reconstruction, Americans loaned billions of dollars to war-torn European nations. By the late 1920s, however, American

Intercollegiate Athletics

College sports spread widely in the late nineteenth century, but by the 1920s violence and cheating seemed to be rampant. Reports of brutality, academic fraud, and illegal payments to recruits prompted the Carnegie Foundation for the Advancement of Higher Education in 1924 to undertake an investigation of college sports. Its 1929 report condemned coaches and alumni supporters for violating the amateur code and recommended the abolition of varsity football, where violence and corruption seemed most widespread. The report had minimal effect. As the career of Red Grange illustrated, college football was immensely popular during the 1920s, and scores of schools built massive stadiums and arenas to attract spectators, bolster alumni allegiance, enhance revenues, and promote school spirit.

From the 1920s to the present, big-time intercollegiate sports, with highly paid coaches and highly recruited athletes, have become one of the nation's major commercial entertainments. At the same time, American higher education has struggled to reconcile conflicts between the commercialism of athletic competition on one hand and the academic mission and ideal of amateurism on the other. No other country developed as extensive a link between high-caliber sport and education as the United States. Supposedly, cultivation of the mind is the objective of higher education. But the economic potential of competition and accompanying urge to win at all costs have spawned expanding athletic departments that include administrators, practice, training, and study facilities, and tutors, as well as multiple coaches and trainers, with the result that athletic programs compete with and sometimes overshadow an institution's academic mission.

Publicity about scandals, fraud, and felonious behavior has sparked controversy in college sports since the 1920s. In 1952, after revelations of point-shaving (fixing the outcome) of basketball games involving colleges in New York City and elsewhere, the American Council on Education (ACE) undertook a study similar to that of the Carnegie Foundation a generation earlier. The ACE's recommendations, including the elimination of football bowl games, went largely unheeded. In 1991, further abuses, especially in admission and academic eligibility, prompted the Knight Foundation Commission on Intercollegiate Athletics to conduct a study that urged college presidents to take the lead in reforming intercollegiate athletics. Few significant changes resulted, even after a follow-up study in 2001.

The most sweeping changes followed court rulings in the 1990s, mandating under Title IX of the Educational Amendments Act of 1972 that women's sports be treated equally with men's sports. Enforcement, however, provoked a backlash that aimed to prevent men's teams from being cut or reduced in roster size in order to satisfy Title IX's gender equity requirements. Also, by 2015, money from television and donations large and small enabled big-time schools and conferences to flex their muscles in a variety of ways. That year, for example, the five power college athletic conferences, the ones with big-time football and men's basketball programs—Big Ten, SEC, Pac 12, Big 12, and ACC—induced the NCAA to grant them autonomy to raise athletic scholarship amounts several thousand dollars to cover "full cost" of college education plus other prerogatives that most schools cannot afford. Recently the NCAA has made efforts to regulate academic standards and reward academic success by monitoring athletes' academic progress, but reform's effectiveness depends on cooperation from member institutions. As long as millions of dollars are involved and sports remain a vital component of college as well as national culture, the system established in the 1920s has shown ability to withstand most pressures for change.

CRITICAL THINKING

- College sports, particularly men's football and basketball, garner massive amounts of money for successful institutions. In many cases, these institutions of higher learning capitalize on the popularity of their athletes (well after they have stopped playing) through restrictions on the use of their images among other things. Some protests to this practice have arisen in recent years. Do institutions of higher education owe anything other than an education to the athletes that make millions of dollars in revenue for them?

---

investors were keeping their money at home, investing instead in the stock market. Europeans, unable to borrow funds and unable to sell goods in the American market because of high tariffs, began to buy less from the United States. Moreover, the Allied nations depended on German war reparations so they could pay their war debts to the United States, and the German government depended on American bank loans to pay those reparations. When the crash choked off American loans, Germany could not meet obligations to the Allies, and in turn the Allies were unable to pay war debts to the United States. The Western economy ground to a halt.

Some Europeans also branded the United States as stingy for its handling of World War I debts and reparations. Twenty-eight nations became entangled in a web of inter-Allied government debts, which totaled $26.5 billion ($9.6 billion of them owed to the U.S. government). Europeans owed private American creditors another $3 billion. Europeans urged Americans to erase these debts as a magnanimous contribution to the war effort. During the war, they angrily charged, Europe had bled while America profited. "There is only one way we could be worse with the Europeans," remarked the humorist Will Rogers, "and that is to have helped them out in two wars instead of one." American leaders, however, insisted on repayment, some pointing out that the victorious European nations had gained vast territory and resources as war spoils. Senator George Norris of Nebraska, emphasizing domestic priorities, declared that the United States could build highways in "every county seat" if only the Europeans would pay their debts.

21-8h Lack of Federal Regulation

Federal policies also underlay the crisis. The government refrained from regulating speculation and only occasionally scolded undisciplined bankers and businesspeople. In keeping with its support of business expansion, the Federal Reserve Board pursued easy credit policies, charging low discount rates (interest on its loans to member banks) even though such loans were financing the speculative mania.

Partly because of optimism and partly because of relatively unsophisticated economic analysis, neither experts nor people on the street realized what really had happened in 1929. Conventional wisdom, based on experiences from previous depressions, held that little could be done to correct economic downturns; they simply had to run their course. So in 1929, people waited for the tailspin to ease, never realizing that the "new era" had come to an end and that the economy, politics, and society would have to be rebuilt.

Summary

Two critical events, the end of the First World War and beginning of the Great Depression, marked the boundaries of the 1920s. In the war's aftermath, traditional customs and values weakened as the American people sought new forms of self-expression and gratification. A host of effects from science and technology—automobiles, electric appliances, and mass media, especially radio—touched the lives of rich and poor alike. Sports and movies made entertainment more accessible. Moreover, the decade's freewheeling consumerism enabled ordinary Americans to emulate wealthier people not only by purchasing more but also by trying to get rich through stock market speculation. The depression that followed the stock market crash stifled these habits, at least for a while. Overseas, meanwhile, U.S. administrations and humanitarian groups worked to preserve the peace even as they sought to expand America's global political and economic power.

Beneath the "new era" lurked two important phenomena rooted in previous eras. One was the continued prejudice and ethnic tensions that had long tainted the American dream. As Klansmen and immigration restrictionists made their voices heard, they encouraged discrimination against racial minorities and slurs against supposedly inferior ethnic groups. Meanwhile, the distinguishing forces of twentieth-century life—technological change, bureaucratization, mass culture, and growth of the middle class—accelerated, making the decade truly "new." Both phenomena would recur as major themes in the nation's history for the rest of the twentieth century.

Suggestions for Further Reading

Patrick Cohrs, *The Unfinished Peace After World War I: America, Britain and the Stabilization of Europe, 1919–1932* (2006)

Lynn Dumenil, *The Modern Temper: American Culture and Society in the 1920s* (1995)

Colin Grant, *Negro with a Hat: The Rise and Fall of Marcus Garvey* (2008)

Owen Gutfreund, *Twentieth-Century Sprawl: Highways and the Reshaping of the American Landscape* (2004)

Maury Klein, *Rainbow's End: The Crash of 1929* (2003)

Lisa McGirr, *The War on Alcohol: Prohibition and the Rise of the American State* (2016)

Nathan Miller, *New World Coming: The 1920s and the Making of Modern America* (2004)

Mae M. Ngai, *Impossible Subjects: Illegal Aliens and the Making of Modern America* (2004)

Martha L. Olney, *Buy Now, Pay Later: Advertising, Credit, and Consumer Durables in the 1920s* (1991)

Thomas R. Pegram, *One Hundred Percent American: The Rebirth and Decline of the Ku Klux Klan in the 1920s* (2011)

George Sanchez, *Becoming Mexican American: Ethnicity, Culture and Identity in Chicano Los Angeles, 1900–1945* (1993)

Susan Thistle, *From Marriage to the Market: The Transformation of Women's Lives and Work* (2006)

The Great Depression and the New Deal, 1929–1939

n 1931, the rain stopped in the Great Plains. Montana and North Dakota became as arid as
the Sonora Desert. Temperatures reached 115 degrees in Iowa. The soil baked. Farmers watched
rich black dirt turn to gray dust.

Then the winds began to blow. Farmers had stripped the Plains of native grasses in the 1920s,
using tractors to plow up fifty thousand acres of new land every day. Now, with nothing to hold
the earth, it began to blow away. The dust storms began in 1934—and worsened in 1935. Dust
obscured the noonday sun; some days it was pitch black at noon. Cattle, blinded by blowing grit,
ran in circles until they died. A seven-year-old boy in Smith Center, Kansas, suffocated in a dust
drift. Boiling clouds of dust filled the skies in parts of Kansas, Colorado, Oklahoma, Texas, and
New Mexico—the Dust Bowl.

In late 1937, on a farm near Stigler, Oklahoma, Marvin Montgomery made a difficult decision.
"The drought and such as that, it just got so hard," he told a congressional committee conducting
hearings at a migratory labor camp in 1940. "I decided it would help me to change countries." So
on December 29, 1937, Montgomery and his wife and four children loaded a secondhand Hudson
automobile with their worldly goods—furniture, bedding, pots and pans—and headed for California.

The Montgomerys were not alone. At least a third of farms in the Dust Bowl were abandoned
in the 1930s, and many families made the westward trek, lured by circulars and newspaper
advertisements promising work in the fields of California. Some three hundred thousand people
migrated to California in the 1930s. Most of these were not displaced and poverty-stricken farm

◁ This 1939 photograph, titled "Mother and Children on the Road," was taken in Tule Lake, California, by
Farm Security Administration photographer Dorothea Lange. The FSA used photos like this one to build
public support for New Deal programs to assist migrant workers and the rural poor. Library of Congress Prints and Photographs
Division[LC-USF34-T01-020993-E]

Chronology

1929	Stock market crash (October); Great Depression begins
1930	Hawley-Smoot Tariff raises rates on imports
	Motion Picture Production Code creates industry censorship of U.S. movies
1931	"Scottsboro Boys" arrested in Alabama
1932	Banks fail throughout nation
	Bonus Army marches on Washington
	Hoover's Reconstruction Finance Corporation tries to stabilize banks, insurance companies, railroads
	Roosevelt elected president
1933	13 million Americans unemployed
	"First Hundred Days" of Roosevelt administration offer major legislation for economic recovery and poor relief
	Adolf Hitler becomes chancellor of Germany
1934	Populist demagogues draw large following
	Indian Reorganization (Wheeler-Howard) Act restores lands to tribal ownership
1935	The "Second New Deal" creates government programs to offer immediate relief, enhance economic security, and guarantee workers' right to organize
	Congress passes first Neutrality Act
1936	9 million Americans unemployed
	United Auto Workers begin sit-down strike against General Motors
1937	Roosevelt's Court-packing plan fails
	Memorial Day massacre of striking steelworkers
	"Roosevelt recession" begins
	Sino-Japanese War breaks out
1938	10.4 million Americans unemployed
	Munich Conference grants part of Czechoslovakia to Germany
1939	Marian Anderson performs at Lincoln Memorial
	Germany invades Poland; Second World War begins

families like the Montgomerys; many were white-collar workers seeking better opportunities in California's cities. It was the plight of families like the Montgomerys, however, captured in federal government–sponsored Farm Security Administration (FSA) photographs and immortalized in John Steinbeck's best-selling 1938 novel *The Grapes of Wrath*, that came to represent the human suffering of the Great Depression.

The Montgomerys' trip was not easy. The family ran out of money somewhere in Arizona and worked in the cotton fields there for five weeks before they moved on. Once in California, "I hoed beets some; hoed some cotton, and I picked some spuds," Montgomery reported, but wages were low, and migrant families found little welcome. As they took over the agricultural labor formerly done by Mexicans and Mexican Americans, they learned that, by doing fieldwork, they had forfeited their "whiteness" in the eyes of many rural Californians. "Negroes and Okies upstairs," read a sign in a San Joaquin Valley movie theater.

Most migrants to rural California lived in squalid makeshift camps, but the Montgomerys were lucky. They got space in housing provided for farmworkers by the FSA. The FSA camp at Shafter in Kern County had 240 tents and 40 small houses. For nine months the Montgomery family of six lived in a fourteen-by-sixteen-foot tent, which rented for 10 cents a day plus four hours of volunteer labor a month. Then they proudly moved into an FSA house, "with water, lights, and everything, yes sir; and a little garden spot furnished." Montgomery, homesick for the farm, told the congressional committee that he hoped to return to Oklahoma, but his seventeen-year-old son, Harvey, saw a different future. "I like California," he said. "I would rather stay out here." And soon there were plentiful employment opportunities in California, not only for Harvey Montgomery but for many other newcomers, in aircraft factories and shipyards mobilizing for the Second World War.

Experience an interactive version of this story in MindTap®.

The Montgomerys' experience shows the human costs of the Great Depression, but statistics are necessary to give a sense of its magnitude. In the 1930s, as nations worldwide plunged into depression, the United States confronted a crisis of enormous proportions. Between 1929 and 1933, the gross national product was cut in half. Corporate profits fell from $10 billion to $1 billion; 100,000 businesses shut their doors altogether. Four million workers were unemployed in January 1930; by November, the number had jumped to 6 million. When President **Herbert Hoover** left office in 1933, 13 million Americans—about one-fourth of the labor force—were idle, and millions more worked only part time. There was no national safety net: no welfare system, no unemployment compensation, no Social Security. And as banks failed by the thousands, with no federally guaranteed deposit insurance, families' savings simply disappeared.

Herbert Hoover, who had been elected president in the prosperity and optimism of the late 1920s, looked first to private enterprise for solutions. By the end of his term, he had extended the federal government's role in managing an economic crisis further than any of his predecessors. Nonetheless, the depression deepened and Americans became increasingly desperate. In the United States the economic catastrophe exacerbated existing racial and class tensions, while in Germany it propelled **Adolf Hitler** to power. Although America's leaders did not really expect the United States to turn to fascism, they also knew that the German people had not anticipated Hitler's rise. By late 1932, the depression seemed more than just "hard times." Many feared it was a crisis of capitalism, even of democracy itself.

In 1932, voters replaced Hoover with a man who promised a New Deal and projected hope in a time of despair. **Franklin Delano Roosevelt** seemed willing to experiment, and although his scattershot approach did not end the economic depression (only the massive mobilization for World War II did that), New Deal programs did alleviate suffering. For the first time, the federal government assumed responsibility for the nation's economy and its citizens' welfare.

Although some Americans saw the depression crisis as an opportunity for major economic change—even revolution—New Deal programs did not fundamentally alter the existing capitalist system or the distribution of wealth. Roosevelt did not directly challenge legal segregation in the South, either—in part because he relied on the votes of southern white Democrats to pass New Deal legislation.

Despite its limits, the New Deal preserved America's democratic experiment through a time of uncertainty and crisis. By decade's end, the widening force of world war shifted America's focus from domestic to foreign policy. But the changes set in motion by the New Deal continued to transform the United States for decades to come.

- 📖 *How did economic hard times during the 1930s affect Americans, and what differences were there in the experiences of specific groups and regions?*

- 📖 *How and why did the power of the federal government expand during the Great Depression, and what were the successes and failures of the New Deal?*

- 📖 *How do the responses of the United States compare to those of other nations during the international crisis of the 1930s?*

22-1 Hard Times, 1929–1933

▷ **How did the Great Depression exacerbate discrimination against minority groups?**

▷ **How did the Great Depression impact lower- and middle-class workers?**

▷ **What methods did Herbert Hoover employ to address the economic crisis?**

▷ **How did Americans respond to the economic crisis of the Great Depression?**

By the early 1930s, as the depression continued to deepen, tens of millions of Americans were desperately poor. In the cities, hungry men and women lined up at soup kitchens. People survived on potatoes, crackers, or dandelion greens; some scratched through garbage cans for bits of food. In West Virginia and Kentucky, hunger was so widespread—and resources so limited—that the American Friends Service Committee distributed food only to those who were at least 10 percent below the normal weight for their height. In November 1932, *The Nation* told its readers that one-sixth of the American population risked starvation over the coming winter. Social workers in New York reported there was "no food at all" in the homes of many of the city's black children. In Albany, New York, a ten-year-old girl died of starvation in her elementary school classroom.

Families, unable to pay rent, were evicted. The new homeless poured into shantytowns, called

Herbert Hoover The thirty-first president of the United States, 1929–1933.

Adolf Hitler German chancellor and Nazi dictator whose efforts to restore his nation's prominence included a brutal program to purify it of Jews and others he deemed "inferior races."

Franklin Delano Roosevelt The thirty-second president of the United States (1933–1945).

"Hoovervilles" in ironic tribute to the formerly popular president. Over a million men took to the road or the rails in desperate search of any sort of work. Teenage boys and girls also left destitute families to strike out on their own. With uncertain futures, many young couples delayed marriage; the average age at marriage rose by more than two years during the 1930s. Married people put off having children, and in 1933 the birth rate sank below replacement rates. (Sales of condoms—at $1 per dozen—did not fall during the depression.) More than a quarter of women who were between the ages of twenty and thirty during the Great Depression never had children.

22-1a Farmers and Industrial Workers

Farmers were hit especially hard by the economic crisis. The agricultural sector, which employed almost one-quarter of American workers, had never shared in the good times of the 1920s. But as urbanites cut back on spending and foreign competitors dumped agricultural surpluses into the global market, farm prices hit rock bottom. Farmers tried to compensate for lower prices by producing more, thus adding to the surplus and depressing prices even further. By 1932, a bushel of wheat that cost North Dakota farmers 77 cents to produce brought only 33 cents. Throughout the nation, cash-strapped farmers could not pay their property taxes or mortgages. Banks, facing their own ruin, foreclosed. In Mississippi, it was reported in 1932, on a single day in April approximately one-fourth of all the farmland in the state was being auctioned off to meet debts. By the middle of the decade, the ecological crisis of the Dust Bowl would drive thousands of farmers from their land.

Unlike farmers, America's industrial workers had seen a slow but steady rise in their standard of living during the 1920s. In 1929, almost every urban American who wanted a job had one, and workers' spending on consumer goods had bolstered the nation's economic growth. But as Americans had less money to spend, sales of manufactured goods plummeted and factories closed—more than seventy thousand

had gone out of business by 1933. As car sales dropped from 4.5 million in 1929 to 1 million in 1933, Ford laid off more than two-thirds of its Detroit workers. The remaining workers at U.S. Steel, America's first billion-dollar corporation, were put on "short hours"; the huge steel company had no full-time workers in 1933. Almost one-quarter of industrial workers were unemployed, and those who managed to hang onto a job saw the average wage fall by almost one-third.

22-1b Marginal Workers

For workers on the lowest rungs of the employment ladder, the depression was a crushing blow. In the South, where opportunities were already most limited for African Americans, jobs that many white men had considered below their dignity before the depression—street cleaner, bellhop, garbage collector—seemed suddenly desirable. In 1930, a short-lived fascist-style organization, the Black Shirts, recruited forty thousand members with the slogan "No Jobs for Niggers Until Every White Man Has a Job!" Northern blacks did not fare much better. As industry cut production, African Americans were the first fired. An Urban League survey of 106 cities found black unemployment rates averaged 30 to 60 percent higher than rates for whites. By 1932, African American unemployment reached almost 50 percent.

Mexican Americans and Mexican nationals trying to make a living in the American Southwest also felt the twin impacts of economic depression and racism. Their wages on California farms fell from a miserable 35 cents an hour in 1929 to a cruel 14 cents an hour by 1932. Throughout the Southwest, Anglo-Americans claimed that foreign workers were stealing their jobs. Campaigns against "foreigners" hurt not only Mexican immigrants but also American citizens of Hispanic descent whose families had lived in the Southwest for centuries, long before the land belonged to the United States. In 1931, the Labor Department announced plans to deport illegal immigrants to free jobs for American citizens. This policy fell hardest on people of Mexican origin. Even

◁ During the 1920s, farmers deep plowed land in the Great Plains, opening new farmland but destroying the deep-rooted grasses that had trapped moisture and held soil even when little rain fell. During the severe drought of the 1930s, soil turned to dust and, swept up by high winds, formed huge dark clouds—such as this dust storm in Baca County, Colorado.

Library of Congress Prints and Photographs Division[LC-USF34-001615-ZE]

those who had immigrated legally often lacked full documentation. Officials often ignored the fact that children born in the United States were U.S. citizens. The U.S. government officially deported 82,000 Mexicans between 1929 and 1935, but a much larger number—almost half a million people—repatriated to Mexico during the 1930s. Some left voluntarily, but many were coerced or tricked into believing they had no choice.

Even before the economic crisis, women of all classes and races were barred from many jobs and were paid significantly less than men. As the economy worsened, discrimination increased. Most Americans already believed that men should be breadwinners and women homemakers. With so many men unemployed, it was easy to believe that women who worked took jobs from men. In fact, men laid off from U.S. Steel would not likely have been hired as elementary schoolteachers, secretaries, "salesgirls," or maids. Nonetheless, when a 1936 Gallup poll asked whether wives should work if their husbands had jobs, 82 percent of the respondents (including 75 percent of the women) answered no. Such beliefs translated into policy. Of fifteen hundred urban school systems surveyed in 1930 and 1931, 77 percent refused to hire married women as teachers, and 63 percent fired female teachers who married while employed.

The depression had a mixed impact on women workers. At first, women lost jobs more quickly than men. Women in low-wage manufacturing jobs were laid off before male employees, who were presumed to be supporting families. Hard times hit domestic workers especially hard, as middle-class families economized by dispensing with household help. Almost one-quarter of women in domestic service—a high percentage of them African American—were unemployed by January 1931. And as jobs disappeared, women of color lost even these poorly paid positions to white women who were newly willing to do domestic labor. Despite discrimination and a poor economy, however, the number of women working outside the home rose during the 1930s. "Women's jobs," such as teaching, clerical work, and switchboard operating, were not hit as hard as "men's jobs" in heavy industry, and women—including married women who previously did not work for wages—increasingly sought employment to keep their families afloat during hard times. Still, by 1940, only 15.2 percent of married women worked outside the home.

22-1c Middle-Class Workers and Families

Although unemployment rates climbed to 25 percent, most Americans did not lose their homes or their jobs during the depression. Professional and white-collar workers did not fare as badly as industrial workers and farmers. Many middle-class families, however, while never hungry or homeless, "made do" with less. "Use it up, wear it out, make it do, or do without," the saying went, and middle-class women cut back on household expenses by canning food or making their own clothes. Newspapers offered imaginative suggestions for cooking cheap cuts of meat ("Liverburgers") or for

△ As the economic depression deepened, manufacturers of consumer goods struggled to sell their products and stay in business. Americans had less money to spend, and even those who were economically secure sought to make dollars stretch further. Here, a woman browses through sale ads in her newspaper.

using "extenders," cheap ingredients to make food go further ("Cracker-Stuffed Cabbage"). Although most families' incomes fell, the impact was cushioned by the falling cost of consumer goods, especially food. In early 1933, for example, a cafe in Omaha offered a ten-course meal, complete with a rose for ladies and a cigar for gentlemen, for 60 cents.

As housewives scrambled to make do, men who could no longer provide well for their families often blamed themselves for their "failures." But even for the relatively affluent, the psychological impact of the depression was inescapable. The human toll of the depression was visible everywhere, and no one took economic security for granted anymore. Suffering was never equal, but all Americans had to contend with years of uncertainty and with fears about the future of their family and their nation.

22-1d Hoover's Limited Solutions

Although Herbert Hoover, "the Great Engineer," had a reputation as a problem solver, the economic crisis was not easily solved, and no one, including Hoover, really knew what to do. Experts and leaders disagreed about the causes of the depression, and they disagreed about the proper course of action as well. Many prominent business leaders believed that financial panics and depressions, no matter how painful, were part of a natural and ultimately beneficial "business cycle." Economic depressions, according to this theory, brought down inflated prices and cleared the way for real economic growth. Herbert Hoover disagreed. "The economic fatalist," he said, "believes that these crises are inevitable. . . . I would remind these pessimists that exactly the same thing was once said of typhoid, cholera, and smallpox." Hoover put his faith in a voluntary system of "associationalism," in which the federal government coordinated efforts of business and professional organizations to solve the nation's economic problems by crafting programs that state and local governments, along with private industry, could then choose—voluntarily—to implement.

While many Americans thought that Hoover was doing nothing to fight the economic downturn, in truth he stretched his core beliefs about the proper role of government to their limit. He tried voluntarism, exhortation, and limited government intervention. First, he sought voluntary pledges from hundreds of business groups to keep wages stable and renew economic investment. But when individual business-people looked at their own bottom lines, few could live up to those promises.

As unemployment climbed, Hoover continued to encourage voluntary responses to mounting need, creating the President's Organization on Unemployment Relief (POUR) to generate private contributions to aid the destitute. Although 1932 saw record charitable contributions, they were nowhere near adequate. By mid-1932, one-quarter of New York's private charities, funds exhausted, had closed their doors. Atlanta's Central Relief Committee could provide only $1.30 per family per week to those seeking help. State and city officials found their treasuries drying up, too. Hoover, however, held firm. "It is not the function of the government to relieve individuals of their responsibilities to their neighbors," he insisted.

Hoover feared that government "relief" would destroy the spirit of self-reliance among the poor. Thus, he authorized federal funds to feed the drought-stricken livestock of Arkansas farmers but rejected a smaller grant to provide food for impoverished farm families. Many Americans were becoming angry at Hoover's seeming insensitivity. When Hoover, trying to restore confidence to the increasingly anxious nation, said, "What this country needs is a good big laugh. . . . If someone could get off a good joke every ten days, I think our troubles would be over," the resulting jokes were not exactly what he had in mind. "Business is improving," one man tells another. "Is Hoover dead?" asks his companion. In the two short years since his election, Hoover had become the most hated man in America.

Hoover eventually endorsed limited federal action to combat the economic crisis, but it was much too little. Federal public works projects, such as the Grand Coulee Dam in Washington, created some jobs. Hoover also signed into law the Hawley-Smoot Tariff (1930), which was meant to support American farmers and manufacturers by raising import duties on foreign goods to a staggering 40 percent. Instead, it hampered international trade as other nations created their own protective tariffs. And as other nations sold fewer goods to the United States, they had less money to repay their U.S. debts or buy American products. Exports of American merchandise continued to slide, falling by more than half from their pre-Great Depression high of $5.2 billion. Fearing the collapse of the international monetary system, Hoover in 1931 announced a moratorium on the payment of First World War debts and reparations.

In January 1932, the administration took its most forceful action, creating the **Reconstruction Finance Corporation (RFC)** to provide federal loans to banks, insurance companies, and railroads, an action Hoover hoped would shore up those industries and halt the disinvestment in the American economy. Here, Hoover had compromised his ideological principles. This was direct government intervention, not "voluntarism." If he would support direct assistance to private industries, why not direct relief to the millions of unemployed?

22-1e Protest and Social Unrest

More and more Americans were asking that question. Although most people met the crisis with bewilderment or quiet despair, social unrest grew as the depression deepened. In scattered incidents, farmers and unemployed workers took direct action against what they saw as the causes of their plight. Others lashed out in anger, scapegoating those even weaker than themselves. Increasing violence raised the specter of popular revolt, and Chicago mayor Anton Cermak told Congress that if the federal government did not send his citizens aid, it would have to send troops instead.

Throughout the nation, tens of thousands of farmers took the law into their own hands. Angry crowds forced auctioneers to accept just a few dollars for foreclosed property, and then returned it to the original owners. In August 1932, a new group, the Farmers' Holiday Association, encouraged farmers to take a "holiday"—to hold back agricultural products to limit supply and drive prices up. In the Midwest, farmers barricaded roads with spiked logs and telegraph poles to stop other farmers' trucks, and then dumped the contents in roadside ditches.

In cities, the most militant actions came from Unemployed Councils, local groups similar to unions for unemployed workers that were created and led by Communist Party members. Communist leaders believed the depression demonstrated capitalism's failure and offered an opportunity for revolution. Few of the quarter-million Americans who joined the local Unemployed Councils sought revolution, but they did demand action. "Fight, Don't Starve," read banners in a Chicago demonstration. Demonstrations often turned ugly. When three thousand members of Detroit Unemployment Councils marched on Ford's River Rouge plant in 1932, Ford security guards opened fire on the crowd, killing four men and wounding fifty. Battles between protesters and police broke out in cities from the East Coast to the West Coast but rarely were covered as national news.

As social unrest spread, so, too, did racial violence. For example, vigilante committees offered bounties to force

Reconstruction Finance Corporation (RFC) Agency set up under the Hoover administration during the Great Depression to make loans to shore up banks and other industries.

African American workers off the Illinois Central Railroad's payroll: $25 for maiming and $100 for killing black workers. Ten men were murdered and at least seven more wounded. The Ku Klux Klan also gained strength. Thirty-eight black men were tortured, hanged, and mutilated by white mobs in the early years of the Great Depression, while local authorities prevented more than a hundred attempted lynchings. Racial violence was not restricted to the South; lynchings also took place in Pennsylvania, Minnesota, Colorado, and Ohio.

22-1f Bonus Army

The worst public confrontation shook the nation in the summer of 1932. More than fifteen thousand unemployed World War I veterans and their families converged on the nation's capital as Congress debated a bill authorizing immediate payment of cash "bonuses" that veterans had been scheduled to receive in 1945. Calling themselves the Bonus Expeditionary Force, or Bonus Army, they set up a sprawling "Hooverville" shantytown just across the river from the Capitol. Concerned about the impact on the federal budget, President Hoover opposed the bonus bill, and after much debate the Senate voted it down.

Most of the Bonus Marchers left Washington after this defeat, but several thousand stayed on. Some were simply destitute, with nowhere to go; others stayed to press their case. The president called them "insurrectionists" and set a deadline for their departure. On July 28, Hoover sent in the U.S. Army, led by General Douglas MacArthur. Four infantry companies, four troops of cavalry, a machine gun squadron, and six tanks converged on the veterans and their families. What followed shocked the nation. Men and women were chased down by horsemen; children were tear-gassed; shacks were set afire. The next day, newspapers carried photographs of U.S. troops attacking their own citizens. Hoover was unrepentant, insisting in a campaign speech, "Thank God we still have a government that knows how to deal with a mob."

While desperation-driven social unrest raised fears of revolution, some saw an even greater danger in the growing disillusionment with democracy itself. As the depression worsened, the appeal of a strong leader—someone who would take decisive action, unencumbered by constitutionally mandated checks and balances—grew. In early 1933, media magnate William Randolph Hearst released the film *Gabriel over the White House*, in which a political hack of a president is possessed by the archangel Gabriel and, divinely inspired, assumes dictatorial powers to end the misery of the Great Depression. More significantly, in February 1933, the U.S. Senate passed a resolution calling for newly elected president Franklin D. Roosevelt to assume "unlimited power." The rise to power of Hitler and his National Socialist Party in depression-ravaged Germany was an obvious parallel, adding to the sense of crisis that would come to a head in early 1933.

△ In the summer of 1932, unemployed veterans of the First World War demanded Congress authorize early payment of promised soldiers' bonuses. This cartoon shows the "Bonus Expeditionary Forces"—doctors, laborers, farmers, merchants, "Americans All"—marching to seek "Justice" in Washington, D.C.

22-2 Franklin D. Roosevelt and the Launching of the New Deal

▷ **What actions did Franklin D. Roosevelt take to address the banking crisis?**

▷ **How did New Deal programs seek to institute economic recovery in industry and agriculture?**

▷ **What attitudes and practices guided the federal government when providing relief for workers?**

▷ **How did the Great Depression impact U.S. foreign policy and international relations?**

In the presidential campaign of 1932, voters were presented with a clear choice. In the face of the Great Depression, incumbent Herbert Hoover held to a platform of limited federal intervention. Democratic challenger Franklin Delano Roosevelt insisted that the federal government had to play a much greater role. He supported direct relief payments for the unemployed, declaring that such governmental aid was not charity but instead "a matter of social duty." He pledged "a new deal for the American people." During the campaign, he was never very explicit about the outlines of his New Deal. His most concrete proposals, in fact, were sometimes contradictory

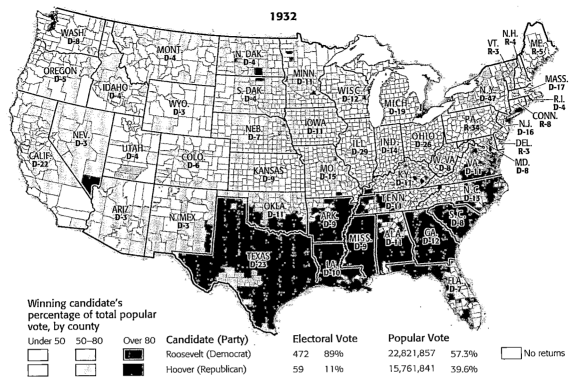

Winning candidate's percentage of total popular vote, by county			Candidate (Party)	Electoral Vote		Popular Vote		
Under 50	50–80	Over 80	Roosevelt (Democrat)	472	89%	22,821,857	57.3%	No returns
			Hoover (Republican)	59	11%	15,761,841	39.6%	

Map 22.1 Presidential Election, 1932

One factor above all decided the 1932 presidential election: the Great Depression. Roosevelt won 42 states and Hoover 6.

(in a nation without national news media, this was less a problem than it would be today). But all understood that he had committed to use the power of the federal government to combat the economic crisis that was paralyzing the nation. Voters chose Roosevelt over Hoover overwhelmingly: 22.8 million to 15.8 million in the popular vote (see Map 22.1).

Franklin Roosevelt, the twentieth-century president most beloved by America's "common people," had been born into a world of old money and upper-class privilege. The talented son of a politically prominent family, he seemed destined for political success. After graduating from Harvard College and Columbia Law School, he had married **Eleanor Roosevelt**, Theodore Roosevelt's niece and his own fifth cousin, once removed. He served in the New York State legislature; was appointed assistant secretary of the navy by Woodrow Wilson; and at the age of thirty-eight, ran for vice president in 1920 on the Democratic Party's losing ticket.

Then, in 1921, Roosevelt was stricken with polio. For two years he was bedridden, fighting one of the most feared diseases of the early twentieth century. He lost the use of his legs but gained, according to his wife Eleanor, a new strength of character that would serve him well as he reached out to depression-scarred America. As

Eleanor Roosevelt Widely popular and influential—and sometimes controversial—First Lady of the United States from 1933 to 1945.

Roosevelt explained it, "If you had spent two years in bed trying to wiggle your big toe, after that anything would seem easy." By 1928, Roosevelt was sufficiently recovered to run for—and win—the governorship of New York and then to accept the Democratic Party's presidential nomination in 1932.

Elected in November 1932, Roosevelt would not take office until March 4, 1933. (The Twentieth Amendment to the Constitution—the so-called Lame Duck Amendment, ratified in 1933—shifted all future inaugurations to January 20.) In this long interregnum, the American banking system reached the verge of collapse.

22-2a Banking Crisis

The origins of the banking crisis lay in the flush years of World War I and the 1920s, when American banks made countless risky loans. After real estate and stock market bubbles burst in 1929 and agricultural prices collapsed, many of these loans went bad, leaving many banks without sufficient funds to cover their customers' deposits. Depositors, afraid of losing their savings in a bank collapse, pulled money out of banks and put it into gold or under mattresses. "Bank runs," in which crowds of angry, frightened customers lined up to demand their money, became a common sight in economically ravaged towns throughout the nation. By Roosevelt's inauguration on March 4, every state in the Union had either suspended banking operations or restricted depositors' access to their money. The new president understood that this was more than a test of his administration. The total collapse of the U.S. banking system would threaten the nation's survival.

Roosevelt (who reportedly saw the film *Gabriel over the White House* several times before his inauguration) used his inaugural address to promise the American people decisive action. Standing in a cold rain on the Capitol steps, he vowed to face the crisis "frankly and boldly." The lines we best remember from his speech are words of comfort: "Let me assert my firm belief," the new president told the thousands gathered on the Capitol grounds and the millions gathered around their radios, "that the only thing we have to fear is fear itself—nameless, unreasoning, unjustified terror." But the only loud cheers that day came when Roosevelt proclaimed that, if need be, "I shall ask the Congress for the one remaining instrument to meet the crisis—broad Executive power to wage a war against the emergency, as great as the power that would be given to me if we were in fact invaded by a foreign foe."

The next day Roosevelt, using powers legally granted by the World War I Trading with the Enemy Act, closed the nation's banks for a four-day "holiday" and summoned Congress to an emergency session. He immediately introduced the Emergency Banking Relief Bill, which was passed sight unseen by unanimous House vote, approved 73 to 7 in the Senate, and signed into law the same day. This bill provided federal authority to reopen solvent banks and reorganize the rest, and authorized federal money to shore up private banks. In his inaugural address, Roosevelt had attacked "unscrupulous money changers," and many critics of the failed banking system had hoped he planned to remove the banks from private hands. Instead, as one North Dakota congressman complained, "the President drove the money changers out of the Capitol on March 4th and they were all back on the 9th." Roosevelt's banking policy was much like Hoover's—a fundamentally conservative approach that upheld the status quo.

The banking bill could save the U.S. banking system only if Americans were confident enough to deposit money in the reopened banks. So Roosevelt, in the first of his radio "Fireside Chats," asked the support of the American people. "We have provided the machinery to restore our financial system," he said. "It is up to you to support and make it work." The next morning, when the banks opened their doors, people lined up—but this time, most waited to deposit money. It was an enormous triumph for the new president. It also demonstrated that Roosevelt, though unafraid to take bold action, was not as radical as some wished or as others feared.

22-2b First Hundred Days

During the ninety-nine-day-long special session of Congress, dubbed by journalists "The First Hundred Days," the federal government took on dramatically new roles. Roosevelt, aided by a group of advisers—lawyers, university professors, and social workers, who were collectively nicknamed "the

△ In November 1930, Franklin D. Roosevelt (1882–1945) read the good news. Reelected governor of New York by 735,000 votes, he immediately became a leading contender for the Democratic presidential nomination. Notice Roosevelt's leg braces, rarely shown because of an unwritten agreement by photographers to shoot him from the waist up.

Brain Trust"—and by the enormously capable First Lady, set out to revive the American economy. These "New Dealers" had no single, coherent plan, and Roosevelt's economic policies fluctuated between attempts to balance the budget and massive deficit spending (spending more than is taken in in taxes and borrowing the difference). But with a strong mandate for action and the support of a Democrat-controlled Congress, the new administration produced a flood of legislation. The first priority was economic recovery. Two basic strategies emerged during the First Hundred Days. New Dealers experimented with national economic planning, and they created a range of "relief" programs to help those in need.

22-2c National Industrial Recovery Act

At the heart of the New Deal experiment in planning were the National Industrial Recovery Act (NIRA) and the Agricultural Adjustment Act (AAA). The NIRA was based on the belief that "destructive competition" had worsened industry's economic woes. Skirting antitrust regulation, the NIRA authorized competing businesses to cooperate in crafting industrywide codes. Thus, for example, automobile manufacturers would cooperate to limit production, establish industrywide prices, and set workers' wages. Competition among manufacturers would no longer drive down prices and wages. With wages and prices stabilized, the theory went, consumer spending would increase, thus allowing industries to rehire workers. Significantly, Section 7(a) guaranteed industrial workers the right to "organize and bargain collectively"—in other words, to unionize.

Individual businesses' participation in this program, administered by the National Recovery Administration (NRA), was voluntary—with one catch. Businesses that adhered to the industrywide codes could display the Blue Eagle, the NRA symbol; the government urged consumers to boycott businesses that did not fly the Blue Eagle. This voluntary program, though larger in scale than any previous government–private sector cooperation, was not very different from Hoover-era "associationalism."

From the beginning, the NRA faced serious problems. As small-business owners had feared, big business easily dominated the NRA-mandated cartels. NRA staff lacked the training and experience to stand up to the representatives of corporate America. The twenty-six-year-old NRA staffer who oversaw the creation of the petroleum industry code was "helped" by twenty highly-paid oil industry lawyers. The majority of the 541 codes eventually approved by the NRA reflected the interests of major corporations, not small-business owners, labor, or consumers. Most fundamentally, the NRA did not deliver economic recovery. In 1935, the Supreme Court put an end to the fragile, floundering system. Using an old-fashioned (what Roosevelt called a "horse-and-buggy") definition of interstate commerce, the Supreme Court found that the NRA extended federal power past its constitutional bounds.

22-2d Agricultural Adjustment Act

The **Agricultural Adjustment Act (AAA)** had a more enduring effect on the United States. Establishing a national system of crop controls, the AAA offered subsidies to farmers who agreed to limit production of specific crops. (Overproduction drove crop prices down.) But to reduce production in 1933, the nation's farmers agreed to destroy 8.5 million piglets and to plow under crops in the fields. Although limiting production did raise agricultural prices, millions of hungry Americans found it difficult to understand the economic theory behind this waste of food.

Government crop subsidies had unintended consequences: they were a disaster for tenant farmers and sharecroppers, for as landlords cut production they turned tenant farmers off their land. In the South, the number of sharecropper farms dropped by almost one-third between 1930 and 1940 and dispossessed farmers—many of them African American—headed to cities and towns. But the subsidies did help many. In the depression-ravaged Dakotas, for example, government payments accounted for almost three-quarters of the total farm income for 1934.

In 1936, the Supreme Court found that the AAA, like the NRA, was unconstitutional. But the AAA (unlike the NRA) was too popular with its constituency—American farmers—to disappear. The legislation was rewritten to meet the Supreme Court's objections, and farm subsidies continue into the twenty-first century.

22-2e Relief Programs

With millions of Americans in desperate poverty, Roosevelt also moved quickly to implement poor relief: $3 billion in federal aid was allocated in 1935. New Dealers, however—like many other Americans—disapproved of direct relief payments. "Give a man a dole and you save his body and destroy his spirit; give him a job and pay him an assured wage and you save both the body and the spirit," wrote Harry Hopkins, Roosevelt's trusted adviser and head of the president's major relief agency, the Federal Emergency Relief Administration (FERA). Thus New Deal programs emphasized "work relief." By January 1934, the Civil Works Administration had hired 4 million people, most earning $15 a week. And the **Civilian Conservation Corps (CCC)** paid unmarried young men (young women were not eligible) $1 a day to do hard outdoor labor: building dams and reservoirs, creating trails in national parks. The program was segregated by race but brought together young men from very different backgrounds. By 1942, the CCC had employed 2.5 million men, including 80,000 American Indians who worked on western Indian reservations.

National Industrial Recovery Act (NIRA) Agency that brought together business leaders to draft codes of "fair competition" for their industries.

National Recovery Administration (NRA) Agency that established industry-wide codes authorized by NIRA and which oversaw individual businesses' voluntary adherence to them. The program was struck down by the Supreme Court in 1935.

Agricultural Adjustment Act (AAA) New Deal program that sought to curb the surplus farm production that depressed crop prices by offering farmers payments for reducing production of seven farm products.

Civilian Conservation Corps (CCC) Government relief program that employed jobless young men in such projects as reforestation, park maintenance, and erosion control.

Table 22.1 New Deal Achievements

Year	Labor	Agriculture and Environment	Business and Industrial Recovery	Relief	Reform
1933	Section 7(a) of NIRA	Agricultural Adjustment Act Farm Credit Act	Emergency Banking Relief Act Economy Act Beer-Wine Revenue Act Banking Act of 1933 (guaranteed deposits) National Industrial Recovery Act	Civilian Conservation Corps Federal Emergency Relief Act Home Owners Refinancing Act Public Works Administration Civil Works Administration	TVA Federal Securities Act
1934	National Labor Relations Board	Taylor Grazing Act			Securities Exchange Act Reciprocal Trade Agreements Act Export-Import Bank
1935	National Labor Relations (Wagner) Act	Resettlement Administration Rural Electrification Administration		Works Progress Administration National Youth Administration	Social Security Act Public Utility Holding Company Act Revenue Act (wealth tax)
1937		Farm Security Administration		National Housing Act	
1938	Fair Labor Standards Act	Agricultural Adjustment Act of 1938			

Source: Adapted from Charles Sellers, Henry May, and Neil R. McMillen, *A Synopsis of American History,* 6th ed. Copyright © 1985 by Houghton Mifflin Company. Reprinted by permission.

Work relief programs rarely addressed the needs of poor women. Mothers of young children were usually classified as "unemployable" and were offered relief instead of jobs. But in North Carolina, for example, the "mother's-aid" grant was one-sixth of the wage paid in a federal works program. While federal relief programs rejected the poor-law tradition that distinguished between the "deserving" and the "undeserving" poor, local officials often did not. As journalist Lorena Hickok reported to Harry Hopkins, "a woman who isn't a good housekeeper is apt to have a pretty rough time of it. And heaven help the family in which there is any 'moral problem.'"

The **Public Works Administration (PWA)**, created by Title II of the National Industrial Recovery Act, used public funds to create jobs for men in the construction industry and building trades. In 1933, Congress appropriated $3.3 billion—or 165 percent of federal revenues for that year—to New Deal public works programs that would strengthen the nation's infrastructure. PWA workers built the Triborough Bridge in New York City, the Grand River

Dam in Oklahoma, school buildings in almost half of the nation's counties, and most of the new sewer systems created during the depression years.

The special session of Congress, convened by FDR in March, adjourned on June 16, 1933, having passed fifteen major pieces of legislation (see Table 22.1). In just over three months, the United States had rebounded from near collapse, returning (in columnist Walter Lippmann's words) from a collection of "disorderly panic-stricken mobs and factions" to "an organized nation confident of our power to provide for our own security and to control our own destiny." And as New Deal programs continued to be passed and implemented, unemployment fell steadily from 13 million in 1933 to 9 million in 1936, farm prices rose, along with wages and salaries, and business failures abated (see Figure 22.1).

Public Works Administration (PWA) New Deal relief agency that appropriated $3.3 billion for large-scale public works projects to provide jobs and stimulate the economy.

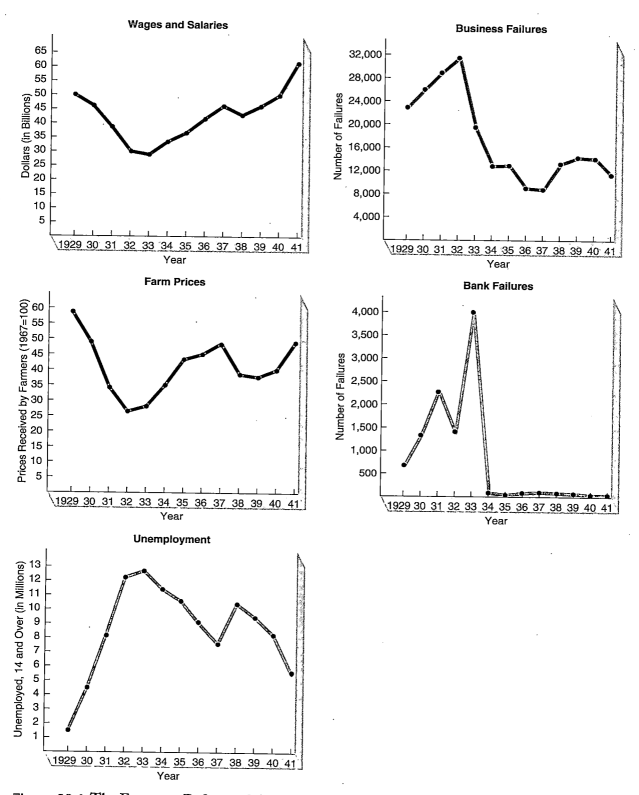

Figure 22.1 The Economy Before and After the New Deal, 1929–1941

The New Deal reduced bank closings, business failures, and unemployment, and it increased farm prices, wages, and salaries. Some of the nation's most persistent economic problems, however, did not disappear until the advent of the Second World War.

22-2f Lowering Tariffs

Internationally, meanwhile, the Roosevelt administration worked to expand trade. Increased trade, Secretary of State Cordell Hull insisted, would not only help the United States pull itself out of the economic doldrums but also boost the chances for global peace. Calling the protective tariff the "king of evils," he successfully pressed Congress to pass the Reciprocal Trade Agreements Act in 1934. This important legislation empowered the president to reduce U.S. tariffs by as much as 50 percent through special agreements with foreign countries. The central feature of the act was the most-favored-nation principle, whereby the United States was entitled to the lowest tariff rate set by any nation with which it had an agreement. If, for example, Belgium and the United States granted each other most-favored-nation status, and Belgium then negotiated an agreement with Germany that reduced the Belgian tariff on German typewriters, American typewriters would receive the same low rate.

In 1934, Hull also helped create the Export-Import Bank, a government agency that provided loans to foreigners for the purchase of American goods. The bank stimulated trade and became a diplomatic weapon, allowing the United States to exact concessions through the approval or denial of loans. But in the short term, Hull's ambitious programs—examples of America's independent internationalism—brought only mixed results.

22-2g U.S. Recognition of the Soviet Union

Economic imperatives also lay behind another major foreign policy decision in these years: the move by the Roosevelt administration to extend diplomatic recognition to the Soviet Union. Throughout the 1920s, the Republicans had refused to open diplomatic relations with the Soviet government, which had failed to pay $600 million for confiscated American-owned property and had repudiated preexisting Russian debts. To many Americans, the communists ranked as godless, radical malcontents bent on destroying the American way of life through world revolution. Nonetheless, in the late 1920s U.S. businesses such as General Electric and International Harvester entered the Soviet marketplace, and Henry Ford signed a contract to build an automobile plant there. By 1930 the Soviet Union had become the largest buyer of American farm and industrial equipment.

Upon entering the White House, Roosevelt concluded that nonrecognition had failed to alter the Soviet system, and he speculated that closer Soviet-American relations might help the economy and also deter Japanese expansion. In 1933, Roosevelt granted U.S. diplomatic recognition to the Soviet Union in return for Soviet agreement to discuss the debts question and to grant Americans in the Soviet Union religious freedom and legal rights.

22-2h Good Neighbor Policy

In Latin America, too, Roosevelt moved to reorient the direction of U.S. policy. He pledged that the United States would be a **"Good Neighbor,"** by which he meant in essence that Washington would be less blatant in its domination—less willing to defend exploitative business practices, less eager to launch military expeditions, and less reluctant to consult with Latin Americans. The policy was not without effect—in Mexico, for example, Roosevelt showed a level of restraint that his predecessors lacked. Overall, though, his administration continued to support and bolster dictators in the region, believing they would promote stability and preserve U.S. economic interests. ("He may be an S.O.B.," Roosevelt supposedly remarked of the Dominican Republic's ruthless leader Rafael Leonidas Trujillo, "but he is our S.O.B.") And when a revolution brought a radical government to power in Cuba in 1933, FDR proved unwilling to let the matter be. Although he refrained from sending U.S. ground troops to Cuba, he instructed the American ambassador in Havana to work with conservative Cubans to replace the new government with a regime more friendly to U.S. interests. With Washington's support, army sergeant Fulgencio Batista took power in 1934.

22-3 Political Pressure and the Second New Deal

▶ Which groups of Americans opposed the New Deal, and why?

▶ Who proposed alternative ways to address the economic crisis, and what did those programs have in common?

▶ How did the programs of the Second New Deal seek to meet Americans' demands for relief and social justice?

Roosevelt's New Deal had enjoyed unprecedented popular and congressional support, but that would not last. The seeming unity of the First Hundred Days masked deep divides within the nation, and once the immediate crisis was averted, the struggle over solutions began in earnest. As some tried to stop the expansion of government power, others pushed for increased governmental action to combat continuing poverty and inequality. Pressure came from all directions as the president considered the next phase of New Deal action.

22-3a Business Opposition

As the economy partially recovered, many wealthy business leaders started publicly criticizing the New Deal. They condemned budget-busting government spending for relief and jobs programs, as well as the regulations and rising taxes that affected them directly. In 1934, several corporate leaders joined with former presidential candidate Al Smith and disaffected conservative Democrats to establish the American Liberty League, an economically conservative organization that waged a highly visible campaign against New Deal "radicalism." Attempting to

"Good Neighbor"
Implemented by President Roosevelt, this Latin American policy stated that no nation had the right to intervene in the affairs of another; it replaced direct U.S. intervention with diplomacy and support for various leaders, businesses, and programs.

CANADA
Ottawa ⊛

ATLANTIC
OCEAN

●San Francisco
UNITED STATES

—40°N—

Washington, D.C.⊛

Roosevelt's Good Neighbor Policy, 1933

U.S. troops, 1917–1922
U.S. investors dominate sugar industry
Revolution of 1933
U.S. abrogates Platt Amendment, 1934
Batista era, 1934–1959

U.S. upholds right of intervention at
Pan American Conference, 1928

U.S. troops, 1915–1934
Financial supervision, 1916–1941

MEXICO

Gulf
of
Mexico

Miami ●

THE
BAHAMAS
⊛Nassau

Constitution of 1917 challenges U.S. interests
Nationalization of foreign oil companies, 1938
U.S.-Mexico agreement settles oil dispute, 1942

⊛Havana
CUBA
Guantánamo●

DOMINICAN
REP.

U.S. financial supervision, 1905–1941
U.S. troops withdrawn, 1924
Trujillo era, 1930–1961

⊛Mexico
City

Belmopan
BELIZE

JAMAICA
Kingston⊛

HAITI⊛
Port-au-
Prince

San Juan
VIRGIN IS. (U.S./U.K.)

—20°N—

⊛Santo
Domingo

PUERTO ●
RICO (U.S.)

U.S. colony since 1917

GUATEMALA
Guatemala City⊛
San Salvador

HONDURAS
⊛Tegucigalpa
NICARAGUA
⊛Managua

Caribbean Sea

U.S. colony
Jones Act grants U.S. citizenship, 1917

EL SALVADOR

●San José

U.S. invasion, 1924
United Fruit Company active

COSTA
RICA
PANAMA

⊛Panama

⊛Caracas
VENEZUELA

⊛Bogotá

GUYANA
Georgetown
⊛   ⊛
Paramaribo

SURINAME
●Cayenne
FRENCH GUIANA (Fr.)

U.S. financial supervision, 1911–1924
U.S. military occupation, 1912–1925
U.S. war against Sandino, 1926–1933
Somoza era, 1936–1979

COLOMBIA

SURINAME

Equator– 0° —

U.S. control of Canal Zone
Declaration of Panama, 1939

⊛Quito
ECUADOR

U.S. oil investments

Amazon R.

PACIFIC
OCEAN

PERU

Lima⊛

BRAZIL

BOLIVIA
⊛La Paz

⊛Brasilia

—20°S—

U.S. copper interests

CHILE

PARAGUAY
⊛Asunción

Paraná R.

Santiago⊛

Buenos Aires⊛

URUGUAY
⊛Montevideo

ARGENTINA

U.S. votes for nonintervention pledge
at Pan-American Conference, 1936

—40°S—

40°W

N

0   500   1000 Km.
0   500   1000 Mi.

80°W   60°W

Map 22.2 The United States and Latin America Between the Wars

The United States often intervened in other nations to maintain its hegemonic power in Latin America, where nationalists
resented outside meddling in their sovereign affairs. The Good Neighbor policy decreased U.S. military interventions, but U.S.
economic interests remained strong in the hemisphere.

splinter the Democratic Party by turning southern whites against the New Deal, the Liberty League also secretly channeled funds to a racist group in the South that circulated pictures of the First Lady with African Americans.

22-3b Demagogues and Populists

While many prominent business leaders fought the New Deal, other Americans (sometimes called "populists") thought the government favored business too much and paid too little attention to the needs of the common people. Unemployment had decreased—but 9 million people were still without work. In 1934, 1.5 million workers went on strike. In 1935, enormous dust storms enveloped the southern plains, killing livestock and driving families like the Montgomerys from their land. Millions of Americans still suffered. As their dissatisfaction mounted, so, too, did the appeal of various demagogues, who played to the prejudices and unreasoning passions of the people.

Father Charles Coughlin, a Roman Catholic priest whose weekly radio sermons reached up to 30 million listeners, spoke to those who felt they had lost control of their lives to distant elites and impersonal forces. Increasingly anti–New Deal, he was also increasingly anti-Semitic, telling his listeners that an international conspiracy of Jewish bankers caused their problems.

Another challenge came from Dr. Francis E. Townsend, a public health officer in Long Beach, California, who was thrown out of work at age sixty-seven with only $100 in savings. His situation was not unusual. With social welfare left to the states, only about 400,000 of the 6.6 million elderly Americans received any sort of state-supplied pension, and many lost both jobs and savings during the depression. Townsend proposed that Americans over the age of sixty should receive a government pension of $200 a month, financed by a new "transaction" (sales) tax. In fact, this plan was fiscally impossible (almost three-quarters of working Americans earned $200 a month or less) and profoundly regressive (because sales tax rates are the same for everyone, they take a larger share of income from those who earn the least). Nonetheless, 20 million Americans, or 1 in 5 adults—concerned about the plight of the elderly and not about details of funding—signed petitions supporting this plan.

Then there was Huey Long, perhaps the most successful populist demagogue in American history. Long was elected governor of Louisiana in 1928 with the slogan "Every Man a King, But No One Wears a Crown." As a U.S. senator, Long initially supported the New Deal but soon decided that Roosevelt had fallen captive to big business. Long countered in 1934 with the Share Our Wealth Society. Declaring that no family needed more than $5 million, he argued that the government should take any wealth over that amount, along with any income beyond $1 million a year, and use those funds to give each American family an annual income of $2,000 and a one-time homestead allowance of $5,000. (Long's plan was fiscally impossible but definitely not regressive.) By mid-1935, Long's movement claimed 7 million members, and few doubted that he aspired to the presidency. But Long was killed by a bodyguard's bullet during an assassination attempt in September 1935.

22-3c Left-Wing Critics

The political left also gained ground as hard times continued. Socialists and communists alike criticized the New Deal for trying to save capitalism instead of working to lessen the inequality of power and wealth in American society. In California, muckraker and socialist Upton Sinclair won the Democratic gubernatorial nomination in 1934 with the slogan "End Poverty in California," while in Wisconsin, the left-wing Progressive Party provided seven of the state's ten representatives to Congress. The U.S. Communist Party also gained support as it campaigned for social welfare and relief. Changing its strategy to disclaim any intention of overthrowing the U.S. government, the party proclaimed that "Communism Is Twentieth Century Americanism" and began to cooperate with left-wing labor unions, student groups, and writers' organizations in a **"Popular Front"** against fascism abroad and racism at home. It continued to fight racial discrimination through the League of Struggle for Negro Rights (founded in the late 1920s to fight lynching), and sent lawyers and funds to support the "Scottsboro Boys," who were falsely accused of raping two white women in Alabama (see "Race and the Limits of the New Deal," Section 22-6d). As one

"Popular Front" Coalition of communist and politically left groups against fascism and racism.

△ Senator Huey Long was probably the most flamboyant member of the U.S. Congress, fond of white silk suits, pink ties, strong whiskey, and women who were not his wife. His appeals to populist anger and resentment led FDR to call him one of the most dangerous men in the nation.

Bettmann/Getty Images

◁ Mary McLeod Bethune, pictured with her friend and supporter Eleanor Roosevelt, became the first African American woman to head a federal agency as director of the Division of Negro Affairs for the National Youth Administration.

Bettmann/Getty Images

black worker who became a communist organizer in Alabama explained, the Communist Party "fought selflessly and tirelessly to undo the wrongs perpetrated upon my race. Here was no dilly-dallying, no pussyfooting on the question of full equality of the Negro people." In 1938, at its high point for the decade, the party had fifty-five thousand members.

22-3d Shaping the Second New Deal

It was not only external critics who pushed Roosevelt to focus on social justice. His administration—largely due to Eleanor Roosevelt's influence—included many progressive activists. **Frances Perkins,** America's first woman cabinet member, came from a social work background, as did Roosevelt's close adviser Harold Ickes. A group of women social reformers who coalesced around the First Lady became important figures in government and in the Democratic Party. And African Americans had an unprecedented voice in this White House. By 1936, at least fifty black Americans held relatively important positions in New Deal agencies and cabinet-level departments. Journalists called these officials—who met on Friday evenings at the home of Mary McLeod Bethune, a distinguished educator who served as director of the Division of Negro Affairs for the National Youth Administration—the "black cabinet." Finally, Eleanor Roosevelt herself worked tirelessly to put social justice issues at the center of the New Deal agenda.

As Roosevelt faced the election of 1936, he understood that he had to appeal to Americans who had seemingly contradictory desires. Those who had been hit hard by the depression looked to the New Deal for help and for social justice. If that help was not forthcoming, Roosevelt would lose their support. Other Americans—not the poorest, but those with a tenuous hold on the middle class—were afraid of the continued chaos and disorder. They wanted security and stability. Still others, with more to lose, were frightened by the populist promises of people like Long and Coughlin. They wanted the New Deal to preserve American capitalism. With these lessons in mind, Roosevelt took the initiative once more.

During the period historians call the Second New Deal, Roosevelt introduced a range of progressive programs aimed at providing, as he said in a 1935 address to Congress, "greater security for the average man than he has ever known before in the history of America." The first triumph of the Second New Deal was an innocuous-sounding but momentous law that Roosevelt called "the Big Bill." The Emergency Relief Appropriation Act provided $4 billion in new deficit spending, primarily to create massive public works programs for the jobless. It also established the Resettlement Administration, which resettled destitute families and organized rural homestead communities and suburban greenbelt towns for low-income workers; the Rural Electrification Administration, which brought electricity to isolated rural areas; and the National Youth Administration, which sponsored work-relief programs for young adults and part-time jobs for students.

22-3e Works Progress Administration

The largest and best-known program funded by the Emergency Relief Appropriation Act was the **Works Progress Administration (WPA),** later renamed the Work Projects

Frances Perkins Served as Secretary of Labor from 1933 to 1945, former Progressive reformer, and first woman cabinet member.

Works Progress Administration (WPA) New Deal agency that hired millions of people to work on public works construction projects, including highways, roads, and public buildings; it also provided jobs for artists, actors, and writers in cultural programs.

Administration. The WPA employed more than 8.5 million people who built 650,000 miles of highways and roads and 125,000 public buildings, as well as bridges, reservoirs, irrigation systems, sewage treatment plants, parks, playgrounds, and swimming pools throughout the nation. Critics labeled these projects "boondoggles" or argued that they were simply to buy political favor, but WPA workers built schools and hospitals, operated nurseries for preschool children, and taught 1.5 million adults to read and write.

The WPA also employed artists, musicians, writers, and actors, commissioning artists to decorate post office walls with murals depicting ordinary life in America, sponsoring theater performances in cities and towns throughout the nation, and hiring fifteen thousand musicians to play in government-sponsored orchestras. Through the Federal Writers' Project (FWP), authors created guidebooks for every state and territory and wrote about the plain people of the United States, including a collection of "slave narratives" from more than two thousand elderly men and women who had been held in bondage before the Civil War. These cultural programs were also controversial, for many of the WPA artists, musicians, actors, and writers created works that showed sympathy for the political struggles of workers and farmers, attempting to recover a tradition of American radicalism by celebrating the lives and labor of America's plain folk.

△ The Works Progress Administration commissioned twenty-six artists to create a mural depicting scenes of life in modern California for San Francisco's Coit Tower, which had been completed in 1933.

Photographs in the Carol M. Highsmith Archive, Library of Congress, Prints and Photographs Division. [LC-DIG-highsm-13594]

22-3f Social Security Act

Big Bill programs and agencies were part of a short-term "emergency" strategy to address the immediate needs of the nation. Roosevelt's long-term strategy centered around the second major piece of Second New Deal legislation, the **Social Security Act**. It created a federal pension system in which eligible workers paid mandatory Social Security taxes on their wages and their employers contributed an equivalent amount; these workers then received federal retirement benefits. The Social Security Act also created several welfare programs, including a cooperative federal-state system of unemployment compensation and Aid to Dependent Children (later renamed Aid to Families with Dependent Children, or AFDC) for needy children in families without fathers present. Over the course of the twentieth century, benefits provided through the Social Security system would save tens of millions of Americans, especially the elderly, from poverty and despair.

Compared with the social security systems already in place in most western European nations, the U.S. Social Security system was fairly conservative. First, the government did not pay for old-age benefits; workers and their employers did. Second, the tax was regressive in that the more workers earned, the less they were taxed proportionally. Finally, the law did not cover agricultural labor, domestic service, and "casual labor not in the course of the employer's trade or business" (for example, janitorial work at a hospital). That meant that people of color, who disproportionately worked as farm laborers, as domestic servants, and in service jobs in hospitals and restaurants, were often ineligible. The act also excluded public-sector employees, so that many teachers, nurses, librarians, and social workers, the majority of whom were women, went uncovered. (Although the original Social Security Act provided no retirement benefits for spouses or widows of covered workers, Congress added these benefits in 1939.) Despite these limits, the Social Security Act was highly significant because the federal government took some responsibility for the economic security of the aged, the temporarily unemployed, dependent children, and people with disabilities.

22-3g Roosevelt's Populist Strategies

As the election of 1936 approached, Roosevelt adopted the populist language of his critics. Denouncing big business's "entrenched greed" and the "unjust concentration of wealth and power," he supported a new tax on business profits and increased taxes on inheritances, large gifts, and profits from the sale of property (see Figure 22.2).

In November 1936, Roosevelt won the presidency by a landslide. The Democrats also won such huge majorities in the House and Senate that some worried the two-party system might collapse. In fact, Roosevelt and the Democrats had forged a powerful "New Deal coalition" that pulled together groups from very

Social Security Act New Deal relief measure that launched a federal retirement benefits system as well as unemployment compensation, aid to low-income children, and other welfare benefits.

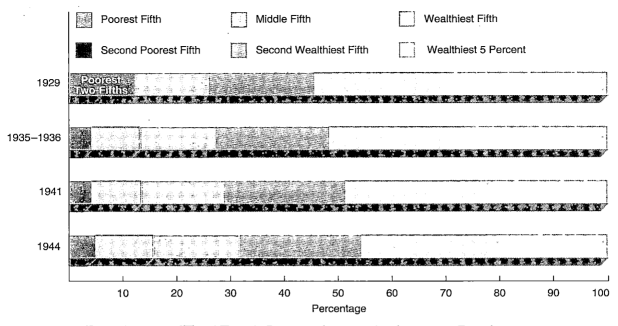

Figure 22.2 Distribution of Total Family Income Among the American People, 1929–1944 (Percentage)

Although the New Deal provided economic relief to the American people, it did not, as its critics so often charged, significantly redistribute income downward from the rich to the poor. *Source: Adapted from U.S. Bureau of the Census, Historical Statistics of the United States, Colonial Times to 1970. Bicentennial Edition, Washington, D.C.: U.S. Government Printing Office, 1975, page 301.*

different backgrounds and with different interests: the urban working class (especially immigrants from southern and eastern Europe and their sons and daughters), organized labor, the eleven states of the Confederacy (the "Solid South"), and northern blacks. By this time, the African American population in northern cities was large enough to constitute voting blocs, and New Deal benefits drew them away from the Republican Party, which they had long supported as the party of Lincoln. This New Deal coalition ensured that Democrats would occupy the White House for most of the next thirty years.

22-4 Labor

▶ **How did federal, state, and local governments intervene in labor relations during the Great Depression?**

▶ **What is the difference between craft and industrial unions, and how did the Great Depression exacerbate tensions between the two?**

▶ **What were the consequences of labor conflicts during the Great Depression?**

National Labor Relations (Wagner) Act Guaranteed workers the rights to organize and bargain collectively and outlawed unfair labor practices.

During the worst years of the depression, American workers continued to organize and to struggle for the rights of labor. Management,

however, fought back. Refusing to recognize unions, some even hired armed thugs to intimidate workers. One business publication declared that "a few hundred funerals will have a quieting influence." As employers refused to negotiate with union representatives, workers walked off the job. Local police or National Guard troops frequently intervened on the side of management, smashing workers' picket lines. Violence erupted in the steel, automobile, and textile industries; among lumber workers in the Pacific Northwest; and among teamsters in the Midwest. In 1934, police met a longshoremen's strike with violence on the docks of San Francisco; two union members were killed, and workers' anger spread to other industries. Eventually, 130,000 workers joined the general strike.

Workers pushed the Roosevelt administration for support, which came in the 1935 **National Labor Relations (Wagner) Act.** This act guaranteed workers the right to organize unions and to bargain collectively. It outlawed "unfair labor practices," such as firing workers who joined unions; prohibited management from sponsoring company unions; and required employers to bargain with labor's elected union representatives to set wages, hours, and working conditions. The Wagner Act also created a mechanism for enforcement: the National Labor Relations Board (NLRB). With federal protection, union membership grew. Organizers in the coalfields told miners that "President Roosevelt wants you to join the union," and join they did—along with workers in dozens of industries. In 1929 union membership stood at 3.6 million; in mid-1938 it surpassed 7 million.

The Wagner Act further alienated business leaders from the New Deal. "No Obedience," proclaimed an editorial in a leading business magazine. The business-sponsored Liberty League insisted—incorrectly—that the Supreme Court would soon find the Wagner Act unconstitutional.

22-4a Rivalry Between Craft and Industrial Unions

The growth and increasing militancy of the labor movement exacerbated an existing division between "craft" and "industrial" unions in the United States. Craft unions represented labor's elite: the skilled workers in a particular trade, such as carpentry. Industrial unions represented all the workers, skilled and unskilled, in a given industry such as automobile manufacture. In the 1930s, it was the industrial unions that had grown dramatically.

Craft unions dominated the American Federation of Labor, the powerful umbrella organization for individual unions. Most AFL leaders offered little support for industrial organizing. Many looked down on the industrial workers, disproportionately immigrants from southern and eastern Europe—"the rubbish at labor's door," in the words of the Teamsters' president. Skilled workers had economic interests different from those of the great mass of unskilled workers, and more conservative craft unionists were often alarmed at what they saw as the radicalism of industrial unions.

In 1935, the industrial unionists made their move. John L. Lewis, head of the United Mine Workers and the nation's most prominent labor leader, resigned as vice president of the AFL. He and other industrial unionists created the Committee for Industrial Organization (CIO); the AFL responded by suspending all CIO unions. By 1938, the slightly renamed **Congress of Industrial Organizations** had 3.7 million members, slightly more than the AFL's 3.4 million. Unlike the AFL, the CIO included women and people of color in its membership. Union membership gave these "marginal" workers greater employment security and the benefits of collective bargaining.

22-4b Sit-Down Strikes

The most decisive labor conflict of the decade came in late 1936, when the United Auto Workers (UAW), an industrial union, demanded recognition from General Motors (GM), Chrysler, and Ford. When GM refused, UAW organizers responded with a relatively new tactic: a "sit-down strike." On December 30, 1936, workers at the Fisher Body plant in Flint, Michigan, went on strike *inside* the Fisher One factory. They refused to leave the building, thus immobilizing a key part of the GM production system. GM tried to force the workers out by turning off the heat. When police attempted to take back the plant, strikers hurled steel bolts, coffee mugs, and bottles. The police tried tear gas. Strikers turned the plant's water hoses on the police.

As the sit-down strike spread to adjacent plants, auto production plummeted. General Motors obtained a court order to evacuate the plant, but the strikers stood firm, risking imprisonment and fines. In a critical decision, Michigan's governor refused to send in the National Guard to clear workers from the buildings. After forty-four days, the UAW triumphed. GM agreed to recognize the union, and Chrysler quickly followed. Ford held out until 1941.

22-4c Memorial Day Massacre

On the heels of this triumph, however, came a grim reminder of the costs of labor's struggle. On Memorial Day 1937, a group of picnicking workers and their families marched toward the Republic Steel plant in Chicago, intending to show support for strikers on a picket line in front of the plant. Police blocked their route and ordered them to disperse. One of the marchers threw something at the police, and the police attacked. Ten men were killed, seven of them shot in the back. Thirty marchers were wounded, including a woman and three children. Many Americans, fed up with labor strife and violence, showed little sympathy for the workers. The anti-labor *Chicago Tribune* blamed the marchers and praised police for repelling "a trained military unit of a revolutionary body."

At great cost, organized labor made great gains during the 1930s. Violence decreased as the NLRB effectively mediated disputes. And unionized workers—about 23 percent of the nonagricultural workforce—saw their standard of living rise. By 1941, the average steelworker could afford to buy a new coat for himself and his wife every six years and, every other year, a pair of shoes for each of his children.

22-5 Federal Power and the Nationalization of Culture

▷ How did the federal government expand its control of and influence over the West?

▷ What was the impact of the Indian Reorganization Act?

▷ How did the federal government respond to widespread poverty in the South?

▷ What role did popular culture play in providing relief during the Great Depression?

In the 1930s, national culture, politics, and policies played an increasingly important role in the lives of Americans from different regions, classes, and ethnic backgrounds as the reach of the national mass media grew and the power of the federal government expanded. During the decade-long economic crisis, political power moved from the state and local level to the White House and Congress, and individual Americans, in far more ways, found their lives bound up with the federal government. By the end of the 1930s, almost 35 percent of the population had received some sort of federal government benefit, whether crop subsidies through the

Congress of Industrial Organizations Association of 3.7 million members of industrial unions; included women and people of color.

The Women's Emergency Brigade and General Motors Sit-Down Strike

During the 1937 sit-down strike by automobile workers in Flint, Michigan, a women's "emergency brigade" of wives, daughters, sisters, and sweethearts demonstrated daily at the plant. When police tried to force the men out of Chevrolet Plant No. 9 by filling it with tear gas, the women used clubs to smash the plant's windows and let in fresh air. Sixteen people were injured that day in the riot between police and strikers. The following day the Women's Emergency Brigade marched again.

CRITICAL THINKING

Using this photograph as visual evidence:
- How did these women attempt to demonstrate the respectability and mainstream nature of their protest?
- How does that message fit with the clubs several still carry?

Bettmann/Getty Images

△ Gerenda Johnson, wife of a striker, leads a march past the GM Chevrolet small parts plant on the day following a violent conflict between police and strikers.

federal AAA or a WPA job or relief payments through FERA. Americans in the 1930s began to look to the federal government to play a major and active role in the life of the nation.

22-5a New Deal in the West

The New Deal changed the American West more than any other region, as federally sponsored construction of dams and other public works projects reshaped the region's economy and environment. During the 1930s, the federal Bureau of Reclamation, an obscure agency created in 1902 to provide irrigation for small farms and ranches, dramatically expanded its mandate to build large multipurpose dams that controlled entire river systems. For example, the Boulder Dam (later renamed for Herbert Hoover) harnessed the Colorado River, providing water to southern California and using hydroelectric power to produce electricity for Los Angeles and southern Arizona. The water from these dams opened new areas to agriculture and allowed western cities to expand; the cheap electricity they produced attracted industry to the region. These federally managed projects also gave the federal government an unprecedented role in the West. Especially after the completion of Washington State's Grand Coulee Dam in 1941, the federal government controlled both a great deal of water and hydroelectric power in the region. And in the West, control of water meant control over the region's future.

The federal government also brought millions of acres of western land under its control in the 1930s as it attempted to combat the environmental disaster of the Dust Bowl and to keep crop and livestock prices from falling further. To reduce pressure on the land from overgrazing, the federal government bought 8 million cattle from farmers in a six-month period in 1934–1935 and transported the healthy cattle out of the region. In 1934, the Taylor Grazing Act imposed new restrictions on ranchers' use of public lands for grazing stock. Federal stock reduction programs probably saved the western cattle industry, but they destroyed the traditional economy of the Navajos by forcing them to reduce the size of sheep herds on their federally protected reservation lands. Despite new restrictions, federal subsidies and AAA crop supports greatly benefited the owners of large farms and ranches, but such programs also increased federal government control in the region. As historian Richard White argues, by the end of the 1930s, "federal bureaucracies were quite literally remaking the American West."

22-5b New Deal for American Indians

New federal activism extended to the West's people as well. Over the past several decades, federal policy toward American Indians, especially those on western reservations, had been disastrous. The Bureau of Indian Affairs (BIA) was riddled with corruption; in its attempts to "assimilate" Native peoples, it had separated children from their parents, suppressed Native languages, and outlawed tribal religious practices. Such BIA-enforced assimilation was not successful. Division of tribal lands had failed to promote individual

landownership—almost half of those living on reservations in 1933 owned no land. In the early 1930s, American Indians were the poorest group in the nation, plagued by epidemics and malnutrition, with an infant mortality rate twice that of white Americans.

In 1933, Roosevelt named one of the BIA's most vocal critics to head the agency. John Collier, founder of the American Indian Defense Agency, meant to completely reverse the course of America's Indian policy, and his initiatives had many positive results. The **Indian Reorganization Act (IRA)** of 1934 went a long way toward ending the forced assimilation of Native peoples and restoring American Indian lands to tribal ownership. It also gave federal recognition to tribal governments. American Indian tribes had regained their status as semisovereign nations, guaranteed "internal sovereignty" in all matters not specifically limited by acts of Congress.

Not all Native peoples supported the IRA. Some saw it as a "back-to-the-blanket" measure based on romantic notions of "authentic" Native American culture. The tribal government structure specified by the IRA was culturally alien—and quite perplexing—to tribes such as the Papagos, whose language had no word for "representative." The Navajo nation also refused to ratify the IRA; in a terrible case of bad timing, the vote took place during the federally mandated destruction of Navajo sheep herds. Eventually, however, 181 tribes organized under the IRA. Collier had succeeded in reversing some of the destructive policies of the past, and the IRA laid the groundwork for future economic development and limited political autonomy among Native peoples.

22-5c New Deal in the South

New Dealers did not set out to transform the American West, but they did intend to transform the American South. Well before the Great Depression, the South was mired in widespread and debilitating poverty. In 1929, the South's per capita income of $365 per year was less than half of the West's $921. More than half of the region's farm families were tenants or sharecroppers with no land of their own. "Sickness, misery, and unnecessary death," in the words of a contemporary study, plagued the southern poor. Almost 15 percent of South Carolina's people could not read or write.

Roosevelt, who sought a cure for his polio in the pools of Warm Springs, Georgia, had seen southern poverty firsthand and understood its human costs. But in describing the South as "the Nation's No. 1 economic problem" in 1938, he was referring to the economic theory that underlay many New Deal programs. As long as its people were too poor to participate in the nation's mass consumer economy, the South would be a drag on national economic recovery.

> **Indian Reorganization Act (IRA)** A 1934 measure that sought to restore Native peoples' lands to tribal ownership and provided federal recognition of tribes as semisovereign nations.

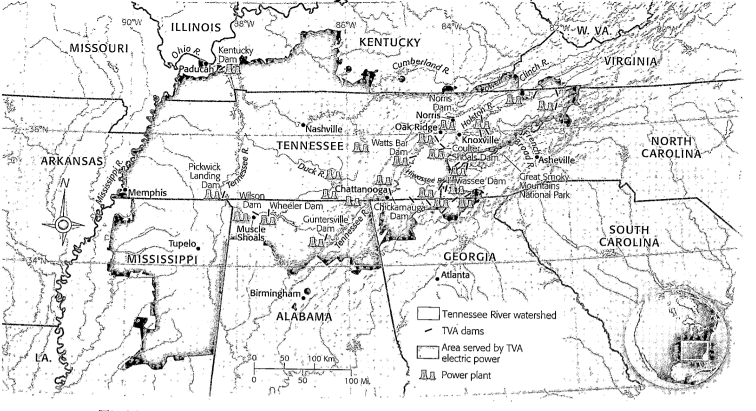

Map 22.3 The Tennessee Valley Authority

To control flooding and generate electricity, the Tennessee Valley Authority constructed dams along the Tennessee River and its tributaries from Paducah, Kentucky, to Knoxville, Tennessee.

The largest federal intervention in the South was the **Tennessee Valley Authority (TVA)**, authorized by Congress during Roosevelt's First Hundred Days. The TVA was created to develop a water and hydroelectric power project similar to the multipurpose dams of the West; dams would not only control flooding but also produce electric power for the region (see Map 22.3). However, confronted with the poverty and hopelessness of the Tennessee River Valley region (which included parts of Virginia, North Carolina, Tennessee, Georgia, Alabama, Mississippi, and Kentucky), the TVA quickly extended its focus. Through the TVA, the federal government promoted economic development, helped bring electricity to rural areas, restored fields worn out from overuse, and fought the curse of malaria.

Although it benefited many poor southerners, over time the TVA proved to be a monumental environmental disaster. TVA strip mining caused soil erosion. Its coal-burning generators released sulfur oxides, which combined with water vapor to produce acid rain. Above all, the TVA degraded the water by dumping untreated sewage, toxic chemicals, and metal pollutants from strip mining into streams and rivers.

Tennessee Valley Authority (TVA) Ambitious plan of economic development that centered on creating an extensive hydroelectric power project in the poor Appalachian area.

During the 1930s, the Roosevelt administration faced a very difficult political situation in the South. The southern senators whose support Roosevelt so desperately needed benefited from the flow of federal dollars to their states. But they were also suspicious of federal intervention and determined to preserve states' rights. Especially when federal action threatened the South's racial hierarchy, they resisted passionately. As the nation's poorest and least educated region, the South would not easily be integrated into the national culture and economy. But New Deal programs began that process and in so doing improved the lives of at least some of the region's people.

22-5d Mass Media and Popular Culture

It was not only federal government programs that broke down regional boundaries and fostered national connections during the 1930s. America's national mass media and popular culture helped millions survive hard times.

Photojournalism magazines *Life* and *Look* began publishing during the 1930s, and each quickly drew millions of readers. But it was the sound of the radio that filled the days and nights of the depression era. Manufacturers rushed to produce cheaper models, and by 1937 Americans were buying radios at the rate of twenty-eight a minute. By the end of the decade, 27.5 million households owned radios, and families listened on average five hours a day. Roosevelt understood the importance of the radio in American life, going directly to the American people with radio "Fireside Chats" throughout his presidency—and Americans ranked him eleventh among America's top "radio personalities" in 1938.

The 1936 Olympic Games

The 1936 Olympic Games that were scheduled to take place in Berlin, under the Nazi regime, created a dilemma for the United States and other nations. Should they go to Berlin? Would participation in the Nazi-orchestrated spectacle lend credence to Hitler's regime? Or would victories won by other nations undermine Hitler's claims about the superiority of Germany's "Aryan race"?

GERMANY
BERLIN·1936
1-16ᵗ AUGUST
OLYMPIC GAMES

Universal History Archive/Universal Images Group/Getty Images

Although the modern Olympic Games had been founded in 1896 with high hopes that they might help unite the nations of the world in peace and understanding, international politics were never far from the surface. Germany had been excluded from the 1920 and 1924 games following its aggression and defeat in World War I, and the International Olympic Committee's choice (in 1931) of Berlin for the XI Olympiad was intended to welcome Germany back into the world community. However, with Hitler's rise to power in 1933, Germany determined to use the games as propaganda for the Nazi state and to demonstrate the superiority of its pure "Aryan" athletes. Soon thereafter, campaigns to boycott the Berlin Olympics emerged in several nations, including Great Britain, Sweden, France, Czechoslovakia, and the United States.

The American people were divided over the question of a boycott. Some U.S. Jewish groups led campaigns against U.S. participation in Berlin, while others took no public position, concerned that their actions might lead to increased anti-Semitic violence within Germany. Jewish athletes made individual decisions

about whether or not to boycott the Olympics. The president of the United States Olympic Committee, Avery Brundage, attributed the boycott movement to a "conspiracy" of Jews and communists and instructed American athletes not to get involved in the "present Jew-Nazi altercation." African Americans, overwhelmingly, opposed boycotting the games. Well aware of Hitler's attitudes toward "mongrel" peoples, many looked forward to demonstrating on the tracks and fields of Berlin just how wrong Hitler's notions of Aryan superiority were. Some also pointed out the hypocrisy of American officials who criticized Germany while ignoring U.S. discrimination against black athletes.

In the end, the United States sent 312 athletes to Berlin; of these, 18 were African American. These African American athletes won fourteen medals, almost one-quarter of the U.S. total of fifty-six. Track and field star Jesse Owens came home with four gold medals. Jewish athletes won thirteen medals in the 1936 Olympics; one of those athletes was American. But German athletes won eighty-nine medals to U.S. athletes' fifty-six, and despite the initial controversy, the XI Olympiad was a

◁ The eleventh summer Olympic Games in Berlin were carefully crafted as propaganda for the Nazi state. And the spectacle of the 1936 games, as represented in the poster above, was impressive. But on the athletic fields, Nazi claims of Aryan superiority were challenged by athletes such as African American Jesse Owens, who is shown at left breaking the Olympic record in the 200-meter race.

Bettmann/Getty Images

(Continued)

public relations triumph for Germany. The *New York Times,* impressed by the spectacle of the games and the hospitality of the Germans, proclaimed that the XI Olympiad had put Germany "back in the fold of nations."

The idealistic vision of nations linked together through peaceful athletic competition hit a low point at the 1936 Olympics. The 1940 Olympic Games, scheduled for Tokyo, were cancelled because of the escalating world war.

CRITICAL THINKING

□ Despite the idealistic intent of the Olympics to link the world's nations together through peaceful athletic competition, politics have gotten in the way on numerous occasions, including in 1936.

□ What other instances can you think of where politics influenced an Olympic competition?

□ Is it possible for international politics not to affect the Olympics and other sporting events that occur on a world stage?

The radio offered Americans many things. In a time of uncertainty, radio gave citizens immediate access—as never before—to the political news of the day and to the actual voices of their elected leaders. During hard times, radio offered escape: for children, the adventures of *Flash Gordon*; for housewives, new soap operas, such as *The Romance of Helen Trent.* Entire families gathered to listen to the comedy of ex-vaudevillians Jack Benny, George Burns, and Gracie Allen.

Radio also gave people a chance to participate—however vicariously—in events they could never have experienced before. Listeners were carried to New York City for performances of the Metropolitan Opera on Saturday afternoons, to the Moana Hotel on the beach at Waikiki through the live broadcast of *Hawaii Calls*, to major league baseball games (begun by the St. Louis Cardinals in 1935) in distant cities. Millions shared the horror of the kidnapping of aviator Charles Lindbergh's son in 1932; black Americans in the urban North and rural South experienced the triumphs of African American boxer Joe Louis ("the Brown Bomber"). Radio lessened the isolation of individuals and communities. It helped create a more homogeneous mass culture as people throughout the nation listened to the same programs; by offering a set of shared experiences, it also lessened the gulfs among Americans from different regions and class backgrounds.

Hollywood movies also offered shared experiences. During the first years of the depression almost one-third of all movie theaters closed, and ticket prices fell from 30 to 20 cents. By the mid-1930s, however, Americans were going to the movies again, and a nation of fewer than 130 million bought 80 million to 90 million movie tickets each week. Many Americans sought escape from grim realities at the movies. Comedies were especially popular, from the slapstick of the Marx Brothers to the sophisticated banter of *My Man Godfrey* or *It Happened One Night.* However, the appeal of upbeat movies was in the context of economic hard times. The song "Who's Afraid of the Big Bad Wolf?" from Disney's *Three Little Pigs* was a big hit in 1933—as the economy hit bottom.

When sales of undershirts plummeted in 1934 after Clark Gable took off his shirt to reveal a bare chest in *It Happened One Night*, it seemed clear that film influenced American attitudes and behavior. But some Americans had long worried about the power of film, criticizing their frequent use of sexual innuendo as well as the gangster movies that drew crowds in the early 1930s. No matter that the gangster hero always met death or destruction; critics argued that these films seemed to glamorize crime. Faced with a boycott

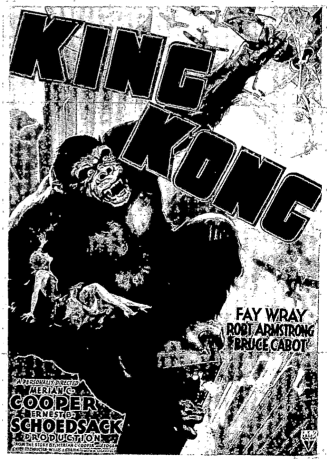

△ *King Kong* broke all box-office records in 1933, as Americans flocked to see the giant ape fighting off airplanes from the top of New York's new Empire State Building—the tallest building in the world.

organized by the Roman Catholic Legion of Decency, in 1934 the film industry established a production code that would determine what American film audiences saw—and did not see—for decades. Pledged the Production Code Administration: "There is no room . . . for pictures which offend against common decency."

Finally, in an unintended consequence, federal policies intended to channel jobs to male heads of households strengthened the power of national popular culture. During Roosevelt's first two years in office, 1.5 million youths lost jobs; many young people who would have gone to work at the age of fourteen in better times decided to stay in school. By the end of the decade, three-quarters of American youth went to high school—up from one-half in 1920—and graduation rates doubled. School was free, classrooms were warm, and education seemed to promise a better future. The exuberant, fad-driven peer cultures that had developed in 1920s high schools and colleges were no more, but consumer-oriented youth culture had not died out. And as more young people went to high school, more participated in that national youth culture. Increasingly, young people listened to the same music. More than ever before, they adopted the same styles of clothing, of dance, of speech. Paradoxically, the hard times of the depression did not destroy youth culture; instead, they caused youth culture to spread more widely among America's young.

22-6 The Limits of the New Deal

▷ How did Franklin D. Roosevelt's actions weaken the effectiveness of the New Deal agenda?

▷ How did the New Deal fail minority groups, and why?

▷ Why did African Americans support Franklin D. Roosevelt?

▷ What role did First Lady Eleanor Roosevelt play in her husband's presidency?

Roosevelt began his second term with great optimism and a strong mandate for reform. Almost immediately, however, the president's own actions undermined his New Deal agenda. Labor strife and racial issues divided the American people. As fascism spread in Europe, the world inched toward war, and domestic initiatives lost ground to foreign affairs and defense. By the end of 1938, New Deal reform had ground to a halt, but it had already had a profound impact on the United States.

22-6a Court-Packing Plan

Following his landslide electoral victory in 1936, Roosevelt set out to safeguard his progressive agenda. The greatest danger he saw was from the U.S. Supreme Court. In ruling unconstitutional both the National Industrial Recovery Act

(in 1935) and the Agricultural Adjustment Act (in 1936), the Court rejected not only specific provisions of hastily drafted New Deal legislation but also the expansion of presidential and federal power such legislation entailed. Only three of the nine justices were consistently sympathetic to New Deal "emergency" measures, and Roosevelt was convinced the Court would invalidate most of the Second New Deal legislation. Citing the advanced age and heavy workload of the nine justices, he asked Congress for authority to appoint up to six new justices to the Supreme Court. But in an era that had seen the rise to power of Hitler, Mussolini, and Stalin, many Americans saw Roosevelt's plan as an attack on constitutional government. Even those sympathetic to the New Deal worried about politicizing the Court. "Assuming, which is not at all impossible," wrote prominent journalist William Allen White, "a reactionary president, as charming, as eloquent and as irresistible as Roosevelt, with power to change the court, and we should be in the devil's own fix." Congress rebelled, and Roosevelt experienced his first major congressional defeat.

The episode had a final, ironic twist. During the long public debate over Court packing, the ideological center of the Supreme Court shifted. Key swing-vote justices began to vote in favor of liberal, pro–New Deal rulings. In short order, the Court upheld both the Wagner Act and the Social Security Act. Moreover, a new judicial pension program encouraged older judges to retire, allowing Roosevelt to appoint seven new associate justices in the next four years, including such notables as Hugo Black, Felix Frankfurter, and William O. Douglas. In the end, Roosevelt got what he wanted from the Supreme Court, but the Court-packing plan damaged his political credibility.

22-6b Roosevelt Recession

Another New Deal setback was the renewed economic recession of 1937–1939, sometimes called the Roosevelt recession. Despite his use of deficit spending, Roosevelt had never abandoned his commitment to a balanced budget. In 1937, confident that the depression had reversed, he began to cut government spending. At the same time, the Federal Reserve Board, concerned about a 3.6 percent inflation rate, tightened credit. The two actions sent the economy into a tailspin: unemployment climbed from 7.7 million in 1937 to 10.4 million in 1938. Soon Roosevelt resumed deficit financing.

The New Deal was in trouble in 1937 and 1938, and New Dealers struggled over the direction of liberal reform. Some urged vigorous trust-busting; others advocated the resurrection of national economic planning as it had existed under the National Recovery Administration. But in the end, Roosevelt rejected these alternatives and chose deficit financing as a means of stimulating consumer demand and creating jobs. And in 1939, with conflict over the world war that had begun in Europe commanding more and more of the nation's attention, the New Deal came to an end. Roosevelt sacrificed further domestic reforms in return for conservative support for his programs of military rearmament and preparedness.

22-6c Election of 1940

No president had ever served more than two terms, and many Americans speculated about whether Franklin Roosevelt would run for a third term in 1940. Roosevelt seemed undecided until that spring, when Adolf Hitler's military advances in Europe apparently convinced him to stay on (see "The Expanding Conflict," Section 23-1a). Roosevelt headed off the predictable attacks from his opponent, Republican Wendell Willkie, by expanding military and naval contracts and thus reducing unemployment. Roosevelt also promised Americans, "Your boys are not going to be sent into any foreign wars."

Roosevelt did not win this election in a landslide, as he had in 1936 (see Map 22.4). But the New Deal coalition held. Once again Roosevelt won in the cities, supported by blue-collar workers, ethnic Americans, and African Americans. He also carried every state in the South. Although New Deal reform was over at home, Roosevelt was still riding a wave of public approval.

22-6d Race and the Limits of the New Deal

While the New Deal directly touched the lives of a great many Americans, not all benefited equally. More than anything else, differences were based on race. The New Deal fell short of equality for people of color for two major reasons.

First was the relationship between local and national power. National programs were implemented at the local level, and where local custom conflicted with national intent, as in the South and West, local custom won. In the South, African Americans received lower relief payments than whites and were paid lower wages in WPA jobs. The situation was

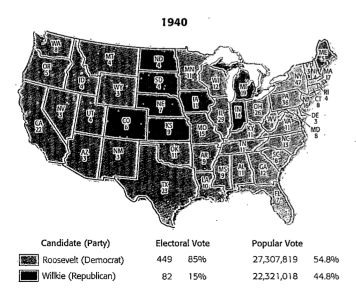

1940

Candidate (Party)	Electoral Vote		Popular Vote	
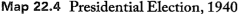 Roosevelt (Democrat)	449	85%	27,307,819	54.8%
Willkie (Republican)	82	15%	22,321,018	44.8%

Map 22.4 Presidential Election, 1940

Roosevelt won an unprecedented third term in the 1940 presidential election. He did not repeat his landslide 1936 victory, in which he won all but two states. But he did capture 38 states in 1940 to Republican Wendell Willkie's 10.

similar in the Southwest. In Tucson, Arizona, for example, Federal Emergency Relief Agency officials divided applicants into four groups—Anglos, Mexican Americans, Mexican immigrants, and Indians—and allocated relief payments in descending order.

Such discriminatory practices were rooted not only in racism but also in the economic interests of whites/Anglos. The majority of African American and Mexican American workers were paid so poorly that they *earned* less than impoverished whites got for "relief." Why would these workers take low-paying private jobs if government relief or government work programs provided more income? Local communities understood that federal programs threatened a political, social, and economic system based on racial hierarchies.

The case of the Scottsboro Boys illustrates the power of racism in the conflict between local and national power in 1930s America. One night in March 1931, a fight broke out between groups of young black and white "hobos" on a Southern Railroad freight train as it passed through Alabama. The black youths won the fight and tossed the whites off the train. Not long afterward, a posse stopped the train, arrested the black youths, and threw them in the Scottsboro, Alabama, jail. The posse also discovered two white women "riding the rails," who claimed that the young men had raped them. Word spread, and the youths were barely saved from a lynch mob. Medical evidence later showed that the women were lying. But within two weeks, eight of the so-called Scottsboro Boys were convicted of rape by all-white juries and sentenced to death. The ninth, a boy of thirteen, was saved from the death penalty by one vote. The case—so clearly a product of southern racism—became a cause célèbre, both in the nation and, through the efforts of the Communist Party, around the world.

The Supreme Court intervened, ruling that Alabama deprived black defendants of equal protection under the law by systematically excluding African Americans from juries and that the defendants had been denied counsel. Alabama, however, staged new trials. Five of the young men were convicted (four would be paroled by 1950, and one escaped from prison). Despite federal action through the Supreme Court, Alabama prevailed. Southern resistance to federal intervention—centered around issues of race—would not yield easily to federal power.

Second, the gains made by people of color under the New Deal were limited by the political realities of southern resistance. Roosevelt needed the support of southern Democrats to pass his legislative program, and they were willing to hold him hostage over race. In 1938, for example, southern Democrats blocked an antilynching bill with a six-week-long filibuster in the Senate. Roosevelt refused to use his political capital to break the filibuster and pass the bill. Politically, he had much to lose and little to gain. He knew that blacks would not desert the Democratic Party, but without southern senators, his legislative agenda was dead. Roosevelt wanted all Americans to enjoy the benefits of democracy, but he had no strong commitment to the cause of civil rights. As the NAACP's Roy Wilkins put it, "Mr. Roosevelt was no friend of the Negro. He wasn't an enemy, but he wasn't a friend."

22-6e African American Support

Why, then, did African Americans support Roosevelt and the New Deal? Because despite discriminatory policies, the New Deal helped African Americans. By the end of the 1930s, almost one-third of African American households survived on income from a WPA job. African Americans held some significant positions in the Roosevelt administration. Finally, there was the First Lady. When the acclaimed black contralto Marian Anderson was barred from performing in Washington's Constitution Hall by its owners, the Daughters of the American Revolution, Eleanor Roosevelt responded by resigning her membership in the DAR; she then helped arrange for Anderson to sing at the Lincoln Memorial on Easter Sunday, 1939. Such public commitment to racial equality was enormously important to African American citizens.

Despite widespread support for Roosevelt and the New Deal, many African Americans were well aware of the limits of New Deal reform. Some concluded that they could depend only on themselves and organized self-help and direct-action movements. In 1934, black tenant farmers and sharecroppers joined with poor whites to form the Southern Tenant Farmers' Union. In the North, the militant Harlem Tenants League fought rent increases and evictions, and African American consumers began to boycott white merchants who refused to hire blacks as clerks. Their slogan was "Don't Buy Where You Can't Work." And the Brotherhood of Sleeping Car Porters,

under the astute leadership of A. Philip Randolph, fought for the rights of black workers.

22-6f An Assessment of the New Deal

Any analysis of the New Deal must begin with Franklin Delano Roosevelt himself. Assessments of Roosevelt varied widely during his presidency: he was passionately hated and just as passionately loved. Roosevelt personified the presidency for the American people. When he spoke directly to Americans in his Fireside Chats, hundreds of thousands wrote to him, sharing their problems, asking for his help, offering their advice.

Eleanor Roosevelt, the nation's First Lady, played a crucial and unprecedented role in the Roosevelt administration. As First Lady, she worked tirelessly for social justice and human rights, bringing reformers, trade unionists, and advocates for the rights of women and African Americans to the White House. Described by some as the conscience of the New Deal, she took public positions—especially on African American civil rights—far more progressive than those of her husband's administration. In some ways she served as a lightning rod, deflecting conservative criticism from her husband to herself. But her public stances also cemented the allegiance of other groups, African Americans in particular, to the New Deal.

Most historians and political scientists consider Franklin Roosevelt a truly great president, citing his courage and buoyant self-confidence, his willingness to experiment, and his capacity to inspire the nation during the most somber days of the depression. Some, who see the New Deal as a squandered opportunity for true political and economic change, charge that Roosevelt lacked vision and courage. They judge Roosevelt by goals that were not his own: Roosevelt was a pragmatist whose goal was to preserve the

◁ Marchers in Washington, D.C., demand freedom for the Scottsboro Boys, young African American men who were falsely accused and convicted of raping two white women in Alabama in 1931. This 1933 march was organized by the International Labor Defense, the legal arm of the Communist Party of the United States of America, which waged a strong campaign on behalf of the nine young men.

Bettmann/Getty Images

system. Nonetheless, Franklin Delano Roosevelt transformed the American presidency, increasing its strength and independence and fostering a more direct connection with the American people.

During his more than twelve years in office, Roosevelt helped to expand the role of the federal government. For the first time, the federal government took primary responsibility for safeguarding the economic security of the American people. New Deal programs pumped money into the economy and saved millions of Americans from hunger and misery. However, as late as 1939, more than 10 million men and women were still jobless, and the nation's unemployment rate stood at 19 percent. In the end, it was not the New Deal, but massive government spending during the Second World War that brought full economic recovery. In 1941, as a result of mobilization for war, unemployment declined to 10 percent, and in 1944, at the height of the war, only 1 percent of the labor force was jobless. World War II, not the New Deal, would reinvigorate the American economy.

22-7 The Approach of War

▶ What methods did the Nazis use to gain control inside and outside of Germany?

▶ How did American isolationist views influence the federal government's response to foreign affairs?

▶ How did Franklin D. Roosevelt's views on foreign affairs evolve during his presidency?

▶ What developments contributed to increased tension between Japan and the United States?

The U.S. domestic struggles—economic, political, and social—took place with in a larger international crisis and, by the late 1930s, a rapidly expanding war. On March 5, 1933, one day after Roosevelt's inauguration, Germany's parliament granted dictatorial powers to the new chancellor, Adolf Hitler, leader of the **Nazi Party**. The act marked the culmination of a stunning rise to power for Hitler, whose Nazis very likely would have remained a fringe party had the Great Depression not hit Germany with such force. Production plummeted 40 percent, and unemployment ballooned to 6 million, meaning that two workers out of five did not have jobs. Together with a disintegrating banking system, which robbed millions of their savings, as well as widespread resentment among Germans over the Versailles peace settlement, the plummeting employment figures brought mass discontent to the country. While the communists preached a workers' revolution, German business executives and property owners threw their support behind Hitler and the Nazis, many of them believing they could manipulate him once he had thwarted the communists. They were wrong.

Like Benito Mussolini, who had gained control of Italy in 1922, Hitler was a fascist. Fascism (called Nazism, or National Socialism, in Germany) was a collection of ideas and prejudices that celebrated supremacy of the state over the individual; of dictatorship over democracy; of authoritarianism over freedom of speech; of a regulated, state-oriented economy over a free-market economy; and of militarism and war over peace. The Nazis vowed not only to revive German economic and military strength but also to cripple communism and "purify" the German "race" by destroying Jews and other people, such as homosexuals and Romani people, whom Hitler disparaged as inferiors. The Nuremberg Laws of 1935 stripped Jews of citizenship and outlawed intermarriage with Germans. Teachers, doctors, and other professionals could not practice their craft, and half of all German Jews were without work.

22-7a German Aggression Under Hitler

Determined to get Germany out from under the Versailles treaty system, Hitler withdrew Germany from the League of Nations, ended reparations payments, and began to rearm. While secretly laying plans for the conquest of neighboring states, he watched admiringly as Mussolini's troops invaded the African nation of Ethiopia in 1935. The next year, Hitler ordered his own troops into the Rhineland, an area that the Versailles treaty had demilitarized. When Germany's timid neighbor France did not resist this act, Hitler crowed, "The world belongs to the man with guts!"

Soon the aggressors joined hands. In 1936, Italy and Germany formed an alliance called the Rome-Berlin Axis. Shortly thereafter, Germany and Japan united against the Soviet Union in the Anti-Comintern Pact. To these events Britain and France responded with a policy of **appeasement**, hoping to curb Hitler's expansionist appetite by permitting him a few territorial nibbles. The policy of appeasing Hitler, though not altogether unreasonable in terms of what could be known at the time, proved disastrous, for the hate-filled German leader continually raised his demands.

Early in 1938, Hitler once again tested the limits of European tolerance when he sent soldiers into Austria to annex the nation of his birth. Then, in September, he seized the largely German-speaking Sudeten region of Czechoslovakia. Appeasement reached its apex that month when France and Britain, without consulting the Czechs, agreed at Munich to allow Hitler this territorial bite, in exchange for a pledge that he would not take more. British prime minister Neville Chamberlain returned home to proclaim "peace in our time," confident that Hitler was satiated. In March 1939, Hitler swallowed the rest of Czechoslovakia (see Map 22.5).

22-7b Isolationist Views in the United States

Americans had watched this buildup of tension in Europe with apprehension. Many sought to distance themselves from the tumult by embracing isolationism, whose key elements were abhorrence of war and fervent opposition to U.S. alliances with other nations. A 1937 Gallup poll found that nearly two-thirds of the respondents thought U.S.

Nazi Party National Socialist German Workers' Party; founded in Germany in 1919, it rose to prominence under the leadership of Adolf Hitler and stressed fascism and anti-Semitism.

appeasement The process of making concessions to pacify, quiet, or satisfy the other party.

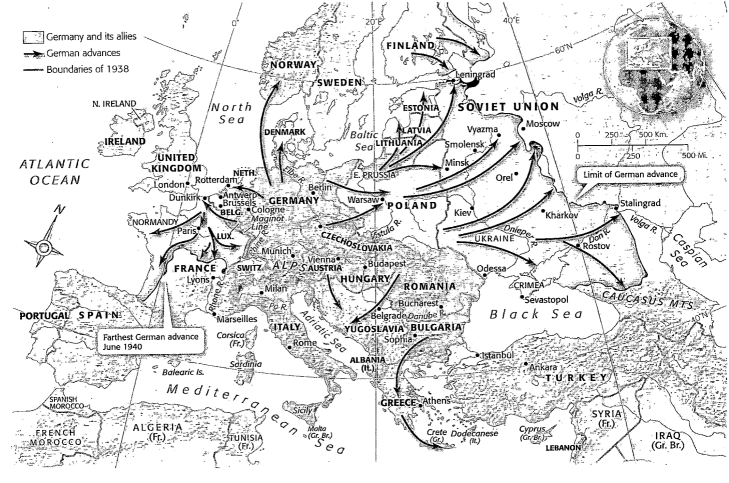

Map 22.5 The German Advance

Hitler's drive to dominate Europe pushed German troops deep into France and the Soviet Union. Great Britain took a beating but held on with the help of American economic and military aid before the United States entered the Second World War in late 1941.

participation in World War I had been a mistake. The vast majority of isolationists opposed fascism and condemned aggression, but they did not think the United States should have to do what Europeans themselves refused to do: block Hitler. Isolationist sentiment was strongest in the Midwest and among anti-British ethnic groups, especially Americans of German or Irish descent, but it was a nationwide phenomenon that cut across socioeconomic, ethnic, party, and sectional lines, and it attracted a majority of the American people.

Some isolationists charged that corporate "merchants of death" had promoted war and were assisting the aggressors. In an era newly critical of business as unemployment rates hovered around 20 percent, a congressional committee headed by Senator Gerald P. Nye held hearings from 1934 to 1936 on the role of business and financiers in the U.S. decision to enter the First World War. The Nye committee did not prove that American munitions makers had dragged the nation into that war, but it did uncover evidence that corporations practicing "rotten commercialism" had bribed foreign politicians to bolster arms sales in the 1920s and 1930s and had lobbied against arms control.

Reflecting the popular desire for distance from Europe's disputes, Roosevelt signed a series of **neutrality acts,** in which Congress sought to protect the nation by outlawing the kinds of contacts that had compromised U.S. neutrality during World War I. The Neutrality Act of 1935 prohibited arms shipments to either side in a war, once the president had declared the existence of belligerency. Roosevelt had wanted the authority to name the aggressor and apply an arms embargo against it alone, but Congress would not grant the president such discretionary power. The Neutrality Act of 1936 forbade loans to belligerents. After a joint resolution in 1937 declared the United States neutral in the Spanish Civil War, Roosevelt embargoed arms shipments to both sides. The Neutrality Act of 1937 introduced the cash-and-carry principle: warring nations wishing to trade with the United States would have to pay cash for their nonmilitary purchases and carry the goods from U.S. ports in their own ships. The act also forbade Americans from traveling on the ships of belligerent nations.

22-7c Roosevelt's Evolving Views

President Roosevelt shared the prevailing popular isolationism in the early 1930s. Although prior to World War I he was an expansionist and interventionist like his older cousin Theodore, during the interwar period FDR talked less about

neutrality acts Laws passed in the mid-1930s to keep the United States out of any European wars.

preparedness and more about disarmament and the horrors of war, less about policing the world and more about handling problems at home. In a passionate speech delivered in August 1936 at Chautauqua, New York, Roosevelt expressed prevailing isolationist opinion and made a pitch for the pacifist vote in the upcoming election: "I have seen war. . . . I have seen blood running from the wounded. I have seen men coughing out their gassed lungs. . . . I have seen the agony of mothers and wives. I hate war." The United States, he promised, would remain unentangled in the European conflict. During the crisis over Czechoslovakia in 1938, Roosevelt endorsed appeasement and greeted the Munich accord with a "universal sense of relief."

At the same time, Roosevelt grew increasingly troubled by the behavior of Germany. When, in November 1938, the Nazi leadership used the shooting of a German diplomat in Paris by a Jewish man (whose parents had just been deported to Poland by the Nazi government) as an excuse to launch *Kristallnacht* (or Crystal Night, after the shattered glass that littered German streets after the attacks on Jewish synagogues, businesses, and homes) and sent tens of thousands of Jews to concentration camps, FDR recalled the U.S. ambassador to Germany and allowed fifteen thousand refugees on visitor permits to remain longer in the United States. But he went no further, and Congress—motivated by economic concerns and spreading anti-Semitism—voted to uphold U.S. immigration restrictions as Jews attempted to flee Hitler's Germany.

Even the tragic voyage of the *St. Louis* did not change government policy. The vessel left Hamburg in mid-1939 carrying 930 desperate Jewish refugees, none of whom had proper immigration documents. Denied entry to Havana, the *St. Louis* headed for Miami, where Coast Guard cutters prevented it from docking. The ship was forced back to Europe, where some refugees took shelter in nations soon to be overrun by Hitler's legions.

Roosevelt, however, had quietly begun readying the country for war. In early 1938, he successfully pressured the House of Representatives to defeat a constitutional amendment proposed by Indiana Democrat Louis Ludlow to require a majority vote in a national referendum before a congressional declaration of war could go into effect (unless the United States were attacked). Later that year, in the wake of the Munich crisis, Roosevelt asked Congress for funds to build up the air force, which he believed essential to deter aggression. In January 1939, the president secretly decided to sell bombers to France, saying privately that "our frontier is on the Rhine." Although the more than five hundred combat planes delivered to France did not deter war, French orders spurred growth of the U.S. aircraft industry.

For Roosevelt and for other Western leaders, Hitler's swallowing of the whole of Czechoslovakia in March 1939 proved a turning point, forcing them to face a stark new reality. Until now, they had been able to explain away Hitler's actions by saying he was only trying to reunite German-speaking peoples. That argument no longer worked. Leaders in Paris and London realized that, if the German leader were to be

stopped, it would have to be by force. When Hitler began eyeing his neighbor Poland, London and Paris announced they would stand by the Poles. The Soviets made a different choice. Soviet leader Joseph Stalin believed that the West's appeasement of Hitler had left him no choice but to cut a deal with Berlin, and he signed a non-aggression pact with Germany in 1939. But Stalin also coveted territory: a top-secret protocol attached to the pact carved eastern Europe into German and Soviet zones and permitted the Soviets to grab the eastern half of Poland and the three Baltic states of Lithuania, Estonia, and Latvia, formerly part of the Russian Empire.

22-7d Poland and the Outbreak of World War II

In the early morning hours of September 1, 1939, German tank columns rolled into Poland. German fighting planes covered the advance, thereby launching a new type of warfare, the *blitzkrieg* (lightning war)—highly mobile land forces and armor combined with tactical aircraft. Within forty-eight hours, Britain and France responded by declaring war on Germany. "It's come at last," Franklin Roosevelt murmured. "God help us all."

U.S. Army Center of Military History

△ German leader Adolf Hitler (1889–1945) is surrounded in this propagandistic painting by images that came to symbolize hate, genocide, and war: Nazi flags with emblems of the swastika, the iron cross on the dictator's pocket, Nazi troops in loyal salute. The anti-Semitic Hitler denounced the United States as a "Jewish rubbish heap" of "inferiority and decadence" that was "incapable of conducting war."

When Europe descended into the abyss of war in September 1939, Roosevelt declared neutrality and pressed for repeal of the arms embargo. Isolationist senator Arthur Vandenberg of Michigan roared back that the United States could not be "an arsenal for one belligerent without becoming a target for the other." After much debate, however, Congress in November lifted the embargo on contraband and approved cash-and-carry exports of arms. Using "methods short of war," Roosevelt thus began to aid the Allies.

22-7e Asian Tensions

In Asia, meanwhile, Japan was on the march. The United States had interests at stake in the region: the Philippines and Pacific islands, religious missions, trade and investments, and the Open Door in China. In traditional missionary fashion, Americans also believed that they were China's special friend and protector. "With God's help," Senator Kenneth Wherry of Nebraska once proclaimed, "we will lift Shanghai up and up, ever up, until it is just like Kansas City." By contrast, the aggressive Japan loomed as a threat to American attitudes and interests. The Tokyo government seemed bent on subjugating China and unhinging the Open Door doctrine of equal trade and investment opportunity.

In the late 1920s, civil war broke out in China when Jiang Jieshi (Chiang Kai-shek) ousted Mao Zedong and his communist followers from the ruling Guomindang Party. Americans applauded this display of anti-Bolshevism and Jiang's conversion to Christianity in 1930. Jiang's new wife, Soong Meiling, also won their hearts. American educated, Madame Jiang spoke flawless English, dressed in Western fashion, and cultivated ties with prominent Americans. Warming to Jiang, U.S. officials abandoned one imperial vestige by signing a treaty in 1928 restoring control of tariffs to the Chinese.

Japan continued to pressure the Chinese (see Map 22.6). In mid-1937, owing to Japanese provocation, the Sino-Japanese War erupted. Japanese forces seized Beijing and cities along the coast. The gruesome bombing of Shanghai intensified anti-Japanese sentiment in the United States. Senator Norris, an isolationist who moved further away from isolationism with each Japanese thrust, condemned the Japanese as "disgraceful, ignoble, barbarous, and cruel, even beyond the power of language to describe." In an effort to help China by permitting it to buy American arms, Roosevelt refused to declare the existence of war, thus avoiding activation of the Neutrality Acts.

22-7f Roosevelt's Quarantine Speech

In a speech denouncing the aggressors on October 5, 1937, the president called for a "quarantine" to curb the "epidemic

Map 22.6 Japanese Expansion Before Pearl Harbor

The Japanese quest for predominance began at the turn of the century and intensified in the 1930s. China suffered the most at the hands of Tokyo's military. Vulnerable U.S. possessions in Asia and the Pacific proved no obstacle to Japan's ambitions for a Greater East Asia Co-Prosperity Sphere.

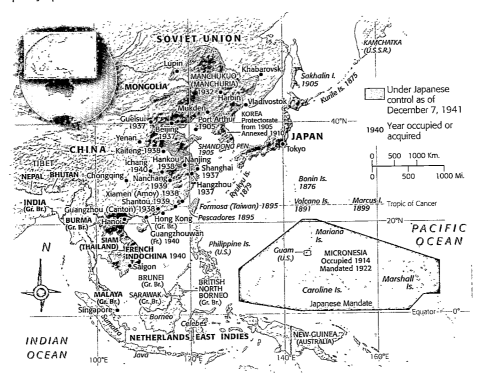

Social Security

The New Deal's Social Security system expanded over subsequent decades, and now covers almost 99 percent of American workers. It has dramatically reduced the poverty rate among the nation's elderly, giving millions a more secure and enjoyable old age, and it provides financial support for the disabled and for dependent children.

Despite its successes, today's Social Security system faces an uncertain future. Its troubles are due in part to decisions made during the 1930s. President Franklin Roosevelt did not want Social Security to be confused with poor relief. Therefore, he rejected the European model of government-funded pensions and instead created a system financed by payments from workers and their employers—a system based on individual accounts. This system, however, presented a short-term problem. If benefits came from their own contributions, workers who began receiving Social Security payments in 1940 would have received less than $1 a month. Therefore, Social Security payments from current workers paid the benefits of those already retired.

Over the years, this system of financing has become increasingly unstable, as an ever-larger pool of retirees has to be supported by those currently in the workforce. People are living longer. In 1935, when the system was created, average life expectancy was lower than sixty-five years, the age one could begin to collect benefits. Today, on average, American men live almost sixteen years past sixty-five, and women come close to twenty more years. In 1935, there were 16 current workers paying into the system for each person receiving retirement benefits. In 2010, there were 2.8 workers per retiree. The 77 million baby boomers born in the 1940s, 1950s, and 1960s are now retiring (though current retirees do not receive full Social Security benefits until age 66). Unless the system is reformed, many argue, the retirement of the baby-boom cohort could even bankrupt the system.

While the stock market was rising rapidly during the 1990s, some proposed that, because Social Security paid only a fraction of what individuals might have earned by investing their

Social Security tax payments in the stock market, Americans be allowed to do just that. Some opponents declared this proposal too risky; others simply pointed to the structure of Social Security retirement. If current workers kept their money to invest, where would benefits for current retirees come from? The stock market's huge drop in 2001 and then the long-lasting economic downturn that began in 2008 (and the losses sustained by private pension funds) slowed the push for privatization. Nonetheless, as baby boomers retire in growing numbers, questions about the future of Social Security remain an important part of the system's legacy.

CRITICAL THINKING

- What should be done to shore up Social Security?
- Is privatization the answer to the looming shortfalls in the Social Security System?
- Should the age of full benefits be raised?
- What other possible solutions are there?

---

of world lawlessness." People who thought Washington had been too gentle with Japan cheered. Isolationists warned that the president was edging toward war. On December 12, Japanese aircraft sank the American gunboat *Panay*, an escort for Standard Oil Company tankers on the Yangtze River. Two American sailors died during the attack. Roosevelt was much relieved when Tokyo apologized and offered to pay for damages.

Japan's declaration of a "New Order" in Asia, in the words of one American official, "banged, barred, and bolted" the Open Door. Alarmed, the Roosevelt administration during the late 1930s gave loans and sold military equipment to Jiang's Chinese government. Secretary Hull declared a moral embargo on the shipment of airplanes to Japan. Meanwhile, the U.S. Navy continued to grow, aided by a billion-dollar congressional appropriation in 1938. In mid-1939, the United States abrogated its trade treaty with Tokyo, yet Americans continued to ship oil, cotton, and machinery to Japan. The administration hesitated to initiate economic sanctions because such pressure might spark a Japanese-American war at a time when Germany posed a more serious threat and the

United States was unprepared for war. When war broke out in Europe in the late summer of 1939, Japanese-American relations were stalemated.

Summary

In the 1930s, a major economic crisis and the approach of another world war threatened the future of the nation. By 1933, almost one-quarter of America's workers were unemployed. Millions of people did not have enough to eat or adequate places to live. Herbert Hoover, elected president in 1928, believed that government should play only a limited role in managing the nation's economy and rejected both public jobs programs and aid to the poor. In the 1932 presidential election, voters turned to the candidate who promised them a "New Deal." President Franklin Delano Roosevelt acted decisively to stabilize America's capitalist system and then worked to ameliorate its harshest impacts on the nation's people.

The New Deal was a liberal reform program that developed within the parameters of America's capitalist and democratic system. The New Deal expanded the role and power of the federal government. Because of New Deal reforms, banks, utilities, stock markets, farms, and most businesses operated under rules set by the federal government. Federal law guaranteed workers' right to join unions without fear of employer reprisals and required employers to negotiate with workers' unions. New Deal programs offered public jobs to the unemployed and guaranteed many Americans the basic protection of a national welfare system.

The New Deal faced challenges from many directions. As the depression wore on, populist demagogues blamed scapegoats or offered overly simple explanations for the plight of the American people. Business leaders attacked the New Deal for its new regulation of business and its support of organized labor. As the federal government expanded its role throughout the nation, tensions between national and local authority sometimes flared up. Both the West and the South were transformed by federal government action, but citizens of both regions were suspicious of federal intervention, and white southerners strongly resisted any attempt to challenge systems of racial discrimination. The political realities of a fragile New Deal coalition and strong opposition shaped—and limited—New Deal programs of the 1930s and the social welfare systems with which Americans still live today.

New Deal programs helped many of America's people live better, more secure lives. And the New Deal fundamentally changed the way that the U.S. government would deal with future economic downturns and with the needs of its citizens in good times and in bad.

Yet the New Deal by itself did not end the Great Depression; it took World War II and the economic boom it created to make that happen. As the crises in Europe and Asia deepened in the last years of the 1930s, the Roosevelt administration sought to keep the United States out of the fray; even after Nazi forces invaded Poland in September 1939, thus sparking a new European struggle, the president declared American neutrality. As he did so, however, he sent aid to the Allies and began preparing the country for war.

Suggestions for Further Reading

Anthony J. Badger, *The New Deal: The Depression Years, 1933–1940* (1989)

Alan Brinkley, *The End of Reform: New Deal Liberalism in Recession and War* (1995)

Alan Brinkley, *Voices of Protest: Huey Long, Father Coughlin, and the Great Depression* (1982)

Lizabeth Cohen, *Making a New Deal: Industrial Workers in Chicago* (1990)

Blanche Wiesen Cook, *Eleanor Roosevelt*, Vols. 1 and 2 (1992, 1999)

Kirsten Downey, *The Woman Behind the New Deal: The Life and Legacy of Frances Perkins—Social Security, Unemployment Insurance* (2009)

Timothy Egan, *The Worst Hard Time* (2005)

Sidney Fine, *Sitdown: The General Motors Strike of 1936–37* (1969)

James E. Goodman, *Stories of Scottsboro* (1994)

Ira Katznelson, *Fear Itself: The New Deal and the Origins of Our Time* (2014)

David M. Kennedy, *Freedom from Fear: The American People in Depression and War* (1999)

Eric Rauchway, *The Great Depression and the New Deal: A Very Short Introduction* (2008)

Jason Scott Smith, *Building New Deal Liberalism: The Political Economy of Public Works, 1933–1956* (2005)

Donald Worster, *Dust Bowl: The Southern Plains in the 1930s* (2004)

MINDTAP
From Cengage

MindTap® is a fully online personalized learning experience built upon Cengage Learning content. MindTap® combines student learning tools—readings, multimedia, activities, and assessments—into a singular Learning Path that guides students through the course and helps students develop the critical thinking, analysis, and communication skills that are essential to academic and professional success.

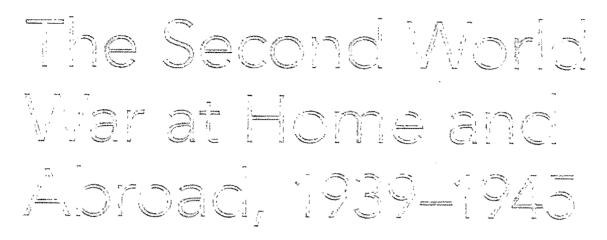

The Second World War at Home and Abroad, 1939–1945

The first wave of planes launched before dawn from Japanese aircraft carriers two hundred and thirty miles north of O'ahu; a second wave followed soon thereafter. At the island's north shore, one group circled leeward toward the battleships anchored at Pearl Harbor; a second swept down the center of the island between the Ko'olau and the Waianae mountain ranges. Most of the people outside that lovely Sunday morning paid them little mind; war games were so common in Hawai'i by that point that even seasoned military men were fooled. Watching planes diving on Pearl Harbor from the control tower at the adjacent army air base, Colonel William Farthing mused, "I wonder what the marines are doing to the navy so early on Sunday morning." Seconds later, as a Japanese bomber dived toward the air base, a rising sun emblazoned on its fuselage, one soldier pointed: "Look! There goes one of the red team." Then the plane dropped a bomb.

On the battleship *West Virginia*, Ship's Cook Third Class Doris Miller was collecting laundry when the general quarters alarm sounded. Miller, a 6'3", three-hundred-pound African American man whom the navy restricted to mess service because of his race, followed officers' orders to report to the bridge. Miller took over a .50-caliber Browning anti-aircraft gun—a weapon he'd never before fired—manning it until he ran out of ammunition and the order came to abandon the sinking ship. At Wheeler Field an army fighter pilot, Second Lieutenant Philip Rasmussen, commandeered an obsolete P-36 and took off to battle the Japanese, still wearing the purple pajamas in which he'd been sleeping. And in Honolulu, seventeen-year-old Daniel Inouye—the son of a Japanese immigrant who would win the Medal of Honor for heroism in the coming war and eventually serve as president pro tempore of the U.S. Senate—headed for the volunteer Red Cross station at Lunalilo School, where he worked for twenty-four hours without rest, treating the wounded and ferrying the dead to a makeshift morgue. Huddled in an air raid shelter, sixteen-year-old Mary Ann Ramsey saw the injured brought in "with filthy black oil covering shredded flesh." As casualties mounted, prostitutes turned

◁ The stricken USS *West Virginia* was one of eight battleships caught in the surprise Japanese attack at Pearl Harbor, Hawai'i, on December 7, 1941. In this photograph, sailors on a launch attempt to rescue a crew member from the water as oil burns around the sinking ship. National Archives

Chronology

1939   ▨ Germany invades Poland; World War II begins

1940   ▨ France and the Low Countries fall to the Germans

1941   ▨ Lend-Lease Act passed by Congress
        ▨ Atlantic Charter issued by Roosevelt and Churchill
        ▨ Japan attacks Pearl Harbor
        ▨ United States enters World War II

1942   ▨ War Production Board created to oversee conversion to military production
        ▨ Allies losing war in Pacific to Japan; U.S. victory at Battle of Midway in June is turning point
        ▨ Office of Price Administration creates rationing system for food and consumer goods
        ▨ United States pursues "Europe First" war policy; Allies reject Stalin's demands for a second front and invade North Africa
        ▨ West Coast Japanese Americans relocated to internment camps
        ▨ Manhattan Project set up to create atomic bomb
        ▨ Congress of Racial Equality established

1943   ▨ Soviet army defeats German troops at Stalingrad
        ▨ Congress passes War Labor Disputes (Smith-Connally) Act following coal miners' strike
        ▨ "Zoot suit riots" in Los Angeles; race riots break out in Detroit, Harlem, and other cities
        ▨ Allies invade Italy
        ▨ Roosevelt, Churchill, and Stalin meet at Tehran Conference

1944   ▨ Allied troops land at Normandy on D-Day, June 6
        ▨ Roosevelt elected to fourth term as president
        ▨ United States retakes Philippines

1945   ▨ Roosevelt, Stalin, and Churchill meet at Yalta Conference
        ▨ British and U.S. forces firebomb Dresden, Germany
        ▨ Battles of Iwo Jima and Okinawa result in heavy Japanese and American losses
        ▨ Roosevelt dies; Truman becomes president
        ▨ Germany surrenders; Allied forces liberate Nazi death camps
        ▨ Potsdam Conference calls for Japan's "unconditional surrender"
        ▨ United States uses atomic bombs on Hiroshima and Nagasaki
        ▨ Japan surrenders

the infamous brothels of Hotel Street into temporary hospital wards and nursed the badly wounded.

Japanese planes sank or severely damaged all eight of America's Pacific Fleet battleships. They destroyed or badly damaged 188 planes, most of them parked nose to tail on the island's airfields. More than 2,400 people died in the two-hour attack, 1,177 from the battleship *Arizona*, which sank within seconds after an armor-piercing bomb hit its forward ammunition compartment. That night the people of Hawai'i spent their first night under martial law, the islands completely dark against the threat of another attack. "Shortly before midnight," wrote one who sat in Honolulu's darkness that night, "the moon began to rise, and a vivid lunar rainbow, the old Hawaiian omen of victory, arched over the dark city."

By December 7, 1941, Europe and Asia were already in flames. Now the United States would join the world war.

Experience an interactive version of this story in MindTap®.

The Second World War marked a turning point in the lives of millions of Americans as well as in the history of the United States. Most deeply affected were those who fought the war, on the beaches and battlefields, in the skies and at sea. For forty-five months, Americans fought abroad to subdue the German, Italian, and Japanese aggressors. Although the war began badly for the United States, by mid-1942 the Allies had halted the Axis powers' advance. In June 1944, American troops, together with Canadian, British, and Free French units, launched a massive invasion across the English Channel, landing at Normandy and pushing into Germany by the following spring. Battered by merciless bombing raids, leaderless after Adolf Hitler's suicide, and pressed by a Soviet advance from the east, the Nazis capitulated in May 1945. In the Pacific, Americans drove Japanese forces back, island by island, toward Japan. America's devastating conventional bombing of Japanese cities, followed by the atomic bombs that demolished Hiroshima and Nagasaki in August 1945 and the Soviet Union's declaration of war on Japan, led to surrender. At the end of the war, prospects for international cooperation seemed bleak. The nations that made up the

"Grand Alliance"—Britain, the Soviet Union, and the United States—had very different visions of the postwar world.

The war was fought far from the United States, but it touched the lives of all Americans. This was a total war, in which the United States mobilized all sectors of American society and economy—industry, finance, agriculture, and labor; the civilian population and the military—to defeat the Axis powers. The federal government, which had the monumental task of managing the war on all fronts, expanded its reach and power.

Committed to becoming the "arsenal of democracy," the United States built a massive war industry that demanded workers for seven-days-a-week, twenty-four-hours-a-day production. These factories created new opportunities for formerly marginal workers: women, African Americans, Latinos. During the war, nearly one of every ten Americans moved permanently to another state, most headed for work in war production centers. After a decade of economic depression, Americans found new prosperity in the midst of global conflagration. The war strengthened unity and national purpose, but it also gave new shape to long-standing prejudices: the United States interned 112,000 Japanese nationals and Japanese Americans in remote "relocation camps" and fought the Axis with a racially segregated military. At war's end, although many Americans grieved for loved ones lost in battle and worried about the stability of the emerging postwar order, the United States had unprecedented power and unmatched prosperity among the world's nations.

▫ *What factors brought the United States into the war?*

▫ *What military, diplomatic, and social factors influenced decisions about how to fight the Second World War?*

▫ *How did World War II transform the United States?*

23-1 America's Entry into the Conflict

▷ **How did Franklin D. Roosevelt draw the United States closer to war?**

▷ **How did American attitudes about involvement in the war evolve after 1939?**

▷ **What was the nature of the relationship between Japan and the United States prior to the bombing of Pearl Harbor?**

When a new European war broke out in 1939, many Americans hoped their country could stand apart. But would it be possible? Roosevelt remarked that the United States could not "draw a line of defense around this country and live completely and solely to ourselves," noting that when Thomas Jefferson had tried that with his 1807 embargo, "the damned thing didn't work," and "we got into the War of 1812." America, the president insisted, could not insulate itself from world war. But even as polls showed that Americans strongly favored the Allies and that most supported aid to Britain and France, the great majority also wanted the United States to remain at peace. Troubled by this conflicting advice—oppose Hitler, aid the Allies, but stay out of the war—the president gradually moved the nation from neutrality to undeclared war against Germany and then, after Japan attacked Pearl Harbor, to full-scale war itself.

From 1939 through 1941, Americans vigorously debated their nation's proper role in the growing war. Groups such as the American Legion, the League of Women Voters, labor unions, and local chapters of the Committee to Defend America by Aiding the Allies and the isolationist America First Committee (both organized in 1940) participated vigorously in the national debate. Most Americans understood the high stakes of U.S. foreign policy, but public interest also was fed by the chilling immediacy of radio news reports. Americans' ethnic affiliations with belligerents and victims of aggression also mattered. African American churches organized anti-Italian boycotts to protest Mussolini's pummeling of Ethiopia, and the German American Bund drew German Americans—in relatively small numbers—to rallies supporting the Nazi cause.

23-1a The Expanding Conflict

As Americans debated, the stakes grew higher. In March 1940, the Soviet Union—which had signed a non-aggression pact with Hitler shortly before Germany invaded Poland in 1939—invaded Finland. In April, Germany conquered Denmark and Norway (see Map 22.5). "The small countries are smashed up, one by one, like matchwood," sighed **Winston Churchill**, who became Britain's prime minister on May 10, 1940—the same day that Germany attacked Belgium, the Netherlands, and France. German divisions pushed French and British forces back to the English Channel, and between May 26 and June 6, more than 300,000 Allied soldiers escaped from Dunkirk to Britain on a flotilla of small boats. The Germans occupied Paris a week later. The French government plunged into disunion and chaos, from which emerged a new regime located in the town of Vichy, France, concluded an armistice with Germany on June 22 and collaborated with the conquering Nazis for the remainder of the war. With France out of the picture, the German Luftwaffe

Winston Churchill British wartime prime minister; close friend of FDR and staunch ally of the United States; served 1940–1945 and 1951–1955.

(air force) launched massive bombing raids against Great Britain in preparation for a full-scale invasion.

Alarmed by the swift defeat of one European nation after another, Americans increasingly questioned isolationist principles. Some liberals left the isolationist fold; it became more and more the province of conservatives. Emotions ran high. Roosevelt called the isolationists "ostriches" and charged that some were pro-Nazi subversives. More significantly, the president worked to prevent the fall of Britain. In May 1940, he ordered the sale of old surplus military equipment to Britain and France. In July, he cultivated bipartisan support by naming Republicans Henry L. Stimson and Frank Knox, ardent backers of aid to the Allies, secretaries of war and the navy, respectively. In September, by executive agreement, the president traded fifty over-age American destroyers for leases to eight British military bases, including Newfoundland, Bermuda, and Jamaica.

Recognizing America's move toward war, Germany, Italy, and Japan signed the Tripartite Pact in late September, 1940. The pact formalized existing alliances among the three nations, formally creating the Axis Powers. It officially recognized two separate spheres of influence, with Japan controlling Greater East Asia and—significantly—made clear that if the United States joined the war it would face enemies in both Europe and the Pacific.

23-1b Supporting the Allies

Also in September, Roosevelt signed into law the hotly debated and narrowly passed **Selective Training and Service Act of 1940**, the first peacetime military draft in American history. All men between the ages of twenty-one and thirty-five were required to register, and President Roosevelt himself read out the first number drawn in the national draft lottery. Meanwhile, Roosevelt won reelection in November 1940 with promises of peace: "Your boys are not going to be sent into any foreign wars." Republican candidate Wendell Willkie, who in the emerging spirit of bipartisanship had not made an issue of foreign policy, snapped, "That hypocritical son of a bitch! This is going to beat me!" And it did.

Roosevelt portrayed America's role as "the arsenal of democracy," and claimed that the United States could stay out of the war by enabling the British to win. To that end, he proposed a "Lend-Lease" bill. Because Britain was broke, the president explained, the United States should lend rather than sell weapons, much as a neighbor lends a garden hose to fight a fire. Most lawmakers needed little persuasion. In March 1941, with pro-British sentiment running high, Congress passed the **Lend-Lease Act** with overwhelming support. The initial appropriation was $7 billion, but by the end of the war the amount had reached $50 billion, more than $31 billion of it for Britain.

To make sure Lend-Lease supplies were delivered safely, Roosevelt ordered the U.S. Navy to patrol halfway across the Atlantic and stationed U.S. troops in Greenland and Iceland. He also sent Lend-Lease aid to the Soviet Union, which Hitler had attacked in June (thereby shattering the 1939 Nazi-Soviet nonaggression pact). If the Soviets could hold off two hundred German divisions in the east, Roosevelt calculated, Britain would gain some breathing room. Churchill, with dark humor, responded: "If Hitler invaded Hell, I would make at least a favorable reference to the Devil in the House of Commons."

23-1c Atlantic Charter

In August 1941, Churchill and Roosevelt met for four days on a British battleship off the coast of Newfoundland. They got along well, trading naval stories and making much of the fact that Churchill was half American (his mother was from New York). This meeting produced the **Atlantic Charter**, a set of war aims reminiscent of Wilsonianism: collective security, disarmament, self-determination, economic cooperation, and freedom of the seas. Churchill later recalled that Roosevelt told him in Newfoundland that he could not ask Congress for a declaration of war against Germany, but "he would wage war" and "become more and more provocative."

Within days of that meeting, German and American ships came into direct contact in the Atlantic. On September 4, a German submarine launched torpedoes at (but did not hit) the American destroyer *Greer*. In response, Roosevelt gave the U.S. Navy authority to fire first when under threat. He also publicly announced what he had promised Churchill in private: American warships would convoy British merchant ships across the ocean. The United States thus entered into an undeclared naval war with Germany. When a German submarine torpedoed the U.S. destroyer *Kearny* off the coast of Iceland a month later, Roosevelt declared that "the shooting has started. And history has recorded who fired the first shot." Later in October, when the destroyer *Reuben James* went down with the loss of more than one hundred American lives, Congress revised the Neutrality Acts (see "Isolationist Views in the United States," Section 22-b) to allow armed American merchant ships to carry weapons to Britain. The United States was edging very close to being a belligerent.

23-1d The Growing Crisis with Japan

It seems ironic, therefore, that the Second World War came to the United States by way of Asia. Roosevelt had wanted

---

Selective Training and Service Act of 1940 Controversial 1940 law that required all men between twenty-one and thirty-five (later expanded to eighteen through forty-five) to register with local draft boards; began the first peacetime military draft in U.S. history.

Lend-Lease Act Program proposed by Roosevelt and enacted by Congress in early 1941 to supply war material to cash-strapped Britain.

Atlantic Charter 1941 agreement between the United States and Great Britain that stated the two countries' war aims; it condemned international aggression, affirmed the right of national self-determination, and endorsed the principles of free trade, disarmament, and collective security.

to avoid war with Japan in order to concentrate American resources on the defeat of Germany. In September 1940, after Germany, Italy, and Japan had signed the Tripartite Pact to form the Axis powers, Roosevelt halted shipments of aviation fuel and scrap metal to Japan. Because the president believed the Japanese would consider a cutoff of oil a life-or-death matter, he did not embargo that vital commodity. But in July 1941 Japanese troops occupied French Indochina, seeking to cut off Western shipments of oil and other supplies to China, with whom Japan was at war, while also positioning Japanese troops to seize much of southeast Asia. In response, Washington froze Japanese assets in the United States, virtually ending trade (including oil) with Japan.

Tokyo proposed a summit meeting between President Roosevelt and Prime Minister Prince Konoye, but the United States rejected the idea. American officials insisted that the Japanese first agree to respect China's sovereignty and territorial integrity and to honor the Open Door policy—in short, to get out of China. For Roosevelt, Europe still claimed first priority, but he supported Secretary Hull's hard-line policy against Japan's pursuit of the Greater East Asia Co-Prosperity Sphere—the name Tokyo gave to the vast Asian region it intended to dominate. Fundamentally, the United States was unwilling to cede control of East Asia to Japan, and Japan understood that U.S. terms required it to abandon its growing empire and claims to power in the region, remaining subject to U.S. economic power.

◁ Men doing exercises as they become part of America's first peacetime military draft in 1940.

Ralph Morse/Getty Images

Roosevelt told his advisers to string out ongoing Japanese-American talks as a way to gain time—time to fortify the Philippines and to deal with the crisis in Europe. But because the United States had broken Japan's diplomatic code through Operation MAGIC, officials knew that Tokyo's patience with diplomacy was waning rapidly. In late November, the Japanese rejected American demands to withdraw from Indochina. On December 6, the United States intercepted a 14-part message to the Japanese embassy in Washington, D.C., along with instructions to destroy their cipher machines once it was received. American officials understood the significance of such instructions and, once the document was fully decrypted, sent warnings to American military installations in the Pacific. However, due to some questionable decisions about how to transmit the material, coupled with technical difficulties, the warnings arrived too late.

23-1e Japan's Surprise Attack

Japan had planned a daring raid on U.S. and British territory in the Pacific, one that required coordinating forces for near-simultaneous attacks on sites stretching over nearly seven thousand miles of the Pacific Ocean. In order to hit the most distant site—the U.S. Territory of Hawai'i—an armada of sixty Japanese ships, with a core of six carriers bearing 360 airplanes, had crossed three thousand miles of the Pacific Ocean in total radio silence. Early in the morning of December 7, some 230 miles north of Honolulu, the carriers unleashed their planes, each stamped with a red sun representing the Japanese flag. They swept down on the unsuspecting American naval base and nearby airfields, dropping torpedoes and bombs and strafing buildings.

In Pearl Harbor, the battleship USS *Arizona* fell victim to a Japanese bomb that ignited explosives below deck, killing more than a thousand sailors. The USS *Nevada* tried to escape the inferno by heading out to sea, but when a second wave of aerial attackers struck the ship the crew ran her aground to avoid blocking the harbor channel. Japanese forces sank or damaged eight battleships and many smaller vessels and destroyed more than 160 aircraft on the ground. By chance, all three of the Pacific Fleet's aircraft carriers were at sea and escaped the bombing.

The attack on Pearl Harbor would become a rallying cry for Americans at war, but on that same day (it was December 8 on the other side of the International Date Line), Japan also attacked the neutral nation of Thailand, as well as Malaya, Shanghai, Singapore, Guam, the Philippines, Hong Kong, Wake Island, and Midway—all of which were Pacific possessions of Western powers. Pearl Harbor was one piece of Japan's broader strategy.

Some critics at the time—and later—charged that Roosevelt had conspired to leave the fleet vulnerable to attack so that the United States could enter the Second World War through the "back door" of Asia. However, historians agree that no evidence supports that claim. American officials did believe, based on decrypted diplomatic cables,

that war was likely on the horizon. But they knew nothing more. The decrypted messages never discussed the coming attacks, and most military commanders in Hawai'i were confident—wrongly—that distance offered protection from Japanese attack.

23-1f Declaration of War

On December 8, referring to the previous day as "a date which will live in infamy," Roosevelt vowed that Americans would never forget "the character of the onslaught against us" and asked Congress to declare war against Japan. A unanimous vote in the Senate and a 388-to-1 vote in the House thrust America into war. Representative Jeannette Rankin of Montana voted no, repeating her vote against entry into the First World War. Britain declared war on Japan, but the Soviet Union did not. Three days later, Germany and Italy, honoring the Tripartite Pact they had signed with Japan in September 1940, declared war against the United States. "Hitler's fate was sealed," Churchill later wrote. "Mussolini's fate was sealed. As for the Japanese, they would be ground to powder. . . . I went to bed and slept the sleep of the saved and thankful."

23-2 The United States at War

▷ Why was the United States unprepared for the military conflict of World War II?

▷ How did the war develop in the Pacific after U.S. entry into World War II?

▷ How did the war in Europe develop after U.S. entry into World War II?

As Japanese bombs fell in the U.S. territory of Hawai'i, American antiwar sentiment evaporated. Some former critics of intervention, seeking a persuasive explanation, turned to the popular children's story *Ferdinand the Bull*. Ferdinand, though huge and powerful, just liked to "sit and smell the flowers"—until the day he was stung by a bee. It was a comforting tale about America's role, but it wasn't true. As the world went to war, the United States had not been, like Ferdinand, just "smell[ing] the flowers." America's embargo of shipments to Japan and refusal to accept Japan's expansionist policies had brought the two nations to the brink of war, and the United States was deeply involved in an undeclared naval war with Germany well before Japan's attack on Pearl Harbor. By December 1941, Roosevelt had long since instituted an unprecedented peacetime draft, created war mobilization agencies, and commissioned war plans for simultaneous struggle in Europe and the Pacific.

23-2a A Nation Unprepared

Nonetheless, the nation was not ready for war. Throughout the 1930s, military funding had been a low priority. In September 1939 (when Hitler invaded Poland and began what would become the Second World War), the U.S. Army ranked forty-fifth in size among the world's armies and could fully equip only one-third of its 227,000 men. The peacetime draft instituted in 1940 expanded the U.S. military to 2 million men, but Roosevelt's 1941 survey of war preparedness, the "Victory Plan," estimated that the United States could not be ready to fight before June 1943.

In December 1941, many analysts thought U.S. victory unlikely. In Europe, the Allies were losing the war (see Map 22.5). Hitler had claimed Austria, Czechoslovakia, Poland, the Netherlands, Denmark, and Norway. Romania was lost, then Greece and Bulgaria. France had fallen in June 1940. Britain fought on, but German planes rained bombs on London. More than 3 million soldiers under German command had penetrated deep into the Soviet Union and Africa. German U-boats controlled the Atlantic from the Arctic to the Caribbean. Within months of America's entry into the war, German submarines sank 216 vessels—some so close to American shores that people could see the glow of burning ships.

23-2b War in the Pacific

In the Pacific, the war was largely America's to fight. The Soviets had not declared war on Japan, and there were too few British troops protecting Great Britain's Asian colonies to make much difference. By late spring of 1942, Japan had captured most European colonial possessions in Southeast Asia: the Dutch East Indies (Indonesia); French Indochina (Vietnam, Laos, and Cambodia); and the British colonies of Malaya, Burma, Western New Guinea, Hong Kong, and Singapore. In the American Philippines, the struggle went on longer, but also in vain. The Japanese attacked the Philippines hours after Pearl Harbor and, finding the entire force of B-17 bombers sitting on the airfields, destroyed U.S. air capability in the region. American and Filipino troops retreated to the Bataan Peninsula, hoping to hold the main island, Luzon, but Japanese forces were superior. In March 1942, under orders from Roosevelt, General Douglas MacArthur, the commander of U.S. forces in the Far East, departed the Philippines for Australia, proclaiming, "I shall return."

Left behind were almost eighty thousand American and Filipino troops. Starving and weakened by disease, they held on for almost another month before surrendering. Those who survived long enough to surrender faced worse horror. Japanese troops, lacking supplies themselves, were not prepared to deal with a large number of prisoners, and most believed the prisoners had forfeited honorable treatment by surrendering. In what came to be known as the Bataan Death March, the Japanese force-marched their captives to prison camps more than 65 miles away, denying them food and water and bayoneting or beating to death those who fell behind. As many as ten thousand Filipinos and six hundred Americans died on the march. Tens of thousands of Filipino civilians also died under Japanese occupation.

As losses mounted, the United States began to strike back. On April 18, sixteen American B-25 bombers appeared in the skies over Japan. The Doolittle raid (named after the mission's leader) did little harm to Japan, but it had an enormous psychological impact, pushing Japanese commander Admiral Isoroku Yamamoto to bold action. Instead of consolidating control close to home, Yamamoto concluded, Japan must move quickly to lure the weakened United States into a "decisive battle." The target was Midway—two tiny islands about one thousand miles northwest of Honolulu, where the U.S. Navy had a base. If Japan could take Midway—not implausible, given Japan's string of victories—it would have a secure defensive perimeter far from the home islands (see Map 23.3). By using Guam, the Philippines, and perhaps even Australia as hostages, Japan believed, it could negotiate a favorable peace agreement with the United States.

Admiral Yamamoto did not know that America's MAGIC code-breaking machines could decipher Japanese messages. This time, surprise was on the side of the United States, and the Japanese fleet found the U.S. Navy and its carrier-based dive-bombers lying in wait. The Battle of Midway in June 1942 was a turning point in the Pacific war. Japanese strategists had hoped that the United States, discouraged by

LET'S GO GET 'EM!

U.S. MARINES

△ "Let's Go Get 'Em!," proclaims this 1942 recruiting poster for the United States Marine Corps. Over the course of the war, 6 percent of servicemen overall were killed or wounded; the casualty ratio for Marines was 13 percent.

Japan's early victories, would withdraw and leave Japan to control the Pacific. That outcome was no longer a possibility. Now Japan was on the defensive.

23-2c "Europe First" Strategy

Despite the importance of these early Pacific battles, America's war strategy was "Europe First." Germany, American war planners recognized, was a greater danger to the United States than Japan. If Germany conquered the Soviet Union, they believed, it might directly threaten the United States. Roosevelt also feared that the Soviet Union, suffering almost unimaginable losses as its military battled Hitler's invading army, might pursue a separate peace with Germany and so undo the Allied coalition. Therefore, the United States would work first with Britain and the USSR to defeat Germany, then deal with an isolated Japan.

British prime minister Winston Churchill and Soviet premier **Joseph Stalin** disagreed vehemently, however, over how to wage the war against Germany. By late 1941, before the fierce Russian winter stalled their onslaught, German troops had nearly reached Moscow and Leningrad (present-day St. Petersburg) and had slashed deeply into Ukraine, taking Kiev. Over a million Soviet soldiers had died defending their country. Stalin pressed for British and American troops to attack Germany from the west, through France, to draw German troops away from the Soviet front. Roosevelt believed "with heart and *mind*" that Stalin was right and promised to open a "second front" to Germany's west before the end of 1942. Churchill, however, blocked this plan. He had not forgotten Stalin's nonaggression pact with Hitler (see "Roosevelt's Evolving Views," Section 22-7c), and British military commanders, remembering the agonies of prolonged trench warfare in World War I, did not want to launch a large-scale invasion of Europe. Churchill promoted air attacks on Germany. He wanted to win control of the North Atlantic shipping lanes and to launch a smaller, safer attack on Axis positions in North Africa; halting the Germans there would protect British imperial possessions in the Mediterranean and the oil-rich Middle East.

Against his advisers' recommendation, Roosevelt accepted Churchill's plan. The U.S. military was not yet ready for a major campaign and Roosevelt needed to show the American public some success in the European war. Thus, instead of coming to the rescue of the USSR, the British and Americans made a joint landing in North Africa in November 1942. American troops, facing relatively light resistance, won quick victories in Algeria and Morocco. In Egypt, the British confronted General Erwin

Joseph Stalin Soviet premier and dictator of the Soviet Union who came to power after the death of Vladimir Lenin in 1924 and ruled until his death in 1953.

War Production Board U.S. government agency that allocated resources, coordinated production among thousands of independent factories, and awarded government contracts for wartime production during World War II.

Rommel and his Afrika Korps in a struggle for control of the Suez Canal and the Middle East oil fields. Rommel's army, trapped between British and American troops, was forced to retreat into northern Tunisia and surrendered after six months. And in Russia, against all odds, the Soviet army hung on, fighting block by block for control of the city of Stalingrad in the deadly cold, to defeat the German Sixth Army in early 1943. Stalingrad, like Midway, was a major turning point in the war. By the spring of 1943, Germany, like Japan, was on the defensive. But relations among the Allies remained precarious. The Soviet Union had lost 1.1 million men in the Battle of Stalingrad. The United States and Britain, however, continued to resist Stalin's demand that they immediately open a second front. The death toll, already in the millions, continued to mount.

23-3 The Production Front and American Workers

▷ **How did the American economy shift to production for the war?**

▷ **What role did the government play in wartime production and labor?**

▷ **What was the nature of wartime labor relations between workers and employers?**

In late December 1940—almost a year before the United States entered the war—Franklin Roosevelt pledged that America would serve as the world's "great arsenal of democracy," making the machines that would win the war for the Allies. After Pearl Harbor, U.S. strategy remained much the same. The United States would prevail through a "crushing superiority of equipment," Roosevelt told Congress. Although the war would be fought on the battlefields of Europe and the Pacific, the nation's strategic advantage lay on the "production front" at home.

Goals for military production were staggering. In 1940, with war looming, American factories had built only 3,807 airplanes. Following Pearl Harbor, Roosevelt asked for 60,000 aircraft in 1942 and double that number in 1943. Plans called for building 16 million tons of shipping and 120,000 tanks. The military needed supplies to train and equip a force that would grow to almost 16 million men. Thus, for the duration of the war, military production took precedence. Turning from consumer desires to military needs, jukebox manufacturer Rock-Ola produced M1 carbines and Eureka Vacuum made gas masks, while automobile plants manufactured tanks and dress factories sewed military uniforms. The **War Production Board**, established in early 1942, had the enormous task of allocating resources and coordinating production among thousands of independent factories.

23-3a Businesses, Universities, and the War Effort

During the war, American businesses overwhelmingly cooperated with government war-production plans. Patriotism was one reason, but generous incentives were another. Major American industries had at first resisted government pressure to shift to military production. In 1940, as the United States produced armaments for the Allies, the American economy had begun to recover from the Great Depression. Consumer spending increased, and industrialists gained confidence: automobile manufacturers, for example, expected to sell 25 percent more cars in 1941 than in 1939. Manufacturers understood that it would be enormously expensive to retool factories to produce planes or tanks instead of cars, and that such retooling would leave them totally dependent on a single client—the federal government. Many major industrialists, such as General Motors head Alfred Sloan, were suspicious of Roosevelt and what they saw as his antibusiness policies.

Government, however, met business more than halfway. The federal government paid for expensive retooling and factory expansions; it guaranteed profits by allowing corporations to charge the government for production costs plus a fixed profit; it created generous tax write-offs and exemptions from antitrust laws. War mobilization did not require America's businesses to sacrifice profits. Instead, corporations doubled their net profits between 1939 and 1943. As Secretary of War Henry Stimson explained, when a "capitalist country" goes to war, it must "let business make money out of the process or business won't work."

Most military contracts went to America's largest corporations, which had the facilities and experience to guarantee rapid, efficient production. From mid-1940 through September 1944, the government awarded contracts totaling $175 billion, with about two-thirds going to the top hundred corporations. General Motors alone received 8 percent of the total. This approach made sense for a nation that wanted enormous quantities of war goods manufactured in the shortest possible time; most small businesses simply did not have the necessary capacity. However, wartime government contracts further consolidated American manufacturing in the hands of a few giant corporations.

23-3b Manhattan Project

Wartime needs also created a new relationship between science and the U.S. military. Millions of dollars went to fund research programs at America's largest universities: $117 million to Massachusetts Institute of Technology alone. Such federally sponsored research programs developed new technologies of warfare, such as vastly improved radar systems and the proximity fuse. The most important government-sponsored scientific research program was the **Manhattan Project**, a $2 billion secret effort to build an atomic bomb. Roosevelt had been convinced by scientists fleeing the Nazis in 1939 that Germany was working to create an atomic weapon, and he resolved to beat them at their own efforts. But secrecy was paramount. The handful of key Congressional leaders who knew about the project hid its funding in the budget of the U.S. Army; almost all of Congress, and even FDR's vice president, remained in the dark.

The Manhattan Project achieved the world's first sustained nuclear chain reaction in 1942 at the University of Chicago, and in 1943 the federal government set up a secret community for atomic scientists and their families at Los Alamos, New Mexico. In this remote, sparsely populated, and beautiful setting, some of America's most talented scientists worked with Jewish refugees from Nazi Germany to develop the weapon that would change the world.

23-3c New Opportunities for Workers

America's new defense factories, running around the clock, required millions of workers. At first, workers were plentiful: 9 million Americans were still unemployed in 1940 when war mobilization began, and 3 million remained without work in December 1941. But during the war, the armed forces took almost 16 million men out of the potential civilian labor pool, forcing industry to look elsewhere for workers. Women, African Americans, Mexican Americans, poor whites from the isolated mountain hollows of Appalachia and the tenant farms of the Deep South—all streamed into jobs in defense plants.

In some cases, federal action eased their path. In 1941, as the federal government poured billions of dollars into war industries, many industries refused to hire African Americans. "The Negro will be considered only as janitors and other similar capacities," one executive notified black applicants. **A. Philip Randolph**, head of the Brotherhood of Sleeping Car Porters, proposed a march on Washington, D.C., to demand equal access to defense industry jobs. Roosevelt, fearing that the march might provoke race riots and that communists might infiltrate the movement, offered the March on Washington movement a deal. In exchange for canceling the march, the president issued Executive Order No. 8802, which prohibited discrimination in the defense industry and established the Fair Employment Practices Committee (FEPC) to deal with violations. Although enforcement was uneven, this official act led hundreds of thousands of black Americans to leave the South, seeking work and new lives in the industrial cities of the North and West.

Mexican workers also filled wartime jobs in the United States. Although the U.S. government had deported Mexicans as unemployment rose during the Great Depression, about 200,000 Mexican workers, or *braceros*, were offered short-term contracts to fill agricultural jobs left vacant as Americans sought well-paid war work. Mexican and Mexican American workers alike faced discrimination and segregation, but they seized the economic opportunities newly available to them. In 1941, the Los Angeles shipyards employed not a single Mexican American; by 1944, 17,000 worked there.

Manhattan Project Secret U.S. government-sponsored research program to develop an atomic bomb during World War II.

A. Philip Randolph Labor leader whose threatened march on Washington led President Roosevelt to issue Executive Order No. 8802, which prohibited racial discrimination in war industries and government jobs.

braceros Seasonal farm laborers from Mexico who were offered short-term contracts under a wartime "temporary worker" measure.

◁ War production plans called for defense factories to build 120,000 new aircraft in 1943. Here, women workers take on "men's jobs" at Vultee Aircraft Corporation, using riveting guns and bucking bars to build the center section of wings for training planes.

Bettmann/Getty Images

Early in the war production boom, employers insisted that women were not suited for industrial jobs. But as labor shortages began to threaten the war effort, employers did an about-face. The government's War Manpower Commission glorified the invented worker "**Rosie the Riveter**," who was featured on posters, in magazines, and in the recruiting jingle "Rosie's got a boyfriend, Charlie / Charlie, he's a marine / Rosie is protecting Charlie / Working overtime on the riveting machine."

Rosie the Riveter was an inspiring image, but she did not represent most women workers. Only 16 percent of female employees worked in defense plants, and women filled only 4.4 percent of "skilled" jobs (such as riveting). Nonetheless, the number of women in the workforce grew by 57 percent, as more than 6 million women took wartime jobs, while other women—including over 400,000 African American domestic workers—moved to higher-paying industrial jobs, often with union benefits.

Workers in defense plants were often expected to work ten days for every day off or to accept difficult night shifts. In an effort to keep employees on the job, both businesses and the federal government offered new forms of support. The West Coast Kaiser shipyards paid very well, but also provided child care, subsidized housing, and health care: the Kaiser Permanente Medical Care Program, a forerunner of today's health maintenance organization (HMO), cost workers a weekly payroll deduction of 50 cents. The federal government also funded child care centers and before- and after-school programs.

Rosie the Riveter Symbol of the woman war worker; the bulging muscles represented her strength as she aided the nation's war effort by taking jobs vacated by men who fought in the war.

23-3d Organized Labor During Wartime

Because America's war strategy relied on industrial production, the federal government tried to prevent the labor strikes that had been so common in the 1930s. Just days after Pearl Harbor, a White House labor-management conference agreed to a no-strike/no-lockout pledge, and in 1942, Roosevelt created the National War Labor Board (NWLB) to settle labor disputes. The NWLB forged a temporary compromise between labor union demands for a "closed shop," in which only union members could work, and management's desire for "open" shops: workers could not be required to join a union, but unions could enroll as many members as possible. Between 1940 and 1945, union membership ballooned from 8.5 million to 14.75 million.

However, the government did not hesitate to restrict union power if it threatened war production. When coal miners in the United Mine Workers union went on strike in 1943 after the NWLB attempted to limit wage increases to a cost-of-living adjustment, railroads and steel mills shut down for lack of coal. Few Americans supported this strike. One air force pilot claimed he'd "just as soon shoot down one of those strikers as shoot down Japs—they're doing as much to lose the war for us." As antilabor sentiment grew, Congress passed the War Labor Disputes (Smith-Connally) Act. This act gave the president authority to seize and operate any strike-bound plant deemed necessary to the national security. It also created criminal penalties for leading strikes and tried to constrain union power by prohibiting unions from contributing to political campaigns during time of war.

23-3e Success on the Production Front

For close to four years, American factories operated twenty-four hours a day, seven days a week, fighting the war on the production front. By war's end, the United States was producing 40 percent of the world's weaponry. Between 1940 and 1945, American factories turned out roughly 300,000 airplanes, 102,000 armored vehicles, 77,000 ships, 20 million small arms, 40 billion bullets, and 6 million tons of bombs. To reach such numbers, American factories had transformed skilled work in industries such as shipbuilding into an assembly-line process of mass production. Henry Ford, now seventy-eight years old, created a massive bomber plant on farmland along Willow Run Creek not far from Detroit. Willow Run's assembly lines, almost a mile long, turned out B-24 Liberator bombers at the rate of one an hour. On the West Coast, William Kaiser used mass-production techniques to cut construction time for Liberty ships—the huge, 440-foot-long cargo ships that transported the tanks and guns and bullets overseas—from 355 to 56 days. (As a publicity stunt, Kaiser's Richmond shipyard, near San Francisco, built one Liberty ship in 4 days, 15 hours, and 26 minutes.) The ships were not well made; their welded hulls sometimes split in rough seas, and one ship even foundered while still docked at the pier. However, as the United States struggled to produce cargo ships faster than German U-boats could sink them, speed of production counted for more than quality.

A visitor to the Willow Run plant described "the roar of the machinery, the special din of the riveting gun absolutely deafening nearby, the throbbing crash of the giant metal presses ... the far-reaching line of half-born skyships growing wings under swarms of workers." His words reveal the might of American industry but also offer a glimpse of the experience of workers, who did dirty, repetitive, and physically exhausting work day after day "for the duration." Although American propaganda during the war badly overreached when comparing the contributions of well-paid war workers to those of men in combat, 102,000 men and women were killed doing war production work during the first two years of the war and more than 350,000 were seriously injured.

23-4 Life on the Home Front

▷ **How did Americans feel the presence of the war in their lives on the home front?**

▷ **What racial and ethnic tensions emerged in the United States during the war?**

▷ **How did the war destabilize families?**

The United States, protected by two oceans from its enemies, was spared the war that other nations experienced (Hawai'i was a U.S. territory and the Philippines a U.S. possession, but neither was part of the nation proper). Americans worried about loved ones fighting in distant places; they grieved the loss of sons and brothers and fathers and husbands and friends. Their lives were often profoundly disrupted. But bombs did not fall on American cities; invading armies did not burn and rape and kill. Instead, war mobilization brought prosperity in the midst of global conflagration.

23-4a Supporting the War Effort

The fighting was distant, but the war was a constant presence in the lives of Americans on "the home front." Although Americans were never so unified as the widespread images of "the greatest generation" suggest, civilians supported the war effort in many ways, and "shared sacrifice" was a powerful ideal and significant reality. During the war, families planted 20 million "victory gardens" to replace food that went to America's fighting men. Housewives saved fat from cooking and returned it to butchers, for cooking fat yielded glycerin to make the gunpowder used in shells or bullets. Children collected scrap metal, aware that the iron in one old shovel blade was enough for four hand grenades and that every tin can helped make a tank or Liberty ship.

Many consumer goods were rationed or unavailable. To save wool for military use, the War Production Board directed that men's suits would have narrow lapels, shorter jackets, and no vests or pant cuffs. Bathing suits, the WPB specified, must shrink by 10 percent. When silk and nylon were diverted from stockings to parachutes, women used makeup on their legs and drew in the "stocking" seam with eyebrow pencil. The Office of Price Administration (OPA), created by Congress in 1942, established a nationwide rationing system for sugar, coffee, gasoline, and other consumer goods. By early 1943, the OPA had instituted a point system for rationing food, and feeding a family required complex calculations. Each citizen—regardless of age—was allotted forty-eight blue points (canned fruits and vegetables) and sixty-four red points (meat, fish, and dairy) a month. In September 1944 a small bottle of ketchup "cost" twenty blue points and sirloin steak thirteen red points a pound (in addition to their cost in dollars and cents), while pork shoulder required only dollars. Sugar was tightly rationed, and people saved for months to make a birthday cake or holiday dessert. Rationed goods were available on the black market, but most Americans understood that sugar produced alcohol for weapons manufacture and meat went to feed "our boys" overseas.

23-4b Propaganda and Popular Culture

Although Americans strongly supported the war, government leaders worried that they would gradually become less willing to sacrifice. The Office of War Information (OWI), created in 1942, used Hollywood filmmakers and New York copywriters to sell the war at home. OWI posters exhorted Americans to save and sacrifice, and reminded them to watch what they said, for "loose lips sink ships."

Popular culture also reinforced wartime messages. Songs urged Americans to "Remember December 7th" or to "Accentuate the Positive." Others made fun of America's enemies ("You're a sap, Mr. Jap / You make a Yankee cranky / You're a sap, Mr. Jap / Uncle Sam is gonna spanky") or, like "Cleanin' My Rifle (and Dreamin' of You)," dealt with the hardship of wartime separation.

Movies drew 90 million viewers a week in 1944—out of a total population of 132 million. During the war "Draftee Duck" joined the army, chickens produced for the war effort at "Flockheed," and audiences sang along with an animated version of the song "Der Fuehrer's Face" ("When der fuehrer says we is de master race/We heil (pffft) heil (pffft) right in der fuehrer's face") in pre-film cartoons. For the most part, Hollywood tried to meet Eleanor Roosevelt's challenge to "Keep 'em laughing," though some films, such as *Bataan* or *Wake Island*, portrayed actual—if sanitized—events in the war. But even at the most frivolous comedies, the war was present. Theaters held "plasma premieres" with free admission to those who donated a half-pint of blood to the Red Cross. Before the film began, audiences sang "The Star-Spangled Banner" and watched newsreels with carefully censored footage of recent combat. On D-Day, June 6, 1944, as Allied troops landed at Normandy, theater managers across the nation led audiences in the Lord's Prayer or the Twenty-third Psalm ("The Lord is my shepherd . . ."). It was in movie theaters that Americans saw the horror of Nazi death camps in May 1945. The Universal newsreel narrator ordered audiences, "Don't turn away. Look."

23-4c Wartime Prosperity

The war disrupted the lives of all Americans and demanded profound sacrifice from some. But it also offered many Americans new prosperity. Per capita income rose from $691 in 1939 to $1,515 at war's end. OPA-administered price controls kept inflation down so that wage increases did not disappear to higher costs. And with little to buy, people saved money.

Fighting World War II cost the United States approximately $304 billion (more than $3 trillion in today's dollars). The national debt skyrocketed from $49 billion in 1941 to $259 billion in 1945 (and was not paid off until 1970). The government did not just defer those costs to later generations. It sold war bonds—thus borrowing money from those who bought them. And wartime legislation increased the number of Americans paying personal income tax from 4 million to 42.6 million—at rates ranging from 6 to 94 percent—and introduced a new system in which employers "withheld" taxes from employee paychecks. For the first time, individual Americans paid more in taxes than corporations.

23-4d A Nation in Motion

Despite hardships and fears, the war offered home-front Americans new opportunities, and millions of Americans took them. More than 15 million civilians moved during the war (see Map 23.1). More than half moved to another state, and half that number moved to another region. Seven hundred thousand black Americans left the South during the war years; in 1943, ten thousand black migrants poured into Los Angeles

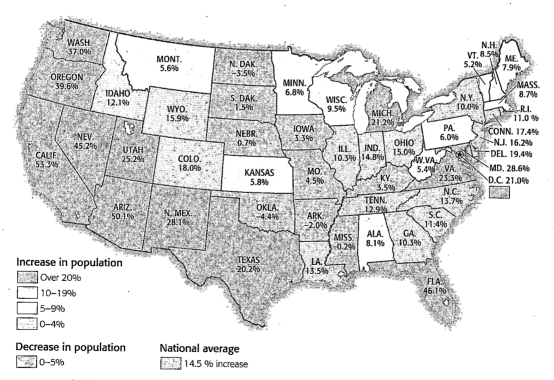

Increase in population
- Over 20%
- 10–19%
- 5–9%
- 0–4%

Decrease in population
- 0–5%

National average
- 14.5 % increase

Map 23.1 A Nation on the Move, 1940–1950

American migration during the 1940s was the largest on record to that time. The farm population dropped dramatically as men, women, and children moved to war-production areas and to army and navy bases, particularly on the West Coast. Well over 30 million Americans (civilian and military) migrated during the war. Many returned to their rural homes after the war, but 12 million migrants stayed in their new locations. Notice the population increases on the West Coast as well as in the Southwest and Florida.

Portraying the Enemy

Racial stereotyping affected how both the Americans and the Japanese waged war. The Americans badly underestimated the Japanese, leaving themselves open for the surprise attack on Pearl Harbor and American forces in the Philippines. And the Japanese, believing Americans were barbarians who lacked a sense of honor, mistakenly expected that the United States would withdraw from East Asia once confronted with Japanese power and determination. This poster, aimed at workers for Texaco oil company, appeared in the first year of the war, not long after Japan's attack on Pearl Harbor.

CRITICAL THINKING

- How is the Japanese soldier portrayed here?
- Why does he urge American workers to take a day off?
- And how might the fact that Japan had launched an immensely successful surprise attack on the United States have shaped this image, or Americans' reactions to it?

Go ahead, please- TAKE DAY OFF!

Galerie Bilderwelt/Hulton Archive/Getty Images

△ American propaganda often portrayed the Japanese enemy as animalistic or subhuman.

every month. More than forty thousand Native Americans left reservations to work in the defense industry. People who had never traveled farther than the next county found themselves on the other side of the country—or of the world. People moved for defense jobs or to be close to loved ones at stateside military postings. Southerners moved north, northerners moved south, and 1.5 million people moved to California.

The rapid influx of war workers to major cities and small towns strained community resources. Migrants crowded into substandard housing—even woodsheds, tents, or cellars—and into trailer parks without adequate sanitary facilities. Disease spread: scabies and ringworm, polio, tuberculosis. Many long-term residents found the newcomers—especially the unmarried male war workers—a rough bunch. In the small town of Lawrence, Kansas, civic leaders bragged of the economic boost a new war plant gave the town but fretted over the appearance of bars, "dirty windowed dispensaries" that sold alcohol to the war workers.

In and around Detroit, where car factories now produced tanks and planes, established residents called war workers freshly arrived from southern Appalachia "hillbillies" and "white trash." A new joke circulated: "How many states are there in the Union? Forty-five. Tennessee and Kentucky moved to Michigan, and Michigan went to hell." Many of these migrants knew little about urban life. One young man from rural Tennessee, unfamiliar with traffic lights and street signs, navigated by counting the number of trees between his home and the war plant where he worked. Some Appalachian "trailer-ites" appalled their neighbors by building outdoor privies or burying garbage in their yards.

23-4e Racial Conflicts

As people from different backgrounds confronted one another under difficult conditions, tensions rose. Widespread racism made things worse. In 1943, almost 250 racial conflicts exploded in forty-seven cities. Outright racial warfare bloodied the streets of Detroit in June. White mobs, undeterred by police, roamed the city, attacking blacks. Blacks hurled rocks at police and dragged white passengers off streetcars. At the end of thirty hours of rioting, twenty-five blacks and nine whites lay dead. Surveying the damage, an elderly black woman said, "There ain't no North anymore. Everything now is South."

The heightened racial and ethnic tensions of wartime also led to riots in Los Angeles in 1943. Young Mexican American gang members, or *pachucos*, had adopted the zoot suit: a long jacket with wide padded shoulders, loose pants "pegged" below the knee, a wide-brimmed hat, and dangling watch chain. With cloth rationed, wearing pants requiring five yards of fabric was a political statement, and some young men wore the zoot suit as a purposeful rejection of wartime ideals of service and sacrifice. Although in fact a high percentage of Mexican Americans served in the armed forces, many white servicemen believed otherwise. Racial tensions were not far from the surface in overcrowded L.A., and rumors that *pachucos* had attacked white sailors quickly led to violence. For four days, mobs of white men—mainly soldiers and sailors—roamed the streets, attacking zoot-suiters and stripping them of their clothes. The city of Los Angeles outlawed zoot suits and arrested men who wore them. The "zoot suit riots" ended only when naval personnel were removed from the city.

23-4f Families in Wartime

The dislocations of war also had profound impacts on the nation's families. Despite policies that exempted married men and fathers from the draft during most of the war, almost 3 million families were broken up. Young children grew up not knowing their fathers. The divorce rate of 16 per 1,000 marriages in 1940 almost doubled to 27 per 1,000 in 1944.

△ Members of the Vega family pose for the camera in uniforms of the Marine Corps, National Guard, and U.S. Navy.

At the same time, hundreds of thousands of men and women were getting married. The number of marriages rose from 73 per 1,000 unmarried women in 1939 to 93 in 1942. Some couples scrambled to get married before the man was sent overseas; others sought military deferments. The birth rate climbed as well: 2.4 million babies were born in 1939 and 3.1 million in 1943. Many were "goodbye babies," conceived with the idea that the father might not survive the war.

On college campuses, some virtually stripped of male students, women complained, along with the song lyrics, "There is no available male." But other young women found an abundance of male company and their elders worried that the war was undermining sexual morality. *Youth in Crisis*, a 1943 newsreel, featured a girl with "experience far beyond her age" necking with a soldier on the street, while *Newsweek* warned of the "victory girls" or "cuddle bunnies" who were said to support the war effort by giving their all to men in uniform. Many young men and women, caught up in the emotional intensity of war, behaved as they never would in peacetime. Often that meant hasty marriages to virtual strangers, especially if a baby was on the way. Despite changes in behavior, taboos against unwed motherhood remained strong, and only 1 percent of births during the war were to unmarried women. Wartime mobility also increased opportunities for same-sex relationships, and gay communities grew in such cities as San Francisco.

In many ways, the war reinforced traditional gender roles that had been weakened during the depression, when many men lost the role of breadwinner. Now men defended their nation while women "kept the home fires burning." Some women took "men's jobs," but most understood that they were "for the duration"—the home-front equivalent to men's wartime military service. Even so, women who worked were frequently blamed for neglecting their children and creating an "epidemic" of juvenile delinquency—evidenced by the "victory girl." Nonetheless, millions of women took on new responsibilities in wartime, whether on the factory floor or within their family.

23-5 The Limits of American Ideals

▷ **How did the American government attempt to balance democratic claims with wartime needs?**

▷ **What was the impact of internment on Japanese Americans during World War II?**

▷ **How did African Americans resist segregation of the military and discrimination during World War II?**

During the war, the U.S. government worked hard to explain to its citizens the reasons for their sacrifices. In 1941, Roosevelt had pledged America to defend "four essential human freedoms"—freedom of speech, freedom of religion, freedom from want, and freedom from fear—and government-sponsored films contrasted democracy and totalitarianism, freedom and fascism, equality and oppression.

Despite such confident proclamations, as America fought the totalitarian regimes of the Axis powers, the nation confronted questions with no easy answers: What limits on civil liberties were justified in the interest of national security? How freely could information flow to the nation's citizens without revealing military secrets to the enemy and costing American lives? How could the United States protect itself against the threat of spies or saboteurs, especially from German, Italian, or Japanese citizens living in the United States? And what about America's ongoing domestic problems—particularly the problem of race? Could the nation address its own citizens' demands for reform as it fought the war against the Axis? The answers to these questions often revealed tensions between the nation's democratic claims and its wartime practices.

For the most part, America handled the issue of civil liberties well. American leaders embraced a "strategy of truth," declaring that citizens of a democratic nation required a truthful accounting of the war's progress. However, the government closely controlled information about military matters. Censorship was serious business, as even seemingly unimportant details might tip off enemies about troop movements or invasion plans: radio stations were forbidden to broadcast weather reports—or even to mention weather conditions—leaving residents without warning of impending storms and sportscasters with no way to explain why play had been suspended or games had been called. During the war, government-created propaganda sometimes dehumanized the enemy, most especially the Japanese. Nonetheless, the American government resorted to hate-mongering much less frequently than during the First World War.

More complex was the question of how to handle dissent and how to guard against the possibility that enemy agents were operating within the nation's borders. The Alien Registration (Smith) Act, passed in 1940, made it unlawful to advocate the overthrow of the U.S. government by force or violence, or to join any organization that did so. After Pearl Harbor, the government used this authority to take thousands of Germans, Italians, and other Europeans into custody as suspected spies and potential traitors. During the war, the government interned 14,426 Europeans in Enemy Alien Camps. Fearing subversion, the government also prohibited ten thousand Italian Americans from living or working in restricted zones along the California coast, including San Francisco and Monterey Bay.

23-5a Internment of Japanese Americans

In March 1942, Roosevelt ordered that all 112,000 foreign-born Japanese and Japanese Americans living in California, Oregon, and the state of Washington (the vast majority of the mainland population) be removed from the West Coast to "relocation centers" for the duration of the war. Each of the Italian and German nationals interned by the U.S. government faced specific, individual charges. That was not the case for Japanese nationals and Japanese Americans. They were imprisoned as a group, under suspicion solely because they were of Japanese descent.

American anger at Japan's "sneak attack" on Pearl Harbor fueled the calls for internment, as did fears that West Coast cities might yet come under enemy attack. Long-standing racism was evident, as the chief of the Western Defense Command warned, "The Japanese race is an enemy race." Finally, people in economic competition with Japanese Americans strongly supported internment. Although Japanese nationals could not become U.S. citizens or own property, American-born Nissei (second generation) and Sansei (third generation), all U.S. citizens, were increasingly successful in business and agriculture. The eviction order forced Japanese Americans to sell property valued at $500 million for a fraction of its worth. West Coast Japanese Americans also lost their positions in the truck-garden, floral, and fishing industries.

The internees were sent to camps carved out of tax-delinquent land in Arkansas's Mississippi River floodplain, to the intermountain terrain of Wyoming and the desert of western Arizona, and to other arid and desolate spots in the West. The camps were bleak and demoralizing. Behind barbed wire stood tar-papered wooden barracks where entire families lived in a single room furnished only with cots, blankets, and a single bare light bulb. Most had no running water. Toilets and dining and bathing facilities were communal; privacy was almost nonexistent. In such difficult circumstances,

Radio News

In radio's early years, stations broadcast little news. Network executives believed their job was to entertain Americans and that current affairs should be left to newspapers. Yet radio could do something that no previous medium of communication could do: it could report not merely what had happened, but what was happening as it happened.

Franklin Roosevelt was among the first to grasp radio's potential in this regard. As governor of New York, he occasionally went on the air, and after becoming president, he commenced his Fireside Chats. With a voice perfectly suited to the medium, he reassured Americans suffering through the depression that, although current conditions were grim, the government was working hard to help them. So successful were these broadcasts that, in the words of one journalist, "The

President has only to look toward a radio to bring Congress to terms."

Across the Atlantic, another leader also understood well the power of radio. Adolf Hitler determined early that he would use German radio to carry speeches directly to the people. His message: Germany had been wronged by enemies abroad and by Marxists and Jews at home. But the Nazis under Hitler's direction would lead the country back to its former greatness. As "Sieg Heil!" thundered over the airwaves, millions of Germans came to see Hitler as their salvation.

In 1938, as events in Europe reached a crisis, American radio networks increased their news coverage. When Hitler annexed Austria in March, NBC and CBS broke into scheduled programs to deliver news bulletins. Then, on the evening of Saturday, March 13, CBS went its rival

one better by broadcasting the first international news roundup, a half-hour show featuring live reports on the annexation from the major capitals of Europe. A new era in American radio was born. In the words of author Joseph Persico, what made the broadcast revolutionary "was the listener's sensation of being on the scene" in far-off Europe.

When leaders from France and Britain met with Hitler in Munich later that year, millions of Americans listened with rapt attention to live radio updates. Correspondents soon became well known, none more so than Edward R. Murrow of CBS. During the Nazi air blitz of London in 1940–1941, Murrow's rich, understated, nicotine-scorched voice kept Americans spellbound. "This—is London," he would begin each broadcast, then proceed to give graphic accounts that tried, as he put it, to "report suffering to people [Americans] who have not suffered."

Murrow was resolutely pro-Allies, and there is little doubt his reports strengthened the interventionist voices in Washington by emphasizing Winston Churchill's greatness and England's bravery. More than that, though, radio reports from Europe made Americans feel more closely linked than before to people living thousands of miles and an ocean away. As American writer Archibald MacLeish said of Murrow's broadcasts, "Without rhetoric, without dramatics, without more emotion than needed be, you destroyed the superstition of distance and of time."

CRITICAL THINKING

◻ Radio broadcasts from Europe in the early days of World War II played an important role in convincing many Americans that intervention was necessary. Does the radio, or specifically today talk radio, continue to be a force in American life?

Library of Congress Prints and Photographs Division [LC-USZ62-119757]

△ Edward R. Murrow at his typewriter in wartime London.

people nonetheless attempted to sustain community life, setting up consumer cooperatives and sports leagues (one Arkansas baseball team called itself the Chiggers), and for many, maintaining Buddhist worship in the face of pressure to adopt Christian beliefs.

Betrayed by their government, many internees were profoundly ambivalent about their loyalty to the United States. Some sought legal remedy, but the Supreme Court upheld the government's action in *Korematsu v. U.S.* (1944). Almost one-quarter of all adults in one Arkansas camp, when asked if they would "swear unqualified allegiance to the United States," answered "no" or expressed some reservation. And almost 6,000 of the 120,000 internees renounced U.S. citizenship and demanded to be sent to Japan. Far more sought to demonstrate their loyalty. The all–Japanese American 442nd Regimental Combat Team, drawn heavily from young men in internment camps, was the most decorated unit of its size. Suffering heavy casualties in Italy and France, members of the 442nd were awarded a Congressional Medal of Honor, 47 Distinguished Service Crosses, 350 Silver Stars, and more than 3,600 Purple Hearts. In 1988, Congress issued a public apology and largely symbolic payment of $20,000 to each of the 60,000 surviving Japanese American internees.

23-5b African Americans and "Double V"

As America mobilized for war, some African American leaders attempted to force the nation to confront the uncomfortable parallels between the racist doctrines of the Nazis and the persistence of Jim Crow segregation in the United States. Proclaiming a "Double V" campaign (victory at home and abroad), groups such as the National Association for the Advancement of Colored People (NAACP) hoped to "persuade, embarrass, compel and shame our government and our nation . . . into a more enlightened attitude toward a tenth of its people." Membership in civil rights organizations soared. The NAACP, 50,000 strong in 1940, had 450,000 members by 1946. And in 1942, civil rights activists, influenced by the philosophy of India's Mohandas Gandhi, founded the Congress of Racial Equality (CORE), which stressed "nonviolent direct action" and staged sit-ins to desegregate restaurants and movie theaters in Chicago and Washington, D.C.

Military service was a key issue for African Americans, who understood the traditional link between the duty to defend one's country and the rights of full citizenship. But the U.S. military remained segregated by race and strongly resisted efforts to use black units as combat troops. As late as 1943, less than 6 percent of the armed forces were African American, compared with more than 10 percent of the population. The marines at first refused to accept African Americans at all, and the navy approximated segregation by assigning black men to service positions in which they would rarely interact with nonblacks as equals or superiors.

23-5c A Segregated Military

Why did the United States fight a war for democracy with a segregated military? The U.S. military understood that its sole priority was to stop the Axis and win the war, and

◁ Families arrive at the Heart Mountain Relocation Center in January 1942. One of the "internment camps" for Japanese Americans and Japanese resident aliens who were incarcerated under Executive Order 9066, Heart Mountain was in a remote area of northwestern Wyoming. Eventually 10,767 people were held in its barren confines, surrounded by barbed wire fence and monitored from nine guard towers.

Myron Davis/Getty Images

the federal government and War Department decided that the midst of world war was no time to try to integrate the armed forces. The majority of Americans (approximately 89 percent of Americans were white) opposed integration, many of them vehemently. As a sign of how deeply racist beliefs penetrated the United States, the Red Cross segregated blood plasma during the war. In most southern states, racial segregation was not simply custom; it was the law. Integration of military installations and training camps, the majority of which were in the South, would have provoked a crisis as federal power contradicted state law. Pointing to outbreaks of racial violence in southern training camps as evidence, government and military officials argued that wartime integration would almost certainly provoke even more racial violence, create disorder within the military, and hinder America's war effort. Such resistance might have been short term, but the War Department did not take that chance. Justifying its decision, the War Department argued that it could not "act outside the law, nor contrary to the will of the majority of the citizens of the Nation." General George C. Marshall, Army Chief of Staff, proclaimed that it was not the job of the army to "solve a social problem that has perplexed the American people throughout the history of this nation. . . . The army is not a sociological laboratory." Hopes for racial justice, so long deferred, were another casualty of the war.

Despite such discrimination, many African Americans stood up for their rights. Lieutenant Jackie Robinson refused to move to the back of the bus while training at the army's Camp Hood, Texas, in 1944—and faced court-martial, even though military regulations forbade racial discrimination on military vehicles, regardless of local law or custom. Black sailors disobeyed orders to return to work after surviving an explosion that destroyed two ships, killed 320 men, and shattered windows 35 miles away—an explosion caused by the navy practice of assigning men who were completely untrained in handling high explosives to load bombs from the munitions depot at Port Chicago, near San Francisco, onto Liberty ships. When they were court-martialed for mutiny, future Supreme Court justice and chief counsel for the NAACP Thurgood Marshall asked why only black sailors did this work. Marshall argued, "This is not fifty men on trial for mutiny. This is the Navy on trial for its whole vicious policy toward Negroes."

As the war wore on, African American servicemen did fight on the front lines, and fought well. The Marine Corps commandant in the Pacific proclaimed that "Negro Marines are no longer on trial. They are Marines, period." The "Tuskegee Airmen," pilots trained at the Tuskegee Institute in Alabama, saw heroic service in all-black units, such as the Ninety-ninth Pursuit Squadron, which won eighty Distinguished Flying Crosses. After the war, African Americans—as some white Americans had feared—called on their wartime service to claim the full rights of citizenship. African Americans' wartime experiences were mixed, but the war was a turning point in the movement for equal rights.

△ During World War II, for the first time, the War Department sanctioned the training and use of African American pilots. These members of the Ninety-ninth Pursuit Squadron—known as "Tuskegee Airmen" because they trained at Alabama's all-black Tuskegee Institute—joined combat over North Africa in June 1943. Like most African American units in the racially segregated armed forces, the men of the Ninety-ninth Pursuit Squadron were under the command of white officers.

23-5d America and the Holocaust

America's inaction in the face of what we now call the Holocaust is a tragic failure, though the consequences are clearer in retrospect than they were at the time. As the United States turned away refugees on the MS *St. Louis* (see "Roosevelt's Evolving Views," Section 22-7c) in early 1939 and refused to relax its immigration quotas to admit European Jews and others fleeing Hitler's Germany, almost no one foresaw that the future would bring death camps like Auschwitz or Treblinka. Americans knew they were turning away people fleeing dire persecution, and while anti-Semitism played a significant role in that decision, it was not unusual to refuse those seeking refuge, especially in the midst of a major economic crisis that seemed to be worsening.

As early as 1942, American newspapers reported the "mass slaughter" of Jews and other "undesirables" (Gypsies, homosexuals, the physically and mentally handicapped) under Hitler. Many Americans, having been taken in by manufactured atrocity tales during World War I, wrongly discounted

△ Millions of civilians were starved, gassed, machine gunned, or worked to death by their Nazi jailers during the war. Here, U.S. Army troops force Nazi Party members to exhume the bodies of two hundred Russian officers and others who were shot by the SS near Wuelfel, while the residents of Hannover watch. Allied troops often compelled local townspeople to watch exhumations of mass graves, attempting to make them confront the atrocities that many insisted they never knew were happening.

these stories. But Roosevelt knew about the existence of Nazi death camps capable of killing up to two thousand people an hour using the gas Zyklon-B.

In 1943, British and American representatives met in Bermuda to discuss the situation but took no concrete action. Many Allied officials, though horrified, saw Hitler's "Final Solution" as just one part of a larger, worldwide holocaust in which tens of millions were dying. Appalled by the reluctance to act, Secretary of the Treasury Henry Morgenthau Jr. charged that the State Department's foot dragging made the United States an accessory to murder. "The matter of rescuing the Jews from extermination is a trust too great to remain in the hands of men who are indifferent, callous, and perhaps even hostile," he wrote bitterly in 1944. Later that year, stirred by Morgenthau's well-documented plea, Roosevelt created the War Refugee Board, which set up refugee camps in Europe and played a crucial role in saving 200,000 Jews from death. But, lamented one American official, "by that time it was too damned late to do too much." By war's end, the Nazis had systematically murdered almost 11 million people.

23-6 Life in the Military

▷ **How was manpower allocated and organized during World War II?**

▷ **What was the nature of the wartime experience for men and women during World War II?**

More than 15 million men and approximately 350,000 women served in the U.S. armed forces during World War II. Eighteen percent of American families had a father, son, or brother in the armed forces. Some of these men (and all of the women) volunteered, eager to defend their nation. But most who served—more than 10 million—were draftees. By presidential order, the military stopped accepting draft-age volunteers in December 1942 as, faced with the challenge of filling the military ranks while maintaining war production and the civilian economy, the Selective Service system and the new War Manpower Commission tried to centralize control over manpower allocation. The draft reached broadly and mostly equitably through the American population during World War II, and most Americans believed that it operated fairly.

23-6a Selective Service

The Selective Service Act did allow deferments, but they did not disproportionately benefit the well-to-do. Almost ten thousand Princeton students or alumni served—as did all four of Franklin and Eleanor Roosevelt's sons—while throughout the nation judges offered minor criminal offenders the choice of the military or jail. The small number of college deferments was more than balanced by deferments for a long list of "critical occupations," including not only war industry workers but also almost 2 million agricultural workers. Most exemptions from military service were for men deemed physically or mentally unqualified to serve. Army physicians discovered what a toll the depression had taken on the nation's youth as draftees arrived with rotted teeth and deteriorated eyesight—signs of malnutrition. Army dentists pulled 15 million teeth and fitted men with dentures; optometrists prescribed 2.5 million pairs of glasses. Hundreds of thousands of men with venereal diseases were cured by sulfa drugs, developed in 1942. Military examiners also found evidence of the impact of racism and poverty. Half of African American draftees had no schooling beyond the sixth grade, and up to one-third were functionally illiterate. Forty-six percent of African Americans and almost one-third of European Americans called for the draft were classified "4-F"—unfit for service.

Nonetheless, almost 12 percent of America's total population served in the military. Regiments were created rapidly, throwing together men from very different backgrounds. Regional differences were profound, and northerners and southerners often—literally—could not understand one another. Ethnic differences complicated things further. Although African Americans and Japanese Americans served in their own separate units, Hispanics, Native Americans, and Chinese Americans served in "white" units. Furthermore, the differences among "whites"—the "Italian" kid from Brooklyn and the one from rural Mississippi (or rural Montana)—were profound. The result was often tension, but many Americans became less prejudiced and less provincial as they served with men unlike themselves.

23-6b Fighting the War

Although military service was widespread, the burdens of combat were not equally shared. Women served their nation honorably and often courageously, but women's roles in the U.S. military were much more restricted than in the British or Soviet militaries, where women served as anti-aircraft gunners and in other combat-related positions. U.S. women served as nurses, in communications offices, and as typists or cooks. The recruiting slogan for the WACs (Women's Army Corps) was "Release a Man for Combat." However, most men in the armed forces never saw combat either; one-quarter never left the United States. The United States had the most extreme "teeth-to-tail" ratio of any of the combatants, with each combat soldier backed up by eight or more support personnel. Japan's ratio was almost one to one. One-third of U.S. military personnel served in clerical positions, filled mainly by well-educated men. African Americans, though assigned dirty and dangerous tasks, were largely kept from combat service. In World War II, lower-class, less-educated white men bore the brunt of the fighting.

For those who fought, combat in World War II was as horrible as anything humans have experienced. Home-front audiences for the war films Hollywood churned out saw men die bravely, shot cleanly through the heart and comforted by their buddies in their last moments. What men experienced was carnage. Less than 10 percent of casualties were caused by bullets. Most men were killed or wounded by mortars, bombs, or grenades. Seventy-five thousand American men remained missing in action at the end of the war, lost at sea or other inaccessible locations or blown into fragments of flesh too small to identify. Combat meant days and weeks of unrelenting rain in malarial jungles, sliding down a mud-slicked hill to land in a pile of putrid corpses. It meant drowning in the waters of the frigid North Atlantic amid burning wreckage of a torpedoed ship. It meant using flamethrowers that burned at 2,000 degrees Fahrenheit on other human beings. It meant being violently ill on a landing craft steering through floating body parts of those who had attempted the landing first, knowing that if you tripped you would likely drown under the sixty-eight-pound weight of your pack, and that if you made it ashore you would likely be blown apart by artillery shells. Service was "for the duration" of the war. Only death, serious injury, or victory offered release. In this hard world, men fought to victory.

In forty-five months of war, close to three hundred thousand American servicemen died in combat. Almost 1 million American troops were wounded, half of them seriously. Medical advances, such as the development of penicillin and the use of blood plasma to prevent shock, helped wounded men survive—but many never fully recovered from those wounds. Between 20 and 30 percent of combat casualties were psychoneurotic, as men were pushed past the limits of endurance. The federal government strictly censored images of American combat deaths for most of the war, consigning them to a secret file known as "the chamber of horrors." Americans at home rarely understood what combat had been like, and many men, upon return, never talked about their experiences in the war.

23-7 Winning the War

▷ What issues emerged among the Allied Powers during World War II?

▷ How did the Allied Powers achieve victory in Europe and the Pacific?

▷ Why did the United States choose to use the atom bomb?

Axis hopes for victory depended on a short war. Leaders in Germany and Japan knew that, if the United States had time to fully mobilize, flooding the theaters of war with armaments

Map 23.2 The Allies on the Offensive in Europe, 1942–1945

The United States pursued a "Europe First" policy: first defeat Germany, then focus on Japan. American military efforts began in North Africa in late 1942 and ended in Germany in 1945 on May 8 (V-E Day).

and reinforcing Allied troops with fresh, trained men, the war was lost. However, powerful factions in the Japanese military and German leadership believed that the United States would concede if it met with early, decisive defeats. Hitler, blinded by racial arrogance, had stated shortly after declaring war on the United States, "I don't see much future for the Americans.... It's a decayed country. . . . American society [is] half Judaized, and the other half Negrified. How can one expect a State like that to hold together." By mid-1942, the Axis powers understood that they had underestimated not only American resolve but also the willingness of other Allies to sacrifice unimaginable numbers of their citizens to stop the Axis advance (see Map 23.2). The chance of an Axis victory grew increasingly slim as the months passed, but though the outcome was virtually certain after spring 1943, two years of bloody fighting lay ahead.

23-7a Tensions Among the Allies

As the war continued, the Allies' suspicions of one another undermined cooperation. The Soviets continued to press Britain and the United States to open a second front to the

west of Germany and so draw German troops away from the USSR, but the United States and Britain continued to delay. Stalin was not mollified by the massive "thousand-bomber" raids on Germany that Britain's Royal Air Force began in 1942, nor by the Allied invasion of Italy in the summer of 1943. With the alliance badly strained, Roosevelt turned to personal diplomacy. The three Allied leaders met in Tehran, Iran, in December 1943. Churchill again proposed a peripheral attack, this time through the Balkans to Vienna. But Stalin had had enough, and this time Roosevelt joined him. The three finally agreed to launch **Operation Overlord**—the cross-channel invasion of France—in early 1944. And the Soviet Union promised to aid the Allies against Japan once Germany was defeated.

23-7b War in Europe

The second front opened in the dark morning hours

Operation Overlord Code name for the largest amphibious invasion in history, in which Allied troops stormed a sixty-mile stretch of the Normandy coast on June 6, 1944 (D-Day).

◁ Allied ships unloading cargo during the first days of the Normandy Invasion, June 1944. As this photograph shows, the scale of the operation was immense: Operation Overlord relied on 326,547 Allied troops, 11,590 aircraft and 6,939 naval vessels.

Regional Council of Basse-Normandie/U.S. National Archives

of June 6, 1944: D-Day. In the largest amphibious landing in history, more than 140,000 Allied troops under the command of American general Dwight D. Eisenhower scrambled ashore at Normandy, France. Thousands of ships ferried the men within one hundred yards of the sandy beaches. Landing craft and soldiers immediately encountered the enemy; they triggered mines and were pinned down by fire from cliffside pillboxes. Meanwhile, 15,500 Allied airborne troops, along with thousands of dummies meant to confuse the German defense, dropped from aircraft. Although heavy aerial and naval bombardment and the clandestine work of saboteurs had softened the German defenses, the fighting was ferocious.

By late July, 1.4 million Allied troops were fighting in France. They spread across the countryside, liberating France and Belgium by the end of August but leaving a path of devastation in their wake. Allied bombing, one British soldier wrote, left villages appearing "dead, mutilated and smothered, a gigantic sightless rubble heap so confounded by devastation as to suggest an Apocalypse." Almost 37,000 Allied troops died in that struggle, and up to 20,000 French civilians were killed. In September, the Allies pushed into Germany. German armored divisions counterattacked in Belgium's Ardennes Forest in December, hoping to push on to Antwerp to halt the flow of Allied supplies through that Belgian port. After weeks of heavy fighting in what

Battle of the Bulge The final German military offensive against the Western Allies in the Ardennes region of Belgium (December 16, 1944–January 25, 1945). Named for the shape of the "bulge" formed by the German forces where they penetrated the Allied lines.

has come to be called the **Battle of the Bulge**—because of the "bulge" created as German troops had pushed back the Allied line—the Allies gained control in late January 1945.

By that point, "strategic" bombing (though not nearly as precise as was publicly claimed) had destroyed Germany's war-production capacity and devastated its economy. In early 1945, the British and Americans began "morale" bombing, killing tens of thousands of civilians in aerial attacks on Berlin and then Dresden. Meanwhile, battle-hardened Soviet troops marched through Poland and cut a path to Berlin. American forces crossed the Rhine River in March 1945 and captured the heavily industrial Ruhr Valley. Several units peeled off to enter Austria and Czechoslovakia, where they met up with Soviet soldiers.

23-7c Yalta Conference

Even as Allied forces faced the last, desperate resistance from German troops in the Battle of the Bulge, Allied leaders began planning the peace. In early 1945, Franklin Roosevelt, by this time very ill, called for a summit meeting to discuss a host of political questions—including what to do with Germany. The three Allied leaders met at Yalta, in the Russian Crimea, in February 1945. Each had definite goals for the shape of the postwar world. Britain, its formerly powerful empire now vulnerable and shrinking, sought to protect its colonial possessions and to limit Soviet power. The Soviet Union, with 21 million dead, wanted Germany to pay reparations to fund its massive rebuilding effort. The Soviets hoped to expand their sphere of influence throughout eastern Europe and to guarantee their national security; Germany, Stalin insisted, must be permanently weakened. Two German invasions in a quarter-century were more than enough.

The United States, like the other powers, hoped to expand its influence and to control the peace. To that end, Roosevelt lobbied for the United Nations Organization, approved in principle the previous year at Dumbarton Oaks in Washington, D.C., through which the United States hoped to exercise influence. The lessons of World War I also shaped American proposals; seeking long-term peace and stability, the United States hoped to avoid the debts-reparations fiasco that had plagued Europe after the First World War. U.S. goals included self-determination for liberated peoples; gradual and orderly decolonization; and management of world affairs by what Roosevelt had once called the Four Policemen: the Soviet Union, Great Britain, the United States, and China. (Roosevelt hoped China might help stabilize Asia after the war; the United States abolished the Chinese Exclusion Act in 1943 in an attempt to consolidate ties between the two nations.) The United States was also determined to limit Soviet influence in the postwar world. Obviously, there was much about which to disagree.

Military positions at the time of the Yalta conference helped shape the negotiations. Soviet troops occupied eastern European nations they had liberated, including Poland, where Moscow had installed a pro-Soviet regime despite a British-supported Polish government-in-exile in London. With Soviet troops in place, Britain and the United States had limited negotiating power over eastern Europe. As for Germany, the Big Three agreed that some eastern German territory would be transferred to Poland and the remainder divided into four zones—the fourth zone to be administered by France, which Britain had pressed to be included in plans for postwar control of Germany, so as to reduce the Soviet zone from one-third to one-quarter. Berlin, within the Soviet zone, would also be divided among the four victors. Yalta marked the high point of the Grand Alliance; in the tradition of diplomatic give-and-take, each of the Allies came away with something it wanted. In exchange for U.S. promises to support Soviet claims on territory lost to Japan in the Russo-Japanese War of 1904–1905, Stalin agreed to sign a treaty of friendship with Jiang Jieshi (Chiang Kai-shek), America's ally in China, rather than with the communist Mao Zedong (Mao Tse-tung), and to declare war on Japan two or three months after Hitler's defeat.

23-7d Harry Truman

Franklin D. Roosevelt, reelected to an unprecedented fourth term in November 1944, did not live to see the war's end. He died on April 12, and Vice President Harry S Truman became president and commander-in-chief. Truman, a senator from Missouri who had replaced former vice president Henry Wallace as Roosevelt's running mate in 1944, was inexperienced in foreign policy. He was not even informed about the top-secret atomic weapons project until after he became president. The day after Roosevelt's death, Truman sought out old friends, Democrats and Republicans, in Congress, to ask their help in this "terrible job." Shortly afterward, he told reporters, "Boys, if you ever pray, pray for me now. I don't know whether

◁ The three Allied leaders— Winston Churchill, Franklin D. Roosevelt, and Joseph Stalin— met at Yalta in February 1945. Having been president for twelve years, Roosevelt showed signs of age and fatigue. Two months later, he died of a massive cerebral hemorrhage.

Franklin D. Roosevelt Library

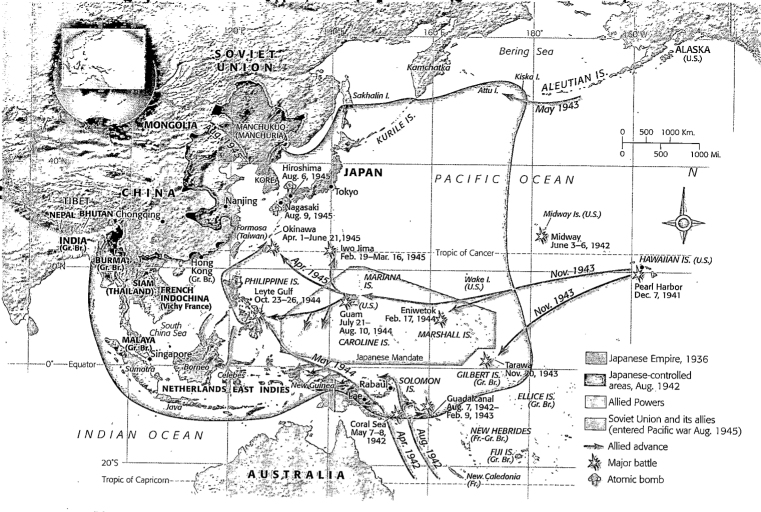

Map 23.3 The Pacific War

The strategy of the United States was to "island-hop"—from Hawai'i in 1942 to Iwo Jima and Okinawa in 1945. Naval battles were also decisive, notably the Battles of the Coral Sea and Midway in 1942. The war in the Pacific ended with Japan's surrender on August 15, 1945 (V-J Day).

you fellows ever had a load of hay fall on you, but when they told me yesterday what had happened, I felt like the moon, the stars, and all the planets had fallen on me." Eighteen days into Truman's presidency, Adolf Hitler killed himself in a bunker in bomb-ravaged Berlin. On May 8, Germany surrendered.

As the great powers jockeyed for influence after Germany's surrender, the Grand Alliance began to crumble. At the Potsdam Conference in mid-July, Truman—a novice at international diplomacy—was less patient with the Soviets than Roosevelt had been. And Truman learned during the conference that a test of the new atomic weapon had been successful. The United States, possessing such a weapon, no longer needed the Soviet Union's help in fighting the Pacific war. Roosevelt had secretly promised Stalin territory from Japan's wartime holdings in exchange for help in defeating Japan; the bomb made those concessions unnecessary. The Allies did agree that Japan must surrender unconditionally. But with the defeat of Hitler and the end of the European war, the wartime bonds among the Allies were strained to breaking.

23-7e The Pacific Campaign

In the Pacific, the war continued. Since halting the Japanese advance in the Battle of Midway in June 1942, American strategy had been to "island-hop" toward Japan, skipping the most strongly fortified islands whenever possible and taking the weaker ones, aiming to strand the Japanese armies on their island outposts. To cut off supplies being shipped from Japan's home islands, Americans also targeted the Japanese merchant marine. Allied and Japanese forces fought savagely for control of tiny specks of land scattered throughout the Pacific. By 1944, Allied troops—from the United States, Britain, Australia, and New Zealand—had secured the Solomon, Gilbert, Marshall, and Mariana Islands. General Douglas MacArthur landed at Leyte to retake the Philippines for the United States in October 1944 (see Map 23.3).

In February 1945, while the Big Three were meeting at Yalta, U.S. and Japanese troops battled for Iwo Jima, an island less than five miles long, located about seven hundred miles south of Tokyo. Twenty-one thousand Japanese defenders occupied the island's high ground.

◁ Navajo "code talkers" in the U.S. Marines were among the first assault forces to land on Pacific beaches. Dodging enemy fire, they set up radio equipment and transmitted vital information to headquarters using a code based on Diné, the Navajo language. In 1942 there was no written version of this complex language and fewer than thirty non-Navajos in the world—none of them Japanese—could understand it. While Navajo Marines made up the majority of the code talkers, members of twenty other tribes and nations served as code talkers in the U.S. military during World War II.

Bettmann/Getty Images

Hidden in a network of caves, trenches, and underground tunnels, they were protected from the aerial bombardment that U.S. forces used to clear the way for an amphibious landing. The stark volcanic island offered no cover, and marines were slaughtered as they came ashore. For twenty days, U.S. forces fought their way, yard by yard, up Mount Suribachi, the highest and most heavily fortified point on Iwo Jima. The struggle for Iwo Jima cost the lives of 6,821 Americans and more than 20,000 Japanese—some of whom committed suicide rather than surrender. Only 200 Japanese soldiers survived.

A month later, American troops landed on Okinawa, an island in the Ryukyus chain at the southern tip of Japan, from which Allied forces planned to invade the main Japanese islands. Fighting raged for two months; death was everywhere. The monsoon rains began in May, turning battlefields into seas of mud filled with decaying corpses. The supporting fleet endured waves of mass kamikaze (suicide) attacks, in which Japanese pilots intentionally crashed bomb-laden planes into American ships. Almost 5,000 seamen perished in these attacks. On Okinawa, 7,374 American soldiers and marines died in battle. Almost the entire Japanese garrison of 100,000 was killed. More than one-quarter of Okinawa's people, or approximately 80,000 civilians, perished as the two powers struggled over their island.

23-7f Bombing of Japan

Even with American forces entrenched just 350 miles from Japan's main islands, Japanese leaders still refused to admit defeat. A powerful military faction was determined to preserve the emperor's sovereignty and to avoid the humiliation of an unconditional surrender. They hung on even while American bombers leveled their cities. On the night of March 9, 1945, 333 American B-29 Superfortresses commanded by General Curtis LeMay dropped a mixture of explosives and incendiary devices on a four-by-three-mile area of Tokyo. Attempting to demonstrate the strategic value of airpower, they created a firestorm, a blaze so fierce that it sucked all the oxygen from the air, producing hurricane-force winds and growing so hot it could melt concrete and steel. Almost 100,000 people were incinerated, suffocated, or boiled to death in canals where they had taken refuge from the fire. Over the following five months, American bombers attacked sixty-six Japanese cities, leaving 8 million people homeless, killing almost 900,000.

Japan, at the same time, was attempting to bomb the U.S. mainland. Thousands of bomb-bearing high-altitude balloons, constructed out of rice paper and potato-flour paste by schoolgirls, were launched into the jet stream. Those that did reach the United States fell on unpopulated areas, occasionally starting forest fires. The only mainland U.S. casualties in the war were five children and an adult on a Sunday school picnic in Oregon who accidentally detonated a balloon bomb that they found in the underbrush. As Admiral Yamamoto had realized at the war's beginning, American resources would far outlast Japan's.

Early in the summer of 1945, Japan began to send out peace feelers through the Soviets. Japan was not, however, willing to accept the "unconditional surrender" terms on

◁ On Okinawa, a wounded GI prays while awaiting evacuation to a field hospital. Medical advances, such as the discovery of penicillin and the use of glucose saline solution to replace lost blood, greatly improved the survival rate for those wounded in combat. But where combat was especially horrific, as it was on Okinawa, psychiatric casualties might outnumber combat deaths three to one.

W. Eugene Smith/Getty Images

which the Allied leaders had agreed at Potsdam, and Truman and his advisers chose not to pursue a negotiated peace. By this time, U.S. troops were mobilizing for an invasion of the Japanese home islands. The experiences of Iwo Jima and Okinawa weighed heavily in the planning; Japanese troops had fought on, well past any hope of victory, and death tolls for Japanese and American troops alike had been enormous. News of the success of the Manhattan Project offered another option, and President Truman took it. Using atomic bombs on Japan, Truman believed, would end the war quickly and save American lives.

Historians still debate Truman's decision to use the atomic bomb. Why would he not negotiate surrender terms? Was Japan on the verge of an unconditional surrender, as some argue? Or was the antisurrender faction of Japanese military leaders strong enough to prevail? Truman knew the bomb could give the United States both real and psychological power in negotiating the peace; how much did his desire to demonstrate the bomb's power to the Soviet Union, or to prevent the Soviets from playing a major role in the last stages of the Pacific war, influence his decision? Did racism or a desire for retaliation play a role? How large were the projected casualty figures for invasion on which Truman based his decision, and were they accurate? No matter the answers to these ongoing debates, bombing (whether conventional or atomic) fit the established U.S. strategy of using machines rather than men whenever possible.

The decision to use the bomb did not seem as

Potsdam Declaration 1945 ultimatum of the Western Allies to Japan to surrender unconditionally or face "prompt and utter destruction."

momentous to Truman as it does in retrospect. The moral line had already been crossed, as the move to wholesale bombing of civilian populations continued throughout the war: The Japanese had bombed the Chinese city of Shanghai in 1937. Germans had "terror-bombed" Warsaw, Rotterdam, and London. British and American bombers had purposely created firestorms in German cities; on a single night in February 1945, 25,000 people perished in the bombing of Dresden. The American bombing of Japanese cities—accomplished with conventional weapons—had already killed close to a million people and destroyed fifty-six square miles of Tokyo alone. What distinguished the atomic bombs from conventional bombs was their power and their efficiency—not that they killed huge numbers of innocent civilians in unspeakably awful ways.

On July 26, 1945, the Allies delivered an ultimatum to Japan: promising that the Japanese people would not be "enslaved," the **Potsdam Declaration** called for the Japanese to surrender unconditionally or face "prompt and utter destruction." Tokyo radio announced that the government would respond with *mokusatsu* (literally, "kill with silence," or ignore the ultimatum). On August 6, 1945, a B-29 bomber named after the pilot's mother, the *Enola Gay*, dropped an atomic bomb above the city of Hiroshima. A flash of dazzling light shot across the sky; then a huge, purplish mushroom cloud boiled forty thousand feet into the atmosphere. Much of the city was leveled by the blast. The bomb ignited a firestorm, and thousands who survived the initial blast burned to death. Approximately 130,000 people were killed. Tens of thousands more would suffer the effects of radiation poisoning.

△ The photo of Hiroshima shown above was taken eight months after the attack. The shock waves and fires caused by the atomic bomb leveled great expanses of the city. Radiation released by the bomb caused lingering deaths for thousands who survived the explosion.

American planes continued their devastating conventional bombing. On August 8, the Soviet Union declared war on Japan. On August 9, the United States dropped a second atomic bomb on Nagasaki, killing at least 60,000 people. Five days later, on August 14, Japan surrendered. Recent histories argue that the Soviet declaration of war played a more significant role in Japan's decision to surrender than America's use of atomic weapons. In the end, the Allies promised that the Japanese emperor could remain as the nation's titular head. Formal surrender ceremonies were held September 2 aboard the battleship *Missouri* in Tokyo Bay. The Second World War was over.

Summary

Hitler once prophesied, "We may be destroyed, but if we are, we shall drag a world with us—a world in flames." In that, Hitler was right. World War II devastated much of the globe. In Asia and in Europe, ghostlike people wandered through rubble, searching desperately for food. One out of nine people in the Soviet Union had perished: a total of at least 21 million civilian and military war dead. The Chinese calculated their war losses at 10 million; the Germans and Austrians at

6 million; the Japanese at 2.5 million. Up to 1 million died of famine in Japanese-controlled Indochina. Almost 11 million people had been systematically murdered in Nazi death camps. Across the globe, the Second World War killed at least 55 million people.

Waging war required the cooperation of Allied nations with very different goals and interests. Tensions among them remained high throughout the war, as the United States and Britain resisted Stalin's demands that they open a second front to draw German soldiers away from the Soviet Union. The United States, meanwhile, was fighting a brutal war in the Pacific, pushing Japanese forces back toward their home islands. By the time Japan surrendered in August 1945, the strains between the Soviet Union and its English-speaking Allies made postwar peace and stability unlikely.

American men and machines were a critical part of the Allied war effort. Although Americans did not join in the perfect unity and shared sacrifice suggested by recent descriptions of "the greatest generation," American servicemen covered the globe, from the Arctic to the tropics. And on the home front, Americans worked around the clock to make the weapons that would win the war. Although they

Nuclear Proliferation

Virtually from the moment of the Hiroshima and Nagasaki atomic bombings, American strategists grappled with the problem of erecting barriers to membership in the "nuclear club." The early focus was on the Soviet Union. How long, analysts wondered, before Stalin gets the bomb? On September 23, 1949, came the answer, as President Truman informed a shocked American public that the Soviets had successfully tested an atomic device.

In the years thereafter, membership in the nuclear club grew, through a combination of huge national investments, espionage, and a black market of willing Western suppliers of needed raw materials and technologies. There were successful detonations by Great Britain (1952), France (1960), China (1964), India (1974), and Pakistan (1998). Israel crossed the nuclear weapon threshold on the eve of the 1967 Six-Day War but to this day has always refused to confirm or deny that it

has the bomb. More recently, creditable reports indicate that North Korea has a small nuclear arsenal and that Iran is working to get one.

If this is a sizable number of nuclear states, it is far fewer than experts predicted in the 1960s. "If three nations made nuclear weapons in the 1970s," one senior British analyst warned then, "ten might do so in the 1980s and thirty in the 1990s." It did not happen, and the main reason is that the five existing nuclear powers committed themselves in the mid-1960s—for a complex set of self-interested reasons—to promoting nonproliferation. Subsequently, the rate of proliferation steadily declined; all told, 22 of 31 states that started down the nuclear path changed course and renounced the bomb. By late 2006, the Treaty on the Non-Proliferation of Nuclear Weapons (NPT), enacted on July 1, 1968, had 187 signatories and was widely hailed as one of the great international agreements of the post-1945 era.

Skeptics took a different view. They noted that three states outside the NPT (Israel, India, and Pakistan) became nuclear powers, and they charged the "original five" with hypocrisy, for doing everything possible to prevent others from obtaining nuclear arms while keeping large stockpiles for themselves. With the world in 2013 awash in some 17,000 nuclear weapons (97 percent of which belong to the United States and Russia), critics feared a new kind of proliferation, in which a terrorist group or other nonstate actor got its hands on one or more bombs. In that nightmare scenario, they warned, the de facto post-Nagasaki international moratorium on the use of nuclear weapons would soon be—literally—blown away.

CRITICAL THINKING

◻ With the rise in non-state terrorism, what actions, if any, should the world's signees of the NPT, particularly the United States and Russia, take regarding existing nuclear stockpiles?

made sacrifices during the war—including almost three hundred thousand who gave their lives—many Americans found that the war had changed their lives for the better. Mobilization for war ended the Great Depression, reducing unemployment practically to zero. War jobs demanded workers, and Americans moved in huge numbers to war-production centers. The influx of workers strained the resources of existing communities and sometimes led to social friction and even violence. But many Americans—African Americans, Mexican Americans, women, poor whites from the South—found new opportunities for employment in well-paid war jobs.

The federal government, in order to manage the nation's war efforts, became a stronger presence in the lives of individual Americans—regulating business and employment; overseeing military conscription, training, and deployment; and even controlling what people could buy to eat or to wear. The Second World War was a powerful engine of social change.

Americans emerged from World War II fully confident that theirs was the greatest country in the world. It was certainly the most powerful. At war's end, only the United States had the capital and economic resources to spur international recovery; only the United States was more prosperous and

more secure than when war began. In the coming struggle to fashion a new world out of the ashes of the old, soon to be called the Cold War, the United States held a commanding position. For better or worse—and clearly there were elements of each—the Second World War was a turning point in the nation's history.

Suggestions for Further Reading

Michael C. C. Adams, *The Best War Ever: America and World War II* (1993)

Tsuyoshi Hasegawa, *Racing the Enemy: Stalin, Truman, and the Surrender of Japan* (2005)

William I. Hitchcock, *The Bitter Road to Freedom: A New History of the Liberation of Europe* (2008)

John Howard, *Concentration Camps on the Homefront: Japanese Americans in the House of Jim Crow* (2008)

David M. Kennedy, *Freedom from Fear: The American People in Depression and War, 1929–1945* (1999)

Warren F. Kimball, *Forged in War: Roosevelt, Churchill, and the Second World War* (1997)

Nelson Lichtenstein, *Labor's War at Home: The CIO in World War II* (1983)

Gerald F. Linderman, *The World Within War: America's Combat Experience in World War II* (1997)

Leisa Meyers, *Creating G.I. Jane: Sexuality and Power in the Women's Army Corps During World War II* (1996)

Williamson Murray and Allan Reed Millett, *A War to Be Won: Fighting the Second World War* (2009)

George Roeder, Jr., *The Censored War: American Visual Experience During World War II* (1993)

James Sparrow, *Warfare State: World War II Americans and the Age of Big Government* (2011)

Ronald Takaki, *Double Victory: A Multicultural History of America in World War II* (2000)

Nancy Beck Young, *Why We Fight: Congress and the Politics of World War II* (2013)

MINDTAP
From Cengage

MindTap® is a fully online personalized learning experience built upon Cengage Learning content. MindTap® combines student learning tools—readings, multimedia, activities, and assessments—into a singular Learning Path that guides students through the course and helps students develop the critical thinking, analysis, and communication skills that are essential to academic and professional success.

The Cold War and American Globalism, 1945–1961

On July 16, 1945, the Deer Team leader parachuted into northern Vietnam, near Kimlung, a village in a valley of rice paddies. Colonel Allison Thomas could not know that the end of the Second World War was just weeks away, but he and the other five members of his Office of Strategic Services (OSS) unit knew their mission: to work with the Vietminh, a nationalist Vietnamese organization, to sabotage Japanese forces that in March had taken direct control of Vietnam from France. After disentangling himself from the banyan tree into which his parachute had slammed him, Thomas spoke a "few flowery sentences" to two hundred Vietminh soldiers assembled near a banner proclaiming, "Welcome to Our American Friends." Ho Chi Minh, head of the Vietminh, ill but speaking in good English, cordially greeted the OSS team and offered supper. The next day Ho denounced the French but remarked that "we welcome 10 million Americans." "Forget the Communist Bogy," Thomas radioed OSS headquarters in China.

A communist who had worked for decades to win his nation's independence from France, Ho joined the French Communist Party after World War I and sought to use it as a vehicle for Vietnamese independence. For the next two decades, living in China, the Soviet Union, and elsewhere, he patiently planned and fought to free his nation from French colonialism. During World War II, Ho's Vietminh warriors harassed both French and Japanese forces and rescued downed American pilots. In March 1945, Ho met with U.S. officials in China, where he read the *Encyclopaedia Americana* and *Time* magazine at an Office of War Information facility. Receiving no aid from his ideological allies in the Soviet Union, Ho hoped that the United States would favor his nation's long quest for liberation from colonialism.

Other OSS personnel soon parachuted into Kimlung, including a male nurse who diagnosed Ho's ailments as malaria and dysentery. Quinine and sulfa drugs restored his health, but Ho

◁ Ho Chi Minh (in shorts) and his chief lieutenant, Gen. Vo Nguyen Giap (in white suit), with members of an Office of Strategic Services (OSS) team at Tan Trao in northern Vietnam, August 1945. Vietnam: Ho Chi Minh (in shorts) and Vo Nguyen Giap (in white suit) with members of an American Office of Strategic Services (OSS) team at Tan Trao in northern Vietnam, August 1945/PICTURES FROM HISTORY/Bridgeman Images

remained frail. As a sign of friendship, the Americans in Vietnam named Ho "OSS Agent 19." Everywhere the Americans went, impoverished villagers thanked them with gifts of food and clothing, despite the devastating famine of 1944–1945 in which at least a million Vietnamese people died. The villagers interpreted the foreigners' presence as a sign of U.S. anticolonial and anti-Japanese sentiments. In early August, the Deer Team began to give Vietminh soldiers weapons training. During many conversations with the OSS members, Ho said he hoped young Vietnamese could study in the United States and that American technicians could help build an independent Vietnam. Citing history, Ho remarked that "your statesmen make eloquent speeches about . . . self-determination. We are self-determined. Why not help us? Am I any different from . . . your George Washington?"

A second OSS unit, the Mercy Team, headed by Captain Archimedes Patti, arrived in the city of Hanoi on August 22. When Patti met Ho—"this wisp of a man," as Patti put it—the Vietminh leader applauded America's assistance and called for future "collaboration." But unbeknownst to these OSS members, who believed that President Franklin D. Roosevelt's general sympathy for eventual Vietnamese independence remained U.S. policy, the new Truman administration in Washington had decided to let France decide the fate of Vietnam. That change in policy explains why Ho never received answers to the several letters and telegrams he sent to Washington—the first dated August 30, 1945.

On September 2, 1945, amid great fanfare in Hanoi, with OSS personnel present, an emotional Ho Chi Minh read his declaration of independence for the Democratic Republic of Vietnam: "All men are created equal; they are endowed by their Creator with certain unalienable Rights; among these are Life, Liberty, and the pursuit of

Happiness." Having borrowed from the internationally renowned American document of 1776, Ho then itemized Vietnamese grievances against France.

By early autumn, both OSS teams had departed Vietnam. In a last meeting with Captain Patti, Ho expressed his sadness that the United States had armed the French to reestablish their colonial rule in Vietnam. Sure, Ho said, U.S. officials in Washington judged him a "Moscow puppet" because he was a communist. But Ho claimed that he drew inspiration from the American struggle for independence and that he was foremost "a free agent," a nationalist. If necessary, Ho insisted, the Vietnamese would go it alone, with or without American or Soviet help. And they did—first against the French and eventually against more than half a million U.S. troops in what became America's longest war up to that time. How different world history might have been had President Harry S Truman responded favorably to Ho Chi Minh's last letter to Washington, dated February 16, 1946, which asked the United States "as guardians and champions of World Justice to take a decisive step in support of our independence."

Experience an interactive version of this story in MindTap®.

Because Ho Chi Minh and many of his nationalist followers had declared themselves communists, U.S. leaders rejected their appeal. Endorsing the containment doctrine to draw the line against communism everywhere, American presidents from Truman to George H. W. Bush believed that a ruthless Soviet Union was directing a worldwide communist conspiracy against peace, free-market capitalism, and political democracy. Soviet leaders from Joseph Stalin to Mikhail Gorbachev protested that a militarized, economically aggressive United States sought nothing less than world domination. This protracted contest between the United States and the Soviet Union acquired the name "the Cold War."

The primary feature of world affairs for more than four decades, the Cold War was fundamentally a bipolar contest between the United States and the Soviet Union over spheres of influence and world power. Decisions made in Washington and Moscow dominated world politics as the capitalist "West" squared off against the communist "East." The contest dominated international relations and eventually took the lives of millions, cost trillions of dollars, spawned doomsday fears, and destabilized one nation after another. On occasion, the two superpowers negotiated at summit conferences and signed agreements to temper their dangerous arms race; at other times they went to the brink of war and armed allies to fight vicious Third World conflicts. Sometimes these allies had their own ideas and ambitions, and they often proved adept at resisting pressure applied on them by one or both of the superpowers. Over time, American and Soviet leaders came to realize that, notwithstanding the immense military might at their disposal, their power to effect change was in key respects limited.

Vietnam was part of the "Third World," a general term for those nations that during the Cold War era wore neither the "West" (the "First World") nor the "East" (the "Second World") label. Sometimes called "developing countries," Third World nations were on the whole nonwhite, nonindustrialized, and located in the southern half of the globe— in Asia, Africa, the Middle East, and Latin America. Many had been colonies of European nations or Japan, and they were vulnerable to the Cold War rivalry that intruded on them. U.S. leaders often interpreted their anticolonialism, political instability, and restrictions on foreign-owned property as Soviet- or communist-inspired, or capable of being exploited by Moscow—in short, as Cold War matters rather than as expressions of profound indigenous nationalism. As an example, Vietnam became one among many sites where Cold War fears and Third World aspirations intersected, prompting American intervention. Such intervention bespoke a globalist foreign policy, meaning that U.S. officials now regarded the entire world as the appropriate sphere for America's influence.

Critics in the United States challenged the architects of the Cold War, questioning their exaggerations of threats from abroad, meddlesome interventions in the Third World, and expensive militarization of foreign policy. But when leaders like Truman described the Cold War in extremist terms as a life-and-death struggle against a monstrous enemy, legitimate criticism became suspect and dissenters were discredited. Critics' searching questions about America's global, interventionist foreign policy and its reliance on nuclear weapons were drowned out by charges that dissenters were "soft on communism," if not un-American. Decision makers in the United States successfully cultivated a Cold War consensus that stifled debate and shaped the mind-set of millions of Americans.

- ▣ Why did relations between the Soviet Union and the United States turn hostile soon after their victory in World War II?

- ▣ When and why did the Cold War expand from a struggle over the future of Europe and central Asia to one encompassing virtually the entire globe?

- ▣ By what means did the Truman and Eisenhower administrations seek to expand America's global influence in the late 1940s and the 1950s?

24-1 From Allies to Adversaries

▷ **What were the respective postwar goals of the Soviet Union and the United States?**

▷ **What issues contributed to escalating tensions between the Soviet Union and the United States and the emergence of the Cold War?**

▷ **How did the personalities of Joseph Stalin and Harry S Truman shape the relationship between the Soviet Union and the United States?**

The Second World War had a deeply unsettling effect on the international system. At its end, Germany was in ruins. Great Britain was badly overstrained and exhausted; France, having endured five years of Nazi occupation, was rent by internal division. Italy also emerged drastically weakened and, in Asia, Japan was decimated and under occupation and China was headed toward a renewed civil war. Throughout Europe and Asia, factories, transportation, and communications links had been reduced to rubble. Agricultural production plummeted, and displaced persons wandered about in search of food and family. How would the devastated economic world be pieced back together? The United States and the Soviet Union, though allies in the war, offered very different answers and models. The collapse of Germany and Japan, moreover, had created power vacuums that drew the two major powers into collision as they sought influence in countries where the Axis aggressors had once held sway. And the political turmoil that many nations experienced after the war also spurred Soviet-American competition. For example, in Greece and China, where civil wars raged between leftists and conservative regimes, the two powers supported different sides.

24-1a Decolonization

The international system also experienced instability because empires were disintegrating, creating the new Third World. Financial constraints and nationalist rebellions forced the imperial states to set their colonies free. Britain exited India (and Pakistan) in 1947 and Burma and Sri Lanka (Ceylon) in 1948. The Philippines gained independence from the United States in 1946. After four years of battling nationalists in Indonesia, the Dutch left in 1949. In the Middle East, Lebanon (1943), Syria (1946), and Jordan (1946) gained independence, while in Palestine British officials faced growing pressure from Zionists intent on creating a Jewish homeland and from Arab leaders opposed to the prospect. In Iraq, too, nationalist agitation increased against the British-installed government. Washington and Moscow paid close attention to this anticolonial ferment, seeing these new or emerging Third World states as potential allies that might provide military bases, resources, and markets. Not all new nations were willing to play along; some chose nonalignment in the Cold War. "We do not intend to be the playthings of others," declared India's leader, Jawaharlal Nehru.

24-1b Stalin's Aims

Driven by different ideologies and different economic and strategic needs in this volatile international climate, the United States and the Soviet Union assessed their most pressing tasks in very different terms. The Soviets, though committed to seeking ultimate victory over the capitalist countries, were most concerned about preventing another invasion of their homeland. It was a territory much less secure than the United States, for reasons both geographic and historical. Its landmass was huge—three times as large as that of the United States—but it had only ten thousand miles of seacoast, much of which was under ice for a large part of the year. Russian leaders both before and after the revolution had made increased maritime access a chief foreign policy aim.

Worse, the geographical frontiers of the USSR were hard to defend. Siberia, vital for its mineral resources, lay six thousand miles east of Moscow and was vulnerable to encroachment by Japan and China. In the west, the border with Poland had generated violent clashes ever since World War I, and eastern Europe had been the launching pad for Hitler's invasion in 1941: the resulting war cost the lives of more than 20 million Soviet citizens and caused massive physical destruction. Henceforth, Soviet leaders determined, they could have no dangers along their western borders.

Overall, however, Soviet territorial objectives were limited. Although many Americans were quick to compare Stalin to Hitler, Stalin did not have the Nazi leader's grandiose plans for world hegemony. In general, his aims resembled those of the czars before him: he wanted to push the USSR's borders to include the Baltic states of Estonia, Latvia, and Lithuania, as well as the eastern part of prewar

Stalin: Ally to Adversary

These two *Look* magazine portrayals of Soviet leader Stalin indicate how quickly the Grand Alliance of World War II disintegrated into the superpower confrontation of the Cold War. In the first piece, from mid-1944, correspondent Ralph Parker writes that Stalin spends half his time writing poetry and the other half reading it to the schoolchildren who clamor to sit on his knee. "Stalin," Parker adds, "is undoubtedly among the best-dressed of all world leaders making Churchill in his siren suit look positively shabby." Four years later, Louis Fischer paints a very different picture. "This small man with drooping shoulders tyrannizes one-fifth of the world," Fischer writes of the Soviet leader, adding that neither Hitler nor any Russian czar was as powerful or as menacing as the "Great Red Father."

CRITICAL THINKING

⸱ What do these two items suggest about American attitudes toward the outside world?

⸱ What do they suggest about the role of the press in U.S. society?

△ "A Guy Named Joe" cover story of *Look* magazine by Ralph Parker, June 27, 1944.

△ "Life Story of Stalin" by Louis Fischer in *Look* magazine, June 8, 1948.

Poland. Fearful of a revived Germany, he sought to ensure pro-Soviet governments in eastern Europe. To the south, Stalin wanted to have a presence in northern Iran, and he pressed the Turks to grant him naval bases and free access out of the Black Sea. The Soviet government promoted economic independence more than trade with other countries; suspicious of their European neighbors, they did not promote rapid rebuilding of the war-ravaged economies of the region or, more generally, expanded world trade.

24-1c U.S. Economic and Strategic Needs

The United States, by contrast, came out of the war secure in its borders. Separated from the other world powers by two vast oceans, the American home base had been virtually immune from attack during the fighting—only an occasional shell from a submarine or a hostile balloon from Japan reached the shores of the continental United States. American casualties were fewer than those of any of the other major combatants—hugely so in comparison with the Soviet Union. With its fixed capital intact, its resources more plentiful than ever, and in lone possession of the atomic bomb, the United States was the strongest power in the world at war's end.

Yet this was no time for complacency, Washington officials reminded one another. Some other power—almost certainly the USSR—could take advantage of the political and economic instability in war-torn Europe and Asia, and eventually seize control of these areas, with dire implications for American security. To prevent this outcome, officials in Washington sought forward bases overseas, in order to keep an airborne enemy at bay. To further enhance U.S. security, American planners, in direct contrast to their Soviet counterparts, sought the quick reconstruction of nations—including the former enemies Germany and Japan—and a world economy based on free trade. Such a system, they reasoned, was essential to preserve America's economic well-being.

The Soviets, on the other hand, refused to join the new World Bank and International Monetary Fund (IMF), created at the July 1944 Bretton Woods Conference by forty-four nations to stabilize trade and finance. They held that the United States dominated both institutions and used them to promote private investment and open international commerce, which Moscow saw as capitalist tools of exploitation. With the United States as its largest donor, the World Bank opened its doors in 1945 and began to make loans to help members finance reconstruction projects; the IMF, also heavily backed by the United States, helped members meet their balance-of-payments problems through currency loans.

24-1d Stalin and Truman

The personalities of the two countries' leaders also mattered. Joseph Stalin, though hostile to the Western powers and capable of utter ruthlessness against his own people (his periodic purges since the 1930s had taken the lives of millions), did not want war. With the huge Russian losses in World War II, he was all too aware of his country's weakness vis-à-vis the United States. For a time at least, he appears to have believed he could achieve his aspirations peacefully, through continued cooperation with the Americans and the British. Over the long term, though, Stalin envisaged more conflict. He believed that Germany and Japan would rise again to threaten the USSR, probably by the 1960s, and his suspicion of the other capitalist powers was boundless. Many have concluded that Stalin was clinically paranoid: the first to do so, a leading Russian neuropathologist in 1927, died a few days later! As historian David Reynolds has noted, this paranoia, coupled with Stalin's xenophobia (fear of anything foreign) and his Marxist-Leninist ideology, created in the Soviet leader a mental map of "them" versus "us" that decisively influenced his approach to world affairs.

Harry Truman had none of Stalin's capacity for deception or ruthlessness, but to a lesser degree he, too, was prone to a "them" versus "us" worldview. Truman often glossed over nuances, ambiguities, and counterevidence; he preferred the simple answer stated in either/or terms. As Winston Churchill, who admired Truman's decisiveness, once observed, the president "takes no notice of delicate ground, he just plants his foot firmly on it." Truman constantly exaggerated, as when he declared in his undelivered farewell address that he had "knocked the socks off the communists" in Korea. Shortly after Roosevelt's death in early 1945, Truman met the Soviet commissar of foreign affairs, V. M. Molotov, at the White House. When the president sharply protested that the Soviets were not fulfilling the Yalta agreement on Poland, Molotov stormed out. Truman had self-consciously developed what he called his "tough method," and he bragged after the encounter that "I gave it to him straight one-two to the jaw." Truman's display of toughness became a trademark of American Cold War diplomacy.

24-1e The Beginning of the Cold War

At what point did the Cold War actually begin? No precise start date can be given. The origins must be thought of as a process, one that arguably began in 1917 with the Bolshevik Revolution and the Western powers' hostile response, but in a more meaningful sense began in mid-1945, as World War II drew to a close. By the spring of 1947, certainly, the struggle had begun.

One of the first Soviet-American clashes came in Poland in 1945, when the Soviets refused to allow the Polish government-in-exile in London to be a part of the communist government that Moscow sponsored. The Soviets also snuffed out civil liberties in the former Nazi satellite of Romania, justifying their actions by pointing to what they claimed was an equivalent U.S. manipulation of Italy. Moscow initially allowed free elections in Hungary and Czechoslovakia, but as the Cold War accelerated and U.S. influence in Europe expanded, the Soviets encouraged communist coups in Hungary (1947) and Czechoslovakia (1948). Yugoslavia stood as a unique case: its independent communist government, led by Josip Broz Tito, successfully broke with Stalin in 1948.

To defend their actions, Moscow officials noted that the United States was reviving their traditional enemy, Germany. Twice in the lifetime of Soviet leaders Germany had wrought enormous suffering on Russia, and Stalin and his associates were determined to prevent a third occurrence. The Soviets also protested that the United States was meddling in Eastern Europe. They cited clandestine American meetings with anti-Soviet groups, repeated calls for elections likely to produce anti-Soviet regimes, and the use of loans to gain political influence (financial diplomacy). Moscow charged that the United States was pursuing a double standard—intervening in the affairs of Eastern Europe but demanding that the Soviet Union stay out of Latin America and Asia. Americans called for free elections in the Soviet sphere, Moscow noted, but not in the U.S. sphere in Latin America, where several military dictatorships ruled.

24-1f Atomic Diplomacy

The atomic bomb also divided the two major powers. The Soviets believed that the United States was practicing "atomic diplomacy"—maintaining a nuclear monopoly to scare the Soviets into diplomatic concessions. Secretary of State James F. Byrnes thought that the atomic bomb gave the United States bargaining power and could serve as a deterrent to Soviet expansion, but Secretary of War Henry L. Stimson thought otherwise in 1945. If Americans continued to have "this weapon rather ostentatiously on our hip," he warned Truman, the Soviets' "suspicions and their distrust of our purposes and motives will increase."

In this atmosphere of suspicion and distrust, Truman refused to turn over the weapon to an international control authority. In 1946, he backed the Baruch Plan, named after its author, financier Bernard Baruch. Largely a propaganda ploy, this proposal provided for U.S. abandonment of its atomic monopoly only after the world's fissionable materials were brought under the authority of an international agency. The Soviets retorted that this plan would require them to shut down their atomic bomb development project while the United States continued its own. Washington and Moscow soon became locked in an expensive and frightening nuclear arms race.

By the middle of 1946, the wartime Grand Alliance was but a fading memory; that year, Soviets and Americans clashed on every front. When the United States turned down a Soviet request for a reconstruction loan but gave a loan to Britain, Moscow upbraided Washington for using its dollars to manipulate foreign governments. The two Cold War powers also backed different groups in Iran, where the United States helped bring the pro-West shah to the throne. Unable to agree on the unification of Germany, the former allies built up their zones independently.

24-1g Warnings from Kennan and Churchill

After Stalin gave a speech in February 1946 that depicted the world as threatened by capitalist acquisitiveness, the American chargé d'affaires in Moscow, **George F. Kennan**, sent a pessimistic "long telegram" to Washington. Kennan asserted that Soviet fanaticism made even a temporary understanding impossible. His widely circulated report fed a growing belief among American officials that only toughness would work with the Soviets. The following month, Winston Churchill delivered a stirring speech in Fulton, Missouri. The former British prime minister warned that a Soviet-erected "iron curtain" had cut off Eastern European countries from the West. With an approving Truman sitting on the stage, Churchill called for an Anglo-American partnership to resist the new menace.

The growing Soviet-American tensions had major implications for the functioning of the United Nations. The delegates who gathered in San Francisco in April 1945 to sign the UN charter had agreed on an organization that would include a General Assembly of all member states, as well as a smaller Security Council that would take the lead on issues of

△ Smiles all around as President Truman waves his hat during his and Winston Churchill's 1946 visit to Fulton, Missouri.

peace and security. Five great powers were given permanent seats on the council—the United States, the Soviet Union, Great Britain, China, and France. These permanent members could not prohibit discussion of any issue, but they could exercise a veto against any proposed action. To be effective on the major issues of war and peace, therefore, the UN needed great-power cooperation of the type that had existed in wartime but was a distant memory by mid-1946. Of the fifty-one founding states, twenty-two came from the Americas and another fifteen from Europe, which in effect gave the United States a large majority in the assembly. In retaliation, Moscow began to exercise its veto in the Security Council.

Some high-level U.S. officials were dismayed by the administration's harsh anti-Soviet posture. Secretary of Commerce Henry A. Wallace, who had been Roosevelt's vice president before Truman, charged that Truman's get-tough policy was substituting atomic and economic coercion for diplomacy. Wallace told a Madison Square Garden audience in September 1946 that "getting tough never brought anything real and lasting—whether for schoolyard bullies or businessmen or world powers. The tougher we get, the tougher the Russians will get." Truman soon fired Wallace from the cabinet, blasting him privately as "a real Commie and a dangerous man" and boasting that he, Truman, had now "run the crackpots out of the Democratic Party."

24-1h Truman Doctrine

East-West tensions escalated further in early 1947, when the British requested American help in Greece to defend their conservative

George F. Kennan American diplomat in Moscow, architect of the Cold War policy of containment.

client-government (a government dependent on the economic or military support of a more powerful country) in a civil war against leftists. In his March 12, 1947, speech to Congress, Truman requested $400 million in aid to Greece and Turkey. He had a selling job to do. The Republican Eightieth Congress wanted less, not more, spending; many of its members had little respect for the Democratic president whose administration the voters had repudiated in the 1946 elections by giving the GOP ("Grand Old Party," the Republican Party) majorities in both houses of Congress. Republican senator Arthur Vandenberg of Michigan, a bipartisan leader who backed Truman's request, bluntly told the president that he would have to "scare hell out of the American people" to gain congressional approval.

With that advice in mind, the president delivered a speech laced with alarmist language intended to stake out the American role in the postwar world. Truman claimed that communism, feeding on economic dislocations, imperiled the world. "If Greece should fall under the control of an armed minority," he gravely concluded in an early version of the domino theory, "the effect upon its neighbor, Turkey, would be immediate and serious (see "Unrelenting Cold War," Section 24-5). Confusion and disorder might well spread throughout the entire Middle East." Truman articulated what became known as the **Truman Doctrine**: "I believe that it must be the policy of the United States to support free peoples who are resisting attempted subjugation by armed minorities or by outside pressures."

Critics correctly pointed out that the Soviet Union was little involved in the Greek civil war, that the communists in Greece were more pro-Tito than pro-Stalin, and that the resistance movement had noncommunist as well as communist members. Nor was the Soviet Union threatening Turkey at the time. Others suggested that such aid should be channeled through the United Nations. Truman countered that, should communists gain control of Greece, they might open the door to Soviet power in the Mediterranean. After much debate, the Senate approved Truman's request by 67 to 23 votes. Using U.S. dollars and military advisers, the Greek government defeated the insurgents in 1949, and Turkey became a staunch U.S. ally on the Soviets' border.

Truman Doctrine U.S. policy designed to contain the spread of communism; began with President Truman's 1947 request to Congress for economic and military aid to the struggling countries of Greece and Turkey to prevent them from succumbing to Soviet pressure.

containment U.S. policy uniting military, economic, and diplomatic strategies to prevent the spread of Soviet communism and to enhance America's security and influence abroad.

24-1i Inevitable Cold War?

In the months after Truman's speech, the term *Cold War* slipped into the lexicon as a description of the Soviet-American relationship. Less than two years had passed since the glorious victory over the Axis powers, and the two Grand Alliance members now found themselves locked in a tense struggle for world dominance. It would last almost half a century. Could the confrontation have been avoided? Not altogether, it seems clear. Even before World War II had ended, perceptive observers anticipated that the United States and the USSR would seek to fill the power vacuum that would exist after the armistice, and that friction would result. The two countries had a history of hostility and tension, and both were militarily powerful. Most of all, the two nations were divided by sharply differing political economies with widely divergent needs and by a deep ideological chasm. Some kind of confrontation was destined to occur.

It is far less clear that the conflict had to result in a Cold War. The "cold peace" that had prevailed from the revolution in 1917 through World War II could conceivably have been maintained into the postwar years as well. Neither side's leadership wanted war. Both hoped—at least in the initial months—that a spirit of cooperation could be maintained. The Cold War resulted from decisions by individual human beings who might well have chosen differently, who might have done more, for example, to maintain diplomatic dialogue, to seek negotiated solutions to complex international problems. For decades, many Americans would wonder if the high price they were paying for victory in the superpower confrontation was necessary.

24-2 Containment in Action

▶ **How did the United States implement containment in western Europe?**

▶ **What domestic and international organizations were created to assist the United States in the area of national security?**

▶ **How did the Soviet Union respond to American containment efforts?**

Having committed themselves to countering Soviet and communist expansion, the Truman team had to figure out just how to fight the Cold War. The policy they chose, **containment**, was in place before the term was coined. George Kennan, having moved from the U.S. embassy in Moscow to the State Department in Washington, published an influential statement of the containment doctrine. Writing as "Mr. X" in the July 1947 issue of the magazine *Foreign Affairs*, Kennan advocated a "policy of firm containment, designed to confront the Russians with unalterable counterforce at every point where they show signs of encroaching upon the interests of a peaceful and stable world." Such counterforce, Kennan argued, would check Soviet expansion and eventually foster a "mellowing" of Soviet behavior. Along with the Truman Doctrine, Kennan's "X" article became a key manifesto of Cold War policy.

24-2a Lippmann's Critique

The veteran journalist Walter Lippmann took issue with the containment doctrine in his slim but powerful book *The Cold War* (1947), calling it a "strategic monstrosity" that failed to distinguish between areas vital and peripheral to U.S. security. If American leaders defined every place on earth as strategically important, Lippmann reasoned, the nation's patience and resources soon would be drained. Nor did Lippmann share Truman's conviction that the Soviet Union was plotting to take over the world. The president, he asserted, put too little emphasis on diplomacy. Ironically, Kennan himself agreed with much of Lippmann's critique, and he soon began to distance himself from the doctrine he had helped to create.

Invoking the containment doctrine, the United States in 1947 and 1948 began to build an international economic and defensive network to protect American prosperity and security, and to advance U.S. hegemony. In Western Europe, the region of primary concern, American diplomats pursued a range of objectives, including economic reconstruction and the fostering of a political environment friendly to the United States. They sought the ouster of communists from governments, as occurred in 1947 in France and Italy, and blockage of "third force" or neutralist tendencies. To maintain political stability in key capitals, U.S. officials worked to keep the decolonization of European empires orderly. In Germany, they advocated the unification of the western zones. At the same time, American culture—consumer goods, music, consumption ethic, and production techniques—permeated European societies. Some Europeans resisted Americanization, but transatlantic ties strengthened.

24-2b Marshall Plan

The first instrument designed to achieve U.S. goals in Western Europe was the **Marshall Plan**. European nations, still reeling economically and unstable politically, lacked the dollars to buy vital American-made goods. Americans, who had already spent billions of dollars on European relief and recovery by 1947, remembered all too well the troubles of the 1930s: global depression, political extremism, and war born of economic discontent. Such cataclysms could not be allowed to happen again; communism must not replace fascism. Western Europe, said one State Department diplomat, was "the keystone in the arch which supports the kind of a world which we have to have in order to conduct our lives."

In June 1947, Secretary of State George C. Marshall announced that the United States would finance a massive European recovery program. Launched in 1948, the Marshall Plan sent $12.4 billion to Western Europe before the program ended in 1951 (see Map 24.1). To stimulate business at home, the legislation required that Europeans spend the foreign aid dollars in the United States on American-made products. The Marshall Plan proved a mixed success; some scholars today even argue that Europe could have revived without it. The program caused inflation, failed to solve a balance-of-payments problem, took only tentative steps toward economic integration, and further divided Europe between "East" and "West." But the program spurred impressive Western European industrial production and investment and

started the region toward self-sustaining economic growth. From the American perspective, moreover, the plan succeeded because it helped contain communism.

24-2c National Security Act

To streamline the administration of U.S. defense, Truman worked with Congress on the **National Security Act of 1947**. The act created the Office of Secretary of Defense (which became the Department of Defense two years later) to oversee all branches of the armed services, the National Security Council (NSC) of high-level officials to advise the president, and the Central Intelligence Agency (CIA) to conduct spy operations and information gathering overseas. By the early 1950s, the CIA had become a significant element in national security policy and had expanded its functions to include covert (secret) operations aimed at overthrowing unfriendly foreign leaders and, as a high-ranking American official put it, a "Department of Dirty Tricks" to stir up economic trouble in "the camp of the enemy." Taken together, the components of the National Security Act gave the president increased powers with which to conduct foreign policy.

In response, Stalin forbade communist satellite governments in Eastern Europe to accept Marshall Plan aid and ordered communist parties in Western Europe to work to thwart the plan. He also created the Cominform, an organization designed to coordinate communist activities around the world. Whereas American planners saw the Marshall Plan as helping their European friends achieve security against a potential Soviet threat, in Stalin's mind it raised anew the specter of capitalist penetration. He tightened his grip on Eastern Europe—most notably, he engineered a coup in Czechoslovakia in February 1948 that ensured full Soviet control of the country—which in turn created more anxiety in the United States. In this way, the U.S.-Soviet relationship became a downward spiral that seemed to gain in velocity with each passing month.

24-2d Berlin Blockade and Airlift

The German problem remained especially intractable. In June 1948, the Americans, French, and British agreed to fuse their German zones, including their three sectors of Berlin. They sought to integrate West Germany (the Federal Republic of Germany) into the Western European economy, complete with a reformed German currency. Fearing a resurgent Germany tied to the American Cold War camp, the Soviets cut off western land access to the jointly occupied city of Berlin, located well inside the Soviet zone. In response to this bold move,

Marshall Plan The Truman administration's proposal for massive U.S. economic aid to speed the recovery of war-torn Europe.

National Security Act of 1947 Act that unified the armed forces under a single agency, later called the Department of Defense. It also established the National Security Council to advise the president on matters of national security and created the Central Intelligence Agency (CIA).

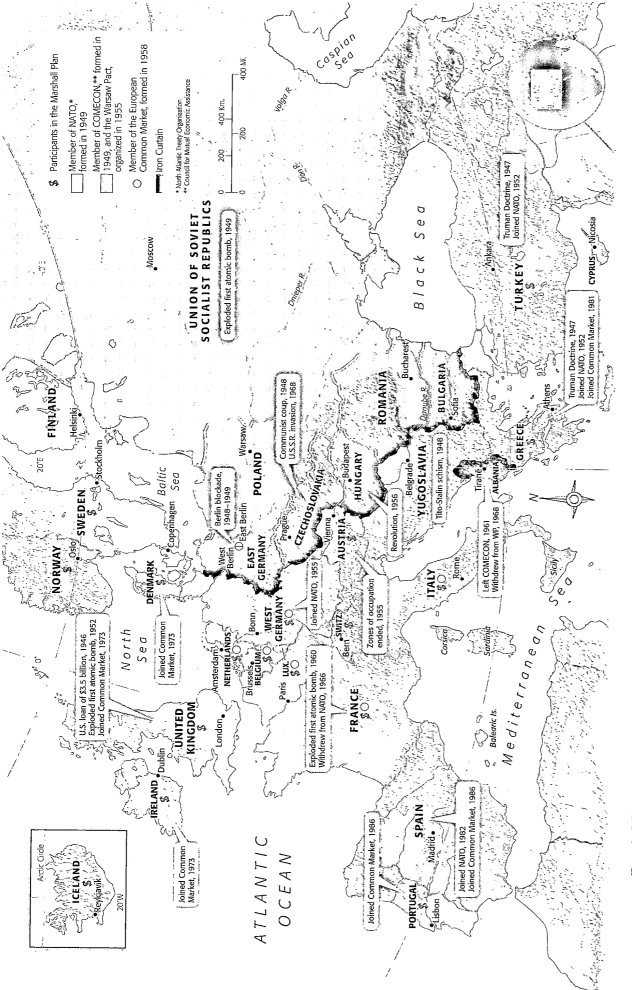

Map 24.1 Divided Europe

After the Second World War, Europe broke into two competing camps. When the United States launched the Marshall Plan in 1948, the Soviet Union countered with its own economic plan the following year. When the United States created NATO in 1949, the Soviet Union answered with the Warsaw Pact in 1955. On the whole, these two camps held firm until the late 1980s.

Map labels

$ Participants in the Marshall Plan

Member of NATO,*
formed in 1949

Member of COMECON,** formed in
1949, and the Warsaw Pact,
organized in 1955

Member of the European
Common Market, formed in 1958

Iron Curtain

* North Atlantic Treaty Organization.
** Council for Mutual Economic Assistance

UNION OF SOVIET
SOCIALIST REPUBLICS

Exploded first atomic bomb, 1949

Moscow

Volga R.

Don R.

Dnieper R.

Caspian Sea

Black Sea

400 Mi.
400 Km.
0 200 400
0 200

FINLAND
Helsinki

SWEDEN
Stockholm

NORWAY
Oslo

Baltic Sea

DENMARK
Copenhagen

Warsaw
POLAND

Berlin blockade,
1948–1949
East Berlin
West Berlin
EAST
GERMANY

Communist coup, 1948
U.S.S.R. invasion, 1968

Prague
CZECHOSLOVAKIA
Vienna
AUSTRIA
Joined NATO, 1955
Zones of occupation
ended, 1955

Budapest
HUNGARY
Revolution, 1956

ROMANIA
Bucharest
Danube R.

BULGARIA
Sofia

Belgrade
YUGOSLAVIA
Tito-Stalin schism, 1948

Tiranë
ALBANIA
Left COMECON, 1961
Withdrew from WP, 1968

GREECE
Athens

TURKEY
Ankara
Truman Doctrine, 1947
Joined NATO, 1952

Truman Doctrine, 1947
Joined NATO, 1952
Joined Common Market, 1981

CYPRUS Nicosia

WEST
GERMANY
Bonn

Exploded first atomic bomb, 1960
Withdrew from NATO, 1966

SWITZ.
Bern

ITALY
Rome

FRANCE
Paris

LUX.
BELGIUM
Brussels
NETHERLANDS
Amsterdam

Joined Common
Market, 1973

UNITED
KINGDOM
London

IRELAND
Dublin

U.S. loan of $3.5 billion, 1946
Exploded first atomic bomb, 1952
Joined Common Market, 1973

North
Sea

ATLANTIC
OCEAN

Mediterranean Sea

Corsica
Sardinia
Sicily
Balearic Is.

Joined Common Market, 1986
PORTUGAL
Lisbon

SPAIN
Madrid
Joined NATO, 1982
Joined Common Market, 1986

20°E
20°W

Arctic Circle
ICELAND
Reykjavík
Joined Common
Market, 1973

△ Under official postwar relief and recovery programs, including the Marshall Plan, the United States shipped billions of dollars' worth of food and equipment to Western European nations struggling to overcome the destruction of the Second World War. Private efforts, such as this one in 1950, also succeeded. The people of Jersey City, New Jersey, sent this snowplow to the mountainous village of Capracotta, Italy.

President Truman ordered a massive airlift of food, fuel, and other supplies to Berlin. Their spoiling effort blunted, the Soviets finally lifted the blockade in May 1949 and founded the German Democratic Republic, or East Germany.

The successful airlift may have saved Harry Truman's political career: he surprised pundits by narrowly defeating Republican Thomas E. Dewey in the presidential election that occurred in the middle of the crisis in November 1948. Safely elected, Truman took the major step of formalizing what was already in essence a military alliance among the United States, Canada, and the nations of Western Europe. In April 1949, twelve nations signed a mutual defense treaty, agreeing that an attack on any one of them would be considered an attack on all, and establishing the **North Atlantic Treaty Organization (NATO)** (see Map 24.1).

The treaty aroused considerable domestic debate, for not since 1778 had the United States entered a formal European military alliance, and some critics, such as Senator Robert A. Taft, Republican of Ohio, claimed that NATO would provoke rather than deter war. Other skeptics argued that the Soviet threat was political, not military. Administration officials themselves did not anticipate a Soviet military thrust against Western Europe, but they responded that, should the Soviets ever probe westward, NATO would function as a

"tripwire," bringing the full force of the United States to bear on the Soviet Union. Truman officials also hoped that NATO would keep Western Europeans from embracing communism or even neutralism in the Cold War. The Senate ratified the treaty by 82 votes to 13, and the United States soon began to spend billions of dollars under the Mutual Defense Assistance Act.

By the summer of 1949, Truman and his advisers were basking in the successes of their foreign policy. Containment was working splendidly, they and many outside observers had concluded. West Germany was on the road to recovery. The Berlin blockade had been defeated, and NATO had been formed. In Western Europe, the threat posed by communist parties seemed lessened. True, there was trouble in China, where the communists under **Mao Zedong** were winning that country's civil war. But that struggle would likely wax and wane for years or even decades to come, and besides, Truman could not

North Atlantic Treaty Organization (NATO) A mutual defense pact between the United States and eleven other nations promising to stand united in the face of military aggression, specifically by the Soviet Union.

Mao Zedong Chinese military and political leader who established the communist People's Republic of China.

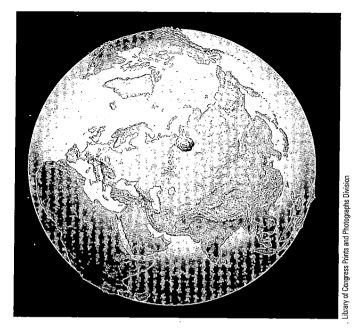

△ Richard Edes Harrison's illustration of the Soviet Union's detonation of an atomic bomb appeared in the October 1949 issue of *Life* magazine. A leading journalist-cartographer of the mid-twentieth century, Harrison was known for incorporating a global perspective in his work. Here, he uses a single cloud of smoke to suggest the potentially far-reaching effects of an isolated bomb explosion.

be held responsible for events there. Just possibly, some dared to think, Harry Truman was on his way to winning the Cold War.

24-2e Twin Shocks

Then, suddenly, in late September, came the "twin shocks," two momentous developments that made Americans feel in even greater danger than ever before—two decades later, they were still dealing with the reverberations. First, an American reconnaissance aircraft detected unusually high radioactivity in the atmosphere. The news stunned U.S. officials: the Soviets had exploded an atomic device. With the American nuclear monopoly erased, Western Europe seemed more vulnerable. At the same time, the communists in China completed their victory in that nation's civil war—the end came more quickly than many expected. Now the world's largest and most populous countries were ruled by communists, and one of them had the atomic bomb. The bipartisan foreign policy of 1945–1948 broke down, as Republicans, bitter over Truman's reelection, declared that traitors in America must have given Stalin the bomb and allowed China to be "lost."

Rejecting calls by Kennan and others for

NSC-68 Secret report by the National Security Council that would characterize U.S. Cold War strategy for decades; it saw the clash between the United States and the Soviet Union as a fight between good and evil and reversed the post–World War II military demobilization, focusing instead on a military buildup.

high-level negotiations, Truman in early 1950 gave the go-ahead to begin production of a hydrogen bomb, the "Super," and ordered his national security team to undertake a thorough review of policy. Kennan bemoaned the militarization of the Cold War and was replaced at the State Department by Paul Nitze. The National Security Council delivered to the president in April 1950 a significant top-secret document labeled **NSC-68**. Predicting continued tension with expansionistic communists all over the world and describing "a shrinking world of polarized power," the report, whose primary author was Nitze, appealed for a much-enlarged military budget and the mobilization of public opinion to support such an increase. The Cold War was about to become a vastly more expensive, more far-reaching affair.

24-3 The Cold War in Asia

▷ **How did the implementation of containment differ in Japan and China?**

▷ **Why did the United States choose to support the French effort to restore colonial rule in Indochina?**

Although Europe was the principal battleground in the early Cold War, Asia gradually became ensnared in the conflict as well. Indeed, it was in Asia that the consequences of an expansive containment doctrine would exact their heaviest price on the United States, in the form of large-scale and bloody wars in Korea and Vietnam. Though always less important to both superpowers than Europe, Asia would be the continent where the Cold War most often turned hot.

From the start, Japan was crucial to U.S. strategy. The United States monopolized Japan's reconstruction through a military occupation directed by General Douglas MacArthur, who envisioned turning the Pacific Ocean into "an Anglo-Saxon lake." Truman did not like "Mr. Prima Donna, Brass Hat" MacArthur, but the general initiated "a democratic revolution from above," as the Japanese called it, that reflected Washington's wishes. MacArthur wrote a democratic constitution, gave women voting rights, revitalized the economy, and destroyed the nation's weapons. U.S. authorities also helped Americanize Japan through censorship; films that hinted at criticism of the United States (for the destruction of Hiroshima, for example) or that depicted traditional Japanese customs, such as suicide, arranged marriages, and swordplay, were banned. In 1951, the United States and Japan signed a separate peace that restored Japan's sovereignty and ended the occupation. A Mutual Security Treaty that year provided for the stationing of U.S. forces on Japanese soil, including a base on Okinawa.

24-3a Chinese Civil War

The administration had less success in China. The United States had long backed the Nationalists of Jiang Jieshi (Chiang Kai-shek) against Mao Zedong's communists. But after the Second World War, Generalissimo Jiang became an unreliable partner who rejected U.S. advice. His government had become corrupt, inefficient, and out of touch with discontented peasants, whom the communists enlisted with promises of land reform. Jiang also subverted American efforts to negotiate a cease-fire and a coalition government. "We picked a bad horse," Truman admitted, privately denouncing the Nationalists as "grafters and crooks." Still, seeing Jiang as the only alternative to Mao, Truman backed him to the end.

American officials divided on the question of whether Mao was a puppet of the Soviet Union. Some considered him an Asian Tito—communist but independent—but most believed him to be part of an international communist movement that might give the Soviets a springboard into Asia. Thus, when the Chinese communists made secret overtures to the United States to begin diplomatic talks in 1945 and again in 1949, American officials rebuffed them. Mao decided to "lean" to the Soviet side in the Cold War. Because China always maintained a fierce independence that rankled the Soviets, before long a Sino-Soviet schism opened. Indeed, Mao deeply resented the Soviets' refusal to aid the communists during the civil war.

Then came Mao's victory in September 1949. Jiang fled to the island of Formosa (Taiwan), and in Beijing (formerly Peking) Mao proclaimed the People's Republic of China (PRC). Truman hesitated to extend diplomatic recognition to the new government, even after the British prime minister asked him, "Are we to cut ourselves off from all contact with one-sixth of the inhabitants of the world?" U.S. officials became alarmed by the 1950 Sino-Soviet treaty of friendship and by the harassment of Americans and their property in China. Truman also chose nonrecognition because a vocal group of Republican critics, the so-called China lobby, pinned Jiang's defeat on the administration. The president insisted that the self-defeating Jiang, despite billions of dollars in American aid, had proven a poor instrument of the

containment doctrine. The administration nonetheless took the politically safe route and rejected recognition. (Not until 1979 did official Sino-American relations resume.)

24-3b Vietnam's Quest for Independence

Mao's victory in China drew urgent American attention to Indochina, the territory in Southeast Asia that had been held by France for the better part of a century. The Japanese had wrested control over Indochina during World War II, but even then Vietnamese nationalists dedicated to independence grew in strength. One leading nationalist, Ho Chi Minh, hoped to use Japan's defeat to assert Vietnamese independence, and he asked for U.S. support. American officials had few kind things to say about French colonial policy, and many were pessimistic that France could achieve a military solution to the conflict. Nevertheless, they rejected Ho's appeals in favor of a restoration of French rule, mostly to ensure France's cooperation in the emerging Soviet-American confrontation. In addition, the Truman administration was wary of Ho Chi Minh's communist politics. Ho, the State Department declared, was an "agent of international communism" who, it was assumed, would assist Soviet and, after 1949, Chinese expansionism. Overlooking the native roots of the nationalist rebellion against French colonialism, and the tenacious Vietnamese resistance to foreign intruders, Washington officials interpreted events in Indochina through a Cold War lens.

Even so, when war between the Vietminh and France broke out in 1946, the United States initially took a hands-off approach. But when Jiang's regime collapsed in China three years later, the Truman administration made two crucial decisions—both of them in early 1950, before the Korean War. First, in February, Washington recognized the French puppet government of Bao Dai, an intelligent but lazy former emperor who had collaborated with both the French and

◁ Mao Zedong was a military theoretician who also involved himself in day-to-day military decision making. He was responsible for, or at least approved, all of the major strategic moves the communists made on their way to power. This image shows him applauding soldiers and other supporters on Tiananmen Square in Beijing.

Apic/Getty Images

the Japanese. In the eyes of many Vietnamese, the United States thus became in essence a colonial power, an ally of the hated French. Second, in May, the administration agreed to send weapons and other assistance to sustain the French in Indochina. From 1945 to 1954, the United States gave $2 billion of the $5 billion that France spent to keep Vietnam within its empire—to no avail. How Vietnam ultimately became the site of a major American war, and how the world's most powerful nation failed to subdue a peasant people who suffered enormous losses, is one of the most remarkable and tragic stories of modern U.S. history.

24-4 The Korean War

▷ **What factors contributed to American involvement in the war between North and South Korea?**

▷ **How did the Korean War change with the entrance of China into the conflict?**

▷ **What were the domestic and international consequences of the Korean War?**

In the early morning of June 25, 1950, a large military force of the Democratic People's Republic of Korea (North Korea) moved across the thirty-eighth parallel into the Republic of Korea (South Korea). Colonized by Japan since 1910, Korea had been divided in two by the victorious powers after Japan's defeat in 1945.

Korean War War between North Korea and South Korea with heavy involvement by the superpowers and by the People's Republic of China, which lasted from 1950 to 1953 and which claimed the lives of millions.

Although the Soviets had armed the North and the Americans had armed the South (U.S. aid had reached $100 million a year), the **Korean War** began as a civil war. Virtually from the moment of the division, the two parts had been skirmishing along their supposedly temporary border while antigovernment (and anti-U.S.) guerrilla fighting flared in the South.

Both the North's communist leader, Kim Il Sung, and the South's president, Syngman Rhee, sought to reunify their nation. Kim's military in particular gained strength when tens of thousands of battle-tested Koreans returned home in 1949 after serving in Mao's army. Displaying the Cold War mentality of the time, however, President Truman claimed that the Soviets had masterminded the North Korean attack. "Communism was acting in Korea just as Hitler, Mussolini, and the Japanese had acted," he said, recalling Axis aggression.

Actually, Kim had to press a doubting Joseph Stalin, who only reluctantly approved the attack after Kim predicted an easy, early victory and after Mao backed Kim. Whatever Stalin's reasoning, his support for Kim's venture remained lukewarm. When the UN Security Council voted to defend South Korea against the invasion from the north, the Soviet representative was not even present to veto the resolution because the Soviets were boycotting the United Nations to protest its refusal to grant membership to the People's Republic of China. During the war, Moscow gave limited aid to North Korea and China, which grew angry at Stalin for reneging on promised Soviet airpower. Stalin, all too aware of his strategic inferiority vis-à-vis the United States, did not want to be dragged into a costly war.

◁ Men of the 3rd Battalion, 34th Infantry Regiment, 35th Infantry Division, take cover to avoid incoming mortar shells, near the Hantan River in central Korea, in April 1951.

Library of Congress, Prints & Photographs Division, Reproduction number LC-USZ62-72424 (b&w film copy neg.)

24-4a U.S. Forces Intervene

The president first ordered General Douglas MacArthur to send arms and troops to South Korea. He did not seek congressional approval—he and his aides feared that lawmakers would initiate a lengthy debate—and thereby set the precedent of waging war on executive authority alone. Worried that Mao might use the occasion to take Formosa, Truman also directed the Seventh Fleet to patrol the waters between the Chinese mainland and Jiang's sanctuary on Formosa, thus inserting the United States again into Chinese politics. After the Security Council voted to assist South Korea, MacArthur became commander of UN forces in Korea. Sixteen nations contributed troops to the UN command, but 40 percent were South Korean and about 50 percent American. In the war's early weeks, North Korean tanks and superior firepower sent the South Korean army into chaotic retreat. The first American soldiers, taking heavy casualties, could not stop the North Korean advance. Within weeks, the South Koreans and Americans had been pushed into the tiny Pusan perimeter at the tip of South Korea (see Map 24.2).

General MacArthur planned a daring amphibious landing at heavily fortified Inchon, several hundred miles behind North Korean lines. After U.S. guns and bombs pounded Inchon, marines splashed ashore on September 15, 1950. The operation was a brilliant success, and the troops soon liberated the South Korean capital of Seoul and pushed the North Koreans back to the thirty-eighth parallel. Even before Inchon, Truman had redefined the U.S. war goal, changing it from the containment of North Korea to the reunification of Korea by force. Communism not only would be stopped; it would be rolled back.

24-4b Chinese Entry into the War

In September, Truman authorized UN forces to cross the thirty-eighth parallel. These troops drove deep into North Korea, and American aircraft began strikes against bridges on the Yalu River, the border between North Korea and China. The Chinese watched warily, fearing that the Americans would next stab at the People's Republic. Mao publicly warned that China could not permit the bombing of its transportation links with Korea and would not accept the annihilation of North Korea itself. MacArthur shrugged off the warnings, and Washington officials agreed with the strong-willed general, drawing further confidence from the fact that, as MacArthur had predicted, the Soviets were not preparing for war.

MacArthur was right about the Soviets, but wrong about the Chinese. Mao, concluding that the "Americans would run more rampant" unless stopped, on October 25 sent Chinese soldiers into the war near the Yalu. Perhaps to lure American forces into a trap or to signal willingness to begin negotiations, they pulled back after a brief and successful offensive against South Korean troops. Then, after MacArthur sent the U.S. Eighth Army northward, tens of thousands of Chinese troops counterattacked on November 26, surprising American forces and driving them pell-mell southward. One

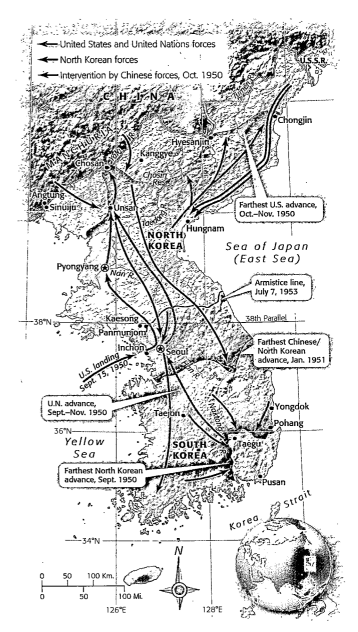

Map 24.2 The Korean War, 1950–1953

Beginning as a civil war between North and South, this war became international when the United States—under the auspices of the United Nations—and the People's Republic of China intervened with their military forces.

U.S. officer termed it "a sight that hasn't been seen for hundreds of years: the men of a whole United States Army fleeing from a battlefield, abandoning their wounded, running for their lives."

24-4c Truman's Firing of MacArthur

By early 1951, the front had stabilized around the thirty-eighth parallel. A stalemate set in. Both Washington and Moscow welcomed negotiations, but MacArthur had other ideas. The theatrical general recklessly called for an attack on China and for Jiang's return to the mainland. Now was the time, he insisted, to smash communism by destroying its Asian flank. Denouncing the concept of limited war (war without nuclear weapons, confined to one place), MacArthur hinted that the president was practicing appeasement. In April, backed by the Joint Chiefs of Staff (the heads of the various armed services), Truman fired MacArthur. The general, who had not set foot in the United States for more than a decade, returned home a hero, with ticker-tape parades and cheers on the lecture circuit. Truman's popularity sagged, but he weathered scattered demands for his impeachment.

Armistice talks began in July 1951, but the fighting and dying went on for two more years. The most contentious point in the negotiations was the fate of prisoners of war (POWs). Defying the Geneva Prisoners of War Convention (1949), U.S. officials announced that only those North Korean and Chinese POWs who wished to go home would be returned. Responding to the American statement that there would be no forced repatriation, the North Koreans denounced forced retention. Both sides undertook "reeducation" or "brainwashing" programs to persuade POWs to resist repatriation.

24-4d Peace Agreement

As the POW issue stalled negotiations, U.S. officials made deliberately vague public statements about using atomic weapons in Korea. American bombers obliterated dams (whose rushing waters then destroyed rice fields), factories, airfields, and bridges in North Korea. Casualties on all sides mounted. Not until July 1953 was an armistice signed. Stalin's death in March and the advent of new leaders in both Moscow and Washington helped ease the way to a settlement that all sides welcomed. The combatants agreed to hand over the POW question to a special panel of neutral nations, which later gave prisoners their choice of staying or leaving. (In the end, 70,000 of about 100,000 North Korean and 5,600 of 20,700 Chinese POWs elected to return home; 21 American and 325 South Korean POWs of some 11,000 decided to stay in North Korea.) The North Korean–South Korean borderline was set near the thirty-eighth parallel, the prewar boundary, and a demilitarized zone was created between the two Koreas.

American casualties totaled 54,246 dead and 103,284 wounded. Close to 5 million Asians died in the war: 2 million North Korean civilians and 500,000 soldiers; 1 million South Korean civilians and 100,000 soldiers; and at least 1 million Chinese soldiers—ranking Korea as one of the costliest wars of the twentieth century.

John Foster Dulles Secretary of state under Dwight D. Eisenhower. He expressed skepticism about merely "containing" communism and spoke instead of rolling it back, but in practice moved cautiously.

24-4e Consequences of the War

The Korean War carried major domestic political consequences. The failure to achieve victory and

the public's impatience with a stalemated war undoubtedly helped to elect Republican Dwight Eisenhower to the presidency in 1952, as the former general promised to "go to Korea" to end the war. The powers of the presidency grew as Congress repeatedly deferred to Truman. The president had never asked Congress for a declaration of war, believing that, as commander-in-chief, he had the authority to send troops wherever he wished. He saw no need to consult Congress—except when he wanted the $69.5 billion Korean War bill paid. In addition, the war, which occurred in the midst of the "who lost China?" debate, inflamed party politics in the United States. Republican lawmakers, including Wisconsin senator Joseph McCarthy, accused Truman and Secretary of State Dean Acheson of being "soft on communism" in failing first to prevent, and then to go all out to win, the war; their verbal attacks strengthened the administration's determination to take an uncompromising position in the negotiations.

The impact on foreign policy was even greater. The Sino-American hostility generated by the war ensured that there would be no U.S. reconciliation with the Beijing government and that South Korea and Formosa would become major recipients of American foreign aid. The alliance with Japan strengthened as the island's economy boomed after filling large procurement orders from the United States. Australia and New Zealand joined the United States in a mutual defense agreement, the ANZUS Treaty (1951). The U.S. Army sent four divisions to Europe, and the administration initiated plans to rearm West Germany. The Korean War also persuaded Truman to do what he had been unwilling to do before the outbreak of hostilities—approve NSC-68. Indeed, the military budget shot up from $14 billion in 1949 to $44 billion in 1953; it remained between $35 billion and $44 billion a year throughout the 1950s. The Soviet Union sought to match this military buildup, and the result was a major arms race between the two nations. In sum, Truman's legacy was a highly militarized U.S. foreign policy active on a global scale.

24-5 Unrelenting Cold War

▶ **How did Cold War policy change during the presidency of Dwight D. Eisenhower?**

▶ **What role did the CIA play in American foreign policy during Eisenhower's presidency?**

▶ **How did Eisenhower respond to the crises in Suez and Hungary?**

The new foreign policy team of President Eisenhower and Secretary of State **John Foster Dulles** largely sustained Truman's Cold War policies. Both brought abundant experience in foreign affairs to their posts. Eisenhower had lived and traveled in Europe, Asia, and Latin America and, as a general during the Second World War, had negotiated with world leaders. After the war, he had served as army chief of staff and NATO supreme commander. Dulles had been closely involved with U.S. diplomacy since the first decade

◁ President Eisenhower *(left)* confers with Secretary of State John Foster Dulles (1888–1959), known for his strong anti-communism and his often self-righteous lecturing style. Dulles once remarked that the United States "is almost the only country strong enough and powerful enough to be moral."

Bettmann/Getty Images

of the century. "Foster has been studying to be secretary of state since he was five years old," Eisenhower observed, exaggerating only slightly. He relied heavily on Dulles to be his emissary abroad. The secretary of state spent so much time traveling to world capitals that critics exclaimed, "Don't do something, Foster, just stand there!"

Eisenhower and Dulles accepted the Cold War consensus about the threat of communism and the need for global vigilance. Although Democrats promoted an image of Eisenhower as a bumbling, passive, aging hero, deferring most foreign policy matters to Dulles, the president in fact commanded the policymaking process and on occasion tamed the more hawkish proposals of Dulles and Vice President Richard Nixon. Even so, the secretary of state's influence was vast. Though polished and authoritative, he impressed people as arrogant, stubborn, and hectoring—and averse to compromise, an essential ingredient in successful diplomacy. Behind closed doors Dulles could show a different side, one considerably more flexible and pragmatic, but there is little evidence

that he saw much utility in negotiations, at least where communists were involved. His assertion that neutrality was an "immoral and short-sighted conception" did not sit well with Third World leaders, who resented being told they had to choose between East and West.

24-5a "Massive Retaliation"

Dulles said that he considered containment too defensive a stance toward communism. He called instead for "liberation," although he never explained precisely how the countries of Eastern Europe could be freed from Soviet control. "Massive retaliation" was the administration's plan for the nuclear obliteration of the Soviet state or its assumed client, the People's Republic of China, if either one took aggressive actions. Eisenhower said that it "simply means the ability to blow hell out of them in a hurry if they start anything." The ability of the United States to make such a threat was thought to provide "deterrence," the prevention of hostile Soviet behavior.

In their "New Look" for the American military, Eisenhower and Dulles emphasized airpower and nuclear weaponry. The president's preference for heavy weapons stemmed in part from his desire to trim the federal budget ("more bang for the buck," as the saying went). Galvanized by the successful test of the world's first hydrogen bomb in November 1952, Eisenhower oversaw a massive stockpiling of nuclear weapons—from 1,200 at the start of his presidency to 22,229 at the end. Backed by its huge military arsenal, the United States could practice "brinkmanship": not backing down in a crisis, even if it meant taking the nation to the brink of war. Eisenhower also popularized the "**domino theory**": that small, weak neighboring nations would fall to communism like a row of dominoes if they were not propped up by the United States.

24-5b CIA as Foreign Policy Instrument

Eisenhower increasingly utilized the Central Intelligence Agency as an instrument of foreign policy. Headed by Allen Dulles, brother of the secretary of state, the CIA put foreign leaders (such as King Hussein of Jordan) on its payroll; subsidized foreign labor unions, newspapers, and political parties (such as the conservative Liberal Democratic Party of Japan); planted false stories in newspapers through its "disinformation" projects; and trained foreign military officers in counterrevolutionary methods. It hired American journalists and professors, secretly funded the National Student Association to spur contacts with foreign student leaders, used business executives as "fronts," and conducted experiments on unsuspecting Americans to determine the effects of "mind control" drugs (the MK-ULTRA program). The CIA also launched covert operations (including assassination schemes) to subvert or destroy governments in the Third World. The CIA helped overthrow the governments of Iran (1953) and Guatemala (1954) but failed in attempts to topple regimes in Indonesia (1958) and Cuba (1961).

The CIA and other components of the American intelligence community followed the principle of plausible deniability: covert operations should be conducted in such a way, and the decisions that launched them concealed so well, that the president could deny any knowledge of them. Thus, President Eisenhower disavowed any U.S. role in Guatemala, even though he had ordered the operation. He and his successor, John F. Kennedy, also denied that they had instructed the CIA to assassinate Cuba's Fidel Castro, whose regime after 1959 became stridently anti-American.

24-5c Nuclear Buildup

Leaders in Moscow soon became aware of Eisenhower's expanded use of covert action as well as his stockpiling of nuclear weapons. They increased their own intelligence activity and tested their first H-bomb in 1953. Four years later, they shocked Americans by firing the world's first intercontinental ballistic missile (ICBM) and then propelling the satellite *Sputnik* into orbit in outer space. Americans felt more vulnerable to air attack and inferior in rocket technology, even though in 1957 the United States had 2,460 strategic weapons and a nuclear stockpile of 5,543, compared with the Soviet Union's 102 and 650. As President Eisenhower said, "If we were to release our nuclear stockpile on the Soviet Union, the main danger would arise not from retaliation but from fallout in the earth's atmosphere." The administration enlarged its fleet of long-range bombers (B-52s) and deployed intermediate-range missiles in Europe, targeted against the Soviet Union. At the end of 1960, the United States began adding Polaris missile-bearing submarines to its navy. To foster future technological advancement, the National Aeronautics and Space Administration (NASA) was created in 1958.

Overall, though, Eisenhower sought to avoid any kind of military confrontation with the Soviet Union and China; notwithstanding Dulles's tough talk of "liberation" and "massive retaliation," the administration was content to follow Truman's lead and emphasize the *containment* of communism. Eisenhower rejected opportunities to use nuclear weapons, and he proved more reluctant than many other Cold War presidents to send American soldiers into battle. He preferred to fight the Soviets at the level of propaganda. Convinced that the struggle against Moscow would in large measure be decided in the arena of international public opinion, he wanted to win the "hearts and minds" of people overseas. The "People-to-People" campaign, launched in 1956, sought to use ordinary Americans and nongovernmental organizations to enhance the international image of the United States and its people.

In the same way, American cultural exchanges and participation in trade fairs in the Eisenhower years were used to create a favorable atmosphere abroad for U.S. political, economic, and military policies. Sometimes, the propaganda war was waged on the Soviets' own turf. In 1959, Vice President Richard Nixon traveled to Moscow to open an American products fair. In the display of a modern American kitchen, part of a model six-room ranch-style house, Nixon extolled capitalist consumerism, while Soviet premier Nikita Khrushchev, Stalin's successor, touted the merits of communism. The encounter became famous as the "kitchen debate."

24-5d Rebellion in Hungary

Eisenhower showed his restraint in 1956 when turmoil rocked parts of Eastern Europe. In February, Khrushchev called for "peaceful coexistence" between capitalists and communists, denounced Stalin, and suggested that Moscow would tolerate different brands of communism. Revolts against Soviet power promptly erupted in Poland and Hungary, testing Khrushchev's new permissiveness. After a new Hungarian government in 1956 announced its withdrawal from the Warsaw Pact (the Soviet military alliance formed in 1955

domino theory Eisenhower's prediction that if Vietnam went communist, then the smaller, neighboring communities of Thailand, Burma, Indonesia, and ultimately all of Asia would fall like dominoes.

Sputnik Soviet satellite that was the world's first successful launch in space in 1957; it dashed the American myth of unquestioned technological superiority.

The People-to-People Campaign

Not long after the start of the Cold War, U.S. officials determined that the Soviet-American confrontation was as much psychological and ideological as military and economic. One result was the People-to-People campaign, a state-private venture initiated by the United States Information Agency (USIA) in 1956, which aimed to win the "hearts and minds" of people around the world. In this program, American propaganda experts sought to channel the energies of ordinary Americans, businesses, civic organizations, labor groups, and women's clubs to promote confidence abroad in the basic goodness of the American people and, by extension, their government. In addition, the campaign was designed to raise morale at home by giving Americans a sense of personal participation in the Cold War struggle. The People-to-People campaign, one USIA pamphlet said, made "every man an ambassador."

Campaign activities resembled the home-front mobilization efforts of World War II. If, during the war, Americans were exhorted by the Office of War Information to purchase war bonds, now they were told that $30 could send a ninety-nine-volume portable library of American books to schools and libraries overseas. Publishers donated magazines and books for free distribution to foreign countries—*Woman's Day*, for example, volunteered six thousand copies of the magazine per month. People-to-People committees organized sister-city affiliations and "pen-pal" letter exchanges, hosted exchange students, and organized traveling "People-to-People delegations" representing their various communities. The travelers were urged to behave like goodwill ambassadors when abroad and to "help overcome any feeling that America is a land that thinks money can buy everything." They were to "appreciate [foreigners'] manners and customs, not to insist on imitations of the American way of doing things."

To extol everyday life in the United States, Camp Fire Girls in more than three thousand communities took photographs on the theme "This is our home. This is how we live. These are my People." The photographs, assembled in albums, were sent to girls in Latin America, Africa, Asia, and the Middle East. The Hobbies Committee, meanwhile, connected people with interests in radio, photography, coins, stamps, and horticulture. One group represented dog owners, in the belief that "dogs make good ambassadors and are capable of hurdling the barriers of language and ideologies in the quest for peace."

Just what effect the People-to-People campaign had on foreign images of the United States is hard to say. The persistence to this day of the widespread impression that Americans are a provincial, materialistic people suggests that skepticism is in order. But alongside this negative image is a more positive one that sees Americans as admirably open, friendly, optimistic, and pragmatic; if the campaign did not erase the former impression, it may have helped foster the latter. Whatever role the People-to-People campaign played in the larger Cold War struggle, it certainly achieved one of its chief objectives: to link ordinary Americans more closely to people in other parts of the world.

CRITICAL THINKING

▫ The People-to-People campaign was meant to cultivate abroad the idea that Americans were good, hard-working people who respected others' cultures and customs. Why was it important to spread this view of Americans in the Cold War atmosphere?

◁ "Make a friend this trip," urges this framed People-to-People poster, delivered to President Eisenhower in May 1957, "for yourself, for your business, for your country." With the president are two of the campaign's leaders, John W. Hanes Jr. and Edward Lipscomb.

Dwight D. Eisenhower Library

with communist countries of Eastern Europe), Soviet troops and tanks battled students and workers in the streets of Budapest and crushed the rebellion.

Although the Eisenhower administration's propaganda had been encouraging liberation efforts, U.S. officials found themselves unable to aid the rebels without igniting a world war. Instead, they promised only to welcome Hungarian immigrants in greater numbers than American quota laws allowed. Even so, the West could have reaped some propaganda advantage from this display of Soviet brute force had not British, French, and Israeli troops—U.S. allies—invaded Egypt during the Suez crisis just before the Soviets smashed the Hungarian uprising (see "Suez Crisis," Section 24-6g).

The turmoil had hardly subsided when the divided city of Berlin once again became a Cold War flash point. The Soviets railed against the placement in West Germany of American bombers capable of carrying nuclear warheads, and they complained that West Berlin had become an escape route for disaffected East Germans. In 1958, Khrushchev announced that the Soviet Union would recognize East German control of all of Berlin unless the United States and its allies began talks on German reunification and rearmament. The United States refused to give up its hold on West Berlin or to break West German ties with NATO. Khrushchev backed away from his ultimatum but promised to press the issue again.

24-5e U-2 Incident

Khrushchev hoped to do just that at a summit meeting planned for Paris in mid-1960. But two weeks before the conference, on May 1, a U-2 spy plane carrying high-powered cameras crashed 1,200 miles inside the Soviet Union. Moscow claimed credit for shooting down the plane, which the Soviets put on display along with Francis Gary Powers, the captured CIA pilot, and the pictures he had been snapping of Soviet military sites. Khrushchev demanded an apology for the U.S. violation of Soviet airspace. When Washington refused, the Soviets walked out of the Paris summit—"a graveyard of lost opportunities," as a Soviet official put it.

While sparring over Europe, both sides kept a wary eye on the People's Republic of China, which denounced the Soviet call for peaceful coexistence. Despite evidence of a widening Sino-Soviet split, most American officials still treated communism as a monolithic world movement. The isolation separating Beijing and Washington stymied communication and made continued conflict between China and the United States likely. In 1954, in a dispute over some miniscule islands off the Chinese coast—Mazu (Matsu) and the chain known as Jinmen (Quemoy)—the United States and the People's Republic of China lurched toward the brink. Taiwan's Jiang Jieshi held these islands and hoped to use them as a launching point for the counterrevolution on the mainland. Communist China's guns bombarded the islands in 1954. Thinking that U.S. credibility was at stake, Eisenhower decided to defend

the outposts; he even hinted that he might use nuclear weapons. Why massive retaliation over such an insignificant issue? "Let's keep the Reds guessing," advised John Foster Dulles. "But what if they guessed wrong?" critics replied.

24-5f Formosa Resolution

In early 1955, Congress passed the Formosa Resolution, authorizing the president to deploy American forces to defend Formosa and adjoining islands. In so doing, Congress formally surrendered to the president what it had informally given up at the time of the Korea decision in 1950: the constitutional power to declare war. Although the crisis passed in April 1955, war loomed again in 1958 over Jinmen and Mazu. This time, after Washington strongly cautioned him not to use force against the mainland, Jiang withdrew some troops from the islands, and China relaxed its bombardments. But Eisenhower's nuclear threats persuaded the Chinese that they, too, needed nuclear arms. In 1964, China exploded its first nuclear bomb.

24-6 The Struggle for the Third World

▶ **How did the United States become involved and intervene in Third World countries?**

▶ **How did Third World countries resist U.S. influence and intervention?**

▶ **What economic and political factors influenced the development of U.S. foreign policy in the Middle East?**

▶ **How did American actions in Vietnam evolve during Eisenhower's presidency?**

In much of the Third World, the process of decolonization that began during the First World War accelerated after the Second World War, when the economically wracked imperial countries proved incapable of resisting their colonies' demands for freedom. A cavalcade of new nations cast off their colonial bonds (see Map 24.3). In 1960 alone, eighteen new African nations did so. From 1943 to 1994, a total of 125 countries became independent (the figure includes the former Soviet republics that departed the USSR in 1991). The emergence of so many new states in the 1940s and after, and the instability associated with the transfer of authority, shook the foundations of the international system. Power was redistributed, creating "near chaos," said one U.S. government report. In the traditional U.S. sphere of influence, Latin America, nationalists once again challenged Washington's dominance.

24-6a Interests in the Third World

By the late 1940s, when Cold War lines were drawn fairly tightly in Europe, Soviet-American rivalry shifted increasingly to the Third World. Much was at stake. The new

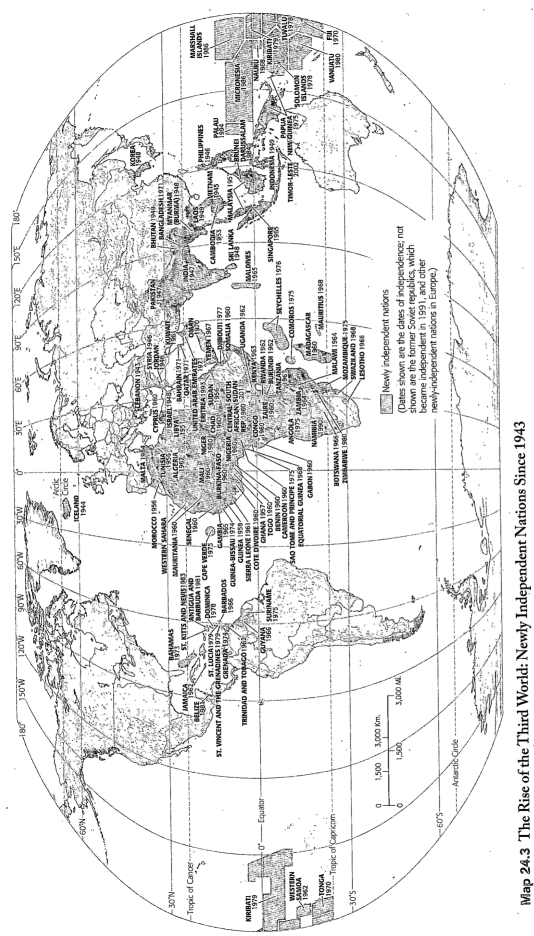

Map 24.3 The Rise of the Third World: Newly Independent Nations Since 1943

Accelerated by the Second World War, decolonization liberated many peoples from imperial rule. New nations emerged in the postwar international system dominated by the Cold War rivalry of the United States and the Soviet Union. Many newly independent states became targets of great-power intrigue but chose nonalignment in the Cold War.

nations could buy American goods and technology, supply strategic raw materials, and invite investments (more than one-third of America's private foreign investments were in Third World countries in 1959). And they could build cultural ties with the United States. Both great powers, moreover, looked to these new states for votes in the United Nations and sought sites within their borders for military and intelligence bases. But often poor and unstable—and rife with tribal, ethnic, and class rivalries—many new nations sought to end the economic, military, and cultural hegemony of the West. Many learned to play off the two superpowers against each other to garner more aid and arms. U.S. interventions—military and otherwise—in the Third World, American leaders believed, became necessary to impress Moscow with Washington's might and to resolve and counter the nationalism and radical anticapitalist social change that threatened American strategic and economic interests.

To thwart nationalist, radical, and communist challenges, the United States directed massive resources—foreign aid, propaganda, development projects—toward the Third World. By 1961, more than 90 percent of U.S. foreign aid was going to developing nations. Washington also allied with native elites and with undemocratic but anticommunist regimes, meddled in civil wars, and unleashed CIA covert operations. These American interventions often generated resentment among the local populace. When some of the larger Third World states—notably India, Ghana, Egypt, and Indonesia—refused to take sides in the Cold War, Secretary of State Dulles declared that neutralism was a step on the road to communism. Both he and Eisenhower insisted that every nation should take a side in the life-and-death Cold War struggle.

American leaders argued that technologically "backward" Third World countries needed Western-induced capitalist development and modernization in order to enjoy economic growth, social harmony, and political moderation. Often these U.S. officials also ascribed stereotyped race-, age-, and gender-based characteristics to Third World peoples, seeing them as dependent, emotional, and irrational, and therefore dependent on the fatherly tutelage of the United States. Cubans, CIA director Allen Dulles told the National Security Council in early 1959, "had to be treated more or less like children. They had to be led rather than rebuffed. If they were rebuffed, like children, they were capable of almost anything." At other times, American officials suggested that Third World countries were weak women—passive and servile, unable to resist the menacing appeals of communists and neutralists.

24-6b Racism and Segregation as U.S. Handicaps

Race attitudes and segregation practices in the United States especially influenced U.S. relations with Third World countries. In 1955, G. L. Mehta, the Indian ambassador to the United States, was refused service in the whites-only section

of a restaurant at Houston International Airport. The insult stung deeply, as did many similar indignities experienced by other Third World diplomats. Fearing damaged relations with India, a large nation whose allegiance the United States sought in the Cold War, John Foster Dulles apologized to Mehta. The secretary thought racial segregation in the United States was a "major international hazard," spoiling American efforts to win friends in Third World countries and giving the Soviets a propaganda advantage. American practices and ideals did not align.

Thus, when the U.S. attorney general appealed to the Supreme Court to strike down segregation in public schools, he underlined that the humiliation of dark-skinned diplomats "furnished grist for the Communist propaganda mills." When the Court announced its *Brown* decision in 1954, the government quickly broadcast news of the desegregation order around the world in thirty-five languages on its Voice of America overseas radio network (see "Supreme Court Victories and School Desegregation," Section 25-4b). But the problem did not go away. For example, after the 1957 Little Rock crisis (see "Federal Authority and States' Rights," Section 25-4e), Dulles remarked that racial bigotry was "ruining our foreign policy. The effect of this in Asia and Africa will be worse for us than Hungary was for the Russians." Still, when an office of the Department of State decided to counter Soviet propaganda by creating for the 1958 World's Fair in Brussels an exhibit titled "The Unfinished Work"—on race relations in the United States and strides taken toward desegregation—southern conservatives kicked up such a furor that the Eisenhower administration closed the display.

American hostility toward revolution also obstructed the quest for influence in the Third World. In the twentieth century, the United States openly opposed revolutions in Mexico, China, Russia, Cuba, Vietnam, Nicaragua, and Iran, among other nations. Preferring, like most other great powers in history, to maintain the status quo, the United States usually supported its European allies or the conservative, propertied classes in the Third World. In 1960, for example, when forty-three African and Asian states sponsored a UN resolution endorsing decolonization, the United States abstained from the vote.

24-6c Development and Modernization

Yet idealism also inspired U.S. policy. Believing that Third World peoples craved modernization and that the American economic model of private enterprise and cooperation among business, labor, and government was best for them, American policymakers launched various "development" projects. Such projects held out the promise of sustained economic growth, prosperity, and stability, which the benefactors hoped would undermine radicalism. In the 1950s, the Carnegie, Ford, and Rockefeller Foundations worked with the U.S. Agency for International Development (AID) to sponsor a Green Revolution, a dramatic increase in agricultural production—for example, by the use of hybrid seeds. The Rockefeller Foundation supported foreign universities' efforts to train national leaders committed to non-radical development; from 1958 to 1969, the philanthropic agency spent $25 million in Nigeria. Before Dean Rusk became secretary of state in 1961, he served as president of the Rockefeller Foundation.

To persuade Third World peoples to abandon radical doctrines and neutralism, American leaders, often in cooperation with the business-sponsored Advertising Council, directed propaganda at developing nations. The United States Information Agency (USIA), founded in 1953, used films, radio broadcasts, the magazine *Free World*, exhibitions, exchange programs, and libraries (in 162 cities worldwide by 1961) to trumpet the theme of "People's Capitalism." Citing America's economic success—contrasted with "slave-labor" conditions in the Soviet Union—the message showcased well-paid American workers, political democracy, and religious freedom. To counter ugly pictures of segregation and white attacks on African Americans and civil rights activists in the South, the USIA applauded success stories of individual African Americans, such as boxers Floyd Patterson and Sugar Ray Robinson. In 1960 alone, some 13.8 million people visited U.S. pavilions abroad, including 1 million at the consumer products exhibit "Tradeways to Peace and Prosperity" in Damascus, Syria.

Undoubtedly, the American way of life appealed to some Third World peoples. They, too, wanted to enjoy American consumer goods, rock music, economic status, and educational opportunities. Hollywood movies offered enticing glimpses of middle-class materialism, and U.S. films dominated many overseas markets. Blue jeans, advertising billboards, and soft drinks flooded these societies. But if foreigners often envied Americans, they also resented them for having so much and wasting so much and for allowing their corporations to extract such high profits from overseas. Americans often received blame for the persistent poverty of the developing world, even though the leaders of those nations made decisions that hindered their own progress, such as pouring millions of dollars into their militaries while their people went hungry. Nonetheless, anti-American resentments could be measured in the late 1950s in attacks on USIA libraries in Calcutta, India; Beirut, Lebanon; and Bogotá, Colombia.

24-6d Intervention in Guatemala

When the more benign techniques of containment—aid, trade, cultural relations—proved insufficient to get Third World nations to line up on the American side in the Cold War, the Eisenhower administration often showed a willingness to press harder, by covert or overt means. Guatemala was an early test case. In 1951, leftist Jacobo

△ In the 1950s, the United States Information Agency—known overseas as the United States Information Service or USIS—sought to generate favorable international perceptions of American ideas and culture, including in what the State Department called "isolated areas." Here, people crowd around a USIS mobile library on a road near Rangoon, Burma, in June 1953.

National Archives and Records Administration

Arbenz Guzmán was elected president of Guatemala, a poor country whose largest landowner was the American-owned United Fruit Company. United Fruit was an economic power throughout Latin America, where it owned 3 million acres of land and operated railroads, ports, ships, and telecommunications facilities. To fulfill his promise of land reform, Arbenz expropriated United Fruit's uncultivated land and offered compensation. The company dismissed the offer and charged that Arbenz posed a communist threat—a charge that CIA officials had already floated because Arbenz employed some communists in his government. The CIA began a secret plot to overthrow Arbenz. He turned to Moscow for military aid, thus reinforcing American suspicions. The CIA airlifted arms into Guatemala, dropping them at United Fruit facilities, and in mid-1954, CIA-supported Guatemalans struck from Honduras. U.S. planes bombed the capital city, and the invaders drove Arbenz from power. The new pro-American regime returned United Fruit's land, but an ensuing civil war staggered the Central American nation for decades.

24-6e The Cuban Revolution and Fidel Castro

Eisenhower also watched with apprehension as turmoil gripped Cuba in the late 1950s. In early 1959, Fidel Castro's rebels, or *barbudos* ("bearded ones"), driven by profound anti-American nationalism, ousted Fulgencio Batista, a longtime U.S. ally who had welcomed North American investors, U.S. military advisers, and tourists to the Caribbean island. Batista's corrupt, dictatorial regime had helped turn Havana into a haven for gambling and prostitution run by organized crime. Cubans had resented U.S. domination ever since the early twentieth century, when the Platt Amendment had compromised their independence. Curbing U.S. influence became a rallying cry of the Cuban revolution, all the more so after the CIA conspired secretly but futilely to block Castro's rise to power in 1958. From the start, Castro sought to roll back the influence of American business, which had invested some $1 billion on the island, and to break the U.S. grasp on Cuban trade.

Castro's increasing authoritarianism, anti-Yankee declarations, and growing popularity in the hemisphere alarmed Washington. In early 1960, after Cuba signed a trade treaty with the Soviet Union, Eisenhower ordered the CIA to organize an invasion force of Cuban exiles to overthrow the Castro government. The agency also began to plot an assassination of the Cuban leader. When Eisenhower drastically cut U.S. purchases of Cuban sugar, Castro seized all North American–owned companies that had not yet been nationalized. Threatened by U.S. decisions designed to bring him and his revolution down, Castro appealed to the Soviet Union, which offered loans and expanded trade. Just before leaving office in early 1961, Eisenhower broke diplomatic relations with Cuba and advised president-elect John F. Kennedy to advance plans for the invasion,

which came—and failed—in early 1961 (see "Bay of Pigs Invasion," Section 26-1e).

24-6f Arab-Israeli Conflict

In the Middle East, meanwhile, the Eisenhower administration confronted challenges posed by ongoing tensions between Arabs and Jews, and by nationalist leaders in Iran and Egypt (see Map 29.2, Section 29-3f). Prior to the end of World War II, only France and Britain among the great powers had been much concerned with this region of the world; they had effectively dominated the area during the prior three decades. But the dissolution of empires and the rise of Cold War tensions drew Washington into the region, as did the deepening tensions in British-held Palestine. From 1945 to 1947, Britain tried to enlist U.S. officials in the effort to find a solution to the vexing question of how to split Palestine between the Arabs and Jews who lived there. The Truman administration rejected London's solicitations, and the British, despairing at the violence between Arabs and Jews and at the rising number of British deaths, in 1947 turned the issue over to the United Nations, which voted to partition Palestine into separate Arab and Jewish states. Arab leaders opposed the decision, but in May 1948 Jewish leaders announced the creation of Israel.

The United States, which lobbied hard to secure the UN vote, extended recognition to the new state mere minutes after the act of foundation. A moral conviction that Jews deserved a homeland after the suffering of the Holocaust, and that Zionism was a worthy movement that would create a democratic Israel, influenced Truman's decision, as did the belief that Jewish votes might swing some states to the Democrats in the 1948 election. These beliefs trumped concerns that Arab oil producers might turn against the United States and that close Soviet-Israeli ties could turn Israel into a pro-Soviet bastion in the Middle East. The Soviet Union did promptly recognize the new nation, but Israeli leaders kept Moscow at arm's length, in part because they had more pressing concerns. Palestinian Arabs, displaced from land they considered theirs, joined with Israel's Arab neighbors to make immediate war on the new state. The Israelis stopped the offensive in bloody fighting over the next six months until a UN-backed truce was called.

Thereafter, U.S. Middle East policy centered on ensuring Israel's survival and cementing ties with Arab oil producers. American companies produced about half of the region's petroleum in the 1950s. Eisenhower consequently sought to avoid actions that might alienate Arab states, such as drawing too close to Israel, and he cultivated close relations with oil-rich Iran. Its ruling shah had granted American oil companies a 40 percent interest in a new petroleum consortium in return for CIA help in the successful overthrow, in 1953, of his rival, and prime minister, Mohammed Mossadegh, who had attempted to nationalize

△ In the years 1948–1950, hundreds of thousands of Jewish refugees arrived in the state of Israel. Legendary war photographer Robert Capa snapped this picture of refugees arriving on a boat in Haifa in 1949. A few years later, while on assignment for *Life* magazine, Capa would be killed by a land mine in Indochina.

foreign oil interests. Nor was it only about petroleum: Iran's position on the Soviet border made the shah a particularly valuable friend.

American officials faced a more formidable foe in Egypt, in the form of Gamal Abdul Nasser, a towering figure in a pan-Arabic movement to reduce Western interests in the Middle East. Nasser vowed to expel the British from the Suez Canal and the Israelis from Palestine. The United States wished neither to anger the Arabs, for fear of losing valuable oil supplies, nor to alienate its ally Israel, which was supported at home by politically active American Jews. But when Nasser declared neutrality in the Cold War, Dulles lost patience.

24-6g Suez Crisis

In 1956, the United States abruptly reneged on its offer to Egypt to help finance the Aswan Dam, a project to provide inexpensive electricity and water for thirsty Nile valley farmland. Secretary Dulles's blunt economic pressure backfired, for Nasser responded by nationalizing the British-owned Suez Canal, intending to use its profits to build the dam. At a mass rally in Alexandria, Nasser expressed the profound nationalism typical of Third World peoples shedding an imperial past: "Tonight our Egyptian canal will be run by Egyptians. Egyptians!" Fully 75 percent of Western Europe's oil came from the Middle

East, most of it transported through the Suez Canal. Fearing an interruption in this vital trade, the British and French conspired with Israel to bring down Nasser. On October 29, 1956, the Israelis invaded Suez, joined two days later by British and French forces.

Eisenhower fumed. America's allies had not consulted him, and the attack had shifted attention from Soviet intervention in Hungary. The president also feared that the invasion would cause Nasser to seek help from the Soviets, inviting them into the Middle East. Eisenhower sternly demanded that London, Paris, and Tel Aviv pull their troops out, and they did. Egypt took possession of the canal, the Soviets built the Aswan Dam, and Nasser became a hero to Third World peoples. French and British influence in the region declined sharply. To counter Nasser, the United States determined to "build up" as an "Arab rival" the conservative King Ibn Saud of Saudi Arabia. Although the monarch renewed America's lease of an air base, few Arabs respected the notoriously corrupt Saud.

24-6h Eisenhower Doctrine

Washington officials worried that a "vacuum" existed in the Middle East—and that the Soviets might fill it. Nasserites insisted that there was no vacuum but rather a growing Arab nationalism that provided the best defense against communism. In an effort to improve the deteriorating

Western position in the Middle East and to protect American interests there, the president in 1957 proclaimed the **Eisenhower Doctrine.** The United States would intervene in the Middle East, he declared, if any government threatened by a communist takeover asked for help. In 1958, fourteen thousand American troops scrambled ashore in Lebanon to quell an internal political dispute that Washington feared might be exploited by pro-Nasser groups or communists. Concentrating the troops in the area of Beirut, Eisenhower said their mission was "not primarily to fight" but merely to show the flag. The restrained use of U.S. military power served to defuse the crisis, as Lebanese officials agreed to work for a peaceful transition to a new leadership. In Dulles's view, the intervention also served to "reassure many small nations that they could call on us in a time of crisis."

Cold War concerns also drove Eisenhower's policy toward Vietnam, where nationalists battled the French for independence. Despite a substantial U.S. aid program initiated under Truman, the French lost steadily to the Vietminh. Finally, in early 1954, Ho's forces surrounded the French fortress at Dien Bien Phu in northwest Vietnam (see Map 26.2, Section 26-4d). Although some of Eisenhower's advisers recommended a massive American air strike against Vietminh positions, perhaps even using tactical atomic weapons, the president moved cautiously. The United States had been advising and bankrolling the French, but it had not committed its own forces to the war. If American airpower did not save the French, would ground troops be required next, and in hostile terrain? As one high-level doubter remarked, "One cannot go over Niagara Falls in a barrel only slightly."

Worrying aloud about a communist victory, Eisenhower pressed the British to help form a coalition to address the Indochinese crisis, but they refused. At home, influential members of Congress—including Lyndon Baines Johnson of Texas, who as president would wage large-scale war in Vietnam—told Eisenhower they wanted "no more Koreas" and warned him against any unilateral U.S. military intervention. Some felt very uneasy about supporting colonialism. The issue became moot on May 7, when the weary French defenders at Dien Bien Phu surrendered.

24-6i Geneva Accords on Vietnam

Peace talks, already under way in Geneva, brought Cold War and nationalist contenders together—the United States, the Soviet Union, Britain, the People's Republic of China, Laos, Cambodia, and the competing Vietnamese regimes of Bao Dai and Ho Chi Minh. John Foster Dulles, a reluctant participant, feared the communists would get

Eisenhower Doctrine The 1957 proclamation that the United States would send military aid and, if necessary, troops to any Middle Eastern nation threatened by "Communist aggression."

the better of any agreement, yet in the end the Vietminh received less than their dominant military position suggested they should. The 1954 Geneva Accords, signed by France and Ho's Democratic Republic of Vietnam, temporarily divided Vietnam at the seventeenth parallel; Ho's government was confined to the North, Bao Dai's to the South. Only after pressure from the Chinese and the Soviets, who feared U.S. intervention in Vietnam without an agreement, did Ho's government agree to this compromise. The seventeenth parallel was meant to serve as a military truce line, not a national boundary, with elections for reunification slated to follow in 1956. Meanwhile, neither North nor South was to join a military alliance or permit foreign military bases on its soil.

Confident that the Geneva agreements ultimately would mean communist victory, the United States from an early point set about trying to undermine them. Soon after the conference, a CIA team entered Vietnam and undertook secret operations against the North, including commando raids across the seventeenth parallel. In the South, the United States helped Ngo Dinh Diem push Bao Dai aside and inaugurate the Republic of Vietnam. A Catholic in a Buddhist nation, Diem was a dedicated nationalist and anticommunist, but he had little mass support. He staged a fraudulent election in South Vietnam that gave him 99 percent of the vote (in Saigon, he received 200,000 more votes than there were registered voters). When Ho and some in the world community pressed for national elections in keeping with the Geneva agreements, Diem and Eisenhower refused, fearing that the popular Vietminh leader would win. From 1955 to 1961, the Diem government received more than $1 billion in American aid, most of it military. American advisers organized and trained Diem's army, and American agriculturalists worked to improve crops. Diem's Saigon regime became dependent on the United States for its very existence, and the culture of South Vietnam became increasingly Americanized.

24-6j National Liberation Front

Diem proved a difficult ally. He acted dictatorially, abolishing village elections and appointing to public office people beholden to him. He threw dissenters in jail and shut down newspapers that criticized his regime. When U.S. officials periodically urged him to implement meaningful land reform, he blithely ignored them. Noncommunists and communists alike began to strike back at Diem's repressive government. In Hanoi, Ho's government initially focused on solidifying its control on the North, but in the late 1950s it began to send aid to southern insurgents, who embarked on a program of terror, assassinating hundreds of Diem's village officials. In late 1960, southern communists, acting at the direction of Hanoi, organized the National Liberation Front (NLF), known as the Vietcong. The Vietcong in turn attracted other anti-Diem groups

△ French troops capture a Vietminh soldier during an operation in the Red River Delta in Tonkin (northern Vietnam) in March 1952. The Vietminh were adept at camouflage, but this soldier could not escape detection while hidden in a dyke.

in the South. And the Eisenhower administration, all too aware of Diem's shortcomings and his unwillingness to follow American advice, continued to affirm its commitment to the preservation of an independent, noncommunist South Vietnam.

Summary

The United States emerged from the Second World War as the preeminent world power. Confident in the nation's immediate physical security, Washington officials nevertheless worried that the unstable international system, an unfriendly Soviet Union, and the decolonizing Third World could upset American plans for the postwar peace. Locked with the Soviet Union in a "Cold War," U.S. leaders marshaled their nation's superior resources to influence and cajole other countries. Foreign economic aid, atomic diplomacy, military alliances, client states, covert operations, interventions, propaganda, cultural infiltration—these and more became the instruments for waging the Cold War, a war that began as a conflict over the future of Europe but soon spread to encompass the globe.

America's claim to international leadership was welcomed by many in Western Europe and elsewhere who feared Stalin's intentions and those of his successors in the Soviet Union. The reconstruction of former enemies Japan and (West) Germany helped those nations recover swiftly and become staunch members of the Western alliance. But U.S. policy also sparked resistance. Communist countries condemned financial and atomic diplomacy, while Third World nations, many of them newly independent, sought to undermine America's European allies and sometimes identified the United States as an imperial coconspirator. On occasion, even America's allies bristled at a United States that boldly proclaimed itself economic master and global policeman, and haughtily touted its hegemonic status.

At home, liberal and radical critics protested that Presidents Truman and Eisenhower exaggerated the communist threat, wasting U.S. assets on immoral foreign ventures; crippled legitimate nationalist aspirations; and displayed racial bias. Still, these presidents and their successors held firm to the mission of creating a nonradical, capitalist, free-trade international order in the mold of domestic America. Determined to

The National Security State

To build a cathedral, someone has observed, you first need a religion, and a religion needs inspiring texts that command authority. For decades, America's Cold War religion has been national security; its texts, the Truman Doctrine, the "X" article, and NSC-68; and its cathedral, the national security state. The word *state* in this case means "civil government." During the Cold War, embracing preparedness for total war, the U.S. government essentially transformed itself into a huge military headquarters that interlocked with corporations and universities. Preaching the doctrine of national security, moreover, members of Congress strove to gain lucrative defense contracts for their districts.

Overseen by the president and his advisory body, the National Security Council, the national security state has had as its core what the National Security Act of 1947 called the National Military Establishment; in 1949, it became the Department of Defense. This department ranks as a leading employer; its payroll by 2007 included 1.4 million people on active duty and almost 600,000 civilian personnel, giving it more employees than Exxon Mobil, Ford, General Motors, and GE combined. Almost 700,000 of these troops and civilians served overseas, in 177 countries covering every time zone. Although spending for national defense declined in the years after the end of the Cold War, it never fell below $290 billion. In the aftermath of the 9/11 terrorist attacks and the invasion of Iraq, the military budget rose again, reaching $439 billion in 2007. By 2016, it topped $600 billion. That figure tops the entire economies of Poland and Belgium and equals the combined military spending of the twenty countries with the next-largest defense budgets. Nor does that sum include tens of billions of dollars in supplementary funds allocated by Congress to pay for operations in Afghanistan and Iraq.

Joining the Department of Defense as instruments of national security policy were the Joint Chiefs of Staff, the Central Intelligence Agency, and dozens more government bodies. The focus of all these entities was on finding the best means to combat real and potential threats from foreign governments. But what about threats from within? The terrorist attacks of September 2001 made starkly clear that enemies existed who, while perhaps beholden to a foreign entity—it need not be a government—launched their attacks from inside the nation's borders. Accordingly, in 2002 President George W. Bush proposed the creation of a Department of Homeland Security (DHS), which would have 170,000 employees and would include all or part of twenty-two agencies, including the Coast Guard, the Customs Service, the Federal Emergency Management Administration (FEMA), and the Internal Revenue Service. It would involve the biggest overhaul of the federal bureaucracy since the Department of Defense was created, and it signified a more expansive notion of national security. By 2017, the number of DHS employees had risen to 240,000.

In 1961, President Eisenhower warned against a "military-industrial complex," while others feared a "garrison state" or a "warfare state." Despite the warnings, by the start of the twenty-first century, the national security state remained vigorous, a lasting legacy of the early Cold War period for a people and a nation.

CRITICAL THINKING

▢ The Department of Homeland Security was established after the attacks of September 11, 2001 to combat homegrown terrorists. Despite this, domestic terrorism has continued to cause American civilians' deaths with the Boston Marathon bombing (2013), Charleston Church shooting (2015), San Bernardino shooting (2015), and Orlando nightclub shooting (2016) as prime examples. What steps should the nation take to avoid future massacres such as these?

contain Soviet expansion, fearful of domestic charges of being "soft on communism," they worked to enlarge the U.S. sphere of influence and shape the world. In their years of nurturing allies and applying the containment doctrine worldwide, Truman and Eisenhower held the line—against the Soviet Union and the People's Republic of China, and against nonalignment, communism, nationalism, and revolution everywhere. One consequence was a dramatic increase in presidential power in the realm of foreign affairs—what the historian Arthur M. Schlesinger Jr. called "the Imperial Presidency"—as Congress ceded constitutional power.

Putting itself at odds with many in the Third World, the United States usually stood with its European allies to slow decolonization and to preach evolution rather than revolution. The globalist perspective of the United States prompted Americans to interpret many troubles in the developing world as Cold War conflicts, inspired if not directed by Soviet-backed communists. The intensity of the Cold War obscured for Americans the indigenous roots of most Third World troubles, as the wars in Korea and Vietnam attested. Nor could the United States abide developing nations' drive for economic independence—for gaining control of their own raw materials and economies. Deeply intertwined in the global economy as importer, exporter, and investor, the United States read challenges from this "periphery" as threats to the American standard of living and a way of life characterized by private enterprise. The Third World, in short, challenged U.S. strategic power by forming a third force in the

Cold War, and it challenged American economic power by seeking a new economic order of shared interests. Overall, the rise of the Third World introduced new actors to the world stage, challenging the bipolarity of the international system and diffusing power.

All the while, the threat of nuclear war unsettled Americans and foreigners alike. In the film *Godzilla* (1956), a prehistoric monster, revived by atomic bomb tests, rampages through Tokyo. Stanley Kramer's popular but disturbing movie *On the Beach* (1959), based on Nevil Shute's best-selling 1957 novel, depicts a nuclear holocaust in which the last humans on earth choose to swallow government-issued poison tablets so that they can die before H-bomb radiation sickness kills them. Such doomsday or Armageddon attitudes contrasted sharply with official U.S. government assurances that Americans would survive a nuclear war. In *On the Beach*, a dying wife asks her husband, "Couldn't anyone have stopped it?" His answer: "Some kinds of silliness you just can't stop." Eisenhower did not halt it, even though he told Khrushchev in 1959 that "we really should come to some sort of agreement in order to stop this fruitless, really wasteful rivalry."

Suggestions for Further Reading

Campbell Craig and Fredrik Logevall, *America's Cold War: The Politics of Insecurity* (2009)

Nick Cullather, *The Hungry World: America's Cold War Battle Against Poverty in Asia* (2013)

Bruce Cumings, *The Korean War: A History* (2010)

Mary L. Dudziak, *Cold War Civil Rights: Race and the Image of American Democracy* (2000)

John Lewis Gaddis, *Strategies of Containment*, 2nd ed. (2005)

Stephen Kinzer, *The Brothers: John Foster Dulles, Allen Dulles, and Their Secret World War* (2013)

Fredrik Logevall, *Embers of War: The Fall of an Empire and the Making of America's Vietnam* (2012)

Geoffrey Roberts, *Stalin's Wars: From World War to Cold War, 1939–1953* (2007)

Marc Trachtenberg, *A Constructed Peace: The Making of the European Settlement, 1945–1963* (1999)

MINDTAP
From Cengage

MindTap® is a fully online personalized learning experience built upon Cengage Learning content. MindTap® combines student learning tools—readings, multimedia, activities, and assessments—into a singular Learning Path that guides students through the course and helps students develop the critical thinking, analysis, and communication skills that are essential to academic and professional success.

America at Midcentury, 1945–1960

saac and Oleta Nelson wrapped themselves in blankets against the predawn winter cold that morning in late January 1951 as they waited for the brilliant flash of light that would shatter the desert darkness. They, along with a hundred or so friends and neighbors from Cedar City, Utah, had driven out to watch the first atomic test on U.S. soil since the end of World War II. "Everybody was really excited," Isaac remembered. "We wanted to help out what little we could" and "show our patriotism." Soon the bomb's red-orange flare lit up the trees on the other side of the valley, more than ten miles away. And later that afternoon, residents of Kanarraville and Cedar City watched as pinkish-tan clouds drifted across the sky.

In the years immediately following World War II, the United States had tested atomic weapons on isolated islands in the South Pacific. U.S. officials were already aware of the dangers of radioactivity, but its unpredictability was driven home by the grisly deaths of crewmembers from a Japanese fishing boat, the *Daigo Fukuryū Maru* (Lucky Dragon 5), that had been unexpectedly caught in the path of fallout from the U.S. Bikini Atoll test in 1954. Despite that knowledge, as the USSR developed its own atomic weapon and the outbreak of hostilities in Korea signaled an escalation of the Cold War, members of the Atomic Energy Commission (AEC) argued that atomic testing outside U.S. borders presented a threat to national security. The danger to American public health and safety, they concluded (in a phrase from 1957 legal testimony), was offset by the threat of "total annihilation" by the Soviet enemy.

In late 1950, President Truman approved use of a large tract of land in Nevada for the nation's nuclear testing. It had meteorological advantages: the prevailing wind blew eastward, away from

◁ In the Nevada desert in May 1955, the U.S. government used its forty-fourth nuclear test explosion to evaluate the survivability of a nuclear blast. These department store mannequins inhabited a small village, built at the cost of a million dollars, its houses stocked with everything from living room furniture to canned soup. *Life* magazine reported: "The condition of the figures—one charred, another only scorched, another almost untouched—showed that the blast, equivalent to 35,000 tons of TNT . . . make[s] clear that even amid atomic holocaust careful planning could save lives." Loomis Dean/Getty Images

population centers of Los Angeles and Las Vegas. Advisers portrayed the land downwind, which stretched across portions of Nevada, Arizona, and Utah, as "virtually uninhabitable." Yet almost 100,000 people occupied farms and small towns in its desert valleys; many were descendants of Mormon settlers who had arrived in the 1840s or members of the Western Shoshone Nation, on whose land the test site lay. And as radioactive clouds from subsequent tests drifted over those small towns and farms, children played in the fallout as if it were snow.

After fallout from "Harry," a thirty-two-kiloton blast, saturated the region in 1953, forty-five hundred of the fourteen thousand sheep on local ranches died. The AEC issued a press release blaming the deaths on "unprecedented cold weather." Lambs were born that spring without wool or skin, their organs covered only by a thin membrane. The commission suppressed veterinary reports that documented lethal levels of radiation. By 1955, the Atomic Energy Commission had mounted a campaign to reassure "downwinders" that the tests posed no danger. AEC medical staff visited small towns armed with blatant and calculated lies: radiation from nuclear tests, they told residents, amounted to only "about one-twentieth of that experienced in an X-ray." That same year, Oleta Nelson stood outside her home, watching a fallout cloud drift across the sky. Within hours, her exposed skin turned bright red. She vomited and had violent diarrhea. A month later, her hair—beautiful, raven black, shoulder length—fell out. It never grew back. Oleta was diagnosed with a brain tumor in 1962. She died in 1965. By that time, the cancer rate for "downwinders" was one and a half times that of the rest of the U.S. population.

Experience an interactive version of this story in MindTap®.

The Cold War did not affect most Americans so directly. Nonetheless, Cold War fears and policies shaped American life during the postwar era in ways both blatant and subtle, even as many people worked hard to leave the difficult years of depression and war behind and create good lives for themselves and their families.

Of all the major nations in the world, only the United States had emerged from World War II stronger and more prosperous. While Europe and Asia had been devastated, America's farms and cities and factories were intact. U.S. production capacity had increased during the war, and despite social tensions and inequalities, the fight against fascism gave Americans a unity of purpose. Victory seemed to confirm their struggles. But sixteen years of depression and war shadowed the U.S. victory, and memories of these experiences would continue to shape the choices Americans made in their private lives, their domestic policies, and their relations with the world.

In the postwar era, the actions of the federal government and the choices made by individual Americans reconfigured American society. Postwar social policies—many of them shaped by Cold War concerns—that sent millions of veterans to college on the GI Bill linked the nation with high-speed interstate highways, fostered the growth of suburbs and the Sunbelt, and disrupted regional isolation helped to create a national middle-class culture that encompassed an unprecedented majority of the nation's citizens. Countless individual decisions—to go to college, to marry young, to have a large family, to move to the suburbs, to start a business—were made possible by these federal initiatives. The cumulative weight of these individual decisions would change the meanings of class and ethnicity in American society. Americans in the postwar era defined a new American Dream—one that centered on the family, on a new level of material comfort and consumption, and on a shared sense of belonging to a common culture. Elite cultural critics roundly denounced this ideal of suburban comfort as "conformism," but many Americans found satisfaction in this new way of life.

Almost one-quarter of the American people did not share in the postwar prosperity—but they were ever less visible to the middle-class majority. Rural poverty continued, and inner cities became increasingly impoverished as more affluent Americans moved to the suburbs and new migrants—poor black and white southerners, new immigrants from Mexico, Puerto Ricans, and Native Americans resettled by the federal government from tribal lands—arrived.

As class and ethnicity became less important in suburbia, race continued to divide the American people. African Americans faced racism and discrimination throughout the nation, but the war had been a turning point in the struggle for equal rights. During this period, African Americans increasingly took direct action, and in 1955 the yearlong Montgomery bus boycott launched the modern civil rights movement. Gradually the federal government began to protect the civil rights of black Americans, including the Supreme Court's school desegregation decision in *Brown v. Board of Education*.

Compared to the dramatic accomplishments of the New Deal, postwar domestic achievements were modest. Truman pledged to expand the New Deal but was stymied by a conservative Congress. **Dwight D. Eisenhower**, elected in 1952 as the first Republican president in twenty years, offered a solid Republican platform, seeking—though rarely attaining—a balanced budget, reduced taxes, and lower levels of government spending. Both presidents focused primarily on the foreign policy challenges of the Cold War.

The economic boom that began with the end of the war lasted twenty-five years, bringing new prosperity to the American people. Although fears—of nuclear war, of returning hard times—lingered, prosperity bred complacency by the late 1950s. At decade's end, people sought satisfaction in their families and in the consumer pleasures newly available to so many.

- *How did the Cold War affect American society and politics?*

- *How did federal government actions following World War II change the nation?*

- *During the 1950s, many people began to think of their country as a middle-class nation. Were they correct?*

25-1 Shaping Postwar America

▷ **What challenges did the United States face as veterans returned from war?**

▷ **What were the consequences of the GI Bill?**

▷ **What factors contributed to suburbanization in the postwar period?**

▷ **How did postwar federal programs contribute to long-term inequality in American society?**

As Americans celebrated the end of World War II and mourned those who would never return, many feared the challenges that lay ahead. The nation had to reintegrate war veterans into civilian society and find

◁ Classroom at the University of Iowa, 1947, where 60 percent of students were war veterans. GI Bill education benefits transformed American universities.

Margaret Bourke-White/The LIFE Picture Collection/Getty Images

places for young families to live. It had to transform a wartime economy to peacetime functions. And it had to contend with the domestic implications of the Cold War and the new global balance of power. Though unemployment rose and a wave of strikes rocked the nation in the immediate aftermath of the war, the economy soon flourished. This strong economy, along with new federal programs, transformed the shape of American society.

25-1a The Veterans Return

In 1945, as Germany and then Japan surrendered, the nation had to demobilize almost 15 million servicemen. Seeking fairness, authorities decided not to demobilize unit by unit, but instead on an individual basis. Each man received a "service score" based on length of time in military service, time overseas, and time in combat—plus the number of his children. Men with the highest scores went home first; those with the lowest numbers were finally demobilized in June 1947.

Veterans' homecomings were often joyful, but in general, Americans were anxious about veterans' return. In one midwestern small town, elected officials estimated that 20 percent of returning veterans would be "debauched and wild," and that many were likely "deadbeats" who "expect too much." Such concerns were so widespread that *Time* magazine, in mid-1945, reassured readers that "the returned overseas soldier is no nerve-shattered civilian-hater who will explode into violent action if he does not get all he thinks he deserves."

GI Bill Popular name for the Servicemen's Readjustment Act (1944), which sought to aid returning veterans—and maintain economic stability—by providing college tuition, job training, unemployment benefits, and low-interest home and farm loans.

Most men found their way—but it was not always easy. Many veterans returned to wives whose lives had gone on without them, to children they barely knew, to a world grown unfamiliar. Some had serious physical injuries. Almost half a million veterans were diagnosed with neuropsychiatric disabilities, and the National Mental Health Act of 1946 passed, in large part, because of awareness of the psychological toll of war on those who fought. In 1946, Americans flocked to the movie *The Best Years of Our Lives*, which won seven Academy Awards for its depiction of three veterans struggling to adjust to the world to which they had returned.

Americans also worried about the economic impact of demobilization. As the end of the war approached and the American war machine slowed, factories had begun to lay off workers. Ten days after the Allied victory over Japan, 1.8 million people nationwide received pink slips, and 640,000 filed for unemployment compensation. How was the shrinking job base to absorb millions of returning veterans?

25-1b The GI Bill

Though the federal government had done little to prepare for U.S. entry into World War II, it had begun planning for demobilization even while some of the war's most difficult battles lay ahead. In the spring of 1944—a year before V-E Day—Congress unanimously passed the Servicemen's Readjustment Act, known as the GI Bill of Rights. The **GI Bill** showed the nation's gratitude to the men who fought, but it also attempted to keep the flood of demobilized veterans (almost all of them male) from swamping the U.S. economy. Roughly half of all veterans received unemployment benefits, meant to stagger veterans' entry into the civilian job market. The GI Bill also provided low-interest loans to buy a house or start a business, and—perhaps most significantly—stipends to cover the cost of college or technical school tuition and living expenses.

The GI Bill, as written, covered all veterans discharged "under conditions other than dishonorable," regardless of race or gender. It was not so inclusive in practice. Congress assigned the Veteran's Administration to administer the GI Bill, even though leaders knew that it didn't have the capacity to manage such a vast program. Thus, left with little oversight, state and local agencies had great control over implementation—and often discriminated against racial and ethnic minorities. And because men and women charged with homosexuality were given "blue" or administrative discharges, the ambiguous wording of the bill ("other than dishonorable") allowed them to be denied benefits, as well.

Nonetheless, the GI Bill offered new opportunities to many, and as individuals grasped these opportunities they changed their own lives and the shape of American society. Almost half of returning veterans used GI education benefits, which cost the nation more than the postwar Marshall Plan. Sub-college programs drew 5.6 million veterans, while 2.2 million attended college, graduate, or professional school. In 1947, about two-thirds of America's college students were veterans. Enrollment swelled at Syracuse University, tripling in a single year. Admissions quotas meant to limit the number of Jewish students largely disappeared, and while racial segregation persisted, Historically Black Colleges ("Negro Colleges") grew and strengthened. Facing the influx of nontraditional students, University of Chicago president Robert Maynard Hutchins protested that the GI Bill would turn universities into "educational hobo jungles," but the flood of students and federal dollars into the nation's colleges and universities created a golden age for higher education, and the resulting increase in well-educated or technically trained workers benefited the American economy.

Education obtained through the GI Bill created social mobility: children of barely literate menial laborers became white-collar professionals. And postwar universities, like the military, brought together people from vastly different backgrounds. The GI Bill helped to create a national middle-class culture, for as colleges exposed people to new ideas and to new experiences, their students tended to become less provincial, less rooted in ethnic or regional cultures.

25-1c Economic Growth

American concerns that economic depression would return with war's end proved unfounded. Adjustment to a peacetime economy was difficult at first, but the economy recovered quickly, fueled by consumer spending. Although Americans had brought home steady paychecks during the war, there was little on which to spend them: no new cars had been built since 1942, and new household appliances were scarce.

Americans had saved their money for four years, and they were ready to buy. Companies like General Motors, which flouted conventional wisdom about a coming depression and expanded its operations just after the war, found millions of eager customers. And because most other factories around the world were in ruins, U.S. corporations expanded their global dominance. Farming was also revolutionized, as increased use of fertilizers and pesticides, along with new machines such as mechanical cotton and tobacco pickers, tripled productivity. Potential profits attracted large investors, and the average size of farms increased from 195 to 306 acres.

25-1d Baby Boom

During the Great Depression, young people had delayed marriage and America's birth rate had plummeted. Marriage and birth rates began to rise as war brought economic recovery. But the end of the war brought a boom. In 1946, the U.S. marriage rate was higher than that of any record-keeping nation (except Hungary) in the history of the twentieth century. The birth rate soared, reversing the downward trend of the past 150 years. "Take the 3,548,000 babies born in 1950," wrote Sylvia F. Porter in her syndicated newspaper column. "Bundle them into a batch, bounce them all over the bountiful land that is America. What do you get?" Porter's answer: "Boom. The biggest, boomiest boom ever known in history. Just imagine how much these extra people, these new markets, will absorb—in food, clothing, in gadgets, in housing, in services. Our factories must expand just to keep pace." Although the **baby boom** peaked in 1957, more than 4 million babies were born every year until 1965 (see Figure 25.1).

25-1e Suburbanization

Where were all these baby boom families to live? Scarcely any new housing had been built since the 1920s. Almost 2 million families were doubled up with relatives in 1948; 50,000 people were living in Quonset huts, and in Chicago housing was so tight that 250 used trolley cars were sold as homes.

A combination of market forces, government actions, and individual decisions solved the housing crisis and, in so doing, changed the way large numbers of Americans lived. In the postwar years, white Americans moved to the suburbs. Their reasons varied. Some moved to escape the crowds and noise of the city. People from rural areas moved closer to city jobs. Some white families moved out of urban neighborhoods because African American families were moving in. Many new suburbanites wanted more political influence and more control over their children's education. More than anything else, however, those who moved wanted to own their own home—and it was the suburbs that offered affordable housing. Although suburban development predated World War II, the massive migration of

baby boom The soaring birth rate that occurred in the United States from 1946 through 1964.

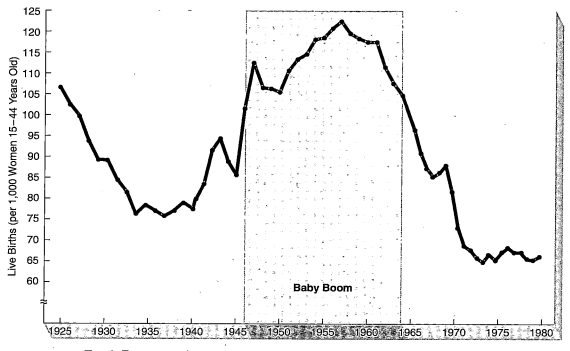

Figure 25.1 Birth Rate, 1945–1964

The birth rate began to rise in 1942 and 1943, but it skyrocketed during the postwar years beginning in 1946, reaching its peak in 1957. From 1954 to 1964, the United States recorded more than 4 million births every year. *Source: Adapted from U.S. Bureau of the Census, Historical Statistics of the United States, Colonial Times to 1970, Bicentennial Edition (Washington, D.C.: U.S. Government Printing Office, 1975), p. 49.*

18 million Americans to the suburbs from cities, small towns, and farms between 1950 and 1960 was on a wholly different scale (see Table 25.1).

In the years following World War II, suburban developers used mass production techniques to create acres of modest suburban houses in what had recently been pastures and fields. In 1947, builder William Levitt adapted Henry Ford's assembly-line methods to revolutionize homebuilding. By 1949, instead of 4 or 5 custom homes per year, Levitt's

Table 25.1 Geographic Distribution of the U.S. Population, 1930–1970 (in Percentages)

Year	Central Cities	Suburbs	Rural Areas and Small Towns
1930	31.8	18.0	50.2
1940	31.6	19.5	48.9
1950	32.3	23.8	43.9
1960	32.6	30.7	36.7
1970	31.4	37.6	31.0

Source: Adapted from U.S. Bureau of the Census, *Decennial Censuses, 1930–1970* (Washington, D.C.: U.S. Government Printing Office).

company built 180 houses a week. They were very basic—four and a half rooms on a 60-by-100-foot lot, all with identical floor plans—the Model Ts of houses. But the same floor plan could be disguised by four different exteriors, and by rotating seven paint colors Levitt guaranteed that only 1 in every 28 houses would be identical. In the Levittown on Long Island, a tree was planted every 28 feet (two and a half trees per house). The basic house, appliances included, sold for $7,990. Other homebuilders quickly adopted Levitt's techniques.

Suburban development could never have happened on such a large scale, however, without federal policies that encouraged it. Federal Housing Administration (FHA) mortgage insurance made low-interest GI mortgages and loans possible. New highways also promoted suburban development. Congress authorized construction of a 37,000-mile chain of highways in 1947 and in 1956 passed the Highway Act to create a 42,500-mile interstate highway system. These highways were built to facilitate commerce and to allow the military to mobilize quickly in case of a threat to national security, but they also allowed workers to live farther and farther from their jobs in central cities.

25-1f Inequality in Benefits

Postwar federal programs did not benefit all Americans equally. First, federal policies often assisted men at the expense of women. The federal Selective Service Act guaranteed that

△ Housing was so tight in the years following World War II that many young couples had to move in with one set of their parents—or accept some unusual housing options. Former marine lieutenant Willard Pedrick and his family made their home in a Quonset hut on the campus of Northwestern University in Evanston, Illinois, where Pedrick was an associate professor in the economics department.

veterans (overwhelmingly men) had priority in postwar hiring. As industry laid off civilian workers to make room for veterans, women lost their jobs at a rate 75 percent higher than men. Many women stayed in the workforce but were pushed into less well-paying jobs. Universities made room for veterans on the GI Bill by excluding qualified women students; a much smaller percentage of college degrees went to women after the war than before.

Inequities were also based on race. Like European American veterans, African American, Native American, Mexican American, and Asian American veterans received educational benefits and hiring preference in civil service jobs following the war. But war workers from these groups were among the first laid off as factories made room for white, male veterans. Federal housing policies also exacerbated racial inequality. Federal loan officers and bankers often labeled African American or racially mixed neighborhoods "high risk" for lending, denying mortgages to members of racial minorities regardless of individual creditworthiness. This practice, called "redlining" because such neighborhoods were outlined in red on lenders' maps, kept African Americans and many Hispanics from buying into the great economic explosion of the postwar

era. White families who bought homes with federally guaranteed mortgages saw their small investments grow dramatically over the years. Discriminatory policies denied most African Americans and other people of color that opportunity.

25-2 Domestic Politics in the Cold War Era

▷ What challenges did Harry S Truman face in managing the transition from a wartime to peacetime economy?

▷ How did the Truman administration seek to continue a New Deal legislative agenda?

▷ Why was there a shift from New Deal liberalism to conservatism after World War II?

Although federal policies and programs shaped American society in the postwar era, domestic politics were not at the forefront of American life. Democratic president Harry Truman attempted to build on the New Deal's liberal agenda, while Republican President Dwight D. Eisenhower called for balanced budgets and business-friendly policies. But both administrations focused on the challenges of the expanding Cold War, and neither came close to the political and legislative activism of the 1930s New Deal.

25-2a Harry S Truman and Postwar Liberalism

Harry Truman, the plainspoken former haberdasher from Missouri, had never expected to be president. In 1944, when Franklin Roosevelt asked him to join the Democratic ticket as the vice-presidential candidate, he almost refused. Roosevelt, the master politician, played hardball. "If he wants to break up the Democratic Party in the middle of the war, that's his responsibility," the president said flatly. "Oh shit," said Truman, "if that's the situation, I'll have to say yes." But the president, with his hands full as America entered its fourth year of war, had little time for his new vice president and left Truman in the dark about everything from the Manhattan Project to plans for postwar domestic policy. When Roosevelt died, suddenly, in April 1945, Truman was unprepared to take his place.

Truman stepped forward, however, placing a sign on his desk that proclaimed, "The Buck Stops Here." Most of Truman's presidency focused on foreign relations, as he led the nation through the last months of World War II and into the new Cold War with the Soviet Union. Domestically, he oversaw the process of reconversion from war to peace and attempted to keep a liberal agenda—the legacy of Roosevelt's New Deal—alive.

In his 1944 State of the Union address, President Roosevelt had offered Americans a "Second Bill of Rights": the right to employment, health care, education, food, and housing. This declaration of government responsibility for the welfare of the nation and its citizens was the cornerstone of postwar liberalism. The Truman administration intended to preserve the federal government's active role in guaranteeing social welfare, promoting social justice, managing the economy, and regulating the power of business corporations. Truman proposed to increase the minimum wage; he supported the **Full Employment Act**, introduced by congressional Democrats in the winter of 1945, which guaranteed work to all who were able and willing, through public-sector employment if necessary.

To pay for his proposed social welfare programs, Truman gambled that full employment would generate sufficient tax revenue and that consumer spending would fuel economic growth. The gamble on economic growth paid off, but Truman quickly learned the limits of his political influence. The conservative coalition of Republicans and southern Democrats that had stalled Roosevelt's New Deal legislation in the late 1930s was even less inclined to support Truman. Congress refused to raise the minimum wage and gutted the Full Employment Act. By the time Truman signed it into law in early 1946, key provisions regarding guaranteed work had virtually disappeared. But the act did reaffirm the federal government's responsibility for managing the economy and created a Council of Economic Advisers to help the president prevent economic downturns.

25-2b Postwar Strikes and the Taft-Hartley Act

The difficulties of converting to a peacetime economy helped to undermine Truman's domestic influence. As the end of wartime price controls sent inflation skyrocketing and people struggled to feed their families, more than 5 million workers went on strike. Unions shut down the coal, automobile, steel, and electric industries, and halted railroad and maritime transportation. The strikes were so disruptive that Americans began hoarding food and gasoline.

By the spring of 1946, Americans were losing patience with the strikes and with the Democratic administration, which many saw as partly responsible. When unions threatened a national railway strike, President Truman made a dramatic appearance before a joint session of Congress. If strikers in an industry deemed vital to national security refused a presidential order to return to work, he announced, he would ask Congress to immediately draft into the armed forces "all workers who are on strike against their government." The Democratic Party, Truman made clear, would not offer unlimited support to organized labor.

Making the most of public anger at the strikes, a group of pro-business Republicans and their conservative Democratic allies worked to restrict the power of labor unions. The 1947 **Taft-Hartley Act** allowed states to adopt right-to-work legislation that outlawed "closed shops" (which required all to join the union if a majority of them favored a union shop). The law also mandated an eighty-day cooling-off period before unions could begin strikes that imperiled national security. Truman vetoed the Taft-Hartley Act; though he had threatened action to avert a national railroad strike, he did not support such limits on union power. But Congress passed the Taft-Hartley Act over Truman's veto. The resulting restrictions limited union growth, especially in the South and West, where states passed right-to-work laws.

As Truman presided over the rocky transition from a wartime to a peacetime economy, he had to deal with massive inflation (briefly hitting 35 percent), shortages of consumer goods, and the wave of postwar strikes that slowed production of eagerly awaited consumer goods and drove prices up further. With powerful congressional opposition, he had little chance of major legislative accomplishments. But his inexperience had contributed to the political impasse. "To err is Truman," people began to joke. Truman's approval rating plunged from 87 percent in late 1945 to 32 percent in 1946.

25-2c 1948 Election

By 1948, it seemed that Republicans would win the White House in November. A confident Republican Party nominated Thomas Dewey, the man Roosevelt had defeated in 1944, as its presidential candidate. The Republicans were counting on schisms in the Democratic Party to give them victory. Former New Dealer Henry A. Wallace was running on the **Progressive Party** ticket advocating friendly relations with the Soviet Union, racial desegregation, and nationalization of basic industries. And when the Democratic Party adopted a pro–civil rights plank in 1948, a group of white southerners had created the States' Rights Democratic Party (the Dixiecrats), which nominated the fiercely segregationist governor Strom Thurmond of South Carolina. If Wallace's candidacy did not destroy Truman's chances, experts said, the Dixiecrats certainly would.

Truman, however, refused to give up. He denounced Henry Wallace for accepting communist support. He also reached out to African American voters in northern cities, becoming the first presidential candidate to campaign in Harlem. In the end, Truman prevailed. African American voters made the difference, giving Truman the electoral votes of key northern states. Roosevelt's New Deal coalition—African Americans, union members, northern urban voters, and most southern whites—had endured.

Full Employment Act Postwar liberal initiative that created mechanisms to help the federal government manage the economy. Although the original bill sought to stimulate economic growth by raising the minimum wage and guaranteeing jobs to those willing and able to work, through public-sector employment if necessary, the act passed without either of these provisions, which were blocked in Congress.

Taft-Hartley Act A 1947 law, passed over Truman's veto, that undermined some of the pro-labor provisions of the 1935 Wagner Act and restricted the power of labor unions.

Progressive Party Party formed from a splintering within the Democratic Party in 1948 by those dissatisfied with Truman. It advocated friendly relations with the Soviet Union, racial desegregation, a ban on monopolies, and nationalization of basic industries.

◁ African American voters were an increasingly important political force in the postwar era. President Truman had political reasons for appealing to black voters, but he also felt a moral obligation to support their struggle for civil rights. Here, a crowd waits to greet the president in 1952.

Cornell Capa/The LIFE Picture Collection/Getty Images

25-2d Truman's Fair Deal

Truman began his new term brimming with confidence. It was time, he believed, for government to fulfill its responsibility to provide economic security for the poor and the elderly. As he worked on his 1949 State of the Union message, he penciled in his intentions: "I expect to give every segment of our population a **fair deal**." Truman, unlike Roosevelt, pushed forward legislation to support the civil rights of African Americans, including the antilynching bill that Roosevelt had given only lukewarm support. He proposed a national health insurance program and federal aid for education. Once again, however, his proposals were defeated. A filibuster by southern conservatives in Congress destroyed his civil rights legislation, the American Medical Association denounced his health insurance plan as "socialized medicine," and the Roman Catholic Church opposed aid to education because it would not include parochial schools.

When the postwar peace proved short-lived and Truman ordered troops to Korea in June 1950, many reservists and National Guardsmen resented being called to active duty. Americans, remembering the shortages of the last war, tried to stockpile sugar, coffee, and canned goods—thus causing inflation. In 1951, the president's approval rating was only 23 percent.

25-2e Eisenhower's Dynamic Conservatism

In 1952 the Republicans insisted "It's Time for a Change," and voters agreed, especially with General Dwight D. Eisenhower as the Republican presidential nominee. Americans hoped that the immensely popular World War II hero could end the Korean War. And Eisenhower appealed to moderates in both parties; the Democrats also had tried to recruit him as their presidential candidate.

With a Republican in the White House for the first time in twenty years, conservatives hoped to roll back such New Deal liberal programs as the mandatory Social Security system. Eisenhower, however, had no such intention. As a moderate Republican, Eisenhower embraced an approach he called "dynamic conservatism": being "conservative when it comes to money and liberal when it comes to human beings." On the liberal side, in 1954 Eisenhower signed legislation that raised Social Security benefits and added 7.5 million workers, mostly self-employed farmers, to the Social Security rolls. The Eisenhower administration also increased funding for education—though increases were motivated by Cold War fears, not liberal principles, in the wake of the Soviet launch of *Sputnik* in 1957 (see "Links to the World: *Sputnik*," Section 26-6).

25-2f Growth of the Military-Industrial Complex

Overall, Eisenhower's administration was unabashedly fiscally conservative and pro-business. The president tried to reduce federal spending and to balance the budget. However, faced with three recessions (in 1953–1954, 1957–1958, and 1960–1961) and the tremendous cost of America's global activities, the Republican administration steadily turned to deficit spending. In 1959, federal spending climbed to $92 billion, about half of which went to defense spending: to support a standing military of 3.5 million men and to develop new weapons for the ongoing Cold War.

Eisenhower worried about this trajectory. In early 1961, as he bid farewell to the nation, the outgoing president condemned this new "conjunction of an immense military establishment and a large arms industry" and warned that its "total influence—economic, political, even

Dwight D. Eisenhower Thirty-fourth president of the United States (1953–1961) and U.S. Army five-star general during World War II; Republican known for his moderate politics, steering a middle course between Democratic liberalism and traditional Republican conservatism.

fair deal Agenda proposed by President Truman that included civil rights, national health care legislation, and federal aid to education.

spiritual"—threatened the nation's democratic process. Eisenhower, the former five-star general and war hero, urged Americans to "guard against . . . the **military-industrial complex.**"

During Eisenhower's presidency, both liberal Democrats and moderate Republicans occupied what historian Arthur M. Schlesinger Jr. called "the vital center." And with the Cold War between the United States and the Soviet Union portrayed as a battle between good and evil and a struggle for the future of the world, criticism of American society seemed suspect—even unpatriotic. British journalist Godfrey Hodgson would later describe this time as an era of "consensus," when Americans were "confident to the verge of complacency about the perfectibility of American society, anxious to the point of paranoia about the threat of communism."

25-3 Cold War Fears and Anticommunism

▶ **What developments contributed to the growth of anticommunist sentiment in the postwar period?**

▶ **How did the federal government attempt to locate communists in American society? What role did Senator Joseph McCarthy (R, WI) play in the postwar red scare?**

▶ **How and why did the search for communists and communist spies become excessive, and what impact did it have on American society?**

International relations profoundly influenced America's domestic politics in the years following World War II. Americans were frightened by the Cold War tensions between the United States and the Soviet Union—and there were legitimate reasons for fear. Reasonable fears, however, spilled over into anticommunist demagoguery and witch hunts. Fear allowed the trampling of civil liberties, the suppression of dissent, and the persecution of thousands of innocent Americans.

---

military-industrial complex Term made famous by President Eisenhower's farewell speech in 1961; it refers to the U.S. military, arms industries, and related government and business interests, which together grew in power, size, and influence in the decades after World War II.

House Un-American Activities Committee Powerful Congressional committee popularly known as HUAC, originally created in 1938, which investigated communist influence in America and contributed to anticommunist hysteria in the postwar United States.

Anticommunism was not new in American society. A Red Scare had swept the nation following the Russian Revolution of 1917, and opponents of America's labor movement had used charges of communism to block unionization through the 1930s. Many saw the Soviet Union's virtual takeover of Eastern Europe in the late 1940s as an alarming parallel to Nazi Germany's takeover of neighboring states. People remembered the

failure of "appeasement" at Munich and worried that the United States was "too soft" in its policy toward the Soviet Union.

25-3a Espionage and Nuclear Fears

In addition, top U.S. government officials knew that the Soviet Union was spying on the United States (as the United States was spying on the Soviet Union). A top-secret project, code-named "Venona," decrypted almost three thousand Soviet telegraphic cables that proved Soviet spies had infiltrated U.S. government agencies and nuclear programs. Intelligence officials resolved to prosecute Soviet spies, but they kept their evidence from the American public so that the Soviets would not realize their codes had been compromised. Thus even legitimate prosecution often appeared as government excess, persecution based on no real evidence.

Fear of nuclear war also contributed to American anticommunism. For four years, the United States alone possessed what seemed the ultimate weapon, but in 1949 the Soviet Union exploded its own atomic device. President Truman, initiating a national atomic civil defense program shortly thereafter, told Americans, "I cannot tell you when or where the attack will come or that it will come at all. I can only remind you that we must be ready when it does come." Children practiced "duck-and-cover" in their school classrooms, learning how to shield themselves "when the bomb falls." *Life* magazine featured backyard fallout shelters. As the stakes of the global struggle increased, Americans worried that the United States was newly vulnerable to attack on its own soil.

25-3b Politics of Anticommunism

At the height of the Cold War, American leaders, including Presidents Truman and Eisenhower, did not always draw a sufficient line between prudent attempts to prevent Soviet spies from infiltrating important government agencies and anticommunist scaremongering for political gain. Truman purposely invoked "the communist threat" to gain support for aid to Greece and Turkey in 1947. Republican politicians "red-baited" Democratic opponents, eventually targeting the Truman administration as a whole. In 1947, President Truman ordered investigations into the loyalty of more than 3 million U.S. government employees. As anticommunist hysteria grew, the government began discharging people deemed "security risks," among them alcoholics, homosexuals, and debtors thought susceptible to blackmail. It rarely had any evidence of disloyalty.

Leading the anticommunist crusade was the **House Un-American Activities Committee** (popularly known as HUAC). Created in 1938 to investigate "subversive and un-American propaganda," the viciously anti–New Deal committee had quickly lost credibility by charging that film stars—including eight-year-old Shirley Temple—were dupes of the Communist Party. In 1947, HUAC attacked Hollywood again. This time it relied on FBI files and on the testimony of Hollywood figures including Walt Disney and Screen Actors Guild president Ronald Reagan, who was also a secret

◁ The Cold War shaped American popular culture as well as foreign policy. Cartoonist Jay Ward's *Rocky and His Friends* premiered on television in 1959. In its first story sequence, "Jet Fuel Formula," Rocky the Flying Squirrel and Bullwinkle J. Moose—urged on by American military leaders—tried to re-create their secret formula for lunar propulsion while evading the tricks and explosive traps of Boris Badenov and Natasha Fatale, spies whose supposed "Pottsylvanian" origins did nothing to mask their heavy Russian accents.

Everett Collection

informant for the FBI, complete with code name. Ten screenwriters and directors, known as the "Hollywood Ten," were sent to prison for contempt of Congress when they refused to "name names" of suspected communists for HUAC. Studios panicked and blacklisted hundreds of actors, screenwriters, directors, even makeup artists who were suspected of communist affiliations. With no evidence of wrongdoing, these men and women had their careers—and sometimes their lives—ruined.

25-3c McCarthyism and the Growing "Witch Hunt"

University professors became targets of the growing "witch hunt" in 1949, when HUAC demanded lists of the textbooks used in courses at eighty-one universities. When the board of regents at the University of California, Berkeley, instituted a loyalty oath for faculty, firing twenty-six who resisted on principle, protests from faculty members across the nation forced the regents to back down. But many professors, afraid of the reach of HUAC, began to downplay controversial material in their courses. In the labor movement, the CIO expelled eleven unions, with more than 900,000 members, for alleged communist domination.

The red panic reached its nadir in February 1950, when a relatively obscure U.S. senator came before an audience in Wheeling, West Virginia, to charge that the U.S. State Department was "thoroughly infested with Communists." Republican Senator **Joseph R. McCarthy** of Wisconsin was not an especially credible source. He made charges and then retracted them, claiming first that there were 205 communists in the State Department, then 57, then 81. He had a severe drinking problem; downing a water glass full of Scotch in a single gulp, he would follow it with a quarter-pound stick of butter, hoping to counteract the effects of the liquor. He had a record of dishonesty as a lawyer and judge in his

hometown of Appleton, Wisconsin. But McCarthy crystallized the anxieties many felt as they faced a new and difficult era in American life, and the anticommunist excesses of this era came to be known as McCarthyism.

With HUAC and McCarthy on the attack, Americans began pointing accusing fingers at one another. The anticommunist crusade was embraced by labor union officials, religious leaders, and the media, as well as by politicians. A bootblack at the Pentagon was questioned by the FBI seventy times because he was alleged to have given $10 during the 1930s to a defense fund for the Scottsboro Boys, who had been represented by an attorney from the Communist Party. Women in New York who lobbied for the continuation of wartime day care programs were denounced as communists by the *New York World Telegram*. "Reds, phonies, and parlor pinks," in Truman's words, seemed to lurk everywhere.

25-3d Anticommunism in Congress

In such a climate, most public figures found it too risky to stand up against McCarthyist tactics. And most Democrats did support the domestic Cold War and its anticommunist actions. In 1950, with bipartisan support, Congress passed the Internal Security (McCarran) Act, which required members of "Communist-front" organizations to register with the government and prohibited them from holding government jobs or traveling abroad. In 1954, the Senate unanimously passed the Communist Control Act (there were two dissenting votes in the House), which effectively made membership in the Communist Party illegal. Its chief sponsor, Democratic senator Hubert H. Humphrey of Minnesota,

Joseph R. McCarthy Wisconsin senator who used the media to stoke anti-communist hysteria, charging that Soviet spies and sympathizers had infiltrated the federal government. He was later discredited.

△ Senator Joseph McCarthy (R, WI), whose name became shorthand for zealous anticommunism. McCarthy was at the forefront of anticommunist witch hunts in postwar America, but he was far from alone.

told his colleagues just before he cast his vote, "We have closed all of the doors. The rats will not get out of the trap."

The anticommunist fervor was fueled by spectacular and controversial trials of Americans accused of passing secrets to the Soviet Union. In 1948, Congressman Richard Nixon of California, a member of HUAC, was propelled onto the national stage when he accused former State Department official Alger Hiss of espionage. In 1950, Hiss was convicted of lying about his contacts with Soviet agents. That same year, **Ethel and Julius Rosenberg** were arrested for passing atomic secrets to the Soviets; they were found guilty of treason and executed in 1953. For decades, many historians believed that the Rosenbergs were primarily victims of a witch hunt. In fact, there was strong evidence of Julius Rosenberg's guilt in cables decrypted at

Ethel and Julius Rosenberg
Couple found guilty of conspiracy to commit espionage and executed in 1953.

the time (as well as evidence that Ethel Rosenberg was less involved than had been charged), but this evidence was not presented at their trial for reasons of national security. The cables remained top secret until 1995, when a Clinton administration initiative opened the files to historians.

25-3e Waning of the Red Scare

Some of the worst excesses of Cold War anticommunism waned when Senator McCarthy was discredited on national television in 1954. McCarthy had used the press masterfully: knowing that newspapers usually buried corrections in their back pages, McCarthy made sensational, headline-worthy accusations just before reporters' deadlines, leaving them no time to verify his claims. But even after journalists knew McCarthy was unreliable they continued to report even his wildest charges. Sensational stories sell papers, and McCarthy had become a celebrity.

But McCarthy eventually miscalculated. When he pushed the Senate to investigate his charge that the U.S. Army was protecting communists within its ranks, both ABC and DuMont broadcast gavel-to-gavel coverage of the resulting Army-McCarthy hearings and Americans watched McCarthy in action. Apparently drunk, he ranted, slurred his words, and browbeat witnesses. Finally, after McCarthy maligned a young lawyer who was not even involved in the hearings, army counsel Joseph Welch intervened. "Have you no sense of decency, sir, at long last?" Welch asked, and the gallery erupted in applause. McCarthy's career as a witch-hunter was over. In December 1954, the Senate voted to "condemn" McCarthy for sullying the dignity of the Senate. He remained a senator, but exhaustion and alcohol took their toll and he died in 1957 at the age of forty-eight. With McCarthy discredited, the most virulent strand of anticommunism had run its course. However, the use of fear tactics for political gain, and the narrowing of American freedoms and liberties, were chilling domestic legacies of the Cold War.

25-4 The Struggle for Civil Rights

▷ **What international and domestic developments contributed to increased support for African American civil rights?**

▷ **How did the federal government simultaneously support and undermine the advancement of African American civil rights?**

▷ **What methods did African Americans use to push for civil rights?**

▷ **In what ways did white Americans respond to the civil rights movement?**

The Cold War—at home and abroad—also shaped African American struggles for social justice and the nation's responses to them. Some African American leaders saw their struggle for equal rights in the United States as part of a larger, international movement. And American diplomats understood that if the United States continued to allow segregation, discrimination, disenfranchisement, and racial violence against its own nonwhite citizens, it would struggle to pull the newly formed African and Asian nations into its sphere of influence. As the Soviet Union was quick to point out, the United States could hardly pose as the leader of the free world or condemn the Soviet Union's record on human rights while it practiced segregation at home. Cold War pressures supported domestic reform: to win the support of nonaligned nations, the United States would have to change its own practices. At the same time, many white Americans saw any criticism of their society as a Soviet-inspired attempt to weaken the United States in the ongoing Cold War. Opponents of the civil rights movement played the communist card, while the FBI and local law enforcement agencies used Cold War fears to claim legitimacy as they investigated civil rights activists. In this heated environment, African Americans struggled to seize the political initiative.

25-4a Black Political Power and Presidential Action

African Americans who had helped win World War II were determined that their lives in postwar America would be better because of their sacrifices. Moreover, politicians like Harry Truman were beginning to pay attention to black aspirations, especially as black voters in some urban-industrial states began to strongly influence the political balance of power.

President Truman had compelling political reasons for supporting African American civil rights. But he also felt a moral obligation. Truman genuinely believed it was only fair that every American, regardless of race, should enjoy the full rights of citizenship. He also was appalled by a resurgence of racial terrorism in the wake of the war, as a revived Ku Klux Klan tried to turn back the clock, threatening, beating, maiming, and murdering Americans who were not willing to accept their old place in the racial hierarchy. Reports that police in Aiken, South Carolina, had gouged out the eyes of a black sergeant just three hours after he had been discharged from the army made Isaac Woodard a national symbol of injustice, as filmmaker Orson Welles and folksinger Woody Guthrie took up his cause.

Popular opinion was beginning to shift, but not enough to prompt congressional action. Instead, Truman used the power of the presidency. In December 1946, he signed an executive order establishing the President's Committee on Civil Rights. The committee's report, *To Secure These Rights*, would become the civil rights movement's agenda for the next twenty years. It called for laws to end lynching and segregation and to guarantee voting rights and equal employment opportunity. For the first time since Reconstruction, a president had acknowledged the federal government's responsibility to protect all its citizens and to strive for racial equality.

In 1948 Truman issued two more executive orders, intended to end racial discrimination in the federal government. One proclaimed a policy of "fair employment" in federal jobs. The other, prompted in part by African American leaders who promised massive draft resistance if the military remained segregated, ordered the armed forces to end racial segregation "as rapidly as possible . . . without impairing efficiency or morale." The military did not readily comply, but by the beginning of the Korean War it had begun to phase out segregated units.

25-4b Supreme Court Victories and School Desegregation

African Americans successfully challenged racial discrimination both in the courts and in state and local legislatures. Northern state legislatures, in response to pressure by civil rights activists, passed measures prohibiting employment discrimination in the 1940s and 1950s. National successes came through the Supreme Court. During the 1940s the NAACP's Legal Defense and Educational Fund, led by Thurgood Marshall, carried forward a plan to destroy the separate but equal doctrine established in *Plessy v. Ferguson* (1896) by insisting on its literal interpretation. In higher education, the NAACP calculated, the cost of true equality in racially separate schools would be prohibitive. "You can't build a cyclotron for one student," the president of the University of Oklahoma acknowledged. NAACP lawsuits won African American students admission to professional and graduate schools at several formerly segregated state universities. The NAACP also won major victories through the Supreme Court in *Smith v. Allwright* (1944), which outlawed the whites-only primaries held by the Democratic Party in some southern states; *Morgan v. Virginia* (1946), which struck down segregation in interstate bus transportation; and *Shelley v. Kraemer* (1948), in which the Court held that racially restrictive covenants (private agreements among white homeowners not to sell to blacks) could not legally be enforced.

Even so, segregation was still standard practice in the 1950s, and blacks continued to suffer disfranchisement, job discrimination, and violence, including the 1951 bombing murder of the Florida state director of the NAACP and his wife. But in 1954, the NAACP won a historic victory that stunned the white South and energized African Americans to challenge segregation on several fronts. ***Brown v. Board of Education of Topeka***, which Thurgood Marshall argued before the high court, incorporated school desegregation cases from several states. The Court's unanimous decision was written by Chief Justice Earl Warren, who, as California's attorney general, had pushed for the internment of Japanese Americans during World War II and had come to regret that action. The

Brown v. Board of Education of Topeka Landmark Supreme Court case (1954) that overturned *Plessy v. Ferguson* (1896); it desegregated public schools by finding that racially separate schools are inherently unequal.

◁ Jackie Robinson cracked the color line in major league baseball when he joined the Brooklyn Dodgers for the 1947 season. Here, in a 1952 game at Ebbetts Field (Brooklyn), one of the greatest base runners of all time steals home plate.

Fred J. Sass/The New York Times Archive

Court concluded that "in the field of public education the doctrine of 'separate but equal' has no place. Separate educational facilities are inherently unequal." But the ruling that overturned *Plessy v. Ferguson* did not demand immediate compliance. A year later, the Court finally ordered school desegregation, but only "with all deliberate speed."

25-4c Montgomery Bus Boycott

By the mid-1950s, African Americans were engaged in a growing grassroots struggle for civil rights in both the North and the South, though southern struggles drew the most national attention. In 1955, Rosa Parks, a department store seamstress and longtime NAACP activist, was arrested when she refused to give up her seat to a white man on a public bus in Montgomery, Alabama. Her arrest gave local black women's organizations and civil rights groups a cause around which to organize a boycott of the city's bus system. They selected **Martin Luther King Jr.**, a recently ordained minister who had just arrived in Montgomery, as their leader. King launched the boycott with a moving speech, declaring, "If we are wrong, the Constitution is wrong. If we are wrong, God Almighty is wrong. If we are wrong, Jesus of Nazareth was merely a utopian dreamer. . . . If we are wrong, justice is a lie."

Martin Luther King Jr. was a twenty-six-year-old Baptist minister with a recent PhD from Boston University. Committed to the transforming potential of Christian love and schooled in the teachings of

Martin Luther King Jr. African American minister and leader of the Civil Rights Movement. His philosophy of civil disobedience fused the spirit of Christianity with the strategy of achieving racial justice through nonviolent resistance.

India's leader Mohandas K. Gandhi, King believed in nonviolent protest and civil disobedience. By refusing to obey unjust and racist laws, he hoped to focus the nation's attention on the immorality of Jim Crow. King persisted in this struggle even as opponents bombed his house and he was jailed for "conspiring" to boycott.

During the yearlong Montgomery bus boycott, blacks young and old rallied in their churches, sang hymns, and prayed that the nation would awaken to the evils of segregation and racial discrimination. They maintained their boycott through heavy rains and the steamy heat of summer, often walking miles a day. One elderly black woman, offered a ride to work by a white reporter, told him, "No, my feets is tired, but my soul is rested." With the bus company near bankruptcy and downtown merchants suffering from declining sales, city officials adopted harassment tactics to bring an end to the boycott. But the black people of Montgomery persevered. Thirteen months after the boycott began, the Supreme Court declared Alabama's bus segregation laws unconstitutional.

25-4d White Resistance

As the civil rights movement won significant victories, white reactions varied. Some communities in border states like Kansas and Maryland quietly implemented the school desegregation order, and many southern moderates advocated a gradual rollback of segregation. But others urged defiance. The Klan experienced another resurgence, and white violence against blacks increased. In August 1955, white men in Mississippi beat, mutilated, and murdered Emmett Till, a fourteen-year-old from Chicago, because they took offense at the way he spoke to a white woman; an all-white jury

△ Reverend Martin Luther King Jr (1929–1968), leader of the African American Civil Rights Movement, delivers a sermon in Atlanta's Ebenezer Baptist Church. King was baptized there as a child and later served with his father, Martin Luther King Sr., as its co-pastor.

Flip Schulke/CORBIS/Corbis via Getty Images

took only sixty-seven minutes to acquit those charged with the crime. Business and professional people created White Citizens' Councils for the express purpose of resisting the school desegregation order. Sometimes called "uptown Ku Klux Klans," the councils brought their economic power to bear against black civil rights activists. In keeping with the program of "massive resistance" proposed by Virginia's U.S. senator, Harry F. Byrd Sr., they pushed through state laws that paid private-school tuition for white children who left public schools to avoid integration and, in Virginia, refused state funding to integrated schools. When FBI director J. Edgar Hoover briefed President Eisenhower on southern racial tensions in 1956, he warned of communist influences among the civil rights activists and even suggested that, if the Citizens' Councils did not worsen the racial situation, their actions might "control the rising tension."

White resistance to civil rights also grew stronger in large northern cities. Chicago's African American population had increased from 275,000 in 1940 to 800,000 in 1960. These

newcomers often found better jobs than they had left, and their numbers gave them political power. But they faced racism and segregation in the North as well. Many department stores and factories refused to hire blacks, who were also denied jobs in skilled trades. Whites welcomed a black family to a Columbus, Ohio, suburb by burning a cross on their front lawn. In 1951 in Cicero, a town adjoining Chicago, several thousand whites who were determined to keep blacks from moving into their neighborhood provoked a race riot. So racially divided was Chicago that the U.S. Commission on Civil Rights in 1959 described it as "the most residentially segregated city in the nation." Detroit and other northern cities were not far behind. And because children attended neighborhood schools, education in the North was in fact often segregated as well, though not by law, as it had been in the South.

25-4e Federal Authority and States' Rights

Unlike Truman, President Eisenhower wanted to avoid taking action on civil rights. Although he disapproved of racial segregation, Eisenhower objected to "compulsory federal law" as a solution, for he believed that race relations would improve "only if [desegregation] starts locally." He also feared that rapid desegregation under his administration would jeopardize Republican inroads in the South. Thus, Eisenhower did not state forthrightly that the federal government would enforce the *Brown* decision as the nation's law. In short, instead of leading, he spoke ambiguously and thereby tacitly encouraged white resistance. In 1956, 101 congressmen and senators from eleven southern states, all Democrats, issued "The Southern Manifesto." This document condemned the *Brown* decision as an "unwarranted exercise of power by the Court," which violated the principle of states' rights, and commended those states that sought to "resist forced integration by any lawful means."

Events in Little Rock, Arkansas, forced the president to act. In September 1957, Arkansas governor Orval E. Faubus defied a court-supported desegregation plan for Little Rock's Central High School. Faubus went on television the night before school began and told Arkansans that "blood would run in the streets" if black students tried to enter the high school the next day. On the second day of school, eight black teenagers tried to enter Central High, but they were turned away by Arkansas National Guard troops the governor had deployed to block their entrance. The ninth student, separated from the others, was surrounded by jeering whites and narrowly escaped the mob with the help of a sympathetic white woman.

It was more than two weeks after school began that the "Little Rock Nine" first entered Central High—and then only because a federal judge intervened. As an angry crowd surrounded the school and television broadcast the scene to the nation and the world, Eisenhower decided to nationalize the Arkansas National Guard (placing it under federal, not state, control) and dispatch one thousand army paratroopers to Little Rock. Troops guarded the students for the rest of the year. Eisenhower's use of federal power in Little Rock was a critical step in America's struggle over racial equality, for he had directly confronted the conflict between federal authority and states' rights. However, state power triumphed the following year, when Faubus closed all public high schools in Little Rock rather than desegregate them. Nonetheless, federal action continued. In 1957, Congress passed the first Civil Rights Act since Reconstruction, creating the United States Commission on Civil Rights to investigate systemic discrimination, such as in voting. Although this measure, like a voting rights act passed three years later, was not fully effective, it was another federal recognition of the centrality of civil rights.

Most important, however, was the growing strength of a new, grassroots civil rights activism. In 1957, Martin Luther King Jr. became the first president of the Southern Christian Leadership Conference (SCLC), organized to coordinate civil rights activities. With the success in Montgomery and the gains won through the Supreme Court and the Truman administration, African Americans were poised to launch a major national movement for civil rights in the years to come.

25-5 Creating a Middle-Class Nation

▶ What factors contributed to the creation of a shared "suburban culture"?

▷ Why was postwar economic growth and prosperity relatively widespread, and what were its limits?

▶ What were the main characteristics of the postwar middle-class culture?

Even as African Americans encountered massive resistance in their struggles for civil rights during the 1950s, in other ways the United States was becoming a more inclusive society. More Americans than ever before participated in a broad middle-class and suburban culture, and divisions among Americans based on class, ethnicity, religion, and regional identity became less important. Old European ethnic identities were fading, as an ever-smaller percentage of America's people were first- or second-generation immigrants. Ever greater numbers of Americans found material comfort and economic security in this time of broadly shared prosperity, with the least economic inequality between the wealthy and the middle class in the past one hundred years.

In the new suburbs, people from different backgrounds worked together to create communities and build schools, churches, and other institutions. Middle-class Americans increasingly looked to powerful national media rather than to regional or ethnic traditions for advice on matters ranging from how to celebrate Thanksgiving to what car to buy to how to raise children. New opportunities for consumption—whether the fads of a powerful teenage culture or the suburban ranch-style house—also tied together Americans from different backgrounds. In the postwar years, a new middle-class way of life was transforming the United States.

25-5a Prosperity for More Americans

During the 1950s, a growing economy gave more Americans than ever before middle-class comforts and economic security (see Figure 25.2). The nation's economic boom was driven by consumer spending, as Americans eagerly bought the cars and kitchen appliances and silk stockings and foodstuffs that had not been available during the war, and industries expanded production to meet consumer demand. Government spending was also important. As the Cold War deepened, the government poured money into defense industries, creating jobs and stimulating the economy. Such spending was made possible, in part, by steep tax rates on the richest Americans—with federal taxes topping out at 91 percent.

Cold War military and aerospace spending changed American society and culture in unintended ways. Weapons development and space programs required highly educated scientists, engineers, and other white-collar workers, so the professional middle class expanded. And as universities received billions of dollars to fund such research, they grew and claimed greater roles in American life. This government-funded research had other unanticipated results: the transistor, invented during the 1950s, made possible both the computer revolution and the transistor radio, without which 1950s youth culture would have looked very different.

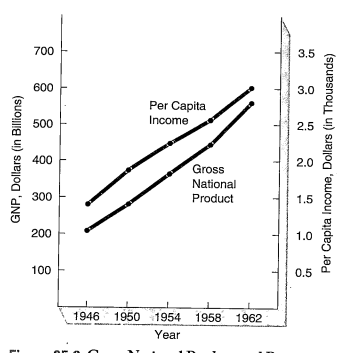

Figure 25.2 Gross National Product and Per Capita Income, 1946–1962

Both gross national product and per capita income soared during the economic boom from 1946 to 1962. Source: Adapted from U.S. Bureau of the Census, Historical Statistics of the United States, Colonial Times to 1970, Bicentennial Edition (Washington, D.C.: U.S. Government Printing Office, 1975), p. 224.

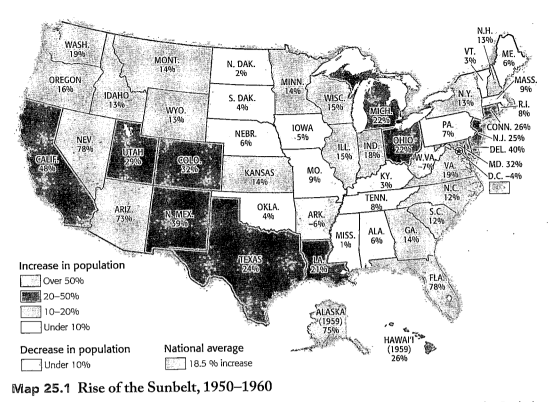

Increase in population
- Over 50%
- 20–50%
- 10–20%
- Under 10%

Decrease in population
- Under 10%

National average
- 18.5 % increase

Map 25.1 Rise of the Sunbelt, 1950–1960

The years after the Second World War saw a continuation of the migration of Americans to the Sunbelt states of the Southwest and the West Coast.

A new era of labor relations also helped bring economic prosperity to more Americans. By 1950, labor and management created a new, more stable relationship. In peaceful negotiations, the United Auto Workers (UAW) and General Motors led the way in providing workers with health insurance, pension plans, and guaranteed cost-of-living adjustments, or COLAs, to protect wages from inflation. The 1950 agreement that *Fortune* magazine called "The Treaty of Detroit" gave GM's workers a five-year contract, with regular wage increases tied to corporate productivity. This was a turning point for the labor movement. In exchange for wages and benefits, organized labor gave up its demands for greater control in corporate affairs. And with wage increases tied to corporate productivity, labor cast its lot with management: workplace stability and efficiency, not strikes, would bring higher wages. During the 1950s, union wages and benefits often rivaled those of college-educated professionals and propelled union families into the ranks of the economic middle class.

25-5b Sunbelt and Economic Growth

Just as labor agreements helped create prosperity for union members and their families, government policies helped bring the nation's poorest region into the American economic mainstream. In the 1930s, Roosevelt had called the South "the nation's No. 1 economic problem." During World War II, new defense industry plants and military training camps channeled federal money to the region, stimulating economic growth. In the postwar era, huge levels of defense spending, especially for the nation's aerospace industry, continued to shift economic development from the Northeast and Midwest to the South and Southwest—the **Sunbelt** (see Map 25.1). Government actions—including generous tax breaks for oil companies, siting of military bases, and awarding of defense and aerospace contracts—were crucial to the region's new prosperity.

The Sunbelt's spectacular growth was also due to agribusiness, the oil industry, real estate development, and recreation. Sunbelt states aggressively—and successfully—sought foreign investment. Industry was drawn to the South by right-to-work laws, which outlawed closed shops, and by low taxes and low heating bills. Air conditioning, which was first used in office buildings during the 1930s, made the hottest summer days bearable (though few residences had even window units before the 1960s). Houston, Phoenix, Los Angeles, San Diego, Dallas, and Miami all boomed; the population of Houston, a center of the aerospace industry and also of oil and petrochemical production, more than tripled between 1940 and 1960. California absorbed no less than one-fifth of

Sunbelt Southern and southwestern states whose rapid economic development brought many new residents during the postwar years.

Moving to Levittown

Builder William Levitt's assembly-line methods created affordable homes for young families—although initially only "Caucasians" were allowed to buy homes in Levittown. Here, truck supervisor Bernard Levey and his family stand in front of their new Levitt-built home in 1950. The Leveys would have received a copy of the Levittown *Homeowners*

Guide, which contained a list of "do's" and "don'ts": for example, residents were not to hang laundry on Sundays, when their neighbors were "most likely to be relaxing on the rear lawn."

CRITICAL THINKING

◻ What does this photograph reveal about the new Levittown development?

◻ Compare the structures you see here (the new home behind the Levey family and one under construction in 1948) with the average new suburban home today. What does their size and layout suggest about the extent of "consumer culture" in the early 1950s?

△ Truck supervisor Bernard Levey standing with his family in front of his new Levitt-built home.

△ Aerial view of a concrete foundation and prefabricated components of a home under construction in the planned community of Levittown, New York, June 1948.

the nation's entire population increase in the 1950s. By 1963, it was the most populous state in the Union.

25-5c A New Middle-Class Culture

By the 1950s, it seemed that America was becoming a middle-class nation. Unionized blue-collar workers gained middle-class incomes, and veterans with GI Bill college educations swelled the growing managerial and professional class. In 1956, for the first time, the United States had more white-collar than blue-collar workers, and in 1957 there were 61 percent more salaried middle-class workers than just a decade earlier. Also for the first time, a majority of families—60 percent—had incomes in the middle-class range (approximately $3,000 to $9,000 a year in the mid-1950s), and the gap between the rich and the middle class shrank dramatically.

However, middle-class identity was not simply a matter of economics. Half of teenagers whose fathers did unskilled menial labor or whose mothers had only a sixth-grade education, a major 1952 survey discovered, believed their family was "middle class" (not working class or lower class). Paradoxically, the strength of unions in the postwar era contributed to a decline in working-class identity: as large numbers of blue-collar workers participated fully in the suburban middle-class culture, the lines separating working class and middle class seemed less important. Increasingly, a family's standard of living mattered more than what sort of work made the standard of living possible. People of color did not share equally in America's postwar prosperity and were usually invisible in American representations of "the good life." However, many middle-income African Americans, Latinos, and Asian Americans did participate in the broad middle-class culture.

25-5d Whiteness and National Culture

The emergence of a national middle-class culture was possible in part because America's population was more homogeneous in the 1950s than before or since. In the nineteenth and early twentieth centuries, the United States had restricted or prohibited immigration from Asia, Africa, and Latin America while accepting millions of Europeans to America's shores. This large-scale European immigration had been shut off in the 1920s, so that by 1960 only 5.7 percent of Americans were foreign born (compared with approximately 15 percent in 1910 and 13.7 percent in 2015). In 1950, 88 percent of Americans were non-Hispanic whites (compared with less than 64 percent in 2010), 10 percent of the population was African American, roughly 2 percent was Hispanic, and Native Americans and Asian Americans each accounted for about one-fifth of 1 percent. But almost all European Americans were at least a generation removed from immigration. Instead of "Italians" or "Russians" or "Jews," they were increasingly likely to describe themselves as "white." In 1959, the addition of two new states, Alaska and Hawai'i, brought more people of Native, Asian, or Pacific origin to the U.S. population.

Although the new suburbs were peopled mostly by white families, these suburbs were usually more diverse than the communities from which their residents had come. America's small towns and urban ethnic enclaves were quite homogeneous and usually intolerant of difference and of challenges to traditional ways. In the suburbs, people from different backgrounds came together: migrants from the city and the country; from different regions of the nation, different ethnic cultures, and different religious backgrounds. It was in the suburbs, paradoxically, that many people encountered different customs and beliefs. But as they joined with neighbors to forge new communities, the new suburbanites frequently adopted the norms of the developing national middle class. They traded the provincial homogeneity of specific ethnic or regional cultures for a new sort of homogeneity: a national white middle-class culture.

25-5e Television

Because many white Americans were new to the middle class, they were uncertain about what behaviors were proper and expected of them. They found instruction, in part, in the national mass media. Women's magazines helped housewives replace the ethnic and regional dishes with which they had grown up with "American" recipes created from national brand name products—such as casseroles made with Campbell's Cream of Mushroom soup. Television also fostered America's shared national culture and taught Americans how to be middle class. Although television sets cost about $300—the equivalent of $2,500 today—almost half of American homes had TVs by 1953. Television ownership rose to 90 percent by 1960, when more American households had a television set than a washing machine or an electric iron.

On television, suburban families like the Andersons (*Father Knows Best*) and the Cleavers (*Leave It to Beaver*) ate dinner at a properly set dining room table. The mothers were always well groomed; June Cleaver did housework in a carefully ironed dress. When children faced moral dilemmas, parents gently but firmly guided them toward correct decisions. Every crisis was resolved through paternal wisdom—and a little humor. In these families, no one ever yelled or hit. These popular family situation comedies portrayed and reinforced the suburban middle-class ideal that so many American families sought.

The "middle-classness" of television programming was due in part to the economics of the television industry. Advertising paid for television programming, and the corporations that bought advertising did not want to offend potential consumers. Thus, although African American musician Nat King Cole drew millions of viewers to his NBC television show, it never found a sponsor. National corporations were afraid that being linked to a black performer like Cole would hurt their sales among whites—especially in the South. Because African Americans made up only about 10 percent of the population and many had limited disposable income, they had little power in this economics-driven system. The *Nat King Cole Show* was canceled within a year; it was a decade before the networks again tried to anchor a show around a black performer.

Television's reach extended beyond the suburbs. People from the inner cities and from isolated rural areas also watched family sitcoms or laughed at the antics of Milton Berle and Lucille Ball. With only network television available—ABC, CBS, and NBC (and, until 1956, DuMont)—70 percent or more of all viewers might be watching the same popular program at the same time. (In the early twenty-first century, the most popular shows might attract 12 percent of the live viewing audience—a group that is steadily shrinking as other viewing platforms develop.) Television gave Americans a shared set of experiences; it also helped create a more homogeneous, white-focused, middle-class culture.

25-5f Consumer Culture

Linked by a shared national culture, Americans also found common ground in a new abundance of consumer goods. After decades of scarcity, Americans had what seemed a dazzling array of consumer goods from which to choose, and they embraced them with unmatched exuberance. Even the most utilitarian objects got two-tone paint jobs or rocket ship details; there was an optimism and vulgar joy in the popularity of turquoise refrigerators, furniture shaped like boomerangs, and cars designed to resemble fighter jets. In this consumer society, people used consumer choices to express their personal identity and to claim status within the broad boundaries of the middle class.

Cars more than anything else embodied the consumer fantasies and exuberance of newly prosperous Americans. Expensive Cadillacs were the first to develop tail fins, and fins soon soared from midrange Chevys, Fords, and Plymouths as well. Americans spent $65 billion on automobiles in 1955—a figure equivalent to almost 20 percent of the gross national product. To pay for all those cars—and for suburban houses with modern appliances—America's consumer debt rose from $5.7 billion in 1945 to $58 billion in 1961.

25-5g Religion

In the same years, Americans turned in unprecedented numbers to organized religion. Membership (primarily in mainline Christian churches) doubled between the end of World War II and the beginning of the 1960s. The uncertainties of the nuclear age likely contributed to the resurgence of religion, and some Americans may have sought spiritual consolation in the wake of the immensely destructive world war. The increasingly important national mass media played a role, as preachers like Billy Graham created national congregations from television audiences, preaching a message that combined the promise of salvation with Cold War patriotism. But along with religious teachings, local churches and synagogues offered new suburbanites a sense of community. They welcomed

◁ Consumer goods reflected a new exuberance during the 1950s, and none more than that decade's automobiles. This candy-pink 1958 Cadillac coupe, complete with swooping tail fins, stands in front of another 1950s institution: a California drive-in.

Car Culture/Getty Images

newcomers, celebrated life's rituals, and supported the sick and the bereaved, who were often far from their extended families and old communities. It is difficult to measure the depth of religious belief in postwar America, but church fellowship halls were near the center of the new postwar middle-class culture.

25-6 Men, Women, and Youth at Midcentury

▷ **What were the dominant postwar attitudes and ideas about gender roles, marriage, and sexuality?**

▷ **How did the postwar economy and culture shape assumptions about men's and women's work?**

▷ **What made the postwar "youth culture" distinctive?**

Most of all, Americans pursued "the good life" and sought refuge from the tensions of the Cold War world through their homes and families. Having survived the Great Depression and a world war, many sought fulfillment in private life rather than public engagement; they saw their commitment to home and family as an expression of faith in the future. However, despite the real satisfactions that many Americans found in family life, both men and women found their life choices limited by powerful social pressures to conform to narrowly defined gender roles.

25-6a Marriage and Families

During the 1950s, few Americans remained single, and most people married very young. By 1959, half of American brides were twenty or younger; their husbands were not much older. This trend toward early marriage was endorsed by experts and approved by most parents, in part as a way to prevent premarital sex. As Americans accepted psychotherapeutic insights in the years following the war, they worried not only that premarital sex might leave the young woman pregnant or ruin her "reputation," but also that the experience could so damage her psychologically that she could never adjust to "normal" marital relations. One popular women's magazine argued, "When two people are ready for sexual intercourse at the fully human level they are ready for marriage. . . . Not to do so is moral cowardice. And society has no right to stand in their way."

Many young couples—still teenagers—found autonomy and freedom from parental authority by marrying and setting up their own household. Most newlyweds quickly had babies—an average of three—completing their family while still in their twenties. Birth control (condoms and diaphragms) was widely available and widely used, for most couples planned the size of their family. But almost all married couples, regardless of race or class, wanted a large family. Two children were the American ideal in 1940; by 1960, most couples wanted four. And though many families looked nothing like television's June, Ward, Wally, and Beaver Cleaver, 87 percent

of children under eighteen lived with two married parents (in 2015, the figure was 61 percent). Fewer children were born outside marriage then; only 3.9 percent of births were to unmarried women in 1950 (compared with about 40 percent of births today). Divorce rates were also lower, escalating from a new high of 9 divorces per 1,000 married couples in 1960 to a peak of 22 in the early 1980s, and down to approximately 16 divorces per 1,000 married couples today.

25-6b Gender Roles in 1950s Families

In these 1950s families, men and women usually took distinct and different roles, with male breadwinners and female homemakers. This division of labor, contemporary commentators insisted, was based on the timeless and essential differences between the sexes. In fact, the economic and social structure and the cultural values of postwar American society largely determined what choices were available to American men and women.

During the 1950s, it was possible for many white families to live in modest middle-class comfort on one (male) salary. (Racial discrimination made this much more difficult for black families.) There were strong incentives for women to stay at home, especially while children were young. Good child care was rarely available, and fewer families lived close to the grandparents or other relatives who had traditionally helped with the children. A new cohort of child care experts, including **Dr. Benjamin Spock**, whose 1946 *Baby and Child Care* sold millions of copies, insisted that a mother's full-time attention was necessary for her children's well-being. Because of hiring discrimination, women who could afford to stay home often did not find the jobs available to them attractive enough to justify a double shift, with paid employment simply added to their responsibilities for cooking and housework. Many women thus chose to devote their considerable energies to family life. America's schools and religious institutions also benefited immensely from their volunteer labor.

25-6c Women and Work

A great number of women, however, found that their lives did not completely match the ideal of 1950s family life. Suburban domesticity left many women feeling isolated, cut off from the larger world of experiences their husbands still inhabited. The popular belief that one should find complete emotional satisfaction in private life put unrealistic pressures on marriages and family relationships. And finally, despite near-universal celebration of women's domestic roles, many women found themselves managing both job and family responsibilities (see Figure 25.3). Twice as many women were employed in 1960 as in 1940, including 39 percent of women with children between the ages of six and seventeen. A majority of these women worked part time

Dr. Benjamin Spock Physician and author of *Baby and Child Care*, the best-selling child-rearing manual for parents of the baby boom generation.

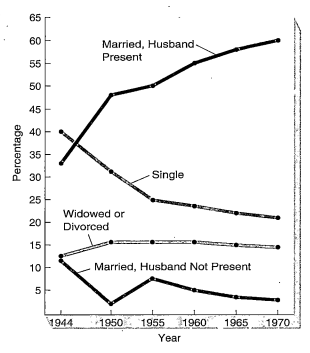

Figure 25.3 Marital Distribution of the Female Labor Force, 1944–1970

The composition of the female labor force changed dramatically from 1944 to 1970. In 1944, 41 percent of women in the labor force were single; in 1970, only 22 percent were single. During the same years, the percentage of the female labor force who had a husband in the home jumped from 34 to 59. The percentage who were widowed or divorced remained about the same from 1944 to 1970. *Source: Adapted from U.S. Bureau of the Census, Historical Statistics of the United States, Colonial Times to 1970, Bicentennial Edition (Washington, D.C.: U.S. Government Printing Office, 1975), p. 133.*

for some specific family goal: a new car, college tuition for the children. They did not see these jobs as violating their primary role as housewife; these jobs were in service to the family, not a means to independence from it.

Whether she worked to supplement a middle-class income, to feed her children, or to support herself, however, a woman faced discrimination in the world of work. Want ads were divided into "Help Wanted—Male" and "Help Wanted—Female" categories. Female full-time workers earned, on average, just 60 percent of what male full-time workers were paid and were restricted to less well-paid "female" fields, as maids, secretaries, teachers, and nurses. Women with exceptional talent or ambition often found their aspirations blocked. A popular book, *Modern Woman: The Lost Sex*, explained that ambitious women and "feminists" suffered from "penis envy." Textbooks for college psychology and sociology courses warned women not to "compete" with men; magazine articles described "career women" as a "third sex." Medical schools commonly limited the admission of women to 5 percent of each class. In 1960, less than 4 percent of lawyers and judges were female. When future Supreme

Court Justice Ruth Bader Ginsburg graduated at the top of her Columbia Law School class in 1959, she could not find a job.

25-6d "Crisis of Masculinity"

While academics and mass media critics alike stressed the importance of "proper" female roles, they devoted equal attention to the plight of the American male. American men faced a "crisis of masculinity," proclaimed the nation's mass-circulation magazines, quoting an array of psychological experts. In a best-selling book, sociologist William H. Whyte explained that postwar corporate employees had become "organization men," succeeding through cooperation and conformity, not through individual initiative and risk. Women, too, were blamed for men's crisis: women's "natural" desire for security and comfort, experts insisted, was stifling men's natural instinct for adventure. Some even linked concerns about masculinity to the Cold War, arguing that, unless America's men recovered masculinity diminished by white-collar work or a suburban, family-centered existence, the nation's future was at risk. At the same time, however, men who did not conform to current standards of male responsibility—husband, father, breadwinner—were forcefully condemned, sometimes in the same magazines that preached the crisis of masculinity. One influential book advocated mandatory psychotherapy for men who reached thirty without having married; such single men were open to charges of "emotional immaturity" or "latent homosexuality."

25-6e Sexuality

Sexuality was complicated terrain in postwar America. Only heterosexual intercourse within marriage was deemed socially acceptable, and consequences for sexual misconduct could be severe. Women who became pregnant outside marriage were often ostracized by friends and family and expelled from schools or colleges. Homosexuality was grounds for dismissal from a job, expulsion from college, even jail. At the same time, a great many Americans were breaking the sexual rules of the era. In his major works on human sexuality, *Sexual Behavior in the Human Male* (1948) and *Sexual Behavior in the Human Female* (1953), Dr. Alfred Kinsey, director of the Institute for Sex Research at Indiana University, informed Americans that, despite the fact that more than 80 percent of his female sample disapproved of premarital sex on "moral grounds," half of these women had had premarital sex. He also reported that at least 37 percent of American men had had "some homosexual experience." Americans made best sellers of Kinsey's dry, quantitative studies—as many rushed to condemn him. One congressman charged Kinsey with "hurling the insult of the century against our mothers, wives, daughters and sisters"; the *Chicago Tribune* called him a "menace to society." Although Kinsey's population samples did not provide a completely accurate picture of American sexual behavior, his findings made many Americans aware that they were not alone in breaking certain rules.

Another challenge to the sexual rules of 1950s America came from Hugh Hefner, who launched *Playboy* magazine in 1953. Within three years, the magazine had a circulation of 1 million. Hefner saw *Playboy* as an attack on America's "ferocious anti-sexuality [and] dark antieroticism" and his nude "playmates" as a means for men to combat what he considered the increasingly "blurred distinctions between the sexes" in a family-centered suburban culture.

25-6f Youth Culture

As children grew up in relative stability and prosperity, a distinctive "youth culture" developed. Youth culture was really a set of subcultures; the culture of white, middle-class, suburban youth was not the same as that of black, urban teens or even of the white working class. Youth culture was, however, distinct from the culture of adults. Its customs and rituals were created within peer groups and shaped by national media—teen magazines, movies, radio, advertising, music—targeted toward this huge potential audience.

The sheer numbers of "baby boom" youth made them a force in American society. People sometimes described the baby boom generation as "a pig in a python," and as this group moved from childhood to youth, communities successively built elementary schools, junior high schools, and high schools. America's corporations quickly learned the power of youth, as children's fads launched multimillion-dollar industries. Slinky, selling for a dollar, began loping down people's stairs in 1947; Mr. Potato Head—probably the first toy advertised on television—had $4 million in sales in 1952. Barbie, introduced by Mattel in 1959, would sell its billionth copy in 1997. In the mid-1950s, when Walt Disney's television show *Disneyland* featured Davy Crockett, "King of the Wild Frontier," every child in America (and more than a few adults) just *had* to have a coonskin cap. When the price of raccoon fur skyrocketed from 25 cents to $8 a pound, many children had to make do with a Davy Crockett lunchbox or toothbrush instead. As these baby boom children grew up, their buying power shaped American popular culture.

By 1960, America's 18 million teenagers were spending $10 billion a year. Seventy-two percent of movie tickets in the 1950s were sold to teenagers, and Hollywood catered to this audience with films that ranged from forgettable B movies like *The Cool and the Crazy* and *Senior Prom* to controversial and influential movies, such as James Dean's *Rebel Without a Cause*. Adults worried that teens would be drawn to romantic images of delinquency in *Rebel Without a Cause*, and teenage boys did copy Dean's rebellious look. The film, however, blamed parents for teenage confusion, drawing heavily on popular psychological theories about sexuality and the "crisis of masculinity." "What can you do when you have to be a man?," James Dean's character implored his father.

Movies helped shape teen fads and fashions, but nothing defined youth culture as much as its music. Young Americans were electrified by the driving energy and beat of Bill Haley and the Comets, Chuck Berry, Little Richard, and Buddy Holly. **Elvis Presley**'s 1956 appearance on TV's *Ed Sullivan Show* touched off a frenzy of teen adulation—and

△ Elvis Presley's first RCA recording, *Heartbreak Hotel*, went to number one on the charts in 1956, and teenage girls went wild for him. Drafted in December 1957, Elvis served in the U.S. Army from 1958 to 1960.

a flood of letters from parents scandalized by his "gyrations." As one reviewer noted, "When Presley executes his bumps and grinds, it must be remembered that even the 12-year-old's curiosity may be overstimulated." Although few white musicians acknowledged the debt, the roots of rock 'n' roll lay in African American rhythm and blues. The raw energy and sometimes sexually suggestive lyrics of early rock music faded as the music industry sought white performers, like Pat Boone, to do blander, more acceptable "cover" versions of music by black artists.

The distinct youth culture that developed in the 1950s made many adults uneasy. Parents worried that the common practice of "going steady" made it more likely that teens would "go too far" sexually. Juvenile delinquency was a major concern. Crime rates for young people had risen dramatically in the years following World War II, but much was "status" crime—curfew violations, sexual experimentation, underage drinking—activities that were criminal because of the person's age, not because of the action itself. Congress held extensive hearings on juvenile delinquency, with experts testifying to the corrupting power of youth-oriented popular culture, comic books in

Elvis Presley Popular rock 'n' roll musician who melded country, gospel, and rhythm and blues influences; his sexually charged style drew young fans and alarmed many adults.

Sputnik

On October 4, 1957, the Soviet Union launched the first human-made satellite into space. *Sputnik*—roughly the size of a basketball, weighing 184 pounds—fell into orbit 500 miles above the earth's surface, emitting a steady beeping sound (A-flat, for 3/10 of a second) that could be picked up not only by sophisticated scientific instruments but by ham radio operators around the world. In the United States, an NBC radio announcer broadcast the beep, telling his listeners: "Listen now for the sound that forevermore separates the old from the new." The Soviets had begun a new era in human history.

Underlining the scientific and psychological triumph that *Sputnik* represented in the ongoing Cold War, Soviets framed it—in Cold War terms—as a triumph of communism. And *Sputnik's* propaganda value was undeniable. In the fall of 1957, Soviet technological and scientific achievement made headlines around the world; the United States, in contrast, offered scenes of racial violence. Radio Moscow, ever eager to make that point, announced the precise moment that *Sputnik* passed over Little Rock, Arkansas, where white mobs had attacked black students attempting to integrate its high school.

Some Americans worried about *Sputnik's* symbolic value. More, however, worried that America had become more vulnerable to Soviet attack. The little beeping sphere mattered little, but the missile that propelled it into outer space was another story. Such a missile could carry a nuclear warhead from

Soviet territory to the United States: the Soviets had created an intercontinental ballistic missile (ICBM). Said Soviet First Secretary Nikita Khrushchev: "[W]e now have all the rockets we need: long range rockets, intermediate-range rockets. And short-range rockets . . . [which] now make it possible to hit a target in any area of the globe."

Khrushchev's claim was more bluster than fact, as U.S. president Eisenhower well knew. American aerial reconnaissance showed that the Soviet missile program was not nearly so advanced or production so prolific. Eisenhower tried to calm the fears of his countrymen, going so far as to play five rounds of golf in the subsequent week. But he was not going to reveal America's top secret program of aerial surveillance.

Within hours of Sputnik's launch, however, Senator Lyndon Johnson (D-TX) had launched a Senate investigation: How had the Republican administration allowed the Soviets to beat the United States into space? Eisenhower, in response to increasing pressure (and surprising the not terribly well funded team in charge of the U.S. satellite program) announced that the United States would have its own satellite in orbit before the end of the year. On December 6, the United States launched a rocket, topped with a grapefruit-sized satellite, from Cape Canaveral, Florida. It rose about four feet into the air and exploded.

U.S. scientists would do better on the next try, successfully launching a satellite into orbit less than two months

later. But the combination of Soviet triumph and U.S. failure left Americans seeking an explanation. One answer seemed to lie in the U.S. educational system. *Life* magazine made the case: "Where there are young minds of great promise, there are rarely the means to advance them." In the heated atmosphere of the Cold War, Congress passed the National Defense Education Act of 1958. "An educational emergency exists," it claimed, which "requires action by the federal government. . . . to help develop as rapidly as possible those skills necessary for national defense."

In the wake of *Sputnik's* launch, federal money began to flow into higher education, funding scientific research and the study of foreign languages and societies. Federal money went to graduate fellowships and, in an attempt to draw more talented students to college, to fund high school college counselors and establish the first college student loan program. In this rise of federal support for American universities, we see a clear link to the world.

CRITICAL THINKING

- In the wake of the Soviet launch of Sputnik, the United States began investing more heavily in higher education through the National Defense Education Act of 1958. With the recent uptick in the use of cyberattacks by foreign governments and non-state entities, should the federal government again take a leading role in the promotion of certain kinds of education?

---

particular. In 1955, *Life* magazine reported, "Some American parents, without quite knowing what it is their kids are up to, are worried that it's something they shouldn't be." Most youthful behavior, however—from going steady to fads in music and dress—fit squarely into the consumer culture that youth shared

with their parents. "Rebellious youth" rarely questioned the logic of postwar American culture.

25-6g Challenges to Middle-Class Culture

Despite the growing reach and power of this middle-class culture, there were pockets of cultural dissent. **Beat** (a word that suggested both "down and out" and "beatific") writers rejected both middle-class social decorum and contemporary literary conventions. Jack Kerouac, author of *On the*

Beat Term used to describe a generation of nonconformist writers, such as Allen Ginsberg, who expressed scorn for the middle-class ideals of conformity, religion, family values, and materialism.

◁ Soviet postcard celebrating the launch of Sputnik I (October 4, 1957) and Sputnik II (November 3, 1957).

Mark Rykoff/Getty Images

Road, traced his inspiration to "weariness with all forms of the modern industrial state." The Beat Generation embraced spontaneity in their art, in their lives sought freedom from the demands of everyday life, and enjoyed a more open sexuality and drug use. Perhaps the most significant beat work was Allen Ginsberg's angry, incantational poem "Howl" (1956), the subject of an obscenity trial whose verdict opened American publishing to a much broader range of works. The mainstream press made fun of the beats, dubbing them and their followers "beatniks" (after *Sputnik,* suggesting their un-Americanness). Although their numbers were small in the 1950s, their rebellion helped shape America's counterculture in the 1960s and 1970s.

25-7 The Limits of the Middle-Class Nation

▷ **What did critics find problematic about the postwar middle-class culture?**

▷ **How did the postwar economy affect the environment?**

▷ **What groups of Americans were left behind in the nation's economic expansion, and why?**

During the 1950s, America's popular culture and mass media celebrated the opportunities available to the nation's people. At the same time, a host of influential critics rushed to condemn the new middle-class culture as a wasteland of conformity, homogeneity, and ugly consumerism.

25-7a Critics of Conformity

These critics were not lone figures crying out in the wilderness. Americans, obsessed with self-criticism even as most participated wholeheartedly in the celebratory "consensus" culture of their age, rushed to buy books like John Keats's *The*

Crack in the Picture Window (1957), which portrayed three families—the "Drones," the "Amiables," and the "Fecunds"—who lived in identical suburban tract houses "vomited" up by developers and sacrificed their remaining individuality in the quest for consumer goods. Some of the most popular fiction of the postwar era, such as J. D. Salinger's *The Catcher in the Rye* and Norman Mailer's *The Naked and the Dead,* was profoundly critical of American society. Americans even made best sellers of difficult academic works, such as David Riesman's *The Lonely Crowd* (1950) and William H. Whyte's *The Organization Man* (1955), both of which criticized the rise of conformity in American life. Versions of these critiques also appeared in mass-circulation magazines like *Ladies' Home Journal* and *Reader's Digest.* Steeped in such cultural criticism, many Americans even understood *Invasion of the Body Snatchers*—a 1956 film in which zombielike aliens grown in huge pods gradually replace a town's human inhabitants—as criticism of suburban conformity and the bland homogeneity of postwar culture.

Most of these critics were attempting to understand large-scale and significant changes in American society. Americans had lost some autonomy as large corporations replaced smaller businesses; they experienced the homogenizing force of mass production and a national consumer culture; they saw distinctions among ethnic groups and even among socioeconomic classes decline in importance. Many wanted to understand these social dislocations better. Critics of the new culture, however, were often elitist and antidemocratic. Many saw only bland conformity and sterility in the emerging middle-class suburban culture and so missed something important. Identical houses did not produce identical souls; instead, inexpensive suburban housing gave healthier, and perhaps happier, lives to millions who had grown up in dank, dark tenements or ramshackle farmhouses without indoor plumbing. In retrospect, however, other criticisms are obvious.

25-7b Environmental Degradation

First, the new consumer culture encouraged wasteful habits and harmed the environment. *BusinessWeek* noted during the 1950s that corporations need not rely on "planned obsolescence," purposely designing a product to wear out so that consumers would have to replace it. Americans replaced products because they were "out of date," not because they did not work, and automakers, encouraging the trend, revamped designs every year. New and inexpensive plastic products and detergents made consumers' lives easier—but were not biodegradable. And America's new consumer society used an ever-larger share of the world's resources. By the 1960s, the United States, with only 5 percent of the world's population, consumed more than one-third of its goods and services.

The rapid economic growth that made the middle-class consumer culture possible exacted environmental costs. Steel mills, coal-powered generators, and internal-combustion car engines burning lead-based gasoline polluted the atmosphere and imperiled people's health. As suburbanites commuted greater distances to their jobs, and neighborhoods were built without public transportation or shopping within walking distance of people's homes, Americans relied on private automobiles, consuming the nonrenewable resources of oil and gasoline and filling cities and suburbs with smog. Vast quantities of water were diverted from lakes and rivers to meet the needs of America's burgeoning Sunbelt cities, including the swimming pools and golf courses that dotted parched Arizona and southern California.

Defense contractors and farmers were among the country's worst polluters. Refuse from nuclear weapons facilities at Hanford, Washington, and at Colorado's Rocky Flats arsenal poisoned soil and water resources for years. Agriculture began employing massive amounts of pesticides and other chemicals. DDT, a chemical used on Pacific islands during the war to kill mosquitoes and lice, was used widely in the United States from 1945 until after 1962, when wildlife biologist Rachel Carson specifically indicted DDT for the deaths of mammals, birds, and fish in her best-selling book *Silent Spring*.

In the midst of prosperity, few understood the consequences of the economic transformation taking place. The nation was moving toward a postindustrial economy in which providing goods and services to consumers was more important than producing goods. Therefore, though union members prospered during the 1950s, union membership grew slowly—because most new jobs were being created not in heavy industries that hired blue-collar workers but in the union-resistant white-collar service trades. Technological advances increased productivity, as automated electronic processes replaced slower mechanical ones—but they pushed people out of relatively well-paid blue-collar jobs into the growing and less well-paid service sector.

25-7c Continuing Racism

Largely oblivious to the environmental degradation and work sector shifts that accompanied economic growth and consumerism, the new middle-class culture also largely ignored those who did not belong to its ranks. Race remained a major dividing line in American society, even as fewer Americans were excluded because of ethnic identity. Racial discrimination stood unchallenged in most of 1950s America. Suburbs, both North and South, were almost always racially segregated. Many white Americans had little or no contact in their daily lives with people of different races—not only because of residential segregation but also because the relatively small populations of nonwhite Americans were not dispersed equally throughout the nation. In 1960, there were 68 people of Chinese descent and 519 African Americans living in Vermont; 181 Native Americans lived in West Virginia; and Mississippi had just 178 Japanese American residents. Most white Americans in the 1950s—especially those outside the South, where there was a large African American population—gave little thought to race. They did not think of the emerging middle-class culture as "white," but as "American," marginalizing people of color in image as in reality (see Map 25.2).

◁ During the Second World War, DDT was used to protect American troops from bug-borne diseases and was hailed as a miracle insecticide. The use of DDT spread in postwar America, but little attention was paid to its often-fatal consequences for birds, mammals, and fish. In 1945, even as children ran alongside, this truck sprayed DDT as part of a mosquito control program at New York's Jones Beach State Park.

Bettmann/Getty Images

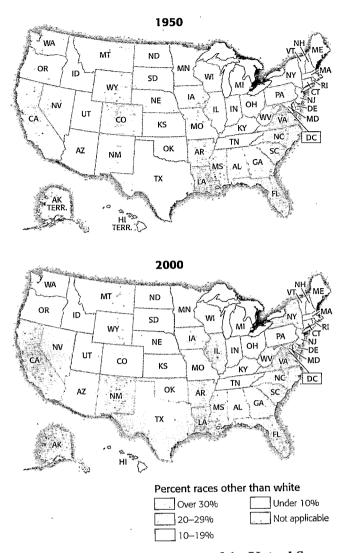

1950

2000

Percent races other than white

Over 30%	Under 10%
20–29%	Not applicable
10–19%	

Map 25.2 Racial Composition of the United States, 1950 and 2000

Compared with present-day America, most states were fairly racially homogeneous in 1950. The exception was the Deep South, where most African Americans still lived. *Source: Adapted from "Demographic Trends in the Twentieth Century," U.S. Census Bureau; www.census.gov/population/www/censusdata/hiscendata.html.*

The new middle-class culture was also indifferent to the plight of the poor. In an age of abundance, more than one in five Americans lived in poverty. One-fifth of the poor were people of color, including almost half of the nation's African American population and more than half of all Native Americans. Two-thirds of the poor lived in households headed by a person with an eighth-grade education or less, one-fourth in households headed by a single woman. More than one-third of the poor were under age eighteen; one-fourth were over age sixty-five. Social Security payments helped the elderly, but many retirees were not yet covered, and

medical costs drove many older Americans into poverty. Few of these people had much reason for hope.

25-7d Poverty in an Age of Abundance

As millions of Americans (most of them white) were settling in the suburbs, the poor were ever more concentrated in the inner cities. African American migrants from the South were joined by poor whites from the southern Appalachians, many of whom moved to Chicago, Cincinnati, Baltimore, and Detroit. Meanwhile, Latin Americans were arriving in growing numbers from Mexico, the Dominican Republic, Colombia, Ecuador, and Cuba. According to the 1960 census, over a half-million Mexican Americans had migrated to the barrios of the Los Angeles–Long Beach area since 1940. And New York City's Puerto Rican population exploded from 70,000 in 1940 to 613,000 in 1960.

All of these newcomers to the cities came seeking better lives and greater opportunities. Because of the strong economy and low unemployment rate, many did gain a higher standard of living. But discrimination limited their advances, and they endured crowded and decrepit housing and poor schools. In addition, the federal programs that helped middle-class Americans sometimes made the lives of the poor worse. For example, the National Housing Act of 1949, passed to make available "a decent home ... for every American family," provided for "urban redevelopment." Redevelopment meant slum clearance. Many poor people lost what housing they had as entire neighborhoods were leveled and replaced with luxury high-rise buildings, parking lots, and even highways.

Rural poverty was a long-standing problem in America, but the growth of large agribusinesses pushed more tenant farmers and owners of small farms off the land. From 1945 to 1961, the nation's farm population declined from 24.4 million to 14.8 million. When the harvesting of cotton in the South was mechanized in the 1940s and 1950s, more than 4 million people were displaced. Southern tobacco growers dismissed their tenant farmers, bought tractors to plow the land, and hired migratory workers to harvest the crops. Many of these displaced farmers traded southern rural poverty for northern urban poverty. And in the West and Southwest, Mexican citizens continued to serve as cheap migrant labor under the *bracero* program. Almost 1 million Mexican workers came legally to the United States in 1959; many more were undocumented workers. Entire families labored, enduring conditions little better than in the Great Depression.

Native Americans were America's poorest people, with an average annual income barely half that of the poverty level. Conditions for Native peoples were made worse by a federal policy implemented during the Eisenhower administration: termination. Termination reversed the Indian Reorganization Act of 1934, allowing Native peoples to terminate their tribal status and so remove reservation lands from federal protection that prohibited their sale. Sixty-one tribes were terminated between 1954 and 1960. Termination could take place only with a tribe's agreement, but pressure was sometimes intense—especially when reservation land

◁ After the war, American Indians lost sacred land to both big corporations and the federal government. In 1948, George Gillette (*left*), chairman of the Fort Berthold, North Dakota, Indian Tribal Council, covers his face and weeps as Secretary of the Interior J. A. Krug signs a contract buying 155,000 acres of tribal land for a reservoir.

AP Photo/William Chaplis

was rich in natural resources. The Klamaths of Oregon, for example, lived on a reservation rich in ponderosa pine, which lumber interests coveted. Enticed by cash payments, almost four-fifths of the Klamaths accepted termination and voted to sell their shares of the forestland. With termination, their way of life collapsed. Many Native Americans left reservation land for the city, joining the influx of other poor Americans seeking jobs and new lives. By the time termination was halted in the 1960s, observers compared the situation of Native Americans to the devastation their forebears had endured in the nineteenth century. Like most of the poor, these Americans were invisible to the growing middle class in the suburbs.

Overall, Americans who had lived through the devastation of the Great Depression and World War II enjoyed the relative prosperity and economic security of the postwar era. But those who had made it to the comfortable middle class often ignored the plight of those left behind. It would be their children—the generation of the baby boom, many reared in suburban comfort—who would see racism, poverty, and the self-satisfaction of postwar suburban culture as a failure of American ideals.

Summary

As the experiences of economic depression and world war receded, Americans worked to create good lives for themselves and their families. People married and had children in record numbers. Millions of veterans used the GI Bill to attend college, buy homes, and start businesses. Although American leaders feared that the nation would lapse back into economic depression after wartime government spending ended, consumer spending brought economic growth. The sustained economic growth of the postwar era, supported by strong labor unions and government policies, lifted a majority of Americans into an expanding middle class and lessened economic inequality.

The Cold War presidencies of Truman and Eisenhower focused on international relations and a global struggle against communism, rather than on domestic politics. Within the United States, Cold War fears provoked an extreme anti-communism that stifled political dissent and diminished Americans' civil liberties and freedoms.

The continuing African American struggle for civil rights drew national attention during the Montgomery bus boycott. African Americans won important victories in the Supreme Court, including the landmark decision in *Brown v. Board of Education*, and both Truman and Eisenhower used federal power to guarantee the rights of black Americans. With these victories, a national civil rights movement began to coalesce, and racial tensions within the nation increased.

Despite continued racial divisions, the United States became in many ways a more inclusive nation in the 1950s, as a majority of Americans participated in a national, consumer-oriented, middle-class culture. This culture largely ignored the poverty that remained in the nation's cities and rural areas, and contributed to rapidly increasing economic degradation. But for the growing number of middle-class Americans who, for the first time, lived in modest material comfort, the American dream seemed a reality.

Suggestions for Further Reading

Glenn C. Altschuler and Stuart M. Blumin, *The GI Bill: A New Deal for Veterans* (2009)

Taylor Branch, *Parting the Waters: America in the King Years, 1954–1963* (1988)

The Pledge of Allegiance

The Pledge of Allegiance that Americans recite in school classrooms and sports stadiums throughout the nation today was shaped by America's Cold War struggle against the Soviet Union. Congress added the phrase "under God" to the existing pledge in 1954, as part of an attempt to emphasize the difference between the God-fearing United States and the "godless communists" of the Soviet Union.

The Pledge of Allegiance was not always an important part of American public life. The original version was written in 1892 by Francis Bellamy, editor of *The Youth's Companion*, to commemorate the four hundredth anniversary of Columbus's arrival in North America. On October 11, 1892, more than 11 million schoolchildren recited the words "I pledge allegiance to my flag and the Republic for which it stands; one nation indivisible, with liberty and justice for all." In 1942, Congress officially adopted a revised version of this pledge as an act of wartime patriotism. The Supreme Court ruled in 1943, however, that schoolchildren could not be forced to say the "Pledge to the Flag."

During the Cold War years, the pledge became more and more important as a way to demonstrate loyalty to the United States. Cold War fears lent force to a campaign by the Knights of Columbus, a Catholic men's service organization, to include "under God" in the pledge. Supporting the bill, President Eisenhower proclaimed that

> in this way we are reaffirming the transcendence of religious faith in America's heritage and future; in this way we shall constantly strengthen those spiritual weapons which forever will be our country's most powerful resource in peace and war. From this day forward, the millions of our schoolchildren will daily proclaim in every city and town, every village and every rural schoolhouse, the dedication of our nation and our people to the Almighty.

Some Americans, citing the doctrine of separation of church and state, have protested the inclusion of "under God" in the nation's pledge. In June 2002, the Ninth District Court (covering California and eight other western states) touched off a major controversy by ruling that the 1954 version of the pledge was unconstitutional because it conveyed a "state endorsement" of a religious belief. Questions about the proper role of religion in American life are sure to remain controversial, a legacy for a people and a nation as America's people become even more diverse in the twenty-first century.

CRITICAL THINKING

☐ The tensions of the Cold War helped to produce the first efforts to identify the United States as a Christian nation encapsulated by the addition of "under God" to the Pledge of Allegiance. In 2002, a federal district court ruled the 1954 version of the pledge to be in violation of the constitutional separation of church and state. The battle over the relationship of the nation to religion continues today. What evidence of this struggle can you identify in the United States today?

Lizabeth Cohen, *A Consumer's Republic: The Politics of Mass Consumption in Postwar America* (2003)

Stephanie Coontz, *The Way We Never Were: American Families and the Nostalgia Trap* (1992)

Thomas Patrick Doherty, *Cold War, Cool Medium: Television, McCarthyism, and American Culture* (2003)

Mary Dudziak, *Cold War Civil Rights: Race and the Image of American Democracy* (2000)

James Gregory, *The Southern Diaspora: How the Great Migrations of Black and White Southerners Transformed the Nation* (2007)

Thomas Hine, *Populuxe* (1986)

Grace Palladino, *Teenagers* (1996)

Michael Sherry, *In the Shadow of War* (1995)

Thomas J. Sugrue, *Sweet Land of Liberty: The Forgotten Struggle for Civil Rights in the North* (2008)

The Tumultuous Sixties, 1960-1968

I t was late at night, and Ezell Blair had a big exam the next day. But there he was with his friends in the dormitory, talking—as they so often did—about injustice, and discrimination, and about living in a nation that proclaimed equality for all but denied full citizenship to some of its people because of the color of their skin. They were complaining about all the do-nothing adults, condemning pretty much the entire black community of Greensboro—and not for the first time—when Franklin McCain said, as if he meant it, "It's time to fish or cut bait." And Joe McNeil said, "Yes, we're a bunch of hypocrites. Come on, let's do it. Let's do it tomorrow." McCain's roommate, David Richmond, agreed. Blair hesitated. "I was thinking about my grades," he said later, just "trying to deal with that architecture and engineering course I was taking."

But Blair was outvoted. The next day, February 1, 1960, after their classes at North Carolina Agricultural and Technical College were over, the four freshmen walked into town. At the F. W. Woolworth's on South Elm Street, one of the most profitable stores in the national chain, each bought a few small things, mostly school supplies. Then, nervously, they sat down on the vinyl-covered stools at the lunch counter and tried to order coffee. These young men—seventeen and eighteen years old—were prepared to be arrested, even physically attacked. But nothing happened. The counter help ignored them as long as possible; they never got their coffee. When one worker finally reminded them, "We don't serve colored here," the four made their point: they had already been served just a few feet away when they made their purchases. Why not at the lunch counter? An elderly white woman came up to the boys and told them how proud she was of them. "We got so much courage and so much pride" from that "little old lady," McCain said later. But still nothing happened. The store closed; the manager turned out the lights. After sitting in near darkness for about forty-five minutes, the

◁ When four freshmen from North Carolina Agricultural and Technical College sat down and tried to order coffee at the whites-only Woolworth's lunch counter in Greensboro, North Carolina, they did not know if they would be arrested or even physically attacked. This photograph is from the second day of the sit-in, when the four were joined by classmates. Bettmann/Getty Images

Chronology

1960
- Sit-ins begin in Greensboro
- Birth control pill approved
- John F. Kennedy elected president
- Young Americans for Freedom write Sharon Statement

1961
- Freedom Riders protest segregation in transportation

1962
- Students for a Democratic Society issues Port Huron Statement
- Cuban missile crisis courts nuclear war

1963
- Civil rights March on Washington for Jobs and Freedom draws more than 250,000
- South Vietnamese leader Diem assassinated following U.S.-sanctioned coup d'état
- John F. Kennedy assassinated; Lyndon B. Johnson becomes president

1964
- Civil Rights Act passed by Congress
- Race riots break out in first of the "long, hot summers"
- Gulf of Tonkin Resolution passed by Congress
- Free Speech Movement begins at University of California, Berkeley
- Lyndon B. Johnson elected president

1965
- Lyndon Johnson launches Great Society programs
- United States commits ground troops to Vietnam and initiates bombing campaign
- Voting Rights Act outlaws practices preventing most African Americans from voting in southern states
- Immigration and Nationality Act lowers barriers to immigration from Asia and Latin America
- Malcolm X assassinated

1966
- National Organization for Women founded

1967
- "Summer of love" in San Francisco's Haight-Ashbury district
- Race riots erupt in Newark, Detroit, and other cities

1968
- Tet Offensive deepens fear of losing war in Vietnam
- Martin Luther King Jr. assassinated
- Robert Kennedy assassinated
- Violence erupts at Democratic National Convention
- Richard Nixon elected president

four men who had begun the sit-in movement got up and walked from the store.

The next day they returned, but they were not alone. Twenty fellow students joined the sit-in. By February 3, sixty-three of the sixty-five seats were taken. On February 4, students from other colleges arrived, and the sit-in spread to the S. H. Kress store across the street. By February 7, there were sit-ins in Winston-Salem; by February 8, in Charlotte; on February 9, sit-ins began in Raleigh. By the third week in February, students were picketing Woolworth's stores in the North, and at lunch counters throughout the South, well-dressed young men and women sat, politely asking to be served. On July 26, 1960, they won. F. W. Woolworth's ended segregation, not only in Greensboro but in all of its stores.

Experience an interactive version of this story in MindTap®.

When these four college freshmen sat down at the Woolworth's lunch counter in Greensboro, they signaled the beginning of a decade of public activism rarely matched in American history. During the 1960s, millions of Americans—many of them young people—took to the streets. Some marched for civil rights or against the war in Vietnam; others lashed out in anger over the circumstances of their lives. Passion over the events of the day revitalized democracy—and threatened to tear the nation apart.

John F. Kennedy, the nation's youngest elected president, told Americans as he took office in 1961, "The torch has been passed to a new generation." Despite his inspirational language, Kennedy had only modest success implementing his domestic agenda. As he began his third year as president, pushed by the bravery of civil rights activists and the intransigence of their white opponents, Kennedy began to offer more active support for civil rights and to propose more ambitious domestic policies. But Kennedy was assassinated in November 1963. His death seemed, to many, the end of an era of hope.

Lyndon Johnson, Kennedy's successor, called on the memory of the martyred president to launch an ambitious program of civil rights and other liberal legislation. Johnson meant to use the power of the federal government to eliminate poverty and to guarantee equal rights to all America's people. He called his vision **the Great Society**.

Despite liberal triumphs in Washington, D.C., and real gains by the African American civil rights movement, social tensions escalated during the mid-1960s. A revitalized conservative movement emerged, and Franklin Roosevelt's old New Deal coalition fractured as white southerners abandoned the Democratic Party. Many African Americans, especially in the North, were angry that poverty and racial discrimination persisted despite the passage of landmark civil rights laws, and their discontent exploded during the "long, hot summers" of the mid-1960s. White youth culture, which seemed intent on rejecting everything an older generation had worked for, created a division that Americans came to call "the generation gap."

Developments overseas also contributed to a growing national instability. After the Cuban missile crisis of 1962 brought the Soviet Union and the United States close to nuclear disaster, President John F. Kennedy and Soviet leader Nikita Khrushchev moved to reduce bilateral tensions in 1963, with the result that Cold War pressures in Europe lessened appreciably. In the rest of the world, however, the superpowers continued their intense competition. Throughout the 1960s, the United States used a variety of approaches—including foreign aid, CIA covert actions, military assaults, cultural penetration, economic sanctions, and diplomacy—in its attempts to win the Cold War, draw unaligned nations into its orbit, and defuse revolutionary nationalism. In Vietnam, Kennedy chose to expand U.S. involvement significantly. Johnson "Americanized" the war, increasing the troop-count to more than half a million in 1968.

By 1968, the war in Vietnam had divided the American people and undermined Johnson's Great Society. With the assassinations of Martin Luther King Jr. and Robert F. Kennedy—two of America's brightest leaders—that spring, with cities in flames, and with tanks in the streets of Chicago in August, the fate of the nation seemed to hang in the balance.

▫ *What were the successes and failures of American liberalism in the 1960s?*

▫ *Why did the United States expand its participation in the war in Vietnam and continue in the war so long?*

▫ *By 1968, many believed the fate of the nation hung in the balance. What did they think was at stake? What divided Americans, and how did they express their differences?*

26-1 Kennedy and the Cold War

▷ **Why did John F. Kennedy capture the attention of the country?**

▷ **What position did John F. Kennedy take on the Cold War and foreign policy?**

▷ **How did Cuba become part of the Cold War tensions between the United States and the Soviet Union?**

President **John F. Kennedy**, was, as writer Norman Mailer observed, "our leading man." Young, handsome, and vigorous, the new chief executive was the first president born in the twentieth century. Kennedy had a genuinely inquiring mind, and as a patron of the arts he brought wit and sophistication to the White House. He was born to wealth and politics: his Irish American grandfather had been mayor of Boston, and his millionaire father, Joseph P. Kennedy, had served as ambassador to Great Britain. In 1946, the young Kennedy, having returned from the Second World War a naval hero (the boat he commanded had been rammed and sunk by a Japanese destroyer in 1943, and Kennedy had saved his crew), continued the family tradition by campaigning to represent Boston in the U.S. House of Representatives. He won easily, served three terms in the House, and in 1952 was elected to the Senate.

26-1a John Fitzgerald Kennedy

As a Democrat, Kennedy inherited the New Deal commitment to America's social welfare system. He generally cast liberal votes in line with the pro-labor sentiments of his low-income, blue-collar constituents. But he avoided controversial issues, such as civil rights and the censure of Joseph McCarthy. Kennedy won a Pulitzer Prize for his *Profiles in Courage* (1956), a study of politicians who had acted on principle, but he shaded the truth when he claimed sole authorship of the book, which had been drafted substantially by aide Theodore Sorensen (though based on more than one hundred pages of notes dictated by Kennedy). In foreign policy, Senator Kennedy endorsed the Cold War policy of containment, and his interest in world affairs deepened as the 1950s progressed. His record as a legislator was not impressive, but he enjoyed an enthusiastic following, especially after his landslide reelection to the Senate in 1958.

Kennedy and his handlers worked hard to cultivate an image of him as a happy and healthy family man. To some extent, it was a ruse. He was a chronic womanizer, and his liaisons continued even after he married Jacqueline Bouvier in 1953. Nor was he the picture of physical vitality

The Great Society President Johnson's vision for America; LBJ believed the federal government must act to alleviate poverty, end racial injustice, and improve the lives of all Americans.

John F. Kennedy Thirty-fifth president of the United States (1961–1963). Assassinated in Dallas, Texas on November 22, 1963.

that his war hero status and youthful handsomeness seemed to project. As a child, he had almost died of scarlet fever, and he spent large portions of his early years in bed, suffering from one ailment after another. He developed severe back problems, made worse by his fighting experience in World War II. After the war, Kennedy was diagnosed with Addison's disease, an adrenaline deficiency that required daily injections of cortisone in order to be contained. At the time, the disease was thought to be terminal; though Kennedy survived, he was often in acute pain. As president, he would require plenty of bed rest and frequent therapeutic swims in the White House pool.

26-1b Election of 1960

Kennedy's rhetoric and style captured the imagination of many Americans. Yet his election victory over Republican

△ Many Americans were enchanted with the youthful and photogenic Kennedys. Here, the president and his family pose outside the Palm Beach, Florida, home of the president's father after a private Easter service, April 14, 1963.

Richard Nixon in 1960 was extraordinarily narrow—118,000 votes out of nearly 69 million cast. Kennedy achieved only mixed success in the South, but he ran well in the Northeast and Midwest. His Roman Catholic faith hurt him in some states, where voters feared he would take direction from the pope, but helped in states with large Catholic populations. As the sitting vice president, Nixon was saddled with the handicaps of incumbency; he had to answer for sagging economic figures and the Soviet downing of a U-2 spy plane. Nixon also looked disagreeable on TV; in televised debates against the telegenic Kennedy, he looked alternately nervous and surly, and the camera made him appear unshaven. Perhaps worse, Eisenhower gave Nixon only a tepid endorsement. Asked to list Nixon's significant decisions as vice president, Eisenhower replied, "If you give me a week, I might think of one."

In a departure from the Eisenhower administration's staid, conservative image, the new president surrounded himself with mostly young advisers of intellectual verve, who proclaimed that they had fresh ideas for invigorating the nation; writer David Halberstam called them "the best and the brightest." Secretary of Defense Robert McNamara (age forty-four) had been an assistant professor at Harvard at twenty-four and later the whiz-kid president of the Ford Motor Company. Kennedy's special assistant for national security affairs, McGeorge Bundy (age forty-one) had become a Harvard dean at thirty-four with only a bachelor's degree. Secretary of State Dean Rusk, the old man in the group at fifty-two, had been a Rhodes Scholar in his youth. Kennedy himself was only forty-three, and his brother Robert, the attorney general, was thirty-five.

It was no accident that most of these "best and brightest" operated in the realm of foreign policy. From the start, Kennedy gave top priority to waging the Cold War. In the campaign, he had criticized Eisenhower's foreign policy as unimaginative, accusing him of missing chances to reduce the threat of nuclear war with the Soviet Union and of weakening America's standing in the Third World. Kennedy and his advisers exuded confidence that they would change things. As national security adviser McGeorge Bundy put it, "The United States is the engine of mankind, and the rest of the world is the caboose." Kennedy's inaugural address suggested no halfway measures: "Let every nation know that we shall pay any price, bear any burden, meet any hardship, support any friend, oppose any foe to assure the survival and the success of liberty."

26-1c Nation Building in the Third World

In reality, Kennedy in office would not be prepared to pay any price or bear any burden in the struggle against communism. He came to understand, sooner than many of his advisers, that there were limits to American power abroad; overall, he showed himself to be cautious and pragmatic in foreign policy. More than his predecessor, he proved willing to initiate dialogue with the Soviets, sometimes using his brother Robert as a secret back channel to Moscow. Yet

Kennedy also sought victory in the Cold War. After Soviet leader Nikita Khrushchev endorsed "wars of national liberation," such as the one in Vietnam, Kennedy called for "peaceful revolution" based on the concept of nation building. The administration set out to help developing nations through the early stages of nationhood with aid programs aimed at improving agriculture, transportation, and communications. Kennedy thus oversaw the creation of the multibillion-dollar Alliance for Progress in 1961 to spur economic development in Latin America. In the same year, he also created the Peace Corps, dispatching thousands of American teachers, agricultural specialists, and health workers, many of them right out of college, to assist authorities in developing nations.

Cynics then and later dismissed the Alliance and the Peace Corps as Cold War tools by which Kennedy sought to counter anti-Americanism and defeat communism in the developing world. The programs did have those aims, but both were also born of genuine humanitarianism. The Peace Corps in particular embodied both the idealistic, can-do spirit of the 1960s and Americans' long pursuit of moral leadership in the world. "More than any other entity," historian Elizabeth Cobbs Hoffman has written, "the Peace Corps broached an age-old dilemma of U.S. foreign policy: how to reconcile the imperatives and temptations of power politics with the ideals of freedom and self-determination for all nations."

It was one thing to broach the dilemma, and quite another to resolve it. Kennedy and his aides considered themselves supportive of social revolution in the Third World, but they could not imagine the legitimacy of communist involvement in any such uprising, or that developing countries might wish to be neutral in the East-West struggle. In addition to largely benevolent programs like the Peace Corps, therefore, the administration also relied on the more insidious concept of counterinsurgency to defeat revolutionaries who challenged pro-American Third World governments. American military and technical advisers trained native troops and police forces to quell unrest.

Nation building and counterinsurgency encountered numerous problems. The Alliance for Progress was only partly successful; infant mortality rates improved, but Latin American economies registered unimpressive growth rates, and class divisions continued to widen, exacerbating political unrest. Americans assumed that the U.S. model of capitalism and representative government could be transferred successfully to foreign cultures. Although many foreign peoples welcomed U.S. economic assistance and craved American material culture, they resented interference by outsiders. And because aid was usually transmitted through a self-interested elite, it often failed to reach the very poor.

26-1d Soviet-American Tensions

Nor did the new president have success in relations with the Soviet Union. A summit meeting with Soviet leader Nikita Khrushchev in Vienna in June 1961 went poorly, with the two leaders disagreeing over the preconditions for peace and stability in the world. Consequently, the administration's first year witnessed little movement on controlling the nuclear arms race or even on getting a superpower ban on testing nuclear weapons in the atmosphere or underground. The latter objective mattered a great deal to Kennedy, who saw a test ban as a prerequisite to preventing additional nations from getting the terrifying weapon. Instead, both superpowers continued testing and accelerated their arms production. In 1961, the U.S. military budget shot up 15 percent; by mid-1964, U.S. nuclear weapons had increased by 150 percent. Government advice to citizens to build fallout shelters in their backyards intensified public fear of devastating war.

If war occurred, many believed it would be over the persistent problem of Berlin. In mid-1961, Khrushchev ratcheted up the tension by demanding an end to Western occupation of West Berlin and a reunification of East and West Germany. Kennedy replied that the United States would stand by its commitment to West Berlin and West Germany. In August, the Soviets—at the urging of the East German regime—erected a concrete and barbed-wire barricade across the divided city to halt the exodus of East Germans into the more prosperous and politically free West Berlin. The Berlin Wall inspired protests throughout the noncommunist world, but Kennedy privately mused that "a wall is a hell of a lot better than a war." The ugly barrier shut off the flow of refugees, and the crisis passed.

26-1e Bay of Pigs Invasion

Yet Kennedy knew that Khrushchev would continue to press for advantage in various parts of the globe. The president was particularly rankled by the growing Soviet assistance to the Cuban government of Fidel Castro. Kennedy once acknowledged that most American allies thought the United States had a "fixation" with Cuba; whether true of the country as a whole, he and his inner circle certainly did. The Eisenhower administration had contested the Cuban revolution and bequeathed to the Kennedy administration a partially developed CIA plan to overthrow Fidel Castro: CIA-trained Cuban exiles would land and secure a beachhead; the Cuban people would rise up against Castro and welcome a new government brought in from the United States.

Kennedy approved the plan, and the attack took place on April 17, 1961, as twelve hundred exiles landed at the swampy Bay of Pigs in Cuba. But no discontented Cubans were there to greet them, only troops loyal to the Castro government. The invaders were quickly surrounded and captured. Kennedy had tried to keep the U.S. participation in the operation hidden—for this reason, he refused to provide air cover for the attackers—but the CIA's role swiftly became public. Anti-American sentiment shot up throughout Latin America. Castro, concluding that the United States would not take defeat well and might launch another invasion, looked even more toward the Soviet Union for a military and economic lifeline.

△ Cuban commandos march from their plane at National Airport in Washington, on May 22, 1961. The commandos were released by Fidel Castro as part of a plan to swap five hundred U.S. tractors or bulldozers for 1214 men captured in the failed Bay of Pigs operation.

Embarrassed by the Bay of Pigs fiasco, Kennedy ratcheted up the pressure on Castro. The CIA soon hatched a project called Operation Mongoose to disrupt the island's trade, support raids on Cuba from Miami, and plot to kill Castro. The agency's assassination schemes included providing Castro with cigars laced with explosives and deadly poison, and an attempt to harpoon him while he was snorkeling at a Caribbean resort. The United States also tightened its economic blockade and undertook military maneuvers in the Caribbean. The Joint Chiefs of Staff sketched plans to spark a rebellion in Cuba that would be followed by an invasion of U.S. troops. "If I had been in Moscow or Havana at that time," defense secretary Robert McNamara later remarked, "I would have believed the Americans were preparing for an invasion."

26-1f Cuban Missile Crisis

McNamara knew whereof he spoke, for both Castro and Khrushchev believed an invasion was coming. This was one reason for the Soviet leader's risky decision in 1962 to secretly deploy nuclear missiles in Cuba: he hoped the presence of such weapons on the island would deter any attack. But Khrushchev also had other motives. Installing atomic weaponry in Cuba would instantly improve the Soviet position in the nuclear balance of power, he believed, and might also force Kennedy to resolve the German problem once and for all. Khrushchev still wanted to oust the West from Berlin, and he also worried that Washington might provide West Germany with nuclear weapons. What better way to prevent such a move than to put Soviet missiles just ninety miles off the coast of Florida? With Castro's support, Khrushchev moved to install the weapons. The world soon faced brinkmanship at its most frightening.

In mid-October 1962, a U-2 plane flying over Cuba photographed the missile sites. The president immediately organized a special Executive Committee (ExComm) of advisers to find a way to force the missiles and their nuclear warheads out of Cuba. Options that the ExComm considered ranged from full-scale invasion to limited bombing to quiet diplomacy. Most participants favored military action, but Kennedy demurred; patiently, he steered the group toward a less confrontational position. McNamara then proposed the formula the president ultimately accepted: a naval quarantine of Cuba.

Kennedy addressed the nation on television on October 22 and demanded that the Soviets retreat. U.S. warships began crisscrossing the Caribbean, while B-52s with nuclear bombs took to the skies. Khrushchev replied that the missiles would be withdrawn if the United States pledged never to attack Cuba. And he added that American Jupiter missiles aimed at the Soviet Union must be removed from Turkey. Edgy advisers predicted war, and for several days the world teetered on the brink of disaster. Then, on October 28, came a compromise. The United States promised not to invade Cuba, secretly pledging to withdraw the Jupiters from Turkey in exchange for the withdrawal of Soviet offensive forces from Cuba. Fearing accidents or some provocative action by Castro that might start a "real fire," Khrushchev decided to settle without consulting the Cubans. The missiles were removed from the island.

Many observers then and later called it Kennedy's finest hour. Tapes of the ExComm meetings recorded during the crisis reveal a deeply engaged, calmly authoritative commander-in-chief, committed to removing the missiles peacefully if possible. Critics claim that Kennedy helped cause the crisis in the first place with his anti-Cuban projects; some contend that quiet diplomacy could have achieved the same result, without the extraordinary tension. Other skeptics assert that Kennedy rejected a diplomatic solution because he feared the Republicans would ride the missiles to victory in the upcoming midterm elections. Still, it cannot be denied that the president handled the crisis skillfully, exercising both restraint and flexibility. At this most tense moment of the Cold War, Kennedy had proven equal to the task.

The **Cuban missile crisis** was a watershed in the Soviet-American relationship. Both Kennedy and Khrushchev acted with greater prudence in its aftermath, taking determined steps toward improved bilateral relations. Much of the hostility drained out of the relationship. In August, the adversaries signed a treaty banning nuclear tests in the atmosphere, the oceans, and outer space. They also installed a coded wire-telegraph "hot line" staffed around the clock by translators and technicians, to allow near-instant communication between the capitals. Both sides refrained from further confrontation in Berlin.

Together, these steps reversed the trend of the previous years and began to build much-needed mutual trust. By the autumn of 1963, Cold War tensions in Europe were subsiding as both sides accepted the status quo of a divided continent and a fortified border. Still, the arms race continued and in some respects accelerated, and the superpower competition in the Third World showed little sign of cooling down.

26-2 Marching for Freedom

▶ **What methods did Americans who fought for civil rights adopt to challenge segregation and disfranchisement in the 1960s?**

▷ **What was the relationship between the federal government and the civil rights movement in the 1960s?**

▶ **How did national coverage of attacks on those struggling for equal rights affect the civil rights movement?**

From the beginning of his presidency, John Kennedy believed that the Cold War was the most important issue facing the American people. But in the early 1960s, young civil rights activists—building on a decades-long struggle—seized the national stage and demanded that the force of the federal government be mobilized behind them. They won victories in their struggle for racial justice, but their gains were paid for in blood.

26-2a Students and the Movement

The Woolworth's lunch counter sit-in begun by the four freshmen from North Carolina A&T marked a turning point in the African American struggle for civil rights. In 1960, six years after the *Brown* decision had declared "separate but equal" unconstitutional, only 10 percent of southern public schools had begun desegregation. Fewer than one in four adult black Americans in the South had access to the voting booth, and water fountains in public places were still labeled

"White Only" and "Colored Only." But one year after the young men had sat down at the all-white lunch counter in Greensboro, more than seventy thousand Americans—most of them college students—had participated in the sit-in movement, challenging segregation at lunch counters in the South and protesting at the northern branches of national chains that practiced segregation in their southern stores.

The young people who created the **Student Nonviolent Coordinating Committee (SNCC)** in the spring of 1960 to help coordinate the sit-in movement were, like Martin Luther King Jr., committed to nonviolence. In the years to come, such young people would risk their lives in the struggle for social justice.

26-2b Freedom Rides and Voter Registration

On May 4, 1961, thirteen members of the Congress of Racial Equality (CORE), a nonviolent civil rights organization formed during World War II, purchased bus tickets in Washington, D.C., for a 1,500-mile trip through the South to New Orleans. This racially integrated group, calling themselves Freedom Riders, meant to show that, despite Supreme Court rulings ordering the desegregation of interstate buses and bus stations, Jim Crow still ruled in the South. These men and women knew they were risking their lives, and some suffered injuries from which they never recovered. One bus was firebombed outside Anniston, Alabama. Riders were badly beaten in Birmingham. In Montgomery, after reinforcements replaced the injured, a mob of more than a thousand whites attacked riders on another bus with baseball bats and steel bars. Police were nowhere to be seen; Montgomery's police commissioner declared, "We have no intention of standing guard for a bunch of troublemakers coming into our city."

News of the violent attacks made headlines around the world. In the Soviet Union, commentators pointed out the "savage nature of American freedom and democracy." One southern business leader, in Tokyo to promote Birmingham as a site for international business development, saw Japanese interest evaporate when photographs of the Birmingham attacks appeared in Tokyo newspapers.

In America, the violence—reported by the national news media—forced Americans to confront the reality of racial discrimination and hatred in their nation. In the south, significant numbers of middle-class whites who rejected Klan violence had nonetheless participated in the "massive resistance" to integration following the *Brown* decision, and even racial moderates remained highly suspicious of interference by the "Yankee" federal government almost a century after the Civil War. The Freedom Rides

Cuban missile crisis Confrontation between the Soviet Union and the United States in 1962 regarding the Soviet deployment of nuclear missiles in Cuba. It put the world on the brink of nuclear disaster until the two nations reached a compromise.

Student Nonviolent Coordinating Committee (SNCC) Civil rights organization founded by young people that played a key role in grassroots organizing in the South in the early 1960s.

made some think differently. The *Atlanta Journal* editorialized: "[I]t is time for the decent people ... to muzzle the jackals." The national and international outcry pushed a reluctant President Kennedy to act. In a direct challenge to southern doctrines of states' rights, Kennedy sent federal marshals to Alabama to safeguard the Freedom Riders and their supporters. At the same time, bowing to white southern pressure, he allowed the Freedom Riders to be arrested in Mississippi.

While some activists pursued these "direct action" tactics, others worked to build black political power in the South. Beginning in 1961, thousands of SNCC volunteers, many of them high school and college students, risked their lives walking the dusty back roads of Mississippi and Georgia, encouraging African Americans to register to vote. Some SNCC volunteers were white, and some were from the North, but many were black southerners, and many were from low-income families. These volunteers understood from experience how racism, powerlessness, and poverty intersected in the lives of African Americans.

26-2c Kennedy and Civil Rights

President Kennedy was generally sympathetic—though not terribly committed—to the civil rights movement, and he realized that racial oppression hurt the United States in the Cold War struggle for international opinion. However, like Franklin D. Roosevelt, he also understood that if he alienated conservative southern Democrats in Congress, his legislative programs would founder. Thus, he appointed five die-hard segregationists to the federal bench in the Deep South and delayed issuing an executive order forbidding segregation in federally subsidized housing (a pledge made in the 1960 campaign) until late 1962. Furthermore, he allowed FBI director J. Edgar Hoover to harass Martin Luther King and other civil rights leaders, using wiretaps and surveillance to gather personal information and circulating rumors of communist connections and of personal improprieties in efforts to discredit their leadership.

But grassroots civil rights activism—and the violence of white mobs—relentlessly forced Kennedy's hand. In September 1962, the president ordered 500 U.S. marshals to protect James Meredith, the first African American student to attempt to enroll at the University of Mississippi. In response, thousands of whites attacked the marshals with guns, gasoline bombs, bricks, and pipes. The mob killed two men and seriously wounded 160 federal marshals. The marshals did not back down, nor did James Meredith. He broke the color line at "Ole Miss."

26-2d Birmingham and the Children's Crusade

In 1961, the Freedom Riders had captured the attention of the nation and the larger Cold War world, and had forced the hand of the president. Martin Luther King Jr., having risen through the Montgomery bus boycott to leadership in the movement, drew a lesson from the Freedom Rides. He and his allies, while still committed to principles of nonviolence, concluded that the only way to advance the

struggle for civil rights was to provoke a crisis that would create pressure for further change. King and his Southern Christian Leadership Conference (SCLC) began to plan a 1963 campaign in one of the most violently racist cities in America: Birmingham, Alabama. Fully aware that their nonviolent protests would draw a violent response, they called their plan "Project C"—for "confrontation." King wanted all Americans to see the racist hate and violence that marred their nation.

Through most of April 1963, nonviolent protests in Birmingham led to hundreds of arrests. Then, on May 2, in a highly controversial action, King and the parents of Birmingham raised the stakes. They put children, some as young as six, on the front lines of protest. As about a thousand black children marched for civil rights, police commissioner Eugene "Bull" Connor ordered his police to train monitor water guns—powerful enough to strip bark from a tree at 100 feet—on them. The water guns mowed the children down. Then police loosed attack dogs. As footage played on the evening news, the nation watched with horror. President Kennedy, once again, was pushed into action. He demanded that Birmingham's white business and political elite negotiate a settlement. Under pressure, they agreed. The Birmingham movement had won a concrete victory. Even more, activists had pushed civil rights to the fore of President Kennedy's political agenda.

26-2e "Segregation Forever!"

The Kennedy administration also confronted the defiant governor of Alabama, George C. Wallace. On June 11, Wallace fulfilled a promise to "bar the schoolhouse door" himself to prevent the desegregation of the University of Alabama. Hearing echoes of Wallace's January 1963 inaugural pledge "Segregation now, segregation tomorrow, segregation forever!" and facing a nation rocked by hundreds of civil rights protests, many of them met with white mob violence, Kennedy committed the power of the federal government to guarantee racial justice—even over the opposition of individual states. The next evening, June 12, in a televised address, Kennedy told the American people, "Now the time has come for this nation to fulfill its promise." A few hours later, thirty-seven-year-old civil rights leader Medgar Evers was murdered—in front of his children—in his driveway in Jackson, Mississippi. The next week, the president asked Congress to pass a comprehensive civil rights bill that would end legal discrimination on the basis of race in the United States.

26-2f March on Washington

On August 28, 1963, a quarter-million Americans gathered in the steamy heat on the Washington Mall. They came from all over America to show Congress their support for Kennedy's civil rights bill; many also wanted federal action to guarantee work opportunities. Behind the scenes, organizers from major civil rights groups—SCLC, CORE, SNCC, the NAACP, the Urban League, and A. Philip Randolph's Brotherhood of Sleeping Car Porters—grappled with growing tensions within the movement. SNCC activists saw Kennedy's

"Project C" and National Opinion

This photograph of a police dog attacking a seventeen-year-old demonstrator during a civil rights march in Birmingham, Alabama, appeared on the front page of the *New York Times* on May 4, 1963, just above a second photograph of a fireman spraying a group that included three teenage girls with a high-pressure fire hose.

The following day, President Kennedy discussed this photo in a meeting in the White House.

CRITICAL THINKING

◻ Some historians argue that photographs not only document history, they make it. Is that statement true in this case?

◻ How does this photograph fit into Martin Luther King's plans for "Project C" (see "Birmingham and the Children's Crusade," Section 26-2d)?

◻ What difference might it make that the *New York Times* editors chose to run this photograph rather than one of the many others taken that day?

△ Mass media coverage helped galvanize public opinion in support of civil rights protesters.

AP Images/Bill Hudson

proposed legislation as too little, too late; they wanted radical action. King and other older leaders counseled the virtues of moderation. The movement was beginning to splinter.

Those divisions were not completely hidden. SNCC's John Lewis proclaimed his "misgiving," asking, "Where is the political party that will make it unnecessary to march on Washington?" What most Americans saw, however, was a celebration of unity. Black and white celebrities joined hands; folksingers sang songs of freedom. Television networks cut away from afternoon soap operas as Martin Luther King Jr., in southern preacher cadences, prophesied a day when "all God's children, black men and white men, Jews and Gentiles, Protestants and Catholics, will be able to join hands and sing in the words of the old Negro spiritual, Free at last!

Free at last! Thank God Almighty, we are free at last!" The 1963 March on Washington for Jobs and Freedom was a moment of triumph, powerfully demonstrating to the nation the determination of its African American citizens to secure equality and justice. But the struggle was far from over. Just days later, white supremacists bombed the Sixteenth Street Baptist Church in Birmingham, killing four black girls.

26-2g Freedom Summer

In the face of violence, the struggle for racial justice continued. During the summer of 1964, more than one thousand white students joined the voter mobilization project in Mississippi. These workers formed Freedom Schools, teaching literacy and constitutional rights, and helped organize the Mississippi

Freedom Democratic Party as an alternative to Mississippi's white-only Democratic Party. Key SNCC organizers also believed that large numbers of white volunteers would focus national attention on Mississippi repression and violence. Not all went smoothly: local black activists were sometimes frustrated when well-educated white volunteers stepped into decision-making roles. Far worse, project workers were arrested, shot at, bombed, and beaten. On June 21, local black activist James Cheney and two white volunteers, Michael Schwerner and Andrew Goodman, were murdered by a Klan mob. Four days later, before their bodies had been found, Walter Cronkite told the nightly news audience that all of America was watching Mississippi. CBS played footage of black and white workers holding hands, singing "We Shall Overcome." That summer, black and white activists risked their lives together, challenging the racial caste system of the Deep South.

26-3 Liberalism and the Great Society

▶ How did Lyndon B. Johnson seek to use the federal government to improve the quality of Americans' lives?

▶ How did different groups of Americans, including political parties, respond to the federal government's active social agenda in the 1960s?

▶ What were the features of the federal government's "War on Poverty"?

By 1963, with civil rights at the top of his domestic agenda, Kennedy seemed to be taking a new path. Campaigning in 1960, he had promised to lead Americans into a "New Frontier," a society in which the federal government would work to eradicate poverty, restore the nation's cities, guarantee health care to the elderly, and provide decent schools for all America's children. But few of Kennedy's domestic initiatives were passed into law, in part because Kennedy did not use his political capital to support them. Lacking a popular mandate in the 1960 election, fearful of alienating southern Democrats in Congress, and without a strong vision of domestic reform, Kennedy let his administration's social policy agenda languish.

Instead, Kennedy focused on less controversial attempts to fine-tune the American economy, believing that continued economic growth and prosperity would solve America's social problems. Kennedy's vision was perhaps best realized in America's space program. As the Soviets drew ahead in the Cold War space race, Kennedy vowed in 1961 to put a man on the moon before decade's end. With billions in new funding, the National Aeronautics and Space Administration (NASA) began the Apollo program. And in February 1962, astronaut John Glenn orbited the earth in the space capsule *Friendship* 7.

Lyndon B. Johnson Thirty-sixth president of the United States (1963–1969); champion of civil rights legislation and the war on poverty, who presided over America's entry into large-scale war in Vietnam.

26-3a Kennedy Assassination

The nation would not learn what sort of president John Kennedy might have become. On November 22, 1963, Kennedy visited Texas, the home state of his vice president, **Lyndon B. Johnson**. In Dallas, riding with his wife, Jackie, in an open-top limousine, Kennedy was cheered by thousands of people lining the motorcade's route. Suddenly, shots rang out. The president crumpled, shot in the head. Tears ran down the cheeks of CBS anchorman Walter Cronkite as he told the nation their president was dead. The word spread quickly, in whispered messages to classroom teachers, by somber announcements in factories and offices, through the stunned faces of people on the street.

That same day, police captured a suspect: Lee Harvey Oswald, a former U.S. Marine (dishonorably discharged) who had once attempted to gain Soviet citizenship. Just two days later, in full view of millions of TV viewers, Oswald himself was shot dead by a shady nightclub owner named Jack Ruby. Americans, already in shock, didn't know what to think. What was Ruby's motive? Was he silencing Oswald to prevent him from implicating others? (The seven-member Warren Commission, appointed by Lyndon Johnson and headed by U.S. Supreme Court Chief Justice Earl Warren, concluded the following year that Oswald had acted alone.) For four days, the tragedy played uninterrupted on American television. Millions of Americans watched their president's funeral: the brave young widow behind a black veil; a riderless horse; three-year-old "John-John" saluting his father's casket. In one awful moment in Dallas, the reality of the Kennedy presidency had been transformed into myth, the man into martyr. People would remember Kennedy less for any specific accomplishment than for his youthful enthusiasm, his inspirational rhetoric, and the romance he brought to American political life. In a peculiar way, he accomplished more in death than in life. In the post-assassination atmosphere of grief and remorse, Lyndon Johnson, sworn in as president aboard *Air Force One*, invoked Kennedy's memory to push through the most ambitious program of legislation since the New Deal.

26-3b Johnson and the Great Society

The new president was a big and passionate man, different from his predecessor in almost every respect. While Kennedy had been raised to wealth and privilege, Johnson had grown up in modest circumstances in the Texas hill country. He was as earthy as Kennedy was elegant, prone to colorful curses and willing to use his physical size to his advantage. Advisers and aides reported that he expected them to follow him into the bathroom and conduct business while he showered or used the toilet. But Johnson had been in national politics most of his adult life. He filled an empty congressional seat from Texas in 1937, and as Senate majority leader from 1954 through 1960, he had learned how to manipulate people and wield power to achieve his ends. Now, as president, he used these political skills in an attempt to unite and reassure the nation. "Let us here highly resolve," he told a joint session of

△ Poverty in America was not only an urban problem, and President Johnson visited poverty-stricken areas throughout the nation during the summer of 1964. Here he talks with the Marlow family of Rocky Mount, North Carolina, on the steps of their farmhouse.

Congress five days after the assassination, "that John Fitzgerald Kennedy did not live—or die—in vain."

Johnson, a liberal in the style of Franklin D. Roosevelt, believed that the federal government must work actively to improve the lives of Americans. In a 1964 commencement address at the University of Michigan, he described his vision of a nation built on "abundance and liberty for all . . . demand[ing] an end to poverty and racial injustice . . . where every child can find knowledge to enrich his mind and to enlarge his talents . . . where every man can renew contact with nature . . . where men are more concerned with the quality of their goals than the quantity of their goods." Johnson called this vision "the Great Society."

26-3c Civil Rights Act

Johnson made civil rights his top legislative priority, and in July he signed into law the **Civil Rights Act of 1964**. This legislation grew from the civil rights protests of the early 1960s: In the wake of violent attacks on civil rights protesters in Birmingham, the Kennedy administration had crafted a bill outlawing *legal* discrimination on the basis of race, color, religion, or national origin in employment, federal programs, voting, and public accommodation. This legislation was hard won, passing only after Kennedy's assassination. In the Senate a "southern bloc" filibustered for 57 days, preventing not only a vote on the bill but any other congressional business. In

the end, growing public support for civil rights, pressure from the Johnson administration, savvy legislative maneuvering, compromise, and a few acts of political heroism brought the bill to a vote.

The Civil Rights Act of 1964 gave the civil rights movement a major legislative victory, in part because it provided means to enforce its provisions: federal authority to withhold funds from public agencies or federal contractors that discriminated, and an Equal Employment Opportunity Commission (EEOC) to investigate claims of job discrimination.

The Civil Rights Act did not only prohibit racial discrimination; it also made it illegal to discriminate on the basis of sex. The original bill had not included sex discrimination. That provision was introduced by a southern congressman who—though he had long supported the pro-women's rights National Woman's Party—meant to undermine the bill. His proposal was met with laughter and jeers by members of the House of Representatives who found the notion of women's legal equality ridiculous. Representative Martha Griffiths, however, saw an opening. In the end, a strange coalition of eleven female representatives (of twelve total), Republicans,

Civil Rights Act of 1964 The most significant civil rights law in modern U.S. history; outlawed legal discrimination based on race color, religion, national origin, and sex, and created means to enforce its provisions.

and anti–civil rights Democrats (who later voted against the bill as a whole) backed the amendment that listed sex as a protected category. (Most liberal Democrats, focused on race, opposed the addition.) In the first years after the bill was passed the EEOC did not take sex discrimination seriously, despite a flood of complaints from women. As one EEOC staffer argued in 1965, complaints about sex discrimination "undermine the efforts on behalf of minority groups" because they divert "attention and resources from the more serious allegations by members of racial, religious, and ethnic communities." Frustrated by such responses, a group of about three hundred prominent women and men came together in 1966 to form the **National Organization for Women (NOW),** an organization created to pressure the EEOC to enforce the law and to work for women's equality in American society. NOW would play a key role in the developing women's movement, which expanded dramatically during the late 1960s and the 1970s (see "The Women's Movement," Section 27-1d).

Many Americans did not believe it was the federal government's job to fight poverty or to end racial discrimination. Racism bolstered opposition to federal action, as it remained powerful, and not only in the South. Throughout the nation, millions of conservative Americans believed that the federal government had been overstepping its constitutional boundaries since the New Deal. They wanted to reinforce local control and states' rights in the face of growing federal power. In the 1964 election, this conservative vision was championed by the Republican candidate, Arizona senator Barry Goldwater.

26-3d Election of 1964

Goldwater had not only voted against the 1964 Civil Rights Act; he also opposed the national Social Security system. Like many conservatives, he believed that individual *liberty,* not equality, was the most important American value. Goldwater's calls for "law and order" drew cheers from voters. He argued that the United States needed a more powerful national military to fight communism; in campaign speeches, he suggested that the United States might use tactical nuclear weapons against its enemies. "Extremism in the defense of liberty is no vice," he told delegates at the 1964 Republican National Convention.

Goldwater's campaign slogan, "In your heart you know he's right," was turned against him by Johnson's supporters: "In your heart you know he's right . . . far right," one punned. Another version warned of Goldwater's willingness to use nuclear weapons: "In your heart you know he might." Johnson campaigned on his record, with an unemployment rate under 4 percent and economic growth at better than 6 percent. But he knew that his support of civil rights had broken apart the New Deal coalition. Shortly after signing the Civil Rights Act of 1964, he told an aide, "I think we just delivered the south to the Republican Party for my lifetime and yours."

The tension between Johnson's support of civil rights and his need for southern Democratic support came to a head at the 1964 Democratic National Convention. Two delegations had arrived from Mississippi, a state in which discriminatory literacy tests and violence disfranchised its black citizens: an official, all-white delegation and a multiracial delegation from the Mississippi Freedom Democratic Party (MFDP). In response, white representatives from southern states threatened to walk out if the MFDP delegates were seated. MFDP delegate Fannie Lou Hamer offered powerful testimony to the convention's credentials committee, concluding, "[If] the Freedom Party is not seated now, I question America." Johnson tried to engineer a compromise, but the MFDP had no interest in political deals. "We didn't come all this way for no two seats," Hamer said, and the delegation walked out.

Johnson lost the MFDP, and he also lost the Deep South—the first Democrat since the Civil War to do so. Yet he won the election by a landslide, and American voters also gave him the most liberal Congress in American history. With the mandate provided by a record 61.1 percent of the popular vote, Johnson launched his Great Society. Congress responded to Johnson's election with the most sweeping reform legislation since 1935.

Civil rights remained a critical issue. In late 1964, Martin Luther King Jr. and other leaders turned to Selma, Alabama—a town with a history of vicious response to civil rights protest—seeking another public confrontation that would mobilize national support and federal action to support voting rights. That confrontation came on March 6, 1965, when state troopers turned electric cattle prods, chains, and tear gas against peaceful marchers as they crossed the Edmund Pettus Bridge on the way to Montgomery. On March 15, the president addressed Congress and the nation, offering full support for a second monumental civil rights bill, the **Voting Rights Act of 1965.** This act outlawed practices that had prevented most black citizens in the Deep South from voting and provided for federal oversight of elections in districts where there was evidence of past discrimination (see Map 26.1). Within two years, African American voter registration in Mississippi jumped from 7 percent to almost 60 percent. Black elected officials became increasingly common in southern states over the following decade.

26-3e Improving American Life

Seeking to improve the quality of American life, the Johnson administration established new student loan and grant programs to help low- and moderate-income Americans

National Organization for Women (NOW) Founded in 1966, a civil rights group for women that lobbied for equal opportunity, filed lawsuits against gender discrimination, and mobilized public opinion against sexism.

Voting Rights Act of 1965 Law that outlawed practices that prevented African Americans in the South from voting, and provided for federal oversight of elections in districts where African Americans had been disfranchised.

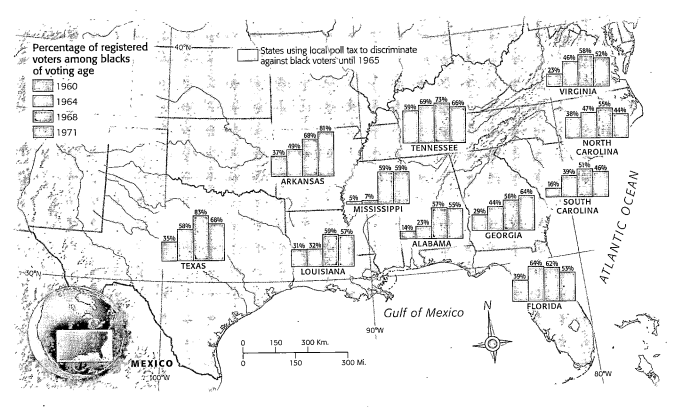

Map 26.1 African American Voting Rights, 1960–1971

After passage of the 1965 Voting Rights Act, African American registration skyrocketed in Mississippi and Alabama, and rose substantially in other southern states. *Source: From* Voter Mobilization and the Politics of Race: The South and Universal Suffrage, 1952–1984 *by Harold W. Stanley. Copyright © 1987 by Praeger Publishers. Reproduced with permission of ABC-CLIO, LLC.*

attend college, and created the National Endowment for the Arts and the National Endowment for the Humanities. The **Immigration Act of 1965** ended the racially-based quotas that had shaped American immigration policy for decades. And Johnson supported important consumer protection legislation, including the 1966 National Traffic and Motor Vehicle Safety Act, which was inspired by Ralph Nader's exposé of the automobile industry, *Unsafe at Any Speed* (1965).

Environmentalists found an ally in the Johnson administration. First Lady Claudia Alta Taylor Johnson (known to all as "Lady Bird") successfully campaigned for laws restricting the billboards and junkyards that had sprung up along the nation's new interstate highway system. Johnson signed "preservation" legislation to protect wilderness areas and supported laws to control environmental pollution.

26-3f War on Poverty

At the heart of Johnson's Great Society was the **War on Poverty**. Johnson and other liberals believed that, in a time of great economic affluence, the nation should devote its resources to programs that could end "poverty, ignorance and hunger as intractable, permanent features of American

society." Beginning in 1964, the Johnson administration passed more than a score of major laws meant to do so (see Table 26.1).

Johnson's goal, in his words, was "to offer the forgotten fifth of our people opportunity, not doles." Thus, many new laws focused on increasing opportunity. Billions of federal dollars went to local governments and school districts to pay for programs meant to improve opportunities for the poor, from preschoolers (Head Start) to high schoolers (Upward Bound) to young adults (Job Corps). The Model Cities program targeted "blighted" urban neighborhoods with federal funds for employment, housing, education, and health. Community Action Programs, working from the assumption that community residents best understood their own needs, channeled federal funds for antipoverty programs directly to neighborhood groups.

Immigration Act of 1965 Law that abolished the national origins quotas of the 1920s, transforming U.S. immigration policy.

War on Poverty Campaign launched by Johnson administration in 1964, based on a set of major laws meant to offer greater opportunity to Americans living in poverty.

Table 26.1 Great Society Achievements, 1964–1966

	1964	1965	1966
Civil Rights	Civil Rights Act Equal Employment Opportunity Commission Twenty-fourth Amendment	Voting Rights Act	
War on Poverty	Economic Opportunity Act Office of Economic Opportunity Job Corps Legal Services for the Poor VISTA		Model Cities
Education		Elementary and Secondary Education Act Head Start Upward Bound	
Environment		Water Quality Act Air Quality Act	Clean Water Restoration Act
New Government Agencies		Department of Housing and Urban Development National Endowments for the Arts and Humanities	Department of Transportation
Other		Medicare and Medicaid Immigration and Nationality Act	

Note: The Great Society of the mid-1960s saw the biggest burst of reform legislation since the New Deal of the 1930s.

◁ Sioux children pledge allegiance to the U.S. flag in a reservation-based Head Start program, Red Shirt, South Dakota, 1965. One of several programs established by the 1964 Economic Opportunity Act, Head Start prepared pre-schoolers from low-income families for grade school.

AP Photo/Sam Myers

The Johnson administration also tried to ensure basic economic safeguards, expanding the existing Food Stamp program and earmarking billions of dollars to construct public housing and subsidize rents. Aid to Families with Dependent Children (AFDC), the basic welfare program created during the New Deal, expanded both benefits and eligibility. And comprehensive health care—a goal of liberals since the 1940s—made progress as, for the first time, federal programs guaranteed health care for those aged sixty-five and older (**Medicare**) and the poor (**Medicaid**).

The War on Poverty was controversial from its beginnings. Leftists believed the government was doing too little to change fundamental structural inequality. Conservatives argued that Great Society programs created dependency among America's poor. Policy analysts noted that some programs were ill conceived and badly implemented. Even supporters acknowledged that programs were vastly underfunded and marred by political compromises. Responding to criticisms, Joseph Califano, one of the "generals" in the War on Poverty, claimed, "Whatever historians of the Great Society say twenty years later, they must admit we tried, and I believe they will conclude that America is a better place because we did."

Decades later, most historians judge the War on Poverty a mixed success. War on Poverty programs offered better housing, health care, and nutrition to the nation's poor. By 1975, for instance, the number of eligible Americans receiving food stamps had increased from 600,000 (in 1965) to 17 million. Poverty among the elderly fell from about 40 percent in 1960 to 16 percent in 1974, due largely to increased Social Security benefits and to Medicare. As federal spending for Social Security, health care, welfare, and education more than doubled between 1965 and 1970, the War on Poverty undoubtedly improved the quality of life for many low-income Americans (see Figure 26.1).

But War on Poverty programs less successfully addressed the root causes of poverty. Neither the Job Corps nor Community Action Programs showed significant results. Economic growth, not Johnson administration policies, was primarily responsible for the dramatic decrease in overall poverty rates—from 22.4 percent of Americans in 1959 to 11 percent in 1973. And one measure of poverty remained unchanged: 11 million Americans in female-headed households remained poor at the end of the decade—the same number as in 1963.

Political compromises that shaped Great Society programs also created long-term problems. For example, Congress accommodated the interests of doctors and hospitals in its Medicare legislation by allowing federal reimbursements of hospitals' "reasonable costs" and doctors' "reasonable charges" in treating elderly patients. With no incentives for doctors or hospitals to hold prices down, the cost of health care rose dramatically. National health care expenditures as a percentage of the gross national product rose by almost 44 percent from 1960 to 1971.

Johnson's Great Society was not an unqualified success, but it was a moment in which many Americans believed they could solve the problems of poverty and disease and discrimination—and that it was necessary to try.

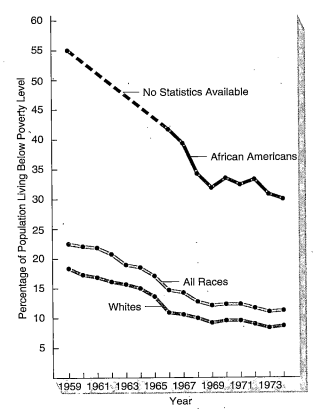

Figure 26.1 Poverty in America for Whites, African Americans, and All Races, 1959–1974

Because of rising levels of economic prosperity, combined with the impact of Great Society programs, the percentage of Americans living in poverty in 1974 was half as high as in 1959. African Americans still were far more likely than white Americans to be poor. In 1959, more than half of all blacks (55.1 percent) were poor; in 1974, the figure remained high (30.3 percent). The government did not record data on African American poverty for the years 1960 through 1965.

26-4 Johnson and Vietnam

▷ **Why did the Johnson administration escalate American involvement in Vietnam?**

▷ **How did the North Vietnamese counter increased U.S. military involvement?**

▷ **What was the nature of American military involvement and the soldier's experience in the war?**

▷ **What divisions emerged within the government over America's presence in Vietnam?**

Johnson's domestic ambitions were threatened from an early point by turmoil overseas. In foreign policy,

Medicare Program providing government health insurance for Americans aged sixty-five and older; created by Congress under President Johnson's leadership in 1965.

Medicaid Program providing health care for the poor; created by Congress under President Johnson's leadership in 1965.

he held firmly to ideas about U.S. superiority and the menace of communism. He saw the world in simple, bipolar terms—them against us—and he saw a lot of "them." But, mostly, he preferred not to see the world beyond America's shores at all. International affairs had never much interested him, and he had little appreciation for foreign cultures. Once, on a visit to Thailand while vice president, he flew into a rage when an aide gently advised him that the Thai people recoil from physical contact with strangers. Dammit, Johnson exploded, he shook hands with people everywhere, and they loved it. At the Taj Mahal in India, Johnson tested the monument's echo with a Texas cowboy yell. And on a trip to Senegal, he ordered that an American bed, a special showerhead, and cases of Cutty Sark be sent along with him. "Foreigners," Johnson quipped early in his administration, only half-jokingly, "are not like the folks I am used to."

26-4a Kennedy's Legacy in Vietnam

Yet Johnson knew from the start that foreign policy, especially regarding Vietnam, would demand his attention. Since the late 1950s, hostilities in Vietnam had increased, as Ho Chi Minh's North assisted and, to a degree, directed the Vietcong guerrillas in the South to advance the reunification of the country under a communist government. President Kennedy had stepped up aid dollars to the Diem regime in Saigon, increased the airdropping of raiding teams into North Vietnam, and launched crop destruction by herbicides to starve the Vietcong and expose their hiding places. Kennedy also strengthened the U.S. military presence in South Vietnam, to the point that by 1963 more than sixteen thousand military advisers were in the country, some authorized to take part in combat alongside the U.S.-equipped Army of the Republic of Vietnam (ARVN).

Meanwhile, opposition to Diem's repressive regime increased, and not just by communists. Peasants objected to programs that removed them from their villages for their own safety, and Buddhist monks, protesting the Roman Catholic Diem's religious persecution, poured gasoline over their robes and ignited themselves in the streets of Saigon. Although Diem was personally honest, he countenanced corruption in his government and concentrated power in the hands of family and friends. He jailed critics to silence them. Eventually, U.S. officials, with Kennedy's approval, encouraged ambitious South Vietnamese generals to remove Diem. On November 1, 1963, the generals struck, murdering Diem. Just a few weeks later, Kennedy himself was assassinated.

The timing of Kennedy's murder ensured that Vietnam would be the most controversial aspect of his legacy. Just what would have happened in Southeast Asia had Kennedy returned from Texas alive can never be known, of course, and the speculation is made more difficult by his contradictory record on the conflict. He expanded U.S. involvement and approved a coup against Diem, but despite the urgings of top advisers he refused to commit American ground forces

to the struggle. Over time, he became increasingly skeptical about South Vietnam's prospects and hinted that he would end the American commitment after winning reelection in 1964. Some authors have gone further and argued that he was ending U.S. involvement even at the time of his death, but the evidence for this claim is thin. More likely, Kennedy arrived in Dallas that fateful day still uncertain about how to solve the Vietnam problem, postponing the truly difficult choices until later.

26-4b Tonkin Gulf Incident and Resolution

Lyndon Johnson, too, was unsure on Vietnam, wanting to do nothing there that could complicate his aim of winning the 1964 election. Yet Johnson also sought victory in the struggle. As a result, throughout 1964 the administration secretly laid plans to expand the war to North Vietnam and never seriously considered negotiating a settlement.

In early August 1964, an incident in the Gulf of Tonkin, off the coast of North Vietnam, drew Johnson's involvement (see Map 26.2). Twice in three days, U.S. destroyers reported coming under attack from North Vietnamese patrol boats. Despite a lack of evidence that the second attack occurred, Johnson ordered retaliatory air strikes against selected North Vietnamese patrol boat bases and an oil depot. He also directed aides to rework a long-existing congressional resolution on the use of force. By a vote of 416 to 0 in the House and 88 to 2 in the Senate, Congress quickly passed the Gulf of Tonkin Resolution, which gave the president the authority to "take all necessary measures to repel any armed attack against the forces of the United States and to prevent further aggression." In so doing, Congress essentially surrendered its warmaking powers to the executive branch. The resolution, Secretary of Defense McNamara later noted, served "to open the floodgates."

26-4c Decision for Escalation

President Johnson, delighted with the broad authority the resolution gave him, used a different metaphor. "Like grandma's nightshirt," he quipped, "it covered everything." He also appreciated what the Gulf of Tonkin affair did for his political standing—his public approval ratings went up dramatically, and his show of force effectively removed Vietnam as a campaign issue for GOP presidential nominee Barry Goldwater. On the ground in South Vietnam, however, the outlook remained grim in the final weeks of 1964, as the Vietcong continued to make gains. U.S. officials responded by laying secret plans for an escalation of American involvement.

In February 1965, in response to Vietcong attacks on American installations in South Vietnam that killed thirty-two Americans, Johnson ordered Operation Rolling Thunder, a bombing program planned the previous fall, which continued, more or less uninterrupted, until October 1968. Then, on March 8, the first U.S. combat battalions came ashore near Danang. The North Vietnamese, however,

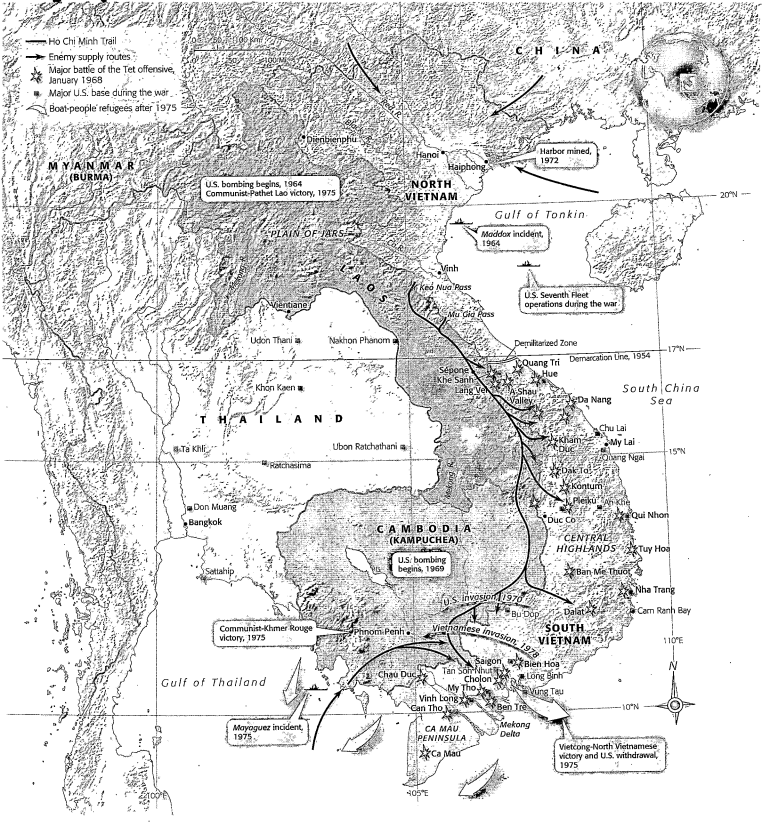

Legend:
- Ho Chi Minh Trail
- Enemy supply routes
- Major battle of the Tet offensive, January 1968
- Major U.S. base during the war
- Boat-people refugees after 1975

CHINA

MYANMAR (BURMA)

Dienbienphu

Hanoi
Haiphong

Harbor mined, 1972

NORTH VIETNAM

U.S. bombing begins, 1964
Communist-Pathet Lao victory, 1975

Gulf of Tonkin

20°N

PLAIN OF JARS

Mekong R.

Vinh

Maddox incident, 1964

Vientiane

Keo Nua Pass

U.S. Seventh Fleet operations during the war

Mu Gia Pass

Udon Thani
Nakhon Phanom

Demilitarized Zone

17°N

Quang Tri
Demarcation Line, 1954

Sépone
Khe Sanh
Lang Ve
Hue

Khon Kaen

A Shau Valley
Da Nang

South China Sea

THAILAND

Ta Khli

Ubon Ratchathani

Chu Lai

Kham Duc
My Lai
Quang Ngai

Ratchasima

15°N

Dak To
Kontum

Don Muang
Bangkok

CAMBODIA (KAMPUCHEA)

Pleiku
An Khe
Qui Nhon

Duc Co

U.S. bombing begins, 1969

CENTRAL HIGHLANDS
Tuy Hoa

Sattahip

Ban Me Thuot

Nha Trang

U.S. invasion, 1970

Bu Dop
Dalat
Cam Ranh Bay

Communist-Khmer Rouge victory, 1975

Phnom Penh

Vietnamese invasion, 1978

SOUTH VIETNAM

110°E

Saigon
Bien Hoa

Gulf of Thailand

Chau Duc

Tan Son Nhut
Cholon
Long Binh

N

My Tho
Vung Tau

Vinh Long
Can Tho

Ben Tre

10°N

Mayaguez incident, 1975

CA MAU PENINSULA

Mekong Delta

Ca Mau

Vietcong-North Vietnamese victory and U.S. withdrawal, 1975

100°E

105°E

Map 26.2 Southeast Asia and the Vietnam War

To prevent communists from coming to power in Vietnam, Cambodia, and Laos in the 1960s, the United States intervened massively in Southeast Asia. The interventions failed, and the remaining American troops made a hasty exit from Vietnam in 1975, when the victorious Vietcong and North Vietnamese took Saigon and renamed it Ho Chi Minh City.

would not give up. They hid in shelters and rebuilt roads and bridges with a perseverance that frustrated and awed American decision makers. They also increased infiltration into the South. In Saigon, meanwhile, coups and countercoups by self-serving military leaders undermined U.S. efforts to turn the war effort around. "I don't think we ought to take this government seriously," Ambassador Henry Cabot Lodge told a White House meeting. "There is simply no one who can do anything."

In July 1965, Johnson convened a series of high-level discussions about U.S. policy in the war. Although these deliberations had about them the character of a charade—Johnson wanted history to record that he agonized over a choice he had in fact already made—they did confirm that the American commitment would be more or less open-ended. On July 28, the president publicly announced a significant troop increase, disclosing that others would follow. By the end of 1965, more than 180,000 U.S. ground troops were in South Vietnam. In 1966, the figure climbed to 385,000. In 1967 alone, U.S. warplanes flew 108,000 sorties and dropped 226,000 tons of bombs on North Vietnam. In 1968, U.S. troop strength reached 536,100 (see Figure 26.2). Each American escalation

brought not victory, but a new North Vietnamese escalation. The Soviet Union and China responded to the stepped-up U.S. involvement by increasing their material assistance to the Hanoi government.

26-4d Opposition to Americanization

The initiation of Rolling Thunder and the U.S. troop commitment "Americanized" the war. What could have been seen as a civil war between North and South, or a war of national reunification, was now clearly an American war against the communist Hanoi government. This "Americanization" of the war in Vietnam came despite deep misgivings on the part of influential and informed voices at home and abroad. In the key months of decision, Democratic leaders in the Senate, major newspapers such as the *New York Times* and the *Wall Street Journal*, and prominent columnists like Walter Lippmann warned against deepening involvement. So did some within the administration, including Vice President Hubert H. Humphrey and Undersecretary of State George W. Ball. Abroad, virtually all of America's allies—including France, Britain, Canada, and Japan—cautioned against escalation and urged a political settlement, on the grounds that no military solution favorable to the United States was possible. Still more remarkable, top U.S. officials themselves shared this pessimism. Most of them knew that the odds of success were not great. They certainly hoped that the new measures would cause Hanoi to end the insurgency in the South, but it cannot be said they were confident.

Why, then, did America's leaders choose war? At stake was "credibility." They feared that, if the United States failed to prevail in Vietnam, friends and foes around the world would find American power less credible. The Soviets and Chinese would be emboldened to challenge U.S. interests elsewhere in the world, and allied governments might conclude that they could not depend on Washington. For at least some key players, too, including the president himself, domestic political credibility and personal credibility were also on the line. Johnson worried that failure in Vietnam would harm his domestic agenda; even more, he feared the personal humiliation that he imagined would inevitably accompany a defeat—and for him, a negotiated withdrawal constituted defeat. As for the stated objective of helping a South Vietnamese ally repulse external aggression, that, too, figured into the equation, but not as much as it would have had the Saigon government—racked with infighting among senior leaders and possessing little popular support—done more to assist in its own defense.

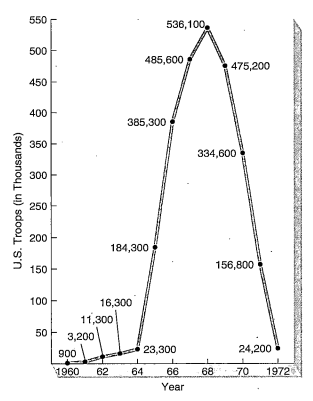

Figure 26.2 U.S. Troops in Vietnam, 1960–1972

These numbers show the Americanization of the Vietnam War under President Johnson, who ordered vast increases in troop levels. President Nixon gradually reversed the escalation, so that by the time of the cease-fire in early 1973, fewer than 25,000 American troops remained in Vietnam. Data are for December 31 of each year. *Source: U.S. Department of Defense*

26-4e American Soldiers in Vietnam

Even as Johnson Americanized the Vietnam War, he sought to keep the publicity surrounding the action as low as possible. Thus, he rejected the Joint Chiefs' view that U.S. reserve forces should be mobilized and a national emergency declared. This decision not to call up reserve units had a momentous impact on the makeup of the American fighting force sent to Vietnam. It forced the military establishment to rely more heavily on the draft, which in turn meant that Vietnam became a young man's war—the average age of soldiers was twenty-two, as compared with twenty-six in World War II. It also became a war of the poor and the working class. Through the years of heavy escalation (1965–1968), college students could get deferments, as could teachers and engineers. (In 1969, the draft was changed so that some students were called up through a lottery system.) The poorest and least-educated young men were less likely to be able to avoid the draft and more likely to volunteer. The armed services recruited hard in poor communities, many of them heavily African American and Latino, advertising the military as an avenue of training and advancement; very often, the pitch worked. Once in uniform, those with fewer skills were far more likely to see combat, and hence to die.

Infantrymen on maneuvers in South Vietnam carried heavy rucksacks into thick jungle growth, where every step was precarious. Booby traps and land mines were a constant threat. Insects swarmed, and leeches sucked at weary bodies. Boots and human skin rotted from the rains, which alternated with withering suns. "It was as if the sun and the land itself were in league with the Vietcong," recalled marine officer Philip Caputo in *A Rumor of War* (1977), "wearing us down,

driving us mad, killing us." The enemy, meanwhile, was hard to find, often burrowed into elaborate underground tunnels or melded into the population, where any Vietnamese might be a Vietcong.

The American forces fought well, and their entry into the conflict in 1965 helped stave off a South Vietnamese defeat. In that sense, Americanization achieved its most immediate and basic objective. But if the stepped-up fighting that year demonstrated to Hanoi leaders that the war would not swiftly be won, it also showed the same thing to their counterparts in Washington. As the North Vietnamese matched each American escalation with one of their own, the war became a stalemate. The U.S. commander, General William Westmoreland, proved mistaken in his belief that a strategy of attrition represented the key to victory—the enemy had a seemingly endless supply of recruits to throw into battle. Under Westmoreland's strategy, the measure of success became the "body count"—that is, the number of North Vietnamese and Vietcong corpses found after battle. From the start, the counts were subject to manipulation by officers eager to convince superiors of the success of an operation. Worse, the American reliance on massive military and other technology—including carpet bombing, napalm (jellied gasoline), and crop defoliants that destroyed entire forests— alienated many South Vietnamese and brought new recruits to the Vietcong.

△ Wounded American soldiers after a battle in Vietnam.

Larry Burrows/Getty Images

26-4f Divisions at Home

Increasingly, Americans divided into those who supported the war and those who did not. As television coverage brought the war—its body counts and body bags, its burned villages and weeping refugees—into homes every night, the number of opponents grew. On college campuses, professors and students organized debates and lectures on American policy. Sometimes going around the clock, these intense public discussions became a form of protest, called "teach-ins" after the sit-ins of the civil rights movement. The big campus and street demonstrations were still to come, but pacifist groups organized early protests.

In early 1966, Senator William Fulbright held televised public hearings on whether the national interest was being served by pursuing the war. What exactly was the threat? senators asked. To the surprise of some, George F. Kennan testified that his containment doctrine was meant for Europe, not the volatile environment of Southeast Asia. America's "preoccupation" with Vietnam, Kennan asserted, was undermining its global obligations. Whether many minds were changed by the Fulbright hearings is hard to say, but they constituted the first in-depth national discussion of the U.S. commitment in Vietnam. They provoked Americans to think about the conflict and the nation's role in it. No longer could anyone doubt that there were deep divisions on Vietnam among public officials, or that two of them, Lyndon Johnson and William Fulbright, formerly close political associates, had broken completely over the war.

Defense secretary Robert McNamara, who despite private misgivings championed the Americanization of the war in 1965, became increasingly troubled by the killing and destructiveness of the bombing. Already in November 1965 he expressed skepticism that victory could ever be achieved, and in the months thereafter he agonized over how the United States looked in the eyes of the world. American credibility, far from being protected by the staunch commitment to the war, was suffering grievous damage, McNamara feared. "The picture of the world's greatest superpower killing or seriously injuring 1,000 noncombatants a week, while trying to pound a tiny backward nation into submission on an issue whose merits are hotly disputed, is not a pretty one," he told Johnson in mid-1967.

But Johnson was in no mood to listen or reconsider. Determined to prevail in Vietnam, he dug in, snapping at "those little shits on the campuses." Although on occasion he halted the bombing to encourage North Vietnam to negotiate (on America's terms), and to disarm critics, such pauses often were accompanied by increases in American troop strength. And the United States sometimes resumed or accelerated the bombing just when a diplomatic breakthrough seemed possible. Hanoi demanded a complete suspension of bombing raids before sitting down at the conference table. And North Vietnamese leaders could not accept American terms, which amounted to abandonment of their determination to achieve an independent, unified Vietnam.

26-5 A Nation Divided

▷ **What factors contributed to urban unrest in the 1960s?**

▷ **What new forms of leadership emerged from the civil rights movement in the 1960s?**

▷ **What causes did the Mexican American civil rights movement embrace during the 1960s?**

▷ **How did young people seek to change their lives and the society in which they lived?**

As Johnson struggled to overcome an implacable foe in Vietnam, his liberal vision of a Great Society faced challenges at home. The divisions among Americans over policy in Vietnam were only one fissure in a society that was fracturing along many different lines: black and white, young and old, radical, liberal, and conservative.

Even as the civil rights movement was winning important victories in the mid-1960s, many African Americans had given up on the promise of liberal reform. In 1964, shortly after President Johnson signed the landmark Civil Rights Act, racial violence erupted in northern cities. Angry residents of Harlem took to the streets after a white police officer shot a black teenager. The following summer, in the predominantly black Watts section of Los Angeles, crowds burned, looted, and battled police for five days and nights. The uprising, which began when a white police officer attempted to arrest a black resident on suspicion of drunken driving, left thirty-four dead and more than one thousand injured. In July 1967, twenty-six people were killed in street battles between African Americans and police and army troops in Newark, New Jersey. A week later, in Detroit, forty-three died as three square miles of the city went up in flames. In 1967 alone, there were 167 violent outbreaks in 128 cities (see Map 26.3).

The "long, hot summers" of urban unrest in the 1960s differed from almost all previous race riots. Past riots were typically started by whites. Here, black residents exploded in anger and frustration over the conditions of their lives. They looted and burned stores, most of them white-owned. But in the process they devastated their own neighborhoods.

In 1968, the National Advisory Commission on Civil Disorders, chaired by Governor Otto Kerner of Illinois, warned that America was "moving towards two societies, one white, one black—separate and unequal," and blamed white racism for the violence. "What white Americans have never fully understood—but what the Negro can never forget—is that white society is deeply implicated in the ghetto. White institutions created it, white institutions maintain it, and white society condones it," concluded the

Map 26.3 Urban Uprisings, 1965–1968

The first major violent black uprising of the 1960s exploded in the Los Angeles neighborhood of Watts in 1965. The bloodiest uprisings of 1967 were in Newark, New Jersey, and Detroit, Michigan. Scores of uprisings erupted in the aftermath of Martin Luther King Jr.'s assassination in 1968.

Kerner Commission. Some white Americans rejected this interpretation. Others, shocked at what appeared to be senseless violence, wondered why African Americans were venting their frustration so destructively just when they were making real progress in the civil rights struggle.

The answer stemmed in part from regional differences. Although the *legal* disfranchisement and discrimination in the South was a clear focal point for civil rights activism, African Americans outside the South also suffered racial discrimination. Increasingly concentrated in the deteriorating ghettos of inner cities, the majority lived in societies as segregated as any in the Deep South. They faced discrimination in housing, in the availability of credit and mortgages, and in employment. The median income of northern blacks was little more than half that of northern

whites, and their unemployment rate was twice as high. Many northern blacks had given up on the civil rights movement, and few believed that Great Society liberalism would solve their plight.

26-5a Black Power

In this climate, a new voice urged blacks to seize their freedom "by any means necessary." Malcolm X, a onetime pimp and street hustler who had converted while in prison to the Nation of Islam faith, offered African Americans a new direction of leadership. Members of the Nation of Islam, commonly known as Black Muslims, espoused black pride and separatism from white society. Their faith, combining elements of traditional Islam with a belief that whites were subhuman "devils" whose race would soon be destroyed, also emphasized the importance of sobriety, thrift, and social responsibility. By the early 1960s, Malcolm X had become the Black Muslims' chief spokesperson, and his advice was straightforward: "If someone puts a hand on you, send him to the cemetery." But Malcolm X was murdered in early 1965 by members of the Nation of Islam who believed he had betrayed their cause by breaking with the Black Muslims to start his own, more racially tolerant organization. In death, Malcolm X became a powerful symbol of black defiance and self-respect.

A year after Malcolm X's death, Stokely Carmichael, SNCC chairman, denounced "the betrayal of black dreams by white America." To be truly free from white oppression, Carmichael proclaimed, blacks had to "stand up and take over"—to elect black candidates, to organize their own schools, to control their own institutions, to embrace "**Black Power.**" That year, SNCC expelled its white members and repudiated both nonviolence and integration. CORE followed suit in 1967.

The best-known black radicals of the era were the Black Panthers, an organization formed in Oakland, California, in 1966. Blending black separatism and revolutionary communism, the Panthers dedicated themselves to destroying both capitalism and "the military arm of our oppressors," the police in the ghettos. In direct contrast to earlier, nonviolent civil rights protesters, who had worn suits and ties or dresses to demonstrate their respectability, male Panthers wore black leather coats, carried weapons, and talked about killing "pigs"—and did kill eleven officers by 1970. Police targeted the Panthers; most infamously, Chicago police murdered local Panther leader Fred Hampton in his bed. However, the Panthers also worked to improve life in their neighborhoods by creating free breakfast and health care programs for children, offering courses in African American history, and demanding jobs and decent housing for the poor.

26-5b Mexican American Activism

In 1965, Mexican Americans made up about 4 percent of the U.S. population, concentrated in the Southwest and California. Although the federal census counted all Hispanics as "white," they were often discriminated against in the job market, pay, housing, schools, and the courts. Organizations such as the League of United Latin American Citizens (LULAC), a middle-class–oriented group founded in 1929, had long sought full assimilation of Hispanic citizens—most of whom were of Mexican origin. But a national Mexican American movement for social justice began outside this growing middle class, first focused on the plight of Mexican and Mexican American migrant farm workers.

Black Power Advocated in 1966 by SNCC president Stokely Carmichael, it promoted black nationalism, self-determination, and greater militance as a means of self-defense.

Grape growers in California relied heavily on migrant farm workers, paying them as little as 10 cents an hour in 1965 (the minimum wage was $1.25), and too frequently the housing they provided lacked running water and indoor toilets. Mexican American and Filipino grape workers launched a strike (*huelga*) against large growers in California's San Joaquin Valley in 1965, and labor organizers César Chávez and Delores Huerta offered leadership. A national consumer boycott of table grapes, led by Chávez and the AFL-CIO-affiliated United Farm Workers (UFW), brought the growers to the bargaining table, winning better wages and working conditions in 1970. The UFW's roots in the Mexican and Mexican American communities were critical to its success, as the union resembled nineteenth-century Mexican *mutualistas*, or cooperative associations, as much as it did a traditional American labor union. Its members founded cooperative groceries, a Spanish-language newspaper, and a theater group; they called on the Virgin de Guadalupe for assistance in their struggle.

△ United Farm Workers leaders César Chávez and Delores Huerta talk during the 1968 grape pickers' strike. The statue of the Virgin Mary, poster for presidential candidate Robert Kennedy, and photograph of Mahatma Gandhi suggest the guiding religious, political, and philosophical underpinnings of the movement.

As migrant workers struggled for a decent standard of living and groups such as LULAC sought assimilation, some young Mexican Americans embraced a different sort of activism. In early March of 1968, about 15,000 students walked out of their high school classrooms in East Los Angeles. This "blowout" protested crumbling school buildings and high dropout rates, the channeling of Mexican Americans into vocational (rather than academic) programs, the lack of Mexican American teachers and administrators, and the absence of Mexican American history and culture in the high school curriculum. The blowout accomplished few immediate gains, but these students helped to launch a broader movement.

26-5c Youth and Politics

By the mid-1960s, 41 percent of Americans were under the age of twenty. These young people spent more time in the world of peer culture than had any previous generation, as three-quarters of them graduated from high school (up from one-fifth in the 1920s) and almost half of them went to college (up from 16 percent in 1940). As this large baby boom generation came of age, many young

△ During award ceremonies at the 1968 Olympic Games in Mexico City, American sprinters Tommie Smith (*center*) and John Carlos (*right*) extend gloved hands skyward to protest racial inequality and express Black Power. In retaliation, U.S. Olympic officials suspended Smith and Carlos.

people took seriously the idea that they must provide democratic leadership for their nation. Black college students had begun the sit-in movement, infusing new life into the struggle for African American civil rights. Mexican American youth had begun to demand recognition of their heritage. Some white college students—from both political left and right—also committed themselves to changing the system.

In the fall of 1960, a group of conservative college students came together at the family estate of William F. Buckley in Sharon, Connecticut, to create Young Americans for Freedom (YAF). Their manifesto, the "Sharon Statement," endorsed Cold War anticommunism and a vision of limited government power directly opposed to New Deal liberalism and its heritage. "In this time of moral and political crises," they wrote, "it is the responsibility of the youth of America to affirm certain eternal truths . . . [F]oremost among the transcendent values is the individual's use of his God-given free will." The YAF planned to capture the Republican Party and move it to the political right; Goldwater's selection as the Republican candidate for president in 1964 demonstrated their early success.

At the other end of the political spectrum, an emerging "New Left" soon joined conservative youth in rejecting liberalism. Whereas conservatives believed that liberalism's activist government encroached on individual liberty, these young Americans believed that liberalism was not enough, that it could never offer true democracy and equality to all America's people. At a meeting in Port Huron, Michigan, in 1962, founding members of Students for a Democratic Society (SDS) proclaimed, "We are people of this generation, bred in at least modest comfort, housed now in the universities, looking uncomfortably to the world we inherit." Their "Port Huron Statement" condemned racism, poverty in the midst of plenty, and the Cold War. Calling for "participatory democracy," SDS sought to wrest power from the corporations, the military, and the politicians and return it to "the people."

26-5d Free Speech Movement

The first indication of the new power of activist white youth came at the University of California, Berkeley. In the fall of 1964, the university administration banned political activity—including recruiting volunteers for civil rights work in Mississippi—from its traditional place along a university-owned sidewalk bordering the campus. When the administration called police to arrest a CORE worker who defied the order, some four thousand students surrounded the police car. Berkeley graduate student and Mississippi Freedom Summer veteran Mario Savio ignited the movement, telling students, "You've got to put your bodies upon the levers . . . [and] you've got to indicate to the people who run it, to the people who own it, that unless you're free, the machine will be prevented from working at all."

Student political groups, left and right, came together to create the **Free Speech Movement (FSM)**. The FSM did win back the right to political speech, but not before state police had arrested almost eight hundred student protesters. Berkeley students took two lessons from the Free Speech Movement. Many saw the administration's actions as a failure of America's democratic promises, and they were radicalized by the experience. But the victory of the FSM also demonstrated to students their potential power. By the end of the decade, the activism born at Berkeley would spread to hundreds of college and university campuses.

26-5e Student Activism

Many student protesters in the 1960s sought greater control over their lives as students, demanding more relevant class offerings, more freedom in selecting their courses of study, and a greater voice in the running of universities. A major target of protest was the doctrine of *in loco parentis*, which until the late 1960s put universities legally "in the place of parents" to their students, allowing control over student behavior that went well beyond the laws of the land. The impact of *in loco parentis* fell heaviest on women, who were subject to strict curfew regulations called parietals, while men had no such rules. Protesters demanded an end to discrimination on the basis of sex, but rejected *in loco parentis* for other reasons as well. A group at the University of Kansas demanded that the administration explain how its statement that "college students are assumed to have maturity of judgment necessary for adult responsibility" squared with the minute regulation of students' nonacademic lives. One young man complained that "a high school dropout selling cabbage in a supermarket" had more rights and freedoms than successful university students. Increasingly, students insisted they should be allowed the full rights and responsibilities of citizens in a democratic society.

Free Speech Movement (FSM) Coalition of student groups at the University of California, Berkeley, that insisted on the right to campus political activity.

doves Term for opponents of American military involvement in Vietnam.

hawks Term for those who favored aggressive pursuit of the Vietnam War.

counterculture Youth movement that promoted drugs, free love, and an alternative way of life opposing the materialism and conformity of mainstream American society.

26-5f Youth and the War in Vietnam

It was the war in Vietnam, however, that mobilized a nationwide student movement. Believing that it was the democratic responsibility of citizens to learn about and speak out on issues of vital national importance, university students and faculty held "teach-ins" about U.S. involvement in Vietnam as the war escalated in 1965. Students for a Democratic Society sponsored the first major antiwar march that year, drawing twenty thousand protesters to Washington, D.C. Local SDS chapters grew steadily as opposition to the war increased. On campuses throughout the nation, students adopted tactics developed in the civil rights movement, picketing ROTC buildings and protesting military research and recruiting done on their campuses. However, despite the visibility of campus antiwar protests, most students did not yet oppose the war: in 1967, only 30 percent of male college students declared themselves "**doves**" on Vietnam, while 67 percent proclaimed themselves "**hawks**." And many young men were, in fact, in Vietnam fighting the war. But as the war continued to escalate, an increasing number of America's youth came to distrust the government that turned a deaf ear to their protests, as well as the university administrations that seemed more a source of arbitrary authority than of democratic education.

26-5g Youth Culture and the Counterculture

But the large baby boom generation would change the nation's culture more than its politics. Although many young people protested the war and marched for social justice, most did not. The sixties' "youth culture" was never homogeneous. Fraternity and sorority life stayed strong on most campuses, even as radicalism flourished. And although there was some crossover, black, white, and Latino youth had different cultural styles: different music, different clothes, even different versions of a youth dialect often incomprehensible to adults. Nonetheless, as potential consumers, young people as a group exercised tremendous cultural authority. Their music and their styles drove American popular culture in the late 1960s.

At the center of youth culture was its music. The Beatles had electrified American teenagers—73 million viewers watched their first television appearance on the *Ed Sullivan Show* in 1964. Bob Dylan promised revolutionary answers in "Blowin' in the Wind"; Janis Joplin brought the sexual power of the blues to white youth; James Brown and Aretha Franklin proclaimed black pride; the psychedelic rock of Jefferson Airplane and the Grateful Dead—along with hallucinogenic drugs—redefined reality. That new reality took brief form in the Woodstock Festival in upstate New York in 1969, as more than 400,000 people reveled in the music and in a world of their own making, living in rain and mud for four days without shelter and without violence.

Some young people hoped to turn youth rebellion into something more than a consumer-based lifestyle, rejecting what they saw as hypocritical middle-class values. They attempted to craft an alternative way of life, or **counterculture**, liberated from competitive materialism and celebrating the legitimacy of pleasure. "Sex, drugs, and rock 'n' roll" became a mantra of sorts, offering these "hippies," or "freaks," a path to a new consciousness. Many did the hard work of creating communes and intentional communities, whether in cities or in hidden stretches of rural America.

John Dominis/The Image Works

△ Hundreds of thousands of young people came together for the Woodstock Music and Art Fair in August 1969. In its coverage, *Time* magazine warned adults that "the children of the welfare state and the atom bomb do indeed march to the beat of a different drummer, as well as to the tune of an electric guitarist," but the local sheriff called them "the nicest bunch of kids I've ever dealt with."

Although the New Left criticized the counterculture as apolitical, many freaks did envision revolutionary change. As John Sinclair, manager of the rock band MC5, explained, mind-blowing experiences with sex, drugs, or music were far more likely to change young peoples' minds than earnest speeches: "Rather than go up there and make some speech about our moral commitment in Vietnam, you just make 'em so freaky they'd never want to go into the army in the first place."

The nascent counterculture had first burst on the national consciousness during the summer of 1967, when tens of thousands of young people poured into the Haight-Ashbury district of San Francisco, the heart of America's psychedelic culture, for the "Summer of Love." As an older generation of "straight" (or Establishment) Americans watched with horror, white youth came to look—and act—more and more like the counterculture. Coats and ties disappeared, as did stockings—and bras. Young men grew long hair, and parents throughout the nation complained, "You can't tell the boys from the girls." Millions used marijuana or hallucinogenic drugs, read underground newspapers, and thought of themselves as alienated from "straight" culture even though they were attending high

school or college and not completely "dropping out" of the Establishment.

Some of the most lasting cultural changes involved attitudes about sex. The mass media were fascinated with "free love," and some people did embrace a truly promiscuous sexuality. More important, however, premarital sex no longer destroyed a woman's "reputation." The birth control pill, distributed since 1960 and widely available to single women by the late 1960s, greatly lessened the risk of unplanned pregnancy, and venereal diseases were easily cured by a basic course of antibiotics. The number of couples living together—"without benefit of matrimony," as the phrase went at the time—increased 900 percent from 1960 to 1970; many young people no longer tried to hide the fact that they were sexually active. Still, 68 percent of American adults disapproved of premarital sex in 1969.

Adults were baffled and often angered by the behavior of youth. A generation that had grown up in the hard decades of depression and war, many of whom saw middle-class respectability as crucial to success and stability, just did not understand. How could young people put such promising futures at risk by having sex without marriage, taking drugs, or opposing the American government over the war in Vietnam?

The British Invasion

The British invasion began in earnest on February 7, 1964. London and Paris had already fallen, reported *Life* magazine, and New York was soon to follow. Three thousand screaming American teenagers were waiting when Pan Am's *Yankee Clipper* touched down at Kennedy Airport with four British "moptops" aboard. "I Want to Hold Your Hand" was already at the top of the U.S. charts, and the Beatles' conquest of America was quick. Seventy-three million people—at that time the largest television audience in history—watched them on the *Ed Sullivan Show* the following Sunday night.

Although the Beatles led the invasion, they did not conquer America alone. The Rolling Stones' first U.S. hit single also came in 1964. The Dave Clark Five appeared on *Ed Sullivan* eighteen times. And there was a whole list of others, some now forgotten, some not: Freddie and the Dreamers, Herman's Hermits, the Animals, the Yardbirds, the Hollies, the Kinks, Gerry and the Pacemakers, Chad and Jeremy, Petula Clark.

The British invasion was, at least in part, the triumphal return of American music, part of a transatlantic exchange that reinvigorated both nations. American rock 'n' roll had lost much of its early energy by the early 1960s, and in England, the London-centered popular music industry was pumping out a highly produced, saccharine version of American pop. But other forms of American music had made their way across the Atlantic, often carried by travelers through port cities like Liverpool, where the Beatles were born. By the late 1950s, young musicians in England's provincial cities were listening to the music of African American bluesmen Muddy Waters and Howlin' Wolf; they were playing cover versions of the early rock 'n' roll of Buddy Holly and Chuck Berry; and they were experimenting with skiffle, a sort of jazz- and blues-influenced folk music played mostly with improvised instruments. None of this music had a large popular audience in the United States, where *Billboard* magazine's

number one hit for 1960 was Percy Faith's "Theme from *A Summer Place*" (a movie starring Sandra Dee and Troy Donahue), and the Singing Nun was at the top of the charts just before the Beatles arrived.

Young British musicians, including John Lennon, Eric Clapton, and Mick Jagger, re-created American musical forms and reinvented rock 'n' roll. By the mid-1960s, the Beatles and the other bands of the British invasion were at the heart of a youth culture that transcended the boundaries of nations. This music not only connected Britain and America but also reached across the Atlantic and the Pacific to link America's youth with young people throughout the world.

CRITICAL THINKING

☐ Music, specifically rock and roll music, was at the heart of the youth culture and the counterculture of the 1960s. It was also a mainstay in many of the protest movements of the era both in the United States and abroad. Why is music so well-suited to the culture of protest?

◁ The Beatles perform on the *Ed Sullivan Show* in February 1964. Although Britain's Queen Mother thought the Beatles "young, fresh, and vital," American parents were appalled when the "long" Beatles haircut swept the nation.

26-6 1968

▷ Why did it seem that the "nation was coming apart" in 1968?

▷ What were the consequences of the Tet Offensive?

▷ How was social unrest a global issue in 1968?

By the beginning of 1968, it seemed that the nation was coming apart. Divided over the war in Vietnam, frustrated by the slow pace of social change, or angry over the racial violence that wracked America's cities, Americans looked for solutions as the nation faced the most serious domestic crisis of the postwar era.

26-6a The Tet Offensive

The year opened with a major attack in Vietnam. On January 31, 1968, the first day of the Vietnamese New Year (Tet), Vietcong and North Vietnamese forces struck all across South Vietnam, capturing provincial capitals (see Map 26.2 in "Opposition to Americanization," Section 26-4d). During the carefully planned offensive, the Saigon airport, the presidential palace, and the ARVN headquarters came under attack. Even the U.S. embassy compound was penetrated by Vietcong soldiers, who occupied its courtyard for six hours. American and South Vietnamese units eventually regained much of the ground they had lost, inflicting heavy casualties and devastating numerous villages.

Although the Tet Offensive did not achieve the resounding battlefield victory that Hanoi strategists had hoped for, the heavy fighting called into question American military leaders' confident predictions in earlier months that the war would soon be won. Had not the Vietcong and North Vietnamese demonstrated that they could strike when and where they wished? If America's airpower, dollars, and half a million troops could not now defeat the Vietcong, could they ever do so? Had the American public been deceived? In February, the highly respected CBS television anchorman Walter Cronkite went to Vietnam to find out. The military brass in Saigon assured him that "we had the enemy just where we wanted him." The newsman recalled, "Tell that to the Marines, I thought—the Marines in the body bags on that helicopter."

26-6b Johnson's Exit

Top presidential advisers sounded notes of despair. Clark Clifford, who had succeeded Robert McNamara as secretary of defense, told Johnson that the war—"a sinkhole"—could not be won, even with the 206,000 additional soldiers requested by Westmoreland. Aware that the nation was suffering a financial crisis prompted by rampant deficit spending to sustain the war and other global commitments, they knew that taking the initiative in Vietnam would cost billions more, further derail the budget, panic foreign owners

△ In early October 1968, as his presidency draws to a close, a weary-looking Lyndon Johnson prepares to address the nation on the war in Vietnam.

of dollars, and wreck the economy. Clifford heard from his associates in the business community; "These men now feel we are in a hopeless bog," he told the president. To "maintain public support for the war without the support of these men" was impossible.

Controversy over the war split the Democratic Party, just as a presidential election loomed in November. Senator Eugene McCarthy of Minnesota and Robert F. Kennedy (now a senator from New York), both strong opponents of Johnson's war policies, forcefully challenged the president in early primaries. Strained by exhausting sessions with skeptical advisers, troubled by the economic implications of escalation, and sensing that more resources would not bring victory, Johnson changed course. During a March 31 television address, he announced a halt to most of the bombing, asked Hanoi to begin negotiations, and stunned his listeners by withdrawing from the presidential race. He had become a casualty of the war, his presidency doomed—as he had always feared it might be—by a seemingly interminable struggle ten thousand miles from Washington. Peace talks began in May in Paris, but the war ground on.

26-6c Assassinations

Less than a week after Johnson's shocking announcement, Martin Luther King Jr. was murdered in Memphis, where he had traveled to support striking sanitation workers. It is still not clear why James Earl Ray, a white forty-year-old drifter and petty criminal, shot King—or whether he acted alone or as part of a conspiracy. By 1968, King, the senior statesman of the civil rights movement, had become an outspoken critic of the Vietnam War and of American capitalism. Despite the continuing power of racism in American society, King was widely respected and honored, and most Americans mourned his death. In the days following his assassination, black rage and grief exploded in 130 cities. Once again, ghetto neighborhoods burned; thirty-four blacks and five whites died. The violence provoked a backlash from whites—primarily urban, working-class people who were tired of violence and who had little sympathy for the demands of black radicals. In Chicago, Mayor Richard Daley ordered police to shoot rioters.

An already shaken nation watched in disbelief as another leader fell to violence only two months later. Antiwar Democratic presidential candidate Robert Kennedy was shot and killed as he celebrated his victory in the California primary. His assassin, Sirhan Sirhan, an Arab nationalist, targeted Kennedy because of his support for Israel.

26-6d Chicago Democratic National Convention

Violence erupted again in August at the Democratic National Convention in Chicago. Thousands of protesters converged on the city: students who'd gone "Clean for Gene," cutting long hair and donning "respectable" clothes to campaign for antiwar candidate Eugene McCarthy; members of America's counterculture drawn by a promise from the anarchist group,

the Yippies, of a "Festival of Life" to counter the "Convention of Death"; members of antiwar groups that ranged from radical to mainstream. Mayor Daley, resolving that no one would disrupt "his" convention, assigned twelve thousand police to twelve-hour shifts and had twelve thousand army troops with bazookas, rifles, and flamethrowers on call as backup. Police attacked peaceful antiwar protesters and journalists. "The whole world is watching," chanted the protesters, as club-swinging police indiscriminately beat people to the ground, and Americans gathered around their television sets, despairing over the future of their nation.

26-6e Global Protest

Although American eyes were focused on the clashes in Chicago, upheavals burst forth around the world that spring and summer. In France, university students protested both rigid academic policies and the Vietnam War. They received support from French workers, who occupied their factories and paralyzed public transport; the turmoil contributed to the collapse of Charles de Gaulle's government the following year. In Italy, Germany, England, Ireland, Sweden, Canada, Mexico, Chile, Japan, and

△ A military truck with civilians waving Czech flags drives past a Soviet truck in Prague on August 21, 1968, shortly after Warsaw Pact troops invaded Czechoslovakia. More than one hundred people were killed in the clashes, and several Prague Spring leaders, including Alexander Dubček, were arrested and taken to Moscow. Dubček's attempts to create "socialism with a human face" are often seen as historical and ideological forerunners to Mikhail Gorbachev's reform policies in the 1980s in the Soviet Union.

Hutton Archive/Getty Images

South Korea, students also protested—sometimes violently—against universities, governments, and the Vietnam War. In Czechoslovakia, hundreds of thousands of demonstrators flooded the streets of Prague, demanding democracy and an end to repression by the Soviet-controlled government. This so-called Prague Spring developed into a full-scale national rebellion before being crushed by Soviet tanks.

Why so many uprisings occurred in so many places simultaneously is not altogether clear. Sheer numbers had an impact. The postwar baby boom experienced by many nations produced by the late 1960s a huge mass of teenagers and young adults, many of whom had grown up in relative prosperity, with high expectations for the future. The expanded reach of global media also mattered. Technological advances allowed the nearly instantaneous transmittal of televised images around the world, so protests in one country could readily inspire similar actions in others. Although the worldwide demonstrations might have occurred even without the Vietnam War, television news footage showing the wealthiest and most industrialized nation carpet-bombing a poor and developing one—whose longtime leader was the charismatic revolutionary Ho Chi Minh—surely helped fuel the agitation.·

26-6f Nixon's Election

The presidential election of 1968, coming at the end of such a difficult year, did little to heal the nation. Democratic nominee Hubert Humphrey, Johnson's vice president, seemed a continuation of the old politics. Republican candidate Richard Nixon, like Goldwater in 1964, called for "law and order"—a phrase some understood as racist code words—to appeal to those who were angry about racial violence and tired of social unrest. Promising to "bring us together," he reached out to those he called "the great, quite forgotten majority—the nonshouters and the nondemonstrators, the millions who ask principally to go their own way in decency and dignity." On Vietnam, Nixon vowed he would "end the war and win the peace." Governor George Wallace of Alabama, who only five years before had vowed, "Segregation forever!" and who proposed using nuclear weapons on Vietnam, ran as a third-party candidate. Wallace carried five southern states, drawing almost 14 percent of the popular vote, and Nixon was elected president with the slimmest of margins (see Map 26.4). Divisions among Americans deepened.

Yet on Christmas Eve 1968—in a step toward fulfilling the pledge John Kennedy had made at the opening of a tumultuous decade—*Apollo* 8 entered lunar orbit. Looking down on a troubled world, the astronauts broadcast photographs of the earth seen from space, a fragile blue orb floating in darkness. As people around the world listened, the astronauts read aloud the opening passages of Genesis, "In the beginning, God created the heaven and the earth ... and God saw that it was good," and many listeners found themselves in tears.

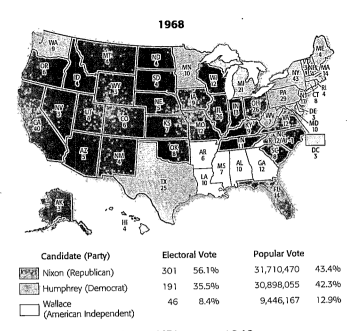

1968

Candidate (Party)	Electoral Vote		Popular Vote	
Nixon (Republican)	301	56.1%	31,710,470	43.4%
Humphrey (Democrat)	191	35.5%	30,898,055	42.3%
Wallace (American Independent)	46	8.4%	9,446,167	12.9%

Map 26.4 Presidential Election, 1968

The popular vote was almost evenly split between Richard M. Nixon and Hubert Humphrey, but Nixon won 31 states to Humphrey's 14 and triumphed easily in electoral votes. George Wallace, the American Independent Party candidate, won 5 states in the Deep South.

Summary

The 1960s began with high hopes for a more democratic America. Civil rights volunteers, often risking their lives, carried the quest for racial equality to all parts of the nation. Gradually, the nation's leaders put their support behind the movement, and the 1964 Civil Rights Act and the 1965 Voting Rights Act were major landmarks in the quest for a more just society. America was shaken by the assassination of President John Kennedy in 1963, but under President Johnson's Great Society, the liberal vision of using government power to improve the lives of the nation's citizens reached new heights.

But throughout this period, the nation was troubled by threats to its stability. The Cold War between the United States and the USSR grew in size and scope during the early 1960s. The world came close to nuclear war in the 1962 Cuban missile crisis, and meanwhile the United States became steadily more involved in the ongoing war in Vietnam. Determined not to let South Vietnam "fall" to communists, Lyndon Johnson in 1965 sent military forces to prevent the victory of communist Vietnamese nationalists led by Ho Chi Minh in that nation's civil war. By 1968, there were more than half a million American ground troops in Vietnam. America's war in Southeast Asia divided the country, undermined

The Immigration Act of 1965

When President Johnson signed the 1965 Immigration Act in a ceremony at the foot of the Statue of Liberty, he stated, "This bill that we sign today is not a revolutionary bill. It does not affect the lives of millions. It will not reshape the structure of our daily lives, or really add importantly to our wealth and power." Johnson believed the act was important in an era of struggle over the role of race in American society because it "repair[ed] a very deep and painful flaw in the fabric of American justice" by ending national origins quotas that all but excluded "Polynesians, orientals, and Negroes" (as Hawai'i's senator Hiram Fong pointed out in 1963). Nevertheless, the president and his advisers saw it as primarily symbolic. They were wrong. This relatively obscure act may have had greater long-term impact on Americans' lives than any other piece of Great Society legislation.

The 1965 Immigration Act ended national quotas (see "Improving American Life," Section 26-3e) and established a policy of family reunification that allowed immediate relatives of U.S. citizens to immigrate to the United States regardless of numerical ceilings on immigration. Those who created the Immigration Act did not expect the numbers of immigrants to rise or the sources of immigration to change. But world events decreed otherwise. As population increased rapidly in many of the world's poorer countries, the continuing prosperity of the United States drew those seeking opportunity. Other immigrants fled political instability, including wars in Southeast Asia and civil conflict in Latin America and Africa. U.S. immigration rates skyrocketed.

Following the National Origins Act of 1924, the percentage of U.S. foreign-born residents had dropped steadily, reaching a low of 5 percent in 1970. In 2014, more than 13 percent of American residents were foreign born—a figure last reached in 1920. (And it's important to note that not all immigration is controlled by legislation, as both figures include unauthorized immigrants—approximately 4 percent of the U.S. population in 2014, according to Pew Research Center estimates.) Moreover, no longer were most immigrants from western Europe. As of 2014 the majorities came from (in order) Mexico, India, China, and the Philippines, followed by El Salvador, Vietnam, Cuba, and Korea.

More than two-thirds of the post-1965 immigrants settled in six states—New York, California, Florida, New Jersey, Illinois, and Texas—but many found their way to parts of America that had previously been much more homogeneous. By the late twentieth century, Spanish-language signs appeared in South Carolina, and Hmong farmers from the mountains of Southeast Asia offered their produce at the farmers' market in Missoula, Montana. The legacy of the 1965 Immigration Act was unintended but profound: the people and the nation are today much more diverse than they otherwise would have been.

CRITICAL THINKING

◻ In keeping with other legislation intended to end legal racism in the United States, the Immigration Act of 1965 addressed "a flaw in the fabric of American Justice"—laws that prevented individuals from immigrating to the United States because of their country of origin (a category usually tied to race or ethnicity). Today, some Americans propose returning to the practice of excluding potential immigrants because of their national origin, religion, or race/ethnicity. What type of immigration policies should the United States have, and why?

Great Society domestic programs, and ultimately destroyed Johnson's presidency.

Despite real gains in civil rights and in attempts to promote justice and to end poverty, divisions among Americans grew in the second half of the decade. Many African Americans turned away from the civil rights movement, seeking more immediate change in their lives. Poor African American neighborhoods burned as violent unrest spread through the nation. Vocal young people—and some of their elders— questioned whether democracy truly existed in the United States. Large numbers of the nation's white youth embraced another form of rebellion, claiming membership in a "counterculture" that rejected white middle-class respectability. With great passion, Americans struggled over the future of their nation.

Suggestions for Further Reading

Beth Bailey, *Sex in the Heartland* (1999)

David Farber, *The Age of Great Dreams* (1994)

Lawrence Freedman, *Kennedy's Wars: Berlin, Cuba, Laos, and Vietnam* (2000)

George C. Herring, *LBJ and Vietnam: A Different Kind of War* (1994)

Peniel Joseph, *Waiting 'Til the Midnight Hour: A Narrative History of Black Power in America* (2006)

Michael Kazin and Maurice Isserman, *America Divided: The Civil War of the 1960s* (1999)

Fredrik Logevall, *Choosing War: The Lost Chance for Peace and the Escalation of War in Vietnam* (1999)

Lisa McGirr, *Suburban Warriors: The Origins of the New American Right* (2001)

Charles Payne, *I've Got the Light of Freedom: The Organizing Tradition and the Mississippi Freedom Struggle* (1995)

Fred Turner, *From Counterculture to Cyberculture: Stewart Brand, The Whole Earth Network, and the Rise of Digital Utopianism* (2006)

Julian Zelizer, *The Fierce Urgency of Now: Lyndon Johnson, Congress, and the Battle for the Great Society* (2015)

MINDTAP
From Cengage

MindTap® is a fully online personalized learning experience built upon Cengage Learning content. MindTap® combines student learning tools—readings, multimedia, activities, and assessments—into a singular Learning Path that guides students through the course and helps students develop the critical thinking, analysis, and communication skills that are essential to academic and professional success.

A Pivotal Era, 1969–1980

On the morning of November 4, 1979, a Sunday, a mob of several thousand young Iranians gathered outside the U.S. embassy in Tehran. They were supporters of Iran's new leader, Ayatollah Ruhollah Khomeini, a shia cleric who had been living in exile in Paris. Most were men, but there were women too, dressed in black and shrouded in chadors. At 10:30, a small group cut the chain that secured the main gate to the embassy compound and made their way inside the grounds. Hundreds followed them. Hearing the commotion and sensing trouble, Bill Daugherty, a CIA officer newly arrived in the country, set about destroying sensitive embassy documents as fast as he could, hand-feeding the papers into a small incinerator in a back room. Soon he could hear the Iranians in the building. Cooly and methodically, he kept going, until the machine seized up and would take no more documents.

By early afternoon, Daugherty and the few dozen other American personnel still present in the embassy had been captured and handcuffed. Though a few (mostly women and African Americans) were released, fifty-two of them languished under Iranian guard. Thus began the Iran hostage crisis, which would last 444 days and go down as one of the defining events in the modern history of U.S.–Iran relations.

Dramatic though were the events of that fall day in the Iranian capital, they were not wholly shocking to outside observers. Early in the year, the U.S.-supported leader of Iran, Shah Mohammad Reza Pahlavi, had been deposed by revolutionary forces loyal to Khomeini, following years of unrest fueled by resentment of the shah's autocratic style and the growing gap

◁ A blindfolded American hostage is paraded by his Iranian captors at the U.S. embassy in Tehran, on
November 1, 1979. Alain Mingam/Gamma-Rapho/Getty Images

Chronology

1969	
	■ Stonewall Inn uprising begins gay liberation movement
	■ *Apollo 11* astronaut Neil Armstrong becomes first person to walk on the moon's surface
	■ National Chicano Liberation Youth Conference held in Denver
	■ Indians of All Tribes occupies Alcatraz Island
	■ Nixon administration begins affirmative action plan

1970	
	■ United States invades Cambodia
	■ Students at Kent State and Jackson State universities shot by National Guard troops
	■ First Earth Day celebrated
	■ Environmental Protection Agency created

1971	
	■ Pentagon Papers published

1972	
	■ Nixon visits China and Soviet Union
	■ CREEP stages Watergate break-in
	■ Congress approves ERA and passes Title IX, which creates growth in women's athletics

1973	
	■ Peace agreement in Paris ends U.S. involvement in Vietnam
	■ OPEC increases oil prices, creating U.S. energy crisis
	■ *Roe v. Wade* legalizes abortion
	■ Agnew resigns; Ford named vice president

1974	
	■ Nixon resigns under threat of impeachment; Ford becomes president

1975	
	■ In deepening economic recession, unemployment hits 8.5 percent
	■ New York City saved from bankruptcy by federal loan guarantees
	■ Congress passes Indian Self-Determination and Education Assistance Act in response to Native American activists

1976	
	■ Carter elected president

1977	
	■ *Regents of the University of California v. Bakke* outlaws quotas but upholds affirmative action
	■ California voters approve Proposition 13

1979	
	■ Three Mile Island nuclear accident raises fears
	■ Camp David accords signed by Israel and Egypt
	■ American hostages seized in Iran
	■ Soviet Union invades Afghanistan
	■ Consumer debt doubles from 1975 to hit $315 billion

between Iran's rich and poor. A succession of U.S. administrations had backed his government, and these close ties had produced deep hostility among the shah's critics on both right and left. For many months before the hostage-taking, the U.S. embassy had been the scene of demonstrations against the American presence in the country, as well as the decision by the Carter administration to allow the ailing shah to travel to the United States for medical treatment; in February 1979, the embassy was attacked and briefly occupied. In response, the Carter administration cut the embassy staff from a pre-revolutionary high of 1400 to about seventy. Most of them now found themselves blindfolded and paraded before the television cameras of the world.

As the days and weeks passed, President Carter became consumed by the crisis. About to begin his campaign for reelection and already facing right-wing accusations of weakness, he groped for some way to free the hostages. It was a political nightmare, made worse be the intense daily attention American media organizations paid to the standoff. Determining that military action was too risky, the White House tried to squeeze Iran through economic sanctions and froze its assets in the United States. It pursued every diplomatic angle, official as well as secret. Nothing worked. The public, initially inclined to rally around the president, grew frustrated.

Finally, on April 11, 1980 Carter approved a high-risk rescue operation, called "Operation Eagle Claw." It failed spectacularly after equipment malfunction in the sandy Iranian desert at a staging area called "Desert One," and during the hasty withdrawal two aircraft collided, killing eight American servicemen. Daugherty and his fellow hostages were not freed until January 1981, after Carter left office and the United States unfroze some Iranian assets and promised not to intervene again in Iran's internal affairs.

How much the crisis contributed to Carter's election defeat is hard to say, but certainly it harmed his prospects. And if he deserves sympathy for his predicament, he can also be criticized for his response to it, a point historian

Gaddis Smith has made well: "President Carter inherited an impossible situation—and he and his advisers made the worst of it." Divided among themselves, they groped for a response to something Americans had scarcely encountered before, at least in sustained fashion: Islamic fundamentalism. It was a harbinger of things to come.

Experience an interactive version of this story in MindTap®.

Most Americans experienced the 1970s as a series of jolts and crises, an era of continuing divisions, betrayed expectations, and new limits. Exposure of Richard Nixon's illegal acts in the political scandal known as "Watergate" shook the faith of Americans not already disillusioned by discovery that the Nixon administration had lied to the public about its conduct of the war in Vietnam. The movements for racial equality and social justice that had flowered in the 1960s became more radical by the early 1970s, as some activists called for social revolution or embraced a form of "cultural nationalism" that emphasized the differences among America's peoples. The United States faced an economic crisis that sent the "misery index" (a combination of the unemployment rate and inflation) skyrocketing and shocked Americans who had grown to expect continued economic growth and widening prosperity. Americans worried about social crisis as the divorce rate soared, as did the rate of violent crime. Environmental crises also challenged the nation: in 1969, Ohio's sludge-filled Cuyahoga River caught fire; in 1979, a partial meltdown at Pennsylvania's Three Mile Island nuclear power plant became America's worst nuclear accident.

Overseas, too, Americans faced challenges. Nixon and his national security adviser, Henry Kissinger, understood that the United States and the Soviet Union, weakened by the costs of their competition and challenged by other nations, faced a world where power was more diffused. Accordingly, even as they pressed for victory in Vietnam, Nixon and Kissinger sought improved relations with the People's Republic of China and the Soviet Union. They failed in Vietnam, but the great-power negotiations bore fruit, and the diplomatic efforts continued under Nixon's successors, Gerald Ford and Jimmy Carter. But Carter's presidency was undermined by international events beyond his control. In the Middle East—a region of growing importance in U.S. foreign policy—Carter helped broker a peace deal between Egypt and Israel but proved powerless to end the hostage crisis in Iran. An economic downturn caused by changes in the global economy and international trade worsened Carter's woes, and on his watch Cold War tensions revived following a Soviet invasion of Afghanistan in 1979.

Despite—and sometimes because of—these crises, the 1970s was a pivotal era in American history. It was a time of triumph for many who sought a more egalitarian American society, as women and people of color fought and won battles against discrimination. It was also a time of major economic transformation. As international economic competition increased, the United States continued to lose well-paid industrial jobs. America's developing postindustrial economy increased economic disparities. Well-educated Americans would soon benefit from new opportunities in technology, finance, and creative fields, while less-educated Americans suffered as low-paid slots in the service sector replaced often-unionized manufacturing jobs. The 1970s economic crisis compounded Americans' loss of confidence in their political leaders; as federal government attempts to manage the economy failed, many Americans rejected the notion of an active federal government. In the 1970s, the growth of a New Deal, Great Society model in which the federal government attempted to protect Americans from the insecurity of the market was challenged by a broad—though contested—turn toward the competitive marketplace as the means to address the political, social, and economic problems of the nation. Thus, as women and racial and ethnic minorities won battles against discrimination, they found increased opportunity to compete in a tough new economy rather than widespread economic and social equality.

- *How did American foreign policy change as a result of involvement in Vietnam?*

- *Why did Americans see this era as an age of limits?*

- *Some historians describe the period between 1968 and 1980 as a time when many Americans lost faith—in their government, in the possibility of joining together in a society that offered equality to all, in the possibility of consensus instead of conflict. Do you agree, or were the struggles and divisions of this era similar to those of previous decades?*

27-1 Rights, Liberation, and Nationalism

▷ How did minority groups embrace cultural nationalism as a means to assert their identity?

▷ What methods did minority groups use to fight for their social and economic rights?

▷ How did the women's movement evolve in the 1960s and 1970s?

▷ What opposition emerged to the efforts of minority groups to obtain equal rights?

The social change movements of the 1960s evolved into new and powerful forms during the 1970s. By the end of the 1960s, as divisions continued to deepen among the American people, movements for social justice and racial equality had become stronger, louder, and often more radical. The civil rights movement splintered as many young African Americans turned away from the tactics of nonviolence, rejected integration in favor of separatism, and embraced a distinct African American culture. By the early 1970s Mexican Americans and Native Americans, inspired by African American claims, had created powerful "Brown Power" and "Red Power" movements that demanded recognition of their own distinct cultures, and the voices of Puerto Rican nationalists had emerged from New York City and Chicago. As women claimed new rights, some feminists—along with gay men and lesbians—called for "liberation." All these claims were controversial, and Americans disagreed both on possible remedies and on the very definition of the problem.

27-1a African American Cultural Nationalism

By the late 1960s many black Americans, disillusioned by the racism that outlasted the end of legal segregation, believed that integration would leave them subordinated in a white-dominated society that did not respect their history or cultural traditions. Mainstream groups such as the NAACP continued to use the nation's courts and ballot boxes to fight for social and political equality, but other activists (like the white youth of the counterculture) looked to culture rather than to narrow political action for social change. Rejecting current European American standards of beauty, young people let their hair grow into "naturals" and "Afros"; they claimed the power of black "soul." Black students and young faculty members sought strength in their own histories and cultural heritages, as colleges and universities met their demands for black studies programs. African traditions were reclaimed—or sometimes created. The new holiday Kwanzaa, invented in 1966 by Maulana Karenga, professor of black studies at California State University, Long Beach, celebrated African heritage. Many African Americans found pride in their history and culture;

the most radical activists gave up on the notion of a larger "American" culture altogether.

27-1b Chicano and Puerto Rican Activism

Mexican Americans, likewise, struggled over the best path to social justice and good lives in the United States. Although growing numbers of the nation's 9 million Mexican Americans (4.3 percent of the U.S. population) were middle class, almost one-quarter of Mexican American families fell below the official poverty line. Almost half of Mexican Americans were functionally illiterate, and dropout rates were phenomenal: in 1974, only 21 percent of Mexican American young men graduated high school.

Confronting widespread discrimination and social inequality, some groups, including the League of United Latin American Citizens (LULAC, founded in 1929) and the new Mexican American Legal Defense and Education Fund (MALDEF, founded in 1968), pursued traditional paths: courts, ballot boxes, and schools. Other groups embraced radical approaches. In northern New Mexico, Reies Tijerina created the Alianza Federal de Mercedes (Federal Alliance of Grants) to fight for the return of land that the organization claimed belonged to local *hispano* villagers (whose ancestors had occupied the territory before it was claimed by the United States) under the 1848 Treaty of Guadalupe Hidalgo. In Denver, former boxer Rudolfo "Corky" Gonzáles drew Mexican American youth to his "Crusade for Justice"; those who gathered there for the National Chicano Liberation Youth Conference in 1969 adopted a manifesto, *El Plan Espiritual de Aztlan*, which condemned the "brutal 'Gringo' invasion of our territories" and declared "the Independence of our ... Nation."

These young activists did not seek equal rights through integration; instead, they wanted to liberate "La Raza" (from *La Raza de Bronze*, "the brown people") from the oppressive force of American society and culture. They also rejected a hyphenated "Mexican-American" identity. The "Mexican American," they explained in *El Plan Espiritual de Aztlan*, "lacks respect for his culture and ethnic heritage ... [and] seeks assimilation as a way out of his 'degraded' social status." These young people called themselves "Chicanos" or "Chicanas"—a term drawn from barrio slang and associated with *pachucos*, the hip, rebellious, and definitely not respectable young men.

Many middle-class Mexican Americans and members of the older generations never embraced the term *Chicano* or the separatist, cultural nationalist agenda of *el movimiento*. Throughout the 1970s, however, younger activists continued to seek "Brown Power" based on a separate and distinct Chicano/Chicana culture. They succeeded in introducing Chicano studies into local high school and college curricula and in creating a strong and unifying sense of cultural identity for Mexican American youth.

Most Latinos in the United States were of Mexican ancestry. The number of Puerto Ricans, however, had expanded steadily since World War II, and by 1970 more than a million Puerto Ricans made their homes in northeastern and midwestern cities, especially New York City and Chicago. Although Puerto Rico was a U.S. commonwealth and Puerto Ricans held U.S. citizenship, migrants often encountered discrimination; by the mid-1970s Puerto Rican households had among the lowest per capita income in the nation. Like black and Chicano youth, young Puerto Ricans embraced cultural nationalism and worked to improve the conditions in their communities. In this case, though, nationalism meant something more: many activists also sought Puerto Rican independence from the United States.

Neither Puerto Rican activism nor the Chicano movement ever had as much national influence as the African American civil rights movement or the Black Power movement. However, both challenged discrimination on the local level and created a basis for political action as the Latino population of the United States grew dramatically over the following decades.

27-1c American Indian Activism

Between 1968 and 1975, American Indian activists forced American society to hear their demands and to reform U.S. government policies toward Native peoples. Many young activists, seeking a return to the "old ways," joined with "traditionalists" among their elders to challenge tribal leaders who advocated assimilation and cooperation with federal agencies.

In November 1969, a small group that called itself "Indians of All Tribes" occupied Alcatraz Island in San Francisco Bay, demanding that the land be returned to Native peoples. The protest, which over time drew more than four hundred people from fifty different tribes or nations, lasted nineteen months and consolidated a new "pan-Indian" approach to activism. Before Alcatraz, protests tended to be concerned with specific local issues on individual reservations. Many of the Alcatraz activists, however, were urban Indians whose lives had been shaped by government policies that led Native peoples to leave reservations and seek jobs in the nation's cities. They were interested in claiming a shared "Indian" identity that transcended tribal differences. These protesters did not succeed in reclaiming Alcatraz Island, but they drew national attention to their struggle and inspired the growing "Red Power" movement. In 1972, members of the radical American Indian Movement occupied a Bureau of Indian Affairs office in Washington, D.C., and then in 1973 a trading post at Wounded Knee, South Dakota, where U.S. Army troops had massacred three hundred Sioux men, women, and children in 1890.

At the same time, more moderate activists, working through such pan-tribal organizations as the National Congress of American Indians and the Native American Rights Fund, lobbied Congress for greater rights and resources to govern themselves and to strengthen their tribal cultures. In response to those demands, Congress and the federal courts returned millions of acres of land to tribal ownership,

△ Calling their movement "Red Power," these American Indian activists dance in 1969 while "reclaiming" Alcatraz Island in San Francisco Bay. Arguing that an 1868 Sioux treaty entitled them to possession of unused federal lands, the group occupied the island until mid-1971.

Ralph Crane/Getty Images

and in 1975 Congress passed the **Indian Self-Determination and Education Assistance Act.** Despite these successes, conditions for most Native Americans remained grim during the 1970s and 1980s: They had higher rates of tuberculosis, alcoholism, and suicide than any other group; nine of ten lived in substandard housing; and the unemployment rate for American Indians hovered around 40 percent.

27-1d The Women's Movement

During the 1950s, even as more and more women joined the paid workforce and participated in the political life of the nation, Americans emphasized women's private roles as wives and mothers; it seemed as if the women's movement that won American women the vote in the 1920s had all but disappeared. But during the 1960s, a "second wave" of the American women's movement emerged, and by the 1970s activists waged a multifront battle for "women's liberation." Feminists did not always agree on methods or goals, but their struggles and successes made the 1970s a pivotal decade for American women.

Indian Self-Determination and Education Assistance Act The 1975 act granted Native American tribes control of federal aid programs on the reservations and oversight of their own schools.

In 1963, the surprise popularity of Betty Friedan's *The Feminine Mystique* signaled there was ample fuel for a revived women's movement. Writing as a housewife and mother (though she had a long history of political activism as well), Friedan described "the problem with no name," the dissatisfaction of educated, middle-class wives and mothers like herself, who—looking at their nice homes and families—wondered guiltily if that was all there was to life. This "problem" was not new; the vague sense of dissatisfaction plaguing housewives had been a staple topic for women's magazines in the 1950s. But Friedan, instead of blaming individual women for failing to adapt to women's proper role, blamed the role itself and the society that created it.

The organized, liberal wing of the women's movement emerged in 1966, with the founding of the **National Organization for Women (NOW)**. NOW was initially a small group of educated, professional women. It served as a traditional lobbying group; its goal was to pressure the EEOC to enforce the 1964 Civil Rights Act (see Section 26-3c "Civil Rights Act"). Racial discrimination was the EEOC's focus, and discrimination on the basis of sex was such a low priority that the topic could be treated as a joke. When a reporter asked EEOC chair Franklin Roosevelt Jr., "What about sex?" Roosevelt laughed, "Don't get me started. I'm all for it." Women who faced workplace discrimination were not amused by such comments, and by 1970, NOW had one hundred chapters with more than three thousand members nationwide.

Another strand of the women's movement developed from the nation's increasingly radical movements for social change and justice. Many women, as they worked for civil rights or against the war in Vietnam, found themselves subordinate to men—making coffee, not policy. As they analyzed inequality in America's social and political structure, these young women began to discuss their own oppression, and the oppression of all women, in American society. In 1968, a group of women gathered outside the Miss America Pageant in Atlantic City to protest the "degrading mindless-boob girlie symbol" represented by the beauty pageant. Although nothing was burned, the pejorative 1970s term for feminists, "bra-burners," came from this event, in which women threw items of "enslavement" (girdles, high heels, curlers, and bras) into a "Freedom Trash Can."

27-1e Feminist Goals and Accomplishments

The feminism embraced by these young activists and others who challenged women's oppression was never a single, coherent set of beliefs. Some argued that the world should be governed by peaceful, noncompetitive values, which they believed were intrinsically female; others claimed that society imposed gender roles and that there were no innate differences between men and women. Most radical feminists, however, practiced what they called

National Organization for Women (NOW) Women's rights organization founded in 1966 that lobbied for equal opportunity, filed lawsuits against gender discrimination, and mobilized public opinion against sexism.

"personal politics." They believed, as feminist author Charlotte Bunch explained, that "there is no private domain of a person's life that is not political, and there is no political issue that is not ultimately personal." Some of these young women began to meet in "consciousness-raising" groups to discuss how, in their personal, everyday lives, women were subordinated by men and by a patriarchal society. By the early 1970s, consciousness-raising groups were meeting in suburban kitchens, college dorm rooms, and churches or synagogues, as women talked about power and patriarchy, romance and marriage, sexuality, abortion, health care, work, and family.

Such conversations left many women convinced that it was crucial to gain the right to control their own bodies. The Boston Women's Health Collective published *Our Bodies, Ourselves* in 1971 (the original edition sold more than 3 million copies), offering women new understanding of their own sexual and reproductive health. And women who sought the right to safe and legal abortions won a major victory in 1973 when the Supreme Court, in a 7-to-2 decision in *Roe v. Wade*, ruled that privacy rights protected a woman's choice to end a pregnancy.

Women's opportunities expanded enormously in the 1970s. When the decade began, help-wanted ads specified "male" or "female." Unmarried women could be denied birth

△ Gloria Steinem, one of the co-founders of *Ms.* magazine, later said of its founding: "I realized as a journalist that there really was nothing for women to read that was controlled by women." *Ms.* premiered in January 1972 and the first issue, with comic book hero Wonder Woman on its cover, sold out within eight days.

control; women were systematically excluded from juries; women (married, divorced, or widowed) frequently could not obtain credit in their own names. U.S. rape law mirrored the claim of a psychiatrist at the University of Kansas student health center: "A woman sometimes plays a big part in provoking her attacker by . . . her overall attitude and appearance"; courts allowed attorneys to use women's sexual histories to discredit them and did not recognize spousal rape. Only 4 percent of American attorneys were female; women made up only 1.3 percent of the military, and there was not a single female general. National Airlines advertisements featured pretty young stewardesses with suggestive captions: "Hi, I'm Linda, and I'm going to FLY you like you've never been flown before." Less than 2 percent of college and university athletic budgets went to women's sports—and women received no athletic scholarships. No woman had ever been named a Rhodes Scholar, served as president of the *Harvard Law Review*, or been ordained as a pastor, rabbi, or (Episcopal) priest. All that would change by the end of the decade.

27-1f Opposition to the Women's Movement

Initially, the nation's elected representatives supported women's claims to equal rights. On March 22, 1972, Senate Republicans and Democrats joined to approve the **Equal Rights Amendment**—the same amendment first proposed by the National Women's Party in the 1920s. By a vote of 82 to 8, senators confirmed that "equality of rights under the law shall not be denied or abridged by the United States or by any State on account of sex." States rapidly fell in line to endorse the amendment; by the end of the year, twenty-two states (of the thirty-eight necessary to amend the Constitution) had ratified the ERA.

While the women's movement encompassed a broad range of women and found many male supporters, it was also met by powerful opposition—much of it from women. Many women believed that middle-class feminists did not understand the realities of their world. They had no desire to be "equal" if that meant giving up traditional gender roles in marriage or going out to work at low-wage, physically exhausting jobs. African American women and Latinas, many of whom had been active in movements for the liberation of their peoples and some of whom had helped create second-wave feminism, often came to regard feminism as a "white" movement that ignored their cultural traditions and needs; some believed the women's movement diverted time and energy away from the fight for racial equality.

Organized opposition to feminism came primarily from conservative, often religiously motivated men and women. As one conservative Christian writer claimed, "The Bible clearly states that the wife is to submit to her husband's leadership . . . just as she would to Christ her Lord." Such beliefs, along with fears about changing gender roles and expectations, fueled the STOP-ERA movement led by Phyllis Schlafly, a lawyer and prominent conservative political activist. Schlafly argued that ERA supporters were "a bunch of bitter women seeking a constitutional cure for their personal problems." She attacked the women's movement as "a total assault on the role of the American woman as wife and mother, and on the family as the basic unit of society." Schlafly and her supporters argued that the ERA would foster federal intervention in personal life, decriminalize rape, force Americans to use unisex toilets, and make women subject to the military draft.

Many women saw feminism as an attack on the choices they had made and felt that by opposing the ERA they were defending their traditional roles. In fighting the ERA, tens of thousands of women became politically experienced; they fed a growing grassroots conservative movement that would come into its own in the 1980s. By the mid-1970s, the STOP-ERA movement had stalled the Equal Rights Amendment. Despite Congress's extension of the ratification deadline, the amendment would fall three states short of ratification and expire in 1982.

27-1g Gay Liberation

In the early 1970s, consensual sexual intercourse between people of the same sex was illegal in almost every state, and until 1973 homosexuality was labeled a mental disorder by the American Psychiatric Association. Homosexual couples did not receive partnership benefits, such as health insurance; they could not adopt children. The issue of gay and lesbian rights divided even progressive organizations: in 1970, the New York City chapter of NOW expelled its lesbian officers. Gay men and lesbians faced discrimination in both private and public life, but unlike most members of racial minorities, they could conceal the identity that made them vulnerable. Remaining "in the closet" offered protection from discrimination and harassment, but also foreclosed the possibility of an openly gay identity or sexual/romantic relationships. Reliance on "the closet" also made it very difficult to organize a political movement. There were small "homophile" organizations, such as the Mattachine Society (named for the Société Mattachine—a medieval musical organization whose members performed in masks, which allowed them to criticize the nobility without fear of reprisal—to evoke the "masked" lives of gay Americans) and the Daughters of Bilitis (after a work of love poems between women), which had worked for gay rights since the 1950s. But the symbolic beginning of the gay liberation movement came on June 28, 1969, when New York City police raided the Stonewall Inn, a gay bar in Greenwich Village, for violating the New York City law that made it illegal for more than three homosexual patrons to occupy a bar at the same time. That night, for the first time, patrons stood up to the police. As word spread through New York's gay community, hundreds more joined the confrontation. The next morning, New

Equal Rights Amendment Proposed constitutional amendment guaranteeing equal rights for women; passed with strong support of both Democrats and Republicans in congress, but fell short of ratification by the states by the congressionally-extended deadline of 1982.

Yorkers found a new slogan spray-painted on neighborhood walls: "Gay Power."

Inspired by the Stonewall riot, some men and women worked openly and militantly for gay rights. They focused on a dual agenda: legal equality and the promotion of Gay Pride. In a version of the identity politics adopted by racial and ethnic communities, some rejected the notion of fitting into straight (heterosexual) culture and helped create distinctive gay communities. By 1973, there were about eight hundred gay organizations in the United States. Centered in big cities and on college campuses, most organizations tried to create supportive environments for gay men and lesbians to come "out of the closet." Once "out," they could use their numbers ("We are everywhere" was a popular slogan) to push for political reform, such as nondiscrimination statutes similar to those that protected women and racial minority groups. By the end of the decade, gay men and lesbians were a political force in cities including New York, Miami, and San Francisco, and they played an increasingly visible role in the social and political life of the nation.

27-1h Affirmative Action

As activists made Americans increasingly aware of discrimination and inequality, policymakers struggled to frame remedies. As early as 1965, President Johnson had acknowledged the limits of civil rights legislation. "You do not take a person who, for years, has been hobbled by chains and liberate him, bring him up to the starting line of a race and then say, 'you are free to compete with all the others,'" Johnson told an audience at Howard University, "and still justly believe that you have been completely fair." In this speech, Johnson called for "not just legal equality . . . but equality as a fact and equality as a result." Here Johnson joined his belief that the federal government must help *individuals* attain the skills necessary to compete in American society to a new concept: equality could be measured by *group* outcomes or results.

Practical issues helped shift emphasis to group outcomes, as well. The 1964 Civil Rights Act had outlawed discrimination, but seemed to stipulate that action could be taken only when an employer "intentionally" discriminated against an individual. This individual, case-by-case approach to equal rights created a nightmare for the Equal Employment Opportunity Commission (EEOC). The tens of thousands of cases filed suggested that racial and sexual discrimination were widespread, but each alleged incident required proof that the employer intended to discriminate against an individual. Some argued that it was possible, instead, to prove discrimination by "results"—by the relative number of African Americans or women, for example, an employer had hired or promoted.

In 1969, the Nixon administration implemented the first major government affirmative action program to promote "equality of results." The Philadelphia Plan (so called because it targeted government contracts in that city) required businesses contracting with the federal government to show (in the words of President Nixon) "affirmative action to meet the goals of increasing minority employment" and set specific numerical "goals," or quotas, for employers. Major government contracts soon required affirmative action for women and members of racial and ethnic minorities, and many large corporations and universities began their own programs.

Supporters saw affirmative action as a remedy for the lasting effects of past discrimination. Critics (some of whom supported racial and sexual equality) argued that attempts to create proportional representation for women and minorities meant discrimination against other individuals who had not created past discrimination, and that group-based remedies violated the principle that individuals should be judged on their own merits. As affirmative action programs began to have an impact in hiring and college admissions, a deepening recession made jobs scarce. Thus, because the job market was not expanding, hiring more minorities and women often meant hiring fewer white men. White working-class men were most adversely affected by the policy, and many resented it. And while women and people of color had new protections, they gained them just as individual competition for jobs became fierce.

27-2 The End in Vietnam

▷ **How did Richard Nixon simultaneously deescalate and expand the war in Vietnam?**

▷ **What were the domestic and international consequences of American involvement in Vietnam?**

▷ **Why does American involvement in Vietnam remain a controversial issue?**

Of all the divisions in American politics and society at the end of the 1960s, none was as pervasive as that over the war in Vietnam. "I'm not going to end up like LBJ," Richard Nixon vowed after winning the 1968 presidential election, recalling that the war had destroyed Johnson's political career. "I'm going to stop that war. Fast." But he did not. He understood that the conflict was generating deep divisions at home and hurting the nation's image abroad, yet—like officials in the Johnson administration—he feared that a precipitous withdrawal would harm American credibility on the world stage as well as his own domestic standing. Anxious to get American troops out of Vietnam, Nixon was at the same time no less committed than his predecessors to preserving an independent, noncommunist South Vietnam. To accomplish these aims, he set upon a policy that at once contracted and expanded the war.

27-2a Invasion of Cambodia

A centerpiece of Nixon's policy was "Vietnamization"—the building up of South Vietnamese forces to replace U.S. forces. Nixon hoped that such a policy would quiet domestic opposition and advance the peace talks under way in Paris since May 1968. Accordingly, the president began to withdraw American troops from Vietnam, decreasing their number from 543,000 in the spring of 1969 to 156,800 by the end

◁ The court-martial of Lieutenant William Calley for his role in the My Lai massacre of more than 300 unarmed Vietnamese civilians, like the war in Vietnam, divided Americans.

of 1971, and to 60,000 by the fall of 1972. Vietnamization did help limit domestic dissent, but it did nothing to end the stalemate in the Paris negotiations. Even as he embarked on this troop withdrawal, Nixon intensified the bombing of North Vietnam and enemy supply depots in neighboring Cambodia, hoping to pound Hanoi into concessions (see Map 26.2 in "Johnson and Vietnam," Section 26-4).

The bombing of neutral Cambodia commenced in March 1969. Over the next fourteen months, B-52 pilots flew 3,600 missions and dropped over 100,000 tons of bombs on that country. At first, the administration went to great lengths to keep the bombing campaign secret. When the North Vietnamese refused to buckle, Nixon turned up the heat: in April 1970, South Vietnamese and U.S. forces invaded Cambodia in search of arms depots and North Vietnamese army sanctuaries. The president announced publicly that he would not allow "the world's most powerful nation" to act "like a pitiful, helpless giant."

27-2b Protests and Counter-demonstrations

Instantly, the antiwar movement rose up, as students on about 450 college campuses went out on strike and hundreds of thousands of demonstrators gathered in various cities to protest the administration's policies. The crisis atmosphere intensified further on May 4, when National Guardsmen in Ohio fired into a crowd of students at Kent State University, killing four young people and wounding eleven. Ten days later, police and state highway patrolmen armed with automatic weapons blasted a women's dormitory at Jackson State, a historically black university in Mississippi, killing two students and wounding nine others. The police claimed they had been shot at, but no evidence of sniping could be found. In Congress, where opposition to the war had been

building over the previous months, Nixon's widening of the war sparked outrage, and in June the Senate terminated the Gulf of Tonkin Resolution of 1964. After two months, U.S. troops withdrew from Cambodia, having accomplished little.

Americans still remained divided on the war. Although a majority told pollsters they thought the original U.S. troop commitment to Vietnam had been a mistake, 50 percent said they believed Nixon's claim that the Cambodia invasion would shorten the war. Angered by the sight of demonstrating college students, many backed the president and the war effort. In Washington, an "Honor America Day" program attracted more than 200,000 people who heard Billy Graham and Bob Hope laud administration policy. Nevertheless, though Nixon welcomed these expressions of support, the tumult over the invasion served to reduce his options on the war. Henceforth, solid majorities could be expected to oppose any new missions for U.S. ground troops in Southeast Asia.

Nixon's troubles at home mounted in June 1971, when the *New York Times* and other newspapers began to publish the **Pentagon Papers,** a top-secret official study of U.S. decisions in the Vietnam War commissioned by former Secretary of Defense Robert McNamara. In 1969 Daniel Ellsberg, a thirty-eight-year-old former Pentagon aide who had contributed to a portion of the study and now felt increasingly disillusioned with the war, gained access to a copy being stored at the Rand Corporation in California. He spent months poring over the forty-seven volumes and determined he

Pentagon Papers A forty-seven-volume U.S. government study from the end of World War II to the Vietnam War, tracing U.S. involvement in Southeast Asia. Released to the press by former Pentagon employee Daniel Ellsberg, the papers revealed military mistakes and a long history of White House lies to Congress, foreign leaders, and the American people.

must disclose their contents to the public. The study showed incontrovertibly, Ellsberg believed, that presidents had repeatedly escalated the American commitment in Vietnam despite pessimistic estimates from their advisers. Perhaps disclosure of this information could force a change in policy. With the help of a Rand colleague, Ellsberg surreptitiously photocopied the entire study, then spent months pleading with antiwar senators and representatives to release it. When they refused, he went to the press.

Nixon secured an injunction to prevent publication, but the Supreme Court overturned the order. Americans learned from this study that political and military leaders frequently had lied to the public about their aims and strategies in Southeast Asia.

Equally troubling was the growing evidence of decay within the armed forces. Morale and discipline among troops had been on the decline even before Nixon took office, and there were growing reports of drug addiction, desertion, racial discord, even the murder of unpopular officers by enlisted men (a practice called "fragging"). Stories of atrocities committed by U.S. troops also began to make their way home. The court-martial and conviction in 1971 of Lieutenant William Calley, who was charged with overseeing the killing of more than three hundred unarmed South Vietnamese civilians in the hamlet of **My Lai** in 1968, got particular attention. An army photographer captured the horror in graphic pictures. For many, the massacre signified the dehumanizing impact of the war on those who fought it.

27-2c Paris Peace Accords

The Nixon administration, meanwhile, stepped up its efforts to pressure Hanoi into a settlement. Johnson had lacked the will to "go to the brink," Nixon told Kissinger, but "I have the will in spades." When the North Vietnamese launched a major offensive across the border into South Vietnam in March 1972, Nixon responded with a massive aerial onslaught against North Vietnam. In December 1972, after an apparent peace agreement collapsed when the South Vietnamese refused to moderate their position, the United States launched a massive air strike on the North—the so-called "Christmas bombing."

But a diplomatic agreement was close. Months earlier, Kissinger and his North Vietnamese counterpart in the negotiations, Le Duc Tho, had resolved many of the outstanding issues. Most notably, Kissinger agreed that North Vietnamese troops could remain in the South after the settlement, while Tho abandoned Hanoi's insistence that the Saigon government of Nguyen Van Thieu be removed. Nixon had instructed Kissinger to make concessions because the president was eager to improve relations with the Soviet Union and China, to win back the allegiance of America's allies, and to restore stability at home. On January 27, 1973, Kissinger and Le Duc Tho signed a cease-fire agreement in Paris, and Nixon compelled a reluctant Thieu to accept it by threatening to cut off U.S. aid while at the same time promising to defend the South if the North violated the agreement. In the accord, the United States promised to withdraw all of its troops within sixty days. North Vietnamese troops would be allowed to stay in South Vietnam, and a coalition government that included the Vietcong eventually would be formed in the South.

The United States pulled its troops out of Vietnam, leaving behind some military advisers. Soon, both North and South violated the cease-fire, and full-scale war erupted once more. The feeble South Vietnamese government, despite holding a clear superiority in the number of tanks and combat-ready troops, could not hold out. Just before its surrender, hundreds of Americans and Vietnamese who had worked for them were hastily evacuated from Saigon. On April 29, 1975, the South Vietnamese government collapsed, and Vietnam was reunified under a communist government based in Hanoi. Shortly thereafter, Saigon was renamed Ho Chi Minh City for the persevering patriot, who had died in 1969.

27-2d Costs of the Vietnam War

The overall costs of the war were immense. More than 58,000 Americans and somewhere between 1.5 to 3 million Vietnamese had died. Civilian deaths in Cambodia and Laos numbered in the hundreds of thousands. The war cost the United States at least $170 billion, and billions more would be paid out in veterans' benefits. The vast sums spent on the war became unavailable for investment in domestic programs. Instead, the nation suffered inflation and retreat from reform, as well as political schism and abuses of executive power. The war also delayed accommodation with the Soviet Union and the People's Republic of China, fueled friction with allies, and alienated Third World nations.

In 1975, communists assumed control and formed repressive governments in Vietnam, Cambodia, and Laos, but beyond Indochina the domino effect once predicted by U.S. officials never occurred. Acute hunger afflicted the people of those devastated lands. Soon refugees—"boat people"— crowded aboard unsafe vessels in an attempt to escape their battered homelands. Many emigrated to the United States, where they were received with mixed feelings by Americans reluctant to be reminded of defeat in Asia. But many Americans faced the fact that the United States, which had relentlessly bombed, burned, and defoliated once-rich agricultural lands, bore considerable responsibility for the plight of the Southeast Asian peoples.

27-2e Debate Over the Lessons of Vietnam

Americans seemed both angry and confused about the nation's war experience. Hawkish observers claimed that America's failure in Vietnam undermined the nation's credibility and tempted enemies to exploit opportunities at the expense of

---

My Lai South Vietnamese village and site of an intended search-and-destroy mission by U.S. soldiers that evolved into a brutal massacre of more than 300 unarmed civilians, including women and children; some were lined up in ditches and shot, with their village then burned to the ground.

The Image of War

The Vietnam War has been called the first "television war." More than ever before (or arguably since), news clips and photos brought Americans and others around the world face to face with the fighting and its victims. On June 8, 1972, as children and their families fled the village of Trang Bang, their bodies seared by napalm, Huynh Cong "Nick" Ut took this iconic photograph that became an antiwar rallying point and symbol of hope. The girl in the center, Phan Thi Kim Phuc, survived the attack but had to endure fourteen months of painful rehabilitation to treat the third-degree burns that covered more than half of her body. Kim later became a Canadian citizen and a Goodwill Ambassador for the United Nations Educational, Scientific and Cultural Organization (UNESCO).

CRITICAL THINKING

☐ Some analysts have argued that a single image can become the voice of popular protest; others say that even indelible images such as this one cannot have that power. What do you think?

Nick Ut/AP Images

U.S. interests. They pointed to a "Vietnam syndrome"—a resulting American suspicion of foreign entanglements—which they feared would inhibit the future exercise of U.S. power. America lost in Vietnam, they asserted, because Americans had lost their guts at home.

Dovish analysts drew different conclusions, denying that the military had suffered undue restrictions. Some blamed the war on an imperial presidency that had permitted strong-willed men to act without restraint and on a weak Congress that had conceded too much power to the executive branch. Make the president adhere to the checks-and-balances system—make him go to Congress for a declaration of war—these critics counseled, and America would become less interventionist. This view found expression in the War Powers Act of 1973, which sought to limit the president's war-making freedom. Henceforth, Congress would have to approve any commitment of U.S. forces to combat action lasting more than sixty days. In the same year, the draft (which

◁ On Memorial Day 2010, a Vietnam veteran prays over the name of a friend, one of the few American women killed in the war. The national Vietnam Veterans Memorial in Washington, D.C., was designed in 1980 by Maya Lin, then an undergraduate at Yale University. Critics called the memorial a "scar" and a "black gash of shame," but it has become the most visited site on the National Mall.

AP Photo/Jose Luis Magana

had been shifted to a lottery system in 1969) came to an end; the U.S. military would henceforth be a volunteer army.

27-2f Vietnam Veterans

Public discussion of the lessons of the Vietnam War was also stimulated by veterans' calls for help in dealing with posttraumatic stress disorder, which afflicted thousands of the 2.8 million Vietnam veterans. Once home, they suffered nightmares and extreme nervousness. Doctors reported that the disorder stemmed primarily from the soldiers' having seen so many children, women, and elderly people killed. Some GIs inadvertently killed these people; some killed them vengefully and later felt guilt. Other veterans heightened public awareness of the war by publicizing their deteriorating health from the effects of exposure to the defoliant Agent Orange and other herbicides they had handled or were accidentally sprayed with in Vietnam. The Vietnam Veterans Memorial, erected in Washington, D.C., in 1982, has kept the issue alive, as have many oral history projects of veterans conducted by school and college students in classes to this day.

27-3 Nixon, Kissinger, and the World

▷ How did Richard Nixon and Henry Kissinger seek to adapt the United States to a more multipolar world?

▷ How did Nixon seek to improve relations with the Soviet Union and China?

▷ How did Nixon and Kissinger seek to assert U.S. influence in the Middle East and Third World countries?

Even as Nixon and Kissinger tried to achieve victory in Vietnam, they understood that the United States had overreached in the 1960s with a military commitment that had caused massive bloodshed, deep domestic divisions, and economic dislocation. The difficulties of the war signified to them that American power was limited and, in relative terms, in decline. This reality necessitated a new approach to the Cold War, and both moved quickly to reorient American policy. In particular, they believed the United States had to adapt to a new, multipolar international system; no longer could that system be defined simply by the Soviet-American rivalry. Western Europe was becoming a major player in its own right, as was Japan. The Middle East loomed increasingly large, due in large part to America's growing dependence on oil from the region. Above all, Americans had to come to grips with the reality of China by rethinking the policy of hostile isolation followed by the United States since the communist takeover in 1949.

They were an unlikely duo—the reclusive, ambitious Californian, born of Quaker parents, and the sociable, dynamic Jewish intellectual who had fled Nazi Germany as a child. Nixon, ten years older, was more or less a career politician, while Kissinger had made his name as a Harvard professor and foreign policy consultant. Whereas Nixon was a staunch Republican, Kissinger had no strong partisan commitments and indeed said disparaging things about Republicans to his Democratic friends. What the two men had in common was a tendency toward paranoia about rivals and a capacity to think in broad conceptual terms about America's place in the world.

In July 1969, Nixon and Kissinger acknowledged the limits of American power and resources when they announced the Nixon Doctrine. The United States, they said, would continue to provide economic aid to allies in Asia

◁ "This was the week that changed the world," Richard Nixon said of his visit to China in February 1972. Many historians agree and consider the China opening Nixon's greatest achievement as president. When he and wife Pat visited the Great Wall, the president reportedly remarked: "This is a great wall."

and elsewhere, but these allies should no longer count on American troops. It was an admission that Washington could no longer afford to sustain its many overseas commitments and therefore would have to rely more on regional allies— including, it turned out, many authoritarian regimes—to maintain an anticommunist world order. Although Nixon did not say so, his doctrine amounted to a partial retreat from the 1947 Truman Doctrine, with its promise to support non-communist governments facing internal or external threats to their existence.

27-3a Détente

If the Nixon Doctrine was one pillar of the new foreign policy, the other was **détente**: measured cooperation with the Soviets through negotiations within a general environment of rivalry, drawn from the French word for "relaxation." Détente's primary purpose, like that of the containment doctrine it resembled, was to check Soviet expansion and limit the Soviet arms buildup, though now that goal would be accomplished through diplomacy and mutual concessions. The second part of the strategy sought to curb revolution and radicalism in the Third World so as to quash threats to American interests. More specifically, the Cold War and limited wars like that in Vietnam were costing too much; expanded trade with friendlier Soviets and Chinese might reduce the huge U.S. balance-of-payments deficit. And improving relations with both communist giants, at a time when Sino-Soviet tensions were increasing, might exacerbate feuding between the two, weakening communism.

The Soviet Union's leadership had its own reasons for wanting détente. The Cold War was a drain on its resources, too, and by the late 1960s defense needs and consumer demands were increasingly at odds. Improved ties with Washington would also allow the USSR to focus more on its

increasingly fractious relations with China and might generate serious progress on outstanding European issues, including the status of Germany and Berlin. Some ideologues in the Moscow leadership remained deeply suspicious of cozying up to the American capitalists, but they did not prevail over advocates of change. Thus, in May 1972, the United States and the USSR agreed in the ABM Treaty (officially the Treaty on the Limitation of Anti-Ballistic Missile Systems) to slow the costly arms race by limiting the construction and deployment of intercontinental ballistic missiles and antiballistic missile defenses.

27-3b Opening to China

While cultivating détente with the Soviet Union, the United States took dramatic steps to end more than two decades of Sino-American hostility. The Chinese welcomed the change because they wanted to spur trade and hoped that friendlier Sino-American relations would make their onetime ally and now enemy, the Soviet Union, more cautious. Nixon reasoned the same way: "We're using the Chinese thaw to get the Russians shook." In early 1972, Nixon made a historic trip to "Red China," where he and the venerable Chinese leaders Mao Zedong and Zhou Enlai agreed to disagree on a number of issues, except one: the Soviet Union should not be permitted to make gains in Asia. Sino-American relations improved slightly, and official diplomatic recognition and the exchange of ambassadors came in 1979.

The opening to communist China and the policy of détente with the Soviet Union reflected Nixon's and Kissinger's belief in the importance of maintaining stability among the great

détente Nixon's foreign policy initiative with the Soviet Union; it focused on mutual cooperation and sought to check expansion and reduce arms buildup through diplomacy and negotiation.

OPEC and the 1973 Oil Embargo

If one date can be said to have marked the relative decline of American power in the Cold War era and the arrival of the Arab nations of the Middle East as important players on the world stage, it would be October 20, 1973. That day, the Arab members of the Organization of Petroleum Exporting Countries (OPEC)—Saudi Arabia, Iraq, Kuwait, Libya, and Algeria—imposed a total embargo on oil shipments to the United States and to other allies of Israel. The move was in retaliation against U.S. support of Israel in the two-week-old Yom Kippur War. The embargo followed a decision by the members three days earlier to unilaterally raise oil prices, from $3.01 to $5.12 per barrel. In December, the five Arab countries, joined by Iran, raised prices again, to $11.65 per barrel, close to a fourfold increase from early October. "This decision," said National Security Adviser Henry Kissinger of the price hike, "was one of the pivotal events in the history of this century."

Kissinger exaggerated, but not by much. Gasoline prices surged across America, and some dealers ran low on supplies. Frustrated Americans endured endless lines at the pumps and shivered in underheated homes. Letters to newspaper editors expressed anger not merely at the Arab governments but also at the major oil companies, whose profits soared. When the embargo was lifted after five months, in March 1974, oil prices stayed high, and the aftereffects of the embargo would linger through the decade. Like no other event could, it confirmed the extent to which Americans no longer exercised full control over their own economic destiny.

Just twenty years before, in the early 1950s, Americans had produced at home all the oil they needed. Detroit automakers had no difficulty selling ever larger gas-guzzlers with ever more outrageous tail fins. By the early 1960s, the picture had begun to change, as American factories and automobiles then were dependent on foreign sources for one out of every six barrels of oil they used. By 1972, the figure had gone up to about two out of six,

or more than 30 percent. Although in absolute terms the amount was massive—U.S. motorists consumed one of every seven barrels used in the world each day—few Americans worried; hence the shock of the embargo. As author Daniel Yergin has put it, "The shortfall struck at fundamental beliefs in the endless abundance of resources, convictions so deeply rooted in the American character and experience that a large part of the public did not even know, up until October 1973, that the United States imported any oil at all."

Although Americans resumed their wasteful ways after the embargo ended, an important change had occurred, whether people understood it or not. The United States had become a dependent nation, its economic future linked to decisions by Arab leaders half a world away.

CRITICAL THINKING

▫ What lessons did the United States learn from the oil embargo?

▫ How did it affect foreign policy and national economic policies?

GAS SHORTAGE!
Sales Limited to
10 GALS. OF GAS.
PER CUSTOMER

Owen Franken/Getty Images

△ A common sight during the oil crisis of 1973–74 was long lines and ominous signs at service stations in the United States. In this image, taken in early 1974, a station in Connecticut makes its point clearly.

powers. In the Third World, too, they sought stability, though there they hoped to get it not by change but by maintaining the status quo. As it happened, events in the Third World would provide the Nixon-Kissinger approach with its greatest test, and not merely because of Vietnam.

In the Middle East, the situation had grown more volatile in the aftermath of the Arab-Israeli Six-Day War in 1967. In that conflict, Israel had scored victories against Egypt and Syria, seizing the Sinai Peninsula and the Gaza Strip from Egypt, the West Bank and East Jerusalem from Jordan, and the Golan Heights from Syria (see Map 29.2). Instantly, Israel's regional position was transformed, as it gained 28,000 square miles and could henceforth defend itself more easily against invading military forces. But the victory came at a price. Gaza and the West Bank were the ancestral home of hundreds of thousands of Palestinians and the more recent home of additional hundreds of thousands of Palestinian refugees from the 1948 Arab-Israeli conflict (see Section 24-6f "Arab-Israeli Conflict,"). Suddenly, Israel found itself governing large numbers of people who wanted nothing more than to see Israel destroyed. When the Israelis began to establish Jewish settlements in their newly won areas, Arab resentment grew even stronger. Terrorists associated with the Palestinian Liberation Organization (PLO) made hit-and-run raids on Jewish settlements, hijacked jetliners, and murdered eleven Israeli Olympic team members at the 1972 Olympic Games in Munich, West Germany. The Israelis retaliated by assassinating PLO leaders.

In October 1973, on the Jewish High Holy Day of Yom Kippur, Egypt and Syria attacked Israel. Their motives were complex, but primarily they sought revenge for the 1967 defeat. Caught by surprise, Israel reeled before launching an effective counteroffensive against Soviet-armed Egyptian forces in the Sinai. In an attempt to punish Americans for their pro-Israel stance, the Organization of Petroleum Exporting Countries (OPEC), a group of mostly Arab nations that had joined together to raise the price of oil, embargoed shipments of oil to the United States and other supporters of Israel. An energy crisis and dramatically higher oil prices rocked the nation. Soon Kissinger arranged a cease-fire in the war, but OPEC did not lift the oil embargo until March 1974. The next year, Kissinger persuaded Egypt and Israel to accept a UN peacekeeping force in the Sinai. But peace did not come to the region, for Palestinians and other Arabs still vowed to destroy Israel, and Israelis insisted on building more Jewish settlements in occupied lands.

27-3c Antiradicalism in Latin America and Africa

In Latin America, meanwhile, the Nixon administration sought to preserve stability and to thwart radical leftist challenges to authoritarian rule. In Chile, after voters in 1970 elected a Marxist president, Salvador Allende, the CIA began secret operations to disrupt Chile and encouraged military officers to stage a coup. In 1973, a military junta ousted Allende and installed an authoritarian regime under General Augusto Pinochet. (Allende was subsequently murdered.) Washington publicly denied any role in the affair that implanted iron-fisted tyranny in Chile for two decades.

In Africa as well, Washington preferred the status quo. Nixon backed the white-minority regime in Rhodesia (now Zimbabwe), while in South Africa he tolerated the white rulers who imposed the segregationist policy of apartheid on blacks and mixed-race "coloureds" (85 percent of the population), keeping them poor, disfranchised, and ghettoized in prisonlike townships. Elsewhere on the continent, Washington built economic ties and sent arms to friendly black nations, such as Kenya and the Republic of the Congo (Léopoldville) (now the Democratic Republic of the Congo). The administration also began to distance the United States from the white governments of Rhodesia and South Africa. America had to "prevent the radicalization of Africa," said Kissinger.

27-4 Presidential Politics and the Crisis of Leadership

▶ How did Nixon's personality and political beliefs shape his domestic policy record and lead to his downfall?

▶ In what ways was Nixon's domestic political agenda both liberal and conservative?

▶ What effect did the "Watergate" crisis have on American society and government?

Richard Nixon's foreign policy accomplishments were overshadowed by his failures at home. He betrayed the public trust and broke laws, large and small. His misconduct, combined with Americans' growing belief that their leaders had lied to them repeatedly about the war in Vietnam, shook Americans' faith in government. This new mistrust joined with conservatives' traditional suspicion of big, activist government to create a crisis of leadership and undermine liberal policies that had governed the nation since the New Deal, even in the Eisenhower era. The profound suspicion of presidential leadership and government action that enveloped the nation by the end of the Watergate hearings would limit what Gerald Ford and Jimmy Carter, Nixon's successors to the presidency, could accomplish.

27-4a Nixon's Domestic Agenda

Richard Nixon was brilliant, driven, politically cunning, able to address changing global realities with creativity. He was also crude, prejudiced against Jews and African Americans, happy to use dirty tricks and presidential power against those he considered his enemies, and driven by a sense of resentment that bordered on paranoia. Despite his tenacity and intelligence, Nixon—the son of a grocer from an agricultural region of southern California—was never accepted by the sophisticated northeastern liberal elite. (After Nixon's election, *Washingtonian* magazine joked that "cottage cheese with ketchup" had replaced elegant desserts at White House dinners.) Nixon loathed the liberal establishment, which loathed him back, and his presidency was driven by that hatred as much as by any strong philosophical commitment to conservative principles.

Nixon's domestic policy initiatives have long confused historians. Much of his agenda was liberal, expanding federal programs to improve society. The Nixon administration pioneered affirmative action. It doubled the budgets of the new National Endowment for the Humanities (NEH) and National Endowment for the Arts (NEA). Nixon supported the ERA, signed major environmental legislation, created the Occupational Safety and Health Administration (OSHA), actively attempted to manage the economy using deficit spending, and even proposed a guaranteed minimum income for all Americans.

At the same time, Nixon pursued a conservative agenda. One of his major legislative goals was "devolution," or shifting federal government authority to states and localities. He promoted revenue-sharing programs that distributed federal funds back to the states to use as they saw fit, thus appealing to those who were angry about, as they saw it, paying high taxes to support liberal "giveaway" programs for poor and minority Americans. As president, Nixon worked to equate the Republican Party with law and order and the Democrats with permissiveness, crime, drugs, radicalism, and the "hippie lifestyle." To capitalize on the backlash against the 1960s movements for social change and consolidate the support of those he called "the silent majority," Nixon fostered division, using his outspoken vice president, Spiro Agnew, to attack war protesters and critics as "naughty children," "effete . . . snobs," and "ideological eunuchs." He appointed four conservative justices to the Supreme Court: Warren Burger, Harry Blackmun, Lewis Powell Jr., and William Rehnquist.

With such a confusing record, was Nixon liberal, conservative, or simply pragmatic? The answer is complicated. For example, when the Nixon administration proposed a guaranteed minimum income for all Americans, including the working poor, his larger goal was to dismantle the federal welfare system and destroy its liberal bureaucracy of social workers (no longer necessary under Nixon's model). And though Nixon doubled funding for the NEA, he redirected awards from the northeastern art establishment—the "elite" that he thought of as an enemy—toward local and regional art groups that sponsored popular art forms, such as representational painting or folk music. Nixon did not reject a powerful role for the federal government, but he was suspicious of federal bureaucrats, social change activists, and intellectual elites.

In addition, recognizing the possibility of attracting white southerners to the Republican Party, Nixon pursued a highly pragmatic "southern strategy." He nominated two southerners for positions on the Supreme Court—one of whom had a segregationist record—and when Congress declined to confirm either nominee,

George McGovern Liberal senator from South Dakota and Democratic candidate for president in 1972.

Nixon protested angrily, saying, "I understand the bitter feelings of millions of Americans who live in the South." After the Supreme Court upheld a school desegregation plan that required a North Carolina school system—still highly segregated fifteen years after the *Brown* decision—to achieve racial integration by removing both black and white children from their neighborhood schools and busing them to schools elsewhere in the county (*Swann v. Charlotte-Mecklenburg*, 1971), Nixon denounced busing as a reckless and extreme remedy. (Neither resistance to busing nor continuing segregation was a purely southern phenomenon, as Boston showed in 1974 when residents protested—sometimes violently—court-ordered busing to combat school segregation.)

27-4b Enemies and Dirty Tricks

Nixon was almost sure of reelection in 1972. His Democratic opponent was **George McGovern**, a progressive senator from South Dakota and strong opponent of the Vietnam War. McGovern appealed to the left and essentially wrote off the middle, declaring, "I am not a centrist candidate." Alabama governor George Wallace, running on a third-party ticket, withdrew from the race after he was paralyzed in an assassination attempt. The Nixon campaign, however, was taking no chances. On June 17, four months before the election, five men tied to the Committee to Re-elect the President (CREEP) were caught breaking into the Democratic National Committee's offices at the Watergate complex in Washington, D.C. The break-in got little attention at the time, and Nixon was swept into office with 60 percent of the popular vote in November. McGovern carried only Massachusetts and the District of Columbia. But even as Nixon triumphed, his downfall had begun.

From the beginning of his presidency, Nixon was obsessed with the idea that, in a time of national turmoil, he was surrounded by enemies. He made "enemies lists," hundreds of names long, that included all black members of Congress and the presidents of most Ivy League universities. The Nixon administration worked, in the words of one of its members, to "use the available federal machinery to screw our political enemies." On Nixon's order, his aide Charles Colson (best known for his maxim "When you've got them by the balls, their hearts and minds will follow") formed a secret group called the Plumbers. Their first assignment was to break into the office of the psychiatrist treating Daniel Ellsberg, the former Pentagon employee who had gone public with the Pentagon Papers, looking for material to discredit him. The Plumbers expanded their "dirty tricks" operations during the 1972 presidential campaign, bugging phones, infiltrating campaign staffs, even writing and distributing anonymous letters falsely accusing Democratic candidates of sexual misconduct. They had already bugged the Democratic National Committee offices and were going back to plant more surveillance equipment when they were caught by the D.C. police at the Watergate complex.

27-4c Watergate Cover-up and Investigation

Nixon was not directly involved in the Watergate break-in. But instead of distancing himself and firing those responsible, he tried to cover it up, ordering the CIA to stop the FBI's investigation, claiming it imperiled national security. At this point, Nixon had obstructed justice—a felony and, under the Constitution, an impeachable crime—but he had also, it seemed, halted the investigation. However, two young, relatively unknown reporters for the *Washington Post*, Carl Bernstein and Bob Woodward, stayed on the story. Aided by an anonymous, highly placed government official whom they code-named Deep Throat (the title of a notorious 1972 X-rated film), they followed a money trail that led straight to the White House. (W. Mark Felt, who was second in command at the FBI in the early 1970s, publicly identified himself as Watergate's Deep Throat in 2005.)

From May to August 1973, the Senate held televised public hearings on the Watergate affair. White House Counsel John Dean, fearful that he was being made the fall guy for the entire Watergate fiasco, gave damning testimony. Then, on July 13, a White House aide told the Senate Committee that Nixon regularly recorded his conversations in the Oval Office. These tape recordings were the "smoking gun" that could prove Nixon's direct involvement in the cover-up—but Nixon refused to turn the tapes over to Congress.

27-4d Impeachment and Resignation

As Nixon and Congress fought over the tapes, Nixon faced scandals on other fronts. In October 1973, Vice President Spiro Agnew resigned, following charges that he had accepted bribes while governor of Maryland. Following constitutional procedures, Nixon appointed and Congress approved Michigan's **Gerald Ford**, the House minority leader, as Agnew's replacement. Meanwhile, Nixon's staff grew increasingly concerned about his excessive drinking and seeming mental instability. Then, on October 24, 1973, the House of Representatives began impeachment proceedings against the president.

Under court order, Nixon began releasing edited portions of the Oval Office tapes to Congress. Although the first tapes revealed no criminal activity, the public was shocked by Nixon's constant obscenities and racist slurs. Finally, in July 1974, the Supreme Court ruled that Nixon must release all the tapes. Despite "mysterious" erasures on two key tapes, the House Judiciary Committee found evidence of three impeachable offenses: obstruction of justice, abuse of power, and contempt of Congress. On August 9, 1974, facing certain impeachment and conviction, Richard Nixon became the first president of the United States to resign his office.

The Watergate scandal shook the confidence of American citizens in their government. It also prompted Congress to reevaluate the balance of power between the executive and legislative branches. New laws intended to restrict presidential power included the War Powers Act and the 1974 Budget and Impoundment Control Act, which made it impossible for the president to disregard congressional spending mandates.

27-4e Ford's Presidency

Gerald Ford, the nation's first unelected president, faced a nation awash in cynicism. The presidency was discredited. The economy was in decline. The nation's people were divided. When, in one of his first official acts as president, Ford issued a full pardon to Richard Nixon, forestalling any attempts to bring criminal charges, his approval ratings plummeted from 71 to 41 percent. Some suggested, with no evidence, that he had struck some sort of sordid deal with Nixon. Ford insisted, for decades, that he had simply acted in the interest of the nation, but shortly before his death in late 2006 he told a reporter that, though few knew it, he and Nixon had been good friends and that he "didn't want to see my real friend have the stigma" of criminal charges.

While Ford was, overall, a decent and honorable man who did his best to end what he called "the long national nightmare," he accomplished little domestically during his two and a half years in office. The Democrats gained a large margin in the 1974 congressional elections and, after Watergate, Congress was willing to exercise its power. Ford almost routinely vetoed its bills—thirty-nine in one year—but Congress often overrode his veto. And Ford had become the object of constant mockery, portrayed as a buffoon and a klutz in political cartoons, comedy monologues, and especially on the new hit television show *Saturday Night Live*. When Ford slipped on the steps exiting *Air Force One*, all major newscasts showed the footage. The irony of portraying Ford—who had turned down a chance to play in the National Football League in order to attend Yale Law School—as physically inept was extraordinary. But as Ford understood, these portrayals began to give the impression that he was a "stumbler," in danger of making blunders of all kinds. Ford caught the fallout of disrespect that Nixon's actions had unleashed. No longer would respect for the office of the presidency prevent the mass media from reporting presidential slips, stumbles, frailties, or misconduct. Ford was the first president to discover how much the rules had changed.

27-4f Carter as "Outsider" President

Jimmy Carter, who was elected in 1976 by a slim margin, initially benefited from Americans' suspicion of politicians. Carter was a one-term governor of Georgia, one of the new southern leaders who were committed to racial equality and integration. He had grown up in the rural Georgia town of Plains, where his family owned a peanut farm, graduated from the U.S. Naval Academy, then served as an engineer in the navy's nuclear submarine program. Carter, a deeply religious born-again Christian, made a virtue of his lack of political experience. Promising the American people, "I will

Gerald Ford Michigan congressman who took the place of Vice President Spiro Agnew when Agnew resigned following charges of corruption. Ford became the thirty-eighth president of the United States when Nixon resigned in 1974.

Jimmy Carter Thirty-ninth president of the United States (1977–1981).

△ Resigning in disgrace as impeachment for his role in the Watergate cover-up became a certainty, Richard Nixon flashes the "V for victory" sign as he leaves the White House for the last time.

never lie to you," he emphasized his distance from Washington and the political corruption of recent times.

From his inauguration, when he broke with the convention of a motorcade and walked down Pennsylvania Avenue holding hands with his wife and close adviser, Rosalynn, and their young daughter, Amy, Carter rejected the trappings of the imperial presidency and emphasized his populist, outsider appeal. But the outsider status that gained him the presidency would make Carter a less effective president. Though he was an astute policymaker, he scorned the sort of deal making necessary to get legislation through Congress.

Carter faced problems that would have challenged any leader: the economy continued to decline, energy shortages had not abated, the American people distrusted their government. More than any other American leader of the post–World War II era, Carter was willing to tell the American people things they did not want to hear. As shortages of natural gas forced schools and businesses to close during the bitterly cold winter of 1977, Carter went on television—wearing a cardigan sweater—to call for "sacrifice" in a new era of limits. Carter tried to model that sacrifice: he had White House thermostats lowered to a daytime temperature of 65 degrees and asked all Americans to do the same. He also tried to shape policy, submitting a detailed, conservation-based energy plan to Congress. And he moved beyond concrete solutions. In the defining speech of his presidency Carter told Americans that the nation suffered from a crisis of the spirit. He talked about the false lures of "self-indulgence and consumption," about "paralysis and stagnation and drift." And he called for a "new commitment to the path of common purpose." But his words failed to inspire Americans to break free of what was then described as a national malaise.

Carter did score some noteworthy domestic accomplishments. He worked to ease burdensome government regulations without destroying consumer and worker safeguards, and created the Department of Energy and the Department of Education. He also established a $1.6 billion "superfund" to clean up abandoned chemical waste sites and placed more than 100 million acres of Alaskan land under the federal government's protection as national parks, national forests, and wildlife refuges.

27-5 Economic Crisis

▷ What were the causes of the economic crisis in the 1970s?

▷ How did the federal government attempt to manage the economic crisis in the 1970s?

▷ How did Americans respond to the economic crisis of the 1970s?

Americans' loss of confidence in their political leaders was intensified by a growing economic crisis. Since World War II, except for a few brief downturns, prosperity had been a fundamental condition of American life. A steadily rising gross national product, based largely on growing rates of productivity, had propelled large numbers of Americans into the economically comfortable middle class. Prosperity had made possible the great liberal initiatives of the 1960s and improved the lives of America's poor and elderly citizens. But in the early 1970s, that long period of economic expansion and prosperity came to an end. Almost every economic indicator drove home bad news. In 1974 alone, the gross national product dropped 2 full percentage points. Industrial production fell 9 percent. Inflation—the increase in costs of goods and services—skyrocketed, and unemployment grew.

27-5a Stagflation and Its Causes

Throughout most of the 1970s, the U.S. economy floundered in a condition that economists dubbed "stagflation": a stagnant economy characterized by high unemployment combined with out-of-control inflation (see Figure 27.1). Stagflation was almost impossible to manage with traditional economic remedies. When the federal government increased spending to stimulate the economy and so reduce unemployment, inflation grew. When the federal government tried to rein in inflation by cutting government spending or tightening the money supply, the recession deepened and unemployment rates skyrocketed.

The causes of the economic crisis were complex. Federal management of the economy was in part to blame: President Johnson had reversed conventional economic wisdom and created inflationary pressure by insisting that the United States could have both "guns and butter" as he waged a very expensive war in Vietnam while greatly expanding domestic spending in his Great Society programs. But America's changing role in the global economy also created problems. After World War II, with most leading industrial nations in ruins, the United States had stood alone at the pinnacle of the global economy. But in the decades that followed, the war-ravaged nations—often with major economic assistance from the United States—had built new, technologically advanced industrial plants. By the early 1970s, both of America's major wartime adversaries, Japan and Germany, had become major economic powers—and major competitors in global trade. U.S. trade laws allowed easy access to American consumers even as those nations restricted American imports. In 1971, for the first time since the end of the nineteenth century, the United States imported more goods than it exported, beginning an era of American trade deficits.

American corporations were also to blame. During the years of global dominance, few American companies saw the need to improve production techniques or educate workers, and thus American productivity—that is, the average

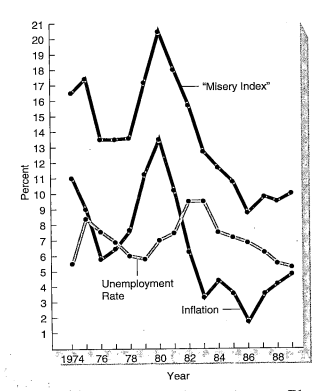

Figure 27.1 "Misery Index" (Unemployment Plus Inflation), 1974–1989

Americans' economic discomfort directly determined their political behavior. When the "misery index" was high in 1976 and 1980, Americans voted for a change in presidents. When economic discomfort declined in 1984 and 1988, Ronald Reagan and George Bush were the political beneficiaries. *Source: Adapted from* Economic Report of the President, 1992 *(Washington, D.C.: 1992), pp. 340, 365.*

output of goods per hour of labor—had begun to decline. As workers' productivity declined, however, their wages rarely did. High labor costs combined with falling productivity made American goods more and more expensive—both for Americans and for consumers in other nations. Even worse, without significant competition from foreign manufacturers, American companies had allowed the quality of their goods to decline. From 1966 to 1973, for example, American car and truck manufacturers had to recall almost 30 million vehicles because of serious defects.

America's global economic vulnerability was driven home by the energy crisis that began in 1973. Americans had grown up with cheap and abundant energy, and their lifestyles showed it. American passenger cars got an average of 13.4 miles per gallon in 1973, when a gallon of gas cost 38 cents (about $2.07 in 2016 dollars); neither home-heating nor household appliances were designed to be energy efficient. The country, however, depended on imported oil for almost one-third of its energy supply. When OPEC cut off oil shipments to the United States, U.S. oil prices rose 350 percent. The increases reverberated through the economy: heating costs, shipping costs, and manufacturing costs increased, and so did the cost of goods and services. Inflation jumped from 3 percent in early 1973 to 11 percent in 1974. Sales of gas-guzzling American cars plummeted as people rushed to buy energy-efficient subcompacts from Japan and Europe. American car manufacturers, stuck with machinery for producing large cars, were hit hard. GM laid off 6 percent of its domestic workforce and put an even larger number on rolling unpaid leaves. As the ailing automobile industry quit buying steel, glass, and rubber, manufacturers of these goods laid off workers, too.

27-5b Attempts to Fix the Economy

American political leaders tried desperately to manage the economic crisis, but their actions often exacerbated it instead. As America's rising trade deficit undermined international confidence in the dollar, the Nixon administration ended the dollar's link to the gold standard; free-floating exchange rates increased the price of foreign goods in the United States and stimulated inflation. President Ford created a voluntary program, Whip Inflation Now (complete with red and white "WIN" buttons), in 1974 to encourage grassroots anti-inflation efforts. Following the tenets of monetary theory, which held that, with less money available to "chase" the supply of goods, price increases would gradually slow down, ending the inflationary spiral, Ford curbed federal spending and encouraged the Federal Reserve Board

to tighten credit—and prompted the worst recession in forty years. In 1975, unemployment climbed to 8.5 percent.

Carter first attempted to bring unemployment rates down by stimulating the economy, but inflation careened out of control; he then tried to slow the economy down—and prompted a major recession during the election year of 1980. One approach pointed in a new direction: both Ford and Carter pinned their hopes less on government regulation than on market competition, and the Carter administration led a bipartisan effort to deregulate airline, trucking, banking, and communications industries. But at the end of the decade, the economy was still in crisis and Americans were losing faith in the American economy and in the ability of their political leaders to manage it.

27-5c Impacts of the Economic Crisis

The economic crisis of the 1970s accelerated the nation's transition from an industrial to a service economy. During the 1970s, the American economy "deindustrialized." Automobile companies laid off workers. Massive steel plants shut down, leaving entire communities devastated. Other manufacturing concerns moved overseas, seeking lower labor costs and fewer government regulations. New jobs were created—27 million of them—but they were overwhelmingly in the lower end of what economists call the "service sector": retail sales, restaurants, warehouse and transportation work. As heavy industries collapsed, formerly highly paid, unionized workers took

△ Long lines of people seeking unemployment benefits formed in this St. Louis suburb after nearby Chrysler auto and truck assembly plants shut down.

jobs in the growing—but not unionized—service sector, most of which paid lower wages and lacked health care benefits. Formerly successful blue-collar workers saw their middle-class standard of living slipping away.

In addition, more people were chasing fewer jobs. Married homemakers looked for work because inflation steadily ate away at their husbands' wages. Baby boomers added pressure; even in the best of times the economy would have been hard pressed to produce jobs for the millions of young people who entered the labor market in the 1970s. Young people graduating from high school or college in the 1970s had been raised with high expectations. Instead, they found new limits.

The economic crisis also helped to shift the economic and population centers of the nation. As the old industrial regions of the North and Midwest went into decline, people fled the "snow belt" or the "rust belt," speeding up the Sunbelt boom already in progress (see Map 27.1). The Sunbelt was where the jobs were. The federal government had invested heavily in the South and West during the postwar era, especially in military and defense industries, and in the infrastructures necessary for them. Never a major center for heavy manufactures, the Sunbelt was primed for the rapid growth of modern industries and services—aerospace, defense, electronics, transportation, research, banking and finance, and leisure. City and state governments competed to lure businesses and investment dollars, in part by preventing the growth of

unions. Atlanta, Houston, and other southern cities marketed themselves as cosmopolitan, sophisticated, and racially tolerant; they bought sports teams and built museums.

This population shift south and west, combined with the flight of middle-class taxpayers to the suburbs, created disaster in northern and midwestern cities. New York City, close to financial collapse by late 1975, was saved only when the House and Senate Banking Committees approved federal loan guarantees. Cleveland defaulted on its debts in 1978, the first major city to do so since Detroit declared bankruptcy in 1933.

27-5d Tax Revolts

Even as stagflation and Sunbelt growth transformed American politics, a "tax revolt" movement emerged in the rapidly growing American West. In California, inflation had driven property taxes up rapidly, hitting middle-class taxpayers hard. In this era of economic decline and post-Watergate suspicion, angry taxpayers saw government as the problem. Instead of calling for wealthy citizens and major corporations to pay a larger share of taxes, voters rebelled against taxation itself. California's Proposition 13, passed by a landslide in 1978, rolled back property taxes and restricted future increases. Within months of Proposition 13's passage, thirty-seven states cut property taxes, and twenty-eight lowered their state income tax rates.

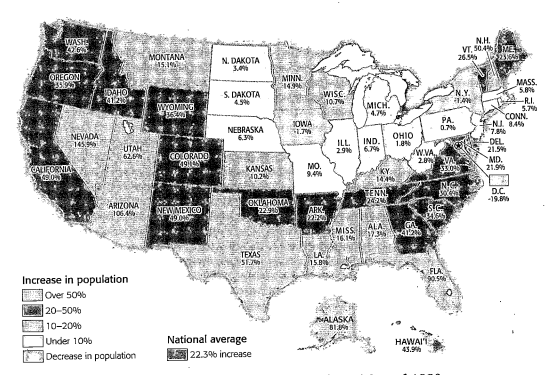

Map 27.1 The Continued Shift to the Sunbelt in the 1970s and 1980s

Throughout the 1970s and 1980s, Americans continued to leave economically declining areas of the North and East in pursuit of opportunity in the Sunbelt. States in the Sunbelt and in the West had the largest population increases. *Source: "Shift to the Sunbelt," Newsweek, September 10, 1990.*

The impact of Proposition 13 and similar initiatives was initially cushioned by state budget surpluses, but as those surpluses turned to deficits, states cut services—closing fire stations and public libraries, ending or limiting mental health services and programs for the disabled. Public schools were hit especially hard. The tax revolt movement signaled the growth of a new conservatism; voters who wanted lower taxes and smaller government would help bring Ronald Reagan to the White House in the election of 1980.

27-5e Credit and Investment

The runaway inflation of the 1970s also changed how Americans managed their money. Before this era, home mortgages and auto loans were the only kind of major debt most Americans would venture. National credit cards had become common only in the late 1960s, and few Americans—especially those who remembered the Great Depression—were willing to spend money they did not have. In the 1970s, however, thriftiness stopped making sense. Double-digit inflation rates meant double-digit declines in the purchasing power of a dollar. It was economically smarter to buy goods before their prices went up—even if it meant borrowing the money. Because debt was paid off later with devalued dollars, the consumer came out ahead. In 1975, consumer debt hit a high of $167 billion; by 1979 that figure had almost doubled, to $315 billion.

The 1970s were also the decade in which average Americans became investors rather than savers. Throughout the 1970s, because of regulations created during the Great Depression, the interest rates that banks could pay on individual savings accounts were capped. An average savings account bearing 5 percent interest actually *lost* more than 20 percent of its value from 1970 through 1980 because of inflation. That same money, invested at market rates, would have grown dramatically. Fidelity Investments, a mutual fund company, saw a business opportunity: its money market accounts combined many smaller investments to purchase large-denomination Treasury bills and certificates of deposit, thus allowing small investors to get the high interest rates normally available only to major investors. Money flooded out of passbook accounts and into money funds, and money market investments grew from $1.7 billion in 1974 to $200 billion in 1982. At the same time, deregulation of the New York Stock Exchange spawned discount brokerage houses, whose low commission rates made it affordable for middle-class investors to trade stocks.

27-6 An Era of Cultural Transformation

▷ Why were Americans uneasy about the state of the environment and technological change?

▷ How did sexual behavior and expectations about the family change during this decade?

▷ How does the emphasis on "diversity" emerge, and how does it differ from affirmative action?

During the 1970s, as Americans struggled with economic recession, government betrayal, and social division, they also transformed critical parts of American culture. The current environmental movement, the growth of technology, the rise of born-again Christianity and a "therapeutic culture," contemporary forms of sexuality and the family, new roles for youth, and America's emphasis on diversity all have roots in this pivotal decade.

27-6a Environmentalism

Just as Americans were forced to confront the end of postwar prosperity, a series of ecological crises drove home the limits on natural resources and the fragility of the environment. In 1969, a major oil spill took place off the coast of Santa Barbara, California; that same year, the polluted Cuyahoga River, flowing through Cleveland, caught fire. Although the energy crisis of the 1970s was due to an oil embargo, not a scarcity of oil, it drove home the real limits of the world's supplies of oil and natural gas. In 1979, human error contributed to a nuclear accident at the Three Mile Island nuclear power plant near Harrisburg, Pennsylvania; in 1980, President Carter declared a federal emergency in the Niagara Falls, New York neighborhood of Love Canal—which had previously served as a dump site for a local chemical manufacturer—after it was discovered that over 30 percent of local residents had suffered chromosomal damage from exposure to toxic chemicals that had leaked from the dump. Public activism during the 1970s produced major environmental regulations and initiatives, from the Environmental Protection Agency (EPA), created (under strong public pressure) in 1970 by the Nixon administration, to eighteen major environmental laws enacted by Congress during the decade.

When 20 million Americans—half of them schoolchildren—gathered in local communities to celebrate the first Earth Day on April 22, 1970, they signaled the triumph of a relatively new understanding of environmentalism. Traditional concerns about preserving "unspoiled" wilderness had joined with a new focus on "ecology," which stressed the connections between the earth and all living organisms, including humans. Central to this movement was a recognition that the earth's resources were finite and must be both conserved and protected from the consequences of human action, such as pollution. In 1971, biologist Barry Commoner insisted, "The present course of environmental degradation . . . is so serious, that, if continued, it will destroy the capability of the environment to support a reasonably civilized human society." Many of those concerned about the strain on earth's resources also identified rapid global population growth as a problem, and state public health offices frequently dispensed contraceptives as a way to stem this new "epidemic."

27-6b Technology

During these years, Americans became increasingly uneasy about the science and technology that had been one source

△ Students at Cerritos College celebrate the first Earth Day, April 22, 1970. More than 20 million Americans participated in local teach-ins, celebrations, and protests to draw attention to environmental issues. By 1990, Earth Day was observed throughout the world, drawing 200 million participants from 141 nations.

Julian Wasser/Getty Images

of America's might. In a triumph of technology, American astronaut **Neil Armstrong** stepped onto the lunar surface on July 20, 1969, as people worldwide watched the grainy television transmission and heard, indistinctly, his first words—"That's one small step for [a] man, one giant leap for mankind." But the advances that could take a man to the moon seemed unable to cope with earthbound problems of poverty, crime, pollution, and urban decay; and the failure of technological warfare to deliver victory in Vietnam came at the same time antiwar protesters were questioning the morality of using such technology. Some Americans joined a movement for "appropriate technology" and human-scale development, but the nation was profoundly dependent on complex technological systems. And it was during the 1970s that the foundation was laid for America's computer revolution. The integrated circuit was created in 1970, and by 1975 the MITS Altair

8800—operated by toggle switches that entered individual binary numbers, boasting 256 bytes of memory, and requiring about thirty hours to assemble—could be mail-ordered from Albuquerque, New Mexico.

27-6c Religion and the Therapeutic Culture

As Americans confronted material limits, they increasingly sought spiritual fulfillment and well-being. Some turned to religion, though not to traditional mainstream Protestantism. Methodist, Presbyterian, and Episcopalian churches all lost members during this era, while membership in evangelical and fundamentalist Christian churches grew dramatically. Protestant evangelicals, professing a personal relationship with their savior, described themselves as "born again" and emphasized the immediate, daily presence of God in their lives. Even some Catholics, such as the Mexican Americans who embraced the *cursillo* movement (a "little course" in faith), sought a more personal relationship with God. Other Americans looked to the variety of beliefs and practices described as "New Age." The New Age movement drew from, and often combined, versions of nonwestern spiritual and religious practices, including Zen Buddhism, yoga, and shamanism, along with insights from Western psychology and a form of spiritually oriented environmentalism. Some desires for spiritual comfort went badly wrong, as when 907 members of the People's Temple, a religious cult led by James Jones, committed "revolutionary suicide" by drinking cyanide-laced Kool-Aid at "Jonestown," the group's compound in Guyana, in 1978.

Also in the 1970s, America saw the full emergence of a "therapeutic" culture. Although some Americans were disgusted with the self-centeredness of the "Me Decade," best-selling books by therapists and self-help gurus insisted that individual feelings offered the ultimate measure of truth; emotional honesty and self-awareness were social goods surpassing the bonds of community, friendship, or family. Self-help books with titles like *I Ain't Much Baby—But I'm All I've Got*, or *I'm OK—You're OK* (first published in 1967, it became a best seller in the mid-1970s) made up 15 percent of all best-selling books during the decade.

27-6d Sexuality and the Family

One such self-help book was *The Joy of Sex* (1972), which sold 3.8 million copies in two years. Sex became much more visible in America's public culture during the 1970s, as network television loosened its regulation of sexual content. At the beginning of the 1960s, married couples in television shows were required to occupy twin beds; in the 1970s, hit television shows included *Three's Company*, a situation comedy based on the then-scandalous premise that a single man shared an apartment with two beautiful female roommates—and got away with it only by pretending to their suspicious landlord

Neil Armstrong First person to set foot on the moon.

that he was gay. *Charlie's Angels*, another major television hit, capitalized on what people called the "jiggle factor" and displayed (for the time) lots of bare female flesh. A major youth fad of the era was "streaking," running naked through public places. Donna Summers's 1975 disco hit "Love to Love You Baby" contained sixteen minutes of sexual moaning. Discos were sites of sexual display, both for gay men and for macho working-class cultures; the hustle (a dance) originated in a Latino section of the Bronx, and the 1977 hit film *Saturday Night Fever* portrayed an Italian American young man who escaped the confines of his family and the limits of his dead-end job in sexually charged dance at a Brooklyn disco. And though very few Americans participated in heterosexual orgies at New York City's Plato's Retreat, many knew about them through a *Time* magazine feature story.

Sexual behaviors had also changed. The 1970s were the era of singles bars and gay bathhouses, and some Americans led sexual lives virtually unrestrained by the old rules. For most Americans, however, the major changes brought about by the "sexual revolution" were a broader public acceptance of premarital sex and a limited acceptance of homosexuality, especially among more educated Americans. More and more heterosexual young people lived together without marriage during the 1970s; the census bureau even coined the term *POSSLQ* ("persons of opposite sex sharing living quarters") to describe the relationship. When First Lady Betty Ford said on 60 *Minutes* that she would not be surprised if her then-seventeen-year-old daughter Susan began a sexual relationship, it was clear that much had changed in the course of a decade.

Changes in sexual mores and in the roles possible for women helped to alter the shape of the American family as well. Both men and women married later than in recent decades, and American women had fewer children. By the end of the 1970s, the birth rate had dropped almost 40 percent from its 1957 peak. Almost one-quarter of young single women in 1980 said that they did not plan to have children. And a steadily rising percentage of babies was born to unmarried women, as the number of families headed by never-married women rose 400 percent during the 1970s. The divorce rate also rose, in part because states implemented "no fault" divorce. Although families seemed less stable in the 1970s than in the previous postwar decades, Americans also developed a greater acceptance of various family forms (the blended family of television's *Brady Bunch*, for example), and many young couples sought greater equality between the sexes in romantic relationships or marriages.

27-6e Youth

Young people gained new freedoms and responsibilities in American society during the 1970s, but they also confronted economic crisis and social upheaval. In 1971, partly in recognition that the eighteen-year-old men who were eligible for the draft were not eligible to vote, Congress passed—and the states quickly ratified—the Twenty-sixth Amendment, which guaranteed the right of eighteen-year-olds to vote. In a similar impulse, twenty-nine states lowered their minimum drinking age. Marijuana use skyrocketed, and several states moved toward decriminalization. As young people graduated from high school or college, they were more likely to live with others their own age than with their parents. In the early part of the decade, some young people established communes—both urban and rural—and attempted to create countercultural worlds outside "the system." Later in the decade, a very different group of young people, partly in reaction to a postindustrial landscape of limited opportunity and the seeming impossibility of political change, created the punk movement, which offered new physical and cultural spaces for youth both through music and its do-it-yourself ethic.

27-6f Diversity

The racial justice and identity movements of the late 1960s and the 1970s made all Americans more aware of differences among the nation's peoples—an awareness made stronger by the great influx of new immigrants, not from Europe but from Latin America and Asia. It was a challenge, however, to figure out how to acknowledge the new importance of "difference" in public policy. The solution developed in the 1970s was the idea of "diversity." Difference was not a problem but a strength; the nation should not seek policies to diminish differences among its peoples but should instead seek to foster the "diversity" of its schools, workplaces, and public culture.

One major move in this direction came in the 1978 Supreme Court decision *Regents of the University of California v. Bakke*. Allan Bakke, a thirty-three-year-old white man with a strong academic record, had been denied admission to the medical school of the University of California at Davis. Bakke sued, charging that he had been denied "equal protection" of the law because the medical school's affirmative action program reserved 16 percent of its slots for racial minority candidates, who were held to lower standards than other applicants. The case set off furious debates nationwide over the legitimacy of affirmative action. In 1978, the Supreme Court, in a split decision, decided in favor of Bakke. Four justices argued that any race-based decision violated the Civil Rights Act of 1964; four saw affirmative action programs as constitutionally acceptable remedies for past discrimination. The deciding vote, though for Bakke, contained an important qualification. A "diverse student body," Justice Lewis Powell wrote, is "a constitutionally permissible goal for an institution of higher education." To achieve the positive quality of "diversity," educational institutions could take race into account when making decisions about admissions.

27-7 Renewed Cold War and Middle East Crisis

▷ **What challenges did Jimmy Carter face in implementing his foreign policy?**

▷ **How did the relationship between the United States and the Middle East develop during Jimmy Carter's presidency?**

▷ **What factors contributed to tense relations between the Soviet Union and the United States?**

When Jimmy Carter took office in 1977, he asked Americans to put their "inordinate fear of Communism" behind them. With reformist zeal, Carter vowed to reduce the U.S. military presence overseas, to cut back arms sales (which had reached the unprecedented height of $10 billion per year under Nixon), and to slow the nuclear arms race. At the time, more than 400,000 American military personnel were stationed abroad, the United States had military links with ninety-two nations, and the CIA was active on every continent. Carter promised to avoid new Vietnams through an activist preventive diplomacy in the Third World and to give more attention to environmental issues as well as relations between rich and poor nations. He especially determined to improve human rights abroad—the freedom to vote, worship, travel, speak out, and get a fair trial. Like his predecessors, however, Carter identified revolutionary nationalism as a threat to America's prominent global position.

27-7a Carter's Divided Administration

Carter spoke and acted inconsistently, in part because in the post-Vietnam years, no consensus existed in foreign policy and in part because his advisers squabbled among themselves. One source of the problem was the stern-faced Zbigniew Brzezinski, a Polish-born political scientist who became Carter's national security adviser. An old-fashioned Cold Warrior, Brzezinski blamed foreign crises on Soviet expansionism. Carter gradually listened more to Brzezinski than to Secretary of State Cyrus Vance, an experienced public servant who advocated quiet diplomacy. Vocal neoconservative intellectuals, such as Norman Podhoretz, editor of *Commentary* magazine, and the Committee on the Present Danger, founded in 1976 by such Cold War hawks as Paul Nitze, who had composed NSC-68 in 1950, criticized Carter for any relaxation of the Cold War and demanded that he jettison détente.

Nitze got his wish. Under Carter, détente deteriorated, and the Cold War deepened. But it did not happen right away. Initially, Carter maintained fairly good relations with Moscow and was able to score some foreign policy successes around the world. In Panama, where citizens longed for control over the Canal Zone, which they believed had been wrongfully taken from them in 1903, Carter reenergized

negotiations that had begun after anti-American riots in Panama in 1964. The United States signed two treaties with Panama in 1977. One provided for the return of the Canal Zone to Panama in 2000, and the other guaranteed the United States the right to defend the canal after that time. With conservatives denouncing the deal as a sellout, the Senate narrowly endorsed both agreements in 1978. The majority agreed with Carter's argument that relinquishing the canal was the best way to improve U.S. relations with Latin America.

27-7b Camp David Accords

Important though it was, the Panama agreement paled next to what must be considered the crowning accomplishment of Carter's presidency: the **Camp David Accords**, the first mediated peace treaty between Israel and an Arab nation. Through tenacious personal diplomacy at a Camp David, Maryland, meeting in September 1978 with Egyptian and Israeli leaders, the president persuaded Israel and Egypt to agree to a peace treaty, gained Israel's promise to withdraw from the Sinai Peninsula, and forged a provisional agreement that provided for continued negotiations on the future status of the Palestinian people living in the occupied territories of Jordan's West Bank and Egypt's Gaza Strip (see Map 29.2). Other Arab states denounced the agreement for not requiring Israel to relinquish all occupied territories and for not guaranteeing a Palestinian homeland. But the accord at least ended warfare along one frontier in that troubled area of the world. On March 26, 1979, Israeli prime minister Menachem Begin and Egyptian president Anwar al-Sadat signed the formal treaty on the White House lawn, with a beaming Carter looking on.

27-7c Soviet Invasion of Afghanistan

Carter's moment of diplomatic triumph did not last long, for soon other foreign policy problems pressed in. Relations with Moscow had deteriorated, with U.S. and Soviet officials sparring over the Kremlin's reluctance to lift restrictions on Jewish emigration from the USSR, and over the Soviet decision to deploy new intermediate-range ballistic missiles aimed at Western Europe. Then, in December 1979, the Soviets invaded Afghanistan. A remote, mountainous country, Afghanistan had long been a source of great-power conflict because of its strategic position. In the nineteenth century, it was the fulcrum of the Great Game, the contest between Britain and Russia for control of Central Asia and India. Following World War II, Afghanistan settled into a pattern of ethnic and factional squabbling; few in the West paid attention until the country spiraled into anarchy in the

Camp David Accords
Agreements that were signed by Egypt's President Sadat and Israel's Prime Minister Begin following twelve days of secret negotiations—arranged by President Carter—at Camp David.

△ Egyptian President Anwar al-Sadat, U.S. President Jimmy Carter, and Israeli Prime Minister Menachem Begin sit together outside the White House on March 26, 1979, ready to sign the peace treaty based on the Camp David Accords of September 1978. The treaty ended the long-standing state of war between Egypt and Israel.

1970s. In late 1979, the Red Army bludgeoned its way into Afghanistan to shore up a faltering communist government under siege by Muslim rebels. Moscow officials calculated that they could be in and out of the country before anyone really noticed, including the Americans.

To their dismay, Carter not only noticed but reacted forcefully—no doubt in part because of the test he faced simultaneously with the hostage crisis in neighboring Iran. He suspended shipments of grain and high-technology equipment to the Soviet Union, withdrew a major new arms control treaty from Senate consideration, and initiated an international boycott of the 1980 Summer Olympics in Moscow. He also secretly authorized the CIA to distribute aid, including arms and military support, to the Mujahidin (Islamic guerillas) fighting the communist government and sanctioned military aid to their backer, Pakistan. Announcing the Carter Doctrine, the president asserted that the United States would intervene, unilaterally and militarily if necessary, should Soviet aggression threaten the petroleum-rich Persian Gulf. This string of measures represented a victory of the hawkish Brzezinski over the pro-détente Vance. Indeed, Carter seemed more ardent than Brzezinski in his denunciations of the Kremlin. He warned aides that the Soviets, unless checked, would likely attack elsewhere in the Middle East, but declassified documents confirm

what critics at the time said: that the Soviet invasion was limited in scope and did not presage a push southwest to the Persian Gulf.

The Iranian revolution, together with the rise of the Mujahidin in Afghanistan, signified the emergence of Islamic fundamentalism as a force in world affairs. Socialism and capitalism, the great answers that the two superpowers offered to the problems of modernization, had failed to solve the problems in Central Asia and the Middle East, let alone satisfy the passions and expectations they had aroused. Nor had they assuaged deeply held feelings of humiliation generated by centuries of Western domination. As a result, Islamic orthodoxy found growing support for its message: that secular leaders such as Nasser in Egypt and the shah in Iran had taken their peoples down the wrong path, necessitating a return to conservative Islamic values and Islamic law. The Iranian revolution in particular expressed a deep and complex mixture of discontent within many Islamic societies.

27-7d Rise of Saddam Hussein

U.S. officials took some consolation from the fact that Iran faced growing friction from the avowedly secular government in neighboring Iraq. Ruled by the Ba'athist Party (a secular and quasi-socialist party with branches in several Arab countries), Iraq had already won favor in Washington

△ In June 1980, midway through the Iran Hostage Crisis, a group of anti-American protesters set fire to a U.S. flag on the roof of the occupied U.S. embassy in Tehran.

for its ruthless pursuit and execution of Iraqi communists. When a Ba'athist leader named Saddam Hussein took over as president of Iraq in 1979 and began threatening the Tehran government, U.S. officials were not displeased; to them, Saddam seemed likely to offset the Iranian danger in the Persian Gulf region. As border clashes between Iraqi and Iranian forces escalated in 1980, culminating in the outbreak of large-scale war in September, Washington policymakers took an officially neutral position but soon tilted toward Iraq.

Jimmy Carter's record in foreign affairs sparked considerable criticism from both left and right. He had earned some diplomatic successes in the Middle East, Africa, and Latin America, but the revived Cold War and the prolonged Iranian hostage crisis had hurt the administration politically. Contrary to Carter's goals, more American military personnel were stationed overseas in 1980 than in 1976; the defense budget climbed and sales of arms abroad grew to $15.3 billion in 1980. On human rights, the president proved inconsistent. He practiced a double standard by applying the human rights test to some nations (the Soviet Union, Argentina, and Chile) but not to U.S. allies (South Korea, the shah's Iran, and the Philippines). Still, if inconsistent, Carter's human rights policy was not unimportant: he gained the release and saved the lives of some political prisoners, and he popularized and institutionalized concern

for human rights around the world. But Carter did not satisfy Americans who wanted a post-Vietnam restoration of the economic dominance and military edge the United States once enjoyed. He lost the 1980 election to the hawkish Ronald Reagan, former Hollywood actor and governor of California.

Summary

The 1970s were a difficult decade for Americans. From the crisis year of 1968 on, it seemed that Americans were ever more polarized—over the war in Vietnam, over the best path to racial equality and equal rights for all Americans, over the meaning of equality, and over the meaning of America itself. As many activists for social justice turned to "cultural nationalism," notions of American unity seemed a relic of the past. And though a new women's movement won great victories against sex discrimination, a powerful opposition movement arose in response.

During this era, Americans became increasingly disillusioned with politics and presidential leadership. Richard Nixon's abuses of power in the Watergate scandal and cover-up, combined with growing awareness that several administrations had lied to the citizenry repeatedly about America's role in Vietnam, produced a profound suspicion of government. A major economic crisis ended the post–World War II

The All-Volunteer Force

On June 30, 1973, the United States ended its military draft. From that date on, the nation relied on an all-volunteer force (AVF). The draft had been in effect, with only a brief interruption in the late 1940s, since the United States had begun to mobilize in 1940 for World War II. Never before had the United States had a peacetime draft. But as the country took on new roles of global leadership after the war, and as the dark shadow of the Cold War grew, the draft became an accepted part of American life. More than 50 million American men had been inducted into the nation's military between the end of World War II and the end of conscription in 1973.

Richard Nixon had promised to end the draft during his presidential campaign in 1968. It was an astute political move, for the draft had become a focus for widespread protest during the failing—and increasingly unpopular—war in Vietnam. Ending the draft was not feasible during the war, but Nixon kept his promise and began planning for an all-volunteer force as soon as he took office. Many Americans supported the shift because they believed it would be more difficult for a president to send an all-volunteer military to war. According to this logic, if people did not support the war, there would be no draft to compel them to fight.

The military, however, was not enthusiastic about Nixon's plan. The war in Vietnam had shattered morale and left much of the nation's military—particularly the army—in disarray. Public opinion of the military was at an all-time low. How were the military services to fill their ranks?

The army, as the largest of the four services, had to draw the largest number of volunteers. It faced a difficult task. Reform was the first step: getting rid of "chickenshit" (unrelated to military skills) tasks such as cutting grass, "Kitchen Police" (KP) and the like, and enhancing military professionalism. The army also turned to state-of-the-art market research and advertising. Discovering that many young men were afraid they would lose their individuality in the army, the army's advertising agency launched a new campaign. Instead of the traditional poster of Uncle Sam proclaiming, "I Want You," the new volunteer army claimed, "Today's Army Wants to Join You."

The AVF had a rough beginning. The army had to recruit about 225,000 new soldiers each year (compared to about 62,500 per year in 2016) and had difficulty attracting enough capable young men and women. Within a decade, however, America's military boasted a higher rate of high school graduates and higher mental "quality" (as measured by standardized tests) than the comparable age population

in the United States. During an era of relative peace, many young men and women found opportunities for education and training through military service. Military service was particularly attractive to capable but economically disadvantaged young people, a high percentage of whom were African American.

The move to a volunteer force had major legacies for the American people. The military understood that, without a draft, it would have to turn to women in order to fill the ranks. The proportion of women in the active military increased from 1.9 percent in 1972 to about 15 percent currently, and the roles they were allowed to fill widened dramatically. At the same time, the nation's understanding of military service changed. With a volunteer force, military service was no longer an obligation of (male) citizenship. Instead, the military had to compete in the national labor market, often portraying military service to potential recruits as "a good job." The implications seemed less urgent in peacetime. But in time of war, the legacy of the move to an AVF is highly charged.

CRITICAL THINKING

□ What does it mean when only a small number of volunteers bears the burden of warfare and most Americans never have to consider the possibility of going to war?

---

expansion that had fueled the growth of the middle class and social reform programs alike, and Americans struggled with the psychological impact of a new age of limits and with the effects of stagflation: rising unemployment rates coupled with high rates of inflation.

Overseas, a string of setbacks—defeat in Vietnam, the oil embargo, and the Iranian hostage crisis—signified the waning of American power during the 1970s. The nation seemed increasingly unable to have its own way on the world stage. Détente with the Soviet Union had flourished for a time, as both superpowers sought to adjust to the new

geopolitical realities; however, by 1980 Cold War tensions were again on the rise. But if the nation's most important bilateral relationship remained that with the USSR, an important change, not always perceptible at the time, was under way: more and more, the focus of U.S. foreign policy was on the Middle East.

Plagued by political, economic, and foreign policy crises, America ended the 1970s bruised, battered, and frustrated. The age of liberalism was long over; the turn toward marketplace solutions had begun, and the elements for a conservative resurgence were in place.

Suggestions for Further Reading

Thomas Borstelman, *The 1970s: A New Global History from Civil Rights to Economic Inequality* (2012)

Jefferson R. Cowie, *Stayin' Alive: The 1970s and the Last Days of the Working Class* (2010)

Donald T. Critchlow, *Phyllis Schlafly and Grassroots Conservatism: A Woman's Crusade* (2005)

Daniel Ellsberg, *Secrets: A Memoir of Vietnam and the Pentagon Papers* (2002)

David Farber, *Taken Hostage: The Iran Hostage Crisis and America's First Encounter with Radical Islam* (2004)

Ken Hughes, *Fatal Politics: The Nixon Tapes, the Vietnam War, and the Casualties of Reelection* (2015)

Nancy MacLean, *Freedom Is Not Enough: The Opening of the American Workplace* (2006)

Rick Perlstein, *Nixonland: The Rise of a President and the Fracturing of America* (2008)

Ruth Rosen, *The World Split Open: How the Modern Women's Movement Changed America* (2000)

Hal Rothman, *The Greening of a Nation: Environmentalism in the U.S. Since 1945* (1997)

Odd Arne Westad, *The Global Cold War: Third World Interventions and the Making of Our Times* (2005)

Natasha Zaretsky, *No Direction Home: The American Family and the Fear of National Decline, 1968—1980* (2007)

Conservatism Revived, 1980–1992

The train to DC was late, and Sheila and Joe Kerley waited with their still-sleepy children for it to arrive at the Charlottesville, Virginia, station, surrounded by people in "Washington for Jesus" T-shirts, singing hymns to pass the time. Joe and Sheila had taken off work for this trip to the nation's capital, Joe from his father-in-law's small plumbing company, Sheila from her position as teacher's aide at the Christian school their children, 6-year-old Joey and 4-year-old Nikki, attended.

On the morning of April 29, 1980, the Kerleys were headed to a Christian rally on the mall in Washington, DC. Joe and Sheila believed strongly in the power of prayer. He'd been a rebellious teenager who'd dropped out of high school in Tennessee; they'd married young, and both of them were certain Joe's conversion had saved their marriage. Once saved, Sheila said, he became "a different person."

The Kerleys were going to the rally because they believed the Equal Rights Amendment would "tear down family life" (though they had difficulty explaining how), and because they didn't want their children taught about evolution, and because they were worried about the threat of communism. More than anything else, though, they believed that the United States was suffering because it had lost God's favor.

That morning, 200,000 people—most of them charismatic, Pentecostal, and evangelical Christians—massed on the national mall. They carried Bibles and American flags, hoisted signs and banners: "The Bible—It's True"; "America Must Repent or Perish." The day began with steady rain, but with the words of an opening prayer, the skies cleared. The air echoed with cries of "Praise the Lord." Groups joined hands to pray. Some men and women spoke in tongues.

◁ In 1988, on the eighth anniversary of the original "Washington for Jesus" rally, President Reagan addressed the crowd gathered for the second such rally by videotape. Cynthia Johnson/Getty Images

Chronology

1980	Reagan elected president
1981	AIDS first observed in United States
	Economic problems continue; prime interest rate reaches 21.5 percent
	"Reaganomics" plan of budget and tax cuts approved by Congress
1982	Unemployment reaches 10.8 percent, highest rate since Great Depression
	ERA defeated after STOP ERA campaign prevents ratification in key states
1983	Reagan introduces SDI
	Terrorists kill U.S. Marines in Lebanon
	U.S. invasion of Grenada
1984	Reagan aids Contras despite congressional ban
	Economic recovery; unemployment rate drops and economy grows without inflation
	Reagan reelected
	Gorbachev promotes reforms in USSR
1986	Iran-Contra scandal erupts
1987	Palestinian *intifada* begins
1988	George H. W. Bush elected president
1989	Tiananmen Square massacre in China
	Berlin Wall torn down
	U.S. troops invade Panama
	Gulf between rich and poor at highest point since 1920s
1990	Americans with Disabilities Act passed
	Communist regimes in Eastern Europe collapse
	Iraq invades Kuwait
	South Africa begins to dismantle apartheid
1991	Persian Gulf War
	USSR dissolves into independent states
	United States enters recession
1992	Annual federal budget deficit reaches high of $300 billion at end of Bush presidency

In the keynote speech Bill Bright, the head of Campus Crusade for Christ, chronicled America's descent into "a world aflame." He recounted a "series of plagues"—the war in Vietnam, racial conflict, Watergate, the rise in divorce, unwed pregnancy, abortion, drug use—and warned: "Unless we repent and turn from our sin, we can expect to be destroyed."

The organizers of the rally had begun with a clearly political purpose, crafting a "Christian Declaration" with a list of legislative goals, including ending legal abortion and cutting spending on social programs. Public opposition from other Christian leaders led them to pull that document. Nonetheless, delegates were sent to lobby their congressional representatives. When James Farmer, the founder of the Congress of Racial Equality, said, "We must fight to defeat their use of religious rhetoric to conceal their rightwing objectives," Reverend Pat Robertson told reporters that the rally was for prayer, not politics. But, he insisted, "Every leader in this city holds his tenure only so long as God wills it, and they have no authority except as God gives it to them. So the Congress and the President are secondary to us. And God was here today to hear us."

Experience an interactive version of this story in MindTap®.

I n the wake of the economic crisis and social divisions of the 1970s, the United States entered a new era of conservatism in the 1980s—one in which the growing religious right would play a critical role. A new conservative coalition comprised of widely different groups joined to elect Ronald Reagan president; his support came from wealthy people who liked his pro-business economic policies; the religious New Right who sought the creation of "God's America"; and white middle- and working-class Americans attracted by Reagan's charisma and his embrace of "old-fashioned" values. The election of Ronald Reagan in 1980 began a twelve-year period of Republican rule, as Reagan was succeeded by his vice president, George Bush, in 1988.

Members of this new coalition had different goals, but all expected the presidential administration to embrace their causes. Reagan did support New Right social issues: he was anti-abortion, he embraced prayer in schools, he ended Republican Party support for the Equal Rights Amendment, and he appointed judges to both the Supreme Court and the federal bench whose rulings strengthened social-conservative agendas. Nonetheless, the Reagan administration focused primarily on the agendas of political and economic conservatives: reducing the size and power of the federal government and creating favorable conditions for business and industry. The U.S. economy recovered from the stagflation that had plagued the nation, and through much of the 1980s, it boomed. But corruption flourished in financial institutions freed from government oversight, and taxpayers paid the bill for bailouts. By the end of the Reagan-Bush era, a combination of tax cuts and massive increases in defense spending left a budget deficit five times larger than when Reagan took office.

The 1980s saw increasing divisions between rich and poor in America. A host of social problems—drugs, violence, homelessness, the growing AIDS epidemic—made life even more difficult for the urban poor, especially as government aid was cut. But for those on the other side of the economic divide, the 1980s were an era of luxury and ostentation. One of the most poignant images from the time was of a homeless man huddled just outside the Reagan White House—the two Americans, divided by a widening gulf.

The most dramatic events of the Reagan-Bush years were not domestic, however, but international. In the span of a decade, the Cold War intensified drastically and then ended. The key figure in the intensification was Reagan, who entered office promising to reassert America's military might and stand up to the Soviet Union, and he delivered on both counts. The key figure in ending the Cold War was Soviet leader Mikhail Gorbachev, who came to power in 1985 determined to address the USSR's long-term economic decline and needed a more amicable superpower relationship to do so. Gorbachev, though no revolutionary—he hoped to reform the Soviet system, not eradicate it—lost control of events as a wave of revolutions in Eastern Europe toppled one communist regime after another. In 1991, the Soviet Union itself disappeared, and the United States found itself the world's lone superpower. The Persian Gulf War of that same year demonstrated America's unrivaled world power and the unprecedented importance of the Middle East in U.S. foreign policy.

⊡ *Ronald Reagan, campaigning for president in 1984, told voters, "It's morning again in America." How might Americans from different backgrounds judge the accuracy of his claim?*

⊡ *What issues, beliefs, backgrounds, and economic realities divided Americans in the 1980s, and how do those divisions continue to shape the culture and politics of contemporary America?*

⊡ *Why did the Cold War intensify and then wane during the decade of the 1980s?*

28-1 A New Conservative Coalition

▷ **Why did the New Deal coalition come to an end?**

▷ **What groups in American society comprised the conservative coalition?**

The 1970s had been a hard decade for Americans: defeat in Vietnam, the resignation of a president in disgrace, the energy crisis, economic "stagflation," and the Iranian hostage crisis. Increasingly, Americans had lost faith in their government and in government-based solutions to the nation's problems. Many turned away from the liberal policies that had dominated American politics since the New Deal. Conservatives, ranging from wealthy business interests to an emerging religious right, saw an opportunity in this national disillusion. In the election year of 1980, when President Carter's public approval rating stood at 21 percent, a diverse set of conservative groups forged a new coalition, coalescing around Republican candidate **Ronald Reagan**. The election of 1980 marked a sea change in American politics. Its victor, Ronald Reagan—as much as any president since Franklin Roosevelt—defined the era over which he presided.

28-1a The End of the New Deal Coalition

The New Deal coalition—the combination of organized labor, urban ethnic and working-class whites, African Americans, and white southerners who, since the days of Franklin Roosevelt, had dependably voted Democratic—had begun to splinter by the late 1960s, as large numbers of white southerners abandoned the Democratic Party. By 1980, the votes of urban working-class white Americans outside the South were also in play. These voters offered a compelling target for conservative organizers such as Richard Viguerie, founder of *Conservative Digest* magazine, who meant to make the white working class the foundation of a new conservative movement.

Changes in the American economy had helped shift working-class politics. Labor unions had traditionally supported and been supported by the Democratic Party; as factories relocated to "right-to-work" states or shut down altogether during the 1970s,

Ronald Reagan Former actor and California governor (1967–1975) who served as the fortieth president of the United States (1981–1989).

union membership fell. Labor offered the Democratic Party smaller numbers, and loyalty to the Democratic Party had less pull on nonunionized workers.

As working-class whites faced new economic limits, government action often seemed incomprehensible or even harmful. New government-mandated affirmative action programs further reduced opportunities for working-class white men in a time of shrinking employment. White working-class parents often saw busing (sending children from racially segregated neighborhoods to other school districts to integrate schools) as government interference that threatened the quality of their children's education and even their safety. Watching the growth of liberal social programs for the poor, some working-class whites felt outraged that they worked hard to support their families while others lived on taxpayer-funded welfare. Racial prejudice played a role here; while the majority of welfare recipients were white, opponents of such government programs frequently portrayed welfare as a transfer of money from hardworking white families to indolent black ones.

Finally, many white working-class Americans were socially conservative. Catholics, who filled many urban ethnic working-class neighborhoods, worried not only about changes in sexual behaviors and women's roles but about government support for social change, including the Supreme Court's recognition of abortion rights in *Roe v. Wade*. As working-class whites felt economically beleaguered and often frustrated by government actions, conservative questions about the proper limits of the liberal state gained a new hearing.

28-1b Growth of the Religious Right

By 1980, a newly powerful movement of social conservatives, based in fundamentalist Christian churches, was poised to influence American politics. Their new prominence surprised many Americans; at the beginning of the decade, historians commonly argued that the 1925 Scopes trial over the teaching of evolution had been the last gasp of fundamentalist Christianity in the United States. They were wrong. Since the 1960s, America's mainline liberal Protestant churches—Episcopalian, Presbyterian, Methodist—had been losing members, while Southern Baptists and other denominations that offered the spiritual experience of being "born again" through belief in Jesus Christ and that accepted the literal truth of the Bible (fundamentalism) had grown rapidly. Fundamentalist and evangelical preachers reached out to vast audiences through television: by the late 1970s, televangelist Oral Roberts was drawing an audience of 3.9 million. Close to 20 percent of Americans identified themselves as fundamentalist Christians in 1980.

Most fundamentalist Christian churches stayed out of the social and political conflicts of the 1960s and early 1970s, arguing that preaching the "pure saving gospel of Jesus Christ" was more important. But in the late 1970s—motivated by what they saw as the betrayal of God's will in an increasingly permissive American society—some influential preachers began to mobilize their flocks for political struggle.

The Moral Majority, founded in 1979 by Jerry Falwell, sought to create a "Christian America," which Falwell believed required fighting against the ERA and women's rights (he called NOW the "National Order of Witches"), gay rights, abortion, pornography, and the teaching of evolution and sex education in public schools.

28-1c Economic Conservatives

America's business community had also developed a strong political presence by the beginning of the 1980s. The Business Roundtable, founded in 1972, brought together chief executive officers from America's largest corporations—the Fortune 500. These corporations controlled billions of dollars and millions of jobs; their leaders meant to leverage this financial power to shape American politics and public policy. CEOs of corporations such as Sears, General Foods, and Westinghouse personally lobbied politicians, as the Roundtable pushed for deregulation and corporate tax breaks and investment credits.

The U.S. Chamber of Commerce, which traced its origins to 1912, had also become more politically active. Unlike the Business Roundtable, which emphasized the quiet influence of powerful CEOs, the U.S. Chamber of Commerce

△ At the Republican National Convention, a delegate from Texas supports Ronald Reagan. Reagan's favorite campaign slogan was "Let's make America great again."

Dick Halstead/The LIFE Images Collection/Getty Images

built a broadly based grassroots movement that celebrated entrepreneurship and welcomed businesses of any size. Attempting to build a mass movement for capitalism, the chamber relied on individual members to persuade their local public schools to adopt its education module, "Economics for Young Americans." By 1981, the chamber had 2,700 local Congressional Action Committees to lobby congressional representatives; they pushed to weaken government regulations, lower taxes, and restrict the power of labor unions. And unlike the Business Roundtable, the chamber joined the religious right in its socially conservative agenda.

28-1d The Election of 1980

As the American presidential election season began in 1980, inflation was in double digits. Mortgage rates approached 14 percent. Oil prices were three times what they'd been at the start of the decade. Unemployment lingered at the then-high rate of 7 percent. And fifty-two American hostages remained in captivity in Iran. None of that offered any advantage to Democratic incumbent Jimmy Carter. Conservative leaders understood their opportunity.

Several strong Republican candidates entered the race, but support quickly coalesced around Ronald Reagan, a former movie star and two-term governor of California. Reagan offered (in marked contrast to Carter) an optimistic vision of America's future. With his Hollywood charm and strong conservative credentials, he succeeded in forging very different sorts of American conservatives into a new political coalition.

Turnout was low on Election Day, but Reagan crushed Carter at the polls. And for the first time since 1952, the Senate majority went to the Republicans.

28-2 Reagan's Conservative Agenda

▷ **What vision of America's future did the Reagan administration offer?**

▷ **What federal programs and policies did the Reagan administration seek to reform, and why?**

▷ **Why did Ronald Reagan appeal to the New Right?**

Reagan's conservative credentials were strong. In the 1940s, as president of Hollywood's Screen Actors Guild, Reagan had been a New Deal Democrat. But in the 1950s, as a corporate spokesman for General Electric, he became increasingly conservative. In 1964, Reagan's televised speech supporting Republican presidential candidate Barry Goldwater catapulted him to the forefront of conservative politics. America, Reagan said, had come to "a time for choosing" between free enterprise and big government, between individual liberty and "the ant heap of totalitarianism."

Elected governor of California just two years later, Reagan became known for his right-wing rhetoric: America should "level Vietnam, pave it, paint stripes on it, and make

a parking lot out of it," Reagan claimed. And in 1969, when student protesters occupied "People's Park" near the University of California in Berkeley, he threatened a "bloodbath" and dispatched National Guard troops in full riot gear. Reagan was often pragmatic, however, about policy decisions. He denounced welfare but presided over reform of the state's social welfare bureaucracy. And he signed one of the nation's most liberal abortion laws.

Ronald Reagan, at age sixty-nine the oldest American to that point elected to the presidency, restored the pomp and circumstance Jimmy Carter had resolutely stripped from the office. For example, Reagan spent $19.4 million for his inaugural balls; Carter's cost $3.5 million. (Private donors pay for these events.) And Reagan, as president, was not especially focused on the details of governing or the specifics of policies and programs. When outgoing president Jimmy Carter briefed him on urgent issues of foreign and domestic policy, Reagan listened politely but took not a single note and asked no questions. Critics argued that his lack of knowledge could prove dangerous—as when he insisted that intercontinental ballistic missiles carrying nuclear warheads could be called back once launched, or when he said that "approximately 80 percent of our air pollution stems from hydrocarbons released by vegetation."

But supporters insisted that Reagan was a great president in large part because he focused on the big picture. When he spoke to the American people, he offered what seemed to be simple truths—and he did it with the straightforwardness of a true believer and the warmth and humor of an experienced actor. Although many—even among Reagan supporters— winced at his willingness to reduce complex policy issues to simple (and often misleading) stories, Reagan was to most Americans the "Great Communicator." He won admiration for his courage after he was seriously wounded in an assassination attempt just sixty-nine days into his presidency. Reagan quipped to doctors preparing to remove the bullet lodged near his heart, "I hope you're all Republicans."

Most important, Reagan had a clear vision for America's future. He and his advisers wanted to roll back fifty years of liberal policies that had made government increasingly responsible for the health of the nation's economy and for the social welfare of its citizens. In the words of David Stockman, a Reagan appointee who headed the Office of Management and Budget, the administration meant to "create a minimalist government" and sever "the umbilical cords of dependency that run from Washington to every nook and cranny of the nation."

28-2a Attacks on Social Welfare Programs

Traditional conservatives believed that the federal government could not solve America's social problems. But a broader and less coherent backlash against Great Society programs strengthened conservatives' hands. Many Americans who struggled to make ends meet during the economic crises of the 1970s and early 1980s resented paying taxes that, they believed, funded government "handouts" to people who did not work. Reagan himself used existing racial tensions to undermine support for welfare, repeatedly describing a "welfare queen" from Chicago's South Side (a primarily African American area) who had collected welfare checks under eighty different last names and defrauded the government of $150,000 (the actual case involved two aliases and $8,000). In 1981, the administration cut welfare programs for the poor by $25 billion. But programs such as Aid to Families with Dependent Children and food stamps were a small part of the budget compared with Social Security and Medicare—social welfare programs that benefited Americans of all income levels, not just the poor. Major budget cuts for these popular, broadly based programs proved impossible. The Reagan administration did shrink the *proportion* of the federal budget devoted to social welfare programs (including Social Security and Medicare) from 28 to 22 percent by the late 1980s—but only because it increased defense spending by $1.2 trillion.

28-2b Pro-Business Policies and the Environment

The Reagan administration also attacked federal environmental, health, and safety regulations that conservatives believed reduced business profits and discouraged economic growth. Administration officials claimed that removing the stifling hand of government regulation would restore the energy and creativity of America's free-market system. However, they did not so much end government's role as deploy government power to aid corporate America.

President Reagan appointed opponents of federal regulations to head the agencies charged with enforcing them—letting foxes guard the chicken coop, critics charged. Environmentalists were appalled when Reagan appointed James Watt, a well-known anti-environmentalist, as secretary of the interior. Watt was a leader in the "Sagebrush Rebellion," which sought to shift publicly owned lands in the West, such as national forests, from federal to state control. Land control issues were complicated: the federal government controlled more than half of western lands—including 83 percent of the land in Nevada, 66 percent in Utah, and 50 percent in Wyoming—and many westerners believed that eastern policymakers did not understand the realities of western life. But states' ability to control land within their borders was not the sole issue; Watt and his group wanted to open western public lands to private businesses for logging, mining, and ranching.

Telling senators in his 1981 confirmation hearing, "I don't know how many generations we can count on until the Lord returns," Watt saw no need to protect national resources and public wilderness for future generations. As interior secretary, he allowed private corporations to acquire oil, mineral, and timber rights to federal lands for minuscule payments. Watt was forced to resign in 1983 after he dismissively referred to a federal advisory panel as "a black . . . a woman, two Jews, and a cripple." But his appointment had already backfired, for his actions reenergized the nation's environmental movement and even provoked opposition from business leaders who understood that uncontrolled strip-mining and clear-cut logging of western lands could destroy lucrative tourism and recreation industries in western states.

28-2c Attacks on Organized Labor

As part of its pro-business agenda, the Reagan administration undercut organized labor's ability to negotiate wages and working conditions. Union power was already waning; labor union membership declined in the 1970s as jobs in heavy industry disappeared, and efforts to unionize the high-growth electronics and service sectors of the economy had failed. Setting the tone for his administration, in August 1981 Reagan intervened in a strike by the Professional Air Traffic Controllers Organization (PATCO). The air traffic controllers—federal employees, for whom striking was illegal—were protesting working conditions they believed compromised the safety of American air travel. Only forty-eight hours into the strike, Reagan fired the 11,350 strikers, stipulating that they could never be rehired by the Federal Aviation Administration.

With the support of Reagan appointees to the National Labor Relations Board and an anti-union secretary of labor, businesses took an increasingly hard line with labor during the 1980s and unions failed to mount an effective opposition. By 1990, only 12 percent of private sector workers were unionized. Yet roughly 44 percent of union families had voted for Reagan in 1980, drawn to his geniality, espousal of old-fashioned values, and vigorous anticommunist rhetoric.

28-2d The New Right

Although Reagan's domestic agenda focused on traditional conservative political and economic goals, New Right issues played an increasingly important role in Reagan-era social policy. It is surprising that the strongly religious New Right was drawn to Reagan, a divorced man without strong ties to religion or, seemingly, his own children. But the non-church-going Reagan lent his support to the New Right, endorsing the anti-abortion cause and supporting prayer in public schools.

Reagan's judicial nominations also pleased the religious New Right. Though the Senate, in a bipartisan vote, refused to confirm Supreme Court nominee Robert Bork after eighty-seven hours of antagonistic hearings, Congress eventually confirmed Anthony M. Kennedy instead. Reagan also appointed Antonin Scalia, who would become a key conservative force on the Court, and Sandra Day O'Connor (the first female appointee) and elevated Nixon appointee William Rehnquist to chief justice. In 1986, the increasingly conservative Supreme Court upheld a Georgia law that punished consensual sex between men with up to twenty years in jail (*Bowers v. Hardwick*); in 1989, the justices ruled that a Missouri law restricting the right to an abortion was constitutional (*Webster v. Reproductive Health Services*), thus encouraging further challenges to *Roe v. Wade*. In federal courts, U.S. Justice Department lawyers argued New Right positions on such social issues, and Reagan's 378 appointees to the federal bench usually ruled accordingly. Overall, however, the Reagan administration did not push a conservative social agenda as strongly as some members of the new Republican coalition had hoped.

28-3 Economic Conservatism

▷ What economic theories and ideas shaped the Reagan administration's economic agenda?

▷ How did implementation of "Reaganomics" affect the American economy and the American people?

▷ What impact did deregulation have on the banking and finance industries?

▷ Who benefited from the economic and financial policies implemented during the Reagan administration?

The U.S. economy was in bad shape at the beginning of the 1980s. In 1981, the economy plunged deeper into recession and unemployment rates jumped. Everyone agreed that something had to be done.

Business elites, conservative economists, and the president himself argued that New Deal remedies, emphasizing government intervention in the economy through spending, had failed. Reagan offered the American people a simple diagnosis of the nation's economic woes. Instead of focusing on the complexities of global competition, deindustrialization, and OPEC's control of oil, Reagan argued that U.S. economic problems were caused by government intrusion in the "free-market" economic system. At fault were intrusive government regulation of business and industry, expensive government social programs that offered "handouts" to nonproductive citizens, high taxes, and deficit spending—in short, government itself. The Reagan administration's economic agenda—often called "Reaganomics"—was closely tied to its larger conservative ideology of limited government: it sought to "unshackle" the free-enterprise system from government regulation and control, to slash spending on social programs, to limit government's use of taxes to redistribute income among the American people, and to balance the budget by reducing the role of the federal government.

28-3a Harsh Medicine for Inflation

Before this new approach could have any real impact, the administration had to solve the continuing problem of inflation. Here the Federal Reserve Bank, an autonomous federal agency, stepped in. In 1981, the Federal Reserve Bank raised interest rates for bank loans to an unprecedented 21.5 percent, battling inflation by tightening the money supply and slowing the economy down. The nation plunged into recession. During the last three months of the year, the gross national product (GNP) fell 5 percent, and sales of cars and houses dropped sharply. With declining economic activity, unemployment soared to 8 percent, the highest level in almost six years.

By late 1982, unemployment had reached 10.8 percent, the highest rate since 1940. For African Americans, it was 20 percent. Many of the unemployed were blue-collar workers in ailing "smokestack industries," such as steel and automobiles. Reagan and his advisers promised that consumers would lift the economy out of the recession by spending their tax cuts. But as late as April 1983, unemployment still stood at 10 percent, and people were angry. Jobless steelworkers paraded through McKeesport, Pennsylvania, carrying a coffin that bore the epitaph "American Dream." Agriculture, too, was faltering and near collapse. Farmers suffered not only from falling crop prices due to overproduction but also from floods, droughts, and burdensome debts with high interest rates. Many lost their property to mortgage foreclosure; others filed for bankruptcy. As the recession deepened, poverty rose to its highest level since 1965.

It was harsh medicine, but the Federal Reserve Bank's plan to end stagflation worked. High interest rates helped drop inflation from 12 percent in 1980 to less than 7 percent in 1982. The economy also benefited from OPEC's 1981 decision to stop engineering an artificial scarcity and increase oil production, thus lowering prices—and inflation.

28-3b Supply-Side Economics

With inflation tamed, proponents of conservative economic policy could develop their pro-business agenda. The Reagan administration's economic policy was based largely on supply-side economics, the theory that tax cuts (rather than government spending) will create economic growth. According to a theory proposed by economist Arthur Laffer—his soon-to-be-famous Laffer curve—at some point rising tax rates discourage people from engaging in taxable activities (such as investing their money): if profits from investments simply disappear to taxes, what is the incentive to invest? As people invest less, the economy slows. Even though tax rates remain high, the government collects less in tax revenue because the economy stalls. Cutting taxes, according to this theory, reverses the cycle and increases tax revenues.

Although economists accepted the Laffer curve's broader principle, almost none believed that U.S. tax rates were anywhere close to the point of disincentive. Even conservative economists were suspicious of supply-side principles. Reagan and his staff, however—on the basis of the unproven assumption that both corporate and personal tax rates in the United States were so high that they discouraged investment—sought a massive tax cut. They argued that American corporations and individuals would invest funds freed up by lower tax rates, producing new plants, new jobs, and new products. This economic growth would more than make up for the tax revenues lost. And as prosperity returned, the profits at the top would "trickle down" to the middle classes and even to the poor.

Reagan proposed to balance the federal budget through economic growth (created by tax cuts) and deep spending cuts, primarily in social programs. Congress cooperated with a three-year, $750 billion tax cut, at that point the largest ever in American history. Cutting the federal budget, however, proved more difficult; while Reagan's plan assumed $100 billion in cuts from programs including Social Security and Medicare, Congress was not about to cut those benefits. Reagan, meanwhile, canceled out domestic spending cuts by dramatically increasing defense spending.

Major tax cuts, big increases in defense spending, small cuts in social programs: the numbers did not add up. The annual federal budget deficit exploded—from $59 billion in 1980 to more than $100 billion in 1982 to almost $300 billion by the end of George H. W. Bush's presidency in 1993. The Republican administrations borrowed money to make up the difference, transforming the United States from the world's largest creditor nation to its largest debtor (see Figure 28.1). The national debt grew to almost $3 trillion. Because an ever-greater share of the federal budget went to pay the interest on this ballooning debt, less was available for federal programs, foreign or domestic.

28-3c Deregulation

Supply-side economics was not the only policy that transformed America's economy in the 1980s. Deregulation, begun under Jimmy Carter and expanded vastly under Reagan (the Federal Register, which contains all federal regulations, shrank from 87,012 pages in 1980 to 47,418 pages in 1986), created new opportunities for American business and industry. The 1978 deregulation of the airline industry lowered ticket prices both short term and long term; airline tickets cost almost 45 percent less in the early twenty-first century (in constant dollars) than in 1978. Deregulation of telecommunications industries created serious competition for the giant AT&T, and long-distance calling became inexpensive.

The Reagan administration loosened regulation of the American banking and finance industries and purposely

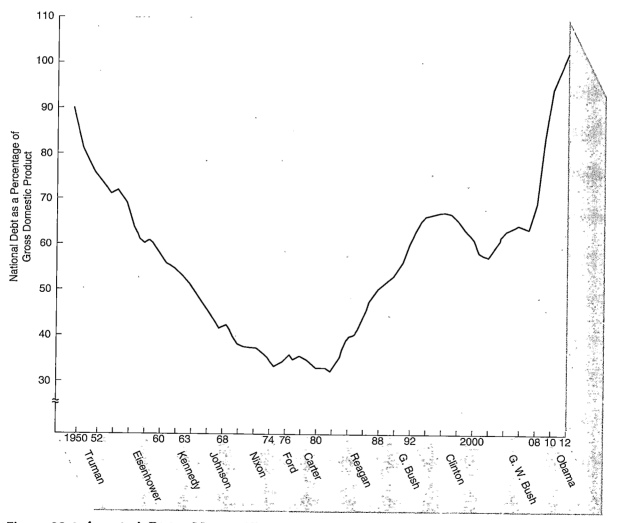

Figure 28.1 America's Rising National Debt, 1974–2012

America's national debt, which rose sporadically throughout the 1970s, soared to record heights during the 1980s. Under President Reagan, large defense expenditures and tax cuts caused the national debt to grow by $1.5 trillion.

Source: Adapted from U.S. Bureau of the Census, Statistical Abstract of the United States (Washington, D.C.: 1992), p. 315.

△ President Ronald Reagan, who created a major budget deficit by pairing large tax cuts with large increases in defense spending, brandishes his "Tax Ax" at a Chamber of Commerce lunch in 1986.

cut the ability of the Securities and Exchange Commission (SEC), which oversees Wall Street, to enforce those regulations. In 1984, the GNP rose 7 percent, the sharpest increase since 1951, and midyear unemployment fell to a four-year low of 7 percent. The economy was booming, but without sparking inflation.

28-3d "Morning in America"

By the presidential election of 1984, the recession was only a memory. Reagan got credit for the recovery. The Democratic candidate, former Vice President Walter Mondale, talked about fairness and compassion; not all Americans, Mondale told the American public, were prospering in Reagan's America. Reagan, in contrast, proclaimed, "It's morning again in America." Television ads showed heartwarming images of American life, as an off-screen narrator told viewers, "Life is better. America is back. And people have a sense of pride they never felt they'd feel again." Reagan won in a landslide, with 59 percent of the vote. Mondale, with running mate Geraldine Ferraro—U.S. congresswoman from New York

and the first woman vice presidential candidate—carried only his home state of Minnesota.

28-3e Junk Bonds and Merger Mania

Reagan's reelection in 1984 guaranteed the continuation of deregulation and pro-business economic policies, which facilitated economic risk taking and new financial practices. On Wall Street, for example, a reclusive bond trader for the firm Drexel Firestone named Michael Milken pioneered the "junk bond" industry and created wildly lucrative investment possibilities. Milken offered financing to debt-ridden or otherwise weak corporations that could not get traditional, low-interest bank loans to fund expansion, using bond issues that paid investors high interest rates because they were high-risk (thus "junk") bonds. Many of these corporations, Milken realized, were attractive targets for takeover by other corporations or investors—who, in turn, could finance takeovers with junk bonds. Such "predators" could use the first corporation's existing debt as a tax write-off, sell off unprofitable units, and lay off employees to create a more efficient—and thus more profitable—corporation. Investors in the original junk bonds could make huge profits by selling their shares to the corporate raiders.

By the mid-1980s, it was no longer only weak corporations that were targeted for these "hostile takeovers"; hundreds of major corporations—including giants Walt Disney and Conoco—fell prey to merger mania. Profits for investors were staggering, and by 1987 Milken, the guru of junk bonds, was earning $550 million a year—about $1,046 a minute—in salary; counting investment returns, Milken's income was about $1 billion a year.

In the 1980s, new conservative economic policies led to large-scale economic reorganization and increased economic growth. Heightened competition and corporate downsizing often created more efficient businesses and industries. Deregulation helped smaller and often innovative corporations challenge the virtual monopolies of giant corporations in fields like telecommunications. And through much of the 1980s, following the "Reagan recession," the American economy boomed.

28-3f The Costs of Economic Conservatism

The conservative policies of the 1980s and the high-risk boom they unleashed also had significant costs. Corporate downsizing meant layoffs for white-collar employees, many of whom (especially those past middle age) had difficulty finding comparable positions. The wave of mergers and takeovers left American corporations as a whole more burdened by debt. It also helped to consolidate sectors of the economy—such as the media—under the control of an ever-smaller number of players.

The high-risk, deregulated boom of the 1980s, furthermore, was rotten with corruption. By the late 1980s, insider trading scandals—in which people used "inside" information about corporations that wasn't available to the general public to make huge profits trading stocks—rocked financial markets and sent some of the most prominent figures on Wall Street to jail (albeit comfortable, "country club" jails). Congress's deregulation of the nation's savings and loan institutions (S&Ls) also fostered corruption and left regular Americans at risk. By ending government oversight of investment practices, while guaranteeing to cover losses from bad S&L investments, Congress left no penalties for failure. S&Ls increasingly put depositors' money into high-risk investments and engaged in shady—even criminal—deals. S&Ls lost billions of dollars in bad investments, sometimes turning to fraud to cover them up. Scandal reached all the way to the White House: Vice President Bush's son Neil was involved in shady S&L deals. The Reagan-Bush administration's bailout of the S&L industry had a total price tag of more than half a trillion dollars.

Finally, during the 1980s, the rich got richer, and the poor got poorer (see Figure 28.2). Ten times as many Americans reported an annual income of $500,000 in 1989 as in 1980. By 1989, CEOs received, on average, 71 times an average worker's pay, up from a 20-to-1 ratio in 1965 (the ratio was 303 to 1 in 2015, down from a 2000 high of 383 to 1). In 1987, the United States had forty-nine billionaires—up from one in 1978. While the number of very wealthy Americans grew, middle-class incomes were stagnant.

Most of the new inequality was due to conservative economic policies, which benefited the wealthy at the expense of middle- and lower-income Americans. Reagan's tax policies decreased the "total effective tax rates"—income taxes plus Social Security taxes—for the top 1 percent of American families by 14.4 percent. But they increased tax rates for the poorest 20 percent of families by 16 percent. By 1990, the richest 1 percent of Americans controlled 40 percent of the nation's wealth; fully 80 percent of wealth was controlled by the top 20 percent. Not since the 1920s had America seen such economic inequality.

28-4 Challenges and Opportunities Abroad

▷ **Why did Ronald Reagan's approach to the Soviet Union shift from his first to his second term in office?**

▷ **How was the Reagan Doctrine implemented in the Caribbean and Latin America?**

▷ **What new challenges did the United States face in developing foreign policy toward the Middle East?**

A key element in Reagan's winning strategy in the 1980 election was his forthright call for the United States to assert itself on the world stage. Though lacking a firm grasp of international issues, history, and geography—friends and associates often marveled at his ability to get even elementary facts wrong—Reagan adhered to a few core principles. One was a deep and abiding anticommunism, which had dictated his worldview for decades and which formed the foundation of his presidential campaign. A second was an underlying optimism about the ability of American power and values to bring positive change in the world. Reagan liked to quote Thomas Paine of the American Revolution: "We have it in our power to begin the world over again." Yet Reagan was also a political pragmatist, particularly as time went on and his administration became mired in scandal. Together, these elements help explain both his aggressive anticommunist foreign policy and his willingness to respond positively in his

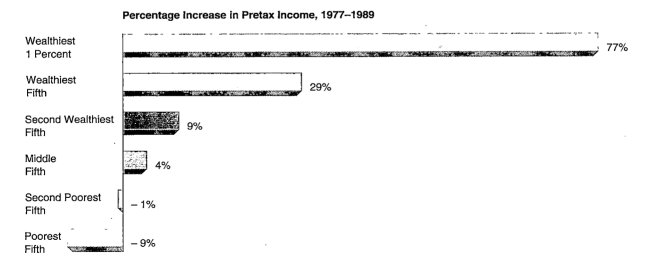

Figure 28.2 While the Rich Got Richer in the 1980s, the Poor Got Poorer

Between 1977 and 1989, the richest 1 percent of American families reaped most of the gains from economic growth. In fact, the average pretax income of families in the top percentage rose 77 percent. At the same time, the typical family saw its income edge up only 4 percent. And the bottom 40 percent of families had actual declines in income. *Source: Data from the New York Times, March 5, 1992.*

second term to Soviet leader Mikhail Gorbachev's call for "new thinking" in world affairs.

28-4a Soviet-American Tension

Initially, toughness vis-à-vis Moscow was the watchword. Embracing the strident anticommunism that characterized U.S. foreign policy in the early Cold War, Reagan and his advisers rejected both the détente of the Nixon years and the Carter administration's focus on extending human rights abroad. Where Nixon and Carter perceived an increasingly multipolar international system, the Reagan team reverted to a bipolar perspective defined by the Soviet-American relationship. Much of the intellectual ballast and moral fervor for this shift toward confrontation with Moscow was provided by **neoconservatives**, a small but influential group composed primarily of academics and intellectuals, many of them former Democrats who believed the party had lost its way after Vietnam and who rejected the old conservatism as backward looking. Key figures in this group included Richard Perle and Paul Wolfowitz, who held mid-level positions in the administration.

In his first presidential press conference, Reagan described a malevolent Soviet Union, whose leaders thought they had "the right to commit any crime, to lie, to cheat." When Poland's pro-Soviet leaders in 1981 cracked down on Solidarity, an independent labor organization, Washington responded by restricting Soviet-American trade and hurling angry words at Moscow. In March 1983, Reagan told an audience of evangelical Christians in Florida that the Soviets were "the focus of evil in the modern world . . . an evil empire." That same year, Reagan restricted commercial flights to the Soviet Union after a Soviet fighter pilot mistakenly shot down a South Korean commercial jet that had strayed some three hundred miles off course into Soviet airspace, killing 269 passengers.

Reagan believed that a substantial military buildup would thwart the Soviet threat and intimidate Moscow. Accordingly, the administration launched the largest peacetime arms buildup in American history, driving up the federal debt. In 1985, when the military budget hit $294.7 billion (a doubling since 1980), the Pentagon spent an average of $28 million an hour. Assigning low priority to arms control talks, Reagan announced in 1983 his desire for a space-based defense shield against incoming ballistic missiles: the **Strategic Defense Initiative (SDI)**. His critics tagged it "Star Wars" and said perfecting such a system was scientifically impossible—some enemy missiles would always get through the shield. Moreover, the critics warned, SDI would have the effect of elevating the arms race to dangerous new levels. But Reagan was undaunted, and in the years that followed, SDI research and development consumed tens of billions of dollars.

28-4b Reagan Doctrine

Because he attributed Third World disorders to Soviet intrigue, the president declared the Reagan Doctrine: the United States would openly support anticommunist movements—"freedom fighters"—wherever they were battling the Soviets or Soviet-backed governments. In Afghanistan, the president continued

Jimmy Carter's policy of providing covert assistance, through Pakistan, to the Mujahidin rebels in their war against the Soviet occupation. CIA director William J. Casey made numerous trips to Pakistan to coordinate the flow of arms and other assistance. When the Soviets stepped up the war in 1985, the Reagan administration sent more high-tech weapons. Particularly important were the Stinger anti-aircraft missiles. Easily transportable and fired by a single soldier, the Stingers turned the tide in the Afghan war by making Soviet jets and helicopters vulnerable below twelve thousand feet. Soviet commanders had no effective response.

The administration also applied the Reagan Doctrine aggressively in the Caribbean and Central America. Senior officials believed that the Soviets and Castro's Cuba were fomenting disorder in the region (see Map 28.1). Accordingly, in October 1983 the president sent U.S. troops into the tiny Caribbean island of Grenada to oust a pro-Marxist government that appeared to be forging ties with Moscow and Havana. In El Salvador, he provided military and economic assistance to a military-dominated government struggling against left-wing revolutionaries. The regime used (or could not control) right-wing death squads, which by the end of the decade had killed forty thousand dissidents and other citizens, as well as several American missionaries who had been working with landless peasants. By then, the United States had spent more than $6 billion there in a counterinsurgency war. In January 1992, the Salvadoran combatants finally negotiated a UN-sponsored peace.

28-4c Contra War in Nicaragua

In nearby Nicaragua, too, the administration made its presence felt. In 1979, leftist insurgents in Nicaragua had overthrown Anastasio Somoza, a longtime ally of the United States and member of the dictatorial family that had ruled the Central American nation since the mid-1930s. The revolutionaries called themselves Sandinistas in honor of Augusto César Sandino—who had headed the nationalistic, anti-imperialist Nicaraguan opposition against U.S. occupation in the 1930s and been assassinated by Somoza henchmen—and they denounced the tradition of U.S. imperialism in their country. When the Sandinistas aided rebels in El Salvador, bought Soviet weapons, and invited Cubans to work in Nicaragua's hospitals and schools and help reorganize the Nicaraguan army, Reagan officials charged that Nicaragua was becoming a Soviet client. In 1981, the CIA began to train, arm, and direct more than ten thousand counterrevolutionaries, known as *contras*, to overthrow the Nicaraguan government.

neoconservatives A small but influential group of intellectuals—typically former Democrats disillusioned with the party after Vietnam—who became part of Republican Ronald Reagan's conservative coalition.

Strategic Defense Initiative (SDI) Reagan's proposed program for developing a high-tech, space-based defense shield that would protect the United States against incoming ballistic missiles; nicknamed "Star Wars" by critics.

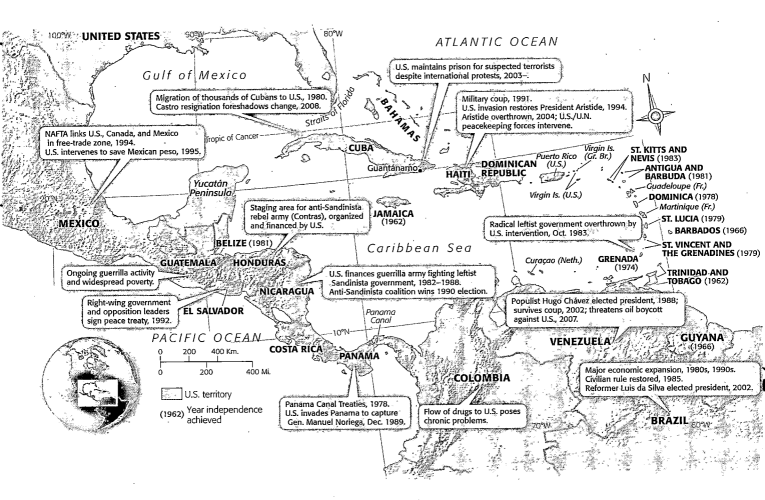

Map 28.1 The United States in the Caribbean and Central America

The United States has often intervened in the Caribbean and Central America. Geographical proximity, economic stakes, political disputes, security links, trade in illicit drugs, and Cuban leader Fidel Castro's longtime defiance of Washington have kept U.S. eyes fixed on events in the region.

Not everyone accepted the administration's interpretation of the stakes. Many Americans, including Democratic leaders in Congress, were skeptical about the communist threat to the region and warned that Nicaragua could become another Vietnam. Consequently, Congress in 1984 voted to stop U.S. military aid to the contras. Secretly, the Reagan administration lined up other countries, including Saudi Arabia, Panama, and South Korea, to funnel money and weapons to the contras, and in 1985 Reagan imposed an economic embargo against Nicaragua. The president might have opted for a diplomatic solution, but he rejected a plan proposed by Costa Rica's president Oscar Arias Sanchez in 1987 to obtain a cease-fire in Central America through negotiations and cutbacks in military aid to all rebel forces. (Arias won the 1987 Nobel Peace Prize.) Three years later, after Reagan had left

Oliver North U.S. Marine colonel who became a central figure in the Iran-contra, arms-for-hostages scandal.

office, all of the Central American presidents at last brokered a settlement; in the national election that followed, the Sandinistas lost to a U.S.-funded party. After nearly a decade of civil war, thirty thousand Nicaraguans had died, and the ravaged economy had dwindled to one of the poorest in the hemisphere.

28-4d Iran-Contra Scandal

Reagan's obsession with defeating the Sandinistas almost caused his political undoing. In November 1986, it became known that the president's national security adviser, John M. Poindexter, and an aide, marine lieutenant colonel **Oliver North**, in collusion with CIA director Casey, had covertly sold weapons to Iran as part of a largely unsuccessful attempt to win the release of several Americans being held hostage by Islamic fundamentalist groups in the Middle East. During the same period, Washington had been condemning Iran as a terrorist nation and demanding that America's allies not trade with the Islamic state. Still more damaging was the revelation that money from the Iran arms deal had been illegally diverted to a fund to aid the contras—this after Congress had unambiguously rejected providing such aid. North later admitted he had illegally destroyed government documents and lied to Congress to keep the operation clandestine.

Although Reagan survived the **Iran-Contra scandal**—it remained unclear just what he did and did not know about the operation—his presidency suffered a major blow. His personal popularity declined, and an emboldened Congress began to reassert its authority over foreign affairs. In late 1992, outgoing President George Bush pardoned several former government officials convicted of lying to Congress. Critics smelled a cover-up, for Bush himself, as vice president, had participated in high-level meetings on Iran-contra deals. As for North, his conviction was overturned on a technicality. In view of its deliberate thwarting of congressional authority, the Iran-contra secret network, the scholar William LeoGrande has argued, "posed a greater threat to democracy in the United States than Nicaragua ever did."

28-4e U.S. Interests in the Middle East

The Iran-contra scandal also pointed to the increased importance in U.S. foreign policy of the Middle East and terrorism (see Map 29.2). As before, the United States had as its main goals in the Middle East preserving access to oil and supporting its ally Israel, while at the same time checking Soviet influence in the region. But in the 1980s American leaders faced new pressures, in the form of a deepened Israeli-Palestinian conflict and an anti-American and anti-Israeli Islamic fundamentalist movement that began to spread after the ouster of the shah of Iran in 1979.

The 1979 Camp David Accords between Israel and Egypt had raised hopes of a lasting settlement involving self-government for the Palestinian Arabs living in the Israeli-occupied Gaza Strip and West Bank. It did not happen, as Israel and the Palestinian Liberation Organization (PLO) remained at odds. In 1982, in retaliation for Palestinian shelling of Israel from Lebanon, Israeli troops invaded Lebanon, reaching the capital, Beirut, and inflicting massive damage. The beleaguered PLO and various Lebanese factions called on Syria to contain the Israelis. Thousands of civilians died in the multifaceted conflict, and a million people became refugees. Reagan made no effort to halt the Israeli offensive, but he agreed to send U.S. Marines to Lebanon to join a peacekeeping force. Soon the American troops became embroiled in a war between Christian and Muslim factions, as the latter accused the marines of helping the Christian-dominated government rather than acting as neutral peacekeepers. In October 1983, terrorist bombs demolished a barracks, killing 241 American servicemen. Sensing the futility of the mission, Reagan pulled the remaining marines out four months later.

28-4f Terrorism

The attack on the marine barracks showed the growing danger of terrorism to the United States and other Western countries. In the 1980s, numerous otherwise powerless groups, many of them associated with the Palestinian cause or with Islamic fundamentalism, relied on terrorist acts to further their political aims. Often they targeted American citizens and property, on account of Washington's support of Israel and U.S. involvement in the Lebanese civil war. Of the 690 hijackings, kidnappings, bombings, and shootings around the world in 1985, for example, 217 were against Americans. Most of these actions originated in Iran, Libya, Lebanon, and the Gaza Strip. In June 1985, for example, Shi'ite

Iran-Contra scandal Scandal in which the Reagan administration illegally sold weapons to Iran to finance contras in Nicaragua.

◁ A U.S. Marine lieutenant stands guard as rescue workers comb the ruins of the American embassy in Beirut after a suicide bombing on April 18, 1983. The attack killed 63, including 17 Americans. The U.S. Marines were there as part of a multinational peacekeeping intervention in Lebanon's Civil War.

Francoise De Mulder/Getty Images

Muslim terrorists from Lebanon hijacked an American jet-liner, killed one passenger, and held thirty-nine Americans hostage for seventeen days. Three years later, a Pan American passenger plane was destroyed over Scotland by a bomb that, investigators later determined, had been concealed in a cassette player. Several organizations claimed responsibility for the bombing, but questions remain about who did it.

Washington, firmly allied with Israel, continued to propose peace plans designed to persuade the Israelis to give back occupied territories and the Arabs to give up attempts to push the Jews out of the Middle East (the "land-for-peace" formula). As the peace process stalled in 1987, Palestinians living in the West Bank began an *intifada* (Arabic for "uprising") against Israeli forces. Israel refused to negotiate, but the United States decided to talk with PLO chief Yasir Arafat after he renounced terrorism and accepted Israel's right to live in peace and security. For the PLO to recognize Israel and, in effect, for the United States to recognize the PLO were major developments in the Arab-Israeli conflict, even as a lasting settlement remained elusive.

In South Africa, too, American diplomacy became more aggressive as the decade progressed. At first, the Reagan administration followed a policy of "constructive engagement"—asking the increasingly isolated government to reform its apartheid system, designed to preserve white supremacy. But many Americans demanded economic sanctions: cutting off imports from South Africa and pressuring some 350 American companies—top among them Texaco, General Motors, Ford, and Goodyear—to cease operations there. Some American cities and states passed divestment laws, withdrawing dollars (such as pension funds used to buy stock) from American companies active in South Africa. Public protest and congressional legislation forced the Reagan administration in 1986 to impose economic restrictions against South Africa. Within two years, about half of the U.S. companies in South Africa had pulled out.

28-4g Enter Gorbachev

Many on the right disliked the South Africa sanctions policy—they believed the main black opposition group, the African National Congress (ANC), was dominated by communists, and they doubted the efficacy of sanctions—and the more extreme among them soon found another reason to be disenchanted with Reagan. A new Soviet leader, Mikhail S. Gorbachev, had come to power, and Reagan, his own popularity sagging, showed a newfound willingness to enter negotiations with the "evil empire." Gorbachev called for a friendlier superpower relationship and a new, more cooperative world system. At a 1985 Geneva summit meeting between the two men, Reagan agreed in principle with Gorbachev's contention that strategic weapons should be substantially reduced, and at a 1986 meeting in Reykjavik, Iceland, they came very close to a major reduction agreement. SDI, however, stood in the way: Gorbachev insisted that the initiative be shelved, and Reagan refused to part with it, despite continuing scientific objections that the plan would cost billions of dollars and never work.

But Reagan and Gorbachev got along well, despite the language barrier and their differing personalities. Reagan's penchant for telling stories rather than discussing the intricacies of policy did not trouble the detail-oriented Gorbachev. As General Colin Powell commented, though the Soviet leader was far superior to Reagan in mastery of specifics, he never exhibited even a trace of condescension. He understood that Reagan was, as Powell put it, "the embodiment of his people's down-to-earth character, practicality, and optimism." And Reagan toned down his strident anti-Soviet rhetoric, particularly as his more hawkish advisers left the administration in the late 1980s.

28-4h *Perestroika* and *Glasnost*

The turnaround in Soviet-American relations stemmed more from changes abroad than from Reagan's decisions. As Reagan said near the end of his presidency, he had been "dropped into

▲ In one of several summit meetings, top Soviet leader Mikhail Gorbachev (b. 1931) and President Ronald Reagan (1911–2004) met in Moscow in May 1988 in hopes of signing a Strategic Arms Reduction Talks (START) agreement. The chemistry of warm friendship that Reagan later claimed characterized his personal relationship with Gorbachev fell short of producing cuts in dangerous strategic weapons. But their cordial interaction encouraged the diplomatic dialogue that helped end the Cold War.

a grand historical moment." Under the dynamic Gorbachev, a younger generation of Soviet leaders came to power in 1985. They began to modernize the highly bureaucratized, decaying economy through a reform program known as *perestroika* ("restructuring") and to liberalize the authoritarian political system through *glasnost* ("openness"). For these reforms to work, however, Soviet military expenditures had to be reduced and foreign aid decreased.

In 1987, Gorbachev and Reagan signed the **Intermediate-Range Nuclear Forces (INF) Treaty**, which banned all land-based intermediate-range nuclear missiles in Europe. Soon began the destruction of 2,800 missiles, including Soviet missiles targeted at Western Europe and NATO missiles aimed at the Soviet Union. Gorbachev also unilaterally reduced his nation's armed forces, helped settle regional conflicts, and began the withdrawal of Soviet troops from Afghanistan. After more than forty chilling years, the Cold War was coming to an end.

28-5 American Society in the 1980s

▷ **What were the origins of the "culture wars" of the 1980s?**

▷ **What social crises did the United States face in the 1980s?**

▷ **How did immigration change American society in the 1970s and 1980s?**

As the Cold War waned, so, too, did Americans' belief that the nation was united by a set of shared, middle-class values. By the 1980s, after years of social struggle and division, few Americans believed in the reality of that vision; many rejected it as undesirable. And though the 1980s were never as contentious and violent as the era of social protest in the 1960s and early 1970s, deep social and cultural divides existed among Americans. A newly powerful group of Christian conservatives challenged the secular culture of the American majority. A growing class of affluent, well-educated Americans seemed a society apart from the urban poor, and new technologies reshaped both work and leisure. At the same time, immigration was dramatically changing the composition of the American population.

28-5a "Culture Wars"

Throughout the 1980s, a coalition of conservative Christians known as the New Right waged campaigns against America's secular culture. Rejecting the "multiculturalist" belief that different cultures and lifestyle choices were equally valid, the New Right worked to make "God's law" the basis for American society. Concerned Women for America, founded by Beverly LaHayes in 1979, attempted to have elementary school readers containing "unacceptable" religious beliefs (including excerpts from *The Diary of Anne Frank* and *The Wizard of Oz*) removed from school classrooms, and

fundamentalist Christian groups once again began to challenge the teaching of evolutionary theory in public schools. The Reagan administration frequently turned to James Dobson, founder of the conservative Focus on the Family organization, for policy advice.

Although the New Right often found an ally in the Reagan White House, many other Americans vigorously opposed a movement they saw as preaching a doctrine of intolerance and threatening basic freedoms—including freedom of religion for those whose beliefs did not accord with the conservative Christianity of the New Right. In 1982, prominent figures from the fields of business, religion, politics, and entertainment founded People for the American Way to support American civil liberties and freedoms, the separation of church and state, and the values of tolerance and diversity. The struggle between the religious right and their opponents for the future of the nation came to be known as the "culture wars."

It was not only organized groups, however, that opposed the agenda of the religious right. Many New Right beliefs ran counter to the way most Americans lived—especially when it came to women's roles. By the 1980s, a generation of girls had grown up expecting freedoms and opportunities that their mothers never had. Legislation such as the Civil Rights Act of 1964 and Title IX had opened both academic and athletic programs to girls and women. In 1960, there were 38 male lawyers for every female lawyer in the United States; by 1983, the ratio was 5.5 to 1. By 1985, more than half of married women with children under three worked outside the home—many from economic necessity. The religious right's insistence that women's place was in the home, subordinated to her husband, contradicted not only the gains made toward sexual equality in American society but also the reality of many women's lives.

28-5b The New Inequality

As Americans fought the "culture wars" of the 1980s, another major social divide threatened the nation. A 1988 national report on race relations looked back to the 1968 Kerner Commission report to claim, "America is again becoming two separate societies," white and black. It argued that African Americans endured poverty, segregation, and crime in inner-city ghettos while most whites lived comfortably in suburban enclaves. In fact, America's separate societies of comfort and hardship were not wholly determined by race. The majority of America's poor were white, and the black middle class was strong and expanding. But people of color made up a disproportionate share of America's poor. In 1980, 33 percent of blacks and 26 percent of Latinos lived in poverty, compared with 10 percent of whites (see Figure 28.3).

Reasons for poverty varied. For people of color,

Intermediate-Range Nuclear Forces (INF) Treaty Treaty signed by U.S. president Reagan and Soviet leader Mikhail Gorbachev banning all land-based intermediate-range nuclear missiles in Europe, and resulting in the destruction of 2,800 missiles.

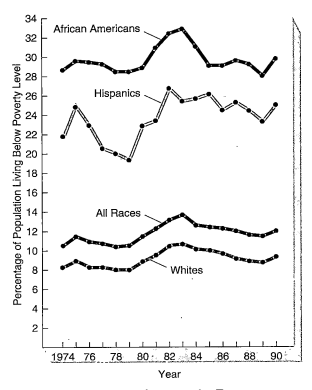

Figure 28.3 Poverty in America by Race, 1974–1990

Poverty in America rose in the early 1980s but subsided afterward. Many people of color, however, experienced little relief during the decade. Notice that the percentage of African Americans living below the poverty level was three times higher than that for whites. It was also much higher for Hispanics.

the legacies of racism played a role. The changing job structure was partly responsible, as the overall number of well-paid jobs for both skilled and unskilled workers decreased, replaced by lower-paid service jobs. New York alone had 234,000 fewer blue-collar workers in 1980 than at the beginning of the 1970s. In addition, families headed by a single mother were more likely to be poor—five times more likely than families of the same race with two parents present. By 1990, a high rate of unwed pregnancy and a rising divorce rate meant that about one-quarter of all children lived in a single-parent household. Racial differences were significant: in 1992, 59 percent of African American children and 17 percent of white children lived in households headed by a single woman, and almost half of black children lived in poverty.

28-5c Social Crises in American Cities

As inequality increased, so, too, did social pathology. In impoverished and often hopeless inner-city neighborhoods, violent crime—particularly homicides and gang warfare—grew alarmingly, as did school dropout rates, crime rates, and child abuse. Some people tried to find escape in hard drugs, especially crack, a derivative of cocaine, which first struck New York City's poorest neighborhoods in 1985. Crack's legacy included destroyed families, abused children, and heavily armed teenage drug dealers. Gang shootouts over drugs were deadly: the toll in Los Angeles in 1987 was 387 deaths, more than half of them innocent bystanders. Shocked by the violence, many states instituted mandatory prison sentences for possessing small amounts of crack. The federal government made penalties for a gram of crack equivalent to those for 100 grams of cocaine, the drug of choice for more affluent,

◁ A homeless man collects donations for the Temple of Rainbow food kitchen in a vacant lot, 1988. Americans increasingly recognized homelessness as a major national problem during the 1980s.

William Foley/Getty Images

Combating the Spread of AIDS

During the 1960s and 1970s, with penicillin offering a quick and painless cure for venereal diseases, and with dependable contraceptives, such as the birth control pill, widely available, nonmonogamous sex had fewer physical risks than at any time in history. But new sexually transmitted diseases appeared during the 1980s. By far the most serious was HIV/AIDS (Human Immunodeficiency Virus/Acquired Immune Deficiency Syndrome). Because AIDS initially was diagnosed in communities of gay men, many heterosexual Americans were slow to understand that they, too, might be at risk. Public health agencies and activist groups worked to raise awareness and promote safe sex.

CRITICAL THINKING

How is the couple in this ad portrayed?
- How does this image complicate widespread assumptions about who is at risk?
- How does this public service advertisement make the case for "safe sex"?

△ Campaigns for "safe sex," such as this New York City subway ad, urged people to use condoms.

white Americans during the 1980s. This war on drugs, along with a crackdown on rapidly rising violent crime and a far more punitive criminal justice system, increased America's prison population almost fourfold. By 2000, young black men were more likely to have been arrested than to have graduated from a four-year college.

Rates of homelessness also grew during the 1980s, in part because of major cuts to low-income housing subsidies. Some of the homeless were impoverished families; many of the people living on the streets had problems with drugs or alcohol. About one-third of the homeless were former psychiatric patients discharged from psychiatric wards in a burst of enthusiasm for "deinstitutionalization." By 1985, 80 percent of the total number of beds in state mental hospitals had been eliminated on the premise that small neighborhood programs would be more responsive to people's needs than large state hospitals. Such local programs failed to materialize. Without adequate medical supervision and medication, many of America's mentally ill citizens wandered the streets.

28-5d The AIDS Epidemic

Another social crisis confronting Americans in the 1980s was the global spread of acquired immune deficiency syndrome, or **AIDS**. Caused by the human immunodeficiency virus (HIV), which attacks cells in the immune system, AIDS leaves its victims susceptible to deadly infections and cancers. The human immunodeficiency virus itself is spread through the exchange of blood or body fluids, often through sexual intercourse or needle sharing by intravenous drug users.

AIDS was first diagnosed in the United States in 1981. During the 1980s it seemed an almost certain death sentence. Politicians were slow to devote resources to combating AIDS, in part because it was initially perceived as a "gay man's disease" and as such drew little concern from many of the nation's leaders. "A man reaps what he sows," declared the Reverend Jerry Falwell of the Moral Majority. A new group, ACT UP (the AIDS Coalition to Unleash Power), staged guerilla, agitprop demonstrations to confront "the system" that was so slow to address the threat of AIDS; ACT UP wrapped the home of conservative senator Jesse Helms in a huge, custom-made condom, and when Northwest Airlines refused to carry passengers with AIDS, the group bought millions of dollars' worth of Northwest tickets—and refused to pay for them. AIDS, along with other sexually transmitted diseases, such as genital herpes and chlamydia, ended an era defined by penicillin and "the Pill," in which sex was freed from the threat of serious disease or unwanted pregnancy.

AIDS Acquired Immune Deficiency Syndrome, first diagnosed in the United States in 1981; it had a very high mortality rate in the 1980s.

28-5e New Immigrants from Asia

Social divisions were further complicated by the arrival of new groups of immigrants. Between 1970 and 1990, the United States absorbed more than 13 million new arrivals, most from Latin America and Asia.

Before the immigration act reforms of 1965, less than 1 percent of Americans were of Asian ancestry; that percentage more than tripled by 1990. The new immigrants came from different nations. Before 1965, more than half of Asian Americans were of Japanese ancestry; Chinese or Filipino Americans made up most of the rest. There were only 603 Vietnamese residents of the United States in 1964. By 1990, the United States had absorbed almost 800,000 refugees from Indochina, casualties of the war in Vietnam and surrounding nations. Immigrants flooded in from South Korea, Thailand, India, Pakistan, Bangladesh, Indonesia, Singapore, Laos, Cambodia, and Vietnam. Japanese Americans became a much smaller portion of the Asian American population, at 15 percent surpassed by Chinese and Filipino Americans and rivaled by the Vietnamese.

Immigrants from Asia tended to be either highly skilled or unskilled. Unsettled conditions in the Philippines in the 1970s and 1980s created an exodus of well-educated Filipinos to the United States. India's economy was not able to support its abundance of well-trained physicians and health care workers, who increasingly found employment in the United States and elsewhere. Korea, Taiwan, and China also lost skilled and educated workers to the United States. Other immigrants from China, however, had few job skills and spoke little or no English. Large numbers of new immigrants crowded into neighborhoods like New York City's Chinatown, where women worked long hours under terrible conditions in the city's nonunion garment industry.

◁ Applicants for visas wait in line at the U.S. embassy in New Delhi, India. In 1985, 140,000 people were on the waiting list for one of 20,000 annual immigrant visas. Many poorer nations, such as India, experienced a "brain drain" of highly educated people to the United States and Western Europe.

Sandro Tucci/Getty Images

Immigrants from Southeast Asia were the most likely to be unskilled and to live in poverty in the United States, though some found opportunities for success.

But even highly educated immigrants often found their options limited. A 1983 study found that Korean immigrants or Korean Americans owned three-quarters of the approximately twelve hundred greengroceries (small stores that sell fresh vegetables and fruit) in New York City. Though often cited as a great immigrant success story, Korean greengrocers usually had descended the professional ladder: 78 percent of them had college or professional degrees.

28-5f The Growing Latino Population

Although immigration from Asia was high, unprecedented rates of immigration coupled with a high birth rate made Latinos the fastest-growing group of Americans. New immigrants from Mexico joined Mexican Americans and other Spanish-surnamed Americans, many of whose families had lived in this land even before it became the United States. In 1970, Latinos comprised 4.5 percent of the nation's population; that percentage jumped to 9 percent by 1990, when one out of three Los Angelenos and Miamians were Hispanic, as were 48 percent of the population of San Antonio and 70 percent of El Paso. Mexican Americans, concentrated in California and the Southwest, made up the majority of this population, but Puerto Ricans, Cubans, Dominicans, and other immigrants from the Caribbean also lived in the United States, clustered principally in East Coast cities.

During the 1980s, people from Guatemala and El Salvador fled civil war and government violence. Many found their way to the United States even though the U.S. government commonly refused to grant them political asylum (about 113,000 Cubans received political refugee status during the 1980s, compared with fewer than 1,400 El Salvadorans) until 1989. Economic troubles in Mexico and throughout Central and South America also produced a flood of a different sort of refugee: undocumented workers who crossed the two-thousand-mile border between the United States and Mexico, seeking economic opportunities. Some were sojourners who moved back and forth between nations. A majority meant to stay. These new Americans created a hybrid culture that became an important part of the American mosaic. "We want to be here," explained Daniel Villanueva, a TV executive in Los Angeles, "but without losing our language and our culture. They are a richness, a treasure that we don't care to lose."

The incorporation of so many newcomers into American society was not always easy, as many Americans believed new arrivals threatened their jobs and economic security, and nativist violence and simple bigotry increased. In 1982, twenty-seven-year-old Vincent Chin was beaten to death in Detroit by an unemployed autoworker and his uncle. American auto plants were losing the competition with Japanese imports, and the two men seemingly mistook the Chinese American Chin for Japanese, reportedly shouting at him, "It's because of you little [expletive deleted] that we're out of work." In New York, Philadelphia, and Los Angeles,

inner-city African Americans boycotted Korean groceries. Riots broke out in Los Angeles schools between black students and newly arrived Mexicans. In Dade County, Florida, voters passed an antibilingual measure that led to the removal of Spanish-language signs on public transportation, while at the state and national level people debated initiatives declaring English the "official" language of the United States. Public school classrooms, however, struggled with practical issues: in 1992, more than one thousand school districts in the United States enrolled students from at least eight different language groups.

Concerned about the flow of illegal aliens into the United States, Congress passed the **Immigration Reform and Control (Simpson-Rodino) Act** in 1986. The act's purpose was to discourage illegal immigration by imposing sanctions on employers who hired undocumented workers, but it also provided amnesty to millions who had immigrated illegally before 1982. As immigration continued at a high rate into the 1990s, however, it would further transform the face of America, offering both the richness of diverse cultures and the potential for continued social conflict.

28-5g New Ways of Life

Many Americans found their ways of life transformed during the 1980s, in large part due to new technologies and new models of distribution and consumption. American businesses made huge capital investments in technology during the 1980s as computers became increasingly central to the workplace. Such new communications technology made it possible to locate large office parks on the outskirts of cities, where building costs were low; these new workplaces fostered the development of "edge cities" or "technoburbs" filled with residents who lived, worked, and shopped outside the old city centers. New single-family homes grew larger and more expensive; the average cost of a new home rose from two and a half times the median household salary in 1980 to more than four times the median salary in 1988, and 42 percent of new homes had three or more bathrooms.

While the very rich embraced ostentation (Donald Trump's $29 million yacht had gold-plated bathroom fixtures) during this decade, people of more modest means also consumed more. Between 1980 and 1988, Wal-mart's sales jumped from $1.6 billion to $20.6 billion. The number of American shopping malls increased by two-thirds during the decade, and supermarkets stocked twice as many different items as they had ten years before. Eating out became common; by the end of the decade McDonald's was serving 17 million people a day, while "nouvelle cuisine" (artfully presented small portions, emphasizing fresh ingredients) appeared in upscale restaurants. The percentage of Americans who were overweight or

Immigration Reform and Control (Simpson-Rodino) Act A 1986 law that sought to discourage illegal immigration by fining employers who hired undocumented workers, but that also provided amnesty and a path to citizenship for millions who had immigrated illegally before 1982.

obese increased dramatically during the 1980s, even as more and more people began to run marathons (or compete in the much more demanding triathlons), tens of millions took aerobics classes or bought actress Jane Fonda's aerobics exercise videos, and the rapidly growing Nike brand launched its new slogan: "Just Do It."

New technology was not restricted to the workplace. Apple, founded by Steve Jobs and Steve Wozniak in 1976, introduced the Apple II computer in 1977; 2.1 million had been sold by 1985. IBM introduced its PC (personal computer) in 1981: for $1,565 (equivalent to $4,080 2015 dollars), purchasers got only 16 kilobytes of RAM. But the industry grew quickly, as did computer capacity, and almost half of American families owned some form of home computer by 1990.

Cable television expanded the choices offered by broadcast TV; about half of all families subscribed by the middle of the decade. When MTV (Music Television) was launched in 1981, only a few thousand cable subscribers in New Jersey had access, but it quickly grew to a national phenomenon. The first generation of MTV stars included Michael Jackson, whose fourteen-minute "Thriller" video premiered there in 1983, and Madonna, whose creative manipulation of her own image, from "Boy Toy" sexuality to celebration of female empowerment in "Express Yourself," infuriated both sides in the decade's culture wars. Newly affordable VCRs also gave consumers more choice. Movie attendance dropped as Americans rented movies to view at home, and children no longer had to wait for the annual and much-anticipated airing of *Cinderella* or *The Wizard of Oz* on television, but could instead watch *The Muppets Take Manhattan* or a host of other child-focused videos on demand—or as often as parents would allow.

28-6 The End of the Cold War and Global Disorder

▶ How did George H. W. Bush respond to events and developments on the international stage?

▶ What movements for democratization emerged in the 1980s?

▶ Why did the United States intervene militarily in the Middle East?

The departure of Ronald Reagan from the presidency coincided with a set of changes in world affairs that would lead in short order to the end of the Cold War and the dawn of a new international system. Reagan's vice president, **George H. W. Bush**, would become president and oversee the transition. The scion of a Wall Street banker who had been a U.S. senator from Connecticut, Bush had attended an exclusive boarding school and then gone on to Yale. An upper-class, eastern Establishment figure of the type that was becoming increasingly rare in the Republican Party, he had the advantage over his rivals for the presidential nomination in that he had been a loyal vice president. And he possessed a formidable résumé—he had been ambassador to the United Nations, chairman of the Republican Party, special envoy to China, and director of the CIA. He had also been a war hero, flying fifty-eight combat missions in the Pacific in World War II and receiving the Distinguished Flying Cross.

28-6a George Herbert Walker Bush

In 1988, the Democratic Party nominated Massachusetts governor Michael Dukakis for president; Vice President Bush, with Reagan's support, gained the Republican nomination. Bush built on Reagan's popularity, the nation's economic prosperity, and international stability. His camp also waged one of the most racially negative campaigns in recent American history, airing a television commercial featuring a black convicted murderer, Willie Horton, who had terrorized a Maryland couple, raping the woman, while on weekend furlough—a temporary release program begun under Dukakis's Republican predecessor but used in the ad to suggest that Dukakis was "soft on crime." Bush defeated Dukakis by 8 percentage points in the popular vote, but the Democrats retained control of both houses of Congress.

From the start, Bush focused most of his attention on foreign policy, but domestic issues demanded his attention. Though the most-quoted line from his presidential campaign was "Read my lips: no new taxes," when confronted with a rapidly growing federal deficit, Bush chose to do what he thought necessary for the good of the nation: he compromised with Congress and raised taxes. Bush believed that government could not solve the nation's social problems, and he praised private charitable organizations as "a thousand points of light" and called for more "hands-on" activism from the American people. Yet he believed government played an important role in the "kinder, gentler nation" he envisioned. In 1990, Bush signed the **Americans with Disabilities Act (ADA)** (see "Legacy for a People and a Nation"). Much to the disappointment of conservatives who opposed increased government regulation, Bush signed the Clean Air Act, which sought to reduce acid rain by limiting emissions from factories and automobiles. And in 1991, after months of contentious debate, Bush and Congress agreed on a civil rights bill that expanded the remedies victims of job discrimination could seek. However, Bush also nominated the highly conservative **Clarence Thomas** to the Supreme Court.

In world affairs, Bush was by nature cautious and reactive, even in the face of huge changes in the international system and much to the chagrin of neoconservatives. Mikhail Gorbachev's reforms in the Soviet Union were now taking

△ President George H. W. Bush signs the Americans with Disabilities Act (ADA) on the White House lawn, July 26, 1990. As he lifted his pen, the president said: "Let the shameful wall of exclusion finally come tumbling down."

on a life of their own, stimulating reforms in Eastern Europe that ultimately led to revolution. In 1989, many thousands of people in East Germany, Poland, Hungary, Czechoslovakia, and Romania, longing for personal freedom, startled the world by repudiating their communist governments and staging mass protests against a despised ideology. In November 1989, Germans scaled the Berlin Wall and then tore it down; the following October, the two Germanys reunited after forty-five years of separation. By then, the other communist governments in Eastern Europe had either fallen or were about to do so.

28-6b Pro-Democracy Movements

Challenges to communist rule in China met with less success. In June 1989, hundreds—perhaps thousands—of unarmed students and other citizens who for weeks had been holding peaceful pro-democracy rallies in Beijing's Tiananmen Square were slaughtered by Chinese armed forces. The Bush administration, anxious to preserve influence in Beijing, did no more than denounce the action, allowing the Chinese government, whose successful economic reforms had won much admiration in the 1980s, to emphatically reject political liberalization.

Elsewhere, however, the forces of democratization proved too powerful to resist. In South Africa, a new government under F. W. de Klerk, responding to increased domestic and international pressure (including from college campuses in the United States, where students erected shantytowns and called for universities to divest their investments in financial institutions with holdings in South Africa), began a cautious retreat from the apartheid system. In February 1990, de Klerk legalized all political parties in South Africa, including the ANC, and ordered the release of Nelson Mandela, a hero to black South Africans, after a twenty-seven-year imprisonment. Then, in a staged process lasting several years, the government repealed its apartheid laws and opened up the vote to all citizens, regardless of color. Mandela, who became South Africa's first black president in 1994, called the transformation of his country "a small miracle."

28-6c Collapse of Soviet Power

In 1990, the Soviet Union itself began to disintegrate. First the Baltic states of Lithuania, Latvia, and Estonia declared independence from Moscow's rule. The following year, the Soviet Union itself ceased to exist, disintegrating into fifteen

△ The 1980s witnessed the rise of organized "divestment campaigns" on American college campuses in opposition to South Africa's apartheid system. Here protestors gather outside their shantytown at the University of Colorado in Boulder in early 1988. Some 80 students lived in shacks and tents built to protest the South African government and the university's investments in that country.

independent successor states—Russia, Ukraine, Belarus, Armenia, Tajikistan, and many others (see Map 28.2). Muscled aside by Russian reformers who thought he was moving too slowly toward democracy and free-market economics, Gorbachev himself lost power. The breakup of the Soviet empire, the dismantling of the Warsaw Pact (the Soviet military alliance formed in 1955 with communist countries of eastern Europe), the repudiation of communism by its own leaders, German reunification, and a significantly reduced risk of nuclear war signaled the end of the Cold War. The Soviet-American rivalry that for half a century had dominated international politics—and circumscribed domestic prospects in both countries—was over.

The United States and its allies had won. The containment policy followed by nine presidents—from Truman through Bush—had many critics over the years, on both the left and the right, but it had succeeded on a most basic level: it had

contained communism for four-plus decades without blowing up the world and without obliterating freedom at home. Two systems competed in this East-West confrontation, and that of the West had clearly triumphed—as anyone who experienced life in both a NATO country and a Warsaw Pact nation quickly realized. Next to the glitz and bustle and well-stocked store shelves of the former were the drab housing projects, polluted skies, and scarce consumer goods of the latter. Over time, the Soviet socialist economy proved less and less able to compete with the American free-market one, less and less able to cope with the demands of the Soviet and Eastern European citizenry.

Yet the Soviet empire might have hobbled along for years more had it not been for Gorbachev, one of the most influential figures of the twentieth century. His ascension to the top of the Soviet leadership was the single most important event in the final phase of the Cold War, and it is hard to imagine the far-reaching changes of the 1985–1990 period without his influence. Through a series of unexpected overtures and decisions, Gorbachev fundamentally transformed the nature of the superpower relationship in a way that could scarcely have been anticipated a few years before. Ronald Reagan's role was less central but still vitally important, not so much because of his hard-line policies in his first term as because of his later willingness to enter into serious negotiations and to treat Gorbachev more as a partner than as an adversary. George H. W. Bush, too, followed this general approach. In this way, just as personalities mattered in starting the Cold War, so they mattered in ending it.

28-6d Costs of Victory

The victory in the Cold War elicited little celebration among Americans. The struggle had exacted a heavy price in money and lives. The confrontation may never have become a hot war on a global level, but the period after 1945 nevertheless witnessed numerous bloody Cold War–related conflicts claiming millions of lives. In the Vietnam War alone, between 1.5 million and 2 million people died, more than 58,000 of them Americans. Military budgets, meanwhile, had eaten up billions upon billions of dollars that could have been allocated to domestic programs. Some Americans wondered whether the steep price had been necessary, whether the communist threat had ever been as grave as officials, from the late 1940s on, had claimed.

Bush proclaimed a "new world order," but for him and his advisers the question was: what happens next? As the Cold War closed, they struggled to describe the dimensions of an international system that they said would be based on democracy, free trade, and the rule of law. The administration signed important arms reduction treaties with the Soviet Union in 1991 and with the post-breakup Russia in 1993, leading to major reductions in nuclear weapons on both sides, but the United States sustained a large defense budget and continued to station large numbers of military forces overseas. As a result, Americans were denied the "peace dividend" that

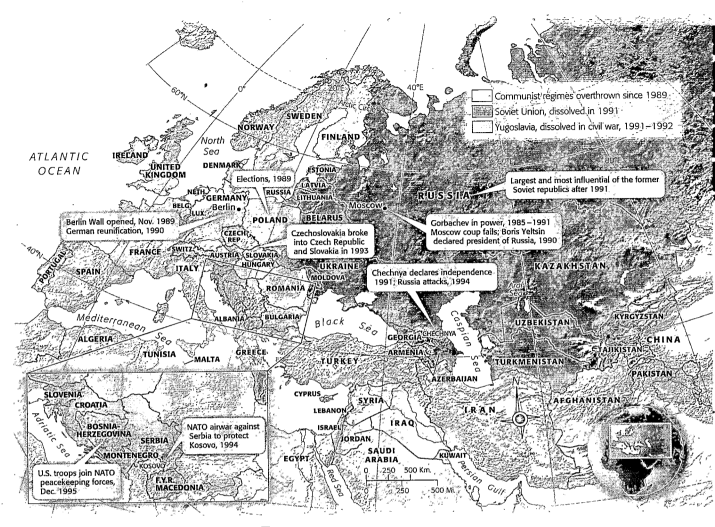

Map 28.2 The End of the Cold War in Europe

When Mikhail Gorbachev came to power in the Soviet Union in 1985, he initiated reforms that ultimately undermined the communist regimes in Eastern Europe and East Germany and led to the breakup of the Soviet Union itself, ensuring an end to the Cold War.

they hoped would reduce taxes and free up funds to address domestic problems.

28-6e Saddam Hussein's Gamble

The strongest test of Bush's foreign policy came in the Middle East. The Iran-Iraq War had ended inconclusively in August 1988, after eight years of fighting and almost four hundred thousand dead. The Reagan administration had assisted the Iraqi war effort with weapons and intelligence, as had many other NATO countries. In mid-1990, Iraqi president Saddam Hussein, facing massive war debts and growing domestic discontent, invaded neighboring Kuwait, hoping thereby to enhance his regional power and his oil revenues and shore up domestic support. He counted on Washington to look the other way. Instead, George Bush condemned the invasion and vowed to defend Kuwait. He was outraged by Hussein's act of aggression and also feared that Iraq might

threaten U.S. oil supplies, not merely in Kuwait but also in petroleum-rich Saudi Arabia next door.

Within weeks, Bush had convinced virtually every important government, including most of the Arab and Islamic states, to sign on to an economic boycott of Iraq. Then, in Operation Desert Shield, Bush dispatched more than 500,000 U.S. forces to the region, where they were joined by more than 200,000 from the allies. Likening Saddam to Hitler and declaring the moment the first post–Cold War "test of our mettle," Bush rallied a deeply divided Congress to authorize "all necessary means" to oust Iraq from Kuwait (by a vote of 250 to 183 in the House and 52 to 47 in the Senate). Although Bush did not invoke the 1973 War Powers Act, numerous observers saw his seeking a congressional resolution of approval as reinforcing the intent of the act. Many Americans believed that economic sanctions imposed on Iraq should be given more time

CNN

When Ted Turner launched CNN, his Cable News Network, on June 1, 1980, few people took it seriously. CNN, with a staff of three hundred—mostly young, mostly inexperienced— operated out of the basement of a converted country club in Atlanta. Dismissed by critics as the Chicken Noodle Network, CNN was at first best known for its on-air errors, as when a cleaning woman walked onto the set and emptied anchor Bernard Shaw's trash during his live newscast. But by 1992, against all expectations, CNN was seen in more than 150 nations worldwide, and Time magazine named Ted Turner its "Man of the Year" for realizing media theorist Marshall McLuhan's vision of the world as a "global village" united by mass media.

Throughout the 1980s, CNN steadily built relations with local news outlets in nations throughout the world. As critical—and sometimes unanticipated—events reshaped the world, CNN reported live from Tiananmen Square and from the Berlin Wall in 1989. Millions watched as CNN reporters broadcast live from Baghdad in the early hours of the Gulf War in 1991. CNN changed not only viewers' experience of these events but diplomacy itself. When the Soviet Union wanted to denounce the 1989 U.S. invasion of Panama, officials called CNN's Moscow bureau instead of the U.S. embassy. During the Gulf War, Saddam Hussein reportedly kept televisions in his bunker tuned to CNN, and U.S. generals relied on its broadcasts to judge the effectiveness of missile attacks. In 1992, President George H. W. Bush noted, "I learn more from CNN than I do from the CIA."

Although Turner's twenty-four-hour news network had a global mission, its American origins were often apparent. During the U.S. invasion of Panama, CNN cautioned correspondents not to refer to the American military forces as "our" troops. Turner himself once sent his staff a memo insisting that anyone who used the word *foreign* instead of *international* would be fined $100. What CNN offered was not so much international news but a global experience: people throughout the world joined in watching the major moments in contemporary history as they unfolded. America's CNN created new links among the world's people. But as *Time* magazine noted (while praising Turner as the "Prince of the Global Village"), such connections "did not produce instantaneous brotherhood, just a slowly dawning awareness of the implications of a world transfixed by a single TV image."

CRITICAL THINKING

☐ If people throughout the world receive news from the same source, why do they all not understand the events and their meaning the same way?

△ A CNN correspondent interviews Israeli deputy foreign minister Benjamin Netanyahu on January 19, 1991. Following an alarm indicating an Iraqi missile attack on Israeli targets, those in the Jerusalem CNN studios had donned gas masks. CNN changed media history in the way its live coverage reported events as they unfolded.

◁ In the Persian Gulf War of early 1991, Operation Desert Storm forced Iraqi troops out of Kuwait. Much of that nation's oil industry was destroyed by bombs and by the retreating Iraqis, who torched oil facilities as they left. Oil wells burned for months, darkening the sky over these American forces and causing environmental damage.

Bruno Barbey/Magnum Photos

to work, but Bush would not wait. "This will not be another Vietnam," the president said, by which he meant it would not be a lengthy and frustrating affair. Victory would come swiftly and cleanly.

28-6f Operation Desert Storm

Operation Desert Storm began on January 16, 1991, with the greatest air armada in history pummeling Iraqi targets. American cruise missiles reinforced round-the-clock bombing raids on Baghdad, Iraq's capital. It was a television war, in which CNN reporters broadcast live from a Baghdad hotel while bombs were falling in the city, and millions of Americans sat transfixed in their living rooms, eyes glued to the TV. In late February, coalition forces under General Norman Schwarzkopf launched a ground war that quickly routed the Iraqis from Kuwait. When the war ended on March 1, at least 40,000 Iraqis had been killed, while the death toll for allied troops stood at 240 (148 of them Americans). Almost one-quarter of the American dead were killed by "friendly fire"—by weapons fired by U.S. or allied troops.

Bush rejected a call from some of his advisers to take Baghdad and topple Saddam Hussein's regime. Coalition members would not have agreed to such a plan—it would go beyond the original objective of forcing Iraq out of Kuwait—and it was also not clear who in Iraq would replace the dictator. Some also warned that the drive to Baghdad could bog down, subjecting U.S. forces to a costly and drawn-out campaign. So Saddam survived in power, though with his authority curtailed. The UN maintained an arms and economic embargo, and the Security Council issued Resolution 687, demanding that Iraq provide full disclosure of all aspects

of its program to develop weapons of mass destruction and ballistic missiles with a range greater than 150 kilometers. In Resolution 688, the Security Council condemned a brutal crackdown by the Iraqi regime against Kurds in northern Iraq and Shi'ite Muslims in the south and demanded access for humanitarian groups. The United States, Britain, and France seized on Resolution 688 to create a northern "no-fly zone" prohibiting Iraqi aircraft flights. A similar no-fly zone was set up in southern Iraq in 1992 and expanded in 1996.

Although in time some would question President Bush's decision to stop short of Baghdad, initially there were few objections. In the wake of Desert Storm, the president's popularity in the polls soared to 91 percent, beating the previous high of 89 percent set by Harry Truman in June 1945 after the surrender of Germany. Cocky White House advisers thought Bush could ride his popularity right through the 1992 election and beyond. In the afterglow of military victory it seemed a good bet, but in the months following the Gulf War the nation entered a full-fledged recession. Unemployment climbed to 8 percent. By late 1991, fewer than 40 percent of Americans felt comfortable with the way the country was going. By the time George H. W. Bush and the Republicans entered the election year of 1992, the glow of military victory in the Gulf War had faded completely.

Summary

When Ronald Reagan left the White House in 1988, succeeded by his vice president, George Bush, the *New York Times* summed up his presidency: "Ronald Reagan leaves no Vietnam War, no Watergate, no hostage crisis. But he

The Americans with Disabilities Act

The Americans with Disabilities Act (ADA), passed by large bipartisan majorities in Congress and signed into law by President George H. W. Bush on July 26, 1990, built on the legacy of America's civil rights movement; President Bush called it "the world's first comprehensive declaration of equality for people with disabilities." But the ADA did more than prohibit discrimination against people with physical and mental disabilities. It mandated that public and private entities—including schools, stores, restaurants and hotels, libraries and other government buildings, and public transportation authorities—provide "reasonable accommodations" to allow people with disabilities to participate fully in the life of their communities and their nation.

In less than two decades, the equal-access provisions of the ADA have changed the landscape of America. Steep curbs and stairs once blocked access to wheelchair users; now ramps and lifts are common. Buses "kneel" for passengers with limited mobility; crosswalks and elevators use audible signals for the sight impaired. At colleges and universities, qualified students (including those with learning disabilities) receive a wide range of assistance or accommodation. The National Park Service's "accessibility" program has enabled people with a whole spectrum of disabilities to travel into the Grand Canyon and on trails in many parks. Lee Page, a wheelchair user and sports fan from Virginia, described the impact of ADA standards for sports stadiums: "We were able to see over the standing spectators as the anthem was sung. I could see the flag and everything that was happening down on the field. . . . I finally felt like a part of the crowd."

At the same time that the ADA has offered greater opportunity to many Americans, regulations covering employment have generated some difficult legal questions. Which conditions are covered by the ADA? (The Supreme Court has ruled that asymptomatic HIV infection is a covered disability and carpal tunnel syndrome is not.) Employers may not discriminate against qualified people who can, with "reasonable" accommodation, perform the "essential" tasks of a job—but what is "reasonable" and what is "essential"? The specific provisions of the ADA will likely continue to be contested and redefined in the courts. But as Attorney General Janet Reno noted, as she celebrated the tenth anniversary of the ADA with a ceremony at Warm Springs, Georgia, where President Franklin Roosevelt had sought therapy for the effects of polio, the true legacy of the ADA is the determination "to find the best in everyone and to give everyone equal opportunity."

CRITICAL THINKING

- Terms such as "reasonable" and "essential" do not give specific guidance. What should employers consider in their efforts to offer equal opportunity?

---

leaves huge question marks—and much to do." George H. W. Bush met the foreign policy promises of the 1980s, as the Soviet Union collapsed and America achieved victory in the decades-long Cold War. He also led the United States into war with Iraq—a war that ended in swift and decisive victory but left Saddam Hussein in power.

During the 1980s, the United States moved from deep recession to economic prosperity. However, deep tax cuts and massive increases in defense spending created huge budget deficits, increasing the national debt from $994 billion to more than $2.9 trillion. This enormous debt would limit the options of subsequent presidential administrations. Pro-business policies, such as deregulation, created opportunities for the development of new technologies and prompted economic growth but also opened the door to corruption and fraud. Policies that benefited the wealthy at the expense of middle-class or poor Americans widened the gulf between the rich and everyone else. And drug addiction, crime, and violence grew during this era, especially in the nation's most impoverished areas.

The 1980s also saw the coalescence of the "culture wars" between fundamentalist Christians who sought to "restore" America to God and opponents who championed separation of church and state and embraced liberal values. The nation shifted politically to the right, though the coalitions of economic and social conservatives that supported Reagan were fragile and did not guarantee continued Republican dominance.

Finally, during the 1980s, the face of America changed. A society that many had thought of as comprised of white and black Americans became ever more diverse. The nation's Latino population grew in size and visibility. New immigrants from Asia arrived in large numbers; though still a small part of the population, they would play an increasingly important role in American society. During the Reagan-Bush years, America had become both more divided and more diverse. In the years to come, Americans and their leaders would struggle with the legacies of the Reagan era.

Suggestions for Further Reading

Elijah Anderson, *Streetwise: Race, Class, and Change in an Urban Community* (1992)

Lou Cannon, *President Reagan: The Role of a Lifetime* (2000)

Robert M. Collins, *Transforming America: Politics and Culture During the Reagan Years* (2006)

Campbell Craig and Fredrik Logevall, *America's Cold War* (2009)

Andrew Hartman, *A War for the Soul of America: A History of the Culture Wars* (2015)

Bradford Martin, *The Other Eighties: A Secret History of America in the Age of Reagan* (2011)

James Patterson, *The Restless Giant: The United States from Watergate to Bush vs. Gore* (2005)

Kim Phillips-Fein, *Invisible Hands: The Making of the Conservative Movement from the New Deal to Reagan* (2009)

Daniel T. Rogers, *Age of Fracture* (2012)

James Graham Wilson, *The Triumph of Improvisation: Gorbachev's Adaptability, Reagan's Engagement, and the End of the Cold War* (2014)

MINDTAP
From Cengage

MindTap® is a fully online personalized learning experience built upon Cengage Learning content. MindTap® combines student learning tools—readings, multimedia, activities, and assessments—into a singular Learning Path that guides students through the course and helps students develop the critical thinking, analysis, and communication skills that are essential to academic and professional success.

Into the Global Millennium: America Since 1992

A t 8:46 AM on that fateful Tuesday morning, Jan Demczur, a window washer, stepped into an elevator in the North Tower of the World Trade Center in New York City. The elevator started to climb, but before it reached its next landing, one of the six occupants recalled, "We felt a muted thud. The whole building shook. And the elevator swung from side to side like a pendulum." None of the occupants knew it, but American Airlines Flight 175 had just crashed into the building, at a speed of 440 miles per hour.

The elevator started plunging. Someone pushed the emergency stop button, and the descent stopped. For several minutes, nothing happened. Then a voice came over the intercom to deliver a blunt message: there had been an explosion. The line went dead, as smoke began to seep through the elevator's doors. Using the wooden handle of Demczur's squeegee, several of the men forced open the doors but discovered they were on the fiftieth floor, five hundred feet above the ground, where this elevator did not stop. In front of them was a wall.

Demczur, a Polish immigrant who once worked as a builder, saw that the wall was made of Sheetrock, a plasterboard he knew could be cut. Using the squeegee, he started to scrape the metal edge against the wall, back and forth, over and over again. When the blade broke and fell down the shaft, he used a short metal handle that he had in his bucket. It took more than an hour, but the six men took turns scraping and poking, and finally burst through to a men's bathroom. Startled firefighters guided them to a stairwell. After an agonizingly slow descent through the heavy smoke, they finally burst onto the street at 10:23 a.m. Five minutes later, the tower collapsed.

It was September 11, 2001.

Only later that day did Demczur learn what had happened: terrorists had hijacked four airliners and turned them into missiles. Two had been flown into the World Trade Center; one had

◁ "The Tribute of Light," dedicated to the memory of the victims of the World Trade Center terrorist attacks, lights up the sky above Lower Manhattan on March 11, 2002, the six-month anniversary of the attacks. The Brooklyn Bridge is seen in the foreground. AP Photo/Daniel P. Derella

Chronology

1992	▣ Violence erupts in Los Angeles over Rodney King verdict
	▣ Major economic recession
	▣ Clinton elected president
1993	▣ Congress approves North American Free Trade Agreement (NAFTA)
1994	▣ Republican "Contract with America"
	▣ Genocide in Rwanda
	▣ U.S. intervention in Haiti
1995	▣ Domestic terrorist bombs Oklahoma City federal building
	▣ U.S. diplomats broker peace for Bosnia
1996	▣ Welfare reform bill places time limits on welfare payments
	▣ Clinton reelected president
1999	▣ NATO bombs Serbia over Kosovo crisis
	▣ Antiglobalization demonstrators disrupt World Trade Organization (WTO) meeting in Seattle
2000	▣ Nation records longest economic expansion in its history
	▣ Supreme Court settles contested presidential election in favor of George W. Bush
2001	▣ Economy dips into recession
	▣ Al Qaeda terrorists attack World Trade Center and Pentagon

	▣ United States attacks Al Qaeda positions in Afghanistan, topples ruling Taliban regime
2003	▣ United States invades Iraq, ousts Saddam Hussein regime
2004	▣ Bush reelected
2005	▣ Hurricane Katrina strikes Gulf Coast
2006	▣ By end of year, U.S. war deaths in Iraq reach three thousand
2007	▣ Major economic recession begins in December
2008	▣ Barack Obama elected president
2009	▣ Obama announces increased U.S. military commitment to Afghanistan; U.S. continues troop drawdown in Iraq
2010	▣ Congress passes Patient Protection and Affordable Care Act
2011	▣ U.S. Navy SEALs kill Osama bin Laden
2012	▣ Obama reelected president
2015	▣ Iran nuclear deal
	▣ Reestablishment of U.S.-Cuba relations
2016	▣ Donald Trump elected president

slammed into the Pentagon in Washington, D.C.; and one had crashed in a field in rural Pennsylvania after passengers tried to wrest control of the plane from the hijackers. Both World Trade Center towers had collapsed, killing close to three thousand people, including Demczur's close friend Roko Camaj, a window washer from Albania.

It was the deadliest attack the United States had ever suffered on its soil, and it would lead to far-ranging changes in American life. But the events of the day sent shock waves well beyond the country's shores, indeed around the globe, and made starkly clear just how interconnected the world had become at the dawn of the twenty-first century. At the World

Trade Center alone, nearly five hundred foreigners from more than eighty countries lost their lives. Sixty-seven Britons died, twenty-one Jamaicans, and twenty-seven Japanese. Mexico lost seventeen of its citizens; India lost thirty-four. Sixteen Canadians perished, as did fifteen Australians and seven Haitians. The tiny Caribbean nation of Trinidad and Tobago counted fifteen deaths.

The list of victims revealed the extraordinary diversity of people who inhabited New York, showing the city once again to be a mélange of world cultures. According to a chaplain at "Ground Zero," the victims' families communicated their grief in well over a hundred languages. Many of the victims were, like Demczur and Camaj, immigrants who had come to New York to seek a better life for themselves and their families; others were there on temporary work visas. But all helped to make the World Trade Center a kind of global city within a city, where some 50,000 people worked and another 140,000 visited on any given day.

A symbol of U.S. financial power, the World Trade Center towers were also—as their very name suggested—a symbol of the globalization of world trade that had been a central phenomenon of the 1980s and 1990s. The towers housed the offices and Wall Street infrastructure of more than four hundred businesses, including some of the world's leading financial institutions—Bank of America, Switzerland's Credit Suisse Group, Germany's Deutsche Bank, and Japan's Dai-Ichi Kangyo Bank.

Experience an interactive version of this story in MindTap®.

One of the buzzwords produced by the 1990s is *globalization*; by most definitions, globalization went beyond trade and investment to include the web of connections—in commerce, communications, and culture—that increasingly bound the world together. The terrorists, who were tied to a radical Islamic group called Al Qaeda, sought to strike a blow at that globalization, yet their attack was also an expression of it. In other words, Al Qaeda depended on the same international technological, economic, and travel infrastructure that had fueled global integration. Cell phones, computers, intercontinental air travel—the plotters made full use of these instruments of globalization in preparing to carry out their attack, then turned four modern jetliners into lethal weapons.

Americans struggled to comprehend the meaning of the attacks. For a broad majority of them, the last decade of the century offered good times. The stock market soared, unemployment dropped, and more Americans than ever before owned their own homes. But the 1990s were also marked by violence and cultural conflict—the first multiethnic uprising in Los Angeles, domestic terrorism in Oklahoma City, shootings by students at their schools, hate crimes that shocked the nation.

These were also years of political volatility and divisions. From the first days of Clinton's presidency, conservative Republicans blocked the Democrats' legislative programs. With a conservative agenda of limited government and "family values," the GOP routed Democrats in the 1994 midterm elections. But Republicans overestimated their power, alienating many voters by forcing the federal government to shut down during the winter of 1995–1996 in a standoff over the federal budget, and Clinton was reelected in 1996. However, Clinton's impeachment over sexual impropriety compromised his ability to lead the nation.

Clinton's successor, George W. Bush, responded to the 9/11 attacks by declaring a "war on terrorism." In so doing, he committed his administration and the nation to a complex and dangerous campaign of undefined scope and duration. Twice within eighteen months, Bush ordered U.S. forces into large-scale military action, first in Afghanistan, where Al Qaeda had its headquarters with the blessing of the ruling Taliban regime, then in Iraq to oust the government of Saddam Hussein. Both operations initially went well militarily, as the Taliban and the Iraqi government were quickly beaten. Al Qaeda, however, did not cease to be a threat, and in Afghanistan fighting eventually resumed. In Iraq, U.S. occupying forces battled a large-scale insurgency. Bush saw his high approval ratings begin to drop, and though he won reelection in 2004, his second term was undermined by continued bloodshed in Iraq and scandal at home. In 2008, Democratic candidate Barack Obama won the presidency on a platform of hope and change. The election of the nation's first African American president was a moment of great symbolic importance, but Obama, who inherited two wars and a major recession, found it difficult to create the domestic transformations he had promised. The depth of the economic crisis drastically limited the scope for substantive policy initiatives, and Obama also operated in a deeply polarized climate. Nevertheless, in his two terms in office, he brought the recession to an end, concluded American combat involvement in Iraq, and got Congress to pass the Patient Protection and Affordable Care Act, the most significant regulatory overhaul of the U.S. healthcare system since 1965. In 2016, a divided nation split the popular and electoral college vote, sending Donald J. Trump to the White House.

globalization The removal of barriers to the flow of capital, goods, and ideas across national borders.

■ *What was "the new economy" of the 1990s, and how did it contribute to the globalization of business?*

■ *Did the attacks of September 11, 2001, change America in fundamental ways? Explain.*

■ *Why did the United States wage wars in Iraq and Afghanistan in the decade after 9/11, and why did it struggle to prevail in both despite its massive technological superiority?*

29-1 Social Strains and New Directions

▷ **What did the Los Angeles riots reveal about the complexity of race relations in the United States?**

▷ **How did the Democrats and Republicans simultaneously compromise with one another and challenge one another on public policy?**

▷ **How did Bill Clinton respond to international events and address foreign policy issues?**

Although the 1990s would be remembered as an era of relative peace and prosperity, the decade did not start that way. Scourges of drugs, homelessness, and crime plagued America's cities. Racial tensions had worsened; the gulf between rich and poor had grown more pronounced. The economy, slowing since 1989, had tipped into recession. Public disillusionment with political leaders ran strong. As the 1992 presidential election year began, Americans were frustrated and looking for a change.

29-1a Turmoil in L.A.

The racial tensions that troubled the nation erupted in the South Central neighborhood of Los Angeles in 1992. The violence in Los Angeles (which the Korean community called Sa-I-Gu, or 4/29, for the date it began) was a multiethnic uprising that left at least fifty-three people dead. Like most such outbreaks, there was an immediate cause. A jury with no African American members had acquitted four white police officers charged with beating a black man, Rodney King, who had fled a pursuing police car at speeds exceeding 110 miles per hour.

Bill Clinton Forty-second president of the United States (1993–2001). Clinton served as the governor of Arkansas for twelve years prior to his election to the U.S. presidency.

Hillary Rodham Clinton Wife of President Bill Clinton, she was directly involved in policymaking during her husband's presidency. She later served as a New York senator (2001–2009), ran for president (2008 and 2016), and served as secretary of state (2009–2013) in the first Obama administration.

The roots of the violence went deeper. After well-paid jobs disappeared during the deindustrialization of the 1970s and 1980s, almost one-third of South Central residents lived in poverty. Tensions increased as new immigrants—Latinos from Mexico and Central America who competed with African American residents for jobs, as well as Koreans who established small businesses—sought a foothold in the area. Outside the legitimate economy, the 40 Crips (an African American gang) and the 18th Street gang (Latino) struggled over territory as the crack epidemic further decimated the neighborhood and the homicide rate soared. Police tactics had alienated most neighborhood residents, and relations were especially strained between African Americans and the new Korean population, as many African American and Latino residents saw high prices in Korean-owned shops as exploitation, while Korean shopkeepers complained of shoplifting, robberies, and violence.

Other sources of the conflict extended well beyond Los Angeles. During the Bush (senior) administration, the nation's economy had grown slowly or not at all. Factory employment was at its lowest level since the recession of 1982, and corporate downsizing meant that well-educated white-collar workers were also losing jobs. In 1992, poverty was at its highest level since 1964.

29-1b Clinton and the "New Democrats"

As the American economy suffered, so did President George H. W. Bush's approval rating. Despite the credit Bush gained for foreign policy—the end of the Cold War and the quick victory in the Gulf War—economic woes and a lack of what he once called the "vision thing" left him vulnerable in the 1992 presidential election. On Election Day, Democratic nominee **Bill Clinton** and his running mate, Tennessee senator Al Gore, swept New England, the West Coast, and much of the industrial Midwest, even making inroads into what had become an almost solidly Republican South and drawing "Reagan Democrats" back into the fold.

Bill Clinton was a larger-than-life figure, a born politician from a small town called Hope who had wanted to be president most of his life. In college during the 1960s he had protested the Vietnam War and (like many of his generation) had maneuvered to keep himself from being sent to Vietnam. Clinton had won a Rhodes Scholarship to Oxford, earned his law degree from Yale, and returned to his home state of Arkansas, where he was elected governor in 1978 at the age of thirty-two. Bill Clinton's wife, **Hillary Rodham Clinton**, was the first First Lady to have a significant career of her own during her married life; they had met when they were both law students at Yale, where Hillary Rodham had made Law Review (an honor not shared by her husband).

Politically, Bill Clinton was a "new Democrat." He, along with other members of the new Democratic Leadership Council, advocated a more centrist—though still socially progressive—position for the Democratic Party. Clinton and his colleagues asked whether large

◁ Presidential candidate and tenor saxophonist Bill Clinton plays Elvis Presley's *Heartbreak Hotel* on the Arsenio Hall show, June 3, 1992. Many Washington commentators deemed it undignified, but Clinton's turn to late-night TV—a first in presidential campaigning—appealed to young and non-white Americans and transformed his campaign.

AP Images/Reed Saxon

government bureaucracies were still appropriate tools for addressing social problems in modern America. They emphasized private-sector economic development rather than public jobs programs, focusing on job training and other policies that they believed would promote opportunity, not dependency. They championed a global outlook in both foreign policy and economic development. Finally, they emphasized an ethic of "mutual responsibility" and "inclusiveness."

Clinton plunged into an ambitious program of reform and revitalization. His major goal was to make health care affordable and accessible for all Americans, including the millions who had no insurance coverage. But special interests mobilized in opposition: the insurance industry worried about lost profits; the business community feared higher taxes to support the uninsured; the medical community was concerned about more regulation, lower government reimbursement rates, and reduced healthcare quality. The administration's healthcare task force, co-chaired by Hillary Rodham Clinton, could not create a political coalition strong enough to defeat these forces. Within a year, the centerpiece of Clinton's fledgling presidency had failed.

29-1c "Republican Revolution" and Political Compromise

With Clinton beleaguered, Republicans mounted a challenge. In September 1994, conservative Republicans championed a new "Contract with America." Developed under the leadership of Georgia congressman **Newt Gingrich**, the "Contract" called for a balanced-budget amendment to the Constitution, reduction of the capital gains tax, a two-year limit on welfare payments (while making unmarried mothers under eighteen ineligible), and increased defense spending.

In the midterm elections, the Republican Party mobilized socially conservative voters, gaining control of both houses of Congress for the first time since 1954 and increasing their share in state legislatures and governorships. Many Republicans believed their ongoing attempts to weaken federal power and to dismantle the welfare state would now succeed.

The Republicans of the 104th Congress, however, had miscalculated. Although many Americans liked the idea of cutting government spending, they opposed cuts to specific programs: Medicare and Medicaid, education and college loans, highway construction, farm subsidies, veterans' benefits, and Social Security. Republicans made a bigger mistake when they issued President Clinton an ultimatum on the federal budget. Clinton refused to accept their terms, and Republicans shut down the federal government in response. An angry public blamed the Republicans.

Such actions showed Clinton's resolve. But Clinton also compromised with those to his political right. He signed the 1996 Personal Responsibility and Work Opportunity Act, a welfare reform measure that required heads of families on welfare to find work within two years (though states could exempt up to 20 percent of recipients), limited welfare benefits to five years over an individual's lifetime, and made many legal immigrants ineligible. He also signed the Telecommunications Act of 1996, which reduced diversity in America's media by permitting companies to own more television and radio stations.

Clinton and Gore were reelected in 1996 (defeating Republican Bob Dole and Reform Party candidate Ross Perot), in part

Newt Gingrich Republican congressman from Georgia (1979–1999) who co-authored the 1994 "Contract with America." Gingrich served as Speaker of the House from 1995–1999, and led the Congressional shutdown of the U.S. federal government that lasted for 27 days in 1995–1996.

◁ Congressman Newt Gingrich (R., GA) led the opposition to President Bill Clinton and the Democratic Party's agenda. Here, at a rally on Capitol Hill in September 1994, Gingrich secures the support of Republican congressional candidates for his "Contract with America."

John Duricka/AP Images

because Clinton stole some of the conservatives' thunder. He declared that "the era of big government is over" and invoked family values, a centerpiece of the Republican campaign. Some of Clinton's actions were true compromises with conservative interests; other times he attempted to reclaim issues from the conservatives, as when he redefined family values as "fighting for the family-leave law or the assault-weapons ban or ... trying to keep tobacco out of the hands of kids."

29-1d Political Partisanship and Domestic Terrorism

Despite widespread economic security and Clinton's moves toward the political center, politics were divisive, often ugly, and sometimes violent during the Clinton era. The political right attacked Clinton with a vehemence not seen since Franklin Roosevelt's New Deal. Hillary Clinton was a frequent target; when she told a hostile interviewer during her husband's first presidential campaign, "I suppose I could have stayed home and baked cookies and had teas. But what I decided to do was pursue my profession, which I entered before my husband was in public life," the *New York Post* called her "a buffoon, an insult to most women."

A political extremism that existed well beyond the bounds of Washington politics exploded into view on April 19, 1995, when 168 children, women, and men were killed in a blast that destroyed the nine-story Alfred P. Murrah Federal Building in downtown Oklahoma City. Many thought the bomb had been set by Middle Eastern terrorists. But evidence from a charred piece of truck axle found two blocks from the explosion led investigators to Timothy McVeigh, a native-born white American and a decorated veteran of the Persian Gulf War. McVeigh was seeking revenge for the deaths of members of the Branch Davidian religious sect,

whom he believed the FBI had deliberately slaughtered in a standoff over firearms charges on that date two years before in Waco, Texas.

In the months that followed, reporters and government investigators discovered networks of militias, tax resisters, and various white-supremacist groups throughout the nation. These groups were united by distrust of the federal government. Many saw federal gun control laws, such as the Brady Bill, signed into law in 1993, as a dangerous usurpation of citizens' right to bear arms. Members of these groups believed that the federal government was controlled by "sinister forces," including Jews, cultural elitists, Queen Elizabeth, and the United Nations.

Inside Washington, partisan politics grew more divisive. Republicans demanded an open-ended investigation of alleged wrongdoings by Bill and Hillary Clinton. The special counsel's investigation, which cost taxpayers $72 million, found no wrongdoing in the Clintons' financial or political affairs, but did offer evidence that Bill Clinton had committed perjury when he testified to a grand jury that he had not engaged in sexual relations with twenty-two-year-old White House intern Monica Lewinsky. In the wake of these charges, in 1998 Clinton became the second president—and the first in 130 years—to be impeached by the House of Representatives. However, the Republican-controlled Senate, responding at least in part to popular opinion, acquitted Clinton. Ironically, both Republican Speaker of the House Newt Gingrich and his successor, Robert Livingston, subsequently resigned when faced with evidence of their own extramarital affairs.

29-1e Clinton's Diplomacy

Internationally, the Clinton team faced less tumult; the United States still occupied a uniquely powerful position on the world stage. The demise of the Soviet Union had created a one-superpower world, in which the United States stood far above other powers in political, military, and economic might. Yet in his first term Clinton was more wary in traditional aspects of foreign policy—great-power diplomacy, arms control, regional disputes—than in facilitating American cultural and trade expansion. He was deeply suspicious of foreign military involvements. The Vietnam debacle had taught him that the American public had limited patience for wars lacking a clear-cut national interest, a lesson he found confirmed by George Bush's failure to gain lasting political strength from the Gulf War victory.

This mistrust of foreign interventions was cemented for Clinton by the difficulties he inherited from Bush in Somalia. In 1992, Bush had sent U.S. Marines to the East African nation as part of a UN effort to ensure that humanitarian supplies reached starving Somalis. But in summer 1993, when Americans came under deadly attack from forces loyal to a local warlord, Clinton withdrew U.S. troops. And to his later regret he did not intervene in Rwanda, where in 1994 the majority Hutus butchered 800,000 of the minority Tutsis in a brutal civil war.

29-1f Balkan Crisis

That Somalia and Rwanda were on the policy agenda at all testified to the growing importance of humanitarian concerns in post–Cold War U.S. policy. Many administration officials argued for using America's power to contain ethnic hatreds, support human rights, and promote democracy worldwide. The notion faced a severe test in the Balkans, which erupted in a series of ethnic wars. Bosnian Muslims, Serbs, and Croats were soon killing one another by the tens of thousands. Clinton talked tough against Serbian aggression and atrocities in Bosnia-Herzegovina, especially the Serbs' "ethnic cleansing" of Muslims through massacres and rape camps.

He occasionally ordered air strikes, but he primarily emphasized diplomacy. In late 1995, American diplomats brokered a fragile peace.

But Yugoslav president Slobodan Milosevic continued the anti-Muslim and anti-Croat fervor. When Serb forces moved to violently rid Serbia's southern province of Kosovo of its majority ethnic Albanians, Clinton was pressed to intervene. Initially he resisted. But reports of Serbian atrocities and a major refugee crisis stirred world opinion and convinced Clinton to respond. In 1999, U.S.-led NATO forces launched a massive aerial bombardment of Serbia. Milosevic withdrew from Kosovo, where U.S. troops joined a UN peacekeeping force. That same year, the International War Crimes Tribunal indicted Milosevic and his top aides for atrocities.

29-1g Agreements in the Middle East

In the Middle East, Clinton took an active role in trying to bring the Palestine Liberation Organization (PLO) and Israel together to settle their differences. In September 1993, the PLO's Yasir Arafat and Israeli prime minister Yitzhak Rabin signed an agreement at the White House for Palestinian self-rule in the Gaza Strip and the West Bank's Jericho. The following year Israel signed a peace accord with Jordan, further reducing the chances of another full-scale Arab-Israeli war. But radical anti-Arafat Palestinians continued terrorist attacks on Israelis, while extremist Israelis killed Palestinians and, in November 1995, Rabin himself. Only after American-conducted negotiations and renewed violence in the West Bank did Israel agree in early 1997 to withdraw its forces from the Palestinian city of Hebron. Thereafter, the peace process alternately sagged and spurted.

The same could be said of international efforts to protect the environment, which gained momentum in the 1990s. The George H. W. Bush administration had opposed many

◁ Villagers flee towards the town of Glogovac, in the Pristina district of central Kosovo, at the height of the Kosovo crisis in 1999.

David Brauchli/Getty Images

provisions of the 1992 Rio de Janeiro Treaty protecting the diversity of plant and animal species, and resisted stricter rules to reduce **global warming**. Clinton, urged on by Vice President Al Gore, signed the 1997 Kyoto Protocol, which aimed to combat emissions of carbon dioxide and other gases that most scientists believe trap heat in the atmosphere. The treaty required the United States to reduce its emissions by 2012 to 7 percent below its 1990 levels. (It failed to meet that target.) But facing strong congressional opposition, Clinton never submitted the protocol for ratification to the Republican-controlled Senate.

29-1h Bin Laden and Al Qaeda

Meanwhile, the administration was increasingly concerned about the threat to U.S. interests by Islamic fundamentalism. In particular, senior officials worried about the rise of **Al Qaeda** (Arabic for "the base"), an international terrorist network led by **Osama bin Laden**, which was dedicated to purging Muslim countries of what it saw as the profane influence of the West and installing fundamentalist Islamic regimes.

The son of a Yemen-born construction tycoon in Saudi Arabia, bin Laden had supported the Afghan Mujahidin in their struggle against Soviet occupation. He then founded Al Qaeda and financed terrorist projects with his substantial inheritance. U.S. officials grew more concerned, particularly as bin Laden focused on American targets. In 1995, a car bomb in Riyadh killed seven people, five of them Americans. In 1998, simultaneous bombings at the American embassies in Kenya and Tanzania killed 224 people, including twelve Americans.

In Yemen in 2000, a boat laden with explosives hit the destroyer USS *Cole*, killing seventeen American sailors. Although bin Laden masterminded and financed these attacks, he eluded U.S. attempts to apprehend him. In 1998, Clinton approved a plan to assassinate bin Laden at an Al Qaeda camp in Afghanistan, but the attempt failed.

Clinton's accomplishments during his two terms in office were modest. Domestic achievements included programs that made life easier for American families. The Family and Medical Leave Act gave employees the right to take time off work to care for ailing relatives or newborn children; health insurance reforms guaranteed that Americans would not lose

global warming, or climate change, is the worldwide increase in average temperatures of the Earth's surface caused by greenhouse gas emissions.

Al Qaeda A radical Islamic group founded in the late 1980s and headed by Osama bin Laden until his death; it relies on an international network of cells to carry out terrorist attacks against the West, particularly the United States and its allies, in the name of Islamic fundamentalism.

Osama bin Laden A wealthy Islamic fundamentalist militant expelled from his native Saudi Arabia in 1991; he took refuge in Sudan, where he financed large-scale construction and agricultural projects and amassed followers of his Al Qaeda terrorist organization. He masterminded several attacks, among them the September 11, 2001, attack on the United States.

health insurance when they changed jobs because of preexisting medical conditions. Clinton also created national parks and monuments that protected 3.2 million acres of American land and made unprecedented progress cleaning up toxic waste dumps throughout the nation. In foreign policy, meanwhile, he brokered a durable if incomplete peace in the Balkans and facilitated negotiations between Palestinian and Israeli officials, but he failed to act quickly or decisively to stop the mass killings in Rwanda.

29-2 Globalization and Prosperity

▷ **What factors contributed to a period of economic prosperity in the 1990s?**

▷ **How did globalization evolve in the 1990s?**

▷ **Why was globalization a controversial development?**

Despite conflicts abroad and partisan struggles in Washington, the majority of Americans experienced the late 1990s as a time of unprecedented peace and prosperity, fueled by the dizzying rise of the stock market. Between 1991 and 1999, the Dow Jones Industrial Average climbed from 3,169 to a high of 11,497 (see Figure 29.1). The booming market benefited the middle class and the wealthy, as mutual funds, 401(k) plans, and other new investment vehicles drew a majority of Americans into the stock market. In 1952, only 4 percent of American households were invested in stocks; by 2000, almost 60 percent were.

At the end of the 1990s, the unemployment rate stood at 4.3 percent—the lowest peacetime rate since 1957. That made it easier to implement welfare reform, and welfare rolls declined 50 percent. Both the richest 5 percent and the least-well-off 20 percent of American households saw their incomes rise almost 25 percent. But that translated to an average gain of $50,000 for the top 5 percent and only $2,880 for the bottom 20 percent, further widening the gap between rich and poor. Still, by decade's end, more than two-thirds of Americans were homeowners—the highest percentage in history.

Just how much credit Clinton deserved for the improved economy is debatable. Presidents typically get too much blame when the economy struggles and too much credit when times are good. The roots of the 1990s boom were in the 1970s, when American corporations began investing in automation, retooling plants to become more energy efficient, and cutting labor costs by moving to the union-weak South and West and to countries such as China and Mexico, where labor was cheap and pollution controls were lax.

29-2a Digital Revolution

Economic growth during the 1980s and 1990s was also driven by new digital technology: the rapid development of computers, fax machines, cell phones, and the Internet. New

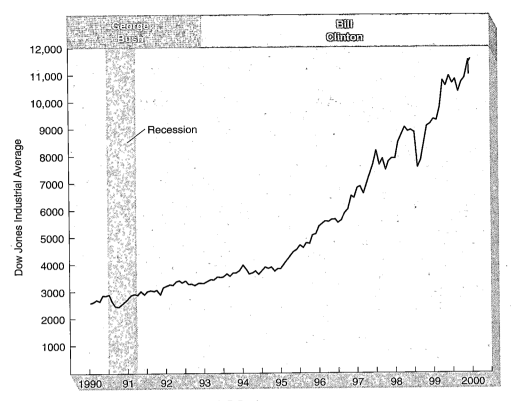

George Bush

Bill Clinton

Recession

Figure 29.1 The American Stock Market

This graph of the Dow Jones Industrial Average, climbing steadily in the bull market of the 1990s, illustrates the great economic expansion of the decade.

companies and industries sprang up, many headquartered in the "Silicon Valley" near San Francisco. By the second half of the 1990s, the Forbes list of the four hundred richest Americans featured high-tech leaders such as Microsoft's Bill Gates, who became the wealthiest person in the world with worth approaching $100 billion at that point, as his company produced the operating software for most personal computers. The high-tech industry had considerable spillover effects, generating improved productivity, new jobs, and sustained economic growth.

◁ Students and their teacher gather around a laptop at an elementary school in Hebei Province, China. This then-innovative tool for learning connected these students to resources that were not easily accessible before.

View Stock/Photoshot

The heart of this technological revolution was the microprocessor. Introduced in 1970 by Intel, the microprocessor miniaturized the central processing unit of a computer, meaning small machines could now perform calculations previously requiring large machines. Computing chores that took a week in the early 1970s took one minute by 2000; the cost of storing one megabyte of information, or enough for 320 pages of text, fell from more than $5,000 in 1975 to 17 cents in 1999 to 0.07 (7/100ths) of a cent in 2009; and while it cost $100,000 to store a gigabyte in 1975, by 2015 the figure was three or four cents. The implications for business were enormous.

29-2b Globalization of Business

Clinton perceived early on that the technology revolution would shrink the world and make it more interconnected. He was convinced that, with the demise of Soviet communism, capitalism—or at least the introduction of market forces, freer trade, and deregulation—was spreading around the globe.

Globalization was not a new phenomenon—it had been under way for a century—but now it had unprecedented momentum. Journalist Thomas L. Friedman asserted that the post–Cold War world was "the age of globalization," characterized by the integration of markets, finance, and technologies. U.S. officials lowered trade and investment barriers, completing George H.W. Bush's **North American Free Trade Agreement (NAFTA)** with Canada and Mexico in 1993, and in 1994 concluding the Uruguay Round of the General Agreement on Tariffs and Trade (GATT), which lowered tariffs for the seventy member nations that accounted for about 80 percent of world trade. The administration also endorsed the 1995 creation of the **World Trade Organization (WTO)** to administer and enforce agreements made at the Uruguay Round. Finally, the president formed a National Economic Council to promote trade missions around the world.

Multinational corporations were the hallmark of this global economy. By 2007, there were 79,000 parent companies worldwide and 790,000 foreign affiliates. Some, such as Nike and Gap, Inc., subcontracted production of certain merchandise to whichever developing countries had the lowest labor costs. Such arrangements created a "new international division of labor" and generated a boom in world exports, which, at $5.4 trillion in 1998, had doubled in two decades. U.S. exports reached $680 billion in 1998, but imports rose even higher, to $907 billion (for a trade deficit of $227 billion). Sometimes the multinationals directly affected foreign policy, as when Clinton in 1995 extended full diplomatic recognition to Vietnam partly in response to pressure from such corporations as Coca-Cola, Citigroup, General Motors, and United Airlines, which wanted to enter that emerging market.

North American Free Trade Agreement (NAFTA) Pact that admitted Mexico to the free-trade zone that the United States and Canada had created earlier.

World Trade Organization (WTO) International organization that regulates the global trading system and provides dispute resolution between member nations.

29-2c The Debate over Globalization

While the administration promoted open markets, labor unions argued that free-trade agreements exacerbated the trade deficit and exported American jobs. Other critics maintained that globalization widened the gap between rich and poor countries, creating a mass of "slave laborers" in poor countries working under conditions that would never be tolerated in the West. Environmentalists charged that globalization also exported pollution to countries unprepared to deal with. Still other critics warned about the power of multinational corporations and the global financial markets over traditional cultures.

Antiglobalization activists staged mass demonstrations and also targeted corporations such as the Gap, Starbucks, Nike, and especially McDonald's, which by 1995 was serving 30 million customers daily in twenty thousand franchises in over one hundred countries. Critics assailed the company's slaughterhouse techniques, alleged exploitation of workers, its high-fat menu, and its role in creating an increasingly homogeneous and sterile world culture. For six years starting in 1996, McDonald's endured hundreds of often-violent protests, including bombings in Rome, Prague, London, Macao, Rio de Janeiro, and Jakarta.

Others decried the violence and the underlying arguments of the antiglobalization campaigners. True, some economists acknowledged, statistics showed that global inequality had grown in recent years. But if one included quality-of-life measurements, such as literacy and health, global inequality

△ McDonald's restaurants circled the globe by the early twenty-first century, exemplifying the globalization of American culture. This Ukrainian woman in Kiev seems to enjoy both her hamburger and a conversation with the human symbol of the fast-food chain, Ronald McDonald.

AP Images/Efrem Lukatsky

had actually declined. And globalization is responsible for only a small percentage of wage and job losses for U.S. workers; the major cause is automation. Other researchers saw no evidence that governments' sovereignty had been seriously compromised or that there was a "race to the bottom" in environmental standards from globalization.

As for creating a homogeneous global culture, McDonald's, others said, tailored its menu and operating practices to local tastes. And although American movies, TV programs, music, computer software, and other "intellectual property" often dominated world markets, foreign competition also made itself felt in America. Millions of American children were gripped by the Japanese Pokémon fad, and satellite television established a worldwide following for European soccer teams. An influx of foreign players added to the international appeal of both the National Basketball Association and Major League Baseball, while in the National Hockey League some 20 percent of players hailed from Europe by the late 1990s.

29-3 9/11 and the War in Iraq

▷ **What domestic and international counterterrorism policies did George W. Bush's administration institute after 9/11?**

▷ **How did George W. Bush's foreign policy actions affect U.S. relations with other nations?**

▷ **Why was the U.S. decision to go to war with Iraq controversial?**

George W. Bush was the unlikely winner of the 2000 presidential election. The strong U.S. economy seemed to favor his opponent, Vice President **Al Gore**, and Gore did win the popular vote (see Map 29.1). But the election came down to the twenty-five electoral votes of Florida, where Bush's brother Jeb was governor. According to the initial tally, Bush won the state—but by so close a margin that a recount was legally required. Thirty-six days later, in the midst of highly contested recount, the Supreme Court voted 5 to 4 along narrowly partisan lines to end the process. Florida's electoral votes—and the presidency—went to **George W. Bush**. Struggles over the election outcome further polarized the nation, and as Bush waited for the January inaugural, critics and comics began referring to him as the "president select."

In view of the close election, many believed that Bush would govern from the center. Some also thought that he was philosophically centrist, as his father had been, and that he had moved to the right only to ensure turnout among evangelical Christians, who made up an increasing portion of the Republican base. From the administration's first days, however, Bush governed from the right, arguably further to the right than any previous administration of modern times.

In international affairs, the administration charted a unilateralist course. Given America's preponderant power, senior Bush officials reasoned, it did not need other countries' help.

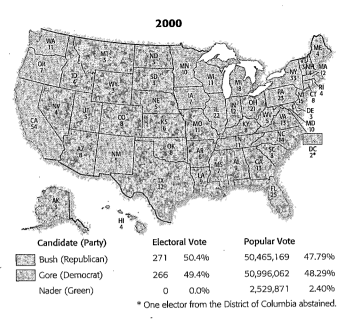

2000

Candidate (Party)	Electoral Vote		Popular Vote	
Bush (Republican)	271	50.4%	50,465,169	47.79%
Gore (Democrat)	266	49.4%	50,996,062	48.29%
Nader (Green)	0	0.0%	2,529,871	2.40%

* One elector from the District of Columbia abstained.

Map 29.1 Presidential Election, 2000

Democratic candidate Al Gore won the popular vote, but George W. Bush succeeded in gaining electoral victory by four votes. Among white males, Bush ran extremely well, while Gore won a majority of minority and women voters. Ralph Nader's Green Party won less than 3 percent of the national vote, but his votes in Florida may have detracted from the Gore tally, helping Bush win the critical electoral votes.

Accordingly, Bush withdrew the United States from the 1972 Anti-Ballistic Missile Treaty with Russia to develop a National Missile Defense system (forbidden under the treaty) broadly similar to Reagan's "Star Wars." The White House also renounced the 1997 **Kyoto Protocol** on controlling global warming and opposed a carefully negotiated protocol to strengthen the 1972 Biological and Toxin Weapons Convention. These decisions and the administration's hands-off policy toward the Israeli-Palestinian peace process caused consternation in Europe.

29-3a 9/11

Then came September 11. On that sunny Tuesday morning, nineteen hijackers seized control of four commercial jets departing from East Coast airports. At 8:46 AM, one plane crashed

Al Gore Longtime Democratic representative (1977–1985) and senator (1985–1993) from Tennessee; vice president under Bill Clinton (1993–2001); unsuccessfully ran for president in the highly contested 2000 race; won a 2007 Nobel Peace Prize for his advocacy and expertise on environmental issues, particularly global warming.

George W. Bush Forty-third president of the United States (2001–2009); governor of Texas from 1995 to 2000, when he resigned upon election to the presidency; son of forty-first President George H. W. Bush.

Kyoto Protocol A protocol setting strict emission targets for industrialized nations. President George W. Bush refused to sign the agreement, making the United States one of only four nations that declined participation.

into the 110-story North Tower of the World Trade Center in New York City. At 9:03 AM, a second plane flew into the South Tower. In less than two hours, both buildings collapsed, killing thousands of office workers, firefighters, and police officers. At 9:43, the third plane crashed into the Pentagon, leaving a huge hole in its west side. The fourth plane was also headed toward Washington, but several passengers—learning of the World Trade Center attacks through cell phone conversations—stormed the cockpit; in the ensuing scuffle, the plane crashed in Somerset County, Pennsylvania, killing all aboard.

More than three thousand people died, making this the deadliest act of terrorism in history. Not since the Japanese assault on Pearl Harbor in 1941 had the United States experienced such a devastating attack on its soil. The hijackers—fifteen Saudi Arabians, two Emiratis, one Lebanese, and, leading them, an Egyptian—had ties to Al Qaeda, Osama bin Laden's radical Islamic organization. Some officials in the Clinton and Bush administrations had warned that an Al Qaeda attack was inevitable, but neither administration made counterterrorism a foreign policy priority.

29-3b Afghanistan War

In an instant, counterterrorism was priority number one. President Bush responded quickly with large-scale military force. Al Qaeda operated out of Afghanistan with the blessing of the ruling Taliban, a repressive Islamic fundamentalist group that had gained power in 1996. In early October, the United States launched a sustained bombing campaign against Taliban and Al Qaeda positions and sent special operations forces to help a resistance organization in northern Afghanistan. Within two months, the Taliban was driven from power, although bin Laden and top Taliban leaders eluded capture.

As administration officials acknowledged, the swift military victory did not end the terrorist threat. Bush spoke of a long struggle against evil forces, in which the nations of the world were either with the United States or against it. Some questioned whether a "war on terrorism" could ever be won in a meaningful sense, given that the foe was a nonstate actor weak in the traditional measures of power—territory and governmental power—and with little to lose. Most Americans, however, were ready to believe. Stunned by September 11, they experienced a renewed sense of national unity and pride. Flag sales soared, and Bush's approval ratings skyrocketed. Citizenship applications from immigrants rose dramatically.

Colin Powell Four-star general, United States Army, who served as national security adviser (1987–1989), chairman of the Joint of Chiefs of Staff (1989–1993), and secretary of state (2001–2005) in the first George W. Bush administration. He was the first African-American to hold each of these positions.

Economic concerns, evident before 9/11, deepened thereafter with a four-day closing of Wall Street and a subsequent sharp drop in stock prices. The week after the markets reopened, the Dow Jones Industrial Average plunged 14.26 percent—the fourth largest weekly drop in percentage terms since 1900. The markets eventually rebounded, but questions remained about the economy's overall health. Such was Bush's political strength after 9/11, however, that neither this economic uncertainty nor the failure to capture Osama bin Laden and top Taliban leaders dented his popularity. In the 2002 midterm elections, Republicans retook the Senate and increased their majority in the House.

29-3c International Responses

Overseas, the president's standing was not nearly so high. Immediately after September 11, there was an outpouring of support from people everywhere. "We are all Americans now," said the French newspaper *Le Monde* after the attacks. Moments of silence in honor of the victims were held in many countries, and governments worldwide announced they would work with Washington against terrorism. But within a year, attitudes changed dramatically. Bush's bellicose stance and good-versus-evil terminology had put off many foreign observers from the start, but they initially swallowed their objections. When the president hinted that America might unilaterally strike Saddam Hussein's Iraq or deal forcefully with North Korea or Iran—the three countries of Bush's "axis of evil"—many allied governments strongly objected.

At issue was not merely the prospect of an American attack on one of these countries but the underlying rationale that would accompany it. Bush and other top officials argued that in an age of terrorism, the United States would not wait for a potential security threat to become real; henceforth, it would strike first. Critics, among them many world leaders, called it recklessly aggressive and contrary to international law, and they wondered what would happen if dictators around the world claimed the same right of preemption.

But Bush was determined, particularly on Iraq. Several of his top advisers, including Secretary of Defense Donald Rumsfeld and Vice President Dick Cheney, had wanted to oust Saddam Hussein for years, indeed since the end of the Gulf War in 1991. After the Twin Towers fell, they folded Iraq into the larger war on terrorism—even though counterterrorism experts saw no link between Saddam and Al Qaeda. For a time, Secretary of State **Colin Powell**, the first African American in that post, kept the focus on Afghanistan, but gradually the thinking in the White House shifted. In November 2001, Bush ordered the Pentagon to initiate war planning for Iraq; by spring 2002, a secret consensus was reached: Saddam Hussein would be removed by force.

29-3d Why Iraq?

In September 2002, Bush challenged the United Nations to enforce its resolutions against Iraq or the United States would act on its own. In subsequent weeks, he and his aides offered shifting reasons for getting tough with Iraq. They said Saddam was a major threat to the United States and its allies, a leader who possessed and would use banned biological and chemical "weapons of mass destruction" (WMDs) and who sought to acquire nuclear weapons. They claimed, contrary to their own intelligence estimates, that he had ties to Al Qaeda and could be linked to the 9/11 attacks. They said that he brutalized his own people and generated regional instability with his tyrannous rule.

Beneath the surface lurked other motivations. Neoconservatives saw in Iraq a chance to use U.S. power to reshape the region in America's image, to oppose tyranny and spread democracy. Ousting Saddam, they said, would enhance the security of Israel, America's key Middle East ally, and likely start a chain reaction that would extend democracy throughout the region. White House political strategists, meanwhile, believed a swift removal of a hated dictator would cement Republican domination in Washington and virtually ensure Bush's reelection. Finally, Bush wanted to prevent an Iraq potentially armed with WMDs from destabilizing an oil-rich region.

29-3e Congressional Approval

Like his father in 1991, Bush claimed he did not need congressional authorization for military action against Iraq; also like his father, he nevertheless sought it. In early October 2002, the House of Representatives voted 296 to 133 and the Senate 77 to 23 to authorize force against Iraq. Many who voted in favor were unwilling to defy a president so close to a midterm election, even though they opposed military action without UN sanction. Critics complained that the president had not presented evidence that Saddam Hussein constituted an imminent threat or was connected to the 9/11 attacks. Bush switched to a less hawkish stance, and in early November, the UN Security Council unanimously approved Resolution 1441, imposing rigorous new arms inspections on Iraq.

Behind the scenes, though, the Security Council was divided over the next move. As the debate continued, and as massive antiwar demonstrations took place around the world, Bush sent about 250,000 soldiers to the region. Britain sent about 45,000 troops.

29-3f Fall of Baghdad

In late February, the United States floated a draft resolution to the UN that proposed issuing an ultimatum to Iraq, but only three of the fifteen Security Council members affirmed support. Bush abandoned the resolution and all further diplomatic efforts on March 17, when he ordered Saddam Hussein to leave Iraq within forty-eight hours or face an attack. Saddam ignored the ultimatum, and on March 19 the United States and Britain launched an aerial bombardment of Baghdad and other areas. A ground invasion followed (see Map 29.2). The Iraqis initially offered stiff resistance, but on April 9, Baghdad fell.

When violence and lawlessness soon erupted, American planners seemed powerless to respond. The plight of ordinary Iraqis deteriorated as the occupation authority proved unable to maintain order. In Baghdad, electricity worked only a few hours each day, and telephone service was non-existent. Decisions by the Coalition Provisional Authority (CPA), headed by Ambassador Paul Bremer, made matters

worse—notably Bremer's move in May to disband the Iraqi army, which left tens of thousands of men, angry and armed, out of work. A multisided insurgency of Saddam loyalists, Iraqi nationalists of various stripes, and foreign Islamic revolutionaries took shape; soon, U.S. occupying forces faced frequent ambushes and hit-and-run attacks. By October 2003, more troops had died from these attacks than had perished in the initial invasion.

The mounting chaos in Iraq and the failure to find weapons of mass destruction had critics questioning the war's validity. The much-derided sanctions and UN inspections, it was now clear, had in fact been successful in rendering Saddam a largely toothless tyrant, with a hollow military and no chemical or biological weapons. Prewar claims of a "rush to war" resounded again. Even defenders of the invasion castigated the administration for its failure to anticipate the occupation problems. In spring 2004, graphic photos showing Iraqi detainees being abused by American guards at Abu Ghraib prison were broadcast worldwide, generating international condemnation.

29-3g Election of 2004

President Bush, facing reelection that fall, expressed disgust at the Abu Ghraib images and fended off charges that he and his top aides knew of and condoned the abuse. Many were skeptical, but voters that fall were prepared to give Bush the benefit of the doubt. His Democratic opponent, Senator **John Kerry** of Massachusetts, a Vietnam veteran who had reluctantly voted for the Iraq resolution in October 2001, had difficulty finding his campaign footing and never articulated a clear alternative strategy on the war. With the electorate deeply split, Bush won reelection with 51 percent of the popular vote to Kerry's 48 percent. The GOP also increased its majorities in the House and Senate.

29-3h America Isolated

Internationally, too, Bush faced criticism, not only on account of Iraq and Abu Ghraib, but also because of his administration's lack of engagement in the Israeli-Palestinian dispute and seeming disdain for diplomacy generally. The White House, critics said, rightly sought to prevent North Korea and Iran from joining the nuclear club but seemed incapable of working imaginatively and multilaterally to make it happen.

Iraq, though, remained the chief problem. The Bush administration denied that the struggle had become a Vietnam-like quagmire, but it seemed uncertain about how to end the fighting. In Congress and the press, calls for withdrawal from Iraq multiplied, but skeptics cautioned it could make things worse, triggering sectarian bloodshed and a collapse of the Baghdad government. The power and regional influence of neighboring Iran would increase, and American credibility would be undermined throughout

John Kerry Senator from Massachusetts (1985–2013) and Vietnam War veteran; Democratic nominee for president in 2004; served as secretary of state (2013–2017) in the second Obama administration.

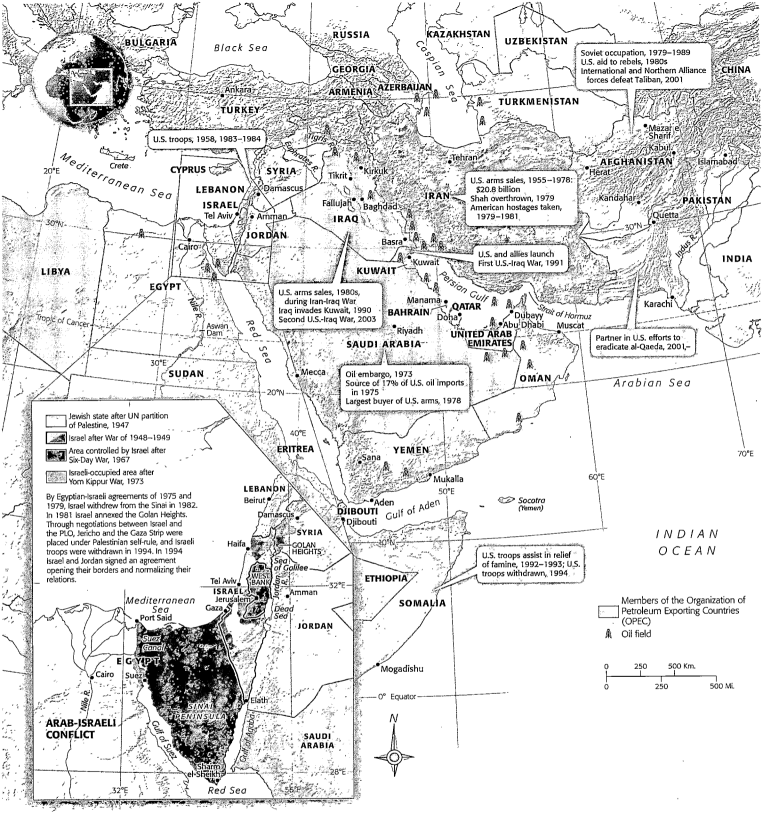

Map 29.2 The Middle East

The nations of the Middle East maintained precarious relations with the United States. To protect its interests, the United States extended large amounts of economic and military aid and sold huge quantities of weapons to the area. At times, Washington ordered U.S. troops to the region. The Arab-Israeli dispute particularly upended order, although the peace process moved forward intermittently.

the Middle East. Some commentators instead called for an increase of U.S. forces in Iraq, and Bush heeded their advice. The "surge" of 2007 contributed to a drastic reduction in violence, as commanders shifted the focus to a counterinsurgency strategy emphasizing protection of the population. But the surge did not achieve meaningful results in its second goal: promoting political reconciliation among the competing factions in Iraq. That objective remained elusive when Bush left office in early 2009.

29-4 Domestic Politics and Foreign Policy in Post– 9/11 America

▷ How did George W. Bush implement a conservative domestic agenda and respond to social crises?

▷ What was the significance of the presidential election of 2008?

▷ How did Barack Obama respond to the international issues he inherited?

While the Bush administration focused on what Bush had labeled "the global war on terrorism" (or GWOT), it also pursued domestic goals. The centerpiece of the Bush domestic agenda, achieved before the attacks of 9/11, was a $1.3 trillion tax cut—the largest in U.S. history. As Bush intended, this tax cut wiped out the $200 billion budget surplus he had inherited from the Clinton administration.

29-4a The Presidency of George W. Bush

Throughout his years as president, George W. Bush embraced conservative ideals, though sometimes in ways that seemed paradoxical. Much of his agenda fit smoothly with conservative principles. Religious conservatives were pleased by the newly prominent role of religion in the political process. The president spoke frequently of his faith; Bush's attorney general, John Ashcroft, a Pentecostal Christian who had stated, prior to his confirmation, that America had "no king but Jesus," held prayer meetings at 8 a.m. every morning in the Justice Department. And Bush appointed the medical director of a Christian pregnancy-counseling center whose website claimed that the "distribution of birth control is demeaning to women, degrading of human sexuality and adverse to human health and happiness" to head the nation's federal family planning program.

Bush was also a strong advocate of economic deregulation. His administration dismantled environmental restrictions on the oil, timber, and mining industries, and as Wall Street developed an incredible array of new and risky financial instruments, he maintained a full hands-off approach to regulation. While he failed to privatize the Social Security system, he did reshape the Supreme Court. Fifty-year-old conservative U.S. Circuit Court judge John Roberts was confirmed as chief justice following the death of Chief Justice William Rehnquist at age eighty, and another strong conservative, fifty-five-year-old Samuel Alito, became junior associate justice following the resignation of Sandra Day O'Connor, who had often voted with the more liberal faction of the court.

At the same time, Bush turned to big government solutions. While Ronald Reagan had tried to abolish the federal Department of Education, Bush dramatically increased the federal government's role in public education in an attempt to fix a "broken system of education that dismisses certain children and classes of children as unteachable." Under his "No Child Left Behind" initiative, schools could only receive federal funding if their state set "high standards" for all students, mandated standardized tests to evaluate their progress, and held failing schools accountable. And while conservatives traditionally argued that the federal government was not responsible for individuals' medical care costs, the Bush administration created an enormously expensive new entitlement program that covered prescription drugs for American seniors, regardless of income, under Medicare.

Although Bush won the presidential election in 2004, growing perceptions of administrative incompetence began to undermine the American people's confidence in the president and his administration. In late August 2005, a major hurricane hit the U.S. Gulf Coast and New Orleans. Hurricane Katrina destroyed the levees that kept low-lying parts of New Orleans from being swamped by water from Lake Pontchartrain and surrounding canals. Floodwater covered 80 percent of New Orleans. More than 1,800 people died in the storm and the floods that followed.

Tens of thousands of people who lacked the resources to flee New Orleans sought shelter at the Superdome. Supplies of food and water quickly ran low and toilets backed up; people wrapped the dead in blankets and waited for rescue. Those outside the Gulf region, watching the suffering crowd of mainly poor, black New Orleanians, began a soul-searching conversation about what Democratic Party leader Howard Dean called the "ugly truth": that poverty remains linked to race in this nation.

29-4b Economic Recession

Economic troubles were also brewing: American home prices—a huge "housing bubble"—were on the verge of collapse. Following the beginnings of deregulation in the financial markets during the 1980s, financial institutions had sought new ways to expand their market and their

"No Child Left Behind" Bush administration initiative intended to improve public schools for all children. This legislation expanded the federal government's role in education; many criticized its reliance on standardized testing for leading teachers to "teach to the test."

Hurricane Katrina Worst natural disaster in U.S. history; resulting flooding destroyed much of New Orleans and the Gulf Coast in August 2005; poor handling of the crisis fueled cries of racism and tarnished the Bush administration.

profits. They began experimenting with "subprime" mortgages for people who, in previous years, would not have qualified for credit. For example, "NINA" loans went to homebuyers with "No Income, No Assets." By 2006, one-fifth of all home loans were subprime. As more Americans bought homes, increased demand and rabid speculation kept housing prices rising. In 2000, a median-priced house "cost" 3 full years of a (median-earning) family's income. At the height of the bubble in 2006, it cost 4.6 years of work. This was good news for lenders: because housing prices kept going up, they saw little risk. If a family defaulted on their mortgage and lost their house, the property could be sold for more—sometimes much more—than the mortgage was worth. Wall Street firms saw an opportunity for rapid short-term profit. They began buying up mortgages, bundling them together, good and bad, into multibillion-dollar packages to sell to investors. These mortgage-backed securities were complex and difficult to value—but because conservatives had cut government oversight (deregulation), large financial institutions got away with risky—and unethical—practices. Some bankers and mortgage rating agencies purposely deceived investors.

This unstable structure began to fail in 2007, as more and more borrowers began to default on their mortgages. People tried to escape unaffordable mortgages by selling their houses, but housing prices dropped rapidly. Increasingly, mortgages were larger than the declining value of houses. And the huge financial institutions that had gambled on mortgage-backed securities did not have enough capital to sustain such losses. America's major financial institutions—indeed, key banks around the world—were on the verge of collapse.

Barack Obama Forty-fourth president of the United States (2009–2017) and the nation's first African American president, who took office in the midst of the worst economic crisis since the Great Depression.

The U.S. economy depends on the availability of credit—for business loans, car loans, home loans, credit cards. This housing crisis paralyzed the credit markets. Businesses couldn't get the loans they needed to buy raw materials or inventory; consumers couldn't get the credit they needed to buy large items, such as cars. And many Americans were already deeply in debt. They had taken out home equity loans against the rising value of their houses; they owed money on several credit cards. In 1981, families saved more than 10 percent of their post-tax income; in 2005, the average family spent more than it earned—and for those under thirty-five, the savings rate was minus 16 percent. As credit tightened, people bought less. Businesses began laying off workers, and the unemployment rate began to climb. Those who were unemployed or worried about their jobs spent less money, and the cycle continued. The Bush administration attempted to prevent the collapse of the financial system by bailing out some of America's largest banks and credit providers—those that were deemed "too big to fail." The Troubled Asset Relief Program (TARP) eventually provided $700 billion in loans to failing institutions, but as "Main Street" recovered more slowly than Wall Street, many Americans were angry that tax dollars had gone to rescue wealthy bankers, none of whom would face prosecution for their misdeeds.

29-4c Barack Obama's Presidency

The presidential election of 2008 was shaped by the growing worldwide economic crisis. As Americans worried about the economy and Bush's approval rating fell to 27 percent, the Democratic candidate, Illinois Senator **Barack Obama**, prevailed over John McCain, the senior senator from Arizona (Map 29.3). Barack Hussein Obama, who would become the nation's first African American president, made

◁ New Orleans police officers and volunteers rescue residents from a flooded neighborhood during the devastation following Hurricane Katrina in August 2005. Katrina destroyed not only New Orleans, but much of the Gulf Coast from Louisiana into Alabama.

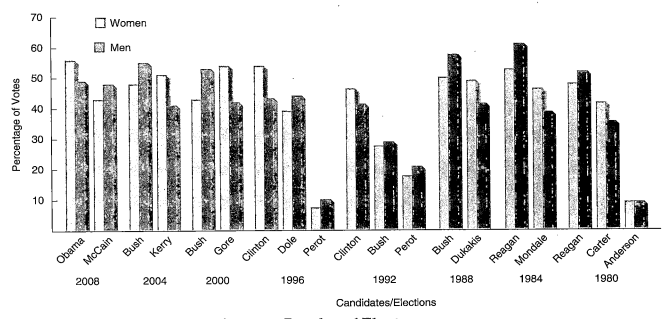

Figure 29.2 The Gender Gap in American Presidential Elections

The gender gap, or the difference in voting patterns between men and women, was first identified in 1980 by National Organization for Women president Eleanor Smeal and has been recognized as an important force in American politics ever since. In virtually every presidential election portrayed here, greater percentages of women (no matter their race or ethnicity, income, level of education, or marital status) than men voted for the Democratic candidate. *Source: Based on data from the Center for American Women and Politics.*

headlines in 2002 by opposing the coming war in Iraq; he caught the nation's attention when he delivered a powerful keynote speech at the 2004 Democratic national convention; three years later, as a first-term senator, he was running for the presidency.

Obama was born in Hawai'i in 1961. His mother was a young white woman from Kansas, his father a Kenyan graduate student at the University of Hawai'i. (The couple divorced when their child was two years old and each married again, giving Barack both African and Indonesian half-siblings.) Obama spent part of his childhood in Indonesia with his mother, attended high school in Hawai'i, and moved to the U.S. mainland for college. After graduating from Harvard Law School, where he served as president of the *Harvard Law Review*, Obama moved to Chicago. There he met and married fellow Harvard Law graduate Michelle Robinson and joined the law school faculty at the University of Chicago.

Obama was an inspirational speaker who offered messages of "hope" and "change." Supporters were passionate about him, expecting in some cases that he would almost miraculously solve the nation's problems and bring bipartisan harmony to a deeply divided Congress (see Figure 29.2). Obama began his presidency with big ideas and ambitious goals, but he also had to confront his inheritance: two unresolved wars, a massive federal deficit, and a major recession that threatened to spin into a global meltdown.

In February 2009, Obama signed legislation creating a $787 billion economic stimulus package in an attempt to

jump-start the economy, and supported expanding TARP and bailing out auto giants GM and Chrysler, both on the verge of failing. The economy began a slow recovery in 2009, but unemployment rates remained high. In 2010, one in eight Americans was receiving food stamps from the government, and Wal-mart pointed to evidence of hard times: a big jump in the purchase of kitchen storage containers for leftovers.

As the recession continued, Republicans won a landslide victory in the 2010 elections, gaining control of the House of Representatives. Spearheading this Republican victory was a new grassroots movement: the Tea Party. The Tea Party mobilized Republican middle-class voters who were angry about big government and expensive federal programs aimed at lower-income Americans, but wealthy conservatives provided essential financial and organizational support.

Obama's victory in 2012 (over Republican Mitt Romney) was narrower than his first, but his coalition held and he drew critical support from the growing Latinx electorate. Treating his election as a mandate, Obama took firmer positions. Despite Obama's renewed political will, however, the nation continued to face fierce struggles over annual debt, budget deficits, taxes, and government expenditures.

Throughout the Obama years, Congress was mired in partisan gridlock, and Republicans frequently stymied administrative actions. Refusing to compromise on the budget in 2013, Republicans shut down the federal government for sixteen days. And after conservative Supreme Court Justice Anton Scalia died in early 2016, Republic Senate leaders

2008

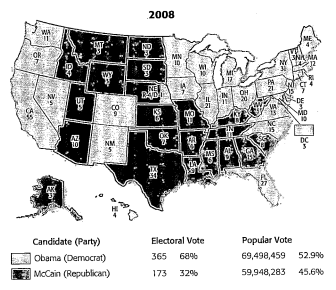

Candidate (Party)	Electoral Vote		Popular Vote	
Obama (Democrat)	365	68%	69,498,459	52.9%
McCain (Republican)	173	32%	59,948,283	45.6%

Map 29.3 Presidential Election, 2008

The economy was the deciding factor in the 2008 election. McCain's claim, in the midst of Wall Street's meltdown in September 2008, that "the fundamentals of our economy are strong" backfired. Americans found Obama's calm and deliberate presence a better bet for dealing with the economic crisis, and gave him victory in November.

refused to consider Merrick Garland, Obama's nominee to the court.

Obama's greatest domestic achievement may have been shepherding the national economy back to health; by the end of his second term, unemployment had dropped from nearly 10 percent to 4.7 percent (see Figure 29.3). During the Obama years, 15.8 million new jobs were created, and in 2014—2015,

real median household income (the inflation-adjusted earning of households in the middle of income distribution) grew 5.2 percent. That said, well-paid manufacturing jobs continued to disappear, replaced by jobs in the service economy, and some who left the job market during the depths of the recession never found a way back into employment.

Obama's most significant achievement was the Affordable Care Act (often called Obamacare). Signed into law in 2010, the ACA is a market-based plan that relies on for-profit insurance companies to provide coverage. The ACA had significant problems in its initial roll out, but by 2016 an additional 20 million Americans had gained insurance as the plan removed lifetime insurance caps, added coverage for preventative care, and prohibited insurance companies from excluding or charging higher premiums to individuals with preexisting medical conditions. In order to pay for this expansion in size and coverage, the plan mandated that all individuals have insurance coverage and taxed the wealthy to subsidize premiums for lower-income Americans. The program drew strong opposition from Republicans, who attempted to repeal it, in full or in part, more than sixty times during Obama's presidency.

Obama committed his presidency to environmental protection. Under his leadership, in 2016 the United States signed the first comprehensive global plan to reduce global warming. He created new national monuments, protecting more than 553 million acres of land and water—more than the past eighteen presidents combined. These monuments conserved the land, but they also celebrated a more inclusive vision of American history, commemorating events central to women, American Indian, African American, and LGBT Americans.

Throughout his presidency, Obama was a measured champion of equal rights and social justice. Some Americans

◁ More than seventy-five thousand people gathered in Chicago's Grant Park to celebrate Barack Obama's election on November 4, 2008.

REUTERS/Gary Hershorn

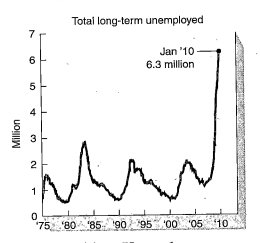

Total long-term unemployed

Jan '10
6.3 million

Figure 29.3 Long-Term Unemployment

Unemployment rates skyrocketed during the recession. But perhaps most striking is the dramatic increase in long-term unemployment. In January 2010, 6.3 million job seekers had been unemployed for twenty-seven weeks or longer. *Source: "Long Term Unemployment" graphs,* New York Times, *February 21, 2010, from http:// www.nytimes.com/2010/02/21/business/economy/21unemployed.html?hp. Reprinted by permission of* The New York Times.

believed that his election signaled the beginning of a "post-racial America." But rising racial tensions, in large part tied to police shootings of black men and the resulting protests, showed how wrong that claim was. Obama, here as in most arenas, emphasized the need for mutual understanding—leaving both advocates for the police and protestors against racialized policing unsatisfied. Under Obama's watch, the Supreme Court guaranteed marriage equality for same-sex couples nationwide; the "Don't Ask, Don't Tell" policy that barred gay men and lesbians from serving openly in the U.S. military was repealed, and women were allowed to join military combat units for the first time. Finally, the Obama years were notable for the grace and dignity with which the president and his family filled their roles.

29-4d Obama and the World

In foreign affairs, Obama focused initially on fulfilling a campaign promise to reduce the nation's involvement in Iraq. U.S. casualty figures continued to decline in 2009, and Obama stuck to a timeline for withdrawal that would have all combat forces out of the country by August 2010. In August 2010, he declared that "the American combat mission in Iraq has ended. Operation Iraqi Freedom is over, and the Iraqi people now have lead responsibility for the security of their country." Though some U.S. troops remained in Iraq as "advise and assist brigades" assigned to noncombat operations, in late 2011 these too were removed. On December 15, 2011, U.S. Defense Secretary Leon Panetta officially pronounced the Iraq War over at a flag-lowering ceremony in Baghdad. The last U.S. troops left Iraqi territory on December 18, 2011, but political stability in the country remained elusive.

Even as he drew down in Iraq, Obama ramped up U.S. involvement in Afghanistan. During the 2008 campaign he had stressed the importance of the ongoing struggle there, and when he took office in early 2009, the situation was deteriorating. The Taliban were regaining a foothold and appeared ready to threaten the existence of the government in Kabul, headed by Hamid Karzai. Obama judged trends to be sufficiently alarming that he ordered 17,000 more American combat troops to Afghanistan even before completion of the first review he'd ordered.

In December, following another policy review, Obama announced a "surge" that would commit 33,000 additional U.S. troops to the struggle (for a total of 100,000), as well as 7,000 troops from NATO members and other allies. He rejected the advice of skeptics such as Vice President Joseph Biden, who questioned whether the surge would work and whether Karzai's government could be counted on to take responsibility for its own security. To placate concerns that he was committing America to an open-ended war, Obama promised that "our troops will begin to come home" by the summer of 2011.

The president didn't make the deadline, but by the summer of 2012 the surge troops had been withdrawn, leaving some 68,000 U.S. forces still in place. Although a constant barrage of drone strikes and special operations raids took a harsh toll on Al Qaeda, it was difficult for the administration to make the case that Afghanistan had achieved stability or that Karzai's government could stand on its own without U.S. assistance.

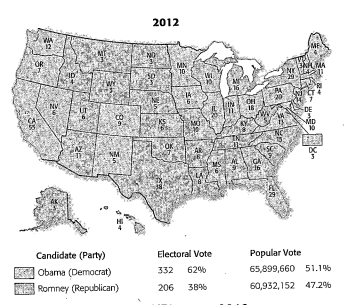

2012

Candidate (Party)	Electoral Vote		Popular Vote	
Obama (Democrat)	332	62%	65,899,660	51.1%
Romney (Republican)	206	38%	60,932,152	47.2%

Map 29.4 Presidential Election, 2012

In the 2012 election, Barack Obama held on to most of his 2008 winning coalition. A fractured Republican party nominated Mitt Romney, who was the first member of the Church of Jesus Christ of Latter-day Saints to run for president as a major political party's candidate.

Notwithstanding the continuing problems in Afghanistan, most voters in the 2012 presidential campaign gave Obama high marks on foreign policy. His trump card was an altogether more dramatic event: the violent death of the mastermind behind the 9/11 attacks, the man who had become the symbolic leader of global *jihad* against the West. In the very early hours of May 2, 2011, American Navy SEALs, in a daring operation later immortalized in the Hollywood film *Zero Dark Thirty*, shot and killed Osama bin Laden in Abbottabad, a garrison town north of Islamabad, Pakistan.

The operation took forty minutes, but the groundwork had been laid years before. Thanks to information acquired by interrogating detainees, CIA analysts identified one of the few Al Qaeda couriers trusted by bin Laden. Eventually, they pinpointed the area of Pakistan in which the courier operated, and in August 2010 they tracked him to a high-walled compound in Abbottabad they speculated was bin Laden's location. On April 29, 2011, Obama gave the go-ahead for the operation, even though there was no certainty bin Laden was there. Three days later, the U.S. commandos swooped down on the compound in stealth helicopters in the dead of a moonless night, moved through the buildings, and shot dead a total of five people, including bin Laden.

In his second term, Obama faced greater pressures abroad, especially with the challenge from ISIL (Islamic State in Iraq and the Levant, also known as ISIS, or Daesh, from the initial letters in the group's earlier Arabic name), a jihadist organization that catapulted onto the global scene in 2013 and 2014 when it conquered significant swaths of territory in Iraq and Syria. Tracing its lineage to the aftermath of the U.S. invasion of Iraq in 2003, ISIS expanded its capabilities after Abu Bakr al-Baghdadi became leader in 2010.

It soon became notorious for its wanton brutality, including mass executions, abductions, and beheadings.

The terror group's rise took U.S. officials by surprise, particularly as the Syrian civil war (which began in 2011 as a broad-based uprising against President Bashar al-Assad) created a power vacuum in parts of the country that ISIS filled. As the fighting raged and a major humanitarian crisis unfolded in Syria, Obama faced intense criticism from some quarters for his unwillingness to intervene more forcefully with American power, even after evidence emerged of Assad's use of banned chemical weapons. Instead, Obama targeted the Islamic State with an American-led bombing campaign and the deployment of a small number of U.S. special forces. The effort gradually achieved results, and by the time Obama left office the amount of ISIS-held territory in Iraq and Syria had been cut in half.

The misery in Syria continued, however, and seemed likely to tarnish Obama's legacy. His supporters hoped his record would be buoyed by other developments, including a landmark nuclear deal with Iran and a diplomatic opening to Cuba, and by the prevention of a 9/11-type attack on American soil on his watch.

29-4e Election of 2016

In 2016, a divided America went to the polls. Although former secretary of state Hillary Clinton won the popular vote by almost 3 million, the electoral college went to businessman and reality TV star Donald Trump, who became the forty-fifth president of the United States. Following a peaceful transfer of power on January 20, 2017, opponents of Trump's agenda gathered in cities throughout the nation. More than half a million people flooded the streets of the nation's capital

◁ On May 1, 2011, photographer Pete Souza captured President Obama and his senior advisers watching in real time the secret raid by American forces against Osama bin Laden's Pakistan compound. Obama had made the decision to launch the attack, but here he can only be spectator like everyone else in the room.

The White House/Getty Images

◁ President-elect Donald Trump delivers his acceptance speech in New York City, November 9, 2016.

for the Women's March on Washington, while up to 4 million more marched in other cities and towns, waving signs and banners, chanting "This is what democracy looks like."

29-5 Americans in the New Millennium

▷ In what ways are Americans divided in recent years? What are the sources of those divisions?

▷ How do American families of the new millennium compare to those of fifty and seventy-five years ago?

▷ What were the consequences of increased connectivity of persons across the globe via technology?

In the twenty-first century, the United States is a nation of extraordinary diversity. For much of the twentieth century, however, it had seemed that the United States was moving in the opposite direction. Very few immigrants had been allowed into the United States from the 1920s through 1965. New technologies, such as radio and television, had a homogenizing effect at first, for these mass media were dependent on reaching the broadest possible audience—a mass market. Although local and ethnic traditions persisted, more and more Americans participated in a shared mass culture. During the last third of the twentieth century, however, those homogenizing trends were reversed. Immigration reform in the mid-1960s opened American borders to large numbers of people from a wider variety of nations than ever before. New technologies—the Internet, and cable and satellite television, with their proliferation of channels—replaced mass markets with niche markets. Everything from cosmetics to cars to politics could be targeted toward specific groups defined by age, ethnicity, class, gender, sexuality, or lifestyle choices.

These changes had mixed results. They may have helped to make Americans' understandings of identity more fluid and more complex. They also created echo chambers, fragmenting the American public into groups whose lifestyle choices, values, and politics were constantly reinforced.

29-5a A Nation Divided

America has become, in fundamental ways, a nation divided. Some of that division is based on concrete differences in circumstances, while some is tied to the political weight Americans give various choices or beliefs.

For example, more than half of American adults see a fundamental conflict between religious belief and science, though two-thirds see no conflict between science and their own beliefs. In the United States, only 32 percent of adults believe that evolution took place solely through natural processes, while 33 percent believe that humans and other living things have existed in their present-day form since the beginning of time. Conflicts have arisen as fundamentalist Christians have struggled to prevent the teaching of evolution in the nation's science classes or to introduce parallel instruction of biblical "creationism" or theories of "intelligent design," which hold that an intelligent creator lies behind the development of life on earth.

Gun ownership has become a key symbolic divide in the American public. According to recent surveys (and such findings are always controversial), approximately 36 percent of American adults either own a firearm or live with someone who does, down from a height of 53 percent in 1994. But who owns such weapons—and why—has changed. Of the somewhere between 265 and 310 million guns in the United States, research suggests that more than half are owned by 3 percent of the population. Many fewer Americans today own guns intended for hunting, while purchases of AR-15 style rifles and of handguns, which

63 percent say they purchased for "protection against people," have risen. Conflicts over Second Amendment rights to gun ownership and potential limits to or regulations of such rights further divide Americans, and the National Rifle Association plays a major role in American politics.

More concrete divisions are tied to the distribution of wealth (see Figure 29.4). Globally, the divide is shocking: in 2015 it took the combined wealth of 3.5 billion people at the bottom of the economic scale to match the wealth owned by 62 individuals at the top (in 2010, it required the combined wealth of 388 billionaires to match that 3.5 billion). And by global standards, even America's poorest five percent are wealthier (in cost-corrected measures) than 68 percent of the globe—although the United States does not measure nearly so well when compared to other developed nations. But within the United States, the economic divide has continued to grow. In 2013, families in the top 1 percent claimed an average income 25 times that of the average family in the bottom 99 percent, the widest gulf in more than three decades. And the divide between the wealthy 1 percent and the super-rich 0.001 percent is growing even faster.

In September 2011, new protests against this growing divide first gained significant attention. New York City's Occupy Wall Street effort was modeled on a variety of international protests, and Occupy was an international movement, but it captured a widespread sense of outrage and frustration within the United States, particularly among well-educated whites, and more than six hundred U.S. communities began local occupations. The movement was often criticized for its lack of clear goals or demands, and it often struggled with its consensus-based governance. But while the U.S. movement faded in 2012—*The New York Times* headlined "The Frenzy that Fizzled"—Occupy drew attention to economic inequality and offered a framework for discussing that divide: "We are the 99%."

Race continues to divide the nation, and despite the diversity of the American public, that divide is most often framed in black and white. Economics play a role: almost a quarter of African Americans live below the poverty line, compared to less than 10 percent of whites. Despite a large black middle class, overall black infant mortality is more than twice the rate for whites; black children are more likely to attend failing schools; and the homicide rate—19.4 per 100,000—falls just below violence-torn Nigeria (and compares to 2.5 per 100,000 for white Americans). According to one 2015 study, young unarmed black men were twice as likely as young unarmed white men to be shot and killed by police officers; of unarmed suspects shot by police in 2015, 41 percent were black.

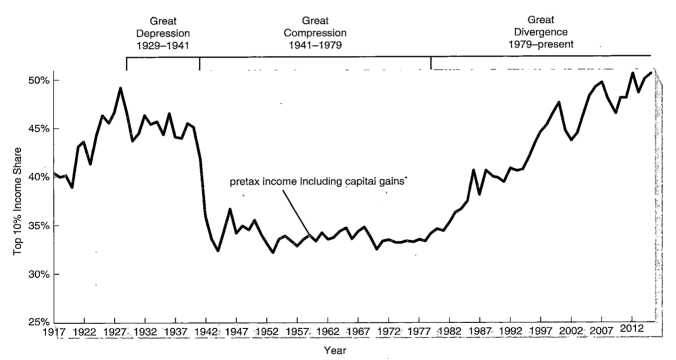

*Income does not include government transfer payments (e.g. Social Security or unemployment).

Figure 29.4 The Great Divergence

This chart shows the share of income received by the top ten percent of American households from 1917 forward. During what economic historians Claudia Golden and Robert Mango labeled "the great compression," Americans' household income was more equal, or compressed. Beginning in the late 1970s, growing income inequality appears as "the great divergence" (economist Paul Krugman's term). In 2015, the top ten percent received slightly more than 50 percent of US household income. Twenty-two percent went to the top one percent of households. *Source:* Emmanuel Saez, "Striking it Richer: The Evolution of Top Incomes in the United States" (Updated with 2015 preliminary estimates), UC Berkeley, June 30, 2016, available at https://eml.berkeley.edu/~saez/saez-UStopincomes-2015.pdf.

◁ Black Lives Matter was created by black community organizers Patrisse Cullors, Alicia Garza, and Opal Tometi in 2013. It became a national and then international movement. Here, students at the University of Washington carry BLM signs in a 2017 protest.

Such losses gave rise to the Black Lives Matter move-ment. BLM emerged first as a hashtag (#BlackLivesMatter) in 2013, after neighborhood watch coordinator George Zimmerman was acquitted for the shooting death of Trayvon Martin, an unarmed 17-year-old who was visiting the gated community where the shooting occurred in Sanford, Florida. BLM moved from online protests to demonstrations in the streets following the police shooting of Michael Brown in 2014 and, focusing on the broader issue of systemic racism, showed significant political force during the 2016 election and in the protests that followed.

In the first decade and a half of the twenty-first century, few people in positions of power paid much attention to the plight of white working-class Americans, whose incomes were stagnating or dropping and whose communities suffered in kind. While no organized protest movement captured their frustrations, increasing suicide rates, along with heroin, opioid, and other prescription drug addictions pointed toward a growing crisis. Fueled by economic concerns, anger over what many perceived as declining status in a more diverse America, and rejection of fundamental social change, these Americans would prove a significant political force in the election of 2016.

29-5b Immigration and the Changing Face of America

On October 17, 2006, the United States population officially passed the 300 million mark, and its people were more diverse than at any time in the nation's history (see Map 29.5). (For comparison, U.S. population was approximately 321 million in 2015; 100 million in 1915; and 200 million in 1967.) During the 1990s, the population of people of color grew twelve times as fast as the white population, fueled by both immigration and birth rates. In 2003, Latinxs moved past African Americans to become the second largest ethnic or racial group in the nation, following non-Hispanic whites (see Figure 29.5). Immigration from Asia also remained high, and according to the 2010 census 5.6 percent of the U.S.

population was Asian or Asian American. Most immigration to the United States is legal, but the number of people in the United States without official documentation peaked in 2007 at 12 million (up from 3 million in 1980), before falling to

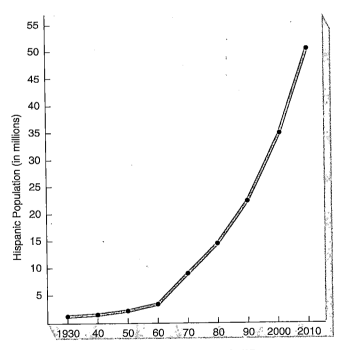

Figure 29.5 The Growth of the U.S. Hispanic Population

"Hispanic" combines people from a wide variety of national origins or ancestries—including all the nations of Central and South America, Mexico, Cuba, Puerto Rico, the Dominican Republic, Spain—as well as those who identify as Californio, Tejano, Nuevo Mexicano, and Mestizo. Source: Adapted from the U.S. Department of Commerce, Economics and Statistics Information, Bureau of the Census, 1993 report "We, the American... Hispanics"; also recent Census Bureau figures for the Hispanic population.

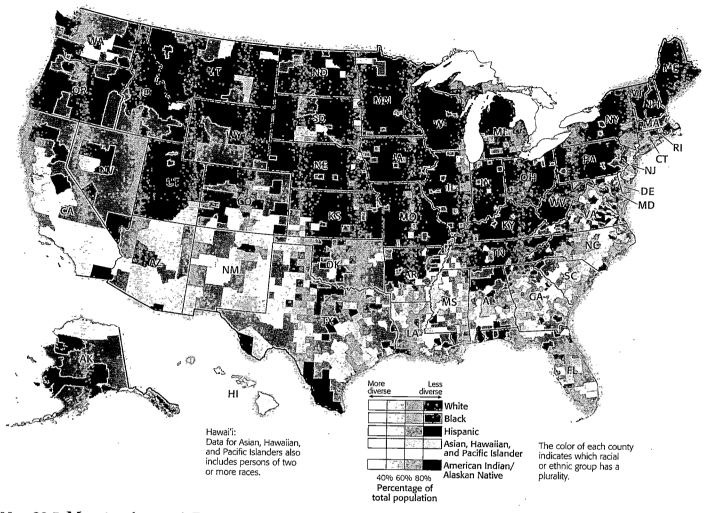

Hawai'i:
Data for Asian, Hawaiian,
and Pacific Islanders also
includes persons of two
or more races.

More diverse   Less diverse

White
Black
Hispanic
Asian, Hawaiian, and Pacific Islander
American Indian/ Alaskan Native

40% 60% 80%
Percentage of
total population

The color of each county
indicates which racial
or ethnic group has a
plurality.

Map 29.5 Mapping America's Diversity

Aggregate figures (more than 12 percent of the U.S. population was black and about 4 percent Asian in 2000, for example) convey America's ethnic and racial diversity. However, as this map shows, members of racial and ethnic groups are not distributed evenly throughout the nation. Source: From The New York Times, © April 1, 2001 The New York Times. All rights reserved. Used by permission and protected by the Copyright Laws of the United States. The printing, copying redistribution, or retransmission of the material without express written permission is prohibited.

about 11 million during the economic recession that began that year, a level that did not rise with economic recovery. Undocumented workers made up almost 8 percent of the U.S. labor force in 2014, including almost 17 percent of agricultural laborers.

These rapid demographic changes have altered the face of America. At a Dairy Queen in the far southern suburbs of Atlanta, six miles from the Gone with the Wind Historical District, teenage children of immigrants from India and Pakistan serve Blizzards and Brownie Earthquakes. In western Kansas, where immigrants from Somalia, Myanmar, Mexico, Sudan, Ethiopia, and Burma now work in Garden City's meatpacking plants, pho is a lunchtime staple on Garden City's main street, a Buddhist prayer space fills the old Kwik Shop, and the Tyson plant offers male and female

prayer rooms to its Muslim employees. Overwhelmingly, Garden City residents have welcomed the new immigrants and their diverse cultures: "This town is so nice," says Ahmed Ali, a young Somali man who works in the meat packing plant. Town leaders credit immigrant workers for the town's vibrant economy and low unemployment rate. But with almost three dozen native languages brought into the town's classrooms, and as children who spent much of their previous lives in the difficult circumstances of refugee camps face difficult adjustments, the town also encounters practical challenges that demand both funding and policy solutions.

Many of America's schools and neighborhoods remain racially segregated and public debates about illegal immigration are heated. At the same time, American popular culture has embraced the influences of this new multiethnic population.

Economics were important: in 2015 the buying power of the growing Latino population exceeded $1.3 trillion, up 167 percent since 2000, while average income for Asian American households tops that for all other groups. But American audiences also crossed racial and ethnic lines as, for example, African American rap and hip-hop attracted large followings of young white men.

29-5c The Changing American Family

The American family takes many different shapes in the twenty-first century (see Figure 29.6). Fewer and fewer American adults are married—barely half in 2015, compared with almost three-quarters in 1960. The median age at marriage continues to rise, reaching 29.2 for men and 27.4 for women in 2015. People are increasingly likely to marry someone of a different race or ethnicity: fewer than 1 percent of couples did so in 1970, compared to more than 15 percent in 2010. About 7 percent of couples live together without marriage, and roughly 14 percent of American adults live alone.

In the early twenty-first century, a vocal antigay movement coexisted with rising support for the legal equality of gay, lesbian, transgendered, and bisexual Americans. Although the federal Defense of Marriage Act (DOMA), passed by Congress in 1996, defined marriage as "only" a union between one man and one woman, many states and private corporations extend domestic partner benefits to gay couples, and in 2002 the American Academy of Pediatrics endorsed adoption by gay couples. Between 2003 and 2013, same-sex marriage was legalized in twelve states, though DOMA prevented the

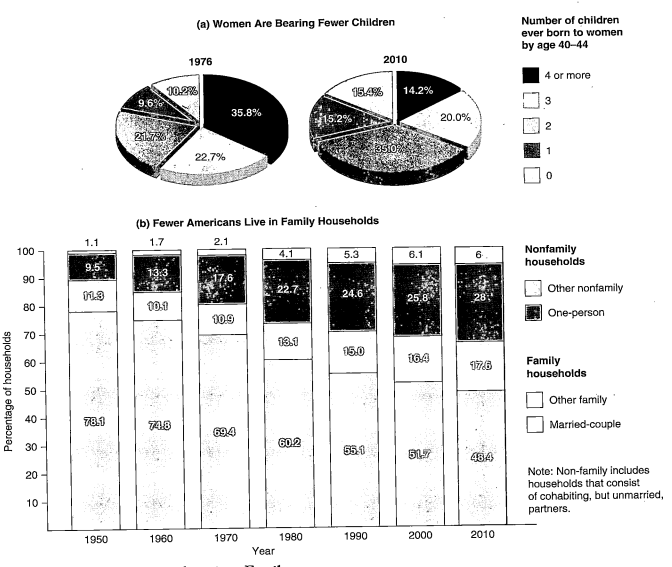

Figure 29.6 The Changing American Family

American households have become smaller, as more people live alone and women have, on average, fewer children. *Source: Adapted from U.S. Bureau of the Census, http://www.census.gov/prod/2002pubs/censr-4.pdf and http://www.census.gov/population/pop-profile/2000 /chap04.pdf.*

American War Dead

In 1991, as the United States prepared to go to war in the Persian Gulf, Defense Secretary Dick Cheney banned the media from photographing American war dead being returned to U.S. soil. The ban imposed by the George H. W. Bush administration may stem from a moment in the 1989 U.S. invasion of Panama, when ABC, CBS, and CNN chose to run coverage of caskets arriving at Dover Air Force Base and President Bush's White House

news conference simultaneously on a split screen, making it appear that the president was not paying appropriate respect to those killed in battle. During the twenty-first-century wars in Iraq and Afghanistan, the George W. Bush administration enforced a blanket ban on media photographs.

Critics argued that the Bush administration was hiding the tragic cost of America's wars, while supporters insisted that the policy protected the

privacy of American military families. The ban was lifted by Robert M. Gates, President Obama's secretary of defense, in 2009, with the support of the U.S. Army. However, media access was granted only when the fallen soldier's family gave permission.

CRITICAL THINKING

▫ In cases such as this, is it possible that what Americans do not see is as important as what they do see?

◁ *Coffins of U.S. military personnel arriving at Dover Air Force Base in Dover, Delaware. This undated photograph was released in response to a Freedom of Information Act request.*

REUTERS/USAF/www.thememoryhole.org/HK

federal government from recognizing any same-sex couples as married. In June 2013 the Supreme Court, in a 5-to-4 decision (*United States v. Windsor*), ruled DOMA unconstitutional, arguing that the legislation "humiliates" children raised by same-sex couples and undermines state power to define marriage. Marriage equality had practical implications: for example, it made legally married same-sex couples eligible for military, health, and other federal benefits.

In the early twenty-first century, babies were almost as likely to be born to unmarried women as to married ones. (In the United States, about 40 percent of babies were born to unmarried women, compared to 54 percent in Sweden and 2 percent in Japan.) Although almost one-third of families with children had only one parent present—most frequently the mother—children also lived in blended families created by second marriages or moved back and forth between households of parents who had joint custody. Based

on current statistical analysis, for couples who married in the mid-1990s the woman's level of education was the clearest predictor of divorce: if the woman graduated from a four-year college, the couple had a 25 percent likelihood of divorce; if she had not, the rate jumped to 50 percent.

In 2016, the leading edge of the baby boom generation turned 70; the median age of the American population was 37.8 in 2015, up from 29.5 in 1967. Although baby boomers are not aging in the same manner as their parents and grandparents—"Sixty is the new forty," the saying goes—the large and growing proportion of older people will have a major impact on American society. As life expectancy increases, the growing number of elderly Americans will put enormous pressure on the nation's healthcare system and family structure—who will care for people when they can no longer live independently?—and strain the Social Security and Medicare systems.

29-5d Violence, Crime, and Incarceration

In past decades, the nation has been haunted by increasingly frequent and inexplicable mass shootings. Americans were shocked in 1999 when two academically successful students at Columbine High School in Colorado murdered thirteen people (and injured twenty-three more) before committing suicide, but students also massacred classmates and teachers in Paducah, Kentucky; Springfield, Oregon; Jonesboro, Arkansas, and on the campuses of Virginia Tech and Okiah College in California. Armed men, most of them young, white, and mentally ill, committed mass murders at coffee shops and nursing homes, at workplaces, hotels, and places of worship, at a mall and a movie theater and an army post and an air force base. Among the most horrific events were a gunman's shooting of ten young girls in a one-room Amish schoolhouse in 2006, the murder of twenty small children and six adults at Sandy Hook Elementary School in Newtown, Connecticut, in 2012, and the slaughter of nine African American worshipers by a 22-year-old white supremacist during a prayer service in Charleston, South Carolina.

Such mass shootings, however, account for less than one-half of 1 percent of gun-related homicides. Shooting deaths, along with other homicides, occur far more frequently in poor, inner-city neighborhoods. In Chicago, for example, close to four hundred school-aged children were shot and killed between 2009 and 2017, and in early 2012 Chicago's death toll exceeded the number of U.S. servicemen and servicewomen killed in Afghanistan. At the same time, the majority of Americans saw rapidly declining rates of violent crime after 1993; according to the FBI, U.S. homicide rates hit a fifty-year low in 2014, and violent crime dropped 16.5 percent between 2006 and 2015.

The U.S. prison population increased dramatically from the mid-1970s through the first decade of the twenty-first century; rates have begun to drop, but still exceed those of almost every nation in the world. In 2008, the U.S. imprisonment rate of 751 per 100,000 compared to Russia's 577, Canada's 117, and Japan's 59. While the United States does have a higher rate of violent (often gun-related) crime than most other developed nations, high incarceration rates are due in part to the length of sentences mandated for nonviolent criminals (including those convicted of drug crimes). Thus it is not so much the number of people sentenced to prison as the length of their sentences that accounts for America's outlier rates. For example, in 2005 the average convicted burglar in Scotland served three and a half months, while his U.S. counterpart stayed in jail fifteen months longer.

While African Americans are still incarcerated at much higher rates than white or Latinx Americans, the racial disparity has begun to shrink. According to the U.S. Bureau of Justice Statistics, the imprisonment rate for black men has dropped 22 percent since 2000, while it has risen slightly for white men; the rate for black women has dropped by almost half, as the rate for white women has grown by 56 percent. In general, although more than nine out of ten inmates are male, women make up the fastest-growing prison population in the United States.

America's prison system, according to the White House Council of Economic Advisors in 2016, costs taxpayers over $80 billion a year; eleven states spent more on their corrections systems than on higher education. Carceral system costs top out at $168,000 per inmate per year in New York City; Kentucky, in contrast, spends less than $15,000. Social costs are extraordinary, as men and women emerging from prison, due in part to their criminal records, are too often unable to become productive members of society or to rejoin stable families and communities.

29-5e Health and Medicine

The leading causes of death in the United States today are heart disease and cancer; almost 1.7 million new cases of cancer were diagnosed in 2016. At the same time, middle-aged whites are dying in increasing numbers not because of these major killers, but due to suicide, alcohol-linked liver disease, and overdoses of prescription opioids and heroin. On the positive side, the CDC reports that new HIV infections are dropping significantly.

Other health issues have become increasingly important. In a rapid change over the course of a decade, more than two-thirds of American adults are now overweight or obese—conditions linked to hypertension, cardiovascular disease, and diabetes. In 1995, no state had an adult obesity rate that hit 20 percent. By 2012, not a single state fell below that 20 percent mark. Twelve states topped 30 percent obesity rates in 2012; three years later, twenty-five states did.

Cigarette smoking continues a slow but steady decline. Slightly less than one-fifth of American adults smoked in 2010, down from about one-third of adults in 1980 and from 42 percent in 1965. According to the Centers for Disease Control, smoking causes one of every five U.S. deaths, and smoking-related medical costs and lost productivity total about $300 billion a year. With clearer understanding of the danger of secondhand smoke, local governments have overwhelmingly banned smoking in public spaces, including restaurants and bars.

In efforts to combat disease and improve quality of life, scientists and medical researchers are making important breakthroughs in a variety of fields, from improved HIV medication to targeted cancer therapies to the development of bionic limbs for amputees. Research on stem cells, the unspecialized cells that can be induced to become cells with specialized functions, is promising. Stem cells may become insulin-producing cells of the pancreas, and thus make possible a cure for diabetes, or they might become dopamine-producing neurons, offering therapy for Parkinson's disease, a progressive disorder of the nervous system that affects over 1 million Americans. Finally, research on the human genome helps to identify the genetic origins of disease and thus paths to more effective treatment.

29-5f Century of Change

The twentieth century had seen more momentous change than any previous century—change that brought enormous benefits to human beings, change that threatened the very existence of the human species. Research in the physical and biological sciences had provided insight into the structure of matter and of the universe. Technology—the application of science—had made startling advances that benefited Americans in nearly every aspect of life: better health, more wealth, more mobility, less drudgery, greater access to information.

Through these advances, Americans at the start of the new century were more connected to the rest of humankind than ever before. This interconnection was perhaps the most powerful product of globalization. A commodities trader in Chicago in February 2010 could send a text message to her fiancé in Tokyo while she spoke on the phone to a trader in Frankfurt, and e-mailed another one in Bombay, all while keeping one eye on NBC's live coverage of the Winter Olympics in Vancouver; within a minute or two, she could receive a reply from her fiancé saying that he missed her, too. If she felt sufficiently lovesick, she could board an airplane and be in Japan the following day.

The world had shrunk to the size of an airplane ticket. In 1955, 51 million people a year traveled by plane. By the turn of the century, 1.6 billion were airborne every year, and 530 million—or about 1.5 million each day—crossed international borders. This permeability of national boundaries brought many benefits, as did the integration of markets and the global spread of information that occurred alongside it.

29-5g Globalization and World Health

But there was a flip side to this growing connectivity, which even advocates of globalization perceived. The rapid increase in international air travel was a particularly potent force for the dissemination of global disease, as flying made it possible for people to reach the other side of the world in far less time than the incubation period for many ailments. Environmental degradation also created major global health threats. In 2003, the World Health Organization (WHO) estimated that nearly one-quarter of the global burden of disease and injury was related to environmental disruption and decline. For example, some 90 percent of diarrheal diseases (such as cholera), which were killing 3 million people a year, resulted from contaminated water. WHO also pointed to globalization and environmental disruption as contributing to the fact that, in the final two decades of the twentieth century, more than thirty infectious diseases were identified in humans for the first time—including AIDS, Ebola virus, hantavirus, and hepatitis C and E. Environmentalists, meanwhile, insisted that the growing interaction of national economies was having a deleterious impact on the ecosystem through climate change, ozone depletion, hazardous waste, and damage to fisheries.

29-5h Confronting Terrorism

In military and diplomatic terms, the years after 9/11 witnessed important changes. The attacks that day brought home what Americans had only dimly perceived before then: that globalization had shrunk the natural buffers that distance and two oceans provided the United States. Al Qaeda, it was clear, had used the increasingly open, integrated, globalized world to give itself new power and reach. It had shown that small cells of terrorists could become true transnational threats—thriving around the world without any single state sponsor or home base. According to American intelligence, Al Qaeda operated in more than ninety countries—including the United States.

How would one go about vanquishing such a foe? Was a decisive victory even possible? These remained open questions in the years after the World Trade Center collapsed.

◁ In this August 25, 2013, photo, inmate firefighters walk along Highway 120 after battling the Rim Fire near Yosemite National Park, California. Caused by a hunter's illegal campfire that got out of control, the blaze was one of the largest in California's history, and the largest ever in the Sierra Nevada mountain range, burning 257,000 acres over a period of nine weeks.

AP Images/Jae C. Hong, File

The "Swine Flu" Pandemic

When United Flight 803 from Washington, D.C., landed at Tokyo's Narita airport on May 20, 2009, Japanese health officials boarded the plane. Garbed in respirator masks, goggles, and disposable scrubs, they used thermal scanners to check passengers for elevated temperatures. Passengers waited anxiously as officials interviewed each person on board, aware that, if any symptoms or suspicious travel patterns were discovered, the entire plane might be quarantined. Japan had already closed its borders to all travelers from Mexico, where the H1N1 "swine flu" virus had emerged about three weeks earlier. Mexico took extraordinary actions, closing schools and businesses and drawing on public health expertise from around the world. Nevertheless, the H1N1 virus had, by mid-May, already spread to more than twenty-two countries. It was much too late to stem the spread of swine flu by isolating travelers from its country of origin.

Soon after a series of deaths in Mexico in late April, the World Health Organization had raised its alert level to stage 5, signaling that officials expected the virus to create the first major flu pandemic in more than forty years. Articles in the world media reminded readers of the flu pandemic of 1918 while emphasizing how much had changed. International air travel had brought the world into much closer contact, with more than 2 billion passengers traveling by airline each year. Health analysts made clear that the "right" pathogen, if it emerged in the "right" place, might spread throughout the world in the space of a day, well before anyone was conscious of the threat it posed.

On the other hand, global connections also offered new tools to combat pandemics: global surveillance of disease, though not equally well developed or dependable in all countries, might head off developing health threats. Individual nations and global organizations pool expertise as they develop vaccines and techniques to cope with pandemics, should one emerge. Because of lessons learned during the 2003 SARS outbreak, Hong Kong provided a model to the rest of the world with its plans for the prevention and management of major outbreaks of infectious disease. Finally, some believe that a global culture where borders present little barrier may facilitate the growth of global immunities to infectious diseases.

People around the world were relieved when the swine flu, after the initial deaths in Mexico, turned out to be no more deadly than a usual flu strain. In previous years, SARS (severe, acute respiratory syndrome) and the H5N1 "bird flu" had also failed to develop into major worldwide heath threats, as did later threats from Ebola. But the World Health Organization and the U.S. Centers for Disease Control cautioned that the emergence of a major pandemic was simply a matter of time, especially as drug-resistant strains of infectious disease emerge. "We live in one world, with one health," observed a UN official. In the era of globalization, diseases do not stop at borders or respect wealth and power, and the links between Americans and the rest of the world's peoples cannot be denied.

CRITICAL THINKING

◻ In this era of globalization, diseases cannot be contained within the borders of one country. What responsibility does the United States have to cooperate with and offer support to other nations when outbreaks of disease occur?

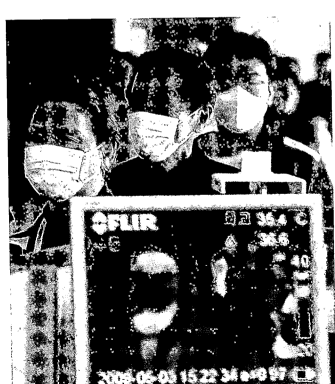

AP Photo/Yonhap, Seo Myung-gon

◁ As the H1N1 virus—"swine flu"—spread rapidly in the spring of 2009, nations around the world attempted to prevent the spread of infection. Here, thermal cameras check the body temperatures of passengers arriving at Incheon International Airport in South Korea.

Unchallenged militarily and seeing no rival great power, the United States felt few constraints about intervening in Afghanistan and then Iraq, but the problems in both countries showed that it could take scant comfort from this superiority. It continued to spend colossal sums on its military, more indeed than the next fourteen highest-spending countries combined (the Pentagon in 2016 spent $600 billion, not including supplemental appropriations for Iraq and Afghanistan). America had taken on military commitments all over the globe, from the Balkans and Iraq to Afghanistan

and Korea (see Table 29.1). Its armed forces looked colossal, but its obligations looked even larger.

And more than ever, Americans debated whether the nation should maintain commitments all over the globe. Was it the case, as proponents of a global posture maintained, that the United States had benefited in countless ways from its post–World War II dominance of the international system, whatever the costs associated with that policy, whatever misadventures that occasionally had resulted? Or could it be, as the critics of "global hegemony" maintained, that the nation

Table 29.1 U.S. Military Personnel on Active Duty in Foreign Countries, 2012[1]

Region/Country[2]	Personnel	Region/Country[2]	Personnel
United States and Territories		Singapore	180
Continental U.S.	1,123,219	Thailand	114
Alaska	21,280	Bahrain	2,902
Hawai'i	49,242	Diego Garcia	516
Guam	5,646	Egypt	292
Puerto Rico	162	Israel	41
Europe		Oman	37
Belgium*	1,165	Pakistan	42
France*	70	Qatar	800
Germany*	45,596	Saudi Arabia	278
Greece*	361	United Arab Emirates	193
Greenland*	138	**Sub-Saharan Africa**	
Hungary	62	Djibouti	139
Italy*	10,916	Kenya	40
Netherlands*	374	South Africa	35
Norway*	90	**Western Hemisphere**	
Portugal*	713	Bahamas, The	50
Russia	67	Brazil	48
Spain*	1,600	Canada	146
Turkey*	1,491	Chile	38
United Kingdom*	9,310	Colombia	64
East Asia and Pacific		Cuba (Guantanamo)	988
Australia	183	Honduras	388
China, People's Republic of	49	Peru	51
Japan	52,692	**Total Worldwide[2]**	1,372,522
Philippines	131	Undistributed[3]	39,157

*NATO countries

[1]Only countries with 30 or more U.S. military personnel are listed.

[2]Includes all regions/countries, not simply those listed.

[3]Undistributed includes Afghanistan, Iraq, Kuwait, Republic of Korea, and any unknown/classified locations.

Source: U.S. Department of Defense, Defense Manpower Data Center (http://siadapp.dmdc.osd.mil/personnel/MILITARY/miltop.htm Accessed July 1, 2013)

Twitter Revolution

When Barack Obama won reelection as president of the United States on November 7, 2012, he celebrated by tweeting a photograph of himself hugging his wife, Michelle. The Tweet read, "Four more years. pic.twitter.com/bAJE6Vom." Almost immediately, it became the most popular Tweet of all time, with more than half a million Retweets.

Twitter, a social networking and microblogging service founded in 2006 by Jack Dorsey and Biz Stone, has become one of the ten most visited websites on the planet, with more than 200 million monthly active users communicating via short bursts of information called Tweets.

Along with Facebook, Flickr, and other social media sites, Twitter has spawned an important structural change in how information spreads. No longer is there a need to rely on the smoke signals and carrier pigeons used by early Americans, or even the phone calls, faxes, and television shows so prized by the Baby Boom generation. In addition to announcing personal opinions and achievements, the new sites have been used to organize protests—indeed, they have been credited with reinventing social activism. Thus the Arab Spring uprisings of 2010–11 and the Iranian election protests of 2009–10 were called "Twitter Revolutions" for the ways they upended the traditional relationship between political authority and popular will and enabled activists to collaborate and coordinate.

That social media and mass political protests are closely connected is a beguiling notion, but also a problematic one. Social networks did not cause these upheavals, and indeed had little connection to the underlying factors behind the protests. In Egypt, for example, the sociopolitical tension between the tiny ruling elite and the mass of the populace had long been acute, prompting many analysts to expect a major upheaval in due course. Egyptian activists, for their part, insisted that old-fashioned grassroots organizing on the ground, not social media, drove their revolution. They further noted that, at the time of the protests, very few Twitter accounts existed in the country.

Yet if Twitter and other social media are not particularly effective at boosting popular *motivation* for a given cause, they can have an outsized impact on increasing *participation*, at least in the short term. The Occupy Wall Street movement of 2011–12, for example, began as a Twitter experiment in July 2011, when the Canadian anti-consumerism magazine *Adbusters* posted the idea of a march in Lower Manhattan. The proposal took hold, and in subsequent months, protesters used Twitter, YouTube, and Facebook to coordinate efforts in cities and towns all over the country as well as abroad.

Twitter has shown other uses as well, including as a de facto emergency communication system for breaking news. The Boston Police, for example, tweeted news of the arrest of a suspect in the 2013 Boston Marathon terrorist attack in order to calm residents' nerves. Researchers are also studying using Twitter to track epidemics and how they spread, while college professors are seeing promising results when they use Twitter to promote student interaction, especially in large lecture classes. For these and other dedicated tweeters, there could be no more fitting legacy of the twentieth century than the Internet and the social media it spawned.

CRITICAL THINKING

- During the 2016 election cycle, George Will, a Washington Post political pundit famously said of Republican nominee and the eventual winner of the election, Donald Trump, "He has an advantage on me. He can say everything he knows about any subject in 140 characters, and I can't." What role have Twitter and other social media outlets played in American politics in the last decade?
- Has social media been beneficial or detrimental to the political process of democracy?

---

could and should draw down its overseas commitments significantly, passing the burdens of regional security in various locales to allied governments, thereby allowing more time, money, and attention to be devoted to improving the lives of Americans at home?

Summary

The 1990s were, for most Americans, good times. A digitized revolution in communications and information—as fundamental as the revolution brought about by electricity and the combustion engine a century earlier, or the steam engine a century before that—was generating prosperity and transforming life in America and around the globe. The longest economic expansion in American history—from 1991 to 2001—meant that most Americans who wanted jobs had them, that the stock market boomed, that the nation had a budget surplus instead of a deficit, and that more Americans than ever before owned their own homes. In addition, America was not only prosperous; it was powerful. With the Soviet Union gone and no other formidable rival on the horizon, the United States stood as the world's lone superpower, its economic and military power daunting to friend and foe alike.

Although America seemed at the apex of power and prosperity, unsettling events troubled the nation, abroad and at home. Just minutes before midnight on December 31, 1999, President Clinton called on the American people not to fear the future, but to "welcome it, create it, and embrace it." The challenges of the future would be greater than Americans imagined as they welcomed the new millennium that night. In 2000, the contested presidential election was decided by the Supreme Court in a partisan 5-to-4 vote; in 2001, the ten-year economic expansion came to an end.

Then, on September 11 of that year, radical Islamic terrorists attacked the World Trade Center and the Pentagon, killing thousands and altering many aspects of American life. The new president, George W. Bush, declared a "war on terrorism," one with both foreign and domestic components. Bush won reelection in 2004, but his fortunes soon waned. The combination of two costly wars abroad and a severe economic crisis at home paved the way for Barack Obama's historic election in 2008, but also shaped the limits and possibilities of Obama's two-term presidency. As he departed the White House for the last time on the morning of January 20, 2017, to attend the inauguration of his successor, it remained to be seen where the wondrous American story would go next.

The world that Americans found in the first years of the twenty-first century was much different from the one they had looked forward to with confidence and high hopes as they celebrated the coming of the new millennium on New Year's Eve 1999. The horror of the terror attacks of September 11, 2001, shook America to its core. Then came two lengthy and inconclusive wars, to be followed in turn by the most severe economic downturn since the Great Depression. By the start of the new decade, Americans were deeply divided over how to respond to the nation's problems. To some, the obstacles seemed impossibly daunting. Yet the American people had faced difficult times before in their history; each time, they had proved their resilience and weathered the storm. As Donald Trump's term began, Americans faced the need to struggle over foreign and domestic policy priorities, over the direction of their nation, with the controlled passion and the commitment to reason that a healthy democracy demands.

Suggestions for Further Reading

Andrew Bacevich, *America's War for the Greater Middle East: A Military History* (2016)

Derek Chollet and James Goldgeier, *America Between the Wars: From 11/9 to 9/11* (2008)

Barbara Ehrenreich, *Nickel and Dimed: On (Not) Getting by in America* (2002)

John F. Harris, *The Survivor: Bill Clinton in the White House* (2005)

Jennifer L. Hochschild, *Facing Up to the American Dream: Race, Class, and the Soul of the Nation* (1995)

Alejandro Portes and Reuben G. Rumbaut, *Immigrant America: A Portrait*, 3rd ed. (2006)

Samantha Power, *"A Problem from Hell": America and the Age of Genocide* (2002)

Emma Sky, *The Unraveling: High Hopes and Missed Opportunities in Iraq* (2015)

Joseph E. Stiglitz, *Globalization and Its Discontents* (2002)

Joby Warrick, *Black Flags: The Rise of ISIS* (2015)

MINDTAP
From Cengage

MindTap® is a fully online personalized learning experience built upon Cengage Learning content. MindTap® combines student learning tools—readings, multimedia, activities, and assessments—into a singular Learning Path that guides students through the course and helps students develop the critical thinking, analysis, and communication skills that are essential to academic and professional success.

Declaration of Independence in Congress, July 4, 1776

When, in the course of human events, it becomes necessary for one people to dissolve the political bonds which have connected them with another, and to assume, among the powers of the earth, the separate and equal station to which the laws of nature and of nature's God entitle them, a decent respect to the opinions of mankind requires that they should declare the causes which impel them to the separation.

We hold these truths to be self-evident: That all men are created equal; that they are endowed by their Creator with certain unalienable rights; that among these are life, liberty, and the pursuit of happiness; that, to secure these rights, governments are instituted among men, deriving their just powers from the consent of the governed; that whenever any form of government becomes destructive of these ends, it is the right of the people to alter or to abolish it, and to institute new government, laying its foundation on such principles, and organizing its powers in such form, as to them shall seem most likely to effect their safety and happiness. Prudence, indeed, will dictate that governments long established should not be changed for light and transient causes; and accordingly all experience hath shown that mankind are more disposed to suffer, while evils are sufferable, than to right themselves by abolishing the forms to which they are accustomed. But when a long train of abuses and usurpations, pursuing invariably the same object, evinces a design to reduce them under absolute despotism, it is their right, it is their duty, to throw off such government, and to provide new guards for their future security. Such has been the patient sufferance of these colonies; and such is now the necessity which constrains them to alter their former systems of government. The history of the present King of Great Britain is a history of repeated injuries and usurpations, all having in direct object the establishment of an absolute tyranny over these states. To prove this, let facts be submitted to a candid world.

He has refused his assent to laws, the most wholesome and necessary for the public good.

He has forbidden his governors to pass laws of immediate and pressing importance, unless suspended in their operation till his assent should be obtained; and, when so suspended, he has utterly neglected to attend to them.

He has refused to pass other laws for the accommodation of large districts of people, unless those people would relinquish the right of representation in the legislature, a right inestimable to them, and formidable to tyrants only.

He has called together legislative bodies at places unusual, uncomfortable, and distant from the depository of their public records, for the sole purpose of fatiguing them into compliance with his measures.

He has dissolved representative houses repeatedly, for opposing, with manly firmness, his invasions on the rights of the people.

He has refused for a long time, after such dissolutions, to cause others to be elected; whereby the legislative powers, incapable of annihilation, have returned to the people at large for their exercise; the state remaining, in the mean time, exposed to all the dangers of invasions from without and convulsions within.

He has endeavored to prevent the population of these states; for that purpose obstructing the laws for naturalization of foreigners; refusing to pass others to encourage their migration hither, and raising the conditions of new appropriations of lands.

He has obstructed the administration of justice, by refusing his assent to laws for establishing judiciary powers.

He has made judges dependent on his will alone, for the tenure of their offices, and the amount and payment of their salaries.

He has erected a multitude of new offices, and sent hither swarms of officers to harass our people and eat out their substance.

He has kept among us, in times of peace, standing armies, without the consent of our legislatures.

He has affected to render the military independent of, and superior to, the civil power.

He has combined with others to subject us to a jurisdiction foreign to our constitution, and unacknowledged by our laws, giving his assent to their acts of pretended legislation:

For quartering large bodies of armed troops among us;

For protecting them, by a mock trial, from punishment for any murders which they should commit on the inhabitants of these states;

For cutting off our trade with all parts of the world;

For imposing taxes on us without our consent;

For depriving us, in many cases, of the benefits of trial by jury;

For transporting us beyond seas, to be tried for pretended offenses;

For abolishing the free system of English laws in a neighboring province, establishing therein an arbitrary government, and enlarging its boundaries, so as to render it at once an example and fit instrument for introducing the same absolute rule into these colonies;

For taking away our charters, abolishing our most valuable laws, and altering fundamentally the forms of our governments;

For suspending our own legislatures, and declaring themselves invested with power to legislate for us in all cases whatsoever.

He has abdicated government here, by declaring us out of his protection and waging war against us.

He has plundered our seas, ravaged our coasts, burned our towns, and destroyed the lives of our people.

He is at this time transporting large armies of foreign mercenaries to complete the works of death, desolation, and tyranny already begun with circumstances of cruelty and perfidy scarcely paralleled in the most barbarous ages, and totally unworthy the head of a civilized nation.

He has constrained our fellow-citizens, taken captive on the high seas, to bear arms against their country, to become the executioners of their friends and brethren, or to fall themselves by their hands.

He has excited domestic insurrection among us, and has endeavored to bring on the inhabitants of our frontiers the merciless Indian savages, whose known rule of warfare is an undistinguished destruction of all ages, sexes, and conditions.

In every stage of these oppressions we have petitioned for redress in the most humble terms; our repeated petitions have been answered only by repeated injury. A prince, whose character is thus marked by every act which may define a tyrant, is unfit to be the ruler of a free people.

Nor have we been wanting in our attentions to our British brethren. We have warned them, from time to time, of attempts by their legislature to extend an unwarrantable jurisdiction over us. We have reminded them of the circumstances of our emigration and settlement here. We have appealed to their native justice and magnanimity; and we have conjured them, by the ties of our common kindred, to disavow these usurpations, which would inevitably interrupt our connections and correspondence. They, too, have been deaf to the voice of justice and of consanguinity. We must, therefore, acquiesce in the necessity which denounces our separation, and hold them, as we hold the rest of mankind, enemies in war, in peace friends.

We, therefore, the representatives of the United States of America, in General Congress assembled, appealing to the Supreme Judge of the world for the rectitude of our intentions, do, in the name and by the authority of the good people of these colonies, solemnly publish and declare, that these United Colonies are, and of right ought to be, FREE AND INDEPENDENT STATES; that they are absolved from all allegiance to the British crown, and that all political connection between them and the state of Great Britain is, and ought to be, totally dissolved; and that, as free and independent states, they have full power to levy war, conclude peace, contract alliances, establish commerce, and do all other acts and things which independent states may of right do. And for the support of this declaration, with a firm reliance on the protection of Divine Providence, we mutually pledge to each other our lives, our fortunes, and our sacred honor.

Articles of Confederation

Whereas the Delegates of the United States of America in Congress assembled did on the fifteenth day of November in the Year of our Lord One Thousand Seven Hundred and Seventy seven, and in the Second Year of the Independence of America agree to certain articles of Confederation and perpetual Union between the States of Newhampshire, Massachusetts Bay, Rhode Island and Providence Plantations, Connecticut, New York, New Jersey, Pennsylvania, Delaware, Maryland, Virginia, North Carolina, South Carolina and Georgia in the Words following, viz. "Articles of Confederation and perpetual Union between the states of Newhampshire, Massachusetts Bay, Rhode Island and Providence Plantations, Connecticut, New York, New Jersey, Pennsylvania, Delaware, Maryland, Virginia, North Carolina, South Carolina and Georgia.

Article I The Stile of this confederacy shall be "The United States of America."

Article II Each state retains its sovereignty, freedom and independence, and every Power, Jurisdiction and right, which is not by this confederation expressly delegated to the United States, in Congress assembled.

Article III The said states hereby severally enter into a firm league of friendship with each other, for their common defence, the security of their Liberties, and their mutual and general welfare, binding themselves to assist each other, against all force offered to, or attacks made upon them, or any of them, on account of religion, sovereignty, trade, or any other pretence whatever.

Article IV The better to secure and perpetuate mutual friendship and intercourse among the people of the different states in this union, the free inhabitants of each of these states, paupers, vagabonds and fugitives from Justice excepted, shall be entitled to all privileges and immunities of free citizens in the several states; and the people of each state shall have free ingress and regress to and from any other state, and shall enjoy therein all the privileges of trade and commerce, subject to the same duties, impositions and restrictions as the inhabitants thereof respectively, provided that such restriction shall not extend so far as to prevent the removal of property imported into any state, to any other state of which the Owner is an inhabitant; provided also that no imposition, duties or restriction shall be laid by any state, on the property of the united states, or either of them.

If any Person guilty of, or charged with treason, felony, or other high misdemeanor in any state, shall flee from Justice, and be found in any of the united states, he shall upon demand of the Governor or executive power, of the state from which he fled, be delivered up and removed to the state having jurisdiction of his offence.

Full faith and credit shall be given in each of these states to the records, acts and judicial proceedings of the courts and magistrates of every other state.

Article V For the more convenient management of the general interests of the united states, delegates shall be annually appointed in such manner as the legislature of each state shall direct, to meet in Congress on the first Monday in November, in every year, with a power reserved to each state, to recall its delegates, or any of them, at any time within the year, and to send others in their stead, for the remainder of the Year.

No state shall be represented in Congress by less than two, nor by more than seven Members; and no person shall be capable of being a delegate for more than three years in any term of six years; nor shall any person, being a delegate, be capable of holding any office under the united states, for which he, or another for his benefit receives any salary, fees or emolument of any kind.

Each state shall maintain its own delegates in a meeting of the states, and while they act as members of the committee of the states.

In determining questions in the united states, in Congress assembled, each state shall have one vote.

Freedom of speech and debate in Congress shall not be impeached or questioned in any Court, or place out of Congress, and the members of congress shall be protected in their persons from arrests and imprisonments, during the time of their going to and from, and attendance on congress, except for treason, felony, or breach of the peace.

Article VI No state without the Consent of the united states in congress assembled, shall send any embassy to, or receive any embassy from, or enter into any conference, agreement, or alliance or treaty with any King, prince or state; nor shall any person holding any office of profit or trust under the united states, or any of them, accept of any present, emolument, office or title of any kind whatever from any king, prince or foreign state; nor shall the united states in congress assembled, or any of them, grant any title of nobility.

No two or more states shall enter into any treaty, confederation or alliance whatever between them, without the consent of the united states in congress assembled, specifying accurately the purposes for which the same is to be entered into, and how long it shall continue.

No state shall lay any imposts or duties, which may interfere with any stipulations in treaties, entered into by the united states in congress assembled, with any king, prince or state, in pursuance of any treaties already proposed by congress, to the courts of France and Spain.

No vessels of war shall be kept up in time of peace by any state, except such number only, as shall be deemed necessary by the united states in congress assembled, for

the defence of such state, or its trade; nor shall any body of forces be kept up by any state, in time of peace, except such number only, as in the judgment of the united states, in congress assembled, shall be deemed requisite to garrison the forts necessary for the defence of such state; but every state shall always keep up a well regulated and disciplined militia, sufficiently armed and accoutred, and shall provide and constantly have ready for use, in public stores, a due number of field pieces and tents, and a proper quantity of arms, ammunition and camp equipage.

No state shall engage in any war without the consent of the united states in congress assembled, unless such state be actually invaded by enemies, or shall have received certain advice of a resolution being formed by some nation of Indians to invade such state, and the danger is so imminent as not to admit of a delay, till the united states in congress assembled can be consulted: nor shall any state grant commissions to any ships or vessels of war, nor letters of marque or reprisal, except it be after a declaration of war by the united states in congress assembled, and then only against the kingdom or state and the subjects thereof, against which war has been so declared, and under such regulations as shall be established by the united states in congress assembled, unless such state be infested by pirates, in which case vessels of war may be fitted out for that occasion, and kept so long as the danger shall continue, or until the united states in congress assembled shall determine otherwise.

Article VII When land-forces are raised by any state for the common defence, all officers of or under the rank of colonel, shall be appointed by the legislature of each state respectively by whom such forces shall be raised, or in such manner as such state shall direct, and all vacancies shall be filled up by the state which first made the appointment.

Article VIII All charges of war, and all other expences that shall be incurred for the common defence or general welfare, and allowed by the united states in congress assembled, shall be defrayed out of a common treasury, which shall be supplied by the several states, in proportion to the value of all land within each state, granted to or surveyed for any Person, as such land and the buildings and improvements thereon shall be estimated according to such mode as the united states in congress assembled, shall from time to time direct and appoint. The taxes for paying that proportion shall be laid and levied by the authority and direction of the legislatures of the several states within the time agreed upon by the united states in congress assembled.

Article IX The united states in congress assembled, shall have the sole and exclusive right and power of determining on peace and war, except in the cases mentioned in the sixth article—of sending and receiving ambassadors—entering into treaties and alliances, provided that no treaty of commerce shall be made whereby the legislative power of the respective states shall be restrained from imposing such imposts and duties on foreigners, as their own people are subjected to, or from prohibiting the exportation or importation of any species of goods or commodities whatsoever—of establishing rules for deciding in all cases, what captures on land or water shall be legal, and in what manner prizes taken by land or naval forces in the service of the united states shall be divided or appropriated—of granting letters of marque and reprisal in times of peace—appointing courts for the trial of piracies and felonies committed on the high seas and establishing courts for receiving and determining final appeals in all cases of captures, provided that no member of congress shall be appointed a judge of any of the said courts.

The united states in congress assembled shall also be the last resort on appeal in all disputes and differences now subsisting or that hereafter may arise between two or more states concerning boundary, jurisdiction or any other cause whatever; which authority shall always be exercised in the manner following. Whenever the legislative or executive authority or lawful agent of any state in controversy with another shall present a petition to congress, stating the matter in question and praying for a hearing, notice thereof shall be given by order of congress to the legislative or executive authority of the other state in controversy, and a day assigned for the appearance of the parties by their lawful agents, who shall then be directed to appoint by joint consent, commissioners or judges to constitute a court for hearing and determining the matter in question: but if they cannot agree, congress shall name three persons out of each of the united states, and from the list of such persons each party shall alternately strike out one, the petitioners beginning, until the number shall be reduced to thirteen; and from that number not less than seven, nor more than nine names as congress shall direct, shall in the presence of congress be drawn out by lot, and the persons whose names shall be so drawn or any five of them, shall be commissioners or judges, to hear and finally determine the controversy, so always as a major part of the judges who shall hear the cause shall agree in the determination: and if either party shall neglect to attend at the day appointed, without showing reasons, which congress shall judge sufficient, or being present shall refuse to strike, the congress shall proceed to nominate three persons out of each state, and the secretary of congress shall strike in behalf of such party absent or refusing; and the judgment and sentence of the court to be appointed, in the manner before prescribed, shall be final and conclusive; and if any of the parties shall refuse to submit to the authority of such court, or to appear to defend their claim or cause, the court shall nevertheless proceed to pronounce sentence, or judgment, which shall in like manner be final and decisive, the judgment or sentence and other proceedings being in

either case transmitted to congress, and lodged among the acts of congress for the security of the parties concerned: provided that every commissioner, before he sits in judgment, shall take an oath to be administered by one of the judges of the supreme or superior court of the state, where the cause shall be tried, "well and truly to hear and determine the matter in question, according to the best of his judgment, without favour, affection or hope of reward:" provided also that no state shall be deprived of territory for the benefit of the united states.

All controversies concerning the private right of soil claimed under different grants of two or more states, whose jurisdictions as they may respect such lands, and the states which passed such grants are adjusted, the said grants or either of them being at the same time claimed to have originated antecedent to such settlement of jurisdiction, shall on the petition of either party to the congress of the united states, be finally determined as near as may be in the same manner as is before prescribed for deciding disputes respecting territorial jurisdiction between different states.

The united states in congress assembled shall also have the sole and exclusive right and power of regulating the alloy and value of coin struck by their own authority, or by that of the respective states—fixing the standard of weights and measures throughout the united states—regulating the trade and managing all affairs with the Indians, not members of any of the states, provided that the legislative right of any state within its own limits be not infringed or violated—establishing and regulating post-offices from one state to another, throughout all the united states, and exacting such postage on the papers passing thro' the same as may be requisite to defray the expences of the said office—appointing all officers of the land forces, in the service of the united states, excepting regimental officers—appointing all the officers of the naval forces, and commissioning all officers whatever in the service of the united states—making rules for the government and regulation of the said land and naval forces, and directing their operations.

The united states in congress assembled shall have authority to appoint a committee, to sit in the recess of congress, to be denominated "A Committee of the States," and to consist of one delegate from each state; and to appoint such other committees and civil officers as may be necessary for managing the general affairs of the united states under their direction—to appoint one of their number to preside, provided that no person be allowed to serve in the office of president more than one year in any term of three years; to ascertain the necessary sums of Money to be raised for the service of the united states, and to appropriate and apply the same for defraying the public expences—to borrow money, or emit bills on the credit of the united states, transmitting every half year to the respective states an account of the sums of money so borrowed or emitted—to build and equip a navy—to agree upon the number of land forces, and to make requisitions from each state for its quota, in proportion to the number of white inhabitants in such state; which requisition shall be binding, and thereupon the legislature of each state shall appoint the regimental officers, raise the men and cloath, arm and equip them in a soldier like manner, at the expence of the united states, and the officers and men so cloathed, armed and equipped shall march to the place appointed, and within the time agreed on by the united states in congress assembled: But if the united states in congress assembled shall, on consideration of circumstances judge proper that any state should not raise men, or should raise a smaller number than its quota, and that any other state should raise a greater number of men than the quota thereof, such extra number shall be raised, officered, cloathed, armed and equipped in the same manner as the quota of such state, unless the legislature of such state shall judge that such extra number cannot be safely spared out of the same, in which case they shall raise, officer, cloath, arm and equip as many of such extra number as they judge can be safely spared. And the officers and men so cloathed, armed and equipped, shall march to the place appointed, and within the time agreed on by the united states in congress assembled.

The united states in congress assembled shall never engage in a war, nor grant letters of marque and reprisal in time of peace, nor enter into any treaties or alliances, nor coin money, nor regulate the value thereof, nor ascertain the sums and expences necessary for the defence and welfare of the united states, or any of them, nor emit bills, nor borrow money on the credit of the united states, nor appropriate money, nor agree upon the number of vessels of war, to be built or purchased, or the number of land or sea forces to be raised, nor appoint a commander in chief of the army or navy, unless nine states assent to the same: nor shall a question on any other point, except for adjourning from day to day be determined, unless by the votes of a majority of the united states in congress assembled.

The congress of the united states shall have power to adjourn to any time within the year, and to any place within the united states, so that no period of adjournment be for a longer duration than the space of six Months, and shall publish the Journal of their proceedings monthly, except such parts thereof relating to treaties, alliances or military operations as in their judgment require secresy; and the yeas and nays of the delegates of each state on any question shall be entered on the Journal, when it is desired by any delegate; and the delegates of a state, or any of them, at his or their request shall be furnished with a transcript of the said Journal, except such parts as are above excepted, to lay before the legislatures of the several states.

Article X The committee of the states, or any nine of them, shall be authorised to execute, in the recess of congress, such

of the powers of congress as the united states in congress assembled, by the consent of nine states, shall from time to time think expedient to vest them with; provided that no power be delegated to the said committee, for the exercise of which, by the articles of confederation, the voice of nine states in the congress of the united states assembled is requisite.

Article XI Canada acceding to this confederation, and joining in the measures of the united states, shall be admitted into, and entitled to all the advantages of this union: but no other colony shall be admitted into the same, unless such admission be agreed to by nine states.

Article XII All bills of credit emitted, monies borrowed and debts contracted by, or under the authority of congress, before the assembling of the united states, in pursuance of the present confederation, shall be deemed and considered as a charge against the united states, for payment and satisfaction whereof the said united states, and the public faith are hereby solemnly pledged.

Article XIII Every state shall abide by the determinations of the united states in congress assembled, on all questions which by this confederation are submitted to them. And the Articles of this confederation shall be inviolably observed by every state, and the union shall be perpetual; nor shall any alteration at any time hereafter be made in any of them; unless such alteration be agreed to in a congress of the united states, and be afterwards confirmed by the legislatures of every state.

AND WHEREAS it hath pleased the Great Governor of the World to incline the hearts of the legislatures we respectively represent in congress, to approve of, and to authorize us to ratify the said articles of confederation and perpetual union. Know Ye that we the under-signed delegates, by virtue of the power and authority to us given for that purpose, do by these presents, in the name and in behalf of our respective constituents, fully and entirely ratify and confirm each and every of the said articles of confederation and perpetual union, and all and singular the matters and things therein contained: And we do further solemnly plight and engage the faith of our respective constituents, that they shall abide by the determinations of the united states in congress assembled, on all questions, which by the said confederation are submitted to them. And that the articles thereof shall be inviolably observed by the states we respectively represent, and that the union shall be perpetual. In Witness whereof we have hereunto set our hands in Congress. Done at Philadelphia in the state of Pennsylvania the ninth Day of July in the Year of our Lord one Thousand seven Hundred and Seventy-eight, and in the third year of the independence of America.

Constitution of the United States of America and Amendments*

Preamble

We the people of the United States, in order to form a more perfect union, establish justice, insure domestic tranquillity, provide for the common defense, promote the general welfare, and secure the blessings of liberty to ourselves and our posterity, do ordain and establish this Constitution for the United States of America.

Article I

Section 1 All legislative powers herein granted shall be vested in a Congress of the United States, which shall consist of a Senate and a House of Representatives.

Section 2 The House of Representatives shall be composed of members chosen every second year by the people of the several States, and the electors in each State shall have the qualifications requisite for electors of the most numerous branch of the State Legislature.

No person shall be a Representative who shall not have attained to the age of twenty-five years, and been seven years a citizen of the United States, and who shall not, when elected, be an inhabitant of that State in which he shall be chosen.

Representatives and direct taxes shall be apportioned among the several States which may be included within this Union, according to their respective numbers, *which shall be determined by adding to the whole number of free persons, including those bound to service for a term of years and excluding Indians not taxed, three-fifths of all other persons.* The actual enumeration shall be made within three years after the first meeting of the Congress of the United States, and within every subsequent term of ten years, in such manner as they shall by law direct. The number of Representatives shall not exceed one for every thirty thousand, but each State shall have at least one Representative; *and until such enumeration shall be made, the State of New Hampshire shall be entitled to choose three, Massachusetts eight, Rhode Island and Providence Plantations one, Connecticut five, New York six, New Jersey four, Pennsylvania eight, Delaware one, Maryland six, Virginia ten, North Carolina five, South Carolina five, and Georgia three.*

When vacancies happen in the representation from any State, the Executive authority thereof shall issue writs of election to fill such vacancies.

The House of Representatives shall choose their Speaker and other officers; and shall have the sole power of impeachment.

Section 3 The Senate of the United States shall be composed of two Senators from each State, *chosen by the legislature thereof,* for six years; and each Senator shall have one vote.

Immediately after they shall be assembled in consequence of the first election, they shall be divided as equally as may be into three classes. The seats of the Senators of the first class shall be vacated at the expiration of the second year, of the second class at the expiration of the fourth year, and of the third class at the expiration of the sixth year, so that one-third may be chosen every second year; and if vacancies happen by resignation or otherwise, during the recess of the legislature of any State, the Executive thereof may make temporary appointments until the next meeting of the legislature, which shall then fill such vacancies.

No person shall be a Senator who shall not have attained to the age of thirty years, and been nine years a citizen of the United States, and who shall not, when elected, be an inhabitant of that State for which he shall be chosen.

The Vice-President of the United States shall be President of the Senate, but shall have no vote, unless they be equally divided.

The Senate shall choose their other officers, and also a President *pro tempore,* in the absence of the Vice-President, or when he shall exercise the office of President of the United States.

The Senate shall have the sole power to try all impeachments. When sitting for that purpose, they shall be on oath or affirmation. When the President of the United States is tried, the Chief Justice shall preside: and no person shall be convicted without the concurrence of two-thirds of the members present.

Judgment in cases of impeachment shall not extend further than to removal from the office, and disqualification to hold and enjoy any office of honor, trust or profit under the United States: but the party convicted shall nevertheless be liable and subject to indictment, trial, judgment and punishment, according to law.

Section 4 The times, places and manner of holding elections for Senators and Representatives shall be prescribed in each State by the legislature thereof; but the Congress may at any time by law make or alter such regulations, except as to the places of choosing Senators.

The Congress shall assemble at least once in every year, and such meeting *shall be on the first Monday in December, unless they shall by law appoint a different day.*

Section 5 Each house shall be the judge of the elections, returns and qualifications of its own members, and a majority of each shall constitute a quorum to do business; but a smaller number may adjourn from day to day, and may be authorized to compel the attendance of absent members, in such manner, and under such penalties, as each house may provide.

---

* Passages no longer in effect are printed in italic type.

Each house may determine the rules of its proceedings, punish its members for disorderly behavior, and with the concurrence of two-thirds, expel a member.

Each house shall keep a journal of its proceedings, and from time to time publish the same, excepting such parts as may in their judgment require secrecy; and the yeas and nays of the members of either house on any question shall, at the desire of one-fifth of those present, be entered on the journal.

Neither house, during the session of Congress, shall, without the consent of the other, adjourn for more than three days, nor to any other place than that in which the two houses shall be sitting.

Section 6 The Senators and Representatives shall receive a compensation for their services, to be ascertained by law and paid out of the treasury of the United States. They shall in all cases except treason, felony and breach of the peace, be privileged from arrest during their attendance at the session of their respective houses, and in going to and returning from the same; and for any speech or debate in either house, they shall not be questioned in any other place.

No Senator or Representative shall, during the time for which he was elected, be appointed to any civil office under the authority of the United States, which shall have been created, or the emoluments whereof shall have been increased, during such time; and no person holding any office under the United States shall be a member of either house during his continuance in office.

Section 7 All bills for raising revenue shall originate in the House of Representatives; but the Senate may propose or concur with amendments as on other bills.

Every bill which shall have passed the House of Representatives and the Senate, shall, before it become a law, be presented to the President of the United States; if he approve he shall sign it, but if not he shall return it with objections to that house in which it originated, who shall enter the objections at large on their journal, and proceed to reconsider it. If after such reconsideration two-thirds of that house shall agree to pass the bill, it shall be sent, together with the objections, to the other house, by which it shall likewise be reconsidered, and, if approved by two-thirds of that house, it shall become a law. But in all such cases the votes of both houses shall be determined by yeas and nays, and the names of the persons voting for and against the bill shall be entered on the journal of each house respectively. If any bill shall not be returned by the President within ten days (Sundays excepted) after it shall have been presented to him, the same shall be a law, in like manner as if he had signed it, unless the Congress by their adjournment prevent its return, in which case it shall not be a law.

Every order, resolution, or vote to which the concurrence of the Senate and House of Representatives may be necessary (except on a question of adjournment) shall be presented to the President of the United States; and before the same shall take effect, shall be approved by him, or being disapproved by him, shall be repassed by two-thirds of the Senate and House of Representatives, according to the rules and limitations prescribed in the case of a bill.

Section 8 The Congress shall have power

To lay and collect taxes, duties, imposts, and excises, to pay the debts and provide for the common defense and general welfare of the United States; but all duties, imposts and excises shall be uniform throughout the United States;

To borrow money on the credit of the United States;

To regulate commerce with foreign nations, and among the several States, and with the Indian tribes;

To establish an uniform rule of naturalization, and uniform laws on the subject of bankruptcies throughout the United States;

To coin money, regulate the value thereof, and of foreign coin, and fix the standard of weights and measures;

To provide for the punishment of counterfeiting the securities and current coin of the United States;

To establish post offices and post roads;

To promote the progress of science and useful arts by securing for limited times to authors and inventors the exclusive right to their respective writings and discoveries;

To constitute tribunals inferior to the Supreme Court;

To define and punish piracies and felonies committed on the high seas and offenses against the law of nations;

To declare war, grant letters of marque and reprisal, and make rules concerning captures on land and water;

To raise and support armies, but no appropriation of money to that use shall be for a longer term than two years;

To provide and maintain a navy;

To make rules for the government and regulation of the land and naval forces;

To provide for calling forth the militia to execute the laws of the Union, suppress insurrections, and repel invasions;

To provide for organizing, arming, and disciplining the militia, and for governing such part of them as may be employed in the service of the United States, reserving to the States respectively the appointment of the officers, and the authority of training the militia according to the discipline prescribed by Congress;

To exercise exclusive legislation in all cases whatsoever, over such district (not exceeding ten miles square) as may, by cession of particular States, and the acceptance of Congress, become the seat of government of the United States, and to exercise like authority over all places purchased by the consent of the legislature of the State, in which the same shall be, for erection of forts, magazines, arsenals, dockyards, and other needful buildings; —and

To make all laws which shall be necessary and proper for carrying into execution the foregoing powers, and all other powers vested by this Constitution in the government of the United States, or in any department or officer thereof.

Section 9 *The migration or importation of such persons as any of the States now existing shall think proper to admit shall not be prohibited by the Congress prior to the year 1808; but a tax or duty may be imposed on such importation, not exceeding $10 for each person.*

The privilege of the writ of habeas corpus shall not be suspended, unless when in cases of rebellion or invasion the public safety may require it.

No bill of attainder or ex post facto law shall be passed.

No capitation, or other direct, tax shall be laid, unless in proportion to the census or enumeration herein before directed to be taken.

No tax or duty shall be laid on articles exported from any State.

No preference shall be given by any regulation of commerce or revenue to the ports of one State over those of another; nor shall vessels bound to, or from, one State, be obliged to enter, clear, or pay duties in another.

No money shall be drawn from the treasury, but in consequence of appropriations made by law; and a regular statement and account of the receipts and expenditures of all public money shall be published from time to time.

No title of nobility shall be granted by the United States: and no person holding any office of profit or trust under them, shall, without the consent of the Congress, accept of any present, emolument, office, or title, of any kind whatever, from any king, prince, or foreign state.

Section 10 No State shall enter into any treaty, alliance, or confederation; grant letters of marque and reprisal; coin money; emit bills of credit; make anything but gold and silver coin a tender in payment of debts; pass any bill of attainder, ex post facto law, or law impairing the obligation of contracts, or grant any title of nobility.

No State shall, without the consent of Congress, lay any imposts or duties on imports or exports, except what may be absolutely necessary for executing its inspection laws: and the net produce of all duties and imposts, laid by any State on imports or exports, shall be for the use of the treasury of the United States; and all such laws shall be subject to the revision and control of the Congress.

No State shall, without the consent of Congress, lay any duty of tonnage, keep troops or ships of war in time of peace, enter into any agreement or compact with another State, or with a foreign power, or engage in war, unless actually invaded, or in such imminent danger as will not admit of delay.

Article II

Section 1 The executive power shall be vested in a President of the United States of America. He shall hold his office during the term of four years, and, together with the Vice-President, chosen for the same term, be elected as follows:

Each State shall appoint, in such manner as the legislature thereof may direct, a number of electors, equal to the whole number of Senators and Representatives to which the State may be entitled in the Congress; but no Senator or Representative, or person holding an office of trust or profit under the United States, shall be appointed an elector.

The electors shall meet in their respective States, and vote by ballot for two persons, of whom one at least shall not be an inhabitant of the same State with themselves. And they shall make a list of all the persons voted for, and of the number of votes for each; which list they shall sign and certify, and transmit sealed to the seat of government of the United States, directed to the President of the Senate. The President of the Senate shall, in the presence of the Senate and House of Representatives, open all the certificates, and the votes shall then be counted. The person having the greatest number of votes shall be the President, if such number be a majority of the whole number of electors appointed; and if there be more than one who have such majority, and have an equal number of votes, then the House of Representatives shall immediately choose by ballot one of them for President; and if no person have a majority, then from the five highest on the list said house shall in like manner choose the President. But in choosing the President the votes shall be taken by States, the representation from each State having one vote; a quorum for this purpose shall consist of a member or members from two-thirds of the States, and a majority of all the States shall be necessary to a choice. In every case, after the choice of the President, the person having the greatest number of votes of the electors shall be the Vice-President. But if there should remain two or more who have equal votes, the Senate shall choose from them by ballot the Vice-President.

The Congress may determine the time of choosing the electors and the day on which they shall give their votes; which day shall be the same throughout the United States.

No person except a natural-born citizen, *or a citizen of the United States at the time of the adoption of this Constitution,* shall be eligible to the office of President; neither shall any person be eligible to that office who shall not have attained to the age of thirty-five years, and been fourteen years a resident within the United States.

In cases of the removal of the President from office or of his death, resignation, or inability to discharge the powers and duties of the said office, the same shall devolve on the Vice-President, and the Congress may by law provide for the case of removal, death, resignation, or inability, both of the President and Vice-President, declaring what officer shall then act as President, and such officer shall act accordingly, until the disability be removed, or a President shall be elected.

The President shall, at stated times, receive for his services a compensation, which shall neither be increased nor diminished during the period for which he shall have been elected, and he shall not receive within that period any other emolument from the United States, or any of them.

Before he enter on the execution of his office, he shall take the following oath or affirmation:—"I do solemnly swear (or affirm) that I will faithfully execute the office of the President of the United States, and will to the best of my ability preserve, protect and defend the Constitution of the United States."

Section 2 The President shall be commander in chief of the army and navy of the United States, and of the militia of the several States, when called into the actual service of the United States; he may require the opinion, in writing, of the principal officer in each of the executive departments, upon any subject relating to the duties of their respective offices, and he shall have power to grant reprieves and pardons for offenses against the United States, except in cases of impeachment.

He shall have power, by and with the advice and consent of the Senate, to make treaties, provided two-thirds of the Senators present concur; and he shall nominate, and by and with the advice and consent of the Senate, shall appoint ambassadors, other public ministers and consuls, judges of the Supreme Court, and all other officers of the United States, whose appointments are not herein otherwise provided for, and which shall be established by law: but Congress may by law vest the appointment of such inferior officers, as they think proper, in the President alone, in the courts of law, or in the heads of departments.

The President shall have power to fill up all vacancies that may happen during the recess of the Senate, by granting commissions which shall expire at the end of their next session.

Section 3 He shall from time to time give to the Congress information of the state of the Union, and recommend to their consideration such measures as he shall judge necessary and expedient; he may, on extraordinary occasions, convene both houses, or either of them, and in case of disagreement between them, with respect to the time of adjournment, he may adjourn them to such time as he shall think proper; he shall receive ambassadors and other public ministers; he shall take care that the laws be faithfully executed, and shall commission all the officers of the United States.

Section 4 The President, Vice-President and all civil officers of the United States shall be removed from office on impeachment for, and on conviction of, treason, bribery, or other high crimes and misdemeanors.

Article III

Section 1 The judicial power of the United States shall be vested in one Supreme Court, and in such inferior courts as the Congress may from time to time ordain and establish. The judges, both of the Supreme and inferior courts, shall hold their offices during good behavior, and shall, at stated times, receive for their services a compensation which shall not be diminished during their continuance in office.

Section 2 The judicial power shall extend to all cases, in law and equity, arising under this Constitution, the laws of the United States, and treaties made, or which shall be made, under their authority;—to all cases affecting ambassadors, other public ministers and consuls;—to all cases of admiralty and maritime jurisdiction;—to controversies to which the United States shall be a party;—to controversies between two or more States;— *between a State and citizens of another State;*—between citizens of different States;—between citizens of the same State claiming lands under grants of different States, and between a State, or the citizens thereof, and foreign states, citizens or subjects.

In all cases affecting ambassadors, other public ministers and consuls, and those in which a State shall be party, the Supreme Court shall have original jurisdiction. In all the other cases before mentioned, the Supreme Court shall have appellate jurisdiction, both as to law and fact, with such exceptions, and under such regulations, as the Congress shall make.

The trial of all crimes, except in cases of impeachment, shall be by jury; and such trial shall be held in the State where said crimes shall have been committed; but when not committed within any State, the trial shall be at such place or places as the Congress may by law have directed.

Section 3 Treason against the United States shall consist only in levying war against them, or in adhering to their enemies, giving them aid and comfort. No person shall be convicted of treason unless on the testimony of two witnesses to the same overt act, or on confession in open court.

The Congress shall have power to declare the punishment of treason, but no attainder of treason shall work corruption of blood, or forfeiture except during the life of the person attainted.

Article IV

Section 1 Full faith and credit shall be given in each State to the public acts, records, and judicial proceedings of every other State. And the Congress may by general laws prescribe the manner in which such acts, records, and proceedings shall be proved, and the effect thereof.

Section 2 The citizens of each State shall be entitled to all privileges and immunities of citizens in the several States.

A person charged in any State with treason, felony, or other crime, who shall flee from justice, and be found in another State, shall on demand of the executive authority of the State from which he fled, be delivered up, to be removed to the State having jurisdiction of the crime.

No person held to service or labor in one State, under the laws thereof, escaping into another, shall, in consequence of any law or regulation therein, be discharged from such service or labor, but shall be delivered up on claim of the party to whom such service or labor may be due.

Section 3 New States may be admitted by the Congress into this Union; but no new State shall be formed or erected within the jurisdiction of any other State; nor any State be formed by the junction of two or more States, or parts of States, without the consent of the legislatures of the States concerned as well as of the Congress.

The Congress shall have power to dispose of and make all needful rules and regulations respecting the territory or other property belonging to the United States; and nothing in this Constitution shall be so construed as to prejudice any claims of the United States, or of any particular State.

Section 4 The United States shall guarantee to every State in this Union a republican form of government, and shall protect each of them against invasion; and on application of the legislature, or of the executive (when the legislature cannot be convened), against domestic violence.

Article V

The Congress, whenever two-thirds of both houses shall deem it necessary, shall propose amendments to this Constitution, or, on the application of the legislatures of two-thirds of the several States, shall call a convention for proposing amendments, which, in either case, shall be valid to all intents and purposes, as part of this Constitution, when ratified by the legislatures of three-fourths of the several States, or by conventions in three-fourths thereof, as the one or the other mode of ratification may be proposed by the Congress; provided *that no amendments which may be made prior to the year one thousand eight hundred and eight shall in any manner affect the first and fourth clauses in the ninth section of the first article;* and that no State, without its consent, shall be deprived of its equal suffrage in the Senate.

Article VI

All debts contracted and engagements entered into, before the adoption of this Constitution, shall be as valid against the United States under this Constitution, as under the Confederation.

This Constitution, and the laws of the United States which shall be made in pursuance thereof; and all treaties made, or which shall be made, under the authority of the United States, shall be the supreme law of the land; and the judges in every State shall be bound thereby, anything in the Constitution or laws of any State to the contrary notwithstanding.

The Senators and Representatives before mentioned, and the members of the several State legislatures, and all executive and judicial officers, both of the United States and of the several States, shall be bound by oath or affirmation to support this Constitution; but no religious test shall ever be required as a qualification to any office or public trust under the United States.

Article VII

The ratification of the conventions of nine States shall be sufficient for the establishment of this Constitution between the States so ratifying the same.

Done in Convention by the unanimous consent of the States present, the seventeenth day of September in the year of our Lord one thousand seven hundred and eighty-seven and of the Independence of the United States of America the twelfth. In witness whereof we have hereunto subscribed our names.

Amendments to the Constitution*

Amendment I

Congress shall make no law respecting an establishment of religion, or prohibiting the free exercise thereof; or abridging the freedom of speech, or of the press; or the right of the people peaceably to assemble, and to petition the government for a redress of grievances.

Amendment II

A well-regulated militia being necessary to the security of a free State, the right of the people to keep and bear arms shall not be infringed.

Amendment III

No soldier shall, in time of peace, be quartered in any house without the consent of the owner, nor in time of war, but in a manner to be prescribed by law.

Amendment IV

The right of the people to be secure in their persons, houses, papers, and effects, against unreasonable searches and seizures, shall not be violated, and no warrants shall issue but upon probable cause, supported by oath or affirmation, and particularly describing the place to be searched, and the persons or things to be seized.

Amendment V

No person shall be held to answer for a capital, or otherwise infamous crime, unless on a presentment or indictment of a grand jury, except in cases arising in the land or naval forces, or in the militia, when in actual service in time of war or public danger; nor shall any person be subject for the same offense to be twice put in jeopardy of life or limb; nor shall be compelled in any criminal case to be a witness against himself, nor be deprived of life, liberty, or property, without due process of law; nor shall private property be taken for public use without just compensation.

Amendment VI

In all criminal prosecutions, the accused shall enjoy the right to a speedy and public trial, by an impartial jury of the State and district wherein the crime shall have been committed,

---

* The first ten Amendments (the Bill of Rights) were adopted in 1791.

which district shall have been previously ascertained by law, and to be informed of the nature and cause of the accusation; to be confronted with the witnesses against him; to have compulsory process for obtaining witnesses in his favor, and to have the assistance of counsel for his defense.

Amendment VII

In suits at common law, where the value in controversy shall exceed twenty dollars, the right of trial by jury shall be preserved, and no fact tried by a jury shall be otherwise reexamined in any court of the United States, than according to the rules of the common law.

Amendment VIII

Excessive bail shall not be required, nor excessive fines imposed, nor cruel and unusual punishments inflicted.

Amendment IX

The enumeration in the Constitution, of certain rights, shall not be construed to deny or disparage others retained by the people.

Amendment X

The powers not delegated to the United States by the Constitution, nor prohibited by it to the States, are reserved to the States respectively, or to the people.

Amendment XI

[Adopted 1798]

The judicial power of the United States shall not be construed to extend to any suit in law or equity, commenced or prosecuted against one of the United States by citizens of another State, or by citizens or subjects of any foreign state.

Amendment XII

[Adopted 1804]

The electors shall meet in their respective States, and vote by ballot for President and Vice-President, one of whom, at least, shall not be an inhabitant of the same State with themselves; they shall name in their ballots the person voted for as President, and in distinct ballots the person voted for as Vice-President, and they shall make distinct lists of all persons voted for as President, and of all persons voted for as Vice-President, and of the number of votes for each, which lists they shall sign and certify, and transmit sealed to the seat of government of the United States, directed to the President of the Senate;—the President of the Senate shall, in the presence of the Senate and House of Representatives, open all the certificates and the votes shall then be counted;—the person having the greatest number of votes for President shall be the President, if such number be a majority of the whole number of electors appointed; and if no person have such majority, then from the persons having the highest numbers not exceeding three on the list of those voted for as President, the House of Representatives shall choose immediately, by ballot, the President. But in choosing the President, the votes shall be taken by States, the representation from each State having one vote; a quorum for this purpose shall consist of a member or members from two-thirds of the States, and a majority of all the States shall be necessary to a choice. And if the House of Representatives shall not choose a President whenever the right of choice shall devolve upon them, before *the fourth day of March* next following, then the Vice-President shall act as President, as in the case of the death or other constitutional disability of the President.

The person having the greatest number of votes as Vice-President shall be the Vice-President, if such number be a majority of the whole number of electors appointed; and if no person have a majority, then from the two highest numbers on the list the Senate shall choose the Vice-President; a quorum for the purpose shall consist of two-thirds of the whole number of Senators, and a majority of the whole number shall be necessary to a choice. But no person constitutionally ineligible to the office of President shall be eligible to that of Vice-President of the United States.

Amendment XIII

[Adopted 1865]

Section 1 Neither slavery nor involuntary servitude, except as a punishment for crime whereof the party shall have been duly convicted, shall exist within the United States, or any place subject to their jurisdiction.

Section 2 Congress shall have power to enforce this article by appropriate legislation.

Amendment XIV

[Adopted 1868]

Section 1 All persons born or naturalized in the United States, and subject to the jurisdiction thereof, are citizens of the United States and of the State wherein they reside. No State shall make or enforce any law which shall abridge the privileges or immunities of citizens of the United States; nor shall any State deprive any person of life, liberty, or property, without due process of law; nor deny to any person within its jurisdiction the equal protection of the laws.

Section 2 Representatives shall be apportioned among the several States according to their respective numbers, counting the whole number of persons in each State, excluding Indians not taxed. But when the right to vote at any election for the choice of Electors for President and Vice-President of the United States, Representatives in Congress, the executive and judicial officers of a State, or the members of the legislature thereof, is denied to any of the male inhabitants of such State, being twenty-one years of age and citizens of the United States, or in any way abridged, except for participation in rebellion, or other crime, the basis of representation therein shall be reduced in the proportion which the number of such male citizens shall bear to the whole number of male citizens twenty-one years of age in such State.

Section 3 No person shall be a Senator or Representative in Congress, or Elector of President and Vice-President, or hold any office, civil or military, under the United States, or under any State, who, having previously taken an oath, as a member of Congress, or as an officer of the United States, or as a member of any State legislature, or as an executive or judicial officer of any State, to support the Constitution of the United States, shall have engaged in insurrection or rebellion against the same, or given aid or comfort to the enemies thereof. Congress may, by a vote of two-thirds of each house, remove such disability.

Section 4 The validity of the public debt of the United States, authorized by law, including debts incurred for payment of pensions and bounties for services in suppressing insurrection or rebellion, shall not be questioned. But neither the United States nor any State shall assume or pay any debt or obligation incurred in aid of insurrection or rebellion against the United States, or any claim for the loss of emancipation of any slave; but all such debts, obligations, and claims shall be held illegal and void.

Section 5 The Congress shall have power to enforce, by appropriate legislation, the provisions of this article.

Amendment XV
[Adopted 1870]

Section 1 The right of citizens of the United States to vote shall not be denied or abridged by the United States or by any State on account of race, color, or previous condition of servitude.

Section 2 The Congress shall have power to enforce this article by appropriate legislation.

Amendment XVI
[Adopted 1913]

The Congress shall have power to lay and collect taxes on incomes, from whatever source derived, without apportionment among the several States, and without regard to any census or enumeration.

Amendment XVII
[Adopted 1913]

Section 1 The Senate of the United States shall be composed of two Senators from each State, elected by the people thereof, for six years; and each Senator shall have one vote. The electors in each State shall have the qualifications requisite for electors of [voters for] the most numerous branch of the State legislatures.

Section 2 When vacancies happen in the representation of any State in the Senate, the executive authority of such State shall issue writs of election to fill such vacancies: Provided, that the Legislature of any State may empower the executive

thereof to make temporary appointments until the people fill the vacancies by election as the Legislature may direct.

Section 3 This amendment shall not be so construed as to affect the election or term of any Senator chosen before it becomes valid as part of the Constitution.

Amendment XVIII
[Adopted 1919; Repealed 1933]

Section 1 After one year from the ratification of this article the manufacture, sale, or transportation of intoxicating liquors within, the importation thereof into, or the exportation thereof from the United States and all territory subject to the jurisdiction thereof, for beverage purposes, is hereby prohibited.

Section 2 The Congress and the several States shall have concurrent power to enforce this article by appropriate legislation.

Section 3 This article shall be inoperative unless it shall have been ratified as an amendment to the Constitution by the legislatures of the several States, as provided by the Constitution, within seven years from the date of the submission thereof to the States by the Congress.

Amendment XIX
[Adopted 1920]

Section 1 The right of citizens of the United States to vote shall not be denied or abridged by the United States or by any State on account of sex.

Section 2 The Congress shall have power to enforce this article by appropriate legislation.

Amendment XX
[Adopted 1933]

Section 1 The terms of the President and Vice-President shall end at noon on the 20th day of January, and the terms of Senators and Representatives at noon on the 3rd day of January, of the years in which such terms would have ended if this article had not been ratified; and the terms of their successors shall then begin.

Section 2 The Congress shall assemble at least once in every year, and such meeting shall begin at noon on the 3rd day of January, unless they shall by law appoint a different day.

Section 3 If, at the time fixed for the beginning of the term of the President, the President-elect shall have died, the Vice-President-elect shall become President. If a President shall not have been chosen before the time fixed for the beginning of his term, or if the President-elect shall have failed to qualify, then the Vice-President-elect shall act as President until a President shall have qualified; and the Congress may by law provide for the case wherein neither a President-elect nor a Vice-President-elect shall have qualified, declaring who shall then act as President, or the manner in which one who is to act shall be selected, and such persons shall act accordingly until a President or Vice-President shall have qualified.

Section 4 The Congress may by law provide for the case of the death of any of the persons from whom the House of Representatives may choose a President whenever the right of choice shall have devolved upon them, and for the case of the death of any of the persons from whom the Senate may choose a Vice-President whenever the right of choice shall have devolved upon them.

Section 5 Sections 1 and 2 shall take effect on the 15th day of October following the ratification of this article.

Section 6 This article shall be inoperative unless it shall have been ratified as an amendment to the Constitution by the Legislatures of three-fourths of the several States within seven years from the date of its submission.

Amendment XXI

[Adopted 1933]
Section 1 The eighteenth article of amendment to the Constitution of the United States is hereby repealed.

Section 2 The transportation or importation into any State, Territory, or Possession of the United States for delivery or use therein of intoxicating liquors, in violation of the laws thereof, is hereby prohibited.

Section 3 This article shall be inoperative unless it shall have been ratified as an amendment to the Constitution by conventions in the several States, as provided in the Constitution, within seven years from the date of submission thereof to the States by the Congress.

Amendment XXII

[Adopted 1951]
Section 1 No person shall be elected to the office of President more than twice, and no person who has held the office of President, or acted as President, for more than two years of a term to which some other person was elected President shall be elected to the office of President more than once. But this article shall not apply to any person holding the office of President when this article was proposed by the Congress, and shall not prevent any person who may be holding the office of President, or acting as President, during the term within which this article becomes operative from holding the office of President or acting as President during the remainder of such term.

Section 2 This article shall be inoperative unless it shall have been ratified as an amendment to the Constitution by the legislatures of three-fourths of the several States within seven years from the date of its submission to the States by the Congress.

Amendment XXIII

[Adopted 1961]
Section 1 The District constituting the seat of Government of the United States shall appoint in such manner as the Congress may direct:

A number of electors of President and Vice-President equal to the whole number of Senators and Representatives in Congress to which the District would be entitled if it were a State, but in no event more than the least populous State; they shall be in addition to those appointed by the States, but they shall be considered for the purposes of the election of President and Vice-President, to be electors appointed by a State; and they shall meet in the District and perform such duties as provided by the twelfth article of amendment.

Section 2 The Congress shall have the power to enforce this article by appropriate legislation.

Amendment XXIV

[Adopted 1964]
Section 1 The right of citizens of the United States to vote in any primary or other election for President or Vice-President, for electors for President or Vice-President, or for Senator or Representative in Congress, shall not be denied or abridged by the United States or any State by reason of failure to pay any poll tax or other tax.

Section 2 The Congress shall have the power to enforce this article by appropriate legislation.

Amendment XXV

[Adopted 1967]
Section 1 In case of the removal of the President from office or of his death or resignation, the Vice-President shall become President.

Section 2 Whenever there is a vacancy in the office of the Vice-President, the President shall nominate a Vice-President who shall take office upon confirmation by a majority vote of both Houses of Congress.

Section 3 Whenever the President transmits to the President pro tempore of the Senate and the Speaker of the House of Representatives his written declaration that he is unable to discharge the powers and duties of his office, and until he transmits to them a written declaration to the contrary, such powers and duties shall be discharged by the Vice-President as Acting President.

Section 4 Whenever the Vice-President and a majority of either the principal officers of the executive departments or of such other body as Congress may by law provide, transmit to the President pro tempore of the Senate and the Speaker of the House of Representatives their written declaration that the President is unable to discharge the powers and duties of his office, the Vice-President shall immediately assume the powers and duties of the office as Acting President.

Thereafter, when the President transmits to the President pro tempore of the Senate and the Speaker of the House of Representatives his written declaration that no inability exists, he shall resume the powers and duties of his office unless the Vice-President and a majority of either the principal officers of the executive department[s] or of such other body as Congress may by law provide, transmit within four days to the President pro tempore of the Senate and the Speaker of the House of Representatives their written declaration that the President is unable to discharge the powers and duties of his office. Thereupon Congress shall decide the issue, assembling within forty-eight hours for that purpose if not in session. If the Congress, within twenty-one days after receipt of the latter written declaration, or, if Congress is not in session, within twenty-one days after Congress is required to assemble, determines by two-thirds vote of both Houses that the President is unable to discharge the powers and duties of his office, the Vice-President shall continue to discharge the same as Acting President; otherwise, the President shall resume the powers and duties of his office.

Amendment XXVI
[Adopted 1971]

Section 1 The right of citizens of the United States, who are eighteen years of age or older, to vote shall not be denied or abridged by the United States or by any State on account of age.

Section 2 The Congress shall have power to enforce this article by appropriate legislation.

Amendment XXVII
[Adopted 1992]

No law, varying the compensation for the services of the Senators and Representatives, shall take effect, until an election of Representatives shall have intervened.

Presidential Elections

Year	Number of States	Candidates	Parties	Popular Vote	% of Popular Vote	Electoral Vote	% Voter Participation
1789	10	**George Washington**	No party			69	
		John Adams	designations			34	
		Other candidates				35	
1792	15	**George Washington**	No party			132	
		John Adams	designations			77	
		George Clinton				50	
		Other candidates				5	
1796	16	**John Adams**	Federalist			71	
		Thomas Jefferson	Democratic-Republican			68	
		Thomas Pinckney	Federalist			59	
		Aaron Burr	Democratic-Republican			30	
		Other candidates				48	
1800	16	**Thomas Jefferson**	Democratic-Republican			73	
		Aaron Burr	Democratic-Republican			73	
		John Adams	Federalist			65	
		Charles C. Pinckney	Federalist			64	
		John Jay	Federalist			1	
1804	17	**Thomas Jefferson**	Democratic-Republican			162	
		Charles C. Pinckney	Federalist			14	
1808	17	**James Madison**	Democratic-Republican			122	
		Charles C. Pinckney	Federalist			47	
		George Clinton	Democratic-Republican			6	
1812	18	**James Madison**	Democratic-Republican			128	
		DeWitt Clinton	Federalist			89	
1816	19	**James Monroe**	Democratic-Republican			183	
		Rufus King	Federalist			34	
1820	24	**James Monroe**	Democratic-Republican			231	
		John Quincy Adams	Independent Republican			1	

Presidential Elections (continued)

Year	Number of States	Candidates	Parties	Popular Vote	% of Popular Vote	Electoral Vote	% Voter Participation
1824	24	John Quincy Adams	Democratic-Republican	108,740	30.5	84	26.9
		Andrew Jackson	Democratic-Republican	153,544	43.1	99	
		Henry Clay	Democratic-Republican	47,136	13.2	37	
		William H. Crawford	Democratic-Republican	46,618	13.1	41	
1828	24	Andrew Jackson	Democratic	647,286	56.0	178	57.6
		John Quincy Adams	National Republican	508,064	44.0	83	
1832	24	Andrew Jackson	Democratic	701,780	54.2	219	55.4
		Henry Clay	National Republican	484,205	37.4	49	
		Other candidates		107,988	8.0	18	
1836	26	Martin Van Buren	Democratic	764,176	50.8	170	57.8
		William H. Harrison	Whig	550,816	36.6	73	
		Hugh L. White	Whig	146,107	9.7	26	
1840	26	William H. Harrison	Whig	1,274,624	53.1	234	80.2
		Martin Van Buren	Democratic	1,127,781	46.9	60	
1844	26	James K. Polk	Democratic	1,338,464	49.6	170	78.9
		Henry Clay	Whig	1,300,097	48.1	105	
		James G. Birney	Liberty	62,300	2.3		
1848	30	Zachary Taylor	Whig	1,360,967	47.4	163	72.7
		Lewis Cass	Democratic	1,222,342	42.5	127	
		Martin Van Buren	Free Soil	291,263	10.1		
1852	31	Franklin Pierce	Democratic	1,601,117	50.9	254	69.6
		Winfield Scott	Whig	1,385,453	44.1	42	
		John P. Hale	Free Soil	155,825	5.0		
1856	31	James Buchanan	Democratic	1,832,955	45.3	174	78.9
		John C. Frémont	Republican	1,339,932	33.1	114	
		Millard Fillmore	American	871,731	21.6		
1860	33	Abraham Lincoln	Republican	1,865,593	39.8	180	81.2
		Stephen A. Douglas	Democratic	1,382,713	29.5	12	
		John C. Breckinridge	Democratic	848,356	18.1	72	
		John Bell	Constitutional Union	592,906	12.6	39	

Year	Number of States	Candidates	Parties	Popular Vote	% of Popular Vote	Electoral Vote	% Voter Participation
1864	36	**Abraham Lincoln**	Republican	2,206,938	55.0	212	73.8
		George B. McClellan	Democratic	1,803,787	45.0	21	
1868	37	**Ulysses S. Grant**	Republican	3,013,421	52.7	214	78.1
		Horatio Seymour	Democratic	2,706,829	47.3	80	
1872	37	**Ulysses S. Grant**	Republican	3,596,745	55.6	286	71.3
		Horace Greeley[b]	Democratic	2,843,446	43.9		
1876	38	**Rutherford B. Hayes**	Republican	4,036,572	48.0	185	81.8
		Samuel J. Tilden	Democratic	4,284,020	51.0	184	
1880	38	**James A. Garfield**	Republican	4,453,295	48.5	214	79.4
		Winfield S. Hancock	Democratic	4,414,082	48.1	155	
		James B. Weaver	Greenback-Labor	308,578	3.4		
1884	38	**Grover Cleveland**	Democratic	4,879,507	48.5	219	77.5
		James G. Blaine	Republican	4,850,293	48.2	182	
		Benjamin F. Butler	Greenback-Labor	175,370	1.8		
		John P. St. John	Prohibition	150,369	1.5		
1888	38	**Benjamin Harrison**	Republican	5,447,129	47.9	233	79.3
		Grover Cleveland	Democratic	5,537,857	48.6	168	
		Clinton B. Fisk	Prohibition	249,506	2.2		
		Anson J. Streeter	Union Labor	146,935	1.3		
1892	44	**Grover Cleveland**	Democratic	5,555,426	46.1	277	74.7
		Benjamin Harrison	Republican	5,182,690	43.0	145	
		James B. Weaver	People's	1,029,846	8.5	22	
		John Bidwell	Prohibition	264,133	2.2		
1896	45	**William McKinley**	Republican	7,102,246	51.1	271	79.3
		William J. Bryan	Democratic	6,492,559	47.7	176	
1900	45	**William McKinley**	Republican	7,218,491	51.7	292	73.2
		William J. Bryan	Democratic; Populist	6,356,734	45.5	155	
		John C. Wooley	Prohibition	208,914	1.5		
1904	45	**Theodore Roosevelt**	Republican	7,628,461	57.4	336	65.2
		Alton B. Parker	Democratic	5,084,223	37.6	140	
		Eugene V. Debs	Socialist	402,283	3.0		
		Silas C. Swallow	Prohibition	258,536	1.9		
1908	46	**William H. Taft**	Republican	7,675,320	51.6	321	65.4
		William J. Bryan	Democratic	6,412,294	43.1	162	
		Eugene V. Debs	Socialist	420,793	2.8		
		Eugene W. Chafin	Prohibition	253,840	1.7		

Presidential Elections (continued)

Year	Number of States	Candidates	Parties	Popular Vote	% of Popular Vote	Electoral Vote	% Voter Participation
1912	48	**Woodrow Wilson**	Democratic	6,296,547	41.9	435	58.8
		Theodore Roosevelt	Progressive	4,118,571	27.4	88	
		William H. Taft	Republican	3,486,720	23.2	8	
		Eugene V. Debs	Socialist	900,672	6.0		
		Eugene W. Chafin	Prohibition	206,275	1.4		
1916	48	**Woodrow Wilson**	Democratic	9,127,695	49.4	277	61.6
		Charles E. Hughes	Republican	8,533,507	46.2	254	
		A. L. Benson	Socialist	585,113	3.2		
		J. Frank Hanly	Prohibition	220,506	1.2		
1920	48	**Warren G. Harding**	Republican	16,143,407	60.4	404	49.2
		James M. Cox	Democratic	9,130,328	34.2	127	
		Eugene V. Debs	Socialist	919,799	3.4		
		P. P. Christensen	Farmer-Labor	265,411	1.0		
1924	48	**Calvin Coolidge**	Republican	15,718,211	54.0	382	48.9
		John W. Davis	Democratic	8,385,283	28.8	136	
		Robert M. La Follette	Progressive	4,831,289	16.6	13	
1928	48	**Herbert C. Hoover**	Republican	21,391,993	58.2	444	56.9
		Alfred E. Smith	Democratic	15,016,169	40.9	87	
1932	48	**Franklin D. Roosevelt**	Democratic	22,821,857	57.4	472	56.9
		Herbert C. Hoover	Republican	15,761,841	39.7	59	
		Norman Thomas	Socialist	884,781	2.2		
1936	48	**Franklin D. Roosevelt**	Democratic	27,752,869	60.8	523	61.0
		Alfred M. Landon	Republican	16,674,665	36.5	8	
		William Lemke	Union	882,479	1.9		
1940	48	**Franklin D. Roosevelt**	Democratic	27,307,819	54.8	449	62.5
		Wendell L. Willkie	Republican	22,321,018	44.8	82	
1944	48	**Franklin D. Roosevelt**	Democratic	25,606,585	53.5	432	55.9
		Thomas E. Dewey	Republican	22,014,745	46.0	99	
1948	48	**Harry S Truman**	Democratic	24,179,345	49.6	303	53.0
		Thomas E. Dewey	Republican	21,991,291	45.1	189	
		J. Strom Thurmond	States' Rights	1,176,125	2.4	39	
		Henry A. Wallace	Progressive	1,157,326	2.4		

Year	Number of States	Candidates	Parties	Popular Vote	% of Popular Vote	Electoral Vote	% Voter Participation[a]
1952	48	Dwight D. Eisenhower	Republican	33,936,234	55.1	442	63.3
		Adlai E. Stevenson	Democratic	27,314,992	44.4	89	
1956	48	Dwight D. Eisenhower	Republican	35,590,472	57.6	457	60.6
		Adlai E. Stevenson	Democratic	26,022,752	42.1	73	
1960	50	John F. Kennedy	Democratic	34,226,731	49.7	303	62.8
		Richard M. Nixon	Republican	34,108,157	49.5	219	
1964	50	Lyndon B. Johnson	Democratic	43,129,566	61.1	486	61.7
		Barry M. Goldwater	Republican	27,178,188	38.5	52	
1968	50	Richard M. Nixon	Republican	33,045,480	43.4	301	60.6
		Hubert H. Humphrey	Democratic	31,850,140	42.7	191	
		George C. Wallace	American Independent	171,422	13.5	46	
1972	50	Richard M. Nixon	Republican	47,169,911	60.7	520	55.2
		George S. McGovern	Democratic	29,170,383	37.5	17	
		John G. Schmitz	American	1,099,482	1.4		
1976	50	James E. Carter	Democratic	40,830,763	50.1	297	53.5
		Gerald R. Ford	Republican	39,147,793	48.0	240	
1980	50	Ronald W. Reagan	Republican	43,904,153	50.7	489	52.6
		James E. Carter	Democratic	35,483,883	41.0	49	
		John B. Anderson	Independent	5,720,060	6.6		
		Ed Clark	Libertarian	921,299	1.1		
1984	50	Ronald W. Reagan	Republican	54,455,075	58.8	525	53.3
		Walter F. Mondale	Democratic	37,577,185	40.6	13	
1988	50	George H. W. Bush	Republican	48,886,097	53.4	426	50.1
		Michael S. Dukakis	Democratic	41,809,074	45.6	111[c]	
1992	50	William J. Clinton	Democratic	44,909,326	43.0	370	55.2
		George H. W. Bush	Republican	39,103,882	37.4	168	
		H. Ross Perot	Independent	19,741,048	18.9		
1996	50	William J. Clinton	Democratic	47,402,357	49.2	379	49.1
		Robert J. Dole	Republican	39,196,755	40.7	159	
		H. Ross Perot	Reform	8,085,402	8.4		
		Ralph Nader	Green	684,902	0.7		
2000	50	George W. Bush	Republican	50,456,169	47.9	271	51.2
		Albert Gore	Democratic	50,996,116	48.4	266	
		Ralph Nader	Green	2,783,728	2.7		

Presidential Elections (continued)

Year	Number of States	Candidates	Parties	Popular Vote	% of Popular Vote	Electoral Vote	% Voter Participation
2004	50	George W. Bush	Republican	62,039,073	50.7	286	55.3
		John F. Kerry	Democratic	59,027,478	48.2	251	
		Ralph Nader	Independent	240,896	0.2		
2008	50	Barack Obama	Democratic	69,498,459	53.0	365	61.7
		John McCain	Republican	59,948,283	46.0	173	
		Ralph Nader	Independent	739,165	0.55		
2012	50	Barack Obama	Democratic	65,907,213	51.07	332	
		Mitt Romney	Republican	60,931,767	47.21	206	
		Gary Johnson	Independent	1,275,804	0.99		
2016	50	Donald J. Trump	Republican	62,984,825	46.1	304	59.7
		Hillary Clinton	Democratic	65,853,516	48.2	227	

Candidates receiving less than 1 percent of the popular vote have been omitted. Thus the percentage of popular vote given for any election year may not total 100 percent.

Before the passage of the Twelfth Amendment in 1804, the electoral college voted for two presidential candidates; the runner-up became vice president.

Before 1824, most presidential electors were chosen by state legislatures, not by popular vote.

[a]Percent of voting-age population casting ballots.

[b]Greeley died shortly after the election; the electors supporting him then divided their votes among minor candidates.

[c]One elector from West Virginia cast her electoral college presidential ballot for Lloyd Bentsen, the Democratic Party's vice-presidential candidate.

Presidents and Vice Presidents

		Office	Term of Service
1st	George Washington	President	1789–1797
	John Adams	Vice President	1789–1797
2nd	John Adams	President	1797–1801
	Thomas Jefferson	Vice President	1797–1801
3rd	Thomas Jefferson	President	1801–1809
	Aaron Burr	Vice President	1801–1805
	George Clinton	Vice President	1805–1809
4th	James Madison	President	1809–1817
	George Clinton	Vice President	1809–1813
	Elbridge Gerry	Vice President	1813–1817
5th	James Monroe	President	1817–1825
	Daniel Tompkins	Vice President	1817–1825
6th	John Quincy Adams	President	1825–1829
	John C. Calhoun	Vice President	1825–1829
7th	Andrew Jackson	President	1829–1837
	John C. Calhoun	Vice President	1829–1833
	Martin Van Buren	Vice President	1833–1837
8th	Martin Van Buren	President	1837–1841
	Richard M. Johnson	Vice President	1837–1841
9th	William H. Harrison	President	1841
	John Tyler	Vice President	1841
10th	John Tyler	President	1841–1845
	None	Vice President	
11th	James K. Polk	President	1845–1849
	George M. Dallas	Vice President	1845–1849
12th	Zachary Taylor	President	1849–1850
	Millard Fillmore	Vice President	1849–1850
13th	Millard Fillmore	President	1850–1853
	None	Vice President	
14th	Franklin Pierce	President	1853–1857
	William R. King	Vice President	1853–1857
15th	James Buchanan	President	1857–1861
	John C. Breckinridge	Vice President	1857–1861
16th	Abraham Lincoln	President	1861–1865
	Hannibal Hamlin	Vice President	1861–1865
	Andrew Johnson	Vice President	1865

Presidents and Vice Presidents (continued)

		Office	Term of Service
17th	Andrew Johnson	President	1865–1869
	None	Vice President	
18th	Ulysses S. Grant	President	1869–1877
	Schuyler Colfax	Vice President	1869–1873
	Henry Wilson	Vice President	1873–1877
19th	Rutherford B. Hayes	President	1877–1881
	William A. Wheeler	Vice President	1877–1881
20th	James A. Garfield	President	1881
	Chester A. Arthur	Vice President	1881
21st	Chester A. Arthur	President	1881–1885
	None	Vice President	
22nd	Grover Cleveland	President	1885–1889
	Thomas A. Hendricks	Vice President	1885–1889
23rd	Benjamin Harrison	President	1889–1893
	Levi P. Morton	Vice President	1889–1893
24th	Grover Cleveland	President	1893–1897
	Adlai E. Stevenson	Vice President	1893–1897
25th	William McKinley	President	1897–1901
	Garret A. Hobart	Vice President	1897–1901
	Theodore Roosevelt	Vice President	1901
26th	Theodore Roosevelt	President	1901–1909
	Charles Fairbanks	Vice President	1905–1909
27th	William H. Taft	President	1909–1913
	James S. Sherman	Vice President	1909–1913
28th	Woodrow Wilson	President	1913–1921
	Thomas R. Marshall	Vice President	1913–1921
29th	Warren G. Harding	President	1921–1923
	Calvin Coolidge	Vice President	1921–1923
30th	Calvin Coolidge	President	1923–1929
	Charles G. Dawes	Vice President	1925–1929
31st	Herbert C. Hoover	President	1929–1933
	Charles Curtis	Vice President	1929–1933
32nd	Franklin D. Roosevelt	President	1933–1945
	John N. Garner	Vice President	1933–1941
	Henry A. Wallace	Vice President	1941–1945
	Harry S Truman	Vice President	1945

		Office	Term of Service
33rd	**Harry S Truman**	President	1945–1953
	Alben W. Barkley	Vice President	1949–1953
34th	**Dwight D. Eisenhower**	President	1953–1961
	Richard M. Nixon	Vice President	1953–1961
35th	**John F. Kennedy**	President	1961–1963
	Lyndon B. Johnson	Vice President	1961–1963
36th	**Lyndon B. Johnson**	President	1963–1969
	Hubert H. Humphrey	Vice President	1965–1969
37th	**Richard M. Nixon**	President	1969–1974
	Spiro T. Agnew	Vice President	1969–1973
	Gerald R. Ford	Vice President	1973–1974
38th	**Gerald R. Ford**	President	1974–1977
	Nelson A. Rockefeller	Vice President	1974–1977
39th	**James E. Carter**	President	1977–1981
	Walter F. Mondale	Vice President	1977–1981
40th	**Ronald W. Reagan**	President	1981–1989
	George H. W. Bush	Vice President	1981–1989
41st	**George H. W. Bush**	President	1989–1993
	J. Danforth Quayle	Vice President	1989–1993
42nd	**William J. Clinton**	President	1993–2001
	Albert A. Gore	Vice President	1993–2001
43rd	**George W. Bush**	President	2001–2009
	Richard B. Cheney	Vice President	2001–2009
44th	**Barack H. Obama**	President	2009–2017
	Joseph R. Biden	Vice President	2009–2017
45th	**Donald J. Trump**	President	2017–
	Michael R. Pence	Vice President	2017–

Justices of the Supreme Court

	Term of Service	Years of Service	Life Span
John Jay	1789–1795	5	1745–1829
John Rutledge	1789–1791	1	1739–1800
William Cushing	1789–1810	20	1732–1810
James Wilson	1789–1798	8	1742–1798
John Blair	1789–1796	6	1732–1800
Robert H. Harrison	1789–1790	—	1745–1790
James Iredell	1790–1799	9	1751–1799
Thomas Johnson	1791–1793	1	1732–1819
William Paterson	1793–1806	13	1745–1806
John Rutledge*	1795	—	1739–1800
Samuel Chase	1796–1811	15	1741–1811
Oliver Ellsworth	1796–1800	4	1745–1807
Bushrod Washington	1798–1829	31	1762–1829
Alfred Moore	1799–1804	4	1755–1810
John Marshall	1801–1835	34	1755–1835
William Johnson	1804–1834	30	1771–1834
H. Brockholst Livingston	1806–1823	16	1757–1823
Thomas Todd	1807–1826	18	1765–1826
Joseph Story	1811–1845	33	1779–1845
Gabriel Duval	1811–1835	24	1752–1844
Smith Thompson	1823–1843	20	1768–1843
Robert Trimble	1826–1828	2	1777–1828
John McLean	1829–1861	32	1785–1861
Henry Baldwin	1830–1844	14	1780–1844
James M. Wayne	1835–1867	32	1790–1867
Roger B. Taney	1836–1864	28	1777–1864
Philip P. Barbour	1836–1841	4	1783–1841
John Catron	1837–1865	28	1786–1865
John McKinley	1837–1852	15	1780–1852
Peter V. Daniel	1841–1860	19	1784–1860
Samuel Nelson	1845–1872	27	1792–1873
Levi Woodbury	1845–1851	5	1789–1851
Robert C. Grier	1846–1870	23	1794–1870
Benjamin R. Curtis	1851–1857	6	1809–1874
John A. Campbell	1853–1861	8	1811–1889
Nathan Clifford	1858–1881	23	1803–1881
Noah H. Swayne	1862–1881	18	1804–1884
Samuel F. Miller	1862–1890	28	1816–1890
David Davis	1862–1877	14	1815–1886

	Term of Service	Years of Service	Life Span
Stephen J. Field	1863–1897	34	1816–1899
Salmon P. Chase	1864–1873	8	1808–1873
William Strong	1870–1880	10	1808–1895
Joseph P. Bradley	1870–1892	22	1813–1892
Ward Hunt	1873–1882	9	1810–1886
Morrison R. Waite	1874–1888	14	1816–1888
John M. Harlan	1877–1911	34	1833–1911
William B. Woods	1880–1887	7	1824–1887
Stanley Mathews	1881–1889	7	1824–1889
Horace Gray	1882–1902	20	1828–1902
Samuel Blatchford	1882–1893	11	1820–1893
Lucius Q. C. Lamar	1888–1893	5	1825–1893
Melville W. Fuller	1888–1910	21	1833–1910
David J. Brewer	1890–1910	20	1837–1910
Henry B. Brown	1890–1906	16	1836–1913
George Shiras Jr.	1892–1903	10	1832–1924
Howell E. Jackson	1893–1895	2	1832–1895
Edward D. White	1894–1910	16	1845–1921
Rufus W. Peckham	1895–1909	14	1838–1909
Joseph McKenna	1898–1925	26	1843–1926
Oliver W. Holmes	1902–1932	30	1841–1935
William D. Day	1903–1922	19	1849–1923
William H. Moody	1906–1910	3	1853–1917
Horace H. Lurton	1910–1914	4	1844–1914
Charles E. Hughes	1910–1916	5	1862–1948
Willis Van Devanter	1911–1937	26	1859–1941
Joseph R. Lamar	1911–1916	5	1857–1916
Edward D. White	1910–1921	11	1845–1921
Mahlon Pitney	1912–1922	10	1858–1924
James C. McReynolds	1914–1941	26	1862–1946
Louis D. Brandeis	1916–1939	22	1856–1941
John H. Clarke	1916–1922	6	1857–1945
William H. Taft	1921–1930	8	1857–1930
George Sutherland	1922–1938	15	1862–1942
Pierce Butler	1922–1939	16	1866–1939
Edward T. Sanford	1923–1930	7	1865–1930
Harlan F. Stone	1925–1941	16	1872–1946
Charles E. Hughes	1930–1941	11	1862–1948
Owen J. Roberts	1930–1945	15	1875–1955
Benjamin N. Cardozo	1932–1938	6	1870–1938
Hugo L. Black	1937–1971	34	1886–1971

Justices of the Supreme Court (continued)

	Term of Service	Years of Service	Life Span
Stanley F. Reed	1938–1957	19	1884–1980
Felix Frankfurter	1939–1962	23	1882–1965
William O. Douglas	1939–1975	36	1898–1980
Frank Murphy	1940–1949	9	1890–1949
Harlan F. Stone	1941–1946	5	1872–1946
James F. Byrnes	1941–1942	1	1879–1972
Robert H. Jackson	1941–1954	13	1892–1954
Wiley B. Rutledge	1943–1949	6	1894–1949
Harold H. Burton	1945–1958	13	1888–1964
Fred M. Vinson	1946–1953	7	1890–1953
Tom C. Clark	1949–1967	18	1899–1977
Sherman Minton	1949–1956	7	1890–1965
Earl Warren	1953–1969	16	1891–1974
John Marshall Harlan	1955–1971	16	1899–1971
William J. Brennan Jr.	1956–1990	34	1906–1997
Charles E. Whittaker	1957–1962	5	1901–1973
Potter Stewart	1958–1981	23	1915–1985
Byron R. White	1962–1993	31	1917–
Arthur J. Goldberg	1962–1965	3	1908–1990
Abe Fortas	1965–1969	4	1910–1982
Thurgood Marshall	1967–1991	24	1908–1993
Warren C. Burger	1969–1986	17	1907–1995
Harry A. Blackmun	1970–1994	24	1908–1998
Lewis F. Powell Jr.	1972–1987	15	1907–1998
William H. Rehnquist	1972–2005	33	1924–2005
John P. Stevens III	1975–2010	35	1920–
Sandra Day O'Connor	1981–2006	25	1930–
Antonin Scalia	1986–2016	30	1936–2016
Anthony M. Kennedy	1988–	—	1936–
David H. Souter	1990–2009	19	1939–
Clarence Thomas	1991–	—	1948–
Ruth Bader Ginsburg	1993–	—	1933–
Stephen Breyer	1994–	—	1938–
John G. Roberts	2005–	—	1955–
Samuel A. Alito, Jr.	2006–	—	1950–
Sonia Sotomayor	2009–	—	1954–
Elena Kagan	2010–	—	1960–
Neil Gorsuch	2017–	—	1967–

Note: Chief justices are in italics.

*Appointed and served one term, but not confirmed by the Senate.

Southwestern natives, importance of
    sheep to, 443
Southwestern slavery, 321
Southwest Ordinance (1790), 198
Soviet Union
    actions of in Europe after
        WWII, 700
    collapse of, 837–838
    communication of Kennedy
        administration with, 758
    declaration of war on Japan, 691
    desire of for détente, 799
    espionage efforts of post-WWII, 734
    German advances into, 1941, 672
    goals of at Yalta Conference,
        686–687
    increased tension during Kennedy
        years, 759
    Lend–Lease aid to, 668
    non-aggression pact with Germany,
        1939, 660
    nuclear capability of, 692
    Reagan's view of in his first
        term, 827
    recognition of Israel by, 718
    response of to U.S. nuclear
        stockpiling, 712
    response of to violence against
        Freedom Riders, 761
    Stalin's territorial goals for after
        WWII, 698–699
    trade agreement with Cuba,
        1960, 718
    U.S. Europe First strategy
        and, 672
    U.S. recognition of, 643
Space program, government
    investment in, 1950s, 740
Spain
    colonization by, 22–23
    colonization contest with
        England, 28
    colonization of North America by,
        35–36
    decline of in 16th century, 23–24
    effect of Amistad case on relations
        with U.S., 249
    effect of influenza pandemic of
        1918 in, 585
    exploration and conquest, 21–22
    participation of in Revolutionary
        War, 168
    Pinckney's Treaty with,
        193–194
    restriction of American trade
        (1780s), 178

territorial expansion in North
    America, 92
use of American *emprasarios* by, 325
Spalding, Eliza, 328
Spalding, Henry, 328
Spanish–American War, motives for,
    562
Spanish Civil War, neutrality of the
    U.S. during, 659
Spanish conquest of the Americas, 3–7
Spanish explorers, 22
Spanish Florida
    Patriot War in, 226
    Pinckney's Treaty and, 198
Spanish flu (influenza pandemic,
    1918), 585
Spanish Louisiana, Haitian refugees in
    (1790s), 203
Spear, Fred, 572 (illus.)
Specie Circular, 345
    collapse of American credit system
        and, 347
Spencer, Herbert, 473
"Spirit of St. Louis," 623 (illus.)
Spirit of the Times (newspaper), 292
Spock, Dr. Benjamin, 745
Spoils system, 342
Sports, 490
    1920s, 622
    effect of globalization on, 855
Sports heroes, 1920s, 623
Sputnik, 712, 733, 748, 749 (illus.)
Squatters, westward expansion
    and, 319
Stafford, Mary, 625 (illus.)
Stages of life, late 19th century, 489
Stagflation
    causes of in 1970s, 805–806
    Federal Reserve Bank plan to
        end, 823
Stalin, Joseph, 685, 699 (illus.)
    death of, 710
    disagreement of with Churchill, 672
    non-aggression pact with Germany,
        1939, 660
    reaction of to the Marshall Plan,
        703
    relationship of with Truman, 700
    reluctant support of Kim in Korean
        War, 708
    territorial aims of after WWII,
        698–699
Stalingrad, battle of (WWII), 672
Stamp Act (1765), 129–130
    colonial resistance to, 131 (map)
    demonstrations against, 130–131

opposition to, 132
repeal of, 134
Standard Oil Company, 472, 473
    (illus.)
    critics of, 473
    Tarbell's history of, 526
Stanton, Edwin M., 385
    Johnson's attempt to remove, 425
Stanton, Elizabeth Cady, 348,
    423, 508
    work of on Thirteenth Amendment,
        415
Starr, Ellen Gates, 527
"The Star-Spangled Banner" (Key),
    226, 238
State-charted banks, 345
State citizenship, 436
State conventions, ratification of
    the U.S. Constitution by, 185,
    186 (table)
State Department, establishment
    of, 188
State governments, limitations on
    authority of (1776–1777), 155
State legislatures, civil rights actions
    of, 737
State of the Union, 1820, 235 (map)
States
    drafting of constitutions,
        154–155
    western land cessions by, 155
State sovereignty, expansion of slavery
    and, 353–354
States' rights
    Confederacy and, 398
    effects of for minorities during New
        Deal, 656–657
    nullification doctrine and, 343
    "The Southern Manifesto," 739
States' Rights Democratic Party, 732.
    See also Dixiecrats
Stationery supplies (18th century), 133
St. Augustine, 36
    settlement of fugitive slaves near, 80
Staunton, Virginia, origination of city
    manager plan in, 529
St. Clair, General Arthur, 197
St. Dominque. *See* Haiti
Steamboats
    commercial importance of, 276
    effect of *Gibbons v. Ogden* on, 236
    use of on the Mississippi River, 233
Steel, Ferdinand L., 255–256
Steel manufacturing, 464, 470
Steel plow, westward expansion and
    invention of, 315